THIRD EDITION

Structured
COBOL 74/85
Fundamentals and Style

Tyler Welburn
Wilson Price

 Mitchell **McGRAW-HILL**

New York St. Louis San Francisco Auckland Bogotá Caracas
Hamburg Lisbon London Madrid Mexico Milan Montreal
New Delhi Oklahoma City Paris San Juan São Paulo Singapore
Sydney Tokyo Toronto Watsonville

To my children: Brent, Veronica, and Keith   *(T.K.W.)*

To my grandchildren: Christopher, Christy, Erica, Katie, and Pamella   *(W.T.P.)*

Structured COBOL

COBOL is an industry language and is not the property of any company or group of organizations. No warranty, expressed or implied, is made by any contributor or by the CODASYL Programming Language Committee as to the accuracy and functioning of the programming system and language. Moreover, no responsibility is assumed by any contributor, or by the committee, in connection therewith.

The authors and copyright holders of the copyrighted material used herein—FLOW-MATIC (trademark of Sperry Rand Corporation), Programming for the UNIVAC I and II, Data Automation Systems, copyrighted 1958, 1959, by Sperry Rand Corporation; IBM Commercial Translator Form No. F 28-8013, copyrighted 1959 by IBM; FACT, DSI 27A5260-2760, copyrighted 1960 by Minneapolis-Honeywell—have specifically authorized the use of this material in whole or in part, in the COBAL specifications. Such authorization extends to the reproduction and use of COBOL specifications in programming manuals or similar publications.

1 2 3 4 5 6 7 8 9 0 VNH VNH 9 5 4 3 2 1 0

ISBN is: 0-07-069166-5
ORDER INFORMATION: Refer to back cover

Sponsoring editors: Raleigh S. Wilson and Steve Mitchell

Editorial Development and Production: BMR
   Copy editor/Proofreader: Karen Richardson
   Page makeup: Cecelia Morales, Arizona Publication Service
   Production coordinator: Jane Granoff
   Technical artist: Cecelia Morales
   Text and cover designer: John Edeen

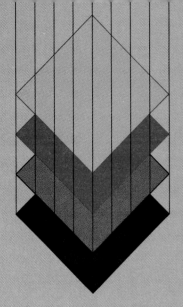

Brief Contents

CONCEPTS MODULE A   **Principles of Data Storage**   1
CHAPTER 1   An Overview of COBOL   12

CONCEPTS MODULE B   **The Program Development Process**   35
CHAPTER 2   Writing a COBOL Program: The IDENTIFICATION, ENVIRONMENT,
and DATA DIVISIONS   52
Chapter 2 Debugging Supplement   88

CONCEPTS MODULE C   **Introduction to Structured Programming Principles**   101
CHAPTER 3   Writing a COBOL Program: The PROCEDURE DIVISION   110
Chapter 3 Debugging Supplement   134

CONCEPTS MODULE D   **Data Storage and Computer Arithmetic**   149
CHAPTER 4   Arithmetic Operations   158
CHAPTER 5   Improving the Appearance of Printed Output   208

CONCEPTS MODULE E   **Principles of Report Design**   255
CHAPTER 6   Report Program Design and Coding   270

CONCEPTS MODULE F   **Structured Design and Documentation Techniques**   319
CHAPTER 7   The IF Statement   338

CONCEPTS MODULE G   **Data Validation Concepts**   377
CHAPTER 8   Data Validation Design and Coding   396
CHAPTER 9   Screen Output and Keyboard Input   446

CONCEPTS MODULE H   **Control-Break Principles**   481
CHAPTER 10   Control-Break Program Design and Coding   490

CONCEPTS MODULE I   **Table-Handling Concepts**   547
CHAPTER 11   Table Processing   562
CHAPTER 12   Advanced Table Processing Techniques   604
CHAPTER 13   Sorting and Merging   642

APPENDIXES

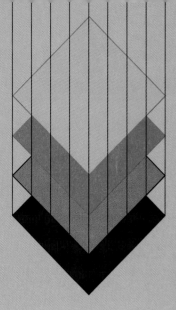

Contents

Preface   xiii

CONCEPTS MODULE A **Principles of Data Storage**   1

A Simple Manual File   2
Data Characteristics   3
Logical Versus Physical Data Entities   5
Module Summary   8
Exercises   8

CHAPTER 1 **An Overview of COBOL**   12

Introducing COBOL   14
The IDENTIFICATION DIVISION: Documenting the Program   18
The ENVIRONMENT DIVISION: Defining the Computer and Input-
    Output   20
The DATA DIVISION: Defining Files, Records, Fields, and Subfields   21
The PROCEDURE DIVISION: Coding the Program Logic   23
Overall Execution of the Program   26
Preparing the Program for Entry into the Computer   28
Chapter Summary   30
Exercises   31
Programming Assignments   34

CONCEPTS MODULE B **The Program Development Process**   35

Four Phases of Program Development   36
The Specification Phase   36
The Design Phase   43
The Coding Phase   44
The Testing Phase   48
Module Summary   49
Exercises   49

CHAPTER 2 **Writing a COBOL Program: The IDENTIFICATION, ENVIRONMENT, and DATA DIVISIONS**   52

Topic: Some COBOL Standards and Practices   54
  Formalizing Conventions and Rules   54
  A Modification to the PATLIST Program   58
Topic: Writing the IDENTIFICATION and ENVIRONMENT Divisions   58
  The IDENTIFICATION DIVISION   58
  The ENVIRONMENT DIVISION   61
Topic: Writing the DATA DIVISION   64
  The FILE SECTION   65
Chapter Summary   73
Style Summary   76
Exercises   77
Programming Assignments   81

Chapter 2   Debugging Supplement   88

Common Errors of Beginning COBOL Programmers   88
A Program With Errors   90
Supplement Summary   97
Exercises   97

CONCEPTS MODULE C **Introduction to Structured Programming Principles**   101

About Structured Programming   102
Structure Charts and Program Modules   102
Representing Program Logic—Flowcharting   104
Representing Program Logic—Pseudocode   106
Module Summary   107
Exercises   108

CHAPTER 3 **Writing a COBOL Program: The PROCEDURE DIVISION**   110

PROCEDURE DIVISION Elements   112
OPEN, CLOSE, and STOP   114
Changing Field Contents by Moving Data   116
The WRITE Statement   120
READ Statement   121
Principles of the PERFORM   123
Conditional Operations   125
Basic Logic of PATLIST2   126
Scope Terminators and the Use of Periods in COBOL-85   127
Chapter Summary   127
Features in COBOL-85 not in COBOL-74   131
Exercises   131
Programming Assignments   133

Chapter 3   Debugging Supplement   134

Compiler Detected Errors   135
Diagnostics From IBM Mainframe COBOL   136
Diagnostics From Ryan-McFarland COBOL   138
Logic Errors   141
Supplement Summary   144
Exercises   144

CONCEPTS MODULE D   **Data Storage and Computer Arithmetic**   149

Internal Coding of Data   150
Signed Numbers and Decimal Points   151
Basic Arithmetic Operations   153
Module Summary   154
Exercises   155

CHAPTER 4   **Arithmetic Operations**   158

Topic: PATDFCT—A Program with Arithmetic Calculations   160
    The Specification Phase of a Programming Task   160
    The Design Phase   163
    The PATDFCT Program Solution   166
Topic: COBOL Arithmetic Statements   172
    A Preview of the Arithmetic Statements   172
    The ADD Statement   173
    The SUBTRACT Statement   177
    The MULTIPLY Statement   178
    The DIVIDE Statement   181
    The COMPUTE Statement   183
    The ON SIZE ERROR Phrase   185
    Selecting the Arithmetic Form to Use   186
    Modifying the PATDFCT Program   188
Topic: Internal Coding of Numeric Data   190
Chapter Summary   192
Features in COBOL-85 not in COBOL-74   194
Exercises   194
Questions Pertaining to PATDFCT   198
Programming Assignments   198

CHAPTER 5   **Improving the Appearance of Printed Output**   208

Topic: Improving the PATDFCT Program   210
    Communicating the Information   210
Topic: PICTURE Clauses   216
    PICTURE Overview   216
    Numeric Editing—Special Insertion   218
    Numeric Editing—Zero Suppression and Replacement   219
    Numeric Editing—Simple Insertion   220
    Numeric Editing—Fixed Insertion   222
    Numeric Editing—Floating Insertion   225
    Describing Alphanumeric-Edited Data-items   227
    Recap of PICTURE Clauses   227
    PICTURE Clause Style Considerations   228
    BLANK WHEN ZERO Clause   229
Topic: The MOVE Statement   229

Capabilities of the MOVE—Preview/Summary   229
Alphanumeric MOVE Operations   231
Numeric MOVE Operations   232
Other MOVE Statement Categories   233
Referring to a Field by Two Different Names   234
Chapter Summary   237
COBOL Picture Symbol Summary   239
Style Summary   243
Features in COBOL-85 not in COBOL-74   243
Exercises   244
Programming Assignments   248

CONCEPTS MODULE E   **Principles of Report Design**   255

Report Areas   256
Printer Specifications   257
Report Design Guidelines   257
Module Summary   266
Exercises   267

CHAPTER 6   **Report Program Design and Coding**   270

Topic: Some Programming Standards   272
The Charge Account Report Program   272
The Program Solution—CHGACCT   278
Topic: Designing a Report Program   283
Programming Specifications for the Payroll Report Program   283
Designing the Structure Chart   287
Writing the Pseudocode and Drawing the Program Flowchart   290
Topic: Coding a Report Program   295
Coding the DATA DIVISION   295
Coding the PROCEDURE DIVISION   298
Some Additional Observations About the PAYROLL Program   305
Chapter Summary   305
Style Summary   307
Features in COBOL-85 not in COBOL-74   307
Exercises   308
Programming Assignments   311

CONCEPTS MODULE F   **Structured Design and Documentation Techniques   319**

A Label Printing Application   320
System and Overall Program Structure Techniques   321
Detailed Program Processing Techniques   325
Module Summary   332
Exercises   334

CHAPTER 7 **The IF Statement**   338

Review of the IF Statement   338
IF Statement—The Relation Condition   340
The IF Statement—Other Condition Types   343
Combined IF Statements   348
Other IF Capabilities   351
Nested IF Statements   353
The EVALUATE Statement—COBOL-85   356
Recap of Nested IF Statements   358
Chapter Summary   359
Style Summary   360
Features in COBOL-85 not in COBOL-74   360
Exercises   362
Programming Assignments   367

CONCEPTS MODULE G **Data Validation Concepts**   377

About Garbage   378
Character Testing   378
Field Checking   380
Record Checking   386
Data Validation Programs   387
Module Summary   392
Exercises   393

CHAPTER 8 **Data Validation Design and Coding**   396

Topic: The Elements of an Editing Task   398
    The INSPECT/REPLACING Statement   398
    The INSPECT/TALLYING Statement   399
    Definition of the Editing Task   400
    Validating Numeric Fields   402
    Validation Modules   405
    Alternative Coding Techniques   409
Topic: The Complete Data Validation Program   412
    Programming Specifications for the Sales-Transaction
        Validation Program   412
    Design Documentation for the Sales-Transaction
        Validation Program   414
    The Complete DATAVAL Program   421
    ENVIRONMENT/DATA DIVISION Coding   425
    PROCEDURE DIVISION Coding   426
Chapter Summary   431
Features in COBOL-85 not in COBOL-74   432
Exercises   433
Programming Assignments   435

CHAPTER 9 **Screen Output and Keyboard Input**   446

Screen I/O With the ACCEPT and DISPLAY   448
A Program to Display the Records of a File   450
The DISPTRA1 Program   452
The SCREEN SECTION   458
Data Entry Program Definition   461
The Data Entry Program   467

Chapter Summary   474
Exercises   476
Programming Assignments   480

CONCEPTS MODULE H   **Control-Break Principles**   481

Sorting Concepts   482
Report Control-Break Concepts   485
Module Summary   487
Exercises   488

CHAPTER 10   **Control-Break Program Design and Coding**   490

Topic: A Single-Level Control-Break Program   492
   Programming Specifications   492
   Program Design   494
   Program Coding   502
Topic: A Multiple-Level Control-Break Program   509
   Programming Specifications   509
   Program Design   513
   Program Coding   522
Chapter Summary   532
Exercises   533
Programming Assignments   536

CONCEPTS MODULE I   **Table-Handling Concepts**   547

About Tables   548
Table-Organization Methods   549
Table-Lookup Methods   551
Multiple-Level Tables   556
Table Data Storage   557
Module Summary   558
Exercises   559

CHAPTER 11   **Table Processing**   562

Establishing a Table   564
Accessing the Table with Subscripts   566
Other Table-Establishment Considerations   569
Establishing a Table with Arguments and Functions   570
Serial Lookups   571
Serial Lookups with Early Exit   582
Binary Search Lookups   584
Chapter Summary   587
COBOL Language Element Summary   587
Style Summary   588
Features in COBOL-85 not in COBOL-74   589
Exercises   589
Programming Assignments   593

CHAPTER 12 **Advanced Table Processing Techniques**   604

Topic: Other Single-Level Table-Lookup Considerations   606
Tables with Range-Step Arguments   606
Separately Defined Table Arguments and Functions   608
Topic: Multiple-Level Tables   611
Two-Level Table Processing   611
Three-Level Table Processing   616
The PERFORM/VARYING/AFTER Statement   618
Input-Loaded Tables   622
Program Example—Processing Using an Input-Loaded Table   623
Chapter Summary   630
Features in COBOL-85 not in COBOL-74   630
Exercises   630
Programming Assignments   633

CHAPTER 13 **Sorting and Merging**   642

Introduction to Sorting   644
Specialized Needs of Sorting—COBOL-74   644
The File to be Sorted   647
Topic: A Sort-Only Program   648
ENVIRONMENT DIVISION Coding   648
DATA DIVISION Coding   650
PROCEDURE DIVISION Coding   651
Recap of Sort Only Programs   654
Topic: A Sort Program with Preprocessing of the Input File   654
DATA DIVISION Coding   657
PROCEDURE DIVISION Coding—COBOL-74   657
PROCEDURE DIVISION Coding—COBOL-85   661
Recap of Sort Programs with Preprocessing of the Input File   662
Topic: A Sort Program with Preprocessing of the Input File and
Postprocessing of the Sorted File   663
ENVIRONMENT DIVISION Coding   666
DATA DIVISION Coding   666
PROCEDURE DIVISION Coding   666
Recap of Sort Programs with Postprocessing of the Sorted File   668
Topic: A Sort Program with Postprocessing of the Sorted File   668
The SORTPOST Program   669
Topic: The MERGE Statement   673
Merging   673
MERGE Statement Deficiency   674
Merging with the SORT Statement   675
Chapter Summary   676
Summary of COBOL-85 Differences   679
Exercises   679
Programming Assignments   681

APPENDIX A **The COBOL Report Writer Feature**   AA-1

APPENDIX B **Other COBOL Clauses and Statements**   AB-1

APPENDIX C **System-Names for Selected COBOL Compilers**   AC-1

APPENDIX D   **Program Interruptions for IBM OS and DOS Systems**   AD-1

APPENDIX E   **Complete COBOL-74 Language Formats**   AE-1

APPENDIX F   **Complete COBOL-85 Language Formats**   AF-1

APPENDIX G   **COBOL Reserved Words**   AG-1

Index   I-1

Preface

Since the second edition of this book, two significant changes have occurred in the COBOL realm. First, COBOL-85—with its block structure capabilities (specifically for structured programming techniques)—is in wide use. Second, high-quality COBOL compilers are available for today's powerful microcomputers. With these, program development and processing are transportable between microcomputers and mainframes. These two changes were prime considerations for adjustments to the third edition in order to maintain the lofty goals of the first two editions.

Computer technology is still an exciting and dynamic field. This text offers beginning COBOL students the firm foundation of important structured programming skills they'll need to enter it. The book combines current COBOL program design and coding techniques with business systems concepts for a practical, thorough introduction.

Goals for the Third Edition

First, we must say that this third edition has benefitted immensely from the observations and criticisms of many users of the second edition. Their experiences provided us with a solid foundation on which to incorporate needed improvements and updating. In addition to maintaining the quality of the second edition, our broad goals were:

- Give COBOL-85 "equal billing" with COBOL-74 without downplaying or slighting either one.

- Further expand the notion of separating general program theory and COBOL programming principles.

- Change the early-chapter topic sequence slightly to provide more versatility in teaching.

- Expand descriptions of debugging and include some debugging examples.

- Include a chapter on screen handling.

Each of these is described in more detail later in this preface.

Key Strengths Retained

In preparing the third edition, we have made a special effort to maintain—and improve—the qualities and features that instructors and students found useful in the second edition. Also, this edition continues to maintain its compatibility with the companion volume, *Advanced Structured COBOL: Batch, On-Line, and Data base Concepts.*

Text Organization

The COBOL syntax is presented within the framework of commonly encountered business-system program models. Concepts are developed step by step—proceeding from the simple to the more complex. Each program category builds upon and adds to the knowledge, techniques, and skills developed in the previous one.

The programs presented here also serve as a ready reference for each application type, and they introduce students to the fact that several traditional application-program categories exist. This permits students to analyze programming tasks in relation to program type and to use common approaches rather than to "reinvent the wheel" for each program. Further, with this method of presentation, coding is never divorced from practical application. The specific integration of concepts, coding, and program models is summarized in Figure 1.

System Concepts Modules

Nine chapters (called *Concepts Modules* and labeled A through I) are included to teach business systems concepts along with the coding. They contain no coverage of the COBOL language *per se*, but instead discuss background information on data concepts, record and report design, data validation, sorting and control breaks, and table handling.

ANS COBOL Orientation

This text is designed for users of American National Standard COBOL—either the 1968, 1974, or 1985 version. Equal treatment is given to both COBOL-74 and COBOL-85 in example programs and program fragments.

Although the text is not oriented toward a specific hardware or compiler vendor, commonly encountered IBM extensions to ANS COBOL are identified and covered.

The only divergence from the Standard is in Chapter 9, which describes screen handling, a topic not yet included in standard COBOL. For this, the Ryan-McFarland version of COBOL-85 is used.

Programming Style Conventions

Over the years, through trial and error, COBOL installations and programmers have developed programming style conventions. The establishment and use of such conventions significantly aid program readability and maintainability. In this text, therefore, applicable style considerations are presented—along with the syntactical coding rules—to provide an introduction to proper coding form. Through presentation of these style conventions, students can quickly learn sound coding practices that might otherwise take years to acquire. Basic programming conventions are introduced with the first program and are expanded upon as appropriate in later examples.

Comprehensive Program Design Documentation

For each text program, a structure chart is presented and the detailed logic is shown in both pseudocode and program flowchart form. (The abbreviated sort programs presented in Chapter 13 omit the detailed logic diagrams, however.)

Structure charts are provided to show overall program organization and module definition. A relaxed, English-like pseudocode is used to make comprehension of the detailed logic easier for the beginning programming student. Since many students are familiar with, and feel comfortable with flowcharts, the logic is also shown in program flowchart form.

Figure 1 Text progression and integration.

Systems concept	Chapter	COBOL coding syntax	Program type	Program name
Data concepts	1	Overview	Read-and-print	PATLIST
Program development	2	IDENTIFICATION DIVISION ENVIRONMENT DIVISION DATA DIVISION	Read-and-print	PATLIST2
Structured programming	3	PROCEDURE DIVISION OPEN PERFORM MOVE READ Nonnumeric literals PERFORM/UNTIL CLOSE STOP Simple IF Figurative constants WRITE ADVANCING integer	Read-and-print (continued)	PATLIST2
Computer arithmetic	4	ADD SUBTRACT MULTIPLY DIVIDE COMPUTE ROUNDED ON SIZE ERROR Numeric literals Assumed decimal point USAGE	Read-calculate-print with totals	PATDFCT PATDFCT2
	5	VALUE clause WRITE/FROM PICTURE BLANK WHEN ZERO MOVE MOVE/CORRESPONDING Data-name qualification REDEFINES	Read-calculate-print with editing, simple headings, and totals	PATDFCT3

Systems concept	Chapter	COBOL coding syntax	Program type	Program name
Report design	6	IF/ELSE Block IF/ELSE 　(COBOL-85) INITIALIZE (COBOL-85)	Read-calculate-print with editing, simple headings, and totals	CHGACC
		ACCEPT/FROM DATE ACCEPT/FROM DAY ACCEPT/FROM TIME READ/INTO ADVANCING identifier ADVANCING PAGE Condition names	Read-calculate-print with page and column headings, and totals	PAYROLL
Structured design	7	IF Relational operators Logical operators 　(AND, OR, NOT) Implied subjects 　and operators EVALUATE (COBOL-85)		
Data validation	8	INSPECT/REPLACING INSPECT/TALLYING	Data validation	DATAVAL
	9	ACCEPT DISPLAY SCREEN SECTION In-line PERFORM 　(COBOL-85)	Full-screen display of data records	DISPTRA1
			Data entry: enter records into a file	DATAENT
Control breaks	10		Control break 　(single-level)	SCTLBRK
			Control break 　(multiple-level)	MCTLBRK
Table handling	11	OCCURS Subscripts INDEXED BY SET PERFORM/VARYING SEARCH KEY Multiple-level	Table processing 　(single-level)	
	12	SEARCH/VARYING PERFORM/VARYING/AFTER	Table loading/ processing (multiple-level)	GROSSPAY
	13	SORT RELEASE RETURN MERGE	Sorting	SORTONLY SORTPRE SORTPP SORTPOST

Clearly Identified Coding Formats and Examples

Whenever COBOL language entries are introduced in the text, they are accompanied by the language format (sometimes shown in a simplified form). The language formats are clearly identified to stand out from the other text.

Complete Programs

Eleven complete programs (and several variations) are included to illustrate the major application program types mentioned. They are shown in a reduced typesize and are arranged to minimize page-flipping while the reader studies the code. As a result, students can more easily grasp the coding interrelationships and thereby more quickly comprehend the program logic.

Portions of the programs are often extracted and discussed in more detail within the body of the text.

Combination Tutorial/Reference Approach

Students often react to COBOL textbooks in one of two ways. Typically, either they feel that the text is a good reference manual but doesn't really explain how to write certain types of programs, or they claim that the book explains things well but is difficult to use as a reference. This text blends tutorial and reference features. Whenever a subject is presented, it is fully covered in one place. However, to guard against information overload, topics are covered on a step-by-step basis and are integrated with programming examples. Furthermore, descriptions are organized to give a "first cut" description, and then go into detail. This makes it possible to skip much of the detail, progress to the next topic (or chapter), and then return at a later date for the fine points.

In the interest of sounding "friendly," the text involves the reader in scenarios. For instance, in the data validation chapter, the reader is to assume that he or she works for the General Merchandise Supply Company, where a new sales transaction system is being set up. One portion of the application is a program to validate the data, which becomes the reader's assignment.

Extensive End of Chapter Material

At the end of each chapter, a chapter summary is presented. Appropriate chapters also contain COBOL language element summaries and style summaries.

Exercises appear after the summaries. Terms for definition and review questions are provided for each chapter. Most chapters also contain syntax/debug exercises.

Range of Programming Assignments

Each chapter includes several programming assignments that relate directly to the material covered within the chapter. Most of the assignments are independent of other assignments. Some are cumulative; for instance, Programming Assignment 4-5 requires that the program of 3-5 be expanded.

Complete test data sets are available for use with the programming assignments.

Numerous Illustrations and Examples

Over 400 figures illuminate the text. The figures include illustrations, diagrams, programming specifications, design documentation, coding, examples, and more.

A Complete Teaching Package

This third edition is not merely a textbook—it is a *teaching package*, designed to provide you, the instructor, with the broadest possible support. The package consists of the following components:

- A comprehensive **Instructor's Guide** containing: (1) chapter objectives, (2) teaching tips, (3) answers to exercises, and (4) test questions.

- A set of **transparency masters**.

- A **solutions/data disk** containing program solutions and data files for each programming assignment in the textbook.

■ A **solutions manual** with listings of the program solution, sample data file, and sample program output for each programming assignment in the text-book.

■ For users of the Ryan-McFarland COBOL-85 software, the **Ryan-McFarland COBOL-85 language** and **Users' manuals**.

Quick-Reference Material on Inside Covers

A mock-up of the IDENTIFICATION and ENVIRONMENT divisions is presented on the inside front cover, together with a checklist of other items that vary with the compiler and computer system being used. This page can be filled in at the beginning of the course and then used as (1) a reminder of the format for coding the first two COBOL divisions and (2) a reference whenever installation-dependent entries must be coded.

For easy reference, the COBOL format notation legend also appears on the inside back cover.

System-Names for Selected Compilers

Syntax for COBOL system-names varies from one compiler to another. To provide helpful additional reference material, implementor-dependent system-names are presented in Appendix C.

Chapter/Topic Organization

Each chapter contains a preliminary overview discussion. Chapters that cover two or more distinct topics have these topics identified as individual entities. Such topic organization clearly identifies the subject of each text segment. This permits easy identification of material that the instructor might choose to skip or cover in a different sequence.

COBOL-85 Software Version Available

This textbook is available with or without software that allows students to complete their assignments on a microcomputer. In order to furnish a compiler with this textbook, Ryan-McFarland produced a special education version of their COBOL-85 which is well suited to the educational environment. It is important to recognize that this version is not a watered-down system that is useless for all except the simplest problems. In fact, the opposite is true; the compiler includes the following powerful features:

1. COBOL programs of up to 800 lines of source code can be compiled.

2. File types supported include sequential, line sequential, relative, and indexed.

3. File size limitation for indexed files is 100 records; for all others, it is 1,000 records.

4. Records in the File Section can be up to 132 bytes in length.

5. Up to four file definitions may be used in any program (that is, four files may be open at one time).

6. Indexed files may include one or two keys.

7. The CALL statement can be implemented to one level. That is, a program can call another, but the called program may not call a third program.

It is important to avoid considering this as "microcomputer COBOL," thereby implying that it is something less than "up-to-snuff" COBOL-85. It is COBOL-85. It is indeed a powerful system for the student.

In addition, the software version of the text includes a data disk that contains the full set of data files for programming assignments of the text.

Expanded and Updated Material

In preparing this revision, we have reconsidered every topic and figure of the second edition in an effort to present the material in as clear and understandable a manner as possible. Similarly, each topic was reassessed for relevance, and additional topic area candidates were considered. Areas in which significant new material appears are as follows.

COBOL-74/COBOL-85

Today's COBOL text can ignore neither the programming techniques required of COBOL-74 nor the features of COBOL-85. The beginning programmer will most likely be performing maintenance on programs written under the constraints of COBOL-74. Obviously, he or she will need to be familiar with the techniques required by that version of COBOL to achieve good structure. On the other hand, that same beginning programmer will likely have COBOL-85 available and, therefore, must be familiar with its rich structured features. Thus, equal billing is given in this book to both versions of COBOL. For every example in which COBOL-85 offers an advantage, two versions of the solution are given. In fact, almost every example program includes a PROCEDURE DIVISION for each COBOL-74 and COBOL-85. In some instances, differences are small; in others, they are significant. For instance, the COBOL-85 EVALUATE statement simplifies the coding of the case structure over using nested IF statements.

Programming Theory and COBOL Practice

The second edition included five system concepts chapters which covered general business systems principles. This approach has been expanded to include 9 concepts modules labeled A through I (almost one for each chapter). Each includes introductory information specifically oriented to the chapter (or chapters) it precedes. For instance, Chapter 1 gives an overview of a program to list data from a file. It is preceded by Concepts Module A (entitled "Principles of Data Storage") that includes topics such as the file/record/field concept and the distinction between physical and logical record. This is information important to understanding the example program of Chapter 1. Similarly, Chapter 3 ("Writing a COBOL Program—the PROCEDURE DIVISION") is preceded by Concepts Module C, which is a brief introduction to good programming practices—including flowcharts and pseudocode.

Topic Sequencing

We each have our own opinions regarding the best time to introduce various topics and the speed with which they should be covered. In this edition, we have attempted to maintain the steady, even pace of the second edition, yet provide more flexibility regarding "advanced" topics. To this end, the IF statement is introduced (in its basic form) in Chapter 3. Descriptions and assignments allow you, the instructor, to leave this topic until later (without a major effort on your part), or include use of conditionals almost from the very beginning of class. Furthermore, the chapter on arithmetic now precedes the chapter on editing, thereby providing "real live" output that requires editing.

Debugging

Debugging tips and suggestions of the second edition have been expanded to two chapter supplements on debugging (following Chapters 2 and 3). These include sample programs (with errors) and post-compile listings, together with diagnostics for IBM mainframe COBOL and for Ryan-McFarland microcomputer COBOL-85. Each is described in detail.

Screen Handling

Unfortunately, COBOL-85 does not include screen-handling syntax. However, most microcomputer COBOL implementations (including the Ryan-McFarland COBOL-85 that accompanies this book) do have a screen section. To provide the student with some experience in writing a program that will interact with the user, a separate chapter is included to cover screen handling. Although designed specifically for the Ryan-McFarland screen implementation, the characteristics are similar to those of other microcomputer screen handling features. Indeed, the principles of user interaction are general in nature.

New Programming Assignments

Additional programming assignments are included, thus further expanding the plethora of the second edition. As in the second edition, the assignments for each chapter offer a range of complexity. Each assignment is fully documented so that it contains explicit instructions for the student. A general background information paragraph has been added to each assignment to provide the student with an insight to the placement of the program in the overall business environment of the hypothetical organization for which it will be written.

Acknowledgements

Our sincere thanks and appreciation go to the following people who have provided assistance in the preparation of all three editions of this book:

Marilyn Bohl
  IBM Corporation
Barbara Comfort
  J. Sergeant Reynolds
    Community College
George Dailey
  Stephen F. Austin State University
Robert H. Doursen
  California Polytechnic State University
Jerome Garfunkel
  Member, ANSI X3J4 and CODASYL
    COBOL Committees
  Jerome Garfunkel Associates, Inc.
Mary Ann Grams
  San Antonio College
Carol C. Grimm
  Palm Beach Junior College
R. Wayne Headrick
  Texas A & M University
Susan Hinrichs
  Missouri Western State College
Ben Kramer
  Massasoit Community College
Sue Krimm
  Los Angeles Pierce College
David M. Kroenke
  Microrim, Inc.
Marjorie Leeson
  Delta College
Sandra Maceyka
  New York Board of Cooperative
    Educational Services at Fairport

Lerond Mallard
  Independant
Anthony Mann
  Central State University
Anne M. McBride
  California State University, Chico
Rosemary Mehrlich
  Systems Plus, Inc.
Eunice Miskimen
  Independant
Donald F. Nelson
  Chairman, CODASYL COBOL
    Committee
  Tandem Computers, Inc.
Mehran Pooya
  University of District of Columbia
Edward Rategan
  College of San Mateo
Cyndi Reese
  Santa Rosa Community College
Brian T. Regan
  Fort Steilacoom Community College
Paul W Ross
  Millersville University
Dan Rota
  Robert Morris College
Joseph Southern
  LaGuardia Community College
George Vlahakis
  Evergreen Valley College

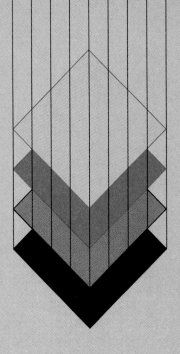

CONCEPTS MODULE **A**

Principles of Data Storage

Module Objectives

The purpose of this concepts module is to provide you with a brief background about the essentials of data storage in the computer. The principles described relate directly to the COBOL topics of both Chapters 1 and 2. From this module, you will learn the following:

- The hierarchy of data: fields, records, and files

- How data is stored, without descriptive formatting information, in the computer's memory

- Two characteristics of a data field that are essential to the COBOL programmer: data class and field length

- The distinction between logical data and physical data

- How data is stored in auxiliary storage devices, such as magnetic disk and tape

Module Outline

A Simple Manual File
Storing Data
Processing Activities

Data Characteristics
Field
Data Class
Field Length

Logical Versus Physical Data Entities
Basic Unit of Computer Storage—The Byte
Data in Memory
Logical Definition of Fields
Data Records in a File
The Storage of Data on Auxiliary Storage Media
The End of File
Terminology—Memory Versus Storage

1

A Simple Manual File
Storing Data

Assume that you have taken a job with Fleetwood Charities (a charitable organization) and that one of your tasks is to keep track of individual patrons (contributors). With hundreds of patrons, it is essential that the data pertaining to them be recorded in an organized way. To accomplish this, the organization maintains a Roladex file with one card for each patron, as shown in Figure A-1. The Roladex cards are ruled and labeled to allocate and identify areas for each person's name, address, city, state, zip code, target contribution, actual contribution, and date of the contribution. Each of these items of information is an element of data about the individual. The collection of all these cards forms a file: the *patron file*.

To simplify access to the card of a particular patron, the cards are arranged in alphabetic order based on the patron's last name. This data is organized and structured; organization and structure are keys to its usefulness.

In data-processing terminology, the area allocated for each data element (such as the name, address, and contribution) is called a **field**. Notice that the field areas in the card are of various sizes to accommodate the varying number of character symbols that may be required for each data element. Each card, containing fields about a single individual, is called a **record**. Note that an important feature of this system is that all of the records in the file have exactly the same format and all contain the same type of data. Hence, we can think of this as the *patron* record. The collection of all these records forms the patron **file**. A file is the collection of all records of a given type arranged in a useful order. The file does not contribute any data above and beyond that in the individual records.

Processing Activities

With the data organized and structured, you can easily manipulate it to provide information needed by the organization. For instance, if the address of Norma Johnson is required, you flip to the portion of the file containing last names starting with the letter J and find the name *Johnson*—much the same as if you were looking it up in a telephone directory.

Another possible processing activity is producing a list of all patrons who have contributed an amount less than their target contribution. The partial report of Figure A-2 is generated by selecting cards of patrons meeting the specified criterion and rearranging this data into a form more convenient to read.

Figure A-1
A single record in a
Rolodex file.

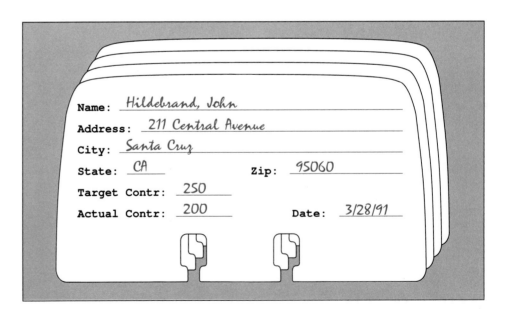

Name:	Hildebrand, John
Address:	211 Central Avenue
City:	Santa Cruz
State: CA	**Zip:** 95060
Target Contr:	250
Actual Contr: 200	**Date:** 3/28/91

Figure A-2
A partial report from the data in the patron file.

```
                    BELOW TARGET REPORT

                              ----Contribution----
              Name            Target       Actual
              ------------------------     ------       ------
              Hazel Anderson              250          100
              Donald Baker               375          300
              J. H. Campbell             200          175
              Harley Davidson            250          100
              F. Englehoff               250          150
              John Hildebrand            250          200
              Jeanette Jones             375            0
              Irwin B. Miller            200          185
              Arnold T. Molitar          200          150
              J. J. Nelson               250            0
              Diane Pratt                375          229
              Howard Arnold Stevenson    200            0
              Eva Zener                  200          190

              TOTALS                    3375         1779
```

Data Characteristics
Field

A **field** (or a subdivision of a field, sometimes referred to as a **subfield**) is the smallest logical data unit in a data-processing system. Fields are composed of adjacent character positions on a data-storage medium; these positions hold letters, digits, and other symbols, which together represent a logical unit of data.

Just what comprises a logical unit of data is a question that is open to a degree of latitude. Look at the name field in the patron file. Evidently, the file designer considered a person's full name to be a logical unit of data. However, often a person's name is broken down into three separate logical units or fields: last name, first name, and middle name (or initial) [see Figure A-3(a)]. The patron record of Figure A-1 includes another field that can reasonably be broken down further: the date of contribution field. In Figure A-3(b), this 6-digit field consists of three fields: month, day, and year. However, since they are normally used together to represent a specific date, it may be more appropriate to consider them subfields of the date-of-contribution field. Actually, there is little distinction between a subfield and a field. As you will learn, the need of an application determines the extent to which fields are broken down.

In writing COBOL programs, data fields have two properties with which you will need to deal: data class and field length.

Figure A-3
A field and its subfields.

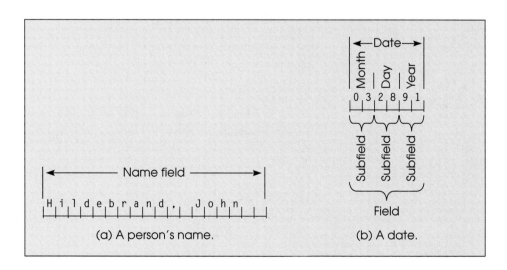

(a) A person's name.

(b) A date.

Data Class   Data class refers to the type of symbols stored within a field. The three basic classes of data follow: numeric, alphabetic, and alphanumeric.

Numeric	Digits 0 (zero) through 9 (can include + and –).
Alphabetic	Letters A through Z (both upper- and lowercase) and space.
Alphanumeric	All numeric characters All alphabetic characters All special characters such as: $ ( ) @ =

Numeric fields are restricted to the digits 0 (zero) through 9. If arithmetic calculations are to be performed with a field, the field *must* be of a numeric data class. The patron record includes two such examples: the target contribution and actual contribution fields. Although fields such as the zip code contain only digits, they are not commonly treated as numeric fields because arithmetic is not normally performed with them. In addition to digits, an arithmetic sign representation of either plus (+) or minus (–) is often present in an arithmetic field.

Alphabetic fields can contain only the letters A through Z and blank spaces. Other characters, such as periods or digits, cannot be included because they are not alphabetic.

Alphanumeric (sometimes termed **alphameric**) fields may contain digits letters, and/or other special characters (such as $, *, and #). Actually, fields consisting of letters and other characters are more commonly encountered than pure alphabetic fields. For instance, the address field includes a house number as well as a street name. Hence, most programmers define all alphabetic fields with an alphanumeric data class.

Field Length   In Figure A-1, the space allocated for the name is sufficient to allow a name of reasonable length. On the other hand, much less space is allocated for the state because state abbreviations are all two letters. (You have probably filled out a form in which it was impossible to squeeze in your address and phone number in the space provided.) Within the computer, fields can range in length from one to many character positions. As with a manual system such as that of Figure A-1, the number of positions allocated for each field depends upon the nature of that field.

Usually, the data files that a program is written to process already exist. This means that the exact layout of the record and the corresponding field lengths are already determined. Hence, any program to process that data must use the precise lengths of the existing fields. If you are creating a new application in which you design the data records, then there are factors that you must take into account; these are described in Concepts Module B.

When performing arithmetic operations in a program, you will usually need to define numeric fields to hold intermediate results. Since these are independent of the input data formats, you must use a degree of judgement in determining the field sizes to ensure that the field size is large enough for the longest result that can occur. When there are just two values involved in a calculation—as when a price is multiplied by a quantity—the maximum field size is easily determined. On the other hand, a sequence of actions such as those necessary to accumulate the total of all the items on an invoice requires judgment and an understanding of the application to determine the needed field width for the result.

Logical Versus Physical Data Entities
Basic Unit of Computer Storage—The Byte

The internal memory of most computers is composed of individual units of storage called **bytes**. Each byte consists of eight binary digits (bits) and can be used in a variety of ways for storing data. With one of the coding techniques, a byte can store one character of data. For instance, the name field shown in Figure A-3(a) is 18 bytes in length and contains a data value consisting of 14 letters, a comma, and blanks. (It is important that you recognize that a blank is a character.) The date field in Figure A-3(b) is six bytes in length and contains a six-position value. As you will learn in Concepts Module C, there are several data format options that you can use (under programmer control).

Data in Memory

The card of Figure A-1 is marked off with appropriate descriptions and lines for the fields—quite convenient for human use. However, if this same data is to be stored in a computer, its form will be very different. Within the computer, fields are stored one after the other in a continuous string with no distinguishing marks or indication between them. For instance, Figure A-4 shows how the record of Figure A-1 might be stored in the computer. Although you can pick out the name and address fields easily, the numbers are run together and are impossible to interpret unless you know something about the record.

For a manual data-processing system such as one using a Roladex file, you can be fairly informal. For example, if a person has a two-line address, you can squeeze both lines into the Address area of the card simply by writing smaller than normal. However, an automated data-processing system requires that explicit standards be set and followed.

Logical Definition of Fields

When using conventional programming languages such as COBOL, you must be keenly aware of the way in which data is stored and how individual fields are made available to you. That is, the string of data in Figure A-4 is of little value if you do not know where one field ends and the other begins. However, consider the format definition of Figure A-5.

Without the formatting information in Figure A-5, the computer can no more extract fields from this record than you can. However, with the format description it is easy to separate out the fields—as is done in Figure A-6.

Figure A-4
A record in computer memory.

```
Hildebrand, John   211 Central AvenueSanta Cruz        CA9506002500200032891
```

Figure A-5
Format description for patron record.

Field	Width	Class
Name	18	Alphanumeric
Street address	18	Alphanumeric
City	17	Alphanumeric
State	2	Alphanumeric
Zip	5	Alphanumeric
Target contribution	4	Numeric
Actual contribution	4	Numeric
Contribution date	6	Alphanumeric
Total record size	74	

Figure A-6
Fields of a record.

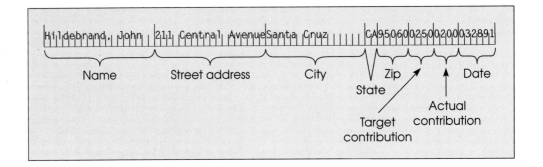

Notice in this example that the only fields identified as numeric are the two contribution fields. As you will learn in Chapter 3, it is common practice to declare a field as numeric only if arithmetic or editing operations might be performed on it.

Data Records in a File

Remember at the beginning of this module, it is noted that a file is simply a collection of records and that the file does not contribute any data beyond that in the individual records. That is, *the data file contains no indication of the field allocations within the record.** Hence, when a record is read into the computer from a disk or tape file, it appears as a single string of characters (such as that in Figure A-4). Any computer program that operates on the patron file must include, in one form or another, some definition describing field subdivisions (such as that in Figure A-5). As you will learn, this is coded into the DATA DIVISION of a COBOL program. Without this information, the computer is no more able to distinguish one field from another than you are.

The Storage of Data on Auxiliary Storage Media

The smallest addressable storage unit in internal computer memory is the byte. In contrast, no such byte addressing is available with auxiliary storage such as disk and tape. Commonly, data is stored on disk or tape in very large blocks without regard to individual fields or even records, and the data is addressable only by block. Thus, if you need a single field from a record stored on disk, the computer must read an entire block of data into memory. The operating system software then extracts the requested record from the block and makes it available to your program which, in turn, has access to individual fields of the record. The size of the block transferred to memory will not necessarily correspond to the size of your record; it will depend upon the characteristics of the disk drive and of the operating system software. This is equally true of the mainframe disk drive and of the personal computer floppy disk with which you are probably familiar.

For instance, the common 360K-byte floppy disk used with personal computers is commonly divided into concentric tracks, each divided (by the disk controlling software) into nine 512-byte sectors as shown in Figure A-7. The sector is the basic unit of storage of the disk. It is sometimes referred to as a **physical record** because its size is determined by the physical characteristics of the disk hardware and the operating system. Since the 512-byte sector size is considerably greater than the 74-byte patron record, it would be possible to store six full records in a single sector, as illustrated in Figure A-8. Hence, the physical record contains six logical records, a logical record being a collection of fields related to the same data entity and arranged in a prescribed format (such as the patron record). If a program requests the third record in a file, disk I/O software reads the physical record and then separates out the requested logical record and makes it available to the program.

---

*In contrast to conventional programming languages such as COBOL, one of the characteristics of a database management system is that descriptive data about the data (such as the format) is included together with the data itself as part of the database.

Figure A-7
Sectors on a floppy disk.

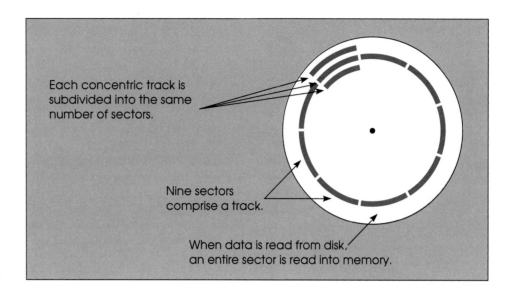

Each concentric track is
subdivided into the same
number of sectors.

Nine sectors
comprise a track.

When data is read from disk,
an entire sector is read into memory.

Figure A-8   Seven records occupying a single sector.

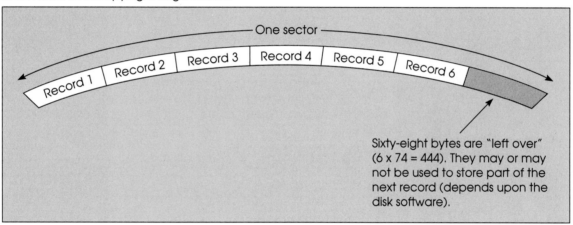

One sector

Record 1   Record 2   Record 3   Record 4   Record 5   Record 6

Sixty-eight bytes are "left over"
(6 x 74 = 444). They may or may
not be used to store part of the
next record (depends upon the
disk software).

Fortunately, we COBOL programmers need not be concerned with this detail since it is done automatically by the disk I/O software. Usually, we need be concerned only with records at the logical level. However, COBOL does provide the person who designs the files with considerable latitude regarding the way in which data is stored on disk or tape. You will learn about that in an advanced COBOL course.

The End of File   If disk storage is a continuous string of data blocks, then you might wonder how the disk software knows when it has reached the last record in a data file. For instance, a program to print a list of contributors from the patron file would read records from disk, one record after the other. Without an indication of the end of the file, it would continue to read data from blocks of disk storage following the patron file. This could be some other data file (with an entirely different format) or even part of a program that had been stored on disk. The disk software prevents this through use of a special **end-of-file** (**EOF**) record that is written when the file is first created. As illustrated in Figure A-9, this EOF record is positioned following the last record in the file. Whenever the disk software is directed to read the next record, it looks to see if that record is the EOF. If it is, then a special indication is given. Programming languages such as COBOL allow you to test for the EOF, as you will learn in Chapter 1.

Figure A-9
The end-of-file (EOF) record.

| Data record 1 | Data record 2 | . . . | Last data record | EOF record |

Terminology—Memory Versus Storage

As you enter the data-processing field, you will find both the words *memory* and *storage* used to describe the hardware components for storing data. In a beginning course, instructors often avoid using the word *memory* because it is easily associated with a human capability. In contrast, the storage units of a computer are more likened to a simple file cabinet that can store data in an orderly fashion than to any human entity. However, in the field the word *memory* is very commonly used, so you should be accustomed to it. In this book, reference to the internal (main) storage unit of the computer most often is as *internal memory* or simply *memory*. Reference to auxiliary storage, such as magnetic tape and disk, is as *auxiliary storage, disk storage,* or *tape storage.*

Module Summary

Data is organized into fields, records, and files. A **field** is a single data item made up of a group of characters (for instance, a person's street address). A **record** is a collection of related fields treated as a unit. A **file** is the collection of all records of a given type.

The basic addressable unit of storage in the computer is the **byte**, which can store a single character: letter, digit, or special character.

A data record in computer memory will appear as a string of characters with no indication of where one field ends and another begins. The COBOL program must provide two items of information regarding each field: the data class and the field length.

The three basic data classes are numeric, alphabetic, and alphanumeric.

Data stored on disk or tape is accessible in large blocks. Each block can consist of many records. The programmer can work at the record level because operating system software automatically makes individual records available to the program.

Logical data characteristics are based upon the application-oriented requirements of a data-processing system; physical data characteristics are dependent upon the data-representation and storage-medium aspects of the computer equipment that is being used. In other words, fields, logical records, and files are determined by the data-processing application (payroll, accounts receivable, inventory control, etc.), but character positions and records blocks are affected by the specific hardware (computer, tape drive, disk storage) being used.

Exercises
Terms for Definition

alphabetic data class _____

alphanumeric data class _____

arithmetic sign _____

auxiliary storage _____

bit _____

byte _____

character position _____

data class _____

EOF record _____

field _____

file _____

internal computer memory _____

logical record _____

numeric data class _____

physical record _____

subfield _____

Review Questions 1. Arrange the following three logical data classifications in order from the largest to the smallest relative to one-another: **field**, **file**, **logical record**.

_____

2. Identify the three classes of data that can be specified for a field, together with the characters encompassed by each data class.

        Class   *Characters*

    a. _____

    b. _____

    c. _____

3. The collection of records of a given type is called a(n) _____ .

4. The smallest unit of addressable internal computer memory is the

   _____ . It contains eight _____ .

5. A record block is sometimes called a(n) _____ record.

6. What are the two properties that must be specified for each data field?

    a. _____

    b. _____

7. Following is an inventory data record.

```
1299JNFIBERGLASS AIR FILTEY15611549015001000120002399
```

The record contains the following fields; write in the space provided the value for each field.

Field	Width	Value from previous record
Part identification	6	_____
Description	20	_____
Source code	5	_____
Quantity on hand	4	_____
Reorder quantity	4	_____
Reorder level	4	_____
Wholesale price (dollars and cents)	5	_____
Retail price (dollars and cents)	5	_____

An Overview of COBOL

Chapter Objectives

This chapter provides you with a broad overview of a complete COBOL program. If you are a beginning programming student, do not expect to understand fully the details of this program after you have read this chapter. Nor should you expect to comprehend all of the interrelationships of the COBOL language. The purpose of this chapter is to introduce you to basic concepts of COBOL. The material presented in this overview chapter will be expanded upon in following chapters. From this chapter, you will learn the following:

- The four broad elements of a COBOL program:

IDENTIFICATION DIVISION	*Documents the program*
ENVIRONMENT DIVISION	*Specifies computer hardware and the data files*
DATA DIVISION	*Defines files, records, and fields*
PROCEDURE DIVISION	*Expresses the program logic*

- The structure of a COBOL program—consisting of divisions, sections, paragraphs, and sentences

- The designation and use of memory areas for input and output operations

- The definition of the format of a record—done in the DATA DIVISION

- The instructions to the computer to carry out the data-processing activities—done in the PROCEDURE DIVISION. Action statements include:

OPEN	*Make data files ready for use*
CLOSE	*End use of data files*
READ	*Copy a record from a data file into memory*
MOVE	*Copy data from one field in memory to another*
WRITE	*Copy a record from memory to an output device*
STOP RUN	*Terminate execution of a program*
PERFORM	*Transfer control to another part of the program*

- The entering of a COBOL program into the computer

Chapter Outline

Introducing COBOL
A Simple Report From the Patron File
Generating Output From Input Data
Broad Elements of a Program

The IDENTIFICATION DIVISION: Documenting the Program

The ENVIRONMENT DIVISION: Defining the Computer and Input-Output
CONFIGURATION SECTION
INPUT-OUTPUT SECTION

The DATA DIVISION: Defining Files, Records, Fields, and Subfields
FILE SECTION
WORKING-STORAGE SECTION

The PROCEDURE DIVISION: Coding the Program Logic
The OPEN and CLOSE Statements
The READ Statement
The MOVE Statement
The WRITE Statement
The STOP RUN Statement
The PERFORM Statement

Overall Execution of the Program

Preparing the Program for Entry Into the Computer
The Coding Form
Area A and Area B Entries

Introducing COBOL
A Simple Report From the Patron File

For your introduction to COBOL, let's consider a simple program to print a list of contributors from the patron file described in Module A. To simplify matters, assume that the city, state, and zip fields are combined into a single field, giving the following input record format:

Field	Width	Class
Name	18	Alphanumeric
Street address	18	Alphanumeric
City/state/zip	24	Alphanumeric
Target contribution	4	Numeric (whole dollars)
Actual contribution	4	Numeric (whole dollars)
Contribution date	6	Alphanumeric
Total record size	74	

As you observed in Module A, notice in the sample data file of Figure 1-1 that it is not possible to identify individual fields without this record format description.

The listing program prints the name and full address of each patron. The listing produced from the input file of Figure 1-1 is shown in Figure 1-2. Notice that there is one line of output for each record of the file; single output lines that correspond to an input record are called **detail lines**. (In later chapters you will learn about heading lines, summary lines, and others.) You can see that data "jammed" together in the input file is separated out so that it is easier to read in the output report. Also, note that not all of the data from the data record is used in printing a detail line.

Figure 1-1
Sample patron data file.

```
Acton, Jocelyn     223 Connecticut StSan Francisco, CA 94107 03500350031891
Anderson, Hazel    1247 Main Street  Woodside, CA 94062      02500100032591
Baker, Donald      1532 Bancroft RoadBerkeley, CA 94703      03750300022891
Broadhurst, Ryan   Route 3           Big Trees, CA 95066     05000500031391
Campbell, J. H.    4892 Powell StreetEmeryville, CA 94608    02000175032391
Davidson, Harley   349 Airport Way   Concord, CA 94519       02500100031791
Drumright, Devon   2817 Laguna StreetOakland, CA 94602       01000105032591
Englehoff, F.      137 Rengstorff Bl.Santa Clara, CA 95051   02500150021591
Erlicht, Beverly   3814 Marina Blvd. San Francisco, CA 94123 02250225013191
Fox, Wylie         35 Crescent CircleOrinda, CA 94563        01000100030191
Grant, Rosalyn P.  4530 17th Street  San Francisco, CA 94114 00750080011591
Hildebrand, John   211 Central AvenueSanta Cruz, CA 95060    02500200032891
Jones, Jeanette    453 Bayview Drive Belvedere, CA 94920     03750000
Lacrosse, Larry    1347 Sacramento   Berkeley, CA 94702      04800520032591
Mattingly, Roscoe  1523 Old Bayshore Mountain View, CA 94043 01800180022891
Miller, Irwin B.   4237 Doppler Blvd.Daly City, CA 94014     02000185010191
Molitar, Arnold T. 125 Wharf Circle  Capitola, CA 95010      02000150032591
Nelson, J. J.      24389 Ballena RoadAlameda, CA 94501       02500000
Pratt, Diane       2201 Pacific Ave. San Francisco, CA 94115 03750229033191
Stevenson, Howard  385 C Street      San Rafael, CA 94901    02000000
Unger, William P.  15062 E. 14th St. San Leandro, CA 94578   03000300031591
Walton, John Jr.   531 Gray Peak RoadBelmont, CA 94002       01500150020391
Winger, Mandy      1987 Dallas Drive Hayward, CA 94545       02250225022891
Zener, Eva         515 Bridgeport AveSausalito, CA 94965     02000190031591
```

Figure 1-2
List of contributors and their
addresses.

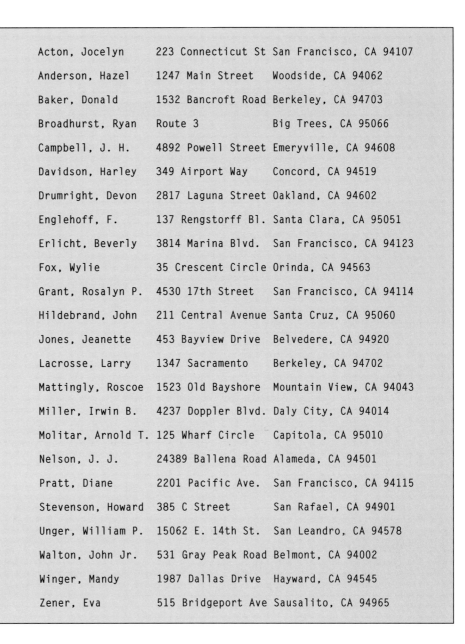

Acton, Jocelyn	223 Connecticut St	San Francisco, CA 94107
Anderson, Hazel	1247 Main Street	Woodside, CA 94062
Baker, Donald	1532 Bancroft Road	Berkeley, CA 94703
Broadhurst, Ryan	Route 3	Big Trees, CA 95066
Campbell, J. H.	4892 Powell Street	Emeryville, CA 94608
Davidson, Harley	349 Airport Way	Concord, CA 94519
Drumright, Devon	2817 Laguna Street	Oakland, CA 94602
Englehoff, F.	137 Rengstorff Bl.	Santa Clara, CA 95051
Erlicht, Beverly	3814 Marina Blvd.	San Francisco, CA 94123
Fox, Wylie	35 Crescent Circle	Orinda, CA 94563
Grant, Rosalyn P.	4530 17th Street	San Francisco, CA 94114
Hildebrand, John	211 Central Avenue	Santa Cruz, CA 95060
Jones, Jeanette	453 Bayview Drive	Belvedere, CA 94920
Lacrosse, Larry	1347 Sacramento	Berkeley, CA 94702
Mattingly, Roscoe	1523 Old Bayshore	Mountain View, CA 94043
Miller, Irwin B.	4237 Doppler Blvd.	Daly City, CA 94014
Molitar, Arnold T.	125 Wharf Circle	Capitola, CA 95010
Nelson, J. J.	24389 Ballena Road	Alameda, CA 94501
Pratt, Diane	2201 Pacific Ave.	San Francisco, CA 94115
Stevenson, Howard	385 C Street	San Rafael, CA 94901
Unger, William P.	15062 E. 14th St.	San Leandro, CA 94578
Walton, John Jr.	531 Gray Peak Road	Belmont, CA 94002
Winger, Mandy	1987 Dallas Drive	Hayward, CA 94545
Zener, Eva	515 Bridgeport Ave	Sausalito, CA 94965

***Generating Output
From Input Data***

Whenever a data record is read into the computer's memory, it is placed in an input area of memory exactly as it is stored in the record. Thus, the 74-byte patron record is read into 74 consecutive bytes of memory. One of the tasks of the programmer is to define this input area and to break it down to the component fields. Similarly, the programmer must define an output area corresponding to the desired printed line.

With both the input and output areas defined, the action of the program as illustrated in Figure 1-3 is to:

1. Read a record into the input area.

2. Move the individual fields to their appropriate positions in the output area.

3. Print the data stored in the output area.

Figure 1-3   The read-move-print sequence.

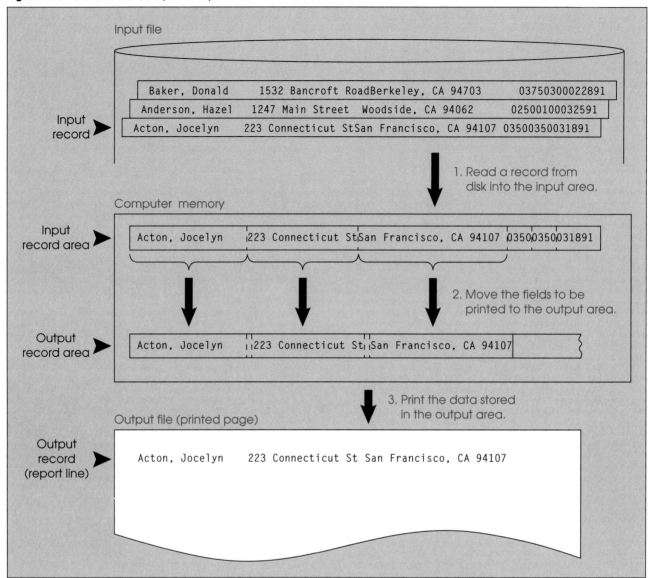

Broad Elements of a Program

From these descriptions, it is evident that a program to process data from a file must include the following elements:

1. Designation of the file from which the data is to be obtained. Almost all computers have more than one disk drive and each drive will likely contain many files.

2. A description of the record format for the data file.

3. A description of the specific sequence of steps (the procedure) to be carried out in processing the data.

This is not unique to COBOL; the same would be necessary in a program written in Pascal, FORTRAN, or BASIC (the description may be subtle for some types of BASIC files). In addition to these three items, virtually all languages have the capability for the programmer to include an identification of the program and its actions. From one language to another, there are significant differences in the way these elements are implemented, but they exist anyway.

In COBOL, these four elements (including identification information) are explicitly identified as separate components or *divisions* of every COBOL program. These components are depicted in Figure 1-4 and are as follows:

- IDENTIFICATION DIVISION   Documents the program.
- ENVIRONMENT DIVISION   Specifies computer hardware and the data files.
- DATA DIVISION   Defines files, records, and fields.
- PROCEDURE DIVISION   Expresses the program logic.

Figure 1-4   COBOL division structure.

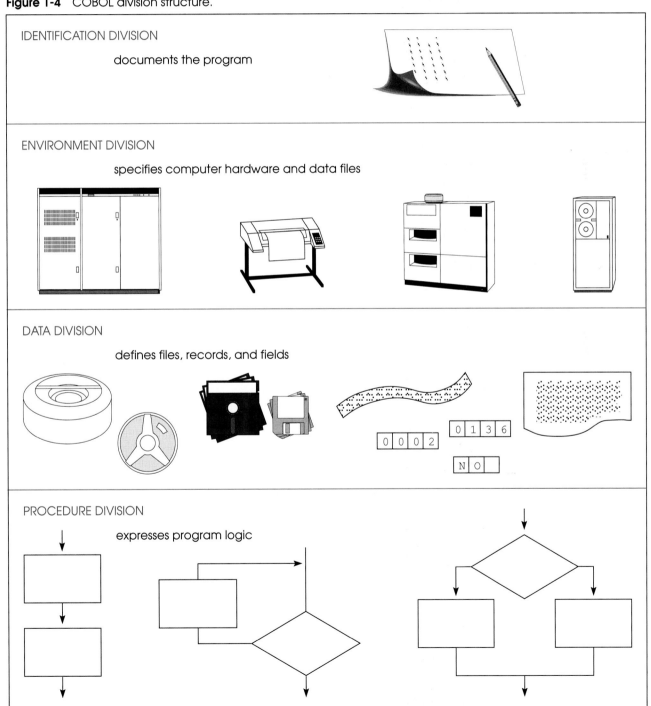

The organization of a COBOL program is somewhat like that of this book. That is, the book is organized by chapters. Each chapter is broken down into major topics, minor headings, paragraphs, and finally, sentences.

An annotated version of the patron list program, which identifies the structural components of the COBOL language, is shown in Figure 1-5. This program forms the basis of discussions that follow. The intent of the following descriptions of this program is two-fold. The first is to give you a broad overview of COBOL. The second is to provide you with enough knowledge so that you can make some meaningful changes to the program. However, you will find many questions unanswered in this first go-around. Do not be concerned with this as you will examine a slightly expanded version of this program in detail in Chapters 2 and 3.

In the program listing, the line numbers to the left are not part of the program; they are included for your reference in studying the program.

The IDENTIFICATION DIVISION: Documenting the Program

The IDENTIFICATION DIVISION is the first division of a COBOL program. This division, comprising the first seven lines of the patron list program, is repeated in Figure 1-6. There is nothing complicated about this division; it simply contains information to document the program. Thus, although this division serves an important function, it has no effect whatever upon the output results that the program produces.

Figure 1-5 Annotated patron list COBOL program.

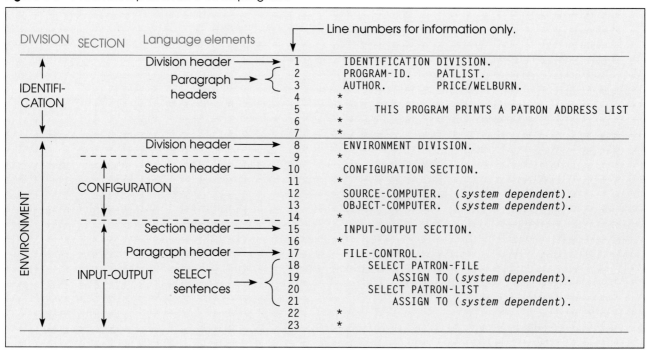

Figure 1-5 (continued)

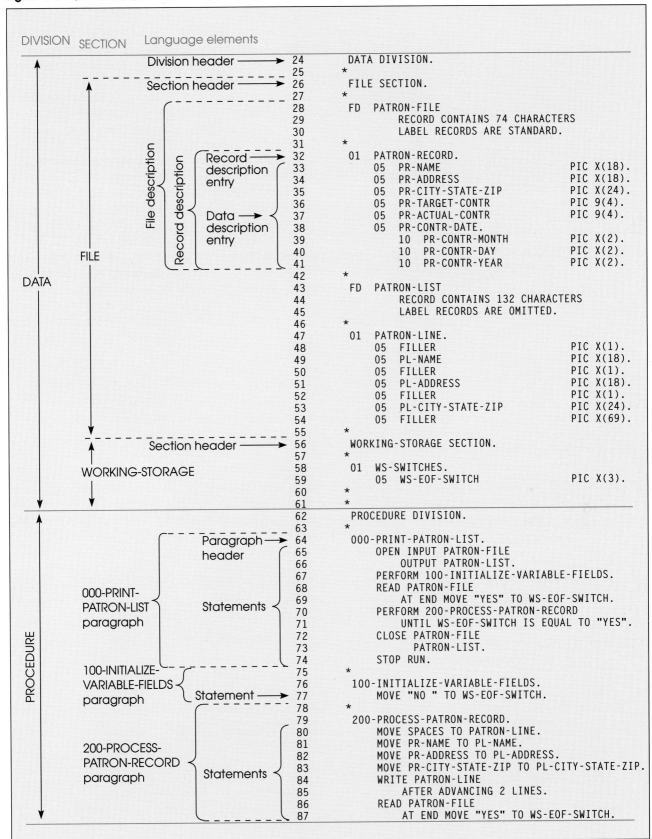

```
                                              24    DATA DIVISION.
                                              25    *
                                              26    FILE SECTION.
                                              27    *
                                              28    FD   PATRON-FILE
                                              29         RECORD CONTAINS 74 CHARACTERS
                                              30         LABEL RECORDS ARE STANDARD.
                                              31    *
                                              32    01   PATRON-RECORD.
                                              33         05   PR-NAME              PIC X(18).
                                              34         05   PR-ADDRESS           PIC X(18).
                                              35         05   PR-CITY-STATE-ZIP    PIC X(24).
                                              36         05   PR-TARGET-CONTR      PIC 9(4).
                                              37         05   PR-ACTUAL-CONTR      PIC 9(4).
                                              38         05   PR-CONTR-DATE.
                                              39              10   PR-CONTR-MONTH  PIC X(2).
                                              40              10   PR-CONTR-DAY    PIC X(2).
                                              41              10   PR-CONTR-YEAR   PIC X(2).
                                              42    *
                                              43    FD   PATRON-LIST
                                              44         RECORD CONTAINS 132 CHARACTERS
                                              45         LABEL RECORDS ARE OMITTED.
                                              46    *
                                              47    01   PATRON-LINE.
                                              48         05   FILLER               PIC X(1).
                                              49         05   PL-NAME              PIC X(18).
                                              50         05   FILLER               PIC X(1).
                                              51         05   PL-ADDRESS           PIC X(18).
                                              52         05   FILLER               PIC X(1).
                                              53         05   PL-CITY-STATE-ZIP    PIC X(24).
                                              54         05   FILLER               PIC X(69).
                                              55    *
                                              56    WORKING-STORAGE SECTION.
                                              57    *
                                              58    01   WS-SWITCHES.
                                              59         05   WS-EOF-SWITCH        PIC X(3).
                                              60    *
                                              61    *
                                              62    PROCEDURE DIVISION.
                                              63    *
                                              64    000-PRINT-PATRON-LIST.
                                              65        OPEN INPUT PATRON-FILE
                                              66             OUTPUT PATRON-LIST.
                                              67        PERFORM 100-INITIALIZE-VARIABLE-FIELDS.
                                              68        READ PATRON-FILE
                                              69             AT END MOVE "YES" TO WS-EOF-SWITCH.
                                              70        PERFORM 200-PROCESS-PATRON-RECORD
                                              71             UNTIL WS-EOF-SWITCH IS EQUAL TO "YES".
                                              72        CLOSE PATRON-FILE
                                              73              PATRON-LIST.
                                              74        STOP RUN.
                                              75    *
                                              76    100-INITIALIZE-VARIABLE-FIELDS.
                                              77        MOVE "NO " TO WS-EOF-SWITCH.
                                              78    *
                                              79    200-PROCESS-PATRON-RECORD.
                                              80        MOVE SPACES TO PATRON-LINE.
                                              81        MOVE PR-NAME TO PL-NAME.
                                              82        MOVE PR-ADDRESS TO PL-ADDRESS.
                                              83        MOVE PR-CITY-STATE-ZIP TO PL-CITY-STATE-ZIP.
                                              84        WRITE PATRON-LINE
                                              85             AFTER ADVANCING 2 LINES.
                                              86        READ PATRON-FILE
                                              87             AT END MOVE "YES" TO WS-EOF-SWITCH.
```

Figure 1-6

The IDENTIFICATION DIVISION for the PATLIST program.

```
1        IDENTIFICATION DIVISION.
2        PROGRAM-ID.    PATLIST.
3        AUTHOR.        PRICE/WELBURN.
4    *
5    *    THIS PROGRAM PRINTS A PATRON ADDRESS LIST
6    *
7    *
```

The first line contains the words IDENTIFICATION DIVISION. This entry is called a **division header**. The first word of each of the other IDENTIFICATION DIVISION lines (except for the comment line) is called a **paragraph header**. This example includes two of the six paragraph headers that may be coded: PROGRAM-ID and AUTHOR.

Each of the words used in the division and paragraph headers of this division is a **reserved word**. Reserved words have special predefined meanings in the COBOL language and must be used only as explicitly allowed by COBOL. Notice that each header is terminated by a period. The COBOL language processor looks for periods to terminate various elements of the program. As you will undoubtedly learn when you begin running programs, omitting a period or a misplaced period will usually cause problems.

Following the predefined paragraph headers are entries that the programmer composes. For example, the programmer has given this program a PROGRAM-ID (the program name) PATLIST—an abbreviation for patron list.

The asterisk character (*) indicates a descriptive comment that conveys only documentation information to the programmer. Since it is ignored by the COBOL system, you can type whatever descriptive comments you like. Note that the * comment is used to produce blank lines, thus separating parts of the program and making it easier to read.

The ENVIRONMENT DIVISION: Defining the Computer and Input-Output

The ENVIRONMENT DIVISION is the link between the predominantly hardware-independent COBOL program and the actual computer and input-output device hardware that the program uses. As shown in Figure 1-7, this division is separated into two sections: the CONFIGURATION SECTION and the INPUT-OUTPUT SECTION. A section-header line is used to identify the beginning of each section.

CONFIGURATION SECTION

Before any COBOL program can be run, it must be converted to the language of the computer on which it will be run. This process, called compiling, is performed by a special compiler program and is described in Concepts Module B.

Figure 1-7   The ENVIRONMENT DIVISION for the PATLIST program.

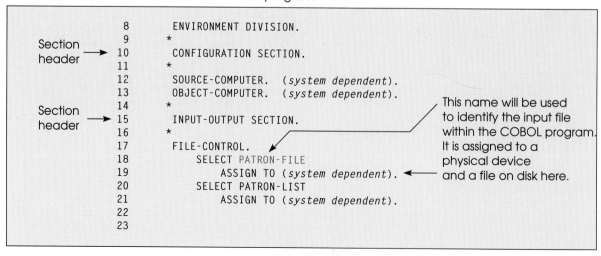

```
                   8        ENVIRONMENT DIVISION.
                   9    *
Section    →      10        CONFIGURATION SECTION.
header            11    *
                  12        SOURCE-COMPUTER.  (system dependent).
                  13        OBJECT-COMPUTER.  (system dependent).
                  14    *
Section    →      15        INPUT-OUTPUT SECTION.
header            16    *
                  17        FILE-CONTROL.
                  18          SELECT PATRON-FILE
                  19            ASSIGN TO (system dependent).
                  20          SELECT PATRON-LIST
                  21            ASSIGN TO (system dependent).
                  22
                  23
```

This name will be used to identify the input file within the COBOL program. It is assigned to a physical device and a file on disk here.

The computers that are to be used to compile and run the COBOL program are specified in the CONFIGURATION SECTION. A SOURCE-COMPUTER paragraph is specified to name the computer model that will be used to compile the COBOL program. The computer model that will actually run the program—in this case, the computer to be used to produce the patron address list—is identified in the OBJECT-COMPUTER paragraph. Although they may differ, the source and object computers are typically the same.

In Figure 1-7, lines 12 and 13 include (*system dependent*) following SOURCE-COMPUTER and OBJECT-COMPUTER. This is not what you would enter in a program; it is simply a message telling you that you must get a name corresponding to the computer you are using. For example, if you were using an IBM 3081, line 12 would read:

```
SOURCE-COMPUTER. IBM 3081.
```

For most compilers, these entries are now treated as comments and are ignored.

INPUT-OUTPUT SECTION

The INPUT-OUTPUT SECTION describes the data files that the program uses. Each file is designated and associated with a hardware input-output device.

The PATLIST program uses two files—the input file (that is, the patron file) containing name-and-address records, and an output report file containing lines of patron data. Even though the program will be sending output to the printer, COBOL considers it as file output. Thus, the word *file* is not limited to a collection of data stored on disk or tape. Two file-control entry sentences—one for each file—exist in the FILE-CONTROL paragraph. Each of these sentences contains two clauses: SELECT and ASSIGN.

The SELECT clause of each file-control entry identifies the file-name that will be used to refer to the data file in the COBOL program. For instance, the patron file has been given (by the programmer) the name PATRON-FILE; all references within the program to the file will be through this name. Words of a COBOL program (such as this name) that the programmer chooses are called **user-defined words**. You will learn about the rules for creating them in Chapter 2.

The corresponding ASSIGN clause specifies a hardware device and/or operating system file name that the operating system will use to refer to the file. For instance, for the Ryan-McFarland compiler available with this book, the ASSIGN for an IBM-PC might take the following form:

```
ASSIGN TO DISK, "D:PATRON.DAT"
```

The file is identified as PATRON.DAT on the D disk drive. Hence, the file referred to in the program as PATRON-FILE is actually the file known to the operating system as PATRON.DAT located on the D disk drive.

The form of the ASSIGN to use for several computers and operating systems is described in Appendix C. Before attempting to run any program, you must obtain the exact form to be used at your installation from an instructor or lab director.

The DATA DIVISION: Defining Files, Records, Fields, and Subfields

As its name implies, the DATA DIVISION is used to describe the data to be processed by the program. The DATA DIVISION for the PATLIST program (shown in Figure 1-8) consists of two sections: the FILE SECTION and the WORKING-STORAGE SECTION. (All programs that you will work with in this book include these two sections.)

The FILE SECTION

Data items (files, records, fields, and subfields) contained in the input and output files are defined in the FILE SECTION. Each file selected in the ENVIRONMENT DIVISION must be described in this section. Thus, the FILE SECTION is made up

Figure 1-8   The DATA DIVISION for the PATLIST program.

```
24          DATA DIVISION.          This is the data file name,
25      *                           as defined in the SELECT clause.
26          FILE SECTION.
27      *
28          FD  PATRON-FILE
29              RECORD CONTAINS 74 CHARACTERS        Record name
30              LABEL RECORDS ARE STANDARD.          Field name
31      *
32          01  PATRON-RECORD.
33              05  PR-NAME              PIC X(18).
34              05  PR-ADDRESS           PIC X(18).    Field length
35              05  PR-CITY-STATE-ZIP    PIC X(24).    and class
36              05  PR-TARGET-CONTR      PIC 9(4).
37              05  PR-ACTUAL-CONTR      PIC 9(4).
38              05  PR-CONTR-DATE.
39                  10  PR-CONTR-MONTH   PIC X(2).
40                  10  PR-CONTR-DAY     PIC X(2).
41                  10  PR-CONTR-YEAR    PIC X(2).
42      *
43          FD  PATRON-LIST
44              RECORD CONTAINS 132 CHARACTERS
45              LABEL RECORDS ARE OMITTED.               The sum of these widths
46      *                                                is equal to this value.
47          01  PATRON-LINE.
48              05  FILLER               PIC X(1).
49              05  PL-NAME              PIC X(18).
50              05  FILLER               PIC X(1).
51              05  PL-ADDRESS           PIC X(18).
52              05  FILLER               PIC X(1).
53              05  PL-CITY-STATE-ZIP    PIC X(24).
54              05  FILLER               PIC X(69).
55      *
56          WORKING-STORAGE SECTION.
57      *
58          01  WS-SWITCHES.
59              05  WS-EOF-SWITCH        PIC X(3).
60
61
```

of file descriptions for all files that the program uses. A **file-description entry** starts with the reserved word FD (which stands for **File D**escription). This word is followed by the file-name and by clauses that describe the file. Notice that the PATRON-FILE clauses tell how many characters the records contain, and whether or not the file contains label records.

After the FD entry for a file, each record format within the file is described. The record format definition of the PATRON-RECORD follows the FD entry. Each element of the record description in this program has either two or three parts:

1. A two-digit level-number (such as 01, 05, or 10, as in these examples) which determines the hierarchy of the element.

2. A user-defined data-name to identify the record or field. You use this name in statements of the PROCEDURE DIVISION when you must refer to the field.

3. A PICTURE clause (usually abbreviated with the reserved word PIC, as in the PATLIST program), which defines the data class and the length of the field.

As in line 32 of the PATLIST program, the level number 01 always signifies a record-description entry. Following the level-number 01 is the user-defined record name: PATRON-RECORD. Following the record description entry is a sequence of entries (termed **data-item description entries**) describing the fields comprising the record. Each must begin with a level number in the range 02 through 49. The use in lines 33 through 38 of the level number 05 (a number that is larger than the 01 of PATRON-RECORD) tells the compiler that these data items are fields that make up the PATRON-RECORD. Observe at lines 38 through 41 that the level numbers 05 and 10 are used. Use of 10, which is larger than 05, indicates that these are subfields of the immediately preceding 05 data item. From the nature of this application, you know that these three subfields are the components of the date field. In this example program, levels 05 and 10 are used; incrementing by 5 is common. However, 02 and 03 are also acceptable.

User-defined data names can be up to 30 characters in length and must contain a letter. You will learn about selecting names in Chapter 2.

Concerning the PIC clause, in line 33 you can see that the entry is X(18). The letter X is a code meaning that the data class is alphanumeric and the 18 (enclosed within parentheses) says that the length of this field is 18 positions. In lines 36 and 37, the PIC code is 9—indicating numeric data class.

Any field that is broken down into subfields must not include a PIC clause. For instance, PR-CONTR-DATE is composed of three subfields, each with its own PIC, thereby defining the size of this date field. Hence, to include a PIC for the PL-CONTR-DATE field would be redundant. Also, the record entry (line 32) does not include a PIC because its size is determined by the fields comprising it. An item with a PIC, which is not broken down further into subfields, is called an **elementary item**.

Beginning with line 43 in Figure 1-8 is the file and record description for the output file PATRON-LIST. Descriptions and remarks about the input FD are equally applicable to this FD. However, since the output line requires that space be inserted between output fields, this record description includes a one-position FILLER between each field. (FILLER is a reserved word which is used to "fill out" the space between fields.)

WORKING-STORAGE SECTION

A program usually requires other fields in addition to those present in the input and output data records. Some examples are fields that are used to accumulate totals or to keep track of program status conditions. Such fields are described in the WORKING-STORAGE SECTION because they are not part of the input or output records described in the FILE SECTION. Because the PATLIST program is a straightforward read-and-print type of program, only one WORKING-STORAGE field (WS-EOF-SWITCH) is required.

Although COBOL includes provisions for defining independent fields within this section, that capability is not used in this book. Instead, all such fields are defined under a working-storage "record," as is done in this example. In line 58, you see WS-SWITCHES, which includes the single elementary item WS-EOF-SWITCH. As you will learn, defining your working variables in this way is an effective method for a meaningful organization.

The PROCEDURE DIVISION: Coding the Program Logic

As you will learn in Concepts Module B, one program design technique widely used in programming is the breaking of a large program into smaller components. Each component, or program module, performs a particular function. Although the small size of the PATLIST program hardly requires modularization, the technique is used here to set the basis for standards that are used throughout the book. The PROCEDURE DIVISION shown in Figure 1-9 consists of the following three modules (identified by their paragraph names):

Figure 1-9
The PROCEDURE DIVISION for
the PATLIST program.

```
62          PROCEDURE DIVISION.
63      *
64          000-PRINT-PATRON-LIST.
65              OPEN INPUT PATRON-FILE
66                   OUTPUT PATRON-LIST.
67              PERFORM 100-INITIALIZE-VARIABLE-FIELDS.
68              READ PATRON-FILE
69                  AT END MOVE "YES" TO WS-EOF-SWITCH.
70              PERFORM 200-PROCESS-PATRON-RECORD
71                  UNTIL WS-EOF-SWITCH IS EQUAL TO "YES".
72              CLOSE PATRON-FILE
73                   PATRON-LIST.
74              STOP RUN.
75      *
76          100-INITIALIZE-VARIABLE-FIELDS.
77              MOVE "NO " TO WS-EOF-SWITCH.
78      *
79          200-PROCESS-PATRON-RECORD.
80              MOVE SPACES TO PATRON-LINE.
81              MOVE PR-NAME TO PL-NAME.
82              MOVE PR-ADDRESS TO PL-ADDRESS.
83              MOVE PR-CITY-STATE-ZIP TO PL-CITY-STATE-ZIP.
84              WRITE PATRON-LINE
85                  AFTER ADVANCING 2 LINES.
86              READ PATRON-FILE
87                  AT END MOVE "YES" TO WS-EOF-SWITCH.
```

000-PRINT-PATRON-LIST.	Control execution of other modules of the program and perform a minimal number of basic operations. Since this is the main module from which control to subordinate modules is transferred, it is commonly called the **mainline module**.
100-INITIALIZE-VARIABLE-FIELDS.	Initialize work variables that control execution of record processing.
200-PROCESS-PATRON-RECORD.	Process one patron record. This module will be executed once for each data record.

Although paragraph-names in the IDENTIFICATION DIVISION and the ENVIRONMENT DIVISION are reserved words, paragraph-names in the PROCEDURE DIVISION are used-defined words. The paragraph-names created for this program were selected to describe the general function of the module. The three digits represent a standard that you will learn about in Concepts Module C.

Each of the paragraphs contains one or more COBOL statements that specify the program instructions. COBOL statements in the PROCEDURE DIVISION designate an operation to take place and therefore begin with a verb: an action word telling the computer to do something. The verbs used in the program, which will be used to identify statements in the program, are:

```
OPEN and CLOSE
READ
MOVE
WRITE
STOP RUN
PERFORM
```

Let's consider each of these.

The OPEN and CLOSE Statements

Each file to be used in a program must be "made ready" before data can be read from or written to it. This is done with the OPEN statement. In Figure 1-9, this is done at lines 65 and 66 with the following OPEN statement:

```
OPEN INPUT PATRON-FILE
     OUTPUT PATRON-LIST.
```

After processing is complete and before the program is terminated, all files that have been opened must be closed. This is done in lines 72 and 73 with the statement:

```
CLOSE PATRON-FILE
      PATRON-LIST.
```

Do not be concerned with the slightly different format of these two statements; that will be described in more detail in Chapter 3. However, do notice that the statement is entered on two lines; the period designates the end of the statement. In later chapters you will learn about the latitude that you have regarding using periods and the recommendations for using them in both 1974 COBOL (COBOL-74) and 1985 COBOL (COBOL-85).

The READ Statement

Once an input file is open, data can be read from it with the READ statement. This is done at lines 68 and 69 (and also at lines 86 and 87) with the statement:

```
READ PATRON-FILE
     AT END MOVE "YES" TO WS-EOF-SWITCH.
```

The verb READ is followed by the name of the file from which the record is to be read. The AT END clause causes a check to be made for an EOF record (refer to Figure A-9). If the record just read is a data record, nothing more happens and execution continues to the next statement. However, if the record read is the EOF, then the MOVE following the AT END is executed and YES is moved to the field WS-EOF-SWITCH. As you will see, this controls the repeated reading and processing of data records.

The MOVE Statement

The operation of moving data from one place in memory to another is done with the MOVE statement, such as that in line 81 of Figure 1-9:

```
MOVE PR-NAME TO PL-NAME.
```

This statement copies data from the input field (PR-NAME) to corresponding positions of the output area (PL-NAME). This program includes a minor variation of the MOVE. In addition to the lines 81 through 83 which move data from one field to another, the MOVE at line 80 moves spaces to the output record (SPACES is a reserved word which represents blank spaces). Notice that when an EOF is encountered when reading a record, the word YES is moved to the working storage field WS-EOF-SWITCH.

The WRITE Statement

The WRITE statement at lines 84 and 85

```
WRITE PATRON-LINE
      AFTER ADVANCING 2 LINES.
```

identifies the output *record* to be written (PATRON-LINE) and causes it to be sent to the printer. (Notice that the READ and WRITE are different in this respect. You READ a file and WRITE a record.) This printed record is the output record into which input data has been moved. The AFTER ADVANCING controls line spacing and results in a double-spaced report, as you can see by referring back to Figure 1-2.

The STOP RUN Statement

The last statement in a program to be executed must be the STOP RUN; it is at line 74 in the mainline module. This statement terminates execution of the program and returns control to the operating system.

The PERFORM Statement

During execution of a program, statements are executed one after the other in the order in which they are encountered. The PERFORM is an exception to this because it causes control to be transferred to statements in another paragraph, as illustrated in Figure 1-10. Because the paragraph is executed out of the normal line of statements, it is often called an **out-of-line** sequence. When the statements of the out-of-line paragraph have been executed, control is returned to the statement following the PERFORM. As you will learn, the PERFORM statement with its out-of-line capabilities forms the basis for programming techniques stressed in this book.

Whereas the PERFORM of line 67 causes a paragraph to be executed one time, the following PERFORM (lines 70 and 71) causes repeated execution (looping) of the 200-PROCESS-PATRON-RECORD paragraph:

```
PERFORM 200-PROCESS-PATRON-RECORD
    UNTIL WS-EOF-SWITCH IS EQUAL TO "YES".
```

That is, this paragraph will be executed repeatedly until the WORKING-STORAGE variable WS-EOF-SWITCH contains YES. (Remember, the AT END clause of the READ statement moves YES into this data item when the EOF record is read.) The logic of this repeated execution is illustrated in Figure 1-11.

Overall Execution of the Program

Throughout this book, you will encounter statements such as, "execution of the MOVE statement causes. . . ." and ". . . this paragraph will be executed repeatedly. . . ." As you will learn in Concepts Module B, the COBOL program statements are not executed directly. They are first converted to the computer's machine language; then the resulting machine language program is executed. Hence, you should always interpret a description such as "this paragraph will be executed repeatedly" as meaning "the machine language program elements resulting from this paragraph will be executed repeatedly."

Execution of a program begins with the first statement following PROCEDURE DIVISION and continues statement by statement until the end of the program is encountered. To illustrate, let's walk through this program (Figure 1-9) to trace the logic flow. For this exercise, assume that the patron file contains two data records (plus the EOF record); the sequence of execution would be as shown on the opposite page.

Figure 1-10   The PERFORM statement.

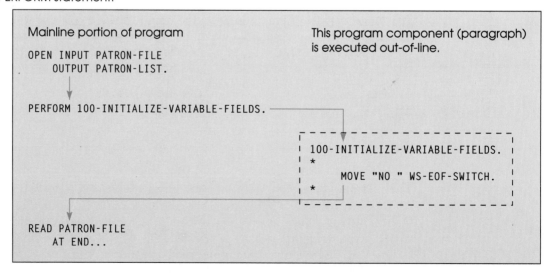

Figure 1-11
Logic of the PERFORM
statement.

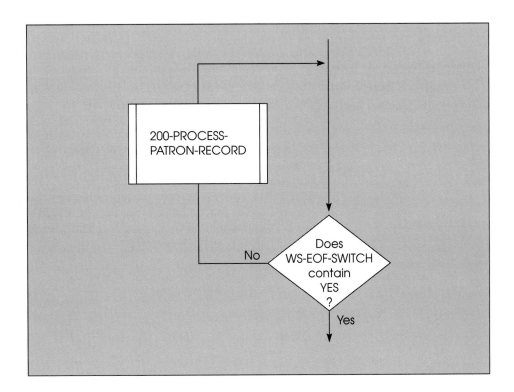

Program line # statement(s)	Action
65–66	Open the input and output files.
67	Transfer control to the 100-INITIALIZE-VARIABLE-FIELDS paragraph.
76–77	Initialize by moving NO to the control field WS-EOF-SWITCH. When completed with this paragraph, return control to line 68.
68–69	Read the first record from the data file. This is a data record (not the EOF), so do not execute the MOVE. Return control to line 70.
70–71	Check to determine if WS-EOF-SWITCH contains YES. It does not, so transfer control to the 200-PROCESS-PATRON-RECORD paragraph at line 79.
80–83	Move spaces to output area. Move data from the input area to the output area.
84–85	Print the line after advancing the paper two lines.
86–87	Read the next (second) record from the data file. This is a data record (not the EOF), so do not execute the MOVE. Execution is at the end of 200-PROCESS-PATRON-RECORD, so return control to line 70.
70–71	Check to determine if WS-EOF-SWITCH contains YES. It does not, so transfer control to the 200-PROCESS-PATRON-RECORD paragraph at line 79.
80–83	Move spaces to output area. Move data from the input area to the output area.
84–85	Print the line after advancing the paper two lines.
86–87	Read the next (third) record from the data file. This is the EOF, so move YES to WS-EOF-SWITCH. Execution is at the end of 200-PROCESS-PATRON-RECORD, so transfer control to line 70.
70–71	Check to determine if WS-EOF-SWITCH contains YES. It does, so do not execute the PERFORM, but continue to the next statement.
72–73	Close the files.
74	Terminate execution of the program.

Preparing the Program for Entry Into the Computer
The Coding Form

When COBOL was first devised, most programs were punched into 80-column cards and read into the computer by special card readers. As a result, the capacity of the card was a determining factor in defining how a COBOL program should be prepared. Even though cards have been widely (although not entirely) replaced by video terminals, the effects of card capacity do remain. For example, a statement in the PROCEDURE DIVISION cannot begin on the line before position (column) 12. In general, it is important that you space over carefully and ensure that your entries are starting in the correct columns. For the sake of convenience, program statements are commonly written on special COBOL coding forms that are vertically ruled with the exact format required by a COBOL program. To give you an idea of how to use a coding form, part of the PATLIST program is shown in Figure 1-12 as it would be written on one. This form is divided into four major fields:

Figure 1-12   The COBOL coding form.

System					Punching Instructions						
Program *PATRON LISTING*				Graphic	Ø	0	1	1	2	Z	Card
Programmer *PRICE / WELBURN*		Date *3/22*		Punch	ZERO	ALPHA	ONE	ALPHA	TWO	ALPHA	Form #

Sequence (PAGE) (SERIAL)	CONT.	A	B	COBOL Statement
1 3 4 6	7	8 12	16 20 24 28	32 36 40 44 48 52 56
0 1		I D E N T I F I C A T I O N	D I V I S I O N .	
0 2	*			
0 3		P R O G R A M - I D .	P A T L I S T .	
0 4		A U T H O R .	P R I C E / W E L B U R N .	
0 5	*			
0 6	*		T H I S P R O G R A M P R I N T S A P A T R O N A D D R E S S L I S T .	
0 7	*			
0 8				
0 9				
1 0		D A T A D I V I S I O N .		
1 1	*			
1 2		F I L E S E C T I O N .		
1 3	*			
1 4		F D P A T R O N - F I L E		
1 5			R E C O R D C O N T A I N S 7 4 C H A R A C T E R S	
1 6			L A B E L R E C O R D S A R E S T A N D A R D .	
1 7	*			
1 8		Ø 1	P A T R O N - R E C O R D .	
1 9			0 5 P R - N A M E	P I C X (1 8) .
2 0			0 5 P R - A D D R E S S	P I C X (1 8) .

Usage	Columns
Sequence number	1–6
Continuation (or * for comment)	7
COBOL statements	8–72
Program identification	73–80 (not shown in Figure 1-12)

With keyboard entry directly into the computer, the Sequence and Identification columns are often not used; we will ignore them. However, some installations do require, as shop standards, that entries be made in one or both of these areas. Referring back to the program listing of Figure 1-5, do not confuse the numbers to the left of each statement with any portion of the coding sheet. These

Figure 1-12 (continued)

System		Punching Instructions	
Program *PATRON LISTING*	Graphic Ø O 1 I 2 Z ZERO ALPHA ONE ALPHA TWO ALPHA	Card	
Programmer *PRICE/WELBURN* Date *3/22*	Punch	Form #	

Sequence (PAGE) (SERIAL)	CONT.	A	B — COBOL Statement
0 1			PROCEDURE DIVISION.
0 2	*		
0 3		000-	PRINT-PATRON-LIST.
0 4			OPEN INPUT PATRON-FILE
0 5			OUTPUT PATRON-LIST.
0 6			PERFORM 100-INITIALIZE-VARIABLE-FIELDS.
0 7			PERFORM 800-READ-PATRON-RECORD.
0 8			PERFORM 200-PROCESS-PATRON-RECORD.
0 9			UNTIL WS-EOF-SWITCH IS EQUAL TO "YES".
1 0			CLOSE PATRON-FILE
1 1			PATRON-LIST.
1 2			STOP RUN.
1 3	*		
1 4		100-	INITIALIZE-VARIABLE-FIELDS.
1 5	*		
1 6			MOVE "NO " TO WS-EOF-SWITCH.
1 7	*		
1 8		200-	PROCESS-PATRON-RECORD.
1 9	*		
2 0			MOVE SPACES TO PATRON-LIST.

Figure 1-13
Simple conventions.

	Letter	Digit
1	*1*	*1*
2	*2*	2
3	*O*	*∅*

numbers were not entered by the programmer. Rather, they are generated by the compiler to identify lines of the program in specifying incorrect statements. Virtually all compilers create such line numbers.

If your program is to be keyed into the computer by someone other than a programmer, it is essential that you provide clear instructions regarding any symbol that might be confused with another symbol. Figure 1-13 shows three pairs of symbols commonly cause problems because of their resemblance to each other.

Notice that they are identified in the Punching Instructions area of the COBOL coding form. The conventions just described are the ones used in this text. However, some programmers slash the letter O instead of the zero. Also, rather than adding a serif to the digit 1, some programmers instead block the letter I by adding serifs at the top and bottom (I).

**Area A and Area B
Entries**

All COBOL statements of the Figure 1-5 program are entered into columns 8–72 (however, the * signifying a comment is entered into column 7). Notice in the coding sheet that column 8 is marked *A* and column 12 is marked *B*. The *A* marks the first position of *Area A* of the COBOL form, which consists of columns 8–11. Similarly, the *B* marks the first position of *Area B*, which includes columns 12–72. These positions are significant because certain COBOL entries must begin in Area A, and others must begin in Area B. Most entries that must begin in Area A will extend into Area B; this is completely acceptable. Relative to the example program in Figure 1-5, the following entries must be started in Area A:

Division headers (IDENTIFICATION, ENVIRONMENT, DATA, and PROCEDURE).

Section headers (including FILE SECTION and WORKING-STORAGE SECTION).

Paragraph headers (including FILE-CONTROL, FD, and 01).

Procedure division paragraph headers.

All other entries must begin in Area B. When entering a program, you must be careful to use the proper number of spaces so that your entry starts in the proper area. *Do not use the tab key to space across* unless you are using an editor especially designed for COBOL that replaces the tab character with an appropriate number of spaces.

In COBOL-74, no program entry can go beyond column 72. However, the COBOL-85 standard does not specify an end to Area B. Hence, you might encounter a compiler that allows a COBOL statement to go beyond column 72. This is an option that the manufacturer of the compiler can take.

Chapter Summary

This completes your "first cut" at COBOL. With this summary view of a simple, but complete, COBOL program, you should be able to make the basic modification to it described in the programming assignment at the end of this chapter. In Chapters 2 and 3, you will learn COBOL language syntax to the level of detail necessary for you to write a variety of COBOL programs.

A COBOL program is made up of reserved words (words with special meaning to the COBOL system) and user-defined words (words defined by the programmer to identify data elements: files, records, and fields).

The four broad elements of a COBOL program:

- IDENTIFICATION DIVISION — Documents the program.

- ENVIRONMENT DIVISION — Specifies computer hardware and the data files.

- DATA DIVISION — Defines files, records, and fields.

- PROCEDURE DIVISION — Expresses the program logic.

The IDENTIFICATION DIVISION is the first entry in the program; this division contains the program identification and documentary information.

The ENVIRONMENT DIVISION is the link between the hardware-independent COBOL program and the actual computer input/output devices, including auxiliary storage units on which data files to be processed are saved. The sample program has two sections: CONFIGURATION SECTION and INPUT-OUTPUT SECTION.

The DATA DIVISION contains descriptions of all data items—files, records, fields, and subfields—used by the COBOL program. The DATA DIVISION for a typical program contains two sections: the FILE SECTION and the WORKING-STORAGE SECTION.

Each record description entry of the DATA DIVISION includes a level number and a user-defined name. A field that is not broken down further (called an elementary item) also includes a PIC clause defining the data class and size.

The WORKING-STORAGE SECTION is used to define fields that are required in the program but are not part of an input or output record.

The PROCEDURE DIVISION contains procedural statements describing the actions to be taken in processing the data. Statements used in this chapter are: OPEN, CLOSE, READ, MOVE, WRITE, STOP RUN, and PERFORM. Looping (repetition) capabilities are provided by the PERFORM/UNTIL.

When entering a COBOL program, you must be aware of Area A (columns 8–11) and Area B (columns 12–72). Division headers, section headers, paragraph headers, and procedure division paragraph headers must begin in Area A. All other entries begin in the Area B.

Exercises
Terms for Definition

Area A _____

Area B _____

comment _____

COBOL division _____

CONFIGURATION SECTION _____

DATA DIVISION _____

division _____

elementary item _____

ENVIRONMENT DIVISION _____

FILE SECTION _____

FILLER _____

IDENTIFICATION DIVISION _____

indicator area _____

INPUT-OUTPUT SECTION _____

paragraph _____

PIC _____

PROCEDURE DIVISION _____

reserved word _____

section _____

sentence _____

user-defined name _____

WORKING-STORAGE SECTION _____

Review Questions   1. List, in correct sequence, the four COBOL divisions and briefly describe the general purpose of each.

     Division/Purpose

    a. _____

      _____

    b. _____

      _____

    c. _____

      _____

    d. _____

      _____

2. Name the DIVISION to which each of the following sections belongs:

    a. WORKING-STORAGE SECTION.   _____

    b. INPUT-OUTPUT SECTION.   _____

    c. FILE SECTION.   _____

    d. CONFIGURATION SECTION.   _____

3. Identify the DIVISION and SECTION (if applicable) to which each of the following paragraphs belongs:

    a. PROGRAM-ID.   _____

    b. OBJECT-COMPUTER.   _____

    c. 000-PRINT-PATRON-LIST.   _____

    d. FILE-CONTROL. _____

    e. SOURCE-COMPUTER. _____

4. The reserved word FD is an abbreviation for what?

_____

5. What type of entry does the level-number 01 signify?

_____

6. What type of entry do the level-numbers 02 through 49 signify?

_____

7. Describe briefly what each of the following COBOL reserved words does:

    a. ASSIGN _____

_____

    b. AT END _____

_____

    c. CLOSE _____

_____

    d. MOVE _____

_____

    e. OPEN _____

_____

    f. PERFORM _____

_____

    g. PERFORM UNTIL _____

_____

    h. READ _____

_____

    i. SELECT _____

_____

    j. STOP RUN _____

_____

    k. WRITE _____

_____

8. For each of the following line numbers, describe what the effect on the program in Figure 1-5 would be if that line were removed.

a. 86, 87 _____

b. 70, 71 _____

c. 67 _____

d. 84, 85 _____

e. 80 _____

f. 50 _____

g. 13 _____

Programming Assignments

Programming Assignment 1-1: Patron Address
Enter, compile, and run the PATLIST program of Figure 1-5.

Programming Assignment 1-2: Patron Address/Contribution List
Input file: The Patron file (PATRON.DAT).

Input-record format:
Note: The following record definition corresponds to the record description in the PATLIST program of Figure 1-5.

Positions	Field name	Data class
1–18	Patron name	Alphanumeric
19–36	Patron street address	Alphanumeric
37–60	Patron city/state/zip	Alphanumeric
61–64	Target contribution	Numeric
65–68	Actual contribution	Numeric
69–74	Contribution date	
69–70	Contribution month	Alphanumeric
71–72	Contribution day	Alphanumeric
73–74	Contribution year	Alphanumeric

Required output:
The program is to print an address list of all contributors in the patron file. The printed report must include the following input fields separated by two spaces.

Output report data items:
Name
Address
City-state-zip
Actual contribution amount

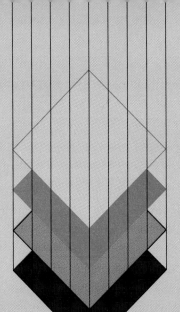

The Program Development Process

Module Objectives

The purpose of this concepts module is to give you an insight to the process of designing and writing a computer program (the program development process). From this module, you will learn the following:

- The four phases of program development: the specification phase, the design phase, the coding phase, and the testing phase.

- The importance of clearly defining exactly what is to be done before proceeding with the programming task (specification phase).

- The use of three commonly used tools for designing a program (solving the problem): structure charts and top-down design, flowcharting, and pseudocode.

- The converting of a design into a computer program in COBOL (the coding phase).

- The process of compiling, whereby the computer converts a COBOL program to machine language.

- The testing phase, during which all aspects of the program are tested to ensure that the program functions as intended.

Module Outline

Four Phases of Program
   Development

The Specification Phase
Determine the Needs of the Users
Input Data Format
Designing a New Data File—Field Length
Illustrative Layouts of the Output Record
Programming Specifications
Approval to Proceed to the Design Phase

The Design Phase
Program Design Tools
Structured Walkthrough

The Coding Phase
Writing the Program
Keying the Program
Compiling the Program
Syntax Errors

The Testing Phase
Debugging

Four Phases of Program Development

From Chapter 1, you have an overview of a COBOL program. You have observed its English-like nature and have seen that you can get an idea of what a program does simply by reading it. Perhaps programming appears to be much easier than you had anticipated. Actually, the task of creating the program (such as that in Figure 1-5 of Chapter 1) is not too difficult once you have mastered the language. A stereotype that many people have is that the programmer sits down, writes the program, then progresses to the next task.

The sequence of steps that you will follow is much more structured than that. Before a program can be written, the precise functions that it is to accomplish must be identified. In many small organizations, or in a large one in which the scope of an application program is limited, the complete program development process is often done by one programmer. On the other hand, for large applications, the process is commonly handled by a group consisting of systems analysts, programmers, and/or programmer/analysts. Most of the programming examples you will experience in this book are relatively small tasks; they would typically be handled by a single programmer in a business environment.

The overall program development process consists of four phases: the specification phase, the design phase, the coding phase, and the testing phase. These are illustrated in Figure B-1. The vehicle for illustrating program development is the patron address listing of Fleetwood Charities described in Chapter 1.

The Specification Phase

Assume that you work as a programmer for the Fleetwood Charities. Your department has been assigned the task of setting up a new patron information system. Stored in the computer's disk storage unit will be a patron file that will contain comprehensive data for each patron, including:

Patron name

Street address

City/state/zip

Target contribution

Actual contribution

Contribution date

Your supervisor has assigned you the task of writing a program to produce an address list of the Fleetwood's patrons. The printed report must identify patrons contributing less than their target amount. (Note that this is an expansion of the PATLIST program of Chapter 1.)

Although you have a "reasonably good idea" of the report your users desire, it is hardly the basis upon which to develop your program. Your cursory perception of the users' needs and what they actually desire may be completely different. In reality, precise documentation is required for (1) the format of the output report to be printed, (2) the nature of the input data to be used, and (3) the general processing actions that the program will follow. So, during the specification phase of the program development process, you will need to do the following:

1. Work with people that will be using the output from your program to determine what they need. From this, determine the input data that will be required to furnish the desired output.

Figure B-1
The program development process.

THE PROGRAM DEVELOPMENT PROCESS

1. The Specification Phase

Programmer/analyst
- meets with user
- documents record layouts and programming specifications
- prepares system flowchart
- obtains approval to proceed

2. The Design Phase

Programmer/analyst prepares program design documentation.

(Completes design review, structure charts, pseudocode, program flowcharts, etc.)

3. The Coding Phase

Programmer writes, keys, and compiles the source program.

4. The Testing Phase

Programmer and others ensure that the program is processing data in accordance with the programming specifications.

2. Obtain the input record format and check to ensure that the data you need to generate the desired output is available. (The term *report* means "printed output from the computer.")

3. Prepare illustrative layouts of the printed report.

4. Define program specifications that describe the overall purpose of the program, identify the inputs and outputs to be processed, and list the major processing operations that are to occur.

5. Obtain approval to proceed to the next step of the program development process. Depending upon organizational requirements, this approval may be required from your supervisor, the requesters of the program output (the users), or both.

The following expands upon these phase elements.

Determine the Needs of the Users

There is little value in developing a program that does not satisfy the needs of the users. Hence, one of your first actions is to find out what they need. (Sometimes users themselves are not too clear on this and the programmer/designer must provide "brainstorming" assistance.) From your meeting with the principal users, you determine that they need a patron list that includes:

■ Patron name

■ An indication of whether or not the patron's contribution is below the target amount

■ Full patron address

With this information, you can design a report form that readily conveys what is needed.

Input Data Format

You might encounter two scenarios when designing a program to fulfill your users' needs. On one hand, the data files from which your program is to extract the data will already exist. In this case, you will usually be restricted to working with the data at hand. You must check that each output item is available in the input data record. For instance, you cannot include the patron telephone number in the report if the telephone number is not stored in the data file. However, sometimes needed output not explicitly stored can be determined from that which is stored. For instance, a registrar might desire a student listing that includes each student's grade point average from a file that does not include that value, but does include the total grade points and units completed for each student. Calculating the desired average from these two quantities is a simple action.

On the other hand, you will sometimes encounter situations in which you must design the entire application and create the data files yourself. In cases such as this, you must carefully assess the anticipated future needs (as well as current needs) of the users.

Once the input files are identified, the exact position of each data item must be identified, since these will be used in the program. For instance, the patron data format can be given to you as the table in Figure B-2(a) or on the record layout form of Figure B-2(b).

When designing an application, you should approach the users to find out what they need. Then you should determine if it is possible to satisfy those needs with the data available or with a reasonable addition to the current data. If the desired output cannot be obtained from available input, then work with the users to reach a satisfactory solution.

Figure B-2 Input data format.

Field	Length	Class	Comments
Name	18	Alphanumeric	
Street address	18	Alphanumeric	
City/state/zip	24	Alphanumeric	
Target contribution	4	Numeric	Whole dollars
Actual contribution	4	Numeric	Whole dollars
Contribution date	6	Alphanumeric	Format *mmyydd*

Note: mmyydd means month/day/year form; for instance, November 29, 1990 would be 112990.

(a) In the form of a table.

Record layout:	Patron record					
Name	Address	City/state/zip	Target contribution	Actual contribution	Contribution date	
					Mo. Day Yr.	
0 1 2 3 4 5 6 7 8 9 10 11 12 13 14 15 16 17 18	19 20 21 22 23 24 25 26 27 28 29 30 31 32 33 34 35 36	37 38 39 40 41 42 43 44 45 46 47 48 49 50 51 52 53 54 55 56 57 58 59 60	61 62 63 64	65 66 67 68	69 70 71 72 73 74	

(b) As a record layout form.

Designing a New Data File—Field Length

In Figure A-1 of Concepts Module A, the space allocated for the name is sufficient to allow a name of reasonable length. On the other hand, much less space is allocated for the state because state abbreviations are all two letters. (You're undoubtedly seen many poorly designed forms by now. For example, you have probably filled out a form in which it was impossible to squeeze in your address and phone number in the space provided.) Within the computer, fields can range in length from one to many character positions (bytes). As with a manual system such as that of Figure A-1, the number of positions allocated for each field depends upon the nature of that field.

It is not difficult to specify the sizes of certain fields because they always consist of a predetermined number of positions. The following are some typical examples.

Field	Width	Example
State abbreviation	2	VT
Social Security number	9	569121991 (hyphens excluded)
Zip code	5	95060
	10	95060-1251 (hyphen included)
Gender (person's sex)	1	M or F

On the other hand, names and quantity fields (including dollar-amount) are not as easy to gauge. For example, how many positions should be provided for the name, address, and city fields of Figure A-1? How much space should be provided for a product description entry in a company inventory file? You do not want such fields so small that you must always abbreviate. However, you should not make them so large that a significant amount of storage space is unused (even with the relatively low cost of today's computer storage). The following table can be used as a guideline in selecting certain alphanumeric field sizes.

Field	This many characters will accommodate...	... this percentage of expected values
Individual last name	11	98%
Individual full name	18	95%
Company name	20	95%
Street address	18	90%
City name	17	99%

Source: Identification Techniques. IBM Publication GC20-1707. Form and Card Design. IBM Publication GC20-8078.

In determining the maximum size of numeric fields, a degree of good judgement must also be used. For instance, a growing company that manufactures electronic instruments might anticipate that they will never have more than 5,000 units of a particular item in stock. Hence, a field width of four would accommodate 9,999 units. Making the width five (an increase of only one position) would most certainly accommodate any unexpected large growth.

Illustrative Layouts of the Output Record

Once you have precisely defined the user's needs, you must lay out the report page format by indicating where each field is to be printed. For this you use a **print chart**, a gridlike form to define an output report to be produced on a computer printer. You can use the print chart to experiment with the order of data items on a line, the amount of space between items, and so forth. Similar to a blueprint for a building, the completed print chart serves as a preview of how the computer-printed report will look. Later in the program development process, it will be used as a reference when writing the program code.

A print chart that you might prepare is shown in Figure B-3. The preprinted numbers running horizontally across the top of the print chart denote the print positions for each report line. The numbers running vertically down the left side of the chart represent the print lines for each page of the report. The series of X's are programmer entries that depict positions on the line where data is to be printed. Hence, this print chart depicts that output will be printed as follows:

Print Position	Field (data item)
2–19	Name
21–38	Address
40–63	City/state/zip
65–66	Double asterisk for under-target patrons

Notice that the printed line is shown twice; that is, one line of X's is shown at line 7 and the second at line 9. The blank line between the two indicates that the report lines are to be double-spaced. This is a common method for indicating line spacing. As an alternative, some programmers simply write a note describing the vertical line-spacing specifications.

Figure B-3 The patron-address list print chart.

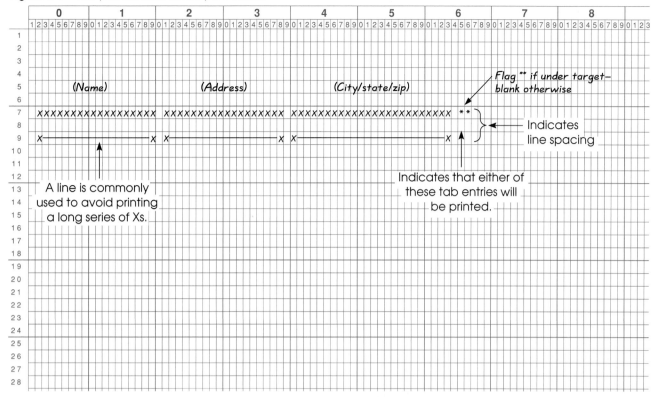

The patron listing of Chapter 1 is an example of **hard-copy output**: output that is printed on a page, thereby providing a permanent copy. Many applications require interaction between the user and the computer via the keyboard and a video display terminal. For instance, a payroll clerk may need to check the actual contribution for a patron by keying in the patron number and having the computer display pertinent patron data on the terminal screen. This is called **soft copy** because no permanent copy is produced; the screen display disappears the instant other information is displayed. Screen layouts are designed in much the same way as printer layouts: by laying everything out on a form. However, rather than use pencil and paper, special screen painting software is commonly used. This allows you to design your screen layout by using the screen as a workpad. When you complete a layout, the software will generate necessary computer code that you can use in your program.

Programming Specifications

With a layout of the name-and-address record and a print chart for the proposed patron-address list, you now have graphic documentation of the input and output that the program should process to produce the patron-address list from the data file.

Before beginning a detailed design of the program, you should prepare a general description of the program functions, an identification of its input and output records, and a list of its processing operations. Together, these items constitute the **programming specifications**. A systems analyst or programmer typically writes such specifications after consultations with the user.

Figure B-4 is a typical set of programming specifications for your application. You would also need to draw an overall representation of the data flow in your system. This is called a **system flowchart** and is shown in Figure B-5.

Figure B-4
The patron-address list
programming specifications.

> ## PROGRAMMING SPECIFICATIONS
>
> **Program name:** PATRON LIST   **Program ID:** PATLIST2
> (with under-target patrons identified)
>
> ---
>
> **Program Description:**
>
> This program is to print an patron address list from
> input patron records. Patrons contributing less than
> their target amount are identified.
>
> **Input File:**
>
> Patron File
>
> **Output File:**
>
> Patron Address List
>
> **List of Program Operations:**
>
> A. Read each input patron record.
>
> B. For each record, print the following fields on
> the employee address list in accordance with the
> format shown on the print chart:
> > Patron name
> > Patron address
> > Patron city/state/zip
> > Two consecutive asterisk characters (**) if the
> > contributed amount is less than the target amount.
>
> C. Double-space each printed line.

Figure B-5
Patron-address list system
flowchart.

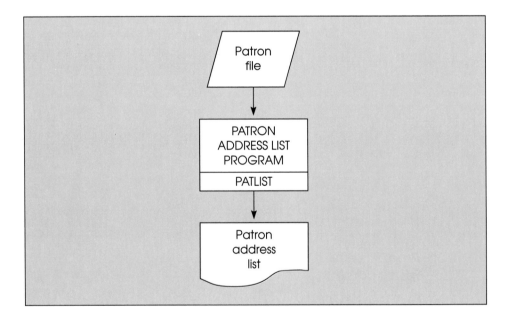

Approval to Proceed to the Design Phase

Before you get into the detail of designing a program, it is important that you review the record layouts and programming specifications with the users who will use the outputs that the program is to produce. This approval process helps to ensure that you have correctly interpreted the application requirements. If errors or problem areas occur within the specifications, they are identified and corrected before you invest program design time and labor in the project.

In many organizations, particularly larger ones, the approval may be formalized by signature—"signing off"—on the specifications or on a special form designed for this purpose. Once approval is gained, you can proceed to the design phase.

In the early phases of most beginning programming courses, students experience relatively little of the specification phase. That is, input data format, output format, and the actions to be performed are clearly defined. Furthermore, there are no users to consult regarding their wishes for the output. The general focus is on learning and using the language effectively. However, in the workplace, the specification phase is critical.

The Design Phase

The first few programs that you write will be relatively basic and you will probably find them fairly easy to visualize. However, most real–life programs are large, complex, and require many conditional operations; thus, they are difficult to visualize. The programmer who begins writing code without first carefully analyzing all aspects of the problem will become hopelessly bogged down.

In some respects, designing a program is much like building a house. Long before the carpenter begins sawing wood and pounding nails, an architect must draw detailed plans regarding the work to be done. Designing and writing a program is no different: the solution must be worked out before detailed coding can begin.

Unfortunately, after receiving a programming assignment, students usually want to code immediately. It is hardly practical to write detailed instructions to the computer for solving a problem if you do not yet know how to solve it yourself.

Program Design Tools

Many program design techniques and tools are available to the program designer. For the programs in this text, three design tools will be used: structure charts, pseudocode, and program flowcharts. These tools are illustrated in Figure B-6 for the PATLIST program.

A **structure chart** is a block representation of a program, showing the components of the program based on the function that each performs. It is founded on the notion that a large problem is more easily solved by breaking it into independent components than by considering it as a single whole. The structure chart is a representation of what the program is to do.

On the other hand, a **flowchart** is a graphical representation of how the problem is to be solved. It pictures the sequence of steps to be taken, points at which either of two actions is taken depending upon a condition, and repetition of an activity (for instance, the COBOL PERFORM-UNTIL). You can see the way in which the program "flows" in the example of Figure B-6(b).

A **pseudocode solution** to a programming problem is an English-like description of the sequence of program actions. It is an alternate to flowcharting in that it provides for the description of the program logic. You can see this by comparing the pseudocode in Figure B-6(c) to the flowchart of Figure B-6(b).

You will learn more about these tools in Module C. They will be used in the design and solution of each example program in this book.

Structured Walkthrough

After completing and checking your program design documentation, it is wise to have someone else check your work. Such checks are valuable because people are often blind to their own errors: it is helpful to have other eyes look over your documentation as a double check. In fact, the process of explaining your design effort to one or more colleagues will often reveal erroneous or questionable design.

An organized design review such as this is called a **structured walkthrough**. (Structured walkthroughs are often also performed later on during the coding phase.) In larger organizations, a walkthrough typically takes the form of a formally scheduled and conducted meeting with perhaps six or so participants. During the walkthrough, both design weaknesses and design errors are identified. Both must be corrected. Once this is completed to the satisfaction of your reviewing colleagues, you are ready to enter the coding phase. While using this book, you will find it valuable if you cooperate with one or more students to review each other's work.

Figure B-6   Common programming tools—the PATLIST program.

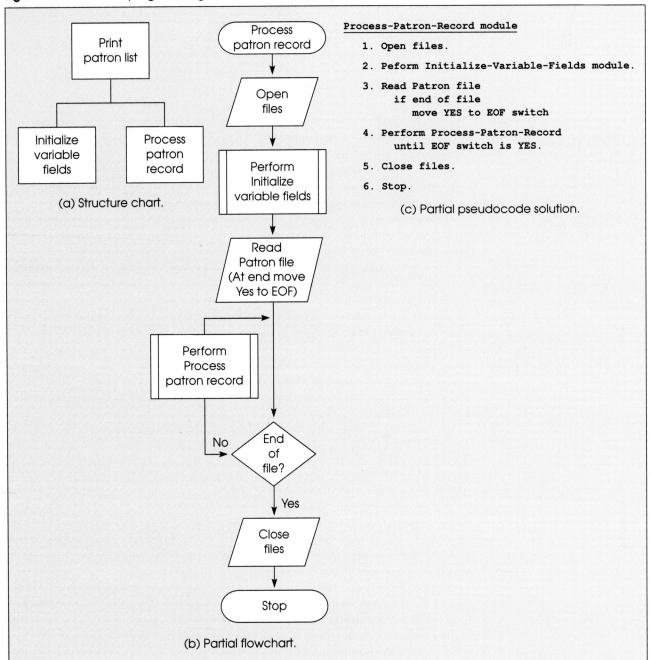

```
Process-Patron-Record module
    1. Open files.
    2. Peform Initialize-Variable-Fields module.
    3. Read Patron file
          if end of file
             move YES to EOF switch
    4. Perform Process-Patron-Record
          until EOF switch is YES.
    5. Close files.
    6. Stop.
```

(c) Partial pseudocode solution.

(a) Structure chart.

(b) Partial flowchart.

The Coding Phase   During the coding phase, you will work from the input and output documentation and the pseudocode or flowchart to prepare a working computer program. If the program design was comprehensively and properly done, the coding phase is a relatively mechanical activity. The actions you will take can be considered in the following three steps:

1. Write the program in COBOL. It is convenient to use special COBOL coding forms in order to position everything properly.

2. Key the program into the computer so that it will be in a computer-readable form.

3. Through special software, convert the COBOL program to the language of the computer on which it will be run.

Let's consider each of these steps in detail.

Writing the Program

With first programs being relatively easy to visualize, it is tempting to combine writing the program and keying it into the computer into a single operation. That is, the beginning student will sometimes be prone to composing the program at the keyboard. This might work with the small, simple programs in the first few chapters of this book, but it can lead to trouble with larger programs. You will find that a COBOL program has many interrelated components that are best laid out and implemented with pencil and paper. Although you can code your program using plain paper, it is simpler if you use COBOL coding forms such as those described in Chapter 1 (see Figure 1-12).

As you code, you will sometimes encounter operations that can be implemented better with a change in design. When this occurs, you should make appropriate adjustments to your design.

Keying the Program

The handprinted coding lines must be transferred to records on a computer-readable storage medium. For this, you will probably be working at a computer terminal with a video display screen. Your COBOL program will be entered directly into the computer and, most likely, will be stored on magnetic disk. If you are using a microcomputer, the program will usually be stored on a floppy disk. The keying process can be under the control of a special program entry utility, an editor, or even a conventional word processor. In some environments, you might punch your program into cards, one statement per card.

Compiling the Program

COBOL was designed specifically for business data-processing using a command syntax that was as nearly English-like as possible. Since the COBOL language is standardized, a COBOL program prepared for use on one make of computer can be run, with little or no modification, on another entirely different computer. Hence, COBOL is said to be *machine-independent*. This independence is in spite of the fact that the internal codes (called the machine-language) of the two computers may be entirely different. The key to program independence is a special type of program called a *language translator*, or **compiler**, that converts your program to the language of the computer you will be using. (Compilers are available from independent software companies as well as computer manufacturers.) Once you have entered your program into a machine-readable form, you must compile it. The computer, under control of the compiler, will read your COBOL program (called the **source program**) and convert the COBOL statements to equivalent machine language instructions for the particular computer. (The exact procedure for doing this depends on the type of computer you are using.) The result of this action, illustrated in Figure B-7, is an **object program** that is ready to be run. You should realize that none of the instructions in your program is being carried out during compiling; the compiler is simply performing the translation operation and creating the object program.

One of the results you will receive from the compiler is a **post-compile listing**, a complete printout of the program. It contains line numbers so that the compiler can identify particular lines that are in error. An edited version of the post-compile listing of the PATLIST2 program is shown in Figure B-8. We will study this program in the next two chapters.

Figure B-7
The compiling process.

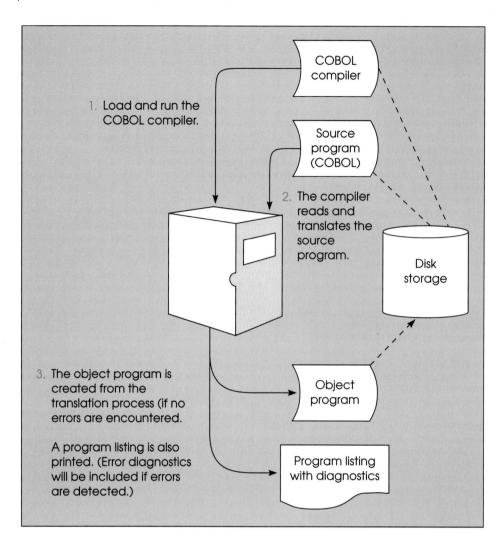

1. Load and run the COBOL compiler.

2. The compiler reads and translates the source program.

3. The object program is created from the translation process (if no errors are encountered.

   A program listing is also printed. (Error diagnostics will be included if errors are detected.)

Figure B-8
A post-compile listing of the PATLIST2 program.

```
 1        IDENTIFICATION DIVISION.
 2
 3        PROGRAM-ID.     PATLIST2.
 4        AUTHOR.         PRICE/WELBURN.
 5        INSTALLATION.   FLEETWOOD CHARITIES.
 6        DATE-WRITTEN.   9/21/90.
 7        SECURITY.       CONFIDENTIAL.
 8
 9     *     THIS PROGRAM PRINTS A PATRON ADDRESS LIST
10     *     AND FLAGS DELINQUENT PATRONS.
11
12
13        ENVIRONMENT DIVISION.
14
15        CONFIGURATION SECTION.
16
17        SOURCE-COMPUTER. (system dependent).
18        OBJECT-COMPUTER. (system dependent).
19
20        INPUT-OUTPUT SECTION.
21
22        FILE-CONTROL.
23            SELECT PATRON-FILE
24                ASSIGN TO (system dependent).
25            SELECT PATRON-LIST
26                ASSIGN TO (system dependent).
27
```

Figure B-8
(continued)

```
28
29        DATA DIVISION.
30
31        FILE SECTION.
32
33        FD  PATRON-FILE
34                RECORD CONTAINS 74 CHARACTERS
35                LABEL RECORDS ARE STANDARD.
36
37        01  PATRON-RECORD.
38            05  PR-NAME                   PIC X(18).
39            05  PR-ADDRESS                PIC X(18).
40            05  PR-CITY-STATE-ZIP         PIC X(24).
41            05  PR-TARGET-CONTR           PIC 9(4).
42            05  PR-ACTUAL-CONTR           PIC 9(4).
43            05  PR-CONTR-DATE.
44                10  PR-CONTR-MONTH        PIC X(2).
45                10  PR-CONTR-DAY          PIC X(2).
46                10  PR-CONTR-YEAR         PIC X(2).
47
48        FD  PATRON-LIST
49                RECORD CONTAINS 132 CHARACTERS
50                LABEL RECORDS ARE OMITTED.
51
52        01  PATRON-LINE.
53            05  FILLER                    PIC X(1).
54            05  PL-NAME                   PIC X(18).
55            05  FILLER                    PIC X(1).
56            05  PL-ADDRESS                PIC X(18).
57            05  FILLER                    PIC X(1).
58            05  PL-CITY-STATE-ZIP         PIC X(24).
59            05  FILLER                    PIC X(1).
60            05  PL-TARGET-FLAG            PIC X(2).
61            05  FILLER                    PIC X(66).
62
63        WORKING-STORAGE SECTION.
64
65        01  WS-SWITCHES.
66            05  WS-EOF-SWITCH             PIC X(3).
67
68
69        PROCEDURE DIVISION.
70
71        000-PRINT-PATRON-LIST.
72            OPEN INPUT PATRON-FILE
73                 OUTPUT PATRON-LIST.
74            PERFORM 100-INITIALIZE-VARIABLE-FIELDS.
75            READ PATRON-FILE
76                AT END MOVE "YES" TO WS-EOF-SWITCH.
77            PERFORM 200-PROCESS-PATRON-RECORD
78                UNTIL WS-EOF-SWITCH IS EQUAL TO "YES".
79            CLOSE PATRON-FILE
80                  PATRON-LIST.
81            STOP RUN.
82
83        100-INITIALIZE-VARIABLE-FIELDS.
84            MOVE "NO " TO WS-EOF-SWITCH.
85
86        200-PROCESS-PATRON-RECORD.
87            MOVE SPACES TO PATRON-LINE.
88            MOVE PR-NAME TO PL-NAME.
89            MOVE PR-ADDRESS TO PL-ADDRESS.
90            MOVE PR-CITY-STATE-ZIP TO PL-CITY-STATE-ZIP.
91            IF PR-ACTUAL-CONTR IS LESS THAN PR-TARGET-CONTR
92                MOVE "**" TO PL-TARGET-FLAG.
93            WRITE PATRON-LINE
94                AFTER ADVANCING 2 LINES.
95            READ PATRON-FILE
96                AT END MOVE "YES" TO WS-EOF-SWITCH.
```

Syntax Errors   As you learned in Chapter 1, COBOL is English-like in its form; you can read a COBOL program and have an idea of what it does without knowing very much about COBOL. However, the rules for writing COBOL statements are very rigorous. For instance, the statement

```
ADD CHARGES-IN, SERVICE-CHARGE GIVING CHARGES-TOTAL
```

is a valid COBOL statement, whereas

```
ADD CHARGES-IN AND SERVICE-CHARGE GIVING CHARGES-TOTAL
```

is incorrect. It does not conform to the COBOL syntax rules. Referring to Figure B-7, the compiler will indicate that this is an error with a diagnostic message.

In general, the type of errors that the compiler can detect are called **syntactical** or **syntax errors**. Just as the author of a composition can make syntax errors in the use of the English language, a programmer can make syntax errors in the use of the COBOL language. Whenever syntax errors are identified by the compiler on the program listing, you must correct the erroneous code of the source program by rekeying the affected entries. Then you must recompile the source program. A compilation in which the compiler does not find any syntax errors is referred to as a *clean compile*. Upon achieving a clean compile, you can begin testing the resulting object program.

The Testing Phase

A distinction exists between editing a novel for correct English grammar and reviewing it for story quality. That is, a novel can be grammatically correct, but still have a bad plot. Similarly, just because you obtain a clean compile does not mean that the program will operate correctly. Your program can include errors that will cause it to execute incorrectly. There are two general types of such errors: logic errors and runtime errors.

Logic errors occur when you tell the computer to perform the wrong operation. For instance, you tell it to subtract the sales tax from the purchase amount rather than add the two. The computer will proceed with no complaint, but the result will be incorrect. Runtime errors occur when you tell the computer to do something it cannot do. For instance, if your program divides total points by a count and the count is 0, you have an operation that the computer cannot perform. When something like this occurs, the computer usually will terminate your program. Programmers commonly refer to this as a program *crash*.

Debugging   The task of finding program errors, or bugs, ordinarily is called **debugging** the program. If you are thorough during the design phase, the number of logic and runtime errors should be relatively few. However, yo*u must never assume that the output you obtain from a computer is correct simply because it is printed by the computer.* The computer does only as you direct it.

It is critical that your test data checks all aspects of your program and exercises every possible option. It is not uncommon for a program to be in production use for months before an especially unusual data combination causes an erroneous sequence of code to be executed. Most of us have seen newspaper articles about a person receiving a monthly $176.87 Social Security check made out for the amount $1,000,176.87, or another person who was continually harassed by the computer for "owing" –1 cent on a charge account.

Finding an error is sometimes very difficult; erroneous results that you see in one part of a program can be the result of an action performed in a completely different part of the program. On the other hand, one of the beauties of program modularization is that modules can often be tested individually, thereby localizing errors and vastly simplifying the debugging process. You will learn more about such techniques later in this book.

Once the program testing is complete, the program can be placed into the production environment and periodically run, thereby performing the task for which it was written.

Module Summary

The program development process typically consists of four phases: the specification phase, the design phase, the coding phase, and the testing phase.

In the **specification phase**, the following documentation is obtained or prepared:

1. Illustrative input and output **record layouts**.

2. **Programming specifications** that briefly describe the program and its operations.

3. **Approval to proceed** to the design phase.

During the **design phase**, programmers commonly prepare a **structure chart** to depict program task relationships on a hierarchical basis. Each of these tasks may then be expressed in **pseudocode** (an English-like program documentation form), depicted graphically in a **program flowchart,** or represented by some other program design and documentation technique. The correctness of the program design is checked by holding a **structured walkthrough** review of the design documentation.

The **coding phase** is that portion of the process in which the design of the preceding phase is converted to a coded program through the following steps:

1. Write the source program.

2. Key in the program.

3. Compile the program.

Failing to follow the language rules (using the wrong syntax) causes the compiler to generate a diagnostic message that pinpoints the incorrect usage. These errors must be corrected and the program recompiled.

Once a clean compile is achieved, the **testing phase** begins, during which the program is tested by running it using data that exercises all elements of the program. Two types of errors can occur: runtime and logic. A runtime error is one that directs the computer to perform an operation of which it is incapable (for example, divide by zero). A logic error is one in which the programmer has directed the computer to do something other than that for which was intended (for example, subtract rather than add).

Exercises

Terms for Definition

clean compile _____

coding _____

compilation process _____

compiler _____

debugging _____

diagnostic messages _____

display screen layout _____

logic error _____

object program _____

print chart _____

program bug _____

program design tools _____

program flowchart _____

programming specifications _____

program testing _____

pseudocode _____

record-layout form _____

report _____

runtime error _____

source program _____

structure chart _____

structured walkthrough _____

syntax errors _____

system flowchart _____

Review Questions   1. Name the four phases of the program development process.

   a. _____

   b. _____

   c. _____

   d. _____

2. During which phase of the program development process is each of the following tasks typically performed?

   a. Key program _____

   b. Write programming specifications _____

   c. Write the program _____

   d. Prepare a pseudocode solution _____

   e. Debug program _____

   f. Prepare a structure chart _____

   g. Test the program _____

   h. Lay out the form of the printed report _____

   i. Compile program _____

    j.   Draw system flowchart _____

    k.   Correct syntactical errors _____

3. A print layout chart is used for what purpose?

    _____

    _____

4. What do you call a chart that depicts the hierarchy of program tasks?

    _____

5. _____ is the generic name for an English-like program documentation language.

6. What is a flowchart?

    _____

    _____

7. A group review of program design or coding is referred to as a(n)

    _____.

8. Distinguish between a source program and an object program.

    _____

    _____

9. Name the three types of errors which can appear in a program.

    a.   _____

    b.   _____

    c.   _____

10. Printed output from running a computer program is often called a(n)

    _____.

11. It is rumored that a computer scientist once said, "Resist the urge to code." What does this mean and why is that a good idea?

    _____

    _____

Writing a COBOL Program: The IDENTIFICATION, ENVIRONMENT, and DATA Divisions

Special Note   *This book addresses two versions of COBOL: the 1974 Standard (COBOL-74) and the 1985 Standard (COBOL-85). The design of COBOL-85 includes features to make the language more compatible with modern programming methods. Any program written with COBOL-74 can be compiled and run under COBOL-85. However, programs using the new features of COBOL-85 are not compatible with COBOL-74 compilers. Beginning with this chapter, significant differences between the two are pointed out. However, the material is organized in such a way that if you have access only to COBOL-74 and do not wish to go into COBOL-85 at this time, you can easily skip the discussions of COBOL-85 with no loss of continuity.*

Chapter Objectives   At this point, you should now have (1) knowledge of data files and processing them, (2) an insight to the basic structure of a COBOL program, and (3) a general understanding of the program development process. In this chapter and the next one, you will be concentrating on the detailed COBOL language specifications necessary to write a COBOL program. From this chapter, you will learn the following:

- The use of some conventions and rules for preparing COBOL programs, including selecting names, positioning and spacing, punctuation, and standardized statement format representation.

- The six permissible paragraphs of the IDENTIFICATION DIVISION.

- The nature of the computer-dependent ENVIRONMENT DIVISION, which consists of two sections: the CONFIGURATION SECTION and INPUT-OUTPUT SECTION.

- The DATA DIVISION that describes the input and output to be processed by the program.

    The file-description entry (FD).
    The record description entry which defines the format of the input or output record.

- The use of level numbers in defining the record, fields within the record, and subfields.

- The PICTURE clause for describing the class and length of data fields.

- The WORKING-STORAGE SECTION in which data-items are defined that are not part of an input or output record.

Chapter Outline   **Topic: Some COBOL Standards and Practices**

Formalizing Conventions and Rules
Reserved Words
User-Defined Words
Positioning, Spacing, and Punctuation
Vertical Spacing of COBOL Coding Lines
COBOL Format Notation

A Modification to the PATLIST Program

Topic: Writing the IDENTIFICATION and ENVIRONMENT Divisions

The IDENTIFICATION DIVISION
PROGRAM-ID Paragraph
AUTHOR Paragraph
INSTALLATION Paragraph
DATE-WRITTEN Paragraph
DATE-COMPILED Paragraph
SECURITY Paragraph
Obsolescence of Entries

The ENVIRONMENT DIVISION
CONFIGURATION SECTION
  SOURCE-COMPUTER Paragraph
  OBJECT-COMPUTER Paragraph
INPUT-OUTPUT SECTION
  FILE-CONTROL Paragraph
Recap of the ENVIRONMENT DIVISION

Topic: Writing the DATA DIVISION

The FILE SECTION
File-Description (FD) Entry
  RECORD CONTAINS Clause
  LABEL RECORDS Clause
  DATA RECORD Clause
  BLOCK CONTAINS Clause
Record-Description Entry
  Level Numbers in Defining the Record, Fields, and Subfields
  Suggested Standards for Indention and Level Numbers
  FILE SECTION Data-Names
  FILLER Entries
  PICTURE Clauses
  About the 9 Picture Symbol
The WORKING-STORAGE SECTION

Topic:	**Some COBOL Standards and Practices**

Formalizing Conventions and Rules

Only very limited reference was made in Chapter 1 to such topics as defining words in COBOL, punctuation, and the forms of COBOL program entries. Let's consider these subjects in more detail before proceeding with details of programming.

Reserved Words

Those words that have predefined meanings in the COBOL language are called **reserved words**. For example, the reserved word PROGRAM-ID signals to the compiler that the next sentence should contain the program-name. For easy reference, a complete list of the reserved words for both COBOL-74 and COBOL-85 is printed on the page facing the inside back cover of this text.

Because reserved words have predefined meanings, they cannot be used as user-defined words. For instance, assume that you used the following entry to define a field of a record.

```
05  RANDOM    PIC X(4).
```

Since the word RANDOM is a reserved word, upon encountering this entry, the compiler would issue a diagnostic message.

User-Defined Words

A **user-defined word** is created by the programmer in accordance with certain rules. Although there are seventeen categories of user-defined words, the PATLIST program uses only three types: program-names, data-names, and procedure-names. A **program-name**—such as PATLIST—is used to identify the program as a whole. **Data-names** are used to identify data files, records, and data-items (fields and subfields). **Procedure-names** are used to identify sections or paragraphs within the PROCEDURE DIVISION.

Although COBOL gives you a great deal of latitude in selecting user-defined words, each must conform to the following rules:

- Be composed only of alphabetic characters (A through Z), digits (0 through 9), and hyphens (-)

- Contain at least one letter [Actually, according to the COBOL standard, procedure-names (though not data-names) may be composed entirely of digits. Such a procedure-name would be a poor choice, however, since it would be less meaningful than a name containing descriptive words.]

- Not exceed 30 characters

- Not begin or end with a hyphen

- Not contain any spaces within the word (that is, embedded blank spaces are not permitted)

- Not be the same as a reserved word

Examples of valid and invalid user-defined words are shown in Figure 2-1. When creating a user-defined word, there is a temptation to use highly abbreviated forms to avoid excessive writing and keying. Do not do this; use names that are meaningful in order to yield a program that is self-documenting. For instance, if a report total field is called REPORT-TOTAL, you have a name that is easy to

Figure 2-1 Valid and invalid user-defined words.

Valid user-defined words	Invalid user-defined words	Reason invalid
NUMBER-1-GRADE	#1-GRADE	# not allowed
GROSS-PAY	GROSS.PAY	. not allowed
GROSSPAY	GROSS PAY	Cannot contain embedded blank
GROSS-PAYROLL	-GROSS-PAYROLL	Cannot begin with hyphen
2ND-QUARTER-EARNINGS	2ND-QUARTER-EARNINGS-	Cannot end with hyphen
YTD-SOCIAL-SECURITY-TAX	YEAR-TO-DATE-SOCIAL-SECURITY-TAX	Cannot contain over 30 characters
X100	100 (as a data name)	Must contain at least one alphabetic character

remember while coding and later reviewing the program. On the other hand, RT or even R-TOTAL could easily be confused with names you have selected for other fields. Also, be careful of abbreviations. For instance, if you abbreviate REPORT using RPRT-TOTAL, it is easy to make a mistake on your abbreviation and use something else when coding the procedures (such as RPT-TOTAL).

COBOL is much like English in that the space is used to separate one word from the next. (Alt hough youcan fig urethisout becauseyourecog nize patterns, the compiler would get nowhere with an equivalent COBOL statement.) Hence, you cannot create a name consisting of two words separated by a space. For instance, REPORT TOTAL is not acceptable, whereas REPORTTOTAL is. But REPORT-TOTAL is much more readable to most people. The hyphen is included as a legal character in forming names so that you can create names that are easier to read and that better document the program. Note that a name such as INPUT-SUMMARY is valid although part of the name (INPUT) is a reserved word.

The use of hyphens in forming words is not limited to user-defined words. Even some of the reserved words contain the hyphen; for example, PROGRAM-ID.

Positioning, Spacing, and Punctuation

All COBOL entries (except comment lines) can be classified as either Area A (positions 8–11) or Area B (positions 12–72) entries. You may start Area A entries anywhere in Area A (traditionally, programmers start them in position 8). You cannot position Area B entries in Area A, but you can begin them anyplace in Area B.

You know from Chapter 1 that spacing and punctuation conventions for COBOL language entries are similar to those we use with English. Following is a summary of these COBOL rules:

- At least one blank space must appear between words. Whenever one blank space is used, any number of blank spaces may be used.

- When a period is shown in the COBOL format notation (described in a following section), the period is required in the coding entry.

- Commas and semicolons can be used to improve readability, but they are ignored by the compiler. For instance, the OPEN statement of PATLIST could be written as follows:

```
OPEN INPUT PATRON-FILE,
     OUTPUT PATRON-LIST.
```

- Whenever a period, comma, or semicolon is used, it must be followed by a blank space.

Although commas and semicolons may be used for documenting type punctuation in a COBOL program, most programmers do not use them very often—it is too easy to make a mistake. For instance, you might mistake a comma for a period or a period for a comma. Actually, if a COBOL program is written with appropriate coding-line alignment, such punctuation usually will not contribute to its readability. You will see in subsequent programs that commas are used only in a few instances.

For neatness and readability, it is a good practice to vertically align various entries of the program. For example, in the PATLIST program of Figure 1-5, all of the PIC clauses are aligned. In examples that follow, vertical alignment will be evident.

Another good style convention to follow regards writing multiple-clause entries using one coding line per clause and indenting when a sentence, statement, or clause extends over multiple lines. Figure 2-2 shows two such examples from the PATLIST program.

Indentions are typically made in four-space units. However, in a PROCEDURE DIVISION module with complex logic, you may find that four-space indents move everything too far to the right. You may wish to use two-space indents in such cases.

Vertical Spacing of COBOL Coding Lines

You can enhance program neatness and readability by inserting blank lines (using vertical spacing) to separate different parts of the program. (Note that this relates to the appearance of the source program, not to the printed program output.) For instance, you can separate each paragraph in the PROCEDURE DIVISION by one or more blank lines, thereby producing a listing that is easier to read. You can use three methods to achieve vertical spacing of the program:

- An asterisk in position 7 produces a **comment line**, causing the entire line to be ignored by the compiler. Leaving the remainder of the line blank, as done in the PATLIST program, achieves vertical spacing.

- Leave a blank line (*see Caution at the top of the next page*).

- A slash character (/) in position 7 is a **page eject** code. When the compiler detects this character while printing your source program, it positions the printer paper to the top of the next page (executes a page eject), then continues printing the program listing.

Figure 2-2
Indenting subsequent lines of a statement.

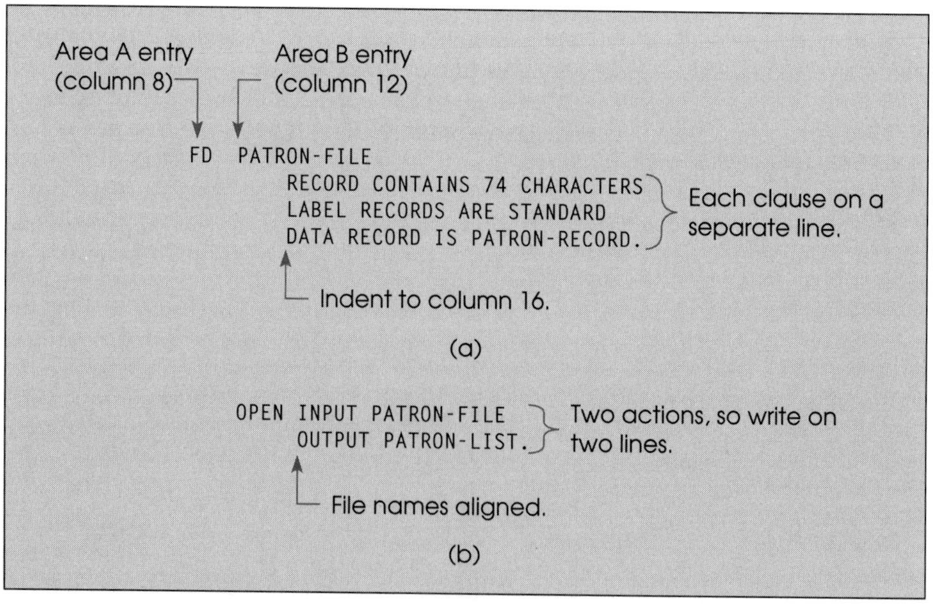

```
Area A entry                 Area B entry
(column 8)                   (column 12)

        FD   PATRON-FILE
                 RECORD CONTAINS 74 CHARACTERS      Each clause on a
                 LABEL RECORDS ARE STANDARD         separate line.
                 DATA RECORD IS PATRON-RECORD.

                    Indent to column 16.

                             (a)

                 OPEN INPUT PATRON-FILE         Two actions, so write on
                      OUTPUT PATRON-LIST.       two lines.

                    File names aligned.

                             (b)
```

Obviously, the blank statement line is simpler to use and provides a cleaner look than a blank comment line. *Caution:* some compilers remove such blanks. Hence, your carefully inserted blanks might disappear. Also, the editor furnished with at least one COBOL compiler terminates the program entry session when the Enter (Return) key is struck twice in succession. Make certain yours does not function this way.

The PATLIST program uses the * for a blank line as something that will always work. All future programs in this book use blank lines (no * in position 7). If your compiler or editor has a problem with blank lines, then use the * in position 7.

The page-eject technique can provide a generous expanse of white space, but should be used only sparingly or else you will have a very bulky program listing. However, if you want the DATA and PROCEDURE divisions to start on new pages, you could precede those division headers with a line containing a slash in position 7.

As a standard for this book, line spacing has been chosen to provide sufficient white space to make listings easily readable, yet not so generous that they consume an excessive amount of space.

- Division headers: preceded by two blank lines and followed by one (except that the PROCEDURE DIVISION is not preceded by any blank lines).

- Section headers: preceded and followed by one blank line.

- FD and 01-level entries: preceded by one blank line.

- Paragraph names (PROCEDURE DIVISION): preceded by one blank line.

COBOL Format Notation

In this chapter and those that follow, you will be looking closely at the precise syntactical format of COBOL language entries. COBOL has a standard **format notation** that was developed to present syntactical rules and requirements. A complete summary of formats is given in Appendix E for COBOL-74 and in Appendix F for COBOL-85. Following is a summary of the meanings for the various symbols used in the format notation. (A table summary is also printed on the inside back cover of this text for quick reference.)

1. Reserved words required in the statement are printed in capital letters and underscored:

   OPEN

2. Reserved words not required in the statement are printed in capital letters but *not* underscored; for instance, IS and THAN can be omitted in the following:

   IS GREATER THAN

3. Names to be supplied by the programmer are indicated in lowercase by forms such as *data–name*, *record–name*, and *paragraph–name*. The word *identifier* is commonly used in place of data–name; for example:

   ACCEPT identifier or ACCEPT data-name

4. When two or more data–names or identifiers are required in a statement, they will be called *identifier–1*, *identifier–2*, and so on:

   DIVIDE identifier-1 BY identifier-2

5. The words *comment-entry* indicate that the entry made by the programmer will be ignored by the compiler and serves solely for documentation (it is a programmer comment):

   INSTALLATION. [comment-entry]...

6. When one of two or more choices is required, the choices will be enclosed within braces, one above the other. For instance, the following means that either *identifier* or *literal* may be used:

DISPLAY { identifier / literal }

7. Brackets are used to enclose an optional part of a statement. For instance,

WRITE record-name [FROM data-name]

can also be used in the following form:

WRITE record-name

8. If the optional component may be one of two or more choices, they will be included in brackets in the same way braces represent a choice. For instance, either HIGH or LOW may be selected or they both may be omitted.

DISPLAY { identifier / literal } [HIGH / LOW]

9. Whenever an element may be used more than one time, an ellipsis (three consecutive dots) is used and the optional portion is enclosed within braces, as illustrated by the following example.

DISPLAY { identifier-1 / literal-1 } . . .

10. If a period is shown in the general form, then it is required in the COBOL entry.

11. All commas and semicolons shown in the general form are optional.

A Modification to the PATLIST Program

One topic in this chapter is not included in the PATLIST program: the IF statement, which provides you with a conditional capability. To that end, the program has been modified to identify patrons who have contributed an amount less than their target contribution. You can see by inspecting Figure 2-3 that these patrons are identified with two asterisks to the right of their output line. As you will see, this requires only two minor changes to PATLIST: one in the DATA DIVISION and the other in the PROCEDURE DIVISION.

Topic: Writing the IDENTIFICATION and ENVIRONMENT Divisions

The IDENTIFICATION DIVISION

Figure 2-4 shows the general format of the IDENTIFICATION DIVISION and an example of each of the six division entries. Notice that the words IDENTIFICATION DIVISION are underlined in the format notation. This means that they are required reserved words. A period follows the word DIVISION. If a period is shown in the format notation, it means that it is required for the COBOL entry. Division headers are always Area A entries, so they should begin in position 8 of the COBOL coding line (they *must* begin somewhere in Area A).

Figure 2-3
The PATLIST2 report with
under-target patrons
identified.

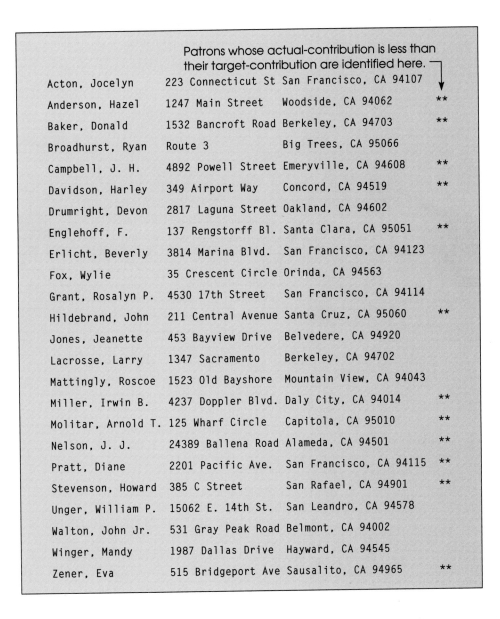

Patrons whose actual-contribution is less than
their target-contribution are identified here.

Acton, Jocelyn	223 Connecticut St San Francisco, CA 94107	
Anderson, Hazel	1247 Main Street Woodside, CA 94062	**
Baker, Donald	1532 Bancroft Road Berkeley, CA 94703	**
Broadhurst, Ryan	Route 3 Big Trees, CA 95066	
Campbell, J. H.	4892 Powell Street Emeryville, CA 94608	**
Davidson, Harley	349 Airport Way Concord, CA 94519	**
Drumright, Devon	2817 Laguna Street Oakland, CA 94602	
Englehoff, F.	137 Rengstorff Bl. Santa Clara, CA 95051	**
Erlicht, Beverly	3814 Marina Blvd. San Francisco, CA 94123	
Fox, Wylie	35 Crescent Circle Orinda, CA 94563	
Grant, Rosalyn P.	4530 17th Street San Francisco, CA 94114	
Hildebrand, John	211 Central Avenue Santa Cruz, CA 95060	**
Jones, Jeanette	453 Bayview Drive Belvedere, CA 94920	
Lacrosse, Larry	1347 Sacramento Berkeley, CA 94702	
Mattingly, Roscoe	1523 Old Bayshore Mountain View, CA 94043	
Miller, Irwin B.	4237 Doppler Blvd. Daly City, CA 94014	**
Molitar, Arnold T.	125 Wharf Circle Capitola, CA 95010	**
Nelson, J. J.	24389 Ballena Road Alameda, CA 94501	**
Pratt, Diane	2201 Pacific Ave. San Francisco, CA 94115	**
Stevenson, Howard	385 C Street San Rafael, CA 94901	**
Unger, William P.	15062 E. 14th St. San Leandro, CA 94578	
Walton, John Jr.	531 Gray Peak Road Belmont, CA 94002	
Winger, Mandy	1987 Dallas Drive Hayward, CA 94545	
Zener, Eva	515 Bridgeport Ave Sausalito, CA 94965	**

Figure 2-4
The IDENTIFICATION
DIVISION.

Format:

IDENTIFICATION DIVISION.
PROGRAM-ID. program-name.
[AUTHOR. [comment entry]. . .]
[INSTALLATION. [comment entry]. . .]
[DATE-WRITTEN. [comment entry]. . .]
[DATE-COMPILED. [comment entry]. . .]
[SECURITY. [comment entry]). . .]

Example:

```
IDENTIFICATION DIVISION.
PROGRAM-ID.   PATLIST.
AUTHOR.       PRICE/WELBURN.
INSTALLATION. FLEETWOOD CHARITIES.
DATE-WRITTEN. 9/21/90
DATE-COMPILED.
SECURITY.     CONFIDENTIAL.
```

Following the division header are the six allowable paragraphs of this division. Referring to the general form in Figure 2-4, notice that:

- All these paragraph headers are reserved words

- Each paragraph-header word is followed by a period

- Only the first paragraph (PROGRAM-ID) is required

Furthermore, each paragraph header is an Area A entry. Let's consider each of them.

PROGRAM-ID Paragraph

The first paragraph in the IDENTIFICATION DIVISION is the **PROGRAM-ID paragraph**. Referring to the general form in Figure 2-4, notice that it is the only required entry of this division. Following the paragraph header, you must enter the program-name. You may have noticed that the name used for the example program is PATLIST (rather than PATRON-LIST). This choice appears to be contrary to the earlier advice of using hyphens and avoiding abbreviations in order to maintain good readability.

The reason the shorter name was selected is that program-names are a special type of user-defined word. A program-name is used by the computer operating system to identify the program. The file-name length restrictions on most operating systems are much less than the generous 30 characters allowed for COBOL words; some operating systems do not allow the hyphen. If you choose a name longer than that allowed by the operating system, the operating system will truncate to the maximum length when storing the program. This can result in two or more programs with the same name and the potential loss of one or more of them. Since most operating systems accommodate eight-character names, that standard is used in this book. You should find out what you can use on your system.

AUTHOR Paragraph

All remaining paragraphs in this division are optional (as indicated by the brackets in the general form), including the AUTHOR paragraph. If it is included in a program, a comment-entry should be written after the AUTHOR paragraph header. Referring to Item 5 (page 57) of the format notation summary, notice that a **comment-entry** is any documenting type entry that you wish to make (it can be any combination of characters acceptable to the computer). Thus, the rules for user-defined words need not be strictly observed when forming a comment-entry. Obviously, its intended use is for entry of the person's name who wrote the program.

INSTALLATION Paragraph

The optional **INSTALLATION paragraph** is used to specify the name of the company or organization data-processing installation for which the program is written. Refer to the example in Figure 2-4. As with the AUTHOR paragraph, this is a comment-entry.

DATE-WRITTEN Paragraph

The date when the COBOL program was written is recorded in the optional **DATE-WRITTEN paragraph**. It usually takes longer than one day to write a COBOL program. Thus, some programmers record the day the program was started; others merely indicate the month and year.

DATE-COMPILED Paragraph

The date when the COBOL program was compiled is placed in the optional **DATE-COMPILED paragraph**. If this comment-entry is left blank, most compilers will insert the actual compiling date automatically.

This is actually redundant information because most compilers automatically print the date and time of the compilation at the top of each page of the program listing. Date and time information is important because when programmers are testing and debugging programs, they usually accumulate a collection of program listings. Inclusion of date information helps to identify the most recent version.

SECURITY Paragraph   The optional **SECURITY paragraph** is often omitted. It does have two occasional uses, though. One is to indicate a governmental security classification: UNCLASSIFIED, CLASSIFIED, SECRET, TOP SECRET, and so on. Another is to provide copyright or trade-secret protection information.

  The only required paragraph in the IDENTIFICATION DIVISION is the PROGRAM-ID paragraph. A minimum-entry IDENTIFICATION DIVISION paragraph would thus contain only the division header and the PROGRAM-ID paragraph. However, the optional paragraphs provide useful documentation.

Obsolescence   Although all the IDENTIFICATION DIVISION optional entries are supported in
of Entries   COBOL-85, they are scheduled to be deleted from the next COBOL standard. Hence, you may wish to use comment lines to encode the same information in your programs, ensuring compatibility with the next COBOL standard.

The ENVIRONMENT DIVISION

Although almost the entire COBOL program can be prepared independent of the specific equipment for which it is written, the coding of the ENVIRONMENT DIVISION is dependent upon the computer, compiler, and/or operating system being used. Each vendor that supplies a COBOL compiler assigns words, called **system-names**, to specific computer models, input/output devices, and other operating features of the environment. The system-names chosen by one vendor usually differ from those selected by another. This somewhat complicates discussion of the ENVIRONMENT DIVISION because many different vendors supply COBOL compilers.

  As you learned in Chapter 1, entries of this division that are dependent on the system you are using are so noted as system-dependent entries. Appendix C presents forms used by several common COBOL systems.

  Regardless of the compiler used, the ENVIRONMENT DIVISION does have a standard format, an abbreviated version of which is illustrated in Figure 2-5. You can see that it consists of two sections: the CONFIGURATION SECTION and the INPUT-OUTPUT SECTION. As indicated, this division and the CONFIGURATION SECTION are required (the INPUT-OUTPUT SECTION is optional, as indicated by the brackets). This is the COBOL-74 standard. In COBOL-85, both sections are optional; in fact, the entire division is optional. You can see this in the general summary of Appendix F.

  As with all division headers, the ENVIRONMENT DIVISION header must begin in Area A and must be terminated with a period.

CONFIGURATION   **SOURCE-COMPUTER Paragraph.**   The **SOURCE-COMPUTER paragraph**
SECTION   defines the computer that will be used to compile the source COBOL program. Following the paragraph header, the system-name for the computer is specified. If your system requires this entry, then you should obtain it from an instructor or lab director. This paragraph is optional in COBOL-85.

Figure 2-5
The ENVIRONMENT DIVISION.

```
Format:

    ENVIRONMENT DIVISION.
    CONFIGURATION SECTION.
    SOURCE-COMPUTER. computer-name.
    OBJECT-COMPUTER. computer-name.
    [INPUT-OUTPUT SECTION.
    FILE-CONTROL.
        SELECT file-name
            ASSIGN TO implementor-name.]
```

OBJECT-COMPUTER Paragraph. The computer that will execute the compiled program is defined in the **OBJECT-COMPUTER paragraph**. Usually the same computer is used for both compilation and execution. This means that the SOURCE-COMPUTER and OBJECT-COMPUTER computer-name entries are typically the same. The standard also allows three other optional entries describing the computer—see Appendix E or F.

INPUT-OUTPUT SECTION

The INPUT-OUTPUT SECTION defines the input and output files to be processed by the program. Although the format notation of Figure 2-5 indicates that this is an optional section, it is required if the program reads input files or writes output files. Since most programs process files, this section is present in almost all programs.

FILE-CONTROL Paragraph. One of the functions of an operating system is to keep track of files stored on disk. For this purpose, each stored file is assigned a name, called a **physical file name**, which the operating system places in its disk directory, together with the location on disk of the file. The name is said to be **external** to the program. Any program processing a file must have access to the file via its physical name. At first glance, it might seem logical to use the physical file name as the reference in the program; for instance, to use the physical file name in the OPEN and READ statements of your program.

There are two reasons for not doing so. First, this method would cause PROCEDURE DIVISION statements to be dependent on the physical file name. If, for a given run, you wanted to use a different data file (one with the same data format but a different name), you would need to change each statement that included the file name. Second, operating system rules for naming files are the result of decisions of the operating system designers and have no relationship to the rules for selecting COBOL names. For instance, many operating systems allow using a period as part of a file name. If the patron file has the physical file name PATRON.DATA, using that in a READ statement such as

```
READ PATRON.DATA
    AT END MOVE "YES" TO END-OF-PATRON-FILE.
```

would cause a syntax error because of the period in PATRON.DATA.

The function of the **FILE-CONTROL paragraph** is to associate each COBOL file-name with the actual file on an I/O device, thus making the rest of the program entirely independent of the physical file name. To do this, the file-control entry contains, as a minimum, two clauses: SELECT and ASSIGN. The SELECT clause introduces the user-defined COBOL file-name, and the ASSIGN clause links the file-name to a particular input/output device and file in a way that is dependent on the computer and compiler.

Figure 2-6(a) illustrates the nature of this link for the IBM mainframe OS environment. Here the connection between the COBOL file-name and the physical file name is as follows:

1. In the SELECT clause, the COBOL file-name PATRON-FILE is assigned to the name UT-S-INFILE. UT-S are identifying codes; INFILE is an arbitrary name selected by the programmer (or assigned by installation standards).

2. In special OS *job control statements* that describe to the operating system what actions to take with this program, INFILE (from UT-S-INFILE of the ASSIGN) is linked to the physical file name PATRON.DATA.

Since the connection between a name within the program and the external physical file name is done outside the COBOL program, processing a different data file requires no change to the COBOL program. It is only necessary to modify the job control statements.

Figure 2-6(b) illustrates another method for achieving this linkage. This method is used by the Ryan-McFarland compiler for the MS-DOS operating system. The same method—as well as minor variations of it—are found in a number of other systems. With this technique, the assignment to disk is explicitly indicated, followed by the physical name of the file. (The physical file name used here is PATRON.DAT, which is consistent with the three-character limit on this part of the file name imposed by MS-DOS.) It is also possible to use a variable name in the ASSIGN, thus allowing the user to enter the physical name of the file when the program is run.

Figure 2-6(c) shows the method used by Microsoft and by several minicomputer COBOL compilers. Here the clause VALUE OF FILE-ID identifies the

Figure 2-6
Linkage between the COBOL program and the physical file.

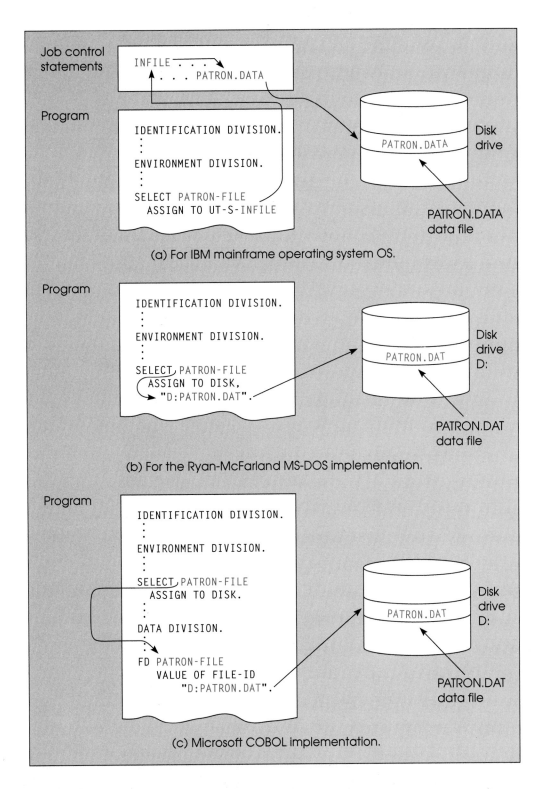

(a) For IBM mainframe operating system OS.

(b) For the Ryan-McFarland MS-DOS implementation.

(c) Microsoft COBOL implementation.

physical file (a variable name can also be used in place of the literal). Notice that this method causes the DATA DIVISION to be nonstandard.

For each file used by the program, there must be a separate file-control entry. Although there is no required order in which they are listed in the FILE-CONTROL paragraph, programmers commonly list the input file (or files) and then the output file (or files).

Recap of the ENVIRONMENT DIVISION

The ENVIRONMENT DIVISION is relatively easy to code; however, you need to obtain the standards for your installation. The division contains two sections: the CONFIGURATION SECTION and the INPUT-OUTPUT SECTION. The former section specifies the computer; the latter identifies the input/output files. In the FILE-CONTROL paragraph of the INPUT-OUTPUT SECTION, a file-control entry is specified for each file used by the program. The file-name is defined in the SELECT clause by a file-control entry and is associated with an input-output device by an ASSIGN clause.

Topic: Writing the DATA DIVISION

The partial DATA DIVISION format is shown in Figure 2-7 and the DATA DIVISION from the PATLIST2 program is shown in Figure 2-8. The **DATA DIVISION header** must appear exactly as shown in Figure 2-7 and must be terminated by a period. The DATA DIVISION consists of two sections: FILE SECTION and WORKING-STORAGE SECTION. (This division is optional in COBOL-85, thus permitting the use of advanced programming techniques. All programs in this book require a DATA DIVISION.)

Figure 2-7 DATA DIVISION format.

```
Format:

        DATA DIVISION.
        FILE SELECTION.
        FD file-name

             [RECORD CONTAINS [ integer-1 TO ] integer-2 CHARACTERS]

             LABEL  { RECORD IS   }  { STANDARD }
                    { RECORDS ARE }  { OMITTED  }

             [ DATA  { RECORD IS   }  data-name-1 [data-name-2]...[data-name-n] ]
                     { RECORDS ARE }

        01 [data-name]

             level-number  { data-name }  [ { PICTURE } IS character-string ]
                           { FILLER    }    { PIC     }

        [ WORKING STORAGE SECTION.

        [77-level-description-entry]...
        [record-description-entry]... ]
```

Figure 2-8
The DATA DIVISION from the
PATLIST2 program.

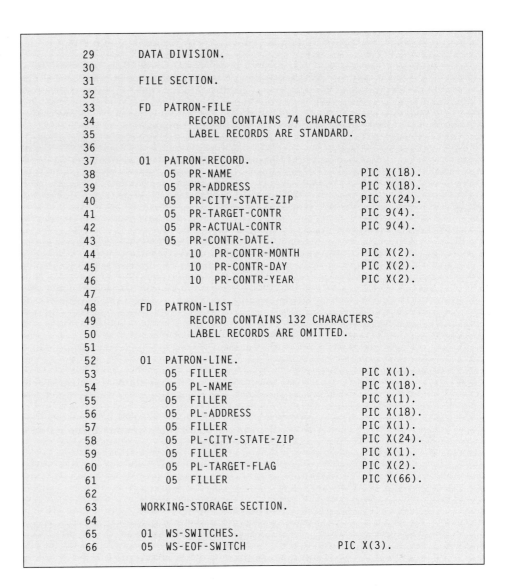

```
29        DATA DIVISION.
30
31        FILE SECTION.
32
33        FD  PATRON-FILE
34                RECORD CONTAINS 74 CHARACTERS
35                LABEL RECORDS ARE STANDARD.
36
37        01  PATRON-RECORD.
38                05  PR-NAME                PIC X(18).
39                05  PR-ADDRESS             PIC X(18).
40                05  PR-CITY-STATE-ZIP      PIC X(24).
41                05  PR-TARGET-CONTR        PIC 9(4).
42                05  PR-ACTUAL-CONTR        PIC 9(4).
43                05  PR-CONTR-DATE.
44                    10  PR-CONTR-MONTH     PIC X(2).
45                    10  PR-CONTR-DAY       PIC X(2).
46                    10  PR-CONTR-YEAR      PIC X(2).
47
48        FD  PATRON-LIST
49                RECORD CONTAINS 132 CHARACTERS
50                LABEL RECORDS ARE OMITTED.
51
52        01  PATRON-LINE.
53                05  FILLER                 PIC X(1).
54                05  PL-NAME                PIC X(18).
55                05  FILLER                 PIC X(1).
56                05  PL-ADDRESS             PIC X(18).
57                05  FILLER                 PIC X(1).
58                05  PL-CITY-STATE-ZIP      PIC X(24).
59                05  FILLER                 PIC X(1).
60                05  PL-TARGET-FLAG         PIC X(2).
61                05  FILLER                 PIC X(66).
62
63        WORKING-STORAGE SECTION.
64
65        01  WS-SWITCHES.
66            05  WS-EOF-SWITCH              PIC X(3).
```

The FILE SECTION

Similar to the FILE-CONTROL paragraph of the ENVIRONMENT DIVISION, the FILE SECTION of the DATA DIVISION is required if files are to be processed. Since all programs in this book process files, this section will appear in all the programs here.

File-Description (FD) Entry

A **file-description (FD) entry** must be specified in the FILE SECTION for each file selected in the FILE-CONTROL paragraph of the ENVIRONMENT DIVISION. The reserved word FD is considered a **level indicator**. COBOL level indicators are two-character alphabetic reserved words used to identify a specific type of file. In addition to the file description (FD) shown in Figures 2-7 and 2-8, the FILE SECTION can contain three other such components: SD (for sorting), RD (for report generation), and CD (for communications). In this chapter, we will focus our attention on the FD.

In most installations, file descriptions of standard data files are stored in separate computer file libraries. These can be accessed from the libraries, making it unnecessary for the programmer to key in the description for each file used in a program.

The two FD entries for the PATLIST2 program have been expanded to include all three allowable clauses in Figure 2-9. Observe that the reserved word FD is written in positions 8 and 9—the Area A. The file-name, however, is an Area B item and has thus been written beginning in position 12. This means that there will always be at least two blank spaces (positions 10 and 11) between the FD indicator and the corresponding file-name. The file-name must be spelled exactly the same as it appears in the SELECT clause.

Notice that because the FD entry contains additional clauses, no period follows after the file-name. The FD clauses are all Area B entries. For readability, the clauses have been indented four spaces so that each begins in position 16. There are three FD clauses in Figure 2-9: RECORD CONTAINS, LABEL RECORDS, and DATA RECORD.

RECORD CONTAINS Clause.   The **RECORD CONTAINS** clause specifies the length of the logical records in the file. The format notation shows the clause enclosed in brackets, which means that this is an optional clause. However, it is a good practice to always include this clause because it (1) provides useful documentation, and (2) will be used by the compiler to check that the same number of positions have been correctly specified for the record. (This latter point will be explained later in this chapter.)

If the file contains variable-length records (a topic not discussed in this book), the TO clause shown in brackets within the format can be used to provide minimum and maximum record lengths. Because PATRON-FILE contains 74-character records, the clause is coded as RECORD CONTAINS 74 CHARACTERS.

In contrast, the approach used with a printer file is different. It is common practice to use a value that is equal to the maximum line length your printer is capable of printing. Then, as report requirements change and the output line becomes wider, you need not change the RECORD CONTAINS clause value. This will serve to ensure that you do not exceed the printer width in your record definition. Consistent with mainframe printers which commonly have print widths of 132 characters, this clause is coded in PATRON-LIST as RECORD CONTAINS 132 CHARACTERS. The actual width of the printed line is 66 positions.

On the other hand, most microcomputer printers have versatile printing capabilities. Minimal printers have print lines of 80 characters. Most others have the ability to use compressed printing, thereby printing as many as 140 characters (or more) on a standard 8 1/2" wide paper. Obviously, you should use a RECORD CONTAINS that is compatible with your printer.

Figure 2-9
The FD entries from the PATLIST2 program.

```
                         ┌─ Must be in Area A.
                         │
                         ▼
            FD   PATRON-FILE
                     RECORD CONTAINS 74 CHARACTERS
                     LABEL RECORDS ARE STANDARD
                     DATA RECORD IS PATRON-RECORD.
                         ▲
                         └─ Must be in Area B.

            FD   PATRON-LIST
                     RECORD CONTAINS 132 CHARACTERS
                     LABEL RECORDS ARE OMITTED
                     DATA RECORD IS PATRON-LINE.
```

LABEL RECORDS Clause.   Frequently in programming, you will encounter language elements that are carry-overs from hardware and/or software limitations that no longer exist. These elements have been carried over to ensure compatibility with earlier systems. The **LABEL RECORDS** clause is one such element. When a data file is stored on magnetic tape it includes, as a first record, a special label record containing data about the file. The programmer had the option to use standard or nonstandard (installation written) labels. The LABEL RECORDS clause was included as a required element in COBOL for the user to identify the label type. As disk storage became predominant, the clause remained a required entry even though disk files do not use labels. This obsolescence is evident by the fact that LABEL RECORDS clause is a required entry in COBOL-74, is an optional entry in COBOL-85, and is scheduled for deletion from the next COBOL standard.

In almost every COBOL program that you encounter, you will see that data files are identified with LABEL RECORDS ARE STANDARD. On the other hand, if you happen to be using punched cards for input, this clause will be LABEL RECORDS ARE OMITTED.

Referring to Figure 2-9, notice that the FD for PATRON-LIST, the printer file, includes LABEL RECORDS ARE OMITTED. Label records do not apply to printers.

DATA RECORD Clause.   The optional **DATA RECORD** clause is used to specify the name of the record (or records) within the file. (Note that in some applications, a file will have records of two or more different formats. Although not consistent with the common definition of files, it is useful for some types of processing.)

The DATA RECORD clause is not included in the PATLIST2 program because the clause serves only a minimal documentation purpose. That is, the record description containing the record-name(s) immediately follows the FD entry. Although included in both COBOL-74 and COBOL-85, it is scheduled for deletion from the next COBOL standard.

It is important to note that a period must be coded, after the last FD clause, to end the sentence. Although the FD clauses are typically written in the sequence shown here, they may be listed in any order.

BLOCK CONTAINS Clause.   Although not used in this program, there is one other clause that you might encounter in the FD: the BLOCK CONTAINS clause. As you learned in Concepts Module A, logical records are commonly blocked into longer physical records. To provide for blocking, the BLOCK CONTAINS clause designates the number of logical records in a physical record (a block). For instance, if a file you are to use has been stored on disk with 20 records per block (it has a blocking factor of 20), you would include the clause:

```
BLOCK CONTAINS 20 RECORDS
```

None of the files you use in this book contains blocked records.

Record-Description Entry   Immediately following the file-description entry, the logical records within the file are specified. Records are defined by specifying a 01-level **record-description entry** to assign a name to the record and then writing data-item descriptions that describe the fields of the record. The general form of this entry is shown in Figure 2-10.

Figure 2-10
The data-item description entry.

```
Format:

                  ┌ data-name ┐  ┌ PICTURE ┐
level-number      │           │  │         │  IS character-string.
                  └ FILLER    ┘  └ PIC     ┘

Examples:
    05  PR-CONTR-DATE.

    10  PR-CONT-MONTH PIC X(2).
    10  PR-CONT-MONTH PICTURE X(2).
    10  PR-CONT-MONTH PICTURE IS X(2).

    05  FILLER        PIC X(66).
```

Level Numbers in Defining the Record, Fields, and Subfields.   To define a record, the level-number 01 is written in Area A and the name of the record (as defined in the DATA RECORDS clause, if used) is written in Area B. The record as a whole is always identified by level-number 01.

Fields and subfields are defined by **data-item description entries** which, as you learned in Chapter 1, have either two or three parts.

1. A two-digit level-number (in the range 02 to 49) which determines the hierarchy of the element. These are always coded in Area B.

2. A user-defined data-name to identify and permit reference to the record or field.

3. A PICTURE clause (usually abbreviated with the reserved word PIC, as it is in the PATLIST2 program), which defines the data class and the length of the field.

As illustrated in the input record description of PATLIST2 as shown in Figure 2-11, level-numbers are assigned on a hierarchical basis. Each subfield has a level-number that is higher in numerical value (which is lower in hierarchical order) than the field to which it is subordinate. If the field or subfield has no lower-level subfields, the data-item description entry also contains a PICTURE clause that describes the field length and data class. In Figure 2-11, PR-CONTR-DATE is the only field that is broken down into subfields; it has no PICTURE clause. Because it consists of components, it is called a **group item**. Any field that has no subordinate subfields is called an **elementary item**. Obviously, a group item does not require PICTURE clause designating a length because its length is the sum of its subordinate elementary item lengths.

Although PATLIST2 shows a field broken down only one level, you can use whatever level is needed for your application. For example, refer to the needs of Silicon Valley Manufacturing for their inventory system and a corresponding partial record description for the product record shown in Figure 2-12. As you will learn in the next chapter, you can operate on the entire inventory code field or to any component of it within the program. For instance, referring to PR-INVENTORY-CODE gives you access to the entire code; PR-PRODUCT-CODE gives you access to the group item composed of PR-ITEM-CODE and PR-PREMIUM-LEVEL; PR-ITEM-CODE gives you access to one of the lowest level subfields.

Suggested Standards for Indention and Level Numbers.   Since level-number 01 is an Area A entry, it should be placed in positions 8 and 9. Level-numbers 02 through 49 cannot be written in Area A, but they may begin in any Area B positions (12 through 72). It is customary to indent each data-item level four spaces to

Figure 2-11
The input record description
for PATRON-RECORD.

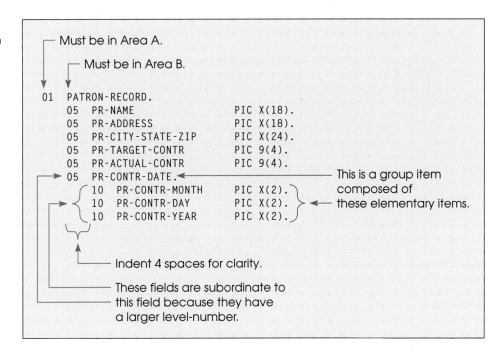

```
        ┌─ Must be in Area A.
        │     ┌─ Must be in Area B.
        ↓     ↓
       01   PATRON-RECORD.
            05   PR-NAME                PIC X(18).
            05   PR-ADDRESS             PIC X(18).
            05   PR-CITY-STATE-ZIP      PIC X(24).
            05   PR-TARGET-CONTR        PIC 9(4).
            05   PR-ACTUAL-CONTR        PIC 9(4).
     ┌───→  05   PR-CONTR-DATE. ←─────────────────── This is a group item
     │         ⌠ 10   PR-CONTR-MONTH    PIC X(2). ⌡        composed of
     │  ┌──→  ⎨  10   PR-CONTR-DAY      PIC X(2). ⎬  ←── these elementary items.
     │  │      ⌡ 10   PR-CONTR-YEAR     PIC X(2). ⌠
     │  │       ⎫
     │  │       ⎭
     │  └──────── Indent 4 spaces for clarity.
     │
     └─────────── These fields are subordinate to
                  this field because they have
                  a larger level-number.
```

Figure 2-12   A field definition and the corresponding COBOL record description (partial).

Inventory control part identification code: 14 positions

Field	Length
Manufacturing plant location	1
Part number	
Product line identification	3
Product code	
Item code	4
Premium level	1
Surface plating	2
Federal standards code	3
Product description	30

```
01   PRODUCT-RECORD.
     05   PR-INVENTORY-CODE.
          10   PR-PLANT-LOCATION          PIC X(1).
          10   PR-PART-NUMBER.
               15   PR-PRODUCT-LINE-ID     PIC X(3).
               15   PR-PRODUCT-CODE.
                    20   PR-ITEM-CODE      PIC X(4).
                    20   PR-PREMIUM-LEVEL  PIC X(1).
               15   PR-SURFACE-PLATING     PIC X(2).
          10   PR-FEDERAL-CODE             PIC X(3).
     05   PR-PRODUCT-DESCRIPTION           PIC X(30).
     .
     .
     .
```

the right of the higher level that precedes it. For example, level 01 begins in position 8, level 05 is indented to position 12, level 10 is indented to position 16, and so forth.

If a record contains many levels, however, these four-space indentions may consume so much of the coding line that little room is left to code the data-item description entry. Two-space indentions may be more practical in such situations.

In Figures 2-11 and 2-12, notice that after the 05 number, level-numbers are assigned in increments of 5 (05, 10, 15, and so on); increments of 10 would work just as well. This leaves numerical gaps so that fields or subfields can be further subdivided at a later time, if necessary.

However, some installations favor consecutive level-number assignment. They maintain that straight numerical order is easier to understand and follow than nonuniformly incremented numbers. Further, when additional subdivisions are merely squeezed into the numerical gaps, the hierarchical four-space indentions will be inconsistent. Advocates of consecutive assignment argue that, since most subdivision changes should also result in indention changes, level-numbers can be easily updated at the same time that the indention changes are being made.

FILE SECTION Data-Names.   The next element in the data-item description entries is the data-name, the user-defined name to which the data item will be referred. Data-names must conform to the rules for user-defined words. In addition, they should be meaningful and descriptive. You probably noticed that a convention was followed in the selection of data-names in the PATLIST2 program. The convention was as follows:

1. The file-name is descriptive and includes a suffix indicating the nature of the file. PATLIST2 uses:

```
PATRON-FILE
PATRON-LIST
```

2. The record-name is derived from the file-name. PATLIST2 uses:

```
PATRON-RECORD
PATRON-LINE
```

Later in this book, you will encounter files that include two or more record descriptions. Naming for such situations is illustrated by the examples.

3. Each field within a record includes a two-letter prefix that relates the field to the record. For example, in PATLIST2 the prefix PR was selected as an abbreviation for PATRON-RECORD and PL for PATRON-LINE. Hence, you know at a glance when checking a PROCEDURE DIVISION that PR-ADDRESS is a field from the input record PATRON-RECORD and that PL-ADDRESS is a field from the output record PATRON-LINE.

4. Each data-name is unique; that is, no two fields are given the same data name. For instance, if you used PR-ADDRESS for both the street address and city-state-zip, there would be no way to distinguish one from the other. However, in Chapter 5 you will learn how you can use duplicate names with appropriate precautions.

Regarding the choice of prefixes, you should use any abbreviation that is meaningful and reminds you that the field is part of a record. Although two-character prefixes are commonly used, three- or four-character prefixes may be required in larger data-processing installations. The key is to make them meaningful without being clumsy. When a common prefix is assigned to all fields within a record, the PROCEDURE DIVISION statements that refer to fields are more meaningful and the program logic is easier to follow than it would be otherwise.

FILLER Entries.   In contrast to the input record, the output record description shown in Figure 2-13 includes FILLER entries in order to provide spacing between fields. The word FILLER is a reserved word; it serves a function in record descriptions analogous to that of zeros in our Arabic numbering system: it is a placeholder. Thus, even though we are not concerned with a particular area of a record, if the area is physically present, it must be accountable. Notice in Figure 2-13(b) that the word FILLER may be omitted in COBOL-85. Since inclusion of the word is optional (and *can* be included), all programs in this book include it in order to maintain compatibility with both standards.

PICTURE Clauses.   Each elementary data-item description must contain a PICTURE clause. This clause is used to specify the data class and length of the field. (It can also describe other attributes, as will be explained in Chapter 5.) A basic PICTURE clause contains the reserved word PICTURE (or the more commonly

Figure 2-13   The output record description for PATRON-LINE.

```
01  PATRON-LINE.                                 01  PATRON-LINE.
    05  FILLER             PIC X(1).                 05                    PIC X(1).
    05  PL-NAME            PIC X(18).                05  PL-NAME           PIC X(18).
    05  FILLER             PIC X(1).                 05                    PIC X(1).
    05  PL-ADDRESS         PIC X(18).                05  PL-ADDRESS        PIC X(18).
    05  FILLER             PIC X(1).                 05                    PIC X(1).
    05  PL-CITY-STATE-ZIP  PIC X(24).                05  PL-CITY-STATE-ZIP PIC X(24).
    05  FILLER             PIC X(1).                 05                    PIC X(1).
    05  PL-TARGET-FLAG     PIC X(2).                 05  PL-TARGET-FLAG    PIC X(2).
    05  FILLER             PIC X(66).                05                    PIC X(66).
```

            (a) COBOL-74 Standard.   (b) Allowable form for COBOL-85 Standard.

used abbreviation PIC) followed by a blank space and an entry described in the general form as *character-string* (see Figure 2-10). The two **picture symbols** with which you are now familiar are X and 9. The picture symbol X defines the field as alphanumeric; the symbol 9 describes a numeric field. Immediately following the symbol is a number, enclosed in parentheses, that indicates the length of the field. Two of the fields from PATRON-RECORD are annotated in Figure 2-14.

Notice that all the picture clauses in the PATLIST2 program are aligned. It really does not matter where the picture clause starts, so long as it is in Area B and there is at least one blank space following the data-name. However, picture clauses within a record-description are easier to read when they are vertically aligned.

Instead of coding the field length as a value within parentheses, the picture symbol can be repeated so that it appears a number of times equal to the length value. The following alternative to the coding of some of the PATLIST2 fields illustrates this:

```
05  PR-TARGET-CONTR    PIC 9999.  equivalent to PIC 9(4)
05  PR-ACTUAL-CONTR    PIC 9999.
05  PR-CONTR-DATE.
    10  PR-CONTR-MONTH  PIC XX.    equivalent to PIC X(2)
    10  PR-CONTR-DAY    PIC XX.
    10  PR-CONTR-YEAR   PIC XX.
```

For picture character-strings that contain only one type of symbol, the use of parentheses is superior to such symbol repetition. It is easier to interpret the field length when expressed as a number, especially for longer fields. Also, you will need to sum the values in a column of picture clauses in order to determine the length of a record. It is easier to do this with the field width enclosed in parentheses than by interpreting the repeated symbols.

Figure 2-14
The PICTURE clause.

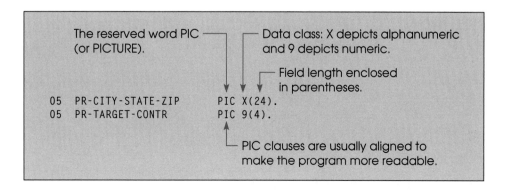

One other point regarding the field lengths is that when a program is compiled, the compiler determines the length of the record by totaling the field lengths expressed in the picture clauses. This occurs whether or not the RECORD CONTAINS clause is included in the FD. However, the advantage of including the RECORD CONTAINS clause is that the compiler compares the computed length to the RECORD CONTAINS length value. If there is a discrepancy, the difference is identified and a diagnostic message is issued.

About the 9 Picture Symbol. Beginning COBOL students sometimes erroneously think that, having used a 9 picture symbol when defining a data-item, the data-item will therefore be able to contain only numeric data. **This is wrong.** For instance, the definition

```
02  PR-ACTUAL-CONTR   PIC 9(4).
```

does not restrict the program from reading alphanumeric data into the field PR-ACTUAL-CONTR during program execution. For instance, if one of the input records contained the name JOHN in the positions for this field, JOHN would be read and stored exactly as if it had been defined X(4). Then of what value is the 9 picture symbol? The answer is that it conveys information to the compiler regarding the following (these are explained in detail in Chapter 5):

1. The types of statements that can operate on a given field. For instance, the compiler will not allow you to add one alphanumeric field to another.

2. The movement of data from a field of one data class to a field of another data class.

The WORKING-STORAGE SECTION

The FILE SECTION of the DATA DIVISION is used to define the files, records, and fields to be read or written by the program. In addition to this input and output data, most programs process other data-items for which memory is required. The WORKING-STORAGE SECTION is used for the definition and storage of these other records and fields. Its format and the WORKING-STORAGE SECTION for PATLIST are shown in Figure 2-15. (When coding the section header, do not forget that a hyphen is required between the words WORKING and STORAGE.) Notice that the general format provides for two types of entries: 77-level and record-description.

If you inspect the WORKING-STORAGE SECTION of a typical COBOL program, you will see that it looks much like the FILE SECTION because it consists of one or more record descriptions. Actually, record-description entries follow the same rules for record description entries in the FILE SECTION. That is, you can have a record broken into fields and subfields to meet the needs of your program. Basically, the level-numbers 01 through 49 can thus be used not only for true record/field/subfield relationships, but also to organize independent fields.

Assignment of level-number 77 signifies that the data-item is an *independent data-item* (a 77-level-entry). That is, it contains no subfields and it is not a subfield

Figure 2-15
The WORKING-STORAGE SECTION.

```
Format:
[WORKING-STORAGE SECTION.
[77-level-entry]...
[record-description-entry]...]

Example from PATLIST:
WORKING-STORAGE SECTION.
01  WS-SWITCHES.
    05  WS-EOF-SWITCH    PIC X(3).
```

of another field. Thus, a 77-level item must be an elementary item. Hence, the two lines of code in Figure 2-15 could have been coded as follows:

```
77  WS-EOF-SWITCH        PIC X(3).
```
⎣— Must be in Area A

Most COBOL programs require a number of independent fields in the WORKING-STORAGE SECTION. A complex program may require many of them. Maintenance programmers have found that it is difficult to work with programs that contain numerous independent items because the collection of such fields typically becomes a haphazard list of data-items with few clues as to the relationship between different fields. This makes the program difficult to understand and modify. Hence, 77-level items are not used in this book. If you use them, remember that they can be used only in WORKING-STORAGE SECTION, not the FILE SECTION.

Instead of using 77-level items, it is better to segregate the WORKING-STORAGE fields into general categories—much like subject matter is organized to build a topic outline. Independent items in WORKING-STORAGE are then reflected not as a random collection of entries, but instead as an organized hierarchical grouping of fields. For this, you can use the record-description-entries of the WORKING-STORAGE SECTION.

Notice in Figure 2-15 that the WORKING-STORAGE SECTION entry names are preceded with the letters WS (meaning WORKING-STORAGE). This is in keeping with the two-letter convention established for fields of the FILE SECTION. In this case, 01-level name WS-SWITCHES is used to indicate fields (one field, in this case) that will be given either of two values. For instance, a value of NO is moved to WS-EOF-SWITCH initially and it is changed to YES when the EOF record is encountered. Such two-state indicator fields are often required for program control; they are commonly called **program switches**, or simply **switches**.

Chapter Summary
Topic: Writing the IDENTIFICATION and ENVIRONMENT Divisions

The IDENTIFICATION DIVISION has six paragraphs, only one of which (PROGRAM-ID) is a required entry. Each paragraph header starts in Area A of the COBOL coding form. The entries following the paragraph header are Area B entries. The PROGRAM-ID entry is a user-defined word; entries for the other paragraphs are comment-entries.

The ENVIRONMENT DIVISION is relatively easy to code, but somewhat difficult to discuss in general because the specific system-names used are dependent upon the particular COBOL compiler being used. The division contains two sections: the CONFIGURATION SECTION and the INPUT-OUTPUT SECTION.

The CONFIGURATION SECTION specifies the computer; its use is optional with many compilers.

The INPUT-OUTPUT SECTION identifies the input/output files. In the FILE-CONTROL paragraph of the INPUT-OUTPUT SECTION, a file-control entry is specified for each file used by the program. The file-name is defined in the SELECT clause by a file-control entry and is associated with an input/output device by an ASSIGN clause.

Topic: Writing the DATA DIVISION

The DATA DIVISION commonly contains two sections: the FILE SECTION and the WORKING-STORAGE SECTION.

In the FILE SECTION, an FD entry must be specified for each file selected in the ENVIRONMENT DIVISION. Following each FD entry, a record-description entry must be coded for each record format contained with the file.

Each record contains data-item description entries for fields within the record. A data-item description entry contains a level-number and a user-defined data-name for the field. If an elementary item is being described, it also contains a picture clause.

COBOL
Programming
Perspective

Initial-Character Printer Forms Control

When a report line is to be printed, the printer must be informed of the line-spacing or line-skipping requirements for the line. That is, the printer must be told whether the line is to be single-spaced, double-spaced, triple-spaced, or printed at the top of the next page.

The first character of the print-line record sent to the printer is used to communicate these **vertical forms-control** requirements. A special ANSI standard exists for this **vertical forms-control character** (ANSI X3.78-1981: Representation of Vertical Carriage Positioning Characters in Information Interchange). This **initial-character** printer forms-control concept is diagrammed below.

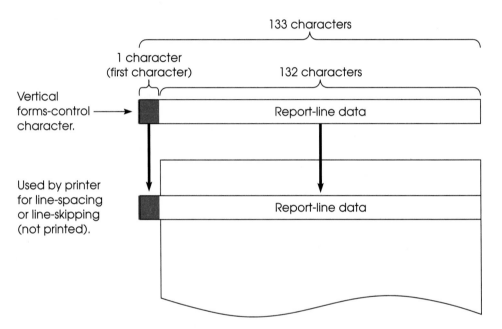

IBM and certain other early COBOL compilers required the programmer to explicitly allocate this forms-control character-position at the beginning of each record directed to the printer. As a result, the coding for a printer **file** using what we can term **explicit forms-control character allocation** would appear as shown below.

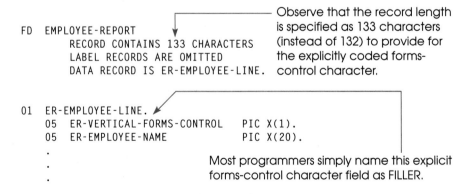

The programs coded in the text use **implicit forms-control character allocation.** That is, although the first-character forms-control character position is still generated by the compiler, the programmer does not provide the position in the program code; it is handled on a basis that is called "transparent to the programmer."

Current IBM mainframe-computer compilers permit either explicit or implicit forms-control character handling. The programmer informs the compiler about which allocation is being used by setting a compiler option to either ADV (implicit) or NOADV (explicit).

Even though explicit allocation of the first-character forms-control character is no longer required by most compilers, many installations with IBM compilers still use the technique. The reason is that they have a large inventory of programs coded with explicit initial-character forms-control character coding. Such installations prefer to keep their coding methods standard for all programs and do not want to tackle the task of converting all the existing programs from explicit to implicit form.

The WORKING-STORAGE SECTION contains data-item descriptions for those fields required by the program that are not defined within the FILE SECTION.

COBOL Language Element Summary

Reserved words have predefined meanings in the COBOL language. A complete list of reserved words is printed facing the inside back cover.

The programmer creates user-defined words in accordance with certain syntactical rules. A user-defined word must

---

- Be composed only of alphabetic characters (A through Z), digits (0 through 9), and hyphens (-)

- Contain at least one letter

- Not exceed 30 characters

- Not begin or end with a hyphen

- Not contain any blank spaces (embedded blanks)

- Not be the same as a reserved word

Comment-entries may be any combination of characters that are acceptable to the computer being used. Comment-entries are used only in the IDENTIFICATION DIVISION and are specified in all paragraphs of that division except the PROGRAM-ID paragraph.

Comment lines contain an asterisk (*) in position 7. They are used to record comments within the COBOL program listing. Words and symbols on comment lines are not treated as COBOL language elements.

Page-eject lines contain a diagonal slash (/) in position 7 and are used to control page skipping within the COBOL program listing (not the report produced by the program).

A **system-name** is a COBOL word that is used to communicate with the operating environment. There are two commonly used types of system-names: **computer-names** and **implementor-names**. A computer-name identifies the computer system being used; an implementor-name refers to a feature or device available on the computer system. System-names are chosen by the compiler vendor.

Level indicators identify a specific type of file-description entry.

Level-numbers indicate either (1) the position of a data-item in the hierarchical structure of a logical record, or (2) special properties of a data-description entry.

PICTURE clauses describe certain characteristics of elementary data-items. This chapter discussed data-class and field-length aspects. Alphanumeric (picture symbol X) and numeric (picture symbol 9) specifications were introduced. Field length can be expressed either by (1) repeating the symbol so that as many symbols are specified as there are characters or digits in the field, or (2) following the X or 9 symbol by the character or digit length enclosed within parentheses. (Additional PICTURE clause specifications are presented in Chapter 5.)

Style Summary
General Coding Conventions

Make user-defined words meaningful and descriptive.

Use hyphens in user-defined words to separate multiple English words and abbreviations.

Do not use commas or semicolons as punctuation.

Provide vertical spacing among divisions, sections, and certain paragraphs by inserting blank lines or blank comment lines (lines with only an asterisk in column 7).

Write only one COBOL sentence, statement, clause, or phrase per coding line.

When a sentence, statement, or clause extends over multiple coding lines, indent each line after the first.

When indention is called for, indent in four-space units. Exceptions are cases in which vertical alignment of entries is desired or when four-space indentions consume too much space on the coding line.

IDENTIFICATION DIVISION Conventions

Limit the program-name to the maximum number of characters allowed by the operating system being used.

ENVIRONMENT DIVISION Conventions

Write the SELECT entry so that the ASSIGN clause begins on a separate line.

Indent the ASSIGN clause four spaces (to position 16).

Sequence the SELECT entries so that the input files are listed first, then the output files.

Do not choose file-names that refer to specific input/output devices (such as CARD-FILE, TAPE-FILE, or DISK-FILE).

DATA DIVISION Conventions

Write each clause of the FD entry on a separate line. Following the file name, indent each clause to position 16.

Use the optional RECORD CONTAINS clause of the FD entry.

Omit the optional DATA RECORDS clause of the FD entry.

Use gap level-number assignment (01, 05, 10, 15, and so on).

Indent each data-item subdivision four spaces (level-number 05 at position 12, level-number 10 at position 16, and so forth). If four-space indentions consume too much space on the coding line, use two-space indentions.

Prefix each data-name of a record with a two-, three-, or four-character abbreviation for that record. The prefix for each record within the program should be unique.

To conserve space on the coding line, use the abbreviation PIC rather than the word PICTURE.

Do not use the optional word IS in the PICTURE clause. It takes up space on the coding line and does not significantly improve program documentation.

Vertically align PICTURE clauses in the record descriptions of the FILE SECTION.

Express the field length in the picture character-string by a number enclosed in parentheses, rather than by the repetition method.

Do not use 77-level items. Instead, organize WORKING-STORAGE independent data-items into collections of logically related fields, using level-numbers 01 through 49.

Summary of Relevant Differences Between COBOL-74 and COBOL-85

The following program elements that are required in COBOL-74 are optional in COBOL-85:

```
ENVIRONMENT DIVISION
    CONFIGURATION SECTION
    SOURCE-COMPUTER paragraph
    OBJECT-COMPUTER paragraph
DATA DIVISION
    LABEL RECORDS clause
    Reserved word FILLER in record definition
```

Exercises

Terms for Definition

COBOL format notation _____

comment-entry _____

comment-line _____

computer-name _____

data-item description entry _____

data-name _____

division header _____

file-control entry _____

file-description entry _____

file-name _____

group item _____

implementor-name _____

independent data-item _____

level indicator _____

level-number _____

paragraph header _____

picture character-string _____

picture symbol _____

procedure-name _____

program-name _____

record-description entry _____

section header _____

system-name _____

Review Questions   1. Identify the COBOL format notation conventions that are used to specify the following language entry types.

Entry type	*Format notation convention*
a. Required reserved word	_____
b. Optional reserved word	_____
c. Programmer-supplied entry	_____
d. Optional feature or entry	_____
e. Alternative entries	_____
f. Entry-repetition permitted	_____

2. The only required paragraph of the IDENTIFICATION DIVISION is the

_____ paragraph.

3. Place a check in the box next to each of the following that is a COBOL reserved word.

☐ ALPHANUMERIC   ☐ FILE
☐ ARE   ☐ FILES
☐ ASSIGN   ☐ GROUP
☐ CHARACTER   ☐ LABEL
☐ CHARACTERS   ☐ MOVE
☐ COBOL   ☐ NUMBERS
☐ CONTAINS   ☐ NUMERIC
☐ DATA   ☐ PICTURE
☐ DATA-NAME   ☐ PICTURE-IS
☐ DATE   ☐ READ
☐ ELEMENTARY   ☐ RUN
☐ EMPLOYEE   ☐ STANDARD
☐ FD   ☐ STOP
☐ FILE-CONTROL   ☐ WORK-AREA
☐ FILE-NAME   ☐ WORK-STORAGE
☐ FILE-SECTION   ☐ WRITE

4. For each of the following that would be invalid as a user-defined word, give the reason that it is not valid.

VALID-USER-DEFINED-WORD _____

VALIDUSERDEFINEDWORD _____

INVALID-USER-DEFINED-WORD _____

A _____

AR-ACCOUNTS-RECEIVABLE-AMOUNTIN _____

AR-PAYMENTS _____

AR PURCHASES _____

AR-CREDITLIMIT _____

AR-E20-20CODE _____

AR-E _____

ARE _____

YTD-SOC-SEC-TAX _____

MTD-S/S-TAX _____

25 _____

25-DOLLARS _____

$25 _____

-25-DOLLARS _____

25DOLLARS50CENTS _____

25.50-DOLLARS _____

5-POUNDS _____

5-LBS _____

5# _____

5. What is the purpose of the CONFIGURATION SECTION of the ENVIRON-
   MENT DIVISION?

   _____

   _____

6. The system-name specified in the SOURCE-COMPUTER and OBJECT-

   COMPUTER paragraphs is called a(n) _____ -name; the
   system-name specified in the ASSIGN clause is called a(n)

   _____ -name.

7. What is the purpose of the FILE-CONTROL paragraph of the INPUT-
   OUTPUT SECTION of the ENVIRONMENT DIVISION?

   _____

   _____

8. Name the two clauses in the file-control entry.

   a. _____

   b. _____

9. If a program has one input file and two output files, _____

   SELECT entries will be required in the _____ paragraph

   of the _____ SECTION of the _____
   DIVISION.

10. If a program has two input files and one output file, _____

    FD entries will be required in the _____ SECTION of the

    _____ DIVISION.

11. Each file-name specified in the _____ entry in the

    _____ DIVISION must have a counterpart entry with the

    exact same file-name in the _____ entry in the

    _____ DIVISION.

12. Why is it recommended that the RECORD CONTAINS clause be specified in
    the FD entry?

    _____

13. Identify the level-numbers for the following types of data-description entries:

    a. Record-description entry _____

    b. Data-item (field) description entry _____

    c. Independent-item description entry _____

14. How can a group data-item be distinguished from an elementary data-item?

    _____

15. What picture symbol is used for the following classes of data?

    a. numeric digits _____

    b. alphanumeric characters _____

16. What are the columns of the following?

    Area A _____   Area B _____

17. Which of the following must start in Area A? Identify by placing a check
    mark in the appropriate box.

    ☐ Division header
    ☐ Section header
    ☐ Paragraph header
    ☐ Entries within a paragraph
    ☐ SELECT clause
    ☐ FD level indicator
    ☐ Clauses within an FD
    ☐ Level 01 entries
    ☐ Level 02 through level 49 entries
    ☐ Level 77 entries

18. A two-state indicator used for program control is commonly referred to by

    programmers as a program _____ .

Programming Assignments

To complete a programming assignment, perform the following tasks:

1. Draw a system flowchart for the problem.
2. Prepare an input record layout.
3. Prepare a print chart to define the printed output.
4. Code the first three divisions of the COBOL program. (You will not be able to code the PROCEDURE DIVISION until you have completed Chapter 3.)

   To minimize the number of extraneous diagnostics, you may find it helpful to include the following "dummy" PROCEDURE DIVISION:

```
PROCEDURE DIVISION.
000-DUMMY.
    STOP RUN.
```

5. Obtain a clean compile for the first three divisions.

Programming Assignment 2-1: Student List

Background information:

The Bayview Institute of Computer Technology maintains comprehensive data on students in computer files. One of the counselors desires to make a brief study of student progress and requires a list of students and the number of units they have completed.

Input file: The Student File (STUDENT.DAT)

Input-record format:

Positions	Field	Data class	Comments
1–2	Record code	Alphanumeric	Code "22"
12–25	Student last name	Alphanumeric	
26–35	Student first name	Alphanumeric	
48–50	Units completed	Numeric	Whole number
51–70	Other data		

Required output:

Printed report, single-spaced, one line for each input record.

Output report-line format:

Positions	Field
4–13	Student first name
15–28	Student last name
32–34	Units completed

Note: Remember, PROCEDURE DIVISION coding is not required for this chapter.

Programming Assignment 2-2: Salesperson List

Background information:

Follow-the-Sun Sales maintain a file of their sales representatives. The sales manager wishes to perform a study of saleperson performance. For this, she needs a list of all salespeople that indicates their territories and their sales. Most of the records have a value of "A" for the Status-code field; those that do not must be identified.

Input file: The Salesperson File (SALESPER.DAT)

Input-record format:

Positions	Field	Data class	Comments
1–2	Record code	Alphanumeric	Code "25"
3–4	Salesperson region	Alphanumeric	
5–8	Salesperson territory	Alphanumeric	
9–11	Salesperson number	Alphanumeric	
12–37	Salesperson name	Alphanumeric	
38	Status code	Alphabetic	
48–50	Product-units sold	Numeric	Whole number
51–79	Other data		

Required output:
Printed report, double-spaced, one line for each input record.

Output report-line format:

Positions	Field
7–8	Salesperson region
12–15	Salesperson territory
19–21	Salesperson number
25–50	Salesperson name
54–56	Product-units sold
65	Status code (only if code not A)

Note: Remember, PROCEDURE DIVISION coding is not required for this chapter.

Programming Assignment 2-3: Company Telephone Directory List
Background information:
The Century-20 Marketing Agency is a fast-moving company that uses automation to the fullest. Virtually all of their activities make use of the computer in one way or another. However, much to the dismay of the personnel director, no one has ever printed a list of employees and their telephone extensions, even though this data is stored in the computer. A company telephone directory *must be* prepared from the employee file.

Input file: The Century-20 Employee File (EMPLOYEE.DAT)

Input-record format:

Positions	Field	Data class	Comments
1–2	Record code	Numeric	Code "26"
8–18	Employee last name	Alphanumeric	
19–27	Employee first name	Alphanumeric	
75–80	Telephone extension	Numeric	

Required output:
Print each employee record two-up (two records on each line) on the output company telephone directory line as specified above. Use single-spacing.

Output report-line format:

Positions	Field
1–11	Employee last name (first record of two)
13–21	Employee first name (first record of two)
25–28	Telephone extension (first record of two)
41–51	Employee last name (second record of two)
53–61	Employee first name (second record of two)
65–68	Telephone extension (second record of two)

Note: Remember, PROCEDURE DIVISION coding is not required for this chapter.

Programming Assignment 2-4: Employee-Address Roster
Background information:
The Temp-Surv Company provides temporary office employees for a wide variety of service companies. Because of their high turnover rate, they need the ability to print an employee-address roster (at frequent intervals) from data in their employee file.

Input file: The Temp-Surv Employee File (EMPLOYEE.DAT)

Input-record format:

Positions	Field	Data class	Comments
1–2	Record code	Alphanumeric	Code "26"
3–7	Employee number	Alphanumeric	
8–28	Employee last name	Alphanumeric	
29–51	Employee address	Alphanumeric	
52–74	Employee city/state/zip	Alphanumeric	
75–78	Other data		

Required output:
For each input employee record, three output employee lines are to be printed.

Example: 50873   WESTERBROOK, ALEXANDER R
                        21065 NORTHWEST 3RD ST
                        OKLAHOMA CITY OK 73118

Single-space each line that applies to the same employee record; double-space between employees.

Output report-line format:

Employee-Name Line	
Positions	**Field**
6–10	Employee number
14–36	Employee name

Note: The output Emlpoyee-name field is two positions longer than the input Employee-name field. Do not worry about this; you will see why it works later.

Employee-Address Line

Positions	Field
14–36	Employee address

Employee City/State/Zip/Telephone Line

Positions	Field
14–36	Employee city/state/zip code

Note: Remember, PROCEDURE DIVISION coding is not required for this chapter.

The next three programming assignments (2-5 through 2-7) are also expanded upon in later chapters.

Programming Assignment 2-5: Nurses' Duty Roster
Background information:

Brooklawn Hospital maintains a file which contains one record for each nurse employed by the hospital. Like many hospitals, Brooklawn has experienced high turnover rates and has difficulty obtaining nurses for special assignments that meet the standards of Brooklawn. The head nurse intends to do a study of the existing nurses' staff. To that end, she requires a printed report from the computer file.

Input file: The Nurses' File (NURSES.DAT)

Input-record format:

Positions	Field	Data class	Comments
1–2	Record type code	Alphanumeric	
3–25	Name (last, first, mi)	Alphanumeric	
26–32	Home telephone number	Alphanumeric	
33–46	Professional specialty	Alphanumeric	Example, Trauma Room
47–52	Date hired	Alphanumeric	Format *yymmdd*
53–55	Salary schedule	Alphanumeric	Row and column
56–93	Other payroll data		Not used in this program
94–96	Ward/duty station	Alphanumeric	
97	Shift code	Numeric	Value of 1, 2, or 3

Required output:

A nurses' assignment roster, double-spaced, one line for each input record.

Output report-line format:

Positions	Field	Comments
1–14	Professional specialty	
20	Shift code	Leave blank if Shift Code is 1; otherwise, print the value.
25–47	Name	
53–55	Ward/duty station	

Note: Remember, PROCEDURE DIVISION coding is not required for this chapter.

Programming Assignment 2-6: Vehicle Rental Application
Background information:
Rent-Ur-Wheels rents various modes of transportation: cars, bicycles, motorcycles, and trucks. The success of their business depends on having a lot of rolling stock and knowing whether or not it is available for rental. To provide this information, the firm maintains a data file which contains one record for each vehicle.

Input file: The Vehicle File (VEHICLE.DAT)

Positions	Field	Data class	Comments
1–4	Vehicle type	Alphanumeric	
5–18	Make of vehicle	Alphanumeric	
19–28	Model	Alphanumeric	
29–35	License number	Alphanumeric	
36–39	Daily rental fee	Numeric	Dollars and cents; code as PIC 9999 for this assignment
40–42	Daily collision ins.	Numeric	Dollars and cents
43–45	Daily liability ins.	Numeric	Dollars and cents
46	Status	Alphanumeric	A = Available R = Rented
47–52	Date due back	Alphanumeric	Format *yymmdd*
53–63	Other data		
64–79	Customer last name	Alphanumeric	
80–89	Customer phone number	Alphanumeric	Includes Area Code

Required output:
Printed report, double-spaced, one line for each vehicle record.

Output report-line format:

Positions	Field
5	Status
10–23	Make of vehicle
26–35	Model
38–41	Vehicle type
45–51	License number

Programming Assignment 2-7: Bookstore Inventory Application
Background information:
Granger and Heatherford, Purveyors of Fine Publications, have finally computerized after years of maintaining manual records of their books. Already designed and installed is an inventory file which contains one record for each book title that they carry. They now need programs to print a variety of reports.

Input file: The Book-Inventory File (GHINVEN.DAT)

Input-record format:

Positions	Field	Data class	Comments
1–18	Title	Alphanumeric	
19–33	Author	Alphanumeric	
34–41	Subject area	Alphanumeric	
42–46	Shelf location	Alphanumeric	
47–50	Unit cost	Numeric	Dollars and cents; code as PIC 9999 for this assignment
51–54	Selling price	Numeric	Same as Unit-cost
55–57	Quantity on hand	Numeric	Whole number
58–60	Reorder level	Numeric	Whole number
61–63	Quantity on order	Numeric	Whole number
64–69	Date of last order	Alphanumeric	Format *mmddyy*

Required output:
Printed report, double-spaced, one line for each input record.

Output report-line format:

Positions	Field
1–8	Subject area
11–25	Author
28–45	Title
47–49	Quantity on hand

Note: Remember, PROCEDURE DIVISION coding is not required for this chapter.

Programming Assignment 2-8: Computer Store Product File
Background information:
Bob and Helen Smith operate their own business, which is called Complete Computers Corporation (or "3C" for short). Their specialty is configuring complete personal computer systems for individuals, but they also advise users on individual components (CPUs, hard disks, monitors, and so forth).

To keep their operating expenses to a minimum, the Smiths do not maintain a large inventory of computer hardware. Instead, they maintain a comprehensive data file which contains information on the physical characteristics, price, and availability of as many computer components as possible. With this information, they can tailor a computer system to each user's requirements and budget. One of the reports they require is a product/vendor summary.

Input file: The CCC Inventory File (CCCINVEN.DAT)

Positions	Field	Data class	Comments
1–5	Product category code	Alphanumeric	
6–20	Product name	Alphanumeric	
21	Product class	Alphanumeric	Value A or B
22–33	Other product data		

Vendors from whom product is available:

34–36	Vendor code for vendor #1	Alphanumeric	
37–42	Price from vendor #1	Numeric	Dollars and cents, code as PIC 999999 for this assignment
43–45	Vendor code for vendor #2	Alphanumeric	
46–51	Price from vendor #2	Numeric	Same as Price #1
52–54	Vendor code for vendor #3	Alphanumeric	
55–60	Price from vendor #3	Numeric	Same as Price #1

Required output:
Printed report, single-spaced, one line for each product record.

Output report-line format:

Positions	Field
1–15	Product name
20–24	Product code
30–32	Vendor code #1
39–41	Vendor code #2
48–50	Vendor code #3

Note: Remember, PROCEDURE DIVISION coding is not required for this chapter.

CHAPTER 2
Debugging Supplement

Supplement Objectives

In the preceding chapter, you learned about coding the IDENTIFICATION, DATA, and ENVIRONMENT divisions. The assignments of that chapter required you to code, compile, and debug these three divisions. When you are first learning a language, it is very easy to make numerous simple mistakes (such as omitting a period or hyphen) that will cause the compiler to indicate an error. The purpose of this supplement is to provide you with the basis for achieving "clean" programs.

Supplement Outline

Common Errors of Beginning COBOL Programmers
Omitted Period
Extra Period
Omitted Hyphen
Extra Hyphen
Omitted Blank Space
Inadvertent Blank Space
Area A/Area B Mistakes
Misspelling

A Program With Errors
Description of the Errors
Diagnostics From IBM Mainframe COBOL
Diagnostics From Ryan-McFarland COBOL

Common Errors of Beginning COBOL Programmers

Beginning COBOL programmers often make similar errors. So that you can guard against them, they are depicted in Figure 2S-1 and are discussed here.

Omitted Period

Whenever a period is shown in the COBOL format notation, it must be there. A period is always required to terminate a division header, section header, paragraph header, FD entry (at the end of the complete entry), and a data-item description. A period is also required at the end of a sentence immediately preceding any of these entries.

Extra Period

A period placed where it should not be can also cause problems. Beginning COBOL programmers sometimes mistakenly place a period between multiclause, multiphrase, or multiline sentences such as the SELECT/ASSIGN file-control entry, the FD entry, the READ/AT END statement, and the WRITE/AFTER ADVANCING statement. Also, a period is sometimes erroneously inserted in a data-item description entry after a data-name, before the picture clause.

Omitted Hyphen

Remember that hyphens are often used in COBOL to join multiple English words into a single COBOL reserved or user-defined word. When a hyphen is specified, it must be used. Required hyphens are often inadvertently omitted from the reserved words PROGRAM-ID, INPUT-OUTPUT, FILE-CONTROL, WORKING-STORAGE, and so forth. Similarly, each user-defined word must be a continuous string of characters. Hyphens must be used rather than blank spaces when forming a user-defined word from multiple English words or abbreviations. As you will

Figure 2S-1   Checklist of common IDENTIFICATION, ENVIRONMENT, and DATA DIVISION syntactical errors.

	Division		
Syntactical errors	*IDENTIFICATION*	*ENVIRONMENT*	*DATA*

Omitted period	`IDENTIFICATION DIVISION.✓`
	`PROGRAM-ID.✓`
	`AUTHOR.✓`
	`INSTALLATION.✓`
	`DATE-WRITTEN.✓`
	`DATE-COMPILED.✓`
	`SECURITY.✓`
		`ENVIRONMENT DIVISION.✓`
		`CONFIGURATION SECTION.✓`
		`SOURCE-COMPUTER.✓`
		`OBJECT-COMPUTER.✓`
		`INPUT-OUTPUT SECTION.✓`
		`FILE-CONTROL.✓`
			`DATA DIVISION.✓`
			`FILE SECTION.✓`
			`WORKING-STORAGE SECTION.✓`
			To terminate FD sentence
			To terminate each data-
			    item description sentence

Extra period		`SELECT file-name ✓`
		`    ASSIGN TO implementor-name`
			`FD   file-name ✓`
			`     RECORD CONTAINS`
			`          integer CHARACTERS`
			`     LABEL RECORDS ARE OMITTED`
			`     DATA RECORD is record name.`
			`02   data-name ✓   PIC X(5).`

Omitted hyphen	`PROGRAM▼ID`
	`DATE▼WRITTEN`
	`DATE▼COMPILED`
		`SOURCE▼COMPUTER`
		`OBJECT▼COMPUTER`
		`INPUT▼OUTPUT`
		`FILE▼CONTROL`
			`WORKING▼STORAGE`
			In data-names

Extra hyphen	`IDENTIFICATION▼DIVISION`	`ENVIRONMENT▼DIVISION`
		`CONFIGURATION SECTION`
		`INPUT-OUTPUT SECTION`
		`ASSIGN TO`
			`RECORD▼CONTAINS`
			`LABEL RECORDS`
			`DATA RECORDS`
			`FILE SECTION`

Omitted blank space			`PIC▼X(5)`
Inadvertent blank space			`PIC X▼(5)`
Incorrect Area A placement			`FD FILE NAME`
Spelling	All reserved words	All reserved words	All reserved words

learn, COBOL-85 scope terminators require a hyphen following the END; for instance, END-READ.

Extra Hyphen   When coding division and section headers, notice that the division or section name is separated from the reserved word DIVISION or SECTION by a blank space—not a hyphen. Because hyphens are used so frequently, there is sometimes a tendency to include them at locations where they should not be present.

Omitted Blank Space   A blank space must be provided between COBOL words (except that a period can follow a COBOL word without an intervening blank space).

Inadvertent Blank Space   An error will never result from the use of extra blank spaces when one is required. That is, whenever one blank space is required, any number of spaces may be coded.

However, sometimes one or more blank spaces are coded where they should not be used. Sometimes a blank space is erroneously coded into a picture character-string, such as X (2). The blank space between the X and the open parenthesis is an error because there should be no blank spaces within the character-string. It should read X(2) without the blank space.

On the other hand, a blank space is required between the reserved word PIC and the beginning of the picture character-string. Hence, PICX(2) is invalid; PIC X(2) is the correct coding.

Area A/Area B Mistakes

The names of all divisions, sections, and paragraphs must start in Area A. Also, the indicator FD and the level-number 01 must begin in Area A. All other COBOL statements used in this book start in Area B.

Misspelling

When a reserved word is used, it must be spelled exactly as specified in the COBOL list of reserved words. Common misspellings are ENVIORNMENT instead of ENVIRONMENT (remember that "iron" is in the word), LABLE rather than LA-BEL, OMITED or OMMITTED for OMITTED, PROCEEDURE instead of PROCE-DURE, and PREFORM in place of PERFORM.

A Program With Errors
Description of the Errors

Each programming assignment in the preceding chapter requires that you create the first three divisions of the program, compile it, and correct all compiler errors. If you make any errors, you will receive appropriate compiler diagnostic messages identifying the statements in error and giving you some idea of what you did wrong. Virtually all compilers classify each diagnostic to show how serious it is. Most have at least the following two categories:

W   *Warning.* A warning calls attention to something that may be a problem. Some compilers will make assumptions concerning the correct form. A warning does not interrupt the compiling, nor does it prevent ultimate execution of the program. However, each warning should be checked and corrected. Ignoring it could lead to execution errors.

E   *Error.* A serious error has been detected that could not be corrected by the compiler. After detecting an E-level error, the incorrect statement is ignored and compilation of the program continues. All E-level errors must be corrected before attempting to run the program.

To give you an idea of how compiler error diagnostics will appear, the first three divisions of PATLIST have been compiled with the following errors:

- PROGRAM-ID entry is written as PROGRAM ID (hyphen omitted).

- SOURCE-COMPUTER is entered, beginning at column 7 (instead of 8).

- A RECORD CONTAINS clause length is shorter than the actual record.

- A SELECT clause is entered, beginning at column 11 (instead of 12).

- The reserved word DAY is used as a field name.

All compilers will detect these five errors. However, the actual form in which the diagnostic is displayed and the overall action taken varies from one compiler to another. The next two sections of this debugging supplement show the actual error messages that you will get from two compilers: IBM mainframe and Ryan-McFarland run on a microcomputer.

Diagnostics From IBM Mainframe COBOL

Figure 2S-2 is the post-compile listing from an IBM mainframe using the Disk Operating System (DOS/VS); it is annotated with the five errors. (Notice that it includes a dummy PROCEDURE DIVISION.) The corresponding compiler diagnostic messages are shown in Figure 2S-3. Each diagnostic consists of three elements:

- The card (line) number of the source program to which the diagnostic refers. For instance, the first message contains 00003 and thus refers to line 00003 (or simply 3) of the source program.

Figure 2S-2
Post-compile listing from IBM
mainframe under DOS/VS.

```
00001          IDENTIFICATION DIVISION.           Hyphen missing
00002
00003          PROGRAM ID.     PATLIST2.
00004          AUTHOR.         PRICE/WELBURN.
00005          INSTALLATION.   FLEETWOOD CHARITIES.
00006          DATE-WRITTEN.   9/21/90.
00007          SECURITY.       CONFIDENTIAL.
00008
00009      *     THIS PROGRAM PRINTS A PATRON ADDRESS LIST
00010      *     AND FLAGS DELINQUENT PATRONS.
00011
00012
00013          ENVIRONMENT DIVISION.
00014
00015          CONFIGURATION SECTION.             Begins in column 7
00016
00017          SOURCE-COMPUTER.   IBM-4381.
00018          OBJECT-COMPUTER.   IBM-4381.
00019
00020          INPUT-OUTPUT SECTION.
00021
00022          FILE-CONTROL.
00023             SELECT PATRON-FILE
00024                 ASSIGN TO SYS010-DA-3340-S.
00025             SELECT PATRON-LIST
00026                 ASSIGN TO SYS005-UR-1403-S.
00027
00028                                              Begins in Area A
00029          DATA DIVISION.
00030
00031          FILE SECTION.
00032
00033          FD  PATRON-FILE
00034                 RECORD CONTAINS 74 CHARACTERS
00035                 LABEL RECORDS ARE STANDARD.
00036
00037          01  PATRON-RECORD.
00038              05  PR-NAME             PIC X(18).
00039              05  PR-ADDRESS          PIC X(18).
00040              05  PR-CITY-STATE-ZIP   PIC X(24).
00041              05  PR-TARGET-CONTR     PIC 9(4).
00042              05  PR-ACTUAL-CONTR     PIC 9(4).
00043              05  PR-CONTR-DATE.                    Reserved
00044                  10  MONTH           PIC X(2).     word
00045                  10  DAY             PIC X(2).
00046                  10  YEAR            PIC X(2).
00047                                                    Wrong
00048          FD  PATRON-LIST                           record
00049                 RECORD CONTAINS 123 CHARACTERS     length
00050                 LABEL RECORDS ARE OMITTED.
00051
00052          01  PATRON-LINE.
00053              05  FILLER              PIC X(1).
00054              05  PL-NAME             PIC X(18).
00055              05  FILLER              PIC X(1).
00056              05  PL-ADDRESS          PIC X(18).
00057              05  FILLER              PIC X(1).
00058              05  PL-CITY-STATE-ZIP   PIC X(24).
00059              05  FILLER              PIC X(1).
00060              05  PL-TARGET-FLAG      PIC X(2).
00061              05  FILLER              PIC X(66).
00062
00063          WORKING-STORAGE SECTION.
00064
00065          01  WS-SWITCHES.
00066              05  EOF-SWITCH          PIC X(3).
00067
00068
00069          PROCEDURE DIVISION.
00070          000-DUMMY.
00071              STOP RUN.
```

Figure 2S-3   Error diagnostics from compiler.

```
CARD   ERROR MESSAGE

00003  ILA1087I-W   ' PROGRAM ' SHOULD NOT BEGIN IN AREA A.
00003  ILA1097I-E   PROGRAM-ID MISSING OR MISPLACED. IF PROGRAM-ID DOES NOT IMMEDIATELY FOLLOW
                    IDENTIFICATION DIVISION, IT WILL BE  IGNORED.
00004  ILA1095I-W   WORD 'SECTION' OR 'DIVISION' MISSING. ASSUMED PRESENT.
00017  ILA1150I-W   ILLEGAL CHARACTER IN COL. 7 CHARACTER  IGNORED.
00017  ILA1150I-W   ILLEGAL CHARACTER IN COL. 7 CHARACTER  IGNORED.
00017  ILA1087I-W   ' OURCE-COMPUTER ' SHOULD NOT BEGIN IN AREA A.
00017  ILA1004I-E   INVALID WORD OURCE-COMPUTER . SKIPPING TO NEXT RECOGNIZABLE WORD.
00025  ILA1087I-W   ' SELECT ' SHOULD NOT BEGIN IN AREA A.
00023  ILA2146I-C   RECORD CONTAINS DISAGREES WITH COMPUTED MAXIMUM. USING COMPUTED MAXIMUM 00072 .
00023  ILA2049I-C   NO VALID OPEN FOR FILE. FILE IGNORED.
00045  ILA1001I-E   NUMERIC LITERAL NOT RECOGNIZED AS LEVEL NUMBER BECAUSE ' DAY 'ILLEGAL AS USED.
                    SKIPPING TO NEXT LEVEL, SECTION OR DIVISION.
00025  ILA2146I-C   RECORD CONTAINS DISAGREES WITH COMPUTED MAXIMUM. USING COMPUTED MAXIMUM 00132 .
00025  ILA2049I-C   NO VALID OPEN FOR FILE. FILE IGNORED.
```

■ An error code that identifies the exact error. If you have an IBM COBOL manual, you can look up this code for a more detailed explanation of the message. Also, the code contains the severity (W, C, or E). In addition to the W and E level diagnostics, IBM mainframe compilers include the C, meaning *conditional*. The C level diagnostic is one in which the compiler has had to make an assumption (which may or may not be correct) in order to continue compiling. An attempt to execute the program will probably not be successful.

■ A brief description of the detected error. The compiler will always find something that is incorrect. However, for some of the errors we can make, it cannot determine exactly what is wrong. Hence, the actual message will sometimes be misleading.

With this background, we can proceed to investigate each of the diagnostics produced by the five program errors shown in Figure 2S-2.

```
00003 ILA1087I-W   ' PROGRAM ' SHOULD NOT BEGIN IN AREA A.
```

At line 3, with the ommission of the hyphen, the compiler sees the word PROGRAM as a separate word (PROGRAM is a reserved word). This is an incorrect usage for it.

```
00003 ILA1097I-E   PROGRAM-ID MISSING OR MISPLACED. IF PROGRAM-ID DOES NOT
                   IMMEDIATELY FOLLOW IDENTIFICATION DIVISION, IT WILL BE
                   IGNORED.
```

The compiler is informing you that the required entry PROGRAM-ID (which must follow IDENTIFICATION DIVISION) is missing.

```
00004 ILA1095I-W   WORD 'SECTION' OR 'DIVISION' MISSING. ASSUMED PRESENT.
```

This is a confusing error because there are no missing sections or divisions. Here is a case in which the missing PROGRAM-ID has caused the compiler some "confusion." These first three diagnostics are all the result of the missing hyphen in PROGRAM-ID; if you make that correction, these messages will disappear.

```
00017 ILA1150I-W   ILLEGAL CHARACTER IN COL. 7 CHARACTER  IGNORED.
```

In line 17, the compiler is telling you that column 7, the continuation column, can contain only a few selected characters and that the letter S is not one of them. It further tells you that it is ignoring this column 7 entry.

```
00017 ILA1087I-W   ' OURCE-COMPUTER ' SHOULD NOT BEGIN IN AREA A.
00017 ILA1004I-E   INVALID WORD OURCE-COMPUTER . SKIPPING TO NEXT
                   RECOGNIZABLE WORD.
```

After discarding the S in column 7, the remainder of the entry in line 17 is meaningless to the compiler and generates these two additional diagnostics. Repositioning SOURCE-COMPUTER to column 8 will take care of these three diagnostics.

```
00025 ILA1087I-W   ' SELECT ' SHOULD NOT BEGIN IN AREA A.
```

At line 25, the compiler has detected the word SELECT beginning in Area A. However, it does recognize what is intended from context, interprets it correctly, and warns you. It is a good idea to correct all such warning messages.

```
00023 ILA2146I-C   RECORD CONTAINS DISAGREES WITH COMPUTED MAXIMUM. USING
                   COMPUTED MAXIMUM 00072 .
```

The record number reference on this message is confusing because it identifies the SELECT statement at line 23, whereas the error relates to entries in the FD. If you total the field lengths of PATRON-RECORD, you will find that they *do* total 74, not 72 as the diagnostic indicates. Hence, the compiler appears to be wrong. However, this is caused by another error, as you will see.

```
00023 ILA2049I-C   NO VALID OPEN FOR FILE. FILE IGNORED.
```

This diagnostic results because the file is not opened in the PROCEDURE DIVISION—remember, this program has only the dummy PROCEDURE DIVISION. For this exercise, you can ignore this message.

```
00045 ILA1001I-E   NUMERIC LITERAL NOT RECOGNIZED AS LEVEL NUMBER BECAUSE
                   ' DAY ' ILLEGAL AS USED. SKIPPING TO NEXT LEVEL,
                   SECTION OR DIVISION.
```

This is a strange message, but it indicates the extent to which the compiler can be confused when a reserved word is misused (the word DAY). Because of this error, the compiler has ignored line 45. Thus, when summing the field lengths, it obtains a record length of 72, not 74. This explains the wrong length record message for line 23. Change the name DAY so that it is not a reserved word and both of the diagnostics will disappear.

```
00025 ILA2146I-C   RECORD CONTAINS DISAGREES WITH COMPUTED MAXIMUM. USING
                   COMPUTED MAXIMUM 00132 .
```

Again, a wrong length record message refers to the SELECT statement of the corresponding record. Change the record length at line 49 from 123 to 132 and this message will disappear.

```
00025 ILA2049I-C   NO VALID OPEN FOR FILE. FILE IGNORED.
```

This diagnostic results because the file is not opened in the PROCEDURE DIVISION—remember, this program has only the dummy PROCEDURE DIVISION.

In this sample set of diagnostics, you have seen two or more messages result from a single error. Occasionally, you will make an error that causes many other valid statements to be flagged as incorrect. When this occurs, if you can find the error, correct it and make another compile to eliminate these excessive messages. Sometimes it is simply not worth the time to attempt finding those messages not resulting from the single catastrophic error.

Diagnostics From Ryan-McFarland COBOL

The Ryan-McFarland COBOL post–compile listing of Figure 2S-4 includes the program PATLIST2. To get a general idea of how to interpret these diagnostics, consider the first one at line 3; this is repeated in Figure 2S-5. As you can see, this collection of messages tells you the following:

1. An E-level error has been detected at line 3.

2. The nature of the error—a brief description is included.

3. The "trouble" starts as indicated by the dollar sign ($) located beneath the letter P in PROGRAM. From this point, the compiler begins ignoring text.

Figure 2S-4   Post-compile listing from Ryan-McFarland MS-DOS compiler.

```
     LINE   DEBUG  PG/LN  A...B.......2.........3.........4.........5.........6.........7..
        1                      IDENTIFICATION DIVISION. ── Hyphen missing
        2                                              ↙
        3                      PROGRAM ID.    PATLIST2.
                                      $
*****  1) E 770: SYNTAX ERROR, EXPECTED WORD: "PROGRAM-ID"  (SCAN SUPPRESSED)  *E*E*E*E*E*E

        4                      AUTHOR.        PRICE/WELBURN.
                                      $
*****  1) I   5: SCAN RESUME *I*I*I*I*I*I*I*I*I*I*I*I*I*I*I*I*I*I*I*I*I*I*I*I*I*I*I*I*I*I*I
***** LAST DIAGNOSTIC AT LINE:    3

        5          INSTALLATION. FLEETWOOD CHARITIES.
        6          DATE-WRITTEN.  9/21/90.
        7          SECURITY.      CONFIDENTIAL.
        8
        9       *      THIS PROGRAM PRINTS A PATRON ADDRESS LIST
       10       *      AND FLAGS DELINQUENT PATRONS.
       11
       12
       13                      ENVIRONMENT DIVISION.
       14   Begins in
       15   Column 7        CONFIGURATION SECTION.
       16             ┐
       17             └──→ SOURCE-COMPUTER.  IBM-PC.
                               $$
*****   1) W  39: INDICATOR AREA CHARACTER  *W*W*W*W*W*W*W*W*W*W*W*W*W*W*W*W*W*W*W*W*W*W*W*W
*****   2) E 159: ENVIRONMENT DIVISION SYNTAX  (SCAN SUPPRESSED)  *E*E*E*E*E*E*E*E*E*E*E*E*E
***** LAST DIAGNOSTIC AT LINE:     4

       18                      OBJECT-COMPUTER.  IBM-PC.
                                      $
*****   1) I   5: SCAN RESUME *I*I*I*I*I*I*I*I*I*I*I*I*I*I*I*I*I*I*I*I*I*I*I*I*I*I*I*I*I*I*I
***** LAST DIAGNOSTIC AT LINE:    17

       19
       20                      INPUT-OUTPUT SECTION.
       21
       22                      FILE-CONTROL.
       23   Begins in           SELECT PATRON-FILE
       24   Area A  ╲              ASSIGN TO DISK, "PATRON.DAT".
       25           ╲────→  SELECT PATRON-LIST
                               $
*****   1) W  61: CLAUSE IN AREA A  *W*W*W*W*W*W*W*W*W*W*W*W*W*W*W*W*W*W*W*W*W*W*W*W*W*W*W*W
***** LAST DIAGNOSTIC AT LINE:    18

       26                          ASSIGN TO PRINTER, "PATLIST.OUT".
       27
       28
       29                  DATA DIVISION.
       30
       31                  FILE SECTION.
       32
       33                  FD  PATRON-FILE
       34                          RECORD CONTAINS 74 CHARACTERS
       35                          LABEL RECORDS ARE STANDARD.
       36
```

Figure 2S-4   (continued)

```
   37                      01   PATRON-RECORD.
   38                           05   PR-NAME                PIC X(18).
   39                           05   PR-ADDRESS             PIC X(18).
   40                           05   PR-CITY-STATE-ZIP      PIC X(24).
   41                           05   PR-TARGET-CONTR        PIC 9(4).
   42                           05   PR-ACTUAL-CONTR        PIC 9(4).
   43                           05   PR-CONTR-DATE.   ← Reserved
   44                                10   MONTH       word  PIC X(2).
   45                                10   DAY               PIC X(2).
                                          $
*****    1) E 384: RESERVED USER WORD   (SCAN SUPPRESSED)  *E*E*E*E*E*E*E*E*E*E*E*E*E*E*E
*****  LAST DIAGNOSTIC AT LINE:     25

   46                                10   YEAR              PIC X(2).
   47
   48                      FD   PATRON-LIST
                                $
*****    1) I   5: SCAN RESUME *I*I*I*I*I*I*I*I*I*I*I*I*I*I*I*I*I*I*I*I*I*I*I*I*I*I*I
*****  LAST DIAGNOSTIC AT LINE:     45    ──── Wrong record length
   49                           RECORD CONTAINS 123 CHARACTERS
   50                           LABEL RECORDS ARE OMITTED.
   51
   52                      01   PATRON-LINE.
   53                           05   FILLER                 PIC X(1).
   54                           05   PL-NAME                PIC X(18).
   55                           05   FILLER                 PIC X(1).
   56                           05   PL-ADDRESS             PIC X(18).
   57                           05   FILLER                 PIC X(1).
   58                           05   PL-CITY-STATE-ZIP      PIC X(24).
   59                           05   FILLER                 PIC X(1).
   60                           05   PL-TARGET-FLAG         PIC X(2).
   61                           05   FILLER                 PIC X(66).
   62
   63                 WORKING-STORAGE SECTION.
   64
   65                 01   WS-SWITCHES.
   66                      05   WS-EOF-SWITCH               PIC X(3).


  E 223:   FILE RECORD SIZE DECLARATION *E*E*E*E*E*E*E*E: PATRON-LIST

  E 173:   FILE DESCRIPTION *E*E*E*E*E*E*E*E*E*E*E*E*E: PATRON-FILE

     5 ERRORS        2 WARNINGS
```

Figure 2S-5   Error caused by omitting hyphen from PROGRAM-ID.

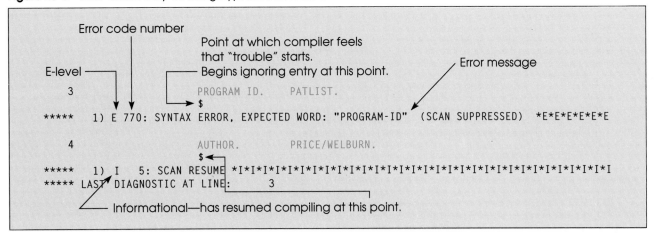

4. The compiler has resumed processing the source program at line 4. This is indicated by the dollar sign under the letter A in AUTHOR and the information line that follows.

Often the brief message included on the diagnostic line is enough to identify the problem for you. However, in some cases, a more extensive description is needed. This is the purpose of the diagnostic code number (for instance, 770 following the E code). The RM-COBOL User Manual lists diagnostic messages (according to these error numbers) with a more extensive description of the error.

Notice that the diagnostic following line 4 has a letter I. In addition to the warning (W) and error (E) diagnostics, RM-COBOL includes I (Informational) messages. They indicate where the compiler has resumed the compiling process after detecting another diagnostic. These messages do not affect the compiling process.

The next diagnostic, generated as a result of beginning SOURCE-COMPUTER in column 7, is shown in Figure 2S-6. Notice that two messages result. The first is a warning, indicating that an incorrect entry has been made in column 7. (The valid entries you have used in this column are * for a comment and / to cause a page eject.) The compiler then inspects Area B and finds OURSE-COMPUTER, which it flags as an invalid entry—an E-level diagnostic. Compiling resumes at line 18.

At line 25, repeated here in Figure 2S-7, the compiler has detected the entry of SELECT in Area A (it must be in Area B). However, in this case, the compiler has detected something that is incorrect and has taken steps to correct it. The program will compile and run properly with this diagnostic. The RM-COBOL compiler has very good features for making minor corrections for you, but occasionally the correction will not be the one you desire. You should always correct these before completing your program.

The next diagnostic, at line 45 (see Figure 2S-4), indicates that the reserved word DAY has been used out of context. This has an unexpected effect on the PROCEDURE DIVISION, as you will learn in the debugging supplement following Chapter 3. However, you are alerted to the fact that there is trouble with this file description by the last diagnostic line in the listing:

```
E 173:   FILE DESCRIPTION  *E*E*E*E*E*E*E*E*E*E*E*E*E:  PATRON-FILE
```

The number 173 is the error code number reference in the RM-COBOL User Guide.

The final error is the incorrect record length entry for the PATRON-LIST file description. Since the compiler only knows whether or not the given record length corresponds to the sum of the field lengths after it scans the entire record, it includes this error message at the end of the listing. Referring to Figure 2S-4, you can see that this message, E 223, is reasonably descriptive.

Figure 2S-6   Error caused by beginning SOURCE-COMPUTER in column 7.

```
           ┌── This message refers to the first $ error indicator.
           │
           │            ┌── Column 7
           │            ▼
    17      │       SOURCE-COMPUTER.  IBM-PC.
           │        $$
*****├─►1) W  39: INDICATOR AREA CHARACTER  *W*W*W*W*W*W*W*W*W*W*W*W*W*W*W*W*W*W*W*W*W*W*W*W
*****├─►2) E 159: ENVIRONMENT DIVISION SYNTAX  (SCAN SUPPRESSED)  *E*E*E*E*E*E*E*E*E*E*E*E*E
           │
           └── This message refers to the second $ error indicator.
```

Figure 2S-7   Error caused by beginning SELECT in column 7.

```
                        ┌── Column 11 (should be in column 12).
                        ▼
    25              SELECT PATRON-LIST
                     $
*****  1) W  61: CLAUSE IN AREA A  *W*W*W*W*W*W*W*W*W*W*W*W*W*W*W*W*W*W*W*W*W*W*W*W*W*W*W

                 Assumes that this is the correct SELECT clause,
                 warns you, then continues compiling.
```

Sometimes you will make an error that causes other quite valid statements to be flagged as incorrect. Although none of these examples illustrates this problem, the Chapter 3 debugging supplement will show you how using the reserved word DAY causes apparently unrelated diagnostic messages for perfectly valid PROCEDURE DIVISION entries. Occasionally, an error will have very serious repercussions, causing many otherwise valid entries to be flagged as in error. Fortunately, the RM-COBOL compiler is well written and this does not occur very frequently.

Supplement Summary

Some of the common errors made by the beginning programmer are: omitting a period when one is required; inserting a period, hyphen, or space where one does not belong; beginning an entry in the wrong column; and misspelling reserved words (or user-defined words).

The compiler produces a post-compile listing, complete with diagnostic messages identifying each error. Sometimes you will need to do a little detective work to find the error causing the diagnostic because an error in one part of the program can cause trouble elsewhere. Occasionally, a single error in one part of the program will cause many correct statements to be flagged with diagnostics.

Exercises

Review Questions

1. Name and describe the two types of errors that are common to most compilers.

   a. _____

   b. _____

2. Assume that you used the name PATRON-FILE in the SELECT of line 18 (of the PATLIST program, Figure 1-5) and PAT-FILE in FD of line 28. How many statements do you think the compiler would flag as in error and what type of message(s) do you think would be issued?

   _____

   _____

   _____

Syntax/Debug Exercises

1. Some or all of the following IDENTIFICATION DIVISION entries are in error. Identify each error and indicate how to correct it.

```
         ┌─── Column 7
         │ 1         2         3         4        1         2         3         4
         ▼ 7890123456789012345678901234567890    7890123456789012345678901234567890

           INDENTIFICATION DIVISION             _____

           PROGRAM ID.    QUIZ.                 _____

           AUTHOR.        THE AUTHOR.           _____

           DATE WRITTEN.  TODAY.                _____

           DATE COMPILED. TOMMORRROW.           _____

           SECURITY-LEVEL. NONE.                _____
```

2. Some or all of the following ENVIRONMENT DIVISION entries are in error. Identify each error and indicate how to correct it. Assume that the system dependent entries are correct.

```
  ┌─ Column 7
  │  1         2         3         4          1         2         3         4
  ▼ 78901234567890123456789012345678 90     78901234567890123456789012345678 90

  ENVIORNMENT DIVISION.                      _____

  CONFIGURATION SECTION.                     _____

  SOURCE COMPUTER.IBM-3081.                  _____

  OBJECT COMPUTER.IBM-4081.                  _____

  INPUT-OUTPUT-SECTION.                      _____

  FILE CONTROL.                              _____

  SELECT INPUT-FILE.                         _____

      ASSIGN TO UT-S-INFILE.                 _____

  SELECT PRINT-FILE                          _____

      ASSIGN TO UT-S-PRTFILE.                _____
```

3. Some or all of the following FD entries are in error. Identify each error and indicate how to correct it.

```
  ┌─ Column 7
  │  1         2         3         4          1         2         3         4
  ▼ 78901234567890123456789012345678 90     78901234567890123456789012345678 90

  FD INPUT-FILE.                             _____

      RECORD CONTAINS 73 CHARACTERS.         _____

      LABLE RECORDS ARE OMITTED.             _____

      DATA-RECORD IS INPUT-RECORD.           _____
```

4. Some or all of the following record-description and data-item description entries of an employee record are in error according to COBOL syntax rules. Identify each error and indicate how to correct it. *Note:* Question 4 is independent of Question 3.

```
      ┌─── Column 7
      │  1              2              3              4              1              2              3              4
      ▼ 7890123456789012345678901234567890123   7890123456789012345678901234567890123
      01  RECORD                                    ─────────────────────────────────
          05  RE-SS-NUM       PIC 9(9)              ─────────────────────────────────
          05  RE-NAME         PIC X(20).            ─────────────────────────────────
          05  RE-ADDRESS PIC  X(24).                ─────────────────────────────────
          05  RE-CITY-STATE   PIC X (24).           ─────────────────────────────────
          05  RE-ZIP          PIC X(10).            ─────────────────────────────────
          05  RE-TELEPHONE    PIC X(13).            ─────────────────────────────────
          05  RE-BIRTHDATE    PIC X(6).             ─────────────────────────────────
          10  RE-BIRTHMONTH   PIC XX.               ─────────────────────────────────
          10  RE-BIRTHDAY     PIC XX.               ─────────────────────────────────
          10  RE-BIRTHYEAR    PIC XX.               ─────────────────────────────────
          05  RE-EMPLOYER     PIC X(30).            ─────────────────────────────────
              10   RE-NAME    PIC X(20).            ─────────────────────────────────
              10   RE-TELEPHONE PIC X(13).          ─────────────────────────────────
```

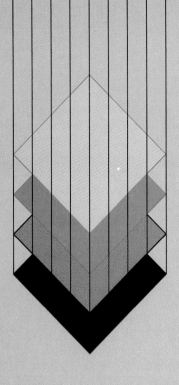

Introduction to Structured Programming Principles

Module Objectives

In Concepts Module B, you learned about the program development process and you had a brief introduction to techniques used during the design phase. This module is devoted to expanding these concepts and building a basis that you can use for an organized, structured approach to program design and coding. From this module, you will learn the following:

- Program modularization, the breaking down of a large program into smaller, independent components.

- The structure chart, a graphical method of displaying the elements of a program in the form of functional elements (modules).

- Modularization as applied to the PATLIST program.

- Using flowcharts to graphically illustrate the logic of a program.

- Using pseudocode (English-like descriptions of actions to be carried out by a program) to develop the logic of a program.

Module Outline

About Structured Programming

Structure Charts and Program Modules
Module-Naming Conventions
Module-Numbering Conventions

Representing Program Logic—Flowcharting

Representing Program Logic—Pseudocode

About Structured Programming

During the first 25 years of computer programming (roughly 1950 to 1975), most programmers designed and wrote programs that were linear. That is, instructions that were to be executed first were placed at the front of the program, immediately followed by those that were to be executed next, with those to be executed last at the end of the program. A program designed and written in this way is called an **unstructured program**. The problem with a linear program of any size is that, as a result of complex logic resulting from many conditional actions, it is not linear at all. Rather, the program can easily become a single mass of code resembling a bowl of spaghetti, with program logic sending execution every which way.

As programmers and managers struggled with the problems that unstructured programs presented, computer scientists were involved in research that contributed to a method of programming that is now called **structured programming**. Today, structured programming is a collection of techniques for program design, documentation, coding, and testing to create proper, reliable, and maintainable software products cost-effectively.

Throughout this book, you will use three tools to assist you in creating good structured programs: structure charts, pseudocode, and flowcharts. Each of these is illustrated in terms of a slightly modified version of the PATLIST program. The new version of the program, called PATLIST2, differs from PATLIST only in that each patron contributing less than the target amount is flagged. You will see the implication of this in the pseudocode and flowchart described later in this chapter.

In Chapter 3, you will expand upon the PROCEDURE DIVISION principles you learned in Chapter 1. This will give you a solid foundation to program the assignments at the end of the chapter. The structure chart, pseudocode, and flowchart that you learn about in this chapter will be almost identical to those that you will need for these programming assignments. Hence, preparing these items for your programs will seem like little more than "filling in the blanks." However, these will serve as a good introduction when you write considerably more complex programs in later chapters.

Structure Charts and Program Modules

In Chapter 1, you were presented with an application need and then the program solution in order to get started quickly. However, all future example program solutions in this book include creation of the structure chart. Let's consider the structure chart for the PATLIST2 program. A listing of the PROCEDURE DIVISION and a corresponding structure chart are shown in Figure C-1. Each of the boxes represents a program **module**, a section of the program that performs a particular function. When implemented in a program, they are commonly referred to as **procedures**. In COBOL, each box generally represents a paragraph in the PROCEDURE DIVISION.

Comparing the structure chart of Figure C-1 to the program, notice that module 100 (lines 82–83 of the program) consists of only one statement. You might wonder about the value of including this as a separate paragraph rather than simply including the MOVE at line 73. The answer is that this first program sets a style convention that will serve you well as programs become more complex and require other operations to be performed in these modules. Also, even though a module may at first involve a single statement, future modifications to the program may require more. The framework of PATLIST can readily accommodate such additions.

All of the actual processing is done in the 200 module (Process-patron-record). The action of processing a patron record consists of the following three basic operations: setting up the output line, printing the line, and obtaining the next record.

Figure C-1   The PATLIST2 program.

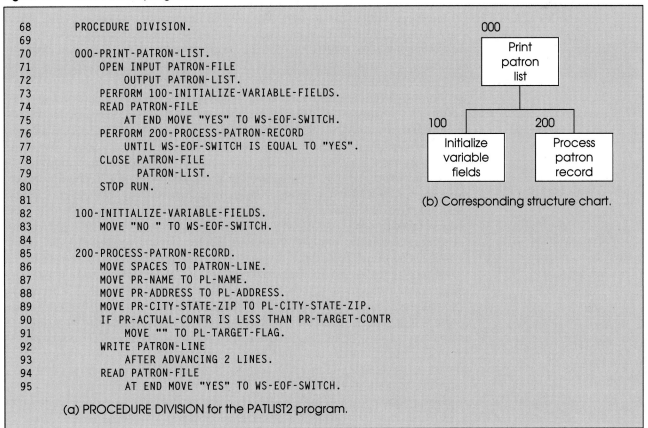

```
68          PROCEDURE DIVISION.
69
70          000-PRINT-PATRON-LIST.
71              OPEN INPUT PATRON-FILE
72                   OUTPUT PATRON-LIST.
73              PERFORM 100-INITIALIZE-VARIABLE-FIELDS.
74              READ PATRON-FILE
75                  AT END MOVE "YES" TO WS-EOF-SWITCH.
76              PERFORM 200-PROCESS-PATRON-RECORD
77                  UNTIL WS-EOF-SWITCH IS EQUAL TO "YES".
78              CLOSE PATRON-FILE
79                    PATRON-LIST.
80              STOP RUN.
81
82          100-INITIALIZE-VARIABLE-FIELDS.
83              MOVE "NO " TO WS-EOF-SWITCH.
84
85          200-PROCESS-PATRON-RECORD.
86              MOVE SPACES TO PATRON-LINE.
87              MOVE PR-NAME TO PL-NAME.
88              MOVE PR-ADDRESS TO PL-ADDRESS.
89              MOVE PR-CITY-STATE-ZIP TO PL-CITY-STATE-ZIP.
90              IF PR-ACTUAL-CONTR IS LESS THAN PR-TARGET-CONTR
91                  MOVE "" TO PL-TARGET-FLAG.
92              WRITE PATRON-LINE
93                  AFTER ADVANCING 2 LINES.
94              READ PATRON-FILE
95                  AT END MOVE "YES" TO WS-EOF-SWITCH.
```

(a) PROCEDURE DIVISION for the PATLIST2 program.

(b) Corresponding structure chart.

Module-Naming Conventions

During the program design phase when the program is broken down into modules, one of the primary objectives is that each module handle a single basic function. Although you will learn more about this in later chapters, you should be aware of it now. Since each program module should handle a specific function, the name chosen for the module should describe the module's function. As shown in Figure C-2, module names that contain a single verb followed by an adjective and an object tend to describe functional modules. So that the module name can be accommodated within the COBOL 30-character user-defined word maximum, it is recommended that module names be composed of a one-word verb followed by a two-word object. By naming modules in this manner, the programmer is forced to consider the true function of the module. The module-naming process can thus be an aid to functional module design.

Figure C-2
Module-naming convention examples.

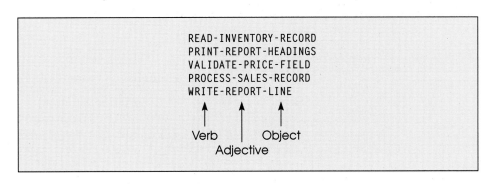

Module-Numbering Conventions

Module numbers are helpful aids to the reading, writing, and debugging of COBOL programs. Trying to locate a particular unnumbered module of a long program can pose difficulties that are much like those encountered when trying to find a certain topic in a book that has no index. Module numbers can be used as reference numbers to aid speedy location. For example, a 3-digit sequence number can be assigned to each module name, and then the modules can be arranged in the program in ascending order according to the number.

A few different module-numbering systems are commonly used. Some employ 3-digit numbers; others use 4-digit numbers. Often a letter code is placed before the numbers to indicate the structure chart level (A represents mainline-level, B the next level, and so on). Sometimes decimal numbers are used. With this method, number 1.3.2 represents the second module subordinate to module 1.3, which, in turn, is the third module below block 1.0. (When the decimal numbering system is used, decimal points are usually expressed as hyphens in the COBOL program procedure-names; decimal points cannot be used in the formation of user-defined words.)

Although specific number ranges for modules (based upon the module's function) can also limit flexibility, they tend to provide for organizational commonality from one program to another. For example, use of consistent module numbers within a data-processing installation helps each programmer to more quickly comprehend programs written by other members of the group. Perhaps more important, consistent module numbering permits one program to be used as a model, or skeleton, for another program with a similar function. As a result, source-program coding time can be significantly reduced when (1) modules are numbered consistently according to function, and (2) modern textediting facilities are used. To that end, a module-numbering convention is used for all programs in this book. A portion of that convention, which is relevant to your first programs, is shown in Figure C-3. This convention is expanded upon in later chapters.

Representing Program Logic— Flowcharting

The structure chart defines what is to be done; after you have completed it, you will determine how the various functions are to be performed. Two tools are commonly used: program flowcharts and pseudocode.

A **program flowchart** is a graphic method of illustrating the program logic; it shows *how* things are to be done—the *logic* of the program. Flowcharts use specific symbols connected by flowlines to represent the various program operations. In the example flowchart of Figure C-4 (for the revised version of PATLIST), you can see the block representations for the various actions. In the flowchart representation, execution of the program will progress as indicated by the series of blocks and the arrows. That is, in the Print-patron-list flowchart (the left-most one), the files are opened, the initialization occurs, and so on according to the representation. Notice that there is a flowchart for each module of the structure chart.

This example flowchart also demonstrates standard symbols that are widely used in flowcharting. As you can see, there are distinct flowchart symbols for these operations: general processing, input/output, predefined process (a paragraph to be performed, in COBOL), decision, and terminal.

Figure C-3
Module-numbering conventions.

Module number	Module function
000	Mainline
100–199	Initialization of variable fields
200–699	General processing

Figure C-4 Flowchart solution to PATLIST2.

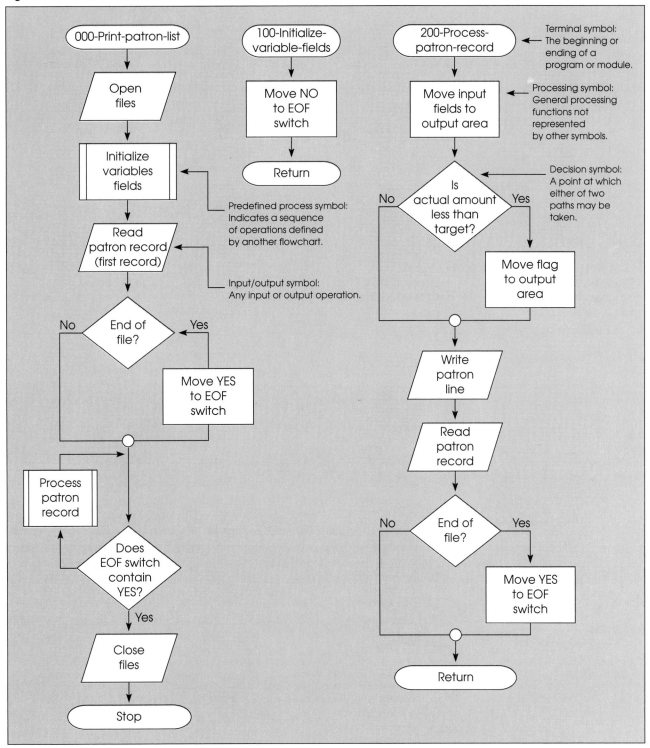

This flowchart also illustrates the three basic structures of modern programming theory: sequence structure, selection structure, looping structure—see Figure C-5. If you inspect the PATLIST2 flowchart of Figure C-4, you will see that it is comprised of combinations of these structures. Notice that the decision in this program is a special case of the selection structure—one of the alternatives is simply omitted. You will be able to flowchart all of your programming assignments

Figure C-5 Three structures of modern programming theory.

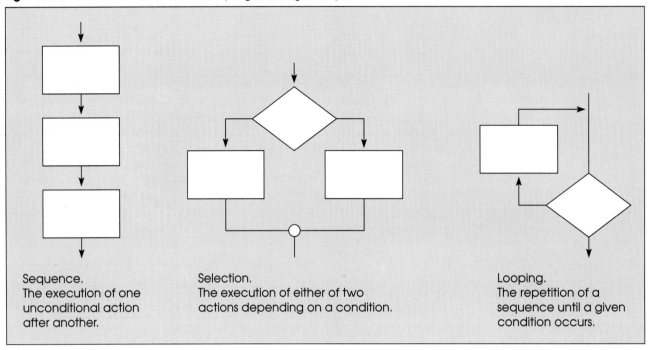

Sequence.
The execution of one
unconditional action
after another.

Selection.
The execution of either of two
actions depending on a condition.

Looping.
The repetition of a
sequence until a given
condition occurs.

using these three basic structures. (It has been proven mathematically that any programming problem can be solved with combinations of these three structures.)

Representing Program Logic— Pseudocode

A **pseudocode** solution to a programming problem is an English-description (using the three structured forms of modern programming theory) of the sequence of program actions. For instance, pseudocode for this program is shown in Figure C-6. Notice that this is not an exact replica of the program. Although it demonstrates separation of the Process-employee-record action from the mainline logic, it does not show the detailed breakdown. During the initial program design, you want to maintain the pseudocode in simple, easy-to-read form. If you write out the

Figure C-6
Pseudocode for PATLIST2.

```
Process-payroll

   1. Open files.
   2. Initialize variables.
   3. Read first patron record.
   4. Repeat Process-patron-record until end of file.
   5. Close files.
   6. Stop the run.

Process-employee-record

   1. Move input patron data to output area.
   2. If actual contribution less than target contribution move flag
      to output line.
   3. Write output line.
   4. Read next patron record.
```

detail in pseudocode, you may as well simply proceed to code the program. The pseudocode allows you to see the overall activities while planning—without getting you bogged down in detail.

Using a word processor to create the pseudocode offers another advantage in that you can easily make changes when the inevitable need for change arises. By comparison, making significant changes to a flowchart usually involves drawing a new one. Still another advantage of pseudocode is that much of the pseudocode can be included in the program as internal documentation describing the program. (All computer languages provide for the inclusion of comments that are ignored by the computer but are retained with the program.) However, with COBOL, such documentation is less important because of COBOL's self-documenting features (as you will learn when you start writing programs). On the other hand, many programmers feel that the program logic is much more evident from the graphic representation of a flowchart than from pseudocode. Both techniques are valuable program design tools.

Module Summary

Structured programming is a collection of techniques for **program design**, **documentation**, **coding**, and **testing** to create proper, reliable, and maintainable software products cost-effectively. The structured programming techniques to which you have been introduced in this chapter include:

- The idea of breaking a program into **independent modules** and arranging them into the form of a **structure chart**.

- **Program logic**, which is comprised entirely of the three basic programming structures:

  - **Sequence:** Execute modules in the specified sequence.

  - **Selection:** Determine which of two actions to take.

  - **Looping:** Repeat an action until the specified condition is met.

Each module should be given a **number** and a **name** which describes what it does. The name should consist of a **verb** and an **object**, to show what is being done. Many computer installations have specific standards for naming and numbering modules. When such standards exist, the programmer must follow them. If there are no such standards, the wise programmer will establish his/her own standards for maximum program clarity and maintainability.

A **program flowchart** is a pictorial diagram of **program logic**, using established symbols to represent specific operations. The advantage of a flowchart is that it very clearly shows the program logic, particularly in situations where conditional statements are nested several levels deep. The disadvantage of a flowchart is that it is difficult to draw in the first place, and very difficult to maintain, since making changes often requires completely redrawing the flowchart.

Pseudocode is a method of expressing program logic in a form which is neither English nor a programming language. The advantage of pseudocode is that it is easy to prepare and to maintain by using a word processor. The disadvantages of pseudocode are that the logic is not as easy to see as in a flowchart, and that the pseudocode may become as wordy as the program itself.

To the beginning programmer, the constraints of structured programming may seem to be obstacles deliberately imposed simply to stifle creativity. In a very simple program, the use of these methods does indeed make the operation more complicated than it needs to be. It is vital to remember that the time to learn correct techniques is in the beginning, and that structured programming techniques mastered now will serve you well when the programs become more challenging.

Exercises

Terms for Definition   looping structure _____

module _____

procedure _____

program flowchart _____

program modularization _____

pseudocode _____

selection structure _____

sequence structure _____

structure chart _____

structured programming _____

Review Question   1. List and describe the function of each of the three basic logic structures.

a. _____

_____

b. _____

_____

c. _____

_____

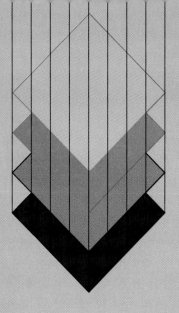

Writing a COBOL Program: The PROCEDURE DIVISION

Chapter Objectives

This chapter expands upon the PROCEDURE DIVISION elements to which you were introduced in Chapter 1. When you complete this chapter, you will be able to program the PROCEDURE DIVISION for program assignments that you started in Chapter 2. From this chapter, you will learn the following:

- The structure of the PROCEDURE DIVISION—consisting of sections (not commonly used), paragraphs, sentences, and statements.

- The use of periods in the PROCEDURE DIVISION.

- Details of how each of the following statements functions:

CLOSE	*Terminate the use of one or more data files in the program.*
IF	*Test a condition to determine the action to take.*
MOVE	*Copy data from one field in memory to another; simple editing of a field.*
OPEN	*Make one or more data files ready for use.*
PERFORM	*Transfer control to another part of the program.*
PERFORM/UNTIL	*Repeatedly execute a procedure until a stated condition is met.*
READ	*Copy a record from a data file into memory; action taken when the file EOF is detected.*
STOP RUN	*Terminate execution of a program.*
WRITE	*Copy a record from memory to an output device with control over line spacing.*

- The basic logic of the PATLIST program and alternate forms.

Topics relating to COBOL-85:

- Scope terminators that signal the end of a conditionally executed sequence of statements.

- The in-line PERFORM that provides for the repeated execution of a sequence of statements without defining it as a separate paragraph.

110

CHAPTER **3**

Chapter Outline

PROCEDURE DIVISION Elements
PROCEDURE DIVISION Header
PROCEDURE DIVISION Sections
PROCEDURE DIVISION Paragraphs
PROCEDURE DIVISION Sentences and Statements
Program Execution

OPEN, CLOSE, and STOP
The OPEN Statement
The CLOSE Statement
The STOP Statement

Changing Field Contents by Moving Data
MOVE Statement
Literals
Figurative Constants
Initializing Fields
A Simple Editing Action With the MOVE

The WRITE Statement
Writing a Record
ADVANCING Phrase

READ Statement
Reading a Record
AT END Phrase

Principles of the PERFORM
The PERFORM Statement
The PERFORM/UNTIL Statement

Conditional Operations
Examples in PATLIST2
The IF Statement

Basic Logic of PATLIST2

Scope Terminators and the Use of Periods in COBOL-85

111

PROCEDURE DIVISION Elements

The PROCEDURE DIVISION of a COBOL program is used to express the logic that the computer is to perform to obtain the specified results. Each procedural step (input, arithmetic, data movement, decision, output, and so forth) is written as an English-like statement. These statements are coded in accordance with the logic design, as expressed by the pseudocode or program flowchart developed for the program. Figure 3-1, which is the PROCEDURE DIVISION of PATLIST2, shows the PROCEDURE DIVISION format and identifies commonly used division elements.

PROCEDURE DIVISION Header

Like other division headers, the PROCEDURE DIVISION header is a required entry and must begin in Area A. It must be spelled exactly as shown in Figure 3-1, must be followed by a period, and must appear on a line by itself.

PROCEDURE DIVISION Sections

Section usage varies from division to division. Remember that the IDENTIFICATION DIVISION does not contain sections. The ENVIRONMENT DIVISION and the DATA DIVISION have certain preassigned (reserved-word) sections that are included in accordance with program needs. PROCEDURE DIVISION sections, which allow two or more paragraphs to be treated as a unit, are optional. It is generally considered good programming style to use sections only when necessary. You will learn about one such need when you study sorting in Chapter 13.

PROCEDURE DIVISION Paragraphs

As with the DATA DIVISION, the PROCEDURE DIVISION is formed by writing paragraphs. A paragraph within the PROCEDURE DIVISION is alternately termed a **procedure** or a **module**. Each paragraph begins with a **procedure-name**, which is coded starting in position 8 of Area A. Procedure-names are user-defined words and must be terminated by a period.

Figure 3-1 The PROCEDURE DIVISION format.

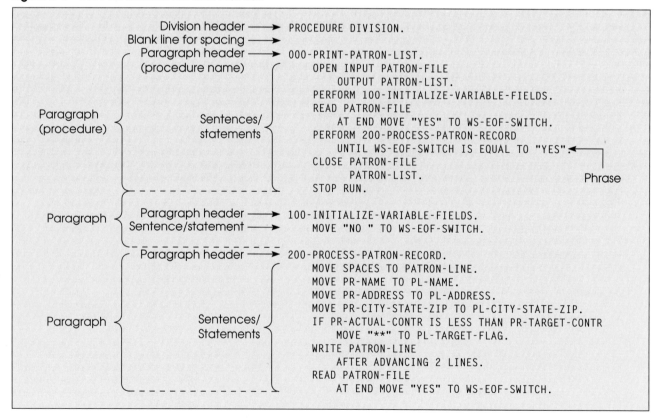

A slight technical difference exists between a procedure and a paragraph. A procedure can contain a group of logically successive paragraphs within the PROCEDURE DIVISION, as in a SECTION. Hence, both section-names and paragraph-names can be procedure-names. When reading this book, you can consider a procedure (and a procedure-name) as being synonymous with a PROCEDURE DIVISION paragraph (and a paragraph-name). The exception is in Chapter 13, where sections are required for sorting.

PROCEDURE DIVISION Sentences and Statements

From the PATLIST2 program, you know that the PROCEDURE DIVISION paragraphs contain one or more statements designating the actions to be carried out during execution of the program. (The verb which begins the statement must be coded in Area B.) A **statement** is a syntactically valid combination of COBOL words that begins with a COBOL verb. For example:

```
MOVE PR-NAME TO PL-NAME
PERFORM 100-INITIALIZE-VARIABLE-FIELDS
```

Through use of the period, one *or more* statements form a **sentence**; thus, a paragraph is composed of one or more sentences, the same as an English paragraph. This is illustrated by the series of MOVE statements in Figure 3-2. From the programmer's perspective, there is little advantage of one of these forms over the other. However, to avoid potential pitfalls, it is suggested that you use a period after each statement. The last section in this book describes an alternate recommended form for users of COBOL-85.

The end of a paragraph is signaled by the start of another paragraph (a paragraph header in Area A) or by the end of the program (no additional statements).

Program Execution

The machine-language instructions generated by the compiler from the COBOL program roughly correspond to statements of the PROCEDURE DIVISION. The first three divisions—IDENTIFICATION, ENVIRONMENT, and DATA—contain only declarative, or definition-type, specifications defining objects on which instructions from the PROCEDURE DIVISION are to operate. As indicated in Chapter 1, even though descriptions in this book refer to execution of the COBOL program, you must keep in mind that the machine-language equivalent of the PROCEDURE DIVISION is being executed.

When the operating system gives control of required computer resources to a program, the first instruction executed will be the machine-language instruction corresponding to the first statement of the PROCEDURE DIVISION. The succeeding statements will then be executed, one by one, in consecutive order until a branching verb is encountered. A branching verb causes control to be transferred to a specific location in the program, rather than simply passing to the next consecutive instruction. When the STOP verb is executed, the computer resources allocated to your COBOL program will be returned to the operating system.

Figure 3-2 A paragraph of one or more sentences.

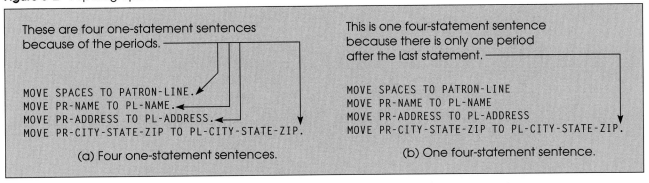

These are four one-statement sentences because of the periods.

```
MOVE SPACES TO PATRON-LINE.
MOVE PR-NAME TO PL-NAME.
MOVE PR-ADDRESS TO PL-ADDRESS.
MOVE PR-CITY-STATE-ZIP TO PL-CITY-STATE-ZIP.
```

(a) Four one-statement sentences.

This is one four-statement sentence because there is only one period after the last statement.

```
MOVE SPACES TO PATRON-LINE
MOVE PR-NAME TO PL-NAME
MOVE PR-ADDRESS TO PL-ADDRESS
MOVE PR-CITY-STATE-ZIP TO PL-CITY-STATE-ZIP.
```

(b) One four-statement sentence.

In Chapter 1, you got a brief introduction to each of the statements used in the PATLIST program. Let's look at them in more detail and in this order: OPEN, CLOSE, STOP RUN, MOVE, WRITE, READ, IF, and PERFORM.

OPEN, CLOSE, and STOP

The OPEN Statement

The first PROCEDURE DIVISION statement of the PATLIST2 program is the OPEN. Each file used by a COBOL program must be "opened" before any other input/output operations involving the file can be executed. The OPEN statement initiates processing for a file. It does *not* cause data records to be read from an input file or written to an output file. It does make available to the program a memory buffer area into which a physical input record can be read or from which a physical output record can be written (this is *not* the record area defined in the COBOL FD). Also, if the use of label records is specified (LABEL RECORDS ARE STANDARD) in the FD entry for the file and if the storage medium uses labels, the OPEN statement causes processing of the label record.

The OPEN statement format is shown in Figure 3-3. In the format, notice that the three lines following the word OPEN are enclosed in braces { }. Recall from the formatting standards described in Chapter 2 that this means that one of the three must be used in the statement.

The reserved word INPUT must precede the name of the input file. Similarly, the reserved word OUTPUT must precede the name of the output file. (The reserved word I-O is used to specify direct-access files upon which both input and output operations may be performed; I-O files are not used in the programs of this text.) If there are multiple files within one of these categories, additional files may be listed following the appropriate reserved word—INPUT, OUTPUT, or I-O—but the reserved word is not repeated.

Notice that the OPEN statement has been written on two lines in conformance with our general style conventions of one phrase per line and indention of statement lines after the first.

Figure 3-4 shows three contrasting OPEN statement coding approaches in which four files are opened. They all do the same thing: open the four named files. Opening all files with a single sentence is commonly done in the mainframe environment because it is more efficient (faster). On the other hand, if one of the file names is misspelled, then some compilers will ignore the entire OPEN statement. As a result, every statement referring to the files will be flagged as in error. However, using one OPEN per sentence causes only statements referring to the misspelled file name to be flagged. Hence, you end up with fewer inappropriate diagnostics on your post-compile listing.

In most file-processing programs, required files are opened at the beginning of the program. However, in some situations, access to the data in a file might be

Figure 3-3
The OPEN statement.

```
Format:

              ⎧ INPUT file-name-1 [file-name-2]...  ⎫
              ⎪                                      ⎪
      OPEN  ⎨ OUTPUT file-name-3 [file-name-4]... ⎬  ...
              ⎪                                      ⎪
              ⎩ I-O file-name-5 [file-name-6]...    ⎭
```

Example from PATLIST2:

```
OPEN INPUT PATRON-FILE
     OUTPUT PATRON-LIST.
```

Figure 3-4
Three equivalent forms for
opening four files.

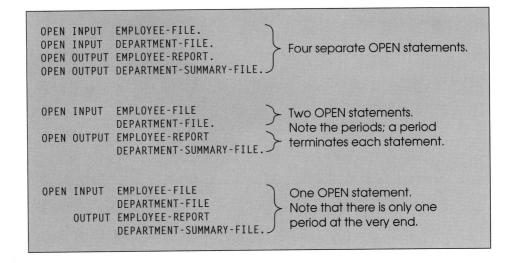

```
OPEN INPUT   EMPLOYEE-FILE.
OPEN INPUT   DEPARTMENT-FILE.                   }  Four separate OPEN statements.
OPEN OUTPUT  EMPLOYEE-REPORT.
OPEN OUTPUT  DEPARTMENT-SUMMARY-FILE.


OPEN INPUT   EMPLOYEE-FILE
             DEPARTMENT-FILE.                   }  Two OPEN statements.
OPEN OUTPUT  EMPLOYEE-REPORT                        Note the periods; a period
             DEPARTMENT-SUMMARY-FILE.           }  terminates each statement.


OPEN INPUT   EMPLOYEE-FILE
             DEPARTMENT-FILE                        One OPEN statement.
      OUTPUT EMPLOYEE-REPORT                        Note that there is only one
             DEPARTMENT-SUMMARY-FILE.           }  period at the very end.
```

required for only a limited time in the program. For such cases, the file should be opened only when it is needed.

The CLOSE Statement   Each file that is opened in a program must be closed before program execution has ended. For most example programs in this book, this takes place immediately prior to terminating program execution. However, as with opening a file, a file can be closed at any point in the program. For instance, if in the middle of a program, you required one-time access to data in a file, you could write a module to open the file, access the data, and close the file. Then you would execute that procedure when needed.

The action of closing a file causes the following to take place with respect to that file:

1. Terminates processing for that file; the file is no longer accessible to the program.

2. Makes the memory buffer area reserved for the input or output activity available to the operating system.

3. If the output is to an auxiliary device, causes the EOF record to be positioned after the last record and causes the last block of data in the memory buffer (this may consist of one or more logical records) to be written to the storage device.

The CLOSE statement is coded with the reserved word CLOSE, followed by the file-name of each file to be closed—as illustrated in Figure 3-5. Unlike the OPEN statement, the reserved words INPUT, OUTPUT, and I/O are not specified (the compiler remembers the designation).

Figure 3-5
The CLOSE statement.

Format:

CLOSE file-name-1 [file-name-2]...

Example from PATLIST2:

```
CLOSE PATRON-FILE
      PATRON-LIST.
```

The STOP Statement

To end program execution, the STOP RUN statement is used. It terminates execution of the program and returns control of computer resources to the operating system. Since the STOP RUN statement is the last statement executed in a COBOL program (that successfully executes), it is commonly referred to as the last *logical* statement, regardless of its physical placement.

Actually, STOP RUN is one of two forms of the STOP statement. If STOP is followed by a literal (instead of RUN), a message is displayed on the computer console and processing is suspended. Execution can be resumed at the statement following STOP by keyboard action. Examples in this book will not use this form of the STOP.

Changing Field Contents by Moving Data

As you know from Chapter 1, you can move data from one field to another. The values you move can also be defined as literals or figurative constants.

MOVE Statement

The MOVE verb is used to transfer data from one area of memory to another. Its format, together with three sample statements from PATLIST2, are shown in Figure 3-6. After the reserved word MOVE, either an identifier or a literal is coded. The term *identifier* means that a field-name from the DATA DIVISION must be coded. The literal can be either a literal or a figurative constant (these are described in the next section of this chapter).

Actually, the word MOVE is a misnomer because the action is one of copying. For instance, in the first example of Figure 3-6, the value stored in the field PR-NAME is copied into the field PL-NAME, as illustrated in Figure 3-7. Notice that the entire field from PR-NAME, including the spaces, is copied into PL-NAME.

Figure 3-6
The MOVE statement.

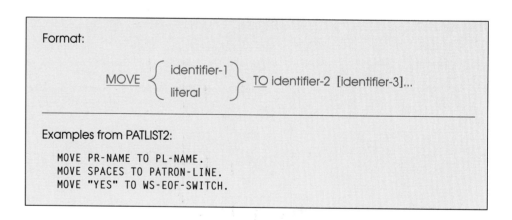

Format:

```
           ⎧ identifier-1 ⎫
MOVE       ⎨              ⎬  TO identifier-2  [identifier-3]...
           ⎩ literal      ⎭
```

Examples from PATLIST2:

```
MOVE PR-NAME TO PL-NAME.
MOVE SPACES TO PATRON-LINE.
MOVE "YES" TO WS-EOF-SWITCH.
```

Figure 3-7
Action of the MOVE STATEMENT.

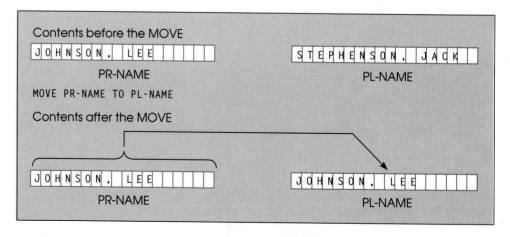

Contents before the MOVE

JOHNSON, LEE   — PR-NAME
STEPHENSON, JACK   — PL-NAME

MOVE PR-NAME TO PL-NAME

Contents after the MOVE

JOHNSON, LEE   — PR-NAME
JOHNSON, LEE   — PL-NAME

The format notation shows a third identifier enclosed in brackets and followed by an ellipsis (three periods). The ellipsis indicates that additional data-names may be written. Thus, one MOVE statement can be used to transfer data from one sending field to one or more receiving fields.

Notice that the MOVE statement initializing WS-EOF-SWITCH moves a literal that includes a space; that is:

```
MOVE "NO " TO WS-EOF-SWITCH.
```

The space is included with NO to make the literal three positions in length: the same as the length of WS-EOF-SWITCH. Actually, the space is not necessary (the literal need not be three positions in length), but we will use it for now. You will learn in Chapter 5 about the way in which the MOVE statement works when the fields are different lengths.

Literals   A value that is included as part of a program and remains fixed is called a **literal**. In mathematics, this is equivalent to a constant. COBOL includes two types of literals: numeric and nonnumeric. For instance, the following MOVE statement includes the nonnumeric literal YES.

```
MOVE "YES" TO WS-EOF-SWITCH.
```

A nonnumeric literal is like an alphanumeric field in that it can consist of any character of the character set (letters, digits, blank spaces, and special characters). For the compiler to distinguish them from data-names, they must be enclosed in quotation marks. The term *nonnumeric* is thus a bit misleading since the literal may contain one or more numeric digits. Indeed, it may be composed entirely of digits. Such a literal is nonnumeric in that it cannot be used in arithmetic calculations.

A nonnumeric literal can range from 1 to 120 characters in length. The quotation marks that enclose the literal act as delimiters to indicate the start and end of the literal value; they are not counted as part of the literal when determining its length.

Because the quotation marks act as delimiters, a quotation mark cannot appear singly as part of the literal itself (for it would be incorrectly interpreted by the compiler as marking the end of the literal). If quotation marks are supposed to be part of the literal, some compilers permit the coding of two delimiters in a row to be interpreted as that single character within the literal.

A numeric literal is simply a number that appears in the PROCEDURE DIVISION. For example, the 2 in the following statement is a numeric literal.

```
WRITE PATRON-LINE
    AFTER ADVANCING 2 LINES
```

Figurative Constants   The word SPACES is a particular type of reserved word called a **figurative constant**. A figurative constant is similar to a literal in that it provides a way of introducing an actual value into a COBOL program. It differs from a literal because the actual value is specified not with the value itself, but instead by a reserved word (such as SPACES). COBOL includes a few figurative constants other than SPACES; one of them is ZERO, which represents the numeric value zero. (It can also be written ZEROS and ZEROES.) You will learn about others in later chapters as appropriate.

Although the word SPACES is used in the PATLIST2 program (the first MOVE statement in the 200-PROCESS-PATRON-RECORD paragraph), the singular form SPACE is equivalent. Both singular and plural forms are provided to permit COBOL coding in accordance with grammatically correct English.

COBOL
Programming
Perspective

Quotation Mark Delimiters for Nonnumeric Literals

Although the ANSI COBOL standard calls for use of quotation marks (") to delimit nonnumeric literals, apostrophes (') are often used instead. When apostrophes are employed as the delimiters, they are typically referred to as **single quotes** to differentiate them from the normal, or **double quote**, marks.

Early IBM computer printers did not have a double-quote character on the print chain. As a result, pre-1968 IBM COBOL compilers used single quotes as the nonnumeric literal delimiters. Current IBM mainframe-computer compilers permit use of either single or double quotes; the programmer informs the compiler which quotes are being used by setting a compiler option to either QUOTE (double quotes) or APOST (single quotes or apostrophes).

Even though double quotes are now available, many installations with IBM compilers still use single quote marks as the delimiters. They do this because they have a large inventory of programs coded with the single quotes. Such installations prefer to keep the delimiter standard for all programs within their library and do not want to tackle the task of converting all the existing programs from single to double quotes.

Double quotes are the prevalent delimiter for users of compilers supplied by vendors other than IBM. However, due to IBM's mainframe-computer dominance, certain other vendors also provide the option to use single quotes.

Regardless of which delimiter is used, once in a while a situation will arise in which the delimiter character should be expressed as data within the nonnumeric literal. For example, suppose the company name DONALD "RED" RICHARDSON'S BROKERAGE were to be expressed as a nonnumeric literal. When double quotes are the delimiter, the quotation marks are not valid within the literal; for single quotes, the apostrophe is prohibited.

To solve such problems, most COBOL compilers permit two adjacent delimiter characters to be specified within a nonnumeric literal. When these adjacent delimiter pairs are encountered within the literal, the compiler properly treats the double occurrence as a single occurrence for the literal data. This means that the above company name example could be specified as follows:

Using double-quote delimiters:

```
"DONALD ""RED"" RICHARDSON'S BROKERAGE"
```

Using single-quote delimiters:

```
'DONALD "RED" RICHARDSON''S BROKERAGE'
```

In both cases, the literal data will be properly represented as:

```
DONALD "RED" RICHARDSON'S BROKERAGE
```

Initializing Fields

When program execution begins, fields defined in the DATA DIVISION contain either (1) unpredictable data left from the previous program that used that area of memory—commonly called **garbage**, or (2) an initialization value used by the operating system to clear storage—typically binary zeros. (The exception to this are fields in the WORKING-STORAGE SECTION defined with a VALUE clause, a topic of Chapter 5).

This means that you must code statements to explicitly initialize all fields that require a specific starting value. In PATLIST2, you see two instances of the need for initialization. One is the program switch WS-EOF-SWITCH. When execution of the program begins, it will contain garbage. (This could *possibly* be "YES", which would cause processing of the data file to be skipped if WS-EOF-SWITCH were not initialized to "NO".)

The other case of initialization is that of the output line area PATRON-LINE. When program execution begins, this entire area will contain garbage. Because the print chart calls for blank spaces between each data column on the report line, those unused areas (the FILLER data-items) must be blanked out or garbage will be printed in these positions of the report.

This area is cleared by the first MOVE statement in the 200-PROCESS-PATRON-RECORD paragraph.

```
MOVE SPACES TO PATRON-LINE
```

You might notice that it is an "overkill" because only the FILLER areas need be blanked; whatever is in data fields (for instance, PL-NAME) will be replaced by the actual data copied from the input record. Instead of blanking just the unused areas, however, it is easier to blank the whole line.

Since the data for each field in the output from one record is replaced by data from the next record, you might wonder about placing this line initialization statement in the 100-INITIALIZE-VARIABLE-FIELDS paragraph. After all, once the FILLER areas are set to spaces, nothing in the program changes them. The answer to this relates to the slow speeds of input/output devices relative to the internal speeds of the computer. In order to allow the operating system to overlap operations, many COBOL systems actually set up two memory buffer areas and automatically switch back and forth between them. Hence, moving spaces to the output line in the initialization procedure would clear only one of them. Then every other printed line would show garbage in the FILLER areas. The simplest solution is to clear the line each time prior to moving data into it.

A Simple Editing Action With the MOVE

Although the input record PATRON-RECORD includes the data field PR-CONTR-DATE (broken down into month, day, and year), it is not printed in the output report. Assume that you wanted to print this date together with appropriate punctuation. For example, the input value:

```
121391
```

would be printed as:

```
12/13/91
```

You can easily do this by setting up the date field in the output area and using a succession of MOVE statements. The necessary statements to do this for the PATLIST2 program are shown in Figure 3-8. Notice that each of the three subfields of the date-of-contribution fields—month, day, and year—were moved individually so that the separating slashes could be inserted where they belong on the

Figure 3-8
A simple editing operation.

```
05  PL-CONTR-DATE.
    10  PL-CONTR-MONTH        PIC X(2).
    10  PL-DATE-SEPARATOR-1   PIC X(1).        Part of the PATRON-LINE
    10  PL-CONTR-DAY          PIC X(2).        record definition.
    10  PL-DATE-SEPARATOR-2   PIC X(1).
    10  PL-CONTR-YEAR         PIC X(2).
        .
        .
        .
MOVE PR-CONTR-MONTH TO PL-CONTR-MONTH.
MOVE PR-CONTR-DAY TO PL-CONTR-DAY.            MOVE statements in the
MOVE PR-CONTR-YEAR TO PL-CONTR-YEAR.         200-PROCESS-PATRON-RECORD
MOVE "/" TO PL-DATE-SEPARATOR-1              paragraph.
              PL-DATE-SEPARATOR-2.
```

output line. The last MOVE, which inserts the slashes, is an example of a literal being copied into multiple (in this case, two) receiving fields.

The WRITE Statement
Writing a Record

When all data to be printed has been moved into the output area (PATRON-LINE in the PATLIST2 program), that line can be written to the output device. Although PATLIST2 prints the output, the WRITE statement is not limited to printing; it can also be used for writing output to any output device. (This determination depends upon entries in the ENVIRONMENT DIVISION.) The WRITE statement, shown in Figure 3-9, is used to cause a record to be transferred from main storage to an output device.

After the reserved word WRITE, you must specify the record-name (**not** the file-name, as is done for the READ statement) of the record to be written as output. You can use the ADVANCING phrase to control vertical forms spacing. Of course, this phrase applies only to report files; that is, those files ultimately directed to a printer device.

ADVANCING Phrase

Because the PATRON-RECORD is directed to a printer file, the ADVANCING phrase is used. Either BEFORE ADVANCING or AFTER ADVANCING could be specified. The former option means that first the line will be written and then the paper form will be advanced (the line is written BEFORE ADVANCING the form). The latter option is used for the reverse situation: the form will be advanced and then the line will be written (the line is written AFTER ADVANCING the form). The AFTER ADVANCING option is most commonly used. (Regardless of whether BEFORE or AFTER is coded, it is important to avoid using both in the same program. Such a combination can lead to program bugs in which one or more lines are printed one top of another.)

Since the print chart for the patron report calls for double-spacing, the integer 2 is specified in the ADVANCING phrase of the PATLIST2 program. After the number of lines, the optional reserved word LINE or LINES is written. When using the integer option, this word makes the WRITE statement a bit more readable, so it is a good idea to include it. Notice that the WRITE statement has been written with the ADVANCING phrase, indented, on a second coding line.

In the ADVANCING phrase, the number of lines can be expressed as an integer number (2 in this example; typically 1, 2, or 3), or as a variable (identifier). You will learn about using the identifier form and other forms in Chapter 5.

Figure 3-9
The WRITE statement.

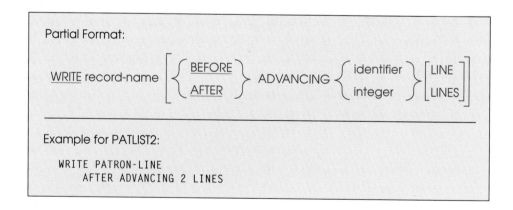

Partial Format:

$$\text{\underline{WRITE} record-name} \left[\begin{Bmatrix} \text{\underline{BEFORE}} \\ \text{\underline{AFTER}} \end{Bmatrix} \text{ADVANCING} \begin{Bmatrix} \text{identifier} \\ \text{integer} \end{Bmatrix} \begin{bmatrix} \text{LINE} \\ \text{LINES} \end{bmatrix} \right]$$

Example for PATLIST2:

```
WRITE PATRON-LINE
    AFTER ADVANCING 2 LINES
```

Figure 3-10
The READ statement.

Format:

> READ file-name
> [AT END imperative-statement]

Example:

```
READ PATRON-FILE
    AT END MOVE "YES" TO WS-EOF-SWITCH.
```

READ Statement
Reading a Record

The READ statement makes a logical record from an input file available to the program. The statement format is shown in Figure 3-10. Notice that, following the reserved word READ, the *file-name*—**not** the record-name—is specified. Although the AT END phrase is shown in brackets and is thus optional, it is required for any program which reads records from the file serially, one after another, until the end of the file is reached. Such *sequential access* is always used for magnetic tape and card files and is commonly used for disk files.

In the PATLIST2 program, executing a READ statement immediately after opening the files will cause the first record of the input PATRON-FILE to be read into the PATRON-RECORD record-description area of the FILE SECTION within the computer's main memory. Whatever was in that area of memory before execution of the READ statement will be overlaid (replaced) by the data transferred from the input file. This processing is illustrated in Figure 3-11. The data read into the FILE SECTION input record-description area remains there until the next READ statement is executed, which then overlays the area with the next record's data. (Although not commonly done, the data in the input area could also be overlaid by explicitly coding instructions to MOVE other data to it.)

AT END Phrase

One characteristic of sequential processing of a data file is that processing begins with the first record and proceeds through to the last. You learned from Concepts Module A that the last data record in a file is followed by a special EOF record. This is convenient because the program can be written to process until the EOF is encountered; no attention need be paid to the number of records in the file. The technique works as well with 50,000 records as with 5 records. The COBOL feature you have used to control this is the AT END phrase of the READ statement

When the AT END phrase is specified, one or more statements must be written after the reserved words AT END. The PATLIST2 program uses the statement:

```
MOVE "YES" TO WS-EOF-SWITCH
```

As illustrated in Figure 3-12, a READ statement with the AT END phrase works as follows:

1. If the next sequential record is obtained from the input file (that is, a data record is present in the file), the program skips the statement(s) after the reserved words AT END until the period terminating the sentence is reached. Program processing then resumes with the next consecutive sentence.

Figure 3-11   The effect of the READ statement.

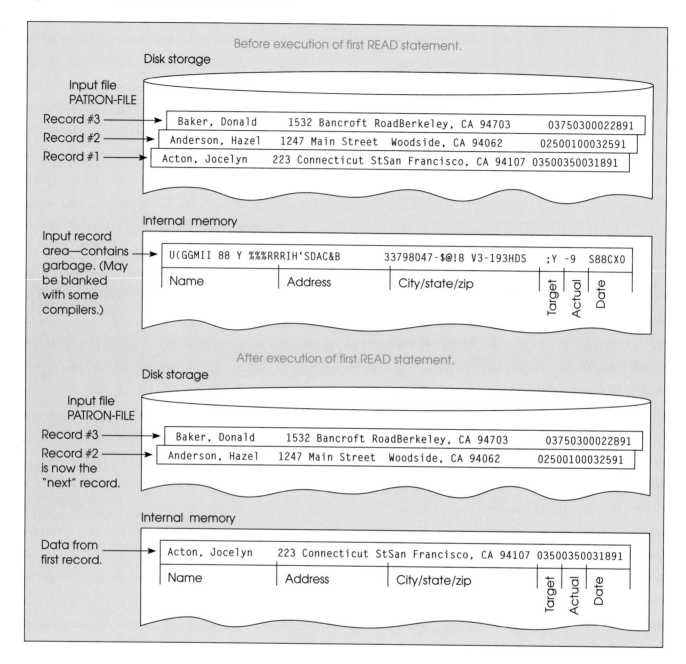

2. If the attempted READ finds that there are no more records in the file to read (that is, end-of-file is detected), the program executes the statement(s) following the reserved words AT END.

Two points about the AT END phrase should be noted. First, the end-of-file condition is not detected when the last data record is read. Instead, end-of-file is identified when the next attempted READ *after* the last data record occurs.

Second, the period following the AT END phrase is very important. It determines exactly which statements are skipped when a record has been read successfully. If you forget it, the compiler will look for the next period, thereby treating all encompassed statements as part of the conditionally executed code.

If you are using COBOL-85, you will learn an alternate recommended set of conventions at the end of this chapter.

Figure 3-12
AT END phrase logic.

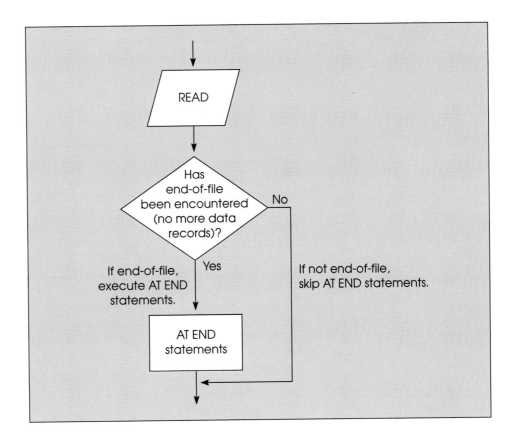

Principles of the PERFORM
The PERFORM Statement

You know from Chapter 1 that the PERFORM causes the computer to transfer control to another paragraph (procedure) in the program. When execution of that paragraph is completed, control is returned to the statement following the PERFORM. This is illustrated in Figure 3-13. Although not illustrated in this program, a performed procedure can perform still another procedure. For instance, the mainline procudure could perform procedure A; from within procudure A, there could be a PERFORM statement referring to procedure B. There is no limit to the number of levels that you can have in a program. (That is, one procedure can call another, which can call a third, and so on.)

The PERFORM/UNTIL Statement

The PERFORM/UNTIL statement operates in a manner similar to the basic PERFORM statement; it transfers control to another procedure of the program and provides for return of control when that procedure has been completed. The

Figure 3-13
Executing a PERFORM.

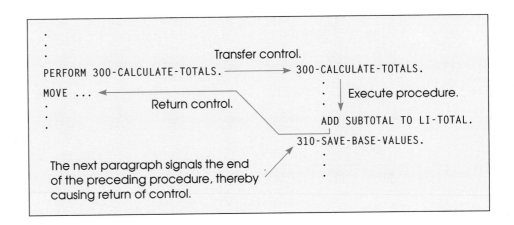

PERFORM/UNTIL statement, illustrated in Figure 3-14, has two important distinctions, however. First, it transfers control *conditionally*, depending upon the status of the condition expressed following the reserved word UNTIL:

1. If the condition is *false*, the specified procedure is performed.

2. If the condition is *true*, the procedure is not performed. Instead, program control continues to the next consecutive statement.

Second, upon return from the performed procedure, it retests the condition rather than proceeding to the next consecutive statement. Thus, the PERFORM/UNTIL statement provides for iterative (repetitive) processing, as illustrated in Figure C-5 (Concepts Module C).

A required element of the PERFORM/UNTIL is that the procedure being performed must eventually change a variable involved in the test condition so that the test condition becomes true. In this example, notice that this is done by the READ statement, the last one in the 200-PROCESS-PATRON-RECORD procedure. If this statement were accidentally omitted from the program, the test condition of the PERFORM/UNTIL would never become true. The consequence of this situation is the subject of a review question at the end of this chapter.

As long as records are being successfully obtained from the input file, the end-of-file switch will remain "NO ". This means that the condition

```
WS-EOF-SWITCH IS EQUAL TO "YES"
```

will be false. The false result thus causes an iteration of the 200-PROCESS-PATRON-RECORD procedure to be performed.

Finally, after the READ statement detects an end-of-file condition, the following will occur:

1. The value "YES" will be moved to the WS-EOF-SWITCH field.

2. Program control will return, as normal, from the 200-PROCESS-PATRON-RECORD procedure to the PERFORM/UNTIL statement.

3. The UNTIL condition of the PERFORM/UNTIL statement is tested and determined to be true.

Figure 3-14   Characteristics of the PERFORM/UNTIL.

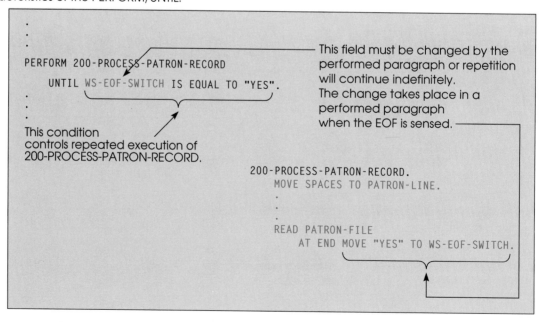

4. Because the UNTIL condition is now satisfied, program execution continues to the next consecutive statement following the PERFORM/UNTIL statement.

Observe that the PERFORM/UNTIL statement has been written to adhere to the style conventions of one phrase per line and an indented second line.

Conditional Operations
Examples in PATLIST2

One way of categorizing prior statement forms is to separate those that cause an action to be taken unconditionally from those that cause an action to be taken depending on some type of condition. For example, consider the READ statement:

```
READ PATRON-FILE
    AT END MOVE "YES" TO WS-EOF-SWITCH.
```

First, it causes a record to be read; then it causes another statement (the MOVE) to be executed *if a condition is true*.

Repeated execution of the 200 module is controlled by a similar type of conditional action using the following PERFORM:

```
PERFORM 200-PROCESS-PATRON-RECORD
    UNTIL WS-EOF-SWITCH IS EQUAL TO "YES".
```

In this case, an action is repeated *until a particular test condition becomes true* (until the value in WS-EOF-SWITCH is "YES").

The PATLIST2 program includes the IF statement, another form that causes something to happen on a conditional basis.

The IF Statement

PATLIST2 uses an IF statement shown in Figure 3-15 to determine whether or not to print two asterisks on the detail line for a patron. There should be no mystery about this form because it functions exactly as its English suggests. That is, if Actual-contribution is less than Target-contribution, the MOVE statement is executed; otherwise, it is skipped.

Although the IF statement's broad range of capabilities aren't described until Chapter 7, its partial format is shown in Figure 3-16.

Figure 3-15   The IF statement from PATLIST2.

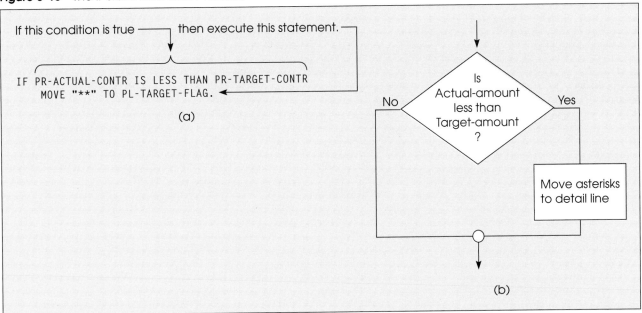

Figure 3-16
Format of the IF statement.

Partial Format:

IF condition statement.

The *condition* is the test element that determines whether or not an action is to be taken. In this program, both the IF and the PERFORM UNTIL have condition forms; these are illustrated in Figure 3-17. Here, two data quantities are linked by relational operators that define the type of comparison to be made. The result of evaluating such relational statements will be either a true or false condition. For instance, if WS-EOF-SWITCH contains YES, the relationship is true; otherwise, it is false.

In addition to the two relational operators illustrated in Figure 3-17, you can also use IS GREATER THAN. In all cases, they execute exactly as the English suggests.

You can also compare a numeric field to a constant value. For instance, if the list of patrons was to include all contributing more than $200, the IF would take the following form:

```
IF PR-ACTUAL-CONTR IS GREATER THAN 200
```

You will learn more about conditional forms in Chapter 7.

Basic Logic of PATLIST2

Let's back off from the details of COBOL for a moment and consider in general terms the processing of data from a file. In a broad sense, we want to repeatedly execute the following sequence of instructions until all data records have been processed:

Do the following until all records have been processed

Read a record
Process the record
Write the results.

Figure 3-17
Conditional forms.

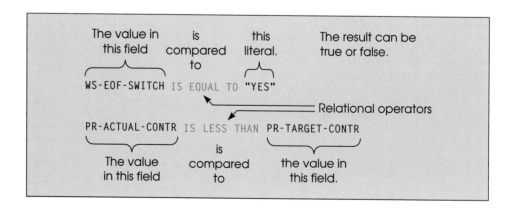

The problem with using this logic in a COBOL program is that the program will attempt to process the EOF record as if it were data. The results will be unpredictable.

Some programming languages get around this problem by allowing the programmer to check on the *next* record before reading it. This "look-ahead" feature allows programming logic that take the following form:

Do the following while the next record is not the EOF

Read a record
Process the record
Write the results.

Unfortunately, COBOL does not have this capability. However, by now you are familiar with the technique used in both PATLIST and PATLIST2 which effectively simulates this look-ahead feature. That is, you have used the following logic:

Read the first record.

Do the following while the current record is not the EOF

Process the record
Write the results
Read a record.

This is commonly called **priming** the input area; the initial read statement is called the **priming read**. All programs in this book use the priming read.

Scope Terminators and the Use of Periods in COBOL-85

With COBOL-74, the accepted practice is to end each statement with a period. However, you will find in Chapter 7 that an IF statement can include more than one statement to be executed on a conditional basis. This range of the IF, called the **scope** of the IF, is signaled to the compiler by using a period after only the last statement of the conditional group. The period serves as a **scope terminator**.

Consistent with the general forms and needs of structured programming principles (and some inabilities of the COBOL-74 form), COBOL-85 includes special entries for identifying the scope of a group of conditionally executed statements. Special **scope terminators** can be used in conjunction with 19 different verbs to signal the end of a conditionally executed sequence of statements. The two statements of PATLIST2 for which scope terminators are appropriate are READ and IF; their corresponding terminators are END-READ and END-IF. A version of PATLIST2 using COBOL-85 is shown in Figure 3-18.

With the scope terminator feature of COBOL-85, there is no reason to use periods within paragraphs. (In fact, they are easy to misuse, thereby resulting in program errors.) Hence, as a standard in this book, all program examples illustrating COBOL-85 will use periods in the PROCEDURE DIVISION only following the paragraph header and following the last statement of a paragraph (both are required).

Chapter Summary

The PROCEDURE DIVISION of a COBOL program expresses the logic that the computer is to follow to obtain the specified results. The PROCEDURE DIVISION may contain user-defined sections, but typically does not. Paragraph-names within

Figure 3-18
COBOL-85 PROCEDURE
DIVISION for PATLIST2.

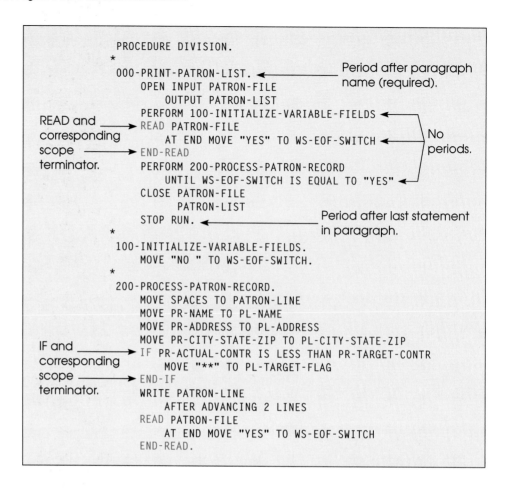

the PROCEDURE DIVISION are user-defined words. Paragraphs and paragraph-names within the PROCEDURE DIVISION are alternatively referred to as **procedures** and **procedure-names**, respectively.

A PROCEDURE DIVISION paragraph contains one or more sentences. A **sentence** contains one or more COBOL statements. A **statement** is a syntactically valid combination of COBOL words that begins with a COBOL verb. Following are the statements described in this chapter:

CLOSE	Terminates processing for one or more files.
IF	Provides a conditional capability; allows an action to be taken or skipped.
MOVE	Copies data from one area of computer memory to another.
OPEN	Makes one or more files ready for processing; must be issued before records of a file can be accessed.
PERFORM	Transfers control to a specified procedure-name and, after the procedure has been executed, returns to the next consecutive statement from which control was transferred.
PERFORM/UNTIL	Operates like a PERFORM statement except that it transfers control conditionally, depending upon the status of the condition expressed in the UNTIL phrase. Upon return, it retests the condition and hence provides iterative processing.

READINGMakes a logical record from an input file available to the program. For sequential input files, it must contain an AT END phrase defining the action to be taken when the file EOF is detected.

STOPTerminates program execution and returns computer control to the operating system.

COBOL-85 Only

END-IFEnds the scope of an IF statement.

END-READEnds the scope of the AT END phrase in a READ statement.

COBOL Language Element Summary

A **COBOL verb** is a word that expresses an action to be taken by a COBOL program. It must begin in Area B.

Nonnumeric literals are used when it is necessary to introduce actual values into a program. They

- Must be enclosed by quotation marks (single or double)
- May contain any characters acceptable to the computer system being used
- Must not exceed 120 characters

Figurative constants are preassigned reserved words that represent actual values.

COBOL Structure Summary

Refer to Figure 3-19 on the following page.

Style Summary

PROCEDURE DIVISION conventions

- Code the OPEN statement with each file-name on a separate line. Vertically align each file-name.
- Code the READ statement with the AT END phrase on a separate line. Indent the AT END phrase four spaces.
- Code the PERFORM/UNTIL statement with the UNTIL phrase on a separate line. Indent the UNTIL phrase four spaces.
- When a MOVE statement will not fit on one coding line, write the reserved word TO and the name of the receiving field on a separate line. Indent the second line four spaces.
- When a MOVE statement has multiple receiving fields, write each receiving field (after the first one) on a separate line. Vertically align each receiving field.
- To ensure optimum efficiency, expand shorter sending-field nonnumeric literals (with blank spaces to the right of the literal data) so that they are equal in length to the receiving field.
- Code the WRITE statement with the ADVANCING phrase on a separate line. Indent the ADVANCING phrase four spaces.
- Code the CLOSE statement with each file-name on a separate line; align the file names.
- In COBOL-85, use periods only at the end of paragraph-names and after the last statement of a paragraph.

Figure 3-19 COBOL Structure Summary chart.

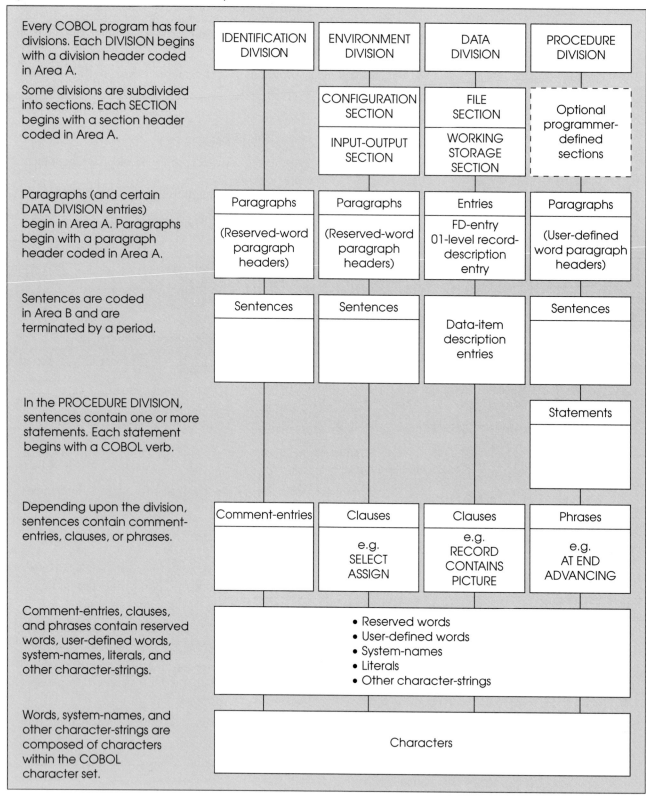

Features in COBOL-85 not in COBOL-74 In COBOL-85, the scope terminators END-READ and END-IF can be used to terminate the conditionally executed statements following the READ/AT END and the IF. All COBOL-85 examples in this book use scope terminators when appropriate.

Exercises
Terms for Definition

COBOL verb _____

conditional statement _____

figurative constant _____

identifier _____

literal _____

mainline procedure _____

nonnumeric literal _____

priming-read _____

procedure-name _____

sentence _____

statement _____

Review Questions

1. The use of sections is _____ in the PROCEDURE DIVISION.

2. A paragraph in the PROCEDURE DIVISION can also be termed a(n) _____ .

3. A procedure-name is a(n) _____ word.

4. A PROCEDURE DIVISION paragraph contains a series of _____ .

5. A syntactically valid combination of COBOL words and symbols beginning with a verb is called a(n) _____ .

6. Procedure-names begin in Area _____ .

7. COBOL verbs begin in Area _____ .

8. A(n) _____ statement must be coded before a data file can be processed.

9. The _____ statement transfers data from one area of computer memory to another.

10. The _____ statement makes a logical record from an input file available to the program.

11. The _____ statement causes a record to be transferred from computer memory to an output device.

12. The _____ statement terminates processing for a file.

13. The _____ statement terminates program execution.

14. The READ statement references the _____ -name; the WRITE statement references the _____ -name.

15. When an UNTIL condition is coded for a PERFORM statement, the condition is tested _____ (before/after) the specified procedure is performed.

16. The COBOL language element used to introduce an actual value into a program is known as a(n) _____ .

17. A nonnumeric literal must be enclosed by _____ and is limited to a length of _____ characters.

18. Preassigned words that represent actual values are known as _____ .

Questions Pertaining to PATLIST2

1. Referring to Figure 3-1, a programmer accidentally omits the last statement of the 200 paragraph of PATLIST2 (READ). Will the compiler detect this omission and give an error diagnostic? What will happen when the program is run?

_____

_____

_____

2. What would happen during execution of PATLIST2 if the data file to be processed contained no data records (it contained only the EOF record)?

_____

_____

_____

3. In PATLIST2, two asterisk characters are moved to the output field PL-TARGET-FLAG if actual-contribution is less than target-contribution. Why isn't it necessary to move two spaces for the others (those where actual-contribution is not less than target-contribution) in order to replace asterisks that may have been moved from the preceding record?

_____

_____

_____

Programming Assignments

To complete a programming assignment started in Chapter 2, perform the following tasks:

1. Draw a structure chart of the PROCEDURE DIVISION for the problem.

2. Prepare program design documentation (such as pseudocode or program flowchart) for the PROCEDURE DIVISION.

3. Add the coding for the PROCEDURE DIVISION to the coding of the first three divisions completed for Chapter 2.

4. Obtain a clean compile of the complete program.

5. Execute the program, using the data file specified by your instructor. Check the output carefully to make sure that your program is working properly.

Special note for Assignment 3-2 (Assignment 2-2 in Chapter 2).
You will need to use the IF statement when moving the Status-code field to the output line. A test condition of IS EQUAL TO (the form you studied in this chapter) functions exactly as the English suggests. You will need to use the test condition IS NOT EQUAL TO. It also functions exactly as the English suggests.

CHAPTER 3
Debugging Supplement

Supplement Objectives

In the Chapter 2 debugging supplement, you learned some guidelines for debugging the first three divisions of a program. As you begin to code the assignments of Chapter 3, you will find that apparently minor errors in the DATA DIVISION can have a significant effect on statements in the PROCEDURE DIVISION. This debugging supplement continues from Chapter 2's. In this supplement, you will learn the following:

- How to recognize the effect in the PROCEDURE DIVISION of errors made in other divisions.

- The nature of logic errors.

  Data-definition errors: incorrect entries in the record definition.
  Logic errors that direct the computer to perform operations other than those you desire, thereby resulting in incorrect output.
  Program errors that direct the computer to perform an action of which it is not capable, thereby causing termination of the program.

- How to use structured walkthroughs to ensure program soundness.

- The creation and use of test data to ensure that a program performs the functions for which it was intended.

Supplement Outline

Compiler-Detected Errors
Avoiding Syntax Errors
The PATLIST2 Program With Errors

Diagnostics From IBM Mainframe COBOL
Incorrect Name for the Output Record
Incorrect Definition of WS-EOF-SWITCH
Using REA Instead of READ
About Making Corrections

Diagnostics From Ryan-McFarland COBOL
Misuse of the Reserved Word DAY
Incorrect Definition of WS-EOF-SWITCH
Using REA Instead of READ
About Making Corrections

Logic Errors
Data-Definition Mistakes
Incorrect Logic
Runtime Errors
Structured Walkthroughs
Program Testing

Compiler-Detected Errors
Avoiding Syntax Errors

As you will learn, there are numerous types of PROCEDURE DIVISION errors you can make that the compiler will detect. These include the common syntactical errors similar to those described in the debugging supplement to Chapter 2. A brief summary of errors for you to guard against in the PROCEDURE DIVISION is included as Figure 3S-1.

Regarding the use of periods, the only *required* periods (COBOL-74) are the following:

1. After the paragraph header.

2. To indicate the scope of a conditionally executed sequence of statements (for example, the last statement following the AT END of a READ).

3. After the last statement of a paragraph.

In COBOL-85, a period must not be used within the scope of a conditionally executed sequence that is terminated by a scope terminator.

Concerning names that you select in a program, you define the following types of names in one part of the program for use in the PROCEDURE DIVISION:

- File-name for a file (defined in the ENVIRONMENT DIVISION)

- Data-name for a record or field (defined in the DATA DIVISION)

- Procedure-name for a paragraph (defined in the PROCEDURE DIVISION)

One of the most common errors is to use a slightly different spelling for a name in the PROCEDURE DIVISION than the defined spelling; the exact spelling must be

Figure 3S-1
Checklist of common PROCEDURE DIVISION syntactical errors.

Syntactical errors	PROCEDURE DIVISION
Omitted period	`PROCEDURE DIVISION`⬈
	To terminate each procedure-name
	To terminate the last sentence of a paragraph
	To terminate scope of IF
Extra period	Premature terminating scope of IF

	`IF FIELD-A IS EQUAL TO FIELD-B`
	`    MOVE PR-INFIELD TO WS-CHECK.`⬈
	`    ADD 1 TO WS-ACCUM.`

Omitted hyphen	In procedure-names

Extra hyphen	`PROCEDURE⌄-DIVISION`
	`AT-END`
	`AFTER-ADVANCING`
	`STOP-RUN`

Omitted blank space	`FIELD-A +FIELD-B` (in COMPUTE statement)
Inadvertent blank space	`MOVE FIELD-⌄A TO FIELD-B.`
Incorrect Area A placement	COBOL statements
Spelling	All reserved words
	All data names as defined in DATA DIVISION

used throughout the program. You can minimize the chances of doing this by not using defining names that are confusing abbreviations of the entities they represent. For instance, EM-SVGS-RPRT is a poor abbreviation for employee savings report; it is too easy to forget your exact abbreviation when coding the PROCEDURE DIVISION. You might incorrectly remember it as EM-SVGS-RPT. Although EM-SAVINGS-REPORT requires more typing, it is much easier to remember. The example program for debugging in this supplement illustrates this error.

The PATLIST2 Program With Errors

For the purpose of illustrating post-compile diagnostics, three errors have been introduced into the PATLIST2 program. They are:

1. **IBM Mainframe COBOL:** The output record name has been entered as PATRON-LIST instead of PATRON-LINE. Note that this is identical to the file name (see line 48).

   Ryan-McFarland COBOL: The reserved word DAY has been used in place of the word PR-CONTR-DAY when defining the input record in the DATA DIVISION. You are familiar with this error from the example of the Chapter 2 debugging supplement. Recall that it was detected by the compiler.

2. The switch WS-EOF-SWITCH is defined in the WORKING-STORAGE SECTION without the two-letter prefix (as EOF-SWITCH).

3. The last statement in the 200 procedure has its verb spelled REA rather than READ.

Diagnostics From IBM Mainframe COBOL

The IBM mainframe post-compile listing is shown in Figure 3S-2; the statements in error are in color. Diagnostics resulting from this compile are shown in Figure 3S-3. Let's consider the effect of each program error on statements in the program.

Incorrect Name for the Output Record

Using PATRON-LIST for the file name and PATRON-LINE for the record name is descriptive, but the names are similar enough that the error at line 52 (using LIST instead of LINE) is an easy one to make. This is a relatively insignificant little error—only two incorrect letters. However, its consequences in the PROCEDURE DIVISION are not insignificant. It results in the name PATRON-LIST being defined twice (lines 48 and 52). Then any reference in the program to the name PATRON-LIST presents the compiler with an ambiguity: which PATRON-LIST is being referenced, the one at line 48 or the one at line 52? This results in the following errors:

25   The SELECT statement requires the unique file-name.

72   The name PATRON-LIST is identified as not unique. Notice, in contrast to the next diagnostic, that the entire statement is not ignored.

79   Because the CLOSE statement refers to the file PATRON-LIST (not unique), the entire statement is discarded. Note that this statement causes two error messages to be generated.

87   By using the wrong spelling on the record name, the correct name (PATRON-LINE) is not defined as indicated in this diagnostic.

93   PATRON-LINE diagnostic: same error as line 87.

You can see that a relatively simple error in the DATA DIVISION can have far-reaching consequences in the PROCEDURE DIVISION. This example is not unusual.

Incorrect Definition of WS-EOF-SWITCH

Referring to line 66 of the listing, notice that there is no indication of misspelling of EOF-SWITCH—its spelling meets all of the rules for user-defined names. Of course, the problem comes when that field is referred to by another name in the

Figure 3S-2   Post-compile listing from IBM mainframe COBOL.

```
00001          IDENTIFICATION DIVISION.                      00048     FD  PATRON-LIST
00002                                                        00049             RECORD CONTAINS 132 CHARACTERS
00003          PROGRAM-ID.    PATLIST2.                      00050             LABEL RECORDS ARE OMITTED.
00004          AUTHOR.        PRICE/WELBURN.                 00051
00005          INSTALLATION.  FLEETWOOD CHARITIES.           00052     01  PATRON-LIST.  ◄── Should be PATRON-LINE.
00006          DATE-WRITTEN.  9/21/90.                       00053         05  FILLER              PIC X(1).
00007          SECURITY.      CONFIDENTIAL.                  00054         05  PL-NAME             PIC X(18).
00008                                                        00055         05  FILLER              PIC X(1).
00009      *     THIS PROGRAM PRINTS A PATRON ADDRESS LIST   00056         05  PL-ADDRESS          PIC X(18).
00010      *     AND FLAGS DELINQUENT PATRONS.               00057         05  FILLER              PIC X(1).
00011                                                        00058         05  PL-CITY-STATE-ZIP   PIC X(24).
00012                                                        00059         05  FILLER              PIC X(1).
00013          ENVIRONMENT DIVISION.                         00060         05  PL-TARGET-FLAG      PIC X(2).
00014                                                        00061         05  FILLER              PIC X(66).
00015          CONFIGURATION SECTION.                        00062
00016                                                        00063     WORKING-STORAGE SECTION.
00017          SOURCE-COMPUTER.  IBM-4381.                   00064
00018          OBJECT-COMPUTER.  IBM-4381.                   00065     01  WS-SWITCHES.
00019                                                        00066         05  EOF-SWITCH          PIC X(3).
00020          INPUT-OUTPUT SECTION.                         00067                    ▲
00021                                                        00068                    └──── Should be WS-OF-SWITCH.
00022          FILE-CONTROL.                                 00069     PROCEDURE DIVISION.
00023              SELECT PATRON-FILE                        00070
00024                  ASSIGN TO SYS010-DA-3340-S.           00071     000-PRINT-PATRON-LIST.
00025              SELECT PATRON-LIST                        00072         OPEN INPUT PATRON-FILE
00026                  ASSIGN TO SYS005-UR-1403-S.           00073              OUTPUT PATRON-LIST.
00027                                                        00074         PERFORM 100-INITIALIZE-VARIABLE-FIELDS.
00028                                                        00075         READ PATRON-FILE
00029          DATA DIVISION.                                00076             AT END MOVE "YES" TO WS-EOF-SWITCH.
00030                                                        00077         PERFORM 200-PROCESS-PATRON-RECORD
00031          FILE SECTION.                                 00078             UNTIL WS-EOF-SWITCH IS EQUAL TO "YES".
00032                                                        00079         CLOSE PATRON-FILE
00033          FD  PATRON-FILE                               00080              PATRON-LIST.
00034              RECORD CONTAINS 74 CHARACTERS             00081         STOP RUN.
00035              LABEL RECORDS ARE STANDARD.               00082
00036                                                        00083     100-INITIALIZE-VARIABLE-FIELDS.
00037          01  PATRON-RECORD.                            00084         MOVE "NO " TO WS-EOF-SWITCH.
00038              05  PR-NAME          PIC X(18).           00085
00039              05  PR-ADDRESS       PIC X(18).           00086     200-PROCESS-PATRON-RECORD.
00040              05  PR-CITY-STATE-ZIP PIC X(24).          00087         MOVE SPACES TO PATRON-LINE.
00041              05  PR-TARGET-CONTR  PIC 9(4).            00088         MOVE PR-NAME TO PL-NAME.
00042              05  PR-ACTUAL-CONTR  PIC 9(4).            00089         MOVE PR-ADDRESS TO PL-ADDRESS.
00043              05  PR-CONTR-DATE.                        00090         MOVE PR-CITY-STATE-ZIP TO PL-CITY-STATE-ZIP.
00044                  10  PR-CONTR-MONTH PIC X(2).          00091         IF PR-ACTUAL-CONTR IS LESS THAN PR-TARGET-CONTR
00045                  10  PR-CONTR-DAY   PIC X(2).          00092             MOVE "**" TO PL-TARGET-FLAG.
00046                  10  PR-CONTR-YEAR  PIC X(2).          00093         WRITE PATRON-LINE
00047                                                        00094             AFTER ADVANCING 2 LINES.
                                                             00095         REA PATRON-FILE
                                                             00096          ▲ AT END MOVE "YES" TO WS-EOF-SWITCH.
                                                                           └── Should be READ.
```

Figure 3S-3   Diagnostics from IBM mainframe compile.

```
CARD    ERROR MESSAGE

00025   ILA2025I-E    FILE-NAME NOT UNIQUE FILE  IGNORED.
00072   ILA3002I-E    ' PATRON-LIST ' NOT UNIQUE. DELETING TILL LEGAL ELEMENT FOUND.
00076   ILA3001I-E    ' WS-EOF-SWITCH ' NOT DEFINED. DISCARDED.
00077   ILA3001I-E    ' WS-EOF-SWITCH ' NOT DEFINED. TEST DISCARDED.
00079   ILA3002I-E    ' PATRON-LIST ' NOT UNIQUE. DELETING TILL LEGAL ELEMENT FOUND.
00079   ILA4002I-E    CLOSE STATEMENT INCOMPLETE. STATEMENT DISCARDED.
00084   ILA3001I-E    ' WS-EOF-SWITCH ' NOT DEFINED. DISCARDED.
00087   ILA3001I-E    ' PATRON-LINE ' NOT DEFINED. DISCARDED.
00093   ILA3001I-E    ' PATRON-LINE ' NOT DEFINED. DISCARDED.
00093   ILA3001I-E    ' REA ' NOT DEFINED. DELETING TILL LEGAL ELEMENT FOUND.
00096   ILA3001I-E    ' WS-EOF-SWITCH ' NOT DEFINED. DISCARDED.
```

PROCEDURE DIVISION, which occurs four times. You see this in the diagnostic NOT DEFINED message for the following program lines:

76   In the AT END clause, a value is moved into WS-EOF-SWITCH, a field that does not exist.

77   The UNTIL controlling repeated execution of the 200 procedure tests WS-EOF-SWITCH.

84   The MOVE statement refers to WS-EOF-SWITCH.

96   Notice in this case that even though the verb at line 95 is unrecognized, the compiler still checks the statement following the AT END. Hence, this diagnostic is identical to that of the corresponding READ at line 76.

Using REA Instead of READ

This is localized and results in a single diagnostic localized to the statement. Interestingly, the diagnostic identifies the error as being at line 93, perhaps as a result of the WRITE diagnostic. The message itself, VERB REQUIRED, is clear; REA is not an acceptable verb. With some errors and combinations of errors, the compiler has difficulty discerning exactly where the problem lies. You will occasionally get strange line references such as this.

About Making Corrections

When you get a post-compile listing with diagnostics, you must inspect each of the messages and write in the corrections adjacent to the statement in error. Then, with an appropriate editor, make the corrections to your program and recompile it.

However, occasionally you will have a relatively minor error in one part of a program that will give you so many diagnostics in the PROCEDURE DIVISION that it will be extremely clumsy working through the listing. For instance, you have seen that the compiler, upon detecting duplication of the word PATRON-LIST, discards those entries. Hence, each reference in the PROCEDURE DIVISION to both PATRON-LIST (duplicated) and PATRON-LINE (undefined) produces a diagnostic. When a situation such as that occurs, giving you several times as many diagnostic lines as program lines, find the problem producing that error, correct it, and run another compile. If you have other errors, you will have a post-compile listing that is far easier to work with than your first.

Diagnostics From Ryan-McFarland COBOL

The RM COBOL post-compile listing beginning with program line 33 is shown in Figure 3S-4. (The first 32 program lines were omitted from this figure because they contain no statements in error.) The actual statements in error are in color. Let's consider the effect of each on subsequent statements in the program.

Misuse of the Reserved Word DAY

You know from the Chapter 2 debugging supplement that using the reserved word DAY in the input record description gives a file description error (see the last line of the listing). Hence, whenever there is reference to this file, a diagnostic will be given. You see this in the diagnostic FILE-NAME INVALID at the following lines in the program:

72   The OPEN statement refers to PATRON-FILE; this name was not defined in the DATA DIVISION because the use of DAY in the record description invalidated the file name. Notice that the compiler ignores everything from that point until the end of that statement. (The scan is resumed at the period.)

75   The READ statement refers to the PATRON-FILE. In this case, notice where the scan resumes—following the AT END clause. The compiler recognizes the AT END (even though the READ has an error) and resumes checking.

79   The CLOSE statement refers to PATRON-FILE; this error is identical in nature to that of the OPEN.

Incorrect Definition of WS-EOF-SWITCH

Referring to line 66 of the listing, notice that there is no indication of misspelling of EOF-SWITCH—this meets all of the rules for user-defined names. Of course, the problem comes when that field is referred to by another name in the PROCEDURE DIVISION, which occurs four times. You see this in the diagnostic IDENTIFIER UNDEFINED at the following lines in the program:

Figure 3S-4   Post-compile listing with diagnostics from Ryan-McFarland COBOL.

```
     LINE    DEBUG    PG/LN    A...B.......2.........3.........4.........5.........6.........7..

      33                       FD  PATRON-FILE
      34                           RECORD CONTAINS 74 CHARACTERS
      35                           LABEL RECORDS ARE STANDARD.
      36
      37                       01  PATRON-RECORD.
      38                           05  PR-NAME                    PIC X(18).
      39                           05  PR-ADDRESS                 PIC X(18).
      40                           05  PR-CITY-STATE-ZIP          PIC X(24).
      41                           05  PR-TARGET-CONTR            PIC 9(4).
      42                           05  PR-ACTUAL-CONTR            PIC 9(4).
      43                           05  PR-CONTR-DATE.
      44                           10  MONTH      Reserved        PIC X(2).
      45                           10  DAY  ◄──── word.           PIC X(2).
                                         $
***** 1) E 384: RESERVED USER WORD   (SCAN SUPPRESSED)  *E*E*E*E*E*E*E*E*E*E*E*E*E*E*E

      46                           10  YEAR                       PIC X(2).
      47
      48                       FD  PATRON-LIST
                                   $
***** 1) I    5: SCAN RESUME *I*I*I*I*I*I*I*I*I*I*I*I*I*I*I*I*I*I*I*I*I*I*I*I*I*I*I*I*I
***** LAST DIAGNOSTIC AT LINE:     44

      49                           RECORD CONTAINS 132 CHARACTERS
      50                           LABEL RECORDS ARE OMITTED.
      51
      52                       01  PATRON-LINE.
      53                           05  FILLER                     PIC X(1).
      54                           05  PL-NAME                    PIC X(18).
      55                           05  FILLER                     PIC X(1).
      56                           05  PL-ADDRESS                 PIC X(18).
      57                           05  FILLER                     PIC X(1).
      58                           05  PL-CITY-STATE-ZIP          PIC X(24).
      59                           05  FILLER                     PIC X(1).
      60                           05  PL-TARGET-FLAG             PIC X(2).
      61                           05  FILLER                     PIC X(66).
      62
      63                       WORKING-STORAGE SECTION.
      64
      65                       01  WS-SWITCHES.
      66                           05  EOF-SWITCH                 PIC X(3).
      67
      68                              ◄────── Should be WS-EOF-SWITCH.
      69                       PROCEDURE DIVISION.
      70
      71    000002            000-PRINT-PATRON-LIST.
      72    000005                OPEN INPUT PATRON-FILE
                                            $
***** 1) E 207: FILE-NAME INVALID  (SCAN SUPPRESSED)   *E*E*E*E*E*E*E*E*E*E*E*E*E*E*E
***** LAST DIAGNOSTIC AT LINE:     47

      73                                OUTPUT PATRON-LIST.
                                                         $
***** 1) I    5: SCAN RESUME *I*I*I*I*I*I*I*I*I*I*I*I*I*I*I*I*I*I*I*I*I*I*I*I*I*I*I*I*I
***** LAST DIAGNOSTIC AT LINE:     71

      74    000008                PERFORM 100-INITIALIZE-VARIABLE-FIELDS.
      75    000011                READ PATRON-FILE
                                       $
***** 1) E 207: FILE-NAME INVALID  (SCAN SUPPRESSED)   *E*E*E*E*E*E*E*E*E*E*E*E*E*E*E
***** LAST DIAGNOSTIC AT LINE:     72

      76    000014                    AT END MOVE "YES" TO WS-EOF-SWITCH.
                                             $                $          $
***** 1) I    5: SCAN RESUME *I*I*I*I*I*I*I*I*I*I*I*I*I*I*I*I*I*I*I*I*I*I*I*I*I*I*I*I*I
***** 2) E 263: IDENTIFIER UNDEFINED   (SCAN SUPPRESSED)  *E*E*E*E*E*E*E*E*E*E*E*E*E*E
***** 3) I    5: SCAN RESUME *I*I*I*I*I*I*I*I*I*I*I*I*I*I*I*I*I*I*I*I*I*I*I*I*I*I*I*I*I
***** LAST DIAGNOSTIC AT LINE:     74
```

Figure 3S-4   (continued)

```
    77    000017                    PERFORM 200-PROCESS-PATRON-RECORD
    78                                 UNTIL WS-EOF-SWITCH IS EQUAL TO "YES".
                                         $                                    $
*****  1) E 263: IDENTIFIER UNDEFINED   (SCAN SUPPRESSED)  *E*E*E*E*E*E*E*E*E*E*E*E*E*E*E
*****  2) I   5: SCAN RESUME *I*I*I*I*I*I*I*I*I*I*I*I*I*I*I*I*I*I*I*I*I*I*I*I*I*I*I*I*I*I*I
***** LAST DIAGNOSTIC AT LINE:    75

    79    000020                    CLOSE PATRON-FILE
                                          $
*****  1) E 207: FILE-NAME INVALID  (SCAN SUPPRESSED)   *E*E*E*E*E*E*E*E*E*E*E*E*E*E*E*E
***** LAST DIAGNOSTIC AT LINE:    77

    80                                 PATRON-LIST.
                                               $
*****  1) I   5: SCAN RESUME *I*I*I*I*I*I*I*I*I*I*I*I*I*I*I*I*I*I*I*I*I*I*I*I*I*I*I*I*I*I*I
***** LAST DIAGNOSTIC AT LINE:    78

    81    000023                    STOP RUN.
    82
    83    000026                 100-INITIALIZE-VARIABLE-FIELDS.
    84    000029                    MOVE "NO " TO WS-EOF-SWITCH.
                                          $              $
*****  1) E 263: IDENTIFIER UNDEFINED   (SCAN SUPPRESSED)  *E*E*E*E*E*E*E*E*E*E*E*E*E*E*E
*****  2) I   5: SCAN RESUME *I*I*I*I*I*I*I*I*I*I*I*I*I*I*I*I*I*I*I*I*I*I*I*I*I*I*I*I*I*I*I
***** LAST DIAGNOSTIC AT LINE:    79

    85
    86    000034                 200-PROCESS-PATRON-RECORD.
    87    000037                    MOVE SPACES TO PATRON-LINE.
    88    000043                    MOVE PR-NAME TO PL-NAME.
    89    000050                    MOVE PR-ADDRESS TO PL-ADDRESS.
    90    000057                    MOVE PR-CITY-STATE-ZIP TO PL-CITY-STATE-ZIP.
    91    000064                    IF PR-ACTUAL-CONTR IS LESS THAN PR-TARGET-CONTR
    92            Should                MOVE "**" TO PL-TARGET-FLAG.
    93    000078   be READ.        WRITE PATRON-LINE
    94                                 AFTER ADVANCING 2 LINES.
    95    000091                    REA PATRON-FILE
                                      $
*****  1) E 465: VERB REQUIRED   (SCAN SUPPRESSED)   *E*E*E*E*E*E*E*E*E*E*E*E*E*E*E*E*E*E
***** LAST DIAGNOSTIC AT LINE:    83

    96    000094                    AT END MOVE "YES" TO WS-EOF-SWITCH.
                                          $          $           $
*****  1) I   5: SCAN RESUME *I*I*I*I*I*I*I*I*I*I*I*I*I*I*I*I*I*I*I*I*I*I*I*I*I*I*I*I*I*I*I
*****  2) E 263: IDENTIFIER UNDEFINED   (SCAN SUPPRESSED)  *E*E*E*E*E*E*E*E*E*E*E*E*E*E*E
*****  3) I   5: SCAN RESUME *I*I*I*I*I*I*I*I*I*I*I*I*I*I*I*I*I*I*I*I*I*I*I*I*I*I*I*I*I*I*I
***** LAST DIAGNOSTIC AT LINE:    94




 E 173:  FILE DESCRIPTION  *E*E*E*E*E*E*E*E*E*E*E*E*E:  PATRON-FILE

    10 ERRORS          0 WARNINGS      FOR PROGRAM PATLIST2
```

76   In the AT END clause, a value is moved into WS-EOF-SWITCH, a field that does not exist.

78   The UNTIL controlling repeated execution of the 200 procedure tests WS-EOF-SWITCH.

84   The MOVE statement refers to WS-EOF-SWITCH.

96   Notice in this case that even though the verb at line 95 is unrecognized, the compiler still resumes the scan following something it recognizes (the AT END). Hence, this diagnostic is identical to that of the corresponding READ at line 76.

Using REA Instead of READ

This is the only error that is localized and results in a single diagnostic localized to the statement. That is, at line 95 you see the message VERB REQUIRED. REA is not an acceptable verb.

About Making Corrections

If you get a post-compile listing such as that in Figure 3S-3, you must inspect each of the diagnostics and write in the corrections adjacent to the statement in error. Then, with an appropriate editor, make the corrections to your program and re-compile it.

Sometimes a minor error in one part of a program will give you so many diagnostics in the PROCEDURE DIVISION that it will be difficult to work through the listing. For instance, you have seen that the compiler, upon detecting the reserved word DAY in the input record, did not resume its scan until it encountered the FD of the next file. If this reserved word had been the first name in the record description, all other field names would be ignored and hence undefined. Every reference to them in the PROCEDURE DIVISION would give a diagnostic. When a situation such as that occurs, giving you several times as many diagnostic lines as program lines, find the problem producing that error, correct it, and run another compile. If you have other errors, you will have a post-compile listing that is far easier to work with than your first.

Logic Errors

Logic errors are those in which you tell the computer to do the wrong thing. Some logic errors will cause the computer to do something that is "against the rules," thus causing your program to terminate (crash). Most others give erroneous results and can only be found by testing.

Data-Definition Mistakes

A common error, and one that is very easy to make, is to use an incorrect field length in the record description. It is critical that the definitions of records and fields in the picture-clause conform to the actual data as it is expressed in the programming specifications (which, in turn, should of course define the actual data characteristics stored in the records). Figure 3S-5 provides an example of how the incorrect definition of a field size will cause processing of misaligned data. For

Figure 3S-5   Example of a data definition error.

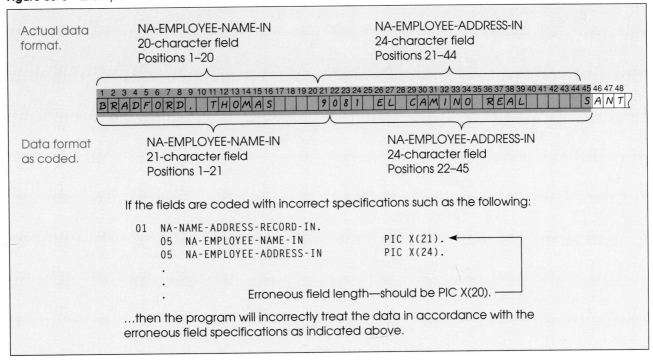

If the fields are coded with incorrect specifications such as the following:

```
01  NA-NAME-ADDRESS-RECORD-IN.
    05  NA-EMPLOYEE-NAME-IN         PIC X(21).
    05  NA-EMPLOYEE-ADDRESS-IN      PIC X(24).
    .
    .
    .
```

Erroneous field length—should be PIC X(20).

...then the program will incorrectly treat the data in accordance with the erroneous field specifications as indicated above.

these two fields, the only detectable error would be that the printed output would appear strange (an extra character at the end of the name, the first character of the address missing, and so on). However, if the shift resulted in nonnumeric data being part of a numeric field involved in an arithmetic operation, the program could crash.

Incorrect Logic

The PROCEDURE DIVISION statements should be written to correspond to the logic expressed in the pseudocode or flowchart (which should, of course, express the correct logic necessary to achieve the required results). If the logic of your program is incorrect, it will not produce the required results. The only way to detect this is through testing, whereby you create a set of test data, determine the exact output that should result from that data, then compare the program output to your expected results.

Problems frequently occur in conditionally executed statements. For instance, assume that you coded the IF statement in PATLIST2 as:

```
IF PR-ACTUAL-CONTR IS GREATER THAN PR-TARGET-CONTR
    MOVE "**" TO PL-TARGET-FLAG.
```

From this, you would obtain a listing of the patrons with some flagged as being below their target (a double asterisk) and others not flagged. Since this report does *not* print the amounts, you would be unable to detect that it was totally incorrect without referring to the original data. On the surface, the incorrect report probably would appear to be quite reasonable.

Too often, beginning programmers feel that they are finished with a program when it compiles error free and produces output when run. Do not fall into this trap.

Consider another example logic error. Assume that you intended to write the following command that adds the quantities IN-CHARGE and SERVICE-CHARGE to give the result TOTAL-CHARGE:

```
ADD IN-CHARGE, SERVICE-CHARGE GIVING TOTAL-CHARGES
```

However, while daydreaming, you subtracted rather than added, as follows:

```
SUBTRACT IN-CHARGE FROM SERVICE-CHARGE GIVING TOTAL-CHARGES
```

To the compiler during the compile and to the computer during program execution, this is a perfectly valid action. The computer has no way of knowing what you *intend* the program to do. The compiler can only check that you wrote the program code in accordance with the syntax requirements of the COBOL language.

Runtime Errors

A runtime error occurs when you direct the computer to do something of which it is not capable. For instance, consider the following statement to divide the total sales by the number of units sold:

```
DIVIDE TOTAL-SALES BY UNITS-SOLD GIVING AVERAGE-PRICE
```

This is perfectly valid syntax and appears to perform the desired calculation (judging from its English form). It will indeed produce the desired result; for instance, if TOTAL-SALES is 1141.44 and UNITS-SOLD is 96, then the calculated result of 11.89 will be stored in AVERAGE-PRICE. However, what if, for some reason, the value in UNITS-SOLD is 0? Since the computer cannot divide by 0, an error will result. When attempting to do this, most computers will generate an error and terminate execution of the program. Your program has *crashed*. If yours is a production program that your company runs at 2:00 A.M. every morning, you should expect a wake-up call from an irate computer operator who probably has an important schedule to maintain.

Structured Walkthroughs

As you learned in Concepts Module B, a structured walkthrough is a formal group review of the work of a programmer or analyst for the purpose of detecting errors or faulty design. Recall that walkthroughs can be conducted at various stages of the program development process: (1) in the specification phase after completion of the programming specifications, (2) in the design phase after completion of each design document, (3) in the coding phase after obtaining a clean compile, and (4) during the testing phase.

Most organizations develop their own standards for conducting structured walkthroughs. The basic guidelines, originally presented in the 1973 IBM publication, *Improved Programming Technologies Management Overview*, are as follows:

1. A walkthrough is not used to review an individual's work performance; it is used to review program quality and project progress.

2. Each person attending a walkthrough must function in the role of either reviewee, reviewer, or recording secretary.

3. The reviewee conducts the meeting, since it is his or her work that will be reviewed.

4. The reviewee is responsible for distributing the material to be reviewed to all the reviewers prior to the meeting.

5. The walkthrough should not exceed two hours.

6. During the walkthrough, problems may be identified, but not corrected.

While you are taking this course, you may or may not participate in a structured walkthrough. With each student having several programming assignments (and with everyone on a different schedule), they are difficult to schedule and coordinate. However, you should at least learn to walk through your programs with another student, looking for potential problems. Without a doubt, you will at some time during this course encounter an error in your program that you simply cannot find, no matter how carefully you look. Often the act of explaining your program to another person makes the error obvious to you. Most of us have had the humbling experience of spending hours attempting to find a bug, only to have a colleague spot it at first glance. It is very easy to become blind to our own mistakes.

Program Testing

The ultimate objective of any program is to process data and produce *correct* output. The only way you can be certain the results are correct and that your program does not contain logic errors is by careful program testing. To test a program, you must:

1. Prepare a set of test data that exercises every aspect of your program. For instance, the test data for the PATLIST2 program must include data with the following characteristics:

   Actual contribution LESS THAN the target contribution

   Actual contribution EQUAL TO the target contribution

   Actual contribution GREATER THAN the target contribution

In addition, it is often a good idea to include zero data amounts. For instance, you might include records for a zero target amount, actual amount, and both. Sometimes zero values give unexpected results. In a program with numerous conditional actions, the test data can be very extensive.

2. Process your test data manually and determine what the computer should print out. For instance, if one of the printed fields for each customer is TOTAL-CHARGE (referring to the preceding ADD example), you would perform the calculation manually and compare your result to that of the computer's. In other words, if your sample values were 156.43 and 2.54 for IN-CHARGE and SERVICE-CHARGE, you would add them to get 158.97. If the computer prints something else, then you have an error.

For large programs, the testing can become complex and time consuming. However, one of the strengths of structured programming using a modular approach is that testing of the program can be done on a structured basis. Such structured testing is sometimes referred to as **top-down** (or **stub**) **testing**.

Because each structured-code module is relatively independent of the others, modules can be tested either one at a time or within a specific group. This means that testing of top-level modules can begin before lower-level modules are completed.

To perform top-down stub testing, dummy procedures are inserted in the program for those modules not yet coded. The dummy procedure contains only the procedure-name header and an EXIT statement (a statement that immediately returns control to the module executing the PERFORM). Although this technique is oriented to programs considerably larger than those you will write in this book, you may find the method helpful toward the end of the course.

Supplement Summary

Errors in a program are best prevented by carefully designing a program, using the good structured techniques described in this book.

An error in the ENVIRONMENT DIVISION or DATA DIVISION can result in diagnostics for many otherwise correct statements in the PROCEDURE DIVISION. If this multiplying effect is great, the best approach is usually to correct the error, then run another compile before proceeding further.

Use extra care in defining input records. If you are off a single position in one field, all fields that follow will be off.

The compiler will not catch logic errors. You must prepare test data that exercises all aspects of your program. Testing is a major element of the programming process.

Exercises
Terms for Definition

logic error _____

program testing _____

runtime error _____

top-down testing _____

Review Questions

1. What is meant by "A clean compile does not mean an error-free program"?

_____

_____

2. What is the difference between a syntax error and a logic error?

_____

_____

_____

Syntax/Debug Exercises

1. The PATLIST2 program includes the following IF statement:

```
IF PR-ACTUAL-CONTR IS LESS THAN PR-TARGET-CONTR
    MOVE "**" TO PL-TARGET-FLAG.
```

What would happen if it were incorrectly entered as follows?

```
IF PR-ACTUAL-CONTR IS LESS THAN PR-ACTUAL-CONTR
    MOVE "**" TO PL-TARGET-FLAG.
```

_____

_____

2. As you will learn in Chapter 7, the IF statement allows the use of the operator NOT. For instance, IS GREATER THAN and IS NOT GREATER THAN are both permissible forms. Would execution of PATLIST2 be any different if the IF statement were as follows? Explain your answer.

```
IF PR-TARGET-CONTR IS NOT GREATER THAN PR-ACTUAL-CONTR
    MOVE "**" TO PL-TARGET-FLAG.
```

_____

_____

3. What is the overall effect on the output for each of the following rearrangements of statements within the 200-Process procedure of the PATLIST2 program? Please explain in the space following.

```
MOVE SPACES TO PATRON-LINE.
MOVE PR-NAME TO PL-NAME.
MOVE PR-ADDRESS TO PL-ADDRESS.
MOVE PR-CITY-STATE-ZIP TO PL-CITY-STATE-ZIP.
WRITE PATRON-LINE
    AFTER ADVANCING 2 LINES.
IF PR-ACTUAL-CONTR IS LESS THAN PR-TARGET-CONTR
    MOVE "**" TO PL-TARGET-FLAG.
READ PATRON-FILE
    AT END MOVE "YES" TO WS-EOF-SWITCH.
MOVE SPACES TO PATRON-LINE.
```

_____

_____

_____

_____

_____

_____

```
MOVE PR-NAME TO PL-NAME.
MOVE PR-ADDRESS TO PL-ADDRESS.
MOVE PR-CITY-STATE-ZIP TO PL-CITY-STATE-ZIP.
IF PR-ACTUAL-CONTR IS LESS THAN PR-TARGET-CONTR
    MOVE "**" TO PL-TARGET-FLAG.
READ PATRON-FILE
    AT END MOVE "YES" TO WS-EOF-SWITCH.
WRITE PATRON-LINE
    AFTER ADVANCING 2 LINES.
```

_____

_____

_____

_____

_____

_____

_____

```
IF PR-ACTUAL-CONTR IS LESS THAN PR-TARGET-CONTR
    MOVE "**" TO PL-TARGET-FLAG.
MOVE SPACES TO PATRON-LINE.
MOVE PR-NAME TO PL-NAME.
MOVE PR-ADDRESS TO PL-ADDRESS.
MOVE PR-CITY-STATE-ZIP TO PL-CITY-STATE-ZIP.
WRITE PATRON-LINE
    AFTER ADVANCING 2 LINES.
READ PATRON-FILE
    AT END MOVE "YES" TO WS-EOF-SWITCH.
READ PATRON-FILE
    AT END MOVE "YES" TO WS-EOF-SWITCH.
```

_____

_____

_____

_____

_____

_____

_____

```
MOVE SPACES TO PATRON-LINE.
MOVE PR-NAME TO PL-NAME.
MOVE PR-ADDRESS TO PL-ADDRESS.
MOVE PR-CITY-STATE-ZIP TO PL-CITY-STATE-ZIP.
IF PR-ACTUAL-CONTR IS LESS THAN PR-TARGET-CONTR
    MOVE "**" TO PL-TARGET-FLAG.
WRITE PATRON-LINE
    AFTER ADVANCING 2 LINES.
```

_____

_____

_____

_____

_____

_____

_____

4. Some or all of the following PROCEDURE DIVISION entries are in error. Identify each error and indicate how to correct it. Assume that all data names have been properly defined in the DATA DIVISION.

```
── Column 7
 1        2         3         4          1        2         3         4
7890123456789012345678901234567890   7890123456789012345678901234567890

000-PROCESS-PAYROLL

OPEN PAYROLL-FILE.

    OUTPUT PAYROLL-REPORT-FILE.

    PREFORM INITIALIZE-VAR-FIELDS.

    READ PAYROLL-FILE

        AT END MOVE "YES" TO EOF-SW.

    PERFORM 200-PROCESS-PAYROLL-RECORD

        UNTIL EOF-SW EQUALS "NO ".

    CLOSE ALL FILES.

    STOP-RUN.

INITIALIZE-VAR-FIELDS

    MOVE "NO" TO EOF-SW.

200-PROCESS-PAYROLL-RECORD

    MOVE PY-RECORD TO PR-RECORD.

    WRITE PAYROLL-REPORT-FILE

        AFTER ADVANCING 2 LINES

    READ PAYROLL-FILE

        AT END MOVE "YES" TO EOF-SW.
```

CONCEPTS MODULE

Data Storage and Computer Arithmetic

Module Objectives

For beginning programmers, the fact that the computer stores data is often sufficient, and little thought is given to the form in which the data is stored. The real world of programming, however, is not so simple. The programmer soon finds that data can be stored in a variety of forms and that the choice of form can have an impact on storage requirements and program efficiency. The purpose of this module is to provide you with your first insight to the way in which data is stored within the computer. From this module, you will learn the following:

- The eight-bit storage byte.

- The two commonly used codes for encoding alphanumeric data: EBCDIC and ASCII.

- How the arithmetic sign is stored together with a numeric field within computer memory.

- Understood decimal point positioning, whereby no actual decimal point is included with numbers.

- The principle of rounding off.

- Basic forms of arithmetic.

- Accumulating and counting.

Module Outline

Internal Coding of Data
Binary Digits
Alphanumeric Data Codes
Numeric Data

Signed Numbers and Decimal Points
Arithmetic Sign for Numeric Data
Assumed Decimal Point
Rounding Off Computed Results

Basic Arithmetic Operations
Arithmetic Terminology
Subtracting One Quantity From Another to Produce a Third
Accumulating
Counting

Internal Coding of Data
Binary Digits

Data is represented within the computer by the electrical or magnetic state of the hardware's circuitry. The basic storage elements that hold data can be in either of two states: *on* or *off*. Any such two-state system is known as a *binary system* and can be used to represent a mathematical binary number system: consisting of only two binary digits: 0 and 1. The words *binary digit* are commonly contracted to **bit**.

The architecture of every digital computer design involves treating a group of bits as a unit for storing coded data. Early computers used a wide variety of methods for grouping bits. One method was to encode a group of four bits so that each addressable storage unit could contain one decimal digit. (A 4-bit number can range in decimal value from 0 to 15.) Another method encoded a group of bits so that each addressable storage unit could contain one alphanumeric character. Still other methods were designed around *words* consisting of 16 bits, 32 bits, or even 64 bits.

In 1964, IBM introduced the System/360 line of computers that featured the 8-bit storage byte. Over the years, the byte has become almost universal as the basic unit of data storage in computers, ranging from the small microcomputers to large mainframes. As used in computers today, the byte can be coded and interpreted in a number of ways, depending upon the types of operations to be performed and the computer instructions that are used.

Alphanumeric Data Codes

With an 8-bit byte, there are 256 combinations of 0 and 1, thereby allowing 256 characters to be encoded. For storage of alphanumeric data, there are two commonly used codes. IBM mainframe-computers (and compatibles)—dating back to the System/360—use the Extended Binary Coded Decimal Interchange Code (EBCDIC). (The acronym EBCDIC is commonly pronounced "eb-see-dick," with the accent on the first syllable.) The American Standard Code for Information Interchange (ASCII) is used by most other manufacturers and is almost universally used with microcomputers, including those from IBM. (ASCII is commonly pronounced "as-key" with the accent on the first syllable.)

From the COBOL programmer's perspective, there is little difference between the two coding forms. That is, each elementary alphanumeric data item causes the compiler to reserve a number of bytes consistent with the field length. For example, the entry

```
05  INVENTORY-CODE    PIC X(5).
```

in an input record will cause the compiler to reserve five bytes for INVENTORY-CODE. If the record read contains the value AL23P for this field, AL23P will be placed, one character per byte, into INVENTORY-CODE in the encoded form of the computer (EBCDIC or ASCII), as illustrated in Figure D-1. It makes no difference to you, the COBOL programmer, whether you are using an EBCDIC or ASCII computer because all encoding is handled automatically by the computer hardware. Hence, this is said to be *transparent* to the programmer.

In COBOL terminology, data that is stored one character per byte is said to be in **display** format. Unless you specify otherwise, all data is stored by your program

Figure D-1
Alphanumeric data in computer memory.

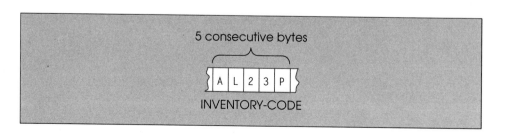

in display format. Any option that the computer selects (unless you specify otherwise) is called a **default option**; hence, display is the default format.

Numeric Data Next, what about numeric fields defined with the 9 picture? Interestingly, the entry

```
05  INVENTORY-QUANT-ONHAND   PIC 9(5).
```

will cause the compiler to reserve five bytes for INVENTORY-QUANT-ONHAND *in exactly the same way as if this were an X picture definition.* As pointed out in Chapter 2, there is no difference in the memory area reserved for these two fields, one with an X picture and the other with a 9 picture. Also, there is no difference in the data that can be stored. The X and 9 pictures only signal to the compiler the types of operations that can be performed on the data in the PROCEDURE DIVISION of the program. For example, you would get a compiler error if you tried to add INVENTORY-CODE to something else. On the other hand, during execution, your program could read alphabetic data into INVENTORY-QUANT-ONHAND without any indication of an error. (You will learn how to protect against this in Chapter 8, Data Validation.)

Signed Numbers and Decimal Points
Arithmetic Sign for Numeric Data

In ordinary arithmetic, we deal with both positive and negative numbers. We represent a negative number by preceding it with a minus sign, and a positive number with either no sign at all or with a plus sign. For instance, –645 is negative and both 645 and +645 are treated as positive. (Technically, 645 is said to be **unsigned**.)

Although including an encoded minus sign preceding the number might seem like a logical way of doing this within the computer, it is not the most common technique. Most computer systems encode the sign directly into one of the digits of the number; hence, it is called an **embedded sign**. The representations of Figure D-2 are examples in which the embedded sign is shown in the rightmost digit of the number. Within the computer, a distinction exists between an unsigned number and a positive number. However, for COBOL arithmetic operations, they are equivalent even though there are some subtle implications within the computer.

One of the implications of the embedded sign to you, the COBOL programmer, is that you need not provide an extra position in the field length definition to accommodate the sign if a number may become negative.

With EBCDIC computers (and most ASCII computers using COBOL), the sign is embedded into the rightmost byte of the field. However, this changes the encoding of that digit in a way that the digit is actually stored as a letter. For instance, –1 is stored as a letter J and +1 as a letter A. Although this is no problem for the computer, it can be confusing to a person inspecting memory contents.

An alternative way of handling sign representation is with a **separate-character sign** in which the plus or minus sign is stored in a separate character position. The position can be either to the left or to the right of the field to which it applies, as illustrated by the examples depicted in Figure D-3. Almost all COBOL compilers written for separate-character sign computers automatically provide for the

Figure D-2
Representation in computer memory of 57382 with embedded signs.

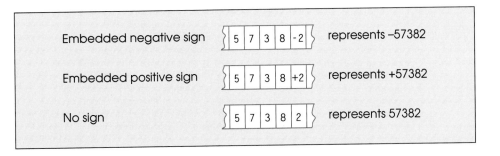

Embedded negative sign	5 7 3 8 -2	represents –57382
Embedded positive sign	5 7 3 8 +2	represents +57382
No sign	5 7 3 8 2	represents 57382

additional sign position so that you, the COBOL programmer, need not be concerned. However, COBOL does provide a DATA DIVISION clause, the SIGN clause, to permit specification of nonstandard sign locations.

Although alphanumeric data in an EBCDIC computer is handled much the same as alphanumeric data in an ASCII computer, there are important differences with numeric data. These differences relate to internal format and to associated arithmetic operations. Since most computers cannot perform arithmetic on data in display format, data format conversions must take place with each arithmetic operation. The way in which an IBM mainframe-computer (EBCDIC) does this is significantly different from the way an ASCII computer does it. Although as CO-BOL programmers we do not care how the computer does arithmetic (so long as it works), there are some factors of which we must be aware—factors which are a result of the evolution of computers. These relate to one method used by IBM in the System/360 architecture for encoding numeric data, a topic discussed at the end of Chapter 4.

Assumed Decimal Point

The preceding discussion of numbers within the computer refers only to whole number quantities. On the other hand, you frequently must deal with fractional values; for instance, dollar and cent amounts such as 257.35. If this quantity were printed in a report, it would occupy six print positions: five for the digits and one for the decimal point. However, if you were to inspect the data field when stored in the computer, you would not see a decimal point. When you define a field that contains a fractional value, you must define the decimal point location as well as the data class and the field length. When the compiler reserves memory for a field, it keeps track of where in memory the field is located, the field length, and the decimal point position. Hence, the number 257.35 would appear in memory as illustrated in Figure D-4. All instructions that the compiler generates to operate on this field take into account the defined decimal point position.

The reason that decimal points are not stored with the data is that arithmetic instructions operate on data by progressing right to left—from one digit to the next. If fields included decimal points, then special circuitry would be required to skip over the point in the position-by-position operation. (It is impossible to "add" one decimal point to another.) For decimal arithmetic, handling decimal point positioning by software (the assumed decimal point) is far less complex than by doing it with hardware.

Figure D-3
Separate sign character.

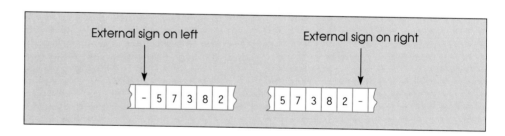

Figure D-4
Assumed decimal point positioning.

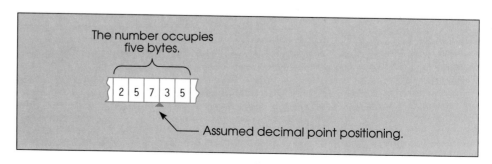

Rounding Off Computed Results If you add the two dollar-and-cent amounts 128.45 and 35.32, your result will be 163.77. The sum has the same number of digits to the right of the decimal point (decimal places) as the two numbers you are adding. On the other hand, if you must calculate the tax on the sum by multiplying it by 0.06, you would get the following result:

$$
\begin{array}{r}
163.77 \\
\times\ \ \ .06 \\
\hline
9.8262
\end{array}
$$

In terms of dollars and cents, how do you handle this? There are two ways. The simplest is simply to discard the excess digits, thus converting 9.8262 to 9.82. This is called **truncation**; the field is truncated to give the desired number of decimal positions.

However, a more realistic action in this case would be to use 9.83, since it is closer to 9.8262 than is 9.82. This is called **rounding off** and is illustrated in Figure D-5. In COBOL, when the result of a calculation produces more positions to the right of the decimal than the picture provides, the result is truncated unless you specify rounding. You will learn how to do this in Chapter 4.

Basic Arithmetic Operations
Arithmetic Terminology

In the discussion of arithmetic statements, it is sometimes convenient to refer to basic arithmetic-element terminology. For your convenience, the basic terms are illustrated in Figure D-6. Notice that each arithmetic operation involves three quantities (four for division). There are two "input" quantities and one result (two for division). For instance, with addition, there are two numbers to be added together and the resulting sum.

To illustrate typical types of calculations and concepts of which you must be aware when doing arithmetic operations on the computer, let's consider some typical examples. These are operations that you will study in Chapter 4, in the context of processing data from the patron data file of Chapter 3.

Figure D-5
Rounding off.

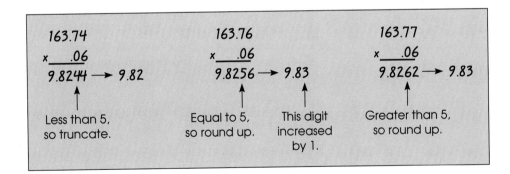

Figure D-6 Arithmetic-element terminology.

Addition	Subtraction	Multiplication	Division
512 Addend + 17 Addend 529 Sum (Total)	236 Minuend − 89 Subtrahend 147 Difference	503 Multiplicand x 8 Multiplier 4024 Product	Quotient Remainder 51 2 5⟌257 Divisor Dividend

Subtracting One Quantity From Another to Produce a Third

Example:

The patron data file includes two numeric fields: the target contribution and the actual contribution. For each patron who is under the targeted amount, you must calculate the deficit. For printed output, you are to include all three quantities.

For this operation, three fields will be required: two for the input quantities and one for the result. The action is the following:

Subtract actual contribution **from** target contribution **giving** deficit.

In an operation such as this, the target and actual fields will not be changed, but the value of the deficit field will be replaced with the newly calculated difference.

Accumulating

Example:

The last line of the patron report must include a total of the deficit amounts for all patrons processed in the preceding example.

For this example, you must compute the total of a series of quantities. The principle of computing a total in a computer program is very similar to the way you would total a column of figures with a pocket calculator. For instance, as each number is entered through keypad, it is added to the value in the calculator display: it is *accumulated* in an *accumulator*. Thus, when you are finished, the accumulator contains the final sum. In computing, the need to accumulate values (such as the contribution for the patron application) is very common.

The accumulating function in a computer program requires two distinct actions (these are equivalent to the actions of accumulating with a pocket calculator). For calculating the patron deficit total, the actions are:

Initialize the deficit total field to 0.

For each deficit value,

> **add** the deficit **to** the deficit total.

Note that in this accumulating operation, the deficit total is both an addend and the sum.

Counting

Frequently too in programming, you must count. For instance, to compute the average value of a data set, you must accumulate the total of the data set and count the number of values processed. To accomplish this, the patron example requires the number of patron records processed.

Example:

The last line of the patron report must also include a count of the number of patrons processed.

This counting example differs from the preceding accumulating example only in that a value 1 is added to the counter (accumulator); that is:

Initialize the counter field to 0.

For each patron with a deficit value,

> **add** 1 **to** the counter.

Module Summary

Information is represented in the computer by circuitry that can be either on or off: a binary representation. The **byte**, a basic unit of storage, consists of eight on-off elements termed **bits** for **binary digits**.

Alphanumeric data is most commonly encoded into the 8-bit byte using either of two codes: EBCDIC (used by IBM-mainframe computers) and ASCII (used by most other computers, including IBM microcomputers).

If you do not explicitly specify otherwise, numeric data is stored one digit per byte in exactly the same form as alphanumeric data.

To store the sign of a number, most computers use a sign that is encoded directly into one of the digits (usually the rightmost); this is called an **embedded sign**.

In COBOL, numeric data that has decimal positions does not include an explicit decimal point. The definition (in the DATA DIVISION) includes an indication of the decimal point location, but it does not include a decimal point. This is called an **assumed decimal point**.

When the number of digits to the right of the decimal point of a number must be reduced—for instance, 9.8262 must be reduced to a dollar and cent amount—two methods can be used. **Truncation** simply involves discarding unwanted digits; thus, 9.8262 becomes 9.82. **Rounding off** requires that the leftmost digit being discarded first be inspected. If it is 5 or larger, increase the last digit retained by 1; thus 9.8262 becomes 9.83. If it is less than 5, truncate; thus, 9.8242 becomes 9.82.

Accumulating is the arithmetic process whereby the total of a series of numbers is computed. In computer programming, this commonly takes the form of an addition operation that is performed each time through a program loop.

Exercises
Terms for Definition

accumulating _____

addend _____

ASCII _____

assumed decimal point _____

binary system _____

bit _____

byte _____

counting _____

default option _____

difference _____

display format _____

dividend _____

divisor _____

EBCDIC _____

embedded sign _____

minuend _____

multiplicand _____

multiplier _____

negative _____

positive _____

product _____

quotient _____

remainder _____

rounding _____

separate-character sign _____

subtrahend _____

sum _____

transparency (to the programmer) _____

truncation _____

unsigned _____

Review Questions

1. What is the difference between accumulating and counting?

   _____

   _____

2. What is the difference between a sum and a total?

   _____

   _____

3. In most computer internal storage systems, a(n) _____

   contains eight _____.

4. Is it necessary for the COBOL programmer to specify the form (EBCDIC or ASCII) in which data is to be stored in the computer? Why or why not?

   _____

   _____

5. Is it necessary for the COBOL programmer to specify that COBOL store data in display format? Why or why not?

   _____

   _____

6. A student says, "A number either is negative or it isn't." Is the student correct? Why or why not?

   _____

   _____

7. For reasons which have their basis in punched-card machine accounting, business data records do not include an actual decimal point in data fields. This practice has both advantages and disadvantages. List as many of each as you can.

_____

_____

_____

_____

_____

_____

_____

_____

_____

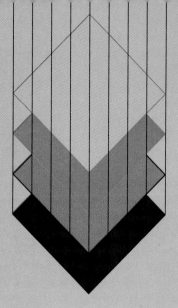

Arithmetic Operations

The PATLIST program of Chapter 3 has shown you how to read data from an input file and rearrange it to give a printed report. Concepts Module D has given you an insight to operating with numeric data in memory. In this chapter, you will learn about arithmetic operations in COBOL; an expansion of the PATLIST program will serve as an introductory vehicle. From this chapter, you will learn the following:

■ Decimal point positioning in numeric fields.

■ Simple editing to improve the appearance of printed numeric output (details of editing are covered in Chapter 5).

■ Designating a sign on a numeric field.

■ Two formats of the ADD statement: ADD/TO and ADD/GIVING.

■ Two formats of the SUBTRACT statement: SUBTRACT/FROM and SUBTRACT/GIVING.

■ Two formats of the MULTIPLY statement: MULTIPLY/BY and MULTIPLY/GIVING.

■ Five formats of the DIVIDE statement.

■ Rounding of calculated results.

■ The COMPUTE statement, which allows calculations to be designated using a form similar to that of algebra.

■ Special methods for internal coding of numeric data.

CHAPTER 4

Chapter Outline

Topic: PATDFCT—A Program with Arithmetic Calculations

The Specification Phase of a Programming Task
Definition of the Problem
Ensure That the Input is Available to Produce the Desired Output
Prepare a Print Chart
Write Program Specifications

The Design Phase
Structure Chart
Pseudocode For PATDFCT
Flowchart For PATDFCT

The PATDFCT Program Solution
Designating a Decimal Point
Arithmetic Operations
Simple Numeric Editing
Multiple Record Description Entries
Processing Logic—The IF Statement
About Signs on Numbers
Numeric Literals

Topic: COBOL Arithmetic Statements

A Preview of the Arithmetic Statements

The ADD Statement
The ADD/TO (Format-1) Statement
The ADD/GIVING (Format-2) Statement

The SUBTRACT Statement
The SUBTRACT/FROM (Format-1) Statement
The SUBTRACT/GIVING (Format-2) Statement
Dealing With Negative Quantities

The MULTIPLY Statement
The MULTIPLY/BY (Format-1) Statement
The ROUNDED Clause
The MULTIPLY/GIVING (Format-2) Statement

The DIVIDE Statement
The DIVIDE/INTO (Format-1) and the DIVIDE/INTO/GIVING (Format-2)
The DIVIDE/INTO/GIVING/REMAINDER (Format-4)
The DIVIDE/BY/GIVING (Format-3) and DIVIDE/BY/GIVING/REMAINDER (Format-5)

The COMPUTE Statement
COMPUTE Statement Processing
COMPUTE Statement Syntax

The ON SIZE ERROR Phrase
Arithmetic Scope Terminators in COBOL-85

Selecting the Arithmetic Form to Use
Arithmetic Verbs
The COMPUTE Statement

Modifying the PATDFCT Program
Introducing Dollar and Cent Amounts
Communicating the Message

Topic: Internal Coding of Numeric Data
Packed-Decimal Data Format
Arithmetic Operations With Packed-Decimal Data
Defining Packed-Decimal in the PICTURE—The USAGE Clause

| Topic: | **PATDFCT—A Program with Arithmetic Calculations** |

The purpose of this Topic is to introduce you to arithmetic operations through a sample programming task. To that end, you will start at the beginning: you will be given the needs of a user. Then you will progress through the program solution. From Concepts Module B, you know that the computer problem-solving process can be broken down into four phases: specification, design, coding, and testing. Let's proceed with the specification phase.

The Specification Phase of a Programming Task
Definition of the Problem

The membership supervisor of Fleetwood Charities wishes to perform a study of contributions from patrons contributing below their targeted amounts. Upon speaking with him, you learn that the report must consist of the following for each patron in the patron file whose contribution is below the target:

Patron name

Contribution date

Target contribution

Actual contribution

Contribution deficit (difference between target and actual)

Percentage of target contribution

In addition to detail lines (one line for each patron under the target), he wants the following printed output—which summarizes data from all of the records—at the end of the report.

The number of below target patrons

The total amount by which these patrons are deficient

Lines that summarize data from preceding records are called **summary lines**.

Ensure That the Input Is Available to Produce the Desired Output

The membership director has given you a precise indication of what he desires from the report. Your first step would be to ensure that the needed data is available from the patron file. The record format of this file is as follows:

Input-record format:

Positions	Field name	Data class
1–18	Patron name	Alphanumeric
19–36	Street address	Alphanumeric
37–60	City/state/zip	Alphanumeric
61–64	Target contribution	Numeric
65–68	Actual contribution	Numeric
69–74	Contribution date	Alphanumeric

Inspecting this, you see that the required output can come from the input record as follows:

Output field	Source
Detail lines:	
Patron name	Input record
Contribution date	Input record
Target contribution	Input record
Actual contribution	Input record
Deficit	Calculate from input actual and target
Percentage contribution	Calculate from input actual and target
Summary line:	
Count	Calculate by counting records
Total deficits	Accumulate calculated deficit amounts

Prepare a Print Chart   The next step is lay out the general format of your report and then prepare a print chart showing all details. In doing this, remember to arrange output fields in an easy-to-read format—think of the end user. Sometimes poorly formatted and difficult-to-read reports go unused even though they contain valuable information.

A finished print chart, together with a partial sample report, are shown in Figure 4-1. (At this point of the design process, you would not yet have a sample copy of the report—the program to produce it is not yet written.)

Figure 4-1   Print chart and partial sample report for PATDFCT.

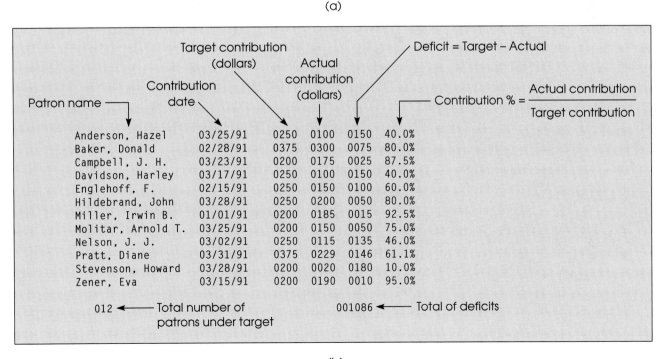

(a)

(b)

Write Program Specifications

The final step in the specification phase is to prepare the programming specifications—a general description of the program function, input and output identification, and a list of processing operations. The programming specifications are shown in Figure 4-2.

   This completes the specification phase. After gaining the approval of the membership supervisor that this indeed satisfies his needs, you can proceed to the design phase.

Figure 4-2
Programming specifications for PATDFCT.

PROGRAMMING SPECIFICATIONS

Program name: DEFICIENT PATRON REPORT   **Program ID:** PATDFCT

Program Description:
   This program is to print a list of patrons and their contributions. Patrons with contributions below target are flagged. A summary is printed at the end of the report.

Input File:
   PATRON.DAT

Output File:
   Patron Summary Report

List of Program Operations:
   A.   Read each patron record.

   B.   For each record in which the actual contribution is less than the target contribution, do the following:

      1.   Calculate the contribution deficiency by subtracting the actual contribution from the target contribution.

      2.   Calculate the percentage contribution by dividing Actual-contribution by Target-contribution, then multiplying by 100.

      3.   Print the following fields on the patron report detail line in accordance with the format shown on the print chart.

            Patron name
            Contribution date
            Target contribution
            Actual contribution
            Contribution deficiency

      4.   Count this record.

      5.   Accumulate (add the deficiency to a deficiency accumulator).

   C.   Double-space each detail line.

   D.   After all input records have been processed, print the following total fields on the summary (total) lines in accordance with the format shown on the print chart:

      1.   Number of patrons under their target amounts.

      2.   The total of their deficits.

The Design Phase
Structure Chart

You will often find that a program you must write is very similar in structure to another; this program is an extension of PATLIST. Thus, it is only logical that you use the structure chart of PATLIST as a starting point [refer to the structure chart of Figure C-1(b)]. This program has the following additional needs:

Action	Module in which action is executed
Initialize accumulators	Done in the existing Initialize module.
Print total line	A new action done after all records are processed—requires a new procedure.

The finished structure chart is shown in Figure 4-3. Notice that in addition to the new 700 module, another module has been added: Process-deficient-patron. When you inspect the program, you will see that this is necessary to accommodate the conditional processing of a patron.

Pseudocode For PATDFCT

The structure chart tells you what must be done; pseudocode will tell you how to do it. The best way to start is to begin with the general and proceed to the specific. Broadly, execution will be:

```
Do initial operations.
Read first record.
Repeat the following until there are no more records.
   If Actual contribution less than target contribution
      process this record.
   Read next record.
Print totals.
```

Figure 4-3
Structure chart for PATDFCT.

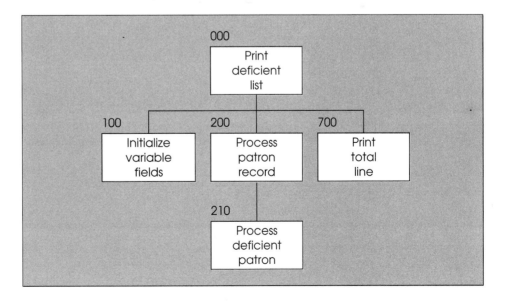

This gives you an overall idea of what your program must do. From the program specifications in Figure 4-2, you can fill in details to produce your pseudocode solution shown in Figure 4-4.

Flowchart For PATDFCT   If you wish to supplement the pseudocode description of your program with a flowchart (or use a flowchart in place of pseudocode), you would first draw the mainline logic (which illustrates the placement of each module). Then you would draw the details of each module; the end result is shown in Figure 4-5. Notice in the 200-Process-patron-record procedure that the logic clearly illustrates performing the 210-Process-deficient-patron procedure only if the Actual-contribution is less than the Target-contribution. As you will see in the program, the code corresponds exactly to the flowchart representation.

Figure 4-4
Pseudocode for PATDFCT.

```
000-Print-deficient-list

  1.   Open files.

  2.   Perform 100-Initialize-variable-fields procedure.

  3.   Read first patron record.

  4.   Repeat 200-Process-patron-record until end of file.

  5.   Perform 700-Print-total-line.

  6.   Close files.

  7.   Stop the run.


100-Initialize-variable-fields

  1.   Set the end-of-file indicator to "NO".


200-Process-patron-record

  1.   If contribution less than target
         perform 210-Process-deficient-patron.

  2.   Read next patron record.


210-Process-deficient-patron

  1.   Clear the output line area.

  2.   Move the following input patron fields to the output area.

         Patron-name
         Contribution-date
         Target-amount
         Actual-amount

  3.   Subtract the Actual-contribution from the Target-contribution
       giving the Deficit.  Move the Deficit to the output record.

  4.   Divide the Actual-contribution by the Target-contribution giving
       the Deficiency-percentage.  Move the Deficiency-percentage to
       the output record.

  5.   Accumulate the Amount-deficient by adding it to the Total-
       amount-deficient.

  6.   Count this record by adding 1 to the Deficient-patron-count.

  7.   Write the detail line (double-spaced).


700-Print-total-line

  1.   Clear the output line area.

  2.   Move the Deficient-patron-count and Total-amount-deficient to
       output line.

  3.   Write the detail line (triple-spaced).
```

Figure 4-5 Flowchart for PATDFCT.

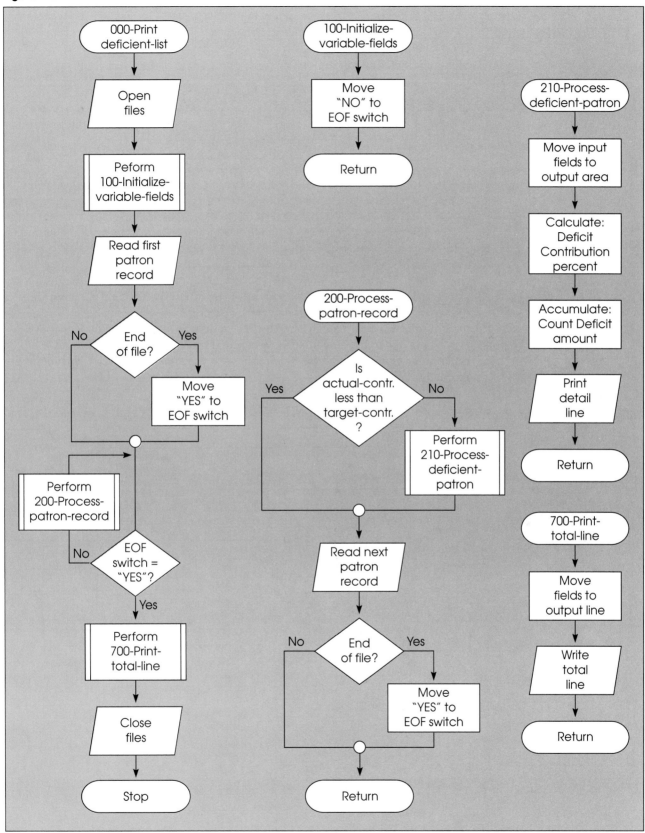

The PATDFCT Program Solution

The first three divisions are shown in Figure 4-6(a); the PROCEDURE Divisions for COBOL-74 and COBOL-85 are shown in Figures 4-6(b) and 4-6(c), respectively. The color lines are the portions of the program of special interest to us now. These illustrate the following topics:

- Designating an understood decimal point

- Basic arithmetic operations

- Inserting a decimal point in the output of numeric data

- Defining two output record formats for the printer output area

In PROCEDURE DIVISION descriptions that follow, you should refer to whichever version is appropriate to your compiler. As you will see, most of the descriptions are common to both, but the line numbers are usually different.

In descriptions that follow which are common to both programs, line number references are included for both. For instance, the paragraph 200-PROCESS-PATRON-RECORD begins at line 104 of the COBOL-74 program and line 105 of the COBOL-85 program. Reference in the text will be line 104/105; the first number is for the COBOL-74 program and the second for the COBOL-85 program.

Designating a Decimal Point

One of the required calculations in this example is to compute the Contribution-percent. In general, a percentage is computed by dividing one number by another and multiplying the result by 100. In this case, the formula together with a sample calculation are:

Figure 4-6 PATDFCT program solution.

```
 1        IDENTIFICATION DIVISION.                          45   01  DEFICIENCY-LINE.
 2                                                          46       05  FILLER                PIC X(1).
 3        PROGRAM-ID.    PATDFCT.                            47       05  DL-NAME               PIC X(18).
 4      *    WRITTEN BY PRICE/WELBURN                        48       05  FILLER                PIC X(2).
 5                                                          49       05  DL-CONTR-MONTH        PIC X(2).
 6      *    THIS PROGRAM PRINTS A LIST OF PATRONS           50       05  DL-SLASH-1            PIC X(1).
 7      *    WHO ARE DEFICIENT IN THEIR CONTRIBUTIONS.       51       05  DL-CONTR-DAY          PIC X(2).
 8                                                          52       05  DL-SLASH-2            PIC X(1).
 9        ENVIRONMENT DIVISION.                              53       05  DL-CONTR-YEAR         PIC X(2).
10                                                          54       05  FILLER                PIC X(4).
11        CONFIGURATION SECTION.                             55       05  DL-TARGET-CONTR       PIC 9(4).
12        SOURCE-COMPUTER.  (system dependent).              56       05  FILLER                PIC X(3).
13        OBJECT-COMPUTER.  (system dependent).              57       05  DL-ACTUAL-CONTR       PIC 9(4).
14                                                          58       05  FILLER                PIC X(3).
15        INPUT-OUTPUT SECTION.                              59       05  DL-AMOUNT-DEFICIENT   PIC 9(4).
16        FILE-CONTROL.                                      60       05  FILLER                PIC X(3).
17                                                          61       05  DL-DEFICIENCY-PERCENT PIC 99.9.
18            SELECT PATRON-FILE                             62       05  DL-PERCENT-SIGN       PIC X(1).
19                ASSIGN TO (system dependent).              63       05  FILLER                PIC X(73).
20                                                          64
21            SELECT DEFICIENCY-LIST                         65   01  TOTAL-LINE.
22                ASSIGN TO (system dependent).              66       05  FILLER                PIC X(4).
23                                                          67       05  TL-DEFICIENT-PATRONS  PIC 9(3).
24        DATA DIVISION.                                     68       05  FILLER                PIC X(38).
25        FILE SECTION.                                      69       05  TL-TOTAL-AMOUNT-DEFICIENT PIC 9(6).
26                                                          70       05  FILLER                PIC X(81).
27        FD  PATRON-FILE                                    71
28            RECORD CONTAINS 74 CHARACTERS                  72   WORKING-STORAGE SECTION.
29            LABEL RECORDS ARE STANDARD.                    73
30                                                          74   01  WS-SWITCHES.
31        01  PATRON-RECORD.                                 75       05  WS-EOF-SWITCH         PIC X(3).
32            05  PR-NAME             PIC X(18).             76
33            05  FILLER              PIC X(42).             77   01  WS-ARITHMETIC-WORK-AREAS.
34            05  PR-TARGET-CONTR     PIC 9(4).              78       05  WS-AMOUNT-DEFICIENT   PIC 9(4).
35            05  PR-ACTUAL-CONTR     PIC 9(4).              79       05  WS-TOTAL-AMOUNT-DEFICIENT PIC 9(6).
36            05  PR-CONTR-DATE.                             80       05  WS-DEFICIENCY-FRACTION PIC V999.
37                10  PR-CONTR-MONTH  PIC X(2).              81       05  WS-DEFICIENCY-PERCENT PIC 99V9.
38                10  PR-CONTR-DAY    PIC X(2).              82       05  WS-DEFICIENT-PATRONS  PIC 9(3).
39                10  PR-CONTR-YEAR   PIC X(2).              83
40
41        FD  DEFICIENCY-LIST
42            RECORD CONTAINS 132 CHARACTERS
43            LABEL RECORDS ARE OMITTED.
44
```

(a) The first three divisions for the PATDFCT program.

FIGURE 4-6   (continued)

```
84   PROCEDURE DIVISION.                              110   210-PROCESS-DEFICIENT-PATRON.
85                                                    111       MOVE SPACES TO DEFICIENCY-LINE.
86   000-PRINT-DEFICIENCY-LIST.                       112       MOVE PR-NAME TO DL-NAME.
87       OPEN INPUT PATRON-FILE                       113       MOVE PR-TARGET-CONTR TO DL-TARGET-CONTR.
88            OUTPUT DEFICIENCY-LIST.                  114       MOVE PR-ACTUAL-CONTR TO DL-ACTUAL-CONTR.
89       PERFORM 100-INITIALIZE-VARIABLE-FIELDS.      115       MOVE PR-CONTR-MONTH TO DL-CONTR-MONTH.
90       READ PATRON-FILE                             116       MOVE PR-CONTR-DAY TO DL-CONTR-DAY.
91           AT END MOVE "YES" TO WS-EOF-SWITCH.      117       MOVE PR-CONTR-YEAR TO DL-CONTR-YEAR.
92       PERFORM 200-PROCESS-PATRON-RECORD            118       MOVE "/" TO DL-SLASH-1, DL-SLASH-2.
93           UNTIL WS-EOF-SWITCH IS EQUAL TO "YES".   119       SUBTRACT PR-ACTUAL-CONTR FROM PR-TARGET-CONTR
94       PERFORM 700-PRINT-TOTAL-LINE.                120           GIVING WS-AMOUNT-DEFICIENT.
95       CLOSE PATRON-FILE                            121       MOVE WS-AMOUNT-DEFICIENT TO DL-AMOUNT-DEFICIENT.
96             DEFICIENCY-LIST.                       122       DIVIDE PR-ACTUAL-CONTR BY PR-TARGET-CONTR
97       STOP RUN.                                    123           GIVING WS-DEFICIENCY-FRACTION.
98                                                    124       MULTIPLY WS-DEFICIENCY-FRACTION BY 100
99   100-INITIALIZE-VARIABLE-FIELDS.                  125           GIVING WS-DEFICIENCY-PERCENT.
100      MOVE "NO " TO WS-EOF-SWITCH.                 126       MOVE WS-DEFICIENCY-PERCENT TO DL-DEFICIENCY-PERCENT.
101      MOVE ZERO TO WS-TOTAL-AMOUNT-DEFICIENT,      127       MOVE "%" TO DL-PERCENT-SIGN.
102              WS-DEFICIENT-PATRONS.                128       WRITE DEFICIENCY-LINE
103                                                   129           AFTER ADVANCING 2 LINES.
104  200-PROCESS-PATRON-RECORD.                       130       ADD WS-AMOUNT-DEFICIENT TO WS-TOTAL-AMOUNT-DEFICIENT.
105      IF PR-ACTUAL-CONTR IS LESS THAN PR-TARGET-CONTR  131   ADD 1 TO WS-DEFICIENT-PATRONS.
106          PERFORM 210-PROCESS-DEFICIENT-PATRON.    132
107      READ PATRON-FILE                             133   700-PRINT-TOTAL-LINE.
108          AT END MOVE "YES" TO WS-EOF-SWITCH.      134       MOVE SPACES TO TOTAL-LINE.
109                                                   135       MOVE WS-DEFICIENT-PATRONS TO TL-DEFICIENT-PATRONS.
                                                      136       MOVE WS-TOTAL-AMOUNT-DEFICIENT
                                                      137           TO TL-TOTAL-AMOUNT-DEFICIENT.
                                                      138       WRITE TOTAL-LINE
                                                      139           AFTER ADVANCING 3 LINES.
```

(b) The PATDFCT PROCEDURE DIVISION—COBOL-74.

```
84   PROCEDURE DIVISION.                              113   210-PROCESS-DEFICIENT-PATRON.
85                                                    114       MOVE SPACES TO DEFICIENCY-LINE
86   000-PRINT-DEFICIENCY-LIST.                       115       MOVE PR-NAME TO DL-NAME
87       OPEN INPUT PATRON-FILE                       116       MOVE PR-TARGET-CONTR TO DL-TARGET-CONTR
88            OUTPUT DEFICIENCY-LIST                  117       MOVE PR-ACTUAL-CONTR TO DL-ACTUAL-CONTR
89       PERFORM 100-INITIALIZE-VARIABLE-FIELDS       118       MOVE PR-CONTR-MONTH TO DL-CONTR-MONTH
90       READ PATRON-FILE                             119       MOVE PR-CONTR-DAY TO DL-CONTR-DAY
91           AT END MOVE "YES" TO WS-EOF-SWITCH       120       MOVE PR-CONTR-YEAR TO DL-CONTR-YEAR
92       END-READ                                     121       MOVE "/" TO DL-SLASH-1, DL-SLASH-2
93       PERFORM 200-PROCESS-PATRON-RECORD            122       SUBTRACT PR-ACTUAL-CONTR FROM PR-TARGET-CONTR
94           UNTIL WS-EOF-SWITCH IS EQUAL TO "YES"    123           GIVING WS-AMOUNT-DEFICIENT
95       PERFORM 700-PRINT-TOTAL-LINE                 124       MOVE WS-AMOUNT-DEFICIENT TO DL-AMOUNT-DEFICIENT
96       CLOSE PATRON-FILE                            125       DIVIDE PR-ACTUAL-CONTR BY PR-TARGET-CONTR
97             DEFICIENCY-LIST                        126           GIVING WS-DEFICIENCY-FRACTION
98       STOP RUN.                                    127       MULTIPLY WS-DEFICIENCY-FRACTION BY 100
99                                                    128           GIVING WS-DEFICIENCY-PERCENT
100  100-INITIALIZE-VARIABLE-FIELDS.                  129       MOVE WS-DEFICIENCY-PERCENT TO DL-DEFICIENCY-PERCENT
101      MOVE "NO " TO WS-EOF-SWITCH                  130       MOVE "%" TO DL-PERCENT-SIGN
102      MOVE ZERO TO WS-TOTAL-AMOUNT-DEFICIENT,      131       WRITE DEFICIENCY-LINE
103              WS-DEFICIENT-PATRONS.                132           AFTER ADVANCING 2 LINES
104                                                   133       ADD WS-AMOUNT-DEFICIENT TO WS-TOTAL-AMOUNT-DEFICIENT
105  200-PROCESS-PATRON-RECORD.                       134       ADD 1 TO WS-DEFICIENT-PATRONS.
106      IF PR-ACTUAL-CONTR IS LESS THAN PR-TARGET-CONTR  135
107          PERFORM 210-PROCESS-DEFICIENT-PATRON     136   700-PRINT-TOTAL-LINE.
108      END-IF                                       137       MOVE SPACES TO TOTAL-LINE
109      READ PATRON-FILE                             138       MOVE WS-DEFICIENT-PATRONS TO TL-DEFICIENT-PATRONS
110          AT END MOVE "YES" TO WS-EOF-SWITCH       139       MOVE WS-TOTAL-AMOUNT-DEFICIENT
111      END-READ.                                    140           TO TL-TOTAL-AMOUNT-DEFICIENT
112                                                   141       WRITE TOTAL-LINE
                                                      142           AFTER ADVANCING 3 LINES.
```

(c) The PATDFCT PROCEDURE DIVISION—COBOL-85.

$$\text{Contribution-percent} = \frac{\text{Contributed-amount}}{\text{Target-amount}} \times 100$$

$$= \frac{185}{200} \times 100$$

$$= .925 \times 100$$

$$= 92.5$$

This result is the exact form in which the value is to be printed (see Figure 4-1). Notice that an intermediate work area will be required that allows for a calculation producing a result with three places to the right of the decimal. This is defined in the WORKING-STORAGE SECTION (line 80) by the following:

```
05  WS-DEFICIENCY-FRACTION    PIC V9(3).
```

Notice the letter V; this signifies to the compiler the location of the understood decimal point. As you learned in Concepts Module D, the field will occupy three bytes of memory; the understood decimal point will not occupy a memory position. However, machine language instructions generated by the compiler will maintain proper decimal positioning.

Arithmetic Operations

In Concepts Module D, you learned some of the basic principles of computer arithmetic operations. To identify the four basic arithmetic operations, COBOL includes the ADD, SUBTRACT, MULTIPLY, and DIVIDE verbs—which do precisely as their names imply. Although there is a variety of each command form, they essentially provide the capabilities of the actions described in Module D. For instance, you will see that the following pseudocode descriptions have COBOL counterparts that are almost identical to these forms:

> **Subtract** actual contribution **from** target contribution **giving** deficit
>
> **add** the deficit **to** the deficit total

The SUBTRACT statement from PATDFCT (at lines 119–120/122-123) corresponds almost exactly to the above pseudocode description; it functions as illustrated in Figure 4-7. [This example shows how the Miller record is processed—see line 7 of Figure 4-1(b).] Notice that the two fields involved in the calculation (PR-ACTUAL-CONTR and PR-TARGET-CONTR) are unchanged by the subtraction. However, the contents of the receiving field (WS-AMOUNT-DEFICIENT) have been replaced with the newly calculated amount (the arithmetic difference).

The ADD statement at line 130/133 of this program is different from the SUBTRACT in that it does not include the GIVING clause. The way in which it functions is illustrated in Figure 4-8. The value in WS-AMOUNT-DEFICIENT is added to the value in WS-TOTAL-AMOUNT-DEFICIENT, with the previous value replaced by the sum.

The counter at line 131/134 works in exactly the same way—except that a numeric literal (the digit 1) is the addend rather than the value of a field.

Calculating the required percentage requires two steps: division and multiplication. This sequence is illustrated in Figure 4-9. In these representations, notice that the implied decimal point is indicated with a small triangle beneath the memory positions.

Figure 4-7
The SUBTRACT-GIVING statement.

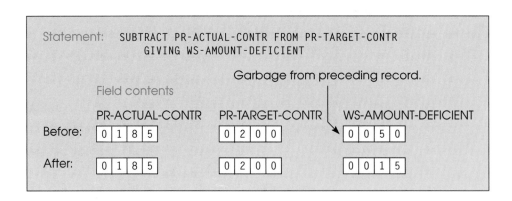

Figure 4-8
The ADD statement.

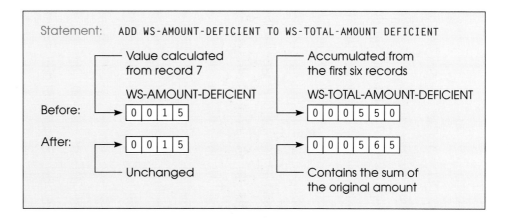

Figure 4-9
Division and multiplication.

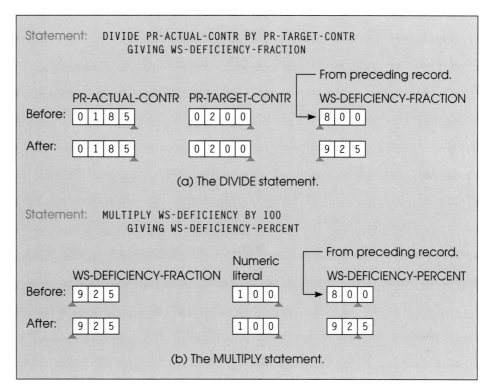

One thing to notice in all of these examples is that there is no indication in the PROCEDURE DIVISION arithmetic statements of decimal point positioning. Once defined in the DATA DIVISION, all decimal positioning and alignment are handled automatically.

Simple Numeric Editing

Although an understood decimal point is adequate for internal operations of the computer, it is totally inadequate for printed output on a report. COBOL handles this with special edit fields that can be defined in the DATA DIVISION describing the type of editing to be done. (This is the main topic of Chapter 5.) At line 61 of PATDFCT, the field DL-DEFICIENCY-PERCENT is defined to include an actual decimal point—as shown in Figure 4-10(a). This is a simple example of a numeric-edited item, a topic you will learn much more about in Chapter 5. The presence of the decimal point signals to the compiler that an actual decimal point is to be

Figure 4-10
A numeric-edited item.

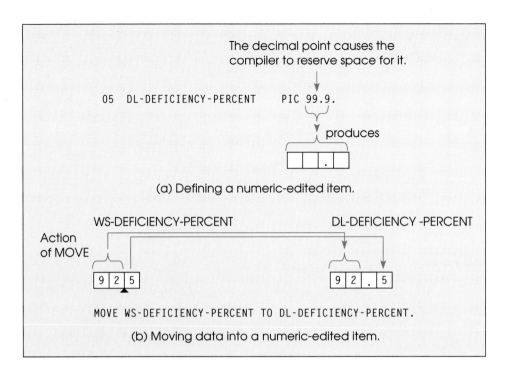

The decimal point causes the compiler to reserve space for it.

05 DL-DEFICIENCY-PERCENT   PIC 99.9.

produces

(a) Defining a numeric-edited item.

WS-DEFICIENCY-PERCENT   DL-DEFICIENCY -PERCENT

Action of MOVE

9 2 5   9 2 . 5

MOVE WS-DEFICIENCY-PERCENT TO DL-DEFICIENCY-PERCENT.

(b) Moving data into a numeric-edited item.

printed on the output. The MOVE statement (line 126/129) positions the data around the decimal point, as illustrated in Figure 4-10(b). Note that this action is automatically done by the MOVE statement.

Multiple Record Description Entries

Referring to the program of Figure 4-6, notice that there are two record descriptions under the DEFICIENCY-LIST file description: DEFICIENCY-LINE beginning line 45 and TOTAL-LINE beginning line 65. Both of these are necessary because the detail line format is different than the total line format. Although it might appear that two separate output lines will result, that is not true here. Whenever there are multiple 01-level record-descriptions within one FD-entry, all the record-descriptions are assigned the same area of storage (132 bytes in this case). You can think of the two record descriptions as being "overlays" on a single area of memory, thereby allowing you to access that area in different ways. Since the record names, DEFICIENCY-LINE, and TOTAL-LINE refer to the same 132 bytes of memory, the following statements will blank the output in exactly the same way:

```
MOVE SPACES TO DEFICIENCY-LINE
MOVE SPACES TO TOTAL-LINE
```

This "reuse" of a single storage area for FILE SECTION records belonging to the same file is termed **implicit redefinition**.

It is important to recognize that this implicit redefinition occurs whenever more than one 01-level record-description entry is specified within an FD-entry in the FILE SECTION. This means that those records occupying the redefined area cannot be built or formatted simultaneously. If they were, then the data for one would overlay that for the other.

Partly because of the restrictions imposed by implicit redefinition, programmers often define records of a file in the WORKING-STORAGE SECTION rather than the FILE SECTION. By doing so, implicit redefinition considerations can be ignored. Such WORKING-STORAGE definition of input and output records is discussed in Chapter 5.

**Processing Logic—
The IF Statement**

The 200-PROCESS-PATRON-RECORD procedure consists of two statements. The IF statement causes the 210-PROCESS-DEFICIENCY-RECORD procedure to be performed if the Actual-contribution is less than the Target-contribution. In either case, the next record is then read by the READ. For example, if PR-ACTUAL-CONTR is 500 and PR-TARGET-CONTR is 600, then the condition is true and the 210 paragraph will be performed, then execution will continue to the READ. If the amounts are 600 and 500, execution will continue to the READ without performing the 210 paragraph.

**About Signs on
Numbers**

In Concepts Module D, you learned that within the computer, numbers can be either signed or unsigned and that the sign is most commonly embedded in the last digit of the number. In COBOL, the default is unsigned. For instance, FIELD-A defined by the entry

```
05  FIELD-A    PIC 9(4).
```

is unsigned, meaning that COBOL will not carry a sign for any number stored in it. Even if a value is placed in it with a sign, that sign will be discarded. For instance, assume that FIELD-B contains 500 and FIELD-A contains 450. Then the statement

```
SUBTRACT FIELD-B FROM FIELD-A.
```

will produce a difference of –50. However, because FIELD-A is defined as unsigned in its picture, COBOL will discard the minus sign (without warning) and the result in FIELD-A will be 50.

Anytime that a field may contain a negative value, then the picture for that field should include an S for sign, as follows:

```
05  FIELD-A    PIC S9(4).
```

For systems that use embedded signs, the S does not occupy any storage space. Hence, this field will still be four bytes in width.

Numeric Literals

The PATDFCT uses numeric literals in two places: the counter in which 1 is added (line 131/134), and in the AFTER ADVANCING clauses of both WRITE statements (lines 129/132 and 139/142). These are examples of whole number numeric literals. In general, you can form numeric literals limited only by the following:

- It can composed only of digits (0 through 9), a sign character (plus or minus), and a decimal point. Thus, it **cannot** include any characters other than digits, an actual decimal point, and a sign. For instance, a V to indicate assumed decimal positioning or a % to indicate a percentage are not allowed.

- It can contain from 1 to 18 digits, for example:

```
0   3   162   5170058770
```

- It can contain at most one decimal point, for example:

```
2.6   387.62   11280.00
```

However, a decimal point must not be used after the last digit of a whole number amount. The compiler would interpret that as indicating the end of a sentence.

■ It can optionally contain either a single plus or a single minus sign, for example:

```
+25   +25.00    -392    -392.79
```

When the sign character is used, it must be the leftmost character of the literal. (When the sign character is not used, the literal is considered to be a positive value.)

■ It must **not** be enclosed in quotes; quotes specify a nonnumeric literal.

Topic:	**COBOL Arithmetic Statements**

A Preview of the Arithmetic Statements

The PATDFCT program has given you an overall idea of the forms of arithmetic statements. Actually, those forms are a representative of the range of formats for the four basic arithmetic statements. That is, you have used a form in which the result replaces one of the input fields, and a form in which both input fields are unchanged and the result is placed in a third field.

Following are basic examples of the four arithmetic statements; notice their similarity of form:

```
ADD FIELD-A TO FIELD-B.
SUBTRACT FIELD-A FROM FIELD-B.
MULTIPLY FIELD-A BY FIELD-B.
DIVIDE FIELD-A INTO FIELD-B.
```

In each case, the value in FIELD-A is "combined" with the value in FIELD-B. FIELD-A is left unchanged; the contents of FIELD-B are replaced with the result of the arithmetic operation.

Each of the four preceding can also be used with the GIVING option, as illustrated by the following:

```
ADD FIELD-A FIELD-B GIVING FIELD-C.
SUBTRACT FIELD-A FROM FIELD-B GIVING FIELD-C.
MULTIPLY FIELD-A BY FIELD-B GIVING FIELD-C.
DIVIDE FIELD-A INTO FIELD-B GIVING FIELD-C.
```

As with the examples you studied in the PATDFCT program, the contents of the input fields (FIELD-A and FIELD-B) are unchanged; the result is placed in the GIVING field (FIELD-C). Regarding the ADD/GIVING, the missing reserved word TO is not a typographical omission; TO is not used in the GIVING form of the ADD.

In coding your DATA DIVISION, you must be aware that all fields upon which arithmetic is performed in the PROCEDURE DIVISION *must be defined as numeric items*. This means that a numeric-edited item (to which you were introduced in the PATDFCT program) *cannot* be used as one of the fields involved in the arithmetic operation. Later in this chapter, you will learn that this does not apply to the field following the GIVING clause because it is not involved in the actual calculation.

The preceding examples gave you an overall idea of the arithmetic tools you have at your disposal. However, each statement has a variety of formats and special features not shown here. These are the topics of the following sections.

The ADD Statement

There are two forms of the ADD statement. Although the COBOL standards call them Format-1 and Format-2, in the text they will also be referred to by the more meaningful designations of ADD/TO and ADD/GIVING, respectively.

The ADD/TO (Format-1) Statement

As you observed in the PATDFCT program, the ADD/TO statement causes the sum to be developed in augend (the second of the two quantities)—thereby erasing the original value of the augend. The ADD/TO statement is typically used within a series of calculations or when accumulating (as in the PATDFCT program).

The ADD/TO format is shown in Figure 4-11. In interpreting this, remember that whenever brackets or braces enclose multiple elements in the format notation, any one of the alternative elements shown may be specified. Notice in the ADD/TO statement that each addend before the word TO can be either an identifier (that is, the data-name of a numeric field) or a numeric literal (an actual numeric value). Hence, from this format you can see that its variations allow you to:

■ Add one field to a second (used in PATDFCT)

■ Add a numeric literal to a field (used in PATDFCT)

■ Add one or more literals and/or fields to a field

■ Add one or more literals and/or fields to two or more fields

The first two cases are used in PATDFCT: WS-AMOUNT-DEFICIENT is added to WS-TOTAL-AMOUNT-DEFICIENT, and 1 is added to WS-DEFICIENT-PATRONS (lines 130/133 and 131/134). The other two variations are shown in Figure 4-12. Note that in these examples, the picture definitions of the fields used are shown; this information is, of course, implied by the memory representation of the data.

In Figure 4-12(a), three addends (SALES-TAX, DELIVERY-CHARGE, and a literal) are being added to the augend (SALES-PRICE). Of course, the original value in SALES-PRICE is replaced by the newly calculated sum.

Although there are only limited situations in which more than one sum is required, an ADD/TO statement can be coded to develop multiple sums. Such processing is handled by specifying more than one field after the word TO, as shown in the example of Figure 4-12(b). In this case, there are two augends: TOTAL-PURCHASES and TOTAL-TAXABLE-PURCHASES.

Figure 4-11
The ADD/TO format.

ADD/TO (Format-1):

$$\text{ADD} \begin{Bmatrix} \text{identifier-1} \\ \text{literal-1} \end{Bmatrix} \begin{bmatrix} \text{identifier-2} \\ \text{literal-2} \end{bmatrix} \ldots \underline{\text{TO}} \text{ identifier-}m \text{ } [\underline{\text{ROUNDED}}]$$

$$\left[\text{identifier-}n \text{ } [\underline{\text{ROUNDED}}] \right] \ldots \text{ } [\text{ON } \underline{\text{SIZE ERROR}} \text{ imperative-statement}]$$

Figure 4-12 Examples of the ADD/TO statement.

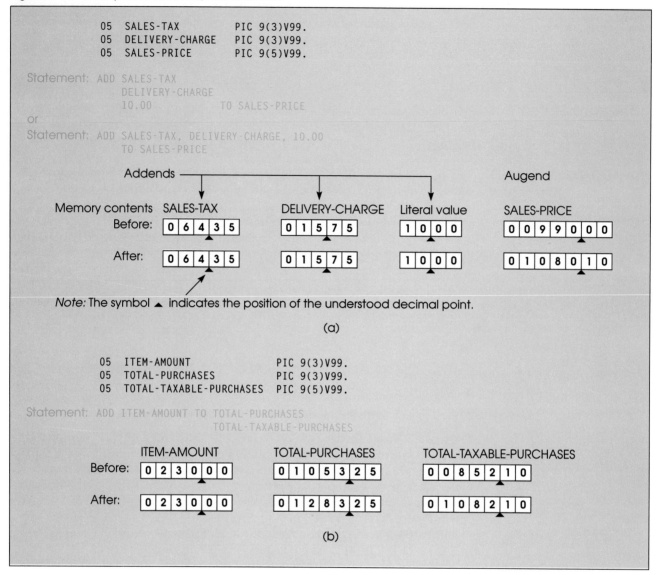

```
        05   SALES-TAX          PIC 9(3)V99.
        05   DELIVERY-CHARGE    PIC 9(3)V99.
        05   SALES-PRICE        PIC 9(5)V99.
Statement: ADD SALES-TAX
                DELIVERY-CHARGE
                10.00              TO SALES-PRICE
or
Statement: ADD SALES-TAX, DELIVERY-CHARGE, 10.00
                TO SALES-PRICE
```

Note: The symbol ▲ indicates the position of the understood decimal point.

(a)

```
        05   ITEM-AMOUNT            PIC 9(3)V99.
        05   TOTAL-PURCHASES        PIC 9(3)V99.
        05   TOTAL-TAXABLE-PURCHASES PIC 9(5)V99.
Statement: ADD ITEM-AMOUNT TO TOTAL-PURCHASES
                            TOTAL-TAXABLE-PURCHASES
```

(b)

Referring to the ADD format, you should recognize that a numeric literal cannot be written after the TO; the augend(s) receive the sum. The sum must be stored in a field—not in a literal.

Both of the Figure 4-12 examples involve data with two digits to the right of the decimal point (typically dollar and cent amounts). Normally, all fields in an ADD or a SUBTRACT statement have the same number of decimal positions. However, this makes no difference to COBOL because the compiler generates code to align decimal points as is appropriate. This is illustrated in Figure 4-13. Notice in the second example that the last digit of RATE-ADJUST is ignored because there is insufficient room for it in BASE-RATE (the field to receive the sum).

Referring to the general format, note that two optional phrases are shown in the ADD/TO format notation: ROUNDED and ON SIZE ERROR. The latter is used for detecting cases in which the calculated quantity will not fit in the result field (positions to the left of the decimal). These two optional phrases can be specified with all arithmetic statements and are explained later in this chapter.

Figure 4-13
Decimal alignment with
the ADD.

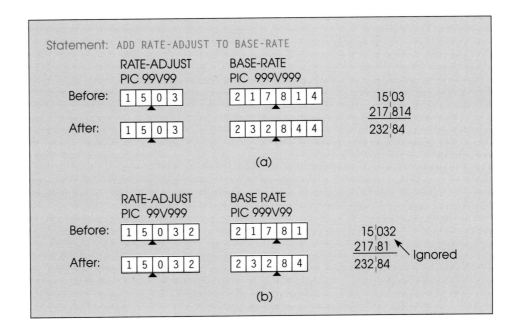

The ADD/GIVING (Format-2) Statement

The ADD/GIVING statement sums two or more quantities without changing any of them and stores the result in a separate field not involved in the calculation. That is, it functions much like the SUBTRACT statement used in PATDFCT. From the general form of the ADD/GIVING in Figure 4-14, notice the following about this statement:

- At least two elements (identifier-1/literal-1 *and* identifier-2/literal-2) must be specified before the reserved word GIVING. Each can be either a numeric field or a numeric literal.

- The reserved word TO, which is required by the ADD/TO statement syntax, is prohibited in the ADD/GIVING statement. (This represents the COBOL-74 standard; the COBOL-85 standard does allow its optional use in a form similar to that of the ADD/TO.) Beginning COBOL programmers using COBOL-74 compilers often inadvertently specify the word TO in the ADD/GIVING statement and receive a diagnostic error message from the compiler.

- The sum of the addition is stored in the field coded after the reserved word GIVING. The field (or fields) that will receive the sum must have a PICTURE specification that is either numeric or numeric edited.

Figure 4-14
The ADD/GIVING format.

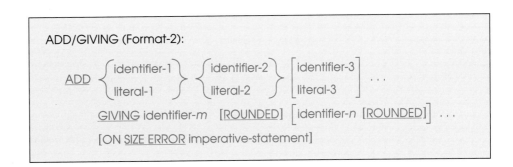

Figure 4-15 ADD/GIVING example.

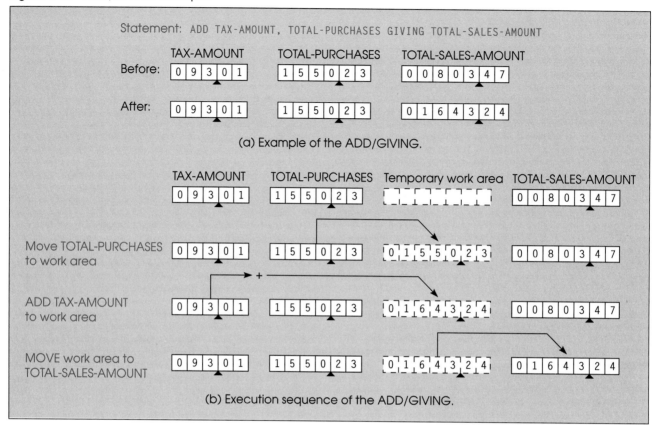

Statement: `ADD TAX-AMOUNT, TOTAL-PURCHASES GIVING TOTAL-SALES-AMOUNT`

(a) Example of the ADD/GIVING.

(b) Execution sequence of the ADD/GIVING.

A simple example of this statement is shown in Figure 4-15(a). (In this example and most that follow, the picture description is not explicitly shown; it is implied by the memory representation.) This ADD statement includes a comma between the two terms to give a visual separation of them; as always, the comma is optional. Figure 4-15(b) should help you conceptualize how the ADD/GIVING works. The arithmetic operations actually take place using a temporary work area in memory. When the arithmetic is completed, the result is moved to the GIVING field.

Inspecting the general form, you can see that any number of values, either literals or data fields, can be added. Also, the resulting sum can be stored in one or more fields; this action is equivalent to the MOVE, which allows you to move (copy) a field into more than one receiving fields. Following are two other examples of the ADD/GIVING:

Example

```
ADD FIELD-A, FIELD-B, FIELD-C, 25.00 GIVING FIELD-TOTAL
```

Action

Sums the contents of fields FIELD-A, FIELD-B, FIELD-C, and the numeric literal 25, then places the result in FIELD-TOTAL.

Example

```
ADD FIELD-A, 25.00 GIVING FIELD-TOTAL, WORK-FIELD
```

Action

Sums the contents of field FIELD-A and the numeric literal 25, then places a copy of the result in both FIELD-TOTAL and WORK-FIELD.

The SUBTRACT Statement

If you understand the ADD statement, you should have little trouble with the SUBTRACT because their general forms are almost the same. Like the ADD, the SUBTRACT has two formats: Format-1 (SUBTRACT/FROM) and Format-2 (SUBTRACT/GIVING).

The SUBTRACT/FROM (Format-1) Statement

Figure 4-16 shows the SUBTRACT/FROM statement format. Its characteristics are illustrated by the following examples:

Example

```
SUBTRACT 20.00 FROM FIELD-B
```

Action

Subtracts the value 20.00 (included in the statement as a numeric literal) from the contents of FIELD-B, with the resulting difference stored in FIELD-B.

Example

```
SUBTRACT FIELD-A FROM FIELD-B
```

Action

Subtracts the contents of FIELD-A from the contents of FIELD-B, with the resulting difference stored in FIELD-B.

Example

```
SUBTRACT FIELD-A, FIELD-B, 12.25 FROM FIELD-C
```

Action

When multiple subtrahends are coded (FIELD-A, FIELD-B, 12.25 in this case), the COBOL compiler handles the computation by first summing the subtrahends and then subtracting that sum from the minuend (or minuends) written after the reserved word FROM. In this example, the contents of FIELD-A, the contents of FIELD-B, and the numeric literal 12.25 are added (using a temporary work area), then this resulting sum is subtracted from FIELD-C.

Example

```
SUBTRACT FIELD-A FROM FIELD-B, FIELD-C
```

Action

Subtracts the contents of FIELD-A from the contents of FIELD-B, with the resulting difference stored in FIELD-B. Then subtracts the contents of FIELD-A from the contents of FIELD-C, with that resulting difference stored in FIELD-C.

Figure 4-16
The SUBTRACT/FROM format.

SUBTRACT/FROM (Format-1):

$$\underline{\text{SUBTRACT}} \left\{ \begin{array}{l} \text{identifier-1} \\ \text{literal-1} \end{array} \right\} \left[\begin{array}{l} \text{identifier-2} \\ \text{literal-2} \end{array} \right] \ldots \underline{\text{FROM}}\ \text{identifier-}m\ [\underline{\text{ROUNDED}}]$$

$$\left[\text{identifier-}n\ [\underline{\text{ROUNDED}}] \right] \ldots [\text{ON}\ \underline{\text{SIZE ERROR}}\ \text{imperative-statement}]$$

As with the ADD, the element following the FROM (the receiving field) cannot be a literal.

The SUBTRACT/GIVING (Format-2) Statement

The SUBTRACT/GIVING statement format is shown in Figure 4-17. As with the ADD/GIVING statement, the GIVING field of this SUBTRACT is not included in the calculation and can thus be either a numeric or a numeric-edited field. One significant syntactical difference exists between the SUBTRACT/GIVING and the ADD/GIVING statements. The word TO is required in the ADD/TO, but *must* be omitted with the ADD/GIVING (except for COBOL-85). With the SUBTRACT, the word FROM is required in both formats.

The following examples of the SUBTRACT/GIVING statement illustrate the general format.

Example

```
SUBTRACT WITH-TAX, FICA, OTHER-DED, 10.00 FROM GROSS-PAY
    GIVING NET-PAY
```

Action

Calculates the sum of 10.00 and the contents of the fields WITH-TAX, FICA, OTHER-DED. Subtracts this sum from the value in GROSS-PAY and stores the result in NET-PAY. The only field changed is NET-PAY.

Example

```
SUBTRACT 1 FROM BONUS-PNTS GIVING CHECK-PNTS, WORK-PNTS
```

Action

The amount 1 is subtracted from the value in BONUS-PNTS; the result is copied into CHECK-PNTS and WORK-PNTS. BONUS-PNTS is not changed.

Dealing With Negative Quantities

As indicated earlier, if a SUBTRACT statement produces a negative result, COBOL will discard the sign unless the receiving field is defined as being signed. This is illustrated in the examples of Figure 14-18. In the first example, both PAYMENT and BALANCE are defined as unsigned. In this case, a number is being subtracted from a smaller number. According to rules of arithmetic, this always calculates a negative number as the difference between the two values. However, the minus sign is discarded by COBOL because BALANCE is defined as unsigned. But, in the second example, both fields are defined as signed by preceding the picture field with the letter S. In this case, signs are carried in both fields and the minus sign on BALANCE resulting from the subtraction is retained.

The MULTIPLY Statement

As with the ADD and SUBTRACT statements, the MULTIPLY statement has two formats, Format-1 and Format-2. These are referred to in the text as MULTIPLY/BY and MULTIPLY/GIVING, respectively.

Figure 4-17
The SUBTRACT/GIVING format.

SUBTRACT/GIVING (Format-2):

$$\underline{SUBTRACT} \left\{ \begin{array}{l} identifier\text{-}1 \\ literal\text{-}1 \end{array} \right\} \left[\begin{array}{l} identifier\text{-}2 \\ literal\text{-}2 \end{array} \right] \ldots \underline{FROM} \left\{ \begin{array}{l} identifier\text{-}m \\ literal\text{-}m \end{array} \right\}$$

$$\underline{GIVING}\ identifier\text{-}n\ [\underline{ROUNDED}]\ \left[identifier\text{-}o\ [\underline{ROUNDED}] \right] \ldots$$

$$[ON\ \underline{SIZE\ ERROR}\ imperative\text{-}statement]$$

Figure 4-18
SUBTRACT examples.

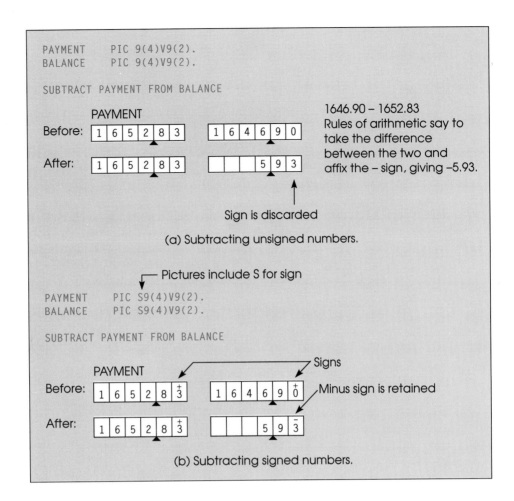

```
PAYMENT      PIC 9(4)V9(2).
BALANCE      PIC 9(4)V9(2).

SUBTRACT PAYMENT FROM BALANCE
```

PAYMENT

Before: [1][6][5][2][8][3]   [1][6][4][6][9][0]

After: [1][6][5][2][8][3]   [ ][ ][ ][5][9][3]

1646.90 – 1652.83
Rules of arithmetic say to take the difference between the two and affix the – sign, giving –5.93.

Sign is discarded

(a) Subtracting unsigned numbers.

Pictures include S for sign

```
PAYMENT      PIC S9(4)V9(2).
BALANCE      PIC S9(4)V9(2).

SUBTRACT PAYMENT FROM BALANCE
```

PAYMENT   Signs

Before: [1][6][5][2][8][3⁺]   [1][6][4][6][9][0⁺]   Minus sign is retained

After: [1][6][5][2][8][3⁺]   [ ][ ][ ][5][9][3⁻]

(b) Subtracting signed numbers.

The MULTIPLY/BY (Format-1) Statement

The MULTIPLY/BY format is shown in Figure 4-19. Notice that the MULTIPLY differs from the ADD and SUBTRACT in that only a single factor (identifier-1/literal-1) can precede the keyword BY. Like the equivalent ADD and SUBTRACT forms, the result is placed in the field following the keyword BY (identifier-2). The following two examples illustrate the general format:

Example

```
MULTIPLY 1.1 BY TAX-RATE
```

Action

The value in TAX-RATE is multiplied by 1.1; the value in TAX-RATE is replaced with the calculated product.

Figure 4-19
The MULTIPLY/BY format.

MULTIPLY/BY (Format-1):

MULTIPLY { identifier-1 / literal-1 } BY identifier-2 [ROUNDED]

[identifier-3 [ROUNDED]] . . . [ON SIZE ERROR imperative-statement]

Example

```
MULTIPLY 1.1 BY BASE-TAX-RATE, COUNTY-RATE, SPECIAL-RATE
```

Action

The values in each of the fields BASE-TAX-RATE, COUNTY-RATE, and SPECIAL-RATE are multiplied by 1.1 and replaced by the respective products.

When listing the factors to the multiplication, you should usually code the longer field (that is, the one with more integer digits) after the word BY to help ensure that the product will fit in the result field.

The ROUNDED Clause

A multiplication in which both fields have digits to the right of the decimal point will almost always have right digits that are discarded, as illustrated by the example of Figure 4-20. By default, COBOL truncates. If you wish the result to be rounded, then you can include the ROUNDED clause, in which case the MULTIPLY statement of Figure 4-20 would be:

```
MULTIPLY TAX-RATE BY TAX-WORK-AREA ROUNDED.
```

The result stored in TAX-WORK-AREA would then be 0019.41 instead of 0019.40.

Note that the ROUNDED clause was not required in any of the ADD or SUBTRACT examples because all elements involved in the calculations were shown with the same number of decimal places. However, anytime the result field for any of these arithmetic statements contains fewer places to the right of the decimal point than the expected calculated result, you should consider the ROUNDED clause.

The MULTIPLY/GIVING (Format-2) Statement

In the MULTIPLY/GIVING general format of Figure 4-21, both factors to the multiplication operation (identifier-1/literal-1 and identifier-2/literal-2) can be either a numeric field or a numeric literal. The product or products (identifier-3, identifier-4, and so on) may be either numeric or numeric-edited fields. The

Figure 4-20
Truncating a product.

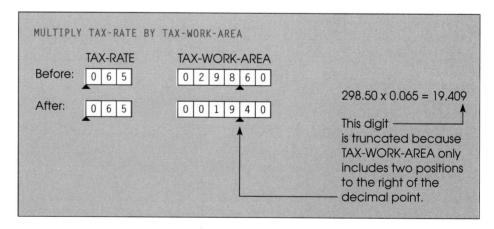

Figure 4-21
The MULTIPLY/GIVING format.

following example of the MULTIPLY/GIVING is the typical way in which this statement is used:

Example

```
MULTIPLY TOTAL-PURCHASES BY TAX-RATE GIVING TAX-AMOUNT
```

Action

The values in TOTAL-PURCHASES and TAX-RATE are multiplied. The original value in TAX-AMOUNT is replaced with the calculated product.

The DIVIDE Statement

The DIVIDE statement is somewhat more complicated in that it has five formats, Format-1 through Format-5. Three of them are DIVIDE/INTO forms and two are DIVIDE/BY forms. The major difference between the INTO and the BY formats is the relative placement of the divisor and dividend within the DIVIDE statement.

The DIVIDE/INTO (Format-1) and the DIVIDE/INTO/GIVING (Format-2)

As you can see by inspecting Figure 4-22, these two DIVIDE statement formats are identical to those of the corresponding MULTIPLY statements. The following two examples illustrate the ways in which you will most commonly use the DIVIDE:

Example

```
DIVIDE TOTAL-UNITS INTO WORK-POINTS
```

Action

The value in TOTAL-UNITS is divided into the value in WORK-POINTS. The original value in WORK-POINTS is replaced with the calculated quotient.

Example

```
DIVIDE TOTAL-UNITS INTO EARNED-POINTS
    GIVING GRADE-POINT-AVERAGE
```

Action

The value in TOTAL-UNITS is divided into the value in EARNED-POINTS and the quotient is stored in GRADE-POINT-AVERAGE.

As with all arithmetic statements, fields listed after the word GIVING are not factors to the division operation; they may be either numeric or numeric-edited fields. The original values of the factors listed before the GIVING are not disturbed.

Figure 4-22
The DIVIDE/INTO and DIVIDE/INTO/GIVING.

DIVIDE/INTO (Format-1):

DIVIDE { identifier-1 / literal-1 } INTO identifier-2 [ROUNDED]

[identifier-3 [ROUNDED]] ... [ON SIZE ERROR imperative-statement]

DIVIDE/INTO (Format-2):

DIVIDE { identifier-1 / literal-1 } INTO { identifier-2 / literal-2 }

GIVING identifier-3 [ROUNDED] [identifier-4 [ROUNDED]] ...

[ON SIZE ERROR imperative-statement]

The DIVIDE/INTO/ GIVING/REMAINDER (Format-4)

As shown in Figure 4-23, the DIVIDE/INTO/GIVING/REMAINDER format permits specification of a field to hold the remainder from the division operation. Otherwise, the arithmetic is like that provided by the DIVIDE/INTO/GIVING format. After the reserved word REMAINDER is coded, the data-name of an elementary numeric field is coded. This field will receive the remainder value.

The REMAINDER phrase is not often specified for DIVIDE operations. The reason for this is also why remainders are not often used in everyday arithmetic—it is much easier to work with remainders expressed as decimal-position values within the quotient. For instance, you would normally express 22/8 as 2.75 rather than as 2, remainder 6.

However, there is one type of situation in which remainders are often used—when working with a counting system that does not cycle at 10. A good example is hours and minutes. For instance, 192 minutes is usually represented as 3 hours 12 minutes rather than 3.2 hours. Notice that if you divide 192 by 60, the quotient is 3 (the number of hours) and the remainder is 12 (the number of minutes). This calculation is implemented in the COBOL statement of Figure 4-24.

The DIVIDE/BY/GIVING (Format-3) and DIVIDE/ BY/GIVING/REMAINDER (Format-5)

As you can see by comparing the general formats of Figure 4-25 to corresponding formats in Figures 4-22 and 4-23, a correspondence occurs between formats of two pairs of the DIVIDE statement:

```
DIVIDE/BY/GIVING            to   DIVIDE/INTO/GIVING
DIVIDE/BY/GIVING/REMAINDER  to   DIVIDE/INTO/GIVING/REMAINDER
```

The differences are (1) the reserved word BY is used rather than the word INTO, and (2) the relative location of the divisor and the dividend are switched. As an example of these forms, the following will perform exactly the same function as the DIVIDE/INTO of Figure 4-24.

```
DIVIDE TOTAL-ELAPSED-TIME BY 60
    GIVING ELAPSED-HOURS REMAINDER ELAPSED-MINUTES
```

Figure 4-23
The DIVIDE/INTO/GIVING/ REMAINDER.

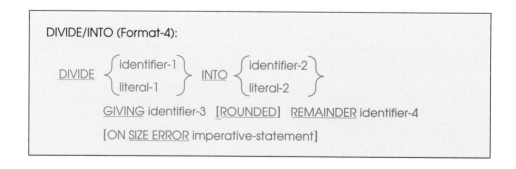

Figure 4-24
Using the REMAINDER phrase.

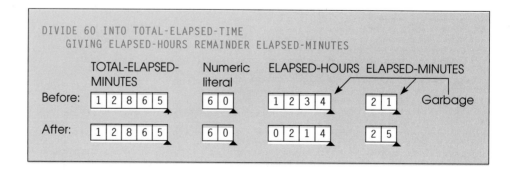

Figure 4-25
The DIVIDE/BY/GIVING and
DIVIDE/BY/GIVING/
REMAINDER.

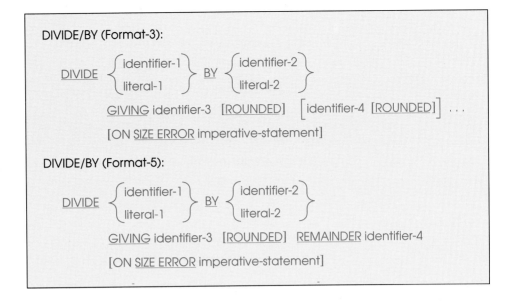

DIVIDE/BY (Format-3):

$$\underline{\text{DIVIDE}} \left\{ \begin{array}{l} \text{identifier-1} \\ \text{literal-1} \end{array} \right\} \underline{\text{BY}} \left\{ \begin{array}{l} \text{identifier-2} \\ \text{literal-2} \end{array} \right\}$$

$$\underline{\text{GIVING}} \text{ identifier-3 } [\underline{\text{ROUNDED}}] \; \left[\text{identifier-4 } [\underline{\text{ROUNDED}}] \right] \; \dots$$

[ON $\underline{\text{SIZE ERROR}}$ imperative-statement]

DIVIDE/BY (Format-5):

$$\underline{\text{DIVIDE}} \left\{ \begin{array}{l} \text{identifier-1} \\ \text{literal-1} \end{array} \right\} \underline{\text{BY}} \left\{ \begin{array}{l} \text{identifier-2} \\ \text{literal-2} \end{array} \right\}$$

$$\underline{\text{GIVING}} \text{ identifier-3 } [\underline{\text{ROUNDED}}] \; \underline{\text{REMAINDER}} \text{ identifier-4}$$

[ON $\underline{\text{SIZE ERROR}}$ imperative-statement]

The COMPUTE Statement

The COMPUTE statement is an alternative to the four basic arithmetic verbs just described. If you have taken most any other computer language (such as BASIC), you will be familiar with the technique employed. It permits the expression of arithmetic calculations in a manner similar to algebraic notation. Figure 4-26 shows the COMPUTE statement, together with examples.

COMPUTE Statement Processing

The five arithmetic operator symbols that may be coded in a COMPUTE statement are:

Operator symbol	Operation
+	addition
−	subtraction
*	multiplication
/	division
**	exponentiation

Figure 4-26
The COMPUTE statement
format and examples.

Format:

$$\underline{\text{COMPUTE}} \text{ identifier-1 } [\underline{\text{ROUNDED}}] \; \left[\text{identifier-2 } [\underline{\text{ROUNDED}}] \right] \; \dots$$

$$= \text{arithmetic-expression } [\text{ON } \underline{\text{SIZE ERROR}} \text{ imperative-statement}]$$

Examples:

```
COMPUTE NEW-BALANCE = BALANCE-FORWARD
                    + CURRENT-PURCHASES
                    + SERVICE-CHARGE
                    - TOTAL-PAYMENT.

COMPUTE INTEREST = PRINCIPAL * RATE * YEARS / 100.

COMPUTE AMOUNT = PRINCIPAL * (1.00 + RATE / 100) ** YEARS.
```

When the arithmetic expression contains more than one arithmetic operator symbol, the operations are executed in a specific order, called the **hierarchy of arithmetic operations** or the **order of precedence**. The order is as follows:

1. Unary operations (reversing the sign of a field)

2. Exponentiation (raising a value to a power)

3. Multiplication and division

4. Addition and subtraction

As an illustration of this hierarchy of operations, consider the following statement:

```
COMPUTE X = A + B / C
```

The sequence of operations is:

1. The division specified by B / C would be carried out.

2. The quotient from that division would be added to the value of A.

3. The result would be placed in X; only the value of X will change.

Some expressions contain two or more additions or subtractions (or multiplications or divisions). When this occurs, the operations within each hierarchy level are executed starting from left to right within the expression. To illustrate, consider the statement:

```
COMPUTE X = A - B / C + D * E
```

The sequence in which the calculations will occur is as follows:

1. B / C (quotient stored in a temporary work area)

2. D * E (product stored in a temporary work area)

3. A – (quotient from Step 1)

4. (difference from Step 3) + (product from Step 2)

Be careful of this hierarchy or else you could get something you had not anticipated. Suppose you wanted to add two fields (A and B) and then divide the sum by another field (C). You would not get the correct result using:

```
COMPUTE X = A + B / C    (Does not give the desired result.)
```

The reason is that the division of B by C would occur before A is added to B.

To override this normal sequence of operations, you would use parentheses—just as in algebra. That is, operations within the innermost set of parentheses are evaluated first and then evaluation proceeds through the outermost set. Equal parentheses levels are evaluated on a left to right basis. Thus, by writing the above statement with parentheses as follows, you would get the desired result:

```
COMPUTE X = (A + B) / C
```

It is a good practice to code parentheses within the arithmetic expression, regardless of whether or not they are actually required to override the normal sequence of operations, for two reasons. First, with complex expressions, it is sometimes difficult to determine exactly when the system will perform each operation. It is simpler and less risky to instead code the parentheses where appropriate to ensure the desired sequence. Second, it is easier to read and understand an arithmetic expression written with parentheses.

COMPUTE Statement Syntax

The identifier coded before the equals sign—that is, the field that will receive the result—must be a numeric or a numeric-edited field. Each field coded within the arithmetic expression—that is, after the equals sign—must be purely numeric (either a numeric field or a numeric literal).

The equals sign and each arithmetic operator sign *must be preceded and followed by a space*. For example, the statement

```
COMPUTE X=A+B
```

is syntactically incorrect. It must instead be coded with spaces to separate the elements of the arithmetic expression; that is:

```
COMPUTE X = A + B
```

In most programming languages, spaces are ignored by the compiler, so they can either be omitted or included to improve readability. So if you know some other language such as BASIC or Pascal, make certain you do not get confused and leave out the spaces.

Although multiply operations are often implied in algebra (the absence of a times sign implies multiplication), all operations must be explicitly coded in the COMPUTE statement arithmetic expression.

When parentheses are coded, they must always appear in pairs and should be coded immediately adjacent to their contents. That is, a left parentheses should have a blank space on the left and no space on the right; a right parentheses should have no space on the left and a blank space on the right.

A **unary operation**—one with only one factor—can be specified to reverse the arithmetic sign of a value within a field. A minus sign coded with no factor to the left is considered to be a **unary arithmetic operator**. For example, the statements

```
COMPUTE X = - B + C
COMPUTE X = A + (- B + C)
```

will cause the value of B to be multiplied by the numeric literal –1 before it is added to C. Remember that unary operations rank highest in the hierarchy of arithmetic operations.

Note that the general format of COMPUTE allows use of the ROUNDED phrase. It works with the COMPUTE in exactly the same way it works with the four arithmetic statements.

The ON SIZE ERROR Phrase

You have probably noticed that all of the arithmetic statement general forms have included the ON SIZE ERROR phrase. When an arithmetic calculation generates a value that exceeds the size of the receiving field, an **arithmetic overflow** condition occurs. In COBOL, it is called a **size error condition**; it is illustrated in Figure 4-27. In this case, the overflow of 1 will be discarded and the resulting sum in TOTAL-AMOUNT will be 0438.86 as shown. COBOL provides no indication of the erroneous result.

Figure 4-27
A size error condition.

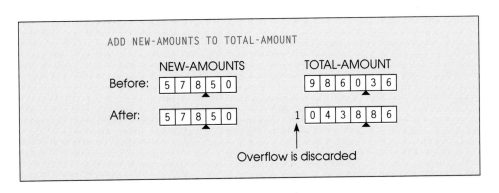

However, this size error condition can be detected and an action taken by including the ON SIZE ERROR phrase as follows:

```
ADD NEW-AMOUNTS TO TOTAL-AMOUNT
    ON SIZE ERROR PERFORM 999-IDENTIFY-SIZE-ERROR
```

Now when the condition of Figure 4-27 occurs, the 999-IDENTIFY-SIZE-ERROR procedure will be performed. When a size error does occur and the phrase is specified, the contents of the receiving field are unpredictable. (That is, the receiving field will typically be unchanged rather than filled with a truncated answer.)

In a normal situation when the result can be accommodated within the answer field (or fields), the ON SIZE ERROR phrase statements are skipped; program processing resumes after the end-of-statement period. Overall, the way in which the ON SIZE ERROR phrase works is virtually identical to the way the AT END phrase of the READ statement functions.

Referring to the general format of any of the arithmetic statements, you can see that any imperative statement can follow the ON SIZE ERROR phrase.

By proper program design and data checking (a topic of Chapter 8), the possibility of size errors can almost always be avoided. A few actions such as calculating running totals (accumulating) can give unexpected results that cause size errors. In such cases, the ON SIZE ERROR (or alternate program logic) should be used. However, use of the ON SIZE ERROR phrase is generally discouraged because it is awkward to handle the exception processing. It is best to check data before calculations to ensure that size error will not occur.

Arithmetic Scope Terminators in COBOL-85

Whenever the ON SIZE ERROR is used, the scope of the statements to be executed must be terminated either with a period or an END scope terminator. This is much like that AT END in the READ. Hence, the preceding example would be coded as follows in COBOL-85:

```
ADD NEW-AMOUNTS TO TOTAL-AMOUNT
    ON SIZE ERROR PERFORM 999-IDENTIFY-SIZE-ERROR
END-ADD
```

The five scope terminators for the arithmetic statements are: END-ADD, END-SUBTRACT, END-MULTIPLY, END-DIVIDE, and END-COMPUTE.

Selecting the Arithmetic Form to Use

Arithmetic Verbs

If you are a little overwhelmed by the vast array of arithmetic forms and are wondering "what to use when," do not be concerned; the proper choice is usually obvious by the application needs.

For instance, the GIVING phrase is typically not applicable when running totals are being accumulated into a WORKING-STORAGE field or when counting or decrementing (counting backwards). Statements without the GIVING phrase are more effective.

On the other hand, the GIVING phrase should be used when all fields in the calculation are needed for later calculations or other uses. For example, suppose that the sum of fields FIELD-A and FIELD-B is required early in the program processing. Then, later on, the original values of FIELD-A and FIELD-B are needed again. If the ADD statement to produce the sum were written without the GIVING phrase as

```
ADD FIELD-A TO FIELD-B
```

the original value of FIELD-B would be lost. Therefore, in this situation, the statement should be written with a GIVING phrase so that a separate field is introduced to hold the sum, for instance:

```
ADD FIELD-A TO FIELD-B GIVING FIELD-C
```

Another situation appropriate for use of the GIVING phrase is when the results of a calculation are to be placed in a numeric-edited field. Remember that a numeric-edited field cannot be used as a field in an arithmetic statement. It may, however, appear in the GIVING phrase. The PATDFCT program contains a case in which this technique could be used to eliminate a MOVE and an intermediate work area. Figure 4-28 includes selected lines from PATDFCT to calculate the percentage (lines 124/127 and 125/128), then move the result to the output area (line 126/129). (The action of the MOVE is illustrated in Figure 4-10.) The alternate MULTIPLY in Figure 4-28 will perform the multiplication and data movement in exactly the same way.

The COMPUTE Statement

Any calculation can be made by either using some combination of the four basic arithmetic verbs or through using the COMPUTE statement. However, if you need a remainder from a divide operation, then the DIVIDE verb is most appropriate because the COMPUTE does not include a REMAINDER phrase. On the other hand, if you must do exponentiation (raising a number to a power), the COMPUTE statement is straightforward.

For the majority of arithmetic operations, though, either the basic arithmetic verbs or the COMPUTE statement can be used. Which should be chosen? There are two schools of thought on this matter.

One view is to always (except for exponentiation) use the four basic arithmetic verbs. Those who advocate this position maintain that the basic verbs are more understandable to most business-oriented programmers; the COMPUTE statement is more mathematically oriented. Further, many have observed that the arithmetic expressions within a COMPUTE statement often become long and complicated. Use of the basic arithmetic verbs ensures that even complex computations are broken down into relatively simple, step-by-step calculations.

A major drawback to the use of the COMPUTE statement is that the COBOL standards do not define the techniques to be used in handling the size, truncation, and rounding aspects of the intermediate results obtained during the calculation. This means that (1) unexpected result values may sometimes occur unless you are aware of the techniques employed by the compiler being used, and (2) even if you are fully cognizant of the approach being followed by a particular vendor's compiler, different results may be obtained when the program is run using another vendor's compiler. As a result, the COMPUTE statement may introduce unexpected results, which thus hinders program portability.

On the other hand, those who favor use of the COMPUTE statement contend that an algebraic expression is more understandable than a string of ADD, SUBTRACT, MULTIPLY, and DIVIDE statements. Further, the COMPUTE statement generally provides more efficient processing, especially for more complicated expressions, than does a string of the individual arithmetic statements.

Figure 4-28
Using a numeric-edited item after a GIVING.

```
        61        05  DL-DEFICIENCY-PERCENT      PIC 99.9.
        .         .
        .         .
        .         .
       124        MULTIPLY WS-DEFICIENCY-FRACTION BY 100
       125            GIVING WS-DEFICIENCY-PERCENT.
       126        MOVE WS-DEFICIENCY-PERCENT TO DL-DEFICIENCY-PERCENT.

   Alternate form:

                  MULTIPLY WS-DEFICIENCY-FRACTION BY 100
                      GIVING DL-DEFICIENCY-PERCENT.
```

Modifying the PATDFCT Program
Introducing Dollar and Cent Amounts

Since Chapter 1, you have worked with the PATRON file on the basis that the input data is in whole dollars, not dollars and cents. Assume that the collections manager of Fleetwood Charities has informed you that the organization would like the PATRON system changed to store and process in terms of dollars and cents. This would mean (1) the data file would have to be reformatted, and (2) the programs to process the data would need to be modified.

Another member of the programming staff has been assigned the task of converting the PATRON file. The new format is to be as follows:

Field	Width	Class	Format
Name	18	Alphanumeric	
Street address	18	Alphanumeric	
City/state/zip	24	Alphanumeric	
Target contribution	6	Numeric	9999V99
Actual contribution	6	Numeric	9999V99
Contribution date	6	Alphanumeric	
Total record size	78		

Your task is to modify the PATDFCT program to accommodate this change to the two numeric fields. A sample of the printed report is shown in Figure 4-29. Obviously, you will need to change the DATA DIVISION to handle the different format for both input and output. The question now is: Will you need to modify the PROCEDURE DIVISION accordingly?

If you inspect this division of the original PATDFCT (Figure 4-6), you will see that there is *no indication of decimal positioning in any of the PROCEDURE DIVISION statements*. Remember, once data is defined in the DATA DIVISION, all decimal positioning and aligned is done *automatically* by COBOL. Hence, there will be no change to the PROCEDURE DIVISION.

In the DATA DIVISION shown in Figure 4-30, the entries that have been modified are shown in color. Notice that appropriate input, output, and work numeric fields are changed to reflect the added decimal places. The RECORD CONTAINS clause (which is optional) is also changed to reflect the increased length of the input record. These are the only modifications necessary to convert PATDFCT to PATDFCT2 to handle the new PATRON data file format.

Figure 4-29
The PATRON deficiency report with dollar and cent amounts.

Anderson, Hazel	03/25/91	0250.00	0101.15	0148.85	40.5%
Baker, Donald	02/28/91	0375.00	0312.50	0062.50	83.3%
Campbell, J. H.	03/23/91	0200.00	0175.00	0025.00	87.5%
Davidson, Harley	03/17/91	0250.00	0100.00	0150.00	40.0%
Englehoff, F.	02/15/91	0250.00	0166.64	0083.36	66.7%
Hildebrand, John	03/28/91	0250.00	0200.00	0050.00	80.0%
Miller, Irwin B.	01/01/91	0200.00	0185.37	0014.63	92.7%
Molitar, Arnold T.	03/25/91	0200.00	0166.66	0033.34	83.3%
Nelson, J. J.	03/02/91	0250.00	0121.98	0128.02	48.8%
Pratt, Diane	03/31/91	0375.00	0229.50	0145.50	61.2%
Stevenson, Howard	03/28/91	0200.00	0020.00	0180.00	10.0%
Zener, Eva	03/15/91	0200.00	0199.95	0000.05	00.0%

```
   012                                        001021.25
```

Figure 4-30
Revised DATA DIVISION:
PATDFCT2.

```
24        DATA DIVISION.
25        FILE SECTION.
26
27        FD  PATRON-FILE
28                RECORD CONTAINS 78 CHARACTERS
29                LABEL RECORDS ARE STANDARD.
30
31        01  PATRON-RECORD.
32            05  PR-NAME                    PIC X(18).
33            05  FILLER                     PIC X(42).
34            05  PR-TARGET-CONTR            PIC 9(4)V99.  ⎫ Input
35            05  PR-ACTUAL-CONTR            PIC 9(4)V99.  ⎬ fields
36            05  PR-CONTR-DATE.
37                10  PR-CONTR-MONTH         PIC X(2).
38                10  PR-CONTR-DAY           PIC X(2).
39                10  PR-CONTR-YEAR          PIC X(2).
40
41        FD  DEFICIENCY-LIST
42                RECORD CONTAINS 132 CHARACTERS
43                LABEL RECORDS ARE OMITTED.
44
45        01  DEFICIENCY-LINE.
46            05  FILLER                     PIC X(1).
47            05  DL-NAME                    PIC X(18).
48            05  FILLER                     PIC X(2).
49            05  DL-CONTR-MONTH             PIC X(2).
50            05  DL-SLASH-1                 PIC X(1).
51            05  DL-CONTR-DAY               PIC X(2).
52            05  DL-SLASH-2                 PIC X(1).
53            05  DL-CONTR-YEAR              PIC X(2).
54            05  FILLER                     PIC X(4).
55            05  DL-TARGET-CONTR            PIC 9(4).99. ◄─┐
56            05  FILLER                     PIC X(3).
57            05  DL-ACTUAL-CONTR            PIC 9(4).99. ◄─┤
58            05  FILLER                     PIC X(3).
59            05  DL-AMOUNT-DEFICIENT        PIC 9(4).99. ◄─┤
60            05  FILLER                     PIC X(3).          ⎫ Output
61            05  DL-DEFICIENCY-PERCENT      PIC 99.9.          ⎬ fields
62            05  DL-PERCENT-SIGN            PIC X(1).          ⎭
63            05  FILLER                     PIC X(64).
64
65        01  TOTAL-LINE.
66            05  FILLER                     PIC X(4).
67            05  TL-DEFICIENT-PATRONS       PIC 9(3).
68            05  FILLER                     PIC X(44).
69            05  TL-TOTAL-AMOUNT-DEFICIENT  PIC 9(6).99. ◄─┘
70            05  FILLER                     PIC X(72).
71
72        WORKING-STORAGE SECTION.
73
74        01  WS-SWITCHES.
75            05  WS-EOF-SWITCH              PIC X(3).
76
77        01  WS-ARITHMETIC-WORK-AREAS.
78            05  WS-AMOUNT-DEFICIENT        PIC 9(4)V99.  ⎫ Work
79            05  WS-TOTAL-AMOUNT-DEFICIENT  PIC 9(6)V99.  ⎬ fields
80            05  WS-DEFICIENCY-FRACTION     PIC V9(3).
```

Communicating the Message

If you compare the report of Figure 4-1 to the report of Figure 4-29, you will notice that Figure 4-1 communicates its information much better because it has been annotated. That is, for purposes of illustration in this text, each of the output quantities includes an appropriate description. On the other hand, the output of Figure 4-29 does not, by itself, convey its message very well. For instance, what are the numbers printed in the third, fourth, and fifth columns? What are the two numbers printed at the bottom of the page? If you were not familiar with the format of the report, you could only guess. Furthermore, all numeric quantities are printed with leading zeros, making the numbers more difficult to read. For example, 0020.00 is clumsier to read than 20.00.

In a nutshell, this report includes all the information requested; however, it communicates that information poorly. An important part of the planning process is the ultimate production of reports that do a good job of communicating the information they present. The next two chapters focus on techniques that allow you to produce high-quality reports.

Topic: Internal Coding of Numeric Data

Packed-Decimal Data Format

In Concepts Module D, you learned about the EBCDIC data coding method for alphanumeric data used in IBM mainframes. In addition to EBCDIC, the IBM System/360 included a special coding method for numeric data (still used today in IBM mainframes). Designers of the System/360 realized that using an entire byte to store one digit was inefficient because each decimal digit can be represented in binary with four bits, or a half-byte (called a *nibble*). This is indeed done in IBM mainframes, using a format called **packed-decimal**—which is illustrated with the five-digit number 57382 in Figure 4-31. Notice in the packed-decimal format that each byte, except the rightmost, contains two digits. The rightmost contains one digit plus the sign. For an application in which large quantities of numeric data were to be stored in a disk file, using packed format can result in a significant reduction in the file size. Over the years, many COBOL applications have been written in which data was stored in packed-decimal format to save disk storage.

However, using packed-decimal format to save disk storage space is becoming a thing of the past. The current trend by software vendors is to include special software as part of the operating system that automatically compresses data to save disk space. These **data compression** routines use sophisticated methods for squeezing the data down to reduce disk storage requirements, then expanding it back to its original form when the data is requested by a program.

Arithmetic Operations With Packed-Decimal Data

Within any computer, special hardware or software features must be included to perform arithmetic on decimal numbers that are stored in an alphanumeric format. For example, the machine language instructions resulting from a simple COBOL ADD verb must convert each number from the display format to a code more amenable to arithmetic before (or during) the addition operation. One of the features of the IBM System/360 (that has carried through to IBM mainframes of today) was that it included special packed-decimal arithmetic instructions optimized to perform arithmetic on packed-decimal data. Hence, using packed-decimal with

Figure 4-31
A five-digit number in display and packed-decimal formats.

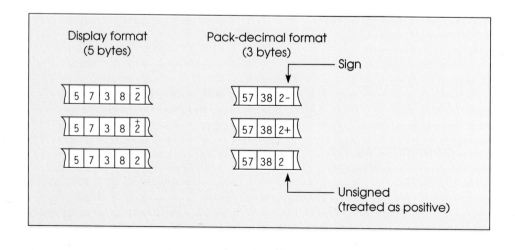

an IBM mainframe not only saves disk storage space, but can also improve the speed of execution of the program. (However, for most business applications, this speed improvement is not very significant.)

On the other hand, most other computers—those designed around the ASCII code—do not have the specialized packed-decimal instructions. To perform arithmetic on packed-decimal data, most of these computers first convert the packed-decimal to display format, perform the arithmetic (which requires further conversion), then convert the results back to packed-decimal as needed. If you are using the Ryan-McFarland compiler that accompanies some versions of this book, you can experiment with this by repeating a sequence of simple arithmetic operations several hundred times (in a loop). You will find that operating on data in display takes 20–30% less time than operating on the same data in packed-decimal.

Although COBOL-74 does not support the packed-decimal format, almost all COBOL-74 compilers do as a nonstandard extension because of the dominance of IBM. COBOL-85 does include support for packed-decimal.

COBOL
Programming
Perspective

About Program Efficiency

The original specifications for COBOL were completed in 1960. For the next 20 years, one of the primary considerations when writing programs was program and file efficiency. Usually, COBOL was a bulky language requiring significant hardware resources and large mainframe computers. Programmers would focus on techniques to save milliseconds in calculational loops and storage positions in internal memory. As magnetic disk storage became available (with low capacities compared to magnetic tape), conserving disk storage became an important factor.

Times have changed. COBOL now runs on microcomputers. These desktop machines have greater capacities than computers on which the original version of COBOL was run. Furthermore, their cost is a small fraction of the cost of the early computers. During the early computer period, the cost of hardware was high relative to the cost of people to use and program the computers. Today the reverse is true: hardware is cheap, supporting personnel are expensive. Many of the sophisticated techniques used in the past to improve the execution speed of a program, or to save a few storage positions in a program or data file, simply are not justified on a cost-effectiveness basis anymore.

Indeed, program modularization techniques that you are learning from this book result in COBOL programs that require more computer storage and are less efficient in their execution than well-written non-modularized programs. However, the key is that computers are less expensive than people. Application programs have become so large and complex that their creation and maintenance represents a major cost of doing business. The focus today is on program simplicity and maintainability. Most large data-processing installations have company or "shop" standards that stress programmer efficiency rather than program efficiency. For instance, the Bank of America conducts its own classes for training COBOL programmers. Their philosophy is: "Do not worry about program efficiency. If necessary, we will get more and faster hardware to handle the job."

Another factor to consider is that of portability. That is, a company writing application software in COBOL will want to sell it to the broadest possible potential customer base, not simply to those with, for instance, IBM mainframes. Techniques to improve execution speed on an IBM mainframe might have exactly the opposite effect on a computer with an entirely different architecture.

This is accentuated with the proliferation of COBOL on mini- and microcomputers. For instance, the Ryan-McFarland Company writes COBOL compilers for a wide range of minicomputers, as well as for the microcomputer. In fact, their overall system is designed in such a way that a program compiled on one computer can be run on any other computer equipped with Ryan-McFarland COBOL. (This is accomplished through use of special software called a *run-time system*.)

On the other hand, you should not be totally oblivious to improving the performance of a program or using techniques that will conserve disk storage. For instance, if you work in an IBM mainframe installation, it would be foolish not to use basic efficiency techniques unique to IBM hardware that can be implemented easily.

Defining Packed-Decimal in the PICTURE—The USAGE Clause

As you learned in Concepts Module D, whenever you define a data item in the DATA DIVISION, it defaults to display format unless you say otherwise. However, if the file from which you must read data contains fields stored in packed-decimal, you must explicitly define them as such in the record description. To do this, you'll utilize the USAGE clause. For instance, the WS-TOTAL-AMOUNT-DEFICIENT field (line 79 in Figure 4-30) would be defined as packed-decimal by the following:

```
05  WS-TOTAL-AMOUNT-DEFICIENT   PIC 9(6)V99  USAGE IS COMP-3.
```

The required key word is USAGE; the word IS is optional. In COBOL, IBM calls the packed-decimal format COMPUTATIONAL-3, or simply COMP-3.

Many non-IBM versions of COBOL, as well as the COBOL-85 standard, use the phrase PACKED-DECIMAL rather than COMP-3. For them, the field definition is:

```
05  WS-TOTAL-AMOUNT-DEFICIENT   PIC 9(6)V99  USAGE IS PACKED-DECIMAL.
```

If you use packed-decimal, be careful not to *misuse* it. That is, you must use it in the input field definitions only if the data is stored on disk in packed-decimal format. There is little to gain by using it in the WORKING-STORAGE SECTION, because its speed improvement for arithmetic operations is not significant in the average business data-processing application. Do not use it in printer output records. Packed-decimal is not used in example programs of this book.

Chapter Summary
Topic: PATDFCT—A Program with Arithmetic Calculations

When multiple 01-level record-description entries are specified within one FD entry, implicit redefinition causes all such records to be assigned to the same area of storage.

A numeric picture field can include an S indicating a signed number and a V indicating an assumed decimal point.

A numeric literal must:

■ Be composed only of digits (0 through 9), a sign character (plus or minus), and a decimal point.

■ Contain at least one digit, but not more than 18 digits.

■ Contain not more than one sign character (plus or minus). When the sign character is used, it must be the leftmost character of the literal. (When the sign character is not used, the literal is considered to be a positive value.)

■ Contain not more than one decimal point. When the decimal point is used, it may be located anywhere in the literal except in the rightmost position.

Numeric fields to accumulate report totals must be specified in the WORKING-STORAGE SECTION; they must be initialized to zero at the start of processing.

Topic: COBOL Arithmetic Statements

Each field to be computed arithmetically must be defined as numeric. Further, the field length, decimal-point location, and arithmetic-sign specifications must be considered. To perform arithmetic calculations, either the basic arithmetic statements—ADD, SUBTRACT, MULTIPLY, and DIVIDE—or the COMPUTE statement can be used. A summary of arithmetic statements is shown Figure 4-32.

Figure 4-32 A summary of arithmetic statements.

Statement	Operand 1	Connector	Operand 2	GIVING	Result	(ROUNDED)	REMAINDER	(ON SIZE ERROR)
ADD/TO (Format-1)	Addend(s) Numeric identifier or Numeric literal	TO	Addend(s)/Sum(s) Numeric identifier			(ROUNDED)		(ON SIZE ERROR) imperative-statement
ADD/GIVING (Format-2)	Addend Numeric identifier or Numeric literal		Addend(s) Numeric identifier or Numeric literal	GIVING	Sum(s) Numeric identifier or Numeric edited literal	(ROUNDED)		(ON SIZE ERROR) imperative-statement
SUBTRACT/FROM (Format-1)	Subtrahend(s) Numeric identifier or Numeric literal	FROM	Minuend(s)/Remainder(s) Numeric identifier			(ROUNDED)		(ON SIZE ERROR) imperative-statement
SUBTRACT/GIVING (Format-2)	Subtrahend(s) Numeric identifier or Numeric literal	FROM	Minuend Numeric identifier or Numeric literal	GIVING	Remainder(s) Numeric identifier or Numeric edited literal	(ROUNDED)		(ON SIZE ERROR) imperative-statement
MULTIPLY/BY (Format-1)	Multiplicand Numeric identifier or Numeric literal	BY	Multiplier/Product(s) Numeric identifier			(ROUNDED)		(ON SIZE ERROR) imperative-statement
MULTIPLY/GIVING (Format-2)	Multiplicand Numeric identifier or Numeric literal	BY	Multiplier Numeric identifier or Numeric literal	GIVING	Product(s) Numeric identifier or Numeric edited literal	(ROUNDED)		(ON SIZE ERROR) imperative-statement
DIVIDE/INTO (Format-1)	Divisor Numeric identifier or Numeric literal	INTO	Dividend(s)/Quotient(s) Numeric identifier			(ROUNDED)		(ON SIZE ERROR) imperative-statement
DIVIDE/INTO/GIVING (Format-2)	Divisor Numeric identifier or Numeric literal	INTO	Dividend Numeric identifier or Numeric literal	GIVING	Quotient(s) Numeric identifier or Numeric edited literal	(ROUNDED)		(ON SIZE ERROR) imperative-statement
DIVIDE/BY/GIVING (Format-3)	Dividend Numeric identifier or Numeric literal	BY	Divisor Numeric identifier or Numeric literal	GIVING	Quotient(s) Numeric identifier or Numeric edited literal	(ROUNDED)		(ON SIZE ERROR) imperative-statement
DIVIDE/INTO/GIVING/REMAINDER (Format-4)	Divisor Numeric identifier or Numeric literal	INTO	Dividend Numeric identifier or Numeric literal	GIVING	Quotient Numeric identifier or Numeric edited literal	(ROUNDED)	REMAINDER Numeric identifier	(ON SIZE ERROR) imperative-statement
DIVIDE/BY/GIVING/REMAINDER (Format-5)	Dividend Numeric identifier or Numeric literal	BY	Divisor Numeric identifier or Numeric literal	GIVING	Quotient Numeric identifier or Numeric edited literal	(ROUNDED)	REMAINDER Numeric identifier	(ON SIZE ERROR) imperative-statement
COMPUTE	Numeric identifier or Numeric edited identifier (ROUNDED)	=	Arithmetic expression					(ON SIZE ERROR) imperative-statement

The optional phrase ROUNDED can be specified for any arithmetic statement answer field that is to be rounded off. The optional phrase ON SIZE ERROR can be specified to provide exception-condition handling when the result will not fit in the answer field.

Generally, the PROCEDURE DIVISION of a program is independent of decimal point positioning. Once defined in the DATA DIVISION, all PROCEDURE DIVISION statements handle all decimal positioning according to the definitions of fields.

Topic: Internal Coding of Numeric Data

In the default display format, all data is stored one character per byte. For numeric data, it is possible to specify packed-decimal, which stores two digits per byte (with the sign in the right half of the rightmost byte). This conserves disk storage for files with a large amount of numeric data. For the IBM mainframe-computers, it provides more efficient arithmetic operations. However, for most ASCII computers, execution is slower than with display format.

Features in COBOL–85 not in COBOL–74

The reserved word TO cannot be used in the ADD/GIVING in COBOL-74; it can optionally be used in COBOL-85.

The scope terminators END-ADD, END-SUBTRACT, END-MULTIPLY, END-DIVIDE, and END-COMPUTE can be used with COBOL-85 to terminate the scope of the statements of the ON SIZE ERROR clause.

Exercises
Terms for Definition

arithmetic overflow _____

detail line _____

end-of-report totals _____

exponentiation _____

hierarchy of arithmetic operations _____

order of precedence _____

size error _____

total line _____

unary arithmetic operator _____

unary operation _____

Review Questions

1. What four properties must be considered when defining a field to be used in arithmetic computations?

   a. _____   c. _____

   b. _____   d. _____

2. A numeric literal can be composed of:

   a. _____

   b. _____

   c. _____

   d. _____

3. A numeric literal must contain at least _____ digit(s), but must not contain more than _____ digits.

4. When an arithmetic sign is specified in a numeric literal, it must appear as the _____ character of the literal.

5. When a decimal point is specified in a numeric literal, it must *not* appear as the _____ character of the literal.

6. Numeric literals may be used in arithmetic statements—except for fields that _____ .

7. An arithmetic statement can contain a numeric-edited item only _____ .

8. Two phrases that can be specified for any arithmetic statement are _____ and _____ .

9. An ADD statement may contain how many addends? _____ .

10. Although the reserved word TO must be specified for the _____ statement, it must be omitted from the _____ statement.

11. The reserved word FROM _____ be specified for the
    (must/must not)

    Format-1 SUBTRACT statement; it _____ be specified for the
    (must/must not)

    Format-2 SUBTRACT statement.

12. The reserved word is _____ specified between the multiplier and the multiplicand of the MULTIPLY statement.

13. When a DIVIDE statement is written with the reserved word operator _____ , the first factor is the dividend; the second factor is the divisor.

14. When a DIVIDE statement is written with the reserved word operator _____ , the first factor is the divisor; the second factor is the dividend.

15. When the reserved word operator BY is specified in a DIVIDE statement, the _____ phrase must be specified.

16. List the hierarchy of arithmetic operations that apply to the COMPUTE statement.

a. _____   c. _____

b. _____   d. _____

17. Identify the value of X after execution of the following COMPUTE statements.

(A = 4; B = 10; C = 2)

COMPUTE statement	Value of X after execution
X = A + B / C	_____
X = (A + B) / C	_____
X ROUNDED = A + (B / C)	_____

18. To detect arithmetic overflows, the _____ phrase should be coded as part of the arithmetic statement.

19. Why must WORKING-STORAGE SECTION fields used for accumulations not contain editing symbols? _____

_____

20. Why should WORKING-STORAGE SECTION fields used for arithmetic typically be coded with the PICTURE symbol S? _____

_____

Syntax/Debug Exercises

1. Suppose it were necessary to divide a 7-position dollars-and-cents field (PIC S99999V99) by 2 and place the answer ROUNDED to the nearest penny, into a dollars-and-cents field named WHOLESALE-AMOUNT. Place a check mark adjacent to the one PICTURE clause that should be specified to provide for the correct rounding, sign handling, and to ensure that a SIZE ERROR cannot occur.

☐ PIC S99999V999   ☐ PIC 99999V999
☐ PIC S9999V99   ☐ PIC 9999V99
☐ PIC S99999V99   ☐ PIC 99999V99
☐ PIC S9999V999   ☐ PIC 9999V99

2. Some of the following arithmetic statements contain syntax errors. For each statement containing a syntax error, rewrite it correctly in the space provided. (Consider each data-item to be a numeric field.)

```
ADD DEPOSIT OLD-BALANCE. _____

ADD DEPOSIT TO OLD-BALANCE. _____
```

```
ADD REG-HOURS PREM-HOURS
    GIVING TOTAL-HOURS. _____

ADD REG-HOURS TO PREM-HOURS
    GIVING TOTAL-HOURS. _____

ADD AMOUNT TO 10. _____

ADD AMOUNT 10
    GIVING ADJ-AMOUNT. _____

ADD DAY-1 DAY-2 DAY-3
    DAY-4 DAY-5 DAY-6
    DAY-7 GIVING WEEK. _____

SUBTRACT CHECK-AMOUNT BALANCE. _____

SUBTRACT CHECK-AMOUNT
    FROM BALANCE. _____

SUBTRACT CHECK-AMOUNT
    SERVICE-CHARGE
    GIVING BALANCE. _____

SUBTRACT CHECK-AMOUNT
    FROM SERVICE-CHARGE
    GIVING BALANCE. _____

MULTIPLY 60 TIMES HOURS. _____

MULTIPLY HOURS BY 60. _____

MULTIPLY 60 BY HOURS. _____

MULTIPLY 60 HOURS
    GIVING MINUTES. _____

MULTIPLY HOURS BY 60
    GIVING MINUTES. _____

DIVIDE MINUTES BY 60. _____

DIVIDE 60 BY MINUTES. _____

DIVIDE MINUTES INTO 60. _____

DIVIDE 60 INTO MINUTES. _____

DIVIDE MINUTES INTO 60
    GIVING HOURS. _____

DIVIDE 60 INTO MINUTES
    GIVING HOURS. _____

DIVIDE MINUTES BY 60
    GIVING HOURS. _____

DIVIDE 60 BY MINUTES
    GIVING HOURS. _____

DIVIDE MINUTES BY 60
    GIVING HOURS
    REMAINDER MINUTES. _____

DIVIDE 60 INTO MINUTES
    REMAINDER MINUTES. _____

DIVIDE AMOUNT BY 2
    GIVING AMT ROUNDED
    AMT-UNROUNDED. _____
```

```
COMPUTE AVERAGE =
     TOTAL-POINTS / NBR.  _____

COMPUTE GROSS-PAY =
     RATE X HOURS.  _____

COMPUTE Y = A+B-C.  _____

COMPUTE R = (S + T) -
            (V / W).  _____
```

Questions Pertaining to PATDFCT

1. What would happen if the two accumulators (WS-DEFICIENT-PATRONS and WS-TOTAL-AMOUNT-DEFICIENT) were not initialized to 0 in PATDFCT (at lines 101 and 102)?

   _____

   _____

2. Would there be any output from PATDFCT if the PATRON file contained no patrons with contributions less than the target amount? Explain your answer.

   _____

   _____

Programming Assignments

Note: In the programming assignment descriptions of numeric input and output quantities, formatting notations as illustrated by the following are used:

nnnnn　　An input numeric field with an assumed decimal point between the third and fourth digits.

nnn.nn　　An output numeric field with a printed decimal point between the third and fourth digits.

Programming Assignment 4-1: Understocked Inventory Report
Background information:
Tools Unlimited is a wholesale company that stocks and sells tools to retailers. Since the company does none of its own manufacturing, its policy is to maintain a sufficient inventory to satisfy customer needs, taking into account the lag-time between placing an order with its manufacturers and delivery of goods. The inventory file includes one record for each item in the inventory. Included in the record is a field containing the quantity-on-hand and another containing the reorder-point. Whenever the quantity-in-hand drops below the reorder-point, an order must be placed to replenish the stock. Management would like a report of all items for which the quantity-on-hand is less than the reorder-point.

Input file: Inventory file (INVEN.DAT)

Input-record format:

Positions	Field	Data class	Comments
1–2	Record code	Numeric	Code 44
4–13	Product identification		Group item
4–7	Product type	Alphanumeric	
8–13	Product number	Alphanumeric	
14–39	Product description	Alphanumeric	
41–46	Unit price (unit cost)	Numeric	Format: 9999V99
48–51	Reorder point	Numeric	Whole number
52–55	Quantity on hand	Numeric	Whole number
56–80	Other data		

Required output:

Print a report, doubled-spaced, with one detail line for each input record for which the quantity-on-hand is less than the reorder-point (for which there is a shortfall). At the end of the report, print a summary line (triple-spaced) for records printed as defined by the following.

Output report-line formats:

Detail line.

Position	Field	Comments
4–14	Product identification	Print in form *xxxx/xxxxxx* (insert a slash between subfields)
17–42	Product description	
45–48	Reorder point	
51–54	Quantity on hand	
58–61	Shortfall quantity	Reorder-level minus Quantity-in-stock

Summary line.

Position	Field
48–50	Number of records with shortfall
55–61	Total shortfall quantity

Programming Assignment 4-2: Salesperson Performance Report

Background information:

The sales manager of Follow-the-Sun Sales has completed her preliminary study of salesperson performance. She now requires a report giving the sales amounts and commissions for each salesperson from the data in the salesperson file.

Input file: Salesperson file (SALESPER.DAT)

Input-record format:

Positions	Field name	Data class	Comments
1–2	Record code	Alphanumeric	Code "25"
3–4	Salesperson region	Alphanumeric	
5–8	Salesperson territory	Alphanumeric	
9–11	Salesperson number	Alphanumeric	
12–37	Salesperson name	Alphanumeric	
38	Status code	Alphabetic	
39–42	Commission rate	Numeric	Format *nnnn*
48–50	Product–units sold	Numeric	Whole number
64–70	Sales revenue	Numeric	Format *nnnnnnnnnn*
71–79	Other data		

Required output:
Print a report, single–spaced, with one detail line for each input record (ignore records that do not have a Status-code value of "A"). At the end of the report, print a summary line (after double–spacing) for these Status-code "A" records.

Output report-line formats:

Detail line.

Positions	Field	Comments
3–4	Salesperson region	
5		Print a hyphen
6–9	Salesperson territory	
12–14	Salesperson number	
17–42	Salesperson name	
45–47	Product–units sold	
50–54	Commission percentage	Format *nn.nn*
60–67	Sales revenue	Format *nnnnnnnn.nn*
74–80	Commission amount	Format *nnnnnnn.nn*

Summary line.

Positions	Field	Comments
58–67	Total amount of sales	Format *nnnnnnn.nn.*
72–80	Total commission amount	Format *nnnnnn.nn.*

Program operations:
1. Process only those records with a Status-code field value of "A".
2. Calculated quantities for detail output are:

   Commission-amount is Sales-revenue times Commission-rate
   Commission-percentage is 100 times Commission-rate

3. Totals are to be accumulated for:

   Amount-of-sales
   Commission-amount

Programming Assignment 4-3: Gross-Pay Report

Background information:

The payroll department of Silicon Manufacturing maintains an employee payroll file with one record for each employee. Data stored includes hours worked and pay rate. A report is required showing the gross pay for each hourly employee and a gross pay total.

Input file: Earnings file (EARNINGS.DAT)

Input-record format:

Positions	Field name	Data class	Comments
11–19	Employee number	Alphanumeric	Social Security number
20–31	Employee last name	Alphanumeric	
32–40	Employee first name	Alphanumeric	
43	Shift differential code	Alphanumeric	
44–48	Hours worked	Numeric	Format *nnnnn*
53	Pay code	Alphabetic	
54–57	Pay rate	Numeric	Format *nnnn*
58–74	Other data		

Required output:

Print a report, doubled-spaced, with a detail line for each hourly employee. At the end of the report, print a summary line (triple-spaced) as defined by the following.

Output report-line formats:

Detail line.

Positions	Field name	Comments
4–14	Employee number	Print in form *xxx–xx–xxxx* (insert hyphens)
17–28	Employee last name	
30–38	Employee first name	
44–49	Hours worked	Format *nn.nnn*
55–61	Gross pay	Format *nnnn.nn*

Summary line.

Positions	Field name	Comments
43–49	Total hours worked	Format *nnnn.nn*
53–61	Total gross pay	Format *nnnnnn.nn*

Program operations:

1. Process only input employee records with a value of "H" for Pay-code.
2. Calculated quantities for detail output are:

   Gross-pay is Pay-rate times Hours-worked.
   If Shift-differential code is "N"
       multiply Gross-pay by 1.1.

3. Totals are to be accumulated for:

   Hours-worked
   Gross-pay

Programming Assignment 4-4: Accounts-Receivable Report

Background information:

One of the critical functions at Silicon Valley Manufacturing is keeping an accurate account of the amounts owed by customers. Each month a report must be prepared from the customer file that summarizes the purchases and payments for each customer. This is called the accounts-receivable report.

Input file: Customer file (CUSTOMER.DAT)

Input-record format:

Positions	Field	Data class	Comments
1–2	Record code		Code "53"
3–7	Customer number		
8–31	Customer name	Alphanumeric	
39–46	Balance forward	Numeric	Format $nnnnnnnn$
47–54	New purchases	Numeric	Format $nnnnnnnn$
71	Special flag	Alphanumeric	
73–80	Payments received	Numeric	Format $nnnnnnnn$

Required output:

A printed report, doubled-spaced, with one detail line for each input record. At the end of the report, print a summary line (triple-spaced) as defined by the following.

Output report-line formats:

Detail line.

Positions	Field name	Comments
1–5	Customer number	
7–30	Customer name	
35–43	Balance forward	Format $nnnnnn.nn$
47–55	New purchases	Format $nnnnnn.nn$
59–67	Payments received	Format $nnnnnn.nn$
71–79	New balance	Format $nnnnnn.nn$

Summary line.

Positions	Field name	Comments
45–55	Total new purchases	Format $nnnnnnnn.nn$
57–67	Total payments received	Format $nnnnnnnn.nn$
69–79	Total of new balances	Format $nnnnnnnn.nn$

Program operations:

1. Process only those customer records with a blank space in the Special-flag field.

2. The New-balance-forward is to be calculated as:

Balance-forward
plus New-purchases
minus Payments-received

3. Totals are to be accumulated for:

New purchases
Payments received
New balance

Programming Assignment 4-5: Nurses' Salary Increase Projection
Background information:
The management of Brooklawn Hospital is currently engaged in salary negotiations with the Nurses' Union. The union has proposed a salary increase of 9%, plus an additional 5% for all employees who work second or third shift. Management wishes to find out just how much impact this proposal will have on current salaries. For this assignment, you must modify the program written for Programming Assignment 2-5 (expanded in Chapter 3) as follows.

Input file: Nurses' file (NURSES.DAT)

Input-record format:
Revise the Other-payroll-data area of the input record (Assignment 2-5) to define the following field:

Positions	Field	Data class	Comments
68–73	Current monthly salary	Numeric	Format *nnnnnn*

Required output:
A printed report, doubled-spaced, with one detail line for each input record. At the end of the report, print a summary line (triple-spaced) as defined by the following.

Output report-line format:

Detail line.

Positions	Field	Comments
1	Professional specialty	
20	Shift code	
25	Name	
49	New base monthly salary	*nnnn.nn*
60	Shift differential	*nnn.nn*
69	New total monthly salary	*nnnn.nn*

Summary line.

Positions	Field	Comments
47	Total of New-base-monthly-salary	*nnnnnn.nn*
67	Total of New-total-monthly-salary	*nnnnnn.nn*

Program operations:
1. Process each record.
2. Calculated quantities for detail output are:

New-base-monthly-salary is
  1.09 times Current-monthly-salary.
Move a value of 0 to the Shift-differential-amount, then
if Shift-code is greater than 1
  calculate the Shift-differential-amount as
    New-base-monthly-salary multiplied by 0.05.
Calculate the New-total-monthly-salary as
  New-base-monthly-salary plus Shift-differential-amount.

3. Totals are to be accumulated for:

New-base-monthly-salary
New-total-monthly-salary

Programming Assignment 4-6: Vehicle Rental Application

Background information:
The daily rental fee charged by Rent-Ur-Wheels does not include any type of insurance. However, in self-defense, the company makes certain forms of insurance available to renters. Collision insurance is available at 5% of the daily rental fee, and liability insurance costs 1.5% of the daily rental fee. To assist the rental clerk in quickly determining the total charges, management has requested a program which will produce a listing showing various combinations of charges. To accomplish this, modify the program written for Programming Assignment 2-6 (expanded in Chapter 3) so that the output appears as follows.

Input file: Vehicle file (VEHICLE.DAT)

Input-record format:
Same as Assignment 2-6.

Required output:
A printed report, double-spaced with one detail line per record according to the following format.

Output report-line format:

Positions	Field name
1–14	Make of vehicle
18–27	Model
31–35	Vehicle type
39–45	License number
49–53	Daily rental fee (no insurance)
57–61	Rental fee including collision insurance
65–69	Rental fee including liability insurance
73–77	Rental fee including both types of insurance

Note: All rental fees printed with the format *nn.nn*.

Programming Assignment 4-7: Bookstore Inventory Application

Background information:

The president of Granger and Heatherford, knowing the value of complete and up-to-date information in business management, has requested that a listing be placed on her desk at 8:00 A.M. each day, showing the status of the firm's salable goods. To accomplish this, you are to modify the program written for Programming Assignment 2-7 (expanded in Chapter 3) as follows:

Input file: Granger/Heatherford inventory file (GHINVEN.DAT)

Input-record format:

Same as Assignment 2-7 (exzcept use PIC 99V99 for unit cost and selling price).

Required output:

1. In addition to the output required in the problem definition of Assignment 2-7, print the selling price and the total value for each title.
2. At the end of the listing, print a total line showing the number of records in the file and the sum of the total values.

Position the new output so that the report appears neat and well balanced. Punctuate all money amounts with a decimal point.

Program operations:

1. Process each input book record.
2. Calculate the Title-total-value as:

   Selling-price times Quantity-on-hand.

3. Totals are to be accumulated for:

   Count of the number of records processed.
   Title-total-value

Programming Assignment 4-8: Stock Brokerage Accounting

Background information:

The stock brokerage firm of Gesellen & Byen keeps track of their clients' investment history by maintaining a file that contains one record for each stock owned by each client. Record format is as follows:

Input file: Investment file (GBINVEST.DAT)

Input-record format:

Positions	Field name	Data class	Comments
1–20	Client name	Alphanumeric	
21–23	Stock symbol	Alphanumeric	
24–29	Number of shares originally purchased	Numeric	Whole number
30–35	Additional shares purchased	Numeric	Whole number
36–41	Number of shares sold	Numeric	Whole number

Required output:

For this assignment, you must do all output format planning.

Each detail line of your report must include:

All input fields

The current number of shares held

The summary line must include:

Total number of shares purchased

Total number of shares sold

Program operations:

1. Process only those investor records for which the additional number of shares purchased is greater than zero.

2. Calculate the Current-shares-held as:

Number-of-shares-originally-purchased
Additional-shares-purchased
Total-number-of-shares-sold

3. Totals are to be accumulated for:

Number of shares purchased
Number of shares sold

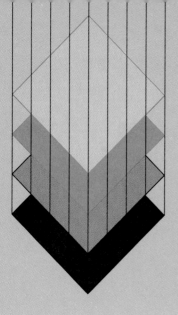

Improving the Appearance of Printed Output

Chapter Objectives

Example programs so far have taken input data and placed it in a form more easily read before printing. However, the form of the data is not very "human-consumable." The focus of this chapter is on making an output report more descriptive and easier to read. From this chapter, you will learn the following:

- The VALUE clause, which allows you to define an initial value in a field of the WORKING-STORAGE SECTION.

- Defining output lines in the WORKING-STORAGE SECTION, then moving them to the output area (defined under the FD) prior to printing.

- The five categories of PICTURE clauses:

    numeric
    alphabetic
    alphanumeric
    numeric-edited
    alphanumeric-edited

- Editing that lets you:

    suppress leading zeros and replace with spaces or asterisks
    insert punctuation such as the decimal point and the comma
    insert a minus or a plus sign
    insert a dollar sign

- Features of the MOVE statement in moving data from one type of field to another (for example, the editing action that occurs when a numeric field is moved to a numeric-edited item).

CHAPTER 5

Chapter Outline

Topic: Improving the PATDFCT Program

Communicating the Information
The VALUE Clause
Output Lines in the WORKING-STORAGE SECTION
Basic Editing

Topic: PICTURE Clauses

PICTURE Overview
Functions of the PICTURE Clause
Basic PICTURE Symbols
Numeric Editing PICTURE Symbols

Numeric Editing—Special Insertion
PICTURE Symbol . (Decimal Point)

Numeric Editing—Zero Suppression and Replacement
PICTURE Symbol Z (Zero Suppression With Blank-Space Replacement)
*PICTURE Symbol * (Zero Suppression With Asterisk Replacement)*

Numeric Editing—Simple Insertion
PICTURE Symbol , (Comma)
PICTURE Symbol / (Slash)
PICTURE Symbol B (Blank Space)
PICTURE Symbol 0 (Zero)

Numeric Editing—Fixed Insertion
PICTURE Symbol – (Fixed Minus Sign)
PICTURE Symbol + (Fixed Plus Sign)
PICTURE Symbol CR (Credit Symbol)
PICTURE Symbol DB (Debit Symbol)
PICTURE Symbol $ (Fixed Currency Sign)

Numeric Editing—Floating Insertion
Floating – (Minus Sign)
Floating + (Plus Sign)
Floating $ (Currency Sign)

Describing Alphanumeric-Edited Data-Items

Recap of PICTURE Clauses
Editing With Hyphens

PICTURE Clause Style Considerations

BLANK WHEN ZERO Clause

Topic: The MOVE Statement

Capabilities of the MOVE— Preview/Summary

Alphanumeric MOVE Operations
Alphanumeric Sending Field to Alphanumeric Receiving Field
Alphanumeric Sending Field to Alphanumeric-Edited Receiving Field
Alphanumeric-Edited Sending Field to Alphanumeric Receiving Field—COBOL-85

Numeric MOVE Operations
Numeric Sending Field to Numeric Receiving Field
Numeric Sending Field to Numeric-Edited Receiving Field
Numeric-Edited Sending Field to Numeric Receiving Field—COBOL-85

Other MOVE Statement Categories
Group Field MOVE Operations
Group Sending Field to Alphanumeric-Edited Receiving Field
Numeric Integer Sending Field to Alphanumeric Receiving Field
Qualification of Data-Names and MOVE/ CORRESPONDING

Referring to a Field by Two Different Names
Calculating Percentage
The REDEFINES Clause

Topic: Improving the PATDFCT Program

Communicating the Information

As pointed out in Chapter 4, the PATDFCT programs contain all of the required information, but they communicate it poorly. There are at least four ways in which the appearance of the PATDFCT2 (Figure 4–30) report could be improved:

1. Include a heading at the top of the page that describes each column of the detail lines. This is called a **column heading**.

2. Include a description of the output quantities on the total line.

3. Replace the leading zeros on all output quantities with spaces; for instance, change 0014.63 to 14.63. This is called **zero suppression**.

4. Insert a comma in the total amount; that is, 1021.25 should print as 1,021.25.

Since these changes to PATDFCT2 do not require any different data or conditions on the output, the modifications to PATDFCT2 will be relatively minor. A printer spacing chart illustrating the desired output format is shown in Figure 5-1(a); the sample report is included in Figure 5-1(b). As you will see, numerous changes will be required in the DATA DIVISION. However, the changes to the PROCEDURE DIVISION will be relatively few. Note that the column heading must be printed prior to beginning the detail processing.

The first three divisions of this program (named PATDFCT3) are shown in Figure 5-2. Two versions of its PROCEDURE DIVISION, one in COBOL-74 and the other in COBOL-85, are included in Figure 5-3. Features of this program are:

1. Setting up output lines in the WORKING-STORAGE SECTION.

2. The VALUE clause.

3. The WRITE/FROM statement.

4. Numeric editing: zero suppression and printing a comma.

5. Alphanumeric editing.

Figure 5-1   Modification to PATDFCT2.

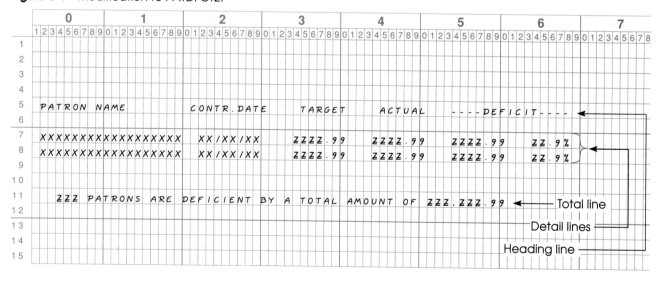

(a) Printer spacing chart for PATDFCT3.

Figure 5-1
(continued)

```
PATRON NAME         CONTR.DATE    TARGET    ACTUAL    ----DEFICIT----

Anderson, Hazel      03/25/91     250.00    101.15     148.85   40.5%

Baker, Donald        02/28/91     375.00    312.50      62.50   83.3%

Campbell, J. H.      03/23/91     200.00    175.00      25.00   87.5%

Davidson, Harley     03/17/91     250.00    100.00     150.00   40.0%

Englehoff, F.        02/15/91     250.00    166.64      83.36   66.7%

Hildebrand, John     03/28/91     250.00    200.00      50.00   80.0%

Miller, Irwin B.     01/01/91     200.00    185.37      14.63   92.7%

Molitar, Arnold T.   03/25/91     200.00    166.66      33.34   83.3%

Nelson, J. J.        03/02/91     250.00    121.98     128.02   48.8%

Pratt, Diane         03/31/91     375.00    229.50     145.50   61.2%

Stevenson, Howard    03/28/91     200.00     20.00     180.00   10.0%

Zener, Eva           03/15/91     200.00    199.95        .05    .0%


     12 PATRONS ARE DEFICIENT BY A TOTAL AMOUNT OF    1,021.25
```

(b) Sample output.

Figure 5-2   The first three divisions for PATDFCT3.

```
1       IDENTIFICATION DIVISION.
2       PROGRAM-ID.    PATDFCT3.
3       *AUTHOR.        PRICE/WELBURN.
4
5       *    THIS PROGRAM PRINTS A LIST OF PATRONS WHO ARE DEFICIENT
6       *    IN THEIR CONTRIBUTIONS.  ALL CONTRIBUTION AMOUNTS ARE
7       *    SHOWN IN DOLLARS AND CENTS.  COLUMN HEADINGS HAVE BEEN
8       *    ADDED TO IDENTIFY THE PRINTED FIELDS.
9
10
11
12      ENVIRONMENT DIVISION.
13
14      CONFIGURATION SECTION.
15
16      SOURCE-COMPUTER.  (system dependent).
17      OBJECT-COMPUTER.  (system dependent).
18
19      INPUT-OUTPUT SECTION.
20
21      FILE-CONTROL.
22          SELECT PATRON-FILE
23              ASSIGN TO (system dependent).
24          SELECT DEFICIENCY-LIST
25              ASSIGN TO (system dependent).
26
27
28      DATA DIVISION.
29
30      FILE SECTION.
31
32      FD  PATRON-FILE
33          RECORD CONTAINS 78 CHARACTERS
34          LABEL RECORDS ARE STANDARD.
35
36      01  PATRON-RECORD.
37          05  PR-NAME              PIC X(18).
38          05  FILLER               PIC X(42).
39          05  PR-TARGET-CONTR      PIC 9(4)V99.
40          05  PR-ACTUAL-CONTR      PIC 9(4)V99.
41          05  PR-CONTR-DATE        PIC X(6).
42
43      FD  DEFICIENCY-LIST
44          RECORD CONTAINS 132 CHARACTERS
45          LABEL RECORDS ARE OMITTED.
46
47      01  DEFICIENCY-LINE          PIC X(132).
48

49      WORKING-STORAGE SECTION.
50
51      01  WS-SWITCHES.
52          05  WS-EOF-SWITCH            PIC X(3).
53
54      01  WS-ARITHMETIC-WORK-AREAS.
55          05  WS-AMOUNT-DEFICIENT      PIC 9(4)V99.
56          05  WS-DEFICIENCY-FRACTION   PIC V9(3).
57
58      01  WS-ACCUMULATORS.
59          05  WS-TOTAL-AMOUNT-DEFICIENT  PIC 9(6)V99.
60          05  WS-DEFICIENT-PATRONS       PIC 9(3).
61
62      01  WS-COLUMN-HEADING-LINE.
63          05  FILLER       PIC X(20)  VALUE " PATRON NAME".
64          05  FILLER       PIC X(14)  VALUE "CONTR.DATE".
65          05  FILLER       PIC X(10)  VALUE "TARGET".
66          05  FILLER       PIC X(09)  VALUE "ACTUAL".
67          05  FILLER       PIC X(15)  VALUE "----DEFICIT----".
68
69      01  WS-DETAIL-LINE.
70          05  FILLER             PIC X(1)   VALUE SPACES.
71          05  DL-NAME            PIC X(18).
72          05  FILLER             PIC X(2)   VALUE SPACES.
73          05  DL-CONTR-DATE      PIC XX/XX/XX.
74          05  FILLER             PIC X(4)   VALUE SPACES.
75          05  DL-TARGET-CONTR    PIC Z(4).99.
76          05  FILLER             PIC X(3)   VALUE SPACES.
77          05  DL-ACTUAL-CONTR    PIC Z(4).99.
78          05  FILLER             PIC X(3)   VALUE SPACES.
79          05  DL-AMOUNT-DEFICIENT  PIC Z(4).99.
80          05  FILLER             PIC X(3)   VALUE SPACES.
81          05  DL-DEFICIENCY-PERCENT  PIC ZZ.9.
82          05  FILLER             PIC X(1)   VALUE "%".
83
84      01  WS-TOTAL-LINE.
85          05  FILLER             PIC X(3)   VALUE SPACES.
86          05  TL-DEFICIENT-PATRONS  PIC Z(3).
87          05  FILLER             PIC X(44)  VALUE
88              " PATRONS ARE DEFICIENT BY A TOTAL AMOUNT OF ".
89          05  TL-TOTAL-AMOUNT-DEFICIENT  PIC ZZZ,ZZZ.99.
90
91
```

Figure 5-3 The PROCEDURE DIVISION for PATDFCT3.

```
92      PROCEDURE DIVISION.                                92      PROCEDURE DIVISION.
93                                                         93
94      000-PRINT-DEFICIENCY-LIST.                         94      000-PRINT-DEFICIENCY-LIST.
95          OPEN INPUT PATRON-FILE                         95          OPEN INPUT PATRON-FILE
96              OUTPUT DEFICIENCY-LIST.                     96              OUTPUT DEFICIENCY-LIST
97          PERFORM 100-INITIALIZE-VARIABLE-FIELDS.        97          PERFORM 100-INITIALIZE-VARIABLE-FIELDS
98          READ PATRON-FILE                               98          READ PATRON-FILE
99              AT END MOVE "YES" TO WS-EOF-SWITCH.        99              AT END MOVE "YES" TO WS-EOF-SWITCH
100         WRITE DEFICIENCY-LINE FROM WS-COLUMN-HEADING-LINE. 100         END-READ
101         PERFORM 200-PROCESS-PATRON-RECORD              101         WRITE DEFICIENCY-LINE FROM WS-COLUMN-HEADING-LINE
102             UNTIL WS-EOF-SWITCH IS EQUAL TO "YES".     102         PERFORM 200-PROCESS-PATRON-RECORD
103         PERFORM 700-PRINT-TOTAL-LINE.                  103             UNTIL WS-EOF-SWITCH IS EQUAL TO "YES"
104         CLOSE PATRON-FILE                              104         PERFORM 700-PRINT-TOTAL-LINE
105             DEFICIENCY-LIST.                           105         CLOSE PATRON-FILE
106         STOP RUN.                                      106             DEFICIENCY-LIST
107                                                        107         STOP RUN.
108     100-INITIALIZE-VARIABLE-FIELDS.                    108
109         MOVE "NO " TO WS-EOF-SWITCH.                   109     100-INITIALIZE-VARIABLE-FIELDS.
110         MOVE ZERO TO WS-TOTAL-AMOUNT-DEFICIENT,        110         MOVE "NO " TO WS-EOF-SWITCH
111             WS-DEFICIENT-PATRONS.                      111         INITIALIZE WS-ACCUMULATORS.
112                                                        112
113     200-PROCESS-PATRON-RECORD.                         113     200-PROCESS-PATRON-RECORD.
114         IF PR-ACTUAL-CONTR IS LESS THAN PR-TARGET-CONTR 114         IF PR-ACTUAL-CONTR IS LESS THAN PR-TARGET-CONTR
115             PERFORM 210-PROCESS-DEFICIENT-PATRON.      115             PERFORM 210-PROCESS-DEFICIENT-PATRON
116         READ PATRON-FILE                               116         END-IF
117             AT END MOVE "YES" TO WS-EOF-SWITCH.        117         READ PATRON-FILE
118                                                        118             AT END MOVE "YES" TO WS-EOF-SWITCH
119     210-PROCESS-DEFICIENT-PATRON.                      119         END-READ.
120         MOVE PR-NAME TO DL-NAME.                       120
121         MOVE PR-TARGET-CONTR TO DL-TARGET-CONTR.       121     210-PROCESS-DEFICIENT-PATRON.
122         MOVE PR-ACTUAL-CONTR TO DL-ACTUAL-CONTR.       122         MOVE PR-NAME TO DL-NAME
123         MOVE PR-CONTR-DATE TO DL-CONTR-DATE.           123         MOVE PR-TARGET-CONTR TO DL-TARGET-CONTR
124         SUBTRACT PR-ACTUAL-CONTR FROM PR-TARGET-CONTR  124         MOVE PR-ACTUAL-CONTR TO DL-ACTUAL-CONTR
125             GIVING WS-AMOUNT-DEFICIENT.                125         MOVE PR-CONTR-DATE TO DL-CONTR-DATE
126         MOVE WS-AMOUNT-DEFICIENT TO DL-AMOUNT-DEFICIENT. 126         SUBTRACT PR-ACTUAL-CONTR FROM PR-TARGET-CONTR
127         DIVIDE PR-ACTUAL-CONTR BY PR-TARGET-CONTR      127             GIVING WS-AMOUNT-DEFICIENT
128             GIVING WS-DEFICIENCY-FRACTION ROUNDED.     128         MOVE WS-AMOUNT-DEFICIENT TO DL-AMOUNT-DEFICIENT
129         MULTIPLY WS-DEFICIENCY-FRACTION BY 100         129         DIVIDE PR-ACTUAL-CONTR BY PR-TARGET-CONTR
130             GIVING DL-DEFICIENCY-PERCENT.              130             GIVING WS-DEFICIENCY-FRACTION ROUNDED
131         WRITE DEFICIENCY-LINE FROM WS-DETAIL-LINE      131         MULTIPLY WS-DEFICIENCY-FRACTION BY 100
132             AFTER ADVANCING 2 LINES.                   132             GIVING DL-DEFICIENCY-PERCENT
133         ADD WS-AMOUNT-DEFICIENT TO WS-TOTAL-AMOUNT-DEFICIENT. 133         WRITE DEFICIENCY-LINE FROM WS-DETAIL-LINE
134         ADD 1 TO WS-DEFICIENT-PATRONS.                 134             AFTER ADVANCING 2 LINES
135                                                        135         ADD WS-AMOUNT-DEFICIENT TO WS-TOTAL-AMOUNT-DEFICIENT
136     700-PRINT-TOTAL-LINE.                              136         ADD 1 TO WS-DEFICIENT-PATRONS.
137         MOVE WS-DEFICIENT-PATRONS TO TL-DEFICIENT-PATRONS. 137
138         MOVE WS-TOTAL-AMOUNT-DEFICIENT                 138     700-PRINT-TOTAL-LINE.
139             TO TL-TOTAL-AMOUNT-DEFICIENT.              139         MOVE WS-DEFICIENT-PATRONS TO TL-DEFICIENT-PATRONS
140         WRITE DEFICIENCY-LINE FROM WS-TOTAL-LINE       140         MOVE WS-TOTAL-AMOUNT-DEFICIENT
141             AFTER ADVANCING 3 LINES.                   141             TO TL-TOTAL-AMOUNT-DEFICIENT
                                                           142         WRITE DEFICIENCY-LINE FROM WS-TOTAL-LINE
                                                           143             AFTER ADVANCING 3 LINES.

              (a) COBOL-74                                                (b) COBOL-85
```

The VALUE Clause

The **VALUE clause** can be included as part of a field definition (in the WORKING-STORAGE SECTION) to establish the initial contents of that field. Its format and several examples are shown in Figure 5-4. (Notice that the first six are taken from PATDFCT3; the line number from Figure 5-2 is included to the left of each of these.) The VALUE clause is typically coded after the PICTURE clause, as shown in the examples. The reserved word VALUE is required, but the word IS is optional and usually omitted (as in all the examples).

The examples of Figure 5-4 illustrate most of the following characteristics of the VALUE clause:

■ A VALUE clause can be used with either alphanumeric or numeric fields.

■ A VALUE clause can be used with a field that is given a specific name or one defined as FILLER. If given a name, that field can be referenced in the PROCE-DURE DIVISION just as any other field. If defined as FILLER, the field cannot be referenced individually. (This is adequate for description lines.)

■ The literal can be shorter than the length defined by the PICTURE clause, but it *cannot* be longer. In line 67, the FILLER field length is 15 characters, exactly the number required for the value (part of the column heading). Remember

Figure 5-4
The VALUE clause.

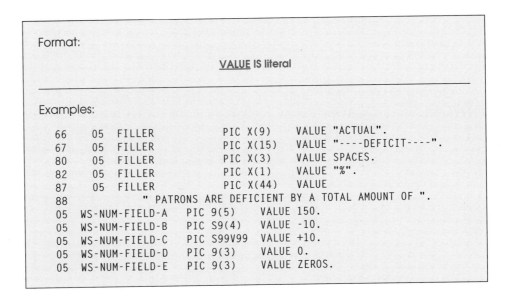

```
Format:

                        VALUE IS literal

Examples:

    66   05  FILLER          PIC X(9)     VALUE "ACTUAL".
    67   05  FILLER          PIC X(15)    VALUE "----DEFICIT----".
    80   05  FILLER          PIC X(3)     VALUE SPACES.
    82   05  FILLER          PIC X(1)     VALUE "%".
    87   05  FILLER          PIC X(44)    VALUE
    88            " PATRONS ARE DEFICIENT BY A TOTAL AMOUNT OF ".
    05  WS-NUM-FIELD-A   PIC 9(5)     VALUE 150.
    05  WS-NUM-FIELD-B   PIC S9(4)    VALUE -10.
    05  WS-NUM-FIELD-C   PIC S99V99   VALUE +10.
    05  WS-NUM-FIELD-D   PIC 9(3)     VALUE 0.
    05  WS-NUM-FIELD-E   PIC 9(3)     VALUE ZEROS.
```

that a numeric literal is limited to a length of 18 digits and a nonnumeric literal is limited to a length of 120 characters. If the literal is long, it can be written on the next line, as in line 88 of Figure 5-4.

■ If an alphanumeric literal is shorter than the field length, it will be positioned to the left in the field and the extra positions to the right will be filled with spaces. For instance, the entry at line 66 includes a PIC X(9), but the literal is only six characters in length. The 9-position FILLER will contain "ACTUALbbb" (where b represents a blank space).

■ If a numeric literal is shorter than the field length, it will be positioned to give the correct numeric value. For example, WS-NUM-FIELD-C will contain a value of +10.00.

■ When a numeric literal is coded with an arithmetic sign (+15 or –208, for example), the numeric PICTURE clause must contain the symbol S.

■ The literal specified in the VALUE clause must be consistent with the category of data defined by the PICTURE clause. That is, if the field is defined as alphanumeric, a nonnumeric literal must be coded; if defined as numeric, a numeric literal must be specified.

■ A figurative constant such as ZERO or SPACE can be used as the literal of a VALUE clause. Recognize, though, that because a blank space is an alphanumeric character, SPACE and SPACES cannot be coded for a numeric field. On the other hand, since a zero can be considered to be either a numeric digit or an alphanumeric character, ZERO, ZEROS, and ZEROES can be specified with either numeric or alphanumeric fields.

Sometimes it is tempting to use the VALUE clause when defining an output line in the FILE SECTION. *This is not valid.* It can be used only with WORKING-STORAGE SECTION fields; its use is prohibited in the FILE SECTION. In addition, the VALUE clause cannot be used with the REDEFINES and OCCURS clauses, topics covered in later chapters.

Perhaps it has occurred to you that the VALUE clause can be used to initialize the two accumulators WS-TOTAL-AMOUNT-DEFICIENT and WS-DEFICIENT-PATRONS and thus remove the initializing MOVE from the 100-INITIALIZE-VARIABLE-FIELDS procedure. If so, you are quite correct. However, this is considered poor programming practice. A good rule to follow is to use the VALUE clause only for items that will not change in the program. Then you know that those fields to which you assign values with the VALUE clause will always be as defined in the WORKING-STORAGE SECTION. As you will learn in Chapter 6, some work areas must be set to zero more than once in a program, an action that can be done only within the PROCEDURE DIVISION.

Output Lines in the WORKING-STORAGE SECTION

In the PATDFCT program, you encountered the notion of defining two different record formats under the DEFICIENCY-LIST File Description (the output file). Recall that this is called implicit redefinition and allows you to have two totally different formats for the single output line. That is one way of taking care of this need. Another way (one that is more practical when printing headings) is the following:

1. Define the output (printer) record as a single 132-position line. (See line 47 of Figure 5-2.)

2. Define each format of output line required by the program as a separate record in the WORKING-STORAGE SECTION. Referring to Figure 5-2, you see three such records: WS-COLUMN-HEADING-LINE (lines 62–67), WS-DETAIL-LINE (lines 69–82), and WS-TOTAL-LINE (lines 84–89).

If you compare the three output line descriptions to the print chart of Figure 5-1, you will see that they coincide exactly. It is important for you to recognize that these generate three separate record areas in memory; this is unlike the implicit redefinition of PATDFCT in which two record descriptions in the FILE SECTION provide two formats for referring to a single area.

The key to using this technique is that prior to printing each line, the appropriate output line must be moved from the WORKING-STORAGE SECTION area to the DEFICIENCY-LINE, the record defined in the output FD. For instance, to print the detail line you would use the following sequence:

```
MOVE WS-DETAIL-LINE TO DEFICIENCY-LINE
WRITE DEFICIENCY LINE
    AFTER ADVANCING 2 LINES
```

Similarly, to print the summary line you would use:

```
MOVE WS-TOTAL-LINE TO DEFICIENCY-LINE
WRITE DEFICIENCY LINE
    AFTER ADVANCING 3 LINES
```

COBOL simplifies this process by providing an optional clause for the WRITE that automatically performs the moving action. This is the WRITE/FROM; the following two WRITE/FROM statements are equivalent to the preceding MOVE-WRITE statement sequences.

```
WRITE DEFICIENCY LINE FROM WS-DETAIL-LINE
    AFTER ADVANCING 2 LINES
WRITE DEFICIENCY LINE FROM WS-TOTAL-LINE
    AFTER ADVANCING 3 LINES
```

Although this form has its conveniences, it will generally not fit into the structured technique of using a single WRITE module for all output from a program.

Basic Editing

In COBOL, the term **edit** refers to the process of suppressing, replacing, and/or inserting characters within a field. You have already seen some simple examples of editing in the PATDFCT2 program. PATDFCT3 includes a few other editing capabilities. The next topic of this chapter is an in-depth look at the editing capabilities included in COBOL.

The three broad editing functions available to you in COBOL are illustrated in PATDFCT3: zero suppression, replacement, and insertion. Consider the total line of Figure 5-2 in which the total amount is printed as 1,021.25. This output format is described by the following numeric-edited field (line 89 of the program).

```
05  TL-TOTAL-AMOUNT-DEFICIENT    PIC ZZZ,ZZZ.99.
```

The MOVE statement

```
MOVE TL-TOTAL-AMOUNT-DEFICIENT
    TO WS-TOTAL-AMOUNT-DEFICIENT
```

moves the numeric field TL-TOTAL-AMOUNT-DEFICIENT to this numeric-edited item, causing the editing to take place as illustrated in Figure 5-5. Notice that leading zeros are suppressed, the Z and 9 characters are replaced with digits of the from field, and the period and comma are inserted. Each of these topics is described in more detail in the next topic of this chapter.

Where the total field is placed in the output area by a MOVE, the field DL-DEFICIENCY-PERCENT (a numeric-edited item) receives its value as a result of the following statement:

```
MULTIPLY WS-DEFICIENCY-FRACTION BY 100
    GIVING DL-DEFICIENCY-PERCENT
```

Remember that this is possible because the GIVING field is not involved in the arithmetic operation. In the PATDFCT2 program, this was accomplished by using a work area for the percentage amount, then moving that result to the output area.

In addition to a numeric editing, COBOL also provides for limited alphanumeric editing. Editing the date field is an example. In PATDFCT2, the date was converted from, for instance, 121390 to 12/13/90 by a succession of MOVE statements. In PATDFCT3, it is done with a combination of the following MOVE and the receiving field picture definition:

```
05  DL-CONTR-DATE                PIC XX/XX/XX.

MOVE PR-CONTR-DATE TO DL-CONTR-DATE
```

Figure 5-5
Numeric editing.

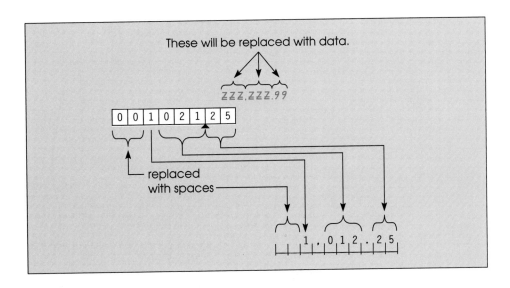

When the MOVE is executed, the action that takes place is illustrated in Figure 5-6.

This concludes the description of the PATDFCT3 program and your preview to the principles of editing. The next topic describes, in detail, the many characteristics of the PICTURE clause.

Topic: PICTURE Clauses

PICTURE Overview
Functions of the PICTURE Clause

As you know, **PICTURE clauses** describe the general characteristics and editing of an elementary data-item. They are used to specify the following attributes:

1. The data class of the field

   ■ Numeric

   ■ Alphabetic

   ■ Alphanumeric

   ■ Numeric-edited

   ■ Alphanumeric-edited

2. The length of the field

3. The location of an assumed decimal point (for numeric fields)

4. Whether or not a numeric field contains an arithmetic sign (to represent positive or negative values)

5. Editing, if any, to be performed on the field

   In previous chapters and in the PATDFCT3 program of this chapter, you have seen examples of a variety of PICTURE symbols. Some of them are specifically for editing operations, such as the Z and the comma. Others are more general in nature. Technically, there are five picture symbol categories: numeric, alphabetic, alphanumeric, numeric-edited, and alphanumeric-edited.

Figure 5-6
Alphanumeric editing.

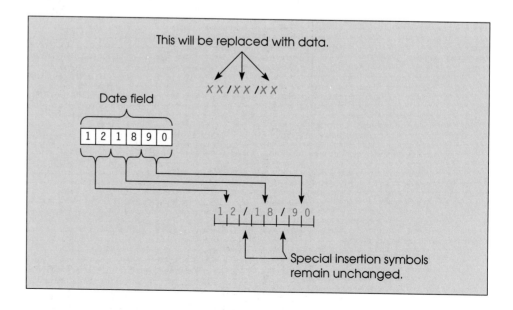

Basic PICTURE Symbols   The first three picture symbol categories are summarized in the table of Figure 5-7. They need no further description because you are familiar with each of them (except for the A) from the preceding chapters.

Numeric Editing PICTURE Symbols   There are five categories of numeric editing symbols: zero suppression and replacement, simple insertion, special insertion, fixed insertion, and floating insertion. These are summarized in Figure 5-8. Let's begin with special insertion, the process of inserting a decimal point.

Figure 5-7
Summary of PICTURE symbols—non-editing.

Data category	Symbol	Meaning
Numeric	9	Numeric digit. Can contain a digit or a sign. A numeric field can range in length from 1 to 18 digits.
	V	Assumed decimal point. When included in a picture, indicates the position of the assumed decimal point in the number. Since the field will not include an actual decimal point, the V does not cause storage space to be reserved. Since a single numeric field value can logically contain only one decimal point, only one V is allowed in a picture character-string. If a V is not present, the decimal point is assumed to be immediately to the right of the rightmost digit position of the field. Hence, a V written as the rightmost symbol of the picture character-string (such as PIC 999V) is redundant.
	S	Arithmetic sign. Must be included if the field might be negative; otherwise, the sign will be discarded. This may or may not cause an extra storage position to be reserved (depending on the COBOL implementation). As a general rule, a signed field should be specified for (1) any input-record numeric fields that either do or might possibly require a sign to be carried, (2) all WORKING-STORAGE fields used for computations, and (3) those output/record numeric fields that receive data from a signed field.
	P	Assumed decimal scaling position (not used in this book).
Alphabetic	A	Alphabetic character. Can contain only letters of the alphabet and the space. As indicated in Concepts Module A, alphanumeric data class is almost always used in place of alphabetic data class.
Alphanumeric	X	Alphanumeric character. Can contain any character in the character set (letters, digits, and special characters).

Figure 5-8
Numeric editing picture symbols by category.

Data category	Symbol	Meaning
Suppression and replacement	Z	Zero suppression with blank space replacement
	*	Zero suppression with asterisk replacement
Simple insertion	,	Comma
	/	Slash (stroke, diagonal)
	B	Blank space
	0	Zero
Special insertion	.	Decimal point
Fixed insertion	–	Minus sign (fixed)
	+	Plus sign (fixed)
	CR	Credit symbol
	DB	Debit symbol
	$	Dollar sign (fixed)
Floating insertion	–	Minus sign (floating)
	+	Plus sign (floating)
	$	Dollar sign (floating)

Numeric Editing—Special Insertion

Although the computer can utilize assumed decimal points for internal processing, human processing usually demands that the decimal point be displayed on the output. Hence, the actual decimal point is almost always specified for report and display screen output. The decimal point is called a **special insertion character** (it is the only one) because, in addition to the insertion editing, it specifies how data from the sending field is decimal-point aligned in the editing field.

PICTURE Symbol . (Decimal Point)

When the **decimal-point editing symbol** is specified, as illustrated in the examples of Figure 5-9, it will be printed, not just assumed. Contrast this actual decimal-point editing picture symbol with the assumed decimal-point V symbol. Recognize that although the assumed decimal-point symbol V does not occupy a storage position, the actual decimal point requires one position.

Figure 5-9
Decimal-point editing examples.

Special Insertion (Decimal-Point) Editing		
Data in storage	Edit field PICTURE	Edited result
103256	PIC 9999.99	1032.56
002500	PIC 9999.99	0025.00
000894	PIC 999.99	000.89
00002	PIC 999.99	000.02
000003	PIC 999.99	000.00
103256	PIC 999.999	103.256
256	PIC 99.9	25.6

Note: ▲ indicates assumed decimal point location.

Since it is mathematically impossible to have more than one decimal point in a decimal value, only one decimal-point symbol can be specified in a picture character-string. Also, because a decimal-point symbol as the rightmost character of a picture character-string might be interpreted by the compiler as an end-of-sentence period, the decimal-point editing symbol cannot be specified there.

Numeric Editing— Zero Suppression and Replacement
PICTURE Symbol Z (Zero Suppression With Blank-Space Replacement)

There are two symbols in this category: Z (zero suppression with blank-space replacement) and * (zero suppression with asterisk replacement).

The lengths of most numeric fields are usually greater than most of the data-entry values recorded in them. When a data value occupies less than the total number of digits of a numeric field, the leftmost positions will contain zeros. These **leading zeros** are alternatively referred to as **leftmost zeros** or **high-order zeros**. Obviously, leading zeros do not affect the value of the data contained in a field. Since they are not needed, they are normally replaced by spaces on printed reports; for instance, 00803 would be printed as 803 preceded by two spaces. This action of replacing leading zeros with spaces is called **zero suppression**. In the value 803, observe that the zero between the eight and the three is not suppressed because it is not a leading zero (it is preceded by a digit other than zero).

As you have seen with preceding examples, COBOL provides for leading zero suppression with blank-space replacement with the symbol Z, probably the most frequently used editing symbol. Examples of its use are shown in Figure 5-10. In the fourth whole number and second assumed decimal examples, notice that nothing is printed for 0 because all positions are replaced with spaces. In this assumed decimal example where a value 0 is edited into ZZZ.ZZ, you can see that the decimal point is suppressed; it would make no sense to leave it with no digits.

Often it is appropriate to zero-suppress all but a certain number of the rightmost positions of a field. For instance, in several examples, a 9 symbol is used to specify unconditional printing of digit positions, regardless of whether the zero is leading or embedded within other digits.

For zero suppression, you can specify any combination of Zs and 9s, but the Z symbols must precede the 9 symbols. In other words, a Z symbol cannot appear to the right of a 9 symbol.

Figure 5-10
Zero suppression and blank-space replacement editing examples.

Zero Suppression and Blank-Space Replacement Editing

With Whole-Number Quantities			With Assumed Decimal Positioning		
Data in storage	Edit field PICTURE	Edited result	Data in storage	Edit field PICTURE	Edited result
10358	PIC ZZZZZ	10358	00002▲	PIC ZZZ.ZZ	.02
00803	PIC ZZZZZ	803	00000▲	PIC ZZZ.ZZ	
00002	PIC ZZZZZ	2	02500▲	PIC ZZZ.99	25.00
00000	PIC ZZZZZ		00089▲	PIC ZZ9.99	0.89
00017	PIC ZZZZ9	17	00089▲	PIC ZZZ.99	.89
00005	PIC ZZZZ9	5	00002▲	PIC ZZZ.99	.02
00000	PIC ZZZZ9	0	00000▲	PIC ZZZ.99	.00

Note: ▲ indicates assumed decimal point location.

Furthermore, you cannot include a combination of Z and 9 symbols to the right of the decimal point. That is, PIC ZZ,ZZZ.Z9 is not valid. The logic behind this is that, on the right-hand side of the decimal point, nonsignificant zeros are the trailing rather than the leading zeros. This is true of all zero suppression operations.

PICTURE Symbol * (Zero Suppression With Asterisk Replacement)

In some cases, leading zeros are considered undesirable, but it is not desirable to leave the positions blank. For instance, on a computer-printed check, blank spaces preceding a dollar amount could be replaced with digits to fraudulently increase the check's value. By replacing leading zeros with asterisks, tampering with the check amount is made more difficult and readability is improved by eliminating leading zeros.

When an asterisk is specified in the picture character-string, leading zeros are replaced by asterisks. In the examples of Figure 5-11, you can see that replacement with asterisk is identical to replacement with space, except that the decimal point is not eliminated with a zero amount. Syntax rules are equivalent to those for the Z symbol: any combination of * symbols and 9 symbols may be specified, but the * symbols must precede the 9 symbols. In other words, an * symbol cannot appear to the right of a 9 symbol.

Numeric Editing— Simple Insertion

There are four simple insertion editing symbols, one of which—the , (comma)—you observed in the PATDFCT3 program. The other three are / (slash), B (blank space), and 0 (zero). Like the period, each of the simple insertion characters, when inserted into a field, requires a separate storage position.

PICTURE Symbol , (Comma)

When we write integer number values in our everyday lives, we place a comma to the left of each group of three digits so that the number is easier to read. The typical use for the comma picture symbol in COBOL is exactly the same. Comma symbols are often used together with Zs or asterisks in a picture character-string. Some examples are shown in Figure 5-12. Just as with everyday usage, if a significant digit does not occur to the left of the comma, the comma is suppressed and replaced by the replacement character.

Although by tradition we often insert commas three digits from one another, comma symbols can be placed anywhere in the picture character-string, except as the rightmost symbol.

Figure 5-11
Zero suppression and asterisk replacement editing examples.

Zero Suppression and Asterisk Replacement Editing					
With Whole-Number Quantities			**With Assumed Decimal Positioning**		
Data in storage	Edit field PICTURE	Edited result	Data in storage	Edit field PICTURE	Edited result
10358	PIC *****	10358	00002	PIC ***.**	***.02
00803	PIC *****	**803	00000	PIC ***.**	***.**
00002	PIC *****	****2	02500	PIC ***.99	*25.00
00000	PIC *****	*****	00089	PIC **9.99	**0.89
00017	PIC ****9	***17	00089	PIC ***.99	***.89
00005	PIC ****9	****5	00002	PIC ***.99	***.02
00000	PIC ****9	****0	00000	PIC ***.99	***.00

Note: ▲ indicates assumed decimal point location.

Figure 5-12
Simple insertion editing—
comma.

Simple Insertion Editing—Comma		
Data in storage	**Edit field PICTURE**	**Edited result**
01234	PIC ZZ,ZZZ	1,234
00234	PIC ZZ,ZZZ	234
00000	PIC ZZ,ZZZ	
00009	PIC ZZZZZ9	0
00009	PIC ZZ,999	009
00009	PIC 99,999	00,009
103256▲	PIC Z,ZZZ.99	1,032.56
003256▲	PIC Z,ZZZ.99	32.56
150028300▲	PIC Z,ZZZ,ZZZ.99	1,500,283.00
000028300▲	PIC Z,ZZZ,ZZZ.99	283.00
003256▲	PIC *,***.99	***32.56
150028300▲	PIC *,***,***.99	1,500,283.00
000028300▲	PIC *,***,***.99	******283.00

Note: ▲ indicates assumed decimal point location.

PICTURE Symbol /
(Slash)

The insertion symbol / is commonly called a **slash**, but is sometimes referred to as a **slant**, **diagonal**, **stroke**, or **virgule**. Probably its most frequent use is as a separator between the month, day, and year subfields of numeric-defined dates.

Suppose we have an input field that contains a date expressed in six-digit month-day-year format (*mmddyy*—two digits for each month, day, and year). Just as decimal points are not typically stored in numeric amount fields in order to conserve storage space, the month/day/year separating slashes are not normally stored in date fields. However, the date would be difficult to read unless we displayed the separating slashes on output reports and screens. For example, without punctuation, the date of Christmas 1988, would read 122588. We can read it much more easily when it is expressed in its customary form of 12/25/88.

The examples of Figure 5-13 illustrate insertion of the slash character to achieve the desired date form. Notice that you can suppress a leading zero month digit so that a date of 030791 would be printed as 3/07/91 (the picture specification could be coded as Z9/99/99). On the other hand, you would not normally suppress the leading day zero because a blank space within the date string (for example, 3/ 7/91) would fragment the date and make it more clumsy to read.

Figure 5-13
Simple insertion editing—
slash.

Simple Insertion Editing—Slash		
Data in storage	**Edit field PICTURE**	**Edited result**
122590	PIC 99/99/99	12/25/90
030791	PIC 99/99/99	03/07/91
030791	PIC Z9/99/99	3/07/91
516	PIC 99/9	51/6

When date formatting, remember that the input date of 6 digits will require 8 positions on output. Also, notice that slash inserting is not limited to date formats. Any number of / symbols can be specified at any location in a picture character-string.

PICTURE Symbol B (Blank Space)

The **blank-space** insertion symbol B does not have as many applications as the comma and the slash, but there are certain situations in which it comes in handy. Suppose, for instance, you want blank spaces (rather than slashes) between the month, day, and year of the date. This could be accomplished by coding PIC 99B99B99 or PIC Z9B99B99, as illustrated in the first example of Figure 5-14. The second example illustrates separating the three parts of a Social Security number. Once again, observe that the nine-digit Social Security field will require eleven output positions.

As with the slash character, any number of B symbols can be specified at any location in a picture character-string.

PICTURE Symbol 0 (Zero)

The insertion symbol 0 (**zero**) has only a few uses. One example can be drawn from the bean business. Beans and many other dry commodities are sold in bulk by hundred-pound units, termed hundredweights and abbreviated CWT (C is the Roman numeral for 100 and WT is a contraction for weight). If each bean sale is recorded in a field called CWTS-SOLD and assigned PIC 9(4), the number of pounds of beans sold would always be a hundred times greater than the value in the CWTS-SOLD field. Suppose a certain output required the number of pounds sold to be expressed in single-pound units rather than hundredweights. To accomplish this conversion without arithmetic, the picture specification could be coded as PIC 999900, as PIC 999,900, or as PIC ZZZ,900 as illustrated in Figure 5-15.

Numeric Editing— Fixed Insertion

Fixed insertion editing symbols are limited to placement at certain locations within the picture character-string. There are five fixed insertion symbols. Four of them— – (fixed minus sign), + (fixed plus sign), CR (credit symbol), and DB (debit symbol)—are conditional picture symbols depending upon the sign of the data field. The fifth fixed insertion symbol is the $ (fixed currency sign).

Figure 5-14
Simple insertion editing— blank space.

Simple Insertion Editing—Blank Space		
Data in storage	Edit field PICTURE	Edited result
112490	PIC 99B99B99	11 24 90
566509224	PIC 999B99B9999	566 50 9224
2468	PIC 989B9B9	2468

Figure 5-15
Simple insertion editing— zero.

Simple Insertion Editing—Zero		
Data in storage	Edit field PICTURE	Edited result
0150	PIC 999900	0015000
0150	PIC ZZZ900	15000
0150	PIC ZZZ,900	15,000
0000	PIC ZZZ,900	000
0000	PIC ZZZ,Z00	00

PICTURE Symbol –
(Fixed Minus Sign)

If a value is negative, then a sign indication symbol must be included in the output field or the sign will not be printed. The **fixed minus sign** allows a minus sign to be printed if the data value is negative. If the value is instead positive or zero, a blank space will appear in the minus-sign location. Several examples are shown in Figure 5-16. Note that you can specify the sign as either the rightmost or the leftmost symbol. As you might expect, only one fixed minus-sign symbol may be coded in a picture characterstring.

It is usually easier to interpret output data when the fixed minus sign is printed to the right of the amount value. This results because leftmost digits of amount fields are typically zero supressed; blank spaces between the minus sign and the number make the value clumsy to read.

PICTURE Symbol +
(Fixed Plus Sign)

The fixed plus sign is similar to the fixed minus sign, except that it always causes a sign to be printed. That is, a plus sign is printed if the data value is positive or zero; a minus sign is printed if the data value is negative. You can see this by referring to the examples of Figure 5-17.

As with the fixed minus sign, you can specify only one fixed plus sign symbol and you must position it as the leftmost or rightmost character of the picture character-string. The fixed plus sign is also normally specified as the rightmost symbol.

PICTURE Symbol CR
(Credit Symbol)

The **credit symbol** occupies two character-positions, but otherwise operates in a manner similar to that of the fixed minus sign. That is, if the data value placed in the field is negative, the letters CR are printed; otherwise, the two positions appear as blank spaces.

In the examples of Figure 5-18, notice that you can either position the CR adjacent to the digit specification or include a blank space between the digits and the CR symbol. Given adequate room on the report line, the space makes for easier reading.

Figure 5-16
Fixed insertion editing—
minus sign.

Fixed Insertion Editing—Minus Sign			
Data in storage	**Sign**	**Edit field PICTURE**	**Edited result**
02345▲	–	PIC ZZ,ZZ9-	2,345-
02345▲	+	PIC ZZ,ZZ9-	2,345
00000▲		PIC ZZ,ZZ9-	0
080056▲	–	PIC Z,ZZZ.99-	800.56-
080056▲	+	PIC Z,ZZZ.99-	800.56
000156▲	–	PIC Z,ZZZ.99-	1.56-
000000▲		PIC Z,ZZZ.99-	.00
02345▲	–	PIC -ZZ,ZZ9	- 2,345
02345▲	+	PIC -ZZ,ZZ9	2,345
00000▲		PIC -ZZ,ZZ9	0
080056▲	–	PIC -Z,ZZZ.99	- 800.56
080056▲	+	PIC -Z,ZZZ.99	800.56
000156▲	–	PIC -Z,ZZZ.99	- 1.56
000000▲		PIC -Z,ZZZ.99	.00

Note: ▲ indicates assumed decimal point location.

Figure 5-17
Fixed insertion editing—
plus sign.

Fixed Insertion Editing—Plus Sign

Data in storage	Sign	Edit field PICTURE	Edited result
02345	+	PIC ZZ,ZZ9+	2,345+
02345	−	PIC ZZ,ZZ9+	2,345−
00000		PIC ZZ,ZZ9+	0+
080056	−	PIC Z,ZZZ.99+	800.56−
080056	+	PIC Z,ZZZ.99+	800.56+
000156	+	PIC Z,ZZZ.99+	1.56+
000000		PIC Z,ZZZ.99+	.00+
02345	+	PIC +ZZ,ZZ9	+2,345
02345	−	PIC +ZZ,ZZ9	−2,345
00000		PIC +ZZ,ZZ9	− 0
080056	−	PIC +Z,ZZZ.99	− 800.56
080056	+	PIC +Z,ZZZ.99	+ 800.56
000156	+	PIC +Z,ZZZ.99	+ 1.56
000000		PIC +Z,ZZZ.99	+ .00

Note: ▲ indicates assumed decimal point location.

Figure 5-18
Fixed insertion editing—
credit (CR).

Fixed Insertion Editing—Credit

Data in storage	Sign	Edit field PICTURE	Edited result
22500	−	PIC ZZZ.99CR	225.00CR
22500	+	PIC ZZZ.99OB	225.00
00000		PIC ZZZ.99CR	.00
22500	−	PIC ZZZ.99BCR	225.00 CR
22500	+	PIC ZZZ.99BCR	225.00

Note: ▲ indicates assumed decimal point location.

A credit symbol typically is used in preference to the minus sign for external and formal reports because it provides a more visually definite indication. For internal reports, the minus sign is commonly used because it uses only one print position and hence conserves valuable space on a print line or display screen.

Only one occurrence of the CR symbol is allowed in a picture character-string and it must occupy the rightmost character-positions.

**PICTURE Symbol DB
(Debit Symbol)**

As you can see by referring to Figure 5-19, the **debit symbol DB** works exactly like the credit symbol: it indicates a negative amount. That is, when DB is specified and the data value is negative, DB will be printed. If the data value is positive or zero, two blank spaces will appear.

The CR or the DB are commonly used in accounting. Which of the two is used in a particular instance depends upon the accounting application.

Figure 5-19
Fixed insertion editing—
debit (DB).

Fixed Insertion Editing—Debit			
Data in storage	**Sign**	**Edit field PICTURE**	**Edited result**
22500	–	PIC ZZZ.99DB	225.00DB
22500	+	PIC ZZZ.99DB	225.00
00000		PIC ZZZ.99DB	.00
22500	–	PIC ZZZ.99BDB	225.00 DB
22500	+	PIC ZZZ.99BDB	225.00

Note: ▲ indicates assumed decimal point location.

PICTURE Symbol $ (Fixed Currency Sign)

The **fixed currency sign** symbol is used to print a dollar sign* preceding a number at a fixed location. The fixed $ can only be specified once and it must be the leftmost symbol of the picture character-string, as illustrated by the examples of Figure 5-20. Notice that if the data value may be negative, provisions must be made for the sign or it will be lost. If the minus insertion symbol is used, it must be positioned to the right.

The fixed dollar sign is commonly used to indicate columnar dollar amounts on the first line and on total lines of formal accounting reports such as balance sheets and income statements.

Numeric Editing— Floating Insertion

Three of the fixed insertion editing symbols can also be specified as **floating insertion symbols**: – (floating minus sign), + (floating plus sign), and $ (floating currency sign). If one of these symbols appears more than once in the leftmost positions of the picture character-string, then it signifies a floating symbol.

Floating – (Minus Sign)

The **floating minus sign** gives you the capability to suppress leading zeros and position the minus sign to the immediate left of the printed number (with no intervening spaces). This is illustrated in Figure 5-21, which also includes two fixed

Figure 5-20
Fixed insertion editing—
dollar sign.

Fixed Insertion Editing—Dollar Sign			
Data in storage	**Sign**	**Edit field PICTURE**	**Edited result**
51207		PIC $ZZZ.99	$512.07
00008		PIC $ZZZ.99	$ .08
00008		PIC $ZZ9.99	$ 0.08
00700	–	PIC $999.99	$007.00
00700	–	PIC $ZZZ.99-	$ 7.00-
00700	–	PIC $ZZZ.99CR	$7.00CR

Note: ▲ indicates assumed decimal point location.

---

*Actually, the currency sign can represent any currency unit: dollars, pounds, francs, marks, and so forth. However, in the United States, the fixed currency sign is commonly referred to as the fixed dollar sign. The currency sign can be changed to other monetary symbols by the developer of the compiler or user option.

Figure 5-21
Floating insertion editing—
minus sign.

Fixed Insertion Editing—Minus Sign			
Data in storage	**Sign**	**Edit field PICTURE**	**Edited result**
108659 ▲	–	PIC --,---.99	-1,086.59
108659 ▲	–	PIC -Z,ZZZ.99	-1,086.59
003000 ▲	–	PIC --,---.99	-30.00
003000 ▲	–	PIC -Z,ZZZ.99	- 30.00
003000 ▲	+	PIC --,---.99	30.00
003000 ▲		PIC --,---.99	30.00
000000 ▲		PIC --,---.99	.00
000000 ▲		PIC --,---.--	

Note: ▲ indicates assumed decimal point location.

minus sign examples for comparison. As you can see, the conditional action of the floating minus sign is exactly the same as that of the fixed minus sign. If the data value is negative, the minus sign is printed; if positive or zero, a blank space will appear.

By comparing the first and second, and the third and fourth examples, you can see that for the floating minus, you simply use the minus sign character wherever you would use the Z character with a fixed minus sign. Be careful to avoid the mistake of making the number of minus symbols exactly equal to the number of zero suppression digits in data value: one extra position is required for the minus sign. For example, the three digit negative number –345 would require PIC – – –9.

As it is with all the floating symbols, if one is specified to the right of the decimal point, then all digit positions to the right of the decimal point must be represented by the floating symbol. Also, when a floating plus or minus sign is used, there must be at least one floating sign symbol to the left of the decimal point. These limitations are illustrated by the following:

Valid	Not valid
PIC – –,– –.– –	PIC – –,– –.– 9
PIC –,– –	PIC .– –

Floating + (Plus Sign) The **floating plus sign** works the same as the floating minus except that a sign (either plus or a minus) is always inserted unless the data value is zero. Examples are shown in Figure 5-22. Notice that, unlike the fixed plus sign, the entire field is blanked for a data value of zero—the sign is suppressed as well.

Floating $ (Currency Sign) With the **floating currency sign** symbol, you can cause a dollar sign to be printed immediately to the left of the first non-suppressed digit of a number. As you can see by referring to Figure 5-23, the floating dollar sign symbol is coded in the left-most position of the picture character-string and repeated for each position through which it should float. (This is the same as the other floating characters.) Notice that if a data value may be negative and the sign is to be indicated, then a minus or CR symbol must be included to the right.

Figure 5-22
Floating insertion editing—
plus sign.

Fixed Insertion Editing—Plus Sign

Data in storage	Sign	Edit field PICTURE	Edited result
01809 ▲	−	PIC ++,+++.99	-180.79
018079 ▲	+	PIC ++,+++.99	+180.79
018079 ▲		PIC ++,+++.99	+180.79
000000 ▲		PIC ++,+++.99	+.00
000000 ▲		PIC ++,+++.++	

Note: ▲ indicates assumed decimal point location.

Figure 5-23
Floating insertion editing—
dollar sign.

Fixed Insertion Editing—Dollar Sign

Data in storage	Sign	Edit field PICTURE	Edited result
004705 ▲		PIC $$,$$$.99	$47.05
004705 ▲		PIC $$,$$$.99	$47.05
004705 ▲	−	PIC $$,$$$.99-	$47.05-
004705 ▲		PIC $$,$$$.99-	$47.05
004705 ▲	−	PIC $$,$$$.99CR	$47.05CR
000007 ▲		PIC $$,$$$.99	$.07
000007 ▲		PIC $$,$$9.99	$0.07
000000 ▲		PIC $$,$$$.99	$.00
000000 ▲		PIC $$,$$$.$$	

Note: ▲ indicates assumed decimal point location.

Whereas the fixed dollar sign is typically used for columnar dollar amounts, the floating dollar sign is generally specified for noncolumnar dollar figures and sometimes on check amounts (although a fixed dollar sign together with asterisk replacement offers better check protection).

Describing Alphanumeric-Edited Data-Items

Only one category exists for alphanumeric editing symbols: simple insertion editing. Three editing symbols can be specified with alphanumeric fields: / (slash), B (blank space), and 0 (zero). The alphanumeric editing symbols are specified and operate exactly like their numeric editing counterparts, except that they are used in conjunction with the alphanumeric picture symbol X rather than the numeric picture symbols. Examples of alphanumeric editing are shown in Figure 5-24.

Recap of PICTURE Clauses

When forming a PICTURE clause, be certain to always choose symbols from one data class: numeric, alphabetic, or alphanumeric. Figure 5-25 lists the picture symbols organized by data class. Symbols cannot be mixed across class lines. For example, if you specified PIC XX,XXX, the COBOL compiler would identify the

Figure 5-24
Alphanumeric editing
examples.

Alphanumeric Editing Examples			
	Data in storage	**Edit field PICTURE**	**Edited result**
Slash	122591	PIC XX/XX/XX	12/25/91
	030792	PIC XX/XX/XX	03/07/92
	ABC	PIC XX/X	AB/C
Blank space	122591	PIC XXBXXBXX	12 25 91
	XYZ	PIC XBXX	X YZ
	ABC123	PIC XBXX/XXX	A BC/123
Zero	A10	PIC XXX0	A100
	12	PIC 0XX	012

clause as invalid because it contains both alphanumeric (X) and numeric editing (the comma) symbols.

Editing With Hyphens

You may have noticed that the hyphen doesn't have an editing symbol. This is because the hyphen and the minus sign are both represented by the same character symbol. Occasionally, there is a need to insert hyphens into a field. A Social Security number field is an example. Also, sometimes numeric dates are represented by using hyphens rather than slashes as the month/day/year separators.

One way to introduce the hyphen into fields is simply by using the MOVE statement, as was done in the PATDFCT2 program. You will learn about another technique, using the INSPECT/REPLACING statement, in Chapter 8.

PICTURE Clause Style Considerations

It was mentioned in the preceding chapter that the parentheses method for forming picture character-strings is more readable than the repetition method. That convention applies when, as in the examples of the preceding chapters, the same picture symbol applies to all the positions of the field.

When editing picture character-strings are formed, however, a clearer indication of the desired editing is conveyed by coding each individual character instead of using the parentheses representation. For example, it is difficult to interpret PIC $Z(2),Z(3).9(2); coding each individual symbol results in the much more readable PIC $ZZ,ZZZ.99.

When an assumed decimal point symbol V appears in a numeric picture character-string, an appropriate convention is to use the parentheses method before the V symbol and to use the repetition method after the V. The specification for a seven-digit dollars-and-cents field, for example, would thus read PIC S9(5)V99.

Figure 5-25
Picture symbols by
data class.

Numeric	Numeric-edited	Alphabetic	Alphanumeric	Alphanumeric-edited	
9	Z	.	A	X	/
S	*	–			0
V	,	+			B
P	/	CR			
	0	DB			
	B	$			

BLANK WHEN ZERO Clause

Although **BLANK WHEN ZERO** is a clause separate from the PICTURE clause, it is closely related because it also controls the output of data.

Sometimes a numeric editing picture clause is specified for a field, but the editing is not wanted when the value of the edited field is zero. As an example, suppose you have a date represented in an input field by a picture character-string of 9(6). For the output report, the editing picture is 99/99/99. However, not all input records have a date present in the input field; when absent, the date field contains zeros. As a result, those records lacking a date would be printed as 00/00/00. Though there is nothing wrong with such rendering, the appearance of the report would be improved by leaving the output date field blank for the zero dates. In other words, the desired processing is to edit the date in accordance with the picture clause, but print nothing if the input field value contains zero.

You can use the BLANK WHEN ZERO clause to achieve the desired result. When this clause is coded for a data-item description entry, it will cause the field to be blanked when a value of zeros is moved to it. As shown in Figure 5-26, the reserved words BLANK WHEN ZERO can be coded after the PICTURE clause. (They could alternatively be coded before the picture clause, but the location shown is convenient and commonly practiced.) The BLANK WHEN ZERO clause is composed of three separate reserved words and thus contains no hyphens. This clause can be used only with numeric and numeric-edited data-items.

There are some common applications of the blank-when-zero effect that can be handled either with the BLANK WHEN ZERO clause or without it. A simple case is when full zero suppression with blank-space replacement is specified. For example, specification of PIC ZZZZ together with a BLANK WHEN ZERO clause is redundant. The same is true for PIC Z,ZZZ since a comma is suppressed whenever no significant digits precede it. As a general rule, if a 9, * 0, $, or a fixed + sign appears in the picture character-string and the blank-when-zero effect is desired, the BLANK WHEN ZERO clause must be coded.

Topic:	The MOVE Statement

Capabilities of the MOVE— Preview/Summary

You have now used the MOVE statement under a variety of circumstances. That is, you have used it to move the contents of one numeric field to another, the contents of one alphanumeric to another, and the contents of numeric and alphanumeric fields to numeric and alpanumeric edit fields. Although the MOVE appears at first glance to be a relatively simple statement, it has a wide variety of capabilities. You have even moved a group item (the record from working storage in PATDFCT3) to an elementary item (the output record).

Figure 5-26
The BLANK WHEN ZERO clause.

```
Format:

                    BLANK WHEN ZERO


Examples:

    05  WS-PRICE      PIC ZZ,ZZZ.99    BLANK WHEN ZERO.
    05  CODE-NUMBER   PIC 99999        BLANK WHEN ZERO.
    05  PL-DATE       PIC 99/99/99     BLANK WHEN ZERO.
```

This Topic focuses explicitly on these and other features of the MOVE statement. Figure 5-27 summarizes (and previews) the many possible MOVE statement combinations. Notice the following about the table as shown here:

■ The action resulting from each type of "from" and "to" field in the MOVE is described in the intersecting box.

■ The notation AN/AN means an alphanumeric to alphanumeric move; similarly, N/N means a numeric to numeric move.

■ The unshaded boxes indicate the most common moves.

■ Some of the moves are noted as ILLEGAL. This means that they cannot be allowed and will be flagged by the compiler. The following are illegal moves that beginning COBOL programmers frequently attempt.

MOVE alphanumeric-field TO numeric or numeric-edited field.

MOVE numeric-field-with-decimal positions TO alphanumeric field.

Figure 5-27   MOVE statement categories.

Sending field	Receiving field				
	Alphanumeric	**Alphanumeric edited**	**Numeric**	**Numeric edited**	**Group**
Alphanumeric	Left justification Receiving field shorter: truncation Receiving field longer: padding with spaces	Same as AN/AN also Editing is performed	ILLEGAL	ILLEGAL	Same as AN/AN
Alphanumeric-edited	Same as AN/AN in COBOL-74. De-editing occurs in COBOL-85.	Same as AN/AN also Editing is performed	ILLEGAL	ILLEGAL	Same as AN/AN
Numeric *Integer*	Same as AN/AN	Same as AN/AN also Editing is performed	Decimal point alignment Receiving field shorter: truncation	Same as N/N also Editing is performed	Same as AN/AN
Noninteger	ILLEGAL	ILLEGAL	Receiving field longer: padding with zeros		
Numeric-edited	Same as AN/AN	Same as AN/AN also Editing is performed	ILLEGAL in COBOL-74 De-editing occurs in COBOL-85	ILLEGAL	Same as AN/AN
Group	Same as AN/AN	Same as AN/AN (No editing is performed)	ILLEGAL	ILLEGAL	Same as AN/AN

Note: Unshaded areas indicate most common MOVE categories.   AN/AN = Alphanumeric to alphanumeric. N/N = Numeric to numeric.

MOVE group field TO numeric or numeric-edited field.

MOVE numeric-edited field TO numeric or numeric-edited field. (*Note:* This is permissible in COBOL-85, as described in a section that follows.)

Let's consider details of some frequently encountered variations of this statement.

Alphanumeric MOVE Operations
Alphanumeric Sending Field to Alphanumeric Receiving Field

When an alphanumeric field is moved to another field, the data in the sending field is normally aligned, or justified in the leftmost position of the receiving field. In other words, the data is moved from the leftmost position of the sending field to the leftmost position of the receiving field. Movement of the remaining positions then continues from left to right.

If the sending and receiving fields are both the same length, they will contain exactly the same data after execution of the MOVE statement. (Remember that the sending field data is not affected by the MOVE processing.)

On the other hand, if the sending and receiving fields are of different lengths, special MOVE statement processing rules apply. Obviously, there are two possibilities: the receiving field shorter than sending field, and the receiving field longer than sending field.

When the sending field is longer, the excess rightmost characters of the sending field are simply chopped off, or **truncated**, in the receiving field. Only those leftmost characters that will fit into the receiving field are thus transferred to the receiving field, as illustrated in Figure 5-28(a).

When the sending field of an alphanumeric MOVE statement is shorter than the receiving field, the excess rightmost positions of the receiving field are filled, or **padded** with blank spaces. This process is illustrated in Figure 5-28(b). Notice that the padding with spaces has the effect of wiping out all of the data that was in the excess positions prior to the move.

Alphanumeric Sending Field to Alphanumeric-Edited Receiving Field

Alphanumeric to alphanumeric-edited MOVE operations are not frequently specified because there are only limited situations in which use of the three alphanumeric editing symbols is appropriate.

When an alphanumeric sending field is moved to an alphanumeric-edited receiving field, the editing occurs in accordance with the picture clause of the receiving field. Hence, the editing characters will be inserted at their specified locations. Otherwise, the justification and truncation or padding follows the same processing rules as described above for an alphanumeric-to-alphanumeric move.

Figure 5-28
Alphanumeric MOVE.

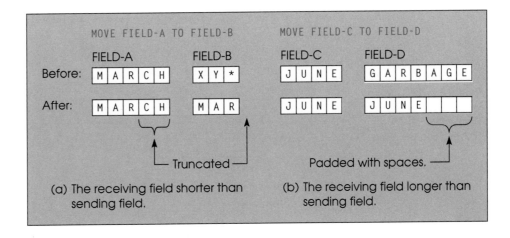

(a) The receiving field shorter than sending field.

(b) The receiving field longer than sending field.

Alphanumeric-Edited Sending Field to Alphanumeric Receiving Field— COBOL-85

Because of the widespread use of data entry via video display terminals, COBOL-85 includes the capability to convert data from its edited form to an unedited form. This action is called **de-editing** and is exactly the reverse of the corresponding edit action. It is done with a MOVE in which the sending field is alphanumeric-edited and the receiving field is alphanumeric. A corresponding de-edit action with numeric data is described later in this section, at which point an example is given.

Numeric MOVE Operations

With numeric MOVE operations, data is always aligned in accordance with the decimal points specified (or implied) in the picture clauses of the sending and receiving fields.

Numeric Sending Field to Numeric Receiving Field

Remember that for purely numeric fields, the decimal point is specified by the assumed decimal point V symbol. If the V is not coded in the picture character-string, the V is considered to be immediately to the right of the rightmost 9.

If either the integer portion or the decimal-position portion of the sending field is longer than its counterpart in the receiving field, a numeric MOVE operation will cause truncation to occur for the receiving portion. If the receiving field integer portion is shorter, the excess leftmost (the **high-order** or **most-significant**) digits will be truncated. If the receiving field decimal-position portion is shorter, the excess rightmost (the **low-order** or **least-significant**) digits will be truncated. Numeric field truncation examples are shown in Figure 5-29(a).

If either the integer portion or the decimal-position portion of the sending field is shorter than its counterpart in the receiving field, a numeric MOVE operation will cause the excess positions in the receiving portion to be padded with zeros. If the receiving field integer portion is longer, zeros will be padded in the excess leftmost digit positions. If the receiving field decimal-position portion is shorter, zeros will be padded in the excess rightmost digit positions. Examples of MOVE operations to longer receiving fields are shown in Figure 5-29(b).

Figure 5-29 Numeric MOVE.

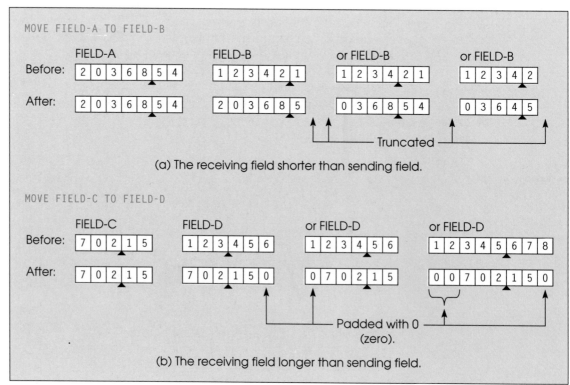

(a) The receiving field shorter than sending field.

(b) The receiving field longer than sending field.

Numeric Sending Field to Numeric-Edited Receiving Field

When a numeric sending field is moved to a numeric-edited receiving field, the editing occurs in accordance with the picture clause of the receiving field. If insertion editing symbols are present, the editing characters will be inserted at their specified locations, thereby augmenting the data character-length within the receiving field. Otherwise, the alignment, truncation, and padding follow the same processing rules as described above for a numeric-to-numeric move.

Numeric-Edited Sending Field to Numeric Receiving Field—COBOL-85

COBOL-85 allows numeric data to be de-edited by moving a numeric-edited field to a numeric receiving field. If the receiving field is properly defined, the resulting action is exactly the opposite of the corresponding edit: all editing insertions are deleted and suppressed zeros are reintroduced. An example of de-editing is shown in Figure 5-30.

Other MOVE Statement Categories
Group Field MOVE Operations

The MOVE operations just described are all elementary field moves. That is, the sending field and the receiving field are both elementary data-items. (Remember that an elementary field is the one with the PICTURE clause; a group field does not contain its own PICTURE clause, but is a collection of elementary data-items.)

Group fields can also be specified in a MOVE statement as either the sending field, the receiving field, or both. When a group field is specified as either the sending or receiving field, the processing rules for an alphanumeric-to-alphanumeric MOVE operation go into effect, even if the sending field is numeric.

Group Sending Field to Alphanumeric-Edited Receiving Field

Although a group to alphanumeric-edited MOVE statement is not a particularly common type, it is a tricky one that can puzzle a beginning programmer. Suppose, for example, that you have a group field called RUN-DATE in which a six-digit numeric date is stored. (This field has three subordinate two-digit elementary fields: MO, DAY, and YR.) To place the run-date in an output-field called OUTRUN-DATE with a picture clause of PIC XX/XX/XX, you code a statement MOVE RUN-DATE TO OUTRUN-DATE. Such a group to alphanumeric-edited MOVE statement is perfectly legal; no syntax error will occur. Unfortunately, you will be disappointed if you expect editing to occur, because the move will be accomplished as if the receiving field were alphanumeric, not alphanumeric-edited. (Contrast this handling with the other sending field combinations shown in the alphanumeric-edited column of Figure 5-27.)

Numeric Integer Sending Field to Alphanumeric Receiving Field

Sometimes it is necessary to move the contents of a numeric integer field (that is, a numeric field without decimal positions or, in other words, a whole number field) to an alphanumeric field. This is permissible and logical since numeric digits may appear in both numeric and alphanumeric fields.

Figure 5-30
De-editing with a numeric-edited sending field and a numeric receiving field MOVE.

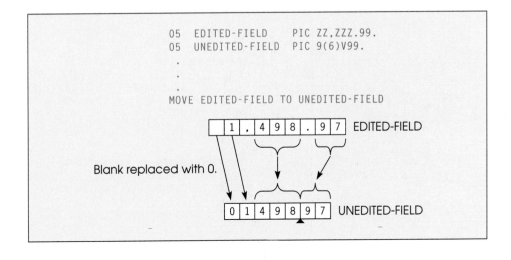

Such a MOVE operates in accordance with the alphanumeric-to-alphanumeric processing rules. That is, the entire number, including leading zeros, will be moved to the receiving field. If the receiving field is longer than the transmitting field, unused positions to the right are blank-space padded.

Qualification of Data-Names and MOVE/ CORRESPONDING

In forming data-names for the programs in this text, each one has been made unique. Use of data-name prefixes for the fields of a record (as was recommended in Chapter 2) almost ensures that all data-names will be different.

However, COBOL does not require that all fields within a program have different names. But, when a data-name is duplicated, there must be a unique data-name at a higher-level field (a data-item with a lower-level number) that can be used to differentiate the fields with the duplicate names. (By definition, then, each 01-level record-description data-name must be unique, since there can be no level-number hierarchically above 01.)

When a field with a duplicate data-name is referenced in the PROCEDURE DIVISION, it must be **qualified** by the data-name that differentiates it at a higher level. Otherwise, the COBOL compiler would not know which one of the fields with the duplicate names was being referenced. An example of duplicate data-names and qualification is shown in Figure 5-31. Notice that in the first three MOVE statements, each duplicated data-name is followed by the reserved word IN (or OF) which is, in turn, followed by the differentiating data-name at the higher level.

Overall, coding with data-name qualification is clumsy and prone to errors, so it is not widely used. However, it does offer an advantage in that a single MOVE CORRESPONDING statement can be used to move all fields with the same data-name. For instance, the example in Figure 5-31 will cause all fields of RECORD-IN with names identical to those in RECORD-OUT to be moved. In this case, the move action will be identical to that of the three moves shown. Notice that the field EMPLOYMENT-CODE will not be moved because it does not have a corresponding field in RECORD-OUT.

Referring to a Field by Two Different Names

There is another topic appropriate to the PATDFCT3 program that does not exactly fall under the category of the MOVE statement, but does provide the ability to access the same data in different forms.

Figure 5-31
Qualification of data-names and the MOVE CORRESPONDING.

```
01   RECORD-IN.
     05   EMPLOYMENT-CODE        PIC X(1).
     05   SS-NUMBER              PIC X(9).
     05   FULL-NAME.
          10   LAST-NAME         PIC X(13).
          10   FIRST-NAME        PIC X(11).
     .
     .
     .
01   RECORD-OUT.
     05   FULL-NAME.
          10   FIRST-NAME        PIC X(11).
          10   LAST-NAME         PIC X(13).
     05   SS-NUMBER              PIC X(9).
     .
     .
     .
     MOVE SS-NUMBER OF RECORD-IN TO SS-NUMBER OF RECORD-OUT
     MOVE FIRST-NAME OF RECORD-IN TO FIRST-NAME OF RECORD-OUT
     MOVE LAST-NAME OF RECORD-IN TO LAST-NAME OF RECORD-OUT

     MOVE CORRESPONDING RECORD-IN TO RECORD-OUT
```

Calculating Percentage Remember that one of the functions of PATDFCT3 was to calculate and print the patron deficiency percentage (deficiency-amount divided by target-contribution times 100). In the program, this was accomplished with the sequence shown in Figure 5-32. Notice that the fractional amount is multiplied by 100 and then moved to DL-DEFICIENCY-PERCENT (by the GIVING) to yield the desired percent.

In general, you will find that COBOL programs frequently deal with percentage fields. As an example, consider an inventory application in which each inventory item is assigned a discount rate; for example, 12.5%. In the data record, the rate would be stored as a three-digit number (125 in this case). What picture should you use for it in the input record? For calculations, you need V999; for output, you need 99V9. If you use V999 for calculations, then you must multiply it by 100 (as in the PATDFCT3 program) prior to moving it to the output area.

Another solution is to use a special DATA DIVISION clause called the REDEFINES, which allows you to describe an area of storage in two or more different ways.

The REDEFINES Clause The PATDFCT3 section of code is rewritten in Figure 5-33 to utilize the REDEFINES clause. This clause causes the three bytes of memory defined for WS-DEFICIENCY-FRACTION as PIC V999 to be given a second name (WS-DEFICIENCY-PERCENT) and picture (PIC 99V9). Remember that the data is stored in memory without the decimal point. If it is referred to as WS-DEFICIENCY-FRACTION, the assumed decimal point will be at the left. If that same data is referred to as WS-DEFICIENCY-PERCENT, the assumed decimal will be between the second and third digits (as desired for a percentage output).

Figure 5-32
Handling decimal-point positioning—the PATDFCT3 program.

```
05   WS-DEFICIENCY-FRACTION        PIC V9(3).  ◄──── Calculation is done
     .                                                —producing a
     .                                                fractional value
     .                                                (for instance, .731),
05   DL-DEFICIENCY-PERCENT         PIC ZZ.9.          which is then
     .                                                multiplied by 100 to
     .                                                produce the percent.
     .
DIVIDE PR-ACTUAL-CONTR BY PR-TARGET-CONTR
     GIVING WS-DEFICIENCY-FRACTION ROUNDED
MULTIPLY WS-DEFICIENCY-FRACTION BY 100  ◄
     GIVING DL-DEFICIENCY-PERCENT
```

Figure 5-33   Using the REDEFINES to handle decimal-point positioning.

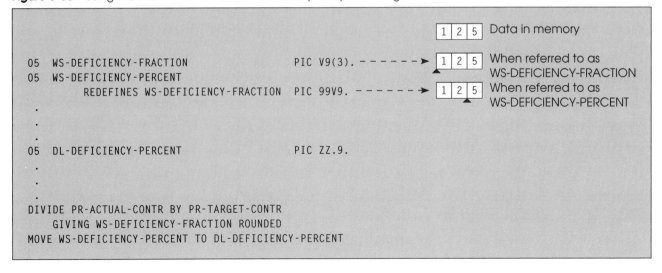

```
                                                        ┌─┬─┬─┐
                                                        │1│2│5│  Data in memory
                                                        └─┴─┴─┘
05   WS-DEFICIENCY-FRACTION              PIC V9(3). ─ ─ ─►┌─┬─┬─┐  When referred to as
05   WS-DEFICIENCY-PERCENT                               │1│2│5│  WS-DEFICIENCY-FRACTION
         REDEFINES WS-DEFICIENCY-FRACTION PIC 99V9. ─ ─ ─►┌─┬─┬─┐  When referred to as
     .                                                   │1│2│5│  WS-DEFICIENCY-PERCENT
     .
     .
05   DL-DEFICIENCY-PERCENT               PIC ZZ.9.
     .
     .
     .
DIVIDE PR-ACTUAL-CONTR BY PR-TARGET-CONTR
     GIVING WS-DEFICIENCY-FRACTION ROUNDED
MOVE WS-DEFICIENCY-PERCENT TO DL-DEFICIENCY-PERCENT
```

The general format and several examples of the REDEFINES are shown in Figure 5-34. Five syntactical rules are used when specifying the REDEFINES clause:

- The REDEFINES clause must be coded immediately after the data-name in the data-item description entry.

- The redefining entry (the field coded with the REDEFINES clause) cannot require more storage positions than the redefined field. In other words, the field with the REDEFINES clause cannot be longer than the redefined field; it must be either equal in length or shorter. *Note*: This restriction does not apply to COBOL-85.

- The redefining entry must immediately follow, at that level-number, the area being redefined.

Figure 5-34 The REDEFINES clause.

Valid REDEFINES entry examples

Valid: The REDEFINES field is shorter than the field being redefined.

```
05  XDATE                     PIC X(6).
05  MONTH REDEFINES XDATE     PIC X(2).
```

Valid: Elementary field REDEFINES group field.

```
05  GROUP-DATE.
    10  MONTH                 PIC X(2).
    10  XDAY                  PIC X(2).
    10  YEAR                  PIC X(2).
05  NUMERIC-DATE
        REDEFINES GROUP-DATE  PIC 9(6).
```

Valid: Group field REDEFINES elementary field.

```
05  NUMERIC-DATE                        PIC 9(6).
05  GROUP-DATE REDEFINES NUMERIC-DATE.
    10  MONTH                           PIC X(2).
    10  XDAY                            PIC X(2).
    10  YEAR                            PIC X(2).
```

Valid: Multiple REDEFINES entries (note that each entry must refer back to the original entry—not to another REDEFINES item).

```
05  ALPHA-DATE                PIC X(6).
05  NUMERIC-DATE
        REDEFINES ALPHA-DATE  PIC 9(6).
05  NUMERIC-MONTH
        REDEFINES ALPHA-DATE  PIC 9(2).
```

Invalid REDEFINES entry examples

Invalid: The REDEFINES field is longer than the field being redefined (valid in COBOL-85).

```
05  MONTH                     PIC X(2).
05  XDATE REDEFINES MONTH     PIC X(6).
```

Invalid: The REDEFINES field is not at the same level as the redefined field.

```
10  ALPHA-DATE                PIC X(6).
05  NUMERIC-DATE
        REDEFINES ALPHA-DATE  PIC 9(6).
```

Invalid: The REDEFINES entry does not immediately follow the field being redefined.

```
05  ALPHA-DATE                PIC X(6).
05  QUANTITY                  PIC S9(5).
05  NUMERIC-DATE
        REDEFINES ALPHA-DATE  PIC 9(6).
```

Invalid: Multiple REDEFINES entries with the second one referencing a REDEFINES item rather than the original redefined item.

```
05  ALPHA-DATE                  PIC X(6).
05  NUMERIC-DATE
        REDEFINES ALPHA-DATE    PIC 9(6).
05  NUMERIC-MONTH
        REDEFINES NUMERIC-DATE  PIC 9(2).
```

■ A field that contains a REDEFINES clause cannot be redefined. (However, the redefined entry can have multiple redefinitions.)

■ The field with the REDEFINES clause cannot contain a VALUE clause.

Again, remember that a field specified with the REDEFINES clause does not define additional areas of storage or different data. Rather, it permits a different name and/or a different PICTURE clause to be assigned to the same area of storage.

Chapter Summary
Topic: Improving the PATDFCT Program

The PICTURE tells the compiler the type of field being defined and the amount of memory to be reserved for it. If the VALUE clause is included (WORKING-STORAGE SECTION only), the compiler will load the field with the value indicated in the clause.

If a program is to have more than one print line, then it is convenient to define each output line as a separate record in the WORKING-STORAGE SECTION. The line can be printed with either the WRITE/FROM or the WRITE by first moving the output line from WORKING-STORAGE to the output field.

The IF/ELSE statement allows either of two actions to be taken, depending upon a condition test. This is the full implementation of the structured programming selection structure.

Topic: PICTURE Clauses

PICTURE clauses describe the following characteristics of fields:

1. Data class
2. Length (number of digits or characters)
3. Assumed decimal-point location (for numeric fields)
4. Arithmetic-sign presence (for numeric fields)
5. Editing to be performed

There are five PICTURE clause categories:

1. Numeric
2. Alphabetic
3. Alphanumeric
4. Numeric-edited
5. Alphanumeric-edited

To form PICTURE clauses, the programmer can use the picture symbols summarized in Figure 5-35. A detailed description of each of these is given in a following section entitled "COBOL Picture Symbol Summary."

Certain other DATA DIVISION clauses are related to PICTURE clauses. The BLANK WHEN ZERO clause can be specified in the data-item description entry for a numeric or numeric-edited field. When a value of zero is transferred to a field specified with the BLANK WHEN ZERO, blank spaces—rather than the normal editing specified in the PICTURE clause—will appear in the field.

Topic: The MOVE Statement

Depending upon the MOVE statement sending and receiving field characteristics, one or more of the following actions may occur: right or left justification, truncation, padding, and/or decimal-point alignment. Common categories with the resulting actions are listed in the four groups on the following pages.

Figure 5-35   Summary of picture symbols.

Data category	Symbol	Meaning	Data category	Symbol	Meaning
Numeric	9	Numeric digit	Numeric-edited (continued)		
	V	Assumed decimal point	Special insertion	.	Decimal point
	S	Arithmetic sign			
	P	Assumed decimal scaling position	Fixed insertion	–	Minus sign (fixed)
				+	Plus sign (fixed)
Alphabetic	A	Alphabetic character		CR	Credit symbol
				DB	Debit symbol
Alphanumeric	X	Alphanumeric character		$	Dollar sign (fixed)
Numeric-edited			Floating insertion	–	Minus sign (floating)
Suppression and replacement	Z	Zero suppression with blank space replacement		+	Plus sign (floating)
				$	Dollar sign (floating)
	*	Zero suppression with asterisk replacement	Alphanumeric-edited	/	Slash (stroke, diagonal)
				B	Blank space
Simple insertion	,	Comma		0	Zero
	/	Slash (stroke, diagonal)			
	B	Blank space			
	0	Zero			

Group 1: **Alphanumeric sending field to alphanumeric receiving field**

or

Numeric integer sending field to alphanumeric receiving field

or

Group sending field

or

Group receiving field

- Left justification in receiving field.

- If the receiving field is shorter, excess rightmost positions from the sending field are truncated.

- If the receiving field is longer, excess rightmost positions in the receiving field are padded with spaces.

Group 2: **Alphanumeric sending field to alphanumeric-edited receiving field**

- Same actions as Group 1.

- Also, editing is performed for the receiving field in accordance with its PICTURE clause.

Group 3: **Numeric sending field to numeric receiving field**

- Decimal-point alignment.

- If the receiving is shorter (on either side of the decimal point), excess sending field digits are truncated.

- If the receiving field is longer (on either side of the decimal point), excess receiving field positions are padded with zeros.

Group 4: **Numeric sending field to numeric-edited receiving field**

■ Same actions as Group 3.

■ Also, editing is performed for the receiving field in accordance with its PICTURE clause.

By the conventions adopted in this book, duplication of data-name should not occur. However, data-names need not be unique. But, when a data-name is duplicated, there must be a unique data-name at a higher-level field (a data-item with a lower-level number) that can be used to qualify the fields with the duplicate names.

The REDEFINES clause is used in the DATA DIVISION to assign more than one data-name and/or PICTURE clause to an area of memory.

COBOL Picture Symbol Summary

Symbol category	Symbol	Description and syntactical requirements
Alphanumeric	X	**Alphanumeric character**
Alphabetic	A	**Alphabetic character**
Numeric	9	**Numeric digit** ■ Each numeric picture character-string must contain at least one 9 symbol. ■ Up to 18 digits may be specified for a numeric field.
	V	**Assumed decimal point** ■ Only one V may be specified within a numeric picture character-string. ■ The V is not counted toward the length of the field. ■ The V is not required for integer (whole number) fields.

	S	**Arithmetic sign.** The S symbol should generally be specified for:
		    Numeric fields in the FILE SECTION that should or may carry an arithmetic sign.
		    Numeric fields in the WORKING-STORAGE SECTION that will be operated on arithmetically.
		■ Only one S may be specified within a numeric picture character-string.
		■ When specified, the S must be the leftmost symbol of the picture character-string.
		■ The S symbol is not usually counted toward the length of the field.
		■ If an S is not specified for a numeric field, the field's contents will be treated as an absolute value.

	P	**Assumed decimal scaling position.** It is a placeholder to scale to the decimal point. It is not used in this book.

COBOL Picture Symbol
Summary (continued)

Symbol category	Symbol	Description and syntactical requirements
Numeric-Edited	Z	**Zero suppression with blank-space replacement.** Normally used to make fields on output reports and displays more readable. ■ Any number (up to 18) of Z symbols may be specified. ■ The Z symbol cannot be preceded by a 9 symbol. ■ If a Z symbol is specified to the right of a decimal point, then all digit positions of the picture character-string must be represented by the Z symbol.
	*	**Zero suppression with asterisk replacement.** Normally used for check protection. ■ Any number of * symbols (up to 18) may be specified. ■ The * symbol cannot be preceded by a 9 symbol. ■ If an * symbol is specified to the right of a decimal point, then all digit positions of the picture character-string must be represented by the * symbol.
	,	**Comma.** Normally used to improve readability when numeric output report or display fields contain over 3 or 4 integer digit positions. ■ Any number of comma symbols may be specified. ■ The comma symbol may be specified at any location, except as the rightmost symbol of the picture character-string.
	/	**Slash.** Normally used to separate the month, day, and year of dates expressed in six-digit format. ■ Any number of slash symbols may be specified. ■ The slash symbol can be specified at any location within the picture character-string.
	B	**Blank space.** Normally used to separate groups of digits and/or letters for readability. ■ Any number of B symbols may be specified. ■ The B symbol can be specified at any location within the picture character-string.
	0	**Zero.** Does not have many applications, but sometimes convenient for appending zeros to the end or beginning of a value. ■ Any number of zero symbols may be specified. ■ The zero symbol can be specified at any location within the picture character-string.

COBOL Picture Symbol
Summary (continued)

Symbol category	Symbol	Description and syntactical requirements
Numeric-Edited (continued)	.	**Decimal Point**. An actual decimal point typically used for display on reports and display screens. ■ Only one decimal point symbol may be specified within a numeric-editing picture character-string. ■ The decimal point cannot be specified as the rightmost character of a picture character-string.
	−	**Fixed minus sign**. Normally specified as the rightmost symbol to identify negative values for signed numeric fields. ■ Only one fixed minus-sign symbol may be specified in a picture character-string. ■ The fixed minus-sign symbol must be specified as either the leftmost or the rightmost symbol of the picture character-string. ■ If the field value is negative, the minus sign will be printed; if the field value is positive or zero, a blank space will appear.
	+	**Fixed plus sign**. Normally specified as the rightmost symbol to identify positive and negative values for signed numeric fields. ■ Only one fixed plus-sign symbol may be specified in a picture character-string. ■ The fixed plus-sign symbol must be specified as either the leftmost or the rightmost symbol of the picture character-string. ■ If the field value is positive or zero, the plus sign will be printed; if the field value is negative, a minus sign will be printed.
	CR	**Credit symbol**. Normally used to identify credit balances on invoices, customer statements, financial statements, and other formal reports. ■ Only one CR symbol may be specified in a picture character-string. ■ The CR symbol must be specified as the rightmost symbol of the picture character-string. ■ If the field value is negative, the CR symbol will be printed; if the field value is positive or zero, two blank spaces will appear.
	DB	**Debit symbol**. Not used very often, except for certain accounting reports. ■ Only one DB symbol may be specified in a picture character-string. ■ The DB symbol must be specified as the rightmost symbol of the picture character-string. ■ If the field value is negative, the DB symbol will be printed; if the field value is positive or zero, two blank spaces will appear.

COBOL Picture Symbol
Summary (continued)

Symbol category	Symbol	Description and syntactical requirements
Numeric-Edited (continued)	$	**Fixed currency sign.** Normally specified to identify dollar amounts on invoices, customer statements, financial reports, and other formal reports.
		■ Only one fixed $ symbol may be specified in a picture character-string.
		■ The fixed $ symbol must be specified as the leftmost symbol of the picture character-string.
	−	**Floating minus sign.** Normally specified to identify negative values for signed numeric fields in those situations in which a minus sign is desired on the lefthand side of a zero-suppressed value.
		■ The floating minus-sign symbol is coded in the leftmost position of the picture character-string and repeated for each position through which the minus sign is to float.
		■ If a floating minus-sign symbol is coded to the right of a decimal point, then all digit positions to the right of the decimal point must be represented by floating minus-sign symbols.
		■ If the field value is negative, the minus sign will be printed; if the field value is positive or zero, a blank space will appear.
	+	**Floating plus sign.** Normally specified to identify positive and negative values for signed numeric fields in those situations in which the plus or minus sign is desired on the left-hand side of a zero-suppressed value.
		■ The floating plus-sign symbol is coded in the leftmost position of the picture character-string and repeated for each position through which the plus or minus sign is to float.
		■ If a floating plus-sign symbol is coded to the right of a decimal point, then all digit positions to the right of the decimal point must be represented by floating plus-sign symbols.
		■ If the field value is positive or zero, the plus sign will be printed; if the field value is negative, a minus sign will be printed. However, if (1) all the digit positions of the picture character-string are represented by the floating plus sign, and (2) the value of the field is zero, then the entire field will appear as blank spaces.

COBOL Picture Symbol
Summary (continued)

Symbol category	Symbol	Description and syntactical requirements
Numeric-Edited (continued)	$	**Floating currency sign.** Normally specified to identify dollar amounts on invoices, customer statements, financial reports, and other formal reports.
		■ The floating currency-sign symbol is coded in the leftmost position of the picture character-string and repeated for each position through which the currency sign is to float.
		■ If a floating currency-sign symbol is coded to the right of a decimal point, then all digit positions to the right of the decimal point must be represented by floating currency-sign symbols.
Alphanumeric-Edited		Refer to the counterpart symbol in the preceding numeric-edited category; the alphanumeric-edited symbols have the same usage and syntactical requirements.
	/	**Slash**
	B	**Blank space**
	0	**Zero**

Style Summary

■ Do not use the alphabetic PICTURE symbol A. Instead, use the symbol X for both alphabetic and alphanumeric fields.

■ When an entire field is defined by the same symbol (or the same symbol plus an S), use the parentheses method to express the field length. For example, a seven-character alphanumeric field can be defined as PIC X(7); an eight-integer, signed numeric field can be defined as PIC S9(8).

■ When a V appears in a numeric picture character-string, use the parentheses method before the V and the repetition method after it. For example, PIC 9(8)V99.

■ If a PICTURE character-string contains editing symbols, code each symbol with the repetition method so that the desired editing is more easily readable. That is, code PIC $ZZ,ZZZ.99– rather than PIC $Z(2),Z(3).9(2)–.

Features in COBOL-85 Not in COBOL-74

The de-editing MOVE (move an edited field to a nonedited field) provides for the removal of editing symbols. With appropriately defined pictures, it works exactly the opposite of an editing move.

The field specified with a REDEFINES clause can be longer than the field being redefined.

Exercises

Terms for Definition   alphabetic data-item _____

alphanumeric data-item _____

alphanumeric-edited data-item _____

check protection _____

edit _____

justified _____

leading zeros _____

numeric data-item _____

numeric-edited data-item _____

truncated _____

zero suppression _____

Review Questions   1. Name the five characteristics of fields that PICTURE clauses describe.

a.   _____

b.   _____

c.   _____

d.   _____

e.   _____

2. List the five data-class categories of PICTURE clauses.

a.   _____

b.   _____

c.   _____

d.   _____

e.   _____

3. Identify the PICTURE symbol and category for each of the following:

PICTURE Category

PICTURE symbol	Alphanumeric	Alphabetic	Numeric	Numeric-Edited	Alphanumeric-Edited	
a. _____	☐	☐	☐	☐	☐	Numeric digit
b. _____	☐	☐	☐	☐	☐	Signed field
c. _____	☐	☐	☐	☐	☐	Assumed decimal point
d. _____	☐	☐	☐	☐	☐	Decimal scaling position
e. _____	☐	☐	☐	☐	☐	Alphabetic character
f. _____	☐	☐	☐	☐	☐	Alphanumeric character
g. _____	☐	☐	☐	☐	☐	Zero suppression with blank-space replacement
h. _____	☐	☐	☐	☐	☐	Zero suppression with asterisk replacement
i. _____	☐	☐	☐	☐	☐	Comma insertion
j. _____	☐	☐	☐	☐	☐	Slash insertion
k. _____	☐	☐	☐	☐	☐	Zero insertion
l. _____	☐	☐	☐	☐	☐	Blank-space insertion
m. _____	☐	☐	☐	☐	☐	Decimal-point insertion
n. _____	☐	☐	☐	☐	☐	Minus sign
o. _____	☐	☐	☐	☐	☐	Plus sign
p. _____	☐	☐	☐	☐	☐	Credit symbol
q. _____	☐	☐	☐	☐	☐	Debit symbol
r. _____	☐	☐	☐	☐	☐	Currency sign

4. Write PICTURE character-strings for the following field specifications.

a. PIC_____   Five integer-digit unsigned numeric.

b. PIC_____   Seven integer-digit signed numeric.

c. PIC_____   Eight-digit (six integers; two decimal places) unsigned numeric.

d. PIC_____   Three-digit (no integers; three decimal places) signed numeric.

e. PIC_____   Two integer-digit representing thousands and hundreds positions (tens and units positions are not stored for the value) unsigned numeric.

f. PIC_____   One digit representing mils position of a cent amount (tens and hundreds decimal places are not stored for the value) unsigned numeric.

g. PIC _____ Twenty-two position alphanumeric.

h. PIC _____ Three integer-digit edited with full leading zero suppression with blank-space replacement.

i. PIC _____ Four-digit dollars-and-cents (two integer positions; two decimal places) edited with a fixed dollar sign and zero suppression with blank-space replacement of the dollar positions.

j. PIC _____ Nine-digit (seven integers; two decimal positions) edited with full zero suppression (print nothing for a zero value) and standard comma insertion.

k. PIC _____ Five-digit dollars-and-cents (three integer positions; two decimal places) edited with a floating dollar sign.

l. PIC _____ Six-digit dollars-and-cents (four integer positions; two decimal places) edited with a fixed dollar sign and zero suppression with asterisk replacement of the dollar positions.

m. PIC _____ Five-digit (all integers) edited with zero suppression with blank-space replacement (of all but the units position) and with a fixed minus sign as the rightmost position (provide standard comma insertion).

n. PIC _____ Six-digit date field edited with slash insertion.

o. PIC _____ Nine-digit Social Security field edited with blank spaces (where hyphens are typically placed).

5. To cause blank spaces to appear in a numeric or numeric-edited field when the value of the data within the _____ field is zero, the clause can be specified.

6. For numeric fields with special or nonstandard arithmetic-sign representation, the _____ clause is specified.

7. When the same data-name is specified for more than one field in the DATA DIVISION, _____ of that data-name is required in the PROCEDURE DIVISION.

8. When the REDEFINES clause is coded, it must immediately follow the _____ in the data-item description entry.

9. When using the REDEFINES clause, the redefining field (the one with the REDEFINES clause) must not be _____ than the redefined field. Also, the redefining entry must immediately _____, at that level-number, the field being redefined.

10. A field specified with a REDEFINES clause cannot contain a(n)

_____ clause or a(n) _____ clause.

Syntax/Debug Exercises

1. Some of the following VALUE clause specifications are not syntactically correct. Place a check mark adjacent to each erroneous entry.

```
☐  05  AMOUNT      PIC S9(5)      VALUE -5.
☐  05  AMOUNT      PIC S9(5)      VALUE 00000.
☐  05  AMOUNT      PIC S9(5)      VALUE ZEROS.
☐  05  AMOUNT      PIC S9(5)      VALUE SPACES
☐  05  AMOUNT      PIC S9(5)      VALUE +555555.
☐  05  AMOUNT      PIC S9(5)      VALUE "81786".
☐  05  AMOUNT      PIC S9(5)      VALUE +3.1416.
☐  05  DOLLARS     PIC S9(3)V99   VALUE +99998.
☐  05  DOLLARS     PIC S9(3)V99   VALUE 99998.
☐  05  DOLLARS     PIC S9(3)V99   VALUE -998.98.
☐  05  DOLLARS     PIC S9(3)V99   VALUE -998V98.
☐  05  DOLLARS     PIC S9(3)V99   VALUE 99.998.
☐  05  CODE-A      PIC 9(4)       VALUE +1234.
☐  05  CODE-A      PIC 9(4)       VALUE 12V34.
☐  05  FIELD-B     PIC X(3)       VALUE SPACES.
☐  05  FIELD-B     PIC X(3)       VALUE ZEROS.
☐  05  FIELD-B     PIC X(3)       VALUE 123.
☐  05  FIELD-B     PIC X(3)       VALUE "123".
☐  05  FIELD-B     PIC X(3)       VALUE "ABC".
```

2. Some of the following PICTURE character-strings are in error. Place a check mark adjacent to each erroneous entry.

```
☐  PIC 9(X)          ☐  PIC ZZ,ZZ,ZZ       ☐  PIC -ZZZ.99-
☐  PIC 9(5)V         ☐  PIC ZZ.ZZ.ZZ       ☐  PIC ZZ,ZZZ.ZZ
☐  PIC S9(5)V99      ☐  PIC ZZ,ZZZ.Z9      ☐  PIC Z9/Z9/99
☐  PIC 9(3)S         ☐  PIC +ZZZ,ZZZ       ☐  PIC XX/XX/XX
☐  PIC S(9)          ☐  PIC ZZZ,Z77+       ☐  PIC 999B99B9999
☐  PIC ZZ,Z99.99     ☐  PIC 99,999.99      ☐  PIC XXXBXXBXXXX
☐  PIC ZZ,ZZ9.ZZ     ☐  PIC $*,***.99CR    ☐  PIC 99900
☐  PIC 9(19)         ☐  PIC $Z,ZZZ.99DR    ☐  PIC XXX00
☐  PIC X(19)         ☐  PIC ----9.99       ☐  PIC +++,++9
```

3. Some of the following MOVE statements are not syntactically correct. Place a check mark adjacent to each erroneous entry.

```
DATA DIVISION.
    .
    .
    .
01  MISCELLANEOUS-FIELDS
    05  NUMERIC-INTEGER-FIELD        PIC 9(7).
    05  NUMERIC-DEC-POSN-FIELD       PIC S9(5)V99.
    05  NUMERIC-EDITED-FIELD         PIC ZZ,ZZZ.99-.
    05  ALPHANUMERIC-FIELD           PIC X(7).
    05  ALPHANUMERIC-EDITED-FIELD    PIC XX/XX/XX.
    .
    .
    .
PROCEDURE DIVISION.
    .
    .
    .
```

```
☐  MOVE ALPHANUMERIC-FIELD TO NUMERIC-INTEGER-FIELD
☐  MOVE NUMERIC-INTEGER-FIELD TO ALPHANUMERIC-FIELD
☐  MOVE NUMERIC-DEC-POSN-FIELD TO ALPHANUMERIC-FIELD
☐  MOVE ALPHANUMERIC-FIELD TO NUMERIC-DEC-POSN-FIELD
☐  MOVE NUMERIC-INTEGER-FIELD TO NUMERIC-EDITED-FIELD
☐  MOVE ALPHANUMERIC-FIELD TO NUMERIC-EDITED-FIELD
☐  MOVE NUMERIC-EDITED-FIELD TO NUMERIC-EDITED-FIELD
☐  MOVE NUMERIC-INTEGER-FIELD TO ALPHANUMERIC-EDITED-FIELD
☐  MOVE NUMERIC-DEC-POSN-FIELD TO MISCELLANEOUS-FIELDS
☐  MOVE ALPHANUMERIC-FIELD TO MISCELLANEOUS-FIELDS
```

4. Some of the following REDEFINES clause specifications are not syntactically correct. Place a check mark adjacent to each erroneous entry.

```
a. ☐   05  FLD-A                          PIC X(5).
        05  FLD-R REDEFINES FLD-A         PIC 9(5).

b. ☐   05  FLD-BPIC 9(5).
        05  FLD-S REDEFINES FLD-B         PIC X(6).

c. ☐   05  FLD-C                          PIC X(6).
        05  FLD-T REDEFINES FLD-C         PIC 9(5).

d. ☐   05  FLD-D                          PIC X(6).
        05  FLD-U REDEFINES FLD-C         PIC 9(6).

e. ☐   05  FLD-E.
            10  FLD-E1                     PIC X(5).
            10  FLD-E2                     PIC S9(5).
        05  FLD-V REDEFINES FLD-E         PIC X(10).

f. ☐   05  FLD-F.
            10    FLD-F1                   PIC X(1).
            10    FLD-F2                   PIC X(2).
            10  FLD-W REDEFINES FLD-F      PIC 9(3).

g. ☐   05  FLD-G                          PIC X(5).
        05  FLD-X REDEFINES FLD-G         PIC 9(5).
        05  FLD-Y REDEFINES FLD-X         PIC 9(3)V99.
```

Programming Assignments

Programming Assignment 5-1: Understocked Inventory Report

You must modify the program of Assignment 4-1 to process every record of the Tools Unlimited inventory file as described by the following.

Output report-line formats:
Heading line.
Use appropriate column headings.

Detail line.

Position	Field	Comments
4–14	Product identification	Print in form *xxxx/xxxxxx* (insert a slash between subfields).
17–42	Product description	
45–49	Reorder point	Insert comma, zero suppress, blank if zero.
52–56	Quantity on hand	Same as reorder point.
60–65	Inventory overage	Insert comma, zero suppress, insert a minus sign to the right if number is negative.

Summary line.
The same data is to be printed as with 4-1.

Position	Field	Comments
13–36	Description	SHORTFALL RECORDS COUNT:
38–40	Number of records with shortfall	Zero suppress
51–58	Description	AMOUNT:
59–64	Total shortfall amount	Insert comma, zero suppress

Program operations:

1. Process every record.
2. Calculate Inventory-overage as

   Quantity-in-stock minus Reorder-level

3. Totals are to be accumulated as in 4-1.

Programming Assignment 5-2: Salesperson Performance Report

You must modify the program of Assignment 4-2 to process every record of the Follow-the-Sun salesperson file, as described by the following.

Output report-line formats:
Heading line.
Use appropriate column headings.

Detail line.

Positions	Field	Comments
3–4	Salesperson region	
5	Hyphen	Print a hyphen.
6–9	Salesperson territory	
12–14	Salesperson number	
17–42	Salesperson name	
45–48	Product-units sold	Zero suppress leading zeros, insert floating minus sign, blank if zero.
50–54	Commission percentage	Suppress leading integer digits, print a decimal point.
55	Percent sign	Print a percent sign.
58–67	Amount of sales	Print a fixed dollar sign, zero suppress with asterisk replacing leading dollar digits, insert a comma, print a decimal point.
72–80	Commission amount	Same as Amount-of-sales.

Summary line.
Insert appropriate descriptions into the summary line.

Positions	Field	Comments
You select	Total amount of sales	Print a fixed dollar sign, zero suppress with asterisk replacing leading dollar digits, insert commas, print a decimal point.
	Total commission amount	Print a fixed dollar sign, zero suppress with asterisk replacing leading dollar digits, insert a comma, print a decimal point.

Programming Assignment 5-3: Gross-Pay Report

You must modify the program of Assignment 4-3 to print the Silicon Valley Manufacturing gross-pay report as follows.

Output report-line formats:
Heading line.
Use appropriate column headings.

Detail line.

Positions	Field name	Comments
4–14	Employee number	Print in form *xxx-xx-xxxx* (insert hyphens).
17–28	Employee last name	
30–38	Employee first name	
44–49	Hours worked	Zero-suppress leading hour digits, print a decimal point.
54–61	Base pay	Zero-suppress leading hour digits, print a decimal point, insert a comma.
66–73	Shift-differential pay	Same as Base-pay (except no comma).
78–85	Gross pay	Same as Base-pay.

Summary line.

Positions	Field name	Comments
30–36	The word TOTALS:	
42–49	Total hours worked	Zero-suppress leading hour digits, print a decimal point, insert a comma.
52–61	Total base pay	Zero-suppress leading hour digits, print a decimal point, insert a comma.
65–73	Total Shift-differential pay	Same as Total base-pay.
76–85	Total gross pay	Same as Total base-pay.
86	Total indication	Print an asterisk.

Program operations:
1. Process as in Assignment 4-3.
2. Calculated quantities for detail output are:

   Base-pay is Hours-worked times Pay-rate.

   If the Shift-differential code equals N, Shift-differential-pay is 0.1 times Base-pay (otherwise it is 0).

   Gross-pay is Base-pay plus Shift-differential-pay.

3. Totals are to be accumulated for:

   Hours-worked

   Base-pay

   Shift-differential-pay

   Gross-pay

Programming Assignment 5-4: Accounts-Receivable Report

You must modify the program of Assignment 4-4 to print the Silicon Valley Manufacturing accounts-receivable report as follows; note that the new report must print two summary lines.

Output report-line formats:
Heading line.
Use appropriate column headings.

Detail line.

Positions	Field name	Comments
1–5	Customer number	
7–30	Customer name	
33–43	Balance forward	Zero-suppress leading dollar digits, insert commas, print a decimal point, print a rightmost fixed minus sign for a negative value.
45–55	New purchases	Same as Balance-forward.
57–67	Payments received	Same as Balance-forward.
69–79	New balance	Same as Balance-forward.

First summary line.

Positions	Field name	Comments
16–28	Description	REPORT TOTALS
30–43	Total balance forward	Zero-suppress leading dollar digits, insert commas, print a decimal point, print a rightmost fixed minus sign for a negative value.
44	Total indication	Print an asterisk (*).
54–67	Total payments received	Same as Total-balance-forward.
68	Total indication	Print an asterisk.

Second summary line.

Positions	Field name	Comments
42–55	Total new purchases	Zero-suppress leading dollar digits, insert commas, print a decimal point, print a rightmost fixed minus sign for a negative value.
56	Total indication	Print an asterisk (*).
66–79	Total new balance	Same as Total-new-purchases.
80	Total indication	Print an asterisk.

Program operations:

1. Process as in Assignment 4-4 (except that all records are to be processed).
2. Totals are to be accumulated for:

   Balance-forward

   Payments-received

   New-purchases

   New-balance

Programming Assignment 5-5: Nurses' Salary Increase Projection

You must modify the program of Assignment 4-5 to process every record of the Brooklawn Hospital file as described by the following.

Output report-line formats:
Heading line.
Use appropriate column headings.

Detail line.

Positions	Field	Comments
1–23	Name	
26–33	Date-hired	Format *mm/dd/yy*
35	Shift code	
37–45	New base	Insert a floating dollar sign, decimal point, insert a comma, suppress leading dollar zeros.
47–53	Shift differential	Insert a floating dollar sign, decimal point, suppress leading dollar zeros.
55–63	New total	Same as New base.

Total line.
Insert a total line that displays the total number of records processed, the number of Shift-code 1 records processed, and the New-total. You plan the format.

Program operations:
1. Process each record.
2. Totals are to be accumulated for:

   Record count

   Shift-code 1 record count

   New-total

Programming Assignment 5-6: Vehicle Rental Application

You must modify the program of Assignment 2-6 (*not* 4-6) to process Rent-Ur-Wheels file records in which the Status field contains "R".

Heading line.
Use appropriate column headings.

Detail line.

Positions	Field	Comments
3–6	Vehicle type	
9–22	Make of vehicle	
25–31	License number	
35–39	Date due back	Format *mm/dd*
42–47	Daily rental fee	Insert decimal point, floating dollar sign.
50–62	Customer phone number	Insert punctuation, for example: (415)555-1234
64–79	Customer last name	

Total line:

Insert a total line that displays the total number of records processed, the average daily rental fee of those records processed, and appropriate description.

Program operations:

1. Process only those records for vehicles that are rented (Status field equal to "R").

2. Totals are to be accumulated for:

   Record count for rented vehicles

   Daily-rental-fee

3. For the summary line. calculate Average-daily-rental-fee as:

   Total of daily-rental-fees divided by Record count for rented vehicles

Programming Assignment 5-7: Bookstore Inventory Application

You must modify the program of Assignment 4-7 for Granger and Heatherford to print more output information. For this assignment, you must do all format planning. The output report must include a column heading line, detail lines, and a summary line with appropriate descriptions.

The detail lines must print the following:

Author

Title

Reorder level

Quantity on order

Date of last order

Quantity on hand

Unit cost

Inventory value (Quantity on hand times Unit cost)

The total line must include:

Total number of books on hand

Total number of books on order

Total inventory value

Use editing that is appropriate to each of the fields.

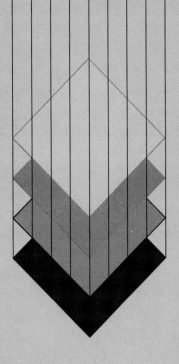

CONCEPTS MODULE

Principles of Report Design

Module Objectives

Throughout this book, emphasis has been placed on designing your printed output so that it clearly illustrates the information you are trying to convey. To this end, each example has utilized a print chart in laying out the printed form. From Chapter 5, you learned about improving the appearance of a report through the use of appropriate description lines and by editing your output fields. This concepts module describes many of the factors that you must consider in the real-world environment of report generation. You should note that the principles described here apply to report generation in general, not simply to report generation using the COBOL programming language. From this module, you will learn the following:

- The printed report page is commonly considered to be comprised of three areas: the heading area, the body area, and the grand-total area.

- Some of the basic guidelines for good report design are:

    Provide heading standard information to identify the report.
    Label all output data and position column headings properly.
    Plan positioning of fields and provide adequate spacing to make the report easy to read.
    Use editing that is appropriate to the application.
    Include page totals when appropriate.

Module Outline

Report Areas
Heading Area
Body Area
Grand-Total Area

Printer Specifications

Report Design Guidelines
Identify the Report and Standardize the Heading-Identification Area
Label All Output Fields
Position Column Headings Properly

Determine Report Width and Length
Consider Margin Requirements
Make the Report Visually Attractive
Allow Sufficient Space for Numeric Results
Consider Intercolumn Space Requirements
Choose Suitable Negative-Value Indication
Use Appropriate Editing
Use Underlining Sparingly
Consider Page Totals for Certain Reports
Use Asterisks to Identify Total Levels
Provide Check Protection for Check Amounts

Report Areas   From Chapter 5, you have seen three types of output lines: column headings positioned at the beginning of the report, detail lines, and total lines positioned at the end of the report. As you have seen, these add significantly to the appearance of the report. However, all of these examples represent a special case not usually encountered in report generation: the output has been limited to a single page. No provisions have been made to accommodate reports covering two or more pages. To address this need, we will consider a report as consisting of three general data areas: the heading area, the body area, and the grand-total area. Figure E-1 identifies each of these areas.

Heading Area   The **heading area** of a report should contain data that will identify the report. Common examples of such data are report title, organization name, report date, and page number. Larger organizations usually print a report-code number on the document to uniquely identify each report and facilitate identification of the computer program that prepared the report.

When dates are printed on reports, it is often appropriate to print two dates: (1) the date to which the report applies (this is called a **period-ending date**), and (2) the date when the computer actually printed or processed the report (the **run date**). Consider, for example, an income statement for the month of October 1991. The period-ending date of 10/31/91 should, of course, be printed in the report heading. But this income statement will probably not be processed until sometime in early November. Provision of a run date—in addition to the period-ending date—is very helpful in case the report is modified, corrected, or revised at a later date.

The bottom part of the heading area usually contains column headings for the detail-line fields printed in the body area below it.

Headings are typically repeated on each page of a report. **Page headings** are the most common type of heading and are repeated on each page of a report. Once in a while, an overall **report heading**, containing prefatory material, is printed before the first page heading.

Figure E-1   Report areas.

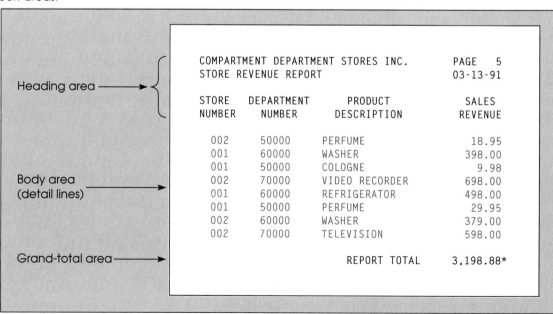

Body Area   The **body area** of a report contains detail lines, summary lines, and/or subtotal lines. As you know from previous examples, a **detail line** is a line that is logically related to an input record, usually on a one-to-one basis. If one or more body lines are printed for each input record, such lines are considered detail lines. A **summary line** is one in which multiple input records (but not all the records of the file) are accumulated or otherwise summarized and printed as one report line. A **subtotal line** presents an accumulation of previously printed detail or summary lines. Subtotal lines are often termed **control-break lines**.

When page totals or other data is printed at the bottom of each page of the report, the area in which it is printed is termed the **page-footing area**.

Grand-Total Area   The **grand-total area** is usually at the end of the report. Commonly printed in this area are items such as record counts, grand totals for columns, and the results of calculations (such as averages, percentages, and so forth) that must be made after all applicable input records have been processed. Descriptive words to identify the total figures are also commonly provided. A report line that contains such data is called a **total line**; you are familiar with total lines from Chapters 4 and 5.

Printer Specifications

Most mainframe-computer line printers provide a maximum of 132 print positions for each horizontal report line. Serial character printers used with microcomputers typically can print from 80–144 characters across the line.

With impact line printers, characters are almost always printed at 10 characters per inch (in typewriting terminology, this is called pica or **10-pitch**). Most serial character printers are capable of printing at other pitch rates; 12 characters per inch (elite or **12-pitch**) and 17 characters per inch (**compressed printing**) are common.

The output of almost all printers is at 6 lines to the vertical inch; a standard 11-vertical-inch form will therefore accommodate a maximum of 66 print lines. (Usually, though, top and bottom margins occupy some of the print lines.) Many of the 6-lines-per-inch printers can also be operator-set to print 8 lines to the inch. In larger data-processing installations, printers are often set at 8 lines per inch to save paper.

Report Design Guidelines

Certain guidelines for report design should be considered when you design a report. Let's consider several basic points.

Identify the Report and Standardize the Heading-Identification Area

Every output report should have a title or some other identifier. If the output is destined to be read or used by someone outside the company or division, the name of the issuing organization should appear on the report. The run date of the report should be specified; the period-ending date should also appear when applicable. A report- and/or program-code identifier that will uniquely identify the report should be assigned and printed on the output. For multipage reports, a page number should be provided. Figure E-2(a) provides an example of appropriate report identification.

Positioning report-identification items in standard locations from one report to the next, a uniform report-heading format makes it easier for the users when working with different reports. For instance, avoid having the report title in the upper left-hand corner of one report and in the lower right-hand heading space of another. Figure E-2(b) shows an example of a standardized heading-identification area that is applied to two different reports.

Figure E-2   Report-identification.

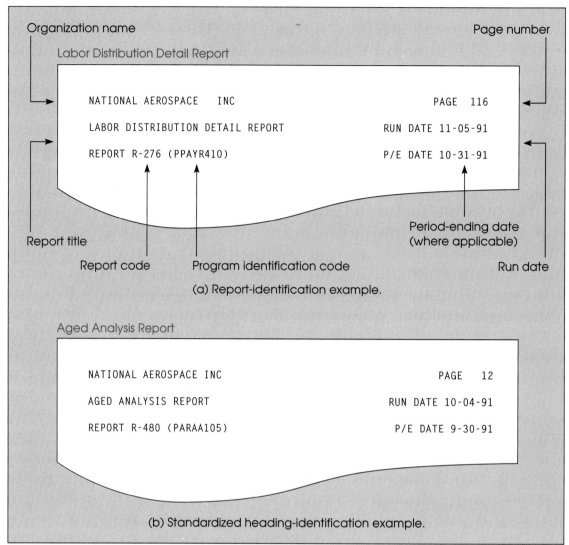

Organization name   Page number

Labor Distribution Detail Report

```
NATIONAL AEROSPACE    INC                              PAGE   116

LABOR DISTRIBUTION DETAIL REPORT              RUN DATE 11-05-91

REPORT R-276 (PPAYR410)                        P/E DATE 10-31-91
```

Report title

Report code   Program identification code

Period-ending date
(where applicable)

Run date

(a) Report-identification example.

Aged Analysis Report

```
NATIONAL AEROSPACE INC                            PAGE    12

AGED ANALYSIS REPORT                         RUN DATE 10-04-91

REPORT R-480 (PARAA105)                       P/E DATE 9-30-91
```

(b) Standardized heading-identification example.

Label All Output Fields   Data fields should not be displayed on a report without a descriptive label that explains what each field is. For detail-line fields, such descriptions will usually take the form of column headings. For the total line and for other exception fields not covered by the column headings, adjacent descriptive words on the same line may be required.

Even though you and the user may be very familiar with the report while it is being developed, data that is printed on reports without identification soon becomes ambiguous and confusing.

Position Column Headings Properly   If a data field beneath a column heading contains a uniform number of characters to be printed on each line, it is probably most attractive to center the column heading above the data span. Typically, however, numeric fields will have blank positions to the left of the value (because of zero suppression) and alphanumeric fields will have blank positions to the right of the printed characters (because the length of the field is usually longer than most of the actual data entries in the field).

Therefore, as depicted in Figure E-3, column headings for numeric fields are usually more visually pleasing when they are offset or justified to the right boundary of the data column; column headings for alphanumeric fields are best positioned at or near the left limit of the data area.

Determine Report Width and Length

The maximum width of traditional computer reports is 132 print positions, printed at 10 characters per inch.

If the report can be accommodated easily in 85 print positions or less, it is a good idea to keep within that number. This permits the user to copy and file the report with a standard 8-1/2-inch-wide paper dimension. However, if your printer prints only the traditional 10 characters per inch, this severely limits the amount of output you can have on a single line. On the other hand, if you have 12 or 17 characters per inch printing available, then you have much more printing capability with this width form.

Computer paper commonly used is 11 inches in length, although 8-1/2–inch length (together with 14-7/8-inch-width) is frequently encountered. With the versatility of serial printers used on microcomputers, the standard 8-1/2 by 11 inch paper is quite common. Figure E-4 illustrates report width and length considerations.

Consider Margin Requirements

If the report is to be bound on the horizontal edges—as is often done with nylon-post binders—a generous top and bottom margin must be provided. Otherwise, some of the report page will be obscured by the binding.

If a report is to be kept in a standard three-ring binder, a left-margin area must be provided for the binder holes. Because of these and other binding considerations, you should investigate binding and filing requirements prior to specifying margin sizes.

Figure E-3
Column-heading positioning example.

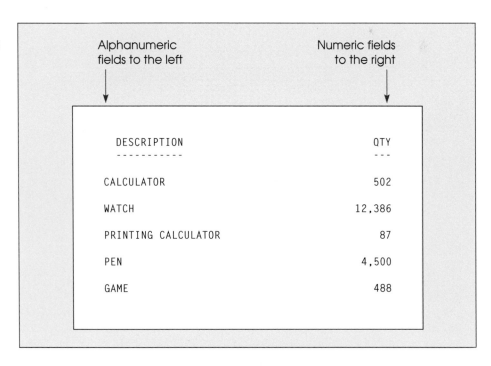

Figure E-4 Report width and length considerations.

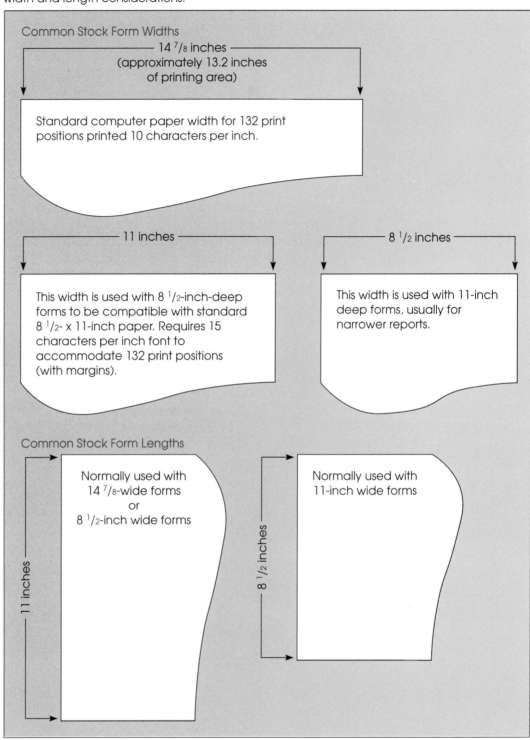

Make the Report Visually Attractive

Do not cram the data together; space the fields across the chosen report width. Provide extra blank lines before and after subtotal and total lines; this **white space** will make the report easier to read. Figure E-5 illustrates typical placement of blank lines.

Allow Sufficient Space for Numeric Results

For numeric amounts that are the result of an arithmetic operation, provide room for the longest possible value that can occur. When just two values are involved in a calculation, the maximum size can be determined by formulas, as shown in Figure E-6.

Figure E-5   Examples of "white space" use.

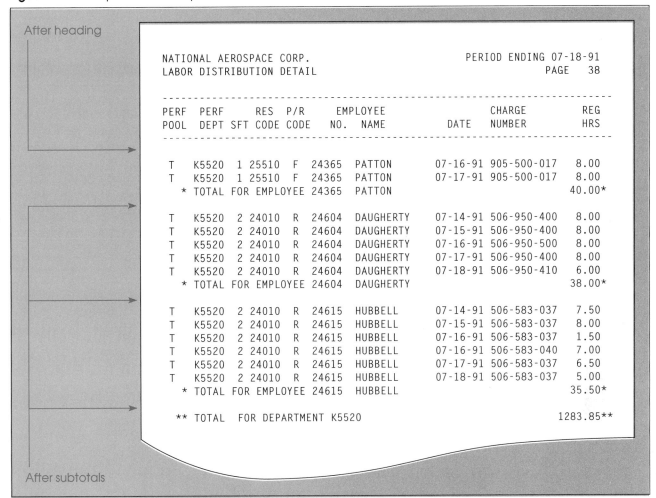

Figure E-6
Result-field digit
requirements for two-factor
arithmetic.

Arithmetic operation	Formula	Worked example	
ADDITION	Longest addend field length + 1	999999 + 99999 1099998	[6 + 1 = 7]
SUBTRACTION	Longest field (minuend or subtrahend) length + 1	99999 – – 1 100000 –	[5 + 1 = 6]
MULTIPLICATION	Sum of multiplier- and multiplicand-field lengths	9999 x 999 9989001	[4 + 3 = 7]
DIVISION Quotient	Dividend-field length	99999 1 ⟌ 99999	[5]
Remainder	Divisor-field length	6 remainder 400 500 ⟌ 3400	[3]

Note: The result-field size should be adjusted for the number of decimal positions (precision) required.

In many situations, however, the total amount will be the result of successive arithmetic operations. For example, the maximum size of a field that is used to accumulate the grand total of account balances will depend upon the number of input records that are being processed. When this is the case, you cannot determine the space required for the maximum value by a formula, but instead you must select it based on your knowledge of the data.

Consider Intercolumn Space Requirements

Determining the number of horizontal print positions that are needed for numeric fields with column totals in the total area requires special consideration. That is, it is the length of the total field, rather than the detail-line field, that is the determining factor. An alternative method, which conserves horizontal space on the detail line, is to stagger the column totals.

Space for negative-number indication (minus signs, credit symbols, and so forth) must also be considered and allocated, when applicable. Figure E-7 depicts these intercolumn space-requirement considerations.

Figure E-7 Intercolumn space-requirement examples.

```
                          Allow space for negative value indication.        Allow enough space between columns
                                                                            on the detail line for the totals.


   NATIONAL AEROSPACE CORP.                                        PERIOD ENDING 07-18-91
   LABOR DISTRIBUTION DETAIL                                                    PAGE    38


   ------------------------------------------------   --------------------------------------
   PERF    EMPLOYEE                       REG    PRM    TOT     REG      PRM
   DEPT    NBR    NAME      DATE          HRS    HRS    HRS     AMOUNT   AMOUNT
   ------------------------------------------------   --------------------------------------

   K5520  25510 PATTON      07-16-91  8.00    .00    8.00    80.88      .00
   K5520  25510 PATTON      07-17-91  8.00    .00    8.00    80.88      .00
      * TOTAL FOR EMP-PATTON           40.00*  .00*  40.00*  404.40*    .00*


   K5520  24604 DAUGHERTY   07-14-91  9.00    .00    9.00    72.90      .00
   K5520  24604 DAUGHERTY   07-14-91  1.00CR  .00    1.00CR   8.10CR
   K5520  24604 DAUGHERTY   07-15-91  8.00    .00    8.00    64.80      .00
   K5520  24604 DAUGHERTY   07-16-91  8.00    .00    8.00    64.80      .00
   K5520  24604 DAUGHERTY   07-17-91  8.00    .00    8.00    64.80      .00
   K5520  24604 DAUGHERTY   07-18-91  6.00    .00    6.00    48.60      .00
      * TOTAL FOR EMP-DAUGHERTY        38.00*  .00*  38.00*  307.80*    .00*


   K5520  24615 HUBBELL     07-14-91  7.50    .00    7.50    72.00      .00
   K5520  24615 HUBBELL     07-15-91  8.00    .00    8.00    76.80      .00
   K5520  24615 HUBBELL     07-16-91  1.50    .00    1.50    14.40      .00
   K5520  24615 HUBBELL     07-16-91  7.00    .00    7.00    67.20      .00
   K5520  24615 HUBBELL     07-17-91  6.50    .00    6.50    62.40      .00
   K5520  24615 HUBBELL     07-18-91  5.00    .00    5.00    48.00      .00
      * TOTAL FOR EMP-HUBBELL          35.50*  .00*  35.50*  340.80*    .00*

   ** TOTAL FOR DEPT-K5520        1283.85**        1400.50**        1768.13**
                                       116.65**         11233.68**
```

Use staggered totals to conserve space on the total line.

Figure E-8
Alternatives for negative-
value indication.

SATISFACTORY
(and appropriate for internal reports):

```
                1.00-
```

BETTER
(for formal reports and customer statements, invoices, etc):

```
          1.00 CR
```

BEST
(for customer statements):

```
     1.00 CR ** CREDIT BALANCE - DO NOT PAY **
```

Choose Suitable Negative-Value Indication

Most numeric amount fields should provide for negative values so that reversals and negative adjustments can be handled. For internal reports, a minus sign symbol (–) is usually adequate to indicate a negative value. The minus sign symbol is convenient to use because it occupies only one character position. However, it is generally preferable to use the CR symbol for formal accounting and other external reports. When displaying a credit balance on a customer's account, it is a good idea to print even further explanation, such as the following:

```
CREDIT BALANCE—DO NOT PAY
```

This message ensures that the value is understood to be negative. Figure E-8 shows examples of negative-value representations.

Use Appropriate Editing

Leading zeros of numeric amount fields should generally be suppressed, but numeric code numbers—such as Social Security and other account numbers—are easier to work with when their leftmost zeros are not suppressed. Insert decimal points when decimal positions are to be printed for an amount. If sufficient space is available on the print line, insert commas into amount fields that contain over three or four integers. Place slashes, or hyphens, in 6-digit dates. Do not print dollar signs except on formal financial reports and checks; for internal reports, the column heading (plus the typical dollar-and-cents placement of the decimal point) should make it clear that the amount is a money figure. Figure E-9 shows editing examples.

Use Underlining Sparingly

It usually consumes printing time and report-line space to underline a field. As a result, most programmer/analysts avoid underlining. Sometimes, however, underlining will be required—as it normally is for formal accounting reports.

Because impact line printers typically do not contain an underscore character, the best way to handle a single underline on such devices is to print a separate line (single-spaced from the previous one) with hyphens in the area to be underlined. For double-underlining, an equals sign (=) can be used.

Serial character printers handle underlining without consuming additional report lines, but usually require extra print time for each underlined character position. Sophisticated page printers provide underlining without sacrificing report space or print time.

Figure E-9
Editing guidelines.

Zero suppression for readability	bbb15.03
Commas for readability of longer numbers	1,250506
Slashes for dates	11//15/91
# *Hyphens* for readability of longer strings of characters	566-50-9224
—underlining (avoid or use sparingly)	<u>400.27</u>
Blank spaces for readability (in lieu of hyphens)	566 50 9224
Negative (or reverse) number indication	
—rightmost fixed-minus sign (commonly used)	500.00-
—floating minus sign	-500.00
—credit symbol	500.00CR
	500.00 CR
—debit symbol	500.00DB
	500.00 DB
—leftmost fixed-minus sign	- 500.00
(rarely used because it is difficult to read)	
Asterisk protection for dollar amounts on checks	$***94.50
Fixed-dollar sign on formal accounting reports	$ 94.50
$ first entry on page for each column, subtotal and total	
$ first entry after each subtotal and total	
Floating dollar sign	$94.50
# *Equals sign* for double underlining	$1,026,782.64
(avoid or use sparingly)	================

Not a COBOL editing symbol.

**Consider Page Totals
for Certain Reports**   For reports that require manual reconciliation and/or modifications to numeric column amounts, consider providing page totals. When handwritten notations must be made to amounts on a report, a column total of the amounts on that page will make it easier for clerks to recompute correct report totals after changes have been made to the detail-line entries. Figure E-10 provides an example.

Figure E-10 Example of a page total.

```
ACCOUNTS RECEIVABLE REPORT                    PERIOD ENDING 05-31-91
                                                        PAGE   15

                                              BALANCE        OVERDUE

     4038 PERCY AND WHITE                    1,289.45         210.58

     4039 CORCORAN, MAUREEN                     28.50            .00

     4041 SARATOGA SCHOOL DISTRICT          12,288.10            .00

     4042 ASSOCIATED STUDENT BODY              33.60            .00

     4043 FENTON, JONES AND PARKER            805.88            .00

     4044 A & W DRAFTING                      112.13         112.13

     4045 E-Z DATA PROCESSING               2,048.00       2,048.00

     4047 CALIFORNIA PRESS                   5,507.28            .00

     4048 TODD WALLACE                         15.48            .00

     4049 ABLE ELECTRONICS                   7,250.44       3,047.37

     4050 YOUNG AND BARSTOW                    506.73            .00

     4051 ALLIED ARTS                         980.41            .00

     4052 WINSTON AND ASSOCIATES            1,877.08            .00


          PAGE TOTAL                       32,743.08*       5,418.08*
```

Use Asterisks to Identify Total Levels

Asterisks, or another symbol, can be used to distinguish totals and subtotals from detail amounts. They also serve to indicate the composition, or level, of the total amount. Figure E-11 shows an example of total-level identification with asterisks. Accountants often refer to these total levels as "one-star," "two-star," and so forth, totals.

Provide Check Protection for Check Amounts

The maximum amount of space allocated for check amounts on preprinted check forms is usually much larger than that required to handle the dollar value of most checks issued. Unused space to the left of the check amount could be altered fraudulently unless some protection method is employed.

One simple method of providing check protection is to fill the amount with leading zeros. For example, if spaces were provided for six dollar digits (plus punctuation commas), a value of $1,234.56 would be printed as $001,234.56. However, such zero-filled amounts are difficult to read. A better approach is to use asterisk protection. With this method, asterisks replace the leading zeros. Our

Figure E-11 Asterisk identification of total levels.

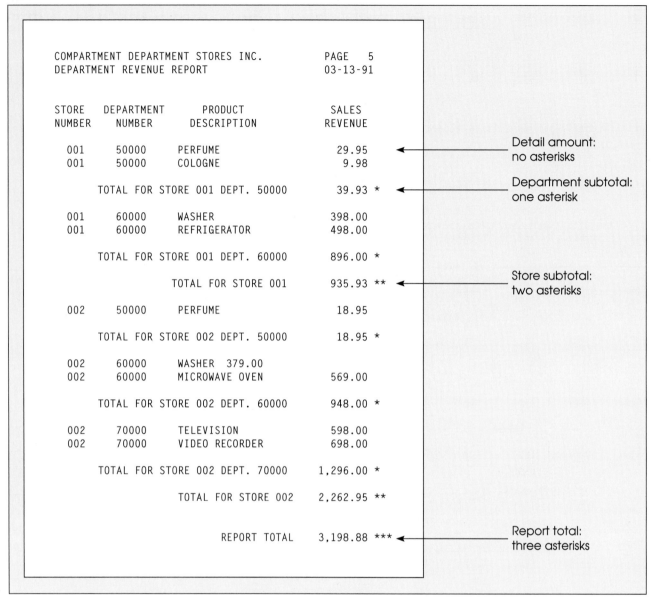

```
COMPARTMENT DEPARTMENT STORES INC.        PAGE   5
DEPARTMENT REVENUE REPORT                 03-13-91


STORE    DEPARTMENT    PRODUCT            SALES
NUMBER     NUMBER     DESCRIPTION        REVENUE

 001       50000      PERFUME              29.95   ◄——  Detail amount:
 001       50000      COLOGNE               9.98            no asterisks

          TOTAL FOR STORE 001 DEPT. 50000  39.93 *  ◄——  Department subtotal:
                                                         one asterisk

 001       60000      WASHER              398.00
 001       60000      REFRIGERATOR        498.00

          TOTAL FOR STORE 001 DEPT. 60000 896.00 *

                  TOTAL FOR STORE 001     935.93 **  ◄——  Store subtotal:
                                                          two asterisks

 002       50000      PERFUME              18.95

          TOTAL FOR STORE 002 DEPT. 50000  18.95 *

 002       60000      WASHER  379.00
 002       60000      MICROWAVE OVEN      569.00

          TOTAL FOR STORE 002 DEPT. 60000 948.00 *

 002       70000      TELEVISION          598.00
 002       70000      VIDEO RECORDER      698.00

          TOTAL FOR STORE 002 DEPT. 70000 1,296.00 *

                  TOTAL FOR STORE 002   2,262.95 **


                      REPORT TOTAL      3,198.88 ***  ◄——  Report total:
                                                            three asterisks
```

example would then appear as the more readable $**1,234.56. An alternate method, but slightly less secure, is to use a floating dollar sign in which the dollar sign is printed immediately to the left of the leftmost significant digit; for instance, $1,234.56.

Module Summary

The three general data areas of a report are: heading, body, and grand-total. The **heading area** generally contains data such as organization name, report title, period-ending date, run date, page number, report number, and column headings. The **body area** contains detail lines, summary lines, and subtotal lines. The **grand-total area** generally contains report column totals, the results of calculations, descriptive words, and record counts. The area at the bottom of each report page in which such data is printed is termed the **page-footing area**.

In designing reports, it is preferable to use an established set of guidelines to maintain consistency in the appearance of your reports. The following are report design guidelines:

- Identify the report.
- Standardize the heading-identification area.
- Label all output fields.
- Position column headings properly.
- Determine report width and length.
- Consider margin requirements.
- Make the report visually attractive.
- Consider placement of filing code and identification numbers.
- Allow sufficient space for numeric results.
- Consider intercolumn space requirements.
- Choose suitable negative-value indication.
- Use appropriate editing.
- Use underlining sparingly.
- Consider page totals for certain reports.
- Use asterisks to identify total levels.
- Provide check protection for check amounts.

Exercises
Terms for Definition

body area _____

control-break line _____

grand-total area _____

heading area _____

page-footing area _____

page headings _____

period-ending _____

report headings _____

run date _____

subtotal line _____

total line _____

Review Questions

1. Identify the three general data areas that you must consider when designing a report.

   a. _____

   b. _____

   c. _____

2. List four report identification items that you should consider when printing on a report.

   a. _____

   b. _____

   c. _____

   d. _____

3. Name the two types of dates that the programmer/analyst should consider when printing on a report.

   a. _____

   b. _____

4. Identify three types of lines that might be found in the body of a report.

   a. _____

   b. _____

   c. _____

5. When page totals or other data are printed at the bottom of each report page, that area is called the _____ area.

6. The end of a report often contains a(n) _____ area.

7. Most mainframe-computer printers provide a maximum of _____ print positions for each horizontal report line.

8. Impact line printers typically print _____ characters per horizontal inch.

9. To be consistent with elite typewriting, many character printers provide for the printing of _____ characters per horizontal inch.

10. The most common line spacings are either _____ or _____ characters per vertical inch.

11. Standard typing paper is _____ inches wide by _____ inches long; the familiar large-size computer paper is _____ inches wide by _____ inches long.

12. Identify two ways that a negative number may be indicated.

   a. _____

   b. _____

13. Digits used in _____ number fields should generally not be

   leading-zero suppressed, whereas it is easier to read _____
   fields when leading-zero suppression is used.

14. Although underlining capabilities are typically present on

   _____ printers, it is often time- and space-consuming to

   underline on _____ printers.

15. When a report requires manual reconciliation, it may be appropriate to

   provide _____ on the report.

16. When multiple total levels are printed on a report, comprehension may be

   aided by the use of _____ to identify total levels.

17. Identify two methods by which a certain degree of check protection may be
   provided for check-amount fields.

   a. _____

   b. _____

Report Program Design and Coding

Chapter Objectives

In Concepts Module E, you learned about many of the factors you must take into account when designing a report. The purpose of this chapter is to apply some of those principles by considering two applications. The first example, a customer charge account report program, closely parallels the PATLIST3 program from Chapter 5. The primary purpose of this program is to illustrate a standard convention for modularizing programs that will be used throughout the remainder of this book. The second example, a payroll report program, incorporates the principles described in Concepts Module E regarding multipage reports. This PAYROLL program code can be used as a model for practically any straightforward read-and-print program with headings and totals. From this chapter, you will learn the following:

- Placing the READ and WRITE statements each in an independent module so that a single statement reads or writes a given file.

- An expansion of the paragraph numbering convention introduced in Chapter 3.

- Using a variable quantity to control line spacing with the WRITE statement.

- The IF/ELSE statement that allows for either of two actions to be taken, depending upon a condition test.

- Report layout and planning.

- Top-down design—an organized approach to program modularization and construction of a structure chart.

- Recommendations for the organization of entries in the WORKING-STORAGE SECTION.

- The ACCEPT/FROM DATE statement which allows you to obtain the current date from the computer operating system.

- The READ/INTO statement (which corresponds to the WRITE/FROM).

- The ADVANCING PAGE option of the WRITE statement, which allows you to position the continuous form paper to the top of a new page.

CHAPTER **6**

Chapter Outline

Topic: Some Programming Standards

The Charge-Account Report Program
The Input File CHGACCT.DAT
The Output Report
Programming Specifications
Independent Module Conventions
Structure Chart
Module Numbering Conventions
Pseudocode and Flowchart

The Program Solution—CHGACCT
The First Three Divisions for the CHGACCT Program
The PROCEDURE DIVISION for the CHGACCT Program
The WRITE Module
The IF/ELSE Statement—COBOL-74
The Block IF and the IF/ELSE Statement—COBOL-85
The INITIALIZE Statement—COBOL-85

Topic: Designing a Report Program

Programming Specifications for the Payroll Report Program
The Input File PAYROLL.DAT
The Output Report
Program Specifications

Designing the Structure Chart
Top-Down Design
Step 1: List Functional Program Modules
Step 2: Describe Overall Program Function
Step 3: Show Major Program Functions
Step 4: Expand First-Level Modules
Initialize-Variable-Fields Module
Print-Report-Headings Module
Read-Payroll-Record Module
Process-Payroll-Record Module
Print-Total-Line Module

Step 5: Identify Common Modules
Step 6: Review Structure Chart
Step 7: Number Each Module

Writing the Pseudocode and Drawing the Program Flowchart
000-Print-Payroll-Report Module
100-Initialize-Variable-Fields Module
200-Process-Payroll-Record Module
700-Print-Total-Line Module
800-Read-Payroll-Record Module
870-Print-Report-Headings Module
880-Write-Report-Top-Line Module
890-Write-Report-Line Module

Topic: Coding a Report Program

Coding the DATA DIVISION
Definition of Records in WORKING-STORAGE
General Control and Work Areas
WS-REPORT CONTROLS Fields
The WS-WORK-AREAS and WS-TOTAL-ACCUMULATOR Fields
The Input and Output Areas

Coding the PROCEDURE DIVISION
The ACCEPT/FROM DATE Statement
The READ Statement INTO Phrase
The WRITE Statement ADVANCING Phrase
Testing for End-of-Page with the IF Statement

Some Additional Observations About the PAYROLL Program

The purpose of this Topic is to further apply some of the principles of the last two chapters and to expand the coding standards that you have been using thus far. This will be done by consideration of another sample program in which the primary focus is on using specialized modules for program output.

The Charge-Account Report Program
The Input File CHGACCT.DAT

The Silicon Valley Distributing Company maintains a data file with one record summarizing charges and payments for each customer; the record format is as follows:

Field	Width	Class	Format
Record code	2	Alphanumeric	
Account number	5	Alphanumeric	
Account name	25	Alphanumeric	
Tax code	1	Alphanumeric	
Balance forward	7	Numeric	S99999V99
Monthly purchase amount	7	Numeric	S99999V99
Number of purchases	4	Numeric	S9(4)
Payments this month	7	Numeric	S99999V99
Total record size	58		

The Output Report

One of the reports generated from this file, the charge account report, is used by the sales manager in her attempt to learn more about the customers. A sample of this report is shown in Figure 6-1. Notice that only two of the input fields are printed; the remainder of the results of calculations using input data.

If you compare this output to that of the PATDFCT3, you will see that they are much the same in overall form. That is, both have a column heading line, detail lines, and a summary line. Hence, you might expect that the programs would be very similar. As you will see, they are considerably different because of the extent to which the charge account program has been modularized to conform to standards that will be used throughout the remainder of this book.

Figure 6-1   Charge account program.

Figure 6-1 (continued)

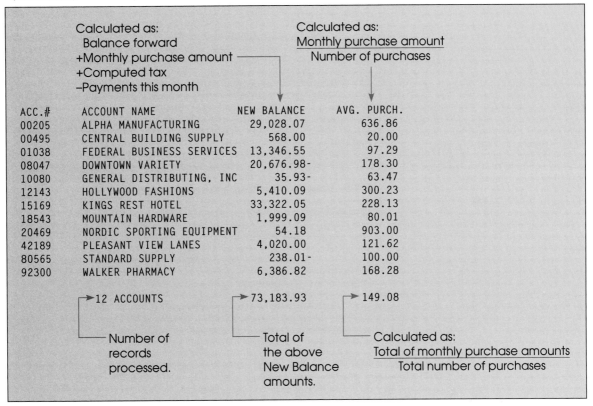

Programming Specifications

The programming specifications are shown in Figure 6-2. Following are particular items you should notice:

- Like the patron deficit programs, this program processes only selected records: those with a Record-code value of 50. Others are ignored.

- The sales-tax-amount depends upon the input field Tax-code. If Tax-code is 9, the applied tax rate is 6%; otherwise, the rate is 7%.

- Although there are numerous calculations, do not be intimidated; they are relatively basic arithmetic operations that you studied in Chapter 4.

Independent Module Conventions

To keep the logic straightforward for previous programs of this text, two identical READ statements were coded in each program; one for the priming read and one for all records after the first. Similarly, in the PATDFCT3 program, three different WRITE statements are used. However, instead of coding such multiple in-line READ or WRITE statements, it is better to include the READ statement in an independent module and the WRITE statement in another. Then whenever an input or output operation is required, the appropriate module can be performed. The advantages are that program logic and debugging are simplified, resulting in program code that is easier to debug and maintain when a common input or output operation for a file is handled at a single location. Furthermore, when records are read or written, certain related functions must typically be included: counting records, counting lines, testing for end-of-file, and so forth. Provision of a common independent module minimizes duplicate coding and precludes the possibility that coding functions are inadvertently omitted or erroneously coded.

With the exception of a special case for the WRITE that you will learn about in Chapter 7, in all this book's future example programs, each input file will utilize a single READ in a separate module and each output file will utilize a single WRITE in a separate module.

Figure 6-2
Programming specifications for the charge account program.

PROGRAMMING SPECIFICATIONS

Program name: CHARGE ACCOUNT REPORT   **Program ID:** CHGACCT

Program Description:

This program is to print a charge account report from input charge account records.

Input File:

CHGACCT.DAT

Output File:

Charge Account Report

List of Program Operations:

A. Read each input charge account record. If the record-code field does not contain a value 50, ignore it and proceed to the next record.

B. For each code-50 record, calculate the new-balance and the average-customer-purchase-amount.

   1. New-balance is to be calculated as follows:

      a. Calculate the sales-tax-amount as follows:

         If the tax-code is equal to 9
            Multiply the purchases-this-month by 0.06
            (a tax rate of 6%)
         Else
            Multiply the purchases-this-month by 0.07
            (a tax rate of 7%).

      b. Add the purchases-this-month and the sales-tax-amount to the balance-forward-from-last-month and subtract the payments-this-month to equal the new-balance.

   2. Average-customer-purchase-amount is to be calculated as follows:

      a. Divide the purchases-this-month-amount by the number-of-purchases-this-month. (Note: The sales-tax-amount is not to be included in this average-customer-purchase-amount computation.)

   3. For each code-50 record, accumulate the following for total output at the end of the report:

      a. Add 1 to the number-of-accounts.

      b. Add the new-balance amount to the total-accounts-receivable.

      c. Add the number-of-purchases-this-month to the total-number-of-purchases-this-month.

      d. Add the purchases-this-month-amount to the total-purchases-this-month-amount.

C. For each code-50 record, print the following fields on the charge account report detail-line in accordance with the format shown on the print chart:

         Account number
         Account name
         Account new-balance
         Account average-purchase-amount

D. Double-space each detail-line.

E. After all the input charge account records have been processed, print the following total fields on the charge account report total-line in accordance with the format shown on the print chart:

   1. Total number of code-50 accounts; to be calculated by counting.

   2. Total accounts receivable for code-50 records; to be calculated by summing the new-balance amounts.

   3. Total average-purchase-amount for code-50 records; to be calculated by dividing total-purchases-this-month-amount by total-number-of-purchases-this-month.

F. Triple-space the total-line from the last detail-line.

Structure Chart   From the overall structure point-of-view, this program is much like the PATDFCT3 program (Figure 5-3). That is, from the mainline module, five actions are carried out (in addition to the file opening and closing):

- Variables are initialized (performed)

- First record is read (in-line statement)

- Column headings are written (in-line statement)

- Data file is processed (repetitive perform)

- Total line is printed (in-line statement)

By removing the previous in-line operations and placing them in separate modules, the form of the structure chart becomes as shown in Figure 6-3. At first glance, this may look much more complicated than those of preceding examples, but it is not. Notice the previous five actions of the mainline module are now shown as independent modules.

Also note that the READ module 800 is performed from two different places in the program: from the mainline module (the priming READ) and from the process module 210 (read the next record). Similarly, the WRITE module is performed from three different places. Any module that appears in more than one place on the structure chart (is performed from more than one module in the program) is called a **common module**. Common modules are identified on the structure chart by shading the upper-right corner as in Figure 6-3.

Module Numbering Conventions   In Concepts Module C, you were introduced to the notion of predetermined numbering ranges for program modules as a method of maintaining commonality from one program to another. Figure 6-4 summarizes the complete range of module numbers used in this book—notice the use of these in the structure chart of Figure 6-3.

Figure 6-3 Structure chart for the charge account program.

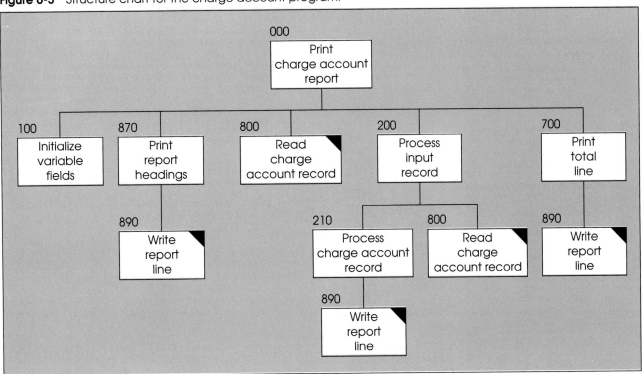

Figure 6-4
Module-numbering
conventions.

Module number	Module function
000	Mainline
100–199	Initialization of variable fields
200–699	General processing
700–799	End-of-run totals, statistics, etc.
800–849	Input (READ, ACCEPT)
850–869	General nonreport output (WRITE, REWRITE, DELETE, DISPLAY)
870–879	Report headings
880–889	Report top-line output (page skipping)
890–899	Report-line output (line spacing)
900–999	Subprogram communication (CALL) and abnormal program termination

**Pseudocode and
Flowchart**

The pseudocode solution for this program is shown in Figure 6-5; the flowchart solution is shown in Figure 6-6. These reflect the additional programming requirements introduced by placing the READ and WRITE statements in separate modules. Also, notice that the program includes a full selection structure: the sales tax rate is either 6% or 7%, depending upon the value in the field Tax-code.

Figure 6-5   Pseudocode for the charge account program.

```
000-Print-charge-account-report module

  1.  Open the files.

  2.  Perform 100-Initialize-variable-fields module.

  3.  Perform 800-Read-charge-account-record module.

  4.  Perform 870-Print-report-headings.

  5.  Perform 200-Process-charge-account-record module until no
      more records.

  6.  Perform 700-Print-total-line module.

  7.  Close the files.

  8.  Stop the run.

100-Initialize-variable-fields module

  1.  Set the end-of-file indicator to "No".

  2.  Set the following accumulators to zero.
          Number-of-accounts
          Total-accounts-receivable
      Total-number-of purchases-this-month
      Total-purchases-this-month-amount.

200-Process-input-record module

  1.  If Record-code is equal to "50"
          perform 210-Process-charge-account-record.

  2.  Perform 800-Read-charge-account-record module.

210-Process-charge-account-record module

  1.  Calculate the Sales-tax as follows:

      If the Tax-code is equal to 9
          Multiply the Purchases-this-month by 0.06
      Else
          Multiply the Purchases-this-month by 0.07.

  2.  Calculate New-balance:
          Add Month-sales-tax-amount,
          Month-purchase-amount,
          Balance-forward
          Subtract Month-payments.

  3.  Move the following fields to the output detail-line:
          Input Account-number
          Input Account-name
          Calculated New-balance.
```

```
  4.  Divide the Number-of-month-purchases into the Month-
      purchase-amount to equal the Average-purchase-amount and
      move it to the Average-purchase-amount in the output
      detail-line.

  5.  Set line spacing to double-space and perform 890-Write-
      report-line.

  6.  Increment accumulators:

      Add 1 to the Number-of-accounts.
      Add the New-balance amount to the Total-accounts-
          receivable.
      Add the Number-of-purchases-this-month to the
          Total-number-of-purchases-this-month.
      Add the Purchases-this-month-amount to the
          Total-purchases-this-month-amount.

700-Print-total-line module

  1.  Calculate Average-purchase amount as Total-purchases-this-
      month-amount divided by Total-number-of-purchases-this-
      month.

  2.  Move the following fields to the output Total-line:
          Number-of-accounts
          Total-accounts-receivable
          Average-purchase.

  3.  Move Total-line to Report-line.

  4.  Move 3 to Line-spacing.

  5.  Perform 890-Write-report-line.

800-Read-charge-account-record module

  1.  Read the next input record.

870-Print-report-headings module

  1.  Move the Column-heading record to Report-line.

  2.  Move zero to Line-spacing indicator.

  3.  Perform 890-Write-report-line.

890-Write-report-line module

  1.  Advance form in accordance with Line-spacing indicator and
      write the Report-line.
```

Figure 6-6 Flowchart for the charge account program (continues on page 278).

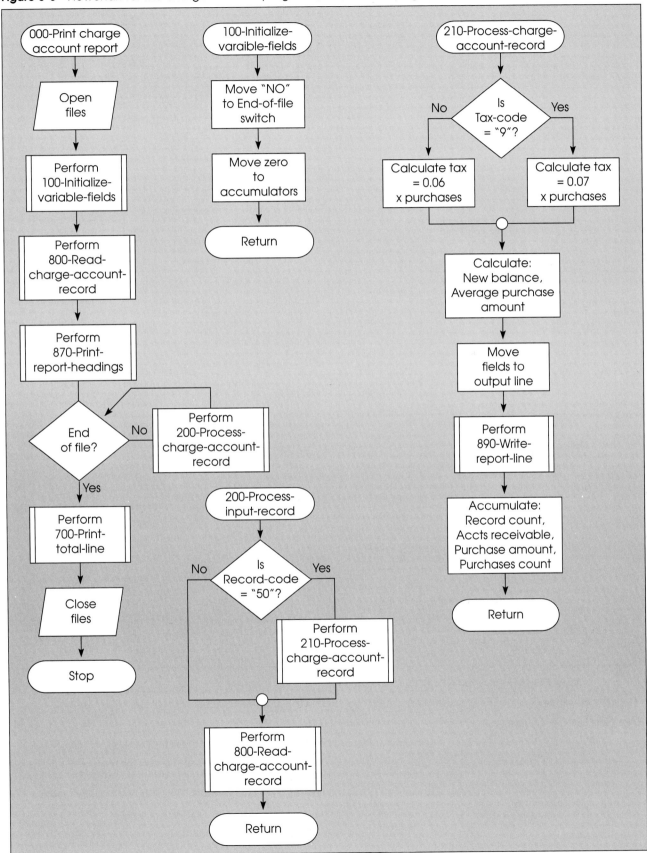

Figure 6-6
(continues from page 277)

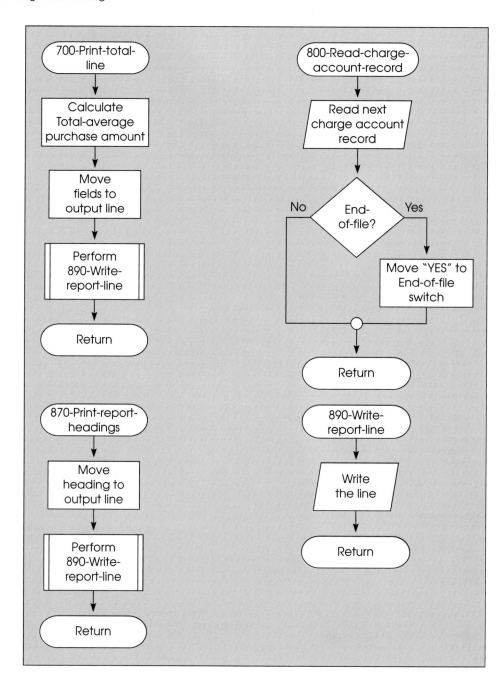

**The Program
Solution—CHGACCT**
**The First Three Divisions
for the CHGACCT
Program**

Referring to Figure 6-7, you can see that the first three divisions of the CHGACCT program are much like those you have seen before. However, there are a few items to which you should direct your attention.

1. All numeric fields in both the input record and in the WORKING-STORAGE SECTION are defined as signed (the PIC field definition contains the letter S). Including the sign picture improves processing efficiency slightly—in addition to making it possible to accommodate negative values (that can occur in this program).

2. Correspondingly, output fields that can be negative include a trailing minus sign (for instance, see DL-NEW-BALANCE on line 89).

Figure 6-7   The first three divisions for the CHGACCT program.

```
1         IDENTIFICATION DIVISION.
2         PROGRAM-ID.    CHGACCT.
3
4      *     WRITTEN BY T. WELBURN.
5      *     SILICON VALLEY DISTRIBUTING COMPANY.
6      *     JAN 12,1986.
7      *     REVISED 8-21-89 BY W. PRICE.
8
9      *     THIS PROGRAM READS RECORDS FROM THE CHARGE ACCOUNT
10     *     FILE.  FOR EACH TYPE "50" RECORD, IT COMPUTES THE
11     *     NEW BALANCE AND AVERAGE PURCHASE AMOUNT FOR THE
12     *     ACCOUNT AND PRINTS A CHARGE ACCOUNT DETAIL LINE.
13
14     *     AFTER ALL INPUT CHARGE ACCOUNT RECORDS HAVE BEEN
15     *     PROCESSED A REPORT TOTAL LINE WILL BE PRINTED.
16
17     *     A COLUMN HEADING LINE IS PRINTED TO IDENTIFY
18     *     COLUMN CONTENTS.
19
20
21        ENVIRONMENT DIVISION.
22
23        CONFIGURATION SECTION.
24
25        SOURCE-COMPUTER.   (system dependent).
26        OBJECT-COMPUTER.   (system dependent).
27
28        INPUT-OUTPUT SECTION.
29
30        FILE-CONTROL.
31            SELECT CHARGE-ACCOUNT-FILE
32                ASSIGN TO (system dependent).
33            SELECT CHARGE-ACCOUNT-REPORT
34                ASSIGN TO (system dependent).
35
36
37        DATA DIVISION.
38
39        FILE SECTION.
40
41        FD  CHARGE-ACCOUNT-FILE
42            RECORD CONTAINS 58 CHARACTERS
43            LABEL RECORDS ARE STANDARD.
44
45        01  CHARGE-ACCOUNT-RECORD.
46            05  CA-RECORD-CODE          PIC X(2).
47            05  CA-ACCOUNT-NUMBER       PIC X(5).
48            05  CA-ACCOUNT-NAME         PIC X(25).
49            05  CA-TAX-CODE             PIC X(1).
50            05  CA-BALANCE-FORWARD      PIC S9(5)V99.
51            05  CA-MONTH-PURCHASE-AMT   PIC S9(5)V99.
52            05  CA-NBR-MONTH-PURCHASES  PIC S9(4).
53            05  CA-MONTH-PAYMENTS       PIC S9(5)V99.
54

55        FD  CHARGE-ACCOUNT-REPORT
56            RECORD CONTAINS 132 CHARACTERS
57            LABEL RECORDS ARE OMITTED.
58
59        01  REPORT-LINE                 PIC X(132).
60
61        WORKING-STORAGE SECTION.
62
63        01  WS-SWITCHES.
64            05  WS-EOF-SWITCH           PIC X(3).
65
66        01  WS-WORK-AREAS.
67            05  WS-BALANCE-WORK         PIC S9(5)V99.
68            05  WS-LINE-SPACING         PIC S9(2).
69
70        01  WS-TOTAL-ACCUMULATORS.
71            05  WS-TOTAL-NBR-ACCOUNTS-ACCUM    PIC S9(4).
72            05  WS-TOTAL-ACCTS-RCVBL-ACCUM     PIC S9(8)V99.
73            05  WS-TOTAL-MONTH-PURCH-AMT-ACCUM PIC S9(7)V99.
74            05  WS-TOTAL-NBR-MONTH-PURCH-ACCUM PIC S9(6).
75
76        01  WS-COLUMN-HEADING-LINE.
77            05  FILLER      PIC X(5)   VALUE SPACES.
78            05  FILLER      PIC X(10)  VALUE "ACC.#".
79            05  FILLER      PIC X(25)  VALUE "ACCOUNT NAME".
80            05  FILLER      PIC X(16)  VALUE "NEW BALANCE".
81            05  FILLER      PIC X(11)  VALUE "AVG. PURCH.".
82
83        01  WS-DETAIL-LINE.
84            05  FILLER           PIC X(5)    VALUE SPACES.
85            05  DL-ACCOUNT-NUMBER PIC X(5).
86            05  FILLER           PIC X(5)    VALUE SPACES.
87            05  DL-ACCOUNT-NAME  PIC X(25).
88            05  FILLER           PIC X(2)    VALUE SPACES.
89            05  DL-NEW-BALANCE   PIC ZZ,ZZZ.99-.
90            05  FILLER           PIC X(5)    VALUE SPACES.
91            05  DL-AVG-PURCHASE  PIC ZZ,ZZZ.99-.
92
93        01  WS-TOTAL-LINE.
94            05  FILLER           PIC X(14)   VALUE SPACES.
95            05  TL-TOTAL-NBR-ACCTS   PIC Z,ZZ9.
96            05  FILLER           PIC X(19)   VALUE " ACCOUNTS".
97            05  TL-TOTAL-ACCTS-RCVBL PIC ZZ,ZZZ,ZZZ.99-.
98            05  FILLER           PIC X(5)    VALUE SPACES.
99            05  TL-AVG-PURCHASE  PIC ZZ,ZZZ.99-.
100
101
```

3. Three output lines are defined in the WORKING-STORAGE SECTION, one for each of the three types of line to be printed: heading, detail, and summary.

4. The accumulators (lines 71–74) have been given a field length that should be sufficient to accommodate the totals they will be accumulating. For instance, CA-MONTH-PURCHASE-AMT is defined as S9(5)V99 (line 51); its corresponding accumulator WS-TOTAL-MONTH-PURCH-AMT-ACCUM is defined as S9(7)V99 (line 73). In determining the size of such an accumulator, you must have at least a rough idea of how much the average monthly purchase amount is and the number of customers to be processed.

The PROCEDURE DIVISION for the CHGACCT Program

The PROCEDURE DIVISION of this program is given in two versions in Figure 6-8: COBOL-74 and COBOL-85.

Consistent with the structure chart representation, notice that the READ statement is included in a separate module (at line 171/166). (In these descriptions, you should refer to whichever version of the program is appropriate to your compiler. Remember from earlier descriptions that in the designation 171/166, the first line number refers to the COBOL-74 version of the program and the second line number to the COBOL-85 version.)

Figure 6-8 The PROCEDURE DIVISION for the CHGACCT program.

```
102        PROCEDURE DIVISION.
103
104        000-PRINT-CHG-ACCT-REPORT.
105            OPEN INPUT CHARGE-ACCOUNT-FILE
106                OUTPUT CHARGE-ACCOUNT-REPORT.
107            PERFORM 100-INITIALIZE-VARIABLE-FIELDS.
108            PERFORM 800-READ-CHARGE-ACCOUNT-RECORD.
109            PERFORM 870-PRINT-REPORT-HEADINGS.
110            PERFORM 200-PROCESS-INPUT-RECORD
111                UNTIL WS-EOF-SWITCH IS EQUAL TO "YES".
112            PERFORM 700-PRINT-TOTAL-LINE.
113            CLOSE CHARGE-ACCOUNT-FILE
114                CHARGE-ACCOUNT-REPORT.
115            STOP RUN.
116
117        100-INITIALIZE-VARIABLE-FIELDS.
118            MOVE "NO " TO WS-EOF-SWITCH.
119            MOVE ZEROS TO WS-TOTAL-NBR-ACCOUNTS-ACCUM
120                         WS-TOTAL-ACCTS-RCVBL-ACCUM
121                         WS-TOTAL-MONTH-PURCH-AMT-ACCUM
122                         WS-TOTAL-NBR-MONTH-PURCH-ACCUM.
123
124        200-PROCESS-INPUT-RECORD.
125            IF CA-RECORD-CODE = "50"
126                PERFORM 210-PROCESS-CHARGE-ACCT-RECORD.
127            PERFORM 800-READ-CHARGE-ACCOUNT-RECORD.
128
129        210-PROCESS-CHARGE-ACCT-RECORD.
130
131        *   DO DETAIL CALCULATIONS
132            IF CA-TAX-CODE = "9"
133                MULTIPLY CA-MONTH-PURCHASE-AMT BY .07
134                    GIVING WS-BALANCE-WORK ROUNDED
135            ELSE
136                MULTIPLY CA-MONTH-PURCHASE-AMT BY .06
137                    GIVING WS-BALANCE-WORK ROUNDED.
138            ADD CA-BALANCE-FORWARD TO WS-BALANCE-WORK.
139            ADD CA-MONTH-PURCHASE-AMT TO WS-BALANCE-WORK.
140            SUBTRACT CA-MONTH-PAYMENTS FROM WS-BALANCE-WORK.
141
142        *   ASSEMBLE AND WRITE DETAIL LINE
143            MOVE CA-ACCOUNT-NUMBER TO DL-ACCOUNT-NUMBER.
144            MOVE CA-ACCOUNT-NAME TO DL-ACCOUNT-NAME.
145            MOVE WS-BALANCE-WORK TO DL-NEW-BALANCE.
146            DIVIDE CA-NBR-MONTH-PURCHASES
147                INTO CA-MONTH-PURCHASE-AMT
148                    GIVING DL-AVG-PURCHASE ROUNDED.
149            MOVE WS-DETAIL-LINE TO REPORT-LINE.
150            MOVE 2 TO WS-LINE-SPACING.
151            PERFORM 890-WRITE-REPORT-LINE.
152
153        *   INCREMENT ACCUMULATORS
154            ADD 1 TO WS-TOTAL-NBR-ACCOUNTS-ACCUM.
155            ADD WS-BALANCE-WORK TO WS-TOTAL-ACCTS-RCVBL-ACCUM.
156            ADD CA-MONTH-PURCHASE-AMT
157                TO WS-TOTAL-MONTH-PURCH-AMT-ACCUM.
158            ADD CA-NBR-MONTH-PURCHASES
159                TO WS-TOTAL-NBR-MONTH-PURCH-ACCUM.
160
161        700-PRINT-TOTAL-LINE.
162            MOVE WS-TOTAL-NBR-ACCOUNTS-ACCUM TO TL-TOTAL-NBR-ACCTS.
163            MOVE WS-TOTAL-ACCTS-RCVBL-ACCUM TO TL-TOTAL-ACCTS-RCVBL.
164            DIVIDE WS-TOTAL-NBR-MONTH-PURCH-ACCUM
165                INTO WS-TOTAL-MONTH-PURCH-AMT-ACCUM
166                    GIVING TL-AVG-PURCHASE ROUNDED.
167            MOVE WS-TOTAL-LINE TO REPORT-LINE.
168            MOVE 3 TO WS-LINE-SPACING.
169            PERFORM 890-WRITE-REPORT-LINE.
170
171        800-READ-CHARGE-ACCOUNT-RECORD.
172            READ CHARGE-ACCOUNT-FILE
173                AT END MOVE "YES" TO WS-EOF-SWITCH.
174
175        870-PRINT-REPORT-HEADINGS.
176            MOVE WS-COLUMN-HEADING-LINE TO REPORT-LINE.
177            MOVE 0 TO WS-LINE-SPACING.
178            PERFORM 890-WRITE-REPORT-LINE.
179
180        890-WRITE-REPORT-LINE.
181            WRITE REPORT-LINE
182                AFTER ADVANCING WS-LINE-SPACING LINES.
```

(a) COBOL-74

```
102        PROCEDURE DIVISION.
103
104        000-PRINT-CHG-ACCT-REPORT.
105            OPEN INPUT CHARGE-ACCOUNT-FILE
106                OUTPUT CHARGE-ACCOUNT-REPORT
107            PERFORM 100-INITIALIZE-VARIABLE-FIELDS
108            PERFORM 800-READ-CHARGE-ACCOUNT-RECORD
109            PERFORM 870-PRINT-REPORT-HEADINGS
110            PERFORM 200-PROCESS-INPUT-RECORD
111                UNTIL WS-EOF-SWITCH IS EQUAL TO "YES"
112            PERFORM 700-PRINT-TOTAL-LINE
113            CLOSE CHARGE-ACCOUNT-FILE
114                CHARGE-ACCOUNT-REPORT
115            STOP RUN.
116
117        100-INITIALIZE-VARIABLE-FIELDS.
118            MOVE "NO " TO WS-EOF-SWITCH
119            INITIALIZE WS-TOTAL-ACCUMULATORS.
120
121        200-PROCESS-INPUT-RECORD.
122            IF CA-RECORD-CODE = "50"
123        *       DO DETAIL CALCULATIONS
124                IF CA-TAX-CODE = "9"
125                    MULTIPLY CA-MONTH-PURCHASE-AMT BY .07
126                        GIVING WS-BALANCE-WORK ROUNDED
127                ELSE
128                    MULTIPLY CA-MONTH-PURCHASE-AMT BY .06
129                        GIVING WS-BALANCE-WORK ROUNDED
130                END-IF
131                ADD CA-BALANCE-FORWARD TO WS-BALANCE-WORK
132                ADD CA-MONTH-PURCHASE-AMT TO WS-BALANCE-WORK
133                SUBTRACT CA-MONTH-PAYMENTS FROM WS-BALANCE-WORK
134
135        *       ASSEMBLE AND WRITE DETAIL LINE
136                MOVE CA-ACCOUNT-NUMBER TO DL-ACCOUNT-NUMBER
137                MOVE CA-ACCOUNT-NAME TO DL-ACCOUNT-NAME
138                MOVE WS-BALANCE-WORK TO DL-NEW-BALANCE
139                DIVIDE CA-NBR-MONTH-PURCHASES
140                    INTO CA-MONTH-PURCHASE-AMT
141                        GIVING DL-AVG-PURCHASE ROUNDED
142                MOVE WS-DETAIL-LINE TO REPORT-LINE
143                MOVE 2 TO WS-LINE-SPACING
144                PERFORM 890-WRITE-REPORT-LINE
145
146        *       INCREMENT ACCUMULATORS
147                ADD 1 TO WS-TOTAL-NBR-ACCOUNTS-ACCUM
148                ADD WS-BALANCE-WORK TO WS-TOTAL-ACCTS-RCVBL-ACCUM
149                ADD CA-MONTH-PURCHASE-AMT
150                    TO WS-TOTAL-MONTH-PURCH-AMT-ACCUM
151                ADD CA-NBR-MONTH-PURCHASES
152                    TO WS-TOTAL-NBR-MONTH-PURCH-ACCUM
153            END-IF
154            PERFORM 800-READ-CHARGE-ACCOUNT-RECORD.
155
156        700-PRINT-TOTAL-LINE.
157            MOVE WS-TOTAL-NBR-ACCOUNTS-ACCUM TO TL-TOTAL-NBR-ACCTS
158            MOVE WS-TOTAL-ACCTS-RCVBL-ACCUM TO TL-TOTAL-ACCTS-RCVBL
159            DIVIDE WS-TOTAL-NBR-MONTH-PURCH-ACCUM
160                INTO WS-TOTAL-MONTH-PURCH-AMT-ACCUM
161                    GIVING TL-AVG-PURCHASE ROUNDED
162            MOVE WS-TOTAL-LINE TO REPORT-LINE
163            MOVE 3 TO WS-LINE-SPACING
164            PERFORM 890-WRITE-REPORT-LINE.
165
166        800-READ-CHARGE-ACCOUNT-RECORD.
167            READ CHARGE-ACCOUNT-FILE
168                AT END MOVE "YES" TO WS-EOF-SWITCH
169            END-READ.
170
171        870-PRINT-REPORT-HEADINGS.
172            MOVE WS-COLUMN-HEADING-LINE TO REPORT-LINE
173            MOVE 0 TO WS-LINE-SPACING
174            PERFORM 890-WRITE-REPORT-LINE.
175
176        890-WRITE-REPORT-LINE.
177            WRITE REPORT-LINE
178                AFTER ADVANCING WS-LINE-SPACING LINES.
```

(b) COBOL-85

Two other features in this program need special attention: the WRITE module and the IF/ELSE statement.

The WRITE Module

The WRITE statement is included in a separate module (at line 180/176). Remember that it must handle writing of all three types of lines: heading, detail, and summary. In the PATDFCT3 program (Figure 5-3), these were done with the following three separate WRITE statements, each slightly different from the other:

```
WRITE DEFICIENCY-LINE FROM WS-COLUMN-HEADING-LINE.
WRITE DEFICIENCY-LINE FROM WS-DETAIL-LINE
    AFTER ADVANCING 2 LINES.
WRITE DEFICIENCY-LINE FROM WS-TOTAL-LINE
    AFTER ADVANCING 3 LINES.
```

In order that all writing (for that file) uses the same WRITE statement, the following is necessary:

1. WRITE rather than WRITE/FROM is used (refer to line 181/177).

2. Because each of the types of output lines requires different line spacing, a variable quantity will be needed for line spacing control.

3. Prior to performing the write module, the output line to be printed must be moved from working-storage to the output line.

Figure 6-9 shows how this method is implemented for printing the detail line. Notice that two MOVE statement are required to set up the writing. You can see corresponding statements for the heading line at lines 176–178/172–174 and for the summary line at program lines 167–169/162–164.

The IF/ELSE Statement—COBOL-74

The charge account problem definition requires that either of two tax rates be used, depending upon the value of the input field Tax-code; this is reflected in the pseudocode and flowchart logic. You have already used the IF statement to execute a statement conditionally. The IF/ELSE is the complete form of the statement. As illustrated in Figure 6-10, it functions exactly as the English suggests. If the tested condition is true, one action is taken; or else (ELSE), the other action is taken. In using the IF/ELSE, be certain to avoid placing a period at the end of the statement preceding the ELSE. If you do, the statement will be terminated and COBOL will interpret ELSE as a separate statement, thereby producing a diagnostic.

Figure 6-9
Printing the detail line.

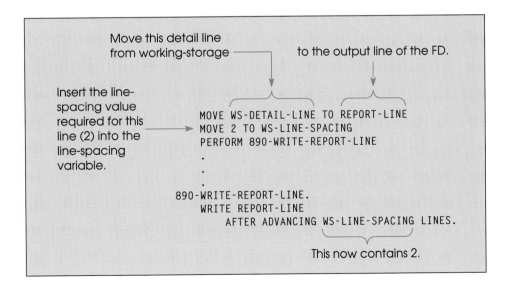

Figure 6-10 The IF/ELSE statement.

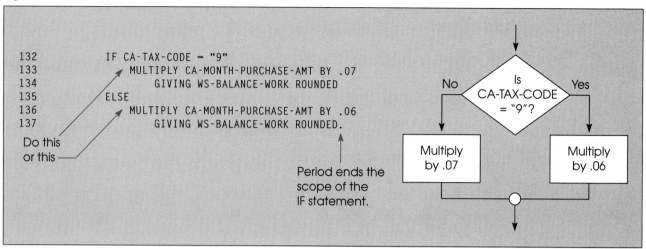

The Block IF and the IF/ELSE Statement—COBOL-85

One major difference exists between the COBOL-74 and the COBOL-85 versions of this program: the way in which the conditional processing of a record is handled. In the COBOL-74 program, a charge-account record is processed in module 210; this module is performed conditionally by the PERFORM at line 126 (Figure 6-8a). Because 210 also contains an IF statement, the separate 210 module is the only way to do this.

On the other hand, the END-IF scope terminator of COBOL-85 provides much more versatility in this respect. In the program of Figure 6-8b, the entire section of record processing code is included within the scope of the IF statement, as illustrated in Figure 6-11. Hence, the separate 210 module is not needed. On the other hand, if you feel more comfortable including the conditional actions as a separate module (210 as in the COBOL-74 form), you can do so.

The charge account problem definition requires that either of two tax rates be used depending upon the value of the input field Tax-code; this is reflected in the pseudocode and flowchart logic. You have already used the IF statement to execute a statement conditionally. The IF/ELSE is the complete form of the statement. As illustrated in Figure 6-12, it functions exactly as the English suggests: if the tested condition is true one action is taken, otherwise (ELSE) the other action is taken. The END-IF terminates the scope of this statement.

The INITIALIZE Statement—COBOL-85

At line 119, you see the statement:

```
INITIALIZE WS-TOTAL-ACCUMULATORS
```

Notice that the identifier WS-TOTAL-ACCUMULATORS is a group item. The action of this statement will be to set all of the elementary numeric items under this group item to zero (these are the accumulators used in the program). The statement is even more versatile than illustrated by this example because the group item initialized can consist of elementary fields of any data class. The initialization involves

Figure 6-11
The scope of the IF statement.

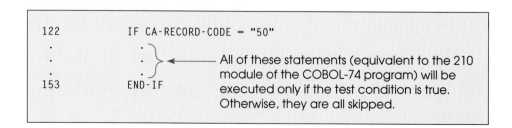

Figure 6-12   The IF/ELSE statement—COBOL-85.

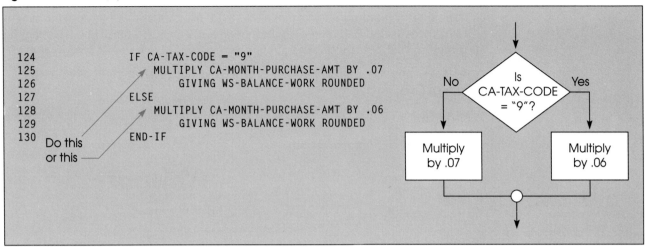

setting numeric and numeric-edited fields to zero, and alphanumeric, alphanumeric-edited, and alphabetic fields to spaces. As shown in the general format of Figure 6-13, you can include the REPLACING/BY clause to provide selective initialization to different values.

Topic: Designing a Report Program

Programming Specifications for the Payroll Report Program
The Input File PAYROLL.DAT

The payroll department of the Universal Business Services Company has created a new payroll file for hourly employees. Each record of the file contains data for one hourly employee as follows:

Positions	Field	Data class	Comments
3–11	Social Security number	Numeric	
12–35	Employee name	Alphanumeric	
36–39	Pay rate	Numeric	Format: S99V99
45–49	Hours worked	Numeric	Format: S999V99

Figure 6-13   Format of the INITIALIZE Statement—COBOL-85.

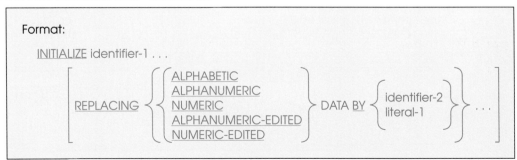

The Output Report   You have been given the task of writing a program to generate a payroll summary report. After meeting with the payroll supervisor, the two of you determine the exact output required and formalize it as the print chart depicted in Figure 6-14 (which also includes a sample report for our convenient reference in evaluating the program). Notice the following about this report:

■ It can consist of multiple pages. Each page includes a complete set of headings lines.

■ Pages are numbered.

Figure 6-14   The payroll program print chart and sample report.

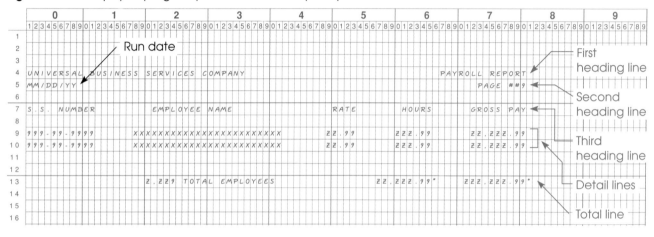

(a)

(b)

- The date that the report was run is printed in the second heading line. As you will see, a special technique is required to obtain the current date from the computer-operating system.

- One detail line is printed for each employee record. All printed values except those in the last column are input quantities. The last column is the gross pay—which is calculated as the hours worked times the pay rate.

- A grand-total line is printed at the end of the report. Accumulations will need to be made for three values: total number of employee payroll records processed, total number of hours worked, and total gross pay.

The print chart of Figure 6-14 shows where everything should be on the report page, but it does not give an indication of how many lines per page should be printed. This determination requires some arithmetic. Assume that the form requirements are as follows:

- A standard 11-inch form length

- Six lines per inch printing

- A 1/2-inch margin at the top of the page

- A 1-inch margin at the bottom of the page

As you can see by referring to Figure 6-15, this results in a line span of 57 lines for each page.

Figure 6-15   Computation of report-line span.

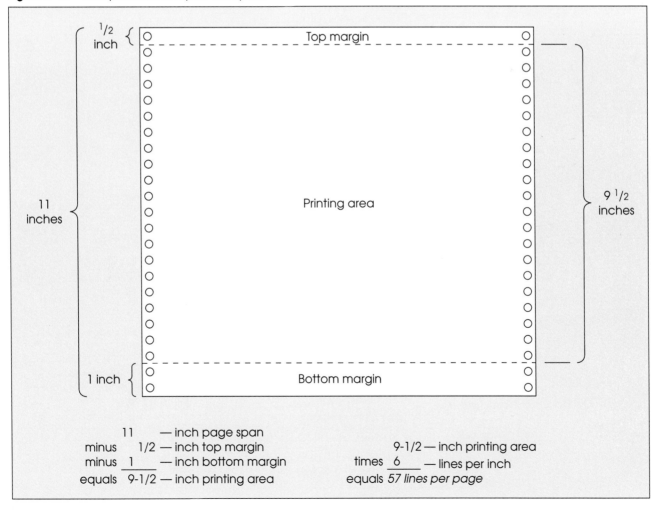

*Program
Specifications*

Having determined the needs of the user and that required input is available for generating the desired output, you can proceed to the program specifications. In Figure 6-16, requirements are described in detail—reflecting the planning of output format. Notice the explicit description of the output format (Items E and F).

Figure 6-16
Programming specifications
for PAYROLL.

PROGRAMMING SPECIFICATIONS

Program name: PAYROLL REPORT   **Program ID:** PAYROLL

Program Description:
　This program is to print a payroll report from input payroll records.

Input File:
　Payroll File

Output File:
　Payroll Report

List of Program Operations:

A.　Read each input payroll record.

B.　For each record:

　1.　Calculate the gross-pay by multiplying the hours-worked by the hourly-rate.

　2.　Print a detail-line containing the following fields in accordance with the format shown on the print-chart:

　　- Employee Social-Security number
　　- Employee name
　　- Employee rate-of-pay
　　- Hours-worked
　　- Gross-pay

　3.　Accumulate the following report totals:

　　a.　Total number of employees listed on the report
　　b.　Total number of hours-worked for all employees
　　c.　Total gross-pay for all employees

C.　Each detail-line should be single-spaced from the previous detail-line.

D.　After all the input payroll records have been processed, the program should print the following total fields on the payroll report total-line in accordance with the format shown on the print chart:

　　- Total number of employees
　　- Total hours-worked
　　- Total gross-pay

E.　Standard 11-inch long continuous forms are to be used as the paper stock. Provide a one-half inch margin at the top of the form and a 1-inch margin at the bottom of the form. Lines are to be printed 6 lines per vertical inch.

F.　Headings are to be printed on the first page of the report. After 57 lines have been used on a report page, the program should skip to the next page and print the headings.

　1.　The run date should be obtained from the operating system and printed on the second heading-line in accordance with the format shown on the print chart.

　2.　The page number should be incremented each time the heading is printed and displayed on the second heading-line in accordance with the format shown on the print chart.

　3.　The first detail-line printed after the headings should be double-spaced from the last heading-line.

Designing the Structure Chart
Top-Down Design

After just working through the CHGACCT program, you probably have a reasonably good idea of the form the structure chart will take for this program. From the structure point-of-view, there is only one difference between these two programs: the repeated printing of heading lines. Hence, you could probably adapt the structure chart of CHGACCT to this program.

However, the structure of programs in this book will become considerably more complex, rendering our previous intuitive approach lacking in doing the job for us. A much more formalized approach is required.

How do you modularize a program? Actually, you will find the process of solving a programming problem very much like building a house. That is, the architect first provides general sketches of the overall house and its placement on the lot. Next, plans are drawn, beginning with the overall and working down to the detail. Only when all of the detailed drawings are complete does actual construction begin.

Similarly, with a programming job, the overall needs and requirements are defined. Then the tasks are broken into subtasks and so on until each is a manageable size. Only after this is complete should the programming begin. This process of working from the general to the specific is commonly called **top-down design**. Let's consider the following seven-step approach to designing a structure chart, using the payroll application as an example.

Step 1: List Functional Program Modules

The programming specifications state that the PAYROLL program must print report headings, process each payroll record, and print a total line.

In accordance with the coding conventions adopted for the CHGACCT program, separate modules will be required to read the payroll records and to print the report lines. In CHGACCT, all lines were printed from a single print module. However, in the PAYROLL program, it will be necessary to use two print modules because of a particular characteristic of the WRITE statement. Hence, as you will learn, two modules will be needed to print the report lines. One print module will write the top, or first, heading line on each page; a second module will be used to write all other lines.

Further, a module to initialize the variable fields in WORKING-STORAGE can be provided. A complete list of the PAYROLL program functions would thus appear as shown in Step 1 of Figure 6-17. When listing functional program modules, they need not be arranged in any particular sequence. The list is merely for reference use while drawing the structure chart to help ensure that all required modules are included.

Notice in the module list that the module-naming conventions introduced earlier in this chapter are followed. Each module name begins with a verb and is followed by a two-word object—the standard used throughout this book. In addition, precise, consistent usage should be observed. Observe the use of the verbs *print* and *write* in the module list. The word *print* is used in this text to describe higher-level modules that either format a report line or handle the printing of more than one line. The word *write* is used for the lower-level, independent common modules that physically WRITE the line.

To facilitate consistent usage among all programmers, many data-processing installations have lists of verbs, together with definitions, for commonly required coding functions.

Step 2: Describe Overall Program Function

In accordance with top-down program development concepts, the top-level block on the structure chart is drawn to describe the overall program function: print payroll report. This is shown in Step 2 of Figure 6-17.

This top-level module, which might be thought of as being at level 0 on the chart, represents the mainline module of the program.

Figure 6-17   Structure chart design (Steps 1–4): Payroll report program.

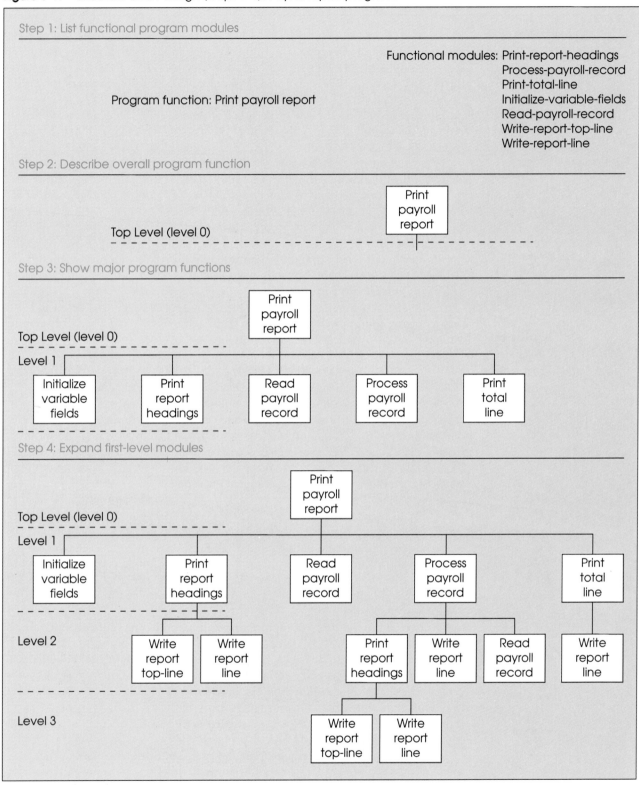

Step 3: Show Major
Program Functions   The modules shown at the first structure chart level from the top are those that relate directly to the overall program function. These are the modules that will be performed from the mainline module. For the PAYROLL program, the following three principal modules can be shown at level 1:

- Print-total-line

- Process-payroll-record

- Initialize-variable-fields

Two other modules shown here at level-1 do not strictly qualify as a major program functions: Read-payroll-record and Print-report-headings. The Read-payroll-record is included because it is the priming-read to obtain the first input payroll record. The Print-report-headings serves a similar function for printing the headings on the first page.

Remember that the purpose of a structure chart is to show how modules relate to one another hierarchically (that is, vertically); sequential (or horizontal) relationships are not necessarily indicated. However, it is easier to relate the structure chart to the program coding when the modules are arranged on the chart from left to right by the order in which the functions will typically occur during program execution. Such a left-to-right arrangement has been incorporated into Step 3 of Figure 6-17, which shows the levels 0 and 1 of the PAYROLL program structure chart.

Step 4: Expand First-Level Modules

Those first-level modules that will perform other modules are expanded to show the performed modules, as illustrated in Step 4 of Figure 6-17. Let's consider each of these first-level modules.

Initialize-Variable-Fields Module. This module is similar in function to that of previous programs in the text. It is executed only once and does not perform any other modules.

Print-Report-Headings Module. There are two conditions under which report headings are printed: at the start of a run (the first page), and after a page has become full and the printer has positioned to a new page. This module as positioned here represents printing the headings for the first page.

This module must in turn perform (1) the write-report-top-line module, which prints the very first heading line on each page, and (2) the write-report-line module, which prints the second and third heading lines. These are shown at level 2.

Read-Payroll-Record Module. The sole function of this module is to read an input record (and to set the end-of-file switch to "YES" when there are no more records in the file). It is identical to the corresponding module of the CHGACCT program. This READ module does not perform any other modules.

Process-Payroll-Record Module. This important processing module performs the following three modules:

- Print-report-headings (when headings are required)

- Write-report-line (to print each detail line)

- Read-payroll-record (to obtain the next input record)

Print-Total-Line Module. This module, executed only once after all payroll records have been processed, performs one other module—print-report-line—to print the grand-total line on the report.

Step 5: Identify Common Modules

As you observed in the CHGACCT program, certain modules—especially those that handle I/O operations—will appear on the structure chart more than once. For this PAYROLL program, the modules Read-payroll-record and Write-report-line each appear twice. These common modules are identified by shading the upper right-hand corner of the common blocks.

Step 6: Review Structure Chart

After you have completed the structure chart, you should review it to verify that it is complete and correct. In doing so, refer to your program specifications to ensure that you have not overlooked any aspect of the program requirements.

Step 7: Number Each Module

Figure 6-18 shows the complete structure chart with common modules identified and module numbers assigned in accordance with the module-numbering conventions of Figure 6-4.

The common modules have been identified by a shaded triangle in the upper right-hand corner. Because the common blocks need be coded only once, parentheses have been affixed to each common block after its first occurrence on the chart. This is simply a small aid to make it easier to check off completed modules during coding (the duplicated blocks with their module numbers in parentheses can be skipped).

Writing the Pseudocode and Drawing the Program Flowchart

Pseudocode for the PAYROLL program is shown in Figure 6-19. A counterpart program flowchart appears in Figure 6-20. Let's consider each of these program modules.

000-Print-Payroll-Report Module

This is the mainline control module. Once the files are opened, it performs the five level-1 modules of the structure chart: 100-Initialize-variable-fields, 800-Read-payroll-record, 870-Print-report-headings, 200-Process-payroll-record, and 700-Print-total-line. After the total line has been printed, the files are closed and the run is stopped.

100-Initialize-Variable-Fields Module

As counterpart initialization modules have done in previous programs of this text, this module handles (1) setting the end-of-file switch to "no" and (2) setting the accumulator fields to zero.

Figure 6-18   Complete structure chart: Payroll report program.

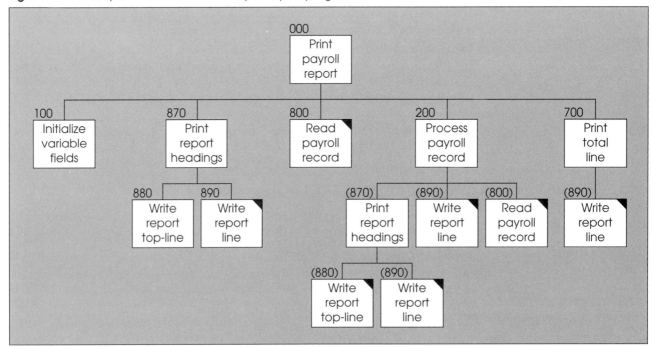

Figure 6-20 (continued)

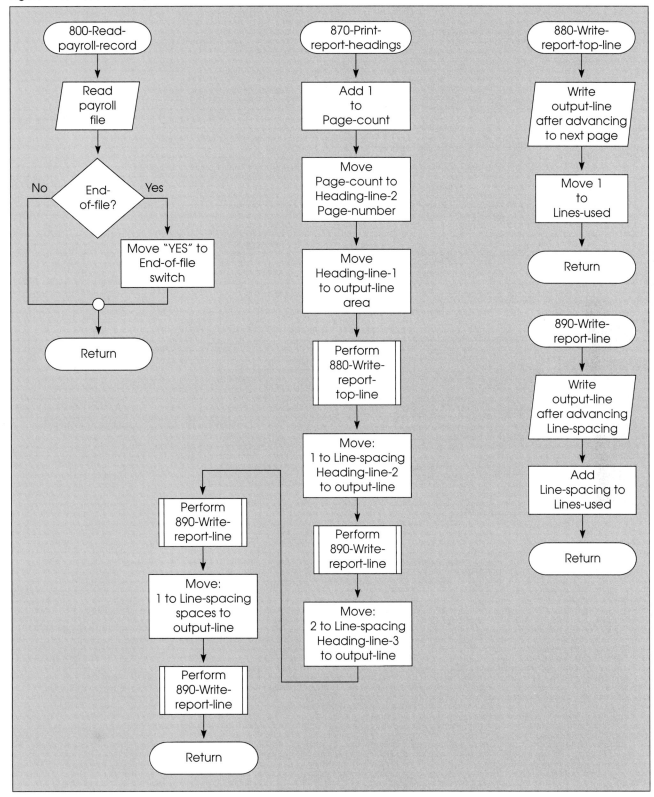

700-Print-Total-Line Module

This module is executed after all the payroll records have been processed. The working-storage fields used to accumulate the report totals—total-employees, total-hours-worked, and total-gross-pay—are moved to the total-line area in working-storage.

A three-step process, similar to that described above for each detail line, is then used to print the total line:

1. The total line is moved from working-storage to the output-line area (in the file section).

2. The line-spacing indicator is set for the proper line spacing (triple-spacing by moving a value 3).

3. The 890-Write-report-line module is performed.

800-Read-Payroll-Record Module

One input employee record is read from the payroll file during each execution of this module. When end-of-file is reached, the end-of-file switch is set to "yes." The PAYROLL program echoes the convention established in the CHGACCT program in that a separate module is used for the READ statement.

870-Print-Report-Headings Module

This module handles the printing of each of the three heading lines. The first thing done in this module is to increment the page number by one because a new report page is being printed. That page-number value is placed in the second heading line.

As indicated previously, printing the first heading line must be done separately from printing other lines (you will learn why later in this chapter). Printing this first line, a two-step process is used:

1. The heading-line is moved from working-storage to the output-line area (in the file section).

2. The 880-Write-report-top-line module is performed to skip to a new report page and print the top line on the page.

A three-step process, similar to that employed for the detail and total lines, is used to print the second and third heading lines:

1. The heading line is moved from working-storage to the output-line area (in the file section).

2. The line-spacing indicator is set for the proper line spacing (single-spacing for the second heading line; double-spacing for the third heading line).

3. The 890-Write-report-line module is performed.

Observe that the programming specifications (Item F.3 of Figure 6-16) call for the first detail line printed after the headings to be double-spaced from the last heading line. However, detail lines are to be single-spaced from one another (per Item C of Figure 6-16). This means that an extra blank line is required *after* the third heading line and *before* the first detail line on each page.

One straightforward way to handle this is to simply print a blank line at the end of this module, as follows:

1. The output-line area (in the file section) is blanked by moving spaces to it.

2. The line-spacing indicator is set for single-spacing.

3. The 890-Write-report-line module is performed.

880-Write-Report-Top-Line Module

This module is used only to print the first heading line on each page. After the write operation, the lines-used indicator is set to 1. This is because one line—the first heading line—will now have been used on the current report page.

890-Write-Report-Line Module This module is used to print all lines—heading, detail, and total—of the report except for the first heading line. It will provide for line spacing (single-, double-, or triple-spacing) in accordance with the value present in the line-spacing indicator field at the time the line is printed.

After printing the line, the value of the line-spacing indicator is added to the lines-used field to keep track of how many lines have been printed on the current page. (Recall that the lines-used field is tested in the 200-Process-payroll-record module to determine when a page is full at which time the continuous form must be positioned to a new page.)

Topic: **Coding a Report Program**

Coding the DATA DIVISION

In the PAYROLL program DATA DIVISION of Figure 6-21, you see nothing new over the concepts of the CHGACCT program (mainly a lot more code). However, there are several items worthy of special note.

Definition of Records in WORKING-STORAGE

You are already familiar from the CHGACCT program with defining the output record as a single 132-byte field. Breakdowns of individual line formats are done in working-storage. For instance, the detail line format description begins at Figure 6-21 line 108. Consistent with the needs of this program, there are five different output records: three heading-line records, one detail-line record, and one total-line record.

The alternative to defining output records in the WORKING-STORAGE SECTION is to use implicit redefinition in the FD. This would be clumsy because you cannot use VALUE clauses in the FILE SECTION; hence, you would need to move each of the descriptive entries (for heading and total lines) each time you needed to write a line. Another advantage is that the WRITE/FROM can, with some COBOL implementations, improve output processing speeds.

Observe in the FILE SECTION coding of Figure 6-21 that the input record PAYROLL-RECORD is also defined as a single field: 49 positions in this case. The individual field breakdown is accomplished in the WORKING-STORAGE SECTION (beginning line 75) in exactly the same way as the output lines. Although this technique does not offer the same multiple-record format advantages for input as it does for output, it is a commonly used method.

However, there is one situation in which it is useful. That is, when the end-of-file has been read, the COBOL standard indicates that the contents of the input area are undefined. Thus, you cannot count on the last record being available. In some applications, you still need reference to the last data record after EOF detection. (An example is described in Chapter 10 for control breaks.) By using a working-storage record area, you will have that last data record available.

For both input and output, another advantage to the separate areas is for debugging when it is necessary to study the contents of the computer's memory to determine what is taking place. A printout of memory contents is commonly called a **memory** or **storage dump**.

A disadvantage of multiple areas is that they consume additional memory within the program. With the current low cost of computer hardware, this is generally not a factor. However, it could be a consideration with large programs on some microcomputers.

General Control and Work Areas

You can see that the WORKING-STORAGE SECTION for each example program is larger than that of the preceding program. Although you can arrange your entries in whatever order you like, your program organization will be enhanced if you use some sort of common pattern. For the programs in this text, the 01-level

Figure 6-21
The DATA DIVISION:
PAYROLL program.

```
36        DATA DIVISION.
37
38        FILE SECTION.
39
40        FD  PAYROLL-FILE
41              RECORD CONTAINS 49 CHARACTERS
42              LABEL RECORDS ARE STANDARD.
43
44        01  PAYROLL-RECORD                    PIC X(49).
45
46        FD  PAYROLL-REPORT
47              RECORD CONTAINS 132 CHARACTERS
48              LABEL RECORDS ARE OMITTED.
49
50        01  REPORT-LINE                       PIC X(132).
51
52        WORKING-STORAGE SECTION.
53
54        01  WS-SWITCHES.
55            05  WS-END-OF-FILE-SWITCH         PIC X(3).
56
57        01  WS-REPORT-CONTROLS.
58            05  WS-PAGE-COUNT                 PIC S9(3).
59            05  WS-LINES-PER-PAGE             PIC S9(2)    VALUE +57.
60            05  WS-LINES-USED                 PIC S9(2).
61            05  WS-LINE-SPACING               PIC S9(2).
62
63        01  WS-WORK-AREAS.
64            05  WS-DATE-WORK.
65                10  WS-YEAR                   PIC 9(2).
66                10  WS-MONTH                  PIC 9(2).
67                10  WS-DAY                    PIC 9(2).
68            05  WS-GROSS-PAY                  PIC S9(5)V99.
69
70        01  WS-TOTAL-ACCUMULATORS.
71            05  WS-TOTAL-EMPLOYEES-ACCUM      PIC S9(4).
72            05  WS-TOTAL-HOURS-WORKED-ACCUM   PIC S9(5)V99.
73            05  WS-TOTAL-GROSS-PAY-ACCUM      PIC S9(6)V99.
74
75        01  PR-PAYROLL-RECORD.
76            05  PR-RECORD-CODE                PIC X(2).
77            05  PR-SOC-SEC-NBR.
78                10  PR-SOC-SEC-NBR-1          PIC 9(3).
79                10  PR-SOC-SEC-NBR-2          PIC 9(2).
80                10  PR-SOC-SEC-NBR-3          PIC 9(4).
81            05  PR-EMPLOYEE-NAME              PIC X(24).
82            05  PR-RATE-OF-PAY                PIC 9(2)V99.
83            05  FILLER                        PIC X(5).
84            05  PR-HOURS-WORKED               PIC 9(3)V99.
85
86        01  H1-HEADING-LINE-1.
87            05  FILLER        PIC X(20)  VALUE "UNIVERSAL BUSINESS S".
88            05  FILLER        PIC X(20)  VALUE "ERVICES COMPANY     ".
89            05  FILLER        PIC X(20)  VALUE "                    ".
90            05  FILLER        PIC X(20)  VALUE "      PAYROLL REPORT".
91
92        01  H2-HEADING-LINE-2.
93            05  H2-MONTH      PIC 9(2).
94            05  FILLER        PIC X(1)   VALUE "/".
95            05  H2-DAY        PIC 9(2).
96            05  FILLER        PIC X(1)   VALUE "/".
97            05  H2-YEAR       PIC 9(2).
98            05  FILLER        PIC X(64)  VALUE SPACES.
99            05  FILLER        PIC X(5)   VALUE "PAGE ".
100           05  H2-PAGE-NBR   PIC ZZ9.
101
102       01  H3-HEADING-LINE-3.
103           05  FILLER        PIC X(20)  VALUE "S.S. NUMBER         ".
104           05  FILLER        PIC X(20)  VALUE "EMPLOYEE NAME       ".
105           05  FILLER        PIC X(20)  VALUE "           RATE     ".
106           05  FILLER        PIC X(20)  VALUE "HOURS      GROSS PAY".
107
108       01  DL-DETAIL-LINE.
109           05  DL-SOC-SEC-NBR.
110               10  DL-SOC-SEC-NBR-1          PIC 9(3).
111               10  FILLER                    PIC X(1)     VALUE "-".
112               10  DL-SOC-SEC-NBR-2          PIC 9(2).
113               10  FILLER                    PIC X(1)     VALUE "-".
114               10  DL-SOC-SEC-NBR-3          PIC 9(4).
115           05  FILLER                        PIC X(6)     VALUE SPACES.
116           05  DL-EMPLOYEE-NAME              PIC X(24).
117           05  FILLER                        PIC X(7)     VALUE SPACES.
118           05  DL-RATE-OF-PAY                PIC ZZ.99.
119           05  FILLER                        PIC X(6)     VALUE SPACES.
120           05  DL-HOURS-WORKED               PIC ZZZ.99.
121           05  FILLER                        PIC X(6)     VALUE SPACES.
122           05  DL-GROSS-PAY                  PIC ZZ,ZZZ.99.
123
124       01  TL-TOTAL-LINE.
125           05  FILLER                        PIC X(19)    VALUE SPACES.
126           05  TL-TOTAL-EMPLOYEES            PIC Z,ZZ9.
127           05  FILLER                        PIC X(32)
128                     VALUE " TOTAL EMPLOYEES                ".
129           05  TL-TOTAL-HOURS-WORKED         PIC ZZ,ZZZ.99.
130           05  FILLER                        PIC X(1)     VALUE "*".
131           05  FILLER                        PIC X(4)     VALUE SPACES.
132           05  TL-TOTAL-GROSS-PAY            PIC ZZZ,ZZZ.99.
133           05  FILLER                        PIC X(1)     VALUE "*".
```

Switches

Report
control fields

Work
areas

Accumulator
(total) fields

Input
record
area

Heading
line
area

Detail
line
area

Total
line
area

record-description entries are arranged in the order illustrated in Figure 6-21: (1) switches, (2) report control fields, (3) work areas, (4) accumulator (total) fields, (5) input-record areas, (6) heading-line areas, (7) detail-line areas, and (8) total-line areas.

WS-REPORT CONTROLS Fields.   You know from the programming specifications that work fields are required in the program to control the following three report functions:

- Sequential page numbering of each report page

- Identification of a full report page so that (1) the page can be skipped over the continuous-form perforations to the top of the next report page, and (2) headings can be printed on the new page

- Variable line spacing (single-, double-, or triple-spacing) with one WRITE statement

The WS-PAGE-COUNT field is used to keep track of the page number of the current report page. It will be incremented each time a new page is headed. Since the programming specifications call for a three-digit page number, WS-PAGE-COUNT has been specified as a three-digit signed numeric field.

The programming specifications call for 57 printed lines per page. To accommodate this need, the WS-LINES-PER-PAGE field is used to hold this line-span value. Observe that its data-item description has been coded with the clause VALUE +57, which means that a value of +57 will be present in the WS-LINES-PER-PAGE field when program execution begins.

To accumulate a running total of the number of lines currently used on each page, the WS-LINES-USED field has been specified. It must accommodate a running total of up to 57, so it has been defined as a two-digit signed numeric field.

As with the CHGACCT program, the WS-LINE-SPACING field is used to keep track of whether single-, double-, or triple-spacing should occur when each line is written.

The WS-WORK-AREAS and WS-TOTAL-ACCUMULATOR Fields.   The work area and accumulator fields you see in Figure 6-21 are similar to their counterparts in previous examples. The programming specifications call for an accumulation of (1) the total number of employees, (2) the total number of hours worked by all employees, and (3) the total gross pay for all employees. Thus, the respective fields WS-TOTAL-EMPLOYEES-ACCUM, WS-TOTAL-HOURS-WORKED-ACCUM, and WS-TOTAL-GROSS-PAY-ACCUM have been defined. The WS-GROSS-PAY field is used as a work area to temporarily hold the product of each employee-rate times hours-worked calculation.

The only "new twist" is the presence of the field WS-DATE-WORK. Later in this chapter, you will see how this is used to obtain the current date from the computer operating system.

The Input and Output Areas   Referring to Figure 6-21, you can see that the WORKING-STORAGE record PR-PAYROLL-RECORD defines the input record. This form is exactly as the definition would have appeared had it been in the FD. Even though it is defined in the WORKING-STORAGE SECTION, the PR prefix for data-names is retained to remind you that this is the PAYROLL-RECORD record definition. Similarly, DL is used to indicate detail line.

For easy identification of the various heading lines, notice that the prefixes H1, H2, and H3 are used (for heading lines 1, 2, and 3, respectively). For convenient reference, the first heading line is repeated on the next page.

This is column 32 ⎯⎯⎯⎯⎯⎯⎯⎯⎯⎯⎯⎯⎯⎯⎯⎯⎯   This is column 72 ⎯⎯⎯⎯⎯

```
01  H1-HEADING-LINE-1.
    05  FILLER          PIC X(20)   VALUE "UNIVERSAL BUSINESS S".
    05  FILLER          PIC X(20)   VALUE "ERVICES COMPANY      ".
    05  FILLER          PIC X(20)   VALUE "                     ".
    05  FILLER          PIC X(20)   VALUE "      PAYROLL REPORT".
```

Observe that these PICTURE clauses are positioned further to the left than the others in the program (they start in position 32). This gives you more room on the same line for entering the literal for the heading. In heading lines H1 and H3 of this program, you can see that the literals are uniformly defined as 20 characters. Hence, the 80-character heading of H1 requires exactly four lines for its definition. Of course, you can refer to the entire line by the group-item name H1-HEADING-LINE-1.

This method is a good one for defining long titles because it is uniform and it makes the counting of spaces between words relatively easy. However, it is not the only way to define a descriptive line; Figure 6-22 shows two other techniques that can be used. Both of these are frequently encountered.

Notice that the second heading line (H1) is set up for the date and page numbers values. The current date will be moved into the date field during the initializing stages of the program. The page number will be changed with each new page.

Coding the PROCEDURE DIVISION

Actually, there is not too much new about the PAYROLL program shown in Figures 6-23 and 6-24; you have learned about most of the underlying principles in the preceding descriptions of the programming specifications. Almost all of the

Figure 6-22
Alternative methods of formatting VALUE clauses for report heading lines.

This method uses nonnumeric literals for words and the figurative constant SPACES for the blank area between the company name and the words PAYROLL REPORT. The method is commonly practiced, but it can be difficult to read and clumsy to modify.

```
01  H1-HEADING-LINE-1.
    05  FILLER          PIC X(35)
            VALUE "UNIVERSAL BUSINESS SERVICES COMPANY".
    05  FILLER          PIC X(31)   VALUE SPACES.
    05  FILLER          PIC X(12)   VALUE "PAYROLL REPORT".
```

This method defines the literal as a single field using the literal continuation capability of COBOL. The approach is very difficult to read and quite error prone.

The first line must be continued all the way to column 72. ⎯⎯⎯⎯⎯⎯⎯⎯

```
01  H1-HEADING-LINE-1.
    05  FILLER          PIC X(80)
            VALUE "UNIVERSAL BUSINESS SERVICES COMPANY
-                                        PAYROLL REPORT".
    "
```

Hyphen in column 7 indicates that this is the continuation of the literal from column 72 of the preceding line.

The literal resumes, following this quote (which can be positioned anywhere in the line.)

Quote ends the literal.

statements have been used in previous programs and thus are familiar to you. However, the following new PROCEDURE DIVISION considerations are introduced:

■ Obtaining the current DATE from the operating system

■ The INTO phrase of the READ statement

■ The ADVANCING PAGE option of the WRITE statement

Figure 6-23   The first three divisions of the PAYROLL program.

```
  1          IDENTIFICATION DIVISION.
  2
  3          PROGRAM-ID.    PAYROLL.
  4
  5      *      WRITTEN BY T. WELBURN.
  6      *      UNIVERSAL BUSINESS SERVICES.
  7      *      JAN 12,1986.
  8      *      REVISED 8-21-89 BY W. PRICE.
  9      *      VALID FOR BOTH COBOL-74 AND COBOL-85.
 10
 11      *      THIS PROGRAM READS PAYROLL RECORDS,
 12      *      COMPUTES THE GROSS PAY FOR EACH EMPLOYEE
 13      *      AND PRINTS AN EMPLOYEE DETAIL LINE
 14      *      FOR EACH PAYROLL RECORD.
 15
 16      *      AFTER ALL INPUT PAYROLL RECORDS HAVE BEEN
 17      *      PROCESSED, A REPORT TOTAL LINE WILL BE PRINTED.
 18
 19
 20          ENVIRONMENT DIVISION.
 21
 22          CONFIGURATION SECTION.
 23
 24          SOURCE-COMPUTER.  (system dependent).
 25          OBJECT-COMPUTER.  (system dependent).
 26
 27          INPUT-OUTPUT SECTION.
 28
 29          FILE-CONTROL.
 30              SELECT PAYROLL-FILE
 31                  ASSIGN TO (system dependent).
 32              SELECT PAYROLL-REPORT
 33                  ASSIGN TO (system dependent).
 34
 35
 36          DATA DIVISION.
 37
 38          FILE SECTION.
 39
 40          FD  PAYROLL-FILE
 41              RECORD CONTAINS 49 CHARACTERS
 42              LABEL RECORDS ARE STANDARD.
 43
 44          01  PAYROLL-RECORD           PIC X(49).
 45
 46          FD  PAYROLL-REPORT
 47              RECORD CONTAINS 132 CHARACTERS
 48              LABEL RECORDS ARE OMITTED.
 49
 50          01  REPORT-LINE              PIC X(132).
 51
 52          WORKING-STORAGE SECTION.
 53
 54          01  WS-SWITCHES.
 55              05  WS-END-OF-FILE-SWITCH    PIC X(3).
 56
 57          01  WS-REPORT-CONTROLS.
 58              05  WS-PAGE-COUNT        PIC S9(3).
 59              05  WS-LINES-PER-PAGE    PIC S9(2)    VALUE +57.
 60              05  WS-LINES-USED        PIC S9(2).
 61              05  WS-LINE-SPACING      PIC S9(2).
 62

 63          01  WS-WORK-AREAS.
 64              05  WS-DATE-WORK.
 65                  10  WS-YEAR              PIC 9(2).
 66                  10  WS-MONTH             PIC 9(2).
 67                  10  WS-DAY               PIC 9(2).
 68              05  WS-GROSS-PAY             PIC S9(5)V99.
 69
 70          01  WS-TOTAL-ACCUMULATORS.
 71              05  WS-TOTAL-EMPLOYEES-ACCUM      PIC S9(4).
 72              05  WS-TOTAL-HOURS-WORKED-ACCUM   PIC S9(5)V99.
 73              05  WS-TOTAL-GROSS-PAY-ACCUM      PIC S9(6)V99.
 74
 75          01  PR-PAYROLL-RECORD.
 76              05  PR-RECORD-CODE               PIC X(2).
 77              05  PR-SOC-SEC-NBR.
 78                  10  PR-SOC-SEC-NBR-1         PIC 9(3).
 79                  10  PR-SOC-SEC-NBR-2         PIC 9(2).
 80                  10  PR-SOC-SEC-NBR-3         PIC 9(4).
 81              05  PR-EMPLOYEE-NAME             PIC X(24).
 82              05  PR-RATE-OF-PAY               PIC 9(2)V99.
 83              05  FILLER                       PIC X(5).
 84              05  PR-HOURS-WORKED              PIC 9(3)V99.
 85
 86          01  H1-HEADING-LINE-1.
 87              05  FILLER          PIC X(20)   VALUE "UNIVERSAL BUSINESS S".
 88              05  FILLER          PIC X(20)   VALUE "ERVICES COMPANY     ".
 89              05  FILLER          PIC X(20)   VALUE "                    ".
 90              05  FILLER          PIC X(20)   VALUE "     PAYROLL REPORT".
 91
 92          01  H2-HEADING-LINE-2.
 93              05  H2-MONTH        PIC 9(2).
 94              05  FILLER          PIC X(1)    VALUE "/".
 95              05  H2-DAY          PIC 9(2).
 96              05  FILLER          PIC X(1)    VALUE "/".
 97              05  H2-YEAR         PIC 9(2).
 98              05  FILLER          PIC X(64)   VALUE SPACES.
 99              05  FILLER          PIC X(5)    VALUE "PAGE ".
100              05  H2-PAGE-NBR     PIC ZZ9.
101
102          01  H3-HEADING-LINE-3.
103              05  FILLER          PIC X(20)   VALUE "S.S. NUMBER        ".
104              05  FILLER          PIC X(20)   VALUE "EMPLOYEE NAME       ".
105              05  FILLER          PIC X(20)   VALUE "         RATE       ".
106              05  FILLER          PIC X(20)   VALUE "HOURS      GROSS PAY".
107
108          01  DL-DETAIL-LINE.
109              05  DL-SOC-SEC-NBR.
110                  10  DL-SOC-SEC-NBR-1     PIC 9(3).
111                  10  FILLER               PIC X(1)    VALUE "-".
112                  10  DL-SOC-SEC-NBR-2     PIC 9(2).
113                  10  FILLER               PIC X(1)    VALUE "-".
114                  10  DL-SOC-SEC-NBR-3     PIC 9(4).
115              05  FILLER               PIC X(6)    VALUE SPACES.
116              05  DL-EMPLOYEE-NAME     PIC X(24).
117              05  FILLER               PIC X(7)    VALUE SPACES.
118              05  DL-RATE-OF-PAY       PIC ZZ.99.
119              05  FILLER               PIC X(6)    VALUE SPACES.
120              05  DL-HOURS-WORKED      PIC ZZZ.99.
121              05  FILLER               PIC X(6)    VALUE SPACES.
122              05  DL-GROSS-PAY         PIC ZZ,ZZZ.99.
123
124          01  TL-TOTAL-LINE.
125              05  FILLER               PIC X(19)   VALUE SPACES.
126              05  TL-TOTAL-EMPLOYEES   PIC Z,ZZ9.
127              05  FILLER               PIC X(32)
128                      VALUE " TOTAL EMPLOYEES               ".
129              05  TL-TOTAL-HOURS-WORKED    PIC ZZ,ZZZ.99.
130              05  FILLER               PIC X(1)    VALUE "*".
131              05  FILLER               PIC X(4)    VALUE SPACES.
132              05  TL-TOTAL-GROSS-PAY   PIC ZZZ,ZZZ.99.
133              05  FILLER               PIC X(1)    VALUE "*".
134
135
```

Figure 6-24 The PROCEDURE DIVISION of the PAYROLL program.

```
136        PROCEDURE DIVISION.
137
138        000-PRINT-PAYROLL-REPORT.
139            OPEN INPUT PAYROLL-FILE
140                OUTPUT PAYROLL-REPORT.
141            PERFORM 100-INITIALIZE-VARIABLE-FIELDS.
142            PERFORM 800-READ-PAYROLL-RECORD.
143            PERFORM 870-PRINT-REPORT-HEADINGS.
144            PERFORM 200-PROCESS-PAYROLL-RECORD
145                UNTIL WS-END-OF-FILE-SWITCH IS EQUAL TO "YES".
146            PERFORM 700-PRINT-TOTAL-LINE.
147            CLOSE PAYROLL-FILE
148                PAYROLL-REPORT.
149            STOP RUN.
150
151        100-INITIALIZE-VARIABLE-FIELDS.
152            MOVE "NO " TO WS-END-OF-FILE-SWITCH.
153            MOVE ZEROS TO WS-TOTAL-EMPLOYEES-ACCUM
154                          WS-TOTAL-HOURS-WORKED-ACCUM
155                          WS-TOTAL-GROSS-PAY-ACCUM
156                          WS-PAGE-COUNT.
157            ACCEPT WS-DATE-WORK FROM DATE.
158            MOVE WS-MONTH TO H2-MONTH.
159            MOVE WS-DAY TO H2-DAY.
160            MOVE WS-YEAR TO H2-YEAR.
161
162        200-PROCESS-PAYROLL-RECORD.
163            IF WS-LINES-USED IS NOT LESS THAN WS-LINES-PER-PAGE
164                PERFORM 870-PRINT-REPORT-HEADINGS.
165            MOVE PR-SOC-SEC-NBR-1 TO DL-SOC-SEC-NBR-1.
166            MOVE PR-SOC-SEC-NBR-2 TO DL-SOC-SEC-NBR-2.
167            MOVE PR-SOC-SEC-NBR-3 TO DL-SOC-SEC-NBR-3.
168            MOVE PR-EMPLOYEE-NAME TO DL-EMPLOYEE-NAME.
169            MOVE PR-RATE-OF-PAY TO DL-RATE-OF-PAY.
170            MOVE PR-HOURS-WORKED TO DL-HOURS-WORKED.
171            MULTIPLY PR-RATE-OF-PAY BY PR-HOURS-WORKED
172                GIVING WS-GROSS-PAY ROUNDED.
173            MOVE WS-GROSS-PAY TO DL-GROSS-PAY.
174            MOVE DL-DETAIL-LINE TO REPORT-LINE.
175            MOVE 1 TO WS-LINE-SPACING.
176            PERFORM 890-WRITE-REPORT-LINE.
177            ADD 1 TO WS-TOTAL-EMPLOYEES-ACCUM.
178            ADD PR-HOURS-WORKED TO WS-TOTAL-HOURS-WORKED-ACCUM.
179            ADD WS-GROSS-PAY TO WS-TOTAL-GROSS-PAY-ACCUM.
180            PERFORM 800-READ-PAYROLL-RECORD.
181
182        700-PRINT-TOTAL-LINE.
183            MOVE WS-TOTAL-EMPLOYEES-ACCUM TO TL-TOTAL-EMPLOYEES.
184            MOVE WS-TOTAL-HOURS-WORKED-ACCUM TO TL-TOTAL-HOURS-WORKED.
185            MOVE WS-TOTAL-GROSS-PAY-ACCUM TO TL-TOTAL-GROSS-PAY.
186            MOVE TL-TOTAL-LINE TO REPORT-LINE.
187            MOVE 3 TO WS-LINE-SPACING.
188            PERFORM 890-WRITE-REPORT-LINE.
189
190        800-READ-PAYROLL-RECORD.
191            READ PAYROLL-FILE INTO PR-PAYROLL-RECORD
192                AT END MOVE "YES" TO WS-END-OF-FILE-SWITCH.
193
194        870-PRINT-REPORT-HEADINGS.
195            ADD 1 TO WS-PAGE-COUNT.
196            MOVE WS-PAGE-COUNT TO H2-PAGE-NBR.
197            MOVE H1-HEADING-LINE-1 TO REPORT-LINE.
198            PERFORM 880-WRITE-REPORT-TOP-LINE.
199            MOVE H2-HEADING-LINE-2 TO REPORT-LINE.
200            MOVE 1 TO WS-LINE-SPACING.
201            PERFORM 890-WRITE-REPORT-LINE.
202            MOVE H3-HEADING-LINE-3 TO REPORT-LINE.
203            MOVE 2 TO WS-LINE-SPACING.
204            PERFORM 890-WRITE-REPORT-LINE.
205            MOVE SPACES TO REPORT-LINE.
206            MOVE 1 TO WS-LINE-SPACING.
207            PERFORM 890-WRITE-REPORT-LINE.
208
209        880-WRITE-REPORT-TOP-LINE.
210            WRITE REPORT-LINE
211                AFTER ADVANCING PAGE.
212            MOVE 1 TO WS-LINES-USED.
213
214        890-WRITE-REPORT-LINE.
215            WRITE REPORT-LINE
216                AFTER ADVANCING WS-LINE-SPACING LINES.
217            ADD WS-LINE-SPACING TO WS-LINES-USED.
```

(a) COBOL-74

```
136        PROCEDURE DIVISION.
137
138        000-PRINT-PAYROLL-REPORT.
139            OPEN INPUT PAYROLL-FILE
140                OUTPUT PAYROLL-REPORT
141            PERFORM 100-INITIALIZE-VARIABLE-FIELDS
142            PERFORM 800-READ-PAYROLL-RECORD
143            PERFORM 870-PRINT-REPORT-HEADINGS
144            PERFORM 200-PROCESS-PAYROLL-RECORD
145                UNTIL WS-END-OF-FILE-SWITCH IS EQUAL TO "YES"
146            PERFORM 700-PRINT-TOTAL-LINE
147            CLOSE PAYROLL-FILE
148                PAYROLL-REPORT
149            STOP RUN.
150
151        100-INITIALIZE-VARIABLE-FIELDS.
152            MOVE "NO " TO WS-END-OF-FILE-SWITCH
153            MOVE ZERO TO WS-PAGE-COUNT
154            INITIALIZE WS-TOTAL-ACCUMULATORS
155            ACCEPT WS-DATE-WORK FROM DATE
156            MOVE WS-MONTH TO H2-MONTH
157            MOVE WS-DAY TO H2-DAY
158            MOVE WS-YEAR TO H2-YEAR.
159
160        200-PROCESS-PAYROLL-RECORD.
161            IF WS-LINES-USED IS NOT LESS THAN WS-LINES-PER-PAGE
162                PERFORM 870-PRINT-REPORT-HEADINGS
163            END-IF
164            MOVE PR-SOC-SEC-NBR-1 TO DL-SOC-SEC-NBR-1
165            MOVE PR-SOC-SEC-NBR-2 TO DL-SOC-SEC-NBR-2
166            MOVE PR-SOC-SEC-NBR-3 TO DL-SOC-SEC-NBR-3
167            MOVE PR-EMPLOYEE-NAME TO DL-EMPLOYEE-NAME
168            MOVE PR-RATE-OF-PAY TO DL-RATE-OF-PAY
169            MOVE PR-HOURS-WORKED TO DL-HOURS-WORKED
170            MULTIPLY PR-RATE-OF-PAY BY PR-HOURS-WORKED
171                GIVING WS-GROSS-PAY ROUNDED
172            MOVE WS-GROSS-PAY TO DL-GROSS-PAY
173            MOVE DL-DETAIL-LINE TO REPORT-LINE
174            MOVE 1 TO WS-LINE-SPACING
175            PERFORM 890-WRITE-REPORT-LINE
176            ADD 1 TO WS-TOTAL-EMPLOYEES-ACCUM
177            ADD PR-HOURS-WORKED TO WS-TOTAL-HOURS-WORKED-ACCUM
178            ADD WS-GROSS-PAY TO WS-TOTAL-GROSS-PAY-ACCUM
179            PERFORM 800-READ-PAYROLL-RECORD.
180
181        700-PRINT-TOTAL-LINE.
182            MOVE WS-TOTAL-EMPLOYEES-ACCUM TO TL-TOTAL-EMPLOYEES
183            MOVE WS-TOTAL-HOURS-WORKED-ACCUM TO TL-TOTAL-HOURS-WORKED
184            MOVE WS-TOTAL-GROSS-PAY-ACCUM TO TL-TOTAL-GROSS-PAY
185            MOVE TL-TOTAL-LINE TO REPORT-LINE
186            MOVE 3 TO WS-LINE-SPACING
187            PERFORM 890-WRITE-REPORT-LINE.
188
189        800-READ-PAYROLL-RECORD.
190            READ PAYROLL-FILE INTO PR-PAYROLL-RECORD
191                AT END MOVE "YES" TO WS-END-OF-FILE-SWITCH
192            END-READ.
193
194        870-PRINT-REPORT-HEADINGS.
195            ADD 1 TO WS-PAGE-COUNT
196            MOVE WS-PAGE-COUNT TO H2-PAGE-NBR
197            MOVE H1-HEADING-LINE-1 TO REPORT-LINE
198            PERFORM 880-WRITE-REPORT-TOP-LINE
199            MOVE H2-HEADING-LINE-2 TO REPORT-LINE
200            MOVE 1 TO WS-LINE-SPACING
201            PERFORM 890-WRITE-REPORT-LINE
202            MOVE H3-HEADING-LINE-3 TO REPORT-LINE
203            MOVE 2 TO WS-LINE-SPACING
204            PERFORM 890-WRITE-REPORT-LINE
205            MOVE SPACES TO REPORT-LINE
206            MOVE 1 TO WS-LINE-SPACING
207            PERFORM 890-WRITE-REPORT-LINE.
208
209        880-WRITE-REPORT-TOP-LINE.
210            WRITE REPORT-LINE
211                AFTER ADVANCING PAGE
212            MOVE 1 TO WS-LINES-USED.
213
214        890-WRITE-REPORT-LINE.
215            WRITE REPORT-LINE
216                AFTER ADVANCING WS-LINE-SPACING LINES
217            ADD WS-LINE-SPACING TO WS-LINES-USED.
```

(b) COBOL-85

The ACCEPT/FROM DATE Statement

To obtain the current date from the operating system, the following ACCEPT/FROM DATE statement is used in the program:

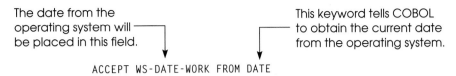

The date from the operating system will be placed in this field.

This keyword tells COBOL to obtain the current date from the operating system.

```
ACCEPT WS-DATE-WORK FROM DATE
```

The date is made available to the program by the operating system as a six-digit, unsigned integer quantity in the *yymmdd* format. (Where *yy* is the two-digit year number of the century, *mm* is the month number, and *dd* is the day number.) The statement moves the date (according to the rules of the MOVE statement) into the field specified in the ACCEPT statement (WS-DATE-WORK in this case). For example, if the current date is March 28, 1991, the contents of WS-DATE-WORK would be as follows:

WS-DATE-WORK

Because the date field is a group-item consisting of three subfields, the year, month, and day are available as shown.

Be aware that some older compilers require that the field to receive the date be an elementary six-digit unsigned numeric integer field. If your compiler has this restriction, you will need to define that field as such, then redefine it in order to obtain the subfields.

The general format of this statement and additional examples are shown in Figure 6-25. Notice that the ACCEPT/FROM statement can also be used to obtain the current day-of-the-year number and the current time. COBOL-85 includes a day-of-the-week option.

When the DAY option is specified, the identifier should be a five-position field. The day number will be stored in what is called a Julianized date format: *yyddd* (where *yy* is the two-digit year number of the century and *ddd* is the three-digit day number from 001 to 365, or 366 during leap year).

Figure 6-25
The ACCEPT/FROM statement.

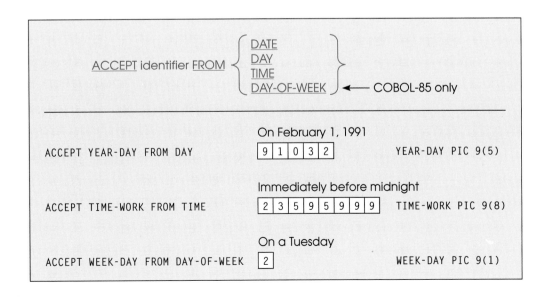

When the TIME option is specified, the identifier should be an eight-position field. The time will be stored in the identifier field in *hhmmsscc* format (where *hh* is the hour number from 00 to 23, *mm* is the minute number from 00 to 59, *ss* is the second number from 00 to 59, and *cc* is hundredths of a second from 00 to 99). Thus, the lowest time value—midnight, the start of a new day—is represented as 00000000. The largest time value occurs immediately before midnight and is represented as 23595999.

When the DAY-OF-WEEK option is specified, the identifier should be a one-position field. The value stored in the identifier field will be a digit from 1 through 7 that corresponds to days of the week from Monday through Sunday. In Figure 6-25, the example returns a value of 2 for Tuesday.

In the PAYROLL program, as with most COBOL programs, we are concerned only with the DATE. So, in the 100-INITIALIZE-VARIABLE-FIELDS module, the DATE is accepted into the WS-DATE-WORK field. Then the month, day, and year portions of the six-digit date are moved individually, two digits at a time, to their respective locations in the H2-HEADING-LINE-2 field. Recognize that the complete six-digit date cannot be moved all at once because the DATE is returned by the operating system in *yymmdd* format but, on the second heading line of the report, it is to be printed in *mm/dd/yy* format.

COBOL Programming Perspective

System Date Handling

The ANS COBOL ACCEPT/FROM DATE statement was not introduced until COBOL-74. Before that, each COBOL compiler vendor chose its own method to retrieve the date from the operating system.

Many COBOL programmers using IBM and IBM-compatible mainframe-computers still use the older, non-ANSI method implemented by IBM in their COBOL compilers: CURRENT-DATE. Because of the prevalence of its use, it is covered here.

CURRENT-DATE is an IBM system-name for an eight-character alphanumeric field that contains the date in *mm/dd/yy* format. To obtain the date, the programmer merely codes a MOVE statement to transfer the CURRENT-DATE to its desired location, as follows:

```
MOVE CURRENT-DATE TO H1-DATE.
```

Observe that, for report headings, the CURRENT-DATE method does not require definition of a separate field (such as the WS-DATE-WORK field of the PAYROLL program) in WORKING-STORAGE to hold the date for reformatting because the CURRENT-DATE is presented in the typically required *mm/dd/yy* format (rather than the *yymmdd* format provided by the ACCEPT/FROM DATE statement). Also, the slashes are already inserted in the CURRENT-DATE.

Because it is simpler to code, most programmers with IBM compilers still use the CURRENT DATE approach. Indeed, many are not even aware of the ANSI COBOL ACCEPT/FROM DATE method. Even if the compiler you are using has both methods available, it is probably better to resist the temptation to use CURRENT-DATE and instead code the ACCEPT/FROM DATE statement so that the program will be in accordance with standard COBOL and hence more portable to other computer systems.

**The READ Statement
INTO Phrase**

From Chapter 5, you are familiar with the WRITE/FROM statement in which the WRITE moves a line from a designated WORKING-STORAGE field to the output line before doing the WRITE. The READ/INTO is effectively the reverse; it reads a data record into the input area, then moves it into a designated WORKING-STORAGE record, as illustrated in Figure 6-26. Note that the following READ-MOVE sequence will accomplish exactly the same thing as the READ/INTO of the PAYROLL program:

```
COBOL-74    READ PAYROLL-FILE
                AT END MOVE "YES" TO WS-END-OF-FILE-SWITCH.
            MOVE PAYROLL-RECORD TO PR-PAYROLL-RECORD.

COBOL-85    READ PAYROLL-FILE
                AT END MOVE "YES" TO WS-END-OF-FILE-SWITCH
            END-READ
            MOVE PAYROLL-RECORD TO PR-PAYROLL-RECORD
```

**The WRITE Statement
ADVANCING Phrase**

From the CHGACCT program, you have already seen a variable used to designate the number of lines to be skipped. For instance, prior to printing the third heading line (which requires double-spacing), the following statement is executed (line 203):

```
MOVE 2 TO WS-LINE-SPACING
```

Figure 6-26
The READ/INTO statement.

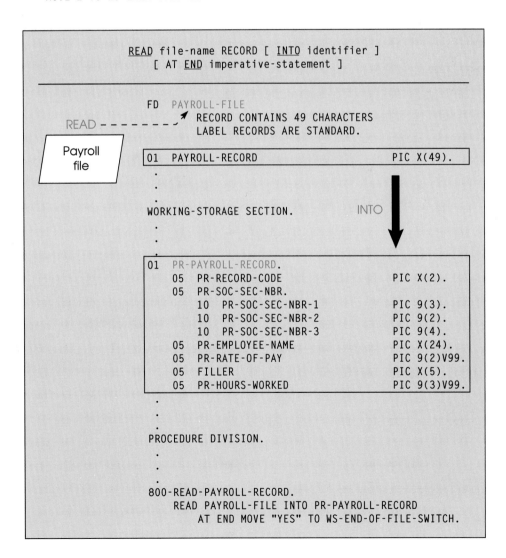

Then at line 215, the following WRITE statement is executed (via a PERFORM):

```
WRITE REPORT-LINE
    AFTER ADVANCING WS-LINE-SPACING LINES
```

Although the line spacing value can have a wide range (typically 0 to 99 depending upon the compiler), it cannot be used to cause the printer to move the form to the beginning of a new report page.

Prior to printing the first heading line, the program must position the form at the top of the next page. You can designate this with the ADVANCING PAGE phrase in a WRITE statement as follows (from lines 210–211 of Figure 6-24):

```
WRITE REPORT-LINE
    AFTER ADVANCING PAGE
```

From the general format of the WRITE statement shown in Figure 6-27, you can see that it allows a variety of forms.

Testing for End-of-Page with the IF Statement

To determine when a page is full, the WS-LINES-USED field must be compared with the WS-LINES-PER-PAGE field. If the value of WS-LINES-USED is equal to the number of lines allotted to the page span, then the 870-PRINT-REPORT-HEADINGS module must be performed to advance the page and print headings on the new page. That is, if WS-LINES-USED contains a value of +57, the headings module must be performed; if it does not, no action regarding headings should be taken.

By now you are quite familiar with the IF statement, which allows for the conditional execution of other statements. Following is the IF from the PAYROLL program (see line 163/161):

```
COBOL-74   IF WS-LINES-USED IS NOT LESS THAN WS-LINES-PER-PAGE
               PERFORM 870-PRINT-REPORT-HEADINGS.

COBOL-85   IF WS-LINES-USED IS NOT LESS THAN WS-LINES-PER-PAGE
               PERFORM 870-PRINT-REPORT-HEADINGS
           END-IF
```

Notice that the IS NOT LESS THAN relational operator is used. In other words, when the two fields become equal, this condition will be true and the heading procedure will be performed. Perhaps you are wondering why the IS NOT LESS THAN test is used rather than the more obvious IS EQUAL TO because they both give the same result. The answer is that you want a new page whenever the line count equals *or exceeds* the maximum allowable. If you were to modify the program at a later date to double-space the detail lines (and increase the line counter by 2 with each detail write), your line counter could progress from 56 to 58, thereby skipping over the equal condition. However, the IS NOT LESS THAN test will always catch such an occurrence.

Figure 6-27
General format of the WRITE statement.

```
Format:

WRITE record-name [FROM identifier-1]

 [                        { { identifier-2 }  [ LINE  ] }  ]
 [ { BEFORE }             { { integer      }  [ LINES ] }  ]
 [ { AFTER  }  ADVANCING  {                             }  ]
 [                        { { mnemonic-name }           }  ]
 [                        { { PAGE          }           }  ]
```

Some Additional Observations About the PAYROLL Program

Signed Fields. The WS-REPORT-CONTROLS fields are all assigned an S symbol in their PICTURE character-string, even though a negative value could never develop in any of these fields. This is done because when a numeric field does not have an S symbol and is either used as (1) a result field for arithmetic operations, or (2) a receiving field for a signed numeric sending field, most COBOL compilers must provide an extra step in the object program code to strip the arithmetic sign from the field. If the S is coded in the result or receiving field, then this extra step is omitted. Thus, more efficient object code is produced when the symbol S is specified in the PICTURE character-string for result fields such as WS-PAGE-COUNT and WS-LINES-USED. You will recall that emphasis in this book has been placed on not sacrificing program simplicity (and ease of maintenance) for program efficiency. However, in this case, program efficiency can be improved with little effort. It's wise to take advantage of such situations.

Assigning a Constant. The maximum number of lines per page is placed in the field WS-LINES-PER-PAGE as the constant value +57. Notice that the only place this field is used in the program is in the condition of the IF, that is:

```
IF WS-LINES-USED IS NOT LESS THAN WS-LINES-PER-PAGE
```

At first thought, defining a separate field for the limit appears unnecessary because the IF could be coded as follows:

```
IF WS-LINES-USED IS NOT LESS THAN +57
```

In general, program maintainability is improved if such constants are defined as fields in working-storage. Then if, at some future date you need to change a value, you can locate it quickly in WORKING-STORAGE. This becomes even more significant if you use the constant in two or more places in the program.

The First Heading Line. Printing the heading line on the first page is handled in somewhat the same way as reading the first data record: it is performed from the mainline module (refer also to the structure chart of Figure 6-18). An alternate method is to initialize the value of WS-LINES-USED to WS-LINES-PER-PAGE (+57). Then during execution, the following will occur (with the omission from the mainline module of line 143):

1. The first record is read.

2. The 800 module will be performed.

3. At line 163/161, the IF condition is true because WS-LINES-USED was initialized to 57. Hence, the headings will be printed for the first page.

Because this is such a common technique (you will probably encounter it on the job), some of the example programs later in this book use it. However, if you use it, be careful because printing of the first page headings is subtly buried in the program logic. This type of action can easily lead to confusion or misinterpretation during program maintenance.

Chapter Summary
Topic: Some Programming Standards

A program module that appears in more than one place on the structure chart (is performed from more than one module in the program) is called a **common module**. Identify common modules on the structure chart by shading the upper-right corner.

A standardized module numbering convention such as that summarized in Figure 6-4 provides for consistency among programs. This helps to standardize code in an installation and results in better program maintainability.

Use only one READ and one WRITE statement for each file—except that you will need two WRITE statements if a top-of-page action is needed. Do this by including each in a separate module. In general, programming code is easier to debug and maintain when a common input or output operation is handled at a single location.

Using the single-WRITE module approach, two actions must take place before performing the WRITE module:

- The output record must be moved from working-storage to the output line.

- The field-name in the AFTER ADVANCING clause must be set to the line spacing value.

Topic: Designing a Report Program

With large programs, an orderly approach to program design is essential. Top-down design is a step-by-step approach of proceeding from the general to the modularized detail until a large, complex task is broken down into a collection of interrelated, basic tasks. Following is a seven-step approach to creating a structure chart:

1. List the functional program modules.

2. Describe the overall program function on the top level of the structure chart.

3. Show the major program functions on the first level of the structure chart.

4. Expand the first-level modules to show the modules that will be performed at lower levels. Expand lower levels until further breakdown is no longer necessary.

5. Identify common modules.

6. Review the structure chart.

7. Number each module.

Once a multipage report format layout is designed and the print chart created, the number of detail lines can be calculated. (This is necessary to control the new page action.) The amount of space required for top and bottom margins and the headings must be subtracted from the form length. The difference is the amount of space available for printing the detail part of the report.

Topic: Coding a Report Program

The READ/INTO option of the READ statement reads a record into the FILE SECTION and then transfers it immediately to a specified record-area (typically in the WORKING-STORAGE SECTION). READ/INTO processing is equivalent to a READ statement followed by a MOVE statement.

To provide report page skipping, the PAGE option of the ADVANCING phrase is used.

To obtain line spacing for a variable number of lines with one WRITE statement, the identifier option of the ADVANCING phrase is specified. The identifier must be a one- or two-digit numeric integer field. When the statement is executed, the printer forms are advanced a number of lines equal to the current value of the identifier field.

The current date, day, or time may be obtained from the operating system by the statement: ACCEPT identifier FROM DATE, DAY, TIME, or (for COBOL-85 only) DAY-OF-WEEK. In each case, the result is moved as an unsigned integer field into the designated identifier as follows:

DATE	*yymmdd*
DAY	*yyddd* (Julianized date format)
TIME	*hhmmsscc*
DAY-OF-WEEK	*d* (Day number 1–7 corresponding to Monday-Sunday)

The IF/ELSE (expansion of the IF statement) provides the full conditional capability to take either of two actions depending upon a test condition (it is the COBOL implementation of the selection structure).

Style Summary
WORKING-STORAGE SECTION

When describing records in the WORKING-STORAGE SECTION that contain primarily constant values for headings, start the PICTURE clauses in position 32 and the VALUE clauses in position 44. This gives you up to 20 positions for the literal. For a long literal, break it up into groups of 20 characters.

Initialize constant fields with VALUE clauses in the WORKING-STORAGE SECTION of the DATA DIVISION; initialize variable fields with PROCEDURE DIVISION statements. Doing so aids program documentation and provides more flexibility for repeated execution of modules.

Define output records in the WORKING-STORAGE SECTION. Such definition (1) allows VALUE clauses to be used for the initialization of constant fields within the record, (2) in some cases, causes output operations to be more efficient, and (3) makes it easier to determine the current output record being processed when referring to a storage dump.

In most cases, define input records in the WORKING-STORAGE SECTION. The advantages of input-record definition in WORKING-STORAGE are not as great as those for output-record definition, but it does (1) permit reference to the fields of a record after the last record in the file has been read, (2) in some cases, cause output operations to be more efficient, and (3) make it easier to determine the current input record being processed when referring to a storage dump.

Arrange your WORKING-STORAGE SECTION entries in an organized way. The following is a recommended order:

1. switches

2. report control fields

3. work areas

4. accumulator (total) fields

5. input-record areas

6. heading-line areas

7. detail-line areas

8. total-line areas

ACCEPT/FROM DATE Statement

If available, use the COBOL-standard ACCEPT/FROM statement rather than other implementor-dependent methods to obtain the calendar date, Julianized date, and time.

WRITE Statement

Use the ADVANCING identifier option of the WRITE statement for line spacing. This permits spacing of a variable number of lines through the use of one common, independent WRITE module.

Avoid use of the WRITE/FROM option for report lines because it is not consistent with the use of common, independent I/O modules.

Features in COBOL-85 Not in COBOL-74

The INITIALIZE statement provides for initializing all elementary items under this group item. The initialization involves setting numeric and numeric-edited fields to zero, and alphanumeric, alphanumeric-edited, and alphabetic fields to spaces.

The DAY-OF-WEEK option can be used in the ACCEPT/FROM statement. COBOL returns a one-digit number ranging from 1 to 7, which represents the days Monday through Sunday.

Exercises

Terms for Definition

common module _____

constant data _____

heading line _____

top-down design _____

variable data _____

Review Questions

1. List the seven steps for preparation of a structure chart.

   a. _____

   b. _____

   c. _____

   d. _____

   e. _____

   f. _____

   g. _____

2. The literal specified in the VALUE clause must be consistent with the

   _____ , _____ , and _____
   of the PICTURE clause with which it is associated.

3. The VALUE clause cannot be specified in the _____.

   SECTION or with a field that contains either a(n) _____ or

   a(n) _____ clause.

4. Identify two reasons why it is usually preferable to define output records in
   the WORKING-STORAGE SECTION, rather than the FILE SECTION.

   a. _____

   b. _____

5. Identify two reasons why it is preferable to define input records in the
   WORKING-STORAGE SECTION, rather than the FILE SECTION.

   a. _____

   b. _____

6. What is a disadvantage of WORKING-STORAGE SECTION definition of
   input and output records?

   _____

7. Most programs that provide for the printing of report headings require report-control fields for which three functions?

   a. _____

   b. _____

   c. _____

8. With the ACCEPT/FROM DATE statement, the field that receives the date should be _____ positions in length; after execution, the field will contain the date in _____ format.

9. With the ACCEPT/FROM DAY statement, the field that receives the day number should be _____ positions in length; after execution, the field will contain the day number in _____ format.

10. When coding the ACCEPT/FROM TIME statement, the field that receives the time should be _____ positions in length; after execution, the field will contain the time in _____ format.

11. A READ statement specified with the INTO phrase is equivalent to the specification of a(n) _____ statement followed by a(n) _____ statement.

12. A WRITE statement specified with the FROM phrase is equivalent to the specification of a(n) _____ statement followed by a(n) _____ statement.

13. To provide for skipping to the top of the next report page, the _____ option of the ADVANCING phrase is used.

14. To provide variable line spacing with one WRITE statement, the _____ option of the ADVANCING phrase is used.

Questions About the Example Programs

CHGACCT—Refer to Figures 6-7 and 6-8

1. REPORT-LINE is defined as a 132-position output line in the FD (program line 59). However, each of the three working-storage output lines (which will be moved to REPORT-LINE) consists of fewer than 132 positions. Explain why this discrepancy is valid.

   _____

   _____

   _____

2. What would occur during execution of the program if the S sign indicator were omitted from the field CA-BALANCE-FORWARD (see line 50)?

_____

_____

_____

3. A beginning programmer surveys CHGACCT and decides that the three output records need not be defined in working-storage, so moves them into the file section so that they implicitly redefine REPORT-LINE. Comment on this.

_____

_____

_____

4. Another programmer forgets the VALUE SPACES clauses in the working-storage record definitions. Describe the appearance of the printed report for each of the three types of lines: column heading, detail, and total.

_____

_____

_____

5. Describe what will occur if the statements initializing the accumulators are omitted (lines 119-122 for COBOL-74 and line 119 for COBOL-85).

_____

_____

_____

6. What will happen if the data file contains no records (only the EOF)?

_____

_____

_____

PAYROLL—Refer to Figures 6-23 and 6-24.

1. Describe the program output if the initial value of WS-LINES-PER-PAGE is accidentally entered as +5 instead of +57.

_____

_____

_____

2. This program includes two counters: WS-PAGE-COUNT and WS-LINES-USED. There is an important conceptual difference between the way in which these accumulators are used in the program. Identify that difference.

_____

_____

_____

3. Describe the printed output if the IF (at line 163/161) were accidentally coded as:

```
IF WS-LINES-USED IS LESS THAN WS-LINES-PER-PAGE
```

_____

_____

_____

4. Describe the printed output if the MOVE statement at line 212 were omitted.

_____

_____

_____

5. Since the report format includes five heading lines (with the blank line preceding the first detail line), there will be 52 detail lines per page. Where will the total line be printed if the data file contains exactly 52 data records?

_____

_____

_____

6. Identify the changes that would be necessary in order to move the field components to the output area using the MOVE/CORRESPONDING statement.

_____

_____

_____

Programming Assignments

Programming Assignment 6-1: Price List
Background information:
The sales manager of Tools Unlimited needs a report—listing each item in the product line and its price—prepared from the inventory file.

Input file: Inventory file (INVEN.DAT)

Input-record format:

Positions	Field	Data class	Comments
1–2	Record code	Numeric	Code 44
4–13	Product identification		Group item
4–7	Product type	Alphanumeric	
8–13	Product number	Alphanumeric	
14–39	Product description	Alphanumeric	
40	Inventory class	Alphanumeric	
41–46	Unit price (unit cost)	Numeric	Format: 9999V99
47–80	Other data		

Output-report format:

```
         0         1         2         3         4         5
   1234567890123456789012345678901234567890123456789012345678901234567
 1
 2
 3
 4
 5                              PRICE LIST (6-1)
 6
 7  PART NUMBER          PART DESCRIPTION                      PRICE
 8
 9  XXXXXXXXXX        XXXXXXXXXXXXXXXXXXXXXXXXXX           Z,ZZZ.99
10  XXXXXXXXXX        XXXXXXXXXXXXXXXXXXXXXXXXXX           Z,ZZZ.99
```

Program operations:

1. Process each input part record—except those with a value "X" for the Inventory-class field.
2. Print the two heading lines on the first page and on each following page of the list.
3. Print an output price list detail line for each part record as specified on the print chart.
4. Single-space each detail line (except double-space between the last heading line and the first detail line on each page, as shown on the print chart). Provide for a span of 57 lines per page.

Programming Assignment 6-2: Earnings Report

Background information:

The personnel manager of Silicon Manufacturing wants a program to print an employee earnings report from data in the earnings file.

Input file: Earnings file (EARNINGS.DAT)

Input-record format:

Positions	Field name	Data class	Comments
11–19	Employee number	Alphanumeric	Social Security number
20–31	Employee last name	Alphanumeric	
32–40	Employee first name	Alphanumeric	
53	Pay code	Alphabetic	
67–74	Year-to-date earnings	Numeric	Format *nnnnnnnn*

Output file:
Earnings Report

Output-report format:

```
          0          1          2          3          4          5
 1234567890123456789012345678901234567890123456789012345

 1
 2
 3
 4  EARNINGS REPORT (6-2)                    MM/DD/YY   PAGE ZZ9
 5
 6     EMPLOYEE          ----EMPLOYEE NAME-----   YEAR-TO-DATE
 7      NUMBER          LAST          FIRST         EARNINGS
 8
 9  999-99-9999       XXXXXXXXXXX  XXXXXXXX       ZZZ,ZZZ.99
10
11  999-99-9999       XXXXXXXXXXX  XXXXXXXX       ZZZ,ZZZ.99
12
13
14                 HOURLY TOTAL EARNINGS     Z,ZZZ,ZZZ.99*
15                 SALARIED TOTAL EARNINGS   Z,ZZZ,ZZZ.99*
```

Program operations:
1. Process each input earnings record.
2. Print the three heading lines on the first page and on each following page of the report.
   a. Print the run date on the first heading line as specified on the print chart.
   b. Accumulate and print the page number on the first heading line as specified on the print chart.
3. For each input employee record, do the following processing:
   a. Print an output earnings detail line, as specified on the print chart.
   b. Accumulate the total earnings for hourly employees (Pay-code is "H") and for non-hourly employees (Pay-code is *not* "H").
4. Double-space each detail line. Provide for a span of 40 lines per page.
5. After all input earnings records have been processed, print two total lines—one for the hourly employees and the other for the non-hourly employees. For the first total line, triple-space from the last detail line as specified on the print chart.

Programming Assignment 6-3: Sales Quota Report
Program description:
The sales manager of Follow-the-Sun Sales wants to know how each member of the sales staff is performing relative to his or her sales quota. For this, a sales quota report must be printed from the salesperson file.

Input file: Salesperson file (SALESPER.DAT)

Input-record format:

Positions	Field name	Data class	Comments
3–4	Salesperson region	Alphanumeric	
5–8	Salesperson territory	Alphanumeric	
9–11	Salesperson number	Alphanumeric	
12–37	Salesperson name	Alphanumeric	
61–70	Sales revenue	Numeric	Format *nnnnnnnnnn*
71–79	Sales quota	Numeric	Format *nnnnnnnnn*

Output-report format:

```
           0          1          2          3          4          5          6          7          8
  123456789012345678901234567890123456789012345678901234567890123456789012345678901234567890
 1
 2
 3
 4 FOLLOW-THE-SUN SALES                                             RUN DATE MM/DD/YY
 5 SALES QUOTA REPORT (6-3)                                                    PAGE ZZ9
 6
 7 REGION-    ----------SALESPERSON----------        SALES          SALES   -PERCENT QUOTA
 8  TERR.    NBR     NAME                             QUOTA          REVENUE  OF QUOTA MADE
 9
10 XX-9999   999  XXXXXXXXXXXXXXXXXXXXXXXXXX    Z,ZZZ,ZZZ.99   ZZ,ZZZ,ZZZ.99      ZZ9%    YES
11
12 XX-9999   999  XXXXXXXXXXXXXXXXXXXXXXXXXX    Z,ZZZ,ZZZ.99   ZZ,ZZZ,ZZZ.99      ZZ9%         YES
13                                                                                        or blank
14
15         TOTAL SALESPERSON  Z,ZZ9*           ZZ,ZZZ,ZZZ.99* ZZZ,ZZZ,ZZZ.99*    ZZ9%*
```

Program operations:
1. Process each input salesperson record.
2. Print the four heading lines on the first page and on each following page of the report.
   a. Print the run date on the first heading line as specified on the print chart.
   b. Accumulate and print the page number on the second heading line as specified on the print chart.
3. For each input salesperson record, do the following processing:
   a. Calculate the percent-of-quota by dividing the sales revenue by the sales quota. Round the percentage to the nearest percentage point.
   b. Print an output detail line as specified on the print chart.
   c. If the salesperson makes his or her quota (Sales-revenue not less than Sales-quota), then print the word "YES" as indicated on the print chart. Otherwise, leave this entry blank.
   d. Accumulate the total number of salespersons, the total sales quota, and the total sales revenue.
4. Double-space each detail line. Provide for a span of 55 lines per page.
5. After all input salesperson records have been processed:
   a. Calculate the total percent-of-quota.
   b. Print the output report total line (triple-spaced from the last detail line) as specified on the print chart.

Programming Assignment 6-4: Aged Analysis Report
Program description:
One of the subsidiaries of Silicon Valley Manufacturing follows standard accounts-receivable procedures of "aging" amounts due. The amount owed by each customer is broken down into categories that identify whether it is a current amount owed, past due by more than 30 days, or past due by more than 60 days. A report

of amounts owed by customers identified by these categories is called an aged analysis report. One is required by the accounting manager.

Input file: Customer file (CUSTOMER.DAT)

Input-record format:

Positions	Field	Data class	Comments
3–7	Customer number		
8–31	Customer name	Alphanumeric	
39–46	Account balance	Numeric	Format *nnnnnnnn*
47–54	Current amount	Numeric	Format *nnnnnnnn*
55–62	Over-30 amount	Numeric	Format *nnnnnnnn*
63–70	Over-60 amount	Numeric	Format *nnnnnnnn*
71–80	Other data		

Output-report format:

```
          0         1         2         3         4         5         6         7         8         9        10
 1234567890123456789012345678901234567890123456789012345678901234567890123456789012345678901234567890123456789 01
 1
 2
 3
 4 EFFICIENT CHIPS MFG. CO                                                   RUN TIME HH:MM:SS   RUN DATE MM/DD/YY
 5 AGED ANALYSIS REPORT (6-4)                                                                           PAGE ZZ9
 6
 7 CUSTOMER                         ACCOUNT          CURRENT          OVER-30          OVER-60
 8 NUMBER        CUSTOMER NAME      BALANCE          AMOUNT           AMOUNT           AMOUNT
 9
10   99999   XXXXXXXXXXXXXXXXXXXXXXXX  ZZZ,ZZZ.99CR     ZZZ,ZZZ.99CR     ZZZ,ZZZ.99CR     ZZZ,ZZZ.99CR
11   99999   XXXXXXXXXXXXXXXXXXXXXXXX  ZZZ,ZZZ.99CR     ZZZ,ZZZ.99CR     ZZZ,ZZZ.99CR     ZZZ,ZZZ.99CR
12
13               PAGE TOTAL   Z,ZZZ,ZZZ.99CR*   Z,ZZZ,ZZZ.99CR*   Z,ZZZ,ZZZ.99CR*   Z,ZZZ,ZZZ.99CR*
14
15             REPORT TOTAL  ZZ,ZZZ,ZZZ.99CR**  ZZ,ZZZ,ZZZ.99CR**  ZZ,ZZZ,ZZZ.99CR**  ZZ,ZZZ,ZZZ.99CR**
```

Program operations:
1. Read each input customer record.
2. Print the four heading lines on the first page and on each following page of the report.
   a. Print the run time on the first heading line as specified on the print chart.
   b. Print the run date on the first heading line as specified on the print chart.
   c. Accumulate and print the page number on the second heading line as specified on the print chart.
3. For each input customer record, do the following processing:
   a. Print an output detail line as specified on the print chart.
   b. Accumulate the total account balance, current amount, over-30 amount, and over-60 amount.
4. Single-space each detail line (except double-space between the last heading line and the first detail line on each page, as shown on the print chart). Provide for a span of 53 lines per page (not counting the page-total line).
5. Print a page-total line at the bottom of each report page as shown on the print chart. The page-total line is to contain a total of the account balances, current amounts, over-30 amounts, and over-60 amounts printed on that page.
6. After all input salesperson records have been processed:
   a. Print the last page-total line.
   b. Print the report total line (double-spaced from the last detail line) as specified on the print chart.

Programming Assignment 6-5: Nurses' Salary Increase Projection

Program description:

The management of Brooklawn Hospital found the pay projections from the program of Assignment 4-5 valuable, but the report was deemed clumsy to read. That program is to be modified as follows:

Input file: Nurses file (NURSES.DAT)

Input-record format: No change over Assignment 4-5.

Output-report format:

```
          0         1         2         3         4         5         6
 1234567890123456789012345678901234567890123456789012345678901234567890123
1
2
3
4  BROOKLAWN HOSPITAL                                      RUN DATE MM/DD/YY
5  SALARY INCREASE PROJECT (6-5)                               PAGE    ZZ9
6
7  PROFESSIONAL                              ------SALARY PROJECTIONS------
8  SPECIALTY         NAME                    BASE      DIFF.      TOTAL
9
10 XXXXXXXXXXXXX  XXXXXXXXXXXXXXXXXXXXXXXX  Z,ZZZ.99  ZZZ.99   Z,ZZZ.99
11
12 XXXXXXXXXXXXX  XXXXXXXXXXXXXXXXXXXXXXXX  Z,ZZZ.99  ZZZ.99   Z,ZZZ.99
13
14
15            TOTAL NURSES      ZZZ*    Z,ZZZ,ZZZ.99*      Z,ZZZ,ZZZ.99*
16       NURSES WITH SHIFT DIFF. ZZZ*
```

Program operations:

1. Process each input customer record.
2. Print the four heading lines on each following page of the report.
3. For each input record, do the following processing:
   a. Print an output detail line as specified on the print chart.
   b. Accumulate totals for the New-base-monthly-salary and the New-total-monthly-salary.
   c. Maintain a count of the number of records processed and the number of nurses receiving a shift differential.
4. Double-space each detail line as shown on the print chart. Provide for a span of 53 lines per page (not counting the total lines).
5. Print the two page total lines as shown on the print chart.

Programming Assignment 6-6: Vehicle Rental Application

Program description:

The program of Assignment 5-6 expanded to include the following:

1. A two-page heading line that includes the date and page number.
2. One or two column heading lines (as appropriate).
3. Detail and summary lines as in Assignment 5-6.
4. Provide for a span of 36 lines per page.

Programming Assignment 6-7: Computer Store Average Prices

Background information:

Complete Computers Corporation (Programming Assignment 2-8) configures personal computer systems for individuals based on specific needs. One of their data files includes information about the variety of computer products they must order to conduct their business. This file includes one record for each product item identifying vendors from which it can be ordered, as well as pertinent pricing information. For each item, the Smiths (owners of the company) have identified two prices to be considered when ordering. First is a target price (one they can reasonably expect to get) and the other is a maximum price (the point beyond which they will begin to lose money). For further costing studies, they want a report that includes some pricing averages.

Input file: The CCC Inventory file (CCCINVEN.DAT)

Input record format:

Positions	Field	Data class	Comments
1–5	Product category code	Alphanumeric	
6–20	Product name	Alphanumeric	
21	Product class	Alphanumeric	Value of A or B.
22–27	Target price	Numeric	Dollars and cents
28–33	Maximum price	Numeric	Dollars and cents
34–60	Other product data		

Output report-line format:

```
          0         1         2         3         4         5
     1234567890123456789012345678901234567890123456789012345678901234567890123
 1
 2
 3
 4   COMPLETE COMPUTERS CORP.                              RUN DATE MM/DD/YY
 5   PRODUCT COMPONENT COST SUMMARY (6-7)                           PAGE ZZ9
 6
 7   PRODUCT                         PRODUCT           TARGET       MAXIMUM
 8   CODE        PRODUCT             CLASS             PRICE         PRICE
 9
10   XXXXX       XXXXXXXXXXXXXXX       X             Z,ZZZ.99      Z,ZZZ.99
11
12   XXXXX       XXXXXXXXXXXXXXX       X             Z,ZZZ.99      Z,ZZZ.99
13
14
15               AVERAGES:   CLASS A                Z,ZZZ.99      Z,ZZZ.99
16                           CLASS B                Z,ZZZ.99      Z,ZZZ.99
```

Program operations:

1. Process each input inventory record.
2. Print the four heading lines on each page of the report.
3. For each input record, do the following processing:
    a. Print an output detail line as specified on the print chart.
    b. Determine whether or not the Product Class is A. If A, accumulate Class A totals for the Target Price and Maximum Price; if not A, accumulate for Class B totals for the Target Price and Maximum Price. (*Note:* This processing causes any record containing other than A or B for this field to be treated as if it were B, an acceptable action for this assignment.)
    c. Maintain a count of the number of Class A records and Class B records.
4. Double–space each detail line as shown on the print chart. Provide for a span of 44 lines per page (not counting the total lines).
5. After the last record is processed, calculate the averages for the prices (the A prices divided by the A count and the B prices divided by the B count).
6. Print the two page total lines as shown on the print chart.

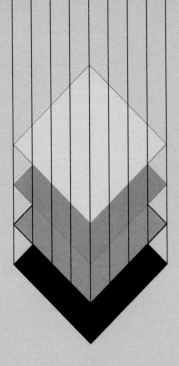

 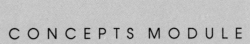

Structured Design and Documentation Techniques

Module Objectives

You are now beginning to see programs that are substantial in size and that include some degree of conditional logic. The topic of the next chapter is the IF statement and its multitude of forms; this will provide the basis for tackling programs with complex logic. A sound approach to program planning and design using available tools will become even more important than it has been with programs so far. The tools you have been using, although widely accepted, are not the only ones available. The purpose of this concepts module is to pause and place structure charts, pseudocode, and flowcharts in their proper perspective, and to focus on some other design tools that are commonly encountered. From this module, you will learn the following techniques:

- Data-flow diagrams
- Hierarchy plus Input-Process-Output (HIPO)
- Nassi-Shneiderman diagrams
- Chapin charts
- Warnier (and Warnier-Orr) diagrams
- Jackson (JSP) diagrams

Module Outline

A Label Printing Application
System and Overall Program Structure Techniques
Structure Charts
Data-Flow Diagrams
HIPO

Detailed Program-Processing Techniques
Traditional Program Flowcharts
Pseudocode
Nassi-Shneiderman Diagrams
Chapin Charts
Warnier (and Warnier-Orr) Diagrams
Jackson (JSP) Diagrams

A Label Printing Application

By now you are probably becoming aware of the fact that programming involves more than simply writing program code. Indeed, you are probably beginning to spend a considerable amount of time designing your program and testing it once it is written. This is not unique to the student environment. In fact, in the business world, far more time is spent in such activities as designing, documenting, and testing than in writing program code.

As you might expect, this has spawned significant effort in the development of techniques and tools to improve the efficiency of the design process. You are familiar with three commonly used tools: structure charts in conjunction with top-down design, pseudocode, and flowcharts. Many other techniques have been advanced to aid in the design and documentation of structured programs. Let's take a brief glance at some of the more commonly known methods.

For the sake of illustration, consider a typical data-processing application: printing mailing labels from a periodical subscriber file. Each subscriber has one record that includes the subscriber name and address; it also includes subscription data, such as an expiration code field indicating whether or not the subscription has expired. The programming specifications for this application are shown in Figure F-1.

Figure F-1
Programming specifications: Subscriber mailing-address label program.

PROGRAMMING SPECIFICATIONS

Program name: MAILING LABELS   **Program ID:** LABELS

Program Description:
This program is to print subscriber mailing labels for current subscribers from subscriber records.

Input File:
Subscriber File

Output File:
Subscriber Labels

List of Program Operations:

   A. Read each input subscriber record.

   B. For each record, check the Expired-code field to see
       if the subscription is current or if it has expired.

      1. If the subscription is current
         (Expired-code = N):

         a. Print a mailing label for the subscriber.

         b. Add 1 to the Labels-printed count.

      2. If the subscription is not current
         (Expired-code not = N):

         a. Do not print a mailing label.

         b. Add 1 to the Expired-subscription count.

   C. After all the input subscriber records have been
       processed, print the following total fields:

      1. The Labels-printed count

      2. The Expired-subscription count

In the sections that follow, several modern design techniques are illustrated with this LABELS program. As you will see, some of the techniques are addressed to overall program structure, whereas others are intended for the expression of more detailed program processing.

System and Overall Program Structure Techniques

Three overall program structure design and documentation techniques are commonly used: structure charts, data-flow diagrams, and HIPO.

Structure Charts

You have been using **structure charts** throughout this text. They graphically show each module (COBOL procedure) required by the program, its hierarchical level, and its relationship to the other program modules. In appearance, a structure chart looks very much like the familiar organization chart that shows the hierarchy of positions within an organization. A structure chart for the LABELS program is shown in Figure F-2.

Remember that a structure chart does not show the sequence in which modules will be executed or the conditional decisions that will cause modules to be performed or skipped. The purpose of a structure chart is to give a concise overview of module hierarchy and structure. It also serves as a table of contents to module location within a program.

Sometimes intermodule communication flow is depicted on the structure chart, as illustrated in Figure F-3. The arrows indicate the direction in which data is passed. The open circles signify the passing of data; the filled circles identify flags or switches.

Data-Flow Diagrams

The use of the **data-flow diagram** for structured design and documentation has been advanced by Edward Yourdon and others within his organization. It is typically used for the design of complete systems. Often called a "bubble chart," the data-flow diagram (DFD) resembles a system flowchart because it is primarily concerned with the flow of data through a program or a system. However, rather than employing special system flowcharting symbols to differentiate physical storage media, clerical activities, programs, subprograms, and the like, the DFD simply uses a circle—or bubble—symbol to represent all data-flow steps.

Figure F-2
Structure chart example.

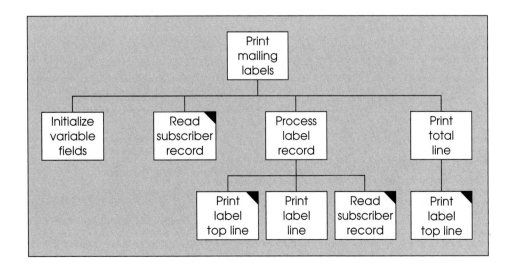

Figure F-3
Structure chart intermodule
communication
conventions.

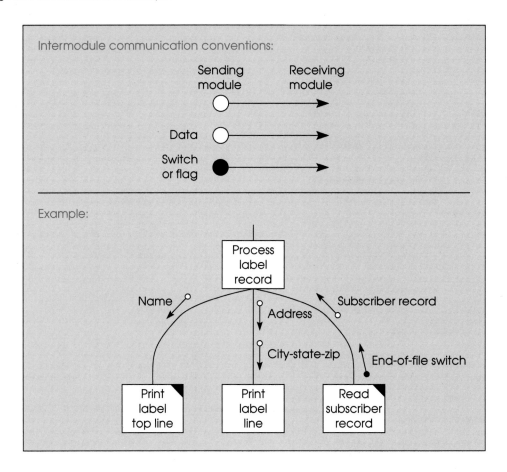

The purpose of the DFD is to show only the logical flow of data, without regard for the following:

1. The physical form (such as disk, tape, and main storage) that the data will take

2. The resources that will operate upon the data (such as people, computers, and programs)

3. The control logic (sequence, selection, or iteration) that will apply to the data

Thus, when used as a structured design technique, the DFD is used as a first step to proper design.

Although data-flow diagrams are not ordinarily used with small, straightforward programs, an illustrative example for the LABELS program is shown in Figure F-4. Use of the DFD is usually applied to the design of complete systems.

HIPO In the early 1970s, IBM Corporation introduced a program design and documentation technique called HIPO. **HIPO** is an acronym for Hierarchy plus Input-Process-Output. The objectives of HIPO are to:

1. Provide a structure by which the functions of a system can be understood

2. State the functions to be accomplished by a program

3. Provide a visual description of the inputs to be used and the outputs to be produced by each program function

Figure F-4   Data-flow diagram example.

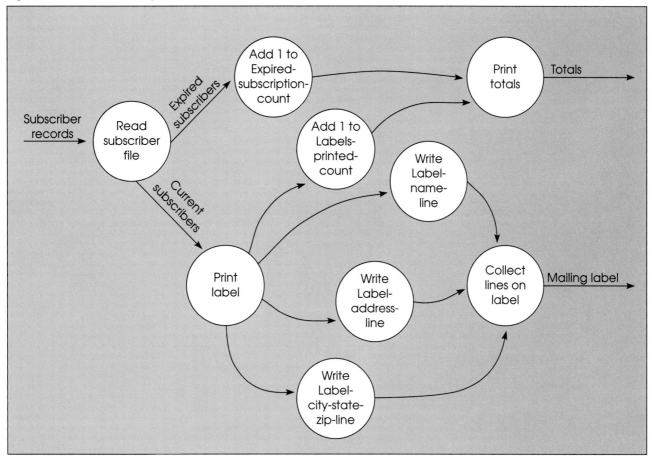

Typical HIPO documentation contains three kinds of diagrams: a **visual table of contents** (often abbreviated and called a **VTOC**), **overview diagrams**, and **detail diagrams**. Figure F-5* depicts and indicates relationships among these three diagrams. A partial HIPO documentation package for the LABELS program is shown in Figure F-6.

HIPO is well suited to the design and development of structured programs because of its top-down modular approach. As a documentation technique, HIPO is strong because it offers three levels of documentation, each of which might be used by different individuals. A manager might require only an overview of the system and thus consult the VTOC and overview diagrams. A programmer needing specific details would probably want information contained on the detail diagrams.

Although HIPO shows program function, it does not indicate detailed program organization and logic as flowcharts do. So, HIPO is often supplemented by pseudocode for detailed logic design and documentation.

---

*Source: *HIPO: A Design Aid and Documentation Technique*. IBM Publication GC20-1851.

Figure F-5   HIPO diagram relationships.

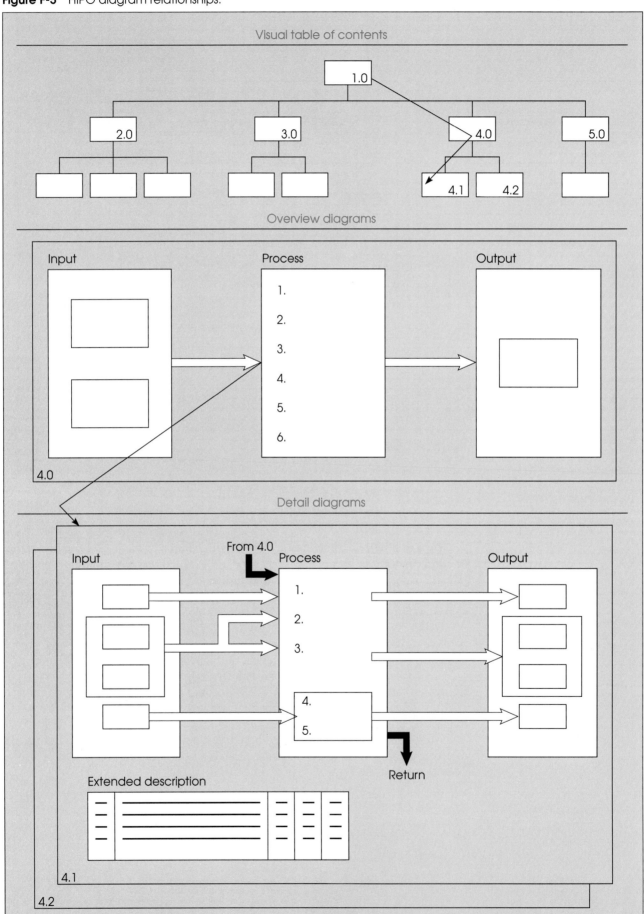

Figure F-6 HIPO example.

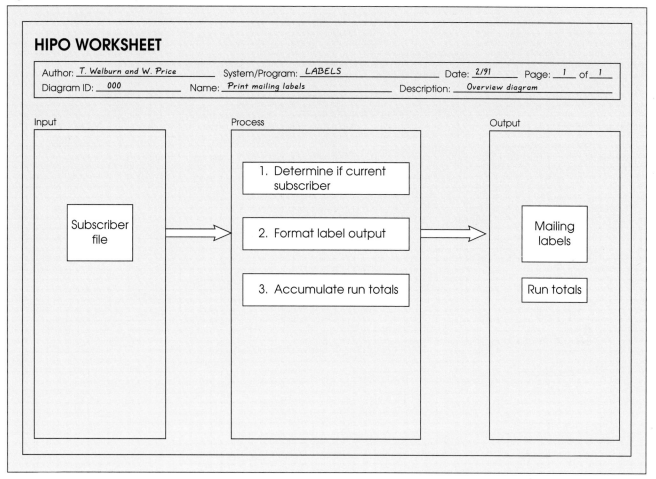

Detailed Program-Processing Techniques

The preceding three methods are used for overall program design and documentation. In contrast, the following techniques are for detailed program processing: traditional program flowcharts, pseudocode, Nassi-Shneiderman diagrams, Chapin charts, Warnier (and Warnier-Orr) diagrams, and Jackson (JSP) diagrams.

Traditional Program Flowcharts

Early in the development of the computer-programming discipline, it was recognized that a method was required to design and document computer-processing operations so that a data-processing function could be converted to computer instructions. A number of techniques were employed: mathematical formulas, written textual material, process charts, decision tables, and flowcharts. Flowcharts quickly became the most widely used method.

The traditional **program flowchart** is a graphic technique specifically developed for the purpose of designing and documenting computer programs. One of the main reasons for the popularity of flowcharts is that they are graphic. That adage, "a picture is worth a thousand words," applies also to the ability of a flowchart to convey complex program logic. A traditional program flowchart of the LABELS program appears in Figure F-7.

Figure F-7
Program flowchart example.

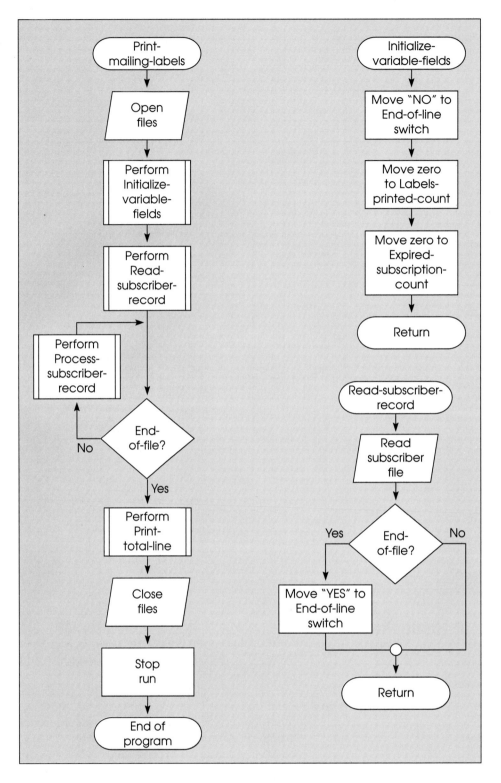

Figure F-7
(continued)

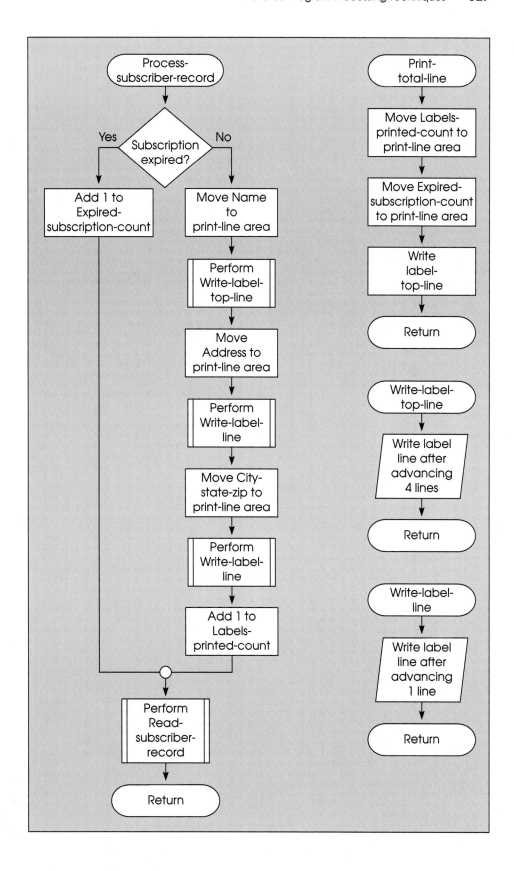

However, traditional program flowcharts are sometimes shunned in structured programming environments. Their drawbacks are the following:

1. They take a long time to draw and, once drawn, they are difficult and time-consuming to change. On the other hand, computer programs are available for the creation and management of flowcharts.

2. They are bulky; their symbols and flowlines consume a significant amount of page space to show the program logic.

3. They do not depict complicated selection and iteration structures in a manner that can be directly translated to structured COBOL code.

Pseudocode

Pseudocode, using an English-like form, has also been used in this text to express detailed program logic. It has become a popular technique because it lends itself to structured programming documentation. That is, the three control structures can be easily represented by relative placement, indention, and key words such as PERFORM, IF, and so on. Pseudocode for the LABELS program is shown in Figure F-8.

Various pseudocode "dialects" are in use. Some tend to be exacting in syntactical requirements; other are more informal. Regardless of the conventions used, however, pseudocode should be (1) well organized, (2) precise enough to code from, and (3) reasonably understandable to nonprogrammers.

One of the primary advantages of pseudocode is that it is well suited to speedy preparation and modification with the use of text-editing programs or word-processing equipment. However, since pseudocode can be very similar to the actual COBOL code, many experienced programmers complain that writing it is time-consuming and redundant.

Nassi-Shneiderman Diagrams

Sometimes referred to as a structured flowchart, the Nassi-Shneiderman diagram is named for Isaac Nassi and Ben Shneiderman, who first described the technique. Like traditional program flowcharts, **Nassi-Shneiderman diagrams** graphically depict the logic to be performed. Unlike traditional program flowcharts, they

Figure F-8   Pseudocode example.

```
000-Print-mailing-labels module

    1.  Open the files.
    2.  Perform Initialize-variable-fields module.
    3.  Perform Read-subscriber-record module.
    4.  Perform Process-subscriber-record module until no more records.
    5.  Perform Print-total-line module.
    6.  Close the files.
    7.  Stop the run.

100-Initialize-variable-fields module

    1.  Set the end-of-file indicator to "No".
    2.  Set the Labels-printed-count to zero.
    3.  Set the Expired-subscription-count to zero.

200-Process-subscriber-record module

    1.  If the Expired-code field is equal to "Y"
            Add 1 to the Expired-subscription-count.
    2.  If the Expired-code field is not equal to "Y"
            Move the Subscriber-name to the print-line
            Perform Write-label-top-line module
            Move the Subscriber-address to the print-line
            Perform Write-label-line module
            Move the Subscriber-city-state-zip to
                the print-line
            Perform Write-label-line module
            Add 1 to the Labels-printed-count.
    3.  Perform Read-subscriber-record module.
```

```
700-Print-total-line module

    1.  Clear the output print-line area.
    2.  Move the Labels-printed-count to the output print-line area.
    3.  Move the Expired-subscription-count to the output print-line
        area.
    4.  Perform Write-label-top-line module.

800-Read-subscriber-record module

    1.  Read a record from the Subscriber-file;
            if there are no more records
                Move "Yes" to the end-of-file indicator.

880-Write-label-top-line module

    1.  Write the output print-line after advancing four spaces to
        the next label.

890-Write-label-line module

    1.  Write the output print-line after single-spacing.
```

contain no flowlines or arrowheads and do not use various symbols and shapes to represent different program functions (such as input/output, processing, and decision). They are called **structured flowcharts** because they depict only the three control structures: sequence, selection, and iteration. A Nassi-Shneiderman diagram for the LABELS program is shown in Figure F-9.

In comparison to traditional program flowcharts, Nassi-Shneiderman diagrams have the advantage of depicting program logic in a graphic form that can be directly translated to structured COBOL code. In addition, they are more compact, easier to draw, and allow for variable rectangle size to accommodate logic descriptions of different lengths. However, they are still difficult to modify and do not lend themselves to preparation with the aid of standard text-editing and word-processing equipment. Some detractors, not impressed with the graphic qualities of the method, dismiss the diagrams as "pseudocode with lines and boxes around it."

Figure F-9
Nassi-Shneiderman diagram example.

Print mailing labels		
Open files		
Initialize-variable-fields → Move "NO" to end-of-file switch		
Move zero to Labels-printed-count		
Move zero to Expired-subscription-count		
Perform Read-subscriber-record		
Perform Process-subscriber-record until End-of-file-switch = "YES"		
Process-subscriber-record → Subscription expired?		
Yes		No
Add 1 to Expired-subscription-count	Move name to print-line area	
	Perform Write-label-top-line	
	Move address to print-line area	
	Perform Write-label-line	
	Move city-state-zip to print-line area	
	Perform Write-label-line	
	Add 1 to Labels-printed-count	
Perform Read-subscriber-record		
Print-total-line → Clear print-line area		
Move Labels-printed-count to print-line area		
Move Expired-subscription-count to print-line area		
Perform Write-label-top-line		
Close files		
Stop run		
Read-Subscriber-record → Read subscriber record		
End-of-file?		
Yes		No
Move "YES" to end-of-file switch		
Write-label-top-line → Write Label-line after advancing 4 lines		
Write-label-line → Write Label-line after advancing 1 line		

Chapin Charts   Originated by Ned Chapin, the **Chapin chart** is a structured flowcharting technique quite similar to Nassi-Shneiderman diagrams. Figure F-10 presents a Chapin chart for the LABELS program logic.

What differentiates a Chapin chart in appearance from a Nassi-Shneiderman diagram is that the Chapin chart represents module-name identifiers and called modules (modules to be performed) within a terminal symbol (an oval). Also, the Chapin chart uniformly depicts "Yes/No" condition-test labels within 45-degree triangles that identify the respective logic path.

As a program design and documentation technique, Chapin charts provide benefits and disadvantages similar to those of Nassi-Shneiderman diagrams.

Figure F-10   Chapin chart example.

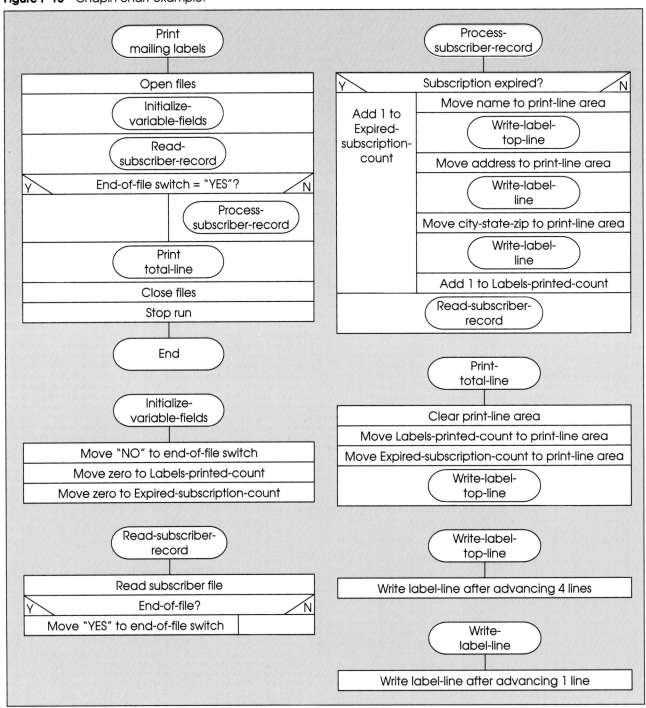

Warnier (and Warnier-Orr) Diagrams

Named for Jean-Dominique Warnier, the **Warnier diagram** depicts program logic with a series of brackets, plus a few other symbols. It can be likened to a structure chart tipped to the left so that it is standing on its side. However, whereas the structure chart shows hierarchical relationships but not process flow, the Warnier diagram indicates both. The Warnier methodology that incorporates Warnier diagrams is called **LCP**, which is an abbreviation for **L**ogical **C**onstruction of **P**rograms, the title of the Warnier book that has been translated from French into English.

Warnier diagrams are often referred to as **Warnier-Orr diagrams** in recognition of the work done by Kenneth Orr in adapting and encouraging use of the technique in structured analysis and design. An example of a Warnier-Orr diagram for the LABELS program is shown in Figure F-11.

The process flow of a Warnier-Orr diagram is presumed to be from left to right and top to bottom. The entries in parentheses below the module and action descriptions represent the number of times that each module or action is to be executed. For example, (1) indicates that a module will be executed once; (0,1) means that—based upon a condition—a module either will be skipped or else executed once. A letter—such as (S)—denotes that a module will be repeated a variable number of

Figure F-11   Warnier-Orr diagram example.

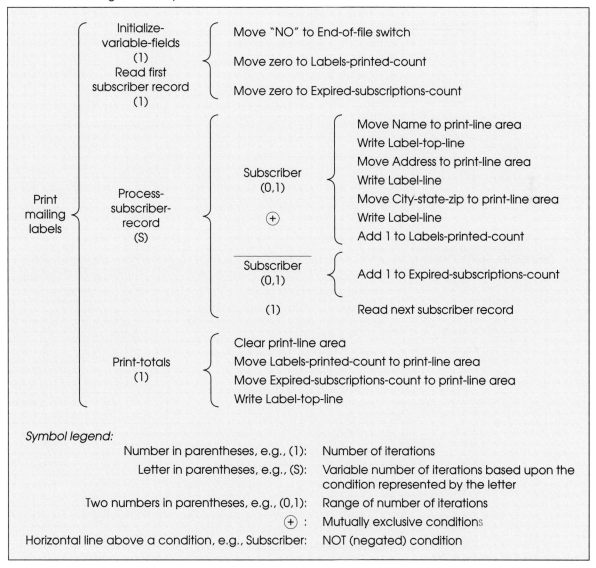

times based upon some value (in Figure F-11, the S represents the number of subscriber records to be processed).

A horizontal line drawn above a description indicates a "not" or negated condition. The plus sign in a circle means that the two adjacent modules are mutually exclusive; only one of the set will be executed during an iteration.

Although probably easier to draw than program flowcharts, Warnier-Orr diagrams also do not lend themselves to easy preparation on text-editing or word-processing equipment.

Jackson (JSP) Diagrams

Michael Jackson's methodology, **Jackson Structured Programming** (usually referred to as **JSP**), uses data-structure design to produce **Jackson (JSP) diagrams**. JSP program design consists of four steps:

1. Draw a data-structure diagram for each input, output, and internal data stream.

2. Combine these separate data structures into one basic program structure.

3. List the operations and allocate them to the program structure.

4. Write the pseudocode.

Figure F-12 shows a JSP diagram for the LABELS program. Step 1 shows the diagrams for the input and output files. Structure types are indicated by a symbol in the upper right-hand corner of the block. The absence of a symbol indicates a sequence structure, a small circle represents a selection structure, and an asterisk identifies the iteration structure. A dash in the middle of a block signifies a null component. Horizontal lines with arrows are used to depict a one-to-one correspondence between the input and the output. In Step 2, the input and output data structures were combined into the basic program structure.

JSP is better known and more widely practiced in Europe than in the United States. A central feature of JSP is that the subject matter of the program—its data input and result—is dealt with first (in Steps 1 and 2 above), whereas the detailed program functions are addressed later (in Steps 3 and 4). JSP does a good job of handling data-structure incompatibilities. Because of this data-structure design approach, different programmers will tend to present similar solutions to the same problem.

Module Summary

As can be inferred from the diversity of techniques surveyed, there are differing views as to appropriate program design and documentation techniques. Most data-processing installations choose a particular method—or combination of methods—as the standard for their organization.

In this text, structure charts are used to indicate overall program organization and module definition. Both traditional program flowcharts and pseudocode are presented to show detailed processing logic. Flowcharts are provided because many students are already familiar with them and feel comfortable about them. Pseudocode is also shown because it does a good job of expressing structured logic.

Probably more important than the specific design and documentation technique chosen is the process of taking two "cuts" at the program design. It is common with many human activities for a person to feel that he or she could do a better job if the task could be done all over again. Thus, the use of a program design technique provides the first "dry run" at tackling the problem; this helps to ensure that the actual program coding will be proper. Of course, the same objective could perhaps be obtained by using none of the design techniques presented, but instead merely coding the program twice. The problem with this approach is that the second coding would probably never happen—because of time requirements, additional schedule pressures, or just plain laziness.

Figure F-12
JSP diagram example.

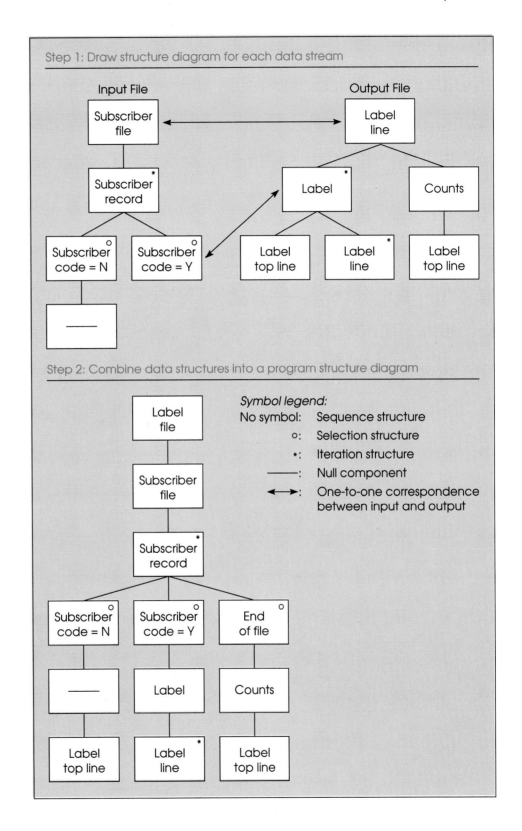

By requiring submission of an initial design in a medium different from actual program code, enforcement of the two-step approach is simplified for most organizations. In addition, each design technique offers its own special graphic and analytic benefits.

To serve as program documentation, all design documents must be maintained and updated concurrent with changes to the actual program code. This requirement is often preached, but rarely practiced unless there are organizational standards and checkpoints enforced to make such updating mandatory.

Exercises

Terms for Definition

Chapin chart _____

data-flow diagram _____

HIPO _____

Jackson (JSP) diagram _____

Nassi-Shneiderman diagram _____

visual table of contents (VTOC) _____

Warnier-Orr diagram _____

Review Questions

1. Match the structured design and documentation technique with its description.

   Structured design and documentation technique
   a. data-flow diagram
   b. HIPO
   c. structure chart
   d. traditional program flowchart
   e. pseudocode
   f. Nassi-Shneiderman diagram
   g. Chapin chart
   h. Warnier-Orr diagram
   i. Jackson (JSP) diagram

   Description

   _____ A structured flowchart with module-name identifiers specified within terminal symbols.

   _____ An English-like form of expressing program logic.

   _____ A design method based upon the structure of the input and output data streams.

   _____ A "bubble-chart" depicting the logical flow of data.

   _____ An overall program design and documentation technique introduced by IBM Corporation in the early 1970s.

_____ A graphic technique, developed early in the computer age, for the design and documentation of program logic.

_____ A structured flowchart diagrammed as a series of rectangles with module names indicated within vertical rectangles. The vertical rectangles define the boundaries of the module.

_____ A method of expressing program logic with brackets and certain other symbols.

_____ A documentation form, resembling an organization chart, for graphically showing the relationship of program modules.

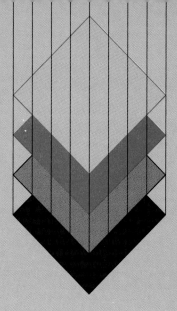

The IF
Statement

Chapter Objectives

In preceding chapters, you used a simple form of the IF statement to determine actions to take. This has provided you with an insight to its basic capabilities. Actually, the IF statement is a powerful COBOL statement that can take many forms. From this chapter, you will learn about its many details:

■ The IF general format, which includes a NEXT SENTENCE option to allow taking no action on the true condition.

■ Four types of condition tests: relation, class, sign, and condition-name.

  Relation condition—compare one quantity to another.
  Class condition—determine if a field is numeric or alphabetic.
  Sign condition—determine if a quantity is negative, zero, or positive.
  Condition-name—substitute a name (providing better documentation) for an equal condition.

■ The AND and OR operators that allow you to combine two or more conditions into a single test.

■ The NOT operator, which allows you to negate a condition (check for the opposite sense).

■ Nested IF statements in which the conditionally executed statements under an IF include other IF statements.

■ For COBOL-85, the EVALUATE statement that simplifies a test in which any one of several alternative actions is to be executed, depending on the results of a test.

CHAPTER **7**

Chapter Outline   Review of the IF Statement
The General Format
About Indenting
Types of Condition

IF Statement—The Relation Condition
Basics of the Relation Condition
Numeric Comparisons
Alphanumeric Comparisons
The NOT Operator

The IF Statement—Other Condition Types
Class Condition
Class Condition—COBOL-85 Additions
Sign Condition
Condition-Name Condition
About the VALUE Clause

Combined IF Statements
The AND Logical Operator
The OR Logical Operator
Complex Conditions

Other IF Capabilities
Negated Conditions
Implied Subjects and Relation Operators

Nested IF Statements
Linear Nested IF
Nonlinear Nested IF
A Word of Caution With Nested IF Statements—COBOL-74

The EVALUATE Statement—COBOL-85
A Basic Form of the EVALUATE Statement
Another Form of the EVALUATE Statement

Recap of Nested IF Statements

337

Review of the IF Statement
The General Format

As you know from previous examples, the IF statement provides you with the capability to code the selection (if-then-else) structure of structured programming theory. The general format of this statement is shown in Figure 7-1. You have used the statement both with and without the ELSE clause.

Basically, you can write the simple IF statement three ways: with both true and false actions, with true actions only, and with false actions only. These are illustrated in Figure 7-2. You are familiar with the first two forms: with both true and false actions (using the ELSE), and with true actions only. The third form of Figure 7-2, with false actions only, uses an IF option called NEXT SENTENCE.

Examples of the IF shown in Figure 7-3 summarize all of the principles you have already learned. Remember that one of the IF characteristics is its scope: the range of statements that are conditionally executed under the IF.

In COBOL-74, the period defines the scope. A misplaced period can cause considerable grief. For instance, in Figure 7-3's Example 2, both the ADD and the MOVE are executed conditionally. However, if you accidentally place a period following the ADD statement, that period will terminate the IF. Hence, only the ADD will be executed conditionally; the MOVE will be executed unconditionally. Even though indenting suggests that it is part of the conditional operation, the compiler ignores all such indenting and ends the IF with the first period it sees.

Figure 7-1
The IF statement format.

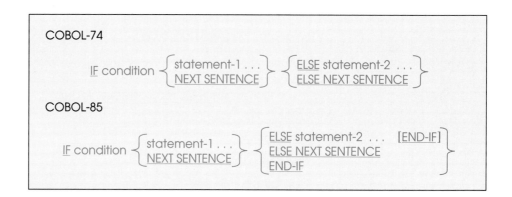

Figure 7-2   The three simple IF configurations.

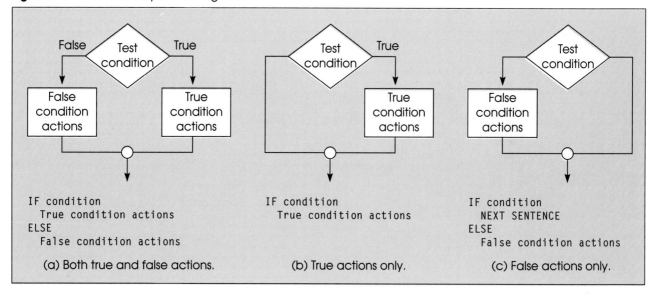

(a) Both true and false actions.   (b) True actions only.   (c) False actions only.

Figure 7-3 Sample IF statements.

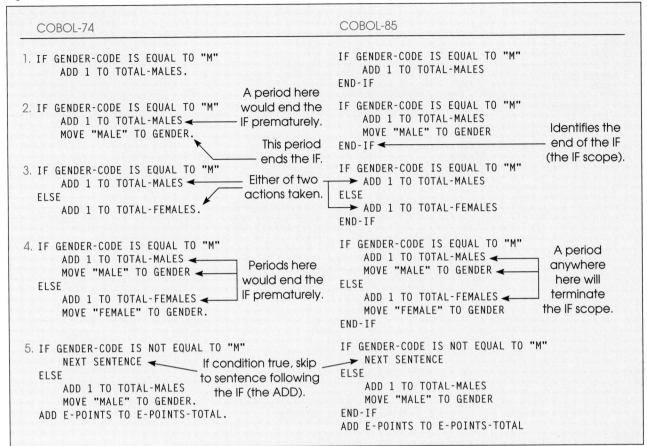

Note that this is *not* a syntax error and will *not* be detected by the compiler. If you are going to make this type of error, you will be luckier if you inadvertently insert a period preceding the ELSE (see Example 4). In this way, the compiler will see the ELSE as a separate statement and give you a diagnostic.

Since COBOL-85 provides the scope terminators, you can very explicitly indicate the scope of an IF using the END-IF. You will have no problem inadvertently terminating the scope of an IF by following the recommended rules for periods in the PROCEDURE DIVISION: use only after the paragraph name and the last statement in the paragraph. If you insert a period following any conditional statement between the IF and END-IF, that period will act as a scope terminator, thereby ending the IF (see the remark to Example 4 of Figure 7-3). Needless to say, you will then have a dangling END-IF—or ELSE and END-IF—which will produce a compiler diagnostic.

Example 5 in Figure 7-3 illustrates the false actions only version of the IF (Figure 7-2(c)) using the NEXT SENTENCE option of the IF. It works this way:

If the value in GENDER-CODE is M:
>The statement following the IF is executed. This statement, NEXT SENTENCE, says, "do nothing—continue on." (A statement that functions this way is called a *null* statement.) Hence, execution continues with the statement following the IF: the ADD statement.

Else (if the value in GENDER-CODE is not M):
>The false condition is executed (the ADD and MOVE), then execution continues with the statement following the IF: the ADD statement.

When coding the NEXT SENTENCE phrase, remember that the words are not hyphenated.

If you compare this example to Examples 2 and 5, you will see that their overall actions are identical, that is:

```
IF GENDER-CODE IS EQUAL TO "M"
```

> If value stored in GENDER-CODE is M, then the condition is true— execute the ADD and MOVE.

```
IF GENDER-CODE IS NOT EQUAL TO "M"
```

> If value stored in GENDER-CODE is M, then the condition is false— execute the ELSE sequence, which is the ADD and MOVE.

Notice that the action to be taken is switched from a true action in Example 2 to a false action in Example 5, simply by changing the sense of the test (from IS EQUAL TO to IS NOT EQUAL TO). In general, any IF requiring a false action can be changed to a true action by changing the sense of the condition. Hence, you might question the value of the false action form and using NEXT SENTENCE. However, there are some instances in which it is useful.

About Indenting

When coding simple IF statements, you should use the form of the examples: start the words IF and ELSE in position 12 and indent the action statement verbs to position 16. Also, place the word ELSE on a line by itself; do not code the word ELSE on the same line with the preceding or following statements. You will find that program modifications often require action statements to be added or deleted. By coding the word ELSE on a line by itself, such changes can be made with minimum IF statement disruption and chance for error.

Recognize that IF statement indention is provided only for program readability and *does not affect execution of the statement*. The IF statement selection control is determined solely by the word ELSE and the end-of-sentence period or, in COBOL-85, the END-IF scope terminator.

Types of Condition

All of the conditions you have used so far have involved comparing one entity to another—looking at the *relation* between two entities. For example, in PATLIST, the relation between actual contribution and target contribution determined whether or not identifying asterisks were printed. Actually, this is one of four types of conditions—relation, class, sign, and condition-name—that can be expressed within an IF statement. The relation is discussed in the next section; the other three are described after that.

IF Statement—The Relation Condition
Basics of the Relation Condition

The relation condition is the most frequently used type. All of the IF statements you have encountered so far use relation conditions. Figure 7-4 shows the relation condition format. As you can see, the element preceding the operator is called the **subject** of the relation and the element following the operator is called the **object**. Usually, the subject is specified as an identifier—that is, a field name—and the object is either an identifier or a literal.

The subject can be tested to determine if it is greater than, less than, equal to, not greater than, not less than, or not equal to the object. COBOL-85 also allows the combination operators—greater than or equal to, and less than or equal to. In all cases, the standard mathematical symbols >, <, and = (reserved words in COBOL) can be used to specify the operator. In this text, the words will always be used.

Relation condition testing compares the subject and object values. The data class of the object of the relation condition should be consistent with the subject. That is, if the subject is numeric, the object should be numeric. If the subject is alphanumeric, the object should be alphanumeric. Although you can use certain

Figure 7-4   Relation condition format.

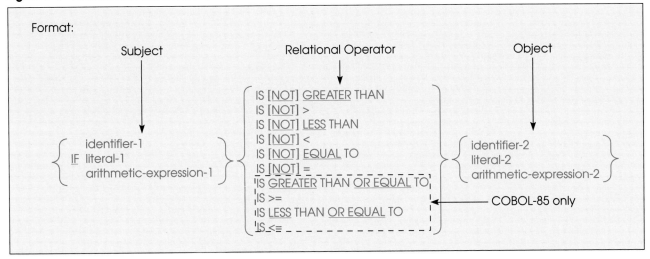

Figure 7-5   Comparison processing table for relation conditions.

Subject field	Object field	
	Numeric data-item **or** **Numeric literal**	**Alphanumeric data-item** **or Nonnumeric literal** **or Group item**
Numeric data-item **or** **Numeric literal**	**Numeric** (algebraic) comparison	**Alphanumeric** (character-by-character) comparison
Alphanumeric data-item **or** **Nonnumeric literal** **or** **Group item**	**Alphanumeric** (character-by-character) comparison	**Alphanumeric** (character-by-character) comparison

other combinations, you must be aware of the specific comparison processing that will occur. A table of comparison processing is shown in Figure 7-5.

Numeric Comparisons   When the subject and object are both defined as numeric data-items, comparison of the two values is made according to their algebraic values. The relative length of the fields does not matter. For example, a three-digit integer field containing 687 is equal to a seven-digit integer field with a value of 0000687. Similarly, 0003.25 is equal to 03.2500; the location of the assumed decimal point *does* affect the comparison values.

Also, arithmetic signs affect the comparison. Positive values are greater than negative values. Thus, +07 is greater than –98.

Alphanumeric Comparisons   The result of alphanumeric comparisons depends upon the collating sequence of the computer being used. **Collating sequence** refers to the order of character values and is determined by the binary value used to code each character. As you would expect, an alphanumeric value of 3 is less than 7. Similarly, the letter R is greater than B in accordance with normal alphabetic sequencing. But, how does a dollar sign ($) compare to an E? Or, which is greater in value—a letter or a digit? Figure 7-6 summarizes the collating sequences of the two commonly used data representation formats: ASCII and EBCDIC. Observe that, with EBCDIC, digits are higher than letters, whereas in ASCII, the converse is true.

Figure 7-6
ASCII and EBCDIC collating
sequences.

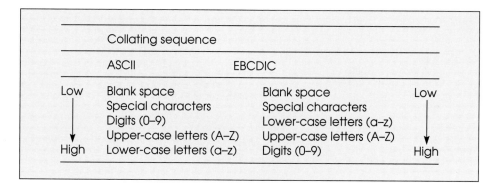

With alphanumeric fields, comparison begins at the leftmost character position and proceeds to the right. Figure 7-7 provides an example of an alphanumeric comparison; note that these fields are equal in length.

When alphanumeric subject and object fields are of different lengths, the shorter field is internally extended on the right with blank spaces until it is the same length as the longer field. Then the comparison takes place as if the fields were equal in length.

The NOT Operator   The PAYROLL program (see Figure 6-24) uses the following IF test to determine when a printed page is full, requiring positioning to a new page.

```
IF WS-LINES-USED IS NOT LESS THAN WS-LINES-PER-PAGE
```

Referring to the IF format of Figure 7-4, you can see that the NOT can be used with any of the operators. When used, the NOT combined with the next keyword are considered to be a single operator. For instance, LESS (the only required word of the operator) is one relational operator; NOT LESS is treated by COBOL as a different operator.

Recall in the discussion of the PAYROLL program that this form was used to ensure that the new-page procedure would be executed whenever WS-LINES-USED equaled or exceeded the WS-LINES-PER-PAGE. Actually, most programmers find this NOT LESS form confusing. A COBOL-74 alternate would be:

```
IF WS-LINES-USED IS LESS THAN WS-LINES-PER-PAGE
    NEXT SENTENCE
ELSE
    PERFORM 870-PRINT-REPORT-HEADINGS.
```

Figure 7-7   Alphanumeric relation condition tests: equal-length fields.

```
05   TRANSACTION-NAME            PIC X(24).
05   MASTER-NAME                 PIC X(24).

IF   TRANSACTION-NAME IS LESS THAN MASTER-NAME
     PERFORM 999-PROCESS-LOW-TRANSACTION.
```

Value in TRANSACTION-NAME field	Value in MASTER-NAME field	Condition test result	Statement executed
JONES	JONES	False	Next sentence
JONES	SMITH	True	999-PROCESS-LOW-TRANSACTION
SMITH	SMITHSON	True	999-PROCESS-LOW-TRANSACTION
THORPE	THORP	False	Next sentence

COBOL-85 provides four other forms that can be used (refer to Figure 7-4) in forming relation conditions. Using this capability, the readability of the program is improved as follows:

```
IF WS-LINES-USED IS GREATER THAN OR EQUAL TO WS-LINES-PER-PAGE
    PERFORM 870-PRINT-REPORT-HEADINGS
END-IF
```

The important thing to remember about these forms is that they all result in the same action.

The IF Statement— Other Condition Types
Class Condition

The **class condition** tests whether a field contains only numeric digits or solely alphabetic characters. As shown in the class condition format of Figure 7-8, a field can be tested to determine if its contents are NUMERIC, ALPHABETIC, NOT NUMERIC, or NOT ALPHABETIC.

For a value to be considered NUMERIC, the field must contain only digits from 0 (zero) through 9. To be considered ALPHABETIC, the field must contain only letters, from A through Z, and blank spaces.

NUMERIC class tests can be made on alphanumeric (PIC X) and numeric (PIC 9) fields; this test is *not* limited to numeric fields. Examples are shown in Figure 7-9. ALPHABETIC class tests can be made on alphanumeric, alphabetic, and group fields. Figure 7-10 provides examples. (*Note:* If you are using COBOL-85, each of the examples that follow would be terminated with an END-IF rather than with a period.)

Class Condition— COBOL-85 Additions

Because COBOL was developed before lowercase letters were commonly represented within the computer, previous versions of the language were unclear as to how lowercase letters should be treated by an ALPHABETIC class test.

Figure 7-8
Class condition format.

Format:

$$IF\ identifier\ IS\ [NOT] \left\{ \begin{array}{c} NUMERIC \\ ALPHABETIC \end{array} \right\}$$

Figure 7-9 NUMERIC class test example.

```
05  PRICE                    PIC 9(3)V99.

IF PRICE IS NUMERIC
    PERFORM 999-VALIDATE-PRICE
ELSE
    PERFORM 999-IDENTIFY-PRICE-ERROR.
```

Value in PRICE field	Class	Condition test result	Statement executed
02999	Numeric	True	999-VALIDATE-PRICE
2999	Alphanumeric*	False	999-IDENTIFY-PRICE-ERROR
0299R	Alphanumeric	False	999-IDENTIFY-PRICE-ERROR
	Alphabetic**	False	999-IDENTIFY-PRICE-ERROR
00000	Numeric	True	999-VALIDATE-PRICE

Note: *leading blank space; **all blanks; ▲ assumed decimal point.

Figure 7-10   ALPHABETIC class test example.

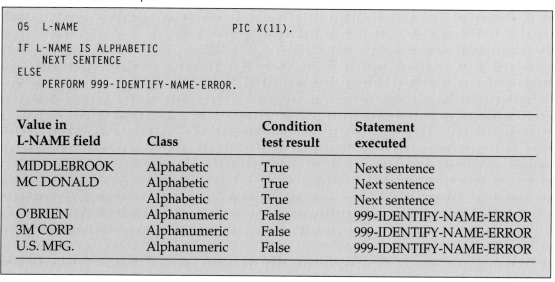

```
05  L-NAME                          PIC X(11).

IF L-NAME IS ALPHABETIC
    NEXT SENTENCE
ELSE
    PERFORM 999-IDENTIFY-NAME-ERROR.
```

Value in L-NAME field	Class	Condition test result	Statement executed
MIDDLEBROOK	Alphabetic	True	Next sentence
MC DONALD	Alphabetic	True	Next sentence
	Alphabetic	True	Next sentence
O'BRIEN	Alphanumeric	False	999-IDENTIFY-NAME-ERROR
3M CORP	Alphanumeric	False	999-IDENTIFY-NAME-ERROR
U.S. MFG.	Alphanumeric	False	999-IDENTIFY-NAME-ERROR

COBOL-85 corrects this situation by introducing two additional class condition operators: ALPHABETIC-UPPER and ALPHABETIC-LOWER. Thus, the alphabetic class conditions and the characters to which they apply are now as follows:

ALPHABETIC	A through Z, a through z, and blank space
ALPHABETIC-UPPER	A through Z and blank space
ALPHABETIC-LOWER	a through z and blank space

Sign Condition   The sign condition tests whether the value of a numeric field is POSITIVE, NEGATIVE, or ZERO. Because it has narrower applicability, the sign test is used much less frequently than relation and class tests.

Figure 7-11 shows the sign condition format and examples. When the value being tested is zero, it is considered to be ZERO, a unique value that is neither positive nor negative.

Figure 7-11
Sign condition format and examples.

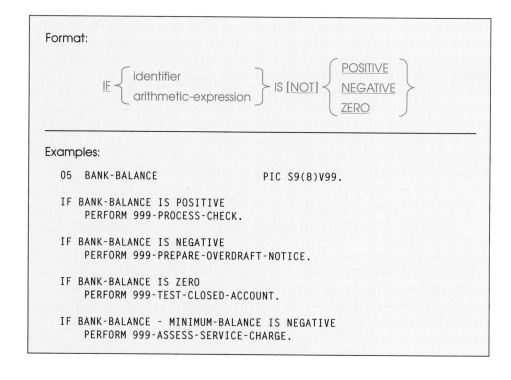

```
Format:

        ⎧ identifier              ⎫          ⎧ POSITIVE ⎫
IF  ⎨                            ⎬  IS [NOT] ⎨ NEGATIVE ⎬
        ⎩ arithmetic-expression  ⎭          ⎩ ZERO     ⎭
```

```
Examples:

    05  BANK-BALANCE                PIC S9(8)V99.

    IF BANK-BALANCE IS POSITIVE
        PERFORM 999-PROCESS-CHECK.

    IF BANK-BALANCE IS NEGATIVE
        PERFORM 999-PREPARE-OVERDRAFT-NOTICE.

    IF BANK-BALANCE IS ZERO
        PERFORM 999-TEST-CLOSED-ACCOUNT.

    IF BANK-BALANCE - MINIMUM-BALANCE IS NEGATIVE
        PERFORM 999-ASSESS-SERVICE-CHARGE.
```

Observe (in the last example of Figure 7-11) that it is sometimes appropriate and convenient to use an arithmetic expression as the subject of a sign condition.

Condition-Name
Condition

A condition-name condition is a special way of writing a relation condition in order to improve its readability. For instance, suppose that you are working on a program in which the field COLOR-CODE can have either of two values: 1 or 2. If code 1 means the color white and code 2 means blue, then you might have a statement such as the following in a program:

```
COBOL-74
IF COLOR-CODE = "1"
    PERFORM 999-PROCESS-SPECIAL
ELSE
    PERFORM 999-PROCESS-NORMAL.
```

```
COBOL-85
IF COLOR-CODE = "1"
    PERFORM 999-PROCESS-SPECIAL
ELSE
    PERFORM 999-PROCESS-NORMAL
END-IF
```

COBOL
Programming
Perspective

Effect of Arithmetic Signs Upon Class Tests

Because of ambiguities involved with the embedded sign form of data representation (see the discussion of arithmetic-sign representation in Concepts Module D), certain intricacies are inherent in NUMERIC class tests.

First, a numeric field that contains an arithmetic sign will be treated differently depending upon how the field is defined in the PICTURE clause. If it is defined as alphanumeric (PIC X(1), for example) or as unsigned numeric (PIC 9(1), for example), a valid signed numeric field will yield a test result of NOT NUMERIC because of the presence of the sign. Of course, if the field were defined as a signed numeric field (PIC S9(1), for example), the field will be considered NUMERIC.

Remember that a signed field with embedded signs will have a signed digit position whose representation is exactly the same as a letter. For example, the data representation for +1 is the same as that for the letter A; the representation for –9 is the same as that for the letter R. So, if you define the numeric field as unsigned (that is, without the S symbol), the system assumes that the data representation is indicating a letter rather than a signed digit.

Second, when a field is defined as signed numeric (PIC S9(1), for example), both a valid signed numeric field and a valid unsigned numeric field will produce the expected test result of NUMERIC.

Examples of such NUMERIC class tests are shown below.

PICTURE clause	Value in field	Embedded sign	Class-test result	Comments
PIC X(5)	12345	+	Not numeric	5+ is same as letter E
or	12345	–	Not numeric	5– is same as letter N
PIC 9(5)	12345	(unsigned)	Numeric	
	1*3X5		Not numeric	* and X are not digits
	12 45		Not numeric	Blank space is not a digit
	1234N		Not numeric	N is not a digit
PIC S9(5)	12345	+	Numeric	
	12345	–	Numeric	
	12345	(unsigned)	Numeric	
	1*3X5		Not numeric	* and X are not digits
	12 45		Not numeric	Blank space is not a digit
	1234N		Numeric	Letter N is same as 5–

If you are like most of us, you would have a hard time remembering whether 1 is the code for white or for blue. The statement is not very self-documenting. However, if it is written as follows, it tells you the color:

```
COBOL-74                                COBOL-85
IF WHITE                                IF WHITE
    PERFORM 999-PROCESS-SPECIAL             PERFORM 999-PROCESS-SPECIAL
ELSE                                    ELSE
    PERFORM 999-PROCESS-NORMAL.             PERFORM 999-PROCESS-NORMAL
                                        END-IF
```

The word WHITE is called a **condition-name condition** and must be defined as a special entry in the DATA DIVISION: an 88-level entry. An example of an 88-level item is shown in Figure 7-12. Each condition-name you use in an IF statement must be defined as an 88-level entry. The 88-level item is coded subordinate to the data-item description entry for the field to which it corresponds.

In the example, COLOR-CODE is a one-character field that contains a code indicating whether the color is white or blue. The two 88-level items following this field definition shows that the condition-name WHITE has been assigned to a value of 1 and the condition-name BLUE has been assigned to a value of 2 in the COLOR-CODE field. That is, when there is a 1 in the field, the condition WHITE is true; when there is a 2 in the field, the condition BLUE is true.

As shown in the condition-name condition format and examples shown in Figure 7-13, 88-level entries are not limited to the simple form of the color-code example. That is, the VALUE clause of an 88-level item may contain multiple values or a range of values. The reserved word THRU is used to define a range of values. For instance, if MONTH-ABBREV contains any one of the four values APR, JUN, SEP, or NOV, then the condition 30-DAY-MONTH is true. Similarly, if MONTH-NBR contains 10, 11, or 12, then the condition QUARTER-4 is true.

The condition-name can be preceded by the word NOT, thereby "switching" the sense of the test. For instance, if you needed to take some action when TEST-PERIOD contained one of the months 1, 2, or 3 (Figure 7-13), you would code:

```
IF QUARTER-1
    PERFORM 999-QUARTER-1-ROUTINE
```

If you needed to take an action when TEST-PERIOD contained other than one of the months 1, 2, or 3, you would code:

```
IF NOT QUARTER-1
    PERFORM 999-OTHER-QUARTER-ROUTINE
```

You will learn more about the NOT operator later.

Figure 7-12
88-level item example.

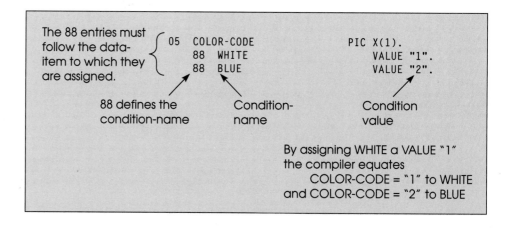

Figure 7-13
VALUE clause format and examples with multiple value and range of value entries.

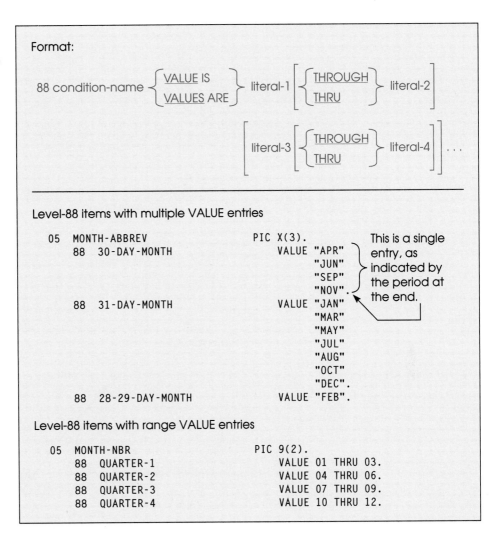

Format:

$$88 \text{ condition-name} \left\{ \begin{array}{l} \underline{\text{VALUE}} \text{ IS} \\ \underline{\text{VALUES}} \text{ ARE} \end{array} \right\} \text{ literal-1} \left[\left\{ \begin{array}{l} \underline{\text{THROUGH}} \\ \underline{\text{THRU}} \end{array} \right\} \text{ literal-2} \right]$$

$$\left[\text{literal-3} \left[\left\{ \begin{array}{l} \underline{\text{THROUGH}} \\ \underline{\text{THRU}} \end{array} \right\} \text{ literal-4} \right] \right] \ldots$$

Level-88 items with multiple VALUE entries

```
    05  MONTH-ABBREV              PIC X(3).
        88  30-DAY-MONTH              VALUE "APR"    This is a single
                                            "JUN"    entry, as
                                            "SEP"    indicated by
                                            "NOV".   the period at
                                                     the end.
        88  31-DAY-MONTH              VALUE "JAN"
                                            "MAR"
                                            "MAY"
                                            "JUL"
                                            "AUG"
                                            "OCT"
                                            "DEC".
        88  28-29-DAY-MONTH           VALUE "FEB".
```

Level-88 items with range VALUE entries

```
    05  MONTH-NBR                 PIC 9(2).
        88  QUARTER-1                 VALUE 01 THRU 03.
        88  QUARTER-2                 VALUE 04 THRU 06.
        88  QUARTER-3                 VALUE 07 THRU 09.
        88  QUARTER-4                 VALUE 10 THRU 12.
```

About the VALUE Clause

Note that there is some ambiguity in the COBOL language about the meaning of the VALUE clause. It is used in two different ways:

- In 01- through 49-level WORKING-STORAGE fields to establish initial values

- In 88-level items to associate values with a condition-name

Recognize that these two uses for VALUE clauses are quite different. For 01- through 49-level items, the VALUE clause causes the field to be **initialized** with the corresponding value; this could be termed an **initializing VALUE clause**. The **condition-name VALUE clause** used with an 88-level item does *not* initialize, however. It instead associates a condition-name with a value.

Recall that you learned special limitations for using the initializing VALUE clauses; in contrast, a condition-name VALUE clause:

- Can be specified in either the FILE SECTION or the WORKING-STORAGE SECTION (initializing VALUE clauses cannot be specified in the FILE SECTION)

- Can be associated with a data-item description that contains a REDEFINES clause

- Can be associated with a data-item description that contains an OCCURS clause (the OCCURS clause is introduced in Chapter 11)

- Can contain multiple values or a range of values

Combined IF Statements

Suppose you are working in a college data-processing department and the program you are preparing requires that students be identified for the dean's list. The requirement is that a student must currently be enrolled in more than 11 units and have a grade point average greater than 3.5. In pseudocode form, you would write:

```
IF current-units greater than 11
AND grade-point-average (GPA) greater than 3.5
    place student on the dean's list
```

You might also have the task of sending special notices to students who are currently enrolled in less than 9 units or have not accumulated more than 30 total units. This pseudocode would take the form:

```
IF current-units less than 9
OR cumulative-units not greater than 30
    send special notice
```

In COBOL, you can build multiple conditions such as these, using the reserved-word **logical operators** AND or OR. In fact, the COBOL form is almost identical to the pseudocode form. IF statements that contain multiple conditions such as these are called **combined IF statements**. The format for a combined IF statement is presented in Figure 7-14.

The AND Logical Operator

When the AND logical operator is used, both conditions must be true for the combined condition to be considered true. If either one or both of the conditions is false, the combined condition is considered false. A graphical way of representing an AND complex condition is called a **Boolean diagram** and is illustrated in Figure 7-15. You can think of this figure as an electric wire with two on-off switches—C (representing current-units) and G (representing GPA). Electricity will flow from point 1 to point 2 only if both switches are on (true); if either is off (false), electricity will not flow. This corresponds to the AND operator: the action is carried out only if both conditions are true.

The AND operator is used in the following statement to satisfy the need for identifying those students taking more than 11 units and having a grade-point average greater than 3.5.

```
COBOL-74
IF  CURRENT-UNITS IS GREATER THAN 11.0
AND GPA IS GREATER THAN 3.5
    PERFORM 999-PLACE-ON-DEANS-LIST.
```

```
COBOL-85
IF  CURRENT-UNITS IS GREATER THAN 11.0
AND GPA IS GREATER THAN 3.5
    PERFORM 999-PLACE-ON-DEANS-LIST
END-IF
```

Figure 7-14
The combined IF statement format.

Format:

$$\text{IF condition} \left\{ \begin{matrix} \underline{\text{AND}} \\ \underline{\text{OR}} \end{matrix} \right\} \text{condition} \left. \right\} \ldots$$

Figure 7-15
Boolean diagram for the AND condition.

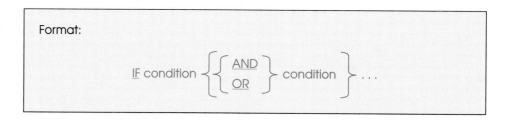

1 ○— C —— R —○ 2   Electricity flows from point 1 to point 2 only if both C and R are **on**. Similarly, the corresponding COBOL action is taken only if both the cumulative-units and GPA requirements are **true**.

Here, if a student is both taking more than 11 units *and* has a GPA greater than 3.5, the statement PERFORM 999-PLACE-ON-DEANS-LIST will be executed. If either one or both of the two conditions is false, the statement will be skipped.

Use of the AND operator is not limited to simply two conditions, as illustrated by this example. For instance, Figure 7-16 provides an example in which five conditions are combined. If all five are true, the true-action statement PERFORM 999-PROCESS-DATE is executed. If any one or more are false, the false-action statement PERFORM 999-IDENTIFY-DATE-ERROR is executed. Observe that different condition types can be combined; the example includes class, relation, and condition-name conditions.

One mistake commonly made by students is to repeat the word IF. For instance, in English you could use either "if first condition and second condition, do. . . ." or else "if first condition and if second condition, do. . . ." The equivalent form is not allowed in COBOL.

The OR Logical Operator

Whereas the AND requires all conditions to be true, the OR is much less restrictive. If any one (or more) of the conditions is true, the combined condition is considered to be true. Only if all conditions are false, is the combined condition considered to be false. This is illustrated by the Boolean diagram of Figure 7-17.

The other combined condition that you encountered at the beginning of this section uses the logical OR and is represented by the following pseudocode:

```
IF current-units less than 9
OR cumulative-units not greater than 30
        send special notice
```

Following is the COBOL equivalent of this pseudocode:

COBOL-74
```
IF  CURRENT-UNITS IS LESS THAN 9.0
OR  CUM-UNITS IS NOT GREATER THAN 30.0
    PERFORM 999-SEND-SPECIAL-NOTICE.
```

COBOL-85
```
IF  CURRENT-UNITS IS LESS THAN 11.0
OR  CUM-UNITS IS NOT GREATER THAN 30.0
    PERFORM 999-SEND-SPECIAL-NOTICE
END-IF
```

Figure 7-16
A combined IF statement with multiple AND operators.

```
05  DATE
    10  T-MONTH                      PIC 9(2).
    10  T-DAY                        PIC 9(2).
    10  T-YEAR                       PIC 9(2).
        88  VALID-YEAR                   VALUE 83 THRU 89.

    IF  DATE IS NUMERIC  ◄──────────────────── A class condition
    AND T-MONTH IS GREATER THAN ZERO ⎫
    AND T-MONTH IS LESS THAN 13      ⎬
    AND T-DAY IS GREATER THAN ZERO   ⎬◄──────── Relation conditions
    AND T-DAY IS LESS THAN 32        ⎭
    AND VALID-YEAR  ◄──────────────────────── A condition-name condition
        PERFORM 999-PROCESS-DATE  ◄────────── If all conditions true, do this
    ELSE
        PERFORM 999-IDENTIFY-DATE-ERROR ◄──── If any of the conditions
                                              false, do this
```

Note: For COBOL-74, add a period at the end of the last line.
For COBOL-85, add the scope terminator END-IF after the last line.

Figure 7-17
Boolean diagram for the OR condition.

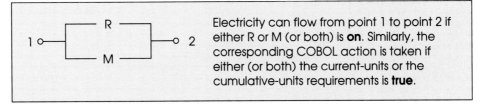

Electricity can flow from point 1 to point 2 if either R or M (or both) is **on**. Similarly, the corresponding COBOL action is taken if either (or both) the current-units or the cumulative-units requirements is **true**.

As with the AND operator, two or more conditions can be linked with an OR operator. When OR is specified, the word IF is not repeated.

Complex Conditions

When the operators AND and OR are both used within the same IF statement, the resulting expression is referred to as a **complex condition**. As an example, assume that you are working on an application and you have been informed that any record for which the following is true must be deleted.

If record-code is equal to 23, *or* update-code is equal to D, *and* balance is zero

This is confusing. In which order must you apply the conditions? Representing this in Boolean diagram form, is it to be interpreted as illustrated to the left in Figure 7-18, or as represented to the right?

If the rules of logic are applied to ordinary English, there is no ambiguity because logic rules say that in a complex form such as this, the *and* association is first made, then the *or* association is made. Hence, this form would be interpreted as in the left diagram of Figure 7-18.

The equivalent COBOL statement is shown in Figure 7-19. Although you and I might be confused in interpreting this, the compiler will not and will perform the conditional evaluation as illustrated in the sample.

Figure 7-18   Dual interpretation of a combined AND and OR.

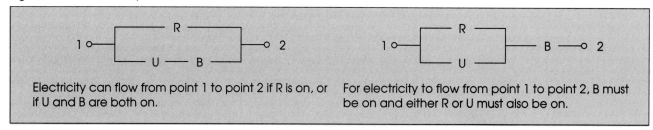

Electricity can flow from point 1 to point 2 if R is on, or if U and B are both on.

For electricity to flow from point 1 to point 2, B must be on and either R or U must also be on.

Figure 7-19   A complex condition IF statement example and its evaluation sequence.

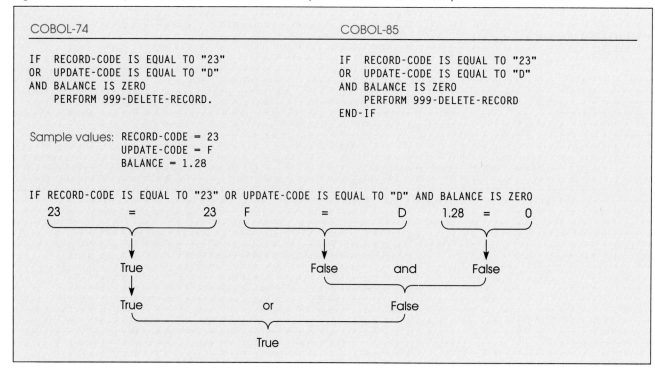

If this is not the way in which you want the condition evaluated, then by using parentheses, you must explicitly tell COBOL the order in which you want the AND and OR operators applied. Thus, to achieve the form of the representation to the right in Figure 7-18, you would use parentheses as shown in Figure 7-20. Evaluation of the condition is illustrated by the same sample values used in Figure 7-19. Notice that the condition evaluates to true in Figure 7-19 but, using the exact same data values, it evaluates to false in Figure 7-20.

Overall, complex conditions tend to be very confusing when you write them and when you later review or modify them. When you use them, *always* use parentheses to explicitly specify the evaluation sequence and to make the condition more understandable.

Other IF Capabilities
Negated Conditions

A **negated condition** is created merely by inserting the operator NOT immediately before the condition. The operator NOT reverses the truth value of the condition to which it is applied. For instance, suppose that the college application (used previously to illustrate the AND) requires that you perform an action for those students not on the dean's list—those with current-units not greater than 11 and GPA not greater than 3.5. For this, you could use the form shown in the Example 3 of Figure 7-21.

When the operator NOT is coded to form a negated condition, the resulting expression is considered a complex condition. (Do not confuse a negated condition NOT—which *precedes the condition*—with the word NOT used within the condition, as in NOT EQUAL TO. These are two distinct entities.) In a condition consisting of all three operators (NOT, AND, and OR), the NOT is evaluated first (from left to right), unless overridden by parentheses.

Figure 7-20 Changing the evaluation sequence with parentheses.

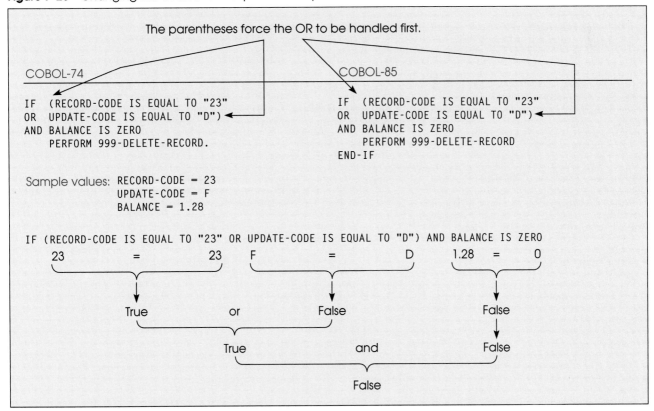

Figure 7-21   Negated condition examples.

	COBOL-74	COBOL-85
1. Negated relation condition	```IF NOT COLOR-CODE = "1" MOVE "BLUE" TO LI-COLOR-CODE.```	```IF NOT COLOR-CODE = "1" MOVE "BLUE" TO LI-COLOR-CODE END-IF```
2. Negated condition-name condition	```IF NOT WHITE MOVE "BLUE" TO LI-COLOR-CODE.```	```IF NOT WHITE MOVE "BLUE" TO LI-COLOR-CODE END-IF```
3. Negated combined IF condition	```IF NOT (CURRENT-UNITS IS GREATER THAN 11.0 AND GPA IS GREATER THAN 3.5)◄ PERFORM 999-PLACE-ON-DEANS-LIST.```	```IF NOT (CURRENT-UNITS IS GREATER THAN 11.0 AND GPA IS GREATER THAN 3.5)◄ PERFORM 999-PLACE-ON-DEANS-LIST END-IF```
4. An alternative to the negated combined IF condition	```IF (CURRENT-UNITS IS GREATER THAN 11.0 AND GPA IS GREATER THAN 3.5) NEXT SENTENCE ELSE PERFORM 999-PLACE-ON-DEANS-LIST.```	```IF (CURRENT-UNITS IS GREATER THAN 11.0 AND GPA IS GREATER THAN 3.5) NEXT SENTENCE ELSE PERFORM 999-PLACE-ON-DEANS-LIST END-IF```

This entire expression is evaluated, then the result is negated (reversed).

As is evident by Example 3 in Figure 7-21, negated conditions are sometimes difficult to understand. Often there is an alternative form that accomplishes the same thing, yet is easier to understand. Example 4 in Figure 7-21 is an equivalent alternative to Example 3.

Implied Subjects and Relation Operators

It is possible to compare one subject with two or more objects and not repeat the subject. For instance, the two IF statements of Figure 7-22 produce exactly the same result. In the second, MONTH is the **implied subject** for the second and third comparisons.

Similarly, **implied relation operators** are also permitted, as illustrated in Figure 7-23. Notice that the relation operator IS LESS THAN is not coded, but rather implied. Implied subjects and relation operators apply only to relation conditions.

Figure 7-22   Implied subject example.

	COBOL-74	COBOL-85
The combined IF statement relation condition—	```IF MONTH IS GREATER THAN ZERO AND MONTH IS LESS THAN "13" AND MONTH IS NOT EQUAL TO "02" PERFORM 999-STANDARD-DAY-CHECK.```	```IF MONTH IS GREATER THAN ZERO AND MONTH IS LESS THAN "13" AND MONTH IS NOT EQUAL TO "02" PERFORM 999-STANDARD-DAY-CHECK END-IF```
may be written with implied subjects—	```IF MONTH IS GREATER THAN ZERO AND LESS THAN "13" AND NOT EQUAL TO "02" PERFORM 999-STANDARD-DAY-CHECK.```	```IF MONTH IS GREATER THAN ZERO AND LESS THAN "13" AND NOT EQUAL TO "02" PERFORM 999-STANDARD-DAY-CHECK END-IF```

Figure 7-23   Implied subject and relation operator example.

	COBOL-74	COBOL-85
| The combined IF statement relation condition— | ```
IF BALANCE IS LESS THAN 10000.00
AND BALANCE IS LESS THAN CREDIT-LIMIT
    PERFORM 999-POST-PAYMENT.
``` | ```
IF BALANCE IS LESS THAN 10000.00
AND BALANCE IS LESS THAN CREDIT-LIMIT
    PERFORM 999-POST-PAYMENT
END-IF
``` |
| may be written with implied subject and relation operator— | ```
IF BALANCE IS LESS THAN 1000.00
AND CREDIT-LIMIT
    PERFORM 999-POST-PAYMENT.
``` | ```
IF BALANCE IS LESS THAN 1000.00
AND CREDIT-LIMIT
    PERFORM 999-POST-PAYMENT
END-IF
``` |

Even though implied subjects and relation operators can be used, it is recommended that you always explicitly code the subjects and operators. Implied subjects and relation operators, like compound conditions, are often misleading and difficult to understand.

Nested IF Statements

When the reserved word IF is specified more than once within an IF statement, the resulting statement is referred to as a **nested IF statement**. Nested IF statements can be classified as linear or nonlinear.

Linear Nested IF

A **linear nested IF** statement is relatively easy to write and understand. Its typical use is when multiple conditions based upon the value of one field exist. For instance, assume that you are working on a payroll application and you encounter a situation in which you must perform operations depending on the transaction-type, as follows:

Transaction-type	Action
NA	Perform Process-name-address
WE	Perform Process-weekly-earnings
YE	Perform Process-yearly-earnings
PD	Perform Process-personnel-data
Any other value	Perform Process-error-transaction

Figure 7-24 includes a flowchart to illustrate this and the required COBOL code to implement it. Notice that the equivalent COBOL-85 code is not shown. The reason is that COBOL-85 includes a special statement (EVALUATE) specifically for handling nested IF statements, and the resulting form is much simpler than the equivalent series of IFs and required END-IFs. The EVALUATE is described in a section that follows.

This form of nested IF is called linear because each ELSE immediately follows each IF condition, one after another. Conditions are tested until a true condition is encountered, in which case the specified action or actions are executed. If no condition is found to be true, the statement following the final else is executed.

A minor variation of this example is a case in which action is to be taken only for values of NA, WE, YE, and PD; anything else is to be ignored. You can modify the code of Figure 7-24 for this task merely by removing the final ELSE and PERFORM (the last two lines).

Figure 7-24
Linear nested IF statement
example—COBOL-74.

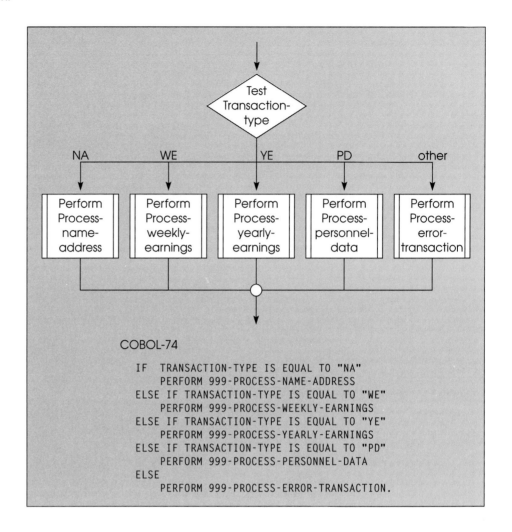

```
COBOL-74

IF  TRANSACTION-TYPE IS EQUAL TO "NA"
        PERFORM 999-PROCESS-NAME-ADDRESS
ELSE IF TRANSACTION-TYPE IS EQUAL TO "WE"
        PERFORM 999-PROCESS-WEEKLY-EARNINGS
ELSE IF TRANSACTION-TYPE IS EQUAL TO "YE"
        PERFORM 999-PROCESS-YEARLY-EARNINGS
ELSE IF TRANSACTION-TYPE IS EQUAL TO "PD"
        PERFORM 999-PROCESS-PERSONNEL-DATA
ELSE
        PERFORM 999-PROCESS-ERROR-TRANSACTION.
```

You can handle indenting for the linear nested IF as shown in the example: the first IF and each ELSE are aligned, and each condition is specified on the same line with its respective ELSE. The action statements are indented four places.

Nonlinear Nested IF The relationship between the IF condition and the ELSE to which it is paired is readily apparent for the linear nested IF. This is because each ELSE immediately follows the IF with which it is associated. The **nonlinear nested IF statement** is somewhat more complicated because (1) a combination of true and false conditions determines the specific action statement group executed, and (2) the ELSE statements may be separated from the IF statement with which it is paired. There are two variations of nonlinear IF statements: one with all action statements after conditions and another with interspersed conditions and action statements.

Figure 7-25 includes the code of a nonlinear nested IF with all action statements after the conditions. With nested IF statements in COBOL-74, each ELSE applies to the first IF that precedes it which has not already been paired with an ELSE. COBOL-85 with its scope terminators clearly identifies the end of the scope of each IF.

For a nonlinear nested IF statement, it is especially important that you indent as an aid to ensuring that the meaning of the statement is clear and understandable. Each ELSE (and END-IF for COBOL-85) should be coded on a separate line and vertically aligned with the IF condition to which it is paired.

In the example of Figure 7-26, action statements have been interspersed with the conditions. Although this might look more complicated, its overall decision structure is the same as that of Figure 7-25, except that some of the tests (IF

Figure 7-25   Nonlinear nested IF example: All action statements after conditions.

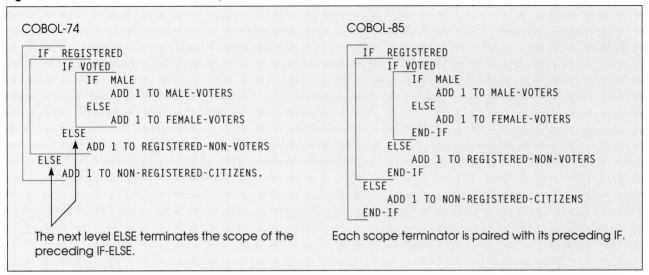

COBOL-74

```
IF  REGISTERED
    IF VOTED
        IF  MALE
            ADD 1 TO MALE-VOTERS
        ELSE
            ADD 1 TO FEMALE-VOTERS
    ELSE
        ADD 1 TO REGISTERED-NON-VOTERS
ELSE
    ADD 1 TO NON-REGISTERED-CITIZENS.
```

The next level ELSE terminates the scope of the
preceding IF-ELSE.

COBOL-85

```
IF  REGISTERED
    IF VOTED
        IF  MALE
            ADD 1 TO MALE-VOTERS
        ELSE
            ADD 1 TO FEMALE-VOTERS
        END-IF
    ELSE
        ADD 1 TO REGISTERED-NON-VOTERS
    END-IF
ELSE
    ADD 1 TO NON-REGISTERED-CITIZENS
END-IF
```

Each scope terminator is paired with its preceding IF.

Figure 7-26   Nonlinear nested IF example: Interspersed condition and action statements.

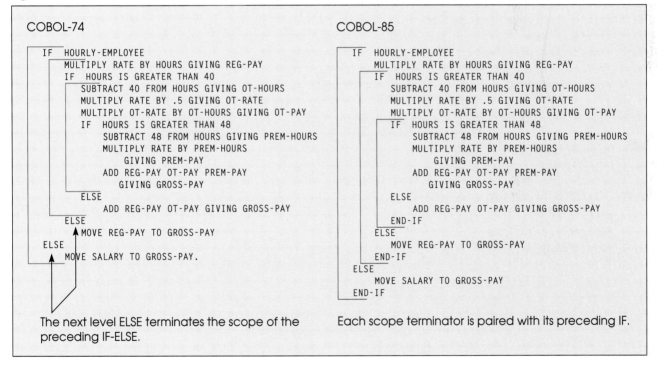

COBOL-74

```
IF  HOURLY-EMPLOYEE
    MULTIPLY RATE BY HOURS GIVING REG-PAY
    IF  HOURS IS GREATER THAN 40
        SUBTRACT 40 FROM HOURS GIVING OT-HOURS
        MULTIPLY RATE BY .5 GIVING OT-RATE
        MULTIPLY OT-RATE BY OT-HOURS GIVING OT-PAY
        IF  HOURS IS GREATER THAN 48
            SUBTRACT 48 FROM HOURS GIVING PREM-HOURS
            MULTIPLY RATE BY PREM-HOURS
                GIVING PREM-PAY
            ADD REG-PAY OT-PAY PREM-PAY
                GIVING GROSS-PAY
        ELSE
            ADD REG-PAY OT-PAY GIVING GROSS-PAY
    ELSE
        MOVE REG-PAY TO GROSS-PAY
ELSE
    MOVE SALARY TO GROSS-PAY.
```

The next level ELSE terminates the scope of the
preceding IF-ELSE.

COBOL-85

```
IF  HOURLY-EMPLOYEE
    MULTIPLY RATE BY HOURS GIVING REG-PAY
    IF  HOURS IS GREATER THAN 40
        SUBTRACT 40 FROM HOURS GIVING OT-HOURS
        MULTIPLY RATE BY .5 GIVING OT-RATE
        MULTIPLY OT-RATE BY OT-HOURS GIVING OT-PAY
        IF  HOURS IS GREATER THAN 48
            SUBTRACT 48 FROM HOURS GIVING PREM-HOURS
            MULTIPLY RATE BY PREM-HOURS
                GIVING PREM-PAY
            ADD REG-PAY OT-PAY PREM-PAY
                GIVING GROSS-PAY
        ELSE
            ADD REG-PAY OT-PAY GIVING GROSS-PAY
        END-IF
    ELSE
        MOVE REG-PAY TO GROSS-PAY
    END-IF
ELSE
    MOVE SALARY TO GROSS-PAY
END-IF
```

Each scope terminator is paired with its preceding IF.

statements) are preceded by action statements. Again, vertical alignment of paired
IF and ELSE (and END-IF for COBOL-85) entries makes the statement more easily understandable.

**A Word of Caution With
Nested IF Statements—
COBOL-74**

In both the examples of nonlinear nested IF statements, each IF required a corresponding ELSE, a result of the application itself. However, what if no action was
to be taken in the example of Figure 7-25 if the voter was not male (the action of
adding 1 to FEMALE-VOTERS was eliminated)? If you wrote the statement as
shown in Figure 7-27(a), you would disappointed when you made a run because
the results would be incorrect. In spite of the way in which you indented, COBOL
would treat the statement as illustrated in Figure 7-27(b).

Figure 7-27   A programming logic error with the nested IF.

```
Incorrect form. . .                              . . . is handled this way.

   IF  REGISTERED                                 IF   REGISTERED
      IF VOTED                                        IF VOTED
          IF  MALE                                        IF  MALE
              ADD 1 TO MALE-VOTERS                            ADD 1 TO MALE-VOTERS
          ELSE                                            ELSE
              ADD 1 TO REGISTERED-NON-VOTERS                 ADD 1 TO REGISTERED-NON-VOTERS
   ELSE                                            ELSE
      ADD 1 TO NON-REGISTERED-CITIZENS.                ADD 1 TO NON-REGISTERED-CITIZENS.

This alignment is misleading.                    The statement will be evaluated as illustrated here.
                                                 There would be no ELSE associated with the first IF.

              (a)                                              (b)
```

In this case, you can avoid the problem by not removing the ELSE and replacing the statement

```
ADD 1 TO FEMALE-VOTERS
```

with

```
NEXT SENTENCE
```

In COBOL-85, there is no problem as long as you use the END-IF scope terminator to terminate each IF—whether or not it includes an ELSE.

The EVALUATE Statement— COBOL-85

A Basic Form of the EVALUATE Statement

The EVALUATE statement (which was incorporated into COBOL by the 1985 standard) is one of the most complex forms in COBOL. In the interest of simplicity, its entire general form is not introduced here. Instead, let's consider two "versions"; these will be relatively straightforward to use.

The first form is equivalent to the linear nested IF of the preceding section. The example illustrated in flowchart form in Figure 7-24 is coded with the EVALUATE in Figure 7-28. Notice that this is almost self-explanatory. Following are important points about this example:

1. In structured programming, this is commonly referred to as the **case structure**; each alternative is considered an allowable **case**.

2. The entry immediately following the keyword EVALUATE (TRANSACTION-TYPE in this case) is called the **selection subject**. It is the entry against which comparisons that follow will be made.

3. The entry immediately following each keyword WHEN is called the **selection object**. This is the entry to which the selection subject is compared.

4. For evaluation purposes, the comparisons are made in exactly the same way as an equal comparison in an IF statement. The first equal condition that occurs causes the corresponding sequence of object statements to be executed. Upon completion of the sequence, control is passed to the END-EVALUATE and execution of the EVALUATE is completed. For instance, if

TRANSACTION-TYPE contains YE, then 999-PROCESS-YEARLY-EARNINGS will be executed. Upon return, control will be passed to the END-EVALUATE.

5. Although only one statement is included for each case in this example (PER-FORM), there may be any number of statements including IF statements or another EVALUATE statement.

6. If none of the preceding WHENs produces an equal condition, then the OTHER option is executed. This option is not required and can be omitted if no action is to be taken when none of the preceding conditions is satisfied.

7. Although not illustrated by this example, a range of values may be specified. For instance, assume that you are testing a numeric quantity in the EVALUATE. If a particular action were required for any value in the range 3 to 7 inclusive, you could write the case as:

```
WHEN 3 THROUGH 7
```

The general form of this limited version of the EVALUATE is shown in Figure 7-29.

Figure 7-28
The EVALUATE statement.

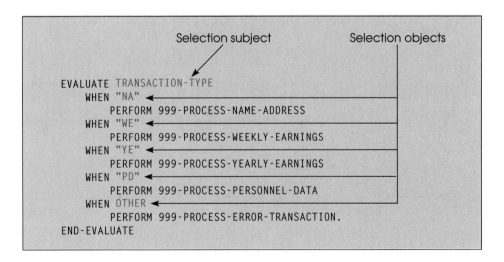

Figure 7-29   Partial general format of the EVALUATE statement.

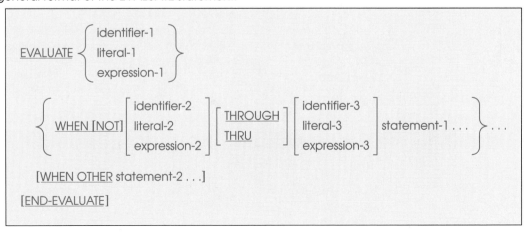

Another Form of the EVALUATE Statement

Situations often arise in programming in which one of several actions is to be taken, but the test conditions for each is quite different from the others. You observed this with the nonlinear nested IF examples in the preceding section. To illustrate the versatility of the EVALUATE, assume that you are working on a program to put into effect the terms of a new union contract. Employees are to be provided with special benefits, depending on their age and seniority with the company as follows:

> If (age 60 or greater) and (seniority 20 or greater)
> perform SPECIAL-BENEFITS-1
>
> If (age 60 or greater) and (seniority less than 20)
> perform SPECIAL-BENEFITS-2
>
> If (age less than 60) and (seniority 20 or greater)
> perform SPECIAL-BENEFITS-3
>
> If (age less than 60) and (seniority less than 20)
> perform STANDARD-BENEFITS-3

Notice that two fields are tested: age and seniority. By arranging the test sequence as in the following pseudocode, the number of comparisons can be minimized:

```
If (age 60 or greater) and (seniority 20 or greater)
   Perform SPECIAL-BENEFITS-1
Else If (age 60 or greater)
   perform SPECIAL-BENEFITS-2
Else If (seniority 20 or greater)
   perform SPECIAL-BENEFITS-3
Else
   perform STANDARD-BENEFITS-3
```

Notice that in the second test, it is not necessary to check the seniority because those with 20 or greater have already been processed following the first If. Likewise, in the third test, it is not necessary to check the age.

This can be coded with the form of the EVALUATE shown in Figure 7-30. If you have any questions about whether or not it will do the job, step through it with sample data values. In studying this example, be aware of the following important points:

1. The selection subject is simply the reserved word TRUE, a logical value. Hence, the selection objects must provide the logical values of either true or false.

2. Execution of this statement involves evaluating the selection objects (following the WHENs) until one is found with a truth value matching the selection subject (TRUE in this case). When that occurs, the corresponding object statements are executed and control passes to the END-EVALUATE.

3. If none of the WHEN subjects is true, then the OTHER option is executed.

Recap of Nested IF Statements

Before the development of structured programming concepts, use of nested IF statements was usually discouraged because they were considered complicated and difficult to understand. However, with structured programming, nested IF statements are often required to provide proper control of statement selection. The complexity of nested IF statements is reduced when (1) the programmer thoroughly understands how the ELSE statement groups are paired with IF conditions, (2) proper indention forms are used when coding the nested IF, and (3) the number of nesting levels is limited to perhaps three or four.

Figure 7-30
Another version of the
EVALUATE statement and its
format.

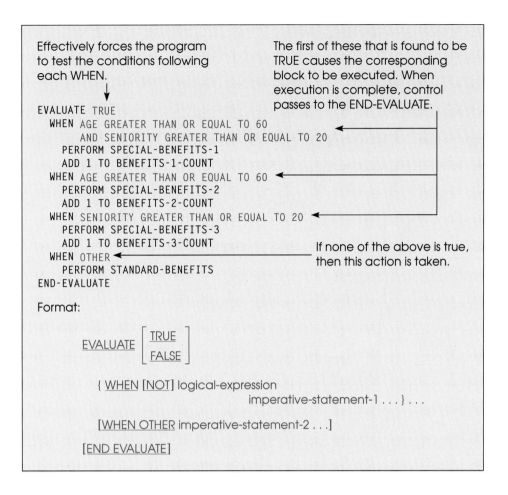

Effectively forces the program
to test the conditions following
each WHEN.

The first of these that is found to be
TRUE causes the corresponding
block to be executed. When
execution is complete, control
passes to the END-EVALUATE.

```
EVALUATE TRUE
    WHEN AGE GREATER THAN OR EQUAL TO 60
        AND SENIORITY GREATER THAN OR EQUAL TO 20
        PERFORM SPECIAL-BENEFITS-1
        ADD 1 TO BENEFITS-1-COUNT
    WHEN AGE GREATER THAN OR EQUAL TO 60
        PERFORM SPECIAL-BENEFITS-2
        ADD 1 TO BENEFITS-2-COUNT
    WHEN SENIORITY GREATER THAN OR EQUAL TO 20
        PERFORM SPECIAL-BENEFITS-3
        ADD 1 TO BENEFITS-3-COUNT
    WHEN OTHER
        PERFORM STANDARD-BENEFITS
END-EVALUATE
```

If none of the above is true,
then this action is taken.

Format:

$$\text{EVALUATE} \begin{bmatrix} \underline{\text{TRUE}} \\ \underline{\text{FALSE}} \end{bmatrix}$$

{ <u>WHEN</u> [<u>NOT</u>] logical-expression
                      imperative-statement-1 . . . } . . .

[<u>WHEN OTHER</u> imperative-statement-2 . . .]

[<u>END EVALUATE</u>]

Chapter Summary

An IF statement can be written as either (1) a simple one-condition statement, (2) a multiple-condition statement combined by logical operators, or (3) a multiple-condition nested IF statement.

A simple IF statement can be written with true actions only, with both true and false actions, or with false actions only. The latter two forms require use of the reserved word ELSE; the false actions only form also uses the reserved words NEXT SENTENCE.

Four types of conditions can be tested with an IF statement: relation, class, sign, and condition-name.

- **Relation conditions** test whether the subject of the condition IS GREATER THAN, IS EQUAL TO, or IS LESS THAN the object. (COBOL-85 also includes IS GREATER THAN OR EQUAL TO and IS LESS THAN OR EQUAL TO.) When the subject and the object are both numeric items, comparisons are made according to their algebraic value. Alphanumeric comparisons depend upon the collating sequence of the computer being used. With alphanumeric fields, comparison begins at the leftmost character position and proceeds to the right. If the fields are not the same length, the shorter field is internally extended with spaces to equal the length of the longer field.

- **Class conditions** test whether a field contains only numeric digits or solely alphabetic characters. Fields that contain only numeric digits (0 through 9) are considered NUMERIC; those containing only alphabetic characters (and may include a blank space) are considered ALPHABETIC.

- **Sign conditions** test whether a numeric field is POSITIVE, NEGATIVE, or ZERO.

■ **Condition-name conditions** are a special way of writing a relation condition that requires an 88-level entry in the DATA DIVISION.

Each 88-level item requires a condition-name VALUE clause in its data-item description. Condition-name VALUE clauses differ from initializing VALUE clauses because a condition-name VALUE clause:

■ Can be used in either the FILE SECTION or the WORKING-STORAGE SECTION

■ Can be associated with a REDEFINES clause

■ Can be associated with an OCCURS clause

■ Can be specified with multiple values or a range of values

A **combined IF statement** contains multiple conditions connected with the logical operators AND or OR.

■ When conditions are joined by the AND operator, all conditions must be true for the true actions to be executed; if one or more conditions are false, the false actions are executed.

■ With the OR operator, if one or more conditions are true, the true actions are executed; if all conditions are false, the false actions are executed.

When both the operators AND and OR are used in the same IF statement, the result is termed a **complex condition**.

A **nested IF statement** contains multiple IF statements. Nested IF statements can be categorized as being linear or nonlinear. A **linear nested IF statement** is one in which each ELSE action immediately follows the condition to which it applies. With a **nonlinear nested IF statement**, multiple IF verbs precede the ELSE actions.

COBOL-85 includes the EVALUATE statement, which allows for compact coding of nested IF conditions.

Style Summary

For relation conditions, make the data class of the subject and the object consistent. That is, when the subject is numeric, the object should be numeric; when the subject is alphanumeric, the object should also be alphanumeric (or a nonnumeric literal).

Use the relation condition words (EQUAL TO, LESS THAN, and GREATER THAN) in preference to the symbols.

If your program requires that you use complex conditions, use parentheses to explicitly specify the evaluation sequence and to make the condition understandable.

Implied subjects and relation operators should not be used in an IF statement. They tend to cause confusion.

Nested IF statements should be limited to three or four levels to prevent them from becoming overly complex. If you are using COBOL-85, use the EVALUATE in place of nested IF statements where appropriate.

Indent elements of your IF statements as illustrated by the examples of this chapter to enhance clarity.

Features in COBOL-85 Not in COBOL-74
Described in this chapter

The following additional relation conditions:

```
IS GREATER THAN OR EQUAL TO
>=
IS LESS THAN OR EQUAL TO
<=
```

The EVALUATE statement to handle multiple-condition testing.

The END-IF scope terminator.

The class conditions ALPHABETIC-UPPER and ALPHABETIC-LOWER, which allow for testing that fields contain only upper-case letters or lower-case letters, respectively.

Not described in this chapter   The optional word THEN can be used in the IF to be more consistent with the if-then-else terminology. Note that it does not affect the execution of the IF statement in any way. Following is an example of its use:

```
IF FA IS GREATER THAN 0
THEN
    ADD 1 TO G-COUNT
ELSE
    ADD 1 TO C-COUNT
END-IF
```

COBOL-85 permits the specification of a user-defined class that can be tested with a class-condition IF statement. The class condition is defined in the SPECIAL-NAMES paragraph of the CONFIGURATION SECTION of the ENVIRONMENT DIVISION and is tested by an IF statement in the PROCEDURE DIVISION. Examples are as follows:

```
ENVIRONMENT DIVISION.
CONFIGURATION SECTION.
    .
    .
    .
SPECIAL-NAMES.
    CLASS VOWEL IS "AEIOU".
    CLASS SPECIAL-LETTER IS "W" THRU "Z".
    .
    .
    .
PROCEDURE DIVISION.
    .
    .
    .
    EVALUATE LETTER-FIELD
        WHEN VOWEL
            PERFORM 999-VOWEL-ROUTINE
        WHEN SPECIAL-LETTER
            PERFORM 999-CONSONANT-ROUTINE
        WHEN OTHER
            PERFORM 999-SPECIAL-ROUTINE
    END-EVALUATE
```

A number of COBOL verbs have exception-condition phrases associated with them. The READ statement AT END phrase is an example. In COBOL-74, these verbs had only a true action and hence can be termed "one-legged" conditions. COBOL-85 provides an alternate, false path for such conditions. Following is a list of verbs you have studied thus far and the alternate path conditions:

Alternate-path condition expression	Verb(s)
NOT AT END	READ
NOT END-OF-PAGE	WRITE
NOT ON SIZE ERROR	ADD, SUBTRACT, MULTIPLY, DIVIDE, COMPUTE

Exercises

Terms for Definition

class condition _____

collating sequence _____

combined IF statement _____

complex condition _____

condition-name condition _____

implied relation operators _____

implied subject _____

linear nested IF statement _____

negated condition _____

nested IF statement _____

nonlinear nested IF statement _____

relation condition _____

sign condition _____

simple IF statement _____

Review Questions

1. An IF statement that contains only one condition is called a(n)

   _____ IF statement; when the logical operators AND or OR

   are used, it is known as a(n) _____ IF statement; an IF
   statement that contains the word IF more than once is termed a(n)

   _____ IF statement.

2. Name the four types of conditions that may be expressed with an IF
   statement.

   a. _____   c. _____

   b. _____   d. _____

3. Identify the three basic relation test operators.

   a. _____   b. _____   c. _____

4. With a relation condition, the element before the relation operator is called

   the _____ ; the element after the operator is termed the

   _____ .

5. When the subject and the object of a relation test are both numeric, comparison of the two values is made according to their _____ value.

6. When the subject and/or object of a relation test are alphanumeric, comparison of the two values is made in accordance with the _____ of the computer system being used.

7. When an alphanumeric comparison is being made and the subject and object are of different lengths, the shorter field is _____.

8. Name the two data classes that can be tested with a class condition.

   a. _____   b. _____

9. Name the three sign conditions that can be tested.

   a. _____   b. _____   c. _____

10. A sign test can be performed only upon _____ fields.

11. A condition-name test requires a level-_____ item in the

    _____ DIVISION.

12. A condition-name VALUE clause may contain one value,

    _____ values, or a(n) _____ of values.

13. Condition-name VALUE clauses _____ (can/cannot) be specified in the FILE SECTION of the DATA DIVISION.

14. When the logical operator _____ is specified in a combined IF statement, all conditions must be true for the true statements to be executed; when the logical operator _____ is specified, one or more conditions must be true for the true statements to be executed.

15. When the operators AND and OR are both used within the same IF statement, the resulting expression is referred to as a(n) _____ condition.

16. When a nested IF statement contains an ELSE immediately following each IF condition, it can be called a(n) _____ nested IF statement.

17. In a nested IF statement, each ELSE applies to:

    _____

    _____

18. Assume that each of the following is stored as an alphanumeric field within your computer. In the space to the right, arrange them into ascending sequence (smallest first, largest last), according to the collating sequence of your computer.

EGG NOODLES _____

BRAN CEREAL _____

7 UP _____

#1 WHOLE WHEAT _____

12PM CAKE MIX _____

Z-BRAN _____

ZBRAN _____

 ZBRAN _____

Z BRAN _____

Bran Cereal _____

All-good Crunch _____

aLL-GOOD CRUNCH _____

19. Following is a list of numeric values stored in your computer. For these, assume the following: (1) they are stored in the appropriate format regarding assumed decimal and sign positioning, and (2) the field length of each is as suggested by the number of digits shown. Arrange them in sequence from the smallest to the largest, as would be determined by the COBOL relation condition. If any two (or more) are equal, place a bracket around them to indicate this.

256 _____

-1 _____

000078.63 _____

-000.95 _____

00000256.000 _____

1000.0 _____

.95 _____

00000.000 _____

-.95 _____

0 _____

20. A programmer must test a field to ensure that it is alphabetic. Instead of using the ALPHABETIC class condition, the programmer decides to use the NOT NUMERIC condition, assuming that they will produce the same result. Comment on this decision.

---

21. Each of the following IF conditions can be written in a different form (for instance, compare Examples 2 and 5 in Figure 7-3). In the space provided, write an equivalent form for each. In all cases, assume that the IF is terminated with either a period or an END-IF.

```
IF FA IS GREATER THAN FB
    ADD 1 TO FA-COUNT
```

```
IF FC IS POSITIVE
    ADD 1 TO FC-COUNT
```

```
IF FF NOT GREATER FE
    ADD 1 TO FE-COUNT
```

```
05  GENDER        PIC X(1).
    88   MASCULINE    VALUE "M".
    88   FEMININE     VALUE "F".
    88   NEUTER       VALUE "N".

IF MASCULINE
    ADD 1 TO M-COUNT
```

```
IF NOT FEMININE
    ADD 1 TO S-COUNT
```

22. Consider the following complex condition (note that the entire condition is written on one line so that you can easily group the parentheses):

```
IF ((FA GREATER 10 OR FB EQUAL 0) AND FC LESS 55) OR FF NOT ZERO
```

For each of the following sets of data values, indicate whether this condition will be true or false by placing a letter T or F in the space provided.

	FA	FB	FC	FF
_____	10	0	0	22
_____	11	0	55	−1
_____	−100	−100	−100	0
_____	−100	−100	−100	−100
_____	0	0	0	0
_____	100	100	100	100

Syntax/Debug Exercise   The following fields are defined in working-storage of a program:

```
05  FIELD-A      PIC X(5).
05  FIELD-B      PIC 9(5).
05  FIELD-C      PIC 9(5).
05  FIELD-D      PIC 9(1).
05  FIELD-E      PIC X(1).
    88   VAL-1       VALUE "A".
    88   VAL-2       VALUE "B".
    88   VAL-3       VALUE "C".
```

Some of the following conditions violate the syntax rules. Identify each that is incorrect and state what is wrong in the space provided.

IF FIELD-E LESS "1" _____

_____

IF FIELD-A IS EQUAL TO FIELD-B _____

_____

IF NOT VAL-1 _____

_____

IF FIELD-E NOT APHABETIC _____

_____

IF FIELD-E IS EQUAL TO VAL-3 _____

_____

IF FIELD-D IS NOT ZERO _____

_____

```
IF  VAL-3
    AND FIELD-B IS GREATER THAN FIELD-D _____
```

_____

```
IF FIELD-B NOT EQUAL TO FIELD-D _____
```

_____

```
IF NOT VAL-1 AND NOT VAL-2 _____
```

_____

```
IF FIELD-A NUMERIC _____
```

_____

```
IF FIELD-E NOT NUMERIC AND NOT ALPHABETIC_____
```

_____

```
IF  FIELD-B GREATER THAN 0
    AND LESS THAN 100 _____
```

_____

```
IF FIELD-B AND FIELD-C GREATER THAN 10. _____
```

_____

```
IF FIELD-B - FIELD-C IS NEGATIVE _____
```

_____

```
IF FIELD-B - FIELD-C IS NUMERIC _____
```

_____

Programming Assignments

Programming Assignment 7-1: Test Grades Report

Background information:

One of the instructors at the Bayview Institute of Computer Technology has decided to automate record keeping for student examinations. Her file contains one record for each exam take by each student. It includes the number of questions on the exam and the number missed by the student. The instructor needs a program to determine and print letter grades based on the raw input.

Input file: Student file (STUDENT.DAT)

Input-record format:

Positions	Field	Data class	Comments
3–11	Student number	Numeric	
12–25	Student last name	Alphanumeric	
26–35	Student first name	Alphanumeric	
52–56	Section number	Numeric	
57–59	Questions asked	Numeric	Whole number
60–62	Questions missed	Numeric	Whole number
63–70	Other data		

Output-report format:

```
          0         1         2         3         4         5         6         7
 1234567890123456789012345678901234567890123456789012345678901234567890123456789012
 1
 2
 3
 4                              TEST  GRADES  REPORT  (7-1)
 5
 6      SECTION    -------STUDENT  NAME-------   QUESTIONS   QUESTIONS   PERCENTAGE   LETTER
 7      NUMBER     LAST  NAME        FIRST  NAME   ASKED      MISSED      CORRECT      GRADE
 8
 9       99999    XXXXXXXXXXXXXX XXXXXXXXXX       ZZ9        ZZ9         ZZ9%          X
10
11       99999    XXXXXXXXXXXXXX XXXXXXXXXX       ZZ9        ZZ9         ZZ9%          X
```

Program operations:
1. Process each input student record.
2. Print the three heading lines on the first page and on each following page of the report.
3. For each input student record, do the following processing:
   a. Calculate the percentage of correct answers by subtracting the questions missed from the questions asked and dividing the remainder by the questions asked.
   b. Assign the letter grade in accordance with the percentage correct, as follows:

100% through	90%	= A
89% through	80%	= B
79% through	70%	= C
69% through	60%	= D
59% through	0%	= F

   c. Print an output detail line as specified on the print chart.
4. Double-space each detail line. Provide for a span of 56 lines per page.

Programming Assignment 7-2: Social Security Tax Report
Background information:
The payroll supervisor at Silicon Valley Manufacturing must prepare a quarterly summary of Social Security tax for all employees. This tax is computed (using 1989 values) as follows:

Earnings	Tax rate
To $48,000	7.51% of earnings
In excess of $48,000	None

Note that tax is calculated for only those earnings up to $48,000. Once an employee's year-to-date earnings reach $48,000, tax is no longer withheld.

Input file: Earnings file (EARNINGS.DAT)

Input-record format:

Positions	Field name	Data class	Comments
11–19	Employee number	Alphanumeric	Social Security number
20–31	Employee last name	Alphanumeric	
32–40	Employee first name	Alphanumeric	
60–66	Current-period earnings	Numeric	Format: *dollars and cents*
67–74	Year-to-date earnings	Numeric	Format: *dollars and cents*

Note: The Year-to-date earnings includes the Current-period earnings amount.

Output-report format:

```
          0         1         2         3         4         5         6         7         8
  1234567890123456789012345678901234567890123456789012345678901234567890123456789012

4 SOCIAL SECURITY TAX REPORT (7-2)                                              PAGE ZZ9

6 SOC. SEC.        ----EMPLOYEE NAME----    YEAR-TO-DATE      THIS PERIOD EARNINGS   S.S. TAX
7 NUMBER        LAST        FIRST            EARNINGS         AMOUNT      TAXABLE     THIS PER.

9 999-99-9999  XXXXXXXXXXXX XXXXXXXXX       ZZZ,ZZZ.99      ZZ,ZZZ.99-  ZZ,ZZZ.99-  Z,ZZZ.99-

11 999-99-9999 XXXXXXXXXXXX XXXXXXXXX       ZZZ,ZZZ.99      ZZ,ZZZ.99-  ZZ,ZZZ.99-  Z,ZZZ.99-
```

Program operations:
1. Process each input employee record.
2. Print the three heading lines on the first page and on each following page of the report.
   a. Accumulate and print the page number on the first heading line as specified on the print chart.
3. For each input employee record, do the following processing:
   a. Determine the Current-period-taxable-amount as follows:
      - If the input Year-to-date-earnings field is equal to or less than $48,000.00, use the Current-period earnings.
      - If the input year-to-date earnings is more than $48,000.00, subtract the Current-period earnings from the Year-to-date-earnings (call this quantity Deficient-amount).
         If Deficient-amount is less than $48,000,
            calculate the Current-period-taxable-amount as 48,000 minus Deficient-amount.
         Else
            Set Current-period-taxable-amount to zero
      - Calculate the Social-security-tax amount will be equal to 7.51% (rounded) of the Current-period-taxable-amount.
   b. Print an output Social-security-tax report detail line as specified on the print chart.
4. Double-space each detail line. Provide for a span of 54 lines per page.

Programming Assignment 7-3: Accounts-Receivable Register
Program description:
The first of each month, Silicon Valley Manufacturing calculates the balance owed by each customer from data in the customer file. Included in the calculations are the prior balance (balance forward), new purchases, payments received, finance charges, and late charges. A bill is printed and mailed to each customer. In addition, a summary called an accounts-receivable register is to be printed for use by the accounting department.

Input file: Customer file (CUSTOMER.DAT)

Input-record format:

Positions	Field	Data class	Comments
3–7	Customer number		
8–31	Customer name	Alphanumeric	
39–46	Balance forward	Numeric	Format: *dollars and cents*
47–54	New purchases	Numeric	Format: *dollars and cents*
73–80	Payments received	Numeric	Format: *dollars and cents*

Output-report format:

Program operations:
1. Process each input customer record.
2. Print the three heading lines on the first page and on each following page of the report.
   a. Print the run date on the first heading line as specified on the print chart.
   b. Accumulate and print the page number on the first heading line as specified on the print chart.
3. For each input customer record, do the following processing:
   a. Calculate the finance charge by subtracting the payments-received amount from the balance-forward amount and multiplying the remainder by 1.5% (the monthly service charge applicable to the unpaid balance).
   b. If the payments-received amount is less than 10% of the balance-forward amount, apply a late charge equal to 1% of the difference. If a late charge is applicable and the late-charge amount is less than $5.00, apply a minimum late charge of $5.00.
   c. Calculate the new balance by subtracting the payments-received amount from the balance-forward amount and adding to the remainder the finance charge, late charge, and new-purchases amounts.
   d. Calculate the minimum-payment amount equal to 10% of the new-balance amount.
   e. Print an output accounts-receivable register detail line as specified on the print chart.

   f. Accumulate the following totals:
- Balance forward
- Payments received
- Finance charge
- Late charge
- New purchases
- New balance
- Minimum payment

   g. Print the account status as follows:
- If the new-balance amount is zero or negative, leave the status field blank.
- If the payments-received amount is equal to or greater than 10% of the balance-forward amount, print "CURRENT."
- If the balance-forward amount is not equal to zero and the payments-received amount is not equal to zero but less than 10% of the balance-forward amount, print "OVERDUE."
- If the balance-forward amount is not equal to zero and the payments-received amount is equal to zero, print "PAST DUE."

4. Double-space each detail line. Provide for a span of 54 lines per page.

5. After all input customer records have been processed, print the two output-report total lines (triple-spaced from the last detail line) as specified on the print chart.

Programming Assignment 7-4: Inventory Reorder Report
Program description:
An inventory reorder report is to be printed from the parts file.

Input file: Inventory file (INVEN.DAT)

Input-record format:

Positions	Field	Data class	Comments
4–13	Product identification	Alphanumeric	
14–39	Product description	Alphanumeric	
40	Inventory class	Alphanumeric	
41–46	Unit price (unit cost)	Numeric	Format: dollars and cents
48–51	Reorder point	Numeric	Whole number
52–55	Quantity on hand	Numeric	Whole number
71–74	Reorder quantity	Numeric	Whole number
75–80	Other data		

Output-report format:

Program operations:

1. Process each input inventory record.
2. Print the four heading lines on the first page and on each following page of the report.
   a. Print the run time and run date on the first heading line as specified on the print chart.
   b. Accumulate and print the page number on the second heading line as specified on the print chart.
3. For each input part record, do the following processing:
   a. If the input inventory-class code is not equal to "A," "B," "C," or "X," print an asterisk (*) in the inventory-class field on the output-report line, but treat the part as an inventory-class "C" item.
   b. Calculate the quantity-available amount by adding the quantity-on-hand amount to the quantity-on-order amount.
   c. If the quantity-available amount is less than the reorder-point amount, calculate the quantity-to-order amount. The quantity-to-order amount should be the reorder-quantity amount unless the quantity-to-order amount is greater, in which case it should be the next higher multiple of the reorder-quantity amount.
   d. If the quantity-available amount is not less than the reorder-point amount, set the quantity-to-order amount to zero.
   e. When the quantity-to-order amount is not equal to zero, print an asterisk in print position 1, as shown on the print chart. Otherwise, leave print position 1 blank.
   f. Calculate the inventory-value amount by multiplying the unit-cost amount by the quantity-on-hand amount.
   g. Calculate the reorder-cost amount by multiplying the unit-cost amount by the quantity-to-order amount.
   h. Print an output inventory reorder report detail line as specified on the print chart.
   i. Accumulate the following totals:
      ■ Inventory value (for each inventory class and for all items as specified on the print chart)
      ■ Reorder cost (for each inventory class and for all items as specified on the print chart)
4. Double-space each detail line. Provide for a span of 53 lines per page.
5. After all input part records have been processed, print the six output-report total lines (triple-spaced from the last detail line) as specified on the print chart.

Programming Assignment 7-5: Nurses' Salary Increase Projection

Background information:

After meeting with the union, the Brooklawn Hospital management has found the report of Assignment 6-5 inadequate to cope with some of the union proposals. These include adjusting pay based on a variety of factors including seniority, parttime/fulltime status, and supervisory responsibility in addition to shift differential. Although the hospital board of trustees agrees with management, the press has supported most of the union proposals as being reasonable. The report of Assignment 6-5 must be expanded further.

Input file: Nurses file (NURSES.DAT)

Input-record format:

The following is the same as the format of Assignment 6-5, except that additional fields have been added as shown.

Positions	Field	Data class	Comments
1–2	Record type code	Alphanumeric	
3–25	Name (last, first, mi)	Alphanumeric	
26–32	Home telephone number	Alphanumeric	
33–46	Professional specialty	Alphanumeric	
47–52	Date hired	Numeric	Format: *yymmdd*
53–55	Salary schedule	Alphanumeric	Row and column
56	Employment code	Alphabetic	F—Fulltime employee
			P—Parttime employee
57	Supervisory code	Alphabetic	Y—Yes, N—No
68–73	Base monthly salary	Numeric	Format: dollars and cents
94–96	Ward/duty station	Alphanumeric	
97	Shift code	Numeric	Value of 1, 2, or 3

Output-report format:

Program operations:

1. Process each input record.
2. Calculated quantities for detail output are:
   a. Projected-base-salary is the Input-base-salary times 1.09.
   b. Benefits-adjustment is:
      30% of Projected-base-salary if Employment-code = "F"
      15% of Projected-base-salary otherwise.
   c. Seniority is to be determined as of 1/1/91. To calculate Years-seniority, subtract the year subfield of Date-hired from 91. Then calculate Seniority-adjustment as the following percentage of the Projected-base-salary:
      None if Years-seniority is less than 10
      3% if the Years-seniority is between 10 and 19 (inclusive)
      7% if the Years-seniority is 20 or greater
   d. Supervisory-adjustment is 10% of the Projected-base-salary if the Supervisory-code contains Y.
   e. Shift-adjustment is calculated as the following percentage of the Projected-base-salary:
      None if Shift-code = 1
      5% if Shift-code = 2
      10% if Shift-code = 3

3. Accumulate the following totals:
    Projected-base-salary
    Benefits-adjustment
    Seniority-adjustment
    Supervisory-adjustment
    Shift-adjustment
4. Double-space each detail line. Provide for a span of 53 lines per page.
5. After all input part records have been processed, print the three output-report total lines (triple-spaced from the last detail line) as specified on the print chart.

Programming Assignment 7-6: Vehicle Rental Summary Report
Background information:
The basic daily rental fee advertised by Rent-Ur-Wheels is only one element of determining the actual daily rate. Customers can receive a variety of discounts (or none at all). Two types of insurance are available and must be factored into the rate. This program is to print a list of all rented vehicles together with the actual daily rate (including any discounts or insurance charges).

Input file: The Vehicle file (VEHICLE.DAT)

Input–record format:
The following is the same as the format of Assignment 2-6, except that additional fields have been inserted as shown.

Positions	Field	Data class	Comments
1–4	Vehicle type	Alphanumeric	
5–18	Make of vehicle	Alphanumeric	
19–28	Model	Alphanumeric	
29–35	License number	Alphanumeric	
36–39	Daily rental fee	Numeric	Dollars and cents
59–60	Number of days rented	Numeric	
61	Insurance code 1	Alphanumeric	Y = Yes Code 1 insurance N = No Code 1 insurance
62	Insurance code 2	Alphanumeric	Y = Yes Code 2 insurance N = No Code 2 insurance
63	Customer discount code	Alphanumeric	Value 1, 2, 3, 9, or blank
64–89	Other data		

Output-report format:

Program operations:
1. Process only those input records with a value R (rented) in the Status field.
2. Calculated quantities for detail output are:
   a. Calculate a discount on the Daily-rental-fee (the Basic Rate on the output report) based on the Customer-discount-code as follows.
      Discount code = 1, give 4%
      Discount code = 2, give 6%
      Discount code = 3 or 9, give 10%
   b. If the Insurance-code-1 field contains Y, calculate a C1-insurance-rate fee of 6.5% the Daily-rental-fee.
   c. Calculate the Net-rate as:
      Daily-rental-fee - Discount + C1-insurance-rate
   d. If the Insurance-code-2 field contains Y, use a C2-insurance-amount of 7.50; otherwise, use zero.
   e. Calculate the Projected-amount as:
      Number-of-days-rented x Net-rate
      Note: Number-of-days-rented is to be printed as Scheduled Days.
3. Accumulate the following totals:
   Number of vehicles currently rented.
   Total number of vehicle days (total of Number-of-days-rented fields).
   Projected gross income (total of Projected-amount fields).
4. Double-space each detail line. Provide for a span of 36 lines per page.
5. After all input records have been processed, print the three output-report total lines (triple-spaced from the last detail line) as specified on the print chart.

Programming Assignment 7-7: Vehicle Rental Summary Report With Date Calculation

Background information:
For a particular study of their operations, Rent-Ur-Wheels has created a special file of typical rentals covering a two-year period. In addition to the output of Assignment 7-6, the Date-returned must be determined from the Date-rented.

Input file: The Vehicle file (VEHICLE.DAT)

Input-record format:
The input-record format is identical to that of Assignment 7-6 with the insertion of the following date field. You might notice that this date is not consistent with the Date-due-back field (positions 51–54) used in earlier assignments. Columns 51–54 are not meaningful in this assignment and must not be used in the date determinations (as described under *Program operations* on the following page).

Positions	Field	Data class	Comments
53–58	Date rented	Numeric	Format *yymmdd*

Output-report format:

```
RENT-UR-WHEELS                                                  RUN DATE MM/DD/YY
DAILY RENTAL SUMMARY (7-7)                                             PAGE ZZ9

LICENSE              RETURN    BASIC          C1 INSUR.   NET   C2 INSUR.   DAYS      RENTAL
NUMBER    MAKE       DATE      RATE     DISC.    RATE     RATE     AMOUNT   RENTED    AMOUNT

XXXXXXX   XXXXXXXXXXXXXXX   XX/XX/XX   ZZ.99   ZZ.ZZ    ZZ.ZZ   ZZ.ZZ    ZZ.ZZ      99     9,999.99

XXXXXXX   XXXXXXXXXXXXXXX   XX/XX/XX   ZZ.99   ZZ.ZZ    ZZ.ZZ   ZZ.ZZ    ZZ.ZZ      99     9,999.99



                                    RENTAL SUMMARY TOTALS:  VEHICLES RENTED    999
                                                            VEHICLE DAYS     9,999
                                                            GROSS RENTAL    99,999.99
```

Program operations:

1. Process each record in the file.
2. Calculated quantities for detail output are the same as those for Assignment 7-6. In addition, the Return-date must be calculated from the Date-rented and the Number-of-days-rented fields. You must add the Number-of-days to the day portion of the Date-rented field, then test to determine if it "overflows" into the next month. Following is a rough form of pseudocode that can be used for this action:

```
Add Day-rented and Number-of-days giving Day-due.
Store 31 in Days-in-the-month work field.
If Month is April, June, September, or November
    store 30 in Days-in-the-month.
If Month is February
    If leap-year store 29 in Days-in-the-month
    Else store 28 in Days-in-the-month.
If Day-due is greater than Days-in-the-month
    subtract Days-in-the-month from Day-due
    add 1 to Month.
    If the Month is 13, adjust Month and Year.
```

You can use division and inspect the remainder to determine if a year is leap year. (Leap year occurs every four years; 1992 is a leap year.)

3. Accumulate the same totals as defined in Assignment 7-6.
   Number of vehicles currently rented.
   Total number of vehicle days (total of Number-of-days-rented fields).
   Projected gross income (total of Projected-amount fields).
4. Double-space each detail line. Provide for a span of 53 lines per page.
5. After all input records have been processed, print the three output-report total lines (triple-spaced from the last detail line) as specified on the print chart.

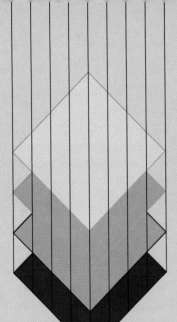

Data Validation Concepts

Module Objectives   One of the important functions of a data-processing department is to protect the integrity of a valuable company asset: the company's data. Once data is entered into the computer, numerous techniques are used so that it does not become corrupted. One of the principal keys to ensuring error-free data is making certain that all data is correct before it is introduced into the files. This is called data validation, the topic of this concepts module. From this module, you will learn the following:

- The nature of character testing (testing for validity of individual characters of fields).

- The variety of methods for field checking, including such actions as checking to ensure that a field is present, checking allowable ranges of numeric fields, checking to ensure that values entered are "reasonable," and checking dates.

- Record checking, which involves ensuring that records are in their proper sequence and correspondence.

- Data validation programs for checking input data. This can be done on-line (data checked as it is entered) or by a batch process (all data is entered and then checked in a "batch").

Module Outline

About Garbage

Character Testing
Class Test
Sign Test

Field Checking
Presence Check
Absence Check
Range Check
Limit Check
Reasonableness Check
Consistency Check
Justification Check
Embedded-Blank Check
Date Check
Self-Checking Numbers
Name-Correspondence Check
Code-Existence Check

Record Checking
Record Sequence Checks
Record-Set Relationship Checks

Data Validation Programs
On-line vs. Batch Data Validation
A Typical Batch Data Validation Application
Handling Errors

About Garbage

That cliché "G.I.G.O." (garbage in—garbage out!) is all too familiar to data-processing personnel and users alike. Although some may lamely try to enlist the phrase as a defense against an input data aberration, the professional programmer/analyst should never utter these words. Rather, the byword should be "G.D.G.I." (garbage doesn't get in). It is the programmer/analyst's responsibility to specify the safeguards and controls necessary to ensure data integrity within the system. This chapter discusses such aspects of control as they relate to data validation during initial input of data to a computer system.

One of the most common mistakes made by the beginning programmer/analyst is the failure to validate data completely at the time of its initial entry into the system. In the vernacular, this is known as letting "garbage," "junk," or "dirty" data into the system. The consequences are severe. Erroneous data spreads throughout the data files of the system like contagious germs. Data that enters the system has an increasing likelihood of becoming infected. As errors compound to epidemic proportions, the system's output is weakened until it is no longer viable. Since this sounds like a case for "General Hospital," the programmer/analyst is well advised to practice preventive medicine—that is, to institute programmed validation checks on data at initial input. There are three general categories of programmed input validation checks: character testing, field checking, and record checking.

Character Testing

The most basic form of data validation control is the testing of individual character positions within a field. There are two forms of **character tests**: class and sign.

Class Test

Class tests are concerned with determining whether data values within a field fall into the **numeric**, **alphabetic**, or **alphanumeric** class. Figure G-1 categorizes character representations according to their class.

Numeric fields should generally be validated to ensure that each digit position is purely numeric. When alphabetic or special characters are present in a numeric field, the data is in error. Thus, a numeric class test helps to ensure the data integrity of the validated numeric field and also of any fields that hold the results of computations involving the field.

Do not get the impression that declaring a field as numeric with PIC 9 will guarantee that the data will always be numeric. Remember from earlier discussions that the picture only tells the compiler the types of actions that can be performed on the data. There are no restrictions on the data that can be entered into a PIC 9 field from, for instance, a READ statement. Furthermore, remember that an alphanumeric field (PIC X) can be tested (using the NUMERIC class test) to determine

Figure G-1
Classes of data.

Data class	Valid characters
Numeric	Digits 0–9
Alphabetic	Letters A–Z, blank space COBOL-85: Letters a–z
Alphanumeric	Digits 0–9 Letters A–Z COBOL-85: Letters a–z Special characters

if it is numeric—that is, contains only digits. It is *not* necessary to define a field as numeric in order to perform a numeric class check on it.

A two-letter state code (such as CA for California, NY for New York, and so forth) is an example of a data element that may be checked to ensure that it is alphabetic. In practice, fields are checked to ensure an alphabetic class much less frequently than they are to validate a numeric class. This is because purely alphabetic-character fields seldom occur. An individual's name, for example, may validly contain an apostrophe or a hyphen. The apostrophe and the hyphen are not alphabetic characters, but instead, special characters of the alphanumeric class.

The term **alphanumeric** encompasses both the numeric and alphabetic classes of data and all special characters. By definition, therefore, all fields can be considered alphanumeric. Hence, there is no need (and no COBOL reserved word available) to test for an alphanumeric class. Figure G-2 provides examples of class-test determinations.

Sign Test   A **sign test** is performed only on fields defined in the DATA DIVISION as numeric (PIC 9). Numeric data can be considered in two categories. Data quantities that actually represent numeric values (such as a quantity-on-hand, or a sale-price) are called **algebraic** because technically they can have a plus or minus sign and can be operated on arithmetically. (Whether or not a given quantity is actually involved in arithmetic in a specific program is beside the point.) On the other hand, numeric codes such as Social Security numbers, telephone numbers, and zip codes are examples of **absolute** values. For them, a sign has absolutely no meaning. Within your program, you may code these as PIC 9 fields or as PIC X fields. However, in some instances, you may find that coding them PIC 9 may simplify the validation.

There are three normal arithmetic sign configurations: positive, negative, and unsigned. (Sometimes a positive sign is used in lieu of an unsigned representation, and vice versa.) The location and coding method used to represent the sign varies depending upon the data-processing equipment, data coding method, and storage medium.

For an absolute value, the sign position should usually be unsigned. However, sometimes absolute numbers are stored with a positive sign if either (1) the data representation method does not have an unsigned format, or (2) it is more convenient to store the number with the positive sign.

Figure G-2
Class-test determinations.

Data element	Data	Class
Name	SMITH	Alphabetic
	JONES	Alphabetic
	O'BRIEN	Alphanumeric
	ANN-MARGRET	Alphanumeric
Maiden name	BROWNbbbbbb	Alphabetic
	bbbbbbbbbb	Alphabetic
U.S. zip code	95130	Numeric
Canadian zip code	K1A 0S9	Alphanumeric
Bank balance	00051327	Numeric
	bbb51327	Alphanumeric
	000513.27	Alphanumeric
	bbb$513.27	Alphanumeric

Note: b = blank space.

An algebraic number that is positive should usually be explicitly signed positive. Positive data received at the time of its initial input is sometimes temporarily unsigned, though. A negative number must contain a negative sign.

Field Checking

In addition to the basic character testing of input data fields, most data elements should be subjected to further, more rigorous checks. These are called **field checks**.

Presence Check

A **presence check** is used to detect missing values in fields. Most input records contain both required and optional fields. For instance, a **key field** uniquely identifies a record. In an employee file, the key field would probably be the employee's Social Security number; in a product file, it would be the product code. Obviously, an employee should not be entered into the employee file—nor a product into the product file—without a value for the key field. In general, a key field is a prime example of a required field—one that, if lacking, causes the input record to be immediately identified as erroneous.

Some fields are present only when their data element is applicable to the data entity. For instance, presence of data in the maiden-name field of an input record is optional because it would not apply to men or unmarried women.

A test for presence should normally be applied to all required fields. Its power is limited, however, since a presence check establishes only that there is data in the field; it does not address the quality or accuracy of the data. Whenever possible, therefore, additional field checks should be applied to each field to help ensure that the data is correct.

Absence Check

The converse of a presence check is an absence check, which is used to ensure that a field or record area is blank. The absence check is typically limited to those situations in which an unused or unassigned area of an input record exists. For example, assume that positions 52 through 57 of a record are not to be used, but something is keyed in position 57. It is likely that the unexplained character belongs in the adjacent field, starting in position 58. An absence check can signal such possible field-alignment errors. Figure G-3 provides examples of presence and absence checks.

Figure G-3 Presence/absence check examples.

Employee-salary record					
SMITH	JOHN			2	000000b
Last name	First name	Middle name	Unassigned area		Monthly salary

Data element	Validation	Result of test on above data
Last name	Must be present	Passes presence test
First name	Must be present	Passes presence test
Middle name	Optional	Untested
Unassigned area	Must be blank	Fails absence test
Monthly salary	Must be present	Passes presence test
	Must be numeric	Fails numeric class test (because of blank space)

Range Check A range check is applied to code numbers to verify that they exist in the coding system being used. For example, the area identification codes assigned to Social Security numbers (the first three digits) range from 001 to 626 and from 700 to 799. A range check applied to these digits can identify certain transposed or otherwise erroneously coded entries. Range-check examples are shown in Figure G-4.

Although these examples suggest that the fields are defined as numeric, such tests can be performed with either numeric or alphanumeric defined data. For instance, assuming that the fields have already been verified to contain only digits, the following will do exactly the same thing:

```
05  TELE-PREFIX        PIC 9(3).    05  TELE-PREFIX        PIC X(3).
    .                                   .
    .                                   .
    .                                   .
IF  TELE-PREFIX LESS THAN 221        IF  TELE-PREFIX LESS THAN "221"
OR  GREATER THAN 299...              OR  GREATER THAN "299"...
```

Limit Check A **limit check** tests a field against maximum and/or minimum values. The limits can be either absolute amounts or percentages. An example of an absolute limit is when all expenditure transactions processed through a petty cash account must be less than $35.00. Similarly, product price changes may be validated against a percentage limit to ensure that a new price is not more than, say, 15 percent above or below the corresponding old price.

Reasonableness Check A **reasonableness check** identifies abnormal data values. In a department store, for instance, a unit sales price of $800 in the notions department or a sales tag indicating a purchase quantity of 10 diamond rings could be identified as an exception condition. As another example, any discounts that are greater than, say, 20 percent of the corresponding list prices can be flagged for investigation. The reasonableness check is similar to the limit check because it requires the establishment of parameters against which data is tested. It differs, however, because the parameters are norms rather than rigid limits.

You must recognize that experimentation may be required to set norms that will best detect invalid transactions while, at the same time, permit valid transactions to be processed routinely. Also, the parameters may need updating from time to time as conditions change. Figure G-5 gives examples of parameters for reasonableness checks.

Figure G-4
Range-check examples.

Data element	Code numbers
Month number	01 through 12
Social Security number (first three digits)	001 through 626, 700 through 799
U.S. telephone prefixes	221 through 998

Figure G-5
Reasonableness-check parameter examples.

Data element	Reasonable value	
	Minimum	Maximum
Number of dependents	0	12
Adult height	58 inches	82 inches
Adult weight	90 pounds	299 pounds
Individual Social Security tax (1989)	$ .00	$3,604.80

It is important to keep in mind that certain values identified as exceptions will, in fact, be valid. Therefore, include provisions in the system to override reasonableness checks to force acceptance of the data into the system. For instance, a data-entry program might display an error message for an input value that does not meet the reasonableness check. However, the program could be designated to allow the operator to override and enter the data anyway.

Consistency Check

A **consistency check** (sometimes called a **relationship check** or a **combination check**) is the consideration of two or more data elements in relation to one another. It can be a powerful means of detecting erroneous data. Suppose that patient diagnosis data is input to a medical-records application and is then checked. If the diagnosis code indicates pregnancy and the sex code specifies male, a prime example of inconsistent data exists. Note that the consistency check does not indicate which of the involved fields is incorrect. It does, though, identify a discrepancy that requires resolution.

Consistency checks are used not only in uncovering errors in data recording, but also in the monitoring of processing operations. Consider a charge account system that uses credit limits of dollar amounts, beyond which the customer is not privileged to incur further debts. Suppose a customer's credit limit is correctly reflected at $500. The customer purchases $750 worth of merchandise, which is charged to the account. In such a situation, there are actually no data errors, but rather an operational problem that was detected by checking the relationship of one field to another.

Justification Check

A **justification check** is used to assure proper alignment of data within a field. Alphabetic and alphanumeric fields are usually left-justified (the first character is in the leftmost position of the field), numeric-integer fields are normally right-justified, and numeric fields with decimal places are typically decimal-point aligned. An alphanumeric field that is present but has a blank space in the leftmost character position fails a normal justification check.

Justification checks are rarely performed on numeric fields. Instead, a numeric field with blank positions would be flagged as erroneous by a numeric class test. The numeric class test is more powerful because it (1) detects both blank *and* non-numeric characters, and (2) checks all positions of the field.

Embedded-Blank Check

An **embedded-blank check** is used to check certain key alphanumeric fields to ensure that blank positions have not been entered inadvertently. An embedded blank is one that has data characters represented within the field—both to the left and to the right of the blank position.

For example, a part number field is an alphanumeric field that often serves as a key field for inventory records. It would not be prudent to allow embedded blanks in part numbers because the blank spaces would cause confusion when entering and retrieving records. So, if embedded-blank spaces are prohibited, detection of an embedded blank will identify an erroneous entry. Figure G-6 shows examples of justification and embedded-blank error conditions.

As with justification checks, embedded-blank tests are not typically made on numeric fields. Since blanks are not numeric digits, a numeric class test will detect embedded blanks. Also, the class test is much easier to code.

Date Check

A **date check** is used to ensure the validity of calendar dates recorded in input transactions. There are two basic formats used to express dates in data-processing systems: Gregorian and Julianized.

A Gregorian date is the one we use daily. The date July 4, 1776, is an example of a Gregorian date representation—it is a date based upon the Gregorian calendar. With a Julianized date, the day is not identified as within a certain month, but rather is assigned a sequential day number within the year in *yyddd* format (where

Figure G-6
Justification and embedded-blank check examples.

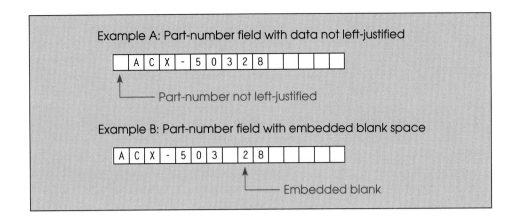

Example A: Part-number field with data not left-justified

A C X - 5 0 3 2 8

Part-number not left-justified

Example B: Part-number field with embedded blank space

A C X - 5 0 3 2 8

Embedded blank

yy signifies the year of the century and *ddd* represents the day number of the year from 001 to 365, or 366 for leap year). Represented in Julianized format, Independence Day appears as 76187.

Gregorian dates are used most frequently for input and output because they are common to our everyday lives and therefore much easier for us to use and understand. Julianized dates are often used internally with data-processing systems. The advantage of a Julianized date is that date-span computations can be made arithmetically without need for adjustments when the dates are not within the same month.

Commonly used Gregorian and Julianized date representations are shown in Figure G-7. Notice that Gregorian dates can be represented in a number of formats. The familiar *mmddyy* format is the one most often used. The leftmost two digits represent a month number from 01 to 12, the middle two digits indicate a day number from 01 to 31, and the rightmost two digits identify the year of the century from 00 to 99. You should be aware, however, that the U.S. military and the people of Europe usually represent six-digit dates in *ddmmyy* format. Also, Gregorian dates are sometimes stored internally in *yymmdd* format, which simplifies comparing two dates to determine which is the earlier of the two. For instance, consider the two dates 12/13/90 and 10/21/91. If these are stored internally as 901213 and 911021, then a single comparison tells you that 911021 (10/21/91) is the larger (later) of the two. (Note that this format parallels our positional numbering system in which the most-significant digit is on the left; the least-significant digit is on the right.)

For Gregorian dates, month numbers are checked to ensure that they are within the range from 01 through 12. Day numbers are, as a minimum, validated against a range of 01 to 31. If increased data integrity is required, a consistency check of day in relation to month can be made (for example, the day range of April, June, September, and November is limited to a span from 01 to 30).

Figure G-7
Date representations.

Date	Type	Data-class
FEBRUARY 15, 1991	Gregorian	Alphanumeric
FEB. 15, 1991	Gregorian	Alphanumeric
021591	Gregorian *mmddyy* format	Numeric
150291	Gregorian *ddmmyy* format	Numeric
910215	Gregorian *yymmdd* format	Numeric
91046	Julianized *yyddd* format	Numeric

Note: d = day digit, *m* = month digit, *y* = year digit.

February presents a special day-range problem. A precise date check for February involves dividing the year by four. If the remainder is zero, the year is a leap year and the acceptable range is then, of course, from 01 to 29—rather than from 01 to 28. There is one exception to this rule, however. If the year ends in 00 (1900, for example), the year is not a leap year unless the four-digit year number is evenly divisible by 400. Thus, 1600 was a leap year, and 2000 will be a leap year, but 1700, 1800, and 1900 were not. Figure G-8 provides examples of date checks.

In addition to checking for valid month/day combinations, it is generally advisable to validate dates for recency. Input transactions to be processed usually have a fairly current date. The further in the past or future the date, the greater the likelihood that a date error has been made. Thus, it is wise to establish a reasonableness check as to how much variance will be permitted before the distant date is identified as an exception condition.

Although any time-limit selection is somewhat arbitrary, it should be based on the data-processing application and processing schedule. Usually, the length of time considered reasonable for past dates is greater than that tolerated for future dates. For example, a sales transaction dated two months in the past may well be reasonable, whereas one dated a week into the future will probably be suspect. Remember that, with all reasonableness checks, a reentry override must be provided to allow exception conditions to be accepted by the system.

Self-Checking Numbers

Self-checking numbers are frequently used in banking, accounts receivable, and other application areas so that account code numbers can be validated. A self-checking number is a code number with a calculated digit—called a **check digit**—appended to it so that clerical, data-entry, and data-transmission errors can be detected by recalculation. For example, suppose that five-digit code numbers are used to identify customer accounts within a charge account system. Whenever any charges, payments, returns, or adjustments are made to an account, it is, of course, necessary to identify the account code number to which each should be posted. Unless some control is exercised over the accuracy of the account codes that are entered into the system, it is probable that undetected errors will happen when recording the code numbers. The following errors frequently occur:

1. **Substitution error.** The wrong digit is entered, as if 7 were keyed as 9.

2. **Simple transposition error.** The correct digits are written, but their positional placement is reversed, as if code number 56789 were entered as 57689.

3. **Double transposition error.** The digits are transposed across a column, as if 56789 were recorded 58769.

Figure G-8
Date-check validity determination examples.

Date (*mm-dd-yy*) format	Validity determination
10-31-91	Valid
10-00-91	Invalid
00-31-91	Invalid
03-16-00	Valid
02-29-91	Invalid
02-29-84	Valid
02-30-84	Invalid

4. **Other transposition error**. The digits are transposed across two or more columns, as if 56789 were input as 59786.

5. **Omission error with right justification**. One or more of the digits is omitted and the resulting short number is justified to the right of the field, as if 56789 were entered as b5689 (b = blank space or other null value in the code position).

6. **Omission error with left justification**. One or more of the digits is omitted and the resulting short number is justified to the left of the field, as if 56789 were entered as 5689b.

7. **Right shift error**. All digits are correctly recorded on the input medium, but the code value is shifted one or more positions to the right of the field boundary, as if 56789 were positioned within the field as b5678.

8. **Left shift error**. All digits are correctly recorded on the input medium, but the code value is shifted one or more positions to the left of the field boundary, as if 56789 were positioned within the field as 6789b.

9. **Insertion error**. One or more extraneous digits are inserted into the code, as if 56789 were keyed as 567289.

Recording errors may cause transaction records to be posted to the wrong account. Severe customer service problems occur when debits and credits are not correctly applied. To counter this situation, you can specify that a check digit be incorporated into the basic code, typically as the terminal digit. A check digit could be formed by simply summing the individual digits of each account number. For account number 40212, for example, the check digit would be 9 (4 + 0 + 2 + 1 + 2 = 9). With this check digit suffixed to the original five-digit code, the full self-checking account number is 402129. Should a clerk make a substitution error when he or she is transcribing or keying any of the digits (for example, 401129), the sum of the digits will not be equal to the check digit 9 (4 + 0 + 1 + 1 + 2 = 8). A check-digit validation routine can thus be employed to detect errors at data-entry time.

Although the sum-of-the-digits method is simple, it has limited value in practice. For instance, it will not detect transposition errors. Other methods are commonly employed that perform more complex calculations to determine a check-digit—one that will provide a much more reliable check.

Name-Correspondence Check

A **name-correspondence check** is sometimes used instead of a self-checking number. For example, Social Security numbers are not self-checking. When posting annual earnings, the Social Security Administration experiences an error rate of up to 10 percent when they use the number alone. To assure that earnings are posted to the correct accounts, each number is verified by checking the first six positions of the last name in the transaction record for correspondence with the name in the master file record. The name-correspondence check does not require computations like self-checking numbers do.

A disadvantage, however, is that the name-correspondence check requires, in addition to the code field, a correspondence field in each transaction record. Further, the master file record must be available when the verification is performed. A self-checking number, on the other hand, can be validated independently. Examples of name-correspondence checks appear in Figure G-9.

Figure G-9 Name-correspondence check examples.

Master record		Transaction record		Correspondence determination
Account number	**Name**	**Account number**	**Name***	
40368	THOMAS	40368	THOMAS	Corresponds
40369	WALLACE	40369	WALLAC*	Corresponds
40370	CARPENTER	40370	ABRAMS	Does not correspond
40380	ADAMS	40380	ADAMS	Corresponds

*First six characters

Code-Existence Check

A **code-existence check** is used to assure that a particular code is valid. Many numeric codes can be validated through the use of range checks or check digits, as mentioned earlier. However, certain codes—particularly those that are alphanumeric or have a relatively low number of entries—require positive matches against a table of valid codes maintained within a program or data file.

Each input code value is then matched by the program against this table. (This function is called a *table-lookup* and is covered in Concepts Module I and Chapters 11 and 12.) If a match is made, the input code is assumed to be valid; if not, the code is identified as in error. Figure G-10 provides an example of a short table that might be used in a code-existence check table.

Record Checking

Not only must the character position and data values of fields be validated, but it is also often necessary to check the sequence, completeness, and status of record group relationships.

Record Sequence Checks

Sequential files are typically arranged in ascending sequence according to the value of the key field (or fields) for the file. **Record sequence checks** should be applied to such files to ensure that the records are truly in the proper sequence.

A key-sequenced sequential file specified for ascending order is out of sequence when a **stepdown-key condition** exists. The key-field value for each record processed should typically be greater than the value of the previous record. A stepdown condition occurs when the key of the current record is less than the key of the previous record. If—as is often the case—duplicate key values are not permitted in the file, an out-of-sequence condition also exists when an **equal-key condition** occurs. Figure G-11 provides examples of record checking.

Figure G-10
Code-existence check
examples.

Fluid container units-of-measure	
Code	**Meaning**
HP	Half-pint
PT	Pint
QT	Quart
HG	Half-gallon
GL	Gallon
HL	Half-liter
LT	Liter
2L	Two-liters
4L	Four-liters

Record-Set Relationship Checks

Sometimes a file contains multiple records for each data-entity. In such cases, a particular record-set arrangement must typically be maintained to ensure that proper processing can be sustained.

For example, in a student-registration system, each student may be required to have one student name-and-address record and from one to seven class records (one for each course in which the student is enrolled). As shown in Figure G-12, errors that can be detected by record-set relationship checks for this example are (1) student name-and-address record present but class record(s) absent, (2) one or more class records present but name-and-address record absent, and (3) too many (over seven) class records present for one name-and-address record. Although the representation of Figure G-12 suggests that these records reside in a single file, they more commonly reside in two different files.

Data Validation Programs

The programmer/analyst must study actual conditions carefully before establishing a data validation plan. The class of each field within the record to be validated must be identified. Numeric class tests should be applied to each numeric field; alphabetic class tests should be performed on any purely alphabetic fields. Additional field checks should be chosen, as appropriate, for each field. When applicable, the order and set requirements of each record within the file should also be validated.

The checks instituted should be rigorous enough to reject a high proportion of the invalid data, but flexible enough to accept all legitimate values.

On-line vs. Batch Data Validation

With today's modern computers, most data entry is done through data-entry stations consisting of video-display terminals (VDTs) equipped with keyboards. There are two ways in which the data being entered can be validated: on-line and batch. When data is entered directly into a system through a terminal, it is commonly checked for validity as it is entered—this is **on-line validation**. For instance, if you stop at your local bank to make a deposit or withdrawal, the teller makes the entry on-line through a terminal connected to the computer. If the teller enters a wrong code, the computer issues a warning immediately, thereby allowing the teller to make the correct entry. In this type of situation, the person entering the data is

Figure G-11
Record sequence-check examples.

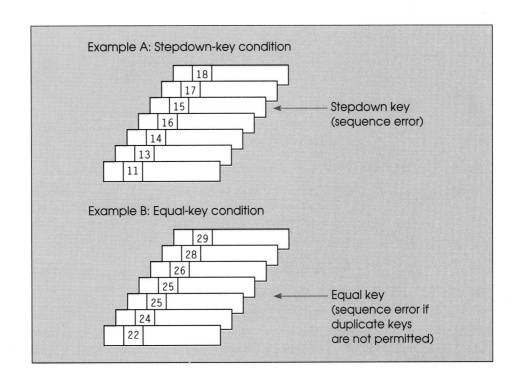

Figure G-12   Record-set relationship check examples.

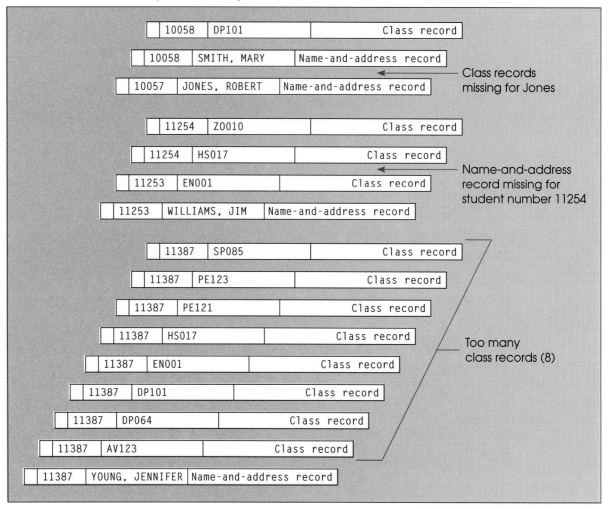

sufficiently knowledgeable of the application to make the proper correction. In on-line applications in which data goes directly into the system, it is imperative that validation be completed on-the-spot and before that transaction is stored.

Other applications are not amenable to validation during data entry. For instance, a company might send its weekly payroll source data (perhaps hand-written) to a service bureau for keying. The service bureau returns one or more tapes or disks containing the keyed data. Usually some validation has been per-formed during entry—for instance, the data-entry program might be designed to allow only digits to be entered into numeric fields. However, there are many other types of errors for which a data-entry person (who is completely unfamiliar with the application) simply does not have the knowledge to handle. For instance, data incorrectly recorded on the source document—yet accurately keyed—might fail checks for such items as range, reasonableness, or code-existence. As a result, in this type of data entry, all data is accepted with the intent of validating it later. A special **data validation program** has the sole purpose of checking to ensure that only valid data is entered into the system. Once detected, erroneous data can be corrected by individuals familiar with the application. This is called **batch validation.**

Data validation programs (both on-line and batch) are often alternatively called **edit programs**. (Recognize that this use of the word *edit* is different from its use in regard to the editing picture symbols.) Some programmers use the term **front-end edit** because data validation programs are typically run as the first processing step after data has been entered into a system—at the beginning of a batch system job stream or as data-entry functions of an on-line system.

***A Typical Batch Data
Validation Application***

Figure G-13 provides an example of a batch payroll system flowchart showing typical front-end placement of a data validation program. Notice that the data validation program has access to the employee **master file**. Access to such a master file is common because the input transaction must be matched to some record in the master file. For instance, a payroll record must not be entered into the system for an employee number not in the employee file.

As the system flowchart of Figure G-13 indicates, most batch data validation programs read an input transaction file and write an audit list and an error list. Sometimes a combined audit/error list is produced.

An **audit list** is a report that shows the contents of each record that has been input to the system; it is usually retained merely for control purposes. The audit

Figure G-13   Example of front-end placement of a data validation program.

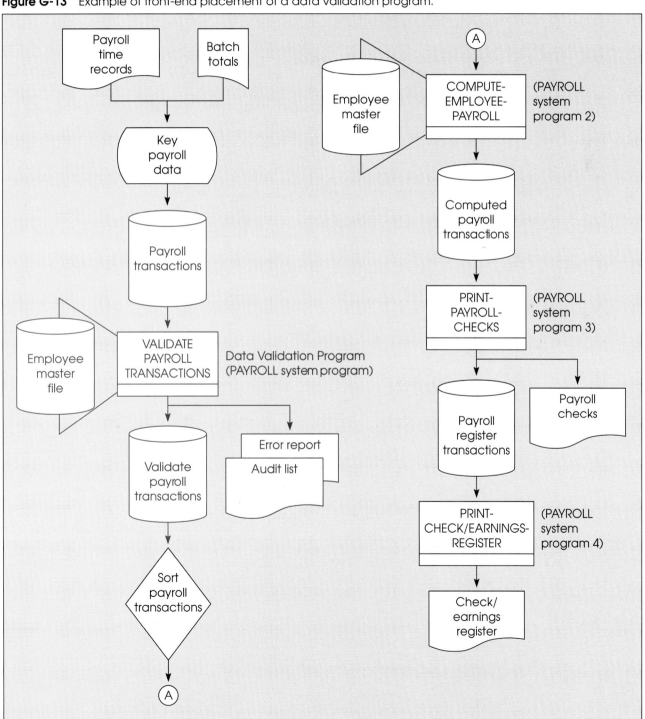

list provides an accounting trail if it is necessary to determine where, or in what form, data originated. An **error list**, on the other hand, is an action document that reports what error or exception conditions have entered the system. Error lists require action to correct or confirm the identified conditions, whereas audit lists need only be retained for reference over a specified period of time. The combined **audit/error list** serves both functions. Voluminous audit lists are often stored on microfiche or some other nonprint storage medium to conserve printing time and expense.

An error list is usually designed with the fields of the input records displayed on the left-hand side of the report; this can be referred to as the **record-image** area. To the right of the record-image area, **error messages** that apply to that record are printed. When report space is limited, **error codes**, rather than descriptive messages, are sometimes used. (You are familiar with both error codes and messages from compiling your programs.) Identification of error conditions by meaningful error messages is obviously preferable to the use of more cryptic error codes. Whenever codes are used, they introduce the need for a legend to explain the meaning of each code symbol.

In addition to messages or codes, the data in error is often highlighted in the record-image area by printing asterisks alongside or below the field in error. Examples of commonly used audit/error list formats are shown in Figure G-14.

Figure G-14
Common audit/error list report formats.

Example A: Audit/error list with error messages and highlighted error fields

```
                          AUDIT/ERROR LIST

        **------------RECORD IMAGE------------**
        STATE  S.S. NUMBER    NAME                 ERROR MESSAGE
        -----  -----------    ------------------   --------------------
         AX    997438475    SMITH, JOHN          INVALID STATE CODE
         **

         AK    998765678    JOHNSON, ROBERT

         AZ    938374 49    JONES, BILL          INVALID SOC. SEC. NBR.
               ********

         CA    998474647                         NAME NOT PRESENT
                            *******************

         CA    9045567828   WALLACE, RUTH
```

Example B: Audit/error list with error codes

```
                          AUDIT/ERROR LIST

        **------------RECORD IMAGE------------**
        STATE  S.S. NUMBER    NAME                 ERROR MESSAGE
        -----  -----------    ------------------   --------------------
         AX    997438475    SMITH, JOHN          S

         AK    998765678    JOHNSON, ROBERT

         AZ    938374 49    JONES, BILL          X

         CA    998474674                         N

         CA    904567828    WALLACE, RUTH
```

Handling Errors   As depicted in Figure G-15, there are two general ways to handle the erroneous transaction records detected by a data validation program. We can call these methods error rejection and error abeyance.

The **error-rejection** approach commonly is used in smaller, simpler, less critical applications. With this method, the "good" transaction records are written to a validated transaction file, whereas the erroneous transactions are identified on the

Figure G-15
Error-handling methods for
data validation programs.

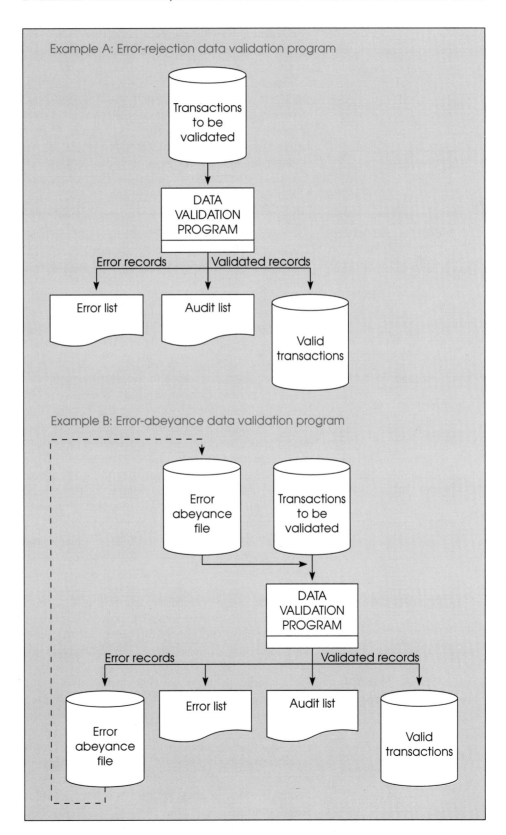

error list and rejected (that is, dropped from further processing). The erroneous records must, of course, be corrected and then reentered into the system in a later processing run.

With the **error-abeyance** method, erroneous transactions are written to an **abeyance**, or **suspense**, file that keeps track of all outstanding error records. Then, when an error is corrected, the original error record is removed from the abeyance file. The obvious advantage of the error-abeyance approach is that the error records are retained on a file to ensure that each discrepancy is resolved and that the correction is actually reentered into the system. However, error-abeyance processing requires more programming effort and processing steps than error-rejection handling.

In the next chapter, you will study a sample sales-transaction validation program. You may think of it as a model data validation program for batch processing. That is, the general program logic used in this example can be applied to practically any data validation program—regardless of the specific application or type of record being validated. To minimize program complexity, the program is designed as an error-rejection (rather than error-abeyance) program. Then in Chapter 9, the same validation techniques are applied to a data-entry program.

Module Summary

Data-processing systems should have safeguards and controls to aid in ensuring the integrity of data within the system. There are three general categories of programmed validation of input data: character testing, field checking, and record checking.

Character Testing

Class tests determine whether positions within a field contain **numeric** or **alphabetic** data. A **sign test** checks whether the value of a numeric field is **positive**, **negative**, or **unsigned**.

Field Checking

Presence checks are used to detect missing fields. **Absence checks** identify extraneous data and misaligned fields. **Range checks** are applied to code numbers to verify that a number is valid. The **limit check** tests a field against maximum and/or minimum values. **Reasonableness checks** identify abnormal (though not necessarily incorrect) values. A **consistency check** is the consideration of two or more data elements in relation to one another. Proper alignment of data within alphanumeric fields is tested by **justification** and **embedded-blank checks**. A **date check** tests the validity of calendar dates. **Self-checking numbers** contain check digits that permit validation of code numbers. A **name-correspondence check** matches a name field in the transaction record with the corresponding field in the master record; if they do not match, the code number upon which the two records were paired may be in error. To assure that a particular code is valid, **code-existence checks** are used.

Record Checking

Record sequence checks are applied to key-sequenced sequential files. When a situation exists in which multiple records are required to form a set of records, the completeness, sequence, and status of the record-set relationships should be validated.

Data Validation Programs

Data validation programs check fields of an input record to help ensure that only valid data enters the system. Such programs often are alternatively called **edit**, or **front-end edit**, **programs**. Most batch data validation programs read an input transaction file and write an **audit list** and an **error list**; combined **audit/error lists** are sometimes produced. Error records are handled by either the **error-rejection** or the **error-abeyance** approach. With the former, errors are rejected from the validated file; with the latter, they are maintained in an error-abeyance file until corrected. Data validation programs often access an existing **master file** for certain validations.

Exercises
Terms for Definition

abeyance file _____

absence check _____

absolute value _____

algebraic value _____

audit/error list _____

audit list _____

character test _____

class test _____

code-existence check _____

combination check _____

consistency check _____

data validation program _____

date check _____

edit program _____

embedded-blank check _____

equal-key condition _____

error-abeyance
   data validation program _____

error codes _____

error messages _____

error-rejection
   data validation program _____

field check _____

front-end edit program _____

Gregorian date _____

Julianized date _____

justification check _____

limit check _____

master file _____

name-correspondence check _____

negative sign representation _____

positive sign representation _____

presence check _____

range check _____   _____

reasonableness check _____

record image _____

record sequence check _____

record-set relationship check _____

relationship check _____

self-checking number _____

sign test _____

stepdown-key condition _____

suspense file _____

unsigned representation _____

Matching Exercise   1. Match the data validation field check with its description by writing the letter of the validation check in the space provided.

a. presence check	g. justification check
b. absence check	h. embedded-blank check
c. range check	i. date check
d. limit check	j. self-checking number
e. reasonableness check	k. name-correspondence check
f. consistency check	l. code-existence check

_____ A check used to help ensure the validity of calendar dates.

_____ A check used to test numeric fields against maximum or minimum values.

_____ A test commonly applied to code-number fields to ensure that the code falls within a permissible span of values.

_____ A check that employs a check digit.

_____ A check used to identify abnormal data values.

_____ A check that considers two or more data elements in relation to one another.

_____ A check (typically employed in lieu of a self-checking number) used— when matching a transaction record to a master record—to ensure that the contents of a key field are correctly recorded.

_____ A check used to test that a required field actually contains data.

_____ A check used to assure proper alignment of data within a field.

_____ A check, typically employing a table-lookup routine, used to assure that a particular code value is valid.

_____ A check applied to unused portions of a record to ensure that data is properly aligned within the field areas.

_____ A check used to test certain key alphanumeric and code fields to ensure that blank positions have not been entered inadvertently.

Review Questions

1. The most commonly required class test is the test for _____ class.

2. A sign test is sometimes performed on fields of _____ class.

3. A numeric field can be considered to contain either a(n)

   _____ or a(n) _____ value.

4. To ensure that the records of a file are properly arranged in ascending or

   descending order, a(n) _____ check is performed.

5. When a file may contain multiple records for each data entity,

   _____ checks should be made.

6. When records with duplicate key values are not allowed within a file, an out-

   of-sequence condition exists when either a(n) _____ or a(n)

   _____ condition is detected. If duplicate key values are
   permitted, an out-of-sequence condition exists when a(n)

   _____ condition is detected.

7. Why are data validation programs sometimes called front-end edits?

   _____

   _____

8. Why is the error-abeyance method of handling erroneous records superior to
   the error-rejection approach?

   _____

   _____

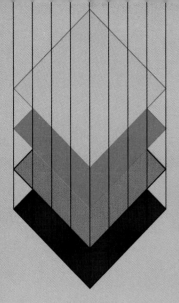

Data Validation Design and Coding

Chapter Objectives

The IF statement you learned earlier provided you with tools to do the data validation operations that you studied in Concepts Module G. Now is the time to put some of these principles to work. From this chapter, you will learn the following:

■ The two forms of the INSPECT statement which allow you to process a field character by character: INSPECT/REPLACING and INSPECT/TALLYING.

Techniques to use in validating data that check:
A given value or a group of values
The presence of an entry in a field
The data class
A range of values
Field justification
Consistency between fields

■ Using alphanumeric definition of numeric fields to avoid error conditions that could terminate execution of the program.

CHAPTER 8

Chapter Outline

Topic: The Elements of an Editing Task

The INSPECT/REPLACING Statement
REPLACING ALL Option
REPLACING LEADING Option
REPLACING FIRST Option

The INSPECT/TALLYING Statement
TALLYING ALL Option
TALLYING LEADING Option

Definition of the Editing Task
The Overall Job
The Validation Portion of the Job
    Input: Alphanumeric Definition of All Input Fields
    Actions to be Taken
    Field Validation Specifications

Validating Numeric Fields
Blanks in Numeric Fields
Zero-Filling of Numeric Fields
Numeric Class Tests

Validation Modules
Record-Code Validation
Date-of-Sale Validation
Department-Number and Item-Number Validation
Item-Description Validation
Employee-Number Validation
Quantity Validation

Price Validation
Type-of-Sale Validation

Alternative Coding Techniques
88-Level Condition-Names for Applicable Validations
Error Messages in WORKING-STORAGE

Topic: The Complete Data Validation Program

Programming Specifications for the Sales-Transaction Validation Program

Design Documentation for the Sales-Transaction Validation Program
000-Val-Sales-Transaction Module
100-Initialize-Variable-Fields Module
200-Val-Sales-Transaction Module
210-Format-Record-Image Module
220-Val-Sales-Trans-Fields Module
310-Val-Record-Code through 390-Val-Type-of-Sale Modules
410-Identify-Error-Type Module
420-Print-Audit-Error-Line Module
700-Print-Report-Totals Module
800-Read-Sales-Trans-Record Module
830-Write-Valid-Sales-Trans Module
870-Print-Report-Headings Module
880-Write-Report-Top-Line Module
890-Write-Report-Line Module

The Complete DATAVAL Program

ENVIRONMENT/DATA DIVISION Coding
Three Files—Effect on the ENVIRONMENT DIVISION
Condition-Name for End-of-File Condition
Error-Switch Control Field
Page Line Span
Redefinition of Input Quantity and Price Fields
Redefinition of Quantity and Price Fields on the Audit/Error Line

PROCEDURE DIVISION Coding
Valid/Invalid Record Control
Testing for End-of-Page
Alternative MOVE Statements to Edited Numeric or Unedited Alphanumeric Fields
Numeric Class Test Before Performing 380-VAL-PRICE Module
Formatting the Error Line
Printing the Error Line
Writing Records to Disk (or Tape)

| **Topic:** | **The Elements of an Editing Task** |

Before proceeding with the task at hand—learning the techniques of data validation—you need to know about the INSPECT statement. With the INSPECT, you can examine a field on a character-by-character basis, an essential task for ensuring the validity of data. There are two primary forms of the INSPECT statement: INSPECT/ REPLACING and INSPECT/TALLYING. (Only commonly used forms of the INSPECT statement are discussed in this chapter. Additional seldom used forms are mentioned in Appendix B.)

The INSPECT/ REPLACING Statement

You use the INSPECT statement with the REPLACING phrase for character translation tasks. It allows you to convert individual characters within a field from one value to another. As shown in the INSPECT/REPLACING format of Figure 8-1, there are three commonly used options: REPLACING ALL, REPLACING LEADING, and REPLACING FIRST.

To simplify the ensuing discussion, the identifiers and literals within the format have been assigned names that describe their function. The field being inspected (identifier-1) is called the **inspected field**. The value that is being sought (identifier-5 or literal-3) is referred to as the **search-field value**. The value to be replaced (identifier-6 or literal-4) is termed the **replacement-field value**.

REPLACING ALL Option

The INSPECT statement with the REPLACING ALL option causes all occurrences of a specified character to be replaced by another character. Suppose that you have a date field with the month, day, and year separated by slashes—but the programming specifications call for hyphen separators. The INSPECT/REPLACING ALL statement shown in Example A of Figure 8-1 will handle this conversion. Each character of the SALE-DATE field is examined from left to right. When a character that is equal to the search-field value (a slash in this case) is found, that character is changed to the replacement-field value (a hyphen in this case).

The inspected field can be either an elementary or a group data-item. Both the search-field value and the replacement-field value can be expressed as either a literal, a figurative constant, or as the data-name of an elementary field. Also, as will be covered later in this chapter, it is important to recognize that the data class of the search-field and replacement-field values must be consistent with that of the inspected field.

Example B of Figure 8-1 shows a situation in which the INSPECT/ REPLACING statement is used to change blank spaces to hyphens within a Social Security number. Here, the search-field value is expressed as a figurative constant and the replacement field value is a data-name.

REPLACING LEADING Option

With the REPLACING LEADING option, only leftmost occurrences of the search-field value are converted to the replacement-field value. This option is commonly used in data validation programs to force unused positions of a numeric field to zeros. When numeric fields are initially entered into a system, the unused leading positions will sometimes contain blank spaces. To use the field for arithmetic operations or numeric editing, however, there should be no blank spaces within the field. As illustrated in Example C of Figure 8-1, the REPLACING LEADING option can be used for this application. (This form of the REPLACING is used in several places of the data validation program that follows.)

Figure 8-1   The INSPECT/REPLACING statement.

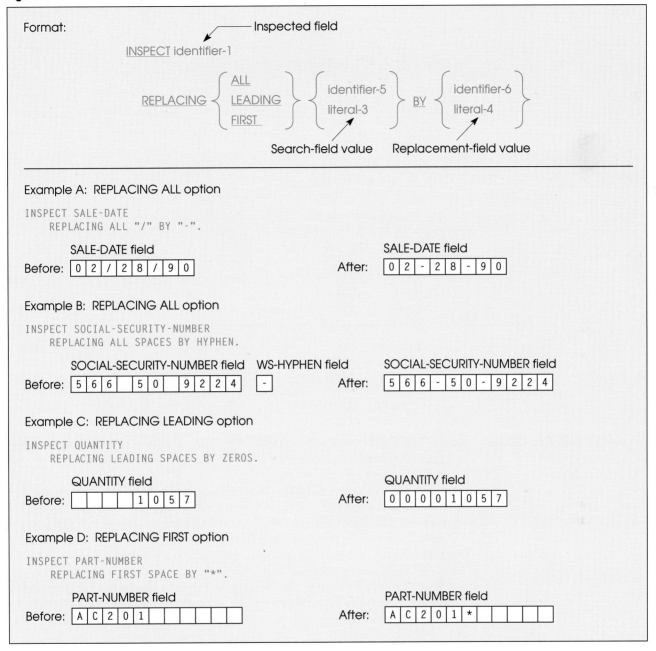

REPLACING FIRST Option

With the REPLACING FIRST option of the INSPECT statement, only the first occurrence of the search field value is replaced by the replacement-field value. Example D of Figure 8-1 provides an example. This FIRST option has considerably fewer uses than the ALL and LEADING options.

The INSPECT/ TALLYING Statement

The INSPECT statement with the TALLYING phrase is used to count the occurrences of certain characters within a field. Its format is shown in Figure 8-2. There are two commonly used INSPECT/TALLYING options: TALLYING/ALL and TALLYING/LEADING.

Figure 8-2
The INSPECT/TALLYING
statement.

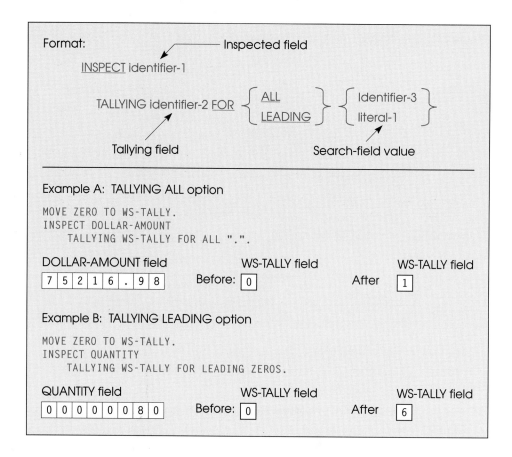

Format:

INSPECT identifier-1 ⟵ Inspected field

TALLYING identifier-2 FOR { ALL / LEADING } { Identifier-3 / literal-1 }

Tallying field ⟶   Search-field value

Example A: TALLYING ALL option

```
MOVE ZERO TO WS-TALLY.
INSPECT DOLLAR-AMOUNT
    TALLYING WS-TALLY FOR ALL ".".
```

DOLLAR-AMOUNT field
| 7 | 5 | 2 | 1 | 6 | . | 9 | 8 |

Before: WS-TALLY field [0]   After: WS-TALLY field [1]

Example B: TALLYING LEADING option

```
MOVE ZERO TO WS-TALLY.
INSPECT QUANTITY
    TALLYING WS-TALLY FOR LEADING ZEROS.
```

QUANTITY field
| 0 | 0 | 0 | 0 | 0 | 0 | 8 | 0 |

Before: WS-TALLY field [0]   After: WS-TALLY field [6]

TALLYING ALL Option

An INSPECT statement with the TALLYING/ALL option counts all occurrences of a character within the inspected field. The count is kept in a field called the **tallying field**.

Suppose a numeric field is one in which entry of a decimal point is permitted. Such a field must be validated to ensure that not more than one decimal point has been keyed. The INSPECT/TALLYING ALL statement shown in Example A of Figure 8-2 will handle this task. Each character of the DOLLAR-AMOUNT field is examined from left to right. Whenever a decimal point is found, the tallying field—WS-TALLY—is incremented by one.

The tallying field must be an elementary numeric-integer field. It is important to recognize that it is your responsibility to properly initialize the tallying field. Such initialization will typically take the form of an immediately preceding statement that moves zeros to the tallying field, as shown in the examples.

TALLYING LEADING Option

With the TALLYING LEADING option of the INSPECT statement, only leftmost occurrences of the search-field value are counted. Example B of Figure 8-2 shows how leading zeros can be tallied within a field.

Definition of the Editing Task
The Overall Job

Now that you have an idea of what the INSPECT statement can do for you, let's consider a typical type of assignment that you might be given as a programmer on the job. Your employer, General Merchandise Supply Company, is setting up a new sales transaction system. At the end of each day, sales transaction data will be entered into a file unedited. Before loading it into the sales transaction file, it must be validated. Your programming supervisor has designed a data validation program (called DATAVAL) to do the following:

■ Read each record from a "raw" data file.

■ For each record, test and validate each field.

■ Write each record that is valid to a new file.

■ Prepare a report that lists each invalid record together with appropriate error messages.

Working as a member of a programming team, you have been assigned the task of writing the modules to perform the validation.

The Validation Portion of the Job

You now know where your portion of the task fits into the overall plan; in order to complete your assignment, you need to know:

■ the input to each module

■ the actions to be taken.

Input: Alphanumeric Definition of All Input Fields. The input to data validation modules consists of the input record itself. Hence, your supervisor provides you with a copy of the input record description shown in Figure 8-3.

In this description, two fields, Quantity and Price (ST-QUANTITY-X and ST-PRICE-X), are defined as alphanumeric and then redefined as numeric. You will see the reason for this as we progress into the validation routines themselves.

Observe that each field has been defined as alphanumeric with the PICTURE symbol X, even if it is actually a numeric field. For example, ST-DEPARTMENT-NUMBER is specified with a picture character-string of X(3), even though it is defined in the programming specifications as a numeric field. In a data validation program, it is a good practice to define numeric fields as alphanumeric rather than numeric.

The reason is that many computer systems cause program processing to be abnormally terminated—that is, the program "blows up"—when arithmetic operations or relation tests are performed on a field that is defined as numeric, but which contains nonnumeric data. This type of program interruption is called a **data exception** or a **decimal-digit error**. Data exceptions are the nemesis of the COBOL programmer; one of the prime functions of a data validation program is to edit numeric fields to ensure that they do not occur.

Figure 8-3
Record description for the DATAVAL program.

```
01  ST-SALES-TRANSACTION-RECORD.
    05  ST-RECORD-CODE              PIC X(2).
    05  ST-DATE-OF-SALE.
        10  ST-MONTH-OF-SALE        PIC X(2).
        10  ST-DAY-OF-SALE          PIC X(2).
        10  ST-YEAR-OF-SALE         PIC X(2).
    05  ST-DEPARTMENT-NUMBER        PIC X(3).
    05  ST-ITEM-NUMBER              PIC X(7).
    05  ST-ITEM-DESCRIPTION.
        10  ST-ITEM-DESC-FIRST-POS  PIC X(1).
        10  ST-ITEM-DESC-REST-POS   PIC X(14).
    05  ST-EMPLOYEE-NUMBER          PIC X(5).
    05  ST-QUANTITY-X               PIC X(5).
    05  ST-QUANTITY REDEFINES ST-QUANTITY-X
                                    PIC S9(5).
    05  ST-PRICE-X                  PIC X(7).
    05  ST-PRICE REDEFINES ST-PRICE-X   PIC S9(5)V99.
    05  ST-TYPE-OF-SALE             PIC X(1).
```

Actions to be Taken.   Each of the input fields must be tested; the logic of the test module (it will be applicable to each field) is shown in Figure 8-4. Notice that for each record found to be invalid you must:

- Move a descriptive error message identifying the type of error to an output message area. The error message receiving field (in working-storage) is defined as AE-ERROR-MESSAGE with a length of 25.

- Perform the procedure 410-IDENTIFY-ERROR-TYPE.

Although not illustrated by this flowchart, some fields have more than one potential error condition. Each will need to be identified and processed by the preceding two-step action.

Field Validation Specifications.   Figure 8-5 summarizes the validation operations you must perform on each field of this sales transaction record. Notice that the tests range from relatively simple (Record-code equal to 27) to fairly extensive (Price subjected to four tests).

In the interest of modular independence, the validation for each field will be coded as an independent module. Let's consider these modules.

Validating Numeric Fields
Blanks in Numeric Fields

There are two general categories of numeric fields that you will encounter in data validation: calculational and non-calculational. A numeric field on which arithmetic, numeric editing, or numeric-IF tests will be required—a *calculational numeric field*—must be defined with 9 picture elements. These fields must contain digits 0–9 only and must always be checked to ensure that they do.

Upon initial data entry, unused positions of calculational numeric fields often contain blank spaces. For instance, when there is no data for a particular numeric field and zero-filling has not been done, a blank numeric field will result. Similarly, if the integer value stored in the field does not require all the digit positions and the field is not zero-filled, blank spaces will be present in the leftmost positions of

Figure 8-4
Test module logic.

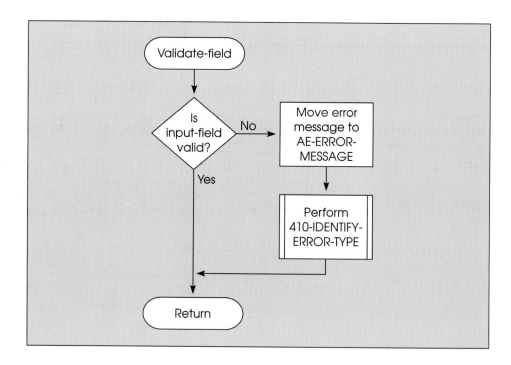

Figure 8-5   Field validation specifications.

Field	Validation type	Validation	Error message
Record-code	code-existence	equal to 27	INVALID RECORD CODE
Date-of-sale	date/range date/range date/class	month: range 01-12 day: range 01-31 year: numeric	INVALID MONTH INVALID DAY YEAR OF NUMERIC
Department-number	class presence	numeric not equal to zero	DEPT NO. NOT NUMERIC DEPT NO. NOT PRESENT
Item-number	class presence	numeric not equal to zero	ITEM NO. NOT NUMERIC ITEM NO. NOT PRESENT
Item-description	presence justification	not equal to spaces if present, first position not equal to a space	ITEM DESC. NOT PRESENT ITEM DESC. NOT LEFT JUST.
Employee-number	range	10001 through 79999	INVALID EMPLOYEE NUMBER
Quantity	class presence	numeric not equal to zero	QUANTITY NOT NUMERIC QUANTITY NOT PRESENT

Price	class
	presence
	sign
	consistency
		numeric
		not equal to zero
		not negative
		if dept. num. is less than
		   500, price must be less
		   than one thousand dollars
			PRICE NOT NUMERIC
			PRICE NOT PRESENT
			PRICE NOT POSITIVE
			PRICE NOT CONSISTENT

Type-of-sale	code-existence	equal to "$", "C", or "R"	INVALID TYPE OF SALE CODE

the field. Remember that blank spaces are not numeric digits. A numeric field must contain only valid digits when it is operated on arithmetically; otherwise, a data exception might occur.

You will also encounter numeric fields on which none of the arithmetic type operations is to be performed; these can be defined with either X or 9 picture elements. A Social Security number is a typical example. Frequently, these fields can contain digits or can be entirely blank (for example, a person's Social Security number is not available when the data is entered).

Zero-Filling of Numeric Fields   To ensure that numeric fields contain no blank spaces, COBOL programmers use the INSPECT statement to force the blank spaces to be replaced by zeros. As shown in Example A of Figure 8-6, an INSPECT statement can be coded to replace ALL spaces within the field by zeros. Although this technique is often used, you should recognize that it handles successfully only those situations in which the numeric field is completely blank or has only leftmost leading spaces.

Figure 8-6
Replacing blank spaces
with zeros.

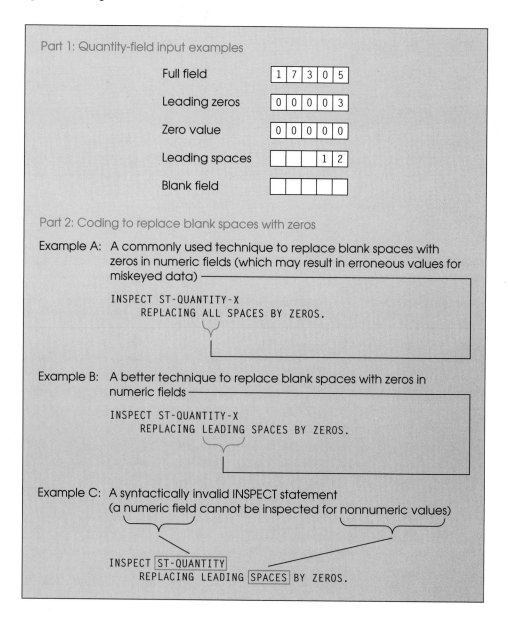

Part 1: Quantity-field input examples

Full field	1 7 3 0 5
Leading zeros	0 0 0 0 3
Zero value	0 0 0 0 0
Leading spaces	1 2
Blank field	

Part 2: Coding to replace blank spaces with zeros

Example A: A commonly used technique to replace blank spaces with zeros in numeric fields (which may result in erroneous values for miskeyed data)

```
INSPECT ST-QUANTITY-X
     REPLACING ALL SPACES BY ZEROS.
```

Example B: A better technique to replace blank spaces with zeros in numeric fields

```
INSPECT ST-QUANTITY-X
     REPLACING LEADING SPACES BY ZEROS.
```

Example C: A syntactically invalid INSPECT statement (a numeric field cannot be inspected for nonnumeric values)

```
INSPECT ST-QUANTITY
     REPLACING LEADING SPACES BY ZEROS.
```

Suppose the numeric data within the field is misaligned or inadvertently contains a blank space—either embedded within the digits or to the right of the value. After all spaces within the field are replaced by zeros, an incorrect value will result. For example, consider the value 1856 misaligned within its field, as shown below.

    1 8 5 6   Incorrectly aligned as: 1 8 5 6

The ALL operator will erroneously convert it to 18560.

Example B of Figure 8-6 shows a simple way to counter this problem: code the operator LEADING instead of ALL. Then only leading, nonsignificant spaces will be converted to zeros. Any additional spaces embedded within the digits or to the left of the digits can then be detected by a NUMERIC class test.

When using the INSPECT, you should guard against a common coding error—the failure to maintain consistency between the data class of the field being inspected and the data class of the character being replaced. Example C of Figure 8-6 shows an invalid statement in which the programmer has specified a numeric field and is trying to replace the SPACES. Recognize that SPACE is a nonnumeric character. For a SPACE to be present in a field, the field should be of alphanumeric data class. A syntax error will occur when a numeric field is coded and a nonnumeric character such as SPACE is specified as the value to be replaced. If the value to be replaced is a nonnumeric character, the field specified in the INSPECT statement must be alphanumeric (PIC X).

Numeric Class Tests   Even after replacing blank spaces within a numeric field by zeros, the field may still contain nonnumeric data. A SPACE is but one nonnumeric character. Other garbage characters such as letters, asterisks, hyphens, and the like must be guarded against. To ensure that a field contains only valid numeric digits, a numeric class test must be made after the zero-filling operation. You will see this in the data validation modules that follow.

Validation Modules
Record-Code Validation

Validation of the Record-code field is the simplest of all; you need only ensure that it contains a value 27. The needed module for this action is shown in Figure 8-7. Notice that if the code is not 27, two actions are taken: the appropriate message is moved to AE-ERROR-MESSAGE and the 410 module is performed.

Date-of-Sale Validation   Referring to Figure 8-5, you see that validation of the date field is much more extensive. All fields must be numeric and the month and day are restricted to their ranges. This added complexity is evident in the 320 module of Figure 8-8.

Here you see that the first action is to replace leading spaces with zeros. Then each component of the date (month, day, and year) is tested separately. The tests for both the month and day involve a numeric test as well as a range test. At first glance, you might feel that the numeric test is not necessary because any quantity with a valid range (between "01" and "12") must therefore be numeric. However, this is *not* necessarily the case because in an alphanumeric field the digit 0 followed

Figure 8-7   Record-code validation.

```
COBOL-74                                          COBOL-85

310-VAL-RECORD-CODE.                              310-VAL-RECORD-CODE.
    IF ST-RECORD-CODE IS NOT EQUAL TO "27"            IF ST-RECORD-CODE IS NOT EQUAL TO "27"
        MOVE "INVALID RECORD CODE" TO AE-ERROR-MESSAGE    MOVE "INVALID RECORD CODE" TO AE-ERROR-MESSAGE
        PERFORM 410-IDENTIFY-ERROR-TYPE.                  PERFORM 410-IDENTIFY-ERROR-TYPE
                                                      END-IF.
```

Figure 8-8   Date-of-sale validation.

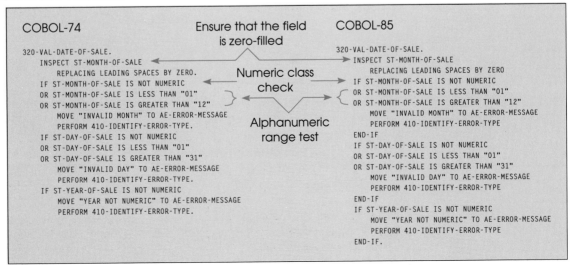

```
COBOL-74                    Ensure that the field    COBOL-85
                              is zero-filled
320-VAL-DATE-OF-SALE.                                320-VAL-DATE-OF-SALE.
    INSPECT ST-MONTH-OF-SALE                             INSPECT ST-MONTH-OF-SALE
        REPLACING LEADING SPACES BY ZERO.                   REPLACING LEADING SPACES BY ZERO
    IF ST-MONTH-OF-SALE IS NOT NUMERIC    Numeric class    IF ST-MONTH-OF-SALE IS NOT NUMERIC
    OR ST-MONTH-OF-SALE IS LESS THAN "01"    check         OR ST-MONTH-OF-SALE IS LESS THAN "01"
    OR ST-MONTH-OF-SALE IS GREATER THAN "12"               OR ST-MONTH-OF-SALE IS GREATER THAN "12"
        MOVE "INVALID MONTH" TO AE-ERROR-MESSAGE               MOVE "INVALID MONTH" TO AE-ERROR-MESSAGE
        PERFORM 410-IDENTIFY-ERROR-TYPE.                       PERFORM 410-IDENTIFY-ERROR-TYPE
    IF ST-DAY-OF-SALE IS NOT NUMERIC    Alphanumeric    END-IF
    OR ST-DAY-OF-SALE IS LESS THAN "01"    range test   IF ST-DAY-OF-SALE IS NOT NUMERIC
    OR ST-DAY-OF-SALE IS GREATER THAN "31"               OR ST-DAY-OF-SALE IS LESS THAN "01"
        MOVE "INVALID DAY" TO AE-ERROR-MESSAGE           OR ST-DAY-OF-SALE IS GREATER THAN "31"
        PERFORM 410-IDENTIFY-ERROR-TYPE.                     MOVE "INVALID DAY" TO AE-ERROR-MESSAGE
    IF ST-YEAR-OF-SALE IS NOT NUMERIC                        PERFORM 410-IDENTIFY-ERROR-TYPE
        MOVE "YEAR NOT NUMERIC" TO AE-ERROR-MESSAGE      END-IF
        PERFORM 410-IDENTIFY-ERROR-TYPE.                 IF ST-YEAR-OF-SALE IS NOT NUMERIC
                                                             MOVE "YEAR NOT NUMERIC" TO AE-ERROR-MESSAGE
                                                             PERFORM 410-IDENTIFY-ERROR-TYPE
                                                         END-IF.
```

by any letter falls between 09 and 10 (this is a result of the collating sequence). Hence, the range check would not detect an incorrect month entry of, for instance, 0P.

If the numeric class tests were not coupled with the nonnumeric range tests and if an invalid character within the range happened to be recorded in that date-of-sale field, the erroneous data would not be detected. So, whenever a numeric range test is handled by an alphanumeric comparison, a numeric class test must also be specified.

Department-Number and Item-Number Validation

The Department-number and Item-number checks both require that the fields be present and that they be numeric. The corresponding code is shown in Figure 8-9. Here you can see that leading spaces are first changed to zeros. Then two tests are performed: numeric and zero. Had the field been empty (filled with blanks), the INSPECT statement would have replaced them all with zeros. Hence, the second test checks for existence of an entry in this field.

Item-Description Validation

The validation specifications require that two tests be made on the Item-description field: there must be an entry (the field must not be blank) and it must be justified (the description must begin in the first position of the field). This is done by breaking the field into two elements, as shown in Figure 8-10.

The 350 module illustrates an easy, efficient way to ensure that an alphanumeric field is properly left-justified. If the first position of the field is blank and any one of the remaining positions is not blank, the field is not left-justified. Recognize that when the field is completely blank, no justification error exists, so it is not identified as such.

Employee-Number Validation

The Employee-number validation is identical to the validation of sales month and day: it must be checked for numeric, and to ensure that it lies within the allowable range. This is done in the 360 module shown in Figure 8-11.

Quantity Validation

The Quantity field is the first of two that are calculational numeric fields. Although it cannot be zero (it must be present), it can be negative. Hence, in Figure 8-12, you can see that the NOT NUMERIC test is performed on ST-QUANTITY (defined with a 9 picture)—refer to the record definition of Figure 8-3. If the test were on ST-QUANTITY-X (defined with an X picture), the sign would give a nonnumeric indication.

Figure 8-9   Department-number and item-number validation.

```
COBOL-74                                          COBOL-85

330-VAL-DEPT-NUMBER.                              330-VAL-DEPARTMENT-NUMBER.
    INSPECT ST-DEPARTMENT-NUMBER                      INSPECT ST-DEPT-NUMBER
        REPLACING LEADING SPACES BY ZEROS.               REPLACING LEADING SPACES BY ZEROS
    IF ST-DEPARTMENT-NUMBER IS NOT NUMERIC            IF ST-DEPARTMENT-NUMBER IS NOT NUMERIC
        MOVE "DEPT. NO. NOT NUMERIC" TO AE-ERROR-MESSAGE     MOVE "DEPT. NO. NOT NUMERIC" TO AE-ERROR-MESSAGE
        PERFORM 410-IDENTIFY-ERROR-TYPE                      PERFORM 410-IDENTIFY-ERROR-TYPE
    IF ST-DEPARTMENT-NUMBER IS EQUAL TO ZERO         END-IF
        MOVE "DEPT. NO. NOT PRESENT" TO AE-ERROR-MESSAGE  IF ST-DEPARTMENT-NUMBER IS EQUAL TO ZERO
        PERFORM 410-IDENTIFY-ERROR-TYPE.                     MOVE "DEPT. NO. NOT PRESENT" TO AE-ERROR-MESSAGE
                                                             PERFORM 410-IDENTIFY-ERROR-TYPE
340-VAL-ITEM-NUMBER.                                  END-IF.
    INSPECT ST-ITEM-NUMBER
        REPLACING LEADING SPACES BY ZEROS.           340-VAL-ITEM-NUMBER.
    IF ST-ITEM-NUMBER IS NOT NUMERIC                     INSPECT ST-ITEM-NUMBER
        MOVE "ITEM NO. NOT NUMERIC" TO AE-ERROR-MESSAGE      REPLACING LEADING SPACES BY ZEROS
        PERFORM 410-IDENTIFY-ERROR-TYPE.             IF ST-ITEM-NUMBER IS NOT NUMERIC
    IF ST-ITEM-NUMBER IS EQUAL TO ZERO                   MOVE "ITEM NO. NOT NUMERIC" TO AE-ERROR-MESSAGE
        MOVE "ITEM NO. NOT PRESENT" TO AE-ERROR-MESSAGE      PERFORM 410-IDENTIFY-ERROR-TYPE
        PERFORM 410-IDENTIFY-ERROR-TYPE.             END-IF
                                                     IF ST-ITEM-NUMBER IS EQUAL TO ZERO
                                                         MOVE "ITEM NO. NOT PRESENT" TO AE-ERROR-MESSAGE
                                                         PERFORM 410-IDENTIFY-ERROR-TYPE
                                                     END-IF.
```

Figure 8-10 Item-description validation.

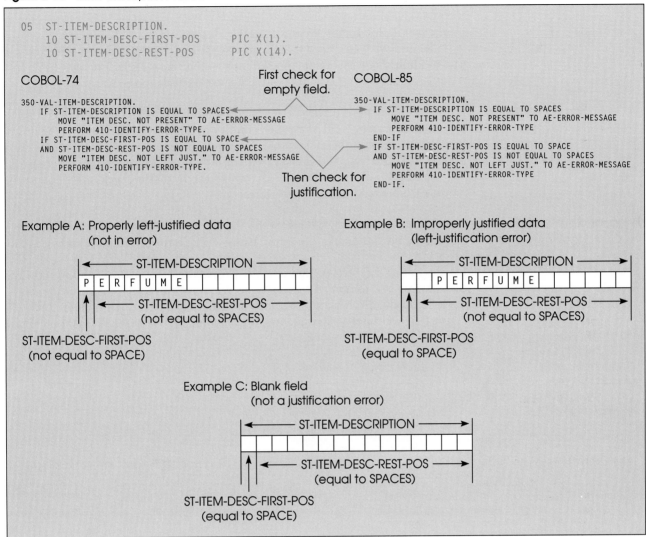

Figure 8-11 Employee-number validation.

```
COBOL-74                                          COBOL-85

360-VAL-EMPLOYEE-NUMBER.                           360-VAL-EMPLOYEE-NUMBER.
    INSPECT ST-EMPLOYEE-NUMBER                         INSPECT ST-EMPLOYEE-NUMBER
        REPLACING LEADING SPACES BY ZEROS.                 REPLACING LEADING SPACES BY ZEROS
    IF ST-EMPLOYEE-NUMBER IS NOT NUMERIC               IF ST-EMPLOYEE-NUMBER IS NOT NUMERIC
    OR ST-EMPLOYEE-NUMBER IS LESS THAN "10001"         OR ST-EMPLOYEE-NUMBER IS LESS THAN "10001"
    OR ST-EMPLOYEE-NUMBER IS GREATER THAN "79999"      OR ST-EMPLOYEE-NUMBER IS GREATER THAN "79999"
        MOVE "INVALID EMPLOYEE NUMBER" TO AE-ERROR-MESSAGE     MOVE "INVALID EMPLOYEE NUMBER" TO AE-ERROR-MESSAGE
        PERFORM 410-IDENTIFY-ERROR-TYPE.                   PERFORM 410-IDENTIFY-ERROR-TYPE
                                                       END-IF.
```

Figure 8-12 Quantity validation.

```
COBOL-74                                          COBOL-85

370-VAL-QUANTITY.                                  370-VAL-QUANTITY.
    IF ST-QUANTITY-X IS NOT NUMERIC                    IF ST-QUANTITY-X IS NOT NUMERIC
        MOVE "QUANTITY NOT NUMERIC" TO AE-ERROR-MESSAGE    MOVE "QUANTITY NOT NUMERIC" TO AE-ERROR-MESSAGE
        PERFORM 410-IDENTIFY-ERROR-TYPE.                   PERFORM 410-IDENTIFY-ERROR-TYPE
    IF ST-QUANTITY-X IS EQUAL TO ZERO              END-IF
        MOVE "QUANTITY NOT PRESENT" TO AE-ERROR-MESSAGE    IF ST-QUANTITY-X IS EQUAL TO ZERO
        PERFORM 410-IDENTIFY-ERROR-TYPE.                   MOVE "QUANTITY NOT PRESENT" TO AE-ERROR-MESSAGE
                                                           PERFORM 410-IDENTIFY-ERROR-TYPE
                                                       END-IF.
```

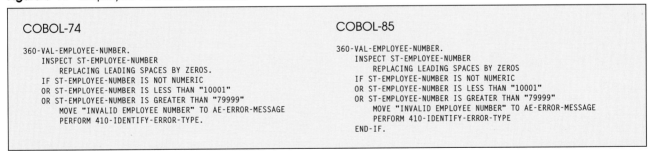

The second IF, the test for a zero value, uses the alphanumeric definition for this field (ST-QUANTITY-X). Actually, either ST-QUANTITY or ST-QUANTITY-X could have been used since the figurative constant ZERO will be interpreted as numeric or alphanumeric by the compiler, depending upon the context.

You might have noticed that the leading spaces are not replaced with zeros in this module. The reason, as you will see, is that zero replacement is done in a module preceding this one to satisfy other needs of the program.

Price Validation

In the 380 module of Figure 8-13, the Price field is checked for a zero condition (presence of a value) and a negative condition. It is also range checked. That is, if the Department-number is less than 500, then the value in this field must be less than $1,000. You can see this test in the third IF of the 380 module in Figure 8-13.

Leading blank replacement, as well as the numeric check, are done in the module from which this one is performed.

Type-of-Sale Validation

The only three allowable values for the Type-of-sale field are $, R, and C; any other entry must be identified as an error. This is done in the 390 module shown in Figure 8-14.

Beginning COBOL programmers often make errors when joining multiple conditions into a combined IF statement. You must carefully consider whether the operator AND or OR should be used and the effect of using the operator NOT. Figure 8-15 contrasts correct and incorrect combinations for the ST-TYPE-OF-SALE field validation.

Figure 8-13 Price validation.

```
COBOL-74                                          COBOL-85

380-VAL-PRICE.                                    380-VAL-PRICE.
    IF ST-PRICE-X IS EQUAL TO ZERO                    IF ST-PRICE-X IS EQUAL TO ZERO
        MOVE "PRICE NOT PRESENT" TO AE-ERROR-MESSAGE      MOVE "PRICE NOT PRESENT" TO AE-ERROR-MESSAGE
        PERFORM 410-IDENTIFY-ERROR-TYPE.                  PERFORM 410-IDENTIFY-ERROR-TYPE
    IF ST-PRICE IS NOT GREATER THAN ZERO              END-IF
        MOVE "PRICE NOT POSITIVE" TO AE-ERROR-MESSAGE  IF ST-PRICE IS NOT GREATER THAN ZERO
        PERFORM 410-IDENTIFY-ERROR-TYPE.                  MOVE "PRICE NOT POSITIVE" TO AE-ERROR-MESSAGE
    IF ST-DEPARTMENT-NUMBER IS LESS THAN "500"            PERFORM 410-IDENTIFY-ERROR-TYPE
    AND ST-PRICE IS GREATER THAN 999.99              END-IF
        MOVE "PRICE NOT CONSISTENT" TO AE-ERROR-MESSAGE IF ST-DEPARTMENT-NUMBER IS LESS THAN "500"
        PERFORM 410-IDENTIFY-ERROR-TYPE.              AND ST-PRICE IS GREATER THAN 999.99
                                                          MOVE "PRICE NOT CONSISTENT" TO AE-ERROR-MESSAGE
                                                          PERFORM 410-IDENTIFY-ERROR-TYPE
                                                      END-IF.
```

Figure 8-14 Type-of-sale validation.

```
COBOL-74                                          COBOL-85

390-VAL-TYPE-OF-SALE.                             390-VAL-TYPE-OF-SALE.
    IF ST-TYPE-OF-SALE IS NOT EQUAL TO "$"            IF ST-TYPE-OF-SALE IS NOT EQUAL TO "$"
    AND ST-TYPE-OF-SALE IS NOT EQUAL TO "C"          AND ST-TYPE-OF-SALE IS NOT EQUAL TO "C"
    AND ST-TYPE-OF-SALE IS NOT EQUAL TO "R"          AND ST-TYPE-OF-SALE IS NOT EQUAL TO "R"
        MOVE "INVALID TYPE OF SALE CODE" TO AE-ERROR-MESSAGE MOVE "INVALID TYPE OF SALE CODE" TO AE-ERROR-MESSAGE
        PERFORM 410-IDENTIFY-ERROR-TYPE.                  PERFORM 410-IDENTIFY-ERROR-TYPE
                                                      END-IF.
```

Figure 8-15 Combined IF operator tests.

390-VAL-TYPE-OF-SALE.	Examples with	
	Valid code "$"	Invalid code "T"

Part A: Correct combined IF test using operators AND and NOT

```
IF ST-TYPE-OF-SALE IS NOT EQUAL TO "$"
AND ST-TYPE-OF-SALE IS NOT EQUAL TO "C"
AND ST-TYPE-OF-SALF IS NOT EQUAL TO "R"
    MOVE "INVALID TYPE OF SALE CODE" TO AE-ERROR-MESSAGE
    PERFORM 410-IDENTIFY-ERROR-TYPE.
```

Valid code "$"	Invalid code "T"
False	True
True	True
True	True
Correct result:	Correct result:
no error identified	error identified

Part B: Incorrect combined IF test using operators OR and NOT

```
IF ST-TYPE-OF-SALE IS NOT EQUAL TO "$"
OR ST-TYPE-OF-SALE IS NOT EQUAL TO "C"
OR ST-TYPE-OF-SALF IS NOT EQUAL TO "R"
    MOVE "INVALID TYPE OF SALE CODE" TO AE-ERROR-MESSAGE
    PERFORM 410-IDENTIFY-ERROR-TYPE.
```

Valid code "$"	Invalid code "T"
False	True
True	True
True	True
Incorrect result:	Correct result:
error identified	error identified

Part C: Correct combined IF test using operator OR

```
IF ST-TYPE-OF-SALE IS EQUAL TO "$"
OR ST-TYPE-OF-SALE is EQUAL TO "C"
OR ST-TYPE-OF-SALE IS EQUAL TO "R"
    NEXT SENTENCE
ELSE
    MOVE "INVALID TYPE OF SALE CODE" TO AE-ERROR-MESSAGE
    PERFORM 410-IDENTIFY-ERROR-TYPE.
```

Valid code "$"	Invalid code "T"
True	False
False	False
False	False
Correct result:	Correct result:
no error identified	error identified

Part D: Incorrect combined IF test using operators AND and NOT

```
IF ST-TYPE-OF-SALE IS NOT EQUAL TO "$"
AND ST-TYPE-OF-SALF IS NOT EQUAL TO "C"
AND ST-TYPE-OF-SALE IS NOT EQUAL TO "R"
    NEXT SENTENCE
ELSE
    MOVE "INVALID TYPE OF SALE CODE" TO AE-ERROR-MESSAGE
    PERFORM 410-IDENTIFY-ERROR-TYPE.
```

Valid code "$"	Invalid code "T"
False	True
True	True
True	True
Incorrect result:	Incorrect result:
error identified	no error identified

Alternative Coding Techniques

The coding presented in the DATAVAL program was written to best explain the logic of a data validation program together with a variety of methods. However, there are some alternative coding techniques that could be incorporated into such a program.

88-Level Condition-Names for Applicable Validations

The IF statement relation-condition tests used for the field validations could be replaced by condition-name tests. This would require specification of 88-level condition-name entries in the input ST-SALES-TRANSACTION-RECORD, as shown in Figure 8-16.

Figure 8-16
Specification of condition-names for field validations.

```
01 ST-SALES-TRANSACTION-RECORD.
   05  ST-RECORD-CODE                    PIC X(2).
       88 VALID-RECORD-CODE                  VALUE "27".
   05  ST-DATE-OF-SALE.
       10  ST-MONTH-OF-SALE              PIC X(2).
           88 VALID-MONTH                    VALUE "01" THRU "12".
       10  ST-DAY-OF-SALE                PIC X(2).
           88 VALID-DAY                      VALUE "01" THRU "31".
       10  ST-YEAR-OF-SALE               PIC X(2).
   05  ST-DEPARTMENT-NUMBER              PIC X(3).
       88 DEPT-NO-NOT-PRESENT                VALUE ZERO.
       88 DEPT-NO-LESS-THAN-500              VALUE "001"
                                                 THRU "499".
   05  ST-ITEM-NUMBER                    PIC X(7).
       88 ITEM-NO-NOT-PRESENT                VALUE ZERO.
   05  ST-ITEM-DESCRIPTION.
       88 ITEM-DESC-NOT-PRESENT              VALUE SPACES.
       10  ST-ITEM-DESC-FIRST-POS        PIC X(1).
           88 ITEM-DESC-FIRST-POS-BLANK      VALUE SPACE.
       10  ST-ITEM-DESC-REST-POS         PIC X(14).
           88 ITEM-DESC-REST-POS-BLANK       VALUE SPACES.
   05  ST-EMPLOYEE-NUMBER                PIC X(5).
       88  VALID-EMPLOYEE-NUMBER             VALUE "10001"
                                                 THRU "79999".
   05  ST-QUANTITY-X                     PIC X(5).
       88  QUANTITY-NOT-PRESENT              VALUE ZERO.
   05  ST-QUANTITY REDEFINES ST-QUANTITY-X
                                         PIC S9(5).
   05  ST-PRICE-X                        PIC X(7).
       88 PRICE-NOT-PRESENT                  VALUE ZEROS.
   05  ST-PRICE REDEFINES ST-PRICE-X     PIC S9(5)V99.
       88 PRICE-1000-DLRS-OR-MORE            VALUE 01000.00
                                                 THRU 99999.99.
   05  ST-TYPE-OF-SALE                   PIC X(1).
       88 VALID-TYPE-OF-SALE                 VALUE "$"
                                                   "C"
                                                   "R".
```

Error Messages in WORKING-STORAGE

Instead of coding the error messages as nonnumeric literals in the PROCEDURE DIVISION, they could be established as data-items in the WORKING-STORAGE SECTION, as seen in Figure 8-17. This technique groups all the error messages into one area of the program listing for easy reference.

As a reference aid, observe that the data-names for each error message incorporate the module number in which the applicable error condition is tested.

Figure 8-18 shows the PROCEDURE DIVISION coding for the validation modules, which incorporates the condition-name tests and WORKING-STORAGE SECTION error messages.

Figure 8-17
Specification of error messages in the WORKING-STORAGE SECTION.

```
01  WS-ERROR-MESSAGES.
    05  WS-220-ERR-1 PIC X(25) VALUE "PRICE NOT NUMERIC".
    05  WS-310-ERR-1 PIC X(25) VALUE "INVALID RECORD CODE".
    05  WS-320-ERR-1 PIC X(25) VALUE "INVALID MONTH".
    05  WS-320-ERR-2 PIC X(25) VALUE "INVALID DAY".
    05  WS-320-ERR-3 PIC X(25) VALUE "YEAR NOT NUMERIC".
    05  WS-330-ERR-1 PIC X(25) VALUE "DEPT. NO. NOT NUMERIC".
    05  WS-330-ERR-2 PIC X(25) VALUE "DEPT. NO. NOT PRESENT".
    05  WS-340-ERR-1 PIC X(25) VALUE "ITEM NO. NOT NUMERIC".
    05  WS-340-ERR-2 PIC X(25) VALUE "ITEM NO. NOT PRESENT".
    05  WS-350-ERR-1 PIC X(25) VALUE "ITEM DESC. NOT PRESENT".
    05  WS-350-ERR-2 PIC X(25) VALUE "ITEM DESC. NOT LEFT JUST".
    05  WS-360-ERR-1 PIC X(25) VALUE "INVALID EMPLOYEE NUMBER".
    05  WS-370-ERR-1 PIC X(25) VALUE "QUANTITY NOT NUMERIC".
    05  WS-370-ERR-2 PIC X(25) VALUE "QUANTITY NOT PRESENT".
    05  WS-380-ERR-1 PIC X(25) VALUE "PRICE NOT PRESENT".
    05  WS-380-ERR-2 PIC X(25) VALUE "PRICE NOT POSITIVE".
    05  WS-380-ERR-3 PIC X(25) VALUE "PRICE NOT CONSISTENT".
    05  WS-390-ERR-1 PIC X(25) VALUE "INVALID TYPE OF SALE CODE".
```

Figure 8-18 Field-validation coding using condition-names and WORKING-STORAGE error messages.

COBOL-74

```
310-VAL-RECORD-CODE.
    IF NOT VALID-RECORD-CODE
        MOVE WS-310-ERR-1 TO AE-ERROR-MESSAGE
        PERFORM 410-IDENTIFY-ERROR-TYPE.

320-VAL-DATE-OF-SALE.
    IF ST-MONTH-OF-SALE IS NOT NUMERIC
    OR NOT VALID-MONTH
        MOVE WS-320-ERR-1 TO AE-ERROR-MESSAGE
        PERFORM 410-IDENTIFY-ERROR-TYPE
    IF ST-DAY-OF-SALE IS NOT NUMERIC
    OR NOT VALID-DAY
        MOVE WS-320-ERR-2 TO AE-ERROR-MESSAGE
        PERFORM 410-IDENTIFY-ERROR-TYPE
    IF ST-YEAR-OF-SALE IS NOT NUMERIC
        MOVE WS-320-ERR-3 TO AE-ERROR-MESSAGE
        PERFORM 410-IDENTIFY-ERROR-TYPE.

330-VAL-DEPT-NUMBER.
    INSPECT ST-DEPARTMENT-NUMBER
        REPLACING LEADING SPACES BY ZEROS.
    IF ST-DEPARTMENT-NUMBER IS NOT NUMERIC
        MOVE WS-330-ERR-1 TO AE-ERROR-MESSAGE
        PERFORM 410-IDENTIFY-ERROR-TYPE.
    IF DEPT-NO-NOT-PRESENT
        MOVE WS-330-ERR-2 TO AE-ERROR-MESSAGE
        PERFORM 410-IDENTIFY-ERROR-TYPE.

340-VAL-ITEM-NUMBER.
    INSPECT ST-ITEM-NUMBER
        REPLACING LEADING SPACES BY ZEROS.
    IF ST-ITEM-NUMBER IS NOT NUMERIC
        MOVE WS-340-ERR-1 TO AE-ERROR-MESSAGE
        PERFORM 410-IDENTIFY-ERROR-TYPE.
    IF ITEM-NO-NOT-PRESENT
        MOVED WS-340-ERR-2 TO AE-ERROR-MESSAGE
        PERFORM 410-IDENTIFY-ERROR-TYPE.

350-VAL-ITEM-DESCRIPTION.
    IF ITEM-DESC-NOT-PRESENT
        MOVE WS-350-ERR-1 TO AE-ERROR-MESSAGE
        PERFORM 410-IDENTIFY-ERROR-TYPE.
    IF ITEM-DESC-FIRST-POS-BLANK
    AND NOT ITEM-DESC-REST-POS-BLANK
        MOVE WS-350-ERR-2 TO AE-ERROR-MESSAGE
        PERFORM 410-IDENTIFY-ERROR-TYPE.

360-VAL-EMPLOYEE-NUMBER.
    IF ST-EMPLOYEE-NUMBER IS NOT NUMERIC
    OR NOT VALID-EMPLOYEE-NUMBER
        MOVE WS-360-ERR-1 TO AE-ERROR-MESSAGE
        PERFORM 410-IDENTIFY-ERROR-TYPE.

370-VAL-QUANTITY.
    IF ST-QUANTITY IS NOT NUMERIC
        MOVE WS-370-ERR-1 TO AE-ERROR-MESSAGE
        PERFORM 410-IDENTIFY-ERROR-TYPE.

380-VAL-PRICE.
    IF PRICE-NOT-PRESENT
        MOVE WS-380-ERR-1 TO AE-ERROR-MESSAGE
        PERFORM 410-IDENTIFY-ERROR-TYPE.
    IF ST-PRICE IS NOT POSITIVE
        MOVE WS-380-ERR-2 TO AE-ERROR-MESSAGE
        PERFORM 410-IDENTIFY-ERROR-TYPE.
    IF DEPT-NO-LESS-THAN-500
    AND PRICE-1000-DLRS-OR-MORE
        MOVE WS-380-ERR-3 TO AE-ERROR-MESSAGE
        PERFORM 410-IDENTIFY-ERROR-TYPE.

390-VAL-TYPE-OF-SALE.
    IF NOT VALID-TYPE-OF-SALE
        MOVE WS-390-TYPE-OF-SALE
        PERFORM 410-IDENTIFY-ERROR-TYPE.
```

COBOL-85

```
310-VAL-RECORD-CODE.
    IF NOT VALID-RECORD-CODE
        MOVE WS-310-ERR-1 TO AE-ERROR-MESSAGE
        PERFORM 410-IDENTIFY-ERROR-TYPE
    END-IF.

320-VAL-DATE-OF-SALE.
    IF ST-MONTH-OF-SALE IS NOT NUMERIC
    OR NOT VALID-MONTH
        MOVE WS-320-ERR-1 TO AE-ERROR-MESSAGE
        PERFORM 410-IDENTIFY-ERROR-TYPE
    END-IF
    IF ST-DAY-OF-SALE IS NOT NUMERIC
    OR NOT VALID-DAY
        MOVE WS-320-ERR-2 TO AE-ERROR-MESSAGE
        PERFORM 410-IDENTIFY-ERROR-TYPE
    END-IF
    IF ST-YEAR-OF-SALE IS NOT NUMERIC
        MOVE WS-320-ERR-3 TO AE-ERROR-MESSAGE
        PERFORM 410-IDENTIFY-ERROR-TYPE
    END-IF.

330-VAL-DEPT-NUMBER.
    INSPECT ST-DEPARTMENT-NUMBER
        REPLACING LEADING SPACES BY ZEROS
    IF ST-DEPARTMENT-NUMBER IS NOT NUMERIC
        MOVE WS-330-ERR-1 TO AE-ERROR-MESSAGE
        PERFORM 410-IDENTIFY-ERROR-TYPE
    END-IF
    IF DEPT-NO-NOT-PRESENT
        MOVE WS-330-ERR-2 TO AE-ERROR-MESSAGE
        PERFORM 410-IDENTIFY-ERROR-TYPE
    END-IF.

340-VAL-ITEM-NUMBER.
    INSPECT ST-ITEM-NUMBER
        REPLACING LEADING SPACES BY ZEROS
    IF ST-ITEM-NUMBER IS NOT NUMERIC
        MOVE WS-340-ERR-1 TO AE-ERROR-MESSAGE
        PERFORM 410-IDENTIFY-ERROR-TYPE
    END-IF
    IF ITEM-NO-NOT-PRESENT
        MOVED WS-340-ERR-2 TO AE-ERROR-MESSAGE
        PERFORM 410-IDENTIFY-ERROR-TYPE
    END-IF.

350-VAL-ITEM-DESCRIPTION.
    IF ITEM-DESC-NOT-PRESENT
        MOVE WS-350-ERR-1 TO AE-ERROR-MESSAGE
        PERFORM 410-IDENTIFY-ERROR-TYPE
    END-IF
    IF ITEM-DESC-FIRST-POS-BLANK
    AND NOT ITEM-DESC-REST-POS-BLANK
        MOVE WS-350-ERR-2 TO AE-ERROR-MESSAGE
        PERFORM 410-IDENTIFY-ERROR-TYPE
    END-IF.

360-VAL-EMPLOYEE-NUMBER.
    IF ST-EMPLOYEE-NUMBER IS NOT NUMERIC
    OR NOT VALID-EMPLOYEE-NUMBER
        MOVE WS-360-ERR-1 TO AE-ERROR-MESSAGE
        PERFORM 410-IDENTIFY-ERROR-TYPE
    END-IF.

370-VAL-QUANTITY.
    IF ST-QUANTITY IS NOT NUMERIC
        MOVE WS-370-ERR-1 TO AE-ERROR-MESSAGE
        PERFORM 410-IDENTIFY-ERROR-TYPE
    END-IF.

380-VAL-PRICE.
    IF PRICE-NOT-PRESENT
        MOVE WS-380-ERR-1 TO AE-ERROR-MESSAGE
        PERFORM 410-IDENTIFY-ERROR-TYPE
    END-IF
    IF ST-PRICE IS NOT POSITIVE
        MOVE WS-380-ERR-2 TO AE-ERROR-MESSAGE
        PERFORM 410-IDENTIFY-ERROR-TYPE
    END-IF
    IF DEPT-NO-LESS-THAN-500
    AND PRICE-1000-DLRS-OR-MORE
        MOVE WS-380-ERR-3 TO AE-ERROR-MESSAGE
        PERFORM 410-IDENTIFY-ERROR-TYPE
    END-IF.

390-VAL-TYPE-OF-SALE.
    IF NOT VALID-TYPE-OF-SALE
        MOVE WS-390-TYPE-OF-SALE
        PERFORM 410-IDENTIFY-ERROR-TYPE
    END-IF.
```

COBOL
Programming
Perspective

Field Definition Guidelines for Data Validation Programs

As mentioned earlier in this chapter, it is a good idea to define all the fields of a record that are input to a data validation program as alphanumeric fields (PIC X). Make all field validations in the input-record area. Use the alphanumeric field for all INSPECT statements and alphanumeric comparisons. In certain cases, however, the alphanumeric field will require redefinition as a numeric field (PIC 9 or S9). Such situations are as follows:

1. **The input field is a signed numeric field.** The input field must be redefined and the signed numeric data-name must be used in the NUMERIC class test. Testing of the alphanumeric data-name will result in an incorrect NOT NUMERIC result for a valid numeric value that carries an arithmetic sign.

2. **A sign test (IF POSITIVE, IF NEGATIVE, or IF ZERO) is to be made on the input field.** The input field must be redefined and the numeric data-name must be used in the sign test. (Remember that COBOL syntax requires a numeric data-name to be referenced in a sign test.) However, recognize that if the data does not pass a NUMERIC class test, that particular field value must *not* be tested with the sign test because a data exception might occur.

3. **The input field is to be moved to a numeric-edited field (such as on the audit/error list).** The input field must be redefined and the numeric data-name must be used as the sending field of the MOVE operation. However, recognize that if the data does not pass a NUMERIC class test, that particular field value must *not* be moved to the numeric-edited field because a data exception might occur.

4. **An input numeric field with decimal positions is to be moved to a numeric field that contains the picture symbol V.** The input field must be redefined and the numeric data-name must be used in the MOVE operation. (Remember that COBOL syntax does not permit an alphanumeric field to be moved to a numeric field with decimal positions.) However, recognize that if the data does not pass a NUMERIC class test, that particular field value must *not* be moved to the numeric field because an incorrect numeric value might result.

5. **You prefer to use a numeric range test** (rather than the alphanumeric range test coupled with a numeric class test described in this chapter). The input field must be redefined and the numeric data-name must be used in the range test. However, recognize that if the data does not pass a NUMERIC class test, the numeric data-name must *not* be tested because a data exception might occur.

Topic:	The Complete Data Validation Program

Programming Specifications for the Sales-Transaction Validation Program

So far, you have looked at one perspective of the data validation report program: the routines to perform the actual verification of data. Let's see how those modules fit into the overall picture. The purpose of the program is two-fold: to create a new file consisting of valid records from the input file, and to identify those records that are incorrect and the reason(s).

Programming specifications for the sales-transaction validation program are shown in Figure 8-19. Observe in the system flowchart that there is one input sales-transaction file and there are two output files: an audit/error list and a valid sales-transaction file on disk.

Figure 8-19 Programming specifications: Sales-transaction validation program.

PROGRAMMING SPECIFICATIONS

Program name: SALES-TRANSACTION VALIDATION   **Program ID:** DATAVAL

Program Description:

This program is to read input sales-transaction records and make certain field validations on each record. An audit/error list is to be printed that lists each record and each error detected. Validated records are written to a disk file of validated-sales-transaction records. At the conclusion of the run, record-count totals are to be printed.

Input File:

Sales-Transaction File

Output Files:

Audit/Error List
Validated Sales-Transaction File

List of Program Operations:

A. Read each input sales-transaction record.

   1. Validate each of the fields within the record as designated in the field validation specifications.

B. For each record that passes all the validation tests, the program is to:

   1. Write the record to the validated-sales-transaction file. The validated-sales-transation file is a disk file. The sales-transaction record format remains the same. (If a record does not pass all the validation tests, do not write that record to the disk file.)

   2. Write an audit-line that contains the record image on the audit/error list.

C. For each record that has one or more errors, write an error-line on the audit/error list for each error detected in that record.

   1. The first error-line for each record is to contain the record image and the error message.

   2. Successive error-lines (if any) for the same record should contain only the error message.

D. Accumulate the following record counts and, after all input sales-transaction records have been processed, print each count on a separate line in accordance with the format shown on the print chart.

  - Total number of records read
  - Total number of valid records
  - Total number of error records

E. Headings are to be printed on each page of the report. On the first page and after 54 lines have been used on a report page, skip to the next page and print the report headings.

   1. The run date is to be obtained from the operating system and printed on the first heading-line in accordance with the format shown on the print chart.

   2. The page number is to be incremented each time the heading is printed and displayed on the second heading-line in accordance with the format shown on the print chart.

F. Line-spacing is to be handled as follows:

   1. The first audit/error-line printed after the headings is to be double-spaced from the last heading-line.

   2. Second and successive error-lines for the same sales-transaction record are to be single-spaced from one another.

   3. The first audit or error line for each sales transaction record is to be double-spaced from the previous line.

   4. The record-count total lines are to be single-spaced from one another. The first record-count total-line is to be triple-spaced from the last detail-line.

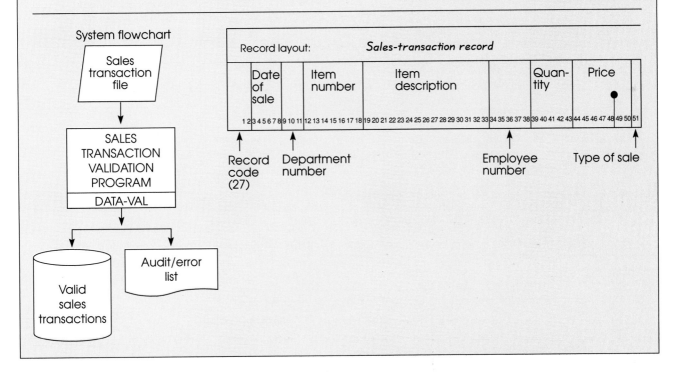

Figure 8-19   (continued)

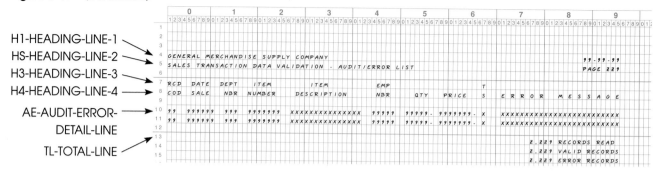

H1-HEADING-LINE-1
HS-HEADING-LINE-2
H3-HEADING-LINE-3
H4-HEADING-LINE-4
AE-AUDIT-ERROR-
DETAIL-LINE
TL-TOTAL-LINE

The program will produce a combined audit/error list. Notice on the print chart that the field values for each input record processed are to be printed in the record-image area on the left-hand side of the report. If any fields of the record are in error, an error message is to be printed to the right in the error-message area. In the output example of Figure 8-20, observe that when there is more than one error for an input record, the second error and all additional errors are printed on a separate line following each preceding error. The record-image area is not repeated. After all input records have been processed, record counts are printed at the end of the report.

Input records that pass all validation checks are written to the output disk file. The output logical record format is exactly the same as the input record format.

Design Documentation for the Sales-Transaction Validation Program

As shown in Figure 8-21, the structure chart for the sales-transaction validation program conforms to the general patterns set by previous programs presented in this text. It contains quite a few more modules, however. Pseudocode for the program is presented in Figure 8-22; the program flowchart appears in Figure 8-23. A review of the logic for each module follows.

Figure 8-20   Sample report output.

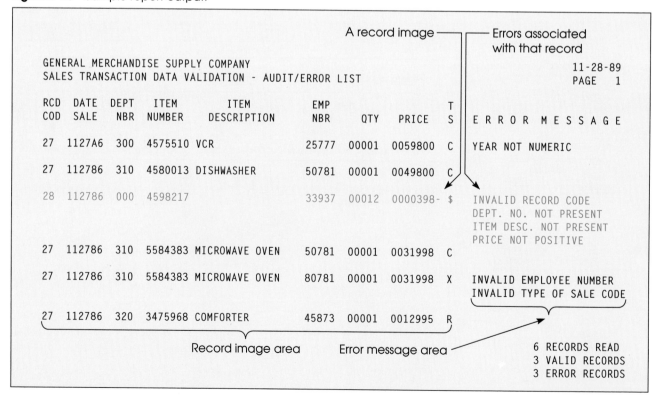

Figure 8-21
Structure chart:
Sales-transaction
validation program.

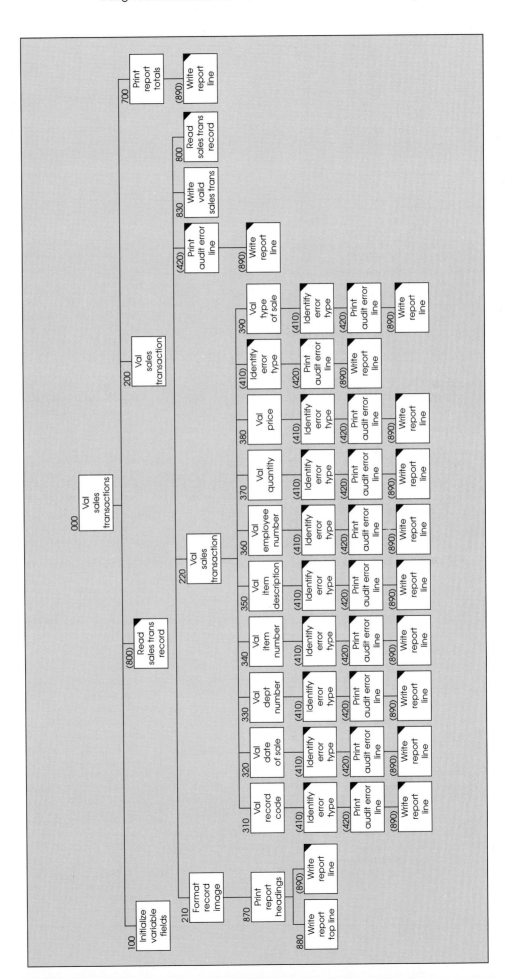

Figure 8-22   Pseudocode: Sales-transaction validation program.

<u>000-Val-Sales-Transactions module</u>

1. Open the files.

2. Perform 100-Initialize-Variable-Fields.

3. Perform 800-Read-Sales-Trans-Record.

4. Perform 200-Val-Sales-Transaction until no more records.

5. Perform 700-Print-Report-Totals.

6. Close the files.

7. Stop the run.

<u>100-Initialize-Variable-Fields module</u>

1. Set the End-of-file indicator to "No".

2. Set the Page-count and Record-count Lines-used fields to zero.

3. Set the Lines-used indicator so that headings for the first page will be triggered.

4. Obtain the date from the operating system and move it to the first heading-line.

<u>200-Val-Sales-Transaction module</u>

1. Move "No" to the Error-Switch.

2. Perform 210-Format-Record-Image.

3. Perform 220-Val-Sales-Trans-Fields.

4. If no errors were detected in the input record
     Add 1 to the Valid-Record count
     Perform 420-Print-Audit-Error-Line
     Move the input Sales-transaction record
        to the output Validated-sales-transaction
        record area
     Write the Validated-sales-transaction record
   Else
     Add 1 to the Error-record count.

5. Perform 800-Read-Sales-Trans-Record.

<u>210-Format-Record-Image module</u>

1. If the report-page is full,
        Perform 870-Print-Report-Headings.

2. Move Spaces to the audit-error-line area.

3. Move each input field to its respective audit-error line field.

<u>220-Val-Sales-Trans-Fields module</u>

1. Perform 310-Val-Record-Code.

2. Perform 320-Val-Date-Of-Sale.

3. Perform 330-Val-Dept-Number.

4. Perform 340-Val-Item-Number.

5. Perform 350-Val-Item-Description.

6. Perform 360-Val-Employee-Number.

7. Perform 370-Val-Quantity.

8. Perform 380-Val-Price.

9. Perform 390-Val-Type-Of-Sale.

<u>310-Val-Record-Code module</u>

<u>320-Val-Date-Of-Sale module</u>

<u>330-Val-Dept-Number module</u>

<u>340-Val-Item-Number module</u>

<u>350-Val-Item-Description module</u>

<u>360-Val-Employee-Number module</u>

<u>370-Val-Quantity module</u>

<u>380-Val-Price module</u>

<u>390-Val-Type-Of-Sale module</u>

For each of the above modules (310- through 390-) the general logic outlined below is used:

1. The validation for that field as designated in the field validation specifications are made.

2. If an error is detected,
        Move the respective error-message
          to the Error-message field in
          the audit-error line.

        Perform 410-Identify-Error-Type.

<u>410-Identify-Error-Type module</u>

1. If this is not the first error-line for this Sales-transaction record
        Move Spaces to the Record-image-area.

2. Move "Yes" to the error-switch.

<u>420-Print-Audit-Error-Line module</u>

1. Move the audit-error-line to the output print-line area.

2. If this is the first line to be printed for this Sales-transaction record,
        Set the line-spacing indicator for
        double-spacing
   Else
        Set the line-spacing indicator for
        single-spacing.

3. Perform 890-Write-Report-Line.

<u>700-Print-Report-Totals module</u>

1. Move spaces to the total-line area.

2. Move the Records-read count field to the output Record-count field.

3. Move the words "Records read" to the output Record-count-description field.

4. Move the Total-line to the output print-line area.

5. Set the Line-spacing indicator for triple-spacing.

6. Perform 890-Write-Report-Line.

7. Move the Valid-records count field to the output Record-count field.

8. Move the words "Valid Records" to the output Record-count-description field.

9. Move the Total-line to the output print-line area.

10. Set the Line-spacing indicator for single-spacing.

11. Perform 890-Write-Report-Line.

12. Move the Error-record count field to the output Record-count field.

13. Move the words "Error Records" to the output Record-count-description field.

14. Move the Total-line to the output print-line area.

15. Perform 890-Write-Report-Line.

<u>800-Sales-Trans-Record module</u>

1. Read a record from the input Sales-transaction file.

2. If there are no more records
        Move "Yes" to the End-of-file indicator.

3. If a record has been read (not end-of-file)
        Add 1 to the Records-read count.

<u>830-Write-Valid-Sales-Trans module</u>

1. Write the output Valid-sales-transaction record area.

<u>870-Print-Report-Headings module</u>

1. Add 1 to the Page-count field.

2. Move the Page-count to the Page-number field in the second heading-line.

3. Move Heading-line 1 to the output print-line area.

4. Perform 880-Write-Report-Top-Line.

5. Move Heading-line-2 to the output print-line area.

6. Set the Line-spacing indicator for single-spacing.

7. Perform 890-Write-Report-Line.

8. Move Heading-line-3 to the output print-line area.

9. Set the Line-spacing indicator for double-spacing.

10. Perform 890-Write-Report-Line.

11. Move Heading-line-4 to the output print-line area.

12. Set the Line-spacing indicator for single-spacing.

13. Perform 890-Write-Report-Line.

<u>880-Write-Report-Top-Line module</u>

1. Advance to the top of the next report page and write the output print-line area.

2. Set the Lines-used indicator to 1.

<u>890-Write-Report-Line module</u>

1. Advance the forms in accordance with the value in the line-spacing indicator field.

2. Add the Line-spacing indicator to the Lines-used field.

Figure 8-23 Flowchart: Sales-transaction validation program.

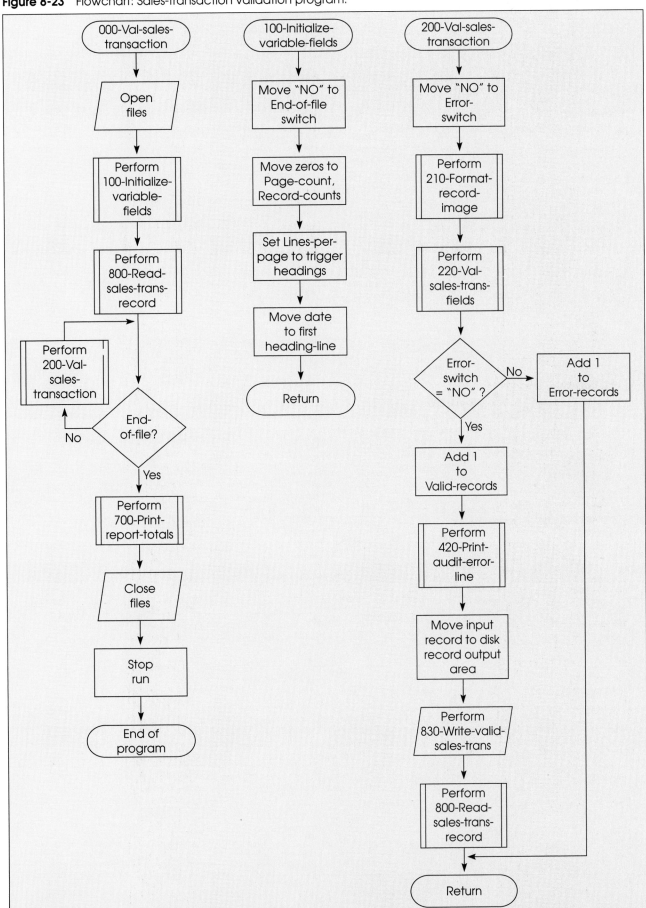

Figure 8-23   (continued)

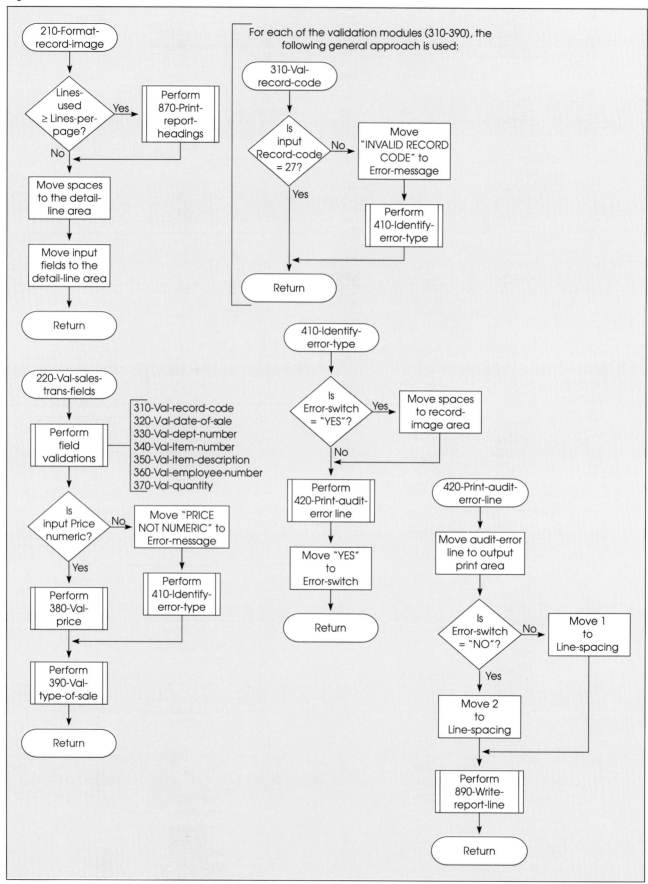

Figure 8-23   (continued)

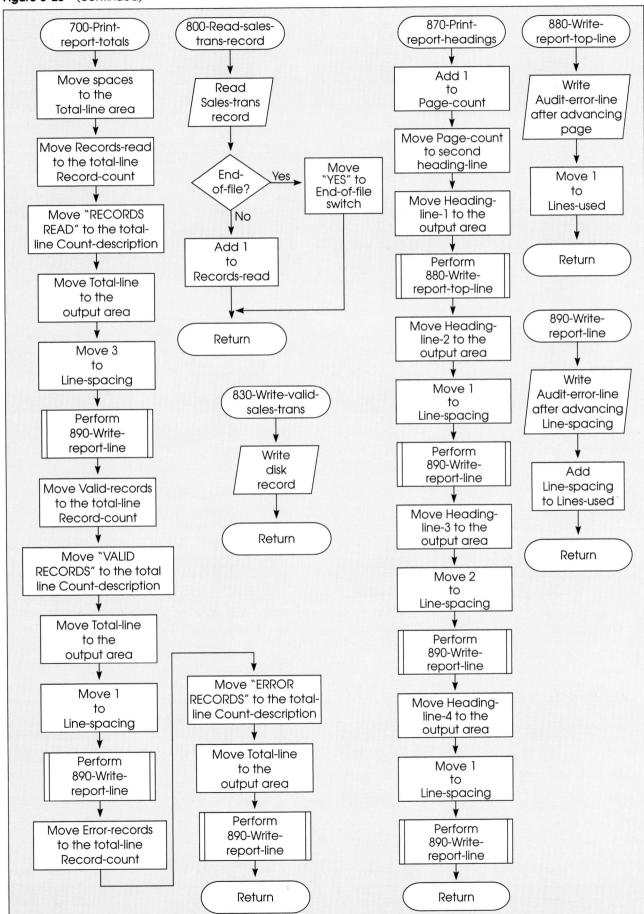

000-Val-Sales-Transaction Module

This is the mainline control module; it performs the four first-level modules of the structure chart: 100-Initialize-variable-fields, 800-Read-sales-trans-record, 200-Val-sales-transaction, and 700-Print-report-totals. The 200-Val-sales-transaction module is performed repeatedly as long as there are input records. After the total lines have been printed and the files have been closed, the run will stop.

100-Initialize-Variable-Fields Module .

The end-of-file switch must be initialized to NO. The page-count field and the fields used for the accumulation of the record-count totals must be set to zeros. The lines-used field is set to a value greater than the line span of the page so that headings for the first page of the audit/error list will be triggered during the first test for page headings. The date is obtained from the operating system and moved to the date area of the first heading line.

200-Val-Sales-Transaction Module

This module performs the 210-Format-record-image and 220-Val-sales-transaction-fields modules. If the input sales-transaction record has no errors, the valid record count is incremented and the 420-Print-audit-error-line module is performed to cause an audit line to be printed. If an error has been detected, the invalid record count is incremented. Finally, the 800-Read-sales-trans-record module is performed to obtain the next input record.

210-Format-Record-Image Module

If the present report page is full, the 870-Print-report-headings module is performed. After the test for headings, each of the input fields is moved to its specified location in the record-image area of the output audit/error list.

220-Val-Sales-Trans-Fields Module

Because no fields have yet been validated for the present input record, the error switch is initialized to NO at the beginning of this module. Then each of the validation modules is performed to check each field of the current input record for errors.

310-Val-Record-Code through 390-Val-Type-of-Sale Modules

Each of these nine modules makes the specified validations of its respective input field. When an error is detected, the appropriate error message is moved to the error-message area of the audit/error list detail line. Then the 410-Identify-error-type module is performed to select the proper format for the error line.

410-Identify-Error-Type Module

This module controls the printing of the record-image area for each error line. The first time this module is performed for each record, the record-image area is to be printed. However, if additional error lines are printed for the same record, the record-image area is not to be reprinted and therefore must be blanked out. The logic of this module controls such processing by testing and setting the error switch.

420-Print-Audit-Error-Line Module

Both audit lines and error lines are printed through this module. Its function is to move the print area to the output area and to set the line-spacing indicator. If this is the first line to be printed for a given input record, the indicator is set for double-spacing; if not, single-spacing is set. The 890-Write-report-line module is then performed.

700-Print-Report-Totals Module   Invoked only once after all records have been processed, this module handles printing of the report totals. For each of the three total lines, the following processing occurs: (1) the total line is formatted; (2) the total line is moved to the output area; (3) the line-spacing indicator is set; and (4) the 890-Write-report-line module is performed.

800-Read-Sales-Trans-Record Module   This module causes the next record to be read from the input sales-transaction file. When end-of-file is detected, the end-of-file indicator is set to YES. Otherwise, each record is tallied to develop the input-transaction record count.

830-Write-Valid-Sales-Trans Module   The valid sales-transaction disk record is in the exact same logical record format as the input sales-transaction record. So, this module simply moves the entire input record to the output disk-record area. Then the valid sales-transaction record is written to disk.

870-Print-Report-Headings Module   The page count of the report is incremented and moved to the second heading line. Then, one by one, each of the four heading lines is moved to the output area, the proper line spacing is set, and the appropriate write module is performed.

880-Write-Report-Top-Line Module   This write module is used only for the first heading line on each page of the report. It causes the printer forms to be skipped to the top of the next page and the top line to be printed. Because the first line of the page is thus used, the lines-used indicator is set to 1.

890-Write-Report-Line Module   This write module is used for all lines of the report other than the first heading line. It provides for variable line spacing in accordance with the value of the line-spacing indicator.

The Complete DATAVAL Program

The first three divisions of the DATAVAL program are shown in Figure 8-24. Note that this code is applicable to both COBOL-74 and COBOL-85. The PROCEDURE DIVISION for the COBOL-74 version is included in Figure 8-25 and for COBOL-85 in Figure 8-26. From earlier studies, you are familiar with all of the COBOL principles used in this program; however, some of the applications involve new twists to previously used principles. Do not be intimidated by the size of this program. Although larger than any previous examples, beyond the data validations elements you just learned about, it is simply a report generation program of the type you learned in Chapter 6. We will first look at some of the forms used in the ENVIRONMENT/DATA DIVISION and then at those of the PROCEDURE DIVISION.

Figure 8-24   First three divisions: Sales-transaction validation program.

```
  1         IDENTIFICATION DIVISION.                            88        01  ST-SALES-TRANSACTION-RECORD.
  2                                                             89            05  ST-RECORD-CODE             PIC X(2).
  3         PROGRAM-ID.    DATAVAL.                             90            05  ST-DATE-OF-SALE.
  4                                                             91                10  ST-MONTH-OF-SALE       PIC X(2).
  5     *     WRITTEN BY T. WELBURN.                            92                10  ST-DAY-OF-SALE         PIC X(2).
  6     *     GENERAL MERCHANDISE SUPPLY COMPANY.               93                10  ST-YEAR-OF-SALE        PIC X(2).
  7     *     MAR  5, 1986.                                     94            05  ST-DEPARTMENT-NUMBER       PIC X(3).
  8     *     REVISED 9-22-89 BY W. PRICE.                      95            05  ST-ITEM-NUMBER             PIC X(7).
  9                                                             96            05  ST-ITEM-DESCRIPTION.
 10     *     THIS PROGRAM WILL READ INPUT SALES TRANSACTION RECORDS  97      10  ST-ITEM-DESC-FIRST-POS     PIC X(1).
 11     *     AND MAKE CERTAIN FIELD VALIDATIONS ON EACH RECORD.      98      10  ST-ITEM-DESC-REST-POS      PIC X(14).
 12     *     AN AUDIT-ERROR LIST WILL BE PREPARED.  EACH VALIDATED   99   05  ST-EMPLOYEE-NUMBER          PIC X(5).
 13     *     RECORD WILL BE WRITTEN TO A DISK FILE.                 100   05  ST-QUANTITY-X               PIC X(5).
 14                                                            101            05  ST-QUANTITY REDEFINES ST-QUANTITY-X
 15     *     EACH RECORD WILL BE PRINTED ON THE AUDIT-ERROR LIST.   102                                   PIC S9(5).
 16     *     IF ANY ERRORS ARE DETECTED FOR A RECORD, EACH ERROR    103   05  ST-PRICE-X                  PIC X(7).
 17     *     WILL BE IDENTIFIED ON THE AUDIT-ERROR LIST.            104   05  ST-PRICE REDEFINES ST-PRICE-X  PIC S9(5)V99.
 18     *     AT THE CONCLUSION OF THE RUN,                          105   05  ST-TYPE-OF-SALE             PIC X(1).
 19     *     RECORD COUNT TOTALS WILL BE PRINTED.                   106
 20                                                            107
 21                                                            108        01  H1-HEADING-LINE-1.
 22         ENVIRONMENT DIVISION.                              109            05  FILLER          PIC X(20)  VALUE "GENERAL MERCHANDISE ".
 23                                                            110            05  FILLER          PIC X(20)  VALUE "SUPPLY COMPANY       ".
 24         CONFIGURATION SECTION.                             111            05  FILLER          PIC X(20)  VALUE "                    ".
 25                                                            112            05  FILLER          PIC X(20)  VALUE "                    ".
 26         SOURCE-COMPUTER.  (system dependent).              113            05  FILLER          PIC X(7)   VALUE "        ".
 27         OBJECT-COMPUTER.  (system dependent).              114            05  H1-MONTH        PIC X(2).
 28                                                            115            05  FILLER          PIC X(1)   VALUE "-".
 29         INPUT-OUTPUT SECTION.                              116            05  H1-DAY          PIC X(2).
 30                                                            117            05  FILLER          PIC X(1)   VALUE "-".
 31         FILE-CONTROL.                                      118            05  H1-YEAR         PIC X(2).
 32             SELECT SALES-TRANSACTION-FILE                  119
 33                 ASSIGN TO (system dependent)               120        01  H2-HEADING-LINE-2.
 34             SELECT AUDIT-ERROR-REPORT                      121            05  FILLER          PIC X(20)  VALUE "SALES TRANSACTION DA".
 35                 ASSIGN TO (system dependent)               122            05  FILLER          PIC X(20)  VALUE "TA VALIDATION - AUDI".
 36             SELECT VALID-SALES-TRANSACTION-FILE            123            05  FILLER          PIC X(20)  VALUE "T/ERROR LIST        ".
 37                 ASSIGN TO (system dependent)               124            05  FILLER          PIC X(20)  VALUE "                    ".
 38                                                            125            05  FILLER          PIC X(12)  VALUE "      PAGE  ".
 39                                                            126            05  H2-PAGE-NBR     PIC ZZ9.
 40         DATA DIVISION.                                     127
 41                                                            128        01  H3-HEADING-LINE-3.
 42         FILE SECTION.                                      129            05  FILLER          PIC X(20)  VALUE "RCD  DATE  DEPT  IT".
 43                                                            130            05  FILLER          PIC X(20)  VALUE "EM        ITEM      ".
 44         FD  SALES-TRANSACTION-FILE                         131            05  FILLER          PIC X(20)  VALUE "   EMP             ".
 45             RECORD CONTAINS 51 CHARACTERS                  132            05  FILLER          PIC X(20)  VALUE "     T             ".
 46             LABEL RECORDS ARE STANDARD.                    133
 47                                                            134        01  H4-HEADING-LINE-4.
 48         01  SALES-TRANSACTION-RECORD     PIC X(51).        135            05  FILLER          PIC X(20)  VALUE "COD  SALE  NBR  NUM".
 49                                                            136            05  FILLER          PIC X(20)  VALUE "BER    DESCRIPTION  ".
 50         FD  AUDIT-ERROR-REPORT                             137            05  FILLER          PIC X(20)  VALUE "  NBR   QTY    PR".
 51             RECORD CONTAINS 132 CHARACTERS                 138            05  FILLER          PIC X(20)  VALUE "ICE  S  ERROR      ".
 52             LABEL RECORDS ARE OMITTED.                     139            05  FILLER          PIC X(20)  VALUE "  M E S S A G E     ".
 53                                                            140
 54         01  AUDIT-ERROR-LINE             PIC X(132).       141        01  AE-AUDIT-ERROR-DETAIL-LINE.
 55                                                            142            05  AE-RECORD-IMAGE-AREA.
 56         FD  VALID-SALES-TRANSACTION-FILE                   143                10  AE-RECORD-CODE         PIC X(2).
 57             RECORD CONTAINS 51 CHARACTERS                  144                10  FILLER                 PIC X(2).
 58             LABEL RECORDS ARE STANDARD.                    145                10  AE-DATE-OF-SALE        PIC X(6).
 59                                                            146                10  FILLER                 PIC X(2).
 60         01  VALID-SALES-TRANSACTION-RECORD  PIC X(51).     147                10  AE-DEPARTMENT-NUMBER   PIC X(3).
 61                                                            148                10  FILLER                 PIC X(2).
 62         WORKING-STORAGE SECTION.                           149                10  AE-ITEM-NUMBER         PIC X(7).
 63                                                            150                10  FILLER                 PIC X(2).
 64         01  WS-SWITCHES.                                   151                10  AE-ITEM-DESCRIPTION    PIC X(15).
 65             05  WS-END-OF-FILE-SWITCH    PIC X(3).         152                10  FILLER                 PIC X(2).
 66                 88  END-OF-FILE             VALUE "YES".   153                10  AE-EMPLOYEE-NUMBER     PIC X(5).
 67             05  WS-ERROR-SWITCH          PIC X(3).         154                10  FILLER                 PIC X(2).
 68                 88  VALID-SALES-TRANS      VALUE "NO ".    155                10  AE-QUANTITY            PIC 99999-.
 69                 88  INVALID-SALES-TRANS    VALUE "YES".    156                10  AE-QUANTITY-X REDEFINES AE-QUANTITY
 70                                                            157                                           PIC X(5).
 71         01  WS-REPORT-CONTROLS.                            158                10  FILLER                 PIC X(1).
 72             05  WS-PAGE-COUNT            PIC S9(3).        159                10  AE-PRICE               PIC 99999V99-.
 73             05  WS-LINES-PER-PAGE        PIC S9(2)  VALUE +54.  160          10  AE-PRICE-X REDEFINES AE-PRICE
 74             05  WS-LINES-USED            PIC S9(2).        161                                           PIC X(7).
 75             05  WS-LINE-SPACING          PIC S9(2).        162                10  FILLER                 PIC X(1).
 76                                                            163                10  AE-TYPE-OF-SALE        PIC X(1).
 77         01  WS-WORK-AREAS.                                 164            05  FILLER                     PIC X(3).
 78             05  WS-DATE-WORK             PIC 9(6).         165            05  AE-ERROR-MESSAGE           PIC X(25).
 79             05  WS-DATE-CONVERSION REDEFINES WS-DATE-WORK. 166
 80                 10  WS-YEAR             PIC 9(2).          167        01  TL-TOTAL-LINE.
 81                 10  WS-MONTH            PIC 9(2).          168            05  FILLER                     PIC X(76).
 82                 10  WS-DAY              PIC 9(2).          169            05  TL-RECORD-COUNT            PIC Z,ZZ9.
 83                                                            170            05  FILLER                     PIC X(1).
 84         01  WS-TOTAL-ACCUMULATORS.                         171            05  TL-RECORD-COUNT-DESCRIPTION  PIC X(13).
 85             05  WS-RECORDS-READ         PIC S9(4).         172
 86             05  WS-VALID-RECORDS        PIC S9(4).         173
 87             05  WS-ERROR-RECORDS        PIC S9(4).
```

Figure 8-25   COBOL-74 PROCEDURE DIVISION: Sales-transaction validation program.

```
174        PROCEDURE DIVISION.                                189
175                                                           190        100-INITIALIZE-VARIABLE-FIELDS.
176        000-VALIDATE-SALES-RECORDS.                        191            MOVE "NO " TO WS-END-OF-FILE-SWITCH.
177            OPEN INPUT SALES-TRANSACTION-FILE              192            MOVE ZEROS TO WS-PAGE-COUNT
178                 OUTPUT AUDIT-ERROR-REPORT                 193                          WS-RECORDS-READ
179                        VALID-SALES-TRANSACTION-FILE.      194                          WS-VALID-RECORDS
180            PERFORM 100-INITIALIZE-VARIABLE-FIELDS.        195                          WS-ERROR-RECORDS.
181            PERFORM 800-READ-SALES-TRANS-RECORD.           196            MOVE WS-LINES-PER-PAGE TO WS-LINES-USED.
182            PERFORM 200-VAL-SALES-TRANSACTION              197            ACCEPT WS-DATE-WORK FROM DATE.
183                UNTIL END-OF-FILE.                         198            MOVE WS-MONTH TO H1-MONTH.
184            PERFORM 700-PRINT-REPORT-TOTALS.               199            MOVE WS-DAY TO H1-DAY.
185            CLOSE SALES-TRANSACTION-FILE                   200            MOVE WS-YEAR TO H1-YEAR.
186                  AUDIT-ERROR-REPORT                       201
187                  VALID-SALES-TRANSACTION-FILE.
188            STOP RUN.
```

Figure 8-25 (continued)

```
202   200-VAL-SALES-TRANSACTION.
203       MOVE "NO " TO WS-ERROR-SWITCH.
204       PERFORM 210-FORMAT-RECORD-IMAGE.
205       PERFORM 220-VAL-SALES-TRANS-FIELDS.
206       IF VALID-SALES-TRANS
207           ADD 1 TO WS-VALID-RECORDS
208           PERFORM 420-PRINT-AUDIT-ERROR-LINE
209           MOVE ST-SALES-TRANSACTION-RECORD
210               TO VALID-SALES-TRANSACTION-RECORD
211           PERFORM 830-WRITE-VALID-SALES-TRANS
212       ELSE
213           ADD 1 TO WS-ERROR-RECORDS.
214       PERFORM 800-READ-SALES-TRANS-RECORD.
215
216   210-FORMAT-RECORD-IMAGE.
217       IF WS-LINES-USED IS NOT LESS THAN WS-LINES-PER-PAGE
218           PERFORM 870-PRINT-REPORT-HEADINGS.
219       MOVE SPACES TO AE-AUDIT-ERROR-DETAIL-LINE.
220       MOVE ST-RECORD-CODE TO AE-RECORD-CODE.
221       MOVE ST-DATE-OF-SALE TO AE-DATE-OF-SALE.
222       MOVE ST-DEPARTMENT-NUMBER TO AE-DEPARTMENT-NUMBER.
223       MOVE ST-ITEM-DESCRIPTION TO AE-ITEM-DESCRIPTION.
224       MOVE ST-EMPLOYEE-NUMBER TO AE-EMPLOYEE-NUMBER.
225       INSPECT ST-QUANTITY-X
226           REPLACING LEADING SPACES BY ZEROS.
227       IF ST-QUANTITY IS NUMERIC
228           MOVE ST-QUANTITY TO AE-QUANTITY
229       ELSE
230           MOVE ST-QUANTITY-X TO AE-QUANTITY-X.
231       INSPECT ST-PRICE-X
232           REPLACING LEADING SPACES BY ZEROS.
233       IF ST-PRICE IS NUMERIC
234           MOVE ST-PRICE TO AE-PRICE
235       ELSE
236           MOVE ST-PRICE-X TO AE-PRICE-X.
237       MOVE ST-TYPE-OF-SALE TO AE-TYPE-OF-SALE.
238
239   220-VAL-SALES-TRANS-FIELDS.
240       PERFORM 310-VAL-RECORD-CODE.
241       PERFORM 320-VAL-DATE-OF-SALE.
242       PERFORM 330-VAL-DEPT-NUMBER.
243       PERFORM 340-VAL-ITEM-NUMBER.
244       PERFORM 350-VAL-ITEM-DESCRIPTION.
245       PERFORM 360-VAL-EMPLOYEE-NUMBER.
246       PERFORM 370-VAL-QUANTITY.
247       IF ST-PRICE IS NUMERIC
248           PERFORM 380-VAL-PRICE
249       ELSE
250           MOVE "PRICE NOT NUMERIC" TO AE-ERROR-MESSAGE
251           PERFORM 410-IDENTIFY-ERROR-TYPE.
252       PERFORM 390-VAL-TYPE-OF-SALE.
253
254   310-VAL-RECORD-CODE.
255       IF ST-RECORD-CODE IS NOT EQUAL TO "27"
256           MOVE "INVALID RECORD CODE" TO AE-ERROR-MESSAGE
257           PERFORM 410-IDENTIFY-ERROR-TYPE.
258
259   320-VAL-DATE-OF-SALE.
260       INSPECT ST-MONTH-OF-SALE
261           REPLACING LEADING SPACES BY ZERO.
262       IF ST-MONTH-OF-SALE IS NOT NUMERIC
263       OR ST-MONTH-OF-SALE IS LESS THAN "01"
264       OR ST-MONTH-OF-SALE IS GREATER THAN "12"
265           MOVE "INVALID MONTH" TO AE-ERROR-MESSAGE
266           PERFORM 410-IDENTIFY-ERROR-TYPE.
267       IF ST-DAY-OF-SALE IS NOT NUMERIC
268       OR ST-DAY-OF-SALE IS LESS THAN "01"
269       OR ST-DAY-OF-SALE IS GREATER THAN "31"
270           MOVE "INVALID DAY" TO AE-ERROR-MESSAGE
271           PERFORM 410-IDENTIFY-ERROR-TYPE.
272       IF ST-YEAR-OF-SALE IS NOT NUMERIC
273           MOVE "YEAR NOT NUMERIC" TO AE-ERROR-MESSAGE
274           PERFORM 410-IDENTIFY-ERROR-TYPE.
275
276   330-VAL-DEPT-NUMBER.
277       INSPECT ST-DEPARTMENT-NUMBER
278           REPLACING LEADING SPACES BY ZEROS.
279       IF ST-DEPARTMENT-NUMBER IS NOT NUMERIC
280           MOVE "DEPT. NO. NOT NUMERIC" TO AE-ERROR-MESSAGE
281           PERFORM 410-IDENTIFY-ERROR-TYPE.
282       IF ST-DEPARTMENT-NUMBER IS EQUAL TO ZERO
283           MOVE "DEPT. NO. NOT PRESENT" TO AE-ERROR-MESSAGE
284           PERFORM 410-IDENTIFY-ERROR-TYPE.
285
286   340-VAL-ITEM-NUMBER.
287       INSPECT ST-ITEM-NUMBER
288           REPLACING LEADING SPACES BY ZEROS.
289       IF ST-ITEM-NUMBER IS NOT NUMERIC
290           MOVE "ITEM NO. NOT NUMERIC" TO AE-ERROR-MESSAGE
291           PERFORM 410-IDENTIFY-ERROR-TYPE.
292       IF ST-ITEM-NUMBER IS EQUAL TO ZERO
293           MOVE "ITEM NO. NOT PRESENT" TO AE-ERROR-MESSAGE
294           PERFORM 410-IDENTIFY-ERROR-TYPE.
295
296   350-VAL-ITEM-DESCRIPTION.
297       IF ST-ITEM-DESCRIPTION IS EQUAL TO SPACES
298           MOVE "ITEM DESC. NOT PRESENT" TO AE-ERROR-MESSAGE
299           PERFORM 410-IDENTIFY-ERROR-TYPE.
300       IF ST-ITEM-DESC-FIRST-POS IS EQUAL TO SPACE
301       AND ST-ITEM-DESC-REST-POS IS NOT EQUAL TO SPACES
302           MOVE "ITEM DESC. NOT LEFT JUST." TO AE-ERROR-MESSAGE
303           PERFORM 410-IDENTIFY-ERROR-TYPE.
304
305   360-VAL-EMPLOYEE-NUMBER.
306       INSPECT ST-EMPLOYEE-NUMBER
307           REPLACING LEADING SPACES BY ZEROS.
308       IF ST-EMPLOYEE-NUMBER IS NOT NUMERIC
309       OR ST-EMPLOYEE-NUMBER IS LESS THAN "10001"
310       OR ST-EMPLOYEE-NUMBER IS GREATER THAN "79999"
311           MOVE "INVALID EMPLOYEE NUMBER" TO AE-ERROR-MESSAGE
312           PERFORM 410-IDENTIFY-ERROR-TYPE.
313
314   370-VAL-QUANTITY.
315       IF ST-QUANTITY-X IS NOT NUMERIC
316           MOVE "QUANTITY NOT NUMERIC" TO AE-ERROR-MESSAGE
317           PERFORM 410-IDENTIFY-ERROR-TYPE.
318       IF ST-QUANTITY-X IS EQUAL TO ZERO
319           MOVE "QUANTITY NOT PRESENT" TO AE-ERROR-MESSAGE
320           PERFORM 410-IDENTIFY-ERROR-TYPE.
321
322   380-VAL-PRICE.
323       IF ST-PRICE-X IS EQUAL TO ZERO
324           MOVE "PRICE NOT PRESENT" TO AE-ERROR-MESSAGE
325           PERFORM 410-IDENTIFY-ERROR-TYPE.
326       IF ST-PRICE IS NOT GREATER THAN ZERO
327           MOVE "PRICE NOT POSITIVE" TO AE-ERROR-MESSAGE
328           PERFORM 410-IDENTIFY-ERROR-TYPE.
329       IF ST-DEPARTMENT-NUMBER IS LESS THAN "500"
330       AND ST-PRICE IS GREATER THAN +00999.99
331           MOVE "PRICE NOT CONSISTENT" TO AE-ERROR-MESSAGE
332           PERFORM 410-IDENTIFY-ERROR-TYPE.
333
334   390-VAL-TYPE-OF-SALE.
335       IF ST-TYPE-OF-SALE IS NOT EQUAL TO "$"
336       AND ST-TYPE-OF-SALE IS NOT EQUAL TO "C"
337       AND ST-TYPE-OF-SALE IS NOT EQUAL TO "R"
338           MOVE "INVALID TYPE OF SALE CODE" TO AE-ERROR-MESSAGE
339           PERFORM 410-IDENTIFY-ERROR-TYPE.
340
341   410-IDENTIFY-ERROR-TYPE.
342       IF INVALID-SALES-TRANS
343           MOVE SPACES TO AE-RECORD-IMAGE-AREA.
344       PERFORM 420-PRINT-AUDIT-ERROR-LINE.
345       MOVE "YES" TO WS-ERROR-SWITCH.
346
347   420-PRINT-AUDIT-ERROR-LINE.
348       MOVE AE-AUDIT-ERROR-DETAIL-LINE TO AUDIT-ERROR-LINE.
349       IF VALID-SALES-TRANS
350           MOVE 2 TO WS-LINE-SPACING
351       ELSE
352           MOVE 1 TO WS-LINE-SPACING.
353       PERFORM 890-WRITE-REPORT-LINE.
354
355   700-PRINT-REPORT-TOTALS.
356       MOVE SPACES TO TL-TOTAL-LINE.
357       MOVE WS-RECORDS-READ TO TL-RECORD-COUNT.
358       MOVE "RECORDS READ" TO TL-RECORD-COUNT-DESCRIPTION.
359       MOVE TL-TOTAL-LINE TO AUDIT-ERROR-LINE.
360       MOVE 3 TO WS-LINE-SPACING.
361       PERFORM 890-WRITE-REPORT-LINE.
362       MOVE WS-VALID-RECORDS TO TL-RECORD-COUNT.
363       MOVE "VALID RECORDS" TO TL-RECORD-COUNT-DESCRIPTION.
364       MOVE TL-TOTAL-LINE TO AUDIT-ERROR-LINE.
365       MOVE 1 TO WS-LINE-SPACING.
366       PERFORM 890-WRITE-REPORT-LINE.
367       MOVE WS-ERROR-RECORDS TO TL-RECORD-COUNT.
368       MOVE "ERROR RECORDS" TO TL-RECORD-COUNT-DESCRIPTION.
369       MOVE TL-TOTAL-LINE TO AUDIT-ERROR-LINE.
370       PERFORM 890-WRITE-REPORT-LINE.
371
372   800-READ-SALES-TRANS-RECORD.
373       READ SALES-TRANSACTION-FILE INTO ST-SALES-TRANSACTION-RECORD
374           AT END MOVE "YES" TO WS-END-OF-FILE-SWITCH.
375       IF NOT END-OF-FILE
376           ADD 1 TO WS-RECORDS-READ.
377
378   830-WRITE-VALID-SALES-TRANS.
379       WRITE VALID-SALES-TRANSACTION-RECORD.
380
381   870-PRINT-REPORT-HEADINGS.
382       ADD 1 TO WS-PAGE-COUNT.
383       MOVE WS-PAGE-COUNT TO H2-PAGE-NBR.
384       MOVE H1-HEADING-LINE-1 TO AUDIT-ERROR-LINE.
385       PERFORM 880-WRITE-REPORT-TOP-LINE.
386       MOVE H2-HEADING-LINE-2 TO AUDIT-ERROR-LINE.
387       MOVE 1 TO WS-LINE-SPACING.
388       PERFORM 890-WRITE-REPORT-LINE.
389       MOVE H3-HEADING-LINE-3 TO AUDIT-ERROR-LINE.
390       MOVE 2 TO WS-LINE-SPACING.
391       PERFORM 890-WRITE-REPORT-LINE.
392       MOVE H4-HEADING-LINE-4 TO AUDIT-ERROR-LINE.
393       MOVE 1 TO WS-LINE-SPACING.
394       PERFORM 890-WRITE-REPORT-LINE.
395
396   880-WRITE-REPORT-TOP-LINE.
397       WRITE AUDIT-ERROR-LINE
398           AFTER ADVANCING PAGE.
399       MOVE 1 TO WS-LINES-USED.
400
401   890-WRITE-REPORT-LINE.
402       WRITE AUDIT-ERROR-LINE
403           AFTER ADVANCING WS-LINE-SPACING.
404       ADD WS-LINE-SPACING TO WS-LINES-USED.
```

Figure 8-26 COBOL-85 PROCEDURE DIVISION: Sales-transaction validation program.

```
174        PROCEDURE DIVISION.
175
176        000-VALIDATE-SALES-RECORDS.
177            OPEN INPUT SALES-TRANSACTION-FILE
178                 OUTPUT AUDIT-ERROR-REPORT
179                        VALID-SALES-TRANSACTION-FILE
180            PERFORM 100-INITIALIZE-VARIABLE-FIELDS
181            PERFORM 800-READ-SALES-TRANS-RECORD
182            PERFORM 200-VAL-SALES-TRANSACTION
183                UNTIL END-OF-FILE
184            PERFORM 700-PRINT-REPORT-TOTALS
185            CLOSE SALES-TRANSACTION-FILE
186                  AUDIT-ERROR-REPORT
187                  VALID-SALES-TRANSACTION-FILE
188            STOP RUN.
189
190        100-INITIALIZE-VARIABLE-FIELDS.
191            MOVE "NO " TO WS-END-OF-FILE-SWITCH
192            INITIALIZE WS-PAGE-COUNT, WS-TOTAL-ACCUMULATORS
193            MOVE WS-LINES-PER-PAGE TO WS-LINES-USED
194            ACCEPT WS-DATE-WORK FROM DATE
195            MOVE WS-MONTH TO H1-MONTH
196            MOVE WS-DAY TO H1-DAY
197            MOVE WS-YEAR TO H1-YEAR.
198
199        200-VAL-SALES-TRANSACTION.
200            MOVE "NO " TO WS-ERROR-SWITCH
201            PERFORM 210-FORMAT-RECORD-IMAGE
202            PERFORM 220-VAL-SALES-TRANS-FIELDS
203            IF VALID-SALES-TRANS
204                ADD 1 TO WS-VALID-RECORDS
205                PERFORM 420-PRINT-AUDIT-ERROR-LINE
206                MOVE ST-SALES-TRANSACTION-RECORD
207                     TO VALID-SALES-TRANSACTION-RECORD
208                PERFORM 830-WRITE-VALID-SALES-TRANS
209            ELSE
210                ADD 1 TO WS-ERROR-RECORDS
211            END-IF
212            PERFORM 800-READ-SALES-TRANS-RECORD.
213
214        210-FORMAT-RECORD-IMAGE.
215            IF WS-LINES-USED IS NOT LESS THAN WS-LINES-PER-PAGE
216                PERFORM 870-PRINT-REPORT-HEADINGS
217            END-IF
218            MOVE SPACES TO AE-AUDIT-ERROR-DETAIL-LINE
219            MOVE ST-RECORD-CODE TO AE-RECORD-CODE
220            MOVE ST-DATE-OF-SALE TO AE-DATE-OF-SALE
221            MOVE ST-DEPARTMENT-NUMBER TO AE-DEPARTMENT-NUMBER
222            MOVE ST-ITEM-DESCRIPTION TO AE-ITEM-DESCRIPTION
223            MOVE ST-EMPLOYEE-NUMBER TO AE-EMPLOYEE-NUMBER
224            INSPECT ST-QUANTITY-X
225                REPLACING LEADING SPACES BY ZEROS
226            IF ST-QUANTITY IS NUMERIC
227                MOVE ST-QUANTITY TO AE-QUANTITY
228            ELSE
229                MOVE ST-QUANTITY-X TO AE-QUANTITY-X
230            END-IF
231            INSPECT ST-PRICE-X
232                REPLACING LEADING SPACES BY ZEROS
233            IF ST-PRICE IS NUMERIC
234                MOVE ST-PRICE TO AE-PRICE
235            ELSE
236                MOVE ST-PRICE-X TO AE-PRICE-X
237            END-IF
238            MOVE ST-TYPE-OF-SALE TO AE-TYPE-OF-SALE.
239
240        220-VAL-SALES-TRANS-FIELDS.
241            PERFORM 310-VAL-RECORD-CODE
242            PERFORM 320-VAL-DATE-OF-SALE
243            PERFORM 330-VAL-DEPT-NUMBER
244            PERFORM 340-VAL-ITEM-NUMBER
245            PERFORM 350-VAL-ITEM-DESCRIPTION
246            PERFORM 360-VAL-EMPLOYEE-NUMBER
247            PERFORM 370-VAL-QUANTITY
248            IF ST-PRICE IS NUMERIC
249                PERFORM 380-VAL-PRICE
250            ELSE
251                MOVE "PRICE NOT NUMERIC" TO AE-ERROR-MESSAGE
252                PERFORM 410-IDENTIFY-ERROR-TYPE
253            END-IF
254            PERFORM 390-VAL-TYPE-OF-SALE.
255
256        310-VAL-RECORD-CODE.
257            IF ST-RECORD-CODE IS NOT EQUAL TO "27"
258                MOVE "INVALID RECORD CODE" TO AE-ERROR-MESSAGE
259                PERFORM 410-IDENTIFY-ERROR-TYPE
260            END-IF.
261
262        320-VAL-DATE-OF-SALE.
263            INSPECT ST-MONTH-OF-SALE
264                REPLACING LEADING SPACES BY ZERO
265            IF ST-MONTH-OF-SALE IS NOT NUMERIC
266            OR ST-MONTH-OF-SALE IS LESS THAN "01"
267            OR ST-MONTH-OF-SALE IS GREATER THAN "12"
268                MOVE "INVALID MONTH" TO AE-ERROR-MESSAGE
269                PERFORM 410-IDENTIFY-ERROR-TYPE
270            END-IF
```

```
271            IF ST-DAY-OF-SALE IS NOT NUMERIC
272            OR ST-DAY-OF-SALE IS LESS THAN "01"
273            OR ST-DAY-OF-SALE IS GREATER THAN "31"
274                MOVE "INVALID DAY" TO AE-ERROR-MESSAGE
275                PERFORM 410-IDENTIFY-ERROR-TYPE
276            END-IF
277            IF ST-YEAR-OF-SALE IS NOT NUMERIC
278                MOVE "YEAR NOT NUMERIC" TO AE-ERROR-MESSAGE
279                PERFORM 410-IDENTIFY-ERROR-TYPE
280            END-IF.
281
282        330-VAL-DEPT-NUMBER.
283            INSPECT ST-DEPARTMENT-NUMBER
284                REPLACING LEADING SPACES BY ZEROS
285            IF ST-DEPARTMENT-NUMBER IS NOT NUMERIC
286                MOVE "DEPT. NO. NOT NUMERIC" TO AE-ERROR-MESSAGE
287                PERFORM 410-IDENTIFY-ERROR-TYPE
288            END-IF
289            IF ST-DEPARTMENT-NUMBER IS EQUAL TO ZERO
290                MOVE "DEPT. NO. NOT PRESENT" TO AE-ERROR-MESSAGE
291                PERFORM 410-IDENTIFY-ERROR-TYPE
292            END-IF.
293
294        340-VAL-ITEM-NUMBER.
295            INSPECT ST-ITEM-NUMBER
296                REPLACING LEADING SPACES BY ZEROS
297            IF ST-ITEM-NUMBER IS NOT NUMERIC
298                MOVE "ITEM NO. NOT NUMERIC" TO AE-ERROR-MESSAGE
299                PERFORM 410-IDENTIFY-ERROR-TYPE
300            END-IF
301            IF ST-ITEM-NUMBER IS EQUAL TO ZERO
302                MOVE "ITEM NO. NOT PRESENT" TO AE-ERROR-MESSAGE
303                PERFORM 410-IDENTIFY-ERROR-TYPE
304            END-IF.
305
306        350-VAL-ITEM-DESCRIPTION.
307            IF ST-ITEM-DESCRIPTION IS EQUAL TO SPACES
308                MOVE "ITEM DESC. NOT PRESENT" TO AE-ERROR-MESSAGE
309                PERFORM 410-IDENTIFY-ERROR-TYPE
310            END-IF
311            IF ST-ITEM-DESC-FIRST-POS IS EQUAL TO SPACE
312            AND ST-ITEM-DESC-REST-POS IS NOT EQUAL TO SPACES
313                MOVE "ITEM DESC. NOT LEFT JUST." TO AE-ERROR-MESSAGE
314                PERFORM 410-IDENTIFY-ERROR-TYPE
315            END-IF.
316
317        360-VAL-EMPLOYEE-NUMBER.
318            INSPECT ST-EMPLOYEE-NUMBER
319                REPLACING LEADING SPACES BY ZEROS
320            IF ST-EMPLOYEE-NUMBER IS NOT NUMERIC
321            OR ST-EMPLOYEE-NUMBER IS LESS THAN "10001"
322            OR ST-EMPLOYEE-NUMBER IS GREATER THAN "79999"
323                MOVE "INVALID EMPLOYEE NUMBER" TO AE-ERROR-MESSAGE
324                PERFORM 410-IDENTIFY-ERROR-TYPE
325            END-IF.
326
327        370-VAL-QUANTITY.
328            IF ST-QUANTITY-X IS NOT NUMERIC
329                MOVE "QUANTITY NOT NUMERIC" TO AE-ERROR-MESSAGE
330                PERFORM 410-IDENTIFY-ERROR-TYPE
331            END-IF
332            IF ST-QUANTITY-X IS EQUAL TO ZERO
333                MOVE "QUANTITY NOT PRESENT" TO AE-ERROR-MESSAGE
334                PERFORM 410-IDENTIFY-ERROR-TYPE
335            END-IF.
336
337        380-VAL-PRICE.
338            IF ST-PRICE-X IS EQUAL TO ZERO
339                MOVE "PRICE NOT PRESENT" TO AE-ERROR-MESSAGE
340                PERFORM 410-IDENTIFY-ERROR-TYPE
341            END-IF
342            IF ST-PRICE IS NOT GREATER THAN ZERO
343                MOVE "PRICE NOT POSITIVE" TO AE-ERROR-MESSAGE
344                PERFORM 410-IDENTIFY-ERROR-TYPE
345            END-IF
346            IF ST-DEPARTMENT-NUMBER IS LESS THAN "500"
347            AND ST-PRICE IS GREATER THAN 999.99
348                MOVE "PRICE NOT CONSISTENT" TO AE-ERROR-MESSAGE
349                PERFORM 410-IDENTIFY-ERROR-TYPE
350            END-IF.
351
352        390-VAL-TYPE-OF-SALE.
353            IF ST-TYPE-OF-SALE IS NOT EQUAL TO "$"
354            AND ST-TYPE-OF-SALE IS NOT EQUAL TO "C"
355            AND ST-TYPE-OF-SALE IS NOT EQUAL TO "R"
356                MOVE "INVALID TYPE OF SALE CODE" TO AE-ERROR-MESSAGE
357                PERFORM 410-IDENTIFY-ERROR-TYPE
358            END-IF.
359
360        410-IDENTIFY-ERROR-TYPE.
361            IF INVALID-SALES-TRANS
362                MOVE SPACES TO AE-RECORD-IMAGE-AREA
363            END-IF
364            PERFORM 420-PRINT-AUDIT-ERROR-LINE
365            MOVE "YES" TO WS-ERROR-SWITCH.
366
```

Figure 8-26 (continued)

```
367    420-PRINT-AUDIT-ERROR-LINE.                              398
368        MOVE AE-AUDIT-ERROR-DETAIL-LINE TO AUDIT-ERROR-LINE  399    830-WRITE-VALID-SALES-TRANS.
369        IF VALID-SALES-TRANS                                 400        WRITE VALID-SALES-TRANSACTION-RECORD.
370            MOVE 2 TO WS-LINE-SPACING                         401
371        ELSE                                                 402    870-PRINT-REPORT-HEADINGS.
372            MOVE 1 TO WS-LINE-SPACING                         403        ADD 1 TO WS-PAGE-COUNT
373        END-IF                                               404        MOVE WS-PAGE-COUNT TO H2-PAGE-NBR
374        PERFORM 890-WRITE-REPORT-LINE.                       405        MOVE H1-HEADING-LINE-1 TO AUDIT-ERROR-LINE
375                                                             406        PERFORM 880-WRITE-REPORT-TOP-LINE
376    700-PRINT-REPORT-TOTALS.                                 407        MOVE H2-HEADING-LINE-2 TO AUDIT-ERROR-LINE
377        MOVE SPACES TO TL-TOTAL-LINE                         408        MOVE 1 TO WS-LINE-SPACING
378        MOVE WS-RECORDS-READ TO TL-RECORD-COUNT              409        PERFORM 890-WRITE-REPORT-LINE
379        MOVE "RECORDS READ" TO TL-RECORD-COUNT-DESCRIPTION   410        MOVE H3-HEADING-LINE-3 TO AUDIT-ERROR-LINE
380        MOVE TL-TOTAL-LINE TO AUDIT-ERROR-LINE               411        MOVE 2 TO WS-LINE-SPACING
381        MOVE 3 TO WS-LINE-SPACING                            412        PERFORM 890-WRITE-REPORT-LINE
382        PERFORM 890-WRITE-REPORT-LINE                        413        MOVE H4-HEADING-LINE-4 TO AUDIT-ERROR-LINE
383        MOVE WS-VALID-RECORDS TO TL-RECORD-COUNT             414        MOVE 1 TO WS-LINE-SPACING
384        MOVE "VALID RECORDS" TO TL-RECORD-COUNT-DESCRIPTION  415        PERFORM 890-WRITE-REPORT-LINE.
385        MOVE TL-TOTAL-LINE TO AUDIT-ERROR-LINE               416
386        MOVE 1 TO WS-LINE-SPACING                            417    880-WRITE-REPORT-TOP-LINE.
387        PERFORM 890-WRITE-REPORT-LINE                        418        WRITE AUDIT-ERROR-LINE
388        MOVE WS-ERROR-RECORDS TO TL-RECORD-COUNT             419            AFTER ADVANCING PAGE
389        MOVE "ERROR RECORDS" TO TL-RECORD-COUNT-DESCRIPTION  420        MOVE 1 TO WS-LINES-USED.
390        MOVE TL-TOTAL-LINE TO AUDIT-ERROR-LINE               421
391        PERFORM 890-WRITE-REPORT-LINE.                       422    890-WRITE-REPORT-LINE.
392                                                             423        WRITE AUDIT-ERROR-LINE
393    800-READ-SALES-TRANS-RECORD.                             424            AFTER ADVANCING WS-LINE-SPACING
394        READ SALES-TRANSACTION-FILE INTO ST-SALES-TRANSACTION-RECORD  425        ADD WS-LINE-SPACING TO WS-LINES-USED.
395            AT END MOVE "YES" TO WS-END-OF-FILE-SWITCH
396            NOT AT END  ADD 1 TO WS-RECORDS-READ
397        END-READ.
```

ENVIRONMENT/DATA DIVISION Coding
Three Files—Effect on the ENVIRONMENT DIVISION

The previous program examples coded in this text have been limited to two files: one input file and one output file. This program is an example with multiple (two) output files. Hence, as you can see in Figure 8-24, there are three file-control entries—three SELECT sentences—in the FILE-CONTROL paragraph. Having three file-control entries means, of course, that three FD entries must be specified in the FILE SECTION of the DATA DIVISION.

Condition-Name for End-of-File Condition

In previous programs of the text, a relation condition was used in the PROCEDURE DIVISION to test for end-of-file. As shown in Figure 8-27, an 88-level condition-name entry—END-OF-FILE—has been affixed to the WS-END-OF-FILE-SWITCH in this program.

By assigning a condition-name in the DATA DIVISION, end-of-file tests can be made in the PROCEDURE DIVISION through specification of convenient and self-documenting condition-name tests.

Error-Switch Control Field

Remember that the program specifications require that for any record in error, the record image together with an error message be printed. However, if a record includes more than one error, the record image must not be repeated on subsequent error message lines. This is accomplished in the PROCEDURE DIVISION by the WS-ERROR-SWITCH field, which is used to keep track of whether or not an error has occurred for each input sales-transaction record. As you will see when

Figure 8-27
Condition-name for end-of-file.

```
          01  WS-SWITCHES.
              05  WS-END-OF-FILE-SWITCH        PIC X(3).
Condition-  →  88  END-OF-FILE                              VALUE "YES".
name entry
              .
              .
              .
Condition-     PERFORM 200-VAL-SALES-TRANSACTION
name test   →     UNTIL END-OF-FILE
```

studying the PROCEDURE DIVISION coding, the field is set to NO before validation begins for each record. When an error is detected, the switch is set to YES.

Page Line Span

Refer to the WS-REPORT-CONTROLS of the WORKING-STORAGE SECTION in Figure 8-24 and you will see that the line-span field, WS-LINES-PER-PAGE (program line 73), has been set to a value of +54, rather than +57 as it was in the PAYROLL program in Chapter 7. The line span has been shortened because the programming specifications call for all lines for the same record to be printed on the same page—not continued from one report page to the next. This concept will be further explained later in this Topic.

Redefinition of Input Quantity and Price Fields

For the purpose of data validation, input fields are commonly defined as alphanumeric, as you have already learned in the preceding Topic. Sometimes, however, numeric-field definition is required. Observe that the alphanumeric ST-QUANTITY-X field has been redefined as a numeric field: ST-QUANTITY. Similarly, the alphanumeric ST-PRICE-X field has been redefined as the numeric ST-PRICE field.

These redefinitions are required because these two numeric fields could be entered as either positive or negative values. When a negative value is entered, a minus sign should be printed on the audit/error list. To provide for the printing of a minus sign, the output audit/error list fields must be defined with a numeric-edited PICTURE character-string.

Remember that an alphanumeric sending field cannot be moved to a numeric-edited receiving field. Hence, the numeric ST-QUANTITY and ST-PRICE data-names must be used to move the input fields to the output report line.

The program specifications also call for a validation of the price field to ensure that it is positive. A convenient way to make such a validation is to use the sign-test form of the IF statement. When making a sign test, a numeric data-name must be specified. As you will see, the ST-PRICE data-name will also be used in the IF-statement sign test prior to executing the 380-VAL-PRICE module.

Redefinition of Quantity and Price Fields on the Audit/Error Line

As mentioned above, if the quantity or price fields are negative, we want to print a minus sign as documentation on the audit/error list. The picture character-strings for AE-QUANTITY and AE-PRICE provide for this negative-value indication. However, if the input ST-QUANTITY or ST-PRICE fields are incorrectly keyed with nonnumeric values, the nonnumeric values must be moved to the AE-QUANTITY-X and the AE-PRICE-X fields. If a field containing nonnumeric characters were moved to a numeric-edited field, a data exception might occur.

In Figure 8-28, notice that the AE-QUANTITY field has been defined before the AE-QUANTITY-X field and that AE-PRICE is coded before AE-PRICE-X. This is because the numeric-edited fields containing the minus signs are one position longer than their respective alphanumeric fields. Remember that a field with a REDEFINES clause must be equal to or shorter in length than the field that it is redefining. Because of this rule, the longer fields AE-QUANTITY and AE-PRICE must be defined before their shorter redefinitions. (*Note:* COBOL-85 does not impose this restriction.)

PROCEDURE DIVISION Coding

The PROCEDURE DIVISION introduces several variations on techniques you have seen in previous example programs. The following topics are described here:

■ Using a switch to control valid/invalid record processing

■ Controlling the report paging (page control)

Figure 8-28 Redefinition of quantity and price fields on the audit/error line.

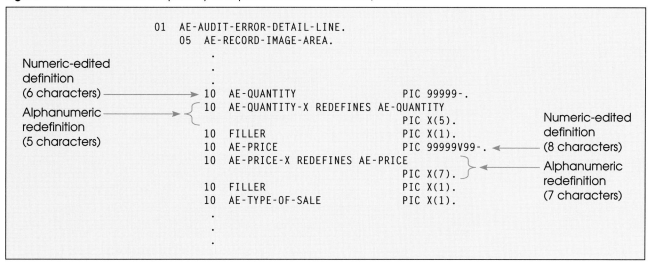

- Selecting the proper move for the Quantity and Price fields: numeric or alphanumeric

- Executing the Price validation module conditionally

- Formatting and printing the error line

- Writing records to disk or tape

In these descriptions, the sections of code that are reproduced are the COBOL-74 versions. The descriptions are equally applicable to the COBOL-85 program.

Valid/Invalid Record Control

Valid/invalid record control is accomplished by means of the switch field WS-ERROR-SWITCH. With each new record, it is given a value of NO. If one or more errors have been found, the field will be set to YES. To understand the sequence of events, assume that a record has been read with an invalid Record-code field. Referring to Figure 8-29, the following will occur:

1. A value of "NO" is moved to WS-ERROR-SWITCH.

2. Control is transferred to the 220-VAL-SALES-TRANS-FIELDS module.

3. Control is transferred to the 310-VAL-RECORD-CODE module.

4. Since the Record-code field is not 27, the IF statement is true—causing control to be transferred to the 410-IDENTIFY-ERROR-TYPE module.

5. A value of "YES" is moved to WS-ERROR-SWITCH.

From the 220-VAL-SALES-TRANS-FIELDS module, each of the validation modules will be executed. For each field that is invalid, YES will be moved to WS-ERROR-SWITCH; this will result in no change to WS-ERROR-SWITCH because it is already YES.

6. Control is ultimately returned to this IF statement.

7. Since VALID-SALES-TRANS is false (this is the condition-name for WS-ERROR-SWITCH contains NO), 1 is added to WS-ERROR-RECORDS. Had no error been detected in any of the fields, WS-ERROR-SWITCH would contain "YES" and VALID-SALES-TRANS would have been true. In that case, the true actions would have been executed.

Figure 8-29
Error-switch control logic.

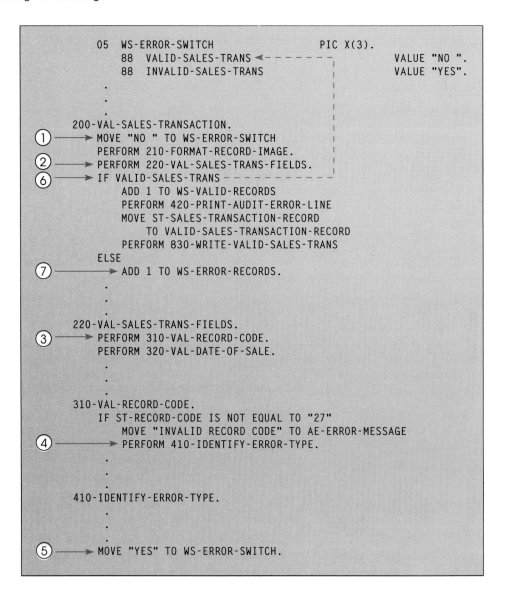

```
                05  WS-ERROR-SWITCH                         PIC X(3).
                    88  VALID-SALES-TRANS ◄ - - - - - - -              VALUE "NO ".
                    88  INVALID-SALES-TRANS                    │       VALUE "YES".
                                .                              │
                                .                              │
                                .                              │
                200-VAL-SALES-TRANSACTION.                     │
      ①────►        MOVE "NO " TO WS-ERROR-SWITCH              │
                    PERFORM 210-FORMAT-RECORD-IMAGE.           │
      ②────►        PERFORM 220-VAL-SALES-TRANS-FIELDS.        │
      ⑥────►        IF VALID-SALES-TRANS - - - - - - - - - - -┘
                        ADD 1 TO WS-VALID-RECORDS
                        PERFORM 420-PRINT-AUDIT-ERROR-LINE
                        MOVE ST-SALES-TRANSACTION-RECORD
                            TO VALID-SALES-TRANSACTION-RECORD
                        PERFORM 830-WRITE-VALID-SALES-TRANS
                    ELSE
      ⑦────►            ADD 1 TO WS-ERROR-RECORDS.
                                .
                                .
                                .
                220-VAL-SALES-TRANS-FIELDS.
      ③────►        PERFORM 310-VAL-RECORD-CODE.
                    PERFORM 320-VAL-DATE-OF-SALE.
                                .
                                .
                                .
                310-VAL-RECORD-CODE.
                    IF ST-RECORD-CODE IS NOT EQUAL TO "27"
                        MOVE "INVALID RECORD CODE" TO AE-ERROR-MESSAGE
      ④────►            PERFORM 410-IDENTIFY-ERROR-TYPE.
                                .
                                .
                                .
                410-IDENTIFY-ERROR-TYPE.
                                .
                                .
                                .
      ⑤────►        MOVE "YES" TO WS-ERROR-SWITCH.
```

Testing for End-of-Page

In the PAYROLL program, the end-of-page test was made before formatting and printing each detail line. Consider what could happen if the end-of-page test were handled in the same way in DATAVAL for a record with two or more errors for one field. If the end-of-page condition occurred immediately after the first error line, the program would skip to the next page and print the headings. The second error line (and any others) would then be printed as the first detail line of the new page, and the record-image area would not be repeated.

This creates clumsy reading. For instance, if a reader of the report were looking at the last record image on the preceding page, he or she might overlook the errors printed on the following page. When viewing the continuation page, the reader would be forced to refer to the preceding page to determine which record contained the errors. Hence, the programming specifications for this program require all the lines for a given record to be printed on the same page.

This potential problem is avoided by performing the end-of-page test only before printing the first line for each input record (see the first statement in the 210 procedure).

An alternative technique is to print, at the bottom of the page, a continuation note that indicates that additional error lines continue on the next page. Then, on the next page, the record-image area would be reprinted on the first line. A continued indication might also appear on the new page. If each field could include many error messages (for instance, 10 or 12), you would probably want to use this method. As you can undoubtedly appreciate, this approach requires more program logic.

The choice of 54 lines as the page line-span is somewhat arbitrary. However, 54 lines will provide a span that both (1) does not leave too much unused space at the bottom of the report when the last record on the page has only one line, and (2) provides sufficient space to print all the error lines on the page when the last record has many errors.

Alternative MOVE Statements to Edited Numeric or Unedited Alphanumeric Fields

Both the Quantity and Price fields are numeric values that can be signed. If they are numeric, they must be printed from a numeric-edited field. However, if they contain nonnumeric characters (and hence are in error), they must be printed from alphanumeric fields, since a move of alphanumeric data to a numeric-edited field could cause a data exception.

This is handled as illustrated in Figure 8-30 for the ST-QUANTITY field (the action with the ST-PRICE field will be the same). If the ST-QUANTITY field of the input sales-transaction record is numeric, it is moved to the AE-QUANTITY field of the AE-AUDIT-ERROR-DETAIL-LINE. If it is not numeric, it is moved to the AE-QUANTITY-X field. This sequence will (1) provide for the appropriate editing of numeric values, (2) display correctly fields that contain invalid nonnumeric characters, and (3) eliminate the possibility of a data exception.

Figure 8-30
Alternate MOVE statements to either edited numeric or unedited alphanumeric fields on the audit/error line.

```
01  ST-SALES-TRANSACTION-RECORD.
        .
        .
        .
    05  ST-QUANTITY-X                    PIC X(5).
    05  ST-QUANTITY REDEFINES ST-QUANTITY-X
                                         PIC S9(5).
        .
        .
        .
01  AE-AUDIT-ERROR-DETAIL-LINE.
        .
        .
        .
        10  AE-QUANTITY                  PIC 99999-.
        10  AE-QUANTITY-X REDEFINES AE-QUANTITY
                                         PIC X(5).
        .
        .
        .
210-FORMAT-RECORD-IMAGE.
        .
        .
        .
    IF ST-QUANTITY IS NUMERIC                        Numeric to numeric-edited
        MOVE ST-QUANTITY TO AE-QUANTITY
    ELSE                                             Alphanumeric to
        MOVE ST-QUANTITY-X TO AE-QUANTITY-X.         alphanumeric
```

Numeric Class Test Before Performing 380-VAL-PRICE Module

Notice in Figure 8-31 that, unlike the other field validation modules, the 380-VAL-PRICE module is performed conditionally. That is, it is not performed unless the ST-PRICE field contains only valid numeric digits. If the ST-PRICE field contains one or more nonnumeric characters, the error is identified and the 380-VAL-PRICE module is skipped.

This conditional execution of the 380-VAL-PRICE module is coded to ensure that a data exception does not occur when making the various numeric and sign-test comparisons specified for the ST-PRICE field. Of course, protection against the data exceptions could alternatively be provided by construction of appropriate nested IF statements. However, the coding shown provides the correct handling and simplifies the logic of the 380-VAL-PRICE module.

Formatting the Error Line

As shown in Figure 8-32, the 410-IDENTIFY-ERROR-TYPE module is used to control the printing of the record-image area for error lines. Remember that the record-image area is to be printed only on the first error line. If there are multiple errors, the second and any following lines should be blank in the record-image area.

The first time the 410-IDENTIFY-ERROR-TYPE module is executed for each record, the WS-ERROR-SWITCH field will contain a value of NO. When the error switch is set to NO, the program logic will leave the record-image data in the record-image area and then set the error switch to YES, since an error has now been detected.

On the second and successive times through this module for the same input record, therefore, the error switch will contain a value of "YES." This will cause the program logic to blank the record-image area so that it will not be displayed on any error lines after the first.

Regardless of whether this is the first or a subsequent error, the 420-PRINT-AUDIT-ERROR-LINE module is performed to control printing of the line.

Figure 8-31

Reason for numeric test prior to performing the price validation module.

```
This logic ensures that the 380-VAL-PRICE module
will not be performed if nonnumeric characters
are present in the ST-PRICE field.

          220-VAL-SALES-TRANS-FIELDS.
                .
                .
                .
          IF ST-PRICE IS NUMERIC
              PERFORM 380-VAL-PRICE
          ELSE
              MOVE "PRICE NOT NUMERIC" TO AE-ERROR-MESSAGE
              PERFORM 410-IDENTIFY-ERROR-TYPE.
                .
                .
Nonnumeric       .
data would  380-VAL-PRICE.
cause a data     IF ST-PRICE-X IS EQUAL TO ZERO
exception            MOVE "PRICE NOT PRESENT" TO AE-ERROR-MESSAGE
here                 PERFORM 410-IDENTIFY-ERROR-TYPE.
            IF ST-PRICE IS NOT GREATER THAN ZERO
                 MOVE "PRICE NOT POSITIVE" TO AE-ERROR-MESSAGE
                 PERFORM 410-IDENTIFY-ERROR-TYPE.
            IF ST-DEPARTMENT-NUMBER IS LESS THAN "500"
and here    AND ST-PRICE IS GREATER THAN +00999.99
                 MOVE "PRICE NOT CONSISTENT" TO AE-ERROR-MESSAGE
                 PERFORM 410-IDENTIFY-ERROR-TYPE.
```

Figure 8-32
Error-line formatting logic.

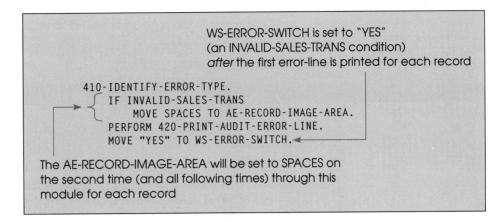

WS-ERROR-SWITCH is set to "YES"
(an INVALID-SALES-TRANS condition)
after the first error-line is printed for each record

```
410-IDENTIFY-ERROR-TYPE.
    IF INVALID-SALES-TRANS
        MOVE SPACES TO AE-RECORD-IMAGE-AREA.
    PERFORM 420-PRINT-AUDIT-ERROR-LINE.
    MOVE "YES" TO WS-ERROR-SWITCH.
```

The AE-RECORD-IMAGE-AREA will be set to SPACES on
the second time (and all following times) through this
module for each record

Figure 8-33
Error-line printing logic.

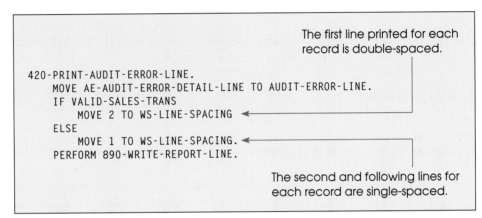

The first line printed for each
record is double-spaced.

```
420-PRINT-AUDIT-ERROR-LINE.
    MOVE AE-AUDIT-ERROR-DETAIL-LINE TO AUDIT-ERROR-LINE.
    IF VALID-SALES-TRANS
        MOVE 2 TO WS-LINE-SPACING
    ELSE
        MOVE 1 TO WS-LINE-SPACING.
    PERFORM 890-WRITE-REPORT-LINE.
```

The second and following lines for
each record are single-spaced.

Printing the Error Line

The 420-PRINT-AUDIT-ERROR-LINE module is used to print both audit lines for valid records and error lines for invalid records. As shown in Figure 8-33, the logic handles the requirement that the first line printed for each input record—either the audit line or the first error line—be double-spaced from the last detail line.

Writing Records to Disk (or Tape)

The WRITE statement coded in the 830-WRITE-VALID-SALES-TRANS module (and included below) is an example of a statement used to write a record to a non-printer device. Although this particular statement is used to write a record to a disk file, the statement to write a record to a tape file is of identical syntax.

```
830-WRITE-VALID-SALES-TRANS.
    WRITE VALID-SALES-TRANSACTION-RECORD.
```

As you can see, this WRITE statement is similar to those used for printer files; the reserved word WRITE is specified and followed by the user-defined record-name. Observe that the ADVANCING phrase is omitted, however, because it applies only to printer files.

Chapter Summary

The INSPECT/REPLACING statement is used for character-translation applications; it has the following options:

- REPLACING ALL: Causes all occurrences of the search-field value within the inspected field to be converted to the replacement-field value.

- REPLACING LEADING: Only leftmost occurrences of the search-field value are converted to the replacement-field value.

■ REPLACING FIRST: Causes only the first occurrence of the search-field value to be converted to the replacement-field value.

The INSPECT/TALLYING statement is used for character-counting applications; it has the following options:

■ TALLYING/ALL: Counts all occurrences of the search-field value within the inspected field.

■ TALLYING/LEADING: Only leftmost occurrences of the search-field value are counted.

For data validation, define all fields as alphanumeric. If operations must be performed on numeric fields requiring numeric definitions (for instance, check the sign), then redefine those fields with the appropriate numeric descriptions.

Prior to validating numeric fields, use the INSPECT/REPLACING to replace leading spaces with zeros.

When validating a numeric field defined with a 9 picture, always perform a numeric test before performing actions that might give a data exception (for instance, doing a sign check).

In the PROCEDURE DIVISION, writing of output is done with the WRITE statement and is independent of the output device (printer or disk/tape). However, there are some differences among the options that can be used with different devices; for instance, the ADVANCING clause is applicable only to printer files.

Define nonarithmetic numeric fields as alphanumeric rather than numeric. A numeric class is usually less efficient because of the need for arithmetic-sign handling and decimal scaling. Also, on some computer systems, numeric fields introduce the possibility that data exceptions may occur and thereby cause abnormal program termination.

Features in COBOL-85 Not in COBOL-74

In COBOL-85, the CONVERTING option of the INSPECT statement is available. It permits the specification of multiple search-character and replacement-character values in one statement. The format and an example are shown below:

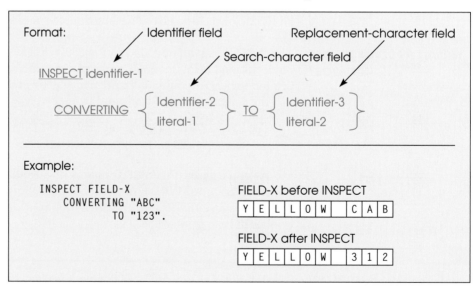

The characters within the search-character and replacement-character fields are matched positionally. The first character of the search-character—when found in the inspected field—is replaced by the first character of the replacement-character field; the second search character is replaced by the second replacement character, and so forth. Thus, as shown in the example above, A is replaced by 1, B is replaced by 2, and so forth.

Exercises

Review Questions

1. The three INSPECT/REPLACING statement options are:

   a. _____   b. _____   c. _____

2. The two INSPECT/TALLYING statement options are:

   a. _____   b. _____

3. Why should nonarithmetic numeric-integer fields generally be specified as alphanumeric rather than as numeric fields?

   _____

   _____

4. For numeric fields that are not zero-filled, why is it advisable to replace LEADING SPACES BY ZEROS rather than ALL SPACES BY ZEROS?

   _____

   _____

5. Explain why a numeric field should be tested for NUMERIC even though all SPACES have been replaced by ZEROS.

   _____

   _____

6. Explain why a numeric range test made with nonnumeric literals also requires a NUMERIC class test.

   _____

   _____

Syntax/Debug Exercises

Each of the following IF statements is based on the field and condition-name definitions of Figure 8-16. (Note that only the IF is shown—conditional actions, not being pertinent to this question, are omitted.) Identify each that is incorrect and rewrite it correctly in the space provided to the right.

```
IF VALID-RECORD-CODE EQUAL "27" _____

IF VALID-MONTH _____

IF VALID-MONTH AND NOT VALID DAY _____

IF ST-MONTH-OF-SALE GREATER 12 _____

IF ST-YEAR-OF-SALE SPACES _____

IF ST-DEPARTMENT-NUMBER EQUAL ZERO _____

IF NOT DEPT-NO-NOT-PRESENT _____

IF ITEM-DESC-FIRST-POS IS EQUAL TO _____

    ITEM-DESC-FIRST-POS-BLANK _____
```

```
IF ST-QUANTITY LESS THAN 10 _____

IF ST-PRICE-X POSITIVE _____

IF ST-TYPE-OF-SALE NOT "R" _____

IF VALID-TYPE-OF-SALE _____

AND ST-TYPE-OF-SALE NOT EQUAL "$" _____
```

Questions About the DATAVAL Program

1. What is the maximum number of output lines that can be printed on a single page by DATAVAL?

   _____

2. Assume that there was a misunderstanding between the system designer and the programmer and the first three fields of the input record were defined as follows:

Field	Columns
Record code	1
Date of sale	2–7
Department number	8–11

   These definitions were used in writing the program. Notice that the field following the Department number will be correctly defined. Also assume that there is to be no Record code validation (the 310 module is not included in the program). Would any records be written to the VALID-SALES-TRANSAC-TION-FILE? If so, describe as best you can the contents of significant fields.

   _____

   _____

   _____

3. Assume that the programmer coded the IF statement in the 210 module as

   ```
   IF WS-LINES-USED IS GREATER THAN WS-LINES-PER-PAGE
   ```

   instead of

   ```
   IF WS-LINES-USED IS NOT LESS THAN WS-LINES-PER-PAGE
   ```

   This would cause the program to function differently than intended in two ways. Describe each.

   a. _____

   b. _____

4. The statement

```
MOVE "NO " TO WS-ERROR-SWITCH
```

has been placed in the 100 module instead of the 200 module. Describe what will happen because of this error.

_____

_____

Programming Assignments

Programming Assignment 8-1: Ledger-Record Validation

Background information:

In any business, keeping an accurate record of money coming in and going out of the company is critical to the operation of the company. Such data is commonly kept in file called a *general ledger file*. In a general ledger system, separate accounts are defined for the variety of fiscal activity. Typical accounts would be salaries, travel, building rental, and petty cash. As financial transactions occur, each is combined with summary data in the appropriate account. Silicon Valley Manufacturing requires that general ledger records be validated. An audit/error list is to be printed that lists each record and identifies, by error code, each error detected.

Input file: Ledger file (LEDGER.ERR)

Input-record format:

Positions	Field	Data class	Comments
1–2	Record code	Alphanumeric	Code LM
4–11	General ledger account number	Numeric	Format: 9999.9999
12–39	Account description	Alphanumeric	
44	Account type	Alphanumeric	
47–56	Account balance	Numeric	Format: 99999999V99
57–79	Other data (no test required)		

Output-report format:

```
          0         1         2         3         4         5         6         7
  1234567890123456789012345678901234567890123456789012345678901234567890123
 1
 2
 3
 4 LEDGER RECORD VALIDATION (8-1)                                AUDIT/ERROR LIST
 5
 6 RC   ACCT NBR      ACCOUNT NAME              AT        BALANCE        ERROR CODES
 7
 8 XX   99999.999  XXXXXXXXXXXXXXXXXXXXXXXXXXXX  9    ZZ,ZZZ,ZZZ.99 -     A B C D E F
 9
10 XX   99999.999  XXXXXXXXXXXXXXXXXXXXXXXXXXXX  9    ZZ,ZZZ,ZZZ.99 -     A B C D E F
```

Program operations:

1. Process each input ledger record.
2. Print the two report-heading lines on the first page and on each following page of the audit/error list.

3. For each input ledger record, print each field of the record and make field validations as specified below. When a field value does not pass the validation, print the applicable error code (shown below in parentheses) at the location specified on the print chart.

a. (Error code A) Validate the record-code field to ensure that it is equal to LM.

b. (Error code B) Validate the account-number field to ensure that it is present.

c. (Error code C) Validate the account-number field to ensure that it is numeric.

d. (Error code D) If the account-name field is present (not equal to spaces), validate it to ensure that it is left-justified.

e. (Error code E) Validate the account-type field to ensure that the account-type field contains either a blank space or a numeric digit within the range of 1 through 6.

f. (Error code F) After replacing any leading blank spaces with zeros, validate the account-balance field and then validate it to ensure that it is numeric.

4. Double-space each audit/error list detail line as specified on the print chart. Provide for a span of 57 lines per page.

Programming Assignment 8-2: Vendor-Record Validation

Background information:

Tools Unlimited has a large number of vendors from whom it makes a wide variety of purchases. A pet project of the purchasing agent has been maintaining data about vendors on a personal computer, using a program written in BASIC by a friend. The time has come to integrate this data with other systems. A program was written to convert the data file to a form compatible with the vendor-control program written in COBOL. These records must be validated. An audit/error list is to be printed that lists each record and identifies, by error code, each error detected. The field in error is also to be highlighted by marking asterisks beneath it in the record-image area of the audit/error list.

Input file: Vendor file (VENDOR.ERR)

Input-record format:

Positions	Field	Data class	Comments
1–2	Record code	Alphanumeric	Code LM
4–11	Vendor number	Numeric	
12–17	Date due	Numeric	Format: *yymmdd*
18–37	Vendor name	Alphanumeric	
67–74	Amount due	Numeric	Dollars and cents

Output-report format:

Program operations:
1. Read each input vendor-transaction record.
2. Print the two report-heading lines on the first page and on each following page of the audit/error list.
   a. Accumulate and print the page number on the first heading line as shown on the print chart.
3. For each input vendor record, print each field of the record and make field validations as specified below. When a field value does not pass the validation, then (a) print the applicable error code (shown in the list below in parentheses) at the location specified on the print chart, and (b) print a row of asterisks beneath the respective field in the record-image area of the audit/error list.
   a. (Error code A) Validate the record-code field to ensure that is equal to VM.
   b. (Error code B) Validate the vendor-number field to ensure that it is present.
   c. (Error code C) Validate the vendor-number field to ensure that it is numeric.
   d. (Error code D) If the date-due field is equal to zero, validate the amount-due field to ensure that it is a negative value (credit balance). If the date due is zero and the amount due is negative, make no further date-due validations (error codes E, F, and G below).
   e. (Error code E) Validate the date-due field to ensure that the month number is within the range of 01 to 12.
   f. (Error code F) Validate the date-due field to ensure that the day number is within the range of 01 to 31.
   g. (Error code G) Validate the date-due field to ensure that the date is not later than the current date plus one year.
   h. (Error code H) If the vendor-name field is present (not equal to spaces), validate it to ensure that it is left-justified.
   i. (Error code 1) After replacing any leading blank spaces with zeros, validate the amount-due field to ensure that it is numeric.
4. Space each audit/error list detail line as specified on the print chart.
   a. Double-space each audit/error line from the previous audit line or error line with asterisks.
   b. Single-space each error line with asterisks from its previous audit/error line. Always print the error line with asterisks on the same report page as its respective audit/error line.
   c. Provide for a span of not more than 57 lines per page.

Programming Assignment 8-3: Earnings-Record Validation
Background information:
Silicon Manufacturing has been the victim of a computer virus intended to destroy the payroll system. Fortunately, one of the programmers detected its presence before much damage was done. However, before processing can be resumed, all records of the earnings file must be validated. An audit/error list is to be printed that lists each record and identifies, by error message, each error detected. Record-count totals are to be printed at the end of the listing.

Input file: Earnings file (EARNINGS.ERR)

Input-record format:

Positions	Field	Data class	Comments
1–2	Record code	Alphanumeric	Code EM
4–6	Plant code	Numeric	
7–10	Department code	Alphanumeric	
11–19	Employee number	Numeric	
20–31	Employee last name	Alphanumeric	
32–40	Employee first name	Alphanumeric	
41	Employee middle initial	Alphanumeric	
44–48	Hours worked	Numeric	Format: 9999V99
49	Sex code	Alphabetic	M or F
50	Marital status	Alphabetic	M, S, or H
51–52	Number of exemptions	Numeric	
53	Pay code	Alphabetic	Blank or H
54–59	Pay rate	Numeric	99V9999 for Hourly 9999V99 for Salaried
60–66	This-period earnings	Numeric	99999V99
67–74	Year-to-date earnings	Numeric	999999V99
75–79	Other data (no test required)		

Output-report format:

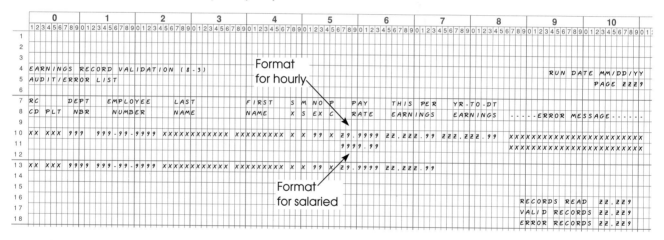

Program operations:

1. Process each input earnings record.
2. Print the four heading lines on the first page and on each following page of the audit/error list.
   a. Print the run date on the first heading line as shown on the print chart.
   b. Accumulate and print the page number on the second heading line as shown on the print chart.
3. For each input earnings record, print each field of the record and make field validations as specified below. When a field value does not pass the validation, print the applicable error message.
   a. Validate the Record-code field to ensure that it is equal to EM. If it is not, print the error message RECORD CODE INVALID.
   b. Validate the Plant-code field to ensure that it is equal to ATL (Atlantic), CTL (Central), MTN (Mountain), or PAC (Pacific). If it is not, print the error message PLANT CODE INVALID.
   c. After replacing any leading blank spaces with zeros, validate the Department-number field to ensure that it is numeric. If it is not, print the error message DEPT NUMBER NOT NUMERIC.

d. Validate the Department-number field to ensure that it is not equal to zero. If it is, print the error message DEPT NUMBER MISSING.

e. After replacing any leading blank spaces with zeros, validate the Employee-number field to ensure that it is numeric. If it is not, print the error message EMP NUMBER NOT NUMERIC.

f. Validate the Employee-number field to ensure that it is not equal to zero. If it is, print the error message EMP NUMBER MISSING.

g. Validate the employee Last-name field to ensure that it is present. If it is not, print the error message LAST NAME MISSING.

h. If there is data in the employee Last-name field, validate to ensure that it is left-justified. If it is not, print the error message LAST NAME NOT LEFT JUST.

i. Validate the employee First-name field to ensure that it is present. If it is not, print the error message FIRST NAME MISSING.

j. If there is data in the employee First-name field, validate to ensure that it is left-justified. If it is not, print the error message FIRST NAME NOT LEFT JUST.

k. Validate the Sex-code field to ensure that it contains either the letter M (male) or F (female). If it does not, print the error message SEX CODE INVALID.

l. Validate the Marital-status field to ensure that it contains either the letter M (married), S (single), or H (head of household). If it does not, print the error message MARITAL STATUS INVALID.

m. After replacing leading blank spaces with zeros, validate the Number-of-exemptions field to ensure that it is numeric. If it is not, print the error message NBR EXEMPTS NOT NUMERIC.

n. Validate the Pay-code field to ensure that it contains either the letter H (hourly) or a blank space (salaried). If it does not, print the error message PAY CODE INVALID.

o. After replacing any leading blank spaces with zeros, validate the Pay-rate field to ensure that it is numeric. If it is not, print the error message PAY RATE NOT NUMERIC.

p. If the Pay-code field indicates an hourly employee and the Pay-rate field is numeric, validate the Pay-rate field to ensure that the value is not less than the minimum wage and not greater than twenty dollars (20.0000). If it is not, print the error message HOURLY RATE INVALID.

q. If the Pay-code field indicates a salaried employee and the Pay-rate field is numeric, validate the Pay-rate field to ensure that the value is equal to or greater than one thousand dollars (1000.00). If it is not, print the error message SALARY AMOUNT INVALID.

r. After replacing leading blank spaces with zeros, validate the This-period-earnings field to ensure that it is numeric. If it is not, print the error message THIS-PR EARN NOT NUMERIC.

s. After replacing leading blank spaces with zeros, validate the Year-to-date earnings field to ensure that it is numeric. If it is not, print the error message YR-DT EARN NOT NUMERIC.

t. If both the This-period-earnings and the year-to-date-earnings fields are numeric, validate the Year-to-date-earnings field to ensure that it is not less than the This-period-earnings field. If it is, print the error message EARNING RELATION INVALID.

4. Accumulate the following record-count totals:
   a. Total number of records read.
   b. Total number of valid records (those that contain no errors).
   c. Total number of error records (those that contain one or more errors).

5. Print audit/error lines as follows:
   a. For each record that passes all the validation tests, write an audit line containing the record-image area on the audit/error list. This line is to be double-spaced from the previous line.
   b. For each record with one or more errors, write one line for each error detected.
      ■ The first error line for each record is to contain the record-image area and the first error detected. This line is to be double-spaced from the previous line.
      ■ Successive error lines for each record are to be single-spaced from the previous line and should contain only the error message (except as specified in Item 6, below).
6. Provide for a span of not more than 57 lines per page.
   a. When it is necessary to continue error messages from one page to another, repeat the record image on the first audit/error line printed on the new page. Print the continuation message (CONTINUED) on that first line.
   b. If there are two or more errors for a record, print at least two lines before skipping to a new page. In other words, do not continue to a new page immediately after just one error line has been printed for a record with multiple errors.
7. After all input earnings records have been processed, print the three output-report total lines (triple-spaced from the last detail line) as specified on the print chart.

Programming Assignment 8-4: Customer-Record Validation
Background information:
One of the older applications of Silicon Valley Manufacturing (a carry-over from the days of punched card processing) uses a file that includes two records for each customer. The first is the customer name record and the second is the customer address record. The data-processing department plans to merge the data from these two files into a single file. However, before doing so, a program is required to print an audit/error list that lists each record and identifies, by error message, each error detected. Record-count totals are to be printed at the end of the listing.

Input file: Customer file (CUSTADDR.ERR)

Input-record formats:

Positions	Field	Data class	Comments
1–2	Record code	Numeric	Code 53
3–7	Customer number	Numeric	
8–31	Customer name	Alphanumeric	
39–46	Account balance	Numeric	Dollars and cents
47–80	Other data (no test required)		

Positions	Field	Data class	Comments
1–2	Record code	Numeric	Code 54
3–7	Customer number	Numeric	
8–31	Customer address	Alphanumeric	
32–44	City	Alphanumeric	
45–46	State	Alphanumeric	
47–51	Zip code	Numeric	
56–65	Telephone number	Numeric	Includes area code
66–75	Customer reference code	Alphanumeric	
76–80	Other data (no test required)		

Output-report format:

```
                0         1         2         3         4         5         6         7         8         9        10
       1234567890123456789012345678901234567890123456789012345678901234567890123456789012345678901234567890
 1
 2
 3
 4  CUSTOMER RECORD VALIDATION (8-4)                                                            RUN DATE MM/DD/YY
 5  AUDIT/ERROR LIST                                                                                  PAGE ZZZ9
 6
 7                 CUSTOMER NAME                    BALANCE                          CUSTOMER
 8  RC    CUST  ----------------------------------------            TELEPHONE     REFERENCE
 9  CD    NBR    CUSTOMER ADDRESS        CITY        ST    ZIP       NUMBER          CODE       ------ERROR MESSAGE-------
10
11  53   99999  XXXXXXXXXXXXXXXXXXXXXXXXX    ZZZ,ZZZ.99-                                        XXXXXXXXXXXXXXXXXXXXXXXXXX
12  54   99999  XXXXXXXXXXXXXXXXXXXXXXXXX XXXXXXXXXXXX XX  99999 (999)999-9999 XXXXXXXXX        XXXXXXXXXXXXXXXXXXXXXXXXXX
13
14  53   99999  XXXXXXXXXXXXXXXXXXXXXXXXX    ZZZ,ZZZ.99-
15  54   99999  XXXXXXXXXXXXXXXXXXXXXXXXX XXXXXXXXXXXX XX  99999 (999)999-9999 XXXXXXXXX
16
17
18                                                                                     RECORDS READ   ZZ,ZZ9
19                                                                                     VALID RECORDS  ZZ,ZZ9
20                                                                                     ERROR RECORDS  ZZ,ZZ9
```

Program operations:

1. Process each input customer record.
2. Print the four heading lines on the first page and on each following page of the audit/error list.
   a. Print the run date on the first heading line as shown on the print chart.
   b. Accumulate and print the page number on the second heading line as shown on the print chart.
3. Validate record-code and record-set relationships.
   a. Validate the record-code field of each record to ensure that it is equal to 53 or 54. If it is not, print the error message INVALID RECORD CODE and make no further validations for that record.
   b. For each customer-number, there should be one 53 record followed by one 54 record. If either record is missing, print a row of asterisks in the record-image area of the audit/error list and print, as appropriate, an error message of either RECORD 53 MISSING or RECORD 54 MISSING.
   c. Check to ensure that there are not duplicate records for one customer number. If either record is duplicated, print the record contents in the record-image area of the audit/error list and print, as appropriate, an error message of either DUPLICATE RECORD 53 or DUPLICATE RECORD 54.
4. For each input customer-name record (record code 53), print each field of the record and make field validations as specified below. When a field value does not pass the validation, print the applicable error message.
   a. Validate the Customer-number field to ensure that it is present and is numeric. If it is not, print the error message CUSTOMER NUMBER NOT NUMERIC.
   b. Validate the customer-name field to ensure that it is present. If it is not, print the error message CUSTOMER NAME MISSING.
   c. If there is data in the customer-name field, validate to ensure that it is left-justified. If it is not, print the error message CUST NAME NOT LEFT JUST.
   d. After replacing leading blank spaces with zeros, validate the account-balance field to ensure that it is numeric. If it is not, print the error message ACCT BALANCE NOT NUMERIC.
5. For each input customer-address record (record code 54), print each field of the record and make field validations as specified below. When a field value does not pass the validation, print the applicable error message.
   a. Validate the customer-address field to ensure that it is present. If it is not, print the error message ADDRESS MISSING.

b.   If there is data in the customer-address field, validate to ensure that it is left-justified. If it is not, print the error message ADDRESS NOT LEFT JUST.

c.   Validate the city field to ensure that it is present. If it is not, print the error message CITY MISSING.

d.   If there is data in the city field, validate to ensure that it is left-justified. If it is not, print the error message CITY NOT LEFT JUST.

e.   Validate the state field to ensure that it contains a two-letter abbreviation. If it does not, print the error message STATE ABBREVIATION INVALID.

f.   Validate the zip code field to ensure that it is numeric. If it is not, print the error message ZIP CODE NOT NUMERIC.

g.   Validate the telephone-number field to ensure that it is numeric. If it is not, print the error message TELEPHONE NBR NOT NUMERIC.

h.   Validate the area-code of the telephone-number to ensure that the first (leftmost) digit is not a zero or a one and that the second (middle) digit is a zero or a one. If either digit is incorrect, print the error message AREA CODE INVALID.

i.   Validate the exchange of the telephone-number to ensure that it is not equal to 555 and that the first (leftmost) and second (middle) digits are not a zero or a one. If it does not pass these tests, print the error message TELEPHONE EXCHANGE INVALID.

j.   Validate the customer-reference-code field to ensure that it is left-justified and contains no embedded-blank spaces. If it is not left-justified or it contains embedded-blank spaces, print the error message CUST REF EMBEDDED BLANKS.

6.   Accumulate the following record-count totals:

a.   Total number of records read.

b.   Total number of valid records (those that contain no errors).

c.   Total number of error records (those that contain one or more errors).

7.   Print audit/error lines as follows:

a.   For each record that passes all the validation tests, write an audit line containing the record-image area on the audit/error list. The first record for a given customer number is to be double-spaced from the previous line. All following lines for that same customer number are to be single-spaced.

b.   For each record with one or more errors, write one line for each error detected.

■   The first error line for each record is to contain the record-image area and the first error detected.

■   Successive error lines for each record are to be single-spaced from the previous line and should contain only the error message (except as specified in Item 8 below).

8.   Provide for a span of not more than 57 lines per page.

a.   When it is necessary to continue error messages from one page to another, repeat the record-image on the first audit/error line printed on the new page. Print the continuation message (CONTINUED) on that first line.

b.   Print at least two lines for each customer number before skipping to a new page. In other words, do not continue to a new page between the first and second line for a given customer number.

9.   After all input customer records have been processed, print the three output-report total lines (triple-spaced from the last detail line) as specified on the print chart.

Programming Assignment 8-5: Nurses' File Validation
Background information:

Several of the programming assignments of preceding chapters have used the nurses' file of the Brooklawn Hospital. The original data-entry program written by the Brooklawn data-processing staff included limited data-checking capabilities.

Consequently, data currently stored in this file contains many errors and inconsistencies. The Brooklawn data-processing staff is rewriting the data-entry programs to include strict data control. Before they are implemented, a data validation program is required to validate the existing file and prepare a report that lists each record and identifies, by error code, each error detected.

Input file: Nurses file—With errors (NURSES.ERR)

Input-record format:

Positions	Field	Data class	Comments
1–2	Record type code	Alphanumeric	
3–13	Last name	Alphanumeric	
14–24	First name	Alphanumeric	
25	Last name	Alphabetic	
26–32	Home telephone number	Alphanumeric	
33–46	Professional specialty	Alphanumeric	For example, Trauma Room
47–52	Date hired	Numeric	Format *yymmdd*
53–55	Salary schedule	Alphanumeric	Row and column
56	Employment code	Alphabetic	F—Fulltime employee P—Parttime employee
57	Supervisory code	Alphabetic	Y—Yes, N—No
68–73	Base monthly salary	Numeric	Format: dollars and cents
94–96	Ward/duty station	Alphanumeric	
97	Shift code	Numeric	Value of 1, 2, or 3

Output-report format:

Program operations:
1. Process each record.
2. Print the four heading lines on the first page and on each following page of the audit/error list.
   a. Print the run date on the first heading line as shown on the print chart.
   b. Accumulate and print the page number on the second heading line as shown on the print chart.

3. For each input record, print each field of the record and make field validations as specified below. When a field value does not pass the validation, print the applicable error message. Fields not identified for validation need not be tested, since they will be replaced when the new system is implemented.

a.   Validate the Record-code field to ensure that it is equal to NU. If it is not, print the error message RECORD CODE INVALID,

b.   Validate the Last-name field to ensure that it is present. If it is not, print the error message LAST NAME MISSING.

c.   If there is data in the employee Last-name field, validate to ensure that it is left-justified. If it is not, print the error message LAST NAME NOT LEFT JUST.

d.   Validate the employee First-name field to ensure that it is present. If it is not, print the error message FIRST NAME MISSING.

e.   If there is data in the employee First-name field, validate to ensure that it is left-justified. If it is not, print the error message FIRST NAME NOT LEFT JUST.

f.   Validate the Middle-initial field to ensure that it is a letter or blank. If it is not, print the error message MIDDLE INITIAL NOT ALPHA.

g.   If there is an entry in the Telephone-number field, check it to ensure that it is numeric. If it is not numeric, print the error message TELE NUM NOT NUMERIC.

h.   Validate the Professional-specialty field to ensure that it is present. If it is not, print the error message PROF SPECIALTY MISSING.

i.   Validate the Date-hired field to ensure that it is present. If it is not, print the error message DATE HIRED MISSING.

j.   If there is data in the Date-hired field check to ensure that it is numeric. If it is not, print the error message DATE HIRED NOT NUM.

k.   If the Date-hired field is numeric, check to ensure that the Year is between 40 (1940) and the current year, inclusive. If it is not, print the error message HIRE YEAR OUT OF RANGE.

l.   If the Date-hired field is numeric, check to ensure that the Month is between 1 and 12. If it is not, print the error message HIRE MONTH INVALID.

m.   If the Date-hired field is numeric, check to ensure that the Day meets the following conditions.

1.   If month is February and the year is not a leap year, the day number must not be greater that 28; if a leap year, the day number must not be greater that 29. (*Note:* Leap year occurs every four years; 1988 and 1992 are leap years.)

2.   If the month is April, June, September, or November the day number must not be greater than 30.

3.   For any other month, the day number must not be greater than 31.

If the Day number does not meet these criterion, print the error message HIRE DAY INVALID.

n.   Validate the Salary-schedule field to ensure that it is present. If it is not, print the error message SALARY SCHEDULE MISSING.

o.   Check to ensure that the Employment-code contains either F or P. If it does not, print the error message INVALID EMPLOYMENT CODE.

p.   Check to ensure that the Supervisory-code contains either Y or N. If it does not, print the error message INVALID SUPER CODE.

q.   After replacing any leading blank spaces with zeros, validate the Base-monthly-salary field to ensure that it is numeric. If it is not, print the error message SALARY NOT NUMERIC.

CHAPTER **9**

Chapter Outline

Screen I/O with the ACCEPT and DISPLAY
The DISPLAY Statement
The ACCEPT Statement

A Program to Display the Records of a File
Programming Specifications For DISPTRA1
Structure Chart and Program Logic

The DISPTRA1 Program
The RM/COBOL-85 SELECT Statement
Using the SET Statement with Conditional Names
The DISPLAY Statement as Used in DISPTRA1
   Editing Output
   Positioning of Displayed Items
   Erasing the Screen
The ACCEPT Statement as Used in DISPTRA1
   The POSITION 0 Option
   The NO BEEP Option
   The UPDATE Option

The SCREEN SECTION
The Sales Transaction Display Program Using a SCREEN SECTION
The DISPLAY and ACCEPT Used with a SCREEN SECTION
Types of SCREEN SECTION Entries
Generalizing the SCREEN SECTION Entries

Data Entry Program Definition
Program Specifications
Program Logic
The In-Line PERFORM—COBOL-85

The Data Entry Program
Program Switches Used in the Data Entry Program
Screen-Name Entries
SCREEN SECTION Picture Entries
Other Notable Screen-Attributes
About Opening the File
The 000-BUILD-DATA-FILE Module
The 050-QUERY-THE-USER
The Data Entry/Validation Modules
Overall Execution—The 200-BUILD-A-RECORD Module

447

Screen I/O with the ACCEPT and DISPLAY

So far in this book, the entire focus has been on batch processing—applications in which transactions are accumulated over time and run periodically. An equally important area is **interactive processing**, whereby the user, working with a keyboard and CRT (cathode ray tube) screen, interacts with the computer directly. For instance, the sales transaction records that you validated in Chapter 8 might be entered directly into the system with immediate checking of each field as it is keyed in. If a field is not valid, the operator is notified and requested to key in the correct value. Hence, the user **interacts** with the computer.

In writing an interactive program, you must carefully design clear, easy-to-read screen displays in much the same way you have already designed printed reports. When designing a report layout, your primary concern is *horizontal* positioning of data. Other than controlling paging, you are not concerned with *vertical* positioning of detail lines because you print one detail line after the other. Your main consideration is one-dimensional layout.

This situation is quite different when doing a screen design because you can position output anywhere on the screen: you must do two-dimensional planning. Monitors commonly used with MS-DOS microcomputers display 25 lines of 80 positions each. Hence, you must designate the line as well as the column in which you want output displayed.

The DISPLAY Statement

In COBOL, the ACCEPT and DISPLAY are used for low-volume, terminal input and output. Although the COBOL-85 standard includes no provisions for screen input and display beyond the simple ACCEPT and DISPLAY, most compilers (including RM/COBOL-85) provide additional features. One of the features that you might be anticipating is the ability to position output anywhere on the screen.

The example of Figure 9-1 illustrates screen positioning of output. Two items are to be displayed: a description (a literal) and the contents of a the data field ST-DEPARTMENT-NUMBER. Figure 9-1(a) shows the exact screen positioning required. The DISPLAY statement of Figure 9-1(b) accomplishes this; the DISPLAY statement format is included in Figure 9-1(c). Note that the DISPLAY consists of three elements:

- The verb DISPLAY

- A literal or data identifier

- One or more **control-options**—entries that control the way in which the output is displayed on the screen

You can see that the two control-options, LINE and POSITION, define the horizontal and vertical positioning of the output on the screen.

In addition to LINE and POSITION, you can use several other options to enhance the screen display. For example, the first three options allow you to display output so as to attract attention.

1. High intensity (HIGH): Information can be displayed with "extra" brightness.

2. Reversed video (REVERSE): Normal display is light characters on a dark background. With reversed video, the area surrounding the displayed characters is lighted and the characters themselves are dark.

3. Blinking (BLINK): Causes the displayed characters to blink on and off on the screen. This is distracting and is used only when it is critical that the user take note of the display.

4. Low intensity (LOW): This is the conventional brightness to which you are accustomed on the screen—it is the default of the DISPLAY verb.

Figure 9-1
Using the DISPLAY
statement.

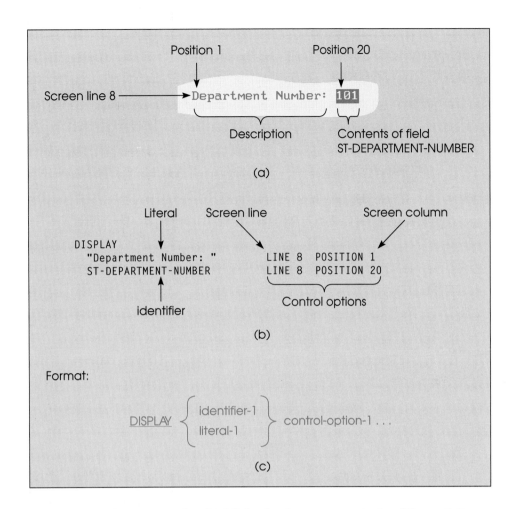

For example, if you wanted to highlight the department number (Figure 9-1) you could use reverse video (light characters on dark) as follows:

```
DISPLAY
    "Department Number: "      LINE 8   POSITION 1
    ST-DEPARTMENT-NUMBER       LINE 8   POSITION 20 REVERSE
```

The ACCEPT Statement Whereas the DISPLAY statement allows you to display information on the screen, the ACCEPT allows you to enter data from the keyboard into the program while simultaneously displaying the entry on the screen. The format of this statement is the same as that of the DISPLAY, as you can see by inspecting the format in Figure 9-2.

The first three options (LINE, POSITION, and REVERSE) function the same as with the DISPLAY. UPDATE allows the current value of ST-ITEM-DESCRIPTION to be offered as a default input value and NO BEEP suppresses the terminal bell. These control-options will be more meaningful to you in the context of the programs that follow.

Figure 9-2
The ACCEPT statement.

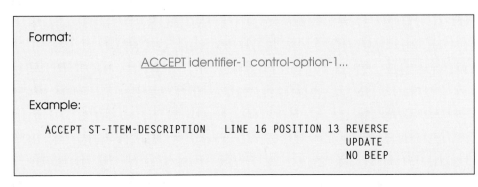

A Program to Display the Records of a File

The first program you will consider displays the contents of a file. Hence, its structure and logic are not much different than some of the first programs you wrote. The file that you will be viewing is a version of the sales transaction file used in Chapter 8. This program allows you to display one record at a time. After viewing a record, you can request that the next record be displayed or that the program be terminated.

Programming Specifications For DISPTRA1

Figure 9-3 consists of the programming specifications for the DISPTRA1 program. As indicated, the program operations are relatively simple. In the input-record format specifications, notice that there are two differences between this version of the sales transaction file and that of Chapter 8. First, the Record-code field has been omitted. Second, the quantity field is designated with a separate sign trailing. This is consistent with the principles of data transportability described in Concepts Module D and Chapter 4.

The screen layout form (equivalent to the print chart) is also included in Figure 9-3. Notice that this form identifies both the line and column positioning for descriptive information (from literals) and data (from identifiers).

Figure 9-3
Program specifications: the DISPTRA1 program.

PROGRAMMING SPECIFICATIONS

Program name: SALES-TRANSACTION DISPLAY   **Program ID:** DISPTRA1

Program Description:
This program is to read each record for an input sales-transaction file and display it on the screen. The user is given the option of displaying the next record or terminating processing.

Input File:
Sales-Transaction File

Program Output:
Program output is softcopy to the screen.

List of Program Operations:
A. Read each input sales-transaction record.
B. For each record:
   1. Format the Date-of-sale, Quantity, and Price for output.
   2. Display all fields on the screen with appropriate screen descriptions.
C. Query user about displaying another record. If user does not wish to continue, terminate processing.

Input file:
Sales transaction file (TRANS1.DAT)

Input-record format:

Positions	Field	Data class	Comments
1-6	Date of sale	Numeric	Format: mmddyy
7-9	Department number	Numeric	
10-16	Item number	Numeric	
17-31	Item description	Alphanumeric	
32-36	Employee number	Numeric	
37-42	Quantity	Numeric	Separate sign (trailing)
43-50	Price	Numeric	Dollars and cents
51	Type of sale	Alphanumeric	Values: $, C, or R

Figure 9-3
(continued)

	1–10	11–20	21–30	31–40	41–50	51–60	61–

```
 5                        S A L E S   T R A N S A C T I O N   D I S P L A Y
 6                        . . . . . . . . . . . . . . . . . . . . . . . . .
 8 D e p a r t m e n t   N u m b e r :   X X X              D a t e :   X X / X X / X X
10 T y p e   o f   s a l e   ( # ,   C ,   o r   R ) :   X        S a l e s p e r s o n   N u m b e r :   X X X X
13 . . . . . . . . . . . . . . . . . . . . . . . I t e m . . . . . . . . . . . . . . . . . . . . . . .
14 N u m b e r        D e s c r i p t i o n               Q u a n t i t y      P r i c e
16 X X X X X X X        X X X X X X X X X X X X X X        - , - , - - 9   Z Z , Z Z Z . 9 9
```

Structure Chart and Program Logic

The structure chart for this program, shown in Figure 9-4, reflects its relatively basic nature. Notice that displaying the record and accepting the user input (about continuing) are shown as separate modules.

As you would expect, the logic is relatively simple, as shown in the pseudocode of Figure 9-5 and the flowchart of Figure 9-6. Notice in the 200 module that after displaying the record, the following sequence of events takes place.

1. The user is queried about displaying another record.

2. Only if the user requests the next record is the 800-Read module performed.

Figure 9-4
Structure chart: the DISPTRA1 program.

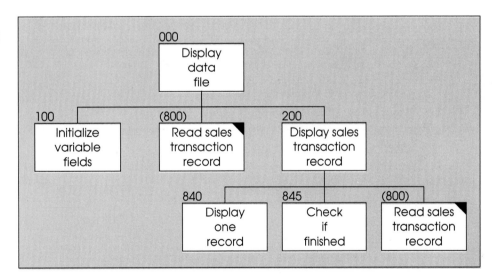

Figure 9-5   Pseudocode: the DISPTRA1 program.

```
000-Display-Data-File module                          2.   Perform 840-Display-1-Record.

1.   Open the file.                                    3.   Perform 845-Check-If-Finished.

2.   Perform 100-Initialize-Variable-Fields.          4.   If Another-record switch is True
                                                               Perform 800-Read-Sales-Trans-Record.
3.   Perform 800-Read-Sales-Trans-Record.

4.   Perform Display-Sales-Trans-Record                800-Read-Sales-Trans-Record module
          until no more processing.
                                                       1.   Read a record from the input Payroll file;
5.   Close the files.                                           if there are no more records
                                                                     Set Another-record switch
6.   Stop the run.                                                 to False.

100-Initialize-Variable-Fields module
                                                       840-Display-1-Record module
1.   Set Another-record switch to True.
                                                       1.   Display the data record.
200-Display-Sales-Trans-Record module
                                                       845-Check-If-Finished module
1.   Move the following fields to output edited fields:
          Date-of-sale                                 1.   Display prompt.
          Quantity
          Price                                        2.   Accept user response into Another-record switch.
```

Figure 9-6 Flowchart: the DISPTRA1 program.

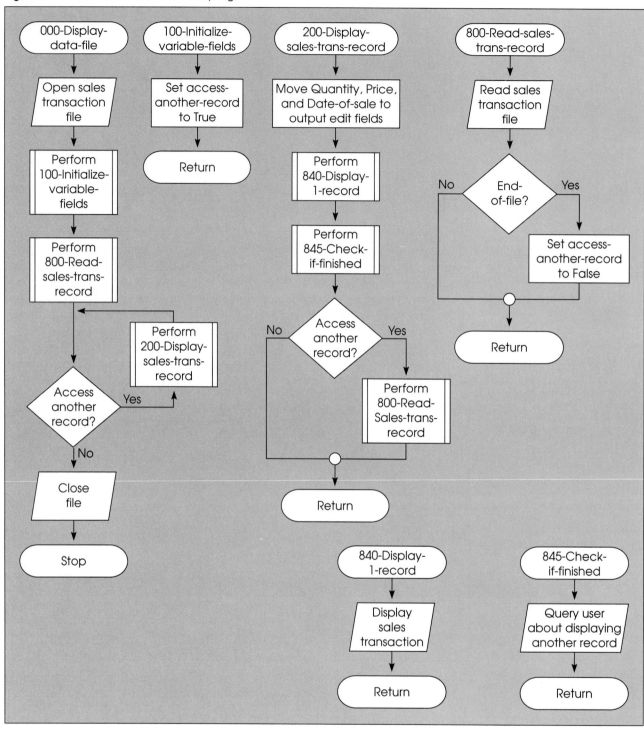

Hence, there are *two* conditions that can cause termination of the program: the user not requesting another record and the end-of-file condition. You will see the implementation of this logic in the program.

The DISPTRA1 Program

The complete program is shown in Figure 9-7. We will focus on these features of this program:

1. The RM/COBOL-85 SELECT statement

2. Using condition-names and the SET statement to change the value of a switch

3. The DISPLAY statement

4. The ACCEPT statement

**The RM/COBOL-85
SELECT Statement**

If you have been using the RM/COBOL-85 compiler, you are already familiar with the SELECT statement entries. The clause

```
ASSIGN TO DISK "TRANS1.DAT"
```

identifies the device as a disk drive (DISK) and the DOS filename (TRANS1.DAT), which is enclosed in quotes. The clause

```
ORGANIZATION IS LINE SEQUENTIAL
```

describes the internal form of the file. It indicates that the records of this file will be processed sequentially in the order they were loaded into the file.

Figure 9-7 The DISPTRA1 program.

```
  1         IDENTIFICATION DIVISION.
  2
  3         PROGRAM-ID. DISPTRA1.
  4
  5     *    Written by Price/Welburn
  6     *    General Merchandise Supply Company
  7     *    September 29, 1989
  8     *    Written for RM/COBOL-85
  9
 10     *    This program displays records from the file TRANS1.DAT.
 11     *    Each record is read and displayed on the screen.
 12     *    After each, the user can request the next one
 13     *    or terminate the program.
 14
 15     *    The program illustrates the DISPLAY and ACCEPT statements.
 16
 17
 18         ENVIRONMENT DIVISION.
 19
 20         CONFIGURATION SECTION.
 21
 22         SOURCE-COMPUTER. IBM-PC.
 23
 24         INPUT-OUTPUT SECTION.
 25
 26         FILE-CONTROL.
 27             SELECT SALES-TRANSACTION-FILE
 28                 ASSIGN TO DISK "TRANS1.DAT"
 29                 ORGANIZATION LINE SEQUENTIAL.
 30
 31
 32         DATA DIVISION.
 33
 34         FILE SECTION.
 35
 36         FD  SALES-TRANSACTION-FILE
 37                 RECORD CONTAINS 50 CHARACTERS
 38                 LABEL RECORDS ARE STANDARD.
 39
 40         01  SALES-TRANSACTION-RECORD        PIC X(50).
 41
 42         WORKING-STORAGE SECTION.
 43
 44         01  WS-SWITCHES.
 45             05  WS-ANOTHER-RECORD           PIC X(1).
 46                 88  ANOTHER-RECORD          VALUE "Y" FALSE "N".
 47
 48         01  WS-DISPLAY-VARIABLES.
 49             05  WS-QUANTITY                 PIC ---,--9.
 50             05  WS-PRICE                    PIC ZZ,ZZZ.99.
 51             05  WS-DATE-OF-SALE             PIC XX/XX/XX.
 52
 53         01  ST-SALES-TRANSACTION-RECORD.
 54             05  ST-DATE-OF-SALE             PIC X(6).
 55             05  ST-DEPARTMENT-NUMBER        PIC X(3).
 56             05  ST-ITEM-NUMBER              PIC X(7).
 57             05  ST-ITEM-DESCRIPTION         PIC X(15).
 58             05  ST-EMPLOYEE-NUMBER          PIC X(5).
 59             05  ST-QUANTITY                 PIC S9(5)
 60                                 SIGN IS TRAILING SEPARATE.
 61             05  ST-PRICE                    PIC 9(5)V99.
```

```
 62             05  ST-TYPE-OF-SALE             PIC X(1).
 63
 64
 65         PROCEDURE DIVISION.
 66
 67         000-DISPLAY-DATA-FILE.
 68             OPEN INPUT SALES-TRANSACTION-FILE
 69             PERFORM 100-INITIALIZE-VARIABLE-FIELDS
 70             PERFORM 800-READ-SALES-TRANS-RECORD
 71             PERFORM 200-DISPLAY-SALES-TRANS-RECORD
 72                 UNTIL NOT ANOTHER-RECORD
 73             CLOSE SALES-TRANSACTION-FILE
 74             STOP RUN.
 75
 76         100-INITIALIZE-VARIABLE-FIELDS.
 77             SET ANOTHER-RECORD TO TRUE.
 78
 79         200-DISPLAY-SALES-TRANS-RECORD.
 80             MOVE ST-QUANTITY TO WS-QUANTITY
 81             MOVE ST-PRICE TO WS-PRICE
 82             MOVE ST-DATE-OF-SALE TO WS-DATE-OF-SALE
 83             PERFORM 840-DISPLAY-1-RECORD
 84             PERFORM 845-CHECK-IF-FINISHED
 85             IF ANOTHER-RECORD
 86                 PERFORM 800-READ-SALES-TRANS-RECORD
 87             END-IF.
 88
 89         800-READ-SALES-TRANS-RECORD.
 90             READ SALES-TRANSACTION-FILE
 91                     INTO ST-SALES-TRANSACTION-RECORD
 92                 AT END SET ANOTHER-RECORD TO FALSE.
 93
 94         840-DISPLAY-1-RECORD.
 95             DISPLAY
 96                 "SALES TRANSACTION DISPLAY" ERASE
 97                                             LINE 5  POSITION 18
 98                 "══════════════════════"    LINE 6  POSITION 18
 99                 "Department Number: "        LINE 8  POSITION 1
100                 ST-DEPARTMENT-NUMBER         LINE 8  POSITION 20 REVERSE
101                 "Date: "                     LINE 8  POSITION 36
102                 WS-DATE-OF-SALE              LINE 8  POSITION 42 REVERSE
103                 "Type of sale ($, C, or R):" LINE 10 POSITION 1
104                 ST-TYPE-OF-SALE              LINE 10 POSITION 28 REVERSE
105                 "Salesperson Number: "       LINE 10 POSITION 35
106                 ST-EMPLOYEE-NUMBER           LINE 10 POSITION 55 REVERSE
107                 "═════════════════Item═════════════════"
108                                             LINE 13 POSITION 1
109                 "Number      Description      Quantity      Price"
110                                             LINE 14 POSITION 1
111                 ST-ITEM-NUMBER               LINE 16 POSITION 1  REVERSE
112                 ST-ITEM-DESCRIPTION          LINE 16 POSITION 13 REVERSE
113                 WS-QUANTITY                  LINE 16 POSITION 34 REVERSE
114                 WS-PRICE                     LINE 16 POSITION 43 REVERSE.
115
116         845-CHECK-IF-FINISHED.
117             DISPLAY
118                 "Do you want to display another record <Y/N>? "
119                                             LINE 20 POSITION 1
120             ACCEPT WS-ANOTHER-RECORD                 POSITION 0  REVERSE
121                                                                  NO BEEP
122                                                                  UPDATE.
```

Using the SET Statement with Conditional Names

By now, you have used program switches in numerous instances. For instance, WS-END-OF-FILE-SWITCH is used in the DATAVAL program to control the repeated processing of input records. The value YES causes repetition; the value NO causes control to pass to the next paragraph. The DATAVAL program also uses a condition-name to improve documentation, as shown in the following statements extracted from the program:

```
05  WS-END-OF-FILE-SWITCH      PIC X(3).
    88  END-OF-FILE                        VALUE "YES".
    .
    .
    .
PERFORM 200-VAL-SALES-TRANS
    UNTIL END-OF-FILE
```

Note that the switch could as well been defined as one character in length (as follows) and the values of Y and N been used as follows.

```
05  WS-END-OF-FILE-SWITCH      PIC X(1).
    88  END-OF-FILE                        VALUE "Y".
    .
    .
    .
MOVE "Y" TO WS-END-OF-FILE-SWITCH
```

RM/COBOL-85 includes an extension of COBOL-85 that is very convenient to use for conditions that can be either true or false. The following example illustrates this feature:

```
05  WS-END-OF-FILE-SWITCH      PIC X.
    88  END-OF-FILE             VALUE "Y"  FALSE "N".
```

This effectively sets up the following corresponding relationships:

Contents of WS-END-OF-FILE-SWITCH	Value of END-OF-FILE
Y	TRUE
N	FALSE

Now instead of saying:

```
MOVE "Y" TO WS-END-OF-FILE-SWITCH
```

You can say:

```
SET END-OF-FILE TO TRUE
```

As implemented in RM/COBOL-85, this format of the SET statement has the general form shown in Figure 9-8. You will see in Chapter 11 that there are other formats of the SET statement.

This technique is used in the DISPTRA1 program, and it is illustrated in Figure 9-9. Notice that the switch is changed through the SET statement and the condition-name, rather than the switch name. At line 85, the switch is tested to determine whether or not another record is to be read. As you will see in the description of the ACCEPT statement, the value of the switch WS-ANOTHER-RECORD is changed by the user response.

Figure 9-8
The RM/COBOL-85 SET
statement format.

```
Format:

SET condition-name-identifier TO  { TRUE  }
                                  { FALSE }
```

Figure 9-9
Using a condition-name with
the SET statement.

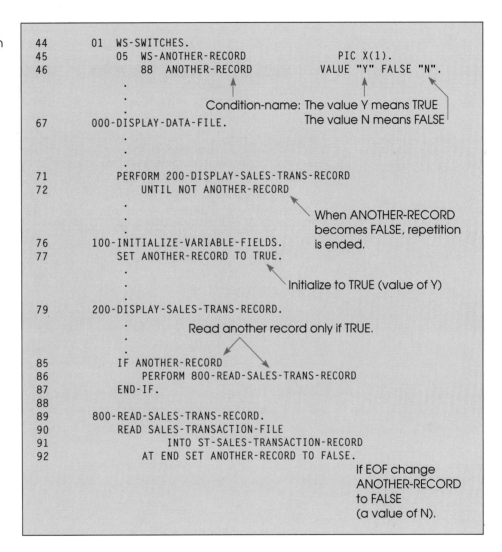

```
44        01  WS-SWITCHES.
45            05  WS-ANOTHER-RECORD           PIC X(1).
46                88  ANOTHER-RECORD          VALUE "Y" FALSE "N".
                          ·
                          ·                Condition-name: The value Y means TRUE
                          ·                The value N means FALSE
67        000-DISPLAY-DATA-FILE.
                          ·
                          ·
                          ·
71            PERFORM 200-DISPLAY-SALES-TRANS-RECORD
72                UNTIL NOT ANOTHER-RECORD
                          ·                    When ANOTHER-RECORD
                          ·                    becomes FALSE, repetition
                          ·                    is ended.
76        100-INITIALIZE-VARIABLE-FIELDS.
77            SET ANOTHER-RECORD TO TRUE.
                          ·
                          ·                    Initialize to TRUE (value of Y)
                          ·
79        200-DISPLAY-SALES-TRANS-RECORD.
                          ·       Read another record only if TRUE.
                          ·
                          ·
85            IF ANOTHER-RECORD
86                PERFORM 800-READ-SALES-TRANS-RECORD
87            END-IF.
88
89        800-READ-SALES-TRANS-RECORD.
90            READ SALES-TRANSACTION-FILE
91                INTO ST-SALES-TRANSACTION-RECORD
92            AT END SET ANOTHER-RECORD TO FALSE.
                                      If EOF change
                                      ANOTHER-RECORD
                                      to FALSE
                                      (a value of N).
```

**The DISPLAY Statement
as Used in DISPTRA1**

In the program, you can see that the entire screen display is accomplished with a single DISPLAY statement in the 840 module. This is almost identical to the form of Figure 9-1, except that many more elements are displayed. If you compare the LINE and POSITION entries in the program (Figure 9-7) to the screen layout of Figure 9-3, you will see that the numbers were taken directly from the layout. A typical screen display resulting from execution of this DISPLAY statement is shown in Figure 9-10.

Editing Output. Notice in the program that identifiers of data to be displayed are those from the input record, except for three fields: Date-of-sale, Quantity, and Price. Because editing is desired to produce a readable display (see the screen layout of Figure 9-3), edit pictures are defined in working-storage and the input fields moved into them before the DISPLAY.

Figure 9-10
Sample screen display for
the DISPTRA1 program.

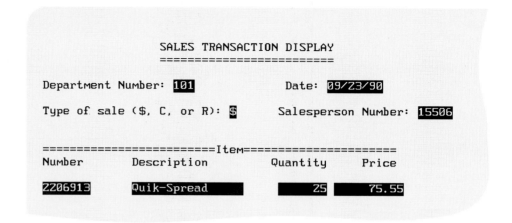

Positioning of Displayed Items.   In the DISPLAY statement of TRANS1.DAT, every displayed item includes LINE and POSITION options. Actually, this is not necessary because after executing a DISPLAY, the cursor remains positioned following the last character displayed. The LINE and POSITION options cause the cursor to be repositioned. Also, another DISPLAY (or ACCEPT) statement causes the cursor to be repositioned to the next line (or elsewhere if LINE and POSITION are used).

Therefore, the data field values that immediately follow the screen descriptions need not include the LINE and POSITION options. For instance, the following two forms are equivalent:

```
"Department Number: "     LINE 8   POSITION 1
ST-DEPARTMENT-NUMBER      LINE 8   POSITION 20 REVERSE
"Department Number: "     LINE 8   POSITION 1
ST-DEPARTMENT-NUMBER      REVERSE
```

Notice that a space is included following the colon after the word *Number*; otherwise, the data would be displayed with no space separating it from the description.

Erasing the Screen.   The first display line includes the ERASE option as follows:

```
DISPLAY
   "SALES TRANSACTION DISPLAY"  ERASE
```

When you run a program, the screen normally contains commands (or their resulting displays) remaining from preceding activities. In sending your program output to the screen, the DISPLAY statement does not check to ensure that the screen is empty. The ERASE option causes the entire screen to be cleared *before* displaying the output.

Where the ERASE alone causes the entire screen to be erased, two other versions allow you to erase only a portion of the screen: ERASE EOL (end of line) and ERASE EOS (end of screen). Consider the following examples:

```
DISPLAY "Sample description"  LINE 9  POSITION 15   ERASE EOL
```

This causes the following to occur:

1. The cursor is positioned at line 9, position 15.

2. The contents of the line from the position of the cursor to the end of the line are changed to blanks.

3. The literal *Sample description* is displayed beginning position 15 of the screen.

The EOS version works in much the same way, except that it clears the remainder of the screen. For example, had the preceding statement included ERASE EOS (instead of EOL) the line would have been clear (as with the EOS) *and* the rest of the screen would have been cleared as well (lines 10 through 25 and columns 1-80).

The ACCEPT Statement as Used in DISPTRA1

If you run the DISPTRA1 program, your screen display will not be limited to the record display of Figure 9-10. It will also include (on line 20) the display shown in Figure 9-11(a) generated from the code of the 845 module shown in Figure 9-11(b). The DISPLAY statement is nothing new. However, the ACCEPT introduces some new principles.

The POSITION 0 Option. You see in the sample display that the cursor is positioned immediately following the prompt to the user. Since another ACCEPT or DISPLAY repositions the cursor to the beginning of the next line, the program must include provisions to prevent this. This is done with the option POSITION 0 included with the ACCEPT.

The NO BEEP Option. Whenever an ACCEPT statement is executed, the computer bell (buzzer) is sounded and the computer awaits data entry from the keyboard. In many situations, the beeping from each ACCEPT is distracting. The NO BEEP option takes care of this by suppressing the sound from the ACCEPT with which it is used.

The UPDATE Option. In Figure 9-11, you see that the user is directed to enter a single letter Y (for Yes to continue) or N (for No to *not* continue). The normal response will be Y in order to display the next record. Hence, the Y is offered as a **default value**, a value that will be used if nothing is entered. In this way, the user need only strike the Enter key to continue displaying records. This is achieved with the UPDATE option, which causes the current value of the identifier to be displayed as the default value. Striking the Enter causes that value to be retained; striking any other key (other than Y) causes a new value to be entered.

In Figure 9-11(b), you can see that the identifier is WS-ANOTHER-RECORD, the program switch defined in the DATA DIVISION (program line 45). Remember that the value Y (equated to the TRUE condition for ANOTHER-RECORD) controls repeated execution of the 200 module.

Figure 9-11
DISPLAY statement.

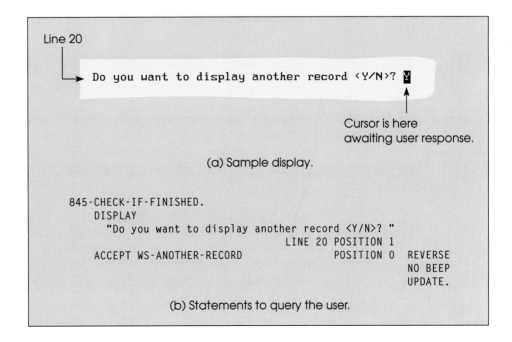

Line 20

Do you want to display another record <Y/N>? ▊

Cursor is here
awaiting user response.

(a) Sample display.

```
845-CHECK-IF-FINISHED.
    DISPLAY
      "Do you want to display another record <Y/N>? "
                                      LINE 20 POSITION 1
    ACCEPT WS-ANOTHER-RECORD              POSITION 0   REVERSE
                                                       NO BEEP
                                                       UPDATE.
```

(b) Statements to query the user.

One thing to remember is that *any* value for WS-ANOTHER-RECORD (other than Y)will be treated as false—not simply N as suggested by the condition-name definition. Thus, if you were to strike the "y" key (without uppercase), the condition would test as false and repeated execution terminated.

The SCREEN SECTION

One of the characteristics of COBOL is that data formatting information is included in the DATA DIVISION, separate from the imperative commands of the PROCEDURE DIVISION. This is convenient for several reasons; one is that it simplifies standardization among programs in a system. For instance, in any program you might write that uses the TRANS1.DAT file for input, you could simply copy the record description from a program library. There is no need to retype it every time it is needed.

However, the use of the ACCEPT and DISPLAY in the DISPTRA1 program requires that the formatting information be included as part of the PROCEDURE DIVISION. In general, this is poor practice because it makes the action of importing a standard screen from a program library clumsy. To remove formatting data for screen I/O from the PROCEDURE DIVISION and place it in the DATA DIVISION, Ryan-McFarland included a SCREEN SECTION with RM/COBOL-85 Release 4.0. Although there is no such section in the COBOL-85 Standard, the Ryan-McFarland implementation is similar to that found in many other COBOL systems.

The Sales Transaction Display Program Using a SCREEN SECTION

In the revised sales transaction display program (DISPTRA2) from Figure 9-12, there is a significant change in the way input and output are handled. In addition to the inclusion of a SCREEN SECTION, the 840-DISPLAY-1-RECORD and 845-CHECK-IF-FINISHED are omitted. Most of the code necessary to control the input and output operations has been shifted from the PROCEDURE DIVISION to the DATA DIVISION.

The SCREEN SECTION is similar to the WORKING-STORAGE SECTION in that "records" are defined using an 01 entry followed by 02–49 level entries. There are some similarities in that both include PIC clauses and VALUE clauses. However, as you can see, there are numerous differences.

The DISPLAY and ACCEPT Used with a SCREEN SECTION

Let's begin with the DISPLAY and ACCEPT at lines 117 and 118; they are the first two statements in the 200-DISPLAY-SALES-TRANS-RECORD module:

```
DISPLAY RECORD-SCREEN
ACCEPT RECORD-SCREEN
```

Notice that *both* of them specify the 01 entry name (see program line 61): the record name in the SCREEN SECTION. As you will learn, some SCREEN SECTION entries react to the DISPLAY and others to the ACCEPT.

Types of SCREEN SECTION Entries

The first 05 entry is repeated in Figure 9-13. The annotations describe, reasonably well, the way in which this works. It may look a little strange to you without the picture clause, but one is simply not needed. Note two minor differences between options of the SCREEN SECTION and the DISPLAY statement. That is, BLANK SCREEN is used in place of ERASE, and the positioning on the line is coded with the word COL (or COLUMN) rather than the word POSITION. Each of the entries in the SCREEN SECTION under *Field descriptions* has the same form (excluding the BLANK SCREEN option).

When a DISPLAY is executed, each literal entry such as this causes output to be displayed on the screen. When an ACCEPT is executed, these literal entries are ignored.

Figure 9-12   Using the SCREEN SECTION: The DISPTRA2 program.

```
  1        IDENTIFICATION DIVISION.                           59        SCREEN SECTION.
  2                                                           60
  3        PROGRAM-ID. DISPTRA2.                              61        01  RECORD-SCREEN.
  4                                                           62      *   Field descriptions
  5      *     Written by Price/Welburn                       63          05  VALUE "SALES TRANSACTION DISPLAY"    BLANK SCREEN
  6      *     General Merchandise Supply Company             64                                                  LINE 5  COL 18.
  7      *     September 29, 1989                             65          05  VALUE  "——————————————————————"      LINE 6  COL 18.
  8      *     Written for RM/COBOL-85                        66          05  VALUE  "Department Number: "          LINE 8  COL 1.
  9                                                           67          05  VALUE  "Date: "                      LINE 8  COL 36.
 10      *     This program displays records from the file TRANS1.DAT.  68          05  VALUE  "Type of sale ($, C, or R):"  LINE 10 COL 1.
 11      *     Each record is read and displayed on the screen.        69          05  VALUE  "Salesperson Number: "    LINE 10 COL 35.
 12      *     After each, the user can request the next one  70          05  VALUE
 13      *     or terminate the program.                      71                 "————————————————Item————————————————————"
 14                                                           72                                                  LINE 13 COL 1.
 15      *     The program illustrates the SCREEN SECTION.    73          05  VALUE
 16                                                           74                 "Number      Description      Quantity      Price"
 17                                                           75                                                  LINE 14 COL 1.
 18        ENVIRONMENT DIVISION.                              76          05  VALUE
 19                                                           77                 "Do you want to display another record <Y/N>? "
 20        CONFIGURATION SECTION.                             78                                                  LINE 20 COL 1.
 21                                                           79      *   Data fields
 22        SOURCE-COMPUTER. IBM-PC.                           80          05  PIC X(3)       FROM ST-DEPARTMENT-NUMBER
 23                                                           81                                                  LINE 8  COL 20 REVERSE.
 24        INPUT-OUTPUT SECTION.                              82          05  PIC XX/XX/XX   FROM ST-DATE-OF-SALE
 25                                                           83                                                  LINE 8  COL 42 REVERSE.
 26        FILE-CONTROL.                                      84          05  PIC X(1)       FROM ST-TYPE-OF-SALE
 27            SELECT SALES-TRANSACTION-FILE                  85                                                  LINE 10 COL 28 REVERSE.
 28                ASSIGN TO DISK, "TRANS1.DAT"               86          05  PIC X(5)       FROM ST-EMPLOYEE-NUMBER
 29                ORGANIZATION LINE SEQUENTIAL.              87                                                  LINE 10 COL 55 REVERSE.
 30                                                           88          05  PIC X(7)       FROM ST-ITEM-NUMBER
 31                                                           89                                                  LINE 16 COL 1  REVERSE.
 32        DATA DIVISION.                                     90          05  PIC X(15)      FROM ST-ITEM-DESCRIPTION
 33                                                           91                                                  LINE 16 COL 13 REVERSE.
 34        FILE SECTION.                                      92          05  PIC ---,--9    FROM ST-QUANTITY
 35                                                           93                                                  LINE 16 COL 34 REVERSE.
 36        FD  SALES-TRANSACTION-FILE                         94          05  PIC ZZ,ZZZ.99  FROM ST-PRICE
 37                RECORD CONTAINS 50 CHARACTERS              95                                                  LINE 16 COL 43 REVERSE.
 38                LABEL RECORDS ARE STANDARD.               96      *   Query user
 39                                                           97          05  PIC X(1)       USING WS-ANOTHER-RECORD
 40        01  SALES-TRANSACTION-RECORD      PIC X(50).       98                                                  LINE 20 COL 46 REVERSE
 41                                                           99                                                  AUTO.
 42        WORKING-STORAGE SECTION.                          100
 43                                                          101
 44        01  WS-SWITCHES.                                  102        PROCEDURE DIVISION.
 45            05  WS-ANOTHER-RECORD         PIC X(1).       103
 46                88  ANOTHER-RECORD        VALUE "Y" FALSE "N".  104        000-DISPLAY-DATA-FILE.
 47                                                          105            OPEN INPUT SALES-TRANSACTION-FILE
 48        01  ST-SALES-TRANSACTION-RECORD.                  106            PERFORM 100-INITIALIZE-VARIABLE-FIELDS
 49            05  ST-DATE-OF-SALE           PIC X(6).       107            PERFORM 800-READ-SALES-TRANS-RECORD
 50            05  ST-DEPARTMENT-NUMBER      PIC X(3).       108            PERFORM 200-DISPLAY-SALES-TRANS-RECORD
 51            05  ST-ITEM-NUMBER            PIC X(7).       109                UNTIL NOT ANOTHER-RECORD
 52            05  ST-ITEM-DESCRIPTION       PIC X(15).      110            CLOSE SALES-TRANSACTION-FILE
 53            05  ST-EMPLOYEE-NUMBER        PIC X(5).       111            STOP RUN.
 54            05  ST-QUANTITY               PIC S9(5)       112
 55                          SIGN IS TRAILING SEPARATE.      113        100-INITIALIZE-VARIABLE-FIELDS.
 56            05  ST-PRICE                  PIC 9(5)V99.    114            SET ANOTHER-RECORD TO TRUE.
 57            05  ST-TYPE-OF-SALE           PIC X(1).       115
 58                                                          116        200-DISPLAY-SALES-TRANS-RECORD.
                                                             117            DISPLAY RECORD-SCREEN
                                                             118            ACCEPT RECORD-SCREEN
                                                             119            IF ANOTHER-RECORD
                                                             120                PERFORM 800-READ-SALES-TRANS-RECORD
                                                             121            END-IF.
                                                             122
                                                             123        800-READ-SALES-TRANS-RECORD.
                                                             124            READ SALES-TRANSACTION-FILE
                                                             125                INTO ST-SALES-TRANSACTION-RECORD
                                                             126                AT END SET ANOTHER-RECORD TO FALSE.
```

Figure 9-13
Defining a literal for screen
display.

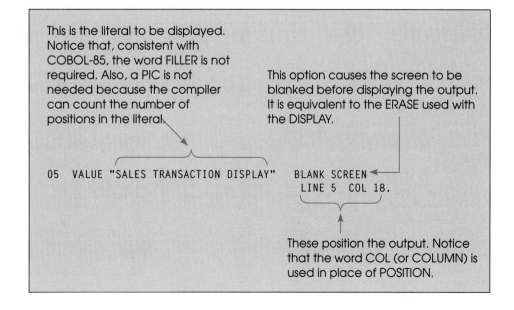

This is the literal to be displayed.
Notice that, consistent with
COBOL-85, the word FILLER is not
required. Also, a PIC is not
needed because the compiler
can count the number of
positions in the literal.

This option causes the screen to be
blanked before displaying the output.
It is equivalent to the ERASE used with
the DISPLAY.

```
05  VALUE "SALES TRANSACTION DISPLAY"    BLANK SCREEN
                                         LINE 5  COL 18.
```

These position the output. Notice
that the word COL (or COLUMN) is
used in place of POSITION.

Next, consider the second of the *Data fields* entries from the SCREEN SECTION; it is repeated in Figure 9-14. (Entries of this SCREEN SECTION are arranged with all Field descriptions first, followed by all Data fields. Their order has no significance when each includes the LINE and COL options.) Since the contents of a field defined elsewhere in the DATA DIVISION are to be printed, a PIC must be included. (A separate numeric-edited item need not be defined as with the DISPLAY because the combination of the screen DISPLAY and this definition serve the purpose.) You can see that each *Data fields* entry includes a picture definition, even if it is exactly the same as the picture by which the field is defined in the FILE SECTION. Do not confuse these two definitions. Each PIC clause in the SCREEN SECTION tells the compiler how to format the screen for that entry and has nothing to do with the PIC clause in the input record description.

When a DISPLAY is executed, the keyword FROM triggers output: the compiler knows that something is to be displayed. When an ACCEPT is executed, the FROM entries are ignored.

The final entry in the SCREEN SECTION is repeated here in Figure 9-15. The USING triggers both the DISPLAY and the ACCEPT. That is, when a DISPLAY is executed, the value of the designated field is displayed. When an ACCEPT is encountered, program execution stops and awaits an entry from the keyboard for any items defined with the USING. This serves the purpose of offering the current value of the field as the default. The AUTO option is included to require the program to accept an entry the moment the key is struck (without striking the Enter key). Note that this is the default action with the ACCEPT without a SCREEN SECTION.

Figure 9-14
Formatting a data field for screen display.

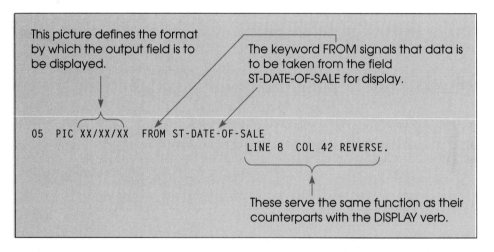

Figure 9-15
The USING—functions for both input and output.

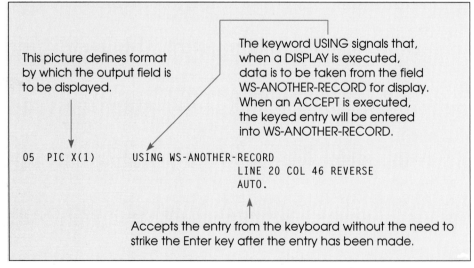

Generalizing the SCREEN SECTION Entries

You can see that the overall form of the SCREEN SECTION is like that of the FILE SECTION and the WORKING-STORAGE SECTION: a 01 entry with subordinate 02-49 entries. The format of the SCREEN SECTION entries is shown in Figure 9-16.

In the SCREEN SECTION of the DISPTRA2 program, only the 01 entry includes a screen-entry-name.

Notice that those entries referred to as control-options with the DISPLAY statements are correspondingly called **screen-attributes** in the SCREEN SECTION. In addition to the LINE, COL, BLANK SCREEN, REVERSE, and AUTO, there are a number of others; the following correspond to options of the DISPLAY:

BLANK LINE corresponds to the ERASE EOL

BLANK REMAINDER corresponds to the ERASE EOS

BLINK corresponds to the BLINK

HIGHLIGHT corresponds to the HIGH

Although the PICTURE clause used in this program looks the same as those used in other sections of the DATA DIVISION, it has a significantly different format, as shown in Figure 9-17.

The element *character-string* is defined in the same way and has the same interpretation as in the other sections of the DATA DIVISION. The element *picture-item* may be any of the following:

FROM identifier

FROM nonnumeric literal

TO identifier

USING identifier

As you have already found, the FROM triggers the DISPLAY and the USING triggers both the ACCEPT and DISPLAY. You will see how the TO is used in the next example program.

Data Entry Program Definition

To illustrate data entry, the next example program combines the screen features of DISPTRA2 and the data validation features of DATAVAL from Chapter 8. That is, the program will permit entry of new records through the keyboard into a data file using screen capabilities. As each field is entered, it is validated using validation modules you studied in the preceding chapter.

Figure 9-16
Screen description entry format.

Format:

level-number [screen-entry-name / FILLER] [screen-attribute]. . .

Figure 9-17
Format of the PICTURE screen-attribute.

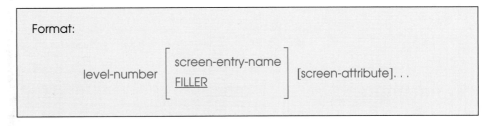

Format:

{ PICTURE / PIC } IS character-string   picture-item

Program Specifications The program specifications for the data entry program DATAENT are shown in Figure 9-18. In these, you see that the operations to be carried out are relatively few—nothing like those in generating the report of DATAVAL. The output record format is identical to that of the display programs you have already studied. This program is actually a "mate" to DISPTRA2 in that it allows the addition of records to the file used by DISPTRA2.

Repeated execution of the record entry is achieved in the same way as repeated record display in the display programs: at the request of the user. Notice that the user must be given the option of saving each data record or ignoring it.

Figure 9-18
Program specifications: the DATAENT program.

PROGRAMMING SPECIFICATIONS

Program name: SALES-TRANSACTION DISPLAY   **Program ID:** DATAENT

Program Description:

This program adds new records to the Sales-transaction file from data entered through the keyboard. Each field is validated as it is entered.

Output File:

Sales-Transaction File (TRANS1.DAT)

List of Program Operations:

A. Accept each input sales-transaction record from the keyboard.

  1. After each field is entered, validate it as designated in the field validation specifications.

  2. If a field is not valid, display an appropriate error message and allow for reentry of that field.

  3. Do not allow data entry to progress to the next field unless the current field value is valid.

B. When data entry for a record is complete, ask the user if the record should be stored to disk. If the response is yes, write the record to disk.

C. Query user about displaying another record. If user does not wish to continue, terminate processing.

==

Output-record format:

Positions	Field	Data class	Comments
1-6	Date of sale	Numeric	Format: mmddyy
7-9	Department number	Numeric	
10-16	Item number	Numeric	
17-31	Item description	Alphanumeric	
32-36	Employee number	Numeric	
37-42	Quantity	Numeric	Separate sign (trailing)
43-50	Price	Numeric	Dollars and cents
51	Type of sale	Alphanumeric	Values: $, C, or R

==

(continued)

Figure 9-18
(continued)

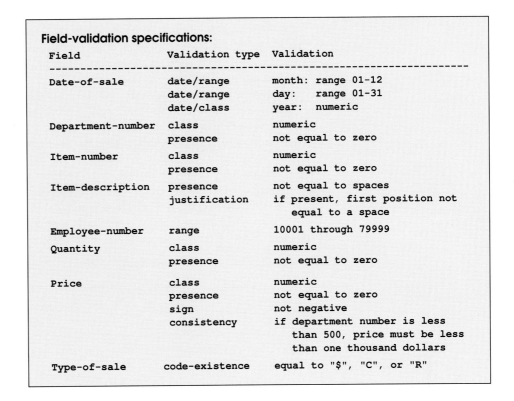

Field-validation specifications:

Field	Validation type	Validation
Date-of-sale	date/range	month: range 01-12
	date/range	day: range 01-31
	date/class	year: numeric
Department-number	class	numeric
	presence	not equal to zero
Item-number	class	numeric
	presence	not equal to zero
Item-description	presence	not equal to spaces
	justification	if present, first position not equal to a space
Employee-number	range	10001 through 79999
Quantity	class	numeric
	presence	not equal to zero
Price	class	numeric
	presence	not equal to zero
	sign	not negative
	consistency	if department number is less than 500, price must be less than one thousand dollars
Type-of-sale	code-existence	equal to "$", "C", or "R"

Normally, a screen chart would be included with the programming specifications. However, the chart is the same as that for the display programs (see Figure 9-3), so it is not duplicated here.

The structure chart for this program is shown in Figure 9-19. From this, you can see that the majority of the modules are for data entry and validation, much the same as DATAVAL.

Figure 9-19 Structure chart: the DATAENT program.

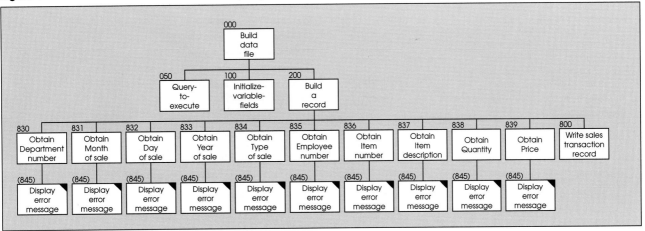

Program Logic The program logic for the data entry program is depicted by the pseudocode of Figure 9-20 and the flowchart of Figure 9-21. Most of this is reasonably straightforward in that it uses principles and techniques that you know from previous examples. However, there are two items that utilize different logic than any you have encountered before.

First is in the mainline module, 000-Build-Data-File. The first action taken is not to open the file, but to query the user. With interactive programs, it is always a good idea to display on the screen an identification of the program and a brief description of what it does. Then give the user the option of continuing or terminating execution immediately in case he or she has run the wrong program. In the logic depicted by both the pseudocode and the flowchart, you can see that the processing operations are done on a conditional basis—only if the user has indicated a desire to execute the program. If not, execution is immediately terminated.

The second item of interest is the logic within the data entry/validation modules (830 through 839). The sequence of actions in each of these is as follows:

1. Initialize the switch Valid-field to False.

2. Repeat the following sequence of statements until Valid-switch is True.

   a. Accept the input field.

   b. If the input field is valid (according to the specifications for that field)
      Move the appropriate error message to a message field
      else
      Set the Valid-field switch to True.

3. Perform the 845-DISPLAY-ERROR-MESSAGE module. This displays the message field if Valid-field is False and clears the screen message line if it is True.

Figure 9-20 Pseudocode: the DATAENT program.

```
000-Build-Data-File module

1.   Perform 050-Query-to-execute.
2.   If Yes-response to continue query
     a.   Perform 100-Initialize-Parameters.
     b.   Open the output file.
     c.   Perform 200-Build-a-Record until no more records to add.
     d.   Close the file.
3.   Stop the run.

050-Query-to-Execute

1.   Move "N" to User-response.
2.   Display an announcement screen.
3.   Query user about continuing.

100-Initialize-Variable-Fields module

1.   Display announcement screen.
2.   Set the No-more-records-to-add switch to False.

200-Build-a-Record module

 1.  Perform 830-Obtain-department-number
 2.  Perform 831-Obtain-month-of-sale
 3.  Perform 832-Obtain-day-of-sale
 4.  Perform 833-Obtain-year-of-sale
 5.  Perform 834-Obtain-type-of-sale
 6.  Perform 835-Obtain-employee-number
 7.  Perform 836-Obtain-item-number
 8.  Perform 837-Obtain-item-description
 9.  Perform 838-Obtain-quantity
10.  Perform 839-Obtain-price
11.  Accept user response to save record
12.  If user response Yes,
         Perform 800-Write-sales-trans-record
13.  Accept user response about another record to add
14.  If no more records
         Set the No-more-records-to-add switch to True.
```

```
800-Write-Sales-Trans-Record Module

1.   Write the output Valid-sales-transaction record area.

830-Obtain-Department-Number module

831-Obtain-Month-of-Sale module

832-Obtain-Day-of-Sale module

833-Obtain-Year-of-Sale module

834-Obtain-Type-of-Sale module

835-Obtain-Employee-Number module

836-Obtain-Item-Number module

837-Obtain-Item-Description module

838-Obtain-Quantity module

839-Obtain-Price module

For each of the above modules (830-839), the general logic outlined
below is used:

1.   Set Valid-field switch to False.
2.   Repeat the following until Valid-field is True.
         Check the field entered.
         If invalid
             move error message to output area
         else
             Set Valid-field switch to True.

845-Display-Error-Message module

1.   Valid-field is True
         Clear message line
     else
         Display error message
         Move Spaces to the Record-image-area.
```

Figure 9-21 Flowchart: the DATAENT program (continued on page 466).

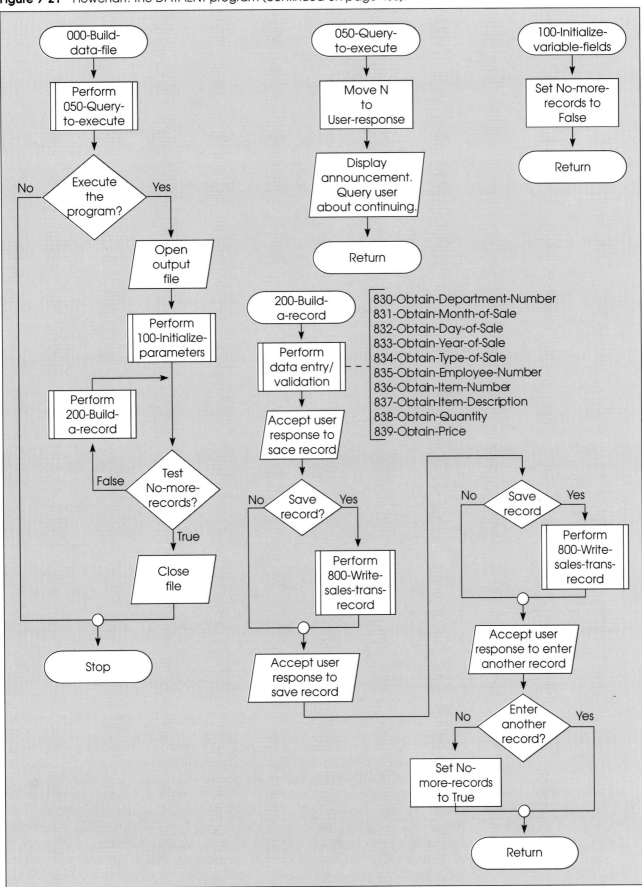

Figure 9-21   (continued from page 465).

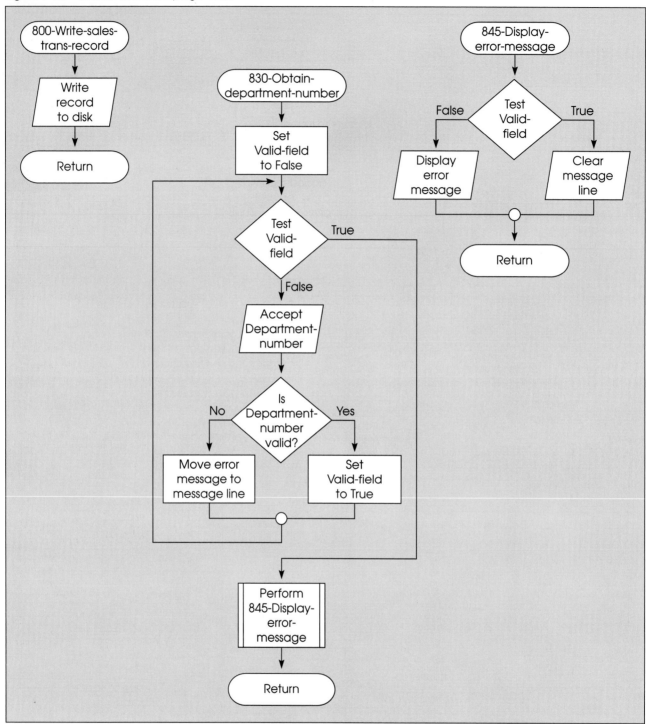

Notice in these modules that a *sequence of statements* is repeated (refer to module 830). In all other programs, you had to perform a separate paragraph to repeat a sequence. COBOL-85 provides an alternative: the in-line PERFORM.

The In-Line PERFORM—
COBOL-85

One of the main focuses of the standards group responsible for the COBOL-85 Standard was to include features more compatible with modern structured programming techniques. With COBOL-74, if you wish to execute a sequence of code repeatedly, you must place that sequence of code in a separate procedure (paragraph). Execution involves transferring control to it (with the PERFORM/ UNTIL), with control being returned when execution of the procedure is completed. Because the procedure to be executed is outside the line of code [see Figure 9-22(a)], it is called an **out-of-line procedure**. An advantage of this out-of-line capability is that a procedure can be performed from two or more different places in the program.

There are many instances when a set of statements to be repeated should remain physically within a module because the action of the sequence is a logical part of that module. However, with COBOL-74 (using structured principles of this text), they must be placed in an out-of-line procedure executed by a PERFORM/UNTIL. Such a use of an out-of-line procedure is clumsy and degrades the readability of the program.

To resolve this problem, COBOL-85 provides an **in-line procedure** capability in which the sequence of code is included directly in the line of code being executed, as illustrated in Figure 9-22(b).* The format of the in-line PERFORM to accomplish this is shown in Figure 9-23.

Execution of this sequence causes the statements from the PERFORM to the END-PERFORM to be executed repeatedly until the condition is true. (The repetitive aspect of this statement is the same as that of the out-of-line PERFORM.) Observe that notation *imperative-statement* means one or more COBOL statements. The END-PERFORM signals the end of the sequence of statements to be performed; it is the scope terminator.

The Data Entry Program

The completed data entry program (DATAENT) is shown in Figure 9-24. You can see that a large portion of this program consists of the SCREEN SECTION in which the variety of screen records are defined for use with both the DISPLAY and

Figure 9-22
Out-of-line and in-line
PERFORM.

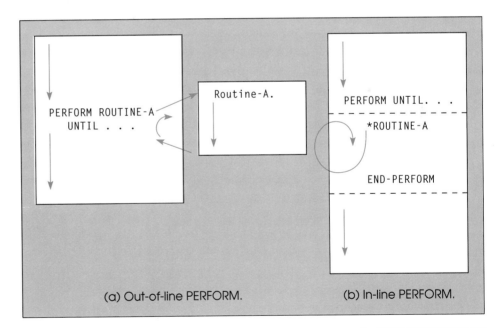

(a) Out-of-line PERFORM.   (b) In-line PERFORM.

Figure 9-23
Format of the in-line
PERFORM.

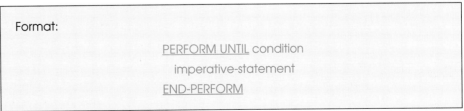

Format:

PERFORM UNTIL condition

imperative-statement

END-PERFORM

---

*This can be coded in COBOL-74 using the GO TO statement, which causes transfer of control *without* the return capabilities of the PERFORM. In accordance with structured programming principles, use of the GO TO branching verb should be avoided.

ACCEPT statements. As you study this program, notice that all screen control and positioning is contained in the SCREEN SECTION—none is coded in the DISPLAY and ACCEPT statements of the PROCEDURE DIVISION. If any changes were to be required for the screen layout, the programmer would make all the changes in the SCREEN SECTION. It would not be necessary to search the PROCEDURE DIVISION for DISPLAY and ACCEPT statements.

Figure 9-24 The DATAENT program.

```
1       IDENTIFICATION DIVISION.
2
3       PROGRAM-ID. DATAENT.
4
5   *       Written by Price/Welburn
6   *       General Merchandise Supply Company
7   *       September 30, 1989
8   *       Written for RM/COBOL-85
9
10  *       This program creates the file TRANS.DAT from data
11  *       entered at the keyboard.  Following are the
12  *       fields of the data record.
13  *           Record code
14  *           Date of sale
15  *           Department number
16  *           Item number
17  *           Item description
18  *           Employee (salesperson) number
19  *           Quantity
20  *           Sale price
21  *           Type of sale
22  *       Each data field is validated as it is entered.
23
24
25      ENVIRONMENT DIVISION.
26
27      CONFIGURATION SECTION.
28
29      SOURCE-COMPUTER. IBM-PC.
30
31      INPUT-OUTPUT SECTION.
32
33      FILE-CONTROL.
34          SELECT SALES-TRANSACTION-FILE
35              ASSIGN TO DISK WS-FILE-NAME
36              ORGANIZATION LINE SEQUENTIAL.
37
38
39      DATA DIVISION.
40
41      FILE SECTION.
42
43      FD  SALES-TRANSACTION-FILE
44          RECORD CONTAINS 50 CHARACTERS
45          LABEL RECORDS ARE STANDARD.
46
47      01  SALES-TRANSACTION-RECORD        PIC X(50).
48
49      WORKING-STORAGE SECTION.
50
51      01  WS-SWITCHES.
52          05  WS-FIELD-VALID-SWITCH       PIC X(1).
53              88  VALID-FIELD         VALUE "Y" FALSE "N".
54          05  WS-CONTINUE-SWITCH          PIC X(1).
55              88  NO-MORE-RECORDS-TO-ADD VALUE "T" FALSE "F".
56          05  WS-RESPONSE                 PIC X(1).
57              88  YES-RESPONSE            VALUE "Y"
58                                                "y".
59
60      01  WS-WORK-VARIABLES.
61          05  WS-FILE-NAME    PIC X(14)  VALUE "TRANS1.DAT".
62          05  WS-USER-MESSAGE             PIC X(50).
63
64      01  ST-SALES-TRANSACTION-RECORD.
65          05  ST-DATE-OF-SALE.
66              10  ST-MONTH-OF-SALE        PIC X(2).
67                  88  VALID-MONTH     VALUE "01" THRU "12".
68              10  ST-DAY-OF-SALE          PIC X(2).
69                  88  VALID-DAY       VALUE "01" THRU "31".
70              10  ST-YEAR-OF-SALE         PIC X(2).
71          05  ST-DEPARTMENT-NUMBER        PIC X(3).
72          05  ST-ITEM-NUMBER              PIC X(7).
73          05  ST-ITEM-DESCRIPTION.
74              10  ST-ITEM-DESC-FIRST-POS  PIC X(1).
75              10                          PIC X(14).
76          05  ST-EMPLOYEE-NUMBER          PIC X(5).
77              88  VALID-EMPLOYEE-NUMBER   VALUE "10001"
78                                              THRU "79999".
79          05  ST-QUANTITY                 PIC S9(5)
80                          SIGN IS TRAILING SEPARATE.
81          05  ST-PRICE                    PIC 9(5)V99.
82          05  ST-TYPE-OF-SALE             PIC X(1).
83              88  VALID-TYPE-OF-SALE      VALUES "$"
84                                                "C"
85                                                "R".
86
87      SCREEN SECTION.
88
89      01  ANNOUNCEMENT-SCREEN.
90          05  VALUE
91          "This program allows you to enter new sales "
92              BLANK SCREEN
93              LINE 5.
94          05  VALUE
95          "transaction records into the file:"
96              LINE 6.
97          05  PIC X(14)  FROM WS-FILE-NAME
98              LINE 8  COL 10.
99          05  VALUE
100         "Do you want to continue <Y/N>? "
101             LINE 10.
102         05  PIC X(1)   USING WS-RESPONSE
103             LINE 10 COL 32
104             REVERSE
105             AUTO.
106
107     01  ACCEPT-RECORD.
108     *   Field descriptions
109         05  VALUE "SALES TRANSACTION ENTRY"    BLANK SCREEN
110                                             LINE 5 COL 18.
111         05  VALUE "======================"  LINE 6  COL 18.
112         05  VALUE "Department Number: "      LINE 8  COL 1.
113         05  VALUE "Date: "                   LINE 8  COL 36.
114         05  VALUE "/  /"                     LINE 8  COL 44.
115         05  VALUE "Type of sale ($, C, or R):" LINE 10 COL 1.
116         05  VALUE "Salesperson Number:"      LINE 10 COL 35.
117         05  VALUE
118         "========================Item===================="
119                                             LINE 13 COL 1.
120         05  VALUE
121         "Number      Description       Quantity    Price"
122                                             LINE 14 COL 1.
123     *   Input fields
124         05  SCR-DEPARTMENT-NUMBER           LINE 8  COL 20
125             PIC 9(3)        TO ST-DEPARTMENT-NUMBER
126             REVERSE.
127         05  SCR-MONTH-OF-SALE               LINE 8  COL 42
128             PIC 99          TO ST-MONTH-OF-SALE
129             REVERSE
130             FULL
131             AUTO.
132         05  SCR-DAY-OF-SALE                 LINE 8  COL 45
133             PIC 99          TO ST-DAY-OF-SALE
134             REVERSE
135             FULL
136             AUTO.
137         05  SCR-YEAR-OF-SALE                LINE 8  COL 48
138             PIC 99          TO ST-YEAR-OF-SALE
139             REVERSE
140             REQUIRED
141             FULL.
142         05  SCR-TYPE-OF-SALE                LINE 10 COL 28
143             PIC X(1)        TO ST-TYPE-OF-SALE
144             REVERSE.
145         05  SCR-EMPLOYEE-NUMBER             LINE 10 COL 55
146             PIC 9(5)        TO ST-EMPLOYEE-NUMBER
147             REVERSE.
148         05  SCR-ITEM-NUMBER                 LINE 16 COL 1
149             PIC 9(7)        TO ST-ITEM-NUMBER
150             REVERSE.
151         05  SCR-ITEM-DESCRIPTION            LINE 16 COL 13
152             PIC X(15)       TO ST-ITEM-DESCRIPTION
153             REVERSE.
154         05  SCR-QUANTITY                    LINE 16 COL 34
155             PIC Z(5)+       TO ST-QUANTITY
156             REVERSE.
157         05  SCR-PRICE                       LINE 16 COL 44
158             PIC ZZZZZ.ZZ  TO ST-PRICE
159             REVERSE.
160
161     01  ERROR-MESSAGE.
162         05  PIC X(50)    FROM WS-USER-MESSAGE LINE 20 COL 1
163             BELL.
164
165     01  CLEAR-MESSAGE.
166         05                               LINE 20 COL 1
167             BLANK REMAINDER.
168
169     01  RESPONSE-SCREEN.
170         05  PIC X(50)    FROM WS-USER-MESSAGE LINE 20 COL 1
171             BLANK REMAINDER.
172         05  PIC X(1)     USING WS-RESPONSE  LINE 20 COL 52
173             REVERSE
174             AUTO.
175
176
```

Figure 9-24   (continued)

```
177        PROCEDURE DIVISION.
178
179        000-BUILD-DATA-FILE.
180            PERFORM 050-QUERY-TO-EXECUTE
181            IF YES-RESPONSE
182                OPEN EXTEND SALES-TRANSACTION-FILE
183                PERFORM 100-INITIALIZE-VARIABLE-FIELDS
184                PERFORM 200-BUILD-A-RECORD
185                    UNTIL NO-MORE-RECORDS-TO-ADD
186                CLOSE SALES-TRANSACTION-FILE
187            END-IF
188            STOP RUN.
189
190        050-QUERY-TO-EXECUTE.
191            MOVE "N" TO WS-RESPONSE
192            DISPLAY ANNOUNCEMENT-SCREEN
193            ACCEPT ANNOUNCEMENT-SCREEN.
194
195        100-INITIALIZE-VARIABLE-FIELDS.
196            SET NO-MORE-RECORDS-TO-ADD TO FALSE.
197
198        200-BUILD-A-RECORD.
199            DISPLAY ACCEPT-RECORD
200
201        * ACCEPT THE DATA
202            PERFORM 830-OBTAIN-DEPARTMENT-NUMBER
203            PERFORM 831-OBTAIN-MONTH-OF-SALE
204            PERFORM 832-OBTAIN-DAY-OF-SALE
205            PERFORM 833-OBTAIN-YEAR-OF-SALE
206            PERFORM 834-OBTAIN-TYPE-OF-SALE
207            PERFORM 835-OBTAIN-EMPLOYEE-NUMBER
208            PERFORM 836-OBTAIN-ITEM-NUMBER
209            PERFORM 837-OBTAIN-ITEM-DESCRIPTION
210            PERFORM 838-OBTAIN-QUANTITY
211            PERFORM 839-OBTAIN-PRICE
212
213        * CHECK TO WRITE IT TO DISK
214            MOVE "Do you want to save this record to the file <Y/N>?"
215                TO WS-USER-MESSAGE
216            MOVE "Y" TO WS-RESPONSE
217            DISPLAY RESPONSE-SCREEN
218            ACCEPT RESPONSE-SCREEN
219            IF YES-RESPONSE
220                MOVE ST-SALES-TRANSACTION-RECORD
221                    TO SALES-TRANSACTION-RECORD
222                PERFORM 800-WRITE-SALES-TRANS-RECORD
223            END-IF
224
225        * CHECK TO CONTINUE
226            MOVE "     Do you want to enter another record <Y/N>?"
227                TO WS-USER-MESSAGE
228            MOVE "Y" TO WS-RESPONSE
229            DISPLAY RESPONSE-SCREEN
230            ACCEPT RESPONSE-SCREEN
231            IF NOT YES-RESPONSE
232                SET NO-MORE-RECORDS-TO-ADD TO TRUE
233            END-IF.
234
235        800-WRITE-SALES-TRANS-RECORD.
236            WRITE SALES-TRANSACTION-RECORD.
237
238        830-OBTAIN-DEPARTMENT-NUMBER.
239            SET VALID-FIELD TO FALSE
240            PERFORM UNTIL VALID-FIELD
241                ACCEPT SCR-DEPARTMENT-NUMBER
242                IF ST-DEPARTMENT-NUMBER = "000"
243                    MOVE "Department number must not be zero"
244                        TO WS-USER-MESSAGE
245                ELSE
246                    SET VALID-FIELD TO TRUE
247                END-IF
248                PERFORM 845-DISPLAY-ERROR-MESSAGE
249            END-PERFORM.
250
251        831-OBTAIN-MONTH-OF-SALE.
252            SET VALID-FIELD TO FALSE
253            PERFORM UNTIL VALID-FIELD
254                ACCEPT SCR-MONTH-OF-SALE
255                IF NOT VALID-MONTH
256                    MOVE "Month number must be between 01 and 12"
257                        TO WS-USER-MESSAGE
258                ELSE
259                    SET VALID-FIELD TO TRUE
260                END-IF
261                PERFORM 845-DISPLAY-ERROR-MESSAGE
262            END-PERFORM.
263
264        832-OBTAIN-DAY-OF-SALE.
265            SET VALID-FIELD TO FALSE
266            PERFORM UNTIL VALID-FIELD
267                ACCEPT SCR-DAY-OF-SALE
268                IF NOT VALID-DAY
269                    MOVE "Day number must be between 01 and 31"
270                        TO WS-USER-MESSAGE
271                ELSE
272                    SET VALID-FIELD TO TRUE
273                END-IF
274                PERFORM 845-DISPLAY-ERROR-MESSAGE
275            END-PERFORM.

276
277        833-OBTAIN-YEAR-OF-SALE.
278            ACCEPT SCR-YEAR-OF-SALE.
279
280        834-OBTAIN-TYPE-OF-SALE.
281            SET VALID-FIELD TO FALSE
282            PERFORM UNTIL VALID-FIELD
283                ACCEPT SCR-TYPE-OF-SALE
284                IF NOT VALID-TYPE-OF-SALE
285                    MOVE "Sale code must be $, C, or R"
286                        TO WS-USER-MESSAGE
287                ELSE
288                    SET VALID-FIELD TO TRUE
289                END-IF
290                PERFORM 845-DISPLAY-ERROR-MESSAGE
291            END-PERFORM.
292
293        835-OBTAIN-EMPLOYEE-NUMBER.
294            SET VALID-FIELD TO FALSE
295            PERFORM UNTIL VALID-FIELD
296                ACCEPT SCR-EMPLOYEE-NUMBER
297                IF NOT VALID-EMPLOYEE-NUMBER
298                    MOVE "Salesperson number must be between 10001 and 79999"
299                        TO WS-USER-MESSAGE
300                ELSE
301                    SET VALID-FIELD TO TRUE
302                END-IF
303                PERFORM 845-DISPLAY-ERROR-MESSAGE
304            END-PERFORM.
305
306        836-OBTAIN-ITEM-NUMBER.
307            SET VALID-FIELD TO FALSE
308            PERFORM UNTIL VALID-FIELD
309                ACCEPT SCR-ITEM-NUMBER
310                IF ST-ITEM-NUMBER IS EQUAL TO ZERO
311                    MOVE "Non-zero item number is required"
312                        TO WS-USER-MESSAGE
313                ELSE
314                    SET VALID-FIELD TO TRUE
315                END-IF
316                PERFORM 845-DISPLAY-ERROR-MESSAGE
317            END-PERFORM.
318
319        837-OBTAIN-ITEM-DESCRIPTION.
320            SET VALID-FIELD TO FALSE
321            PERFORM UNTIL VALID-FIELD
322                ACCEPT SCR-ITEM-DESCRIPTION
323                IF ST-ITEM-DESC-FIRST-POS IS EQUAL TO SPACE
324                    MOVE "First position must not be blank"
325                        TO WS-USER-MESSAGE
326                ELSE
327                    SET VALID-FIELD TO TRUE
328                END-IF
329                PERFORM 845-DISPLAY-ERROR-MESSAGE
330            END-PERFORM.
331
332        838-OBTAIN-QUANTITY.
333            SET VALID-FIELD TO FALSE
334            PERFORM UNTIL VALID-FIELD
335                ACCEPT SCR-QUANTITY
336                IF ST-QUANTITY IS EQUAL TO ZERO
337                    MOVE "Entry must be greater than zero"
338                        TO WS-USER-MESSAGE
339                ELSE
340                    SET VALID-FIELD TO TRUE
341                END-IF
342                PERFORM 845-DISPLAY-ERROR-MESSAGE
343            END-PERFORM.
344
345        839-OBTAIN-PRICE.
346            SET VALID-FIELD TO FALSE
347            PERFORM UNTIL VALID-FIELD
348                ACCEPT SCR-PRICE
349                EVALUATE TRUE
350                    WHEN ST-PRICE IS EQUAL TO ZERO
351                        MOVE "Entry must be greater than zero"
352                            TO WS-USER-MESSAGE
353                    WHEN    ST-DEPARTMENT-NUMBER IS LESS THAN "500"
354                        AND ST-PRICE IS GREATER THAN 999.99
355                        MOVE "Price not consistent with department code"
356                            TO WS-USER-MESSAGE
357                    WHEN OTHER
358                        SET VALID-FIELD TO TRUE
359                END-EVALUATE
360                PERFORM 845-DISPLAY-ERROR-MESSAGE
361            END-PERFORM.
362
363        845-DISPLAY-ERROR-MESSAGE.
364            IF VALID-FIELD
365                DISPLAY CLEAR-MESSAGE
366            ELSE
367                DISPLAY ERROR-MESSAGE
368            END-IF.
```

Program Switches Used in the Data Entry Program

There are three program switches used in this program to control various aspects of its execution. WS-FIELD-VALID-SWITCH is defined with the true/false condition-name VALID-FIELD. It is set to TRUE or FALSE to indicate whether the field being inspected is valid or invalid and controls error message display and repetition of the input/validation process for each field.

WS-CONTINUE-SWITCH is defined with the true/false condition-name NO-MORE-RECORDS-TO-ADD. It is set to TRUE or FALSE to indicate whether or not another record is to be entered. This switch is analogous to the WS-ANOTHER-RECORD switch of the sales transaction display programs and the WS-EOF-SWITCH of all the earlier programs.

WS-RESPONSE is defined with the condition-name YES-RESPONSE, which is given the values "Y" and "y". Because of this, when the user is queried, he or she need not worry about whether the shift key is down or up when responding to a query.

Screen-Name Entries

In the display programs, you dealt with only one screen-name entry: RECORD-SCREEN, the name of the screen record itself. You will recall that none of the entries subordinate to this 01 included names—they were not necessary for that application. However, if the needs of a program require reference to individual elements of a screen definition, then those elements can be given screen-names. For example, the screen entry for the Department-number is shown in Figure 9-25.

Here the screen-name of the area on the screen where the field ST-DEPART-MENT-NUMBER is to be displayed is SCR-DEPARTMENT-NUMBER. Screen-names for each of the display areas are necessary in the DATAENT program because each field is to be validated as it is entered. You will see how this is incorporated in the program.

SCREEN SECTION Picture Entries

Remember that the PIC clause you use for screen entries defines the characteristics of the screen area used for the data element. For instance, PIC 9(3) used for SCR-DEPARTMENT-NUMBER (lines 124 and 125) describes this as a numeric item—just as in the other sections. However, when used defining an input quantity (signified by the TO and USING) *it controls the data that can be entered.* That is, because the field is defined as PIC 9, RM/COBOL will allow only digits and spaces to be entered (a sign can be entered if the picture includes sign capabilities). This is in contrast to PIC definitions in the FILE SECTION and data entered into the program via the READ statement. If any other characters are entered, RM/COBOL automatically displays an error message and positions the cursor within the field for reentry of the data. As a result, the data validation code need not include numeric checks.

For the Quantity and Price fields, you can see that these PIC definitions are numeric edited. The only advantage to doing this is that if you make an error during entry of the data, the program will redisplay it according to the picture you have used.

Figure 9-25
Giving a screen-name to an elementary item.

This is the screen-name. It identifies a position on the screen and is not a data element in the usual sense.

```
05   SCR-DEPARTMENT-NUMBER                    LINE 8   COL 20
        PIC 9(3)          TO ST-DEPARTMENT-NUMBER
        REVERSE.
```

The data entered with execution of the ACCEPT is entered TO this field.

Other Notable Screen-Attributes

There are three items in ACCEPT-RECORD (beginning line 107) of the SCREEN SECTION that warrant further comment. First is the way in which the date is handled. Notice that the month, day, and year are accepted as three separate fields sandwiched around two slashes (line 114). So that the operator sees a continuous transition from one component of the date to the next, the AUTO attribute is used for the month and day. When the two digits are typed, they are automatically accepted without the need for striking the Enter key. If there is no error, entry immediately progresses to the next date component.

The field SCR-YEAR-OF-SALE includes two other attributes: REQUIRED and FULL. The REQUIRED entries specifies that an entry must be made into this field before the ACCEPT can be completed; a blank entry is not allowed. The FULL field means that sufficient characters must be keyed in to fill the field. For instance, typing only the digit 9 would not be acceptable. However, a field designated as FULL can be left empty.

About Opening the File

In contrast to the preceding data display programs, notice that this program does not identify the file in the FILE-CONTROL paragraph. As shown in Figure 9-26, a data-name is used. That field is assigned the alphanumeric value TRANS1.DAT in the WORKING-STORAGE SECTION. One of the exercises at the end of this chapter requires that you make the necessary modifications so that the user can enter the name of the file to be created.

Because records are to be added to an existing file (TRANS1.DAT), a special version of the OPEN statement must be used. That is, the file cannot be opened for OUTPUT because opening for OUTPUT creates a new file; if there is an existing file by that name, it is destroyed. Although opening for INPUT does open an existing file, it only allows input, not output.

This dilemma is resolved in COBOL with the following OPEN EXTEND (refer to line 182 of the program in Figure 9-24).

```
OPEN EXTEND SALES-TRANSACTION-FILE
```

When the EXTEND option is used, the following takes place:

- The designated file is located on the disk and is opened as with the INPUT option.

- Access to the file is positioned at the end of the file.

The file is then ready for output; all records written will be added to the end of the file.

Figure 9-26
Designating the file name.

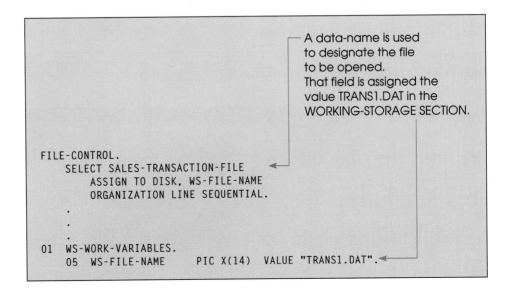

A data-name is used to designate the file to be opened.

That field is assigned the value TRANS1.DAT in the WORKING-STORAGE SECTION.

```
FILE-CONTROL.
    SELECT SALES-TRANSACTION-FILE
        ASSIGN TO DISK, WS-FILE-NAME
        ORGANIZATION LINE SEQUENTIAL.
        .
        .
        .
01  WS-WORK-VARIABLES.
    05  WS-FILE-NAME     PIC X(14) VALUE "TRANS1.DAT".
```

The 000-BUILD-DATA-FILE Module

You can see a direct correspondence between the statements of this module and the pseudocode/flowchart logic. The user is queried from the 050-QUERY-TO-EXECUTE module. If YES-RESPONSE is True (the result of execution of the 050 module), execution of the program continues. Otherwise, control is passed directly to the STOP RUN, thereby terminating execution.

The 050-QUERY-THE-USER

This module queries the user, thereby providing the opportunity to abort the program. The DISPLAY and ACCEPT sequence for ANNOUNCEMENT-SCREEN produce the display depicted in Figure 9-27. Referring to the ANNOUNCEMENT-SCREEN record in the SCREEN SECTION, you can see the following:

- Most of the entries include the LINE attribute, but not the COL. If COL is omitted, the compiler defaults to a value COL 1.

- The 05 items activated by the DISPLAY statement are those with VALUE, FROM, and USING.

- The name of the file to be processed is available from the field WS-FILE-NAME defined in the WORKING-STORAGE SECTION. Notice that it is displayed by way of the FROM.

- Only the last entry is activated by the ACCEPT statement (it has the attribute USING). The user response is accepted into the field WS-RESPONSE through this entry.

Prior to executing the DISPLAY/ACCEPT, a value N is moved into the switch WS-RESPONSE to serve as the default value. In other examples, Y was offered as a default so that the user need only strike the Enter key for repeated execution. However, to execute the program, it is a good idea to require a more positive action (striking the letter Y), as opposed to the more automatic action of striking the Enter key.

The Data Entry/Validation Modules

To investigate the data entry/validation modules, let's examine the 839 module for the Price field. That module, together with other appropriate coding, is shown in Figure 9-28.

Entry into the in-line PERFORM is forced by setting the condition-name VALID-FIELD to FALSE. The first statement within the scope of the PERFORM is:

```
ACCEPT SCR-PRICE
```

This positions the cursor at the Price field (LINE 16 COLUMN 44) and awaits data entry. Notice that the screen-name of this item is used, rather than the record-name ACCEPT-RECORD. Had the record-name been used, entry for *all* of the input fields

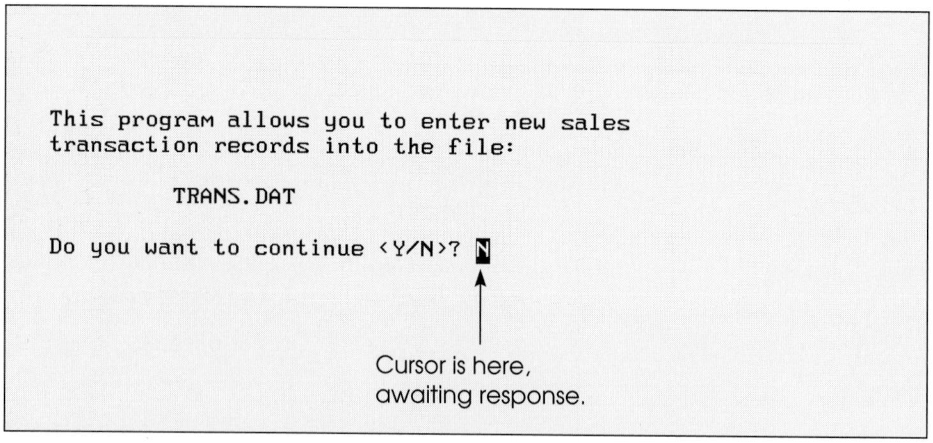

Figure 9-27
The announcement screen.

```
This program allows you to enter new sales
transaction records into the file:

        TRANS.DAT

Do you want to continue <Y/N>? ▊
                                ↑
                        Cursor is here,
                        awaiting response.
```

Figure 9-28
Accepting and validating
the Price field.

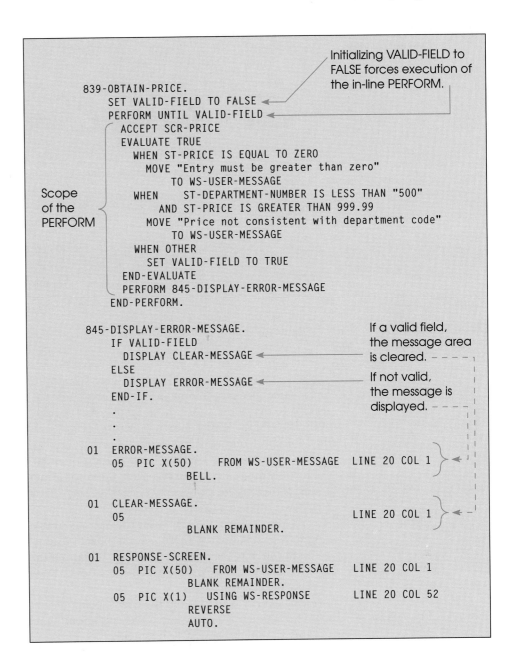

would have been activated (one field after the other). Because each field is validated as it is entered, each is referred to by its elementary-item screen-name.

For the Price field, there are three actions to be taken, depending upon the entry. To accommodate this, an EVALUATE statement is used. If either error condition occurs, an appropriate message is moved to WS-USER-MESSAGE, a 50-position message area defined in the WORKING-STORAGE SECTION. If neither of the error conditions is detected, VALID-FIELD is set to TRUE. This switch serves two purposes. First, it controls the display action of the 845 module (refer to Figure 9-28). Second, it controls repetition of the in-line PERFORM. For example, consider the following sequence for an entry of 0 for Price.

1. Upon executing the EVALUATE, the first option is selected and the error message is moved to the message area.

2. The 845 module is performed, yielding the screen shown in Figure 9-29.

3. Control is returned to the PERFORM. Since VALID-FIELD is not TRUE (it is FALSE), this sequence is executed again. The ACCEPT statement positions the cursor at this screen field to await reentry of the data value (see Figure 9-29).

Figure 9-29
Error message display with
an invalid entry for the
Price field.

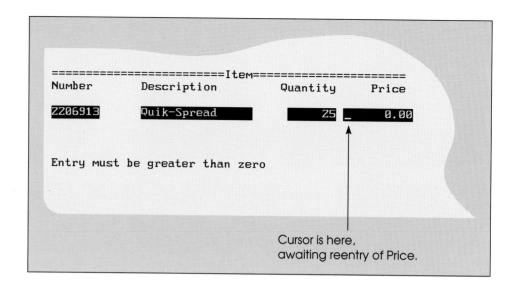

Overall Execution—The 200-BUILD-A-RECORD Module

In building a new record, the 200 module: (1) displays the field description screen, (2) executes each of the data entry/validation modules, (3) writes the record to disk (conditionally), and (4) queries the user about continuing. The logic of the write and query components should be relatively straightforward for you now. Notice that the same message-line field WS-USER-MESSAGE used for the error messages is used to query the user. These display/accept actions are controlled through the RESPONSE-SCREEN shown in Figure 9-28.

A shortcoming of this program is that once the user begins entering a record, there is no way to "back up" and change a field after progressing to the next one. The only alternative is to complete the record, then not save it. Unfortunately, all data for the record previously entered is lost. This is not very "user friendly." There are two ways this can be corrected.

One way is to give the user the options of saving the record, correcting it, or ignoring it. Actually, there is a method of doing this that is a relatively simple modification to the existing program. Executing this is left as an exercise at the end of the chapter. The exercise description includes a brief explanation of how you can make the change.

The other way to avoid the user's losing the entire record because of a mistake is to separate data entry and data validation. That is, allow all fields to be entered using the single ACCEPT statement:

```
ACCEPT ACCEPT-RECORD
```

In this form, the single ACCEPT is not completed until *all* fields have been entered. During the entry process, it is possible to "back up" to previous fields (for correcting mistakes) by using the cursor arrow keys. After the user enters the last field, the ACCEPT is completed and the fields can be validated—as done in the DATAVAL program. However, the program must include provisions to allow the user to reenter the invalid entries. This could be accomplished with the same technique described in Question 12 of the Questions About Example Programs set.

Chapter Summary

Two forms of both the ACCEPT and DISPLAY statements have been described in this chapter: with one or more data-names and with a screen-name.

The ACCEPT-data-name allows for the data entry into one or more fields. The DISPLAY-data-name can display literals and/or data from identifiers. Both the ACCEPT and DISPLAY in this format can include the following control-options:

LINE	Identifies the screen line on which the screen input field is to be positioned.
POSITION	Identifies the screen column on which the screen input field is to be positioned.
ERASE	Clear the entire screen to spaces.
ERASE EOL	Clear from the position of the cursor to the end of the line.
ERASE EOS	Clear from the position of the cursor to the end of the line and all lines that follow.
REVERSE	Show the area of the screen defined by the field (or literal for the DISPLAY) in reversed video.
BLINK	Cause characters in the area of the screen defined by the field (or literal for the DISPLAY) to blink on and off.
HIGH	Cause characters in the area of the screen defined by the field (or literal for the DISPLAY) to be shown in high intensity (extra bright).

The following options are usable only with the ACCEPT:

PROMPT	Causes underscore characters to be positioned on the screen at positions from which data is to be entered.
NO BEEP	Suppresses the computer sound (the bell).

The SCREEN SECTION provides for the screen layout definition. Its basic structure is like that of the other sections of the DATA DIVISION in that it consists of an 01 entry followed by subordinate entries with level numbers ranging from 02 to 49. Each elementary item can include a level-number, a screen-name, and one or more screen-attributes. Screen-attributes described in this chapter are as follows:

LINE	Same as ACCEPT-data-name version.
COL (or COLUMN)	Same as POSITION of ACCEPT-data-name.
BLANK	Same as ERASE of ACCEPT-data-name.
BLANK LINE	Same as ERASE EOL of ACCEPT-data-name.
BLANK REMAINDER	Same as ERASE EOS of ACCEPT-data-name.
REVERSE	Same as ACCEPT-data-name version.
BLINK	Same as ACCEPT-data-name version.
HIGH	Same as ACCEPT-data-name version.
AUTO	Same as ACCEPT-data-name version.
BELL	Rings the BELL when the item is displayed (DISPLAY only).
REQUIRED	During an ACCEPT, an entry must be made in the field; it cannot be left empty.
FULL	During an ACCEPT, does not allow a partial entry to be made into a field. The field must either be left empty or be full.

PIC | Defines the screen format of a screen-name. (*Note:* The PIC cannot be used in the same screen description item as the VALUE.) Must include format definition (for instance 999.99) and a picture item. Picture-item may be any of the following:

> FROM identifier
> FROM nonnumeric-literal
> TO identifier
> USING identifier

The FROM and the USING signify an item that is active during a DISPLAY; the TO and the USING signify an item that is active during an ACCEPT.

If the screen-name of an ACCEPT or DISPLAY refers to a group-item, then all elementary-items subordinate to that group item are active.

A condition-name can be defined with true and false conditions. Then changing its value is done by setting it (using the SET statement) to either TRUE or FALSE.

The in-line PERFORM provides for the repeated execution of a sequence of statements without the use of another paragraph.

Exercises
Terms for Definition

control-option _____

default value _____

hardcopy output _____

in-line procedure _____

interactive processing _____

out-of-line procedure _____

reversed video _____

screen-attribute _____

softcopy output _____

Review Questions

1. Write DISPLAY-data-name statements in the space provided to do each of the following.

   a. Display the message "To be continued"

   _____

   b. Clear the screen, then display the message "To be continued"—starting in line 4, column 7.

   _____

   c. Clear line 9, then display the description "The year is:" followed by the value in the variable LAST-YEAR. The data is to be in reverse display.

      _____

      _____

   d. Clear the screen from line 12 down, then display the description "Maximum allowable entry" at line 15, column 20, and the value of the field AMOUNT at line 16, column 30 blinking.

      _____

      _____

2. Write ACCEPT-data-name statements in the space provided to do each of the following.

   a. Accept a keyboard entry into the data-name ITEM-DESCRIPTION beginning line 7, column 6. Include an appropriate prompt.

      _____

   b. Accept a keyboard entry into the data-name MAX-VALUE from the last position of the cursor. Use reverse video.

      _____

   c. Accept entries into the data-names UNIT-NUMBER (line 10, column 12) and DESCRIPTION (line 10, column 30). The DESCRIPTION field must be highlighted. Use only one DISPLAY statement.

      _____

      _____

3. Write elementary-item entries for the SCREEN SECTION to define each of the DISPLAY actions in question 1.

   a. _____

      _____

   b. _____

      _____

   c. _____

      _____

   d. _____

      _____

4. Write elementary-item entries for the SCREEN SECTION to define each of following.

a. Clear the screen, display the message "Enter the code:" and then accept an entry into the field FILE-CODE, which is defined with PIC X(5). The message is to begin in line 5, column 20 and the input screen field must immediately follow. Use reverse on the input.

_____

_____

_____

b. Clear line 15, then display the message "Should this be saved <Y/N>?". Accept as a response into SAVE-SWITCH a single character input. Offer the letter N as a default.

_____

_____

_____

c. Accept a dollar and cent amount (less than $100, but not less than zero) into the field PAYMENT. Offer the original value in PAYMENT as the default. This is a required field. It must have a screen-name of SCR-PAYMENT and be positioned beginning line 5, column 25.

_____

_____

_____

Questions About Example Programs

1. What will happen in the DISPTRA1 program if the user responds with "y" instead of "Y"?

_____

_____

2. What would be the significance of forgetting to perform the 100-INITIALIZE-VARIABLE-FIELDS module from the mainline module of the DISPTRA1 program?

_____

_____

3. Would the display be changed in any way if the order of the display entries (lines 97 through 114 in the DISPTRA1 program) were changed? Explain your answer and any exceptions (if exceptions exist).

_____

_____

4. Would it make any difference in overall program execution if the user query SCREEN SECTION entry of the DISPTRA2 program (Figure 9-12, lines 97–99) were positioned before the *Data fields* entries (line 79)? Explain your answer.

   _____

   _____

5. If the BLANK SCREEN entry were accidentally omitted from the DISPTRA2 program (line 63) how would the screen look when the program was run?

   _____

   _____

6. What would be the consequence of accidentally using TO in place of USING at line 97 of the DISPTRA2 program?

   _____

   _____

7. What would be the consequence of accidentally use FROM in place of USING at line 97 of the DISPTRA2 program?

   _____

   _____

8. What do you think would happen in the DATAENT program (Figure 9-24) if the END-IF at line 187 were accidentally omitted?

   _____

   _____

9. What changes would be needed in the DATAENT program to make both lowercase and uppercase C and R acceptable as valid entries for Type-of-sale?

   _____

   _____

10. The REQUIRED screen-attribute is used for the field SCR-YEAR-OF-SALE. Why is that same attribute not used for the fields SCR-MONTH-OF-SALE and SCR-DAY-OF-SALE?

    _____

    _____

11. Modify the 050 module and the ANNOUNCEMENT-SCREEN record of DATAENT to allow the user to enter the name of the file to be created. Note that the file name is assigned to the WORKING-STORAGE SECTION entry WS-FILE-NAME.

12. The DATAENT program does not allow the user to go back and correct fields in which an incorrect entry has been made. Modify the 200 module to do the following.

    Provide the user the alternatives of

    1. Writing the record to disk.

2. Changing entries in fields currently on the screen. For this, the entire sequence of PERFORMs for data entry/validation must be executed again. This means that previous contents of the field must be offered as defaults, thus requiring that the TO attributes in the ACCEPT-RECORD screen record be changed to USING.

3. Ignoring the screen contents (not writing to disk).

Because of the USING in ACCEPT-RECORD, it will be necessary to initialize all fields in ST-SALES-TRANSACTION-RECORD. Otherwise, the previous record fields will be offered as default values for each new record to be entered.

Modify the program for corrections.

Programming Assignments

Each of the programming assignments of this chapter refers to assignment definitions of Chapter 8. The first four involve displaying data from existing files. The next four involve data entry. There are two options for coding the data entry programs. One is to use the exact data format of the input file described in Chapter 8. The other is to modify the format slightly to provide for the SEPARATE sign as was done in examples of this chapter. If you do the latter, you will need to create a new file for whichever assignment you choose. This is a simple matter: you need only open the file for OUTPUT rather than for EXTEND. If you wish, you can write a separate (almost trivial) program to create the file and then add records to it, as with the program in this chapter.

Programming Assignment 9-1: Ledger-Record Display
Prepare a program to display the data from the Ledger file (LEDGER.DAT) as described in Assignment 8-1.

Programming Assignment 9-2: Vendor-Record Display
Prepare a program to display the data from the Vendor file (VENDOR.DAT) as described in Assignment 8-2.

Programming Assignment 9-3: Earnings-Record Display
Prepare a program to display the data from the Earnings file (EARNING.DAT) as described in Assignment 8-3.

Programming Assignment 9-4: Customer-Record Display
Prepare a program to display the data from the Customer file (CUSTADDR.DAT) as described in Assignment 8-4.

Programming Assignment 9-5: Ledger-Record Validation
Prepare a data entry/validation program for the file described in Assignment 8-1.

Programming Assignment 9-6: Vendor-Record Validation
Prepare a data entry/validation program for the file described in Assignment 8-2.

Programming Assignment 9-7: Earnings-Record Validation
Prepare a data entry/validation program for the file described in Assignment 8-3.

Programming Assignment 9-8: Customer-Record Validation
Prepare a data entry/validation program for the file described in Assignment 8-4.

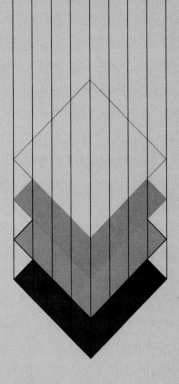

Control-Break Principles

Module Objectives

In Chapter 6, you learned about the many requirements of printing useful reports. Both the example programs and the programming assignments require that totals be printed at the end of the report. Most applications require that reports include such totals and also subtotals based on groupings of records (for instance, subtotals for sales of each department in a store). Programming of this type is called control-break programming because special action is taken in progressing from one group of records to the next. This concepts module is an introduction to control-break principles. From this module, you will learn the following:

■ The need for sorting (arranging records of a file in a desired order) in control-break programming.

■ Single- and multiple-level control-break programming.

Module Outline

Sorting Concepts
Field Type
What Is Sorting?
The Sort Key
    Multiple-Field Sort Keys
    Significance of Fields Within the Sort Key
    Sequence of Sort-Key Field Values

Report Control-Break Concepts
Single-Level Control-Break Reports
Multiple-Level Control-Break Reports

Sorting Concepts
Field Type

Fields can be classified as either indicative or control, in accordance with the function served within the record. Typically, most fields within a record are of the **indicative** type; they contain descriptive, reference-type, or quantitative data about the data entity to which they apply. Fields used to store an address, an inventory code, or a rate-of-pay are examples of indicative fields.

Control fields are used to either explicitly identify a data entity or to sequence the data for a record within a report or list. An important type of control field is a key field. The **key field** is used to explicitly identify a logical record and to relate it to a data entity. For example, if a record contains information about a machine part, its key field is the part number. A record for an employee will probably use a Social Security or employee number field as its key field.

The key field usually serves as the basis for the organization for the file. That is, records are arranged in sequence according to the value of the key field. In the patron list example of earlier chapters, the name field uniquely identifies the data entity and hence can be considered the key field. Also observe that the data within a Roladex file (refer to Concepts Module A) is usually organized according to the first letter of the last name.

Sometimes indicative fields are used as a control field for certain record-sequencing applications. For example, a zip code might be used as a control field when preparing output to be mailed.

What Is Sorting?

Sorting is the process of arranging items according to a certain **order** or **sequence**. The records of a file are generally stored according to the value of a predefined field or set of fields. For example, programming assignments of earlier chapters use the Silicon Valley Manufacturing employee earnings file. The key field to this file is the employee Social Security number. Records in that file would normally be arranged in order by the Social Security number, with the smallest number first in the file and the largest last.*

The Sort Key

The field, or group of fields, that contains the value used to sequence the file is called the **sort key**. In the employee earnings file, the sort key is the employee Social Security number field.

Multiple-Field Sort Keys.   Files are sometimes sorted in different sequences to produce different outputs. For example, remember the sales transaction file of the last two chapters. Its fields include an employee (salesperson) number and an item number. You might need to write a program listing the transactions in name sequence. Since each salesperson will have many records, you must list the records for each salesperson in order by the item number. Consequently, you will need

---

*For records stored on magnetic tape, the records must be placed on the tape in the desired order. However, for magnetic disk storage, this ordering can occur in either of two ways. On one hand, it may be a result of physical placement, as with tape. On the other, it may be the result of indexes to the file that give access to the records in the desired order—in spite of their physical placement (which is quite immaterial). You will learn about using indexes in an advanced COBOL course. All references to sorting and sorted files in this Concepts Module should be interpreted as making the records of a file available in a desired sequence, whether or not they are physically rearranged within the file.

Figure H-1
Example of a multiple-field
sort key.

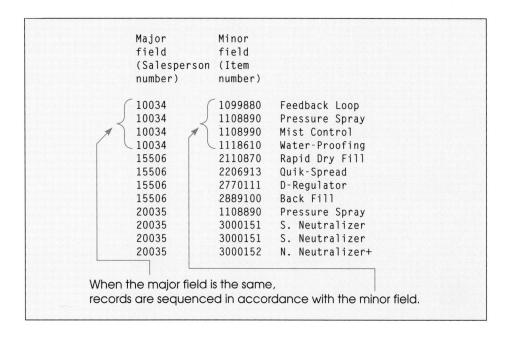

When the major field is the same,
records are sequenced in accordance with the minor field.

to sort the records on both the salesperson number field and the item number field. This is an example of a multiple-field sort key—one that contains two or more fields.

Significance of Fields Within the Sort Key. When a sort key contains more than one field, the most-significant field—the one that determines the overall order of the file—is termed the **major field**. The least-significant field is called the **minor field**. Thus, in the sales transaction example, the salesperson number is the major field and the item number is the **minor** field. Figure H-1 depicts this relationship.

A sort key will often contain more than two fields. For example, consider the situation in which a given salesperson might have several records in the file with the same item number. Then the records might be arranged by order of salesperson number, the prime order. Within each employee group, they would be arranged by item number, and within each item number by date of sale. Now the salesperson number is the major field, the item number the **intermediate** field, and the date of sale the minor field.

Sometimes there are more than three sort-key fields. In such instances, the intermediate fields could be classified as **intermediate-1**, **intermediate-2**, and so on.

Sequence of Sort-Key Field Values. Each sort-key field can be classified as to whether it is ordered in ascending or descending value sequence. It is far more common to arrange sort-key fields in **ascending** value sequence, since that pertains to our normal numerical and alphabetical orders. In certain instances, though, it is more convenient to use outputs arranged in **descending** order. For example, the telephone company prepares a list of subscribers who owe them money for overdue bills. Users might prefer that this report be listed in descending order by amount owed, so that the larger past-due amounts are at the top of the list. Figure H-2 shows an example of how such a report would look.

When descending order is used, there typically will be both ascending and descending fields in the sort key. An example is provided in Figure H-3, which depicts a dean's list. Here is a situation in which the major field, grade-point average (GPA), is listed in descending order so that the highest GPA appears at the top of the list. The student-name field is the minor field, arranged in ascending

Figure H-2
Descending sequence sort-key example.

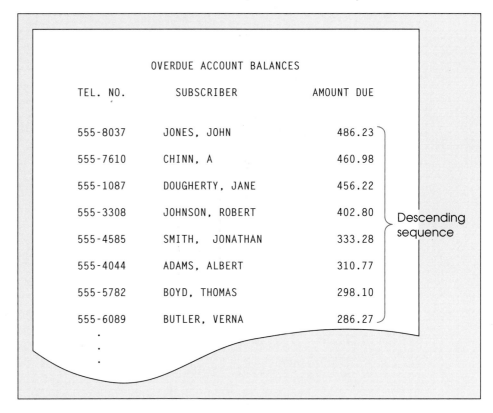

```
              OVERDUE ACCOUNT BALANCES

      TEL. NO.        SUBSCRIBER        AMOUNT DUE


      555-8037     JONES, JOHN            486.23

      555-7610     CHINN, A               460.98

      555-1087     DOUGHERTY, JANE        456.22

      555-3308     JOHNSON, ROBERT        402.80
                                                    Descending
      555-4585     SMITH,   JONATHAN      333.28    sequence

      555-4044     ADAMS, ALBERT          310.77

      555-5782     BOYD, THOMAS           298.10

      555-6089     BUTLER, VERNA          286.27
```

Figure H-3
Ascending and descending sequence sort-key example.

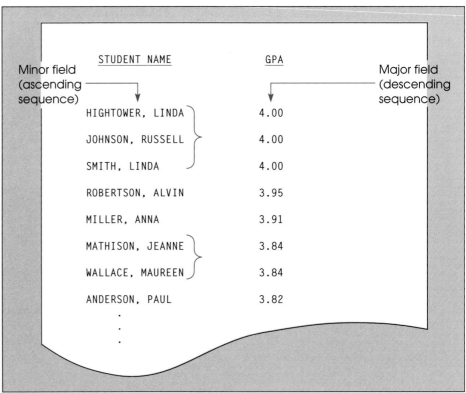

```
                   STUDENT NAME              GPA

Minor field                                            Major field
(ascending                                             (descending
sequence)                                              sequence)
               HIGHTOWER, LINDA           4.00

               JOHNSON, RUSSELL           4.00

               SMITH, LINDA               4.00

               ROBERTSON, ALVIN           3.95

               MILLER, ANNA               3.91

               MATHISON, JEANNE           3.84

               WALLACE, MAUREEN           3.84

               ANDERSON, PAUL             3.82
```

order, so that alphabetical order will prevail among two or more students with identical grade-point averages.

Report Control-Break Concepts

Before a report is printed, records are typically sorted into an appropriate sequence for presentation of the listing. Although record sorting takes a bit of computer time, an appropriate report sequence makes a report much easier to understand and use. It is also common to provide control totals on reports prepared from sorted records.

Consider a sales transaction record for a department store chain that includes the following fields:

Store number

Department number

Product description

Sales revenue

Even without sorting the records, a sales report could be prepared with a report total, as shown in Figure H-4.

Single-Level Control-Break Reports

It is likely, though, that the general manager of the department store chain would also want to know the total sales revenue from each of the chain's stores. The most efficient way to process such a report is to sort the sales transaction records by store number and to print totals whenever all the records for a given store have been printed. This would be an example of a **single-level control-break report**, with the store number as the **control field**. It would appear as shown in Figure H-5.

Because control-break reports must be in sequence according to the value of their control fields, the control-key fields usually comprise or are part of the sort key. There are sometimes additional minor fields in the sort key that are used for sequencing entries within **control groups**, but which do not cause control breaks.

Figure H-4
Unsequenced sales report without control breaks.

```
              COMPARTMENT DEPARTMENT STORES
                     SALES REPORT

       STORE     DEPARTMENT      PRODUCT          SALES
      NUMBER      NUMBER       DESCRIPTION       REVENUE

       002        50000        PERFUME            18.95
       001        60000        WASHER            398.00
       001        50000        COLOGNE             9.98
       002        70000        VIDEO RECORDER    698.00
       002        60000        MICROWAVE OVEN    569.00
       001        60000        REFRIGERATOR      498.00
       001        50000        PERFUME            29.95
       002        60000        WASHER            379.00
       002        70000        TELEVISION        598.00

                         REPORT TOTAL      3,198.88*
```

Figure H-5
Single-level control-break
example.

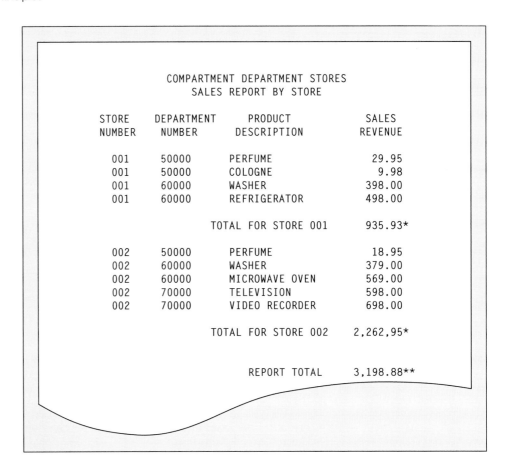

```
              COMPARTMENT DEPARTMENT STORES
                 SALES REPORT BY STORE

    STORE    DEPARTMENT     PRODUCT            SALES
   NUMBER      NUMBER      DESCRIPTION         REVENUE

    001        50000       PERFUME             29.95
    001        50000       COLOGNE              9.98
    001        60000       WASHER             398.00
    001        60000       REFRIGERATOR       498.00

                     TOTAL FOR STORE 001      935.93*

    002        50000       PERFUME             18.95
    002        60000       WASHER             379.00
    002        60000       MICROWAVE OVEN     569.00
    002        70000       TELEVISION         598.00
    002        70000       VIDEO RECORDER     698.00

                     TOTAL FOR STORE 002    2,262.95*


                         REPORT TOTAL       3,198.88**
```

Multiple-Level Control-Break Reports

Perhaps the general manager then distributes the report to each store manager. The store manager is probably interested in looking at the sales revenue for each of his or her departments. Hence, a report sorted by department number within store number (the major field is store number; the minor field is department number) would be appropriate, as shown in Figure H-6. This is an example of a **multiple-level control-break report**. The control fields are also store number and department number. Notice that the store totals are a summation of all the department totals.

If each store manager then sent a copy of the report to the department managers, the department managers would probably like to see the report sequenced by salesperson number within department within store. This would permit the department managers to easily determine how each of their salespeople is performing.

Also, buyers at the main office might be interested in seeing the report organized by product within department, regardless of salesperson or store, so that they could more easily spot product sales trends. Then, too, maybe someone in the advertising department would like to see sales totals sequenced by product within date, so that the effectiveness of advertising campaigns could be judged.

For practically all data-processing applications, a given set of records may require sequencing and reporting in a variety of formats, depending upon the user of the report. Most business reports have control totals based upon the sequence of the report. Thus, control-break programs are very common. In Chapter 10, you will learn how to design and program them. In all cases, the data files for the programming assignments are already sorted in the proper order. The topic of sorting (commonly taught in an advanced COBOL course) is deferred until Chapter 13.

Figure H-6
Multiple-level control-break example.

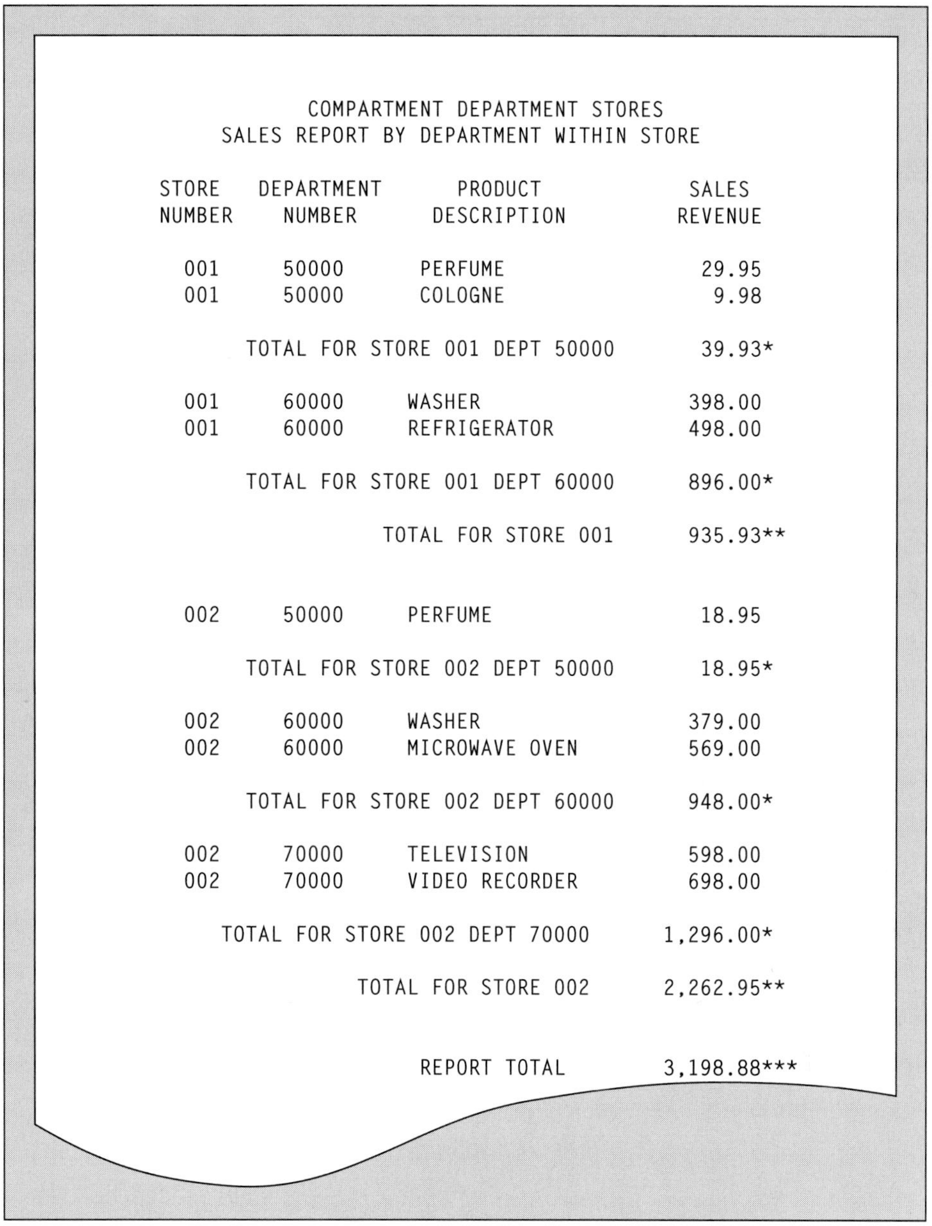

```
                  COMPARTMENT DEPARTMENT STORES
               SALES REPORT BY DEPARTMENT WITHIN STORE

       STORE    DEPARTMENT      PRODUCT          SALES
       NUMBER    NUMBER       DESCRIPTION        REVENUE

        001      50000         PERFUME            29.95
        001      50000         COLOGNE             9.98

            TOTAL FOR STORE 001 DEPT 50000        39.93*

        001      60000         WASHER            398.00
        001      60000         REFRIGERATOR      498.00

            TOTAL FOR STORE 001 DEPT 60000       896.00*

                    TOTAL FOR STORE 001          935.93**


        002      50000         PERFUME            18.95

            TOTAL FOR STORE 002 DEPT 50000        18.95*

        002      60000         WASHER            379.00
        002      60000         MICROWAVE OVEN    569.00

            TOTAL FOR STORE 002 DEPT 60000       948.00*

        002      70000         TELEVISION        598.00
        002      70000         VIDEO RECORDER    698.00

         TOTAL FOR STORE 002 DEPT 70000        1,296.00*

                 TOTAL FOR STORE 002           2,262.95**


                    REPORT TOTAL              3,198.88***
```

Module Summary

Sorting is the process of arranging items according to a certain order or sequence. Records of a file are generally stored according to a certain predefined sequence. The field, or group of fields, that contains the value used to sequence the file is called the **sort key**. When a sort key contains more than one field, the most-significant field is termed the **major field**; the least-significant field is called the **minor field**. Other fields of the sort key, if present, are known as **intermediate fields**. Each sort-key field can be arranged according to either **ascending** or **descending** values within the field.

A **control break** is an important data-processing concept often used in the preparation of reports with **control totals**. A report with just one control field is a **single-level control-break report**; a **multiple-level control-break report** contains two or more control fields.

Exercises

Terms for Definition

ascending value order _____

control break _____

control totals _____

descending value order _____

intermediate field _____

major field control field _____

minor field control group _____

multiple-level control break _____

sequence _____

single-level control break _____

sort key _____

sorting _____

Review Questions

1. The process of arranging items according to a certain order or sequence is called _____.

2. The field, or group of fields, that contains the value used to sequence a file is called the _____.

3. The most-significant field used to sequence a file is called the _____ field.

4. The least-significant field used to sequence a file is called the _____ field.

5. A given field can be arranged in either _____ or _____ order.

6. Sequenced reports with subtotals and totals based upon control fields are called _____ reports.

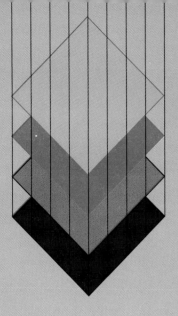

Control-Break Program Design and Coding

Chapter Objectives
In previous programs of this text, we have been concerned only with individual records of a file; the relationship of one record to another record within the file was of no concern. Control-break programs require the records to be in proper sequence. Furthermore, program logic must compare the control field of each record to the control field of the previous record. Although control-break programs are not overly complex, they can be very difficult to program for a person not trained in their design and coding. From this chapter, you will learn the following:

- Nested PERFORM statements, whereby a module repeatedly executed by a PERFORM/UNTIL itself contains a PERFORM/UNTIL to repeatedly execute another module.

- Triggering a control break by comparing the value of the previous record's control field to that of the newly read record.

- The use of intermediate-level accumulators that must be cleared at a control break.

- Processing a period-ending-date record preceding other data records in the file.

CHAPTER 10

Chapter Outline

Topic: A Single-Level Control-Break Program

Programming Specifications

Program Design
Single-Level Control-Break Logic
  Record Sequence
  Test for Control Break
  Test for End-of-Page
Design Documentation

Program Coding
The WORKING-STORAGE SECTION
Coding the PROCEDURE DIVISION
  200-PROCESS-SALES-REP-GROUP Module
  300-PRINT-DETAIL-LINE Module
  310-PRINT-SALES-REP-TOTAL-LINE Module
  700-PRINT-REPORT-TOTAL-LINE Module
  800-READ-SALES-RECORD Module
  870-PRINT-REPORT-HEADINGS Module
  880-WRITE-REPORT-TOP-LINE and 890-WRITE-REPORT-LINE Modules
  Line-Spacing Logic

Topic: A Multiple-Level Control-Break Program

Programming Specifications
Input-Record Layouts
Print Chart

Program Design
Multiple-Level Control-Break Logic
  Nesting of PERFORM/UNTIL Statements
  Control Total Line-Printing Modules
Design Documentation

Program Coding
The FD Entry
The WORKING-STORAGE SECTION
  WS-CONTROL-FIELDS Area
  WS-TOTAL-ACCUMULATORS Area
  Period-Ending Date Record-Description
  Report-Line Changes
Coding the PROCEDURE DIVISION
  000-PRINT-SALES-REPORT Module
  110-PROCESS-DATE-RECORD Module
  200-PROCESS-MAJOR-STATE-GROUP Module Through 220-PROCESS-MINOR-REP-GROUP Module
  310-PRINT-SALES-REP-TOTAL-LINE Module Through 330-PRINT-STATE-TOTAL-LINE Module
  800-READ-SALES-RECORD Module
  Alternate Coding for Control Group Modules—COBOL-85

491

| Topic: | A Single-Level Control-Break Program |

Programming Specifications

Pyramid Sales Company needs a **single-level control-break program** to print its sales report. [The program will be named SCTLBRK (for **S**ingle-level **C**on**T**ro**L**-**BR**ea**K** sales report).] The programming specifications are shown in Figure 10-1.

Notice on the print chart that there are four heading-line formats, one detail-line format, and one report total-line format. The sales-representative total line is the **control total line**.

Figure 10-1 Programming specifications: Single-level control-break sales report program.

PROGRAMMING SPECIFICATIONS

Program name: SINGLE-LEVEL CONTROL-BREAK SALES REPORT   **Program ID:** SCTLBRK

Program Description:

This program is to read input sales records, compute the sales revenue for each record, and print a sales-report detail-line for each sales record.

When the sales-representative number changes, a sales-representative control-total line is to be printed. After all input sales records have been processed, a report-total line is to be printed.

Input File:

Sales File

Output File:

Sales Report (single-level)

List of Program Operations:

A. Read each input sales record.

B. For each sales record, the program is to:

1. Compute the sales-revenue amount by multiplying the unit-price field by the quantity-sold field.

2. Print a detail-line that contains the following fields in accordance with the format shown on the print-chart.

   - Sales-representative number
   - State
   - Branch
   - Date-of-sale
   - Product-code
   - Product-description
   - Unit-price
   - Quantity-sold
   - Sales-revenue

3. Accumulate the following totals:

   - Total sales-revenue for each sales-representative
   - Total sales-revenue for all sales-representatives

C. Whenever the sales-representative number changes, the program is to print a sales-representative control-total line containing the following fields in accordance with the format shown on the print chart:

   - Sales-representative number
   - The words "SALES REP. TOTAL"
   - Total sales-revenue for that sales-representative
   - One asterisk (*)

D. After all the input sales records have been processed, the program is to print the following total fields on the report-total line in accordance with the format shown on the print chart:

   - The words "REPORT TOTAL"
   - Total sales-revenue for all sales-representatives
   - Two asterisks (**)

E. Headings are to be printed on each page of the report. On the first page and after 54 lines have been used on a report page, skip to the next page and print the report headings.

1. The run date is to be obtained from the operating system and printed on the second heading-line in accordance with the format shown on the print chart.

2. The page number is to be incremented each time the heading is printed and displayed on the second heading-line in accordance with the format shown on the print chart.

F. Line-spacing is to be handled as follows:

1. The first detail-line printed after the headings is to be double-spaced from the last heading-line.

2. Detail-lines for the same sales-representative are to be single-spaced from one another.

3. Each sales-representative control-total line is to be double-spaced from the previous detail-line.

4. The first detail-line for each sales-representative is to be triple-spaced from the previous control-total line.

5. The report-total line is to be triple-spaced from the last sales-representative control-total line.

Figure 10-1   (continued)

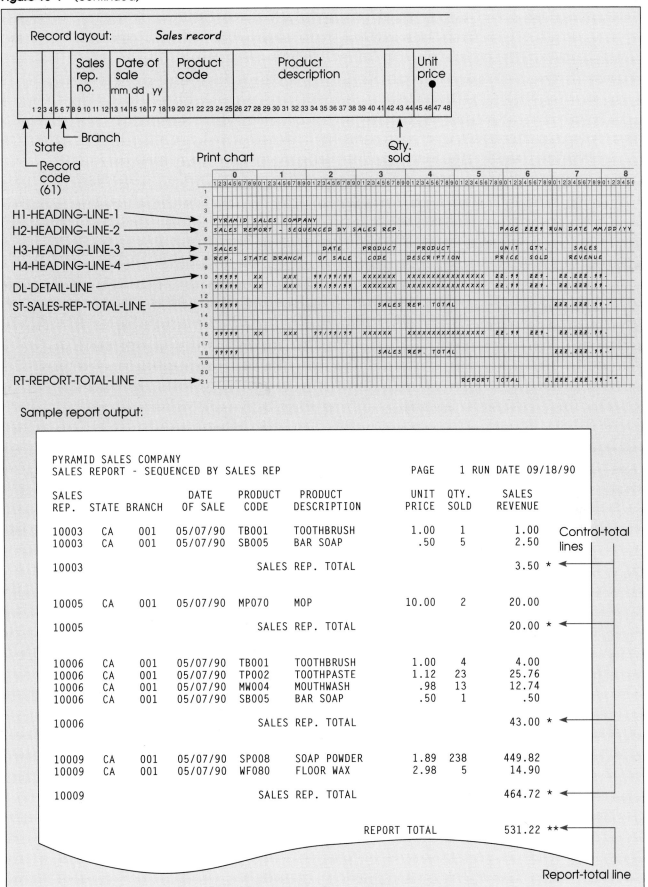

As shown in Figure 10-2, the sales-representative number in the input sales record is the **control field**. When the value of the control field changes from one value to another, a **control break** occurs. The control break must trigger the printing of the control total line for the group of records—the **control group**—with the same sales-representative number.

Certain design considerations applicable to single-level control-break programs have not been encountered in previous programs presented in this text. Let's look at them.

Program Design
Single-Level Control-
Break Logic

The general logic for a single-level control-break program is summarized in Figure 10-3. Observe that the mainline module adheres to the same general pattern that has been used in previous programs. The Process-control-group module handles the test for a control break. In a control-break test, the control field of the **current record** being processed is compared to the control field of the **previous record**. As long as they are equal, the Print-detail-line module will be performed. When a control break occurs, printing of detail lines is suspended and the control total line is printed.

The Print-control-total-line module returns control to the Process-control-group module, but there are no further statements to be executed there, so program control returns to the mainline module. If End-of-file has not been reached, the Process-control-group module is again performed to process the next group of records.

When designing a control-break program, you must give special attention to the record sequence, the test for control break, and the test for end-of-page.

Figure 10-2   Example of sales-representative control breaks.

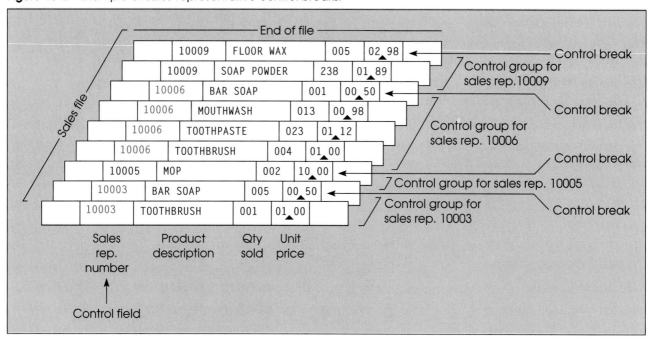

Figure 10-3 Summarized single-level control-break logic.

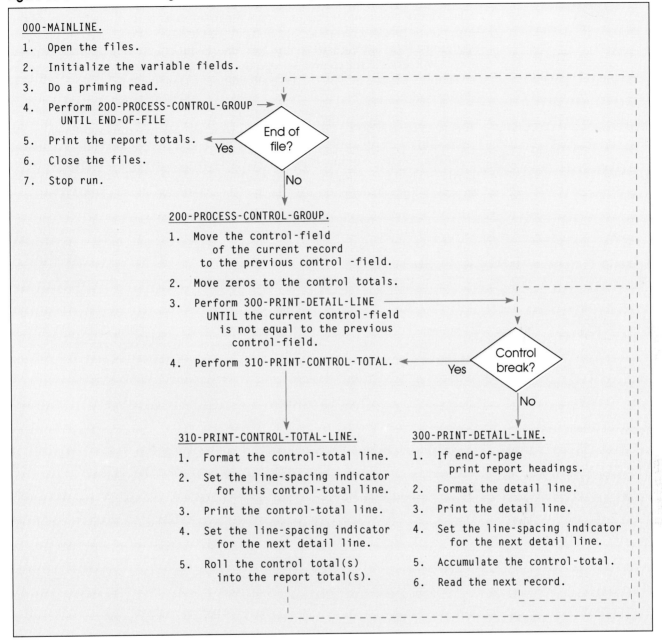

```
000-MAINLINE.

1.  Open the files.

2.  Initialize the variable fields.

3.  Do a priming read.

4.  Perform 200-PROCESS-CONTROL-GROUP
        UNTIL END-OF-FILE

5.  Print the report totals.

6.  Close the files.

7.  Stop run.
```

End of file? Yes No

```
200-PROCESS-CONTROL-GROUP.

1.  Move the control-field
        of the current record
        to the previous control-field.

2.  Move zeros to the control totals.

3.  Perform 300-PRINT-DETAIL-LINE
        UNTIL the current control-field
        is not equal to the previous
        control-field.

4.  Perform 310-PRINT-CONTROL-TOTAL.
```

Control break? Yes No

```
310-PRINT-CONTROL-TOTAL-LINE.            300-PRINT-DETAIL-LINE.

1.  Format the control-total line.       1.  If end-of-page
                                                 print report headings.
2.  Set the line-spacing indicator
        for this control-total line.     2.  Format the detail line.

3.  Print the control-total line.        3.  Print the detail line.

4.  Set the line-spacing indicator       4.  Set the line-spacing indicator
        for the next detail line.                for the next detail line.

5.  Roll the control total(s)            5.  Accumulate the control-total.
        into the report total(s).
                                         6.  Read the next record.
```

Record Sequence.   Remember that the input records for a control-break program must be sorted into control-field sequence. For this sales report, the sales records must be sorted into ascending order in accordance with the values contained in the Sales-representative-number field. In the program's design, we will assume that the file has been sorted and the records are in the desired sequence. (You will learn how to sort in Chapter 13.)

Test for Control Break. There are two tricky things about testing for control breaks. At the beginning of program processing, the program logic must bypass the false control break that will occur when the first record is read. Then, after all the input records have been processed and end-of-file has been reached, the program logic must force out the final control total line. Failure to provide for these requirements will result in the common programming control-break program bugs shown in Figure 10-4. The SCTLBRK program will be designed so that these two errors do not occur.

Test for End-of-Page. This sales report program has two different line formats printed in the body of the report: a detail line and a control total line. Whenever more than one type of line is printed in the body of a report, a question arises regarding when to test for the skip to headings for a new page. For a control-break program, it is usually best to test for headings only when a detail-line is printed.

Figure 10-4 Common control-break program bugs.

```
PYRAMID SALES COMPANY
SALES REPORT - SEQUENCED BY SALES REP                    PAGE    1 RUN DATE 09/18/90

                  SALES              DATE    PRODUCT  PRODUCT          UNIT   QTY.    SALES
                  REP.  STATE BRANCH OF SALE CODE     DESCRIPTION      PRICE  SOLD    REVENUE

                  10003                               SALES REP. TOTAL                  .00*

                  10003  CA    001  05/07/90 TB001    TOOTHBRUSH       1.00   1       1.00
                  10003  CA    001  05/07/90 SB005    BAR SOAP          .50   5       2.50

                  10003                               SALES REP. TOTAL               3.50*

                  10005  CA    001  05/07/90 MP070    MOP             10.00   2      20.00

                  10005                               SALES REP. TOTAL              20.00*


                  10006  CA    001  05/07/90 TB001    TOOTHBRUSH       1.00   4       4.00
                  10006  CA    001  05/07/90 TP002    TOOTHPASTE       1.12  23      25.76
                  10006  CA    001  05/07/90 MW004    MOUTHWASH         .98  13      12.74
                  10006  CA    001  05/07/90 SB005    BAR SOAP          .50   1        .50

                  10006                               SALES REP. TOTAL              43.00*

                  10009  CA    001  05/07/90 SP008    SOAP POWDER      1.89 238     449.82
                  10009  CA    001  05/07/90 WF080    FLOOR WAX        2.98   5      14.90


                                                     REPORT TOTAL               66.50**
```

False control break triggered by the first record

Missing control-total-line for the last control group (Sales rep 10009)

May cause erroneous report total

A test for headings should thus be omitted when the control total line is printed. Such processing will ensure that control totals are not printed by themselves on a separate page. It is easier to read a report when the totals are together on the same page with the last detail line for the control group.

However, when designing the report, you must ensure that there is enough room to print the control totals should they be needed when the bottom of the page is reached. So, although the programming specifications state that a line span of up to 57 lines is available, we will design the program to test—before each detail line is printed—whether 55 lines or more have been used on the page. If so, a new page will be started. If not, that detail line, plus a possible double-spaced total line, will still fit within the 57-line page span (54 lines used, plus 1 single-spaced detail line, plus 2 lines for the double-spaced control-total line equal 57 lines).

Design Documentation   A structure chart for the sales report program is shown in Figure 10-5. The pseudocode and program flowchart are shown in Figures 10-6 and 10-7, respectively.

Figure 10-5
Structure chart: Single-level control-break sales report program.

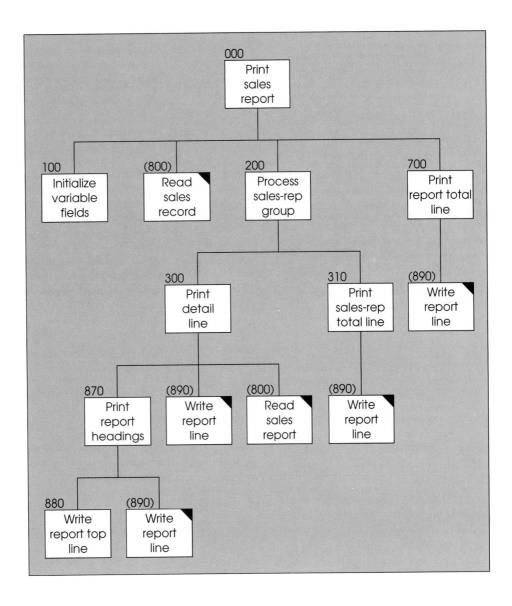

Figure 10-6 Pseudocode: Single-level control-break sales report program.

<u>000-Print-Sales-Report module</u>

1. Open the files.
2. Perform 100-Initialize-Variable-Fields.
3. Perform 800-Read-Sales-Record.
4. Perform 200-Process-Sales-Rep-Group
   until no more records.
5. Perform 700-Print-Report-Total-Line.
6. Close the files.
7. Stop the run.

<u>100-Initialize-Variable-Fields module</u>

1. Set the End-of-file indicator to "No".
2. Set the Page-count field to zero.
3. Set the lines-used indicator so that headings for the first page will be triggered.
4. Obtain the date from the operating system and move it to the second heading-line.
5. Set the Total-accumulator fields to zero.

<u>200-Process-Sales-Rep-Group module</u>

1. Move the input Sales-rep field
   to the Previous-sales-rep field.
2. Move zero to the Total-sales-rep-sales-revenue field.
3. Perform 300-Print-Detail-Line
   until the Sales-rep field in the current input record
   is not equal to the Previous-sales-rep field.
4. Perform 310-Print-Sales-Rep-Total-Line.

<u>300-Print-Detail-Line module</u>

1. If the report page is full,
   Perform 870-Print-Report-Headings.
2. Move the input Sales-rep
   to the detail-line Sales-rep.
3. Move the input State
   to the detail-line State.
4. Move the input Branch
   to the detail-line Branch.
5. Move the input Date-of-sale
   to the detail-line Date-of-sale.
6. Move the input Product-code
   to the detail-line Product-code
7. Move the input Product-description
   to the detail-line Product-description.
8. Move the input Unit-price
   to the detail-line Unit-price.
9. Move the input Quantity-sold
   to the detail-line Quantity-sold.
10. Multiply the input Unit-price by the input Quantity-sold to equal the Sales-revenue.
11. Move the Sales-Revenue
    to the detail-line Sales-revenue.
12. Move the detail-line
    to the output print-line area.
13. Perform 890-Write-Report-Line.
14. Set the Line-spacing indicator for single-spacing.
15. Add the Sales-revenue for this record
    to the Total-sales-rep-sales-revenue.
16. Perform 800-Read-Sales-Record.

<u>310-Print-Sales-Rep-Total-Line module</u>

1. Move the Previous-sales-rep
   to the sales-rep-total-line Sales-rep.
2. Move the Total-sales-rep-sales-revenue
   to the sales-rep-total-line Sales-revenue.
3. Move the sales-rep-total-line
   to the output print-line area.
4. Set the Line-spacing indicator for double-spacing.
5. Perform 890-Write-Report-Line.
6. Set the Line-spacing indicator for triple-spacing.
7. Add the Total-sales-rep-sales-revenue
   to the Total-report-sales-revenue.

<u>700-Print-Report-Total-Line module</u>

1. Move the Total-report-sales-revenue
   to the report-total-line Sales-revenue.
2. Move the report-total-line
   to the output print-line area.
3. Set the Line-spacing indicator for triple-spacing.
4. Perform 890-Write-Report-Line.

<u>800-Read-Sales-Record module</u>

1. Read a record from the input Sales file.
2. If there are no more records
   Move "Yes" to the end-of-file indicator
   Move High-values to the input-record Sales-rep field.

<u>870-Print-Report-Headings module</u>

1. Add 1 to the Page-count.
2. Move the Page-count
   to the Page-number field in the second heading-line.
3. Move Heading-line-1 to the output print-line area.
4. Perform 880-Write-Report-Top-Line.
5. Move Heading-line-2 to the output print-line area.
6. Set the Line-spacing indicator for single-spacing.
7. Perform 890-Write-Report-Line.
8. Move Heading-line-3 to the output print-line area.
9. Set the Line-spacing indicator for double-spacing.
10. Perform 890-Write-Report-Line.
11. Move Heading-line-4 to the output print-line area.
12. Set the Line-spacing indicator for single-spacing.
13. Perform 890-Write-Report-Line.
14. Set the Line-spacing indicator for double spacing.

<u>880-Write-Report-Top-Line module</u>

1. Advance to the top of the next report page
   and write out the output print-line area.
2. Set the Lines-used indicator to 1.

<u>890-Write-Report-Line module</u>

1. Advance the forms in accordance with the value in the Line-spacing indicator field
   and write the output print-line area.
2. Add the Line-spacing indicator to the Lines-used field.

Figure 10-7 Program flowchart: Single-level control-break sales report program (continued on pages 500–501).

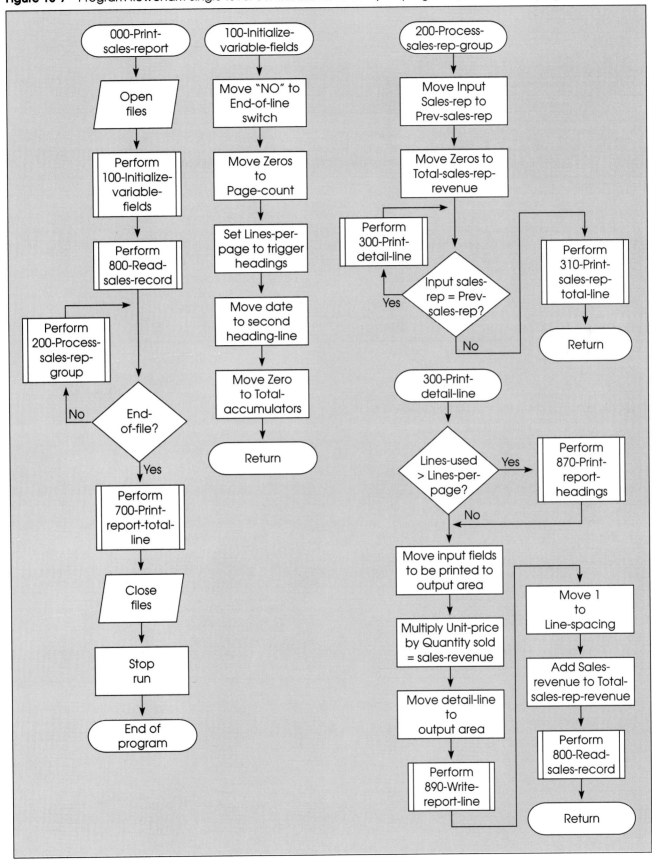

Figure 10-7
(continued from page 499)

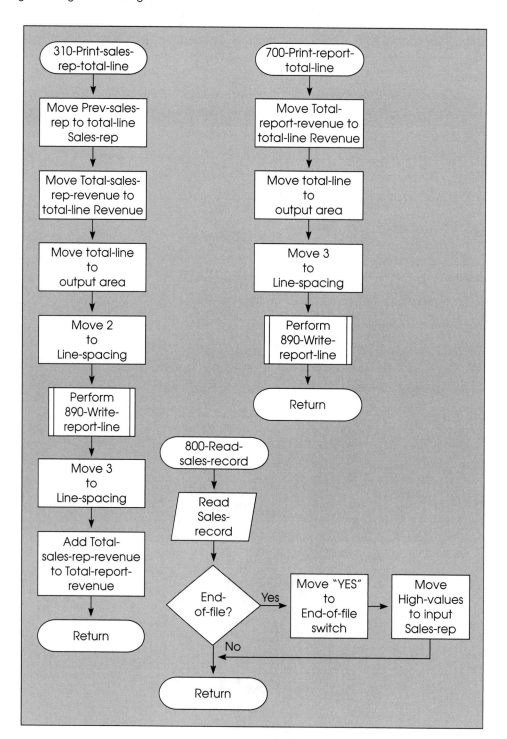

Figure 10-7
(continued)

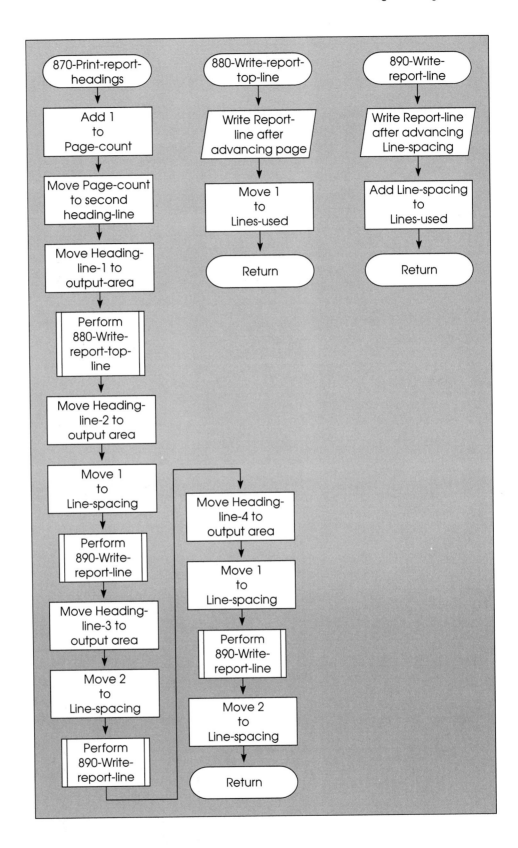

Program Coding   The complete program is shown in Figures 10-8, 10-9 (COBOL-74 PROCEDURE DIVISION), and 10-10 (COBOL-85 PROCEDURE DIVISION).

The WORKING-STORAGE SECTION   There is one new 01-level entry in the WORKING-STORAGE SECTION—the WS-CONTROL-FIELDS entry. Within this group item, the elementary WS-PREVIOUS-SALES-REP field has been specified. This field will be used to hold the Sales-representative-number for the record processed immediately before the current record.

Figure 10-8   First three divisions: Single-level control break program (SCTLBRK).

```
1          IDENTIFICATION DIVISION.                          77    01  WS-TOTAL-ACCUMULATORS.
2          PROGRAM-ID.  SCTLBRK.                             78        05  WS-TOTAL-SALES-REP-ACCUM      PIC S9(6)V99.
3          *                WRITTEN BY T. WELBURN.           79        05  WS-TOTAL-REPORT-ACCUM         PIC S9(7)V99.
4          *                PYRAMID SALES COMPANY.           80
5          *                FEB 27,1986.                     81    01  SR-SALES-RECORD.
6          *                REVISED 9-18-89 BY W. PRICE.     82        05  SR-RECORD-CODE                PIC X(2).
7                                                            83        05  SR-STATE                      PIC X(2).
8          *         THIS PROGRAM READS SALES RECORDS,       84        05  SR-BRANCH                     PIC X(3).
9          *         COMPUTES THE SALES REVENUE FOR EACH SALES RECORD   85        05  SR-SALES-REP                  PIC X(5).
10         *         AND PRINTS A SALES DETAIL LINE          86        05  SR-DATE-OF-SALE               PIC X(6).
11         *         FOR EACH SALES RECORD.                  87        05  SR-PRODUCT-CODE               PIC X(7).
12                                                           88        05  SR-PRODUCT-DESCRIPTION        PIC X(16).
13         *         WHEN THE SALES REP NUMBER CHANGES,      89        05  SR-QUANTITY-SOLD              PIC S9(3).
14         *         A SALES-REP TOTAL LINE IS PRINTED.      90        05  SR-UNIT-PRICE                 PIC 9(2)V99.
15                                                           91
16         *         AFTER ALL INPUT SALES RECORDS HAVE BEEN PROCESSED,   92    01  H1-HEADING-LINE-1.
17         *         A REPORT-TOTAL LINE WILL BE PRINTED.    93        05             PIC X(21)    VALUE "PYRAMID SALES COMPANY".
18                                                           94
19                                                           95    01  H2-HEADING-LINE-2.
20         ENVIRONMENT DIVISION.                             96        05             PIC X(20)    VALUE "SALES REPORT - SEQUE".
21                                                           97        05             PIC X(20)    VALUE "NCED BY SALES REP.  ".
22         CONFIGURATION SECTION.                            98        05             PIC X(23)    VALUE "              PAGE".
23                                                           99        05  H2-PAGE-NBR   PIC ZZZ9.
24         SOURCE-COMPUTER.  (system dependent).            100        05  PIC X(10)   VALUE    " RUN DATE ".
25         OBJECT-COMPUTER.  (system dependent).            101        05  H2-MONTH      PIC 9(2).
26                                                          102        05  PIC X(1)   VALUE "/".
27         INPUT-OUTPUT SECTION.                            103        05  H2-DAY        PIC 9(2).
28                                                          104        05             PIC X(1)     VALUE "/".
29         FILE-CONTROL.                                    105        05  H2-YEAR       PIC 9(2).
30             SELECT SALES-FILE                            106
31                 ASSIGN TO (system dependent).            107    01  H3-HEADING-LINE-3.
32             SELECT SALES-REPORT                          108        05             PIC X(20)    VALUE "SALES              ".
33                 ASSIGN TO (system dependent).            109        05             PIC X(20)    VALUE " DATE     PRODUCT   ".
34                                                          110        05             PIC X(20)    VALUE "PRODUCT         UN".
35                                                          111        05             PIC X(20)    VALUE "IT QTY.    SALES  ".
36         DATA DIVISION.                                   112
37                                                          113    01  H4-HEADING-LINE-4.
38         FILE SECTION.                                    114        05             PIC X(20)    VALUE "REP. STATE BRANCH  ".
39                                                          115        05             PIC X(20)    VALUE " OF SALE    CODE   D".
40         FD  SALES-FILE                                   116        05             PIC X(20)    VALUE "ESCRIPTION      PRI".
41             RECORD CONTAINS 48 CHARACTERS                117        05             PIC X(20)    VALUE "CE SOLD    REVENUE ".
42             LABEL RECORDS ARE STANDARD.                  118
43                                                          119    01  DL-DETAIL-LINE.
44         01  SALES-RECORD.                                120        05  DL-SALES-REP            PIC X(5).
45             05  PIC X(48).                               121        05                          PIC X(3)    VALUE SPACES.
46                                                          122        05  DL-STATE                PIC X(2).
47         FD  SALES-REPORT                                 123        05                          PIC X(4)    VALUE SPACES.
48             RECORD CONTAINS 132 CHARACTERS               124        05  DL-BRANCH               PIC X(3).
49             LABEL RECORDS ARE OMITTED.                   125        05                          PIC X(3)    VALUE SPACES.
50                                                          126        05  DL-DATE-OF-SALE         PIC XX/XX/XX.
51         01  SALES-REPORT-LINE.                           127        05                          PIC X(2)    VALUE SPACES.
52             05  PIC X(132).                              128        05  DL-PRODUCT-CODE         PIC X(7).
53                                                          129        05                          PIC X(2)    VALUE SPACES.
54         WORKING-STORAGE SECTION.                         130        05  DL-PRODUCT-DESCRIPTION  PIC X(16).
55                                                          131        05                          PIC X(2)    VALUE SPACES.
56         01  WS-SWITCHES.                                 132        05  DL-UNIT-PRICE           PIC ZZ.99.
57             05  WS-END-OF-FILE-SWITCH      PIC X(3).     133        05                          PIC X(2)    VALUE SPACES.
58                 88  END-OF-FILE              VALUE "YES".134        05  DL-QUANTITY-SOLD        PIC ZZ9-.
59                                                          135        05                          PIC X(2)    VALUE SPACES.
60         01  WS-CONTROL-FIELDS.                           136        05  DL-SALES-REVENUE        PIC ZZ,ZZZ.99-.
61             05  WS-PREVIOUS-SALES-REP      PIC X(5).     137
62                                                          138    01  ST-SALES-REP-TOTAL-LINE.
63         01  WS-REPORT-CONTROLS.                          139        05  ST-SALES-REP      PIC X(5).
64             05  WS-PAGE-COUNT            PIC S9(4).      140        05                    PIC X(28)  VALUE SPACES.
65             05  WS-LINES-PER-PAGE        PIC S9(2)  VALUE +54.   141        05                    PIC X(16)  VALUE "SALES REP. TOTAL".
66             05  WS-LINES-USED            PIC S9(2).      142        05                    PIC X(20)  VALUE SPACES.
67             05  WS-LINE-SPACING          PIC S9(2).      143        05  ST-SALES-REVENUE  PIC ZZZ,ZZZ.99-.
68                                                          144        05                    PIC X(1)   VALUE "*".
69         01  WS-WORK-AREAS.                               145
70             05  WS-DATE-WORK             PIC 9(6).       146    01  RT-REPORT-TOTAL-LINE.
71             05  WS-DATE-REFORMAT REDEFINES WS-DATE-WORK. 147        05             PIC X(50)   VALUE SPACES.
72                 10  WS-YEAR              PIC 9(2).       148        05             PIC X(12)   VALUE "REPORT TOTAL".
73                 10  WS-MONTH             PIC 9(2).       149        05             PIC X(5)    VALUE SPACES.
74                 10  WS-DAY               PIC 9(2).       150        05  RT-SALES-REVENUE  PIC Z,ZZZ,ZZZ.99-.
75             05  WS-SALES-REVENUE         PIC S9(5)V99.   151        05             PIC X(2)    VALUE "**".
76                                                          152
                                                            153
```

Figure 10-9 COBOL-74 PROCEDURE DIVISION: Single-level control break program (SCTLBRK).

```
154     PROCEDURE DIVISION.
155
156     000-PRINT-SALES-REPORT.
157         OPEN INPUT SALES-FILE
158             OUTPUT SALES-REPORT.
159         PERFORM 100-INITIALIZE-VARIABLE-FIELDS.
160         PERFORM 800-READ-SALES-RECORD.
161         PERFORM 200-PROCESS-SALES-REP-GROUP
162             UNTIL END-OF-FILE.
163         PERFORM 700-PRINT-REPORT-TOTAL-LINE.
164         CLOSE SALES-FILE
165             SALES-REPORT.
166         STOP RUN.
167
168     100-INITIALIZE-VARIABLE-FIELDS.
169         MOVE "NO " TO WS-END-OF-FILE-SWITCH.
170         MOVE ZEROS TO WS-PAGE-COUNT.
171         ACCEPT WS-DATE-WORK FROM DATE.
172         MOVE WS-MONTH TO H2-MONTH.
173         MOVE WS-DAY TO H2-DAY.
174         MOVE WS-YEAR TO H2-YEAR.
175         PERFORM 870-PRINT-REPORT-HEADINGS.
176         MOVE ZEROS TO WS-TOTAL-SALES-REP-ACCUM
177                       WS-TOTAL-REPORT-ACCUM.
178
179     200-PROCESS-SALES-REP-GROUP.
180         MOVE SR-SALES-REP TO WS-PREVIOUS-SALES-REP.
181         MOVE ZEROS TO WS-TOTAL-SALES-REP-ACCUM.
182         PERFORM 300-PRINT-DETAIL-LINE
183             UNTIL SR-SALES-REP IS NOT EQUAL TO WS-PREVIOUS-SALES-REP.
184         PERFORM 310-PRINT-SALES-REP-TOTAL-LINE.
185
186     300-PRINT-DETAIL-LINE.
187         IF WS-LINES-USED IS NOT LESS THAN WS-LINES-PER-PAGE
188             PERFORM 870-PRINT-REPORT-HEADINGS.
189         MOVE SR-SALES-REP TO DL-SALES-REP.
190         MOVE SR-STATE TO DL-STATE.
191         MOVE SR-BRANCH TO DL-BRANCH.
192         MOVE SR-DATE-OF-SALE TO DL-DATE-OF-SALE.
193         MOVE SR-PRODUCT-CODE TO DL-PRODUCT-CODE.
194         MOVE SR-PRODUCT-DESCRIPTION TO DL-PRODUCT-DESCRIPTION.
195         MOVE SR-UNIT-PRICE TO DL-UNIT-PRICE.
196         MOVE SR-QUANTITY-SOLD TO DL-QUANTITY-SOLD.
197         MULTIPLY SR-UNIT-PRICE BY SR-QUANTITY-SOLD
198             GIVING WS-SALES-REVENUE ROUNDED.
199         MOVE WS-SALES-REVENUE TO DL-SALES-REVENUE.
200         MOVE DL-DETAIL-LINE TO SALES-REPORT-LINE.
201         PERFORM 890-WRITE-REPORT-LINE.
202         MOVE 1 TO WS-LINE-SPACING.
203         ADD WS-SALES-REVENUE TO WS-TOTAL-SALES-REP-ACCUM.
204         PERFORM 800-READ-SALES-RECORD.

205
206     310-PRINT-SALES-REP-TOTAL-LINE.
207         MOVE WS-PREVIOUS-SALES-REP TO ST-SALES-REP.
208         MOVE WS-TOTAL-SALES-REP-ACCUM TO ST-SALES-REVENUE.
209         MOVE ST-SALES-REP-TOTAL-LINE TO SALES-REPORT-LINE.
210         MOVE 2 TO WS-LINE-SPACING.
211         PERFORM 890-WRITE-REPORT-LINE.
212         MOVE 3 TO WS-LINE-SPACING.
213         ADD WS-TOTAL-SALES-REP-ACCUM TO WS-TOTAL-REPORT-ACCUM.
214
215     700-PRINT-REPORT-TOTAL-LINE.
216         MOVE WS-TOTAL-REPORT-ACCUM TO RT-SALES-REVENUE.
217         MOVE RT-REPORT-TOTAL-LINE TO SALES-REPORT-LINE.
218         MOVE 3 TO WS-LINE-SPACING.
219         PERFORM 890-WRITE-REPORT-LINE.
220
221     800-READ-SALES-RECORD.
222         READ SALES-FILE INTO SR-SALES-RECORD
223             AT END MOVE "YES" TO WS-END-OF-FILE-SWITCH
224                 MOVE HIGH-VALUES TO SR-SALES-REP.
225
226     870-PRINT-REPORT-HEADINGS.
227         ADD 1 TO WS-PAGE-COUNT.
228         MOVE WS-PAGE-COUNT TO H2-PAGE-NBR.
229         MOVE H1-HEADING-LINE-1 TO SALES-REPORT-LINE.
230         PERFORM 880-WRITE-REPORT-TOP-LINE.
231         MOVE H2-HEADING-LINE-2 TO SALES-REPORT-LINE.
232         MOVE 1 TO WS-LINE-SPACING.
233         PERFORM 890-WRITE-REPORT-LINE.
234         MOVE H3-HEADING-LINE-3 TO SALES-REPORT-LINE.
235         MOVE 2 TO WS-LINE-SPACING.
236         PERFORM 890-WRITE-REPORT-LINE.
237         MOVE H4-HEADING-LINE-4 TO SALES-REPORT-LINE.
238         MOVE 1 TO WS-LINE-SPACING.
239         PERFORM 890-WRITE-REPORT-LINE.
240         MOVE 2 TO WS-LINE-SPACING.
241
242     880-WRITE-REPORT-TOP-LINE.
243         WRITE SALES-REPORT-LINE
244             AFTER ADVANCING PAGE.
245         MOVE 1 TO WS-LINES-USED.
246
247     890-WRITE-REPORT-LINE.
248         WRITE SALES-REPORT-LINE
249             AFTER ADVANCING WS-LINE-SPACING.
250         ADD WS-LINE-SPACING TO WS-LINES-USED.
```

Figure 10-10 COBOL-85 PROCEDURE DIVISION: Single-level control break program (SCTLBRK).

```
154     PROCEDURE DIVISION.
155
156     000-PRINT-SALES-REPORT.
157         OPEN INPUT SALES-FILE
158             OUTPUT SALES-REPORT
159         PERFORM 100-INITIALIZE-VARIABLE-FIELDS
160         PERFORM 800-READ-SALES-RECORD
161         PERFORM 200-PROCESS-SALES-REP-GROUP
162             UNTIL END-OF-FILE
163         PERFORM 700-PRINT-REPORT-TOTAL-LINE
164         CLOSE SALES-FILE
165             SALES-REPORT
166         STOP RUN.
167
168     100-INITIALIZE-VARIABLE-FIELDS.
169         MOVE "NO " TO WS-END-OF-FILE-SWITCH
170         MOVE ZEROS TO WS-PAGE-COUNT
171         ACCEPT WS-DATE-WORK FROM DATE
172         MOVE WS-MONTH TO H2-MONTH
173         MOVE WS-DAY TO H2-DAY
174         MOVE WS-YEAR TO H2-YEAR
175         PERFORM 870-PRINT-REPORT-HEADINGS
176         INITIALIZE WS-TOTAL-ACCUMULATORS.
177
178     200-PROCESS-SALES-REP-GROUP.
179         MOVE SR-SALES-REP TO WS-PREVIOUS-SALES-REP
180         MOVE ZEROS TO WS-TOTAL-SALES-REP-ACCUM
181         PERFORM 300-PRINT-DETAIL-LINE
182             UNTIL SR-SALES-REP IS NOT EQUAL TO WS-PREVIOUS-SALES-REP
183         PERFORM 310-PRINT-SALES-REP-TOTAL-LINE.
184
185     300-PRINT-DETAIL-LINE.
186         IF WS-LINES-USED IS NOT LESS THAN WS-LINES-PER-PAGE
187             PERFORM 870-PRINT-REPORT-HEADINGS
188         END-IF
189         MOVE SR-SALES-REP TO DL-SALES-REP
190         MOVE SR-STATE TO DL-STATE
191         MOVE SR-BRANCH TO DL-BRANCH
192         MOVE SR-DATE-OF-SALE TO DL-DATE-OF-SALE
193         MOVE SR-PRODUCT-CODE TO DL-PRODUCT-CODE
194         MOVE SR-PRODUCT-DESCRIPTION TO DL-PRODUCT-DESCRIPTION
195         MOVE SR-UNIT-PRICE TO DL-UNIT-PRICE
196         MOVE SR-QUANTITY-SOLD TO DL-QUANTITY-SOLD
197         MULTIPLY SR-UNIT-PRICE BY SR-QUANTITY-SOLD
198             GIVING WS-SALES-REVENUE ROUNDED
199         MOVE WS-SALES-REVENUE TO DL-SALES-REVENUE
200         MOVE DL-DETAIL-LINE TO SALES-REPORT-LINE
201         PERFORM 890-WRITE-REPORT-LINE
202         MOVE 1 TO WS-LINE-SPACING
203         ADD WS-SALES-REVENUE TO WS-TOTAL-SALES-REP-ACCUM
204         PERFORM 800-READ-SALES-RECORD.

205
206     310-PRINT-SALES-REP-TOTAL-LINE.
207         MOVE WS-PREVIOUS-SALES-REP TO ST-SALES-REP
208         MOVE WS-TOTAL-SALES-REP-ACCUM TO ST-SALES-REVENUE
209         MOVE ST-SALES-REP-TOTAL-LINE TO SALES-REPORT-LINE
210         MOVE 2 TO WS-LINE-SPACING
211         PERFORM 890-WRITE-REPORT-LINE
212         MOVE 3 TO WS-LINE-SPACING
213         ADD WS-TOTAL-SALES-REP-ACCUM TO WS-TOTAL-REPORT-ACCUM.
214
215     700-PRINT-REPORT-TOTAL-LINE.
216         MOVE WS-TOTAL-REPORT-ACCUM TO RT-SALES-REVENUE
217         MOVE RT-REPORT-TOTAL-LINE TO SALES-REPORT-LINE
218         MOVE 3 TO WS-LINE-SPACING
219         PERFORM 890-WRITE-REPORT-LINE.
220
221     800-READ-SALES-RECORD.
222         READ SALES-FILE INTO SR-SALES-RECORD
223             AT END MOVE "YES" TO WS-END-OF-FILE-SWITCH
224                 MOVE HIGH-VALUES TO SR-SALES-REP
225         END-READ.
226
227     870-PRINT-REPORT-HEADINGS.
228         ADD 1 TO WS-PAGE-COUNT
229         MOVE WS-PAGE-COUNT TO H2-PAGE-NBR
230         MOVE H1-HEADING-LINE-1 TO SALES-REPORT-LINE
231         PERFORM 880-WRITE-REPORT-TOP-LINE
232         MOVE H2-HEADING-LINE-2 TO SALES-REPORT-LINE
233         MOVE 1 TO WS-LINE-SPACING
234         PERFORM 890-WRITE-REPORT-LINE
235         MOVE H3-HEADING-LINE-3 TO SALES-REPORT-LINE
236         MOVE 2 TO WS-LINE-SPACING
237         PERFORM 890-WRITE-REPORT-LINE
238         MOVE H4-HEADING-LINE-4 TO SALES-REPORT-LINE
239         MOVE 1 TO WS-LINE-SPACING
240         PERFORM 890-WRITE-REPORT-LINE
241         MOVE 2 TO WS-LINE-SPACING.
242
243     880-WRITE-REPORT-TOP-LINE.
244         WRITE SALES-REPORT-LINE
245             AFTER ADVANCING PAGE
246         MOVE 1 TO WS-LINES-USED.
247
248     890-WRITE-REPORT-LINE.
249         WRITE SALES-REPORT-LINE
250             AFTER ADVANCING WS-LINE-SPACING
251         ADD WS-LINE-SPACING TO WS-LINES-USED.
```

In the WS-WORK-AREAS entry, the WS-SALES-REVENUE field has been created to hold the product of the quantity sold times the unit price for each input sales record.

In the WS-TOTAL-ACCUMULATORS group item, the WS-TOTAL-SALES-REP-ACCUM and WS-TOTAL-REPORT-ACCUM fields have been defined to accumulate the running totals for each sales representative and for the report total, respectively.

The input record description—SR-SALES-RECORD—and the seven output report-line formats—Hl-HEADING-LINE-1, H2-HEADING-LINE-2, H3-HEAD-ING-LINE-3, H4-HEADING-LINE-4, DL-DETAIL-LINE, ST-SALES-REP-TOTAL-LINE, and RT-REPORT-TOTAL-LINE—have each been coded in accordance with the programming specifications.

Coding the PROCEDURE DIVISION

Because several new programming techniques are incorporated into this program, let's consider each module of the program. As you can see, the first two modules—000-PRINT-SALES-REPORT and 100-INITIALIZE-VARIABLE-FIELDS—are quite similar to corresponding modules of other programs you have studied. However, most of the others have a new twist or two. In the descriptions that follow, only the COBOL-74 versions of the modules are shown. There is absolutely no logic difference between COBOL-74 and COBOL-85. The only consistent differences are the absence of periods at the end of each statement and the use of the END-IF scope terminators.

200-PROCESS-SALES-REP-GROUP Module

```
200-PROCESS-SALES-REP-GROUP.
    MOVE SR-SALES-REP TO WS-PREVIOUS-SALES-REP.
    MOVE ZEROS TO WS-TOTAL-SALES-REP-ACCUM.
    PERFORM 300-PRINT-DETAIL-LINE
        UNTIL SR-SALES-REP IS NOT EQUAL TO WS-PREVIOUS-SALES-REP.
    PERFORM 310-PRINT-SALES-REP-TOTAL-LINE.
```

This module is entered from the 000-PRINT-SALES-REPORT module through a PERFORM/UNTIL END-OF-FILE statement. Observe that this module also contains a PERFORM/UNTIL statement. This is commonly called a **nested** PERFORM/UNTIL relationship.

Due to the nested PERFORM/UNTIL, recognize that this module will be entered only for the first record of each Sales-representative control group—that is, only after a new Sales-representative-number is encountered in the input file. Whenever processing for a new Sales-representative control group is started, it is necessary to reinitialize the previous Sales-representative field and the Sales-representative total-accumulator field in WORKING-STORAGE.

Hence, the first statement in this module moves the sales-representative-number from the input-record area to the WS-PREVIOUS-SALES-REP field. For the first record, this initialization is required to avert the false control break that would otherwise occur when the first record is processed. For following control groups, the reinitialization is needed to maintain proper control-break processing.

The second statement sets the WS-TOTAL-SALES-REP-ACCUM field to zero. Since a new control group is beginning, it is necessary to refresh the total accumulator to a value of zero.

The next statement,

```
PERFORM 300-PRINT-DETAIL-LINE
    UNTIL SR-SALES-REP IS NOT EQUAL TO WS-PREVIOUS-SALES-REP
```

will cause detail lines to be printed until an input record with a different Sales-representative-number is read. When the current Sales-representative-number is not equal to the previous one, a control break has occurred. Program control will then leave the PERFORM/UNTIL statement and proceed to the next consecutive statement (PERFORM 310-PRINT-SALES-REP-TOTAL-LINE), which will cause the control-break total line to be printed.

After the control break, program control returns to the PERFORM/UNTIL statement in the mainline module. Unless end-of-file has been detected, the 200-PROCESS-SALES-REP-GROUP module will again be performed to process the records for the next sales representative.

300-PRINT-DETAIL-LINE Module

```
300-PRINT-DETAIL-LINE.
    IF WS-LINES-USED IS NOT LESS THAN WS-LINES-PER-PAGE
        PERFORM 870-PRINT-REPORT-HEADINGS.
    MOVE SR-SALES-REP TO DL-SALES-REP.
    MOVE SR-STATE TO DL-STATE.
    MOVE SR-BRANCH TO DL-BRANCH.
    MOVE SR-DATE-OF-SALE TO DL-DATE-OF-SALE.
    MOVE SR-PRODUCT-CODE TO DL-PRODUCT-CODE.
    MOVE SR-PRODUCT-DESCRIPTION TO DL-PRODUCT-DESCRIPTION.
    MOVE SR-UNIT-PRICE TO DL-UNIT-PRICE.
    MOVE SR-QUANTITY-SOLD TO DL-QUANTITY-SOLD.
    MULTIPLY SR-UNIT-PRICE BY SR-QUANTITY-SOLD
        GIVING WS-SALES-REVENUE ROUNDED.
    MOVE WS-SALES-REVENUE TO DL-SALES-REVENUE.
    MOVE DL-DETAIL-LINE TO SALES-REPORT-LINE.
    PERFORM 890-WRITE-REPORT-LINE.
    MOVE 1 TO WS-LINE-SPACING.
    ADD WS-SALES-REVENUE TO WS-TOTAL-SALES-REP-ACCUM.
    PERFORM 800-READ-SALES-RECORD.
```

The processing for this module conforms to the general logic used in the record-processing module of the PAYROLL program. The following functions are handled:

1. An end-of-page test is made and, if headings are required, the Report-headings module is performed.

2. The input fields to be printed are moved to the detail-line area.

3. The detail-line calculation (unit price times quantity equals sales revenue) is made. The product is developed in a temporary work-area field—WS-SALES-REVENUE—and then moved to the detail-line area.

4. The detail-line area in WORKING-STORAGE is moved to the report-line area in the FILE SECTION and the Write-report-line module is performed.

5. The WS-LINE-SPACING field is set to single-space the next detail line.

6. The Sales-revenue amount for the detail record is added to the total Sales-revenue-accumulator field for the sales representative.

One difference from previous programs, however, is that the line-spacing field is set *after*—rather than *before*—the detail printed. This matter will be explained later when the line-spacing logic is discussed.

310-PRINT-SALES-REP-TOTAL-LINE Module

```
310-PRINT-SALES-REP-TOTAL-LINE.
    MOVE WS-PREVIOUS-SALES-REP TO ST-SALES-REP.
    MOVE WS-TOTAL-SALES-REP-ACCUM TO ST-SALES-REVENUE.
    MOVE ST-SALES-REP-TOTAL-LINE TO SALES-REPORT-LINE.
    MOVE 2 TO WS-LINE-SPACING.
    PERFORM 890-WRITE-REPORT-LINE
    MOVE 3 TO WS-LINE-SPACING.
    ADD WS-TOTAL-SALES-REP-ACCUM TO WS-TOTAL-REPORT-ACCUM.
```

This module is entered from the 200-PROCESS-SALES-RECORD module whenever a control break occurs. At the time this module is entered, all the detail lines for a given sales representative have been printed and the total sales revenue for that representative has been accumulated and is present in the WS-TOTAL-SALES-REP-ACCUM field.

The first five statements in this module handle formatting and printing of the control total line as follows:

1. The WS-PREVIOUS-SALES-REP field is moved to its respective field in the control total line. Notice that the Sales-representative-number from the previous record—not the current record—is moved to the control total line. Remember that the current record caused the control break; this control total is for the Sales-representative-number of the previous record.

2. The total sales revenue for the sales representative is moved from the accumulator field in WORKING-STORAGE to its respective field in the WORKING-STORAGE SECTION.

3. The control total-line area is moved to the Report-line area in the FILE SECTION, the Line-spacing field is set, and the Write-report-line module is performed.

4. The total sales revenue for the sales representative is added to the grand total of sales revenue for the report as a whole.

5. The Line-spacing field is set to triple-spacing because the programming specifications call for the first detail line after a control break to be triple-spaced from the control total line.

700-PRINT-REPORT-TOTAL-LINE Module

```
700-PRINT-REPORT-TOTAL-LINE.
    MOVE WS-TOTAL-REPORT-ACCUM TO RT-SALES-REVENUE.
    MOVE RT-REPORT-TOTAL-LINE TO SALES-REPORT-LINE.
    MOVE 3 TO WS-LINE-SPACING.
    PERFORM 890-WRITE-REPORT-LINE.
```

This module is entered from the mainline module. It is executed only once—after all input records have been processed and all Sales-representative control total lines have been printed. Logic for this module is similar to that for the other Print-report-total modules presented in this text.

800-READ-SALES-RECORD Module

```
800-READ-SALES-RECORD.
    READ SALES-FILE INTO SR-SALES-RECORD
        AT END MOVE "YES" TO WS-END-OF-FILE-SWITCH
                MOVE HIGH-VALUES TO SR-SALES-REP.
```

As has been done in other read modules presented in this text, a record is read from the input file. If end-of-file is detected, the WS-END-OF-FILE-SWITCH is set to an END-OF-FILE condition.

In this module, one other action is taken at end-of-file time. The Sales-representative-number field in the input-record area is set to HIGH-VALUES. HIGH-VALUES is a figurative constant that can be used to set an alphanumeric field to its highest possible value. This setting is made in order to force out the final control total line, the one for the last Sales-representative-number processed.

By setting the input Sales-representative-number field to a different value when end-of-file is detected, PERFORM/UNTIL iterations in the 200-PROCESS-SALES-REP-GROUP module will cease and the control break for the last control total line will occur. Program control will then return to the mainline module,

where the END-OF-FILE condition will be detected and thus cause PERFORM/
UNTIL iterations of the 200-PRINT-SALES-REP-GROUP module to cease. After
that, the report totals will be printed and the program run will stop.

870-PRINT-REPORT-HEADINGS Module

```
870-PRINT-REPORT-HEADINGS.
    ADD 1 TO WS-PAGE-COUNT.
    MOVE WS-PAGE-COUNT TO H2-PAGE-NBR.
    MOVE H1-HEADING-LINE-1 TO SALES-REPORT-LINE.
    PERFORM 880-WRITE-REPORT-TOP-LINE.
    MOVE H2-HEADING-LINE-2 TO SALES-REPORT-LINE.
    MOVE 1 TO WS-LINE-SPACING.
    PERFORM 890-WRITE-REPORT-LINE.
    MOVE H3-HEADING-LINE-3 TO SALES-REPORT-LINE.
    MOVE 2 TO WS-LINE-SPACING.
    PERFORM 890-WRITE-REPORT-LINE.
    MOVE H4-HEADING-LINE-4 TO SALES-REPORT-LINE.
    MOVE 1 TO WS-LINE-SPACING.
    PERFORM 890-WRITE-REPORT-LINE.
    MOVE 2 TO WS-LINE-SPACING.
```

This Report-headings module is different from the counterpart module of previous programs in only one respect. In the PAYROLL and DATAVAL programs,
remember that a dummy blank line was printed at the end of the Report-headings
module so that the first detail line on each page was properly double-spaced from
the last heading line. Observe that, in this program, the WS-LINE-SPACING field
is set for double-spacing, but the report-line area is not cleared, nor is the Write
module performed. This processing will be fully explained in the discussion of line-
spacing logic that follows.

880-WRITE-REPORT-TOP-LINE and 890-WRITE-REPORT-LINE Modules.

The coding for these two write modules is exactly the same as that used in the
PAYROLL and DATAVAL programs. You have seen this code a sufficient number of times that it need not be repeated here.

Line-Spacing Logic.

The line-spacing logic for this program is a bit more complicated than that coded in previous programs. The complicating factor is that,
although detail lines are normally single-spaced (except for the first detail line after
the column headings, which is double-spaced), the programming specifications call
for the first detail line after each control total line to be triple-spaced.

Of course, this spacing could be accomplished on a straightforward basis by
simply printing a dummy blank double-spaced line at the end of the 310-PRINT
SALES-REP-TOTAL-LINE module (after the control total line has been printed).
These two blank lines, plus the single-spaced detail line, would provide the
specified triple-spacing after the control total line.

As a rule, printing blank lines is not the best way to do it. The line-spacing
technique used in this SCTLBRK program eliminates the need to print blank lines,
while retaining the desired spacing. It is commonly used and, once understood, is
easily recognized in a program.

It is only the detail line that has varying line-spacing requirements: single-
spacing after another detail line, double-spacing after the column-heading line, and
triple-spacing after the control total line. Remember that spacing for each heading
line is constant and that the control total line is always double-spaced from the last
detail line of the group. Hence, the three-step line-printing process introduced in
Chapter 6 must be altered slightly for printing the detail line.

Figure 10-11 diagrams the logic used to handle the line spacing. At points A, B, C, and D, the WS-LINE-SPACING field is set immediately before performing the 890-WRITE-DETAIL-LINE module. This is in accordance with the three-step process used in previous programs of this text. However, notice at point E (in the 310-PRINT-SALES-REP-TOTAL-LINE module), that the WS-LINE-SPACING field

Figure 10-11   Line-spacing logic.

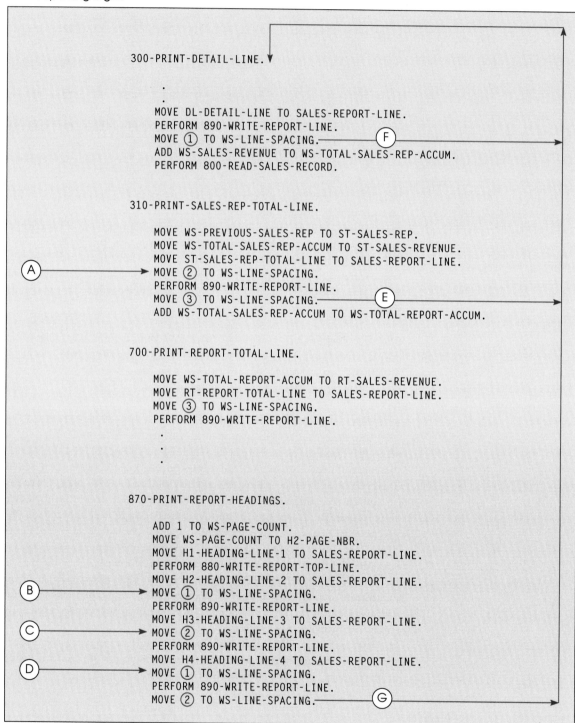

is set to 3 after the line has been printed. The setting is made at this time so that when the next detail line is written in the 300-PRINT-DETAIL-LINE module, the WS-LINE-SPACING field will be set properly for triple-spacing.

This approach means that the WS-LINE-SPACING field must *not* be set for single-spacing *before* printing the detail line in the 300-PRINT-DETAIL-LINE module. If it were, this detail-time single-space setting would override the total-time triple-space setting and all detail lines would end up single-spaced. Therefore, at point F in the figure, WS-LINE-SPACING is set to single-spacing after the detail line has been printed. This will properly set the line-spacing indicator back to single-spacing for the next detail line; single-spacing will thus continue—for all detail lines—until the next control total line or a new report heading is printed. (The next control total line will be properly double-spaced by the normal three-step line-printing process.)

Observe also that this type of logic has eliminated the need for printing of the dummy blank line at the end of the 870-PRINT-REPORT-HEADINGS module (as shown at point G in the figure). By setting the line-spacing indicator to 2 at the end of the headings routine and by not resetting the indicator until after each detail line is printed, the proper double-spacing of the first detail line after the last heading line is provided for.

Topic: A Multiple-Level Control-Break Program

To illustrate a **multiple-level control-break program**, the single-level sales report program will be used as a base. In addition to having more than one control break, this program will incorporate into the heading a period-ending date obtained from an input date record.

Since much of the programming specifications, design documentation, and coding for this multiple-level control-break sales report program will duplicate that of the single-level control-break sales report program, all modifications and new material are identified by shading in the applicable illustrations.

Programming Specifications

Rather than printing only sales-representative control totals, as was done in the single-level SCTLBRK program, this program prints sales-representative totals within branch-office totals within state totals. A report total is also printed. The name of the program is MCTLBRK (for Multiple-level ConTroL-BReaK sales report). The programming specifications are shown in Figure 10-12.

Input-Record Layouts

The input sales record format is exactly the same as it is for the single-level sales report program. However, another input record to carry the period-ending date record must be provided. As mentioned in the programming specifications, this period-ending date record must be sequenced as the first record of the input file.

Print Chart

On the first heading line of the output report, a field for the period-ending date (together with a caption to identify it) has been added. Thus, the report will show both the period-ending date to which the report applies and the run date on which the report is actually printed.

Figure 10-12   Programming specifications: Multiple-level control-break sales report program
(continued on pages 511–512)

PROGRAMMING SPECIFICATIONS

Program name: MULTIPLE-LEVEL CONTROL-BREAK   **Program ID:** MCTLBRK
SALES REPORT

Program Description

This program is to read input sales records, compute the sales revenue for each record, and print a sales-report detail-line for each sales record.

Sales-representative control-total lines are printed for each sales-representative within each branch within each state. Branch control-total lines are printed for each branch within each state. A state control-total line is printed for each state. After all input-sales records have been processed, a report-total line is to be printed.

Input File:

Sales File

Output File:

Sales Report (multiple-level)

List of Program Operations:

A. Read records from the input sales-file.

   1. The first record is to be a period-ending date record.

     a. The period-ending date is to be extracted from the date record and stored in the period-ending date field of the first heading-line.

   2. If the first record is not a period-ending date record, the program processing should terminate.

B. For each sales record, the program is to:

   1. Compute the sales-revenue amount by multiplying the unit-price field by the quantity-sold field.

   2. Print a detail-line that contains the following fields in accordance with the format shown on the print-chart.

     - Sales-representative number
     - State
     - Branch
     - Date-of-sale
     - Product-code
     - Product-description
     - Unit-price
     - Quantity-sold
     - Sales-revenue

   3. Accumulate the following totals:

     - Total sales-revenue for each sales-representative
     - Total sales-revenue for each branch
     - Total sales-revenue for each state
     - Total sales-revenue for all sales-representatives

C. Whenever the sales-representative number (within branch and within state) changes, the program is to print a sales-representative control-total line containing the following fields in accordance with the format shown on the print chart:

   - State
   - Branch
   - Sales-representative number
   - The words "SALES REP. TOTAL"
   - Total sales-revenue for that sales-representative
   - One asterisk (*)

D. Whenever the branch (within state) changes, the program is to print a branch control-total line containing the following fields in accordance with the format shown on the print chart:

   - State
   - Branch
   - The words "BRANCH TOTAL"
   - Total sales-revenue for that branch
   - Two asterisks (**)

E. Whenever the state changes, the program is to print a state control-total line containing the following fields in accordance with the format shown on the print chart:

   - State
   - The words "STATE TOTAL"
   - Total sales-revenue for that state
   - Three asterisks (***)

F. After all the input sales records have been processed, the program is to print the following total fields on the report-total line in accordance with the format shown on the print chart:

   - The words "REPORT TOTAL"
   - Total sales-revenue for all sales-representatives
   - Four asterisks (****)

G. Headings are to be printed on each page of the report. On the first page and after 54 lines have been used on a report page, skip to the next page and print the report headings.

   1. The period-ending date is to be obtained from the date record as described in operation A.1, above, and printed on the first heading-line in accordance with the format shown on the print chart.

   2. The run date is to be obtained from the operating system and printed on the second heading-line in accordance with the format shown on the print chart.

   3. The page number is to be incremented each time the heading is printed and displayed on the second heading-line in accordance with the format shown on the print chart.

H. Line-spacing is to be handled as follows:

   1. The first detail-line printed after the headings is to be double-spaced from the last heading-line.

   2. Detail-lines for the same sales-representative are to be single-spaced from one another.

   3. Each control-total line is to be double-spaced from the previous line.

   4. The first detail line for each sales-representative is to be triple-spaced from the previous control-total.

   5. The report-total line is to be triple-spaced from the last state-control-total line.

Figure 10-12 (continues on page 512)

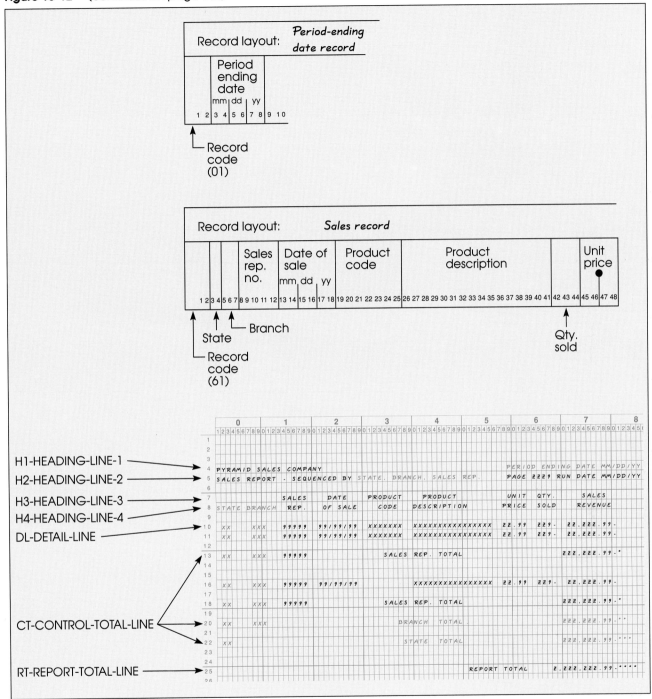

Figurre 10-12   (continued from page 511)

Sample report output:

```
PYRAMID SALES COMPANY                           PERIOD ENDING DATE 09/20/90
SALES REPORT - SEQUENCED BY STATE, BRANCH, SALES REP.    PAGE    1 RUN DATE 09/26/90

              SALES   DATE     PRODUCT   PRODUCT          UNIT  QTY.    SALES
STATE BRANCH  REP.    OF SALE  CODE      DESCRIPTION      PRICE  SOLD   REVENUE

 CA    001   10003   05/07/90  TB001     TOOTHBRUSH        1.00   1      1.00
 CA    001   10003   05/07/90  SB005     BAR SOAP           .50   5      2.50

 CA    001   10003                       SALES REP. TOTAL                3.50 *


 CA    001   10005   05/07/90  MP070     MOP              10.00   2     20.00

 CA    001   10005                       SALES REP. TOTAL               20.00 *

 CA    001                               BRANCH TOTAL                   23.50 **


 CA    002   10063   05/07/90  SB005     BAR SOAP           .50   5      2.50

 CA    002   10063                       SALES REP. TOTAL                2.50 *


 CA    002   10069   05/07/90  SP008     SOAP POWDER       1.89  238   449.82
 CA    002   10069   05/07/90  WF080     FLOOR WAX         2.98   5     14.90

 CA    002   10069                       SALES REP. TOTAL              464.72 *

 CA    002                               BRANCH TOTAL                  467.22 **

 CA                                      STATE TOTAL                   490.72 ***


 NV    017   20006   05/07/90  SB005     BAR SOAP           .50   1       .50

 NV    017   20006                       SALES REP. TOTAL                 .50 *


 NV    017   20009   05/07/90  SP008     SOAP POWDER       1.89   1      1.89
 NV    017   20009   05/07/90  WF080     FLOOR WAX         2.98   1      2.98

 NV    017   20009                       SALES REP. TOTAL                4.87 *

 NV    017                               BRANCH TOTAL                    5.37 **


 NV    018   20033   05/07/90  TB001     TOOTHBRUSH        1.00   1      1.00
 NV    018   20033   05/07/90  SB005     BAR SOAP           .50   5      2.50

 NV    018   20033                       SALES REP. TOTAL                3.50 *


 NV    018   20039   05/07/90  WF080     FLOOR WAX         2.98   2      5.96

 NV    018   20039                       SALES REP. TOTAL                5.96 *

 NV    018                               BRANCH TOTAL                    9.46 **

 NV                                      STATE TOTAL                    14.83 ***


                                         REPORT TOTAL                  505.55 ****
```

A few words of explanation are probably useful with regard to the control fields that are to be printed on each control total line. For a sense what is involved, you should refer to Figure 10-13, which shows an example of the multiple-level control groups for the input sales records. Notice that breaks occur when: (1) the Sales-representative-number changes, (2) the Branch-number changes, and (3) the State changes.

A Sales-representative control total line applies to that Sales-representative-number within that branch within that state. A branch control total line applies to that branch within that state. A state control total line applies to that state.

Therefore, on the sales-representative control total line, the applicable state, branch, and sales-representative-number should be printed. On the branch control total line, the state and branch—but not the sales-representative-number—should be displayed. On the state control-break line, only the state should be shown.

Program Design
Multiple-Level
Control-Break Logic

When there is more than one control-break level, program logic complexity is increased in two areas: the nesting of PERFORM/UNTIL statements to process each control level and the need to provide additional control total line-printing modules.

Nesting of PERFORM/UNTIL Statements. To design a multiple-level control-break program, the most inclusive control field—**the major control field**—must be identified. Then, in order of decreasing significance, each additional control field must be identified down to the **minor control field**. In the multiple-level sales report, we have:

State field: the major control field

Branch field: intermediate control field

Sales-representative-number field: the minor control field

Figure 10-13 Example of multiple-level control groups.

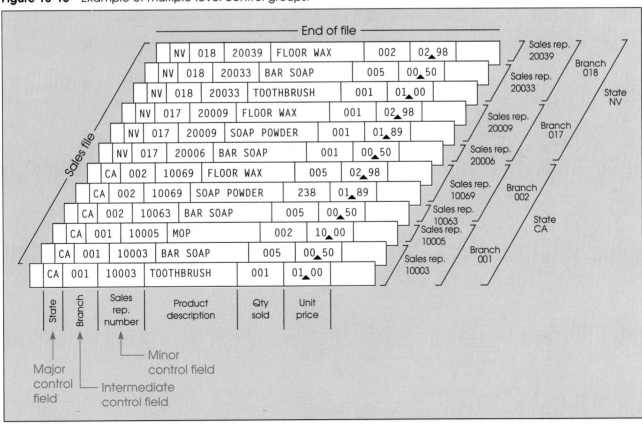

In this regard, notice that the arrangement of the Sales-representative-number, Branch, and State fields has been changed on the print chart to show them in major to minor sequence, from left to right. Reports are usually easier to read and understand when control fields are arranged in major-field to minor-field order across a line. (The single-level sales report shows its major field—Sales-representative-number—on the left for ease of reference, also.) The additional control total lines for branch and state totals are also shown on the print chart.

In the nested PERFORM/UNTIL control-break logic, the major control field must always be tested first. The nesting then proceeds in decreasing significance down through the minor control field. One tricky aspect of multiple-level control-break tests is that at each level, not only its respective control field must be checked, but all higher-level (more major) control fields must also be tested for a control break.

For example, at the major level only the major control field—State—is tested. However, when checking for an intermediate branch control break, not only the Branch field, but also the State field must be tested for a change. Similarly, when checking for a Sales-representative control break, the State, Branch, and sales-representative-number fields must all be tested.

Figure 10-14 provides an example of why all more significant control fields must be tested at each level (words are used in the Branch and Sales-representative field instead of code numbers to simplify the explanation). If only the minor Sales-representative field were tested after processing the Smith in Chicago, the Smiths in Springfield would be lumped together in the same Sales-representative control group because their names are the same. By testing all three fields at the minor level, it is clear that a State control break has occurred between the first and second records. Further, if only the intermediate branch field were tested after processing the Smith in Springfield, Illinois; the Jones in Springfield, Massachusetts, would be combined into the same Branch control group, even though the branches are in different states.

When a control break is detected, control total lines must be printed as follows:

1. A major field (State) control break triggers minor (Sales-representative), intermediate (Branch), and then major (State) control totals.

2. An intermediate field (Branch) control break triggers minor (Sales-representative), and then intermediate (Branch) control totals.

3. A minor field (Sales-representative) control break triggers only minor (Sales-representative) totals.

Figure 10-14 Example of need for proper control-break testing hierarchy.

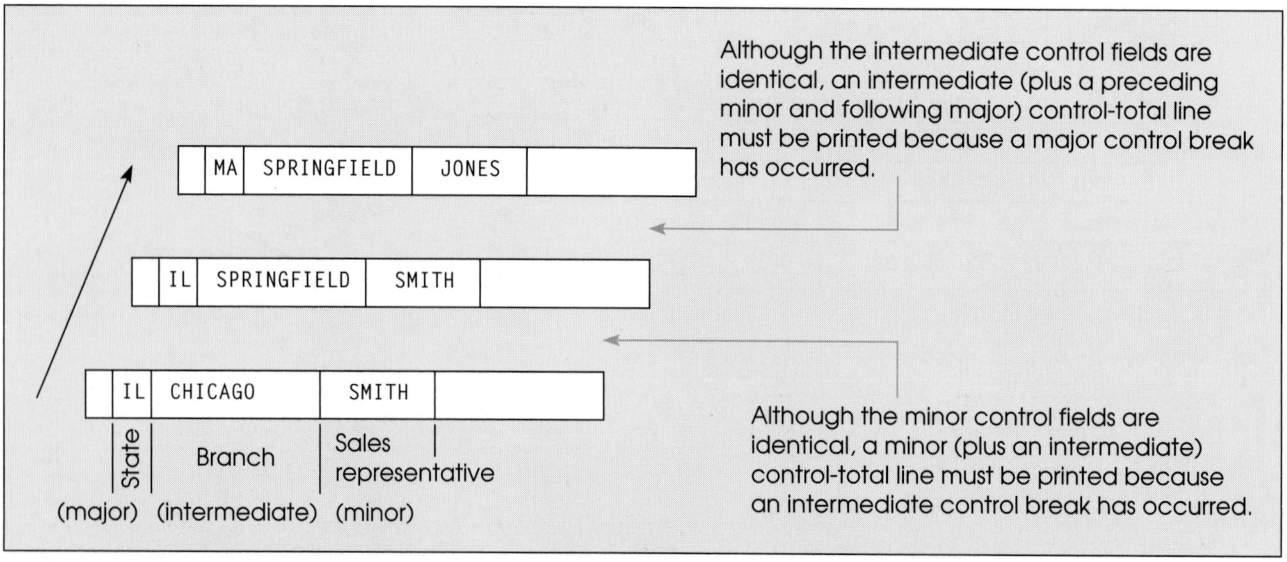

Figure 10-17   Pseudocode: Multiple-level control-break sales report program.

<u>000-Print-Sales-Report module</u>

1. Open the files.
2. Perform 100-Initialize-Variable-Fields.
3. Perform 110-Process-Date-Record.
4. Perform 200-Process-Major-State-Group until no more records.
5. Perform 700-Print-Report-Total-Line.
6. Close the files.
7. Stop the run.

<u>100-Initialize-Variable-Fields module</u>

1. Set the End-of-file indicator to "No".
2. Set the Page-count field to zero.
3. Set the Lines-used indicator so that headings for the first page will be triggered.
4. Obtain the date from the operating system and move it to the second heading-line.
5. Set the Total-accumulator fields to zero.

<u>110-Process-Date-Record module</u>

1. Perform 800-Read-Sales-Record.
2. If a date-record has been read (Record-code = 01)
   Move the input Period-ending-date to the Period-ending-date in the first heading-line.
   Perform 800-Read-Sales-Record
   Else
   Set the End-of-file indicator to "Yes".

<u>200-Process-Major-State-Group module</u>

1. Move the input State field to the Previous-state field.
2. Move zero to the Total-state-sales-revenue field.
3. Perform 210-Process-Inter-Branch-Group
      until the State field in the current input record
         is not equal to the Previous-state field.
4. Perform 330-Print-State-Total-Line.

<u>210-Process-Inter-Branch-Group module</u>

1. Move the input Branch field to the Previous-branch field.
2. Move zero to the Total-branch-sales-revenue field.
3. Perform 220-Process-Minor-Rep-Group
      until the Branch field in the current input record
         is not equal to the Previous-branch field
      or   the State field in the current input record
         is not equal to the Previous-state field.
4. Perform 320-Print-Branch-Total-Line.

<u>220-Process-Minor-Rep-Group module</u>

1. Move the input Sales-rep field
      to the Previous-sales-rep field.
2. Move zero to the Total-sales-rep-revenue field.
3. Perform 300-Print-Detail-Line
      until the Sales-rep field in the current input record
         is not equal to the Previous-sales-rep field
      or   the Branch field in the current input record
         is not equal to the Previous-branch field
      or   the State field in the current input record
         is not equal to the Previous-state field.
4. Perform 310-Print-Sales-Rep-Total-Line.

<u>300-Print-Detail-Line module</u>

1. If the report page is full,
      Perform 870-Print-Report-Headings.
2. Move the input Sales-rep
      to the detail-line Sales-rep.
3. Move the input State
      to the detail-line State.
4. Move the input Branch
      to the detail-line Branch.
5. Move the input Date-of-sale
      to the detail-line Date-of-sale.
6. Move the input Product-code
      to the detail-line Product-code.
7. Move the input Product-description
      to the detail-line Product-description.
8. Move the input Unit-price
      to the detail-line Unit-price.
9. Move the input Quantity-sold
      to the detail-line Quantity-sold.
10. Multiply the input Unit-price by the input Quantity-sold
      to equal the Sales-revenue.
11. Move the Sales-Revenue to the detail-line Sales-revenue.
12. Move the detail-line to the output print-line area.
13. Perform 890-Write-Report-Line.
14. Set the Line-spacing indicator for single-spacing.
15. Add the Sales-revenue for this record
      to the Total-sales-rep-sales-revenue.
16. Perform 800-Read-Sales-Record.

<u>310-Print-Sales-Rep-Total-Line module</u>

1. Move the Previous-state
      to the control-total-line State.
2. Move the Previous-branch
      to the control-total-line Branch.
3. Move the Previous-sales-rep
      to the control-total-line Sales-rep.
4. Move the words "SALES REP." to the control-total-line.
5. Move the Total-sales rep-sales-revenue
      to the control-total-line Sales-revenue.
6. Move one asterisk (*) to the control-total-line.
7. Move the control-total-line to the output print-line area.
8. Set the Line-spacing indicator for double-spacing.
9. Perform 890-Write-Report-Line.
10. Set the Line-spacing indicator for triple-spacing.
11. Add the Total-sales-rep-sales-revenue
      to the Total-branch-sales-revenue.

<u>320-Print-Branch-Total-Line module</u>

1. Blank the Sales-rep field in the control-total-line.
2. Move the word "BRANCH" to the control-total-line.
3. Move the Total-branch-sales-revenue
      to the control-total-line Sales-revenue.
4. Move two asterisks (**) to the control-total-line.
5. Set the Line-spacing indicator for double-spacing.
6. Move the control-total-line
      to the output print-line area.
7. Perform 890-Write-Report-Line.
8. Set the Line-spacing indicator for triple-spacing.
9. Add the Total-branch-sales-revenue
      to the Total-state-sales-revenue.

<u>330-Print-State-Total-Line module</u>

1. Blank the Branch field in the control-total-line.
2. Move the word "STATE" to the control-total-line.
3. Move the Total-state-sales-revenue
      to the control-total-line Sales-revenue.
4. Move three asterisks (***) to the control-total-line.
5. Set the Line-spacing indicator for double-spacing.
6. Move the control-total-line to the output-line area.
7. Perform 890-Write-Report-Line.
8. Set the Line-spacing indicator for triple-spacing.
9. Add the Total-state-sales-revenue
      to the Total-report-sales-revenue.

<u>700-Print-Report-Total-Line module</u>

1. Move the Total-report-sales-revenue
      to the report-total-line Sales-revenue.
2. Move the report-total-line to the output print-line area.
3. Set the Line-spacing indicator for triple-spacing.
4. Perform 890-Write-Report-Line.

<u>800-Read-Sales-Record module</u>

1. Read a record from the input Sales file.
2. If there are no more records
      Move "YES" to the end-of-file indicator
      Move High-values to the input-record Sales-rep Branch, and State fields.

<u>870-Print-Report-Headings module</u>

1. Add 1 to the Page-count.
2. Move the Page-count
      to the Page-number field in the second heading-line.
3. Move Heading-line-1 to the output print-line area.
4. Perform 880-Write-Report-Top-Line.
5. Move Heading-line-2 to the output print-line area.
6. Set the Line-spacing indicator for single-spacing.
7. Perform 890-Write-Report-Line.
8. Move Heading-line-3 to the output print-line area.
9. Set the Line-spacing indicator for double-spacing.
10. Perform 890-Write-Report-Line.
11. Move Heading-line-4 to the output print-line area.
12. Set the Line-spacing indicator for single-spacing.
13. Perform 890-Write-Report-Line.
14. Set the Line-spacing indicator for double-spacing.

<u>880-Write-Report-Top-Line module</u>

1. Advance to the top of the next report page
      and write out the output print-line area.
2. Set the Lines-used indicator to 1.

<u>890-Write-Report-Line module</u>

1. Advance the forms in accordance with the value in the Line-spacing indicator field
      and write the output print-line area.
2. Add the Line-spacing indicator to the Lines-used field.

Figure 10-18   Program flowchart: Multiple-level control-break sales report program (continued on pages 519–521).

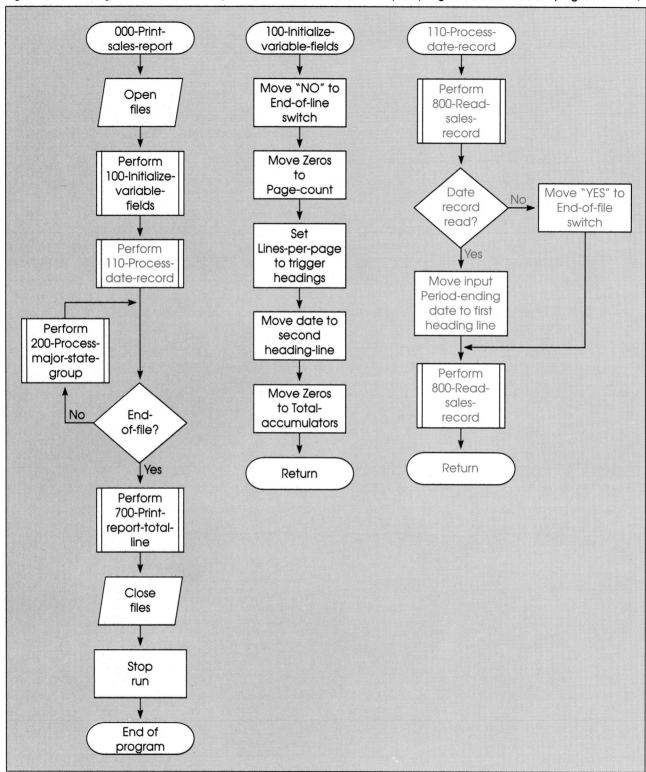

Figure 10-18   (continued from page 518)

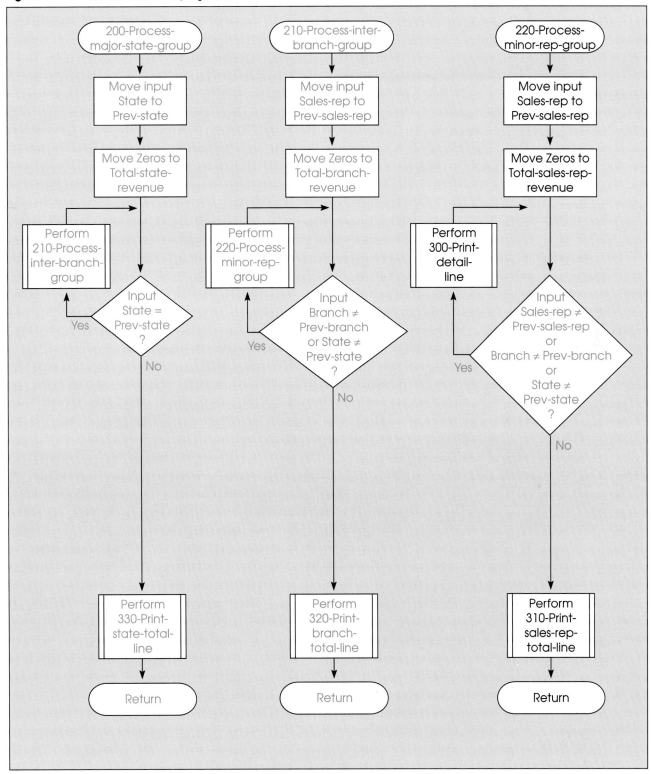

Figure 10-18   (continued from page 518)

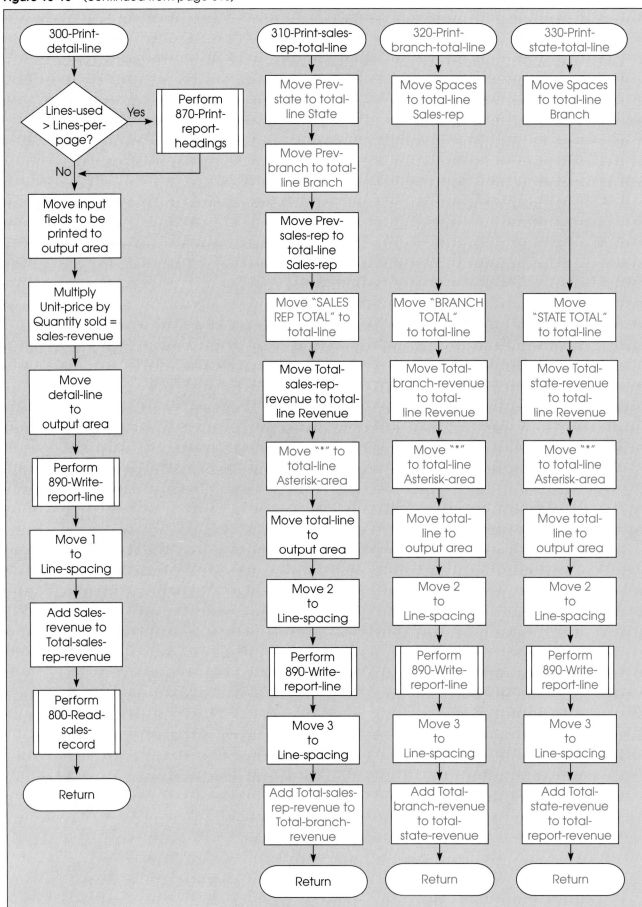

Figure 10-18 (continued from page 518)

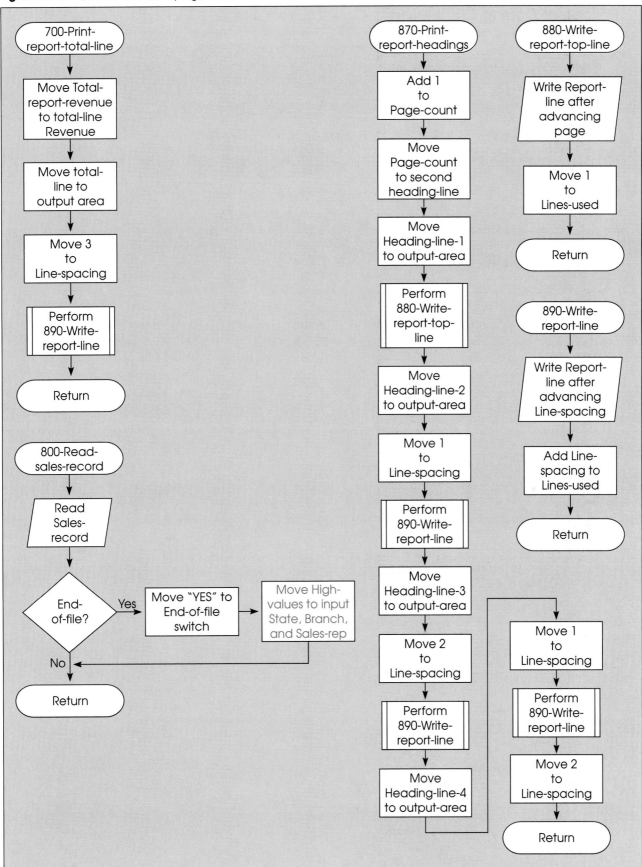

Program Coding   The first three divisions of the MCTLBRK program are shown in Figure 10-19; the COBOL-74 and COBOL-85 versions are shown in Figures 10-20 and 10-21, respectively. This program differs from the SCTLBRK program as described in the following sections.

Figure 10-19   First three divisions: Multiple-level control break program (MCTLBRK).

```
  1      IDENTIFICATION DIVISION.
  2      PROGRAM-ID.  MCTLBRK.
  3      *           WRITTEN BY T. WELBURN.
  4      *           PYRAMID SALES COMPANY.
  5      *           FEB 27, 1986.
  6      *           REVISED 9-25-89 BY W. PRICE      1974 STANDARD.
  7
  8      *           THIS PROGRAM READS SALES RECORDS,
  9      *           COMPUTES THE SALES REVENUE FOR EACH SALES RECORD
 10      *           AND PRINTS A SALES DETAIL LINE
 11      *           FOR EACH SALES RECORD.
 12
 13      *           TOTAL LINES ARE PRINTED BY SALES-REP
 14      *           WITHIN BRANCH WITHIN STATE.
 15
 16      *           AFTER ALL INPUT SALES RECORDS HAVE BEEN PROCESSED,
 17      *           A REPORT TOTAL LINE WILL BE PRINTED.
 18
 19
 20      ENVIRONMENT DIVISION.
 21
 22      CONFIGURATION SECTION.
 23
 24      SOURCE-COMPUTER.  (system dependent).
 25      OBJECT-COMPUTER.  (system dependent).
 26
 27      INPUT-OUTPUT SECTION.
 28
 29      FILE-CONTROL.
 30          SELECT SALES-FILE
 31              ASSIGN TO (system dependent).
 32          SELECT SALES-REPORT
 33              ASSIGN TO (system dependent).
 34
 35
 36      DATA DIVISION.
 37
 38      FILE SECTION.
 39
 40      FD  SALES-FILE
 41          RECORD CONTAINS 8 TO 48 CHARACTERS
 42          LABEL RECORDS ARE OMITTED.
 43
 44      01  SALES-RECORD.
 45          05  FILLER                    PIC X(48).
 46
 47      FD  SALES-REPORT
 48          RECORD CONTAINS 132 CHARACTERS
 49          LABEL RECORDS ARE OMITTED.
 50
 51      01  SALES-REPORT-LINE.
 52          05  FILLER                    PIC X(132).
 53
 54      WORKING-STORAGE SECTION.
 55
 56      01  WS-SWITCHES.
 57          05  WS-END-OF-FILE-SWITCH     PIC X(3).
 58              88  END-OF-FILE                       VALUE "YES".
 59
 60      01  WS-CONTROL-FIELDS.
 61          05  WS-PREVIOUS-STATE         PIC X(2).
 62          05  WS-PREVIOUS-BRANCH        PIC X(3).
 63          05  WS-PREVIOUS-SALES-REP     PIC X(5).
 64
 65      01  WS-REPORT-CONTROLS.
 66          05  WS-PAGE-COUNT             PIC S9(4).
 67          05  WS-LINES-PER-PAGE         PIC S9(2)  VALUE +54.
 68          05  WS-LINES-USED             PIC S9(2).
 69          05  WS-LINE-SPACING           PIC S9(2).
 70
 71      01  WS-WORK-AREAS.
 72          05  WS-DATE-WORK              PIC 9(6).
 73          05  WS-DATE-REFORMAT REDEFINES WS-DATE-WORK.
 74              10  WS-YEAR               PIC 9(2).
 75              10  WS-MONTH              PIC 9(2).
 76              10  WS-DAY                PIC 9(2).
 77          05  WS-SALES-REVENUE          PIC S9(5)V99.
 78
 79      01  WS-TOTAL-ACCUMULATORS.
 80          05  WS-TOTAL-SALES-REP-ACCUM  PIC S9(6)V99.
 81          05  WS-TOTAL-BRANCH-ACCUM     PIC S9(6)V99.
 82          05  WS-TOTAL-STATE-ACCUM      PIC S9(6)V99.
 83          05  WS-TOTAL-REPORT-ACCUM     PIC S9(7)V99.
 84
 85      01  SR-SALES-RECORD.
 86          05  SR-RECORD-CODE            PIC X(2).
 87          05  SR-STATE                  PIC X(2).
 88          05  SR-BRANCH                 PIC X(3).
 89          05  SR-SALES-REP              PIC X(5).
 90          05  SR-DATE-OF-SALE           PIC X(6).
 91          05  SR-PRODUCT-CODE           PIC X(7).
 92          05  SR-PRODUCT-DESCRIPTION    PIC X(16).
 93          05  SR-QUANTITY-SOLD          PIC S9(3).
 94          05  SR-UNIT-PRICE             PIC 9(2)V99.
 95
 96      01  DR-DATE-RECORD REDEFINES SR-SALES-RECORD.
 97          05  DR-RECORD-CODE            PIC X(2).
 98              88  DATE-RECORD                       VALUE "01".
 99          05  DR-PERIOD-ENDING-DATE     PIC X(6).
100          05  FILLER                    PIC X(40).
101
102      01  H1-HEADING-LINE-1.
103          05  FILLER          PIC X(20)  VALUE "PYRAMID SALES COMPAN".
104          05  FILLER          PIC X(20)  VALUE "Y                   ".
105          05  FILLER          PIC X(20)  VALUE "                  PE".
106          05  FILLER          PIC X(17)  VALUE "RIOD ENDING DATE ".
107          05  H1-PER-END-DATE PIC XX/XX/XX.
108
109      01  H2-HEADING-LINE-2.
110          05  FILLER          PIC X(20)  VALUE "SALES REPORT - SEQUE".
111          05  FILLER          PIC X(20)  VALUE "NCED BY STATE, BRANC".
112          05  FILLER          PIC X(20)  VALUE "H, SALES REP.    PA".
113          05  FILLER          PIC X(03)  VALUE "GE ".
114          05  H2-PAGE-NBR     PIC ZZZ9.
115          05  FILLER          PIC X(10)  VALUE    " RUN DATE ".
116          05  H2-MONTH        PIC 9(2).
117          05  FILLER          PIC X(1)   VALUE "/".
118          05  H2-DAY          PIC 9(2).
119          05  FILLER          PIC X(1)   VALUE "/".
120          05  H2-YEAR         PIC 9(2).
121
122      01  H3-HEADING-LINE-3.
123          05  FILLER          PIC X(20)  VALUE "          SALES ".
124          05  FILLER          PIC X(20)  VALUE " DATE    PRODUCT    ".
125          05  FILLER          PIC X(20)  VALUE " PRODUCT          UN".
126          05  FILLER          PIC X(20)  VALUE "IT QTY.    SALES ".
127
128      01  H4-HEADING-LINE-4.
129          05  FILLER          PIC X(20)  VALUE "STATE BRANCH REP.  ".
130          05  FILLER          PIC X(20)  VALUE " OF SALE  CODE    D".
131          05  FILLER          PIC X(20)  VALUE "ESCRIPTION      PRI".
132          05  FILLER          PIC X(20)  VALUE "CE SOLD    REVENUE ".
133
134      01  DL-DETAIL-LINE.
135          05  FILLER                    PIC X(1)   VALUE SPACES.
136          05  DL-STATE                  PIC X(2).
137          05  FILLER                    PIC X(4)   VALUE SPACES.
138          05  DL-BRANCH                 PIC X(3).
139          05  FILLER                    PIC X(3)   VALUE SPACES.
140          05  DL-SALES-REP              PIC X(5).
141          05  FILLER                    PIC X(2)   VALUE SPACES.
142          05  DL-DATE-OF-SALE           PIC XX/XX/XX.
143          05  FILLER                    PIC X(2).
144          05  DL-PRODUCT-CODE           PIC X(7).
145          05  FILLER                    PIC X(2)   VALUE SPACES.
146          05  DL-PRODUCT-DESCRIPTION    PIC X(16).
147          05  FILLER                    PIC X(2).
148          05  DL-UNIT-PRICE             PIC ZZ.99.
149          05  FILLER                    PIC X(2)   VALUE SPACES.
150          05  DL-QUANTITY-SOLD          PIC ZZ9-.
151          05  FILLER                    PIC X(2)   VALUE SPACES.
152          05  DL-SALES-REVENUE          PIC ZZ,ZZZ.99-.
153
154      01  CT-CONTROL-TOTAL-LINE.
155          05  FILLER                    PIC X(1)   VALUE SPACES.
156          05  CT-STATE                  PIC X(2).
157          05  FILLER                    PIC X(4)   VALUE SPACES.
158          05  CT-BRANCH                 PIC X(3).
159          05  FILLER                    PIC X(3)   VALUE SPACES.
160          05  CT-SALES-REP              PIC X(5).
161          05  FILLER                    PIC X(15)  VALUE SPACES.
162          05  CT-TOTAL-DESCRIPTION      PIC X(10)  JUSTIFIED RIGHT.
163          05  FILLER                    PIC X(6)   VALUE " TOTAL".
164          05  FILLER                    PIC X(20)  VALUE SPACES.
165          05  CT-SALES-REVENUE          PIC ZZZ,ZZZ.99-.
166          05  CT-ASTERISKS              PIC X(3).
167
168      01  RT-REPORT-TOTAL-LINE.
169          05  FILLER                    PIC X(50)  VALUE SPACES.
170          05  FILLER                    PIC X(12) VALUE "REPORT TOTAL".
171          05  FILLER                    PIC X(5)   VALUE SPACES.
172          05  RT-SALES-REVENUE          PIC Z,ZZZ,ZZZ.99-.
173          05  FILLER                    PIC X(4)   VALUE "****".
174
175
```

Figure 10-20   COBOL-74 PROCEDURE DIVISION: Multiple-level control break program (MCTLBRK).

```
176     PROCEDURE DIVISION.
177
178     000-PRINT-SALES-REPORT.
179         OPEN INPUT SALES-FILE
180             OUTPUT SALES-REPORT.
181         PERFORM 100-INITIALIZE-VARIABLE-FIELDS.
182         PERFORM 110-PROCESS-DATE-RECORD.
183         PERFORM 200-PROCESS-MAJOR-STATE-GROUP
184             UNTIL END-OF-FILE.
185         PERFORM 700-PRINT-REPORT-TOTAL-LINE.
186         CLOSE SALES-FILE
187             SALES-REPORT.
188         STOP RUN.
189
190     100-INITIALIZE-VARIABLE-FIELDS.
191         MOVE "NO " TO WS-END-OF-FILE-SWITCH.
192         MOVE ZEROS TO WS-PAGE-COUNT.
193         MOVE WS-LINES-PER-PAGE TO WS-LINES-USED.
194         ACCEPT WS-DATE-WORK FROM DATE.
195         MOVE WS-MONTH TO H2-MONTH.
196         MOVE WS-DAY TO H2-DAY.
197         MOVE WS-YEAR TO H2-YEAR.
198         MOVE ZEROS TO WS-TOTAL-REPORT-ACCUM.
199
200     110-PROCESS-DATE-RECORD.
201         PERFORM 800-READ-SALES-RECORD.
202         IF DATE-RECORD
203             MOVE DR-PERIOD-ENDING-DATE TO H1-PER-END-DATE
204             PERFORM 800-READ-SALES-RECORD
205         ELSE
206             MOVE "YES" TO WS-END-OF-FILE-SWITCH.
207
208     200-PROCESS-MAJOR-STATE-GROUP.
209         MOVE SR-STATE TO WS-PREVIOUS-STATE.
210         MOVE ZEROS TO WS-TOTAL-STATE-ACCUM.
211         PERFORM 210-PROCESS-INTER-BRANCH-GROUP
212             UNTIL SR-STATE IS NOT EQUAL TO WS-PREVIOUS-STATE.
213         PERFORM 330-PRINT-STATE-TOTAL-LINE.
214
215     210-PROCESS-INTER-BRANCH-GROUP.
216         MOVE SR-BRANCH TO WS-PREVIOUS-BRANCH.
217         MOVE ZEROS TO WS-TOTAL-BRANCH-ACCUM.
218         PERFORM 220-PROCESS-MINOR-REP-GROUP
219             UNTIL SR-BRANCH IS NOT EQUAL TO WS-PREVIOUS-BRANCH
220                 OR SR-STATE IS NOT EQUAL TO WS-PREVIOUS-STATE.
221         PERFORM 320-PRINT-BRANCH-TOTAL-LINE.
222
223     220-PROCESS-MINOR-REP-GROUP.
224         MOVE SR-SALES-REP TO WS-PREVIOUS-SALES-REP.
225         MOVE ZEROS TO WS-TOTAL-SALES-REP-ACCUM.
226         PERFORM 300-PRINT-DETAIL-LINE
227             UNTIL SR-SALES-REP IS NOT EQUAL TO WS-PREVIOUS-SALES-REP
228                 OR SR-BRANCH IS NOT EQUAL TO WS-PREVIOUS-BRANCH
229                 OR SR-STATE IS NOT EQUAL TO WS-PREVIOUS-STATE.
230         PERFORM 310-PRINT-SALES-REP-TOTAL-LINE.
231
232     300-PRINT-DETAIL-LINE.
233         IF WS-LINES-USED IS NOT LESS THAN WS-LINES-PER-PAGE
234             PERFORM 870-PRINT-REPORT-HEADINGS.
235         MOVE SR-SALES-REP TO DL-SALES-REP.
236         MOVE SR-STATE TO DL-STATE.
237         MOVE SR-BRANCH TO DL-BRANCH.
238         MOVE SR-DATE-OF-SALE TO DL-DATE-OF-SALE.
239         MOVE SR-PRODUCT-CODE TO DL-PRODUCT-CODE.
240         MOVE SR-PRODUCT-DESCRIPTION TO DL-PRODUCT-DESCRIPTION.
241         MOVE SR-UNIT-PRICE TO DL-UNIT-PRICE.
242         MOVE SR-QUANTITY-SOLD TO DL-QUANTITY-SOLD.
243         MULTIPLY SR-UNIT-PRICE BY SR-QUANTITY-SOLD
244             GIVING WS-SALES-REVENUE ROUNDED.
245         MOVE WS-SALES-REVENUE TO DL-SALES-REVENUE.
246         MOVE DL-DETAIL-LINE TO SALES-REPORT-LINE.
247         PERFORM 890-WRITE-REPORT-LINE.
248         MOVE 1 TO WS-LINE-SPACING.
249         ADD WS-SALES-REVENUE TO WS-TOTAL-SALES-REP-ACCUM.
250         PERFORM 800-READ-SALES-RECORD.

251
252     310-PRINT-SALES-REP-TOTAL-LINE.
253         MOVE WS-PREVIOUS-STATE TO CT-STATE.
254         MOVE WS-PREVIOUS-BRANCH TO CT-BRANCH.
255         MOVE WS-PREVIOUS-SALES-REP TO CT-SALES-REP.
256         MOVE "SALES REP." TO CT-TOTAL-DESCRIPTION.
257         MOVE WS-TOTAL-SALES-REP-ACCUM TO CT-SALES-REVENUE.
258         MOVE "*  " TO CT-ASTERISKS.
259         MOVE CT-CONTROL-TOTAL-LINE TO SALES-REPORT-LINE.
260         MOVE 2 TO WS-LINE-SPACING.
261         PERFORM 890-WRITE-REPORT-LINE.
262         MOVE 3 TO WS-LINE-SPACING.
263         ADD WS-TOTAL-SALES-REP-ACCUM TO WS-TOTAL-BRANCH-ACCUM.
264
265     320-PRINT-BRANCH-TOTAL-LINE.
266         MOVE SPACES TO CT-SALES-REP.
267         MOVE "BRANCH" TO CT-TOTAL-DESCRIPTION.
268         MOVE WS-TOTAL-BRANCH-ACCUM TO CT-SALES-REVENUE.
269         MOVE "** " TO CT-ASTERISKS.
270         MOVE CT-CONTROL-TOTAL-LINE TO SALES-REPORT-LINE.
271         MOVE 2 TO WS-LINE-SPACING.
272         PERFORM 890-WRITE-REPORT-LINE.
273         MOVE 3 TO WS-LINE-SPACING.
274         ADD WS-TOTAL-BRANCH-ACCUM TO WS-TOTAL-STATE-ACCUM.
275
276     330-PRINT-STATE-TOTAL-LINE.
277         MOVE SPACES TO CT-BRANCH.
278         MOVE "STATE" TO CT-TOTAL-DESCRIPTION.
279         MOVE WS-TOTAL-STATE-ACCUM TO CT-SALES-REVENUE.
280         MOVE "***" TO CT-ASTERISKS.
281         MOVE CT-CONTROL-TOTAL-LINE TO SALES-REPORT-LINE.
282         MOVE 2 TO WS-LINE-SPACING.
283         PERFORM 890-WRITE-REPORT-LINE.
284         MOVE 3 TO WS-LINE-SPACING.
285         ADD WS-TOTAL-STATE-ACCUM TO WS-TOTAL-REPORT-ACCUM.
286
287     700-PRINT-REPORT-TOTAL-LINE.
288         MOVE WS-TOTAL-REPORT-ACCUM TO RT-SALES-REVENUE.
289         MOVE RT-REPORT-TOTAL-LINE TO SALES-REPORT-LINE.
290         MOVE 3 TO WS-LINE-SPACING.
291         PERFORM 890-WRITE-REPORT-LINE.
292
293     800-READ-SALES-RECORD.
294         READ SALES-FILE INTO SR-SALES-RECORD
295             AT END MOVE "YES" TO WS-END-OF-FILE-SWITCH
296                 MOVE HIGH-VALUES TO SR-STATE
297                                     SR-BRANCH
298                                     SR-SALES-REP.
299
300     870-PRINT-REPORT-HEADINGS.
301         ADD 1 TO WS-PAGE-COUNT.
302         MOVE WS-PAGE-COUNT TO H2-PAGE-NBR.
303         MOVE H1-HEADING-LINE-1 TO SALES-REPORT-LINE.
304         PERFORM 880-WRITE-REPORT-TOP-LINE.
305         MOVE H2-HEADING-LINE-2 TO SALES-REPORT-LINE.
306         MOVE 1 TO WS-LINE-SPACING.
307         PERFORM 890-WRITE-REPORT-LINE.
308         MOVE H3-HEADING-LINE-3 TO SALES-REPORT-LINE.
309         MOVE 2 TO WS-LINE-SPACING.
310         PERFORM 890-WRITE-REPORT-LINE.
311         MOVE H4-HEADING-LINE-4 TO SALES-REPORT-LINE.
312         MOVE 1 TO WS-LINE-SPACING.
313         PERFORM 890-WRITE-REPORT-LINE.
314         MOVE 2 TO WS-LINE-SPACING.
315
316     880-WRITE-REPORT-TOP-LINE.
317         WRITE SALES-REPORT-LINE
318             AFTER ADVANCING PAGE.
319         MOVE 1 TO WS-LINES-USED.
320
321     890-WRITE-REPORT-LINE.
322         WRITE SALES-REPORT-LINE
323             AFTER ADVANCING WS-LINE-SPACING.
324         ADD WS-LINE-SPACING TO WS-LINES-USED.
```

Figure 10-21   COBOL-85 PROCEDURE DIVISION: Multiple-level control break program (MCTLBRK).

```
176        PROCEDURE DIVISION.
177
178        000-PRINT-SALES-REPORT.
179            OPEN INPUT SALES-FILE
180                 OUTPUT SALES-REPORT
181            PERFORM 100-INITIALIZE-VARIABLE-FIELDS
182            PERFORM 110-PROCESS-DATE-RECORD
183            PERFORM 200-PROCESS-MAJOR-STATE-GROUP
184                UNTIL END-OF-FILE
185            PERFORM 700-PRINT-REPORT-TOTAL-LINE
186            CLOSE SALES-FILE
187                  SALES-REPORT
188            STOP RUN.
189
190        100-INITIALIZE-VARIABLE-FIELDS.
191            MOVE "NO " TO WS-END-OF-FILE-SWITCH
192            MOVE ZEROS TO WS-PAGE-COUNT
193            MOVE WS-LINES-PER-PAGE TO WS-LINES-USED
194            ACCEPT WS-DATE-WORK FROM DATE
195            MOVE WS-MONTH TO H2-MONTH
196            MOVE WS-DAY TO H2-DAY
197            MOVE WS-YEAR TO H2-YEAR
198            MOVE ZEROS TO WS-TOTAL-REPORT-ACCUM.
199
200        110-PROCESS-DATE-RECORD.
201            PERFORM 800-READ-SALES-RECORD
202            IF DATE-RECORD
203                MOVE DR-PERIOD-ENDING-DATE TO H1-PER-END-DATE
204                PERFORM 800-READ-SALES-RECORD
205            ELSE
206                MOVE "YES" TO WS-END-OF-FILE-SWITCH
207            END-IF.
208
209        200-PROCESS-MAJOR-STATE-GROUP.
210            MOVE SR-STATE TO WS-PREVIOUS-STATE
211            MOVE ZEROS TO WS-TOTAL-STATE-ACCUM
212            PERFORM 210-PROCESS-INTER-BRANCH-GROUP
213                UNTIL SR-STATE IS NOT EQUAL TO WS-PREVIOUS-STATE
214            PERFORM 330-PRINT-STATE-TOTAL-LINE.
215
216        210-PROCESS-INTER-BRANCH-GROUP.
217            MOVE SR-BRANCH TO WS-PREVIOUS-BRANCH
218            MOVE ZEROS TO WS-TOTAL-BRANCH-ACCUM
219            PERFORM 220-PROCESS-MINOR-REP-GROUP
220                UNTIL SR-BRANCH IS NOT EQUAL TO WS-PREVIOUS-BRANCH
221                OR SR-STATE IS NOT EQUAL TO WS-PREVIOUS-STATE
222            PERFORM 320-PRINT-BRANCH-TOTAL-LINE.
223
224        220-PROCESS-MINOR-REP-GROUP.
225            MOVE SR-SALES-REP TO WS-PREVIOUS-SALES-REP
226            MOVE ZEROS TO WS-TOTAL-SALES-REP-ACCUM
227            PERFORM 300-PRINT-DETAIL-LINE
228                UNTIL SR-SALES-REP IS NOT EQUAL TO WS-PREVIOUS-SALES-REP
229                OR SR-BRANCH IS NOT EQUAL TO WS-PREVIOUS-BRANCH
230                OR SR-STATE IS NOT EQUAL TO WS-PREVIOUS-STATE
231            PERFORM 310-PRINT-SALES-REP-TOTAL-LINE.
232
233        300-PRINT-DETAIL-LINE.
234            IF WS-LINES-USED IS NOT LESS THAN WS-LINES-PER-PAGE
235                PERFORM 870-PRINT-REPORT-HEADINGS
236            END-IF
237            MOVE SR-SALES-REP TO DL-SALES-REP
238            MOVE SR-STATE TO DL-STATE
239            MOVE SR-BRANCH TO DL-BRANCH
240            MOVE SR-DATE-OF-SALE TO DL-DATE-OF-SALE
241            MOVE SR-PRODUCT-CODE TO DL-PRODUCT-CODE
242            MOVE SR-PRODUCT-DESCRIPTION TO DL-PRODUCT-DESCRIPTION
243            MOVE SR-UNIT-PRICE TO DL-UNIT-PRICE
244            MOVE SR-QUANTITY-SOLD TO DL-QUANTITY-SOLD
245            MULTIPLY SR-UNIT-PRICE BY SR-QUANTITY-SOLD
246                GIVING WS-SALES-REVENUE ROUNDED
247            MOVE WS-SALES-REVENUE TO DL-SALES-REVENUE
248            MOVE DL-DETAIL-LINE TO SALES-REPORT-LINE
249            PERFORM 890-WRITE-REPORT-LINE
250            MOVE 1 TO WS-LINE-SPACING
251            ADD WS-SALES-REVENUE TO WS-TOTAL-SALES-REP-ACCUM
252            PERFORM 800-READ-SALES-RECORD.
```

```
253
254        310-PRINT-SALES-REP-TOTAL-LINE.
255            MOVE WS-PREVIOUS-STATE TO CT-STATE
256            MOVE WS-PREVIOUS-BRANCH TO CT-BRANCH
257            MOVE WS-PREVIOUS-SALES-REP TO CT-SALES-REP
258            MOVE "SALES REP." TO CT-TOTAL-DESCRIPTION
259            MOVE WS-TOTAL-SALES-REP-ACCUM TO CT-SALES-REVENUE
260            MOVE "*  " TO CT-ASTERISKS
261            MOVE CT-CONTROL-TOTAL-LINE TO SALES-REPORT-LINE
262            MOVE 2 TO WS-LINE-SPACING
263            PERFORM 890-WRITE-REPORT-LINE
264            MOVE 3 TO WS-LINE-SPACING
265            ADD WS-TOTAL-SALES-REP-ACCUM TO WS-TOTAL-BRANCH-ACCUM.
266
267        320-PRINT-BRANCH-TOTAL-LINE.
268            MOVE SPACES TO CT-SALES-REP
269            MOVE "BRANCH" TO CT-TOTAL-DESCRIPTION
270            MOVE WS-TOTAL-BRANCH-ACCUM TO CT-SALES-REVENUE
271            MOVE "** " TO CT-ASTERISKS
272            MOVE CT-CONTROL-TOTAL-LINE TO SALES-REPORT-LINE
273            MOVE 2 TO WS-LINE-SPACING
274            PERFORM 890-WRITE-REPORT-LINE
275            MOVE 3 TO WS-LINE-SPACING
276            ADD WS-TOTAL-BRANCH-ACCUM TO WS-TOTAL-STATE-ACCUM.
277
278        330-PRINT-STATE-TOTAL-LINE.
279            MOVE SPACES TO CT-BRANCH
280            MOVE "STATE" TO CT-TOTAL-DESCRIPTION
281            MOVE WS-TOTAL-STATE-ACCUM TO CT-SALES-REVENUE
282            MOVE "*** " TO CT-ASTERISKS
283            MOVE CT-CONTROL-TOTAL-LINE TO SALES-REPORT-LINE
284            MOVE 2 TO WS-LINE-SPACING
285            PERFORM 890-WRITE-REPORT-LINE
286            MOVE 3 TO WS-LINE-SPACING
287            ADD WS-TOTAL-STATE-ACCUM TO WS-TOTAL-REPORT-ACCUM.
288
289        700-PRINT-REPORT-TOTAL-LINE.
290            MOVE WS-TOTAL-REPORT-ACCUM TO RT-SALES-REVENUE
291            MOVE RT-REPORT-TOTAL-LINE TO SALES-REPORT-LINE
292            MOVE 3 TO WS-LINE-SPACING
293            PERFORM 890-WRITE-REPORT-LINE.
294
295        800-READ-SALES-RECORD.
296            READ SALES-FILE INTO SR-SALES-RECORD
297                AT END MOVE "YES" TO WS-END-OF-FILE-SWITCH
298                    MOVE HIGH-VALUES TO SR-STATE
299                                        SR-BRANCH
300                                        SR-SALES-REP
301            END-READ.
302
303        870-PRINT-REPORT-HEADINGS.
304            ADD 1 TO WS-PAGE-COUNT
305            MOVE WS-PAGE-COUNT TO H2-PAGE-NBR
306            MOVE H1-HEADING-LINE-1 TO SALES-REPORT-LINE
307            PERFORM 880-WRITE-REPORT-TOP-LINE
308            MOVE H2-HEADING-LINE-2 TO SALES-REPORT-LINE
309            MOVE 1 TO WS-LINE-SPACING
310            PERFORM 890-WRITE-REPORT-LINE
311            MOVE H3-HEADING-LINE-3 TO SALES-REPORT-LINE
312            MOVE 2 TO WS-LINE-SPACING
313            PERFORM 890-WRITE-REPORT-LINE
314            MOVE H4-HEADING-LINE-4 TO SALES-REPORT-LINE
315            MOVE 1 TO WS-LINE-SPACING
316            PERFORM 890-WRITE-REPORT-LINE
317            MOVE 2 TO WS-LINE-SPACING.
318
319        880-WRITE-REPORT-TOP-LINE.
320            WRITE SALES-REPORT-LINE
321                AFTER ADVANCING PAGE
322            MOVE 1 TO WS-LINES-USED.
323
324        890-WRITE-REPORT-LINE.
325            WRITE SALES-REPORT-LINE
326                AFTER ADVANCING WS-LINE-SPACING
327            ADD WS-LINE-SPACING TO WS-LINES-USED.
```

The FD Entry   One of several significant differences that this program exhibits over previous programs is that it reads records of two entirely different formats: the date record (the first one) and the data records that follow. These two records are of different lengths: 8 positions and 48 positions, respectively. Consequently, COBOL must be so informed in the FD for the input file. This is done in the RECORD CONTAINS clause as follows:

```
FD  SALES-FILE
    RECORD CONTAINS 8 TO 48 CHARACTERS
    LABEL RECORDS ARE OMITTED.
```

The WORKING-STORAGE SECTION

Similarly, the FILE SECTION coding matches that of the SCTLBRK program. There are a few additions and changes to the WORKING-STORAGE SECTION, however.

WS-CONTROL-FIELDS Area

```
01  WS-CONTROL-FIELDS.
    05  WS-PREVIOUS-STATE          PIC X(2).
    05  WS-PREVIOUS-BRANCH         PIC X(3).
    05  WS-PREVIOUS-SALES-REP      PIC X(5).
```

Because this program has three control fields, two additional fields must be added to the WS-CONTROL-FIELDS group item. Thus, the WS-PREVIOUS-STATE and WS-PREVIOUS-BRANCH fields have been specified to hold the state and branch fields, respectively, from the previous record.

Observe that the elementary control fields have been arranged in major to minor order. That is, the major control field, WS-PREVIOUS-STATE, is coded first; the intermediate control field, WS-PREVIOUS-BRANCH, is second; and the minor control field, WS-PREVIOUS-SALES-REP, is specified last. Although such major through minor ordering is not necessary, it is logically sound and aids program readability by specifying the fields in such sequence. Further, this arrangement of control fields can simplify input-record sequence-checking logic, should it be required.

WS-TOTAL-ACCUMULATORS Area

```
01  WS-TOTAL-ACCUMULATORS.
    05  WS-TOTAL-SALES-REP-ACCUM    PIC S9(6)V99.
    05  WS-TOTAL-BRANCH-ACCUM       PIC S9(6)V99.
    05  WS-TOTAL-STATE-ACCUM        PIC S9(6)V99.
    05  WS-TOTAL-REPORT-ACCUM       PIC S9(7)V99.
```

Because this program has three control totals, two additional fields must be added to the WS-TOTAL-ACCUMULATORS group item. Hence, the WS-TOTAL-BRANCH-ACCUM and WS-TOTAL-STATE-ACCUM fields have been specified to accumulate the branch and state totals, respectively. Notice that the control total fields have been specified in minor to major order. As mentioned with regard to the control fields, a specific order is not necessary. However, arrangement of the accumulator fields in minor to major sequence aids program readability because it depicts the hierarchy of totals as they will be printed on the report.

Period-Ending Date Record-Description

```
01  SR-SALES-RECORD.
    05  SR-RECORD-CODE            PIC X(2).
    05  SR-STATE                  PIC X(2).
    05  SR-BRANCH                 PIC X(3).
    05  SR-SALES-REP              PIC X(5).
    05  SR-DATE-OF-SALE           PIC X(6).
    05  SR-PRODUCT-CODE           PIC X(7).
    05  SR-PRODUCT-DESCRIPTION    PIC X(16).
    05  SR-QUANTITY-SOLD          PIC S9(3).
    05  SR-UNIT-PRICE             PIC 9(2)V99.

01  DR-DATE-RECORD REDEFINES SR-SALES-RECORD.
    05  DR-RECORD-CODE            PIC X(2).
        88  DATE-RECORD                        VALUE "01".
    05  DR-PERIOD-ENDING-DATE     PIC X(6).
    05  FILLER                    PIC X(40).
```

The DR-DATE-RECORD record-description entry defines the input period-ending date record. Notice that the 01-level DR-DATE-RECORD entry has been coded with a REDEFINES clause. This means that the date record will occupy the same 48 storage locations that the SR-SALES-RECORD does.

This redefinition has been specified because the READ/INTO statement used to read records from the input file causes all input records to be stored in the SR-SALES-RECORD area. No confusion between the two different record formats will occur because, according to the programming specifications, the date record must be the first record of the file. The period-ending date can be moved to the heading-line area for storage. Hence, there will be no need to retain the date record in storage. As a result, the same input-record storage area can be used to process both the date record and the sales records.

Report-Line Changes.   The following changes have been made to the report lines.

H1-HEADING-LINE-1
The constant words "PERIOD ENDING DATE" have been added, together with the variable field H1-PERIOD-ENDING-DATE.

H2-HEADING-LINE-2
To reflect the multiple-level control-break sequence, the report title has been changed to "SALES REPORT - SEQUENCED BY STATE, BRANCH, AND SALES REP."

H3-HEADING-LINE-3 and H4-HEADING-LINE-4
The column heading changes for the repositioned control fields state, branch, and sales representative-have been reflected in these lines.

DL-DETAIL-LINE
The relative placement of the DL-SALES-REP, DL-STATE, and DL-BRANCH fields has been changed to reflect the arrangement specified on the print chart.

CT-CONTROL-TOTAL-LINE
This control total line is equivalent to the ST-SALES-REP-TOTAL-LINE of the single-level sales report. As shown in Example A of Figure 10-22, this single report-line format will be used for all three control total lines. The record-prefix has been changed to CT and the CT-STATE and CT-BRANCH fields have been added so that the applicable state and branch can be displayed on each control total line.

Also, the constant words that described the single-level total—"SALES REP TOTAL"—has been shortened to just the word "TOTAL" so that it can be used for all three control totals. A variable field, CT-TOTAL-DESCRIPTION, has been added to display the description of which total is being printed: state, branch, or sales representative.

Further, the CT-ASTERISKS field has been established so that either one, two, or three asterisks can be displayed on the control total line in accordance with the level of the total (sales representative, branch, or state, respectively).

Of course, instead of using just one common control total line, a separate line for each of the three control total lines could have been specified, as shown in Example B of Figure 10-22. By providing for all three lines with just one record-description entry, a coding shortcut has been taken. (In the PROCEDURE DIVISION, though, additional statements must be provided to move the appropriate description and correct number of asterisks to the line.)

Figure 10-22   Alternative methods of defining control total lines.

```
Example A:  Common control-total line           Example B:  Separate control-total line
            record-definition                               record-definition

01  CT-CONTROL-TOTAL-LINE.                       01  RT-SALES-REP-TOTAL-LINE.
    05  FILLER              PIC X(1)   VALUE SPACES.       05  FILLER              PIC X(1)   VALUE SPACES.
    05  CT-STATE            PIC X(2).                      05  RT-STATE            PIC X(2).
    05  FILLER              PIC X(4)   VALUE SPACES.       05  FILLER              PIC X(4)   VALUE SPACES.
    05  CT-BRANCH           PIC X(3)                       05  RT-BRANCH           PIC X(3).
    05  FILLER              PIC X)3)   VALUE SPACES.       05  FILLER              PIC X(3)   VALUE SPACES.
    05  CT-SALES-REP        PIC X(5).                      05  RT-SALES-REP        PIC X(5).
    05  FILLER              PIC X(15)  VALUE SPACES.       05  FILLER              PIC X(15)  VALUE SPACES.
    05  CT-TOTAL-DESCRIPTION PIC X(10) JUSTIFIED RIGHT.    05  FILLER              PIC X(16)
    05  FILLER              PIC X(6)   VALUE " TOTAL".                             VALUE "SALES REP. TOTAL".
    05  FILLER              PIC X(20)  VALUE SPACES         05  FILLER              PIC X(20)  VALUE SPACES.
    05  CT-SALES-REVENUE    PIC ZZZ,ZZZ.99-.               05  RT-SALES-REVENUE    PIC ZZZ,ZZZ.99-.
    05  CT-ASTERISKS        PIC X(3).                      05  FILLER              PIC X(1)   VALUE "*".
    05  FILLER              PIC X(49)  VALUE SPACES.        05  FILLER              PIC X(51)  VALUE SPACES.

                                                  01  BT-SALES-REP-TOTAL-LINE.
                                                      05  FILLER              PIC X(1)   VALUE SPACES.
                                                      05  BT-STATE            PIC X(2).
                                                      05  FILLER              PIC X(4)   VALUE SPACES.
                                                      05  BT-BRANCH           PIC X(3).
                                                      05  FILLER              PIC X(23)  VALUE SPACES.
                                                      05  FILLER              PIC X(16)
                                                                              VALUE "    BRANCH TOTAL".
                                                      05  FILLER              PIC X(20)  VALUE SPACES.
                                                      05  BT-SALES-REVENUE    PIC ZZZ,ZZZ.99-.
                                                      05  FILLER              PIC X(2)   VALUE "**".
                                                      05  FILLER              PIC X(50)  VALUE SPACES.

                                                  01  ST-SALES-REP-TOTAL-LINE.
                                                      05  FILLER              PIC X(1)   VALUE SPACES.
                                                      05  ST-STATE            PIC X(2).
                                                      05  FILLER              PIC X(30)    VALUE SPACES.
                                                      05  FILLER              PIC X(16)
                                                                              VALUE "     STATE TOTAL".
                                                      05  FILLER              PIC X(20)  VALUE SPACES.
                                                      05  ST-SALES-REVENUE    PIC ZZZ,ZZZ.99-.
                                                      05  FILLER              PIC X(3)   VALUE "***".
                                                      05  FILLER              PIC X(49)  VALUE SPACES.
```

Given the print chart for this sales report, the shortcut is acceptable. If the three total lines were significantly different in format, however, it would be better to describe each line as a separate 01-level item.

RT-REPORT-TOTAL-LINE
The number of asterisks following the report total has been increased from two to four in accordance with the print-chart specifications. The length of the FILLER area following the CT-ASTERISKS field has been correspondingly decreased.

Coding the
PROCEDURE DIVISION   Many of the PROCEDURE DIVISION modules of MCTLBRK are unchanged from SCTLBRK; others have some basic changes. Also, some new modules have been added. Let's consider the new ones and those with significant coding changes.

000-PRINT-SALES-REPORT Module

```
000-PRINT-SALES-REPORT.
    OPEN INPUT SALES-FILE
         OUTPUT SALES-REPORT.
    PERFORM 100-INITIALIZE-VARIABLE-FIELDS.
    PERFORM 110-PROCESS-DATE-RECORD.
    PERFORM 200-PROCESS-MAJOR-STATE-GROUP
        UNTIL END-OF-FILE.
    PERFORM 700-PRINT-REPORT-TOTAL-LINE.
    CLOSE SALES-FILE
          SALES-REPORT.
    STOP RUN.
```

Notice that the point in the mainline module where the priming read typically appears instead contains a statement to perform a Process-date-record module. Acquisition of the period-ending date record and the priming read for the sales records will take place there. This is explained in the next topic: the 110-PROCESS-DATE-RECORD module.

110-PROCESS-DATE-RECORD Module

```
110-PROCESS-DATE-RECORD.
    PERFORM 800-READ-SALES-RECORD.
    IF DATE-RECORD
        MOVE DR-PERIOD-ENDING-DATE TO H1-PER-END-DATE
        PERFORM 800-READ-SALES-RECORD
    ELSE
        MOVE "YES" TO WS-END-OF-FILE-SWITCH.
```

The purpose of this module is to obtain the date record and transfer it to the appropriate field in the first heading line. Since the programming specifications call for the first record of the sales file to be the period-ending date record, the 800-READ-SALES-RECORD module is performed.

After the read module is performed, the program logic checks to see if a period-ending date record was actually read. This is accomplished by the IF DATE-RECORD test. If that first record read into storage is correctly coded as a date record (that is, if the DR-RECORD-CODE field is equal to "01"), the date will be moved from the DR-PERIOD-ENDING-DATE field to the H1-PER-END-DATE field. After that, the read module is performed once again; this second read operation will serve as the priming read for the regular sales-record processing.

On the other hand, if the record is not coded as a date record, WS-END-OF-FILE switch is set to "YES". Remember that the programming specifications call for the program run to be canceled if the date record is not present. This premature setting of the end-of-file switch to an END-OF-FILE condition will provide an orderly termination of the program run and skip the processing of the remaining records in the sales file.

You might question why the priming read was (1) coded in this module rather than in the mainline module (as it typically has been for the programs in this text), and (2) coded to be executed conditionally upon finding the date record. The reason is to properly handle empty file processing. Suppose, due to an operations error, that there were no records at all in the sales file. The first read operation (the attempt to read a date record) would read the end-of-file marker and cause the end-of-file switch to be set. The second execution (the priming read) would be an attempt to read beyond the end of the input file and cause an abnormal program termination—the program would "bomb out."

Hence, only the first read operation in a program can be executed unconditionally. All read operations after the first must be executed conditionally (dependent on the fact that end-of-file has not yet been reached) to properly handle empty file processing. (A PERFORM/UNTIL END-OF-FILE statement also provides such conditional read-module processing. If end-of-file has already been reached when a PERFORM/UNTIL END-OF-FILE statement is encountered, the PERFORM is not executed. Program control instead flows to the next consecutive statement.)

An alternative to coding the conditional priming read in the date-processing module (as has been done in the MCTLBRK program) would be to code—in the mainline module—a conditional priming read such as IF NOT END-OF-FILE PERFORM 800-READ-SALES-RECORD.

200-PROCESS-MAJOR-STATE-GROUP Module
Through 220-PROCESS-MINOR-REP-GROUP Module

```
200-PROCESS-MAJOR-STATE-GROUP.
    MOVE SR-STATE TO WS-PREVIOUS-STATE.
    MOVE ZEROS TO WS-TOTAL-STATE-ACCUM.
    PERFORM 210-PROCESS-INTER-BRANCH-GROUP
        UNTIL SR-STATE IS NOT EQUAL TO WS-PREVIOUS-STATE.
    PERFORM 330-PRINT-STATE-TOTAL-LINE.

210-PROCESS-INTER-BRANCH-GROUP.
    MOVE SR-BRANCH TO WS-PREVIOUS-BRANCH.
    MOVE ZEROS TO WS-TOTAL-BRANCH-ACCUM.
    PERFORM 220-PROCESS-MINOR-REP-GROUP
        UNTIL SR-BRANCH IS NOT EQUAL TO WS-PREVIOUS-BRANCH
            OR SR-STATE IS NOT EQUAL TO WS-PREVIOUS-STATE.
    PERFORM 320-PRINT-BRANCH-TOTAL-LINE.

220-PROCESS-MINOR-REP-GROUP.
    MOVE SR-SALES-REP TO WS-PREVIOUS-SALES-REP.
    MOVE ZEROS TO WS-TOTAL-SALES-REP-ACCUM.
    PERFORM 300-PRINT-DETAIL-LINE
        UNTIL SR-SALES-REP IS NOT EQUAL TO WS-PREVIOUS-SALES-REP
            OR SR-BRANCH IS NOT EQUAL TO WS-PREVIOUS-BRANCH
            OR SR-STATE IS NOT EQUAL TO WS-PREVIOUS-STATE.
    PERFORM 310-PRINT-SALES-REP-TOTAL-LINE.
```

The words MAJOR, INTER (for intermediate), and MINOR have been added to these nested PERFORM/UNTIL modules to clarify the control-level hierarchy. In each module, the following processing occurs:

1. Because a new control group is being started at that level, the control-field value from the current record is moved to its previous control field in WORKING-STORAGE.

2. The total accumulator for that control level is reset to zero (because a new control group accumulation is beginning for that level).

3. Until there is a control break at that level, the next lower-level nested module is performed. (At the 220-PROCESS-MINOR-REP-GROUP level, there is no lower-level nested module; the 300-PRINT-DETAIL LINE module is performed.)

4. After a control break, the control total line-printing module for that control level is performed.

310-PRINT-SALES-REP-TOTAL-LINE Module
Through 330-PRINT-STATE-TOTAL-LINE Module

```
310-PRINT-SALES-REP-TOTAL-LINE.
    MOVE WS-PREVIOUS-STATE TO CT-STATE.
    MOVE WS-PREVIOUS-BRANCH TO CT-BRANCH.
    MOVE WS-PREVIOUS-SALES-REP TO CT-SALES-REP.
    MOVE "SALES REP." TO CT-TOTAL-DESCRIPTION.
    MOVE WS-TOTAL-SALES-REP-ACCUM TO CT-SALES-REVENUE.
    MOVE "*  " TO CT-ASTERISKS.
    MOVE CT-CONTROL-TOTAL-LINE TO SALES-REPORT-LINE.
    MOVE 2 TO WS-LINE-SPACING.
    PERFORM 890-WRITE-REPORT-LINE.
    MOVE 3 TO WS-LINE-SPACING.
    ADD WS-TOTAL-SALES-REP-ACCUM TO WS-TOTAL-BRANCH-ACCUM.

320-PRINT-BRANCH-TOTAL-LINE.
    MOVE SPACES TO CT-SALES-REP.
    MOVE "BRANCH" TO CT-TOTAL-DESCRIPTION.
    MOVE WS-TOTAL-BRANCH-ACCUM TO CT-SALES-REVENUE.
    MOVE "** " TO CT-ASTERISKS.
    MOVE CT-CONTROL-TOTAL-LINE TO SALES-REPORT-LINE.
    MOVE 2 TO WS-LINE-SPACING.
    PERFORM 890-WRITE-REPORT-LINE.
    MOVE 3 TO WS-LINE-SPACING.
    ADD WS-TOTAL-BRANCH-ACCUM TO WS-TOTAL-STATE-ACCUM.

330-PRINT-STATE-TOTAL-LINE.
    MOVE SPACES TO CT-BRANCH.
    MOVE "STATE" TO CT-TOTAL-DESCRIPTION.
    MOVE WS-TOTAL-STATE-ACCUM TO CT-SALES-REVENUE.
    MOVE "***" TO CT-ASTERISKS.
    MOVE CT-CONTROL-TOTAL-LINE TO SALES-REPORT-LINE.
    MOVE 2 TO WS-LINE-SPACING.
    PERFORM 890-WRITE-REPORT-LINE.
    MOVE 3 TO WS-LINE-SPACING.
    ADD WS-TOTAL-STATE-ACCUM TO WS-TOTAL-REPORT-ACCUM.
```

Each of these three modules handles the following control-break line-printing tasks:

1. The appropriate control fields are moved to the control total line area.

2. A description of the control total line being printed ("SALES REP", "BRANCH", "STATE") is moved to the control total line area.

3. The appropriate control total accumulation is moved to the control total line area.

4. The proper number of asterisks to designate the control total level is moved to the control total line area.

5. The control total line area is moved from WORKING-STORAGE to the output-line area in the FILE SECTION.

6. The WS-LINE-SPACING field is set to double-space the control total line from the previous report line.

7. The 890-WRITE-REPORT-LINE module is performed.

8. The WS-LINE-SPACING field is set to triple-spacing for the next detail line.

9. The control total accumulation for that level is rolled to the next higher-level control total accumulation.

Item 8, above, deserves more explanation. Remember that the first detail line for a particular sales representative is to be triple-spaced from the last control-break line printed. Therefore, the WS-LINE-SPACING field is set for triple-spacing immediately after each control total line is printed in case there are no subsequent (more major) control total lines to be printed before the next detail line. If one or more additional control total lines are to be printed, the triple-space setting is superseded by the next setting of the WS-LINE-SPACING for double-spacing (Item 6, page 530) when the more major control total line is subsequently printed.

800-READ-SALES-RECORD Module

```
800-READ-SALES-RECORD.
    READ SALES-FILE INTO SR-SALES-RECORD
        AT END MOVE "YES" TO WS-END-OF-FILE-SWITCH
            MOVE HIGH-VALUES TO SR-STATE
                              SR-BRANCH
                              SR-SALES-REP.
```

When end-of-file is reached, each of the three control fields must be set to HIGH-VALUES to trigger the control breaks for the last record.

Alternate Coding for Control Group Modules—COBOL-85.

In the MCTLBRK program, repeated execution of the branch-level processing is achieved by PERFORMing the 210-PROCESS-INTER-BRANCH-GROUP from the 200 module. Similarly, repeated execution of the sales representative-level processing is achieved by PERFORMing the 220-PROCESS-MINOR-REP-GROUP from the 210 module. Separate modules are necessary with COBOL-74 because the PERFORM/UNTIL is the only vehicle for repeated processing of a sequence of statements.

If you inspect the 200-220 modules of Figure 10-21 (the COBOL-85 PROCEDURE DIVISION), you will see that the code is identical to that of the COBOL-74 version except for the reduced use of periods. However, there is another way that this can be coded using the in-line PERFORM. (If you skipped Chapter 9, you should read the section on this statement. Its format is shown in Figure 9-23.)

Figure 10-23 shows how you can position all of the statements in-line (in a single module) to process each level. Note that there are two in-line loops, one within the other; they are called **nested loops** (corresponding to nested PERFORM). Following is a description of the actions during execution.

1. Upon entering this module, the two MOVE statements are executed, then execution "falls into" the outer loop controlled by the first in-line PERFORM.

```
PERFORM UNTIL SR-STATE IS NOT EQUAL TO WS-PREVIOUS-STATE
```

The scope of the loop is defined by the corresponding END-PERFORM. Control will remain within this loop until the PERFORM condition is satisfied.

Figure 10-23   Using the in-line PERFORM for total processing.

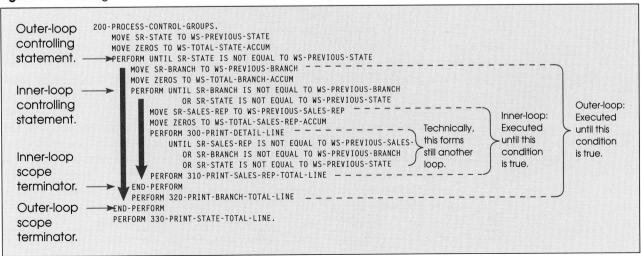

2. The two MOVE (Branch level) statements are executed, then execution "falls into" the inner loop controlled by the second in-line PERFORM.

```
PERFORM UNTIL SR-BRANCH IS NOT EQUAL TO WS-PREVIOUS-BRANCH
        OR SR-STATE IS NOT EQUAL TO WS-PREVIOUS-STATE
```

The scope of this loop is defined by its corresponding END-PERFORM. Control will remain within this inner loop until this PERFORM condition is satisfied.

Notice that one of the statements within this loop is a PERFORM statement to repeatedly execute another paragraph (300-PRINT-DETAIL-LINE). Technically, we have a three-level loop, two controlled by in-line PERFORM statements and a third controlled by an out-of-line PERFORM.

3. When the inner-loop condition is satisfied (the condition becomes true), execution will continue to the statement following the inner-loop scope terminator. The 320-PRINT-BRANCH-TOTAL-LINE module will be performed and immediate control is back to the outer loop. The outer-loop condition is again tested to determine if the outer loop should be repeated or execution should continue to the statement following the outer-loop scope terminator.

You should step through this carefully, while comparing it to the form in Figure 10-21 to ensure that they both do the same thing. Which of these forms is better is a matter of opinion. Some programmers feel that the separation of multiple paragraphs provides better documentation and is more easily understood. Others, especially those who have used other structured languages, prefer the in-line PERFORM version.

Chapter Summary

Control-break programs require that the input records be in proper control-field sequence for the control breaks. The program logic must compare the control fields of the current record to those of the previous record. When the values are different, a **control break** occurs. As the result of a control break, a **control total line** is typically printed, which contains accumulations—**control totals**—of certain detail-line fields for that **control group** of records.

A **single-level control-break program** has one control field that triggers one type of control break. The SCTLBRK program is an example of a single-level control-break program.

A **multiple-level control-break program** has two or more control fields that trigger two or more levels of control breaks. The MCTLBRK program is an example of a multiple-level control-break program.

When there is more than one control-break level, program logic complexity is increased in two areas: (1) the nesting of PERFORM/UNTIL statements to process each control level, and (2) the need to provide additional control total line-printing modules.

In nested PERFORM/UNTIL control-break logic, the major control field must always be tested first. The nesting then proceeds in decreasing significance down through the minor control fields. One tricky aspect of multiple-level control-break tests is that at each level, not only must its respective control field be checked, but all higher-level (more major) control fields must also be tested for a control break.

Period-ending date records are often used to provide a period-ending date on a report. When a date record is required within a program, the program logic must test the record code to ensure that the date record is actually present. Otherwise, erroneous processing may occur.

Exercises

Terms for Definition

control total _____

control total line _____

major control field _____

minor control field _____

multiple-level control-break program _____

nested loop _____

nested PERFORM _____

period-ending date record _____

rolling the total _____

Review Questions

1. Control-break programs require that the input records be

   _____.

2. Control-break program logic requires that the _____ field(s)

   of the _____ record be compared to that (those) of the

   _____ record.

3. Control-field accumulations are termed _____.

4. A report line that contains the control group accumulations is called the

   _____ line.

5. A single-level control-break program has _____ control
   field(s).

6. A multiple-level control-break program has _____ control
   field(s).

7. For multiple-level control breaks, the _____ control field

   must be tested first; the _____ control field must be tested
   last.

8. When a period-ending date record is present within a data file, it is typically

   specified to be the _____ record within the file.

9. When a period-ending date record is specified to be within a file, the program

   logic should check for its _____.

1. In writing the SCTLBRK program (Figure 10-9), a programmer became confused and made the first statement of the 200-PROCESS-SALES-REP-GROUP

   ```
   MOVE HIGH-VALUES TO WS-PREVIOUS-SALES-REP
   ```

   instead of:

   ```
   MOVE SR-SALES-REP TO WS-PREVIOUS-SALES-REP
   ```

   Describe how this will affect the running and/or the output of the program.

   _____

   _____

   _____

2. The programmer of Question 1 is having a tough day. After recognizing the error, he or she (whichever you desire) realized that the correct statement is:

   ```
   MOVE SR-SALES-REP TO WS-PREVIOUS-SALES-REP
   ```

   After some deep thought, this programmer decided to place it in the 800-READ-SALES-RECORD module following the READ statement. (This is *not* a good choice.) Describe what this will do to the program output.

   _____

   _____

   _____

3. In a final, desperate attempt, the programmer moved this MOVE statement so that it immediately preceded the READ statement. The reasoning was that the current number should be saved immediately prior to reading the next one. Comment about this action.

   _____

   _____

   _____

4. Would you hire the programmer of Questions 1, 2 and 3? _____

   _____

5. Assume that the Sales file of the SCTLBRK program is not correctly sorted and that in one portion of the file, the sequence of the Salesperson-representative field is as follows:

   ```
   10006
   10006
   10009
   10006
   10009
   10009
   10014
   ```

Describe the output relative to the group total lines that will be printed.

_____

_____

_____

6. In the 200-PROCESS-MAJOR-STATE-GROUP module of the MCTLBRK program (Figure 10-20 or 10-21), assume that the statement

```
MOVE ZEROS TO WS-TOTAL-STATE-ACCUM
```

has been omitted. How would this affect the output of the program?

_____

_____

_____

7. Because the MCTLBRK program reads two types of records (the date record and sales records), two input formats are defined in working-storage (Figure 10-19). DR-DATE-RECORD redefines the SR-SALES-RECORD area. Is it _necessary_ that the REDEFINES be used or could DR-DATE-RECORD be a separate area? Explain your answer.

_____

_____

_____

8. In the 800-READ-SALES-RECORD module of the MCTLBRK program (Figure 10-20 or 10-21), HIGH-VALUES is moved to the fields SR-STATE, SR-BRANCH, and SR-SALES-REP in the AT END option of the READ. Describe the consequences of omitting this MOVE.

_____

_____

_____

9. Assume that the Sales file for the MCTLBRK program has been sorted incorrectly. For the MCTLBRK program, the Sales file must be sorted by Sales-representative-number within Branch within State within Record-code. However, it was incorrectly sorted within State within Branch within Sales-representative-number within Record-code. Note that only the Date record will be positioned properly; the others will be exactly reversed. Furthermore, assume that there are at least two records for each salesperson. Describe the appearance of the report, especially relating to the group total lines.

_____

_____

_____

Programming Assignments

Programming Assignment 10-1: Account Balance Report

Background information:

Programming Assignment 9-1 describes a general ledger file in which separate accounts are defined for the variety of fiscal activity of a company. Group total reports, both single-level and multiple-level, are commonly prepared from data in a general ledger file. For a particular application, Silicon Valley Manufacturing requires an account balance report. Single-level control totals are to be printed whenever the first (leftmost) digit of the account number changes. A report total is also to be printed.

Input file: General Ledger file (LEDGER.DAT)

Input-record format:

Positions	Field	Data class	Comments
1–2	Record code	Alphanumeric	Code LM
4–11	General ledger account number	Numeric	Format: 9999V9999
12–39	Account name	Alphanumeric	
44	Account type	Alphanumeric	
47–56	Account balance	Numeric	Format: 99999999V99 (may be negative)

Output-report format:

```
                    0         1         2         3         4         5         6
          1234567890123456789012345678901234567890123456789012345678901234567890 1234
 1
 2
 3
 4          ****                    ACCOUNT  BALANCE  REPORT  (10-1)              ****
 5
 6          ACCOUNT  NUMBER         ACCOUNT  NAME                      ACCOUNT  BALANCE
 7
 8              9999.9999        XXXXXXXXXXXXXXXXXXXXXXXXXXXX         ZZZ,ZZZ.99-
 9              9999.9999        XXXXXXXXXXXXXXXXXXXXXXXXXXXX         ZZZ,ZZZ.99-
10
11                              TOTAL  FOR  ACCOUNT  9XXX         Z,ZZZ,ZZZ.99-*
12
13
14              9999.9999        XXXXXXXXXXXXXXXXXXXXXXXXXXXX         ZZZ,ZZZ.99-
15
16                              TOTAL  FOR  ACCOUNT  9XXX         Z,ZZZ,ZZZ.99-*
17
18
19                              REPORT  TOTAL                   ZZ,ZZZ,ZZZ.99-**
```

Program operations:

1. Process each input ledger record.
2. Print the two heading lines on the first page and on each following page of the report.

3. The input ledger records have already been sequenced by the account-number field. For each input ledger record, do the following processing:
   a. Print an output detail line as specified on the print chart.
   b. Accumulate the account balance.
4. Whenever the first (leftmost) digit of the account-number field changes, print a control total line as shown on the print chart. The following fields should be printed on the control total line:
   a. The words TOTAL FOR ACCOUNTS.
   b. The first digit of the account number followed by the letters XXX (to indicate that this total applies to all accounts beginning with that number).
   c. The total account balance for such account numbers (followed by a single asterisk).
5. Accumulate the control totals into a report total. After all input records have been processed, print the report total line.
6. Provide for a span of 55 lines per page. Do not permit a control total line to be printed at the top of a new page. (That is, do not print a control total line on a report page that does not contain at least one detail line for the control group to which it applies.) Line spacing is to be handled as follows:
   a. Single-space each detail line [except (1) double-space between the last heading line and the first detail page, and (2) triple-space between the control total line and the first detail line for the next control group].
   b. Triple-space the report total line from the preceding control total line.

Programming Assignment 10-2: Daily Cash Requirements Report
Background information:
In the new vendor file of Tools Unlimited (Programming Assignment 9-2), each vendor record will contain the amount owed to that vendor and the date that it is due. In order for Tools Unlimited to manage its resources efficiently, the financial officer needs a report showing how much owed money comes due each day. This will give management a picture of how much cash will be required on a daily basis. In order to produce the report, the vendor file will be sorted on the Date-due field. Multiple-level control totals are to be printed whenever the Date-due field changes. The totals are to reflect the amount due for each day, each month, and each year. A report total is also to be printed.

Input file: Vendor file (VENDOR.DAT)

Input-record format:

Positions	Field	Data class	Comments
1–2	Record code	Alphanumeric	Code LM
4–11	Vendor number	Numeric	
12–17	Date due	Numeric	Format: *yymmdd*
18–37	Vendor name	Alphanumeric	
67–74	Amount due	Numeric	Dollars and cents (may be negative)

Output-report format:

```
          0          1          2          3          4          5          6          7
 1234567890123456789012345678901234567890123456789012345678901234567890123456789 0
 1
 2
 3
 4 DAILY CASH REQUIREMENTS REPORT (10-2)                                      PAGE ZZ9
 5
 6         DATE DUE        VENDOR                                      AMOUNT
 7         YY MO DA        NUMBER            VENDOR NAME                 DUE
 8
 9         YY MM DD    99999999      XXXXXXXXXXXXXXXXXXXX        ----,----.99
10               DD    99999999      XXXXXXXXXXXXXXXXXXXX        ----,----.99
11                        TOTAL DUE ON YY-MM-DD            Z,ZZZ,ZZZ.99*
12
13                        TOTAL DUE IN YY-MM            ZZ,ZZZ,ZZZ.99**
14
15                        TOTAL DUE IN 19YY            ZZZ,ZZZ,ZZZ.99***
16
17
18                        TOTAL DUE                    ZZZ,ZZZ,ZZZ.99****
```

Program operations:

1. Process each input vendor record.
2. Print the three heading lines on the first page and on each following page of the report.
   a. Accumulate and print the page number on the first heading line as shown on the print report.
3. The input vendor records have already been sequenced by the Date-due field. For each input vendor record, do the following processing:
   a. On the detail line, provide group indication for the year and month of the Date-due field. That is, print the year only on the first detail line of each page and on the first detail line when the year changes. Print the month only on the first detail line of each page and on the first detail line when the month and/or year changes.
   b. Print an output detail line as specified on the print chart.
   c. Accumulate the Amount-due field.
4. Print control total lines as follows:
   a. Whenever the Date-due changes, print a day control total line (one-asterisk total) as shown on the print chart.
   b. Whenever the month and/or year of the Date-due changes, print a month control total line (two-asterisk total) as shown on the print chart.
   c. Whenever the year of the Date-due changes, print a year control total line (three-asterisk total) as shown on the print chart.
5. Accumulate the year control totals into a report total. After all input records have been processed, print the report total line.
6. Provide for a span of 54 lines per page. Do not permit control total lines to be printed at the top of a new page. (That is, do not print a control total line on a report page that does not contain at least one detail line for the control group to which it applies.) Line spacing is to be handled as follows:
   a. Single-space each detail line [except (1) double-space between the last heading line and the first detail line on each page, and (2) double-space between the control total line and the first detail line for the next control group].
   b. Single-space the day control total line from the preceding detail line (as shown on the print chart).

c. Double-space the month control total line from the preceding day control total line (as shown on the print chart).
d. Double-space the year control total line from the preceding month control total line (as shown on the print chart).
e. Triple-space the report total line from the preceding year control total line.

Programming Assignment 10-3: Departmental Earnings Report
Background information:
The employee earnings file of Silicon Valley Manufacturing has been used for a variety of programming assignments in preceding chapters. Since each employee earnings record includes a Plant-code and a Department-number, group-total reports can be prepared. In particular, the payroll department supervisor needs a multiple-level control total report in which totals are printed whenever the plant or department number changes. A report total is also required.

Input file: Earnings fiile (EARNINGS.DAD)

Input-record format:

Positions	Field	Data class	Comments
1–2	Record code	Numeric	Code 01
3–8	Period ending date	Numeric	Format: *mmddyy*
9–74	Not used		

Positions	Field	Data class	Comments
1–2	Record code	Alphanumeric	Code EM
4–6	Plant code	Numeric	
7–10	Department code	Alphanumeric	
11–19	Employee number	Numeric	
20–31	Employee last name	Alphanumeric	
32–40	Employee first name	Alphanumeric	
44–48	Hours worked	Numeric	Format: 999V99
49	Sex code	Alphabetic	M or F
50	Marital status	Alphabetic	M, S, or H
51–52	Number of exemptions	Numeric	
53	Pay code	Alphabetic	Blank or H
54–59	Pay rate	Numeric	99V9999 for Hourly 9999V99 for Salaried
60–66	This-period earnings	Numeric	99999V99
67–74	Year-to-date earnings	Numeric	999999V99

Output-report format:

```
          0              1              2              3              4              5              6              7
 1234567890123456789012345678901234567890123456789012345678901234567890123456789012345678901

 4  DEPARTMENTAL  EARNINGS  REPORT  (10-3)                              PERIOD  ENDING  MM/DD/YY
 5  SEQUENCED  BY  EMPLOYEE  NUMBER                                         RUN  DATE  MM/DD/YY
 6     WITHIN  DEPARTMENT  WITHIN  PLANT                                           PAGE  ZZZ9

 8                                         XXXXXXXX  PLANT

10  PLANT     DEPT     EMPL  NUMBER      LAST  NAME      FIRST  NM        THIS  PER       YEAR-TO-DT

12  XXX      9999     999-99-9999      XXXXXXXXXXXX  XXXXXXXXX      ZZ,ZZZ.99      ZZZ,ZZZ.99
13                    999-99-9999      XXXXXXXXXXXX  XXXXXXXXX      ZZ,ZZZ.99      ZZZ,ZZZ.99

15                     TOTAL  FOR  DEPT  9999                   ZZZ,ZZZ.99   Z,ZZZ,ZZZ.99 *

17                     TOTAL  FOR  PLANT  XXXXXXXX      Z,ZZZ,ZZZ.99  ZZ,ZZZ,ZZZ.99 **

20                     REPORT  TOTAL                 Z,ZZZ,ZZZ.99  ZZ,ZZZ,ZZZ.99 ***
```

Program operations:

1. Process each input record.
2. Print the five heading lines on the first page and on each following page of the report.
   a. The first record of the file should be the period-ending date record. The period-ending date is to be extracted from the date record and stored in the first heading line as shown on the print chart. If the period-ending date record is not present as the first record of the file, terminate the program processing.
   b. Print the run date on the second heading line as shown on the print chart.
   c. Accumulate and print the page number on the third heading line as shown on the print chart.
   d. Print the plant identification (as explained in Item 3, below) on the fourth heading line.
3. The input earnings records have already been sequenced by Employee-number within Department within Plant within Record-code. Whenever a new Plant control group is started, skip to a new report page. In other words, the first Plant control group will, of course, begin on the first page; each following Plant control group should also begin on a fresh page.
   a. The abbreviation stored in the Plant field should be converted to the complete plant identification as follows:
      ATL = ATLANTIC
      CTL = CENTRAL
      MTN = MOUNTAIN
      PAC = PACIFIC
   b. The applicable plant identification should be printed on the fourth heading line of each page.
4. For each input earnings record, do the following processing:
   a. On the detail line, provide group indication for the Plant and Department-number fields. That is, print the Plant field only on the first detail line of each page and on the first detail line when the Plant changes. Print the Department-number field only on the first detail line of each page and on the first detail line when the value of the Department-number and/or plant field changes.

b. Print an output detail line as specified on the print chart.
c. Accumulate the This-period-earnings and Year-to-date-earnings fields.
5. Print control total lines as follows:
   a. Whenever the Department-number and/or Plant changes, print a Department-number control total line (one-asterisk total) as shown on the print chart.
   b. Whenever the Plant changes, print a Plant control total line (two-asterisk total) as shown on the print chart. Print the Plant identification on this line as explained in Item 3.a, page 540.
6. Accumulate the Plant control totals into a report total. After all input records have been processed, print the report total line.
7. Provide for a span of 54 lines per page. Do not permit control total lines to be printed at the top of a new page. (That is, do not print a control total line on a report page that does not contain at least one detail line for the control group to which it applies.) Line spacing is to be handled as follows:
   a. Single-space each detail line [except (1) double-space between the last heading line and the first detail line on each page, and (2) double-space between the control total line and the first detail line for the next control group].
   b. Double-space the Department-number control total line from the preceding detail line (as shown on the print chart).
   c. Double-space the Plant control total line from the preceding department-number control total line (as shown on the print chart).
   d. Triple-space the report total line from the preceding Plant control total line.

Programming Assignment 10-4: Territory Sales Report
Background information:
The Salesperson file of Follow-the-Sun Sales has been used in a variety of programming assignments, beginning in Chapter 2. Since each salesperson record includes fields for the territory and region to which the salesperson belongs, you might guess that the sales manager would like a report with appropriate breakdowns. To satisfy this requirement, a multiple-level report is needed that prints control totals whenever the region or territory changes. A report total is also to be printed.

Input file: Salesperson file (SALESPER.DAD)

Input-record format:

Positions	Field	Data class	Comments
1–2	Record code	Numeric	Code 01
3–8	Period ending date	Numeric	Format: *mmddyy*
9–79	Not used		

Positions	Field	Data class	Comments
1–2	Record code	Numeric	Code 25
3–4	Salesperson region	Alphanumeric	
5–8	Salesperson territory	Numeric	
9–11	Salesperson number	Numeric	
12–37	Salesperson name	Numeric	
61–70	Sales revenue	Numeric	Dollars and cents
71–79	Sales quota	Numeric	Dollars and cents

Output-report format:

```
                0           1           2           3           4           5           6           7           8
      1234567890123456789012345678901234567890123456789012345678901234567890123456789012345678901
 1
 2
 3
 4  TERRITORY SALES REPORT (10-4)                                      PERIOD ENDING DATE:   MM/DD/YY
 5  SEQUENCED BY SALESPERSON                 XXXXXXXXXXXX REGION                RUN DATE:     MM/DD/YY
 6    WITHIN TERRITORY WITHIN REGION                                               PAGE ZZZ9
 7
 8                         SALESPERSON  SALES REVENUE       SALES QUOTA    PCTG        VARIANCE
 9
10  REGION XX TERRITORY 9999    (CONTINUED)
11
12      999 XXXXXXXXXXXXXXXXXXXXXXXXXX  ZZ,ZZZ,ZZZ.99   ZZ,ZZZ,ZZZ.99  ZZZ.9%   ZZ,ZZZ,ZZZ.99-
13      999 XXXXXXXXXXXXXXXXXXXXXXXXXX  ZZ,ZZZ,ZZZ.99   ZZ,ZZZ,ZZZ.99  ZZZ.9%   ZZ,ZZZ,ZZZ.99-
14
15          TERRITORY 9999 TOTAL  ZZZ,ZZZ,ZZZ.99 ZZZ,ZZZ,ZZZ.99 ZZZ.9% ZZZ,ZZZ,ZZZ.99-*
16
17              REGION XX TOTAL   ZZZ,ZZZ,ZZZ.99 ZZZ,ZZZ,ZZZ.99 ZZZ.9% ZZZ,ZZZ,ZZZ.99-**
18
19
20                REPORT TOTAL   ZZZ,ZZZ,ZZZ.99 ZZZ,ZZZ,ZZZ.99 ZZZ.9% ZZZ,ZZZ,ZZZ.99-***
```

Program operations:

1. Process each input record.
2. Print the four heading lines on the first page and on each following page of the report.
   a. The first record of the file should be the Period-ending date record. The Period-ending date is to be extracted from the date record and stored in the first heading line as shown on the print chart. If the Period-ending date record is not present as the first record of the file, terminate the program processing.
   b. Print the run date on the second heading line as shown on the print chart.
   c. Accumulate and print the page number on the third heading line as shown on the print chart.
   d. Print the name of the Region (as explained in Item 3, below) on the second heading line.
3. The input salesperson records have already been sequenced by Salesperson-number within Territory within Region within Record-code. Whenever a new Region control group is started, skip to a new report page. In other words, the first Region control group will, of course, begin on the first page; each following Region control group should also begin on a fresh page.
   a. The abbreviation stored in the Region field should be converted to the complete region name as follows:
      NE = NORTHEASTERN
      SE = SOUTHEASTERN
      MW = MIDWESTERN
      NW = NORTHWESTERN
      SW = SOUTHWESTERN
   b. The applicable region name should be printed on the second heading line of each page.
4. Whenever a new Territory control group is started, print a control heading line that prints out the Region and Territory as shown on the print chart. If a Territory is being continued from one report page to another, print the word (CONTINUED) as shown on the print chart.
5. For each input salesperson record, do the following processing:
   a. Print an output detail line as specified on the print chart.
   b. Accumulate the Sales-revenue, Sales-quota, and Variance fields.

6. Print control total lines as follows:
   a. Whenever the Region and/or Territory changes, print a Territory control total line (one-asterisk total) as shown on the print chart.
   b. Whenever the Region changes, print a Region control total line (two-asterisk total) as shown on the print chart.
7. Accumulate the Region control totals into a report total. After all input records have been processed, print the report total line.
8. Provide for a span of 54 lines per page.
   a. Do not permit control heading lines to be printed at the bottom of a page. (That is, do not print a control heading line to be printed unless there is also room for at least two detail lines to be printed for that control group.)
   b. Do not permit control total lines to be printed at the top of a new page. (That is, do not print a control total line on a report page that does not contain at least one detail line for the control group to which it applies.)
9. Line spacing is to be handled as follows:
   a. Single-space each detail line (except double-space after each control heading line).
   b. Double-space the Territory control total line from the preceding detail line (as shown on the print chart).
   c. Double-space the Region control total line from the preceding Territory control total line (as shown on the print chart).
   d. Triple-space the report total line from the preceding Region control total line (as shown on the print chart).

Programming Assignment 10-5: Budget Summary for Nurses—Single-Level Control Break

Background information:

As do most organizations, Brooklawn Hospital controls expenditures through budget codes that define categories to which each expenditure is to be charged. For budgetary purposes, each employee is charged to a cost center (depending upon the manager under whom the employee works) and each is given a budget code depending on the type of function performed. Management needs a report that summarizes by cost center.

Input file: Nurses file (NURSES.DAT)

Input-record format:
The following are fields from the nurses file that are applicable to this program.

Positions	Field	Data class	Comments
3–25	Name (last, first, mi)	Alphanumeric	
33–46	Professional specialty	Alphanumeric	For example, Trauma Room
47–52	Date hired	Numeric	Format *yymmdd*
58–60	Cost center	Numeric	
68–73	Base monthly salary	Numeric	Format: dollars and cents
74–97	Other data		

Output-report format:

```
              0                 1                 2                 3                 4                 5                 6
      1 2 3 4 5 6 7 8 9 0 1 2 3 4 5 6 7 8 9 0 1 2 3 4 5 6 7 8 9 0 1 2 3 4 5 6 7 8 9 0 1 2 3 4 5 6 7 8 9 0 1 2 3 4 5 6 7 8 9 0 1 2 3 4 5 6 7 8 9 0 1 2 3 4
  1
  2
  3
  4   BROOKLAWN COST CENTER SUMMARY (10-5)                                                    PAGE ZZ9
  5
  6   COST                                      DATE                                          BASE
  7   CTR    EMPLOYEE NAME                       HIRED    SPECIALTY                            SALARY
  8
  9   XXX    XXXXXXXXXXXXXXXXXXXXXXXX  XX/XX/XX  XXXXXXXXXXXXXXXX   Z,ZZZ.99
 10          XXXXXXXXXXXXXXXXXXXXXXXX  XX/XX/XX  XXXXXXXXXXXXXXXX   Z,ZZZ.99
 11
 12
 13
 14          TOTAL FOR COST CENTER XXX                              ZZZ,ZZZ.99*
 15
 16
 17          REPORT TOTAL                                        Z,ZZZ,ZZZ.99**
```

Program operations:
1. Process each input record.
2. Print the three heading lines on the first page and on each following page of the report.
3. The input records are in sequence by the Cost-center field. For each record, do the following:
   a. Print an output detail line as specified on the print chart. On the detail line, provide group indication for the cost center. That is, print the Cost-center field only on the first detail line for that cost center or on the first detail line of each page.
   b. Accumulate the Base-monthly-salary field.
4. Whenever the cost center changes, print a control total line (one-asterisk total) as shown on the print chart.
5. Accumulate the cost center control totals into a report total. After all input records have been processed, print the report total line.
6. Provide for a span of 54 lines per page. Do not permit control total lines to be printed at the top of a new page. (That is, do not print a control total line on a report page that does not contain at least one detail line for the control group to which it applies.) Line spacing is to be handled as follows:
   a. Single-space each detail line [except (1) double-space between the last heading line and the first detail line on each page, and (2) double-space between the control total line and the first detail line for the next control group].
   b. Triple-space the report total line from the preceding year control total line.

Programming Assignment 10-6: Budget Summary for Nurses— Two-Level Control Break
Background information:
Instead of a single-level grouping by cost center, Brooklawn management requires a two-level grouping by cost center, then by budget code.

Input file: Nurses file (NURSES.DAT)

Input-record format:

In addition to the fields defined for Assignment 10-5, you must use the following.

Positions	Field	Data class	Comments
61–64	Budget code	Numeric	Whole number

Output-report format:

```
         0         1         2         3         4         5         6
1234567890123456789012345678901234567890123456789012345678901234
 1
 2
 3
 4 BROOKLAWN COST CENTER SUMMARY (10-6)        RUN DATE: MM/DD/YY
 5 BUDGET SUMMARY                                 PAGE:  ZZ9
 6 COST CENTER XXX -- XXXXXXXXX
 7
 8      EMPLOYEE NAME              HIRED  SPECIALTY        SALARY
 9
10 BUDGET CODE XXXX   (CONTINUED)
11
12     XXXXXXXXXXXXXXXXXXXXXXXX XX/XX/XX XXXXXXXXXXXXXX   Z,ZZZ.99
13     XXXXXXXXXXXXXXXXXXXXXXXX XX/XX/XX XXXXXXXXXXXXXX   Z,ZZZ.99
14
15
16     BUDGET TOTAL FOR BUDGET CODE XXXX        ZZZ,ZZZ.99*
17
18     BUDGET TOTAL FOR COST CENTER XXX         ZZZ,ZZZ.99**
19
20
21     REPORT TOTAL                           Z,ZZZ,ZZZ.99***
```

Program operations:

1. Process each input record.
2. Print the four heading lines on the first page and on each following page of the report.
   a. Print the run date on the second heading line as shown on the print chart.
   b. Accumulate and print the page number on the third heading line as shown on the print chart.
   c. On the third heading line, print the Cost-center value and the name of the manager of that cost center (as explained in item 3 following).
3. The input records are in sequence by budget code within cost center. Whenever a new cost center control goup is started, skip to a new report page. In other words, the first cost center control group will begin on the first page; each following cost center control group should also begin on a fresh page.
   a. The cost center code on the third heading line must be supplemented by the name of the manager. Normally, this would be available from another file. For this program, use the following:

Cost center	Manager
100	JOHNSON
104	STEVENS
112	HAMILTON
199	MORALES

4. Whenever a new budget code control group is started, print a control heading line that prints out the budget code as shown on the print chart. If a budget code is being continued from one report page to another, print the word (CONTINUED) as shown on the print chart.

5. For each input record, do the following processing:
   a. Print an output detail line as specified on the print chart.
   b. Accumulate the Base-monthly-salary field.

6. Print control total lines as follows:
   a. Whenever the cost center and/or budget code changes, print a budget code control total line (one-asterisk total) as shown on the print chart.
   b. Whenever the cost center changes, print a cost center control total line (two-asterisk total) as shown on the print chart.

7. Accumulate the cost center control totals into a report total. After all input records have been processed, print the report total line.

8. Provide for a span of 54 lines per page.
   a. Do not permit a control heading line (see line 10 of the spacing chart) to be printed at the bottom of a page. That is, do not print a control heading line unless there is also room for at least two detail lines to be printed for that control group.
   b. Do not permit control total lines to be printed at the top of a new page. (That is, do not print a control total line on a report page that does not contain at least one detail line for the control group to which it applies.)

9. Line spacing is to be handled as follows:
   a. Single-space each detail line (except double-space after each control heading line).
   b. Double-space the budget code control total line from the preceding detail line (as shown on the print chart).
   c. Double-space the cost center control total line from the preceding budget code control total line (as shown on the print chart).
   d. Triple-space the report total line from the preceding cost center control total line (as shown on the print chart).

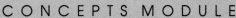

Table Handling Concepts

Module Objectives

The focus of this module is to provide you with some theory regarding table usage in order to lay the basis for later table-processing concepts. From this module, you will learn the following.

- Precisely what a table is from the data-processing perspective and the commonly used terminology.

- The methods for arranging entries of a table: random, sequential, usage-frequency, and positional.

- Computer-techniques for finding a desired entry in a table (table lookup): serial, binary, and positional searching.

- Single- and multiple-level tables.

- Creating a table.

Module Outline

About Tables

Table-Organization Methods
Random Organization
Sequential Organization
Usage-Frequency Organization
Positional Organization

Table-Lookup Methods
Serial Search
Binary Search
Positional Addressing

Multiple-Level Tables

Table Data Storage

About Tables

The word *table* has a number of meanings in the English language. In data-processing terminology, a commonly encountered definition of table is:

Table:
A collection of data in which each item is uniquely identified by a label, by its position relative to the other items, or by some other means.

Consider the familiar income tax table, a logarithmic table, a mileage table, or an airlines schedule. These are all tables used to present information in tabular form for a common reason: to provide data that is concise, yet easy to read and understand.

Tables are similarly used in programming. They allow data to be stored compactly and referenced or retrieved efficiently by a program.

Let's take an example. Suppose we have input records containing a month-number field in which months are represented by two-digit codes. On output, however, we want to print the month names in alphabetic format as three-character abbreviations. A table can be established within a program to accomplish this task. Figure I-1 shows how the table could be formed and indicates the terminology used for its components.

A table contains **table entries**. A table entry may contain a **table argument** and one or more **table functions**. The month-table example includes 12 table entries. Each table entry contains a table argument—the month number—and one table function—the month-name abbreviation for the month represented by the month number.

The field used to locate the appropriate table entry—in this case, the month-number field of the input record—is called the **search argument**.

Figure I-1
Table components.

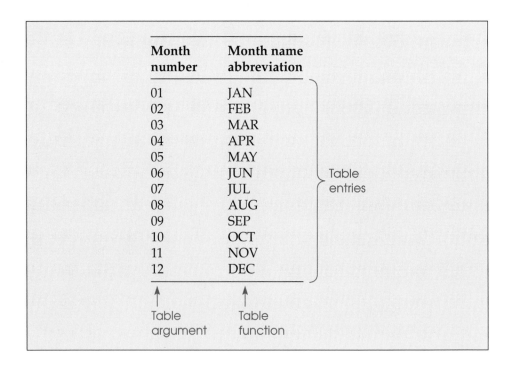

Figure I-2
Table with two functions.

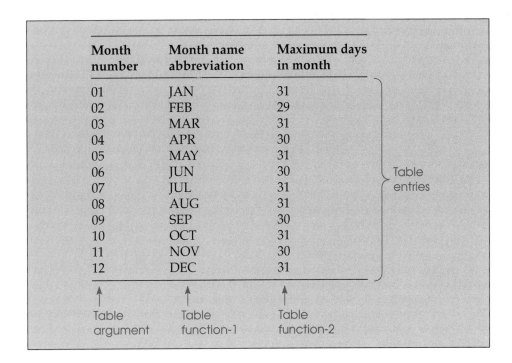

Month number	Month name abbreviation	Maximum days in month	
01	JAN	31	
02	FEB	29	
03	MAR	31	
04	APR	30	
05	MAY	31	
06	JUN	30	Table entries
07	JUL	31	
08	AUG	31	
09	SEP	30	
10	OCT	31	
11	NOV	30	
12	DEC	31	
↑ Table argument	↑ Table function-1	↑ Table function-2	

Table entries can have more than one table function. For example, in addition to the month abbreviation, suppose that the maximum number of days in each month is required for data validation purposes. Figure I-2 shows the month table expanded so that it contains two table functions.

Table-Organization Methods

When a program table is designed, the table-entry arguments can be organized using four methods: randomly, sequentially, by usage-frequency, and positionally.

Random Organization

A table of hypothetical soft-drink product codes, together with their associated flavors, or product names, is shown in Example A of Figure I-3. The product-code numbers are the table arguments; the flavor names are the table functions. The table entries have merely been listed in random product-code number order. Thus, **random organization** establishes table-entry location haphazardly—without concern for the values or characteristics of the table arguments.

Sequential Organization

When a table is arranged according to the collating sequence of its table arguments, it is said to be of **sequential organization**. Example B of Figure I-3 shows the soft-drink table again. This time, though, the table entries are arranged in ascending sequence according to the value of the product code. As an alternative, the table entries could be arranged in descending product-code sequence. Ascending order is used much more frequently, however.

Usage-Frequency Organization

Sometimes a table will have some entries that are frequently referred to and others that receive only occasional reference. If a few table entries are expected to receive a significant percentage of references (often called "hits") in relation to all

Figure I-3
Table-organization examples.

Example A: Random table organization		Example B: Sequential table organization	
Product code (Table argument)	**Soft drink flavor (Table function)**	**Product code (Table argument)**	**Soft drink flavor (Table function)**
110	ORANGE	100	LEMON-LIME
300	GINGER ALE	110	ORANGE
320	CREME SODA	120	CHERRY COLA
120	CHERRY COLA	130	STRAWBERRY
200	ROOT BEER	140	GRAPE
310	SELTZER	150	FRUIT PUNCH
500	COLA	200	ROOT BEER
100	LEMON-LIME	300	GINGER ALE
150	FRUIT PUNCH	310	SELTZER
140	GRAPE	320	CREME SODA
130	STRAWBERRY	500	COLA

Example C: Usage-frequency table organization		Example D: Positional table organization	
Product code (Table argument)	**Soft drink flavor (Table function)**	**Month name abbreviation**	**Maximum days in month**
500	COLA	JAN	31
100	LEMON-LIME	FEB	29
200	ROOT BEER	MAR	31
120	CHERRY COLA	APR	30
110	ORANGE	MAY	31
300	GINGER ALE	JUN	30
140	GRAPE	JUL	31
150	FRUIT PUNCH	AUG	31
130	STRAWBERRY	SEP	30
320	CREME SODA	OCT	31
310	SELTZER	NOV	30
		DEC	31

Table function-1 ↑   Table function-2 ↑

other entries, program-processing time will be reduced by placing the frequently used entries at the beginning of the table. As shown in Example C of Figure I-3, the soft-drink table can be arranged in the order of normal sales volume patterns. That is, the most popular flavors—cola, lemon-lime, and so forth—are positioned at the start of the table; the low-volume drinks are placed at the end of the table. This type of arrangement is known as **usage-frequency organization**.

Positional Organization   A table of **positional organization** requires entries with an unbroken sequence of numeric table arguments. Thus, a table is not a suitable candidate for positional organization if it contains either (1) alphabetic or other special characters, or (2) large gaps between the numeric code values (as the soft-drink product tables does). Such tables typically require too many null entries to maintain the positional organization. In other words, the unused code numbers would necessitate plugging the table with too many "dummy" table entries.

The month table discussed earlier can be considered to be a positionally organized table. It contains an unbroken sequence of numeric table arguments from 01 to 12. When a table is organized positionally, there is no need to explicitly store the table argument in the table; the table argument value can be implicitly determined by its relative position in the table. In other words, the ninth table entry can be considered to have a table argument of nine. Example D of Figure I-3 shows the month table as a positionally organized table without an explicit table argument.

When the table arguments are not included in the table, storage space is conserved. Positional organization is the only table-organization method that offers this benefit.

Table-Lookup Methods

A table is established and organized so that a program can efficiently access and retrieve data fields that relate to a given search argument. The process of using the search argument to locate the table entry is termed **table lookup**. There are three general table-lookup methods: serial search, binary search, and positional addressing.

Serial Search

A **serial search** compares the search argument with the table argument of the first table entry. If they are equal, the appropriate table entry has been located. If they do not match, the program logic causes the search argument to be compared to each remaining table argument, one by one, until either (1) a table argument that matches the search argument is found, or (2) the end of the table is reached. This logic is diagrammed in Figure I-4.

A serial search is the most commonly used lookup method and the only one that can be used with tables of random or usage-frequency organization. For a sequentially organized table, a programming enhancement can be incorporated into the serial search. It is called **serial search with early exit**.

For certain applications, a search argument may have no matching table argument. This can happen when either (1) there are erroneously coded or keyed search arguments, or (2) the table contains only exception entries for certain items that require special handling.

Figure I-4   Serial search logic example.

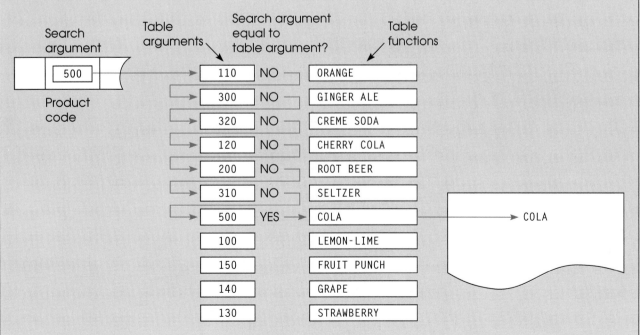

For a table with random or usage-frequency organization, the entire table must be searched before it can be determined that a search argument has no corresponding table argument. Figure I-5 illustrates this requirement. The length of time required to make such a search increases with the number of table entries. That is, the longer the table, the longer the time required to reach the end of the table and thus determine that there is no corresponding table argument.

Figure I-6 shows how processing time can be reduced by using a sequentially organized table together with a serial search with early exit. This reduces the number of comparisons required to determine that a search argument has no corresponding table argument.

Instead of just checking for an equal condition between search and table argument, early exit logic first tests to see if the search argument is greater than the table argument. If the search argument is higher, the equal table argument has clearly not yet been reached in the table. This means that the next table entry must be checked.

On the other hand, if the search argument is not greater than the table argument, the program logic then tests to see if the arguments are equal. If they do match, the table entry has, of course, been located.

However, if the search argument and table argument are *not* equal (is smaller), the search argument does not have a corresponding table argument. This results from organizing the table arguments in ascending sequence. Consequently, the lookup can be terminated, since it is known that no match will be found further on in the table.

By reducing the number of table entries checked, this early exit processing results in fewer comparisons and thus decreases program-processing time. Remember that early exit processing requires that the table be organized sequentially.

Binary Search

When a table contains numerous table entries, a serial search for arguments whose entries are located deep in the table becomes time-consuming. For sequentially organized tables, a binary search can be used instead of a serial search. With longer tables, a binary search will substantially reduce the average amount of time required to locate a table entry.

Figure I-5 Serial search with no corresponding table argument.

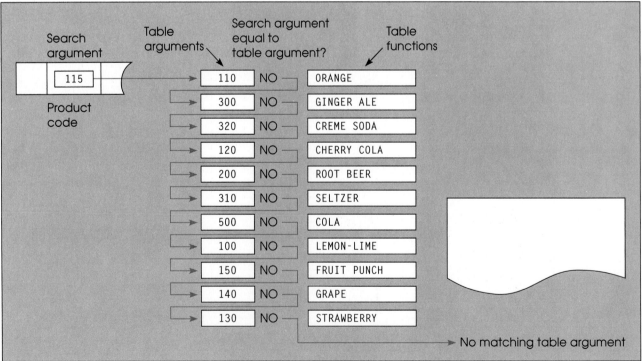

Figure I-6   Serial search with early exit example.

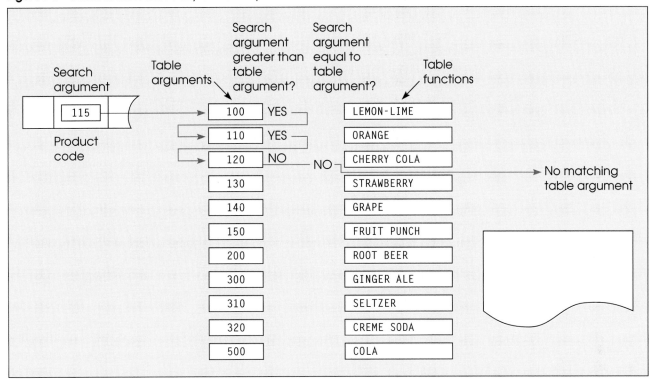

The **binary search** technique is diagrammed in Figure I-7. Notice that the first comparison is made against the table argument in the middle of the table (rather than the first argument, as is done with the serial search). Then, either the top half or the bottom half of the table is searched, depending upon the relationship of the search argument to the midpoint table argument.

Figure I-7   Binary search example.

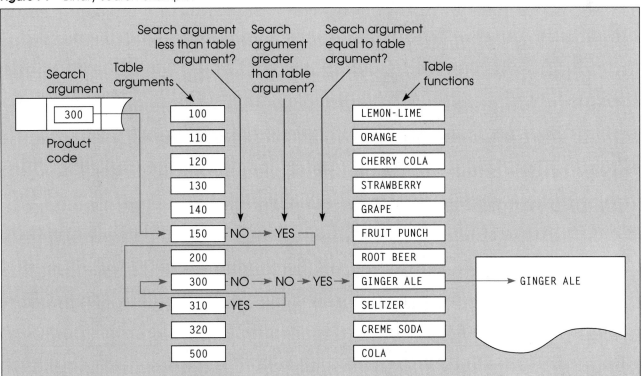

If the search argument is of lesser value than the middle table argument, the first half of the table becomes the search area. Conversely, if the search argument is greater than the midpoint argument, the last half of the table is checked.

Next, the search argument is compared with the argument of the middle entry in the selected half of the table to determine their relationship. Depending upon the result of that comparison, the table is again split in half and the middle entry of that portion of the table is checked. This halving process is repeated until either an equal table argument is found or there are no remaining portions of the table to divide.

Remember that a binary search requires a table of sequential organization and cannot, of course, be used with a table organized randomly or by usage frequency. As will be explained in the next section, there is no need to use a binary search for a positionally organized table.

A binary search is much quicker than a serial search for large tables. Notice in Figure I-8 that the average number of comparisons required for the serial search of a 1000-entry table is 500, whereas the maximum number of comparisons for a binary search is only 10. However, since there is some "overhead" required to initialize and execute a binary search, it is not as efficient for smaller tables. As a rule of thumb, binary searches should be applied only to sequentially organized tables with over 50 table entries.

Positional Addressing

No search is required when **positional addressing** is used. As a result, it provides the fastest retrieval of table data. However, it can be used only with positionally organized tables. With positional addressing, the search argument specifies the

Figure I-8 Number of comparisons required for serial and binary searches.

| Number of table entries | Serial search | | Binary search |
	Maximum number of comparisons	Average number of comparisons	Maximum number of comparisons
50	50	25	6
100	100	50	7
500	500	250	9
1,000	1,000	500	10
2,000	2,000	1,000	11
5,000	5,000	2,500	13
10,000	10,000	5,000	14

Formula to compute maximum number of binary search comparisons (x = maximum number of comparisons required):

$$2^x > \text{number of table entries}$$

Example to solve for x with 50 table entries:

$2^1 = 2$ [< number of table entries]
$2^2 = 4$ [< number of table entries]
$2^3 = 8$ [< number of table entries]
$2^4 = 16$ [< number of table entries]
$2^5 = 32$ [< number of table entries]
→ $2^6 = 64$ [> number of table entries]

———— Maximum number of comparisons required = 6

relative position (or an indication of the relative position) of the corresponding table entry. Thus, the table argument is directly located without the need for a matching operation, as shown in Figure I-9.

Remember that positional addressing applies only to positionally organized tables that require an unbroken sequence of numeric table arguments. The argument values need not start at one, however. As shown in Figure I-10, if the first table entry corresponds to an arbitrarily chosen table argument value of 27,

Figure I-9   *Positional addressing example.*

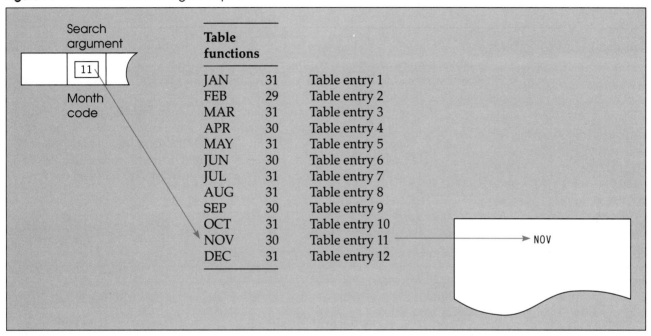

Figure I-10   *Other positional addressing examples.*

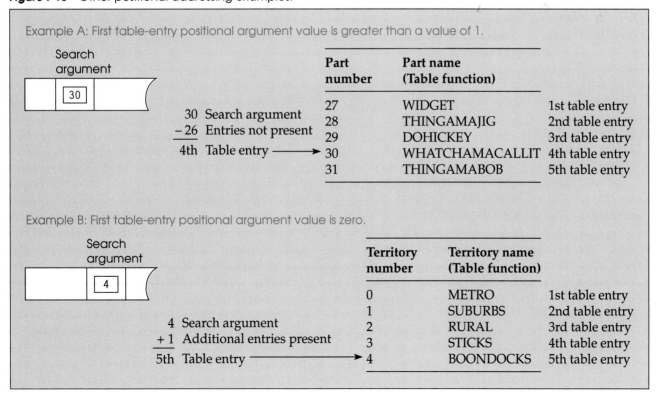

the matching table entry could be determined by subtracting a value of 26 from the search argument value. When the first table entry's argument value is zero, the corresponding table entry can be found by adding one to the search argument value.

Before attempting to access a positionally addressed table, it is imperative that the search argument be validated to ensure that it is within the range of the table. For example, when positionally addressing the month-name table, it is mandatory that the search argument value be greater than 0 and less than 13. If an out-of-range value is used, erroneous processing occurs.

Figure I-11 summarizes table-organization and table-lookup characteristics.

Multiple-Level Tables

The tables discussed so far are all examples of **single-level (one-dimensional)** tables. Some applications require tables with two or more dimensions. Such tables can be termed **multiple-level**, or **multidimensional** tables. A multiple-level table has, in effect, tables within table entries.

A federal income tax withholding table, as shown in Figure I-12, is an example of a two-level table. The first level pertains to amount of earnings ("wages"); the second level applies to number of exemptions ("withholding allowances") claimed.

An example of a three-level table is shown in Figure I-13. Notice that the price depends upon three items: the product code, the quantity ordered, and the type of customer.

Figure I-11 Summary of table-organization and table-lookup characteristics.

Table organization	Lookup method			
	Serial search	Serial search with early exit	Binary search	Positional addressing
Random	Same lookup efficiency as for sequential organization			
Sequential	Lookup may be slow if number of table entries is large	Improves serial search when many search arguments do not have matching table argument	Most efficient sequential lookup for longer tables (differential increases as table gets longer)	
Usage-frequency	Efficient lookup if great majority of search arguments are just a few table entries			
Positional				Immediate lookup

Figure I-12   Two-level table example.

WEEKLY PAYROLL PERIOD
SINGLE PERSONS — UNMARRIED HEADS OF HOUSEHOLD

And the wages are—		And the number of withholding allowances claimed is—										
At least	Less than	0	1	2	3	4	5	6	7	8	9	10 or more
		The amount of income tax to be withheld will be—										
340	350	48.00	42.00	36.00	31.00	25.00	19.00	13.00	7.00	1.00	0	0
350	360	50.00	44.00	38.00	32.00	26.00	20.00	14.00	8.00	2.00	0	0
360	370	51.00	45.00	39.00	34.00	28.00	22.00	16.00	10.00	4.00	0	0
370	380	53.00	47.00	41.00	35.00	29.00	23.00	17.00	11.00	5.00	0	0
380	390	54.00	48.00	42.00	37.00	31.00	25.00	19.00	13.00	7.00	1.00	0
390	400	56.00	50.00	44.00	38.00	32.00	26.00	20.00	14.00	8.00	3.00	0
400	410	58.00	51.00	45.00	40.00	34.00	28.00	22.00	16.00	10.00	4.00	0
410	420	61.00	53.00	47.00	41.00	35.00	29.00	23.00	17.00	11.00	6.00	0
420	430	64.00	54.00	48.00	43.00	37.00	31.00	25.00	19.00	13.00	7.00	1.00
430	440	67.00	56.00	50.00	44.00	38.00	32.00	26.00	20.00	14.00	9.00	3.00

Level-1 table arguments

Level-2 table arguments

Figure I-13   Three-level table example.

Level-2 table arguments

Product-code	Quantity ordered							
	1		2–6		7–12		13–up	
	Regular customers	Government and educational customers	Regular customers	Government and educational customers	Regular customers	Government and educational customers	Regular customers	Government and educational customers
A1818	$110.00	$102.00	$100.00	$ 92.00	$ 95.00	$ 86.00	$ 90.00	$ 81.00
A2418	128.00	115.00	117.00	105.00	111.00	100.00	106.00	95.00
A3018	139.00	125.00	127.00	114.00	120.00	108.00	114.00	103.00
A2424	149.00	134.00	136.00	122.00	129.00	116.00	123.00	111.00
A3024	161.00	146.00	148.00	132.00	139.00	125.00	131.00	118.00
A3624	173.00	158.00	159.00	141.00	149.00	144.00	142.00	128.00
A4824	200.00	180.00	182.00	164.00	173.00	156.00	164.00	148.00

Level-1 table arguments

Level-3 table arguments

Table Data Storage

Table data can be coded directly into a computer program or read into the program as input records. The former approach is sometimes called a **hard-coded table**; the latter method uses an **input-loaded table**. Figure I-14 contrasts these two sources.

When a table is coded directly into a program, it is cumbersome to make additions, deletions, or modifications to the table. Usually, a programmer must make the changes and then the program must be recompiled.

Figure I-14 Hard-coded and input-loaded tables.

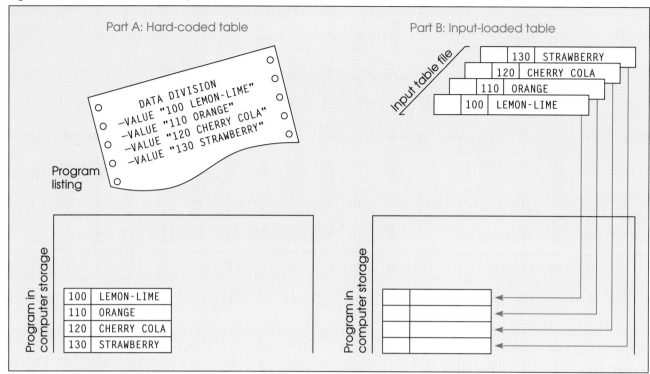

Input-loaded tables are better suited to volatile data. The frequent changes or updates to a table can be processed, as required, by control clerks or other authorized personnel.

However, with input-loaded tables, it is more difficult to ensure that unauthorized or erroneous changes not be made. Further, the correct table must be loaded each time the program is run. Therefore, more controls—both program and manual—are required to ensure correct and accurate processing.

Thus, a hard-coded table is less flexible than an input-loaded table. This quality can be either beneficial or detrimental, depending upon the application. Sensitive or security-dependent data-items, such as salaries by job level or confidential data, are best handled as hard-coded tables. Tables containing routine, normal business data-items may fare better as input-loaded tables.

Module Summary

In programming, a **table** is used to store data compactly for rapid retrieval. A table contains a **table entry** for each data entity represented. Each table entry may contain a **table argument** and one or more **table functions**. The field used to locate the table entry is termed the **search argument**.

Tables can be organized at **random**, in **sequential** order, by **usage frequency**, or by **positional** location within the table. There are three general table-lookup methods: **serial search**, **binary search**, and **positional addressing**. A table with only one **dimension** is termed a **single-level** table; one with two or more dimensions is called a **multiple-level** table. Table data may be **hard-coded** into a program or **input-loaded** into the program each time the program is run.

Exercises

Terms for Definition

binary search _____

hard-coded table _____

input-loaded table _____

multi-dimensional table _____

multiple-level table _____

one-dimensional table _____

positional addressing _____

positional organization _____

random organization _____

search argument _____

sequential organization _____

serial search _____

serial search with early exit _____

single-level table _____

table _____

table argument _____

table entry _____

table function _____

table lookup _____

usage-frequency organization _____

Review Questions

1. A table entry may contain a table _____ and one or more table _____.

2. The field, typically derived from input data, that is used to locate the appropriate table entry is called the _____.

3. If table entries are listed haphazardly within the table, the table can be said to be of _____ organization.

4. When a table is arranged in accordance with the collating sequence of its table arguments, it is of _____ organization.

5. With _____ organization, the most frequently encountered table entries are placed at the beginning of the table.

6. A table of _____ organization requires entries with an unbroken sequence of numeric table arguments.

7. The most commonly used table-lookup method is a(n) _____ search.

8. A table-lookup method that provides relatively quick lookups for longer

   tables is called a(n) _____ search.

9. A(n) _____ lookup requires no search and hence provides rapid retrieval of table data.

10. A(n) _____ lookup can be performed only when the table is organized sequentially.

11. A(n) _____ lookup can be performed only when the table is organized positionally.

12. A serial search with early exit can be used only when a table is organized

    _____ .

13. Before a(n) _____ lookup is performed, it is imperative that the search argument be validated to ensure that it is within the range of the table.

14. A table with two or more dimensions is often referred to as a(n)

    _____ table.

15. When table entries are coded directly into the program, the table can be called

    a(n) _____ table; when table entries are read into program

    storage, the table can be called a(n) _____ table.

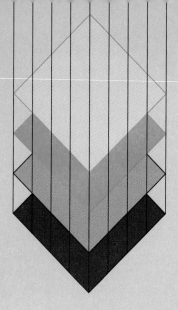

Table Processing

Chapter Objectives

Table processing is an important COBOL subject that has many aspects. Fundamental table-processing concepts are described in this chapter; more advanced table-processing considerations are covered in the next chapter. From this chapter, you will learn the following:

- Directly accessing a positionally organized table without the need for searching.

- The OCCURS clause, which specifies how many times a field or group of fields is repeated.

- Accessing a table, using subscripts to identify the particular element of the table that is desired.

- Defining a table consisting of arguments and functions.

- The PERFORM/VARYING statement, which uses automatic counting for the control of a processing loop.

- The coding necessary to perform serial table lookup.

- The SEARCH statement, which is specifically designed for table lookup.

- Early exit from a table lookup searching loop.

- Performing a binary search using the SEARCH/ALL statement.

Chapter Outline

Establishing a Table
A Simple Table—Months of the Year
The OCCURS Clause

Accessing the Table with Subscripts
What is a Subscript?
Literal Subscripts
Variable Subscripts
About COMP USAGE for Subscripts

Other Table-Establishment Considerations
Uniform Field Lengths
Naming the Table Data-Items That Contain the Data Values

Establishing a Table with Arguments and Functions

Serial Lookups
PERFORM/UNTIL Statement Driver
   DATA DIVISION Coding
   PROCEDURE DIVISION Coding
   Improved Lookup Coding
PERFORM/VARYING Statement Driver
SEARCH Statement Driver
   The INDEXED BY Clause
   The SET Statement
   The Format-1 (Serial) SEARCH Statement

Serial Lookups with Early Exit
DATA DIVISION Coding
PROCEDURE DIVISION Coding

Binary Search Lookups
The KEY Clause
The Format-2 (Binary) SEARCH Statement
   The ALL Clause

563

Establishing a Table
A Simple Table—
Months of the Year

Tables are defined in the WORKING-STORAGE SECTION of the DATA DIVISION and are accessed in the PROCEDURE DIVISION. As depicted in Figure 11-1, suppose that you want to define a table of three-letter calendar-month abbreviations so that input records containing a month number from 01 to 12 can be processed and printed out with the corresponding month abbreviation.

This table-processing task can be efficiently processed by (1) establishing a **positionally organized table** in WORKING-STORAGE, and (2) coding PROCEDURE DIVISION statements to handle the logic.

A month-abbreviation table is best established as a **hard-coded table** (rather than an **input-loaded table**, which will be discussed in the next chapter) because the months of the year are (1) stable—rather than volatile—data entities (the present month names have been with us for a long time and can be expected to stay that way for some time into the future), and (2) the number of table entries is limited (twelve).

To establish a hard-coded table, you must first code the table data in VALUE clauses within the WORKING-STORAGE SECTION. Such coding for the month-abbreviation table is shown in Figure 11-2. Observe that a 01-level group item, MT-MONTH-ABBREVIATION-DATA, is established to contain the table data as a whole. (The prefix MT has been assigned to signify that this is the **Month Table**.) Within the group item for the table, the twelve table entries have been specified. Each entry is defined as a three-character alphanumeric field, and assigned its corresponding month abbreviation through use of a VALUE clause. With COBOL-74, you must include the reserved word FILLER; with COBOL-85, FILLER may be omitted. Although all examples that follow include the word FILLER, it can be omitted with COBOL-85.

Actually, it is not necessary to define each table entry as a separate data-item. Instead, multiple entries could be assigned to a data-item, as shown in Figure 11-3. However, it is usually better to define each table entry separately because the separate data-items make the table entries easier to read and modify should additions, changes, or deletions to the table become necessary.

The OCCURS Clause

After the hard-coded table data has been established with VALUE clauses, the table must be redefined with an OCCURS clause, as shown in Figure 11-4. This redefinition is required to permit efficient access to the table entries in the PROCEDURE DIVISION.

Figure 11-1   Month-abbreviation table application.

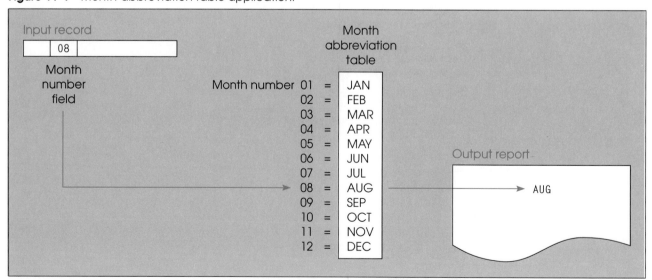

Figure 11-2 Establishing table data in WORKING-STORAGE: Recommended method.

```
COBOL-74                                        COBOL-85

01  MT-MONTH-ABBREVIATION-DATA.                  01  MT-MONTH-ABBREVIATION-DATA.
    05  FILLER         PIC X(3)    VALUE "JAN".      05              PIC X(3)    VALUE "JAN".
    05  FILLER         PIC X(3)    VALUE "FEB".      05              PIC X(3)    VALUE "FEB".
    05  FILLER         PIC X(3)    VALUE "MAR".      05              PIC X(3)    VALUE "MAR".
    05  FILLER         PIC X(3)    VALUE "APR".      05              PIC X(3)    VALUE "APR".
    05  FILLER         PIC X(3)    VALUE "MAY".      05              PIC X(3)    VALUE "MAY".
    05  FILLER         PIC X(3)    VALUE "JUN".      05              PIC X(3)    VALUE "JUN".
    05  FILLER         PIC X(3)    VALUE "JUL".      05              PIC X(3)    VALUE "JUL".
    05  FILLER         PIC X(3)    VALUE "AUG".      05              PIC X(3)    VALUE "AUG".
    05  FILLER         PIC X(3)    VALUE "SEP".      05              PIC X(3)    VALUE "SEP".
    05  FILLER         PIC X(3)    VALUE "OCT".      05              PIC X(3)    VALUE "OCT".
    05  FILLER         PIC X(3)    VALUE "NOV".      05              PIC X(3)    VALUE "NOV".
    05  FILLER         PIC X(3)    VALUE "DEC".      05              PIC X(3)    VALUE "DEC".
```

Figure 11-3
Establishing table data in WORKING-STORAGE: *Not* recommended method.

```
01   MT-MONTH-ABBREVIATION-DATA.
     05  FILLER              PIC X(36)
         VALUE "JANFEBMARAPRMAYJUNJULAUGSEPOCTNOVDEC".
```

Figure 11-4
Redefinition of table data with the OCCURS clause.

```
Format:

                        OCCURS integer TIMES


Example:

    01   MT-MONTH-ABBREVIATION-DATA.
         05  FILLER           PIC X(3)        VALUE "JAN".
         05  FILLER           PIC X(3)        VALUE "FEB".
         05  FILLER           PIC X(3)        VALUE "MAR".
         05  FILLER           PIC X(3)        VALUE "APR".
         05  FILLER           PIC X(3)        VALUE "MAY".
         05  FILLER           PIC X(3)        VALUE "JUN".
         05  FILLER           PIC X(3)        VALUE "JUL".
         05  FILLER           PIC X(3)        VALUE "AUG".
         05  FILLER           PIC X(3)        VALUE "SEP".
         05  FILLER           PIC X(3)        VALUE "OCT".
         05  FILLER           PIC X(3)        VALUE "NOV".
         05  FILLER           PIC X(3)        VALUE "DEC".
    01   MR-MONTH-ABBREVIATION-TABLE
             REDEFINES MT-MONTH-ABBREVIATION-DATA.
         05  MT-MONTH-ABBREVIATION        OCCURS 12 TIMES
                                          PIC X(3).
```

The OCCURS clause is used to specify how many times a particular field or group of fields is repeated. The integer number specified in the OCCURS clause identifies the number of repetitions. The OCCURS clause can be used with any data-item that has a level-number from 02 through 49; it cannot be affixed to a 01-level or 77-level item. Another restriction is that a data-item with an OCCURS clause cannot contain a VALUE clause.

The prohibition that a data-item cannot contain both an OCCURS and a VALUE clause explains why a hard-coded table must first be defined with the appropriate VALUE-clause data and then redefined with the OCCURS clause.

As a result, the coding for the MT-MONTH-ABBREVIATION-DATA specifies 36 character-positions containing the 12 three-letter month abbreviations. The MT-MONTH-ABBREVIATION-TABLE then redefines those same 36 storage positions as 12 occurrences of a three-character field called MT-MONTH-ABBREVIATION.

Accessing the Table with Subscripts

Whenever an OCCURS clause is associated with a data-item, either a subscript or an index must be used when referring to that item in the PROCEDURE DIVISION. Subscripts are described next; indexes are described later in the chapter.

What is a Subscript?

A **subscript** is used to refer to a specific occurrence of a repeated field defined with the OCCURS clause. The subscript identifies which occurrence of the field is being referenced. In the month-abbreviation table, for example, JAN is occurrence 1, FEB is occurrence 2, MAR is occurrence 3, and so on. This is depicted in Figure 11-5.

Subscripts are coded within parentheses and used in the PROCEDURE DIVISION. There are two ways that a subscript can be expressed—as a literal or as a variable.

Literal Subscripts

A **literal subscript** is coded as an integer numeric literal. Figure 11-6 shows how the month abbreviation AUG could be extracted from the table with a literal subscript and placed in an output-report line field called RL-MONTH-ABBREVIATION. The occurrence number of 8 is simply coded in parentheses following the data-name MT-MONTH-ABBREVIATION.

Literal subscripts have limited use because they must be hard-coded into the program logic. Consider our need to convert a month-number field (IN-MONTH-NUMBER) to a month-abbreviation field on a report line (RL-MONTH-ABBREVIATION). Using literal subscripts, you would need to code rather tedious and lengthy logic, as shown in Figure 11-7. And this application has only 12 table entries! It is not uncommon for a table to have hundreds—or even thousands—of entries. As you will see, variable subscripts offer much more flexibility.

Figure 11-5
Depiction of table specifications.

MT-MONTH-ABBREVIATION-DATA	MT-MONTH-ABBREVIATION-TABLE
JAN	MT-MONTH-ABBREVIATION occurrence 1
FEB	MT-MONTH-ABBREVIATION occurrence 2
MAR	MT-MONTH-ABBREVIATION occurrence 3
APR	MT-MONTH-ABBREVIATION occurrence 4
MAY	MT-MONTH-ABBREVIATION occurrence 5
JUN	MT-MONTH-ABBREVIATION occurrence 6
JUL	MT-MONTH-ABBREVIATION occurrence 7
AUG	MT-MONTH-ABBREVIATION occurrence 8
SEP	MT-MONTH-ABBREVIATION occurrence 9
OCT	MT-MONTH-ABBREVIATION occurrence 10
NOV	MT-MONTH-ABBREVIATION occurrence 11
DEC	MT-MONTH-ABBREVIATION occurrence 12

Figure 11-6
Example of table accessing
with a literal subscript.

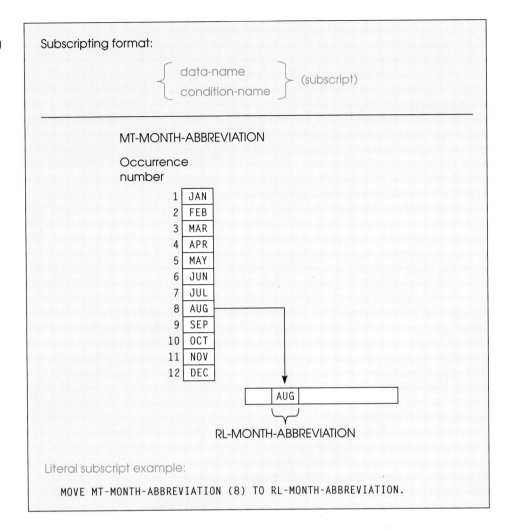

Subscripting format:

$$\left.\begin{array}{l} \text{data-name} \\ \text{condition-name} \end{array}\right\} \text{(subscript)}$$

MT-MONTH-ABBREVIATION

Occurrence
number

1	JAN
2	FEB
3	MAR
4	APR
5	MAY
6	JUN
7	JUL
8	AUG
9	SEP
10	OCT
11	NOV
12	DEC

AUG

RL-MONTH-ABBREVIATION

Literal subscript example:

```
MOVE MT-MONTH-ABBREVIATION (8) TO RL-MONTH-ABBREVIATION.
```

Figure 11-7   Coding for table accessing with literal subscripts.

COBOL-74

```
IF IN-MONTH-NUMBER IS EQUAL TO 1
    MOVE MT-MONTH-ABBREVIATION (1) TO RL-MONTH-ABBREVIATION
ELSE IF IN-MONTH-NUMBER IS EQUAL TO 2
    MOVE MT-MONTH-ABBREVIATION (2) TO RL-MONTH-ABBREVIATION
ELSE IF IN-MONTH-NUMBER IS EQUAL TO 3
    MOVE MT-MONTH-ABBREVIATION (3) TO RL-MONTH-ABBREVIATION
ELSE IF IN-MONTH-NUMBER IS EQUAL TO 4
    MOVE MT-MONTH-ABBREVIATION (4) TO RL-MONTH-ABBREVIATION
ELSE IF IN-MONTH-NUMBER IS EQUAL TO 5
    MOVE MT-MONTH-ABBREVIATION (5) TO RL-MONTH-ABBREVIATION
ELSE IF IN-MONTH-NUMBER IS EQUAL TO 6
    MOVE MT-MONTH-ABBREVIATION (6) TO RL-MONTH-ABBREVIATION
ELSE IF IN-MONTH-NUMBER IS EQUAL TO 7
    MOVE MT-MONTH-ABBREVIATION (7) TO RL-MONTH-ABBREVIATION
ELSE IF IN-MONTH-NUMBER IS EQUAL TO 8
    MOVE MT-MONTH-ABBREVIATION (8) TO RL-MONTH-ABBREVIATION
ELSE IF IN-MONTH-NUMBER IS EQUAL TO 9
    MOVE MT-MONTH-ABBREVIATION (9) TO RL-MONTH-ABBREVIATION
ELSE IF IN-MONTH-NUMBER IS EQUAL TO 10
    MOVE MT-MONTH-ABBREVIATION (10) TO RL-MONTH-ABBREVIATION
ELSE IF IN-MONTH-NUMBER IS EQUAL TO 11
    MOVE MT-MONTH-ABBREVIATION (11) TO RL-MONTH-ABBREVIATION
ELSE IF IN-MONTH-NUMBER IS EQUAL TO 12
    MOVE MT-MONTH-ABBREVIATION (12) TO RL-MONTH-ABBREVIATION
```

COBOL-85

```
EVALUATE IN-MONTH-NUMBER
    WHEN 1
        MOVE MT-MONTH-ABBREVIATION (1) TO RL-MONTH-ABBREVIATION
    WHEN 2
        MOVE MT-MONTH-ABBREVIATION (2) TO RL-MONTH-ABBREVIATION
    WHEN 3
        MOVE MT-MONTH-ABBREVIATION (3) TO RL-MONTH-ABBREVIATION
    WHEN 4
        MOVE MT-MONTH-ABBREVIATION (4) TO RL-MONTH-ABBREVIATION
    WHEN 5
        MOVE MT-MONTH-ABBREVIATION (5) TO RL-MONTH-ABBREVIATION
    WHEN 6
        MOVE MT-MONTH-ABBREVIATION (6) TO RL-MONTH-ABBREVIATION
    WHEN 7
        MOVE MT-MONTH-ABBREVIATION (7) TO RL-MONTH-ABBREVIATION
    WHEN 8
        MOVE MT-MONTH-ABBREVIATION (8) TO RL-MONTH-ABBREVIATION
    WHEN 9
        MOVE MT-MONTH-ABBREVIATION (9) TO RL-MONTH-ABBREVIATION
    WHEN 10
        MOVE MT-MONTH-ABBREVIATION (10) TO RL-MONTH-ABBREVIATION
    WHEN 11
        MOVE MT-MONTH-ABBREVIATION (11) TO RL-MONTH-ABBREVIATION
    WHEN 12
        MOVE MT-MONTH-ABBREVIATION (12) TO RL-MONTH-ABBREVIATION
END-EVALUATE
```

Variable Subscripts   A **variable subscript** uses the value contained in a field to identify the occurrence number. Like the literal subscript, it is coded within parentheses and follows the data-name being referenced. As shown in Figure 11-8, the actual value contained in the IN-MONTH-NUMBER field can be used to indicate which of the 12 occurrences of MT-MONTH-ABBREVIATION should be moved to the RL-MONTH-ABBREVIATION field.

This example clearly illustrates how just the one statement using a variable subscript

```
MOVE MT-MONTH-ABBREVIATION (IN-MONTH-NUMBER) TO RL-MONTH-ABBREVIATION
```

replaces the lengthy IF statement required for a literal subscript (as shown in Figure 11-7). This retrieval of data from a positionally organized table through use of a subscripted (or indexed) data-name is called **positional addressing**.

Variable subscripts must be elementary numeric-integer fields defined in the DATA DIVISION. The length of a field used for a subscript must be sufficient to contain the number of occurrences specified in the OCCURS clause.

When the program is executing the statement containing the subscript, the value of the subscript field should be greater than zero and not greater than the number of occurrences of the field being referenced, as specified in the OCCURS clause. For example, if IN-MONTH-NUMBER contained a value less than one or greater than thirteen, the subscript would be outside the range of the table and hence could cause either erroneous results or program termination (depending upon the compiler and operating system). So, before an input field is used as a subscript field, it is imperative that its value be validated to ensure that it is within the proper range. Such a validation could be performed in a prior data validation program, in the using program, or both.

Figure 11-9 provides an example of this type of range-check validation for the subscript used in the month-abbreviation table. With this logic, whenever an

Figure 11-8
Example of table accessing with a variable subscript.

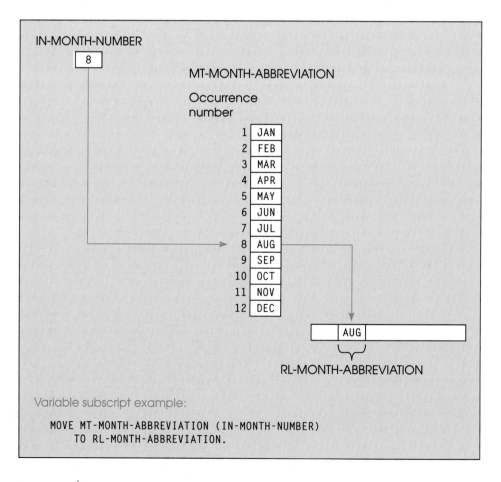

invalid month number is detected in the IN-MONTH-NUMBER field, the error condition is identified by the printing of three asterisks in the RL-MONTH-ABBRE-VIATION field.

About COMP USAGE for Subscripts

Recall from Chapter 4 that the USAGE clause can control the internal format in which data is stored. For whole number quantities, USAGE COMP results in a pure binary form that is very efficient for arithmetic operations. Although program efficiency should not be a primary consideration in program design, here is a case in which subscripting operations can be speeded up with no sacrifice of program "quality."

That is, if a dedicated subscript field is established within WORKING-STOR-AGE, you can define it with a USAGE COMP clause. In fact, you can take that one step further by using the synchronized phrase to most effectively position the binary number in memory. Then the usage clause becomes USAGE COMP SYNC (or USAGE COMP SYNCHRONIZED). You will see this clause used in a later example. However, sometimes—as is the case with our IN-MONTH-NUMBER field—an existing field within a record is used as the subscript field. In such situations, the preexisting usage of the field must, of course, be maintained.

Other Table-Establishment Considerations

With regard to the establishment of hard-coded tables, a couple of other points should be discussed: data-field lengths and data-names.

Uniform Field Lengths

Data values for a given table element are not always of equal lengths. For example, suppose you wanted to establish a table of full month names rather than abbreviations. The shortest table entry (May) has only three characters, whereas the longest (September) is nine letters in length. So that the OCCURS clause can properly identify the repetition of fields, all entries must be as long as the longest entry. Figure 11-10 shows an example of such coding. Notice that each element is defined with PIC X(9). The shorter month names will be left-justified and padded with rightmost blank spaces by the compiler when inserted into their assigned areas.

Figure 11-9
Example of variable-subscript range validation.

```
       IF IN-MONTH-NUMBER IS NOT NUMERIC
           MOVE ZERO TO IN-MONTH-NUMBER.
       IF IN-MONTH-NUMBER IS GREATER THAN ZERO
       AND IN-MONTH-NUMBER IS NOT GREATER THAN 12
           MOVE MT-MONTH-ABBREVIATION (IN-MONTH-NUMBER)
               TO RL-MONTH-ABBREVIATION
       ELSE
           MOVE "***" TO RL-MONTH-ABBREVIATION.
```

Figure 11-10
Table entries padded to a uniform length.

```
       01  MT-MONTH-NAME-DATA.
           05  FILLER          PIC X(9)    VALUE "JANUARY".
           05  FILLER          PIC X(9)    VALUE "FEBRUARY".
           05  FILLER          PIC X(9)    VALUE "MARCH".
           05  FILLER          PIC X(9)    VALUE "APRIL".
           05  FILLER          PIC X(9)    VALUE "MAY".
           05  FILLER          PIC X(9)    VALUE "JUNE".
           05  FILLER          PIC X(9)    VALUE "JULY".
           05  FILLER          PIC X(9)    VALUE "AUGUST".
           05  FILLER          PIC X(9)    VALUE "SEPTEMBER".
           05  FILLER          PIC X(9)    VALUE "OCTOBER".
           05  FILLER          PIC X(9)    VALUE "NOVEMBER".
           05  FILLER          PIC X(9)    VALUE "DECEMBER".
       01  MT-MONTH-NAME-TABLE REDEFINES MT-MONTH-NAME-DATA.
           05  MT-MONTH-NAME                OCCURS 12 TIMES
                                            PIC X(9).
```

Naming the Table Data-Items That Contain the Data Values

In the month-abbreviation and month-name tables, notice that each of the elementary data-items with a VALUE clause is not given a user-defined name. The absence of a name (or the word FILLER) is usually appropriate for hard-coded table data-items because the data is normally accessed only by reference to the redefined data-name with the OCCURS clause; the elementary field with the VALUE clause is never cited.

User-defined data-names, however, may be preferable in a limited number of situations. Suppose a default table entry is to be chosen if, say, the subscript value is out of range. Figure 11-11 illustrates how use of a user-defined data-name facilitates selection of the default table entry. (Of course, a literal subscript could alternatively be used for the default table entry. However, the literal subscript can pose maintenance problems. Should the default entry change its relative location within the table because of table-entry additions or deletions, the literal subscript will require updating to reflect the new occurrence number.)

Establishing a Table with Arguments and Functions

Positionally organized tables, such as the month-abbreviation table, do not contain table arguments. (Implicitly, the relative occurrence number of the entry serves as the argument.) For table lookups, however, a table must contain a table argument for each entry. Hence, unlike the month-abbreviation table that contained only table functions, most tables contain one table argument and one or more table functions.

For example, suppose you have input records with two-character state abbreviations and want to look up the complete state name so that it can be printed on the output. To accomplish this, a 51-entry (50 states plus the District of Columbia) table is required. The table argument is the state abbreviation; the table function is the full name of the state. Figure 11-12 shows coding for such a table. Observe that each of the 51 entries contains the two-letter state abbreviation, followed immediately by the state name. The entries are in alphabetical order according to the table argument (state abbreviation). Hence, the state table can be considered an example of a sequentially organized table.

Data-names associated with the table have been assigned a prefix of ST- (for state table). The field length is defined as 22 [PIC X(22)]—corresponding to the longest name (District of Columbia).

Figure 11-11
Table-entry value defined with a table name.

```
                          05  IN-PURCHASE-AMOUNT    PIC S9(7)V99.
                          05  IN-TAX-RATE-CODE       PIC 9(1).
                           .
                           .
                           .
              01  TT-TAX-RATE-DATA.
                  05  FILLER                PIC V9999    VALUE .0600.
                  05  FILLER                PIC V9999    VALUE .0610.
          ──────▶  05  TT-DEFAULT-RATE       PIC V9999    VALUE .0625.
                  05  FILLER                PIC V9999    VALUE .0633.
                  05  FILLER                PIC V9999    VALUE .0650.
              01  TT-TAX-RATE-TABLE-REDEFINES  TT-TAX-RATE-DATA.
                  05  TT-TAX-RATE                  OCCURS 5 TIMES
                                                   PIC V9999.
                           .
                           .
                           .
                  IF IN-TAX-RATE-CODE IS GREATER THAN ZERO
                  AND IN-TAX-RATE-CODE IS NOT GREATER THAN 5
                      MULTIPLY IN-PURCHASE-AMOUNT
                            BY TT-TAX-RATE (IN-TAX-RATE-CODE)
                  ELSE
                      MULTIPLY IN-PURCHASE-AMOUNT BY TT-DEFAULT-RATE.
```

Figure 11-12 Establishing a table with both a table argument and a table function.

```
State abbreviation                             State name
(table argument data)                          (table function data)

01  ST-STATE-DATA.                                      05   FILLER    PIC X(22) VALUE "NDNORTH DAKOTA".
    05  FILLER    PIC X(22) VALUE "AKALASKA".           05   FILLER    PIC X(22) VALUE "NENEBRASKA".
    05  FILLER    PIC X(22) VALUE "ALALABAMA".          05   FILLER    PIC X(22) VALUE "NHNEW HAMPSHIRE".
    05  FILLER    PIC X(22) VALUE "ARARKANSAS".         05   FILLER    PIC X(22) VALUE "NJNEW JERSEY".
    05  FILLER    PIC X(22) VALUE "AZARIZONA".          05   FILLER    PIC X(22) VALUE "NMNEW MEXICO".
    05  FILLER    PIC X(22) VALUE "CACALIFORNIA".       05   FILLER    PIC X(22) VALUE "NVNEVADA".
    05  FILLER    PIC X(22) VALUE "COCOLORADO".         05   FILLER    PIC X(22) VALUE "NYNEW YORK".
    05  FILLER    PIC X(22) VALUE "CTCONNECTICUT".      05   FILLER    PIC X(22) VALUE "OHOHIO".
    05  FILLER    PIC X(22) VALUE "DCDISTRICT OF COLUMBIA".  05  FILLER  PIC X(22) VALUE "OKOKLAHOMA".
    05  FILLER    PIC X(22) VALUE "DEDELAWARE".         05   FILLER    PIC X(22) VALUE "OROREGON".
    05  FILLER    PIC X(22) VALUE "FLFLORIDA".          05   FILLER    PIC X(22) VALUE "PAPENNSYLVANIA".
    05  FILLER    PIC X(22) VALUE "GAGEORGIA".          05   FILLER    PIC X(22) VALUE "RIRHODE ISLAND".
    05  FILLER    PIC X(22) VALUE "HIHAWAII".           05   FILLER    PIC X(22) VALUE "SCSOUTH CAROLINA".
    05  FILLER    PIC X(22) VALUE "IAIOWA".             05   FILLER    PIC X(22) VALUE "SDSOUTH DAKOTA".
    05  FILLER    PIC X(22) VALUE "IDIDAHO".            05   FILLER    PIC X(22) VALUE "TNTENNESSEE".
    05  FILLER    PIC X(22) VALUE "ILILLINOIS".         05   FILLER    PIC X(22) VALUE "TXTEXAS".
    05  FILLER    PIC X(22) VALUE "ININDIANA".          05   FILLER    PIC X(22) VALUE "UTUTAH".
    05  FILLER    PIC X(22) VALUE "KSKANSAS".           05   FILLER    PIC X(22) VALUE "VAVIRGINIA".
    05  FILLER    PIC X(22) VALUE "KYKENTUCKY".         05   FILLER    PIC X(22) VALUE "VTVERMONT".
    05  FILLER    PIC X(22) VALUE "LALOUISIANA".        05   FILLER    PIC X(22) VALUE "WAWASHINGTON".
    05  FILLER    PIC X(22) VALUE "MAMASSACHUSETTS".    05   FILLER    PIC X(22) VALUE "WIWISCONSIN".
    05  FILLER    PIC X(22) VALUE "MDMARYLAND".         05   FILLER    PIC X(22) VALUE "WVWEST VIRGINIA".
    05  FILLER    PIC X(22) VALUE "MEMAINE".            05   FILLER    PIC X(22) VALUE "WYWYOMING".
    05  FILLER    PIC X(22) VALUE "MIMICHIGAN".    01  ST-STATE-TABLE REDEFINES ST-STATE-DATA.
    05  FILLER    PIC X(22) VALUE "MNMINNESOTA".        05   ST-STATE-ENTRY            OCCURS 51 TIMES.
    05  FILLER    PIC X(22) VALUE "MOMISSOURI".             10   ST-STATE-ABBREVIATION    PIC X(2).
    05  FILLER    PIC X(22) VALUE "MSMISSISSIPPI".          10   ST-STATE-NAME            PIC X(20).
    05  FILLER    PIC X(22) VALUE "MTMONTANA".      Redefined
    05  FILLER    PIC X(22) VALUE "NCNORTH CAROLINA".  table argument          Redefined
                                                                                table function
```

Notice in the table redefinition that the OCCURS clause has been specified at the group level for the ST-STATE-ENTRY data-item. Specification of the OCCURS clause at the group level causes all elementary fields within the group to occur that number of times. An alternative approach is the subject of a question at the end of the chapter.

Serial Lookups

In COBOL, three alternative statements can be used to drive the logic that steps through a table for a **serial lookup**: the PERFORM statement with the UNTIL phrase, the PERFORM statement with the VARYING phrase, or the SEARCH statement. An example of each of these lookup "drivers" is illustrated in examples that follow.

Regardless of which statement (or which programming language, for that matter) is used, four functions must be handled to perform a table lookup:

1. Initializing the field (in COBOL, the subscript or the index) used to step through the table.

2. Testing for correspondence between the search argument and the table argument.

3. Testing to determine if the end of the table has been reached.

4. Incrementing (or decrementing) the subscript or the index.

These functions are shown in flowchart form in Figure 11-13. Coding examples for a serial table lookup using each of the three table-lookup drivers will be presented.

PERFORM/UNTIL Statement Driver

An example of a serial table lookup using a PERFORM/UNTIL statement driver is shown in Figure 11-14. Observe that an additional 01-level entry—ST-TABLE-CONTROLS—has been established in the DATA DIVISION. It contains two fields that are used to control the lookup process: ST-ENTRY-FOUND-SWITCH and ST-SUBSCRIPT. Although it is not necessary to set aside a separate 01-level entry such as this, establishment of a dedicated area—near the table—for these fields is an aid to good program organization and facilitates program maintenance.

DATA DIVISION Coding.   The ST-ENTRY-FOUND-SWITCH is used to keep track of when either the desired table entry is found or when the end of the table has been reached. The condition-name ST-STILL-LOOKING—a switch value of "NO"—is used to indicate the condition in which the entry has not yet been located. If the entry is located, the switch is set to "YES"—the ST-ENTRY-FOUND condition. To signal the ST-END-OF-TABLE condition, the switch is set to "END".

The ST-SUBSCRIPT field is used, of course, as the subscript to step through the table. Notice that it has been assigned a picture clause of PIC S9(4) with COMP SYNC usage (remember that the word USAGE is optional). Specification as a signed field and with COMP SYNC usage provides processing efficiency.

PROCEDURE DIVISION Coding.   Since a table-lookup action is one that may be executed from several places in a program, it makes sense to code it as a separate module, then PERFORM that module when needed. Thus, we must deal with two sections of code. One section is the lookup module itself, which contains the

Figure 11-13   Serial table-lookup logic.

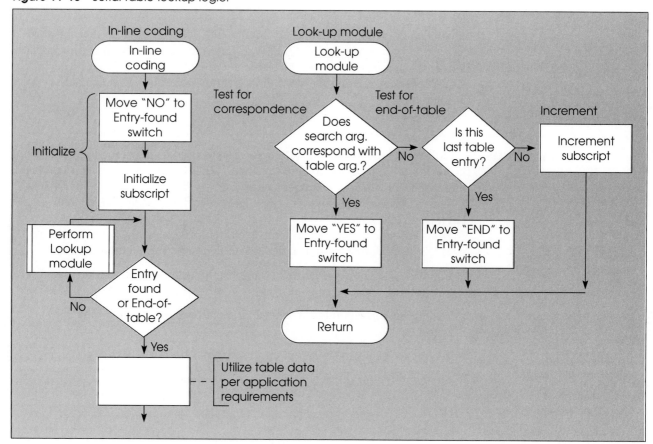

Figure 11-14   Serial table-lookup coding: PERFORM/UNTIL driver.

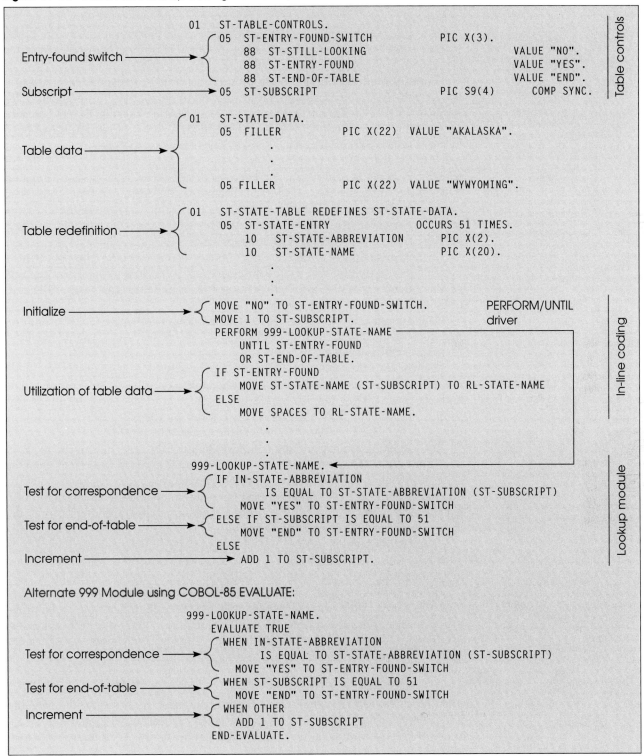

Alternate 999 Module using COBOL-85 EVALUATE:

required code to search the table. The other section is that portion of the code in the program that transfers control to the lookup module and accesses the table data upon return. We can think of the latter as the *in-line coding*.

In-line coding. Before performing the lookup module, the first step (in the in-line coding) is to initialize the table control fields in preparation for the table lookup. The ST-ENTRY-FOUND-SWITCH is set to "NO" and the ST-SUBSCRIPT is set to 1. Then the table-lookup module—999-LOOKUP-STATE-NAME—is performed.

The PERFORM/UNTIL statement is coded so that iterations of the table-lookup module will continue until either the entry is found or the end of the table is reached.

Lookup module. In the lookup module, a test for correspondence between the search argument and the table argument is made. If the IN-STATE-ABBREVIATION field is equal to the ST-STATE-ABBREVIATION field as subscripted by the ST-SUBSCRIPT field, the desired state abbreviation has been located and the ST-ENTRY-FOUND-SWITCH is thus set to "YES".

If the search argument is not equal to the table argument, an end-of-table test is made. Because the table contains 51 entries, the ST-SUBSCRIPT field is compared to 51. If the subscript is equal to 51, it means that the search argument has been compared against all 51 table entries, but no table argument matches the search argument. Therefore, to indicate that the end of the table has been reached, the ST-ENTRY-FOUND-SWITCH is set to "END".

If neither the correspondence nor the end-of-table occurs, the subscript is incremented in preparation for the next iteration of this lookup module. Iteration of this module continues until either the search argument is matched or the end-of-table is detected.

Lookup module—COBOL-85. The COBOL-85 version of the look-up modules functions identically to the COBOL-74 version. The EVALUATE statement allows for slightly cleaner code.

Return to in-line coding. After execution returns to the next consecutive statement following the PERFORM/UNTIL, the table data is extracted from the table and used. You can see that if a table argument matching the search argument was found, the ST-STATE-NAME field subscripted by the ST-SUBSCRIPT field is moved to the RL-STATE-NAME field in the report line.

If a matching table argument is not located, the IN-STATE-ABBREVIATION field is moved to the report-line field. Failure to locate a match will occur when the state abbreviation is miskeyed or if the field contains a foreign designator, such as a Canadian province. Of course, in most cases, failure to make a match should trigger the identification of an error condition. The unmatched-argument processing shown was chosen to simplify the example.

Some programmers retrieve the table data in the lookup module, rather than after return to the in-line coding, as has been shown in the example. However, by waiting until return to the in-line coding, the same lookup module can be used for different lookup data needs. That is, the lookup routine will be needed at multiple points in the program when either (1) the same function must be transferred to different receiving fields at different times, or (2) multiple functions, needed at different times, are present. Hence, the approach shown in which the table data is retrieved in the in-line coding is recommended and is used for the examples in this text.

Improved Lookup Coding.   The lookup coding just discussed is adequate and will provide proper processing. It was presented first because it is straightforward and will help to contrast a few finer coding points. Figure 11-15 shows the same lookup with three improvements.

Table limit field in WORKING-STORAGE. Observe that a field for the number of table entries has been added to the ST-TABLE-CONTROLS area. This table limit field—ST-NUMBER-OF-ENTRIES—has been assigned a VALUE of +51 to indicate that there are 51 entries in the table.

ST-NUMBER-OF-ENTRIES can be used to advantage in the end-of-table test in the PROCEDURE DIVISION instead of the numeric literal 51. Since this field will be compared to the subscript, it has been given a picture clause of PIC S9(4) and a COMP SYNC usage so that it will be consistent with the ST-SUBSCRIPT field.

Figure 11-15 Improved serial table-lookup coding.

```
                               01  ST-TABLE-CONTROLS.
                                   05  ST-ENTRY-FOUND-SWITCH      PIC X(3).
                                       88 ST-STILL-LOOKING                   VALUE "NO".
                                       88 ST-ENTRY-FOUND                     VALUE "YES".
                                       88 ST-END-OF-TABLE                    VALUE "END".
Table limit                        05  ST-SUBSCRIPT              PIC S9(4)   COMP SYNC.
in WORKING-STORAGE ──────────────► 05  ST-NUMBER-OF-ENTRIES     PIC S9(4) VALUE +51
                                                                            COMP SYNC.


                               01  ST-STATE-DATA.
                                   05  FILLER               PIC X(22) VALUE "AKALASKA".
                                                 .
                                                 .
                                                 .
                                   05  FILLER               PIC X(22) VALUE "WYWYOMING".

                               01  ST-STATE-TABLE REDEFINES ST-STATE-DATA.
                                   05  ST-STATE-ENTRY            OCCURS 51 TIMES.
                                       10 ST-STATE-ABBREVIATION  PIC X(2).
                                       10 ST-STATE-NAME          PIC X(20).
                                                 .
                                                 .
                                                 .
                               MOVE "NO" TO ST-ENTRY-FOUND-SWITCH.            PERFORM/UNTIL
                               MOVE 1 TO ST-SUBSCRIPT.                        driver
                               PERFORM 999-LOOKUP-STATE-NAME ─────────────┐
Single UNTIL condition ──────────► UNTIL NOT ST-STILL-LOOKING.             │
                               IF ST-ENTRY-FOUND                           │
                                   MOVE ST-STATE-NAME (ST-SUBSCRIPT TO RL-STATE-NAME │
                               ELSE                                        │
                                   MOVE SPACES TO RL-STATE-NAME.           │
                                                 .                         │
                                                 .                         │
                                                 .                         │
                               999-LOOKUP-STATE-NAME. ◄────────────────────┘
                               IF IN-STATE-ABBREVIATION
                                       IS EQUAL TO ST-STATE-ABBREVIATION (ST-SUBSCRIPT)
                                   MOVE "YES" TO ST-ENTRY-FOUND-SWITCH
Improved
end-of-table test ─────────────► ELSE IF ST-SUBSCRIPT IS NOT LESS THAN ST-NUMBER-OF-ENTRIES
                                   MOVE "END" TO ST-ENTRY-FOUND-SWITCH
                               ELSE
                                   ADD 1 TO ST-SUBSCRIPT.
```

Alternate 999 Module using COBOL-85 EVALUATE:

```
                               999-LOOKUP-STATE-NAME.
                               EVALUATE TRUE
                                 WHEN IN-STATE-ABBREVIATION
                                       IS EQUAL TO ST-STATE-ABBREVIATION (ST-SUBSCRIPT)
                                   MOVE "YES" TO ST-ENTRY-FOUND-SWITCH
Improved
end-of-table test ─────────────► WHEN ST-SUBSCRIPT IS NOT LESS THAN ST-NUMBER-OF-ENTRIES
                                   MOVE "END" TO ST-ENTRY-FOUND-SWITCH
                                 WHEN OTHER
                                   ADD 1 TO ST-SUBSCRIPT
                               END-EVALUATE.
```

Program maintenance tasks are eased by using a field within a table control area, rather than a PROCEDURE DIVISION literal for the end-of-table test. Table entries must often be added or deleted, thereby changing the table size. Suppose, for example, that a state were added to the union. This would require increasing the table size—and the table limit in the end-of-table test—to 52 entries. It is much easier to change one table limit coded at a standard spot near the table in the DATA DIVISION, rather than to search through the PROCEDURE DIVISION looking for places where the table limit has been specified with the literal 51.

Single UNTIL condition. Observe that the combined condition ST-ENTRY-FOUND OR ST-END-OF-TABLE can be replaced by the single negated condition NOT ST-STILL-LOOKING. This is cleaner, more easily understood code.

End-of-table test relation operator. Notice also that the IS EQUAL TO operator has been replaced by a NOT LESS THAN operator. It is a good defensive programming practice to form a relationship test that will also end iterations should the subscript erroneously—due to a programming bug—get set to a value beyond the range of the table.

PERFORM/VARYING Statement Driver

Figure 11-16 shows the format for the PERFORM statement with the VARYING phrase. A PERFORM/VARYING statement driver can be used as an alternative to the PERFORM/UNTIL statement for a serial table lookup. Notice that both initializing and incrementing the subscript are handled by the PERFORM/VARYING statement itself; you need not code separate statements to handle these functions.

When the PERFORM/VARYING statement is executed, the field specified in the VARYING phrase is first initialized to the value specified in the FROM phrase. Then, the condition coded in the UNTIL phrase is tested. Like the PERFORM/UNTIL statement, if the condition is false—has not yet occurred—the named procedure is performed. When the condition is true, program control flows to the next consecutive statement.

A state-name lookup using the PERFORM/VARYING statement is shown in Figure 11-17. There is one tricky thing about using PERFORM/VARYING for a lookup module. If the subscript is being used after return to the in-line coding (which is typically the case when the lookup module is coded as an independent module, as is done in this text), then it must be decremented by 1 to reset it to the proper occurrence number. Hence, the statement SUBTRACT 1 FROM ST-SUBSCRIPT is needed in the state-name lookup coding.

Figure 11-16
PERFORM/VARYING
statement format.

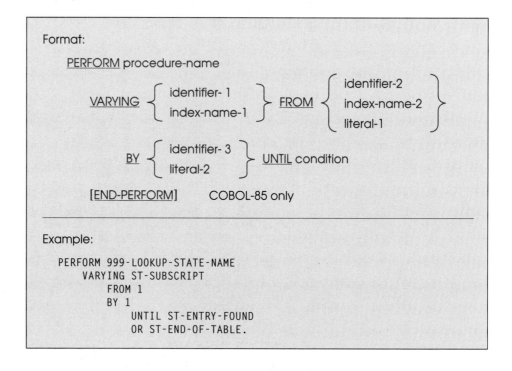

```
Format:

    PERFORM procedure-name

    VARYING  { identifier-1  }  FROM  { identifier-2   }
             { index-name-1  }        { index-name-2   }
                                      { literal-1      }

          BY { identifier-3 }  UNTIL condition
             { literal-2    }

    [END-PERFORM]    COBOL-85 only
```

```
Example:

    PERFORM 999-LOOKUP-STATE-NAME
        VARYING ST-SUBSCRIPT
            FROM 1
            BY 1
                UNTIL ST-ENTRY-FOUND
                OR ST-END-OF-TABLE.
```

Figure 11-17   Serial table-lookup coding: PERFORM/VARYING driver.

```
                          01  ST-TABLE-CONTROLS.
                              05  ST-ENTRY-FOUND-SWITCH        PIC X(3).
                                  88  ST-STILL-LOOKING                     VALUE "NO ".
                                  88  ST-ENTRY-FOUND                       VALUE "YES".
                                  88  ST-END-OF-TABLE                      VALUE "END".
                              05  ST-SUBSCRIPT                PIC S9(4)    COMP SYNC.
                              05  ST-NUMBER-OF-ENTRIES        PIC S9(4)    VALUE +51
                                                                          COMP SYNC.

                          01  ST-STATE-DATA.
                              05  FILLER          PIC X(22) VALUE "AKALASKA".
                                         .
                                         .
                                         .
                              05  FILLER          PIC X(22) VALUE "WYWYOMING".

                          01  ST-STATE-TABLE REDEFINES ST-STATE-DATA.
                              05  ST-STATE-ENTRY              OCCURS 51 TIMES.
                                  10  ST-STATE-ABBREVIATION   PIC X(2).
                                  10  ST-STATE-NAME           PIC X(20).
                                         .
                                         .                                PERFORM/VARYING
                                         .                                driver
     Initialize ─────────────────→  MOVE "NO" TO ST-ENTRY-FOUND-SWITCH.
                                     PERFORM 999-LOOKUP-STATE-NAME ─────────────────┐
                                         VARYING ST-SUBSCRIPT                        │
                                    ┌──→ FROM 1                                      │
     Increment ─────────────────────→  BY 1                          Decrement by 1 │
                                             UNTIL NOT ST-STILL-LOOKING.   ┌─────────┤
                                     IF ST-ENTRY-FOUND                     │         │
                                         SUBTRACT 1 FROM ST-SUBSCRIPT  ←───┘         │
                                         MOVE ST-STATE-NAME (ST-SUBSCRIPT) TO RL-STATE-NAME
                                     ELSE                                            │
                                         MOVE SPACES TO RL-STATE-NAME.              │
                                         .                                          │
                                         .                                          │
                                     999-LOOKUP-STATE-NAME.  ←──────────────────────┘
                                         IF IN-STATE-ABBREVIATION
                                               IS EQUAL TO ST-STATE-ABBREVIATION (ST-SUBSCRIPT)
     No ELSE here because               MOVE "YES" TO ST-ENTRY-FOUND-SWITCH
     no incrementing in             ELSE IF ST-SUBSCRIPT IS NOT LESS THAN ST-NUMBER-OF-ENTRIES
     lookup module ──────────────→      MOVE "END" TO ST-ENTRY-FOUND-SWITCH.
```

Alternate 999 Module using COBOL-85 EVALUATE:

```
                                     999-LOOKUP-STATE-NAME.
                                         EVALUATE TRUE
                                            WHEN IN-STATE-ABBREVIATION
                                                  IS EQUAL TO ST-STATE-ABBREVIATION (ST-SUBSCRIPT)
                                               MOVE "YES" TO ST-ENTRY-FOUND-SWITCH
                                            WHEN ST-SUBSCRIPT IS NOT LESS THAN ST-NUMBER-OF-ENTRIES
     WHEN OTHER option                         MOVE "END" TO ST-ENTRY-FOUND-SWITCH
     not needed ─────────────────→     END-EVALUATE.
```

Decrementing by one is required because of the manner in which the BY phrase logic is handled. Figure 11-18 illustrates the PERFORM/VARYING statement logic. Observe that the VARYING field is incremented after each iteration of the performed module. This means that, after the match occurs, the subscript will be incremented upon return to the PERFORM/VARYING statement. Then the UNTIL condition will be tested and found to be satisfied (the NOT ST-STILL-LOOKING condition is true; the entry has been found). As a result, after program control flows to the next consecutive statement in the in-line coding, the subscript will be pointing to the next higher, rather than the matching, table entry. (Of course, decrementing is not applicable when the table data is extracted in the lookup module.)

SEARCH Statement Driver

The SEARCH statement is specifically designed for table lookup. However, to use it, an index must be associated with the table in the DATA DIVISION. Index formats are shown in Figure 11-19.

The INDEXED BY Clause. When the INDEXED BY clause is coded with the OCCURS clause, a user-defined index-name is specified. This index-name is then used in the PROCEDURE DIVISION like a subscript to identify a specific occurrence within the table.

There are four important differences between indexes and subscripts. First, when an index-name is specified in the INDEXED BY clause, the compiler automatically provides for the index. The programmer does not code a separate data-item in the DATA DIVISION, as is done for a variable subscript.

Figure 11-18 PERFORM/VARYING statement logic.

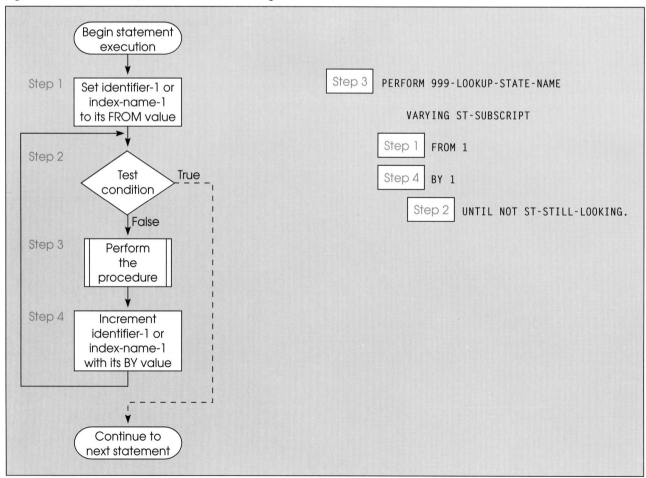

Figure 11-19
Index formats.

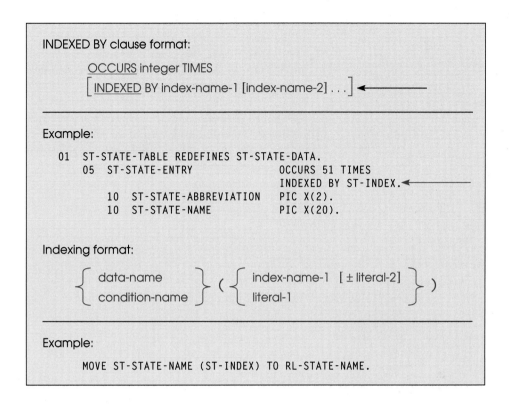

INDEXED BY clause format:

```
    OCCURS integer TIMES
    [ INDEXED BY index-name-1 [index-name-2] . . . ]
```

Example:

```
01  ST-STATE-TABLE REDEFINES ST-STATE-DATA.
    05  ST-STATE-ENTRY                OCCURS 51 TIMES
                                      INDEXED BY ST-INDEX.
        10  ST-STATE-ABBREVIATION  PIC X(2).
        10  ST-STATE-NAME          PIC X(20).
```

Indexing format:

```
    {  data-name       }  (  { index-name-1 [ ± literal-2] }  )
    {  condition-name  }     { literal-1                    }
```

Example:

```
    MOVE ST-STATE-NAME (ST-INDEX) TO RL-STATE-NAME.
```

Second, indexes contain **displacement values**, whereas subscripts are used for the storage of **occurrence numbers**. Displacement refers to the number of positions away from the starting position of the table. Using the month-abbreviation table as an example, Figure 11-20 contrasts subscript occurrence numbers with index displacement values.

Third, since index values are different from normal occurrence values, an index cannot be initialized with the MOVE statement like a subscript is. Similarly, arithmetic statements—such as ADD and SUBTRACT—cannot be used to increment or decrement an index. Instead, the SET statement is provided to initialize, increment, and decrement the index. (If you are using RM/COBOL-85 and studied Chapter 9, you already saw a Ryan-McFarland implementation of this statement.)

Figure 11-20
Subscript occurrence numbers contrasted with index displacement values.

Table entry	Occurrence number (subscript value)	Displacement (index value)
JAN	1 (First occurrence)	0 (Zero bytes away from
FEB	2	3 the start of the table)
MAR	3	6
APR	4	9
MAY	5	12
JUN	6	15
JUL	7	18
AUG	8	21
SEP	9	24
OCT	10	27
NOV	11	30
DEC	12	33

Fourth, indexes can be specified with **relative indexing** by coding, after the index-name, a plus or minus sign followed by an integer literal. For example, the ST-STATE-NAME field could be indexed by (ST-INDEX + 1) to access the next, rather than the current, entry in the table. Relative addressing is seldom used, but is convenient for certain applications.

The SET Statement.   The SET statement format is shown in Figure 11-21. Format-1 is used for initializing an index. This format converts occurrence numbers to index displacement values, and vice versa. Format-2 is used for incrementing and decrementing an index.

Figure 11-21   SET statement format.

Format-1:

$$\text{\underline{SET}} \left\{ \begin{array}{l} \text{identifier-1 [identifier-2]} \dots \\ \text{index-name-1 [index-name-2]} \dots \end{array} \right\} \text{\underline{TO}} \left\{ \begin{array}{l} \text{identifier-3} \\ \text{index-name-3} \\ \text{integer-1} \end{array} \right\}$$

Format-2:

$$\text{SET index-name-1 [index-name-2]} \dots \left\{ \begin{array}{l} \text{\underline{UP BY}} \\ \text{\underline{DOWN BY}} \end{array} \right\} \left\{ \begin{array}{l} \text{identifier-1} \\ \text{integer-1} \end{array} \right\}$$

Examples:

```
SET ST-INDEX TO 1. ◄─────────────── Initializes index
SET ST-INDEX UP BY 1. ◄─────────────── Increments index
SET ST-INDEX DOWN BY 1. ◄─────────────── Decrements index
```

Form: SET receiving-field TO sending-field

Receiving-field	Sending-field		
	Integer or numeric identifier	**Index**	**Index data-item**
Index	Index set to index value corresponding to occurrence number of sending-field	Index set to index value corresponding to occurrence number of sending-field	Index data-item moved to index data-item without conversion
Numeric identifier	Illegal	Numeric identifier set to occurrence number corresponding to index value	Illegal
Index data-item	Illegal	Index moved to index data-item without conversion	Index data-item moved to index data-item without conversion

The Format-1 (Serial) SEARCH Statement. After a table has been established with the INDEXED BY clause, the SEARCH statement can be used to look up table entries. The Format-1 SEARCH statement is used for a serial search; its format is shown in Figure 11-22.

When a Format-1 SEARCH statement is executed, the table specified as identifier-1 is stepped through, entry by entry, until the condition expressed in the WHEN phrase is satisfied. Once a true condition occurs, the search ends. If end-of-table is reached, the condition has not been satisfied, and thus the action or actions specified in the AT END phrase are executed. If multiple WHEN phrases are specified, the search will end whenever any one of the conditions is satisfied; this effect is similar to conditions joined in an OR relationship.

With the SEARCH statement, therefore, index incrementing is handled automatically; the test for correspondence is accomplished by the WHEN phrase; and the end-of-table processing is specified in the AT END phrase. Initializing the index must be handled by coding a SET statement—typically immediately before the SEARCH statement—as is shown in the state table-lookup example that appears in Figure 11-23.

Because the ST-STILL-LOOKING condition is not applicable to a SEARCH statement lookup, it has been omitted from the ST-ENTRY-FOUND-SWITCH specifications. The lookup iterations are driven automatically by the SEARCH statement; there is no need to initialize the switch to the still-looking condition. After execution of the SEARCH statement, the entry-found switch will be set to either "YES" or "END".

Figure 11-22
Serial (Format-1) SEARCH
statement format.

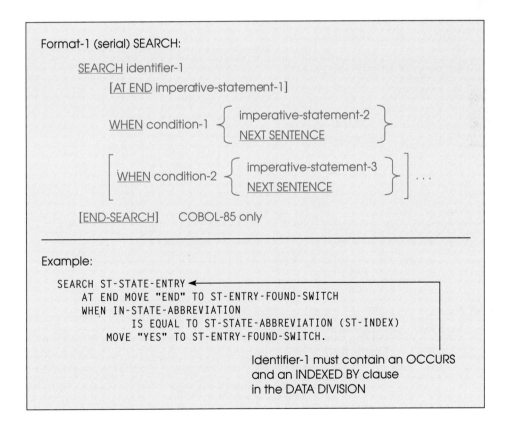

Figure 11-23   Serial table-lookup coding: SEARCH driver.

```
                                   01  ST-TABLE-CONTROLS.
                                       05  ST-ENTRY-FOUND-SWITCH        PIC X(3).
(No subscript field needed                 88  ST-ENTRY-FOUND                VALUE "YES".
because an index must be used)             88  ST-END-OF-TABLE               VALUE "END".

(No table-limit field needed       01  ST-STATE-DATA.
with SEARCH statement)                 05  FILLER               PIC X(22) VALUE "AKALASKA".
                                           .
                                           .
                                           .
                                       05  FILLER               PIC X(22) VALUE "WYWYOMING".

                                   01  ST-STATE-TABLE REDEFINES ST-STATE-DATA.
                                       05  ST-STATE-ENTRY               OCCURS 51 TIMES
Index definition                                                        INDEXED BY ST-INDEX.
                                           10  ST-STATE-ABBREVIATION    PIC X(2).
                                           10  ST-STATE-NAME            PIC X(20).
                                           .
                                           .
                                   PERFORM 999-LOOKUP-STATE-NAME.
                                   IF ST-ENTRY-FOUND
                                       MOVE ST-STATE-NAME (ST-INDEX) TO RL-STATE-NAME
                                   ELSE
                                       MOVE SPACES TO RL-STATE-NAME.
                                           .
                                           .
                                           .
                                   999-LOOKUP-STATE-NAME.
                                       SET ST-INDEX TO 1.                         SEARCH
Initialize                             SEARCH ST-STATE-ENTRY                      driver
Test for end-of-table                    AT END MOVE "END" TO ST-ENTRY-FOUND-SWITCH
Test for correspondence                  WHEN IN-STATE-ABBREVIATION
                                             IS EQUAL TO ST-STATE-ABBREVIATION (ST-INDEX)
                                           MOVE "YES" TO ST-ENTRY-FOUND-SWITCH.
```

Alternate COBOL-85 999 Module:

```
                                   999-LOOKUP-STATE-NAME.
                                       SET ST-INDEX TO 1
                                       SEARCH ST-STATE-ENTRY
                                         AT END MOVE "END" TO ST-ENTRY-FOUND-SWITCH
                                         WHEN IN-STATE-ABBREVIATION
                                             IS EQUAL TO ST-STATE-ABBREVIATION (ST-INDEX)
Add the scope terminator                   MOVE "YES" TO ST-ENTRY-FOUND-SWITCH
(not necessary in this example)        END-SEARCH.
```

Serial Lookups with Early Exit

In certain table-processing situations, not all search arguments will have matching table arguments. Some examples are tables used to validate the existence of a code and cases in which a default value is assigned to nonmatching search arguments. When a sequentially organized table has a significant number of search arguments that are not matched in the table arguments, a **serial lookup with early exit** will provide a more efficient serial search. Coding for such a lookup of the state table is shown in Figure 11-24. (Early exit processing cannot be used for tables organized randomly or by usage frequency.)

Figure 11-24   Serial table lookup with early exit coding.

```
                                01  ST-TABLE-CONTROLS.
                                    05  ST-ENTRY-FOUND-SWITCH      PIC X(3).
(No table limit field               88  ST-STILL-LOOKING                  VALUE "NO".
needed because of                   88  ST-ENTRY-FOUND                    VALUE "YES".
dummy end-of-table entry)           88  ST-END-OF-TABLE                   VALUE "END".

                                01  ST-STATE-DATA.
                                    05  FILLER                 PIC X(22) VALUE "AKALASKA".
                                                .
                                                .
                                                .
                                    05  FILLER                 PIC X(22) VALUE "WYWYOMING".
Dummy end-of-table entry            05  FILLER                 PIC X(22) VALUE HIGH-VALUES.

                                01  ST-STATE-TABLE REDEFINES ST-STATE-DATA.
                                    05  ST-STATE-ENTRY             OCCURS 52 TIMES
                                                                  INDEXED BY ST-INDEX.
                                        10  ST-STATE-ABBREVIATION  PIC X(2).
                                        10  ST-STATE-NAME          PIC X(20).
                                                .
                                                .
                                                .
                                    MOVE "NO" TO ST-ENTRY-FOUND-SWITCH.
                                    PERFORM 999-LOOKUP-STATE-NAME
                                        VARYING ST-INDEX
                                            FROM 1
                                            BY 1
                                                UNTIL NOT ST-STILL-LOOKING.
                                    IF ST-ENTRY-FOUND
                                        SET ST-INDEX DOWN BY 1
                                        MOVE ST-STATE-NAME (ST-INDEX) TO RL-STATE-NAME
                                    ELSE
                                        MOVE SPACES TO RL-STATE-NAME.
                                                .
                                                .
                                                .
                                    999-LOOKUP-STATE-NAME.
                                        IF IN-STATE-ABBREVIATION
The table argument is lower                 IS GREATER THAN ST-STATE-ABBREVIATION (ST-INDEX)
than the search argument                NEXT-SENTENCE
                                        ELSE IF IN-STATE-ABBREVIATION
                                                IS EQUAL TO ST-STATE-ABBREVIATION (ST-INDEX)
Arguments match                         MOVE "YES" TO ST-ENTRY-FOUND-SWITCH
Arguments match                         ELSE
All remaining table arguments           MOVE "END" TO ST-ENTRY-FOUND-SWITCH.
are higher in value
```

Alternate 999 Module using COBOL-85 EVALUATE:

```
                                    999-LOOKUP-STATE-NAME.
                                        EVALUATE IN-STATE-ABBREVIATION
No action if table argument             WHEN GREATER THAN ST-STATE-ABBREVIATION (ST-INDEX)
lower than search argument

                                        WHEN EQUAL TO ST-STATE-ABBREVIATION (ST-INDEX)
Arguments match                             MOVE "YES" TO ST-ENTRY-FOUND-SWITCH
                                        WHEN OTHER
All remaining table arguments               MOVE "END" TO ST-ENTRY-FOUND-SWITCH
are higher value                        END-EVALUATE.
```

DATA DIVISION Coding

Observe that the number of entries in the table has been increased to 52. This results from the **dummy end-of-table entry**, containing HIGH-VALUES, that has been added as the last table entry. As will be explained in the PROCEDURE DIVISION coding, this final table entry will facilitate detection of the end of the table. When a dummy end-of-table entry is provided together with appropriate lookup logic, there is no need for a field—such as ST-NUMBER-OF-ENTRIES—to specify the number of table entries.

A dummy end-of-table entry is sometimes used for serial lookups without early exit, also. The advantage of a dummy end-of-table entry is that it eliminates the need to maintain the number-of-entries field. This, in turn, removes the chance that a program bug might arise due to the programmer's failure to update the number-of-entries field when entries are added to or deleted from the table.

PROCEDURE DIVISION Coding

In the lookup module, observe that the first IF statement of the correspondence test checks to see if the search argument IS GREATER THAN the table argument. If this condition is true, it means that the search argument is a higher value and, if present, will be located further on in the list of table entries. In other words, there are still more table entries to be searched. Hence, the subscript is incremented, that iteration of the lookup module is exited, and the module will be performed again.

If the search argument is not greater, it is tested to see if it IS EQUAL TO the table argument. If it is, the matching table entry has been found, so the entry-found switch is set to "YES" and the lookup module is exited. Recognize that this nested-IF equal relation test will be executed only once during any lookup—when either the matching table argument is found or the end-of-table is reached. (When stepping through the table, the lookup module will always exit from the prior greater-than relation test until the last iteration.)

If the search argument is neither greater than nor equal to the table argument, it means that—since the table arguments are in ascending sequence—a matching table argument will not be found in the table. In this case, the entry-found switch is set to "END" and the lookup module is exited. Again, recognize that this nested-IF less-than relation test will be either executed only once (when end-of-table is reached) during a lookup or not at all (when a matching table argument is located).

The dummy end-of-table entry is required to ensure that this processing will be correctly handled when the search argument is greater in value than the last actual table argument; the HIGH-VALUES dummy entry will force this action to be taken. (When HIGH-VALUES is used for a dummy table entry, you must be careful to ensure that the search and table arguments are defined as alphanumeric fields; otherwise, a data exception might occur when the correspondence test is made.)

Binary Search Lookups

A **binary search** can either be coded by the programmer or handled through the Format-2 SEARCH statement. However, not only is the programmer-coded logic complex, but the SEARCH statement can provide more efficient processing. As a result, almost all programmers use the SEARCH statement when a binary search is needed. A binary search requires specification of (1) the KEY clause in the DATA DIVISION and (2) the ALL phrase in the SEARCH statement in the PROCEDURE DIVISION.

The KEY Clause

When a table is to be used in a binary search, the KEY clause must be specified to indicate whether the table arguments are arranged in ASCENDING or DESCENDING sequence. The KEY clause format and an example for the state table are shown in Figure 11-25.

Recognize that specification of the KEY clause does not actually cause the table arguments to be arranged in ascending or descending order. It is the programmer's

Figure 11-25
KEY clause format.

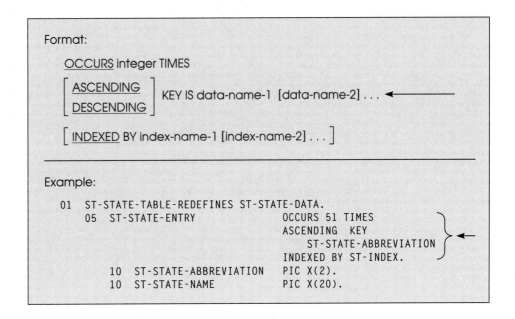

```
Format:

    OCCURS integer TIMES

    ⎡ ASCENDING  ⎤
    ⎢           ⎥  KEY IS data-name-1 [data-name-2] . . .  ◄──────────
    ⎣ DESCENDING ⎦

    [ INDEXED BY index-name-1 [index-name-2] . . . ]
```
_____
```
Example:

    01  ST-STATE-TABLE-REDEFINES ST-STATE-DATA.
        05  ST-STATE-ENTRY              OCCURS 51 TIMES    ⎫
                                        ASCENDING  KEY     ⎬ ◄──
                                            ST-STATE-ABBREVIATION ⎭
                                        INDEXED BY ST-INDEX.
            10  ST-STATE-ABBREVIATION  PIC X(2).
            10  ST-STATE-NAME          PIC X(20).
```

responsibility to make certain that the table is actually arranged in accordance with the KEY clause specifications.

The Format-2 (Binary) SEARCH Statement

The Format-2 SEARCH statement is used to provide a binary search. Its format is shown in Figure 11-26.

Figure 11-26
Binary (Format-2) SEARCH statement format.

```
Format-2 (binary) SEARCH:

SEARCH ALL identifier-1 [AT END imperative-statement-1]

              ⎧             ⎧ IS EQUAL TO ⎫ ⎧ identifier-3            ⎫ ⎫
    WHEN      ⎨ data-name-1 ⎨             ⎬ ⎨ literal-1               ⎬ ⎬
              ⎩             ⎩ IS =        ⎭ ⎩ arithmetic-expression-1 ⎭ ⎭
                condition-name-1

    ⎡         ⎧             ⎧ IS EQUAL TO ⎫ ⎧ identifier-4            ⎫ ⎫ ⎤
    ⎢ AND     ⎨ data-name-2 ⎨             ⎬ ⎨ literal-2               ⎬ ⎬ ⎥ . . .
    ⎣         ⎩             ⎩ IS =        ⎭ ⎩ arithmetic-expression-2 ⎭ ⎭ ⎦
                condition-name-2

              ⎧ imperative-statement-2 ⎫
              ⎨ NEXT SENTENCE          ⎬
              ⎩                        ⎭
```
_____
```
Example:

    ┌──► SEARCH ALL ST-STATE-ENTRY ◄────────────────────┐
    │        AT END MOVE "END" TO ST-ENTRY-FOUND-SWITCH │
    │        WHEN ST-STATE-ABBREVIATION (ST-INDEX)      │
    │             IS EQUAL TO IN-STATE-ABBREVIATION     │
    │        MOVE "YES" TO ST-ENTRY-FOUND-SWITCH.       │
```

The first data-name in each
WHEN phrase must be
indexed by the index
associated with identifier-1

Identifier-1 must contain an OCCURS,
an INDEXED BY, and a KEY clause
in the DATA DIVISION

The ALL Clause.   Specification of the reserved word ALL in the SEARCH statement triggers the binary search logic. Because a binary search is more complicated than a serial search, the Format-2 SEARCH statement imposes some coding restrictions that do not apply to the Format-1 SEARCH. The WHEN phrase requires specification of the indexed-key field as the first entry and the condition test is limited to an EQUAL relationship. If multiple WHEN conditions are required, they must be connected with AND operators. This means that all WHEN conditions must be satisfied for the SEARCH to end prior to end-of-table. Unlike the Format-1 SEARCH statement, if multiple WHEN conditions are coded for a binary search, the reserved word WHEN is not repeated.

When ALL is specified to obtain a binary search, index initialization is handled automatically by the SEARCH statement. Thus, the programmer need not code a SET statement as he or she must do for the Format-1 serial SEARCH statement.

Figure 11-27 shows coding for a binary search state-table lookup. Observe that the fields coded in the WHEN statement are transposed from that shown for the Format-1 serial SEARCH lookup (Figure 11-23). This coding change is required to comply with the requirement that the data-name with the index be specified first.

Figure 11-27   Binary search table-lookup coding: SEARCH ALL driver.

```
                     01  ST-TABLE-CONTROLS.
                         05  ST-ENTRY-FOUND-SWITCH        PIC X(3).
                             88 ST-ENTRY-FOUND                VALUE "YES".
                             88 ST-END-OF-TABLE               VALUE "END".

                     01  ST-STATE-DATA.
                         05  FILLER              PIC X(22) VALUE "AKALASKA".
                             .
                             .
                             .
                         05  FILLER              PIC X(22) VALUE "WYWYOMING".

                     01  ST-STATE-TABLE REDEFINES ST-STATE-DATA.
                         05  ST-STATE-ENTRY           ⎧  OCCURS 51 TIMES
Key definition ─────────────────────────────────→  ⎨  ASCENDING KEY
                                                     ⎩      ST-STATE-ABBREVIATION
                                                        INDEXED BY ST-INDEX.
                             10  ST-STATE-ABBREVIATION   PIC X(2).
                             10  ST-STATE-NAME           PIC X(20).
                                 .
                                 .
                     PERFORM 999-LOOKUP-STATE-NAME.
                     IF ST-ENTRY-FOUND
                         MOVE ST-STATE-NAME (ST-INDEX) TO RL-STATE-NAME
                     ELSE
                         MOVE SPACES TO RL-STATE-NAME.
                             .
                             .
(Initialization of index not needed      .
for binary search) ───────────────  999-LOOKUP-STATE-NAME.
                                                                        SEARCH ALL
ALL phrase for binary search ──────→  SEARCH ALL ST-STATE-ENTRY ←──────── driver
                                          AT END MOVE "END" TO ST-ENTRY-FOUND-SWITCH
                                          WHEN IN-STATE-ABBREVIATION (ST-INDEX)
                                                  IS EQUAL TO ST-STATE-ABBREVIATION
                                              MOVE "YES" TO ST-ENTRY-FOUND-SWITCH.
```

Chapter Summary

Tables are defined in the WORKING-STORAGE SECTION of the DATA DIVISION and accessed in the PROCEDURE DIVISION. Hard-coded table data is specified with VALUE clauses and then redefined with an OCCURS clause.

Whenever an OCCURS clause is associated with a data-item, either a subscript or an index must be used when referring to that item in the PROCEDURE DIVISION. The subscript or index is used to reference a specific occurrence of a repeated field defined with the OCCURS clause. When used to identify a specific occurrence of a repeated field, the subscript or index is enclosed in parentheses following the name of a field specified with the OCCURS clause (or a field within a group field specified with an OCCURS clause).

A **literal subscript** is an actual integer occurrence number coded within parentheses. A **variable subscript** is much more powerful and thus more frequently used. It is a programmer-defined field; the value contained within the field is used to identify the occurrence number. An **index** is defined in an INDEXED BY clause coded in conjunction with an OCCURS clause.

A **serial lookup** is used to retrieve data from a **sequentially, usage-frequency**, or **randomly organized table**. Four functions must be accommodated in a serial lookup: (1) **initializing** the subscript or index field, (2) **testing for correspondence** between the search argument and the table argument, (3) **testing for end-of-table**, and (4) **incrementing** (or decrementing) the subscript or index. A serial table lookup can be coded with either a (1) **PERFORM/UNTIL statement driver**, (2) **PERFORM/VARYING statement driver**, or (3) **SEARCH statement driver**. Either subscripts or indexes can be used with the PERFORM/UNTIL and PERFORM/VARYING drivers; the SEARCH statement requires an index.

A **serial lookup with early exit** requires that the table be of sequential organization. It is typically coded with either a PERFORM/UNTIL or PERFORM/VARYING statement driver.

A **binary search lookup** also requires that the table be of sequential organization. It is usually coded with a SEARCH statement driver by specifying the KEY clause—together with the OCCURS and INDEXED BY clauses—in the DATA DIVISION data-item description for the table. Then, in the PROCEDURE DIVISION, the ALL phrase is coded to obtain the binary search.

COBOL Language Element Summary

The **OCCURS clause** is used to indicate how many times a particular field, or group of fields, is repeated. The integer coded in the OCCURS clause specifies the number of repetitions. The OCCURS clause:

- Can be used with any data-item description that has a level-number from 02 through 49 (it cannot be used with a 01-level or 77-level item).

- Cannot be used with a data-item that contains a VALUE clause (COBOL-74 restriction only).

A **literal subscript** is an integer numeric literal coded within parentheses to identify a specific occurrence of a repeated field. The value of the literal must not be less than 1 nor greater than the number of occurrences specified in the OCCURS clause for the field being referenced.

A **variable subscript** is a programmer-defined field; the value contained within it is used to identify a specific occurrence of a repeated field. A field used for a subscript must:

- Be an elementary numeric-integer field defined in the DATA DIVISION.

- Contain enough digit positions to accommodate the number of occurrences specified in the OCCURS clause for the field being referenced.

At execution time, the subscript field must contain a value not less than 1 nor greater than the number of occurrences specified in the OCCURS clause for the field being referenced.

An **index** is used much like a subscript, but there are four important differences.

- The index-field area is automatically provided by the compiler when an index-name is specified in the INDEXED BY clause. The programmer does not code a data-item, as must be done for a subscript field.

- Indexes contain **displacement** values; subscripts contain occurrence values.

- Initializing, incrementing, and decrementing of an index must be done with a SET statement. Subscripts are modified by MOVE, ADD, and SUBTRACT statements.

- **Relative indexing** is permitted for indexes.

Style Summary
Table Source

Table data should typically be hard-coded into the program if (1) there are security considerations, or (2) it seldom changes.

Table data should typically be loaded from input records when it is volatile, voluminous, and not sensitive to security considerations.

Table Establishment

Determine the optimum method of table organization for the table: sequential, usage-frequency, or positional.

Arrange the table arguments adjacent to the table function or functions to ease programmer checking, debugging, and maintenance functions.

When hard-coding the table data with VALUE clauses, try to specify a separate data-item for each table entry. This will also ease programmer checking, debugging, and maintenance functions. (If the table entries are long or of varying usages, separate data-items may be required for certain fields of each entry.)

The table coding must contain a REDEFINES clause when the table data has been hard-coded with VALUE clauses. This redefinition portion of the table description will always contain one or more OCCURS clauses.

Indexes usually provide more efficient processing than subscripts. Thus, in most cases, the INDEXED BY clause should be specified and the index should be used in the PROCEDURE DIVISION.

If the table is organized sequentially and contains over 50 entries or so, consider specifying the ASCENDING KEY or DESCENDING KEY clause in accordance with its table-argument sequence, so that a binary search can be made.

For ease of reference, establish table control fields immediately before the table. Fields to be specified in this area will include (1) an entry-found switch, (2) a subscript field (when an index is not used), and (3) a number-of-table-entries field (unless the SEARCH statement or a dummy end-of-table entry is used).

When a subscript is used, processing efficiency will usually be enhanced by specifying COMP SYNC usage. Depending upon the number of entries in the table, specify a picture clause of PIC S9(4) or PIC S9(9).

Table Lookups

Since lookups must sometimes be made at multiple locations in a program, always code the lookup logic as a separate, independent module. (This is similar to the convention that calls for I/O modules to be coded as independent modules.)

Unless your application has some specific needs that are not compatible with the SEARCH statement, use it for serial and binary lookups.

- If the table is organized sequentially and contains over 50 entries or so, use SEARCH ALL to obtain a binary search.

- When doing a serial search, remember to set the index to 1 in the lookup module immediately before the SEARCH statement is specified.

Features in COBOL-85 Not in COBOL-74

VALUE clause permitted with an OCCURS clause. In COBOL-74, a VALUE clause could not be specified within a data-item description that contained an OCCURS clause or was subordinate to an OCCURS clause. COBOL-85 drops this restriction.

Relative subscripting introduced. In COBOL-74, relative indexing is permitted, but relative subscripting is not. COBOL-85 provides for relative subscripting; a variable subscript can be augmented or decremented by literal. For example, given a subscript field named SUBSCRIPT, (SUBSCRIPT + 1) can be coded to reference the next table entry; (SUBSCRIPT − 1) can be coded to reference the immediately prior table entry.

Exercises
Terms for Definition

binary search _____

displacement value _____

dummy end-of-table entry _____

hard-coded table _____

index _____

input-loaded table _____

literal subscript _____

occurrence number _____

PERFORM/UNTIL driver _____

PERFORM/VARYING driver _____

positional addressing _____

positionally organized table _____

randomly organized table _____

relative indexing _____

SEARCH driver _____

SEARCH ALL driver _____

sequentially organized table _____

serial lookup _____

serial lookup with early exit _____

subscript _____

table limit field _____

usage-frequency organized table _____

variable subscript _____

Review Questions

1. To establish a hard-coded table, the table data is entered with

   _____ clauses in the _____ of the
   DATA DIVISION.

2. After hard-coded table data has been established, it must be

   _____ with a data-item description entry containing a(n)

   _____ clause.

3. The OCCURS clause can be specified with level numbers _____

   through _____; it cannot be specified with level-numbers

   _____ and _____.

4. A data-item containing an OCCURS clause cannot contain a(n)

   _____ clause.

5. When an OCCURS clause is associated with a data-item, either a(n)

   _____ or a(n) _____ must be used when
   referring to that data-name in the PROCEDURE DIVISION.

6. Subscripts can be expressed as _____ or

   _____.

7. The value of a subscript is used to identify which _____ of
   the data-item is being referenced.

8. It is generally most efficient to define subscripts with _____
   usage.

9. When a statement containing a subscript is being executed, the value
   contained within the subscript field should not be less than

   _____ nor greater than _____.

10. Specification of an OCCURS clause at the group level causes

    _____.

11. Name three statements that can be used to drive a serial lookup.

    a. _____

    b. _____

    c. _____

12. When a PERFORM/VARYING statement is used as the table-lookup driver
    and the located table function is retrieved after return to the in-line coding,

    the subscript or index must be _____.

13. Data can be accessed from a table with a(n) _____ or a
    subscript.

14. Index-names are defined in the _____ clause.

15. Subscripts are used for the storage of _____ numbers; indexes contain _____ values.

16. Subscripts are usually initialized by a(n) _____ statement; indexes are initialized by a(n) _____ statement.

17. Index data-items may be established by specifying _____ usage.

18. Index data-items cannot be specified with _____ or _____ clauses.

19. When a SEARCH statement reaches the end of the table and the condition expressed in the WHEN phrase has not been satisfied, the _____ phrase is executed.

20. Execution of a SEARCH statement ends when either

_____

or

_____.

21. Identifier-1 specified immediately after the SEARCH verb must be the name of a data-item that contains both a(n) _____ clause and a(n) _____ clause in its data-item description.

22. For a binary search, the _____ clause must be specified for the table in the DATA DIVISION and the _____ phrase must be coded in the SEARCH statement in the PROCEDURE DIVISION.

23. If multiple WHEN phrases are specified for a serial SEARCH, the conditions are in a(n) _____ relationship.

24. If multiple WHEN conditions are specified for a binary SEARCH, the conditions are in a(n) _____ relationship.

Questions Pertaining to Chapter Program Segments

1. Explain what would happen during execution of the sequence in Figure 11-14 if the portion of the condition test OR ST-END-OF-TABLE were omitted.

_____

_____

2. Explain what would happen during execution of the sequence in Figure 11-14 if the last ELSE and the statement ADD 1 TO ST-SUBSCRIPT of the 999 module were omitted.

_____

_____

3. What would be the consequence in the code of Figure 11-15 of accidentally using a VALUE +50 instead of +51 for ST-NUMBER-OF-ENTRIES?

_____

_____

4. What would be the consequence in the code of Figure 11-15 of accidentally using a VALUE +52 instead of +51 for ST-NUMBER-OF-ENTRIES?

_____

_____

5. In the PERFORM varying of Figure 11-17, a programmer accidentally used FROM 2 instead of FROM 1. What is the consequence of this?

_____

_____

6. In coding the lookup of Figure 11-24, a programmer used OCCURS 51 TIMES instead of OCCURS 52 TIMES. Will this be detected by the compiler? Explain the consequences during execution.

_____

_____

7. The DATA DIVISION entries of Figure 11-12 establish the state abbreviation/ name table. That is not the only way to do it. Assume that you are shown the following redefinition of that table in a program. Explain how the value entries would need to be arranged to be compatible with this redefinition.

```
01  ST-STATE-TABLE REDEFINES ST-STATE-DATA.
    05  ST-STATE-ABBREVIATION   PIC X(2) OCCURS 51 TIMES.
    05  ST-STATE-NAME           PIC X(20) OCCURS 51 TIMES.
```

_____

_____

8. Would accessing the state abbreviation/name table in the PROCEDURE DIVISION be any different if it is defined as in Figure 11-12 as opposed to being defined as in Question 7? Justify your answer.

_____

_____

Syntax/Debug
Exercises

```
01  RT-REGION-DATA.
    05  FILLER      PIC X(14)  VALUE "GSGREAT SMOKEY".
    05  FILLER      PIC X(14)  VALUE "RVRIM VIEW".
    05  FILLER      PIC X(14)  VALUE "MEMETROPOLITAN".
    05  FILLER      PIC X(14)  VALUE "HIHINTERLANDS".
    05  FILLER      PIC X(14)  VALUE "LVLAKE VIEW".
01  RT-REGION-TABLE REDEFINES RT-REGION-DATA.
    05  RT-REGION-ENTRY         OCCURS 5 TIMES.
        10  RT-REGION-ABBR      PIC X(2).
        10  RT-REGION-NAME      PIC X(12).
```

The statements that follow refer to the preceding table definition. In the space provided, you are to identify each statement as valid or invalid—if invalid, give the reason. In all cases, assume that other fields mentioned are properly defined (for instance, assume that HOLD-AREA is appropriately defined in working-storage).

1. `MOVE RT-REGION-ENTRY TO HOLD-AREA`

2. `MOVE RT-REGION-NAME TO OUT-AREA`

3. `MOVE "NEW VIEW" TO RT-REGION-NAME (5)`

4. `MOVE RT-REGION-DATA TO SAVE-TABLE`

5. `MOVE RT-REGION-NAME (RT-REGION-ABBR) TO OUT-AREA`

6. `MOVE RT-REGION-NAME (HIGH-VALUES) TO ERROR-MESSAGE`

7. `MOVE RT-REGION-NAME ("HI") TO OUT-AREA`

8. `MOVE RT-REGION-NAME (6) TO OUT-AREA`

9. `MOVE RT-REGION-NAME (ITEM) TO OUT-AREA`

10. `MOVE RT-REGION-NAME (COUNTER) TO OUT-AREA1`
    `ADD 5 TO COUNTER`
    `MOVE RT-REGION-NAME (COUNTER) TO OUT-AREA2`

11. `SET RT-INDEX TO 1`
    `MOVE RT-REGION-NAME (RT-INDEX) TO OUT-AREA`

Programming Assignments

Programming Assignment 11-1: Department-Name Lookup
Background information:
The personnel manager at Silicon Valley Manufacturing would like an employee listing that includes each employee's name, department number, and department name. This can be generated from the Earnings file but, since the record includes only the department number, a table lookup will be required.

Input file: Earnings file (EARNINGS.DAT)

Input-record format:

Positions	Field	Data class	Comments
1–2	Record code	Alphanumeric	Code EM
4–6	Plant code	Numeric	
7–10	Department code	Alphanumeric	
11–19	Employee number	Numeric	
20–31	Employee last name	Alphanumeric	
32–40	Employee first name	Alphanumeric	
41–74	Other data		

Output-report format:

```
          0         1         2         3         4         5         6
 1234567890123456789012345678901234567890123456789012345678901234567890123 4
1
2
3
4 (11-1)    LAST NAME     FIRST NAME           DEPT    DEPARTMENT NAME
5
6          XXXXXXXXXXXX  XXXXXXXXX             9999    XXXXXXXXXXXXXXXXXX
7
8          XXXXXXXXXXXX  XXXXXXXXX             9999    XXXXXXXXXXXXXXXXXX
```

Table data:

Department number	Department name
1000	Administration
1100	Purchasing
1200	Personnel
1300	Advertising
1350	Public Relations
1900	Training
2000	Research and Development
3000	Finance
3500	Data Processing
4000	Manufacturing

Program operations:

1. Process each input earnings record.
2. Print the heading line on the first page and on each following page of the report.
3. For each earnings record, do the following processing:
   a. Use the input department-number field to look up the department name. If the input department number cannot be located in the table, print NO SUCH DEPT NBR in the department-name field of the output report.
   b. Print the detail line in accordance with the print-chart specifications.
4. Double-space each detail line. Provide for a span of 57 lines per page.

Programming Assignment 11-2: Degree-Program Lookup

Background information:

The registrar at the Bayview Institute of Computer Technology would like a list of students and their degree programs. Since the Student file only includes the student's major code (not the degree program), the major code will need to be used for lookup to determine the degree program.

Input file: Student file (STUDENT.DAT)

Input-record format:

Positions	Field	Data class	Comments
1–2	Record code	Numeric	Code 22
12–25	Student last name	Alphanumeric	
26–35	Student first name	Alphanumeric	
39–41	Major code	Numeric	
42–70	Other data		

Output-report format:

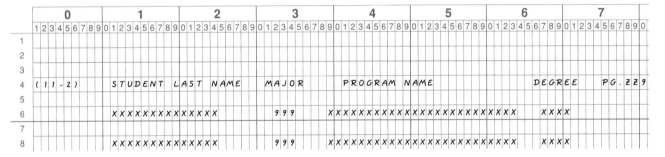

Table data:

Major code	Degree program and degree
100	Accounting (B.S.)
110	Administrative Management (B.S.)
120	Business & Humanities (B.A.)
130	Business Economics (B.A.)
140	Finance (B.S.)
150	Human Relations (B.A.)
160	International Management (B.S.)
170	Industrial Management (B.S.)
180	Marketing (B.S.)
190	Transportation (B.S.)
200	Prelegal Studies (B.A.)
250	Administration of Justice (B.A.)
300	Health Services Mgmt. (B.S.)
400	Hotel & Rest. Mgmt. (B.S.)
500	Information Systems (B.S.)
510	Telecommunications Mgmt. (B.S.)
600	Medical Record Mgmt. (B.S.)
700	Political Science (B.A.)
750	Public Administration (B.A.)
800	Security Management (B.S.)

Program operations:
1. Process each input student record.
2. Print the heading line on the first page and on each following page of the report.
    a. Accumulate and print the page number on the heading line as specified on the print chart.
3. For each student record, do the following processing:
    a. Use the input major-code field to look up the name of the major and the type of degree. If the input major code cannot be located in the table, print MAJOR CODE NOT IN TABLE in the program-name field of the output report and print asterisks in the degree field of the output report.
    b. Print the detail line in accordance with the print-chart specifications.
4. Double-space each detail line. Provide for a span of 57 lines per page.

Programming Assignment 11-3: Region- and Territory-Name Lookup
Background information:

Most of the employees of Follow-the-Sun Sales complain that all reports concerning sales representatives list the computer codes for Region and Territory. The Region is not bad because the codes are easy to recognize; for example, NE means Northeast. On the other hand, the Territory codes are a nuisance; no one ever remembers, for instance, that 1300 is the code for Hawkeye or that 4900 is the code for Mountain. To satisfy this complaint, a program is required that will print the region name and territory name for each salesperson. The staff is hoping that the structure of this program will be incorporated into other salesperson and territory assignment programs.

Input file: Salesperson file (SALESPER.DAT)

Input-record format:

Positions	Field	Data class	Comments
1–2	Record code	Numeric	Code 25
3–4	Salesperson region	Alphanumeric	
5–8	Salesperson territory	Numeric	
9–11	Salesperson number	Numeric	
12–37	Salesperson name	Numeric	
38–79	Other data		

Output-report format:

Table data:

Region

Code	Name
NE	Northeastern
NW	Northwestern
MW	Midwestern
SE	Southeastern
SW	Southwestern

Territory

Code	Name	Code	Name	Code	Name
0100	Midnight Sun	1800	Bluegrass	3500	Empire
0200	Yellowhammer	1900	Pelican	3600	Buckeye
0300	Opportunity	2000	Bay	3700	Sooner
0400	Grand Canyon	2100	Old Line	3800	Beaver
0500	Golden	2200	Pine Tree	3900	Keystone
0600	Centennial	2300	Wolverine	4000	Ocean
0700	Constitution	2400	North Star	4100	Palmetto
0800	Capitol	2500	Show-me	4200	Coyote
0900	Diamond	2600	Magnolia	4300	Volunteer
1000	Sunshine	2700	Treasure	4400	Lone Star
1100	Peach	2800	Tarheal	4500	Beehive
1200	Aloha	2900	Sioux	4600	Old Dominion
1300	Hawkeye	3000	Cornhusker	4700	Green Mountain
1400	Gem	3100	Granite	4800	Evergreen
1500	Prairie	3200	Garden	4900	Badger
1600	Hoosier	3300	Enchantment	5000	Mountain
1700	Sunflower	3400	Sagebrush	5100	Equality

Program operations:
1. Process each input salesperson record.
2. Print the two heading lines on the first page and on each following page of the report.
    a. Print the run date on the first heading line as specified on the print chart.
    b. Accumulate and print the page number on the first heading line as specified on the print chart.
3. For each salesperson record, do the following processing:
    a. Use the input region field to look up the name of the region. If the input region code cannot be located in the table, print asterisks in the region-name field of the output report.
    b. Use the input territory field to look up the name of the territory. If the input territory code cannot be located in the table, print asterisks in the territory-name field of the output report.
    c. Print the detail line in accordance with the print-chart specifications.
4. Double-space each detail line. Provide for a span of 57 lines per page.

Programming Assignment 11-4: International Mailing List Lookup
Background information:

Assignment 8-4 involved performing data validation on the double-record Customer-name and Address file. (Records are stored in pairs: the first record is the Customer name record and the second is the Customer address record.) Although this file will soon be converted to a single record file, a mailing list from the current file is required that includes the country (United States or Canada). Unfortunately, the country name is not included in the record. However, the record does include the two-letter state or province abbreviation from which the country can be determined by table lookup.

Input file: Customer file (CUSTADDR.DAT)

Input-record format:

Positions	Field	Data class	Comments
1–2	Record code	Numeric	Code 53
3–7	Customer number	Numeric	
8–31	Customer name	Alphanumeric	
32–80	Other data		

Positions	Field	Data class	Comments
1–2	Record code	Numeric	Code 54
3–7	Customer number	Numeric	
8–31	Customer address	Alphanumeric	
32–44	City	Alphanumeric	
45–46	State	Alphanumeric	
47–52	Canadian zip code	Alphanumeric	
47–51	U. S. zip code	Alphanumeric	
53–80	Other data		

Output-report format:

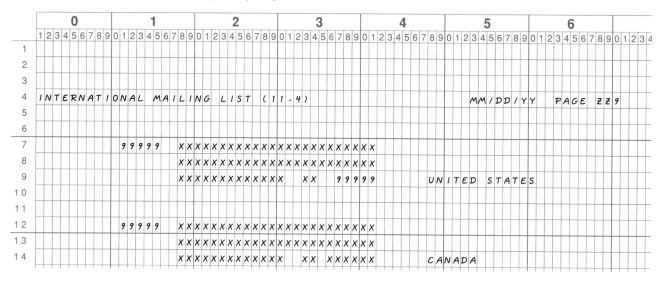

Table data:

United States state abbreviations						Canadian province abbreviations	
AK	HI	ME	NJ	SD		AB	NS
AL	IA	MI	NM	TN		BC	ON
AR	ID	MN	NV	TX		LB	PE
AZ	IL	MO	NY	UT		MB	PQ
CA	IN	MS	OH	VA		NB	SK
CO	KS	MT	OK	VT		NF	YT
CT	KY	NC	OR	WA		NT	
DC	LA	ND	PA	WI			
DE	MA	NE	RI	WV			
FL	MD	NH	SC	WY			
GA							

Program operations:
1. Process each input customer record.
2. Print the heading line on the first page and on each following page of the report.
   a. Print the run date on the first heading line as specified on the print chart.
   b. Accumulate and print the page number on the first heading line as specified on the print chart.
3. For each customer-record pair (record 53 plus 54), do the following processing:
   a. Use the input state field of the 54-record to determine whether the abbreviation is for a state in the United States or a province in Canada.
      - If the input state abbreviation is for a state in the United States, print the word USA in the country-field area on the output report. A state will have a five digit numeric zip code in positions 47 through 51 of the input 54-record. Print the numeric zip code in print positions 37 through 41 of the destination line on the report.
      - If the input state abbreviation is for a province in Canada, print the word CANADA in the country-field area on the output report. A province will have a six-character alphanumeric zip code in positions 47 through 52 of the input 54-record. Print the alphanumeric zip code in print positions 36 through 41 of the destination line on the report.
      - If the input state abbreviation cannot be located in the table data, print asterisks in the country-name field of the output report and do not print the input zip code field.
   b. Print the set of three detail lines for each customer-record set in accordance with the print-chart specifications.
4. Triple-space between customer-record sets. Single-space the lines for a given customer. Print 11 customers per page.

Programming Assignment 11-5: Nurses' Annuity Lookup
Background information:
Employees of Brooklawn Hospital can participate in a special annuity program for long-term savings. To give the employee maximum flexibility, Brooklawn has an approved list of institutions with which it does business. Each employee's participation is indicated by an Annuity-fund field in the data record. The personnel manager of Brooklawn needs a report listing the participation of each employee.

Input file: Nurses file (NURSES.DAT)

Input-record format:

Positions	Field	Data class	Comments
3–25	Name (last, first, mi)	Alphanumeric	
56	Employment code	Alphabetic	
61–64	Budget code	Numeric	
74–75	Annuity code	Alphabetic	
76–80	Annuity withholding	Numeric	Format: dollars and cents
81–97	Other data		

Table data:

Annuity company		Annuity company	
Code	**Name**	**Code**	**Name**
AF	Ace High Income Fund	IB	International Brokers
AM	AmWest	IE	Integrated Equity
AP	Associated Planners	JA	Johnson and Associates
CI	Century Investments	LN	Lincoln National Investment
DF	Drexel, Drexel, & Fox	MF	Monarch Insurance
DI	Decade Investments Group	MI	Mutual Fund of Idaho
FF	Future Fund	RP	Research Plus
FS	Futura Securities	SS	Soyanora Securities
GA	Golden Age Securities	TB	Tres Bien Fund
HM	Hawkeye Mutual	TE	Transportations Equities

Output-report format:

```
        0         1         2         3         4         5         6         7
1234567890123456789012345678901234567890123456789012345678901234567890123456789012
 1
 2
 3
 4 BROOKLAWN HOSPITAL ANNUITY SUMMARY (11-5)                        PAGE ZZ9
 5
 6
 7   EMPLOYEE NAME            B/C    ANNUITY SELECTION              AMOUNT
 8
 9   XXXXXXXXXXXXXXXXXXXXXXX  XXXX   XXXXXXXXXXXXXXXXXXXXXXXXXXXXX  ZZZ.ZZ    PARTTIME
10
11   XXXXXXXXXXXXXXXXXXXXXXX  XXXX   XXXXXXXXXXXXXXXXXXXXXXXXXXXXX  ZZZ.ZZ
```

Program operations:
1. Process each input record.
2. Print the two heading lines on the first page and on each following page of the report.
   a. Accumulate and print the page number on the first heading line as specified on the print chart.
3. For each employee record, use the input Annuity-program field to look up the name of the annuity company. Print the detail line in accordance with the print-chart specifications.

    a. If the input annuity program code cannot be located in the table, print the words INVALID ANNUITY CODE in the annuity selection positions of the output report. Leave the amount entry blank.

    b. If the employee has no entry for the Annuity-program field, then that employee is not participating so leave both the annuity selection and amount fields blank.

    c. If the employee is parttime (Employment-code field contains P), print PARTTIME as shown in the print chart; otherwise leave these positions blank.

4. Double-space each detail line. Provide for a span of 57 lines per page.

Programming Assignment 11-6: Complete Computers Corporation Vendor Lookup

Background information:

In their inventory file, the Complete Computer Corporation of Chapter 2 stores data designating up to three vendors from whom each product can be obtained. The Smiths (owners of the company) desire a report indicating the vendor with the best price for each product.

Input file: The CCC Inventory file (CCCINVEN.DAT)

Input record format:

Positions	Field	Data class	Comments
6–20	Product name	Alphanumeric	
28–33	Maximum price	Numeric	Dollars and cents

Vendors from whom product is available:

34–36	Vendor code for vendor #1	Alphanumeric	
37–42	Price from vendor #1	Numeric	Dollars and cents
43–45	Vendor code for vendor #2	Alphanumeric	
46–51	Price from vendor #2	Numeric	Dollars and cents
52–54	Vendor code for vendor #3	Alphanumeric	
55–60	Price from vendor #3	Numeric	Dollars and cents

Table data:

Vendor Code	Name	Vendor Code	Name
ABA	Abacus Systems	MFM	MicroFine Monitors
ASP	Aspen, Incorporated	NAT	National Telecom Systems
BIC	Burlington International	NPC	National Partial Conductor
DIA	Diamond Hardware	OH	OH Products
EVH	Everhope Corporation	OPM	Optical Memory
GAT	Gates Supply	QUI	Quicksilver Accelerator
GCS	General Computer Supply	RWI	Raleigh Wilson, Inc.
GS	General Kahn	SCS	Specific Computer Supply
HAR	Harbor Circuits	SGM	Shortgrass Memories
HFC	High Flyers Disk	SKS	Standby Keypunch Systems
MEG	Mega-Systems, Incorporated	STD	Standard Keyboards
VAC	Vacuum Tubes, Anonymous	UPS	Universal Power Systems

Output-report format:

```
           0         1         2         3         4         5         6         7
  1234567890123456789012345678901234567890123456789012345678901234567890123456789012

4 COMPLETE COMPUTERS BEST PRICE SUMMARY (11-6)                    PAGE ZZ9
6     PRODUCT           VENDOR                        PRICE     TARGET
8   XXXXXXXXXXXXXX    XXXXXXXXXXXXXXXXXXXXXXXXXX    Z,ZZZ.99   Z,ZZZ.99    ***
10  XXXXXXXXXXXXXX    XXXXXXXXXXXXXXXXXXXXXXXXXX    Z,ZZZ.99   Z,ZZZ.99     ↑
```

If lowest price exceeds maximum allowable price.

Program operations:
1. Process each input record.
2. Print the two heading lines on the first page and on each following page of the report.
   a. Accumulate and print the page number on the first heading line as specified on the print chart.
3. For each inventory record, do the following processing:
   a. Find the vendor with the lowest price of the three. This is the one that will be used for report output. You must be aware that some records will not have entries for all three vendors. However, every record will have at least one vendor and an associated price which is greater than zero.
   b. Look up the name of the lowest price vendor in the table.
   c. Print the detail line as shown in the print chart. Use the lowest priced vendor name and price.
   d. If the price exceeds the Maximum-price field, print three asterisks to the right on the output line as shown in the print chart.
4. Double-space each detail line. Provide for a span of 57 lines per page.

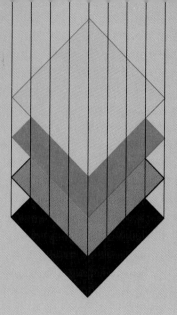

Advanced Table-Processing Techniques

Chapter Objectives

Chapter 11 presented the basic table-processing operations. This chapter introduces more advanced table-handling concepts and techniques that you, as a COBOL programmer, should know. From this chapter, you will learn the following:

- Tables with separately defined arguments and functions.

- Creating multiple-level tables.

- Processing multiple-level tables.

- Other formats and capabilities of the SEARCH statement, including the AFTER phrase for processing multiple-level tables.

- Loading a table from an input file and precautions to take to ensure that it is valid.

CHAPTER 12

Chapter Outline

Topic: Other Single-Level Table-Lookup Considerations

Tables with Range-Step Arguments

Separately Defined Table Arguments and Functions
Subscripts for Separately Defined Arguments and Functions
Indexes for Separately Defined Arguments and Functions
    The SEARCH/VARYING Statement

Topic: Multiple-Level Tables

Two-Level Table Processing
A Two-Level Table with No Explicit Table Arguments
    Establishing a Two-Level Table
    Accessing a Two-Level Table
A Two-Level Table with One (Top-Level) Explicit Argument
A Two-Level Table with Two Explicit Arguments

Three-Level Table Processing

The PERFORM/VARYING/AFTER Statement
PERFORM/VARYING with One AFTER Phrase
PERFORM/VARYING with Two AFTER Phrases

Input-Loaded Tables
Separate Table File or Combined Table and Data File
Table Sequence
Table Limits

Program Example—Processing Using an Input-Loaded Table
Program Documentation
DATA DIVISION Coding
PROCEDURE DIVISION Coding—Loading the Table
    COBOL-74 Solution
    COBOL-85 Solution
    Closing the Table File

Topic:	**Other Single-Level Table-Lookup Considerations**

In addition to the single-level table principles you learned in Chapter 11, you should be familiar with two other single-level table lookup considerations. They are: (1) the handling of tables with range-step arguments and (2) situations in which the arguments and functions are defined in separate tables.

Tables with Range-Step Arguments

Sometimes there will not be a one-to-one correspondence between the search argument value and the table argument value. This situation occurs when one table function (or set of table functions) applies to a range of argument values. A common example of this is an income tax table in which a range of earned income dollar amounts pertain to a specific tax bracket.

Similarly, a range of birth dates applies to each one of the twelve signs of the zodiac. A zodiac-sign table used for a lookup of the sunsign for a given birth date would thus be an example of a **range-step table**.

Suppose you want to use the month and day of birth field to look up the applicable zodiac sign, as shown in Figure 12-1. A range-step lookup generally is best handled as a variation of a serial lookup with early exit. Remember that a table with sequentially organized argument values is required for such a lookup.

The highest numerical value for each sunsign date range should be used as the table argument; the table function is, of course, the sunsign name. Also, since the date range for Capricorn spans from one year to the next, it requires two entries: one for the last day of December and one for the last day of the sunsign period. When establishing the table, the thirteen entries must be listed in numerical order according to the four-digit *mmdd* date value.

Instead of testing just for an equal condition in the lookup module (as was done for the lookups in the last chapter), the correspondence test looks for a search argument that is less than or equal to the table argument value.

As shown in Figure 12-2, a sunsign match occurs when IN-BIRTH-MONTH-DAY is less than or equal to the ZT-SIGN-END-DATE being tested. Observe that, to minimize SEARCH statement coding and comparisons, this less than or equal to relationship is coded with the NOT GREATER THAN operator in the WHEN phrase.

Figure 12-1   Zodiac-sign lookup example.

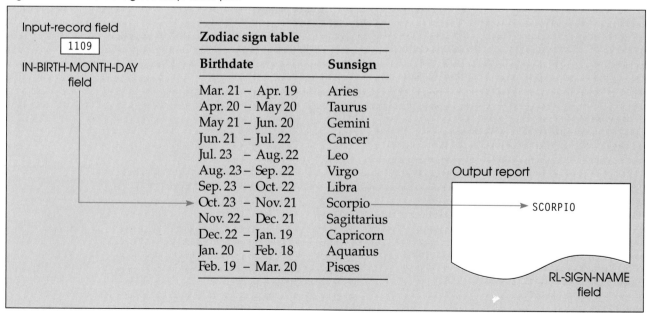

Figure 12-2   Range-step zodiac-sign lookup.

```
                    01  ZT-TABLE-CONTROLS
                        05  ZT-ENTRY-FOUND-SWITCH          PIC X(3).
                            88  ZT-ENTRY-FOUND                        VALUE "YES".
                            88  ZT-END-OF-TABLE                       VALUE "END".

                    01  ZT-ZODIAC-SIGN-DATA.
                        05  FILLER      PIC X(15)     VALUE "0119CAPRICORN".
                        05  FILLER      PIC X(15)     VALUE "0218AQUARIUS".
                        05  FILLER      PIC X(15)     VALUE "0320PISCES".
                        05  FILLER      PIC X(15)     VALUE "0419ARIES".
                        05  FILLER      PIC X(15)     VALUE "0520TAURUS".
                        05  FILLER      PIC X(15)     VALUE "0620GEMINI".
                        05  FILLER      PIC X(15)     VALUE "0722CANCER".
                        05  FILLER      PIC X(15)     VALUE "0822LEO".
                        05  FILLER      PIC X(15)     VALUE "0922VIRGO".
                        05  FILLER      PIC X(15)     VALUE "1022LIBRA".
                        05  FILLER      PIC X(15)     VALUE "1121SCORPIO".
                        05  FILLER      PIC X(15)     VALUE "1221SAGITTARIUS".
                        05  FILLER      PIC X(15)     VALUE "1231CAPRICORN".
                    01  ZT-ZODIAC-SIGN-TABLE REDEFINES ZT-ZODIAC-SIGN-DATA.
                        05  ZT-ZODIAC-SIGN-ENTRY      OCCURS 13 TIMES
                                                      INDEXED BY ZT-INDEX.

                            10  ZT-SIGN-END-DATE          PIC X(4).
                            10  ZT-SIGN-NAME              PIC X(11).
                             .
                             .
                             .
(Test for valid date)   ⎰  IF IN-BIRTH-MONTH-DAY IS NUMERIC
                        ⎨  AND IN-BIRTH-MONTH-DAY IS NOT LESS THAN "0101"
                        ⎱  AND IN-BIRTH-MONTH-DAY IS NOT GREATER THAN "1231"
                               PERFORM 999-LOOKUP-SIGN-NAME
                           ELSE
                               MOVE "END" TO ZT-ENTRY-FOUND-SWITCH.
                           IF ZT-ENTRY-FOUND
                               MOVE ZT-SIGN-NAME (ZT-INDEX) TO RL-SIGN-NAME
                           ELSE
                               MOVE SPACES TO RL-SIGN-NAME.
                             .
                             .
                             .
                    999-LOOKUP-SIGN-NAME.
                        SET ZT-INDEX TO 1.
                        SEARCH ZT-ZODIAC-SIGN-ENTRY
                            AT END MOVE "END" TO ZT-ENTRY-FOUND-SWITCH
Test for search argument less than
or equal to table argument  ⎰ WHEN IN-BIRTH-MONTH-DAY
                            ⎱     IS NOT GREATER THAN ZT-SIGN-END-DATE (ZT-INDEX)
                                MOVE "YES" TO ZT-ENTRY-FOUND-SWITCH.
```

COBOL-85:
The same form is adequate in this case. However, COBOL-85 provides
more versatility with the END-SEARCH scope terminator.

```
                    999-LOOKUP-SIGN-NAME.
                        SET ZT-INDEX TO 1
                        SEARCH ZT-ZODIAC-SIGN-ENTRY
                            AT END MOVE "END" TO ZT-ENTRY-FOUND-SWITCH
                            WHEN IN-BIRTH-MONTH-DAY
                                    IS NOT GREATER THAN ZT-SIGN-END-DATE (ZT-INDEX)
                                MOVE "YES" TO ZT-ENTRY-FOUND-SWITCH
                        END-SEARCH.
```

Separately Defined Table Arguments and Functions

In the example of the state table in Chapter 11 and the zodiac-sign table just presented, each table argument was combined with its table function and defined in the same table entry. This is a good approach because the physically adjacent placement of argument and function makes it relatively easy for you to see the relationship. This helps to ensure that the correct functions are associated with each table argument when the table is created or updated. Sometimes, however, you will find it more convenient to define the table arguments separately from the table functions. (Separate definition is much simpler when the argument and function are of different usages.) As an illustration, the arguments and functions of Figure 12-3 are separately defined.

Figure 12-3
Lookup (using subscripts) from separately defined model and price tables.

```
           01  MT-TABLE-CONTROLS.
               05  MT-ENTRY-FOUND-SWITCH      PIC X(3).
                   88  MT-STILL-LOOKING                      VALUE "NO".
                   88  MT-ENTRY-FOUND                        VALUE "YES".
                   88  MT-END-OF-TABLE                       VALUE "END".
               05  MT-SUBSCRIPT              PIC S9(4) COMP SYNC.
               05  MT-NUMBER-OF-ENTRIES      PIC S9(4) VALUE +7
                                                       COMP SYNC.
           01  MT-MODEL-DATA.
               05  FILLER        PIC X(7)   VALUE "RS16".
               05  FILLER        PIC X(7)   VALUE "RS20".
               05  FILLER        PIC X(7)   VALUE "RS24".
Model      05  FILLER        PIC X(7)   VALUE "LS12-12".
table      05  FILLER        PIC X(7)   VALUE "LS12-16".
               05  FILLER        PIC X(7)   VALUE "LS16-16".
               05  FILLER        PIC X(7)   VALUE "LS16-20".
           01  MT-MODEL-TABLE REDEFINES MT-MODEL-DATA.
               05  MT-MODEL-CODE            OCCURS 7 TIMES
                                           PIC X(7).
           01  PT-PRICE-DATA
               05  FILLER        PIC 9(3)V99 VALUE 098.99.
               05  FILLER        PIC 9(3)V99 VALUE 148.00.
               05  FILLER        PIC 9(3)V99 VALUE 178.00.
Price      05  FILLER        PIC 9(3)V99 VALUE 109.98.
table      05  FILLER        PIC 9(3)V99 VALUE 179.00.
               05  FILLER        PIC 9(3)V99 VALUE 198.99.
               05  FILLER        PIC 9(3)V99 VALUE 298.00.
           01  PT-PRICE-TABLE REDEFINES PT-PRICE-DATA.
               05  PT-MODEL-PRICE           OCCURS 7 TIMES
                                           PIC 9(3)V99.
                   .
                   .
                   .
           MOVE "NO" TO MT-ENTRY-FOUND-SWITCH.
           PERFORM 999-LOOKUP-MODEL-NAME
               VARYING MT-SUBSCRIPT
                   FROM 1
                   BY 1
                       UNTIL NOT MT-STILL-LOOKING.
           IF MT-ENTRY-FOUND
               SUBTRACT 1 FROM MT-SUBSCRIPT
               MOVE PT-MODEL-PRICE (MT-SUBSCRIPT) TO RL-MODEL-PRICE
           ELSE
               MOVE ZEROS TO RL-MODEL-PRICE.
```

Same subscript field and occurrence value relate to both argument and function

```
           999-LOOKUP-MODEL-NAME.
               IF IN-MODEL-CODE IS EQUAL TO MT-MODEL-CODE (MT-SUBSCRIPT)
                   MOVE "YES" TO MT-ENTRY-FOUND-SWITCH
               ELSE IF MT-SUBSCRIPT IS NOT LESS THAN MT-NUMBER-OF-ENTRIES
                   MOVE "END" TO MT-ENTRY-FOUND-SWITCH.
```

Subscripts for Separately Defined Arguments and Functions

When you use subscripts with lookups for separately defined arguments and functions, there are no coding differences from that required for combined arguments and functions. This is shown in the PROCEDURE DIVISION coding of Figure 12-3.

Even though the arguments and functions are defined separately, the same subscript value is nevertheless used for both tables because the occurrence numbers must still correspond.

Indexes for Separately Defined Arguments and Functions

On the other hand, if you use an index in accessing a table consisting of separately defined arguments and functions, you must be a little more careful. That is, when table arguments and functions are defined separately, the index you use to refer to the argument must be different from the index you use to refer to the function. This results from the fact that you must specify a unique index-name for each OCCURS clause.

The SEARCH/VARYING Statement. You can use a SEARCH statement with the VARYING phrase to conveniently handle table lookups for separately defined indexed arguments and functions. Figure 12-4 shows the SEARCH/VARYING statement format. Except for the VARYING phrase, it is identical to the Format-1 serial SEARCH statement introduced in the last chapter. Recognize that the VARYING phrase is limited to Format-1; it cannot be used with the Format-2 binary SEARCH statement.

As shown in Figure 12-5, specification of PT-PRICE-INDEX in the VARYING phrase causes it to be incremented as in previous examples, and it also causes MT-MODEL-INDEX to be incremented in unison. The VARYING phrase of the SEARCH statement is typically used for separately defined arguments and functions, with separate indexes, as coded in the example. When used in this manner, the processing is relatively straightforward.

However, you should be aware of a few SEARCH/VARYING nuances. Observe that either an index-name or an identifier can be specified as the object of the VARYING phrase. The following rules apply to the incrementing action of the object of the VARYING phrase.

Figure 12-4
SEARCH/VARYING statement format.

Format:

```
SEARCH identifier-1 [ VARYING { identifier-2
                                index-name-1 } ]

[AT END imperative-statement-1]

WHEN condition-1 { imperatuve-statement-2
                   NEXT SENTENCE }

[ WHEN condition-2 { imperatuve-statement-3
                     NEXT SENTENCE } ] ...
```

Example:

```
SEARCH MT-MODEL-CODE VARYING PT-PRICE-INDEX
    AT END MOVE "END" TO MT-ENTRY-FOUND-SWITCH
    WHEN IN-MODEL-CODE
            IS EQUAL TO MT-MODEL-CODE (MT-MODEL-INDEX)
    MOVE "YES" TO MT-ENTRY-FOUND-SWITCH.
```

Figure 12-5 Lookup (using indexes with a SEARCH/VARYING driver) from separately defined model and price tables.

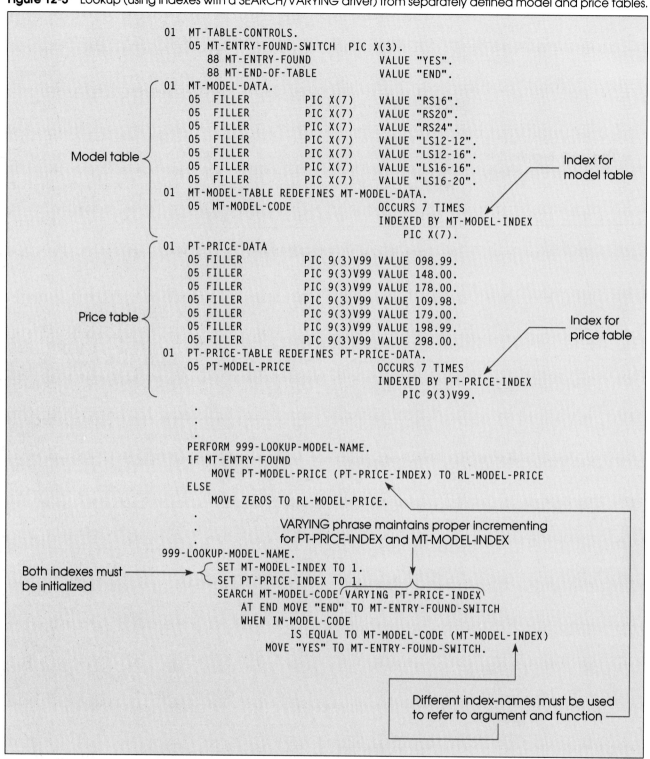

■ When an index-name (an index named in an INDEXED BY clause) is specified
(as it is in Figure 12-5), the index-name is incremented by the same relative
number of occurrences and, at the same time, as the index-name associated
with identifier-1 (the SEARCH index) is incremented.

- When an identifier with INDEX usage (an index data-item) is specified, the index data-item is incremented by *the same displacement value*, and at the same time, as the index-name associated with identifier-1 is incremented.

- When the identifier does not have INDEX usage, it must be an elementary numeric field (of any other usage). The field is then incremented by 1 at the same time as the index-name associated with identifier-1 is incremented.

Topic: Multiple-Level Tables

All the table examples presented in this and the previous chapter have been examples of **single-level** or **one-dimensional tables**. Although single-level tables are used much more frequently, some applications require the use of **multiple-level tables**.

COBOL can handle multiple-level tables with either two or three levels. A **two-level table** is sometimes referred to as a **two-dimensional table**; a **three-level table** may be called a **three-dimensional table**.

Multiple-level tables have tables within table entries. In other words, a two-level table contains two OCCURS clauses—one nested within the other. A three-level table has three nested OCCURS clauses. Do not confuse a table that has multiple functions with a multiple-level table. For example, a table that contains a part number, part description, and a part price for each part is a single-level table with one table argument and two table functions—not a multiple-level table.

Two-Level Table Processing

Two-level tables may have zero, one, or two explicit table arguments. The coding for each type will be discussed in relation to a table of pay rates by shift and within job classification.

A Two-Level Table with No Explicit Table Arguments

An example of a two-level table of pay rates for various job classification codes during each of three shifts is shown in Example A of Figure 12-6. Notice that the hourly pay rate depends upon two factors; job classification and shift worked. In effect, three-occurrence shift pay-rate table is within each of the seven job classification entries. You can think of each job classification entry as a **table row** and of each shift pay-rate entry as a **table column**.

Figure 12-6   Rate-of-pay table.

Example A: Rate-of-pay table data				Example B: Rate-of-pay table occurrences			
	Rate of pay				**Rate of pay**		
Job classification	**Shift 1 (days)**	**Shift 2 (swing)**	**Shift 3 (grave)**	Job classification	**Shift 1 (days)**	**Shift 2 (swing)**	**Shift 3 (grave)**
1	9.64	10.60	11.09	1	(1,1)	(1,2)	(1,3)
2	8.93	9.82	10.27	2	(2,1)	(2,2)	(2,3)
3	7.12	7.83	8.19	3	(3,1)	(3,2)	(3,3)
4	6.80	7.48	7.82	4	(4,1)	(4,2)	(4,3)
5	6.07	6.68	6.98	5	(5,1)	(5,2)	(5,3)
6	5.41	5.95	6.22	6	(6,1)	(6,2)	(6,3)
7	4.39	4.83	5.04	7	(7,1)	(7,2)	(7,3)

7 rows

3 columns per row

Thus, the top-level (row) table argument is the job classification number. The second-level table argument is the shift number. The hourly pay-rate amount for each shift within each job classification is the table function.

Because the job classification numbers are an unbroken string of consecutive values (from 1 to 7), the table row entries can be organized positionally. Similarly, the three shift pay-rate entries (from shift 1 to 3) can be organized positionally.

Example B of Figure 12-6 shows, in parentheses, the occurrence number notation for each table function. The first number within each set of parentheses refers to the table row—the job classification occurrence number. The second number refers to the table column—the pay-rate occurrence number—within the row. In order to look up a particular pay rate, a search argument containing both the job classification and the shift code is required.

Suppose, as shown in Part A of Figure 12-7, that a pay rate is to be looked up from the positional search argument subscript fields of IN-JOB-CLASS and IN-SHIFT-CODE. What coding is necessary to establish and process this table?

Establishing a Two-Level Table. As shown in the DATA DIVISION coding of Part B of Figure 12-7, a two-level table contains two OCCURS clauses; one nested inside the other. Notice that the more inclusive, top-level, table entry RT-JOB-CLASS-ROW has been specified as a 05-level data-item, whereas the nested second-level entry RT-RATE-OF-PAY has been specified at level-10.

Accessing a Two-Level Table. Whenever a two-level table is accessed, the name of the elementary table entry must be followed by two subscripts or two indexes (or a combination of both) coded within parentheses. For instance, with the RT-RATE-TABLE positional addressing example, to refer to a particular rate-of-pay for a given shift and job classification requires the coding: RT-RATE-OF-PAY (IN-JOB-CLASS, IN-SHIFT-CODE). Notice that a comma and a blank space have been used to separate the two entries within the parentheses. (Earlier versions of COBOL required the comma; for COBOL-74 and COBOL-85, it is optional. However, it serves as good documentation in this case.)

When coding two subscripts or indexes for a data-item, the more inclusive, top-level one (the one that applies to the row) must be coded first; the second-level item (the one that applies to the column) is coded last.

Refer to the PROCEDURE DIVISION coding in Part B of Figure 12-7. Because positional addressing is used, notice that the two search argument fields are first validated to ensure that they are within the proper range. If both fields contain valid occurrence values, the designated rate is retrieved from the table. If either or both fields are invalid, a value of zero is used in this example to fill the field to which the pay rate should have been transferred.

A Two-Level Table with One (Top-Level) Explicit Argument

As previously mentioned, only certain applications are able to employ positionally organized tables. Table arguments usually must be explicitly represented within the table data. As shown in Part A of Figure 12-8, for example, suppose that the job classification codes are two-character alphanumeric codes instead of consecutive digits. This situation requires a two-level table with an explicit table argument at the row level. Most two-level tables fall into this category.

Part B of Figure 12-8 shows the coding required to look up the pay rate with an explicit table argument at the top level. The INDEXED BY clause has been specified at the top level. Observe that the lookup for this two-level table with one explicit argument at the row level is essentially a single-level search followed by positional addressing of the column within the row.

Figure 12-7   Two-level rate-of-pay table lookup (positional addressing at both levels).

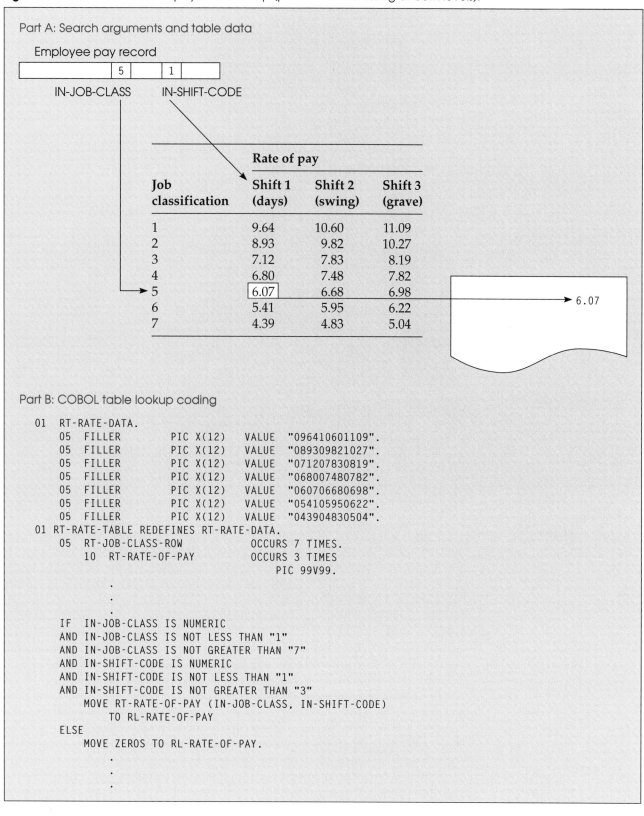

Part A: Search arguments and table data

Employee pay record

IN-JOB-CLASS   IN-SHIFT-CODE

Job classification	Rate of pay		
	Shift 1 (days)	Shift 2 (swing)	Shift 3 (grave)
1	9.64	10.60	11.09
2	8.93	9.82	10.27
3	7.12	7.83	8.19
4	6.80	7.48	7.82
5	6.07	6.68	6.98
6	5.41	5.95	6.22
7	4.39	4.83	5.04

6.07

Part B: COBOL table lookup coding

```
01  RT-RATE-DATA.
    05  FILLER          PIC X(12)    VALUE  "096410601109".
    05  FILLER          PIC X(12)    VALUE  "089309821027".
    05  FILLER          PIC X(12)    VALUE  "071207830819".
    05  FILLER          PIC X(12)    VALUE  "068007480782".
    05  FILLER          PIC X(12)    VALUE  "060706680698".
    05  FILLER          PIC X(12)    VALUE  "054105950622".
    05  FILLER          PIC X(12)    VALUE  "043904830504".
01  RT-RATE-TABLE REDEFINES RT-RATE-DATA.
    05  RT-JOB-CLASS-ROW            OCCURS 7 TIMES.
        10  RT-RATE-OF-PAY          OCCURS 3 TIMES
                                    PIC 99V99.
        .
        .
        .
    IF  IN-JOB-CLASS IS NUMERIC
    AND IN-JOB-CLASS IS NOT LESS THAN "1"
    AND IN-JOB-CLASS IS NOT GREATER THAN "7"
    AND IN-SHIFT-CODE IS NUMERIC
    AND IN-SHIFT-CODE IS NOT LESS THAN "1"
    AND IN-SHIFT-CODE IS NOT GREATER THAN "3"
        MOVE RT-RATE-OF-PAY (IN-JOB-CLASS, IN-SHIFT-CODE)
            TO RL-RATE-OF-PAY
    ELSE
        MOVE ZEROS TO RL-RATE-OF-PAY.
        .
        .
        .
```

Figure 12-8 Two-level rate-of-pay table lookup (top-level serial SEARCH followed by positional addressing).

Part A: Rate-of-pay table data

	Rate of pay		
Job classification	Shift 1 (days)	Shift 2 (swing)	Shift 3 (grave)
A1	9.64	10.60	11.09
A2	8.93	9.82	10.27
B1	7.12	7.83	8.19
C1	6.80	7.48	7.82
C2	6.07	6.68	6.98
C3	5.41	5.95	6.22
C4	4.39	4.83	5.04

Part B: COBOL table-lookup coding

```
01  RT-TABLE-CONTROLS.                              PERFORM 999-LOOKUP-RATE.
    05  RT-ENTRY-FOUND-SWITCH    PIC X(3).          IF  RT-ENTRY-FOUND
        88  RT-ENTRY-FOUND             VALUE "YES". AND IN-SHIFT-CODE IS NUMERIC
        88  RT-END-OF-TABLE            VALUE "END". AND IN-SHIFT-CODE IS NOT LESS THAN "1"
01  RT-RATE-DATA.                                   AND IN-SHIFT-CODE IS NOT GREATER THAN "3"
    05  FILLER     PIC X(12)  VALUE "A1096410601109".    MOVE RT-RATE-OF-PAY (RT-CLASS-INDEX, IN-SHIFT-CODE)
    05  FILLER     PIC X(12)  VALUE "A2089309821027".        TO RL-RATE-OF-PAY
    05  FILLER     PIC X(12)  VALUE "B1071207830819".  ELSE
    05  FILLER     PIC X(12)  VALUE "C1068007480782".      MOVE ZEROS TO RL-RATE-OF-PAY.
    05  FILLER     PIC X(12)  VALUE "C2060706680698".          .
    05  FILLER     PIC X(12)  VALUE "C3054105950622".          .
    05  FILLER     PIC X(12)  VALUE "C4043904830504".          .
01  RT-RATE-TABLE REDEFINES RT-RATE-DATA.           999-LOOKUP-RATE.
    05  RT-JOB-CLASS-ROW       OCCURS 7 TIMES            SET RT-CLASS-INDEX TO 1.
                               INDEXED BY RT-CLASS-INDEX.    SEARCH RT-JOB-CLASS-ROW
        10  RT-JOB-CLASSIFICATION   PIC X(2).                 AT END MOVE "END" TO RT-ENTRY-FOUND-SWITCH
        10  RT-RATE-OF-PAY     OCCURS 3 TIMES                 WHEN IN-JOB-CLASSIFICATION
                               PIC 99V99.                         IS EQUAL TO RT-JOB-CLASSIFICATION (RT-CLASS-INDEX)
                                                                MOVE "YES" TO RT-ENTRY-FOUND-SWITCH.
        .
        .
        .
```

A Two-Level Table with Two Explicit Arguments

Sometimes a two-level table will have two explicit arguments. Assume, as shown in Part A of Figure 12-9, that the shift codes—instead of being coded 1 through 3—are represented by alphanumeric codes of D for day shift, S for swing shift, and G for graveyard shift. Here we have an example of a two-level table with explicit table arguments at both levels.

Part B of Figure 12-9 shows the coding to look up the pay rate with two explicit table arguments. The INDEXED BY clause has been specified at both the job classification and the shift level. In the lookup module, two SEARCH statements are coded. The first is used to find the job classification row; the second to find the appropriate pay rate for the specific shift column within the pay-rate row. Notice in the COBOL-85 version of the lookup module that the scope terminators allow the second search to be executed conditionally under the WHEN of the first search.

In actual practice, two explicit arguments are not often contained within a two-level table. Although there can be any number of row entries, all rows must be the same length. Because the column entries for the rows must therefore contain a uniform number of occurrences, they are typically treated as positional entries by converting the search argument to a positional value. For example, the alphanumeric shift codes D, S, and G could have been converted to 1, 2, and 3, respectively, and the numeric value used as a subscript. Then the RT-SHIFT-CODE field could have been omitted from the table. This would result in a table with one explicit argument at the row level, as is usually the case for a two-level table. (Look-up coding is then handled as shown in Figure 12-8.)

Figure 12-9 Two-level rate-of-pay table lookup (serial SEARCH at both levels).

Part A: Rate-of-pay table data

Job classification	Rate of pay		
	Shift "D" (days)	Shift "S" (swing)	Shift "G" (grave)
A1	9.64	10.60	11.09
A2	8.93	9.82	10.27
B1	7.12	7.83	8.19
C1	6.80	7.48	7.82
C2	6.07	6.68	6.98
C3	5.41	5.95	6.22
C4	4.39	4.83	5.04

Part B: COBOL table-lookup coding

```
01  RT-TABLE-CONTROLS.
    05  RT-ENTRY-FOUND-SWITCH      PIC X(3).
        88  RT-ENTRY-FOUND                     VALUE "YES".
        88  RT-END-OF-TABLE                    VALUE "END".
01  RT-RATE-DATA.
    05  FILLER        PIC X(17)    VALUE "A1D0964S1060G1109".
    05  FILLER        PIC X(17)    VALUE "A2D0893S0982G1027".
    05  FILLER        PIC X(17)    VALUE "B1D0712S0783G0819".
    05  FILLER        PIC X(17)    VALUE "C1D0680S0748G0782".
    05  FILLER        PIC X(17)    VALUE "C2D0607S0668G0698".
    05  FILLER        PIC X(17)    VALUE "C3D0541S0595G0622".
    05  FILLER        PIC X(17)    VALUE "C4D0439S0483G0504".
01  RT-RATE-TABLE REDEFINES RT-RATE-DATA.
    05  RT-JOB-CLASS-ROW           OCCURS 7 TIMES
                                   INDEXED BY RT-CLASS-INDEX.
        10  RT-JOB-CLASSIFICATION      PIC X(2).
        10  RT-SHIFT-ENTRY         OCCURS 3 TIMES
                                   INDEXED BY RT-SHIFT-INDEX
                                   PIC X(1).
            15  RT-SHIFT-CODE      PIC X(1).
            15  RT-RATE-OF-PAY     PIC 99V99.
            .
PERFORM 999-LOOKUP-RATE.
IF RT-ENTRY-FOUND
    MOVE RT-RATE-OF-PAY (RT-CLASS-INDEX, RT-SHIFT-CODE)
        TO RL-RATE-OF-PAY
ELSE
    MOVE ZEROS TO RL-RATE-OF-PAY.
            .
            .
```

```
999-LOOKUP-RATE.                          Alternate COBOL-85 lookup coding.
    SET RT-CLASS-INDEX TO 1.
    SEARCH RT-JOB-CLASS-ROW               300-LOOKUP-RATE.
        AT END MOVE "END" TO RT-ENTRY-FOUND-SWITCH    SET RT-CLASS-INDEX TO 1
        WHEN IN-JOB-CLASSIF-CODE IS EQUAL TO          SEARCH RT-JOB-CLASS-ROW
                RT-JOB-CLASSIFICATION (RT-CLASS-INDEX)     AT END MOVE "END" TO RT-ENTRY-FOUND-SWITCH
            MOVE "YES" TO RT-ENTRY-FOUND-SWITCH.           WHEN IN-JOB-CLASSIF-CODE IS EQUAL TO
    IF RT-ENTRY-FOUND                                          RT-JOB-CLASSIFICATION (RT-CLASS-INDEX)
        SET RT-SHIFT-INDEX TO 1                            SET RT-SHIFT-INDEX TO 1
        SEARCH RT-SHIFT-ENTRY                              SEARCH RT-SHIFT-ENTRY
            AT END MOVE "END" TO RT-ENTRY-FOUND-SWITCH         AT END MOVE "END" TO RT-ENTRY-FOUND-SWITCH
            WHEN IN-SHIFT-CODE IS EQUAL TO                     WHEN IN-SHIFT-CODE IS EQUAL TO
                RT-SHIFT-CODE (RT-CLASS-INDEX, RT-SHIFT-INDEX)     RT-SHIFT-CODE (RT-CLASS-INDEX, RT-SHIFT-INDEX)
                MOVE "YES" TO RT-ENTRY-FOUND-SWITCH.              MOVE "YES" TO RT-ENTRY-FOUND-SWITCH
                                                          END-SEARCH
                                                      END-SEARCH.
```

Three-Level Table Processing

Three-level table processing is similar to two-level table processing except that—because there is one more level—a three-level table contains three nested OCCURS clauses. It also requires the specification of three subscripts and/or indexes to reference the elementary occurrences within the table.

Just as two-level tables may have from zero to two explicit table arguments, a three-level table may have from zero to three explicit table arguments. As an example of three-level table processing, let's consider a table with three explicit table arguments.

Part A of Figure 12-10 shows the flight fare-schedule for a hypothetical (low-price) airline. A schematic representation of how the COBOL table can be constructed is shown in Part B. Notice that the airport code for the departure point has been used as the top-level table argument. The airport code for the arrival point is the second-level table argument. A class-of-service code (B=Business class, C=Coach, F=First class, S=Super saver) serves as the third-level table argument. The fare amount is the table function. Thus, to determine a fare, you need: (1) the departure point, (2) the arrival point, and (3) the class.

Observe in the diagram that all of the three table arguments have been arranged in ascending sequence. This means that their sequence differs from the original table (as shown in Part A of Figure 12-10). Although sequential table

Figure 12-10   Flight fare-schedule table.

Part A: Flight fare-schedule

Departure point	Arrival point	Class of service	Fare
Atlanta (ATL)	Chicago (ORD)	First class	$ 385.00
		Coach	275.00
Chicago (ORD)	Atlanta (ATL)	First class	385.00
		Coach	275.00
	Los Angeles (LAX)	First class	715.00
		Coach	565.00
		Super saver	375.00
	New York (LGA)	Business class	360.00
		Coach	255.00
	San Francisco (SFO)	First class	715.00
		Coach	565.00
		Super saver	375.00
Los Angeles (LAX)	Chicago (ORD)	First class	715.00
		Coach	565.00
		Super saver	375.00
	New York (LGA)	First class	750.00
		Coach	595.00
		Super saver	415.00
	San Francisco (SFO)	Coach	60.00
New York (LGA)	Chicago (ORD)	Business class	360.00
		Coach	255.00
	Los Angeles (LAX)	First class	750.00
		Coach	595.00
		Super saver	415.00
San Francisco (SFO)	Los Angeles (LAX)	Coach	60.00

Figure 12-10 (continued)

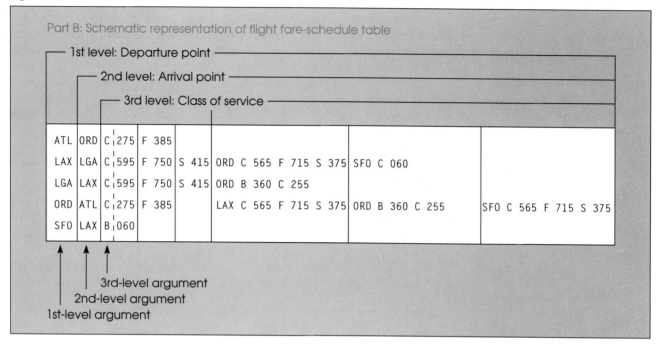

Part B: Schematic representation of flight fare-schedule table

organization is not required, it provides a specific order for the table entries and—with appropriate early-exit lookup coding—could improve processing efficiency.

COBOL coding for the three-level flight fare-schedule table lookup with a SEARCH statement driver is shown in Figure 12-11. The input record contains the search-argument fields IN-DEPARTURE-POINT, IN-ARRIVAL-POINT, and IN-CLASS-OF-SERVICE. When the three-level search argument is matched, the fare amount is moved to the output report-line field RL-FARE. If a match is not found,

Figure 12-11 Three-level flight fare-schedule table lookup.

```
01  FT-TABLE-CONTROLS.
    05  FT-ENTRY-FOUND-SWITCH    PIC X(3).
        88  FT-ENTRY-FOUND           VALUE "YES".
        88  FT-END-OF-TABLE          VALUE "END".
    05  FT-ERROR-MESSAGE  PIC X(40).

01  FT-FLIGHT-DATA.
    05  FILLER PIC X(63)
        VALUE "ATLORDC275F385".
    05  FILLER PIC X(63)
        VALUE "LAXLGAC595F750S415ORDC565F715S375SF0C060".
    05  FILLER PIC X(63)
        VALUE "LGALAXC595F750S415ORDB360C255".
    05  FILLER PIC X(63)
        VALUE "ORDATLC275F385     LAXC565F715S375ORDB360C255
            "SF0C565F715S375".
    05  FILLER PIC X(63)
        VALUE "SFOLAXB060".

01  FT-FLIGHT-TABLE REDEFINES FT-FLIGHT-DATA.
    05  FT-DEPARTURE-ENTRY          OCCURS 5 TIMES.
                                    INDEXED BY FT-DEPART-INDEX.
        10  FT-DEPARTURE-POINT          PIC X(3).
        10  FT-ARRIVAL-ENTRY        OCCURS 4 TIMES
                                    INDEXED BY FT-ARRIVAL-INDEX.
            15  FT-ARRIVAL-POINT        PIC X(3).
            15  FT-CLASS-ENTRY      OCCURS 3 TIMES
                                    INDEXED BY FT-CLASS-INDEX.
                20  FT-CLASS-OF-SERVICE  PIC X(1).
                20  FT-FARE              PIC 9(3).
          .
          .
    PERFORM 997-LOOKUP-FLIGHT-DEPARTURE.
    IF FT-ENTRY-FOUND
        MOVE FT-FARE
            (FT-DEPART-INDEX, FT-ARRIVAL-INDEX, FT-CLASS-INDEX)
            TO RL-FARE
    ELSE
        MOVE SPACES TO RL-FARE
        MOVE FT-ERROR-MESSAGE TO RL-ERROR-MESSAGE.
          .
          .
          .


997-LOOKUP-FLIGHT-DEPARTURE.
    SET FT-DEPART-INDEX TO 1.
    SEARCH FT-DEPARTURE-ENTRY
        AT END MOVE "END" TO FT-ENTRY-FOUND-SWITCH
        WHEN IN-DEPARTURE-POINT
                IS EQUAL TO FT-DEPARTURE-POINT (FT-DEPART-INDEX)
            MOVE "YES" TO FT-ENTRY-FOUND-SWITCH.
    IF FT-ENTRY-FOUND
        PERFORM 998-LOOKUP-FLIGHT-ARRIVAL
    ELSE
        MOVE "NO SUCH DEPARTURE POINT" TO FT-ERROR-MESSAGE.

998-LOOKUP-FLIGHT-ARRIVAL.
    SET FT-ARRIVAL-INDEX TO 1.
    SEARCH FT-ARRIVAL-ENTRY
        AT END MOVE "END" TO FT-ENTRY-FOUND-SWITCH
        WHEN IN-ARRIVAL-POINT IS EQUAL TO
                FT-ARRIVAL-POINT (FT-DEPART-INDEX,
                                  FT-ARRIVAL-INDEX)
            MOVE "YES" TO RT-ENTRY-FOUND-SWITCH.
    IF FT-ENTRY-FOUND
        PERFORM 999-LOOKUP-FLIGHT-CLASS
    ELSE
        MOVE "NO SUCH ARRIVAL FROM DEPARTURE POINT"
            TO FT-ERROR-MESSAGE.

999-LOOKUP-FLIGHT-CLASS.
    SET FT-CLASS-INDEX TO 1.
    SEARCH FT-CLASS-ENTRY
        AT END MOVE "END" TO FT-ENTRY-FOUND-SWITCH
        WHEN IN-CLASS-OF-SERVICE IS EQUAL TO
                FT-CLASS-OF-SERVICE (FT-DEPART-INDEX,
                                     FT-ARRIVAL-INDEX,
                                     FT-CLASS-INDEX)
            MOVE "YES" TO RT-ENTRY-FOUND-SWITCH.
    IF NOT FT-ENTRY-FOUND
        MOVE "NO SUCH SERVICE BETWEEN REQUESTED POINTS"
            TO FT-ERROR-MESSAGE.
```

one of three error messages identifying the unmatched argument is printed in the RL-ERROR-MESSAGE field.

For this example, a COBOL-85 alternate using nested SEARCH statements is not shown. The reason is that the alternative code (resulting because of the three different error messages) is confusing and difficult to follow. Using three separate modules is a simple and straightforward approach.

Although this flight fare-schedule example has been shown with the class of service as an explicit table argument, many COBOL programmers would instead assign a numerical code (1 through 4) to the four classes of service and then organize them positionally.

The PERFORM/VARYING/AFTER Statement

A PERFORM/VARYING statement with the AFTER phrase is convenient to use for those table-processing applications in which each occurrence of a multiple-level table must be completed for processing. Table-handling tasks for which the PERFORM/VARYING/AFTER statement is appropriate include multiple-level table initializing, copying, totaling, and printing.

The PERFORM/VARYING/AFTER statement format is illustrated in Figure 12-12. As it is with the VARYING phrase, all identifiers, data-names, and literals

Figure 12-12
PERFORM/VARYING/AFTER statement format.

Format:

PERFORM procedure-name-1 [{ THROUGH / THRU } procedure-name-2]

VARYING identifier-1 FROM { data-name-1 / index-name-1 / literal-1 }

BY { data-name-4 / literal-1 } UNTIL condition-1

AFTER identifier-2 FROM { data-name-2 / index-name-2 / literal-2 }

BY { data-name-5 / literal-3 } UNTIL condition-2

[AFTER identifier-3 FROM { data-name-3 / index-name-3 / literal-3 }

BY { data-name-6 / literal-6 } UNTIL condition-3]

Example:

```
PERFORM 999-ZERO-REVENUE-TABLE
    VARYING ST-YEAR-INDEX FROM 1 BY 1
        UNTIL ST-YEAR-INDEX IS GREATER THAN 5
    AFTER ST-MONTH-INDEX FROM 1 BY 1
        UNTIL ST-MONTH-INDEX IS GREATER THAN 12.
```

specified in the AFTER phrase must be numeric items; the condition specified after the reserved word UNTIL can be any valid relation, class, sign, or condition-name condition.

Typically, one AFTER phrase is coded for two-level table processing; two AFTER phrases are used for three-level tables.

PERFORM/VARYING with One AFTER Phrase

Part A of Figure 12-13 depicts a table used to record sales revenue, by month, over a five-year period. It is a two-level table. The top-level table-entry is the year. Each year entry contains twelve second-level month entries.

The COBOL coding required to define and initialize this two-level sales revenue table is shown in Part B of Figure 12-13. Observe, in the DATA DIVISION coding, that the table has been set up with explicit table arguments for the top-level year entries and implicit (positional) arguments for the second-level month entries.

The PROCEDURE DIVISION coding illustrates how you would use the PERFORM/VARYING/AFTER statement to initialize the sales revenue table. The 999-ZERO-REVENUE-TABLE procedure is executed 60 times so that each of the 60 ST-REVENUE occurrences is set to zero.

The AFTER clause sets up an iteration within the VARYING iteration. This processing action is depicted in Figure 12-14, which shows a flowchart for the PERFORM/VARYING statement with one AFTER phrase. The flowchart is annotated to reflect the sales revenue table processing.

Given the PERFORM/VARYING/AFTER coding (as shown in Part B of Figure 12-13), notice that the ST-REVENUE entries are zeroed month by month within

Figure 12-13 Two-level table initialization with the PERFORM/VARYING/AFTER statement.

Part A: Sales revenue table

	Year	Jan.	Feb.	Mar.	Apr.	May	Jun.	Jul.	Aug.	Sep.	Oct.	Nov.	Dec.
(Current year)	1990												
(Previous year)	1989												
(Two years ago)	1988												
(Three years ago)	1987												
(Four years ago)	1986												

Part B: COBOL coding for sales revenue table

```
01  ST-SALES-REVENUE-TABLE.
     05  ST-YEAR-ENTRY          OCCURS 5 TIMES
                                INDEXED BY ST-YEAR-INDEX.
        10  ST-YEAR               PIC X(4).
        10  ST-REVENUE          OCCURS 12 TIMES
                                INDEXED BY ST-MONTH-INDEX
                                  PIC S9(9)V99.
           .
           .
           .
     PERFORM 999-ZERO-REVENUE-TABLE
        VARYING ST-YEAR-INDEX FROM 1 BY I
           UNTIL ST-YEAR-INDEX IS GREATER THAN 5
        AFTER ST-MONTH-INDEX FROM 1 BY 1
           UNTIL ST-MONTH-INDEX IS GREATER THAN 12.
           .
           .
           .
 999-ZERO-REVENUE-TABLE.
     MOVE ZEROS TO ST-REVENUE (ST-YEAR-INDEX, ST-MONTH-INDEX).
```

Figure 12-14   PERFORM/VARYING logic with one AFTER phrase.

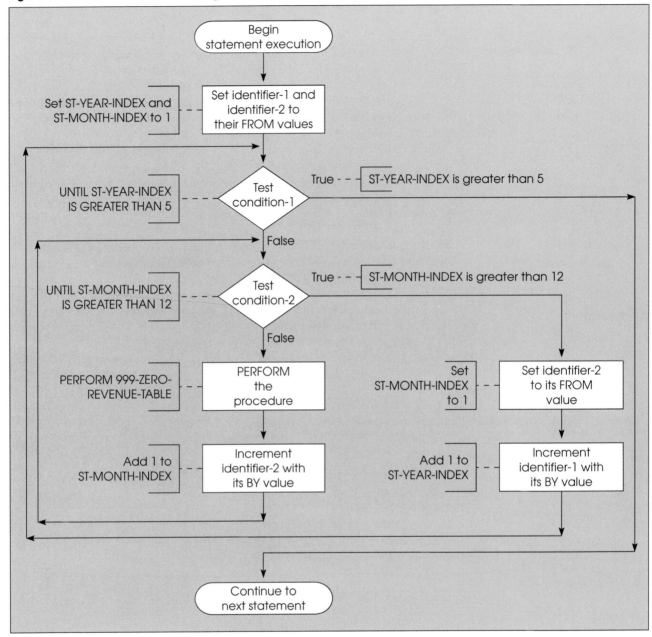

each year. That is, the direction of processing provided by the coding is from left to right across each row entry and then from top to bottom through each row.

PERFORM/VARYING
with Two AFTER Phrases

Figure 12-15 shows the sales revenue table expanded to be a three-level table. This provides an example of a PERFORM/VARYING statement with two AFTER phrases. As shown in the DATA DIVISION coding for the three-level sales revenue coding, there are still 5 top-level year entries and 12 second-level month entries. However, within each month entry, 31 third-level day entries have been added. Thus, there are 1,860 ST-REVENUE entries within the table (31 days times 12 months times 5 years).

As depicted in Figure 12-16, the PERFORM/VARYING/AFTER statement coded within the PROCEDURE DIVISION will cause the 999-ZERO-REVENUE-TABLE procedure to be executed 1,860 times. The ST-REVENUE occurrences will be zeroed from day to day within each month and then from month to month within each year.

Figure 12-15
Three-level table initialization
with the PERFORM/VARYING/
AFTER statement.

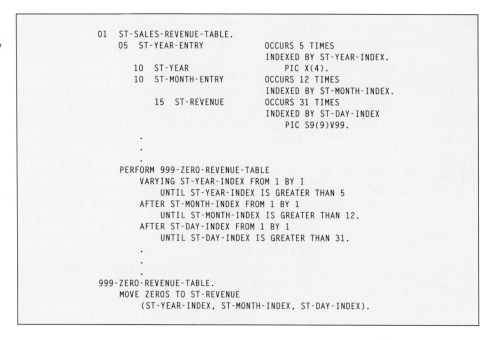

```
01   ST-SALES-REVENUE-TABLE.
     05  ST-YEAR-ENTRY              OCCURS 5 TIMES
                                    INDEXED BY ST-YEAR-INDEX.
         10   ST-YEAR                  PIC X(4).
         10   ST-MONTH-ENTRY        OCCURS 12 TIMES
                                    INDEXED BY ST-MONTH-INDEX.
              15   ST-REVENUE       OCCURS 31 TIMES
                                    INDEXED BY ST-DAY-INDEX
                                        PIC S9(9)V99.
                   .
                   .
                   .
     PERFORM 999-ZERO-REVENUE-TABLE
         VARYING ST-YEAR-INDEX FROM 1 BY I
             UNTIL ST-YEAR-INDEX IS GREATER THAN 5
         AFTER ST-MONTH-INDEX FROM 1 BY 1
             UNTIL ST-MONTH-INDEX IS GREATER THAN 12.
         AFTER ST-DAY-INDEX FROM 1 BY 1
             UNTIL ST-DAY-INDEX IS GREATER THAN 31.
                   .
                   .
                   .
     999-ZERO-REVENUE-TABLE.
         MOVE ZEROS TO ST-REVENUE
             (ST-YEAR-INDEX, ST-MONTH-INDEX, ST-DAY-INDEX).
```

Figure 12-16   PERFORM/VARYING logic with two AFTER phrases.

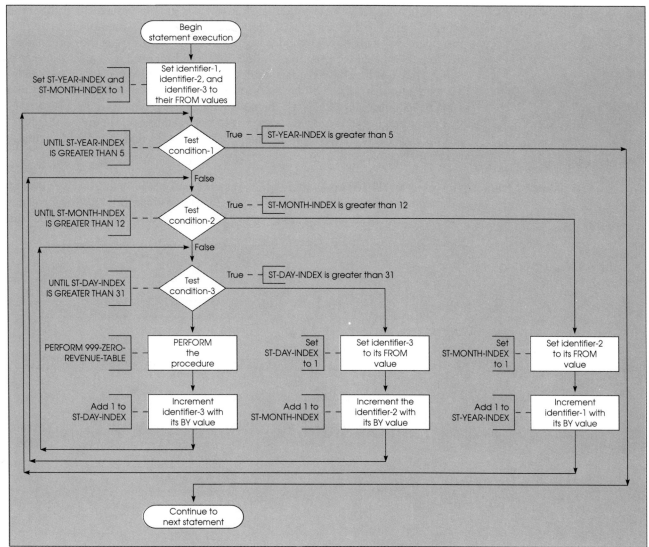

Input-Loaded Tables

Rather than hard-coding table data directly into the COBOL program with VALUE clauses, table data is instead often loaded into the program at run time from records stored tape or disk. When tables are loaded from input records, each record typically contains the data for one table entry. A program with an input-loaded table must contain program logic to read the table records and build the table in the WORKING-STORAGE SECTION. This table-loading process is depicted in Figure 12-17.

Separate Table File or Combined Table and Data File

Generally, the records used to build the table are stored in a separate file which is completely independent of any data file. When a program must load a table file to be used for processing a data file, you essentially "have a program within another program." That is, you will need a complete set of definition and processing statements for the table file. You will code appropriate SELECT, FD, OPEN, READ, and CLOSE statements strictly for the table file.

Once in a while, an input file will include both the table and the data. In that situation, the table records must physically precede the data records to be processed. The program logic must check the record codes of the input records carefully so that it can determine (1) if the table records are actually present in the file, and (2) when the table records have ended and the processing of the regular data records is to begin.

Table Sequence

If the table organization is sequential or positional, it is imperative that the input records be arranged in the proper sequence. Although it is possible to code program logic that would dynamically sequence the table entries as they are loaded, such logic is time-consuming to code and hence seldom used in commercial applications. As a result, table records are typically stored in the correct sequence. Once in a while, table records will be used for other purposes and thus be stored in a different sequence; in such cases, the table records must be sorted before loading.

Even though the records are expected to be in the correct sequence, the table-loading logic must check the record sequence to ensure that the records actually are in the required sequence.

Table Limits

With an input-loaded table, there is always the chance that—because of additions to the table—the number of table entries will exceed the number of occurrences provided for the table as specified in the OCCURS clause. When designing the

Figure 12-17
Depiction of table-loading process.

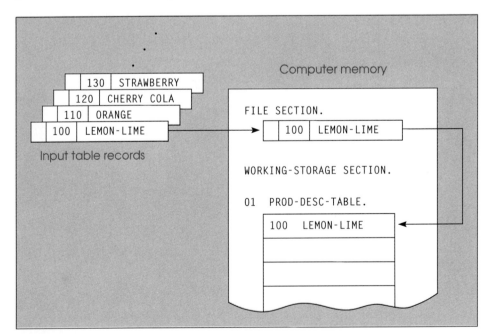

program, therefore, you must be certain to specify an OCCURS value large enough to accommodate a reasonable number of table-entry additions.

Then, in the table-loading routine, your program logic must check the table limits before adding each entry. For example, if 105 entries were present for a table defined with an OCCURS clause specifying 100 occurrences, severe processing bugs would occur unless the program logic diagnosed and reported the error.

Figure 12-18 summarizes the general logic requirements for loading a single-level table.

Program Example— Processing Using an Input-Loaded Table

In both this chapter and Chapter 11, you learned about table-processing techniques by studying portions of programs. You have not seen a full example program that uses a table. Let's consider one now.

This example is designed around the shift pay-rate example described earlier in this chapter (see Figure 12-9). However, whereas the earlier example involves a hard-coded table, this application uses a table that is loaded from a separate table file. Since the table file is in the exact format of the table definition in the DATA DIVISION of Figure 12-9, the section of code used in that example can be used in this program. (The hard-coded VALUE clauses will be omitted, of course.) Once the table is loaded, an employee hours-worked file is processed and the gross pay calculated for each employee.

To minimize logic requirements so that you can concentrate on the table-loading and processing aspects, no report headings are specified for the stock-status report. Furthermore, the normal report summaries are also omitted.

Program Documentation

A full set of programming specifications is shown in Figure 12-19. Notice the following about this application:

- There are two input files: the pay-rate table file and the employee time-worked file.

- If the table is not loaded properly (there are too few or too many table records), processing is to be terminated.

- When processing an employee record, if there is no entry in the table for that employee's job-classification code and shift code, then

    - the pay rate is set to zero for pay calculations

    - the word INVALID is printed on the output report in place of the pay rate.

You see the program structure in the structure chart of Figure 12-20 and the logic in the pseudocode of Figure 12-21. The first three divisions of the finished program are included in Figure 12-22; the PROCEDURE DIVISION is included in Figure 12-23 (COBOL-74) and Figure 12-24 (COBOL-85).

Figure 12-18   General table-loading logic.

```
1.  Initialize the table-loading subscript or index.

2.  [For sequentially organized tables only] Initialize a previous-
    table-argument field to an appropriate initial value (typically
    LOW-VALUES).

3.  Do a priming-read to obtain the first table record.

4.  Perform the load-table module until the end of the table records
    is reached or the table area in storage is full.

5.  Test to see that a minimum number of table entries has been
    loaded. If not, issue an incomplete table load message.
```

```
Load-table module

1.  Test the subscript or index occurrence number to determine if the
    number of table entries loaded is greater than the number of table
    entries provided by the OCCURS clause. If so, issue a table full
    message and suspend table loading.

2.  [For sequentially organized tables only] Test the table argument
    of the input record to determine if it is equal to or less than
    the previous argument loaded. If so, issue a table out-of-
    sequence message and suspend table loading.

    a.  If the table argument is in sequence, store the argument in
        the previous-argument field.

3.  Store the table entry from the input record in the table within
    storage.

4.  Increment the subscript or index.

5.  Read the next table record.
```

Figure 12-19
Program specifications:
GROSSPAY program.

PROGRAMMING SPECIFICATIONS

Program name: GROSS PAY REPORT   **Program ID:** GROSSPAY

Program Description:

This program prepares an employee gross pay report. The overall
operational steps are:
    Load an employee pay rate table from a pay rate file
    Process each employee record from a time-worked file.

Input Files:

    Pay rate (table)
    Employee time-work

Output File:

Employee gross pay

List of Program Operations:

A. Load the pay rate file into the program table.

    1. If the number of records in the table file is not equal
        to the number of row entries in the program table
        terminate processing.

B. Process each employee record from the Employee time-worked
    file.

    1. Look up the employee pay rate in the pay rate file using the
        job classification code and pay code.

        a. If entry not found in table,
                set pay rate to 0
                move INVALID to output line.

        b. Calculate gross pay as:
                pay rate times hours worked

        c. Print a single-spaced detail line containing the
            following fields in accordance with the print chart.

            Department code
            Employee number
            Job classification
            Shift code
            Hourly rate
            Hours worked
            Gross pay

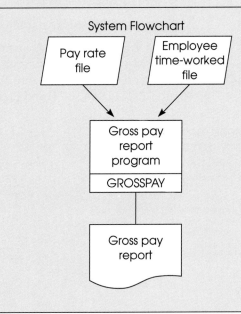

System Flowchart

Figure 12-19 (continued)

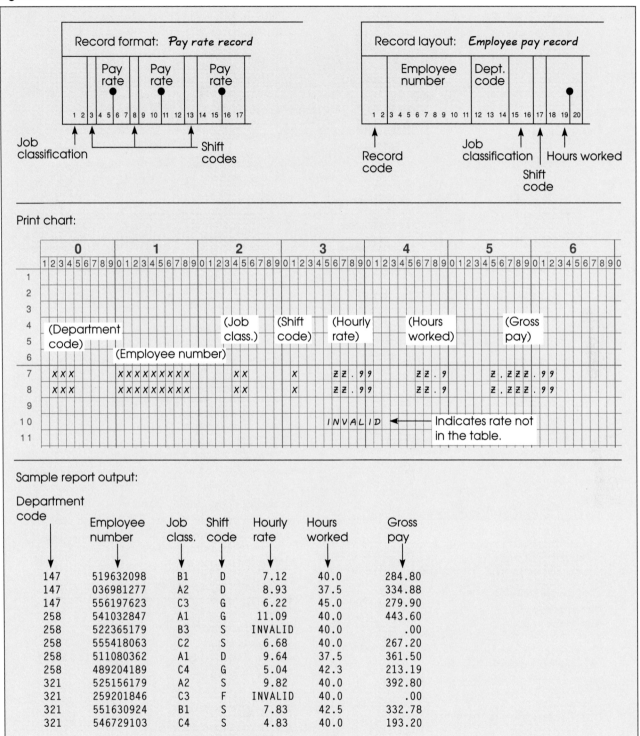

Figure 12-20
Structure chart: GROSSPAY
program.

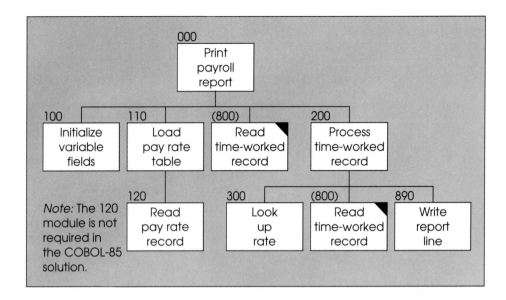

Figure 12-21 Pseudocode: GROSSPAY program.

<u>000-Print-Payroll-Report module</u>

1. Open employee time-worked and report files.
2. Perform 100-Initialize-Variable-Fields.
3. Perform 110-Load-Pay-Rate-Table.
4. If table not loaded
     Move error message to output
     Perform 890-Write-Report-Line
   else
     Perform 800-Read-Time-Worked record
     Perform Process-Payroll record
      until no more records.
5. Close the files.
6. Stop the run.

<u>100-Initialize-Variable-Fields module</u>

1. Set the following to NO
     End-of-table-file switch
     End-of-data-file switch
2. Set Table-loaded switch to space.

<u>110-Load-Pay-Rate-Table module</u>

1. Open pay-rate file.
2. Read first table record
     at end move ERR to Table-loaded-switch
          move YES to End-of-table-file switch.
3. Set Classification-index to 1.
4. Perform 120-Read-Pay-Rate-Record module
     varying Table-entry-counter
     from 1 by 1
     until table loaded or error.

<u>120-Read-Pay-Rate-Record module</u>

1. Move pay rate record to table.
2. Read next table record
     at end move YES to End-of-table-switch.
3. If End-of-table and Correct-table-count
     move YES to Table-loaded-switch.
4. If End-of-table and not Correct-table-count
     move ERR to Table-loaded-switch.
5. If not End-of-table and Correct-table-count
     move ERR to Table-loaded-switch.
6. If not End-of-table and not Correct-table-count
     increment index to next table entry.

<u>200-Process-Payroll-Record module</u>

1. Perform 300-Lookup-Table.
2. If table entry found
     Move table rate to WS-rate
   else
     Move zero to WS-rate
     Move INVALID to output-rate
3. Multiply the WS-rate by Hours-worked to give
   Gross-pay.
4. Move the Gross-pay to the detail-line.
5. Move input fields to detail-line.
6. Move the detail-line to the output-line area.
7. Perform 890-Write-Report-Line.
8. Add 1 to Total-employees.
9. Perform 800-Read-Payroll-Record.

<u>800-Read-Payroll-Record module</u>

1. Read a record from the input Payroll file;
     if EOF move YES to the end-of-file switch.

<u>890-Write-Report-Line module</u>

1. Write the print-line area
     after advancing 1.

Figure 12-22   First three divisions: GROSSPAY program.

```
 1       IDENTIFICATION DIVISION.                              61       WORKING-STORAGE SECTION.
 2                                                             62
 3       PROGRAM-ID.    GROSSPAY.                              63       01  WS-DATA-FILE-SWITCH.
 4       *              WRITTEN BY PRICE/WELBURN.              64           05  WS-END-OF-DATA-FILE-SWITCH    PIC X(3).
 5       *              GLOBAL AIRCRAFT INDUSTRIES.            65               88  END-OF-DATA-FILE                      VALUE "YES".
 6       *              OCT 2,1989.                            66
 7                                                             67       01  WS-WORK-AREAS.
 8       *              THIS PROGRAM PREPARES AN EMPLOYEE GROSS PAY   68           05  WS-RATE-OF-PAY              PIC 99V99.
 9       *              REPORT. THE OVERALL OPERATIONAL STEPS ARE:   69           05  WS-GROSS-PAY               PIC S9(5)V99.
10       *              LOAD AN EMPLOYEE PAY RATE TABLE FROM  70           05  WS-TABLE-ENTRY-COUNTER     PIC 9.
11       *                 A PAY RATE FILE                    71               88  CORRECT-COUNT                        VALUE 7.
12       *              PROCESS EACH EMPLOYEE RECORD FROM A    72
13       *                 TIME-WORKED FILE                   73       01  RT-TABLE-CONTROLS.
14                                                             74           05  WS-END-OF-TABLE-FILE-SWITCH   PIC X(3).
15       *              FOR EACH EMPLOYEE, THE PAY RATE IS DETERMINED   75               88  END-OF-TABLE-FILE                VALUE "YES".
16       *              FROM THE TABLE USING THE JOB CLASSIFICATION   76           05  WS-TABLE-LOADED-SWITCH     PIC X(3).
17       *              AND SHIFT CODES FROM THE EMPLOYEE RECORD. GROSS   77               88  TABLE-LOADED                     VALUE "YES".
18       *              PAY IS CALCULATED AS HOURS-WORKED TIME PAY RATE.   78               88  TABLE-ERROR                      VALUE "ERR".
19                                                             79               88  TABLE-LOAD-CONTINUE              VALUE SPACES.
20                                                             80           05  RT-ENTRY-FOUND-SWITCH      PIC X(3).
21       ENVIRONMENT DIVISION.                                 81               88  RT-ENTRY-FOUND                   VALUE "YES".
22                                                             82               88  RT-END-OF-TABLE                  VALUE "END".
23       CONFIGURATION SECTION.                                83
24                                                             84       01  RT-RATE-TABLE.
25       SOURCE-COMPUTER.  (system dependent).                 85           05  RT-JOB-CLASS-ROW           OCCURS 7 TIMES
26       OBJECT-COMPUTER.  (system dependent).                 86                                          INDEXED BY RT-CLASS-INDEX.
27                                                             87               10  RT-JOB-CLASSIFICATION   PIC X(2).
28       INPUT-OUTPUT SECTION.                                 88               10  RT-SHIFT-ENTRY          OCCURS 3 TIMES
29                                                             89                                          INDEXED BY RT-SHIFT-INDEX.
30       FILE-CONTROL.                                         90                   15  RT-SHIFT-CODE       PIC X(1).
31           SELECT PAY-RATE-FILE                              91                   15  RT-RATE-OF-PAY      PIC 99V99.
32               ASSIGN TO (system dependent).                 92
33           SELECT TIME-WORKED-FILE                           93       01  TW-TIME-WORKED-RECORD-WS.
34               ASSIGN TO (system dependent).                 94           05  TW-RECORD-CODE             PIC X(2).
35           SELECT GROSS-PAY-REPORT                           95           05  TW-EMPLOYEE-NBR            PIC X(9).
36               ASSIGN TO (system dependent).                 96           05  TW-DEPT-CODE               PIC X(3).
37                                                             97           05  TW-JOB-CLASSIF-CODE        PIC X(2).
38                                                             98           05  TW-SHIFT-CODE              PIC X(1).
39       DATA DIVISION.                                        99           05  TW-HOURS-WORKED            PIC 99V9.
40                                                            100
41       FILE SECTION.                                        101       01  DL-DETAIL-LINE.
42                                                            102           05  FILLER                     PIC X(1)    VALUE SPACES.
43       FD  PAY-RATE-FILE                                    103           05  DL-DEPT-CODE               PIC X(3).
44           RECORD CONTAINS 17 CHARACTERS                    104           05  FILLER                     PIC X(5)    VALUE SPACES.
45           LABEL RECORDS ARE STANDARD.                      105           05  DL-EMPLOYEE-NBR            PIC X(9).
46                                                            106           05  FILLER                     PIC X(5)    VALUE SPACES.
47       01  PAY-RATE-RECORD             PIC X(17).           107           05  DL-JOB-CLASSIF-CODE        PIC X(2).
48                                                            108           05  FILLER                     PIC X(5)    VALUE SPACES.
49       FD  TIME-WORKED-FILE                                 109           05  DL-SHIFT-CODE              PIC X(1).
50           RECORD CONTAINS 20 CHARACTERS                    110           05  DL-VALID-HOURLY-RATE.
51           LABEL RECORDS ARE STANDARD.                      111               10  FILLER                 PIC X(5)    VALUE SPACES.
52                                                            112               10  DL-RATE-OF-PAY         PIC ZZ.99.
53       01  TIME-WORKED-RECORD          PIC X(20).           113               10  FILLER                 PIC X(5)    VALUE SPACES.
54                                                            114           05  DL-INVALID-HOURLY-RATE REDEFINES DL-VALID-HOURLY-RATE.
55       FD  GROSS-PAY-REPORT                                 115               10  FILLER                 PIC X(4).
56           RECORD CONTAINS 132 CHARACTERS                   116               10  DL-INVALID-RATE-MESSAGE  PIC X(7).
57           LABEL RECORDS ARE OMITTED.                       117               10  FILLER                 PIC X(4).
58                                                            118           05  DL-HOURS-WORKED            PIC ZZ.9.
59       01  REPORT-LINE                 PIC X(132).          119           05  FILLER                     PIC X(5)    VALUE SPACES.
60                                                            120           05  DL-GROSS-PAY               PIC Z,ZZZ.99.
                                                              121
                                                              122
```

DATA DIVISION Coding

Inspecting the first three divisions in Figure 12-22, you can see that nothing is really new to you. Some points that you might notice:

- The FILE-CONTROL paragraph specifies three files. Correspondingly, the FILE SECTION includes definitions for each.

- The RT-TABLE-CONTROLS record of the WORKING-STORAGE SECTION includes three switches for table processing. As you will see, two of these are used during the table load; the other is used during table access.

- The table record RT-RATE-TABLE corresponds exactly to that of the earlier example (Figure 12-9). However, it does not include the hard-coded entries because this table is loaded from a file.

- The pay rate field (DL-VALID-HOURLY-RATE) in the detail line record is redefined to provide the ability to print the actual hourly rate or the word INVALID (rate not in the table).

Figure 12-23 COBOL-74 PROCEDURE DIVISION: GROSSPAY program.

```
123         PROCEDURE DIVISION.
124
125         000-PRINT-PAYROLL-REPORT.
126             OPEN INPUT TIME-WORKED-FILE
127                  OUTPUT GROSS-PAY-REPORT.
128             PERFORM 100-INITIALIZE-VARIABLE-FIELDS.
129             PERFORM 110-LOAD-PAY-RATE-TABLE.
130             IF NOT TABLE-LOADED
131                 MOVE "TABLE LOAD ERROR - RUN ABORTED" TO REPORT-LINE
132                 PERFORM 890-WRITE-REPORT-LINE
133             ELSE
134                 PERFORM 800-READ-TIME-WORKED-RECORD
135                 PERFORM 200-PROCESS-TIME-WORKED-RECORD
136                     UNTIL END-OF-DATA-FILE.
137             CLOSE TIME-WORKED-FILE
138                   GROSS-PAY-REPORT.
139             STOP RUN.
140
141         100-INITIALIZE-VARIABLE-FIELDS.
142             MOVE "NO" TO WS-END-OF-DATA-FILE-SWITCH.
143             MOVE "NO" TO WS-END-OF-TABLE-FILE-SWITCH.
144             MOVE SPACES TO WS-TABLE-LOADED-SWITCH.
145
146         110-LOAD-PAY-RATE-TABLE.
147             OPEN INPUT PAY-RATE-FILE.
148             READ PAY-RATE-FILE
149                 AT END MOVE "ERR" TO WS-TABLE-LOADED-SWITCH
150                     MOVE "YES" TO WS-END-OF-TABLE-FILE-SWITCH.
151             SET RT-CLASS-INDEX TO 1.
152             PERFORM 120-READ-PAY-RATE-RECORD
153                 VARYING WS-TABLE-ENTRY-COUNTER
154                     FROM 1 BY 1
155                         UNTIL NOT TABLE-LOAD-CONTINUE.
156             CLOSE PAY-RATE-FILE.
157
158         120-READ-PAY-RATE-RECORD.
159             MOVE PAY-RATE-RECORD TO RT-JOB-CLASS-ROW (RT-CLASS-INDEX).
160             READ PAY-RATE-FILE
161                 AT END MOVE "YES" TO WS-END-OF-TABLE-FILE-SWITCH.
162             IF END-OF-TABLE-FILE AND CORRECT-COUNT
163                 MOVE "YES" TO WS-TABLE-LOADED-SWITCH.
164             IF END-OF-TABLE-FILE AND NOT CORRECT-COUNT
165                 MOVE "ERR" TO WS-TABLE-LOADED-SWITCH.
166             IF NOT END-OF-TABLE-FILE AND CORRECT-COUNT
167                 MOVE "ERR" TO WS-TABLE-LOADED-SWITCH.
168             IF NOT END-OF-TABLE-FILE AND NOT CORRECT-COUNT
169                 SET RT-CLASS-INDEX UP BY 1.

170
171         200-PROCESS-TIME-WORKED-RECORD.
172             PERFORM 300-LOOKUP-RATE.
173             IF RT-ENTRY-FOUND
174                 MOVE SPACES TO DL-VALID-HOURLY-RATE
175                 MOVE RT-RATE-OF-PAY (RT-CLASS-INDEX, RT-SHIFT-INDEX)
176                     TO WS-RATE-OF-PAY, DL-RATE-OF-PAY
177             ELSE
178                 MOVE ZEROES TO WS-RATE-OF-PAY
179                 MOVE "INVALID" TO DL-INVALID-RATE-MESSAGE.
180             MOVE TW-EMPLOYEE-NBR TO DL-EMPLOYEE-NBR.
181             MOVE TW-DEPT-CODE TO DL-DEPT-CODE.
182             MOVE TW-JOB-CLASSIF-CODE TO DL-JOB-CLASSIF-CODE.
183             MOVE TW-SHIFT-CODE TO DL-SHIFT-CODE.
184             MOVE TW-HOURS-WORKED TO DL-HOURS-WORKED.
185             MULTIPLY WS-RATE-OF-PAY BY TW-HOURS-WORKED
186                 GIVING WS-GROSS-PAY ROUNDED.
187             MOVE WS-GROSS-PAY TO DL-GROSS-PAY.
188             MOVE DL-DETAIL-LINE TO REPORT-LINE.
189             PERFORM 890-WRITE-REPORT-LINE.
190             PERFORM 800-READ-TIME-WORKED-RECORD.
191
192         300-LOOKUP-RATE.
193             SET RT-CLASS-INDEX TO 1.
194             SEARCH RT-JOB-CLASS-ROW
195                 AT END MOVE "END" TO RT-ENTRY-FOUND-SWITCH
196                 WHEN TW-JOB-CLASSIF-CODE IS EQUAL TO
197                     RT-JOB-CLASSIFICATION (RT-CLASS-INDEX)
198                     MOVE "YES" TO RT-ENTRY-FOUND-SWITCH.
199             IF RT-ENTRY-FOUND
200                 SET RT-SHIFT-INDEX TO 1
201                 SEARCH RT-SHIFT-ENTRY
202                     AT END MOVE "END" TO RT-ENTRY-FOUND-SWITCH
203                     WHEN TW-SHIFT-CODE IS EQUAL TO
204                         RT-SHIFT-CODE (RT-CLASS-INDEX, RT-SHIFT-INDEX)
205                         MOVE "YES" TO RT-ENTRY-FOUND-SWITCH.
206
207         800-READ-TIME-WORKED-RECORD.
208             READ TIME-WORKED-FILE INTO TW-TIME-WORKED-RECORD-WS
209                 AT END MOVE "YES" TO WS-END-OF-DATA-FILE-SWITCH.
210
211         890-WRITE-REPORT-LINE.
212             WRITE REPORT-LINE
213                 AFTER ADVANCING 1.
```

Figure 12-24 COBOL-85 PROCEDURE DIVISION: GROSSPAY program.

```
123         PROCEDURE DIVISION.
124
125         000-PRINT-PAYROLL-REPORT.
126             OPEN INPUT TIME-WORKED-FILE
127                  OUTPUT GROSS-PAY-REPORT
128             PERFORM 100-INITIALIZE-VARIABLE-FIELDS
129             PERFORM 110-LOAD-PAY-RATE-TABLE
130             IF NOT TABLE-LOADED
131                 MOVE "TABLE LOAD ERROR - RUN ABORTED" TO REPORT-LINE
132                 PERFORM 890-WRITE-REPORT-LINE
133             ELSE
134                 PERFORM 800-READ-TIME-WORKED-RECORD
135                 PERFORM 200-PROCESS-TIME-WORKED-RECORD
136                     UNTIL END-OF-DATA-FILE
137             END-IF
138             CLOSE TIME-WORKED-FILE
139                   GROSS-PAY-REPORT
140             STOP RUN.
141
142         100-INITIALIZE-VARIABLE-FIELDS.
143             MOVE "NO" TO WS-END-OF-DATA-FILE-SWITCH
144             MOVE "NO" TO WS-END-OF-TABLE-FILE-SWITCH
145             MOVE SPACES TO WS-TABLE-LOADED-SWITCH.
146
147         110-LOAD-PAY-RATE-TABLE.
148             OPEN INPUT PAY-RATE-FILE
149             READ PAY-RATE-FILE
150                 AT END MOVE "ERR" TO WS-TABLE-LOADED-SWITCH
151                     MOVE "YES" TO WS-END-OF-TABLE-FILE-SWITCH
152             END-READ
153             SET RT-CLASS-INDEX TO 1
154             PERFORM VARYING WS-TABLE-ENTRY-COUNTER
155                 FROM 1 BY 1
156                     UNTIL NOT TABLE-LOAD-CONTINUE
157     *           Inline loop
158                 MOVE PAY-RATE-RECORD
159                     TO RT-JOB-CLASS-ROW (RT-CLASS-INDEX)
160                 READ PAY-RATE-FILE
161                     AT END MOVE "YES" TO WS-END-OF-TABLE-FILE-SWITCH
162                 END-READ
163                 EVALUATE TRUE
164                     WHEN END-OF-TABLE-FILE AND CORRECT-COUNT
165                         MOVE "YES" TO WS-TABLE-LOADED-SWITCH
166                     WHEN END-OF-TABLE-FILE AND NOT CORRECT-COUNT
167                         MOVE "ERR" TO WS-TABLE-LOADED-SWITCH
168                     WHEN NOT END-OF-TABLE-FILE AND CORRECT-COUNT
169                         MOVE "ERR" TO WS-TABLE-LOADED-SWITCH
170                     WHEN OTHER
171                         SET RT-CLASS-INDEX UP BY 1
172                 END-EVALUATE
173             END-PERFORM
174             CLOSE PAY-RATE-FILE.

175
176         200-PROCESS-TIME-WORKED-RECORD.
177             PERFORM 300-LOOKUP-RATE
178             IF RT-ENTRY-FOUND
179                 MOVE SPACES TO DL-VALID-HOURLY-RATE
180                 MOVE RT-RATE-OF-PAY (RT-CLASS-INDEX, RT-SHIFT-INDEX)
181                     TO WS-RATE-OF-PAY, DL-RATE-OF-PAY
182             ELSE
183                 MOVE ZEROES TO WS-RATE-OF-PAY
184                 MOVE "INVALID" TO DL-INVALID-RATE-MESSAGE
185             END-IF
186             MOVE TW-EMPLOYEE-NBR TO DL-EMPLOYEE-NBR
187             MOVE TW-DEPT-CODE TO DL-DEPT-CODE
188             MOVE TW-JOB-CLASSIF-CODE TO DL-JOB-CLASSIF-CODE
189             MOVE TW-SHIFT-CODE TO DL-SHIFT-CODE
190             MOVE TW-HOURS-WORKED TO DL-HOURS-WORKED
191             MULTIPLY WS-RATE-OF-PAY BY TW-HOURS-WORKED
192                 GIVING WS-GROSS-PAY ROUNDED
193             MOVE WS-GROSS-PAY TO DL-GROSS-PAY
194             MOVE DL-DETAIL-LINE TO REPORT-LINE
195             PERFORM 890-WRITE-REPORT-LINE
196             PERFORM 800-READ-TIME-WORKED-RECORD.
197
198         300-LOOKUP-RATE.
199             SET RT-CLASS-INDEX TO 1
200             SEARCH RT-JOB-CLASS-ROW
201                 AT END MOVE "END" TO RT-ENTRY-FOUND-SWITCH
202                 WHEN TW-JOB-CLASSIF-CODE IS EQUAL TO
203                     RT-JOB-CLASSIFICATION (RT-CLASS-INDEX)
204                     SET RT-SHIFT-INDEX TO 1
205                     SEARCH RT-SHIFT-ENTRY
206                         AT END MOVE "END" TO RT-ENTRY-FOUND-SWITCH
207                         WHEN TW-SHIFT-CODE IS EQUAL TO
208                             RT-SHIFT-CODE (RT-CLASS-INDEX, RT-SHIFT-INDEX)
209                             MOVE "YES" TO RT-ENTRY-FOUND-SWITCH
210                     END-SEARCH
211             END-SEARCH.
212
213         800-READ-TIME-WORKED-RECORD.
214             READ TIME-WORKED-FILE INTO TW-TIME-WORKED-RECORD-WS
215                 AT END MOVE "YES" TO WS-END-OF-DATA-FILE-SWITCH.
216
217         890-WRITE-REPORT-LINE.
218             WRITE REPORT-LINE
219                 AFTER ADVANCING 1.
```

PROCEDURE DIVISION Coding—Loading the Table

Most of the coding in this program should be "old hat" to you by now (the table search is the code described in Figure 12-9). However, loading the table can be confusing because of the need to make certain that it is loaded properly before proceeding with processing. Two checks should be made when the table is loaded: (1) ensure that exactly seven records—the number of job-classification codes—are in the table file, and (2) validate the numeric fields. The latter requires data validation techniques that you learned in Chapter 8. To keep this program short so that you can focus on table processing, data validation is omitted.

As illustrated by the general table-loading logic of Figure 12-18, the sequence of actions in loading a table is:

1. Read the first table record.

2. Repeat the following until the table is loaded (or load error occurs):

   a. Count the record.

   b. Move the record to the table.

   c. Read the next table record.

The important point here is that the priming read is used (as with processing a data file). Consequently, the "next record" is not counted until the loop is repeated. This is essential to the following logic for ensuring that the table is properly loaded.

With seven job-classification codes, seven records must be in the pay-rate file; the program must ensure that there are no more and no less. If, as each record is read, it is counted, then following are the four conditions that might occur.

1. End-of-file detected and record count is 7.

   Implication: Valid condition—table is properly loaded.
   Action: Proceed to process the employee data file.

2. End-of-file *not* detected and record count is 7.

   Implication: Invalid condition—file contains more than seven records.
   Action: Print error message and terminate processing.

3. End-of-file detected and record count is *not* 7.

   Implication: Invalid condition—file contains fewer than seven records.
   Action: Print error message and terminate processing.

4. End-of-file *not* detected and record count is *not* 7.

   Implication: Valid condition—table loading not complete.
   Action: Continue loading table (increment to next table entry).

Note that these four possibilities are mutually exclusive (only one can occur for any given pass through the loop).

COBOL-74 Solution. For this test, you could code a nested IF statement—however, it can be confusing. A simple and straightforward approach of using four separate IF statements is used in the 120-READ-PAY-RATE-RECORD module of Figure 12-23. Notice that when this sequence of code is executed, each of the four IF statements will be executed each time—not very "efficient." However, it is simple and easy to understand—an important characteristic of an otherwise confusing sequence of code.

COBOL-85 Solution. The EVALUATE statement is put to good use in this case. Other ways of doing this might result in "more efficient" code, but this spells out each action and serves as good documentation in telling you exactly the conditions under which each action takes place.

Closing the Table File.   Notice that the table file is closed as soon as the loading action is complete (or a load error has been detected). Once the table is loaded, access to the file is no longer required, so the file is closed. Whenever a file is required at only a certain point in a program, it is good programming practice to open it at the point required and close it when it is no longer needed.

Chapter Summary
Topic: Other Single-Level Table-Lookup Considerations

When there is not a one-to-one correspondence between the search argument value and the table argument value, a **range-step table** will result. A range-step table must be of sequential organization; the table arguments are usually arranged in ascending sequence. Typically, only the highest argument value for each range step is stored in the table. In the table lookup, the test for correspondence must thus check for an equal-to or less-than condition.

Sometimes table arguments and table functions are defined in separate tables. When subscripts are employed in the table lookup, the same subscript can be used for both tables. However, if the tables are processed with indexes, separate index-names must be defined and used for each table. The SEARCH/VARYING statement can be used to conveniently handle table lookups for separately defined indexed arguments and functions.

Topic: Multiple-Level Tables

Multiple-level tables contain tables within table entries. A **two-level** or **two-dimensional table** contains two OCCURS clauses, one nested inside the other. A **three-level** or **three-dimensional table** has three nested OCCURS clauses.

Whenever a multiple-level table is accessed, the name of the table entry must be followed by multiple subscripts or indexes. A two-level table requires two subscripts and/or indexes within the parentheses; a three-level table needs three. The PERFORM/VARYING/AFTER statement can be used to handle multiple-level table initialization, copying, totaling, and printing tasks.

Rather than hard-coding table data directly into the program, input-loaded tables are often used. When tables are loaded from input records, each record typically contains the data for one table entry. When processing input-loaded tables, the programmer must provide appropriate logic to handle table sequence checking and table limit considerations.

If the table organization is sequential, the program logic should check to ensure that the table records are actually in the required sequence.

The table-loading logic should always check the table limit to see that the number of table entries provided by the OCCURS clause in the program is not exceeded by the number of actual entries present in the input table file.

Features in COBOL-85 Not in COBOL-74

COBOL-74 provides for processing tables of up to three levels; COBOL-85 provides for processing tables of up to seven levels. In addition to table definition in the DATA DIVISION, this includes an expansion of the number of AFTER phrases allowed in the PERFORM/VARYING/AFTER.

Exercises
Terms for Definition

Combined table/data file _____

Range-step table _____

Separate table file _____

Table column _____

Table row _____

Three-dimensional table _____

Three-level table _____

Two-dimensional table _____

Two-level table _____

Review Questions

1. When there is not a one-to-one correspondence between search arguments

   and table functions, a(n) _____ table can be constructed.

2. Under what condition is it necessary to use separately defined arguments and functions in a table?

   _____

   _____

3. To provide for lookup and retrieval from tables with separately defined arguments and functions, a SEARCH statement with the

   _____ phrase can be used.

4. COBOL-74 can handle multiple-level tables with up to _____ levels.

5. A three-level table contains _____ nested OCCURS clauses.

6. When an elementary field—whose own data-item description does not contain an OCCURS clause—is subordinate to two group fields that do

   contain OCCURS clauses, _____ subscripts and/or indexes must be coded within parentheses in the PROCEDURE DIVISION to identify the specific occurrence.

7. Name four multiple-level table-processing tasks for which it might be appropriate to use the PERFORM/VARYING/AFTER statement.

   a. _____

   b. _____

   c. _____

   d. _____

8. For two-level tables, the PERFORM/VARYING/AFTER statement is typi-

   cally coded with _____ AFTER phrase(s); for three-level

   tables, _____ AFTER phrase(s) are generally used.

9. Rather than hard-coding table data into a program, the table data can be

   _____.

10. When coding a program to load a table with sequential organization from

    input records, the programmer should include logic to _____ the input table records.

11. To ensure that excess table records do not wipe out part of a program, the programmer should include logic to test the _____ when coding a program that loads table records.

Questions About Chapter Examples

1. In the program segment of Figure 12-2, what would happen if the clause OCCURS 13 TIMES were coded as OCCURS 12 TIMES?

_____

_____

2. In the program segment of Figure 12-3, what would happen if the SUBTRACT statement were omitted?

_____

_____

3. Give an "educated guess" as to what would happen in the program segment of Figure 12-5 if the statement

```
MOVE PT-MODEL-PRICE (PT-PRICE-INDEX) TO RL-MODEL-PRICE
```

were accidentally coded as follows:

```
MOVE PT-MODEL-PRICE (MT-MODEL-INDEX) TO RL-MODEL-PRICE
```

_____

_____

4. The DATA DIVISION of the program segment in Figure 12-7 has been changed as follows. Study it carefully and compare it to the code in Figure 12-7.

```
01   RT-RATE-DATA.
     05   FILLER        PIC X(12)   VALUE  "096408930712068006070541 0439".
     05   FILLER        PIC X(12)   VALUE  "106009820783074806680595 0483".
     05   FILLER        PIC X(12)   VALUE  "110910270819078206980622 0504".
01 RT-RATE-TABLE REDEFINES RT-RATE-DATA.
     05   RT-RATE-OF-PAY             OCCURS 3 TIMES.
          10   RT-JOB-CLASS-ROW      OCCURS 7 TIMES
                                     PIC 99V99.
```

What changes will be needed in the PROCEDURE DIVISION code to process the table in this form?

_____

_____

_____

5. The GROSSPAY program (Figure 12-22) is designed to work with a table of a set size: seven job classifications and three pay codes. What changes would need to be made to the program if the number of job classifications were changed from seven to eight?

_____

_____

_____

6. What changes would need to be made to the program if the number of shifts were changed from three to four?

_____

_____

_____

7. In answering Questions 5 and 6, you can see that a fixed size table is not too practical in an environment in which the size of an input-loaded table can change. To generalize this application, a designer decides to change both OCCURS clauses (lines 85 and 88) to OCCURS 10 TIMES. This will allow for up to 10 classifications and 10 pay codes. The input table file will contain a number of records equal to the number of job classification codes. The records will be identical to those of the example program, except they may have more (or fewer) shift-code/pay-rate pairs (not to exceed 10). Describe the changes that would need to be made to the PROCEDURE DIVISION code to accommodate this.

_____

_____

_____

Programming Assignments

Programming Assignment 12-1: GROSSPAY Modification
Modify the GROSSPAY program to accommodate the change described in the preceding Question 7.

Programming Assignment 12-2: Sunsign Name Lookup
Background information:
The dean of students at the Hillside Institute of Astrology and Related Computer Studies has concluded that it would be nice to print a report listing each student and his or her birthdate and sunsign. The program to do this will need a table of dates and corresponding signs.

Input file: Student file (STUDENT.DAT)

Input-record format:

Positions	Field	Data class	Comments
1–2	Record code	Numeric	Code 22
12–25	Student last name	Alphanumeric	
26–35	Student first name	Alphanumeric	
65–70	Date of birth	Numeric	Format: *mmddyy*

Output-report format:

Table data:

Birth date	Zodiac sign name	Birth date	Zodiac sign name
Mar 21–Apr 19	Aries	Sep 23–Oct 22	Libra
Apr 20–May 20	Taurus	Oct 23–Nov 21	Scorpio
May 21–Jun 20	Gemini	Nov 22– Dec 21	Sagittarius
Jun 21–Jul 22	Cancer	Dec 22–Jan 19	Capricorn
Jul 23–Aug 22	Leo	Jan 20–Feb 18	Aquarius
Aug 23–Sep 22	Virgo	Feb 19–Mar 20	Pisces

Program operations:
1. Process each input student record.
2. Print the heading line on the first page and on each following page of the report.
3. For each student record, do the following processing:
   a. Use the month and day of the input date-of-birth field to look up the sunsign name. If the date of birth is invalid, print asterisks in the sunsign-name field of the output report.
   b. If the birth date is on the cusp (the first or last day of each sunsign period), print an asterisk in print position 58, as shown on the print chart.
   c. Print the detail line in accordance with the print-chart specifications.
4. Double-space each detail line. Provide for a span of 57 lines per page.

Programming Assignment 12-3: Load Parts Table
Background information:
For certain processing activities, Tools Unlimited would like to build a table in memory from their inventory file. Each entry of the table is to consist of the Part-number as an argument and the Part-description and Price as corresponding functions. The table produced by this program will be used in conjunction with other programs.

Input file: Inventory file (INVEN.DAT)

Input-record format:

Positions	Field	Data class	Comments
1–2	Record code	Numeric	Code 44
4–13	Part number	Alphanumeric	
14–39	Part description	Alphanumeric	
40	Inventory class	Alphanumeric	
41–46	Unit price	Numeric	Dollars and cents
47–80	Other data		

Output-report format:

```
                    0         1         2         3         4         5         6         7
          1234567890123456789012345678901234567890123456789012345678901234567890123456789012345678901
 1
 2
 3
 4  PARTS TABLE LIST (12-3)                                                          PAGE ZZ9
 5
 6  TABLE OCCURRENCE      PART NUMBER        PART DESCRIPTION                             PRICE
 7
 8         Z9           XXXXXXXXXX        XXXXXXXXXXXXXXXXXXXXXXXXXX                  Z,ZZZ.99
 9
10         Z9           XXXXXXXXXX        XXXXXXXXXXXXXXXXXXXXXXXXXX                  Z,ZZZ.99
```

Program operations:

1. Process each input inventory record.
2. Print the heading line on the first page and on each following page of the report.
    a. Accumulate and print the page number on the heading line as specified on the print chart.
3. Load the appropriate fields from each record into a parts table that contains 75 table entries. The table argument is the part number. The table functions are the part description and price.
    a. Check the sequence of each record to ensure that the part numbers are not duplicated and are in ascending sequence. If the records are out of sequence, print an error message TABLE RECS OUT OF SEQUENCE in the part-description field on the output report.
    b. Check to ensure that not more than 75 parts table records are in the file. If there are, print an error message OVER 75 TABLE RECORDS in the part-description field on the output report.
    c. Check to ensure that at least 15 parts table records are in the file. If there are not, print an error message LESS THAN 15 TABLE RECORDS in the part-description field on the output report.
4. After all the table records have been loaded, print the parts table list as specified on the print chart.
    a. Print the table occurrence number at which each entry is loaded.
    b. Print the detail line in accordance with the print-chart specifications.
5. Double-space each detail line. Provide for a span of 57 lines per page.

Programming Assignment 12-4: Federal Income Tax Computation

Background information:

A federal income tax register report is to be printed. To determine the tax amount, the taxable income for each employee must be used as the search argument in a table lookup.

Input file: Earnings file (EARNINGS.DAT)

Input-record format:

Positions	Field	Data class	Comments
1–2	Record code	Alphanumeric	Code EM
4–6	Plant code	Numeric	
7–10	Department code	Alphanumeric	
11–19	Employee number	Numeric	
20–31	Employee last name	Alphanumeric	
32–40	Employee first name	Alphanumeric	
41	Employee middle initial	Alphanumeric	
44–48	Hours worked	Numeric	Format: 999V99
49	Sex code	Alphabetic	M or F
50	Marital status	Alphabetic	M, S, or H
51–52	Number of exemptions	Numeric	
53	Pay code	Alphabetic	Blank or H
54–59	Pay rate	Numeric	99V9999 for Hourly 9999V99 for Salaried
60–66	This–period earnings	Numeric	99999V99
67–74	Year–to–date earnings	Numeric	999999V99

Output-report format:

```
          0         1         2         3         4         5         6         7         8
 1234567890123456789012345678901234567890123456789012345678901234567890123456789012345678901234567890
 1
 2
 3
 4 FEDERAL  INCOME  TAX  REGISTER  (12-4)                                    MM/DD/YY   PAGE  ZZZ9
 5
 6    EMPLOYEE    ------EMPLOYEE-NAME----  M  NO.   THIS PER.  ANNUALIZED    TAXABLE          TAX
 7     NUMBER     LAST          FIRST      S  EX.   EARNINGS   EARNINGS      EARNINGS       AMOUNT
 8
 9 999-99-9999  XXXXXXXXXXXX  XXXXXXXX     X  99  ZZ,ZZZ.99  ZZZ,ZZZ.99  ZZZ,ZZZ.99  ZZ,ZZZ.99
10
11 999-99-9999  XXXXXXXXXXXX  XXXXXXXX     X  99  ZZ,ZZZ.99  ZZZ,ZZZ.99  ZZZ,ZZZ.99  ZZ,ZZZ.99
```

Note: The table on the following page, to be used for this assignment, is for the year 1985. The "tax simplification" of 1989 reduced the number of categories. The 1985 table is better as a COBOL application.

Table data:

TABLE 7—If the Payroll Period With Respect to an Employee is Annual	
(a) SINGLE person—including head of household	**(b) MARRIED person**

(a) SINGLE person—including head of household

If the amount of wages is:	The amount of income tax to be withheld shall be:	
Not over $1,420 0		
Over— But not over—		of excess over—
$1,420 —$4,370	. . 12%	—$1,420
$4,370 —$9,600	. . $354.00 plus 15%	—$4,370
$9,600 —$15,200	. . $1,138.50 plus 19%	—$9,600
$15,200 —$22,900	. . $2,202.50 plus 25%	—$15,200
$22,900 —$28,930	. . $4,127.50 plus 30%	—$22,900
$28,930 —$34,450	. . $5,936.50 plus 34%	—$28,930
$34,450	. . $7,813.30 plus 37%	—$34,450

(b) MARRIED person

If the amount of wages is:	The amount of income tax to be withheld shall be:	
Not over $2,500 0		
Over— But not over—		of excess over—
$2,500 —$10,000	. . 12%	—$2,500
$10,000 —$19,950	. . $900.00 plus 17%	—$10,000
$19,950 —$24,560	. . $2,591.50 plus 22%	—$19,950
$24,560 —$30,080	. . $3,605.70 plus 25%	—$24,560
$30,080 —$35,590	. . $4,985.70 plus 28%	—$30,080
$35,590 —$46,620	. . $6,528.50 plus 33%	—$35,590
$46,620	. . $10,168.40 plus 37%	—$46,620

Program operations:

1. Process each input earnings record.
2. Print the three heading lines on the first page and on each following page of the report.
   a. Print the run date on the first heading line as specified on the print chart.
   b. Accumulate and print the page number on the first heading line as specified on the print chart.
3. For each earnings record, do the following processing:
   a. Calculate the annualized earnings by multiplying the this-period-earnings field by 12 (the pay periods are monthly; 12 monthly pay periods per year).
   b. Calculate the taxable earnings by multiplying the number of withholding exemptions by $1,000.00 (the personal deduction) and subtract the product from the annualized earnings.
   c. Calculate the annualized federal tax amount from the tax table in accordance with the value of the marital status field. (An S in the marital status field indicates single; an H means head of household; M indicates married.)
   d. Divide the annualized federal tax amount by 12 to equal the federal tax withholding amount for this-period earnings.
   e. Print the detail line in accordance with the print-chart specifications.
4. Double-space each detail line. Provide for a span of 57 lines per page.

Programming Assignment 12-5: Load, Analyze, and Print Temperature Log

Background information:
The data-processing supervisor of the city of Coastaltown, U.S.A. is a meteorology buff and keeps an accurate record of daily high and low temperatures. He wants a report listing daily temperature highs and lows, monthly highs and lows, and the high and low for the year.

Input file: Temperature file (TEMPER.DAT)
Note: This file cannot be processed with the limited use RM compiler because the number of data records exceeds the record count restrictions of this compiler.

Positions	Field	Data class	Comments
3–6	Date	Numeric	*mmdd*
9–11	HIgh temperature	Numeric	Whole number
13–15	Low termperature	Numeric	Whole number

Output-report format:

Low-temperature line

High-temperature line

Example of month-highest indication

Example of month-lowest indication

Program operations:

1. Read each input temperature record. Load the high and low temperatures into a table at the appropriate date location.
   a. If a record has an invalid date, bypass that record; no error message need be printed.
   b. If there is more than one record for any one date, identify the error condition by storing asterisks (***) for that day's temperatures.
2. After all temperatures have been loaded, determine the following:
   a. The highest high temperature for each month
   b. The lowest low temperature for each month
3. Print the annual temperature log as specified on the print chart.
   a. Print the heading line on the first page and on each following page of the report.
      ■ Print the run-date on the first heading line as specified on the print chart.
      ■ Accumulate and print the page number on the first heading line as specified on the print chart.
   b. Print the set of six detail lines for each of the twelve months in accordance with the print chart specifications.
      ■ Left-justify the zero-suppressed temperature adjacent to the hyphen that separates the day number from the temperature. For example, a temperature of 9 degrees on January 1st should be printed as 1-9; a temperature of 32 degrees on January 1st should be printed as 1-32.
      ■ Print the letter H immediately to the right of the highest temperature for each month. Print the letter L immediately to the left of the lowest temperature for each month.
      ■ If the temperatures are missing for a given date, print hyphens in the temperature areas for that date.

c. Print the following information at the end of the report.
   - The temperature and date for the hottest day of the year
   - The temperature and date for the coldest day of the year
   - The total number of days for which valid temperature readings are present within the table
d. Line spacing is to be handled as specified on the print chart. Print 4 months per page; quintuple space between month entries. Print the report footing data on the last page.

Programming Assignment 12-6: Vehicle Insurance Lookup
Background information:

The management of Rent-Ur-Wheels has found it necessary to require a special surcharge that is based on the vehicle type and make. They desire a report listing the daily rental rate and surcharge rate for each vehicle.

Input file: Vehicle file (VEHICLE.DAT)

Positions	Field	Data class	Comments
1–4	Vehicle type	Alphanumeric	
5–18	Make of vehicle	Alphanumeric	
29–35	License number	Alphanumeric	
36–39	Daily rental fee	Numeric	Dollars and cents
40–89	Other data		

Output-report format:

```
         0         1         2         3         4         5         6
 1234567890123456789012345678901234567890123456789012345678901234567890234
 1
 2
 3
 4 RENT-UR-WHEELS  VEHICLE  SURCHARGE  RATES  (12-6)              PAGE  ZZ9
 5
 6
 7    LICENSE       MAKE              TYPE    RATE    SUR.      TOTAL
 8
 9    XXXXXXX     XXXXXXXXXXXXXX     XXXX    ZZ.99   Z.99     ZZ.99
10
11    XXXXXXX     XXXXXXXXXXXXXX     XXXX    ZZ.99   Z.99     ZZ.99
```

Vehicle surcharge table:

Make	Type				
	STD	**LUX**	**VAN**	**SPTS**	**TRCK**
CHEVROLET	2.35	2.97	2.62	2.88	2.61
CHRYSLER	2.50	3.03	2.85	2.99	2.87
FORD	2.38	3.02	2.81	3.02	2.85
OLDSMOBILE	2.62	3.14	2.75	2.92	2.72
NISSAN	2.89	3.26	3.00	3.07	2.99
TOYOTA	2.21	2.82	2.61	2.75	2.63
BMW	2.92	3.31	3.15	3.20	3.14
MERCEDES	3.12	3.57	3.33	3.40	3.32

Program operations:
1. Process each input record.
2. Print the heading line on the first page and on each following page of the report.
   a. Accumulate and print the page number on the heading line as specified on the print chart.
3. For each vehicle record, do the following processing:
   a. Use the vehicle Make and Type to look up the surcharge. If either field is not found in the table, print four asterisks in place of the surcharge output field; do not print a total for that record.
   b. Print the detail line in accordance with the print-chart specifications.
4. Double-space each detail line. Provide for a span of 57 lines per page.

Programming Assignment 12-7: Complete Computers Corporation Vendor Lookup

Background information:
This assignment is identical to that of Assignment 11-6, except that the table is to be loaded from a file.

Input table file: Vendor table file (VENDOR.TBL)

Positions	Field	Data class
1–3	Vendor code	Alphanumeric
4–30	Vendor name	Alphanumeric

Output-report format:
On the first page, list the table file (Vehicle type and make) with appropriate column headings. Do not be concerned with multiple pages. After printing the table, skip to a new page for program output, which is to be identical to that of Assignment 11-6.

Program operations:
1. Load and print the table file. Your array should have a capacity of 25 table entries.
2. Process each input record.
3. Print the two heading lines on the first page and on each following page of the report.
   a. Accumulate and print the page number on the first heading line as specified on the print chart.
4. For each inventory record, do the following processing:
   a. Find the vendor with the lowest price of the three. This is the one that will be used for report output. You must be aware that some records will not have entries for all three vendors. However, every record will have at least one vendor and an associated price which is greater than zero.
   b. Look up the name of the lowest price vendor in the table.
   c. Print the detail line as shown in the print chart. Use the lowest priced vendor name and price.
   d. If the price exceeds the Maximum-price field, print three asterisks to the right on the output line as shown in the print chart.
5. Double-space each detail line. Provide for a span of 57 lines per page.

Sorting and Merging

Chapter Objectives

In Chapter 10, you learned how to write control-break programs. Recall that in order to do control-break processing, records of a file must be in sequence on the control-break fields. For instance, the MCTLBRK program processes a file of sales records, each containing information about one sale including the product sold, the salesperson number, the branch office, and the state. For the report, *major* totals are computed by state, *intermediate* totals by branch office, and *minor* totals for each salesperson. However, before this report can be run, records of the file must be in sequence by state, then within each state group by branch office, and finally within each branch office group by salesperson.

The purpose of this chapter is to learn how to use the SORT statement to arrange records of a file into a desired sequence. From this chapter, you will learn the following:

- Basic principles of the SORT statement and its format.

- Using the SORT statement to sort a file without taking any other actions.

- Using the SORT statement to preprocess records of the file prior to sorting it.

- Using the SORT statement to sort a file and then execute processing actions on records of the sort file (postprocessing).

- Using the SORT statement to preprocess the file prior to sorting it and then execute processing actions on the sort file (postprocessing).

- Using the MERGE statement to combine two files.

CHAPTER 13

Chapter Outline

Introduction to Sorting

Specialized Needs of Sorting—
COBOL-74
Sections in the PROCEDURE DIVISION
The GO TO Statement
The EXIT Statement

The File to be Sorted

Topic: A Sort-Only Program

ENVIRONMENT DIVISION Coding
SELECT Statement for the Sort-Work File

DATA DIVISION Coding
The SD Entry
The Record-Description Entry
　Field Specifications
　Multiple Record-Definition Entries

PROCEDURE DIVISION Coding
The SORT Statement
　The ASCENDING/DESCENDING KEY Phrase
　The USING Phrase
　The GIVING Phrase

Recap of Sort-Only Programs

**Topic: A Sort Program with
Preprocessing of the Input File**

DATA DIVISION Coding

PROCEDURE DIVISION Coding—
COBOL-74
The SORT Statement
　The INPUT PROCEDURE Phrase
Structured Coding Problems Introduced by
the INPUT PROCEDURE Phrase
　Need for Sections
　Module Structure and Numbering Requirements
　Need for GO TO and EXIT Statements
The INPUT PROCEDURE Logic: 2000-IP-SELECT-
INV-RECORDS SECTION
　The RELEASE Statement

PROCEDURE DIVISION Coding—
COBOL-85
Module Numbering
The SORT Statement
　The INPUT PROCEDURE Phrase
The INPUT PROCEDURE Logic
　The RELEASE Statement

Recap of Sort Programs with
Preprocessing of the Input File

**Topic: A Sort Program with
Preprocessing of the Input File and
Postprocessing of the Sorted File**

ENVIRONMENT DIVISION Coding

DATA DIVISION Coding

PROCEDURE DIVISION Coding
The SORT Statement
　The OUTPUT PROCEDURE Phrase
The OUTPUT PROCEDURE Logic
　The RETURN Statement
Notes Regarding the INPUT PROCEDURE

Recap of Sort Programs with
Postprocessing of the Sorted File

**Topic: A Sort Program with
Postprocessing of the Sorted File**

The SORTPOST Program

Topic: The MERGE Statement

Merging

MERGE Statement Deficiency

Merging with the SORT Statement

Introduction to Sorting

Because records of files frequently must be arranged and rearranged in certain sequences for reports, record matching, and the like, **sorting** is a common processing function within commercial data-processing systems. The actual sort logic is typically written and packaged as a generalized utility program so that it can be used to sort various types of records with varying **sort-key** fields.

There are two general approaches to the handling of sort programs within COBOL data-processing installations. One approach is to use the utility sort program directly; such a sort is generally referred to as either a **stand-alone sort** or an **external sort**. The other method is to use the COBOL SORT statement within a COBOL program; this approach is called either a **COBOL sort** or an **internal sort.***

When you use a stand-alone sort to sort a specific group of records into a given sequence, you supply specifications, usually called **parameters**, to the utility sort program. These provide information such as the length of the records to be sorted, the location of the sort-key fields within the record, the data representation for each field, and whether each field is to be arranged in ascending or descending sequence.

To use the COBOL SORT statement in a program, you need to specify much of this same information. SORT-related entries are required in three of the four divisions. The formats of these entries are shown in Figure 13-1.

Specialized Needs of Sorting—COBOL-74

Since COBOL was not specifically designed as a structured language, it includes some features that are not compatible with structured programming techniques. Three of them are: (1) sections in the PROCEDURE DIVISION, (2) the GO TO statement, and (3) the EXIT statement. Since you have not needed them, they have not been described in this book. However, you need them now (if you are using COBOL-74).

If you refer to the general format in Figure 13-1, you will see that two clauses refer to procedures: INPUT PROCEDURE and OUTPUT PROCEDURE. COBOL-74 requires that these procedure names be the names of sections, not paragraphs. Thus, if you are to use the SORT statement with COBOL-74, you need to know about PROCEDURE DIVISION sections and also about the GO TO and EXIT statements.

However, COBOL-85 does allow procedure reference in the SORT statement to be a paragraph name. Hence, the COBOL-85 program examples in this chapter do not use the aforementioned non-structured COBOL language elements.

Sections in the PROCEDURE DIVISION

As you have observed, a **program module** can be defined as a contiguous group of statements referred to as a unit. Throughout this book, the word *module* has been synonymous with COBOL paragraph. If a module (paragraph) is to be performed, you code a statement such as:

```
PERFORM 100-INITIALIZE-VARIABLE-FIELDS
```

This statement causes control to be transferred to a paragraph; when execution of

---

*Unfortunately, the terms *external* and *internal* sometimes cause confusion because their usage by COBOL programmers differs from that used in a computer science context. That is, when a COBOL programmer uses the terms *internal* and *external*, he or she is referring to the sort as being inside or outside a COBOL program, respectively. In computer science courses, an internal sort is typically programmer-coded logic with the sort done entirely in main memory; an external sort is one performed in work areas on disk or tape storage. In commercial data-processing installations, sorting is almost always done through packaged sort logic on disk storage; internal and programmer-coded sorts are rarely used.

Figure 13-1 SORT-related formats.

```
SORT Formats:

        ENVIRONMENT DIVISION.
        INPUT-OUTPUT SECTION.
        FILE-CONTROL.
                SELECT sort-file name
                        ASSIGN TO implementor-name.


        DATA DIVISION.
        FILE SECTION.

        ⌈
        │       SD sort-file-name
        ⌊
                ⌈ RECORD CONTAINS [integer TO] integer-2 CHARACTERS ⌉

                ⌈       ⌈ RECORD IS   ⌉                                  ⌉
                │ DATA ⟨               ⟩ data-name-1 [data-name-2] . . . │ .
                ⌊       ⌊ RECORDS ARE ⌋                                  ⌋

                { record-description-entry } . . . ⌉ . . .
                                                   ⌋


        PROCEDURE DIVISION.

                                   ⌈ ASCENDING  ⌉
          SORT sort-file-name ON  ⟨              ⟩ KEY data-name-1 [data-name-2] . . .
                                   ⌊ DESCENDING ⌋

                ⌈         ⌈ ASCENDING  ⌉                                          ⌉
                │ ON     ⟨              ⟩ KEY data-name-3 [data-name-4] . . .     │ . . .
                ⌊         ⌊ DESCENDING ⌋                                          ⌋

                ⌈ INPUT PROCEDURE IS section-name-1    ⌉
               ⟨                                        ⟩
                ⌊ USING file-name-1 [file-name-3] . . . ⌋

                ⌈ OUTPUT PROCEDURE IS section-name-2 ⌉
               ⟨                                      ⟩
                ⌊ GIVING file-name-2                  ⌋

          RELEASE record-name [FROM identifier]

          RETURN file-name RECORD [INTO identifier]
                AT END imperative-statement
```

that paragraph is completed, control is returned.

Actually, COBOL includes means by which two *or more* paragraphs can be treated as a module and performed by a single PERFORM statement. These have not been introduced in this book because their use tends to be inconsistent with good structured programming practices. However, the COBOL-74 SORT statement requires, for certain actions, that a PROCEDURE DIVISION section be designated for actions to be taken.

In Figure 13-2, you can see that the printing of an address label is done in three consecutive paragraphs. In Example A, these are executed with three consecutive PERFORM statements. In Example B, they are defined as the PRINT-MAILING-LABEL section and are executed by a single PERFORM. As illustrated here, one or more paragraphs may be organized into a section and given a section-name. A section-name can be thought of as a "super-procedure-name." In general, a section-name can be referenced as the procedure-name for a PERFORM statement just like a paragraph-name.

Figure 13-2   PROCEDURE DIVISION sections.

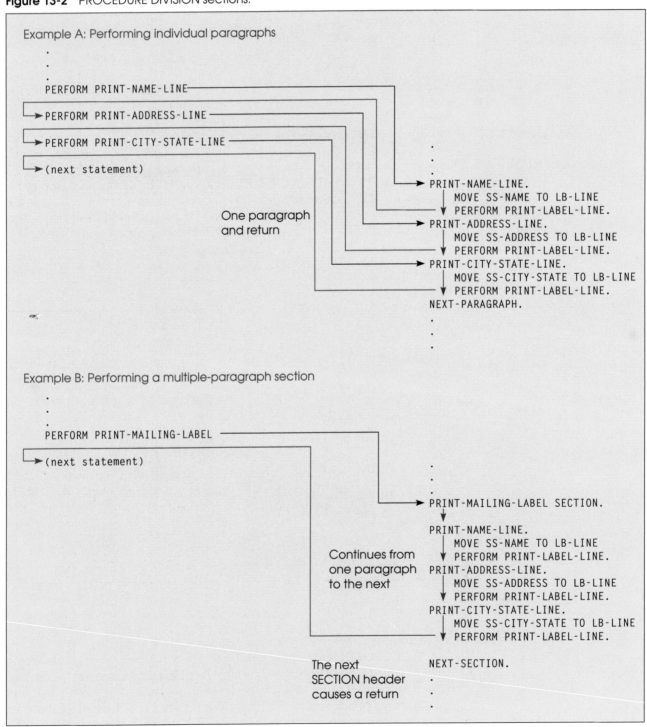

The GO TO Statement   The GO TO statement allows you to transfer control of the program in much the same way as a PERFORM. That is, you could code

```
GO TO 250-CHECK-CONTROL-FIELDS.
```

much as you would code

```
PERFORM 250-CHECK-CONTROL-FIELDS.
```

However, the significant difference is that there are no provisions for returning to the paragraph from which the transfer is made. Once control is transferred to a paragraph, execution continues from that point on. The overuse of this statement is considered *the* taboo in structured COBOL programming. (Structured languages do not even include a GO TO type of statement.) However, as you will see, the nature of the COBOL-74 SORT statement requires use of the GO TO for certain actions.

The EXIT Statement   Right now, you probably have a problem thinking of a situation in which it would be useful to have a paragraph that does nothing: a **null paragraph**. However, there is indeed a need for such a paragraph with the COBOL-74 SORT statement. The reserved word EXIT provides a null statement for a dummy PROCEDURE DIVISION paragraph—one that contains no other statements. When EXIT is used, it must be the only statement in the paragraph and must be followed by a period. Such a paragraph would take the following form:

```
PARAGRAPH-TO-DO-NOTHING.
    EXIT.
```

The File to be Sorted   So that the primary focus of this chapter can be on sort-program coding, the same file is used for all four sample programs. It is an inventory file and has a record format shown in Figure 13-3. In all four examples, the sorting will be on three fields as follows:

Major field: Warehouse code (columns 3–4)

Intermediate field: Inventory value (columns 46–54)

Minor field: Part number (columns 5–19)

Remember, this means that all records with the same warehouse code (major field) will be grouped together. Within each group, the records will be in sequence by inventory value (the intermediate field), and so on. If you need to clarify this, refer to Figure 13-4.

Figure 13-3   Format for the Inventory record.

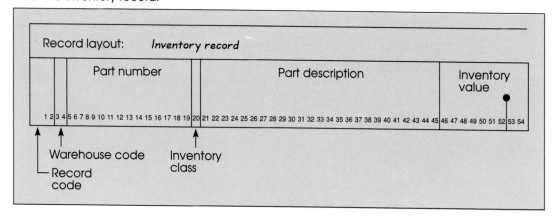

Figure 13-4   Inventory records sorted on Warehouse code, Inventory value, and Part number.

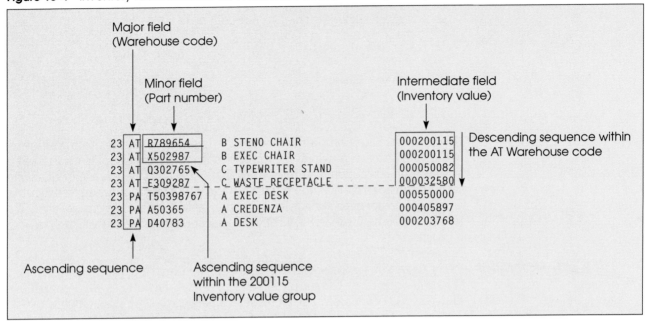

All of the preceding example programs have been introduced with complete program documentation in order to lay a solid foundation for overall program design and coding. This has served as a consistent example of how you should design and code your own programs. By now, you should be quite experienced with these concepts. So in order to concentrate on sort-related topics, the inventory program documentation will be somewhat abbreviated.

Topic: A Sort-Only Program

Programming specifications and a system flowchart for a program to sort an inventory file are shown in Figure 13-5. Observe that the only function of this program is to sort the records of the file into sequence in accordance with the values present in the warehouse-code, inventory-value, and part-number fields.

This program is named SORTONLY (to indicate that this is an example of a sort-only program). The program coding is shown in Figure 13-6. The ENVIRONMENT, DATA, and PROCEDURE DIVISION statements that apply to the sorting function are identified on the program listing and will be discussed in this Topic.

ENVIRONMENT DIVISION Coding

Notice in the system flowchart (as shown in Figure 13-5) that a **sort-work file** has been depicted. This is necessary because sort programs require an area in which to rearrange the records during the sorting process. This sort-work file must be specified in the COBOL program.

Figure 13-5
Programming
documentation: Sort-only
inventory-record program.

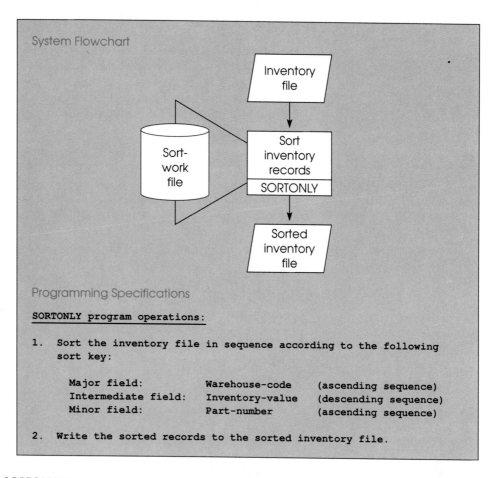

System Flowchart

Programming Specifications

SORTONLY program operations:

1. Sort the inventory file in sequence according to the following
    sort key:

    Major field: Warehouse-code   (ascending sequence)
    Intermediate field: Inventory-value   (descending sequence)
    Minor field: Part-number   (ascending sequence)

2. Write the sorted records to the sorted inventory file.

Figure 13-6   COBOL coding: SORTONLY program.

```
 1        IDENTIFICATION DIVISION.               34        DATA DIVISION.
 2                                               35
 3        PROGRAM-ID.    SORTONLY.               36        FILE SECTION.
 4        *              WRITTEN BY T. WELBURN.  37
 5        *              SILICON VALLEY MANUFACTURING COMPANY.  38    FD  INVENTORY-FILE                  Input
 6        *              MAR 28, 1986.           39            RECORD CONTAINS 54 CHARACTERS   file
 7        *              REVISED 10/3/89 BY W. PRICE.  40       LABEL RECORDS ARE STANDARD.    to be
 8                                               41                                            sorted
 9        *              THIS IS A SORT-ONLY PROGRAM.  42    01  IR-INVENTORY-RECORD.
10                                               43            05  FILLER              PIC X(54).
11        *              SORT STATEMENT PHRASES SPECIFIED ARE:  44
12        *                 USING                45    FD  SORTED-INVENTORY-FILE         Sorted
13        *                 GIVING               46            RECORD CONTAINS 54 CHARACTERS   output
14                                               47            LABEL RECORDS ARE STANDARD.    file
15                                               48
16        ENVIRONMENT DIVISION.                  49    01  SI-INVENTORY-RECORD.
17                                               50            05  FILLER              PIC X(54).
18        CONFIGURATION SECTION.                 51
19                                               52    SD  SORT-FILE
20        SOURCE-COMPUTER. (system dependent).   53            RECORD CONTAINS 54 CHARACTERS.
21        OBJECT-COMPUTER. (system dependent).   54
22                                               55    01  SR-SORT-RECORD.              Sort-
23        INPUT-OUTPUT SECTION.                  56            05  FILLER              PIC X(2).   work
24                                               57            05  SR-WAREHOUSE-CODE   PIC X(2).   file
25        FILE-CONTROL.                          58            05  SR-PART-NUMBER      PIC X(15).
26            SELECT INVENTORY-FILE              59            05  FILLER              PIC X(26).
27                ASSIGN TO (system dependent).  60            05  SR-INVENTORY-VALUE  PIC S9(7)V99.
28            SELECT SORTED-INVENTORY-FILE       61
29                ASSIGN TO (system dependent).  62
30            SELECT SORT-FILE                   63        PROCEDURE DIVISION.
31                ASSIGN TO (system dependent).  64
32                                               65        000-SORT-INVENTORY-RECORDS.
33                                               66            SORT SORT-FILE              SORT
                                                 67                ASCENDING KEY  SR-WAREHOUSE-CODE   state-
                                                 68                DESCENDING KEY SR-INVENTORY-VALUE  ment
                                                 69                ASCENDING KEY  SR-PART-NUMBER
                                                 70                    USING  INVENTORY-FILE
                                                 71                    GIVING SORTED-INVENTORY-FILE.
                                                 72            STOP RUN.
```

SELECT Statement for the Sort-Work File

As shown in Figure 13-7, the SELECT statement for a sort-work file is coded much like that for any other type of file. However, some computer-operating systems have a special implementor-name that must be specified in the ASSIGN clause. (For this requirement, you should check Appendix C or the reference manual for your specific compiler.) Because most COBOL programs contain only one sort-work file per program, and because an application-dependent file-name does not offer much meaning for this file, the user-defined file-name of SORT-FILE is often chosen for the sort-work file.

DATA DIVISION Coding

Like other files, the sort-work file must be described in the FILE SECTION of the DATA DIVISION. However, whereas an FD entry is used for regular files, an SD (**S**ort-file **D**escription) entry is required to describe a sort-work file.

The SD Entry

An SD entry, shown in Figure 13-8, has the same syntax as an FD entry, except that you do not specify the LABEL RECORDS clauses. The operating system or compiler predefines the label record handling. Another clause that you will commonly find in the FD is the BLOCK CONTAINS. Remember from Chapter 2 that this clause is used when multiple data records (logical records) are grouped together for storage on disk as a physical record. This clause is never included in the SD (regardless of the input file) because the sort program determines the optimum block size for the sort-work file.

As with the FD entry, the RECORD CONTAINS clause is optional. However, as discussed in Chapter 2, the benefits of specifying the RECORD CONTAINS clause suggest that it be coded.

The Record-Description Entry

Just as one or more 01-level record-description entries follow an FD entry, record-description entries for the records to be sorted follow the SD entry. However, you should be aware of two special considerations for the sort-file record-description entries.

Field Specifications. Within the record-description entry for a sort-file record, you must specify each of the fields that will be used to determine the record sequence. That is, you must name the sort-key fields (SR-WAREHOUSE-CODE, SR-INVENTORY-VALUE, and SR-PART NUMBER for the SORTONLY program).

As was coded for the SR-SORT-RECORD description, it is common practice to affix data-names to only the sort-key fields; all other areas are simply referred to as FILLER. The reason for this is that the sort-file record is typically used only for

Figure 13-7
SELECT statement for the sort-work file.

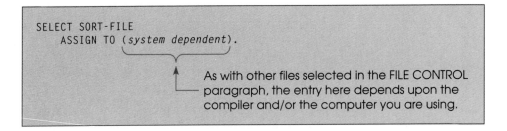

```
SELECT SORT-FILE
    ASSIGN TO (system dependent).
```

As with other files selected in the FILE CONTROL paragraph, the entry here depends upon the compiler and/or the computer you are using.

Figure 13-8
SD entry format.

```
Format:

   [ SD sort-file-name

        [ RECORD CONTAINS [integer-1 TO] integer-2 CHARACTERS ]

        [ DATA  { RECORD IS   }  data-name-1 [data-name-2] ... ]
                { RECORDS ARE }

        { record-description-entry } ...  ] ...
```

```
Example:

   SD  SORT-FILE
           RECORD CONTAINS 54 CHARACTERS.

   01  SR-SORT-RECORD.
       05  FILLER                      PIC X(2).
       05  SR-WAREHOUSE-CODE           PIC X(2).
       05  SR-PART-NUMBER              PIC X(15).
       05  FILLER                      PIC X(26).
       05  SR-INVENTORY-VALUE          PIC S9(7)V99.
```

the sort; definitions for fields that are not part of the sort key are not required and serve little purpose. Thus, although the nonsort-key fields can be specifically named in the sort-file record with a user-defined word, they are usually described only in the input- and/or output-area record-descriptions.

Multiple Record-Definition Entries.   Although a sort file may contain more than one 01-level record-description entry, multiple entries are seldom coded. The reason stems from the record-sorting requirement that sort-key fields must be in the same relative position for each record of the sort. Given this requirement—together with the practice of naming nonsort-key fields as FILLER—even if multiple record-types were being sorted, their record-definition entries would match. As a result, more than one record-definition entry is rarely required for a sort-work file.

PROCEDURE DIVISION Coding

The PROCEDURE DIVISION for the SORTONLY program is very short. It contains only two statements: SORT and STOP.

The SORT Statement

The SORT statement is used to specify the name of the sort-work file, the sort-key fields, the input-file processing, and the output-file processing. As shown in Figure 13-9, after the verb SORT, the name of the sort-work file is specified.

Figure 13-9 SORT statement format.

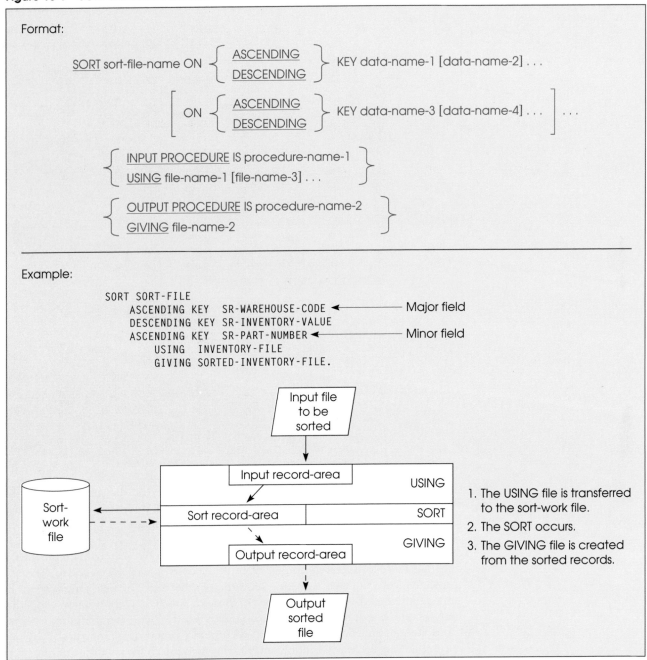

Format:

SORT sort-file-name ON { ASCENDING / DESCENDING } KEY data-name-1 [data-name-2] . . .

[ON { ASCENDING / DESCENDING } KEY data-name-3 [data-name-4] . . .] . . .

{ INPUT PROCEDURE IS procedure-name-1 / USING file-name-1 [file-name-3] . . . }

{ OUTPUT PROCEDURE IS procedure-name-2 / GIVING file-name-2 }

Example:

```
SORT SORT-FILE
    ASCENDING KEY  SR-WAREHOUSE-CODE  ◄───────── Major field
    DESCENDING KEY SR-INVENTORY-VALUE
    ASCENDING KEY  SR-PART-NUMBER ◄───────────── Minor field
        USING  INVENTORY-FILE
        GIVING SORTED-INVENTORY-FILE.
```

Input file to be sorted

Input record-area   USING

Sort-work file

Sort record-area   SORT

Output record-area   GIVING

Output sorted file

1. The USING file is transferred to the sort-work file.
2. The SORT occurs.
3. The GIVING file is created from the sorted records.

The ASCENDING/DESCENDING KEY Phrase.   After the sort-work file-name, you must include the phrase ASCENDING KEY or DESCENDING KEY, depending upon whether the sort-key field is to be arranged in ascending or descending sequence. In this phrase, you list each of the sort-key fields in major through minor field order. That is, if there is more than one field in the sort key, you list the major field first, and list additional fields in order of decreasing significance. This is independent of whether the ASCENDING or DESCENDING option is chosen for a field.

You may mix ASCENDING KEY and DESCENDING KEY sort-key fields within the same SORT statement, as has been done in the SORTONLY program. The reserved words ASCENDING KEY and DESCENDING KEY may be specified for each field or merely coded only for the first field and whenever there is a change from ASCENDING to DESCENDING or vice versa.

Although the optional reserved word ON may be specified, notice in the SORT statement format that it contributes little meaning and is thus usually omitted. Additional KEY phrase coding examples are shown in Figure 13-10. Although the COBOL standard does not place a limit on the number of KEY fields that may be specified, the sort program that the compiler uses will have a certain limit—perhaps a dozen fields or so. Should you need to know the maximum number of fields that can be listed, check the COBOL reference manual for your compiler.

Once in a while, a field that contains mixed-sign representations is a sort-key field. For example, suppose a balance-due field is specified as a KEY field. Most records will have a positive balance-due amount; a few records will have a negative value—a credit balance—in the field; and perhaps an unsigned, assumed positive, representation inadvertently exists in certain fields. In this situation, you must be sure to specify such a field as an elementary item with a signed numeric PICTURE in the sort record. If you defined the field as a group or an alphanumeric item, it would be sorted according to its character value rather than its algebraic value. Depending upon the specific sign representations that the computer system uses, the character-value sequence could cause positive values to be considered lower than negative values; unsigned values might be considered higher than positive values.

The SORT statement will provide correct algebraic sequencing when a signed numeric field is referenced in the KEY phrase. That is, unsigned values are considered equal to positive values and negative values are considered lower in sequence than positive values.

Also, the USAGE of a sort-key field affects the sort sequencing. As an example, recognize that packed fields must be treated differently from unpacked fields during the sort. You will get incorrect sorting results if you do not use the correct USAGE for each KEY field.

Figure 13-10

KEY phrase examples.

```
Example A: ASCENDING KEY specified once

    SORT SORT-FILE
        ASCENDING KEY DEPARTMENT-NUMBER
                      EMPLOYEE-NUMBER
                 .
                 .
                 .


Example B: ASCENDING KEY specified for each sort-key field

    SORT SORT-FILE
        ASCENDING KEY TERRITORY-CODE
        ASCENDING KEY SALES-REP-NUMBER
        ASCENDING KEY PRODUCT-CODE
                 .
                 .
                 .


Example C: Both ASCENDING KEY and DESCENDING KEY phrases specified

    SORT SORT-FILE
        DESCENDING KEY GRADE-POINT-AVERAGE
        ASCENDING KEY  LAST-NAME
                       FIRST-NAME
                       MIDDLE-NAME
                 .
                 .
                 .
```

The USING Phrase.   After the KEY phrase is coded, the USING phrase is specified to name the input file that is to be sorted. When the USING phrase is coded, the SORT statement causes the named file to be opened, transferred to the sort-work file, and closed. In the SORTONLY program, the INVENTORY-FILE is named in the USING phrase as the input file to be sorted.

Observe that OPEN and CLOSE statements have not been coded for the INVENTORY-FILE because these functions are handled automatically by the SORT statement for the USING file. In fact, a syntactical error would occur if the programmer explicitly coded an OPEN and/or a CLOSE statement for a USING file.

According to the standard, notice in the USING phrase format notation that multiple input files can be listed so that two or more files can be sorted together. However, some COBOL compilers do not actually provide this capability. This is another area in which you must check the reference manual for the specific compiler being used.

The GIVING Phrase.   The GIVING phrase provides you with the ability to name the sorted output file that is to be created. When it is coded, the SORT statement causes the named file to be opened, handles the transfer of records from the sort-work file to it, and provides for the closing of the file. In the SORTONLY program, the SORTED-INVENTORY-FILE will be created as the sorted output file.

Just as it is with the USING file, you must not code OPEN and CLOSE statements for a GIVING file. These functions are handled automatically by the SORT statement.

Recap of Sort-Only Programs

Sort-only programs utilize the USING and GIVING phrases of the SORT statement. Actually, sort-only programs are seldom written. It is much quicker to code the parameter specifications for a stand-alone sort and, as will be discussed in the COBOL Programming Perspective in this chapter, a sort-only program does not offer the input/output processing advantages that are provided by the other COBOL sort options.

However, a SORT statement that has both the USING and GIVING phrases is sometimes coded within a program that handles other processing for one of the files. Such a statement might be specified (1) to sort a USING file that has been previously opened, processed, and closed within a program, or (2) for a GIVING file that will subsequently be opened, processed, and closed.

Topic: A Sort Program with Preprocessing of the Input File

Programming documentation for a sort program with preprocessing of the input file is shown in Figure 13-11; this program also sorts the input-inventory file. Notice that the specifications for this program are identical to those for the SORTONLY program, except that only those inventory records that carry an inventory class code of "N" are to be sorted and written to the output-sorted inventory file.

This program is named SORTPRE to indicate that it is an example of a sort program with preprocessing of the input file. The structure chart for this program is shown in Figure 13-12. When a SORT statement is present within a program, observe that the structure chart requires a dummy block to represent the sort function.

COBOL coding for the SORTPRE program appears in Figure 13-13. Here you can see that two versions of the PROCEDURE DIVISION are included: one for COBOL-74 and the other for COBOL-85. Although the SORT statement itself is identical for the two, the way in which the input procedure is implemented is significantly different.

Figure 13-11
Programming
documentation: Sort
program with preprocessing
of the input-inventory file.

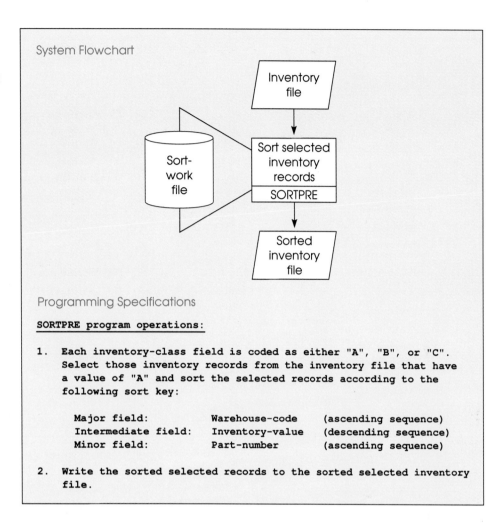

System Flowchart

Programming Specifications

SORTPRE program operations:

1. Each inventory-class field is coded as either "A", "B", or "C".
    Select those inventory records from the inventory file that have
    a value of "A" and sort the selected records according to the
    following sort key:

Major field:	Warehouse-code	(ascending sequence)
Intermediate field:	Inventory-value	(descending sequence)
Minor field:	Part-number	(ascending sequence)

2. Write the sorted selected records to the sorted selected inventory
    file.

Figure 13-12
Structure chart: Sort program
with preprocessing of the
input-inventory file.

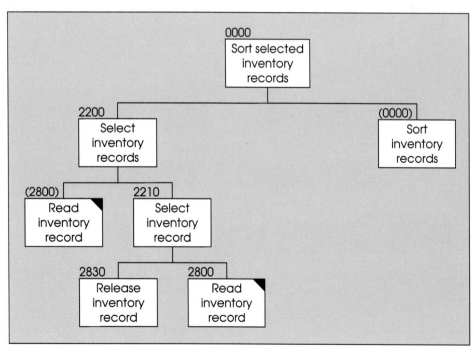

Figure 13-13   COBOL coding: SORTPRE program.

```
  1        IDENTIFICATION DIVISION.                    36        DATA DIVISION.
  2                                                    37
  3        PROGRAM-ID.    SORTPRE.                     38        FILE SECTION.
  4        *              WRITTEN BY T. WELBURN.       39
  5        *              SILICON VALLEY MANUFACTURING COMPANY.   40        FD  INVENTORY-FILE
  6        *              MAR 28, 1986.                41            RECORD CONTAINS 54 CHARACTERS
  7        *              REVISED 10/3/89 BY W. PRICE. 42            LABEL RECORDS ARE STANDARD.
  8                                                    43
  9        *              THIS IS A SORT PROGRAM WITH PREPROCESSING   44        01  IR-INVENTORY-RECORD.
 10        *                 OF THE INPUT FILE.        45            05  FILLER                PIC X(19).
 11                                                    46            05  IR-INVENTORY-CLASS-CODE  PIC X(1).
 12        *              SORT STATEMENT PHRASES SPECIFIED ARE   47            05  FILLER                PIC X(34).
 13        *                 INPUT PROCEDURE           48
 14        *                 GIVING                    49        FD  SORTED-INVENTORY-FILE
 15                                                    50            RECORD CONTAINS 54 CHARACTERS
 16                                                    51            LABEL RECORDS ARE STANDARD.
 17        ENVIRONMENT DIVISION.                       52
 18                                                    53        01  SI-INVENTORY-RECORD.
 19        CONFIGURATION SECTION.                      54            05  FILLER                PIC X(54).
 20                                                    55
 21        SOURCE-COMPUTER.  (system dependent).       56        SD  SORT-FILE
 22        OBJECT-COMPUTER.  (system dependent).       57            RECORD CONTAINS 54 CHARACTERS.
 23                                                    58
 24        INPUT-OUTPUT SECTION.                       59        01  SR-SORT-RECORD.
 25                                                    60            05  FILLER                PIC X(2).
 26        FILE-CONTROL.                               61            05  SR-WAREHOUSE-CODE     PIC X(2).
 27                                                    62            05  SR-PART-NUMBER        PIC X(15).
 28            SELECT INVENTORY-FILE                   63            05  FILLER                PIC X(26).
 29                ASSIGN TO (system dependent).       64            05  SR-INVENTORY-VALUE    PIC S9(7)V99.
 30            SELECT SORTED-INVENTORY-FILE            65
 31                ASSIGN TO (system dependent).       66        WORKING-STORAGE SECTION.
 32            SELECT SORT-FILE                        67
 33                ASSIGN TO (system dependent).       68        01  WS-SWITCHES.
 34                                                    69            05  WS-END-OF-FILE-SWITCH   PIC X(3).
 35                                                    70                88  END-OF-FILE             VALUE "YES".
                                                       71
                                                       72
```

(a) The first three divisions.

```
 73        PROCEDURE DIVISION.                         73        PROCEDURE DIVISION.
 74                                                    74
 75        0000-ML-SORT-INV-RECORDS SECTION.           75        0000-SORT-INVENTORY-RECORDS.
 76                                                    76            OPEN INPUT INVENTORY-FILE.
 77        0000-SORT-INVENTORY-RECORDS.                77            SORT SORT-FILE
 78            OPEN INPUT INVENTORY-FILE.              78                ASCENDING KEY   SR-WAREHOUSE-CODE
 79            SORT SORT-FILE                          79                DESCENDING KEY SR-INVENTORY-VALUE
 80                ASCENDING KEY   SR-WAREHOUSE-CODE   80                ASCENDING KEY   SR-PART-NUMBER
 81                DESCENDING KEY SR-INVENTORY-VALUE   81                    INPUT PROCEDURE IS 2000-SELECT-INV-RECORDS
 82                ASCENDING KEY   SR-PART-NUMBER      82                    GIVING SORTED-INVENTORY-FILE.
 83                    INPUT PROCEDURE IS  2000-IP-SELECT-INV-RECORDS   83            CLOSE INVENTORY-FILE.
 84                    GIVING SORTED-INVENTORY-FILE.   84            STOP RUN.
 85            CLOSE INVENTORY-FILE.                   85
 86            STOP RUN.                               86        2000-SELECT-INV-RECORDS.
 87                                                    87            MOVE "NO" TO WS-END-OF-FILE-SWITCH.
 88        2000-IP-SELECT-INV-RECORDS SECTION.         88            PERFORM 2800-READ-INVENTORY-RECORD.
 89                                                    89            PERFORM 2200-SELECT-INVENTORY-RECORD
 90        2200-IP-SELECT-INV-RECORDS.                 90                UNTIL END-OF-FILE.
 91            MOVE "NO" TO WS-END-OF-FILE-SWITCH.     91
 92            PERFORM 2800-READ-INVENTORY-RECORD.     92        2200-SELECT-INVENTORY-RECORD.
 93            PERFORM 2210-SELECT-INVENTORY-RECORD    93
 94                UNTIL END-OF-FILE.                  94            IF IR-INVENTORY-CLASS-CODE IS EQUAL TO "A"
 95            GO TO 2999-EXIT.                        95                MOVE IR-INVENTORY-RECORD TO SR-SORT-RECORD
 96                                                    96                PERFORM 2850-RELEASE-INVENTORY-RECORD.
 97        2210-SELECT-INVENTORY-RECORD.               97            PERFORM 2800-READ-INVENTORY-RECORD.
 98            IF IR-INVENTORY-CLASS-CODE IS EQUAL TO "A"   98
 99                MOVE IR-INVENTORY-RECORD TO SR-SORT-RECORD   99        2800-READ-INVENTORY-RECORD.
100                PERFORM 2830-RELEASE-INVENTORY-RECORD.   100            READ INVENTORY-FILE
101            PERFORM 2800-READ-INVENTORY-RECORD.    101                AT END MOVE "YES" TO WS-END-OF-FILE-SWITCH.
102                                                   102
103        2800-READ-INVENTORY-RECORD.                103        2850-RELEASE-INVENTORY-RECORD.
104            READ INVENTORY-FILE                     104            RELEASE SR-SORT-RECORD.
105                AT END MOVE "YES" TO WS-END-OF-FILE-SWITCH.
106
107        2830-RELEASE-INVENTORY-RECORD.
108            RELEASE SR-SORT-RECORD.
109
110        2999-EXIT.
111            EXIT.
```

Mainline procedure

INPUT PROCEDURE

Mainline program

INPUT PROCEDURE

Input components

(b) The PROCEDURE DIVISION—COBOL-74.   (c) The PROCEDURE DIVISION—COBOL-85.

DATA DIVISION Coding

The DATA DIVISION coding for the SORTPRE program differs from the SORTONLY program in just two ways. First, the input IR-INVENTORY-RECORD record-description entry has been specified with the IR-INVENTORY-CLASS-CODE field explicitly defined as an elementary field, rather than merely being part of the 54-character FILLER area. This definition is required because this inventory class-code field must be tested to determine whether or not the record should be written to the sort-work file. (Of course, if desired, all the fields of the IR-INVENTORY-RECORD could have been explicitly defined.)

Second, because the USING phrase is not specified in the SORT statement for this program, the WS-END-OF-FILE-SWITCH is required and has thus been defined in the WORKING-STORAGE SECTION.

Although WORKING-STORAGE SECTION definition of input and output records has been generally recommended in this text, notice that FILE SECTION definition has been used in this chapter. This has been done to keep these sort programs shorter and more straightforward so that you can focus upon the sort-related processing. However, WORKING-STORAGE SECTION record-definition is recommended for more complex sort programs.

PROCEDURE DIVISION Coding—COBOL-74
The SORT Statement

The SORT statement for this program is identical to that in the SORTONLY program, except that the USING phrase has been replaced by an INPUT PROCEDURE phrase.

The INPUT PROCEDURE Phrase. To provide for the processing of input records before they are sorted, the INPUT PROCEDURE phrase must be specified. The SORT statement gives control to the INPUT PROCEDURE before the actual sorting takes place. You can think of the INPUT PROCEDURE phrase as operating like a PERFORM statement. That is, control is passed to the procedure and then returned when execution of the procedure has been completed. However, there is one significant syntactical difference: a section-name—not a paragraph-name—must be specified after the reserved words INPUT PROCEDURE IS.

A few other rules apply to the INPUT PROCEDURE; these dictate the organization of the INPUT PROCEDURE in COBOL-74 programs.

- The section-name coded can only be referenced by a SORT statement. That is, it cannot be named in a PERFORM or a GO TO statement.

- Within the INPUT PROCEDURE, program control cannot be transferred to procedures outside it. In other words, PERFORM or GO TO statements within the input procedure (section) cannot name a section or a paragraph that is not itself within the INPUT-PROCEDURE section.

- An INPUT PROCEDURE cannot contain a SORT statement.

Unlike the USING phrase, notice that OPEN and CLOSE statements *must* be coded for the input file when an INPUT PROCEDURE is specified.

Structured Coding Problems Introduced by the INPUT PROCEDURE Phrase

Three items introduced by the INPUT PROCEDURE phrase are in conflict with good structured coding principles you have used throughout this book: (1) the need for sections, (2) module structure and numbering requirements, and (3) the need for GO TO and EXIT statements.

Need for Sections.   Because the INPUT PROCEDURE must be a SECTION, it is logical (and often necessary) to also group the other paragraphs of the program into sections. Notice that two sections have been established in the SORTPRE program: 0000-ML-SORT-INV-RECORDS and 2000-IP-SELECT-INV-RECORDS. (The abbreviations ML and IP following the module numbers are used to identify these sections as mainline and input procedure, respectively.)

Module Structure and Numbering Requirements.   SORT statement syntax, together with the need for sections, combine to impose certain coding requirements that do not lend themselves to optimal structured code. The need to keep all INPUT PROCEDURE paragraphs within the SECTION also causes module-numbering problems.

To be as consistent as possible with the module-numbering system used elsewhere in the text, notice that a section-number digit has been prefixed to the recommended three-digit module number. That is, all the procedure-names within the mainline section begin with 0 (0*nnn*-), the procedure-names within the record-processing section start with 2 (2*nnn*-), and so on. After the section-digit prefix, the recommended three-digit module number appears. This means that when the SORT statement is present in a program, a four-digit module number will be used.

Need for GO TO and EXIT Statements.   To properly structure the coding within the INPUT PROCEDURE, the GO TO and EXIT statements must be used, as will be explained below.

The INPUT PROCEDURE Logic: 2000-IP-SELECT-INV-RECORDS SECTION

This section is like a small program of its own. Its logic is shown in Figure 13-14. When the SORT statement of module 0000-SORT-INV-RECORDS is encountered, this SECTION is executed. The logic of this procedure, which uses a priming-read, is as follows:

1. A record is read from the input INVENTORY-FILE.

2. The IR-INVENTORY-CLASS-CODE field is tested to see if it is equal to an "A."

3. If the class-code is an "A," the input INVENTORY-RECORD is moved to the SR-SORT-RECORD area and the record is released to the SORT-FILE.

The above steps are repeated until all of the records have been read from the INVENTORY-FILE. After end-of-file has been detected, program control transfers back to the SORT statement. Upon return to the SORT statement, the actual sorting of the records contained in the SORT-FILE occurs.

Observe that a GO TO statement is coded at the end of the 2200-SELECT-INVENTORY-RECORD paragraph. This GO TO statement is required so that, after end-of-file has been reached, the remainder of the modules in the SECTION will be skipped for a proper return to the SORT statement. The need to get to the end of the section means that a paragraph, 2999-EXIT, must be established to provide a procedure-name for the GO TO statement. Because it is a dummy module—no program operations are to be executed—the null statement EXIT has been specified within the paragraph.

Figure 13-14   INPUT PROCEDURE logic: COBOL-74 SORTPRE program.

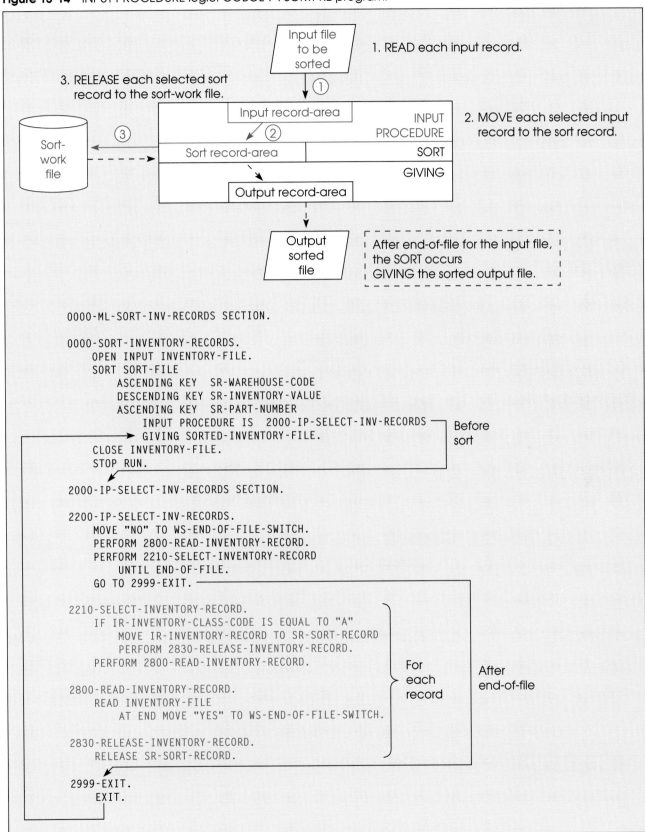

```
0000-ML-SORT-INV-RECORDS SECTION.

0000-SORT-INVENTORY-RECORDS.
    OPEN INPUT INVENTORY-FILE.
    SORT SORT-FILE
        ASCENDING KEY   SR-WAREHOUSE-CODE
        DESCENDING KEY  SR-INVENTORY-VALUE
        ASCENDING KEY   SR-PART-NUMBER
            INPUT PROCEDURE IS  2000-IP-SELECT-INV-RECORDS
            GIVING SORTED-INVENTORY-FILE.
    CLOSE INVENTORY-FILE.
    STOP RUN.

2000-IP-SELECT-INV-RECORDS SECTION.

2200-IP-SELECT-INV-RECORDS.
    MOVE "NO" TO WS-END-OF-FILE-SWITCH.
    PERFORM 2800-READ-INVENTORY-RECORD.
    PERFORM 2210-SELECT-INVENTORY-RECORD
        UNTIL END-OF-FILE.
    GO TO 2999-EXIT.

2210-SELECT-INVENTORY-RECORD.
    IF IR-INVENTORY-CLASS-CODE IS EQUAL TO "A"
        MOVE IR-INVENTORY-RECORD TO SR-SORT-RECORD
        PERFORM 2830-RELEASE-INVENTORY-RECORD.
    PERFORM 2800-READ-INVENTORY-RECORD.

2800-READ-INVENTORY-RECORD.
    READ INVENTORY-FILE
        AT END MOVE "YES" TO WS-END-OF-FILE-SWITCH.

2830-RELEASE-INVENTORY-RECORD.
    RELEASE SR-SORT-RECORD.

2999-EXIT.
    EXIT.
```

Before sort

For each record

After end-of-file

The RELEASE Statement.   The RELEASE statement format is illustrated in Figure 13-15. It is used to transfer a record from the sort-work file record-area to the sort-work file. Its function is similar to that of a WRITE operation to an output file. Like the WRITE statement, it has a FROM phrase. In accordance with our structured coding conventions for input/output operations, the RELEASE statement should be coded as an independent module. The RELEASE statement can be specified only within an INPUT PROCEDURE.

Notice that the IR-INVENTORY-RECORD is moved to the SR-SORT-RECORD area in the 2210-SELECT-INVENTORY-RECORD module before the 2830-RELEASE-INVENTORY-RECORD is performed. You must either MOVE the input-record fields to the sort-work record-area or use the FROM option of the RELEASE statement to transfer the record. Sometimes the input-record format will differ from that of the sort record. When this situation exists, the MOVE statement approach must be used so that the field areas can be reformatted, as shown in Figure 13-16.

Figure 13-15
RELEASE statement format.

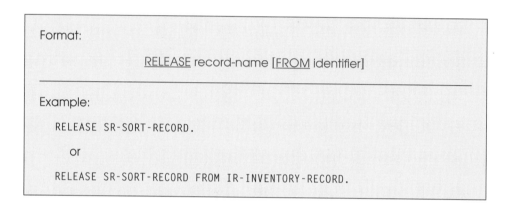

```
Format:

         RELEASE record-name [FROM identifier]


Example:

    RELEASE SR-SORT-RECORD.

      or

    RELEASE SR-SORT-RECORD FROM IR-INVENTORY-RECORD.
```

Figure 13-16   Example of sort-work file reformatting.

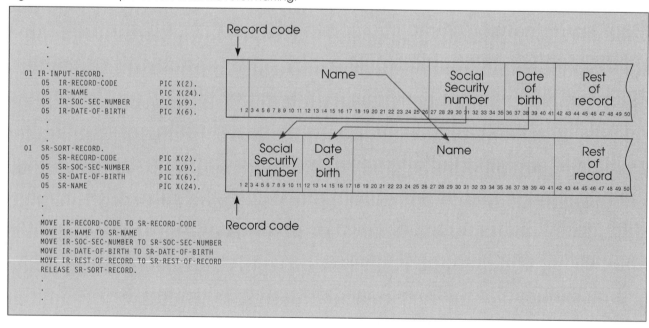

PROCEDURE DIVISION Coding—COBOL-85
Module Numbering

As you will see, sort procedures are virtually small programs within a program. For the sake of program simplicity and good documentation, it is helpful to keep various components of the program together—for instance, all mainline elements together, and all sort procedure elements together. To that end, another digit has been added to the module numbers. All modules associated with the mainline will have their conventional numbers preceded by a 0. Thus, the 000 mainline module will be 0000 and an 890 module to print a report summary line (not done in this program) would be 0890. Sort input procedure modules will be preceded with the digit 2, and sort output procedure modules with the digit 3. Otherwise, the recommended three-digit module number is used.

The SORT Statement

The SORT statement for this program is identical to that in the SORTONLY program, except that the USING phrase has been replaced by an INPUT PROCEDURE phrase.

The INPUT PROCEDURE Phrase.   To provide for the processing of input records before they are sorted, the INPUT PROCEDURE phrase must be specified. The SORT statement gives control to the INPUT PROCEDURE before the actual sorting takes place. You can think of the INPUT PROCEDURE phrase as operating like a PERFORM statement. That is, control is passed to the procedure and then returned when execution of the procedure has been completed.

Unlike the USING phrase, notice that OPEN and CLOSE statements *must* be coded for the input file when an INPUT PROCEDURE is specified.

The INPUT PROCEDURE Logic

The INPUT PROCEDURE (the paragraphs numbered in the 2000s) is like a small program of its own. Its logic is depicted in Figure 13-17. When the SORT statement of module 0000-SORT-INV-RECORDS is encountered, this SECTION is executed. The logic of this procedure, which uses a priming-read, is as follows:

1. A record is read from the input INVENTORY-FILE.

2. The IR-INVENTORY-CLASS-CODE field is tested to see if it is equal to an "A."

3. If the class-code is an "A" the input INVENTORY-RECORD is moved to the SR-SORT-RECORD area and the record is released to the SORT-FILE.

The above steps are repeated until all of the records have been read from the INVENTORY-FILE. After end-of-file has been detected, program control transfers back to the SORT statement. Upon return to the SORT statement, the actual sorting of the records contained in the SORT-FILE occurs.

The RELEASE Statement.   The RELEASE statement format is illustrated in Figure 13-15 (it is included in the COBOL-74 description). It transfers a record from the sort-work file record-area to the sort-work file. Its function is similar to that of a WRITE operation to an output file. Like the WRITE statement, it has a FROM phrase. In accordance with our structured coding conventions for input/output operations, the RELEASE statement should be coded as an independent module. The RELEASE statement can be specified only within an INPUT PROCEDURE.

Notice that the IR-INVENTORY-RECORD is moved to the SR-SORT-RECORD area in the 2210-SELECT-INVENTORY-RECORD module before the 2830-RELEASE-INVENTORY-RECORD is performed. You must either MOVE the input-record fields to the sort-work record-area or use the FROM option of the RELEASE statement to transfer the record. Sometimes the input-record format will differ from that of the sort record. When this situation exists, the MOVE statement approach must be used so that the field areas can be reformatted, as shown in Figure 13-16 (it is included in the COBOL-74 description).

Figure 13-17 INPUT PROCEDURE logic: COBOL-85 SORTPRE program.

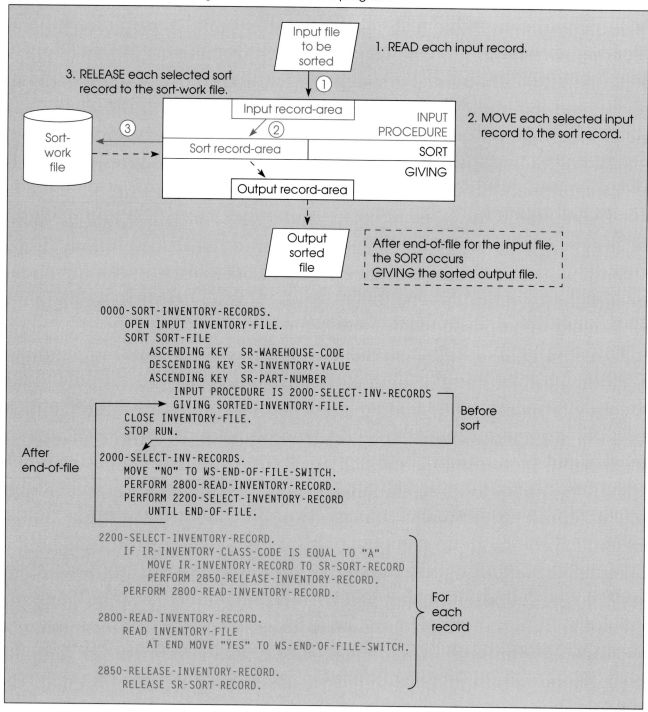

1. READ each input record.

3. RELEASE each selected sort record to the sort-work file.

2. MOVE each selected input record to the sort record.

After end-of-file for the input file, the SORT occurs GIVING the sorted output file.

```
0000-SORT-INVENTORY-RECORDS.
    OPEN INPUT INVENTORY-FILE.
    SORT SORT-FILE
        ASCENDING KEY  SR-WAREHOUSE-CODE
        DESCENDING KEY SR-INVENTORY-VALUE
        ASCENDING KEY  SR-PART-NUMBER
            INPUT PROCEDURE IS 2000-SELECT-INV-RECORDS
            GIVING SORTED-INVENTORY-FILE.
    CLOSE INVENTORY-FILE.
    STOP RUN.

2000-SELECT-INV-RECORDS.
    MOVE "NO" TO WS-END-OF-FILE-SWITCH.
    PERFORM 2800-READ-INVENTORY-RECORD.
    PERFORM 2200-SELECT-INVENTORY-RECORD
        UNTIL END-OF-FILE.

2200-SELECT-INVENTORY-RECORD.
    IF IR-INVENTORY-CLASS-CODE IS EQUAL TO "A"
        MOVE IR-INVENTORY-RECORD TO SR-SORT-RECORD
        PERFORM 2850-RELEASE-INVENTORY-RECORD.
    PERFORM 2800-READ-INVENTORY-RECORD.

2800-READ-INVENTORY-RECORD.
    READ INVENTORY-FILE
        AT END MOVE "YES" TO WS-END-OF-FILE-SWITCH.

2850-RELEASE-INVENTORY-RECORD.
    RELEASE SR-SORT-RECORD.
```

Before sort

After end-of-file

For each record

Recap of Sort Programs with Preprocessing of the Input File

Preprocessing of an input file is used when any one of the following program functions is required:

1. To select certain records from the input file and to sort only those selected records (as is done in the SORTPRE program).

2. To create additional records to be included in the sorted file.

3. To change any characteristics of the input record (record length, field size, field location, field values, or the like) before the sort.

4. To validate, or edit, the records prior to sorting.

5. To list the input records prior to sorting.

6. To count the records of the input file.

The INPUT PROCEDURE phrase must be coded within the SORT statement to provide for preprocessing of the input file.

Topic: | **A Sort Program with Preprocessing of the Input File and Postprocessing of the Sorted File**

Programming documentation for a sort program with both preprocessing of the input file and postprocessing of the sorted file is shown in Figure 13-18. Again, this program sorts the input-inventory file discussed in the last two Topics. The specifications for this program are identical to those for the SORTPRE program, except that this program also lists the sorted inventory records.

This program is named SORTPP (to indicate that it is an example of a sort program with both preprocessing and postprocessing). Its structure chart is shown in Figure 13-19. COBOL coding appears in Figure 13-20.

Figure 13-18 Programming documentation: Sort with preprocessing of the input-inventory file and postprocessing of the sorted file.

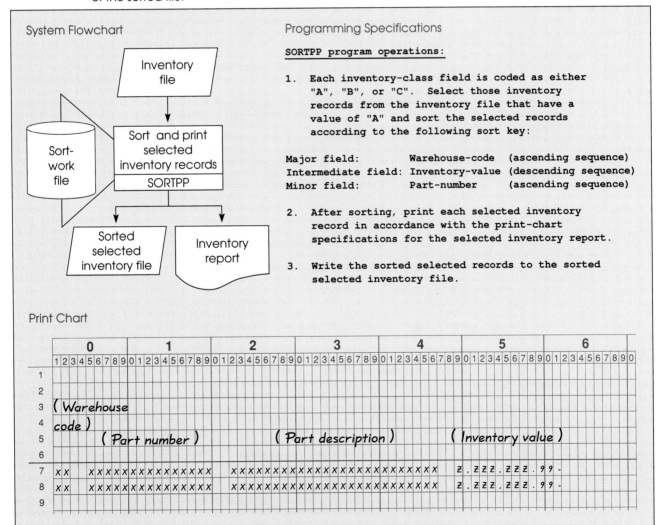

Figure 13-19
Structure chart: Sort with preprocessing of the input-inventory file and postprocessing of the sorted file.

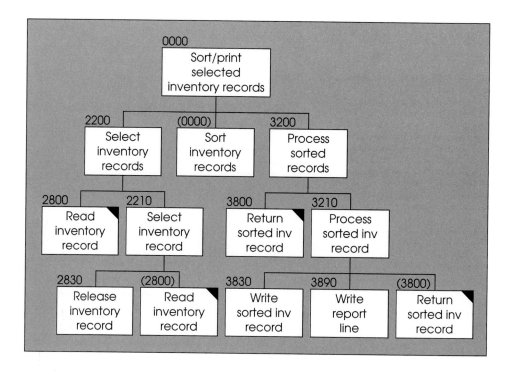

Figure 13-20   COBOL coding: SORTPP program.

```
1          IDENTIFICATION DIVISION.
2
3          PROGRAM-ID.    SORTPP.
4      *          WRITTEN BY T. WELBURN.
5      *          SILICON VALLEY MANUFACTURING COMPANY.
6      *          MAR 28, 1986.
7      *          REVISED 10/3/89 BY W. PRICE.
8
9      *          THIS IS A SORT PROGRAM WITH PREPROCESSING
10     *              OF THE INPUT FILE AND POSTPROCESSING
11     *              OF THE SORTED OUTPUT FILE
12
13     *          SORT STATEMENT PHRASES SPECIFIED ARE:
14     *              INPUT PROCEDURE
15     *              OUTPUT PROCEDURE
16
17
18         ENVIRONMENT DIVISION.
19
20         CONFIGURATION SECTION.
21
22         SOURCE-COMPUTER.  (system dependent).
23         OBJECT-COMPUTER.  (system dependent).
24
25         INPUT-OUTPUT SECTION.
26
27         FILE-CONTROL.
28             SELECT INVENTORY-FILE
29                 ASSIGN TO (system dependent).
30             SELECT INVENTORY-REPORT-FILE
31                 ASSIGN TO (system dependent).
32             SELECT SORTED-INVENTORY-FILE
33                 ASSIGN TO (system dependent).
34             SELECT SORT-FILE
35                 ASSIGN TO (system dependent).
36
37
38         DATA DIVISION.
39
40         FILE SECTION.
41
42         FD  INVENTORY-FILE
43             RECORD CONTAINS 54 CHARACTERS
44             LABEL RECORDS ARE STANDARD.
45
46         01  IR-INVENTORY-RECORD.
47             05  FILLER                    PIC X(19).
48             05  IR-INVENTORY-CLASS-CODE   PIC X(1).
49             05  FILLER                    PIC X(34).
50
51         FD  INVENTORY-REPORT-FILE
52             RECORD CONTAINS 132 CHARACTERS
53             LABEL RECORDS ARE OMITTED.
54
55         01  RL-REPORT-LINE.
56             05  RL-WAREHOUSE-CODE         PIC X(2).
57             05  FILLER                    PIC X(2).
58             05  RL-PART-NUMBER            PIC X(15).
59             05  FILLER                    PIC X(2).
60             05  RL-PART-DESCRIPTION       PIC X(25).
61             05  FILLER                    PIC X(2).
62             05  RL-INVENTORY-VALUE        PIC Z,ZZZ,ZZZ.99-.
63             05  FILLER                    PIC X(71).
64
65         FD  SORTED-INVENTORY-FILE
66             RECORD CONTAINS 54 CHARACTERS
67             LABEL RECORDS ARE STANDARD.
68
69         01  SI-INVENTORY-RECORD.
70             05  SI-RECORD-CODE            PIC X(2).
71             05  SI-WAREHOUSE-CODE         PIC X(2).
72             05  SI-PART-NUMBER            PIC X(15).
73             05  SI-INVENTORY-CLASS-CODE   PIC X(1).
74             05  SI-PART-DESCRIPTION       PIC X(25).
75             05  SI-INVENTORY-VALUE        PIC S9(7)V99.
76
77         SD  SORT-FILE
78             RECORD CONTAINS 54 CHARACTERS.
79
80         01  SR-SORT-RECORD.
81             05  FILLER                    PIC X(2).
82             05  SR-WAREHOUSE-CODE         PIC X(2).
83             05  SR-PART-NUMBER            PIC X(15).
84             05  FILLER                    PIC X(26).
85             05  SR-INVENTORY-VALUE        PIC S9(7)V99.
86
87         WORKING-STORAGE SECTION.
88
89         01  WS-SWITCHES.
90             05  WS-END-OF-FILE-SWITCH     PIC X(3).
91                 88  END-OF-FILE                     VALUE "YES".
92
93
```

(a) The first three divisions.

Figure 13-20 (continued)

```
94    PROCEDURE DIVISION.
95
96    0000-ML-SORT-INV-RECORDS SECTION.                    Mainline
97                                                         procedure
98    0000-SORT-INV-RECORDS.
99        OPEN INPUT INVENTORY-FILE
100            OUTPUT INVENTORY-REPORT-FILE
101                SORTED-INVENTORY-FILE.
102       SORT SORT-FILE
103           ASCENDING KEY  SR-WAREHOUSE-CODE
104           DESCENDING KEY SR-INVENTORY-VALUE
105           ASCENDING KEY  SR-PART-NUMBER
106               INPUT PROCEDURE IS  2000-IP-SELECT-INV-RECORDS
107               OUTPUT PROCEDURE IS 3000-OP-PROCESS-SORTED-RECORDS.
108       CLOSE INVENTORY-FILE
109             INVENTORY-REPORT-FILE
110             SORTED-INVENTORY-FILE.
111       STOP RUN.
112
113   2000-IP-SELECT-INV-RECORDS SECTION.
114                                                         INPUT
115   2200-SELECT-INVENTORY-RECORDS.                        PROCEDURE
116       MOVE "NO " TO WS-END-OF-FILE-SWITCH.
117       PERFORM 2800-READ-INVENTORY-RECORD.
118       PERFORM 2210-SELECT-INVENTORY-RECORD
119           UNTIL END-OF-FILE.
120       GO TO 2999-EXIT.
121
122   2210-SELECT-INVENTORY-RECORD.
123       IF IR-INVENTORY-CLASS-CODE IS EQUAL TO "A"
124           PERFORM 2830-RELEASE-INVENTORY-RECORD.
125       PERFORM 2800-READ-INVENTORY-RECORD.
126
127   2800-READ-INVENTORY-RECORD.
128       READ INVENTORY-FILE
129           AT END MOVE "YES" TO WS-END-OF-FILE-SWITCH.
130
131   2830-RELEASE-INVENTORY-RECORD.
132       RELEASE SR-SORT-RECORD FROM IR-INVENTORY-RECORD.
133
134   2999-EXIT.
135       EXIT.
136
137   3000-OP-PROCESS-SORTED-RECORDS SECTION.
138                                                         OUTPUT
139   3200-PROCESS-SORTED-RECORDS.                          PROCEDURE
140       MOVE "NO " TO WS-END-OF-FILE-SWITCH.
141       PERFORM 3800-RETURN-SORTED-INV-RECORD.
142       PERFORM 3210-PROCESS-SORTED-INV-RECORD
143           UNTIL END-OF-FILE.
144       GO TO 3999-EXIT.
145
146   3210-PROCESS-SORTED-INV-RECORD.
147       MOVE SR-SORT-RECORD TO SI-INVENTORY-RECORD.
148       MOVE SPACES TO RL-REPORT-LINE.
149       MOVE SI-WAREHOUSE-CODE TO RL-WAREHOUSE-CODE.
150       MOVE SI-PART-NUMBER TO RL-PART-NUMBER.
151       MOVE SI-PART-DESCRIPTION TO RL-PART-DESCRIPTION.
152       MOVE SI-INVENTORY-VALUE TO RL-INVENTORY-VALUE.
153       PERFORM 3830-WRITE-SORTED-INV-RECORD.
154       PERFORM 3890-WRITE-REPORT-LINE.
155       PERFORM 3800-RETURN-SORTED-INV-RECORD.
156
157   3800-RETURN-SORTED-INV-RECORD.
158       RETURN SORT-FILE
159           AT END MOVE "YES" TO WS-END-OF-FILE-SWITCH.
160
161   3830-WRITE-SORTED-INV-RECORD.
162       WRITE SI-INVENTORY-RECORD.
163
164
165   3890-WRITE-REPORT-LINE.
166       WRITE RL-REPORT-LINE
167           AFTER ADVANCING 1 LINE.
168
169   3999-EXIT.
170       EXIT.
```

(b) The PROCEDURE-DIVISION—COBOL-74.

```
94    PROCEDURE DIVISION.
95
96    0000-SORT-INV-RECORDS.                               Main
97        OPEN INPUT INVENTORY-FILE                        program
98            OUTPUT INVENTORY-REPORT-FILE
99                SORTED-INVENTORY-FILE
100       SORT SORT-FILE
101           ASCENDING KEY  SR-WAREHOUSE-CODE
102           DESCENDING KEY SR-INVENTORY-VALUE
103           ASCENDING KEY  SR-PART-NUMBER
104               INPUT PROCEDURE IS  2000-SELECT-INVENTORY-RECORDS
105               OUTPUT PROCEDURE IS 3000-PROCESS-SORTED-RECORDS
106       CLOSE INVENTORY-FILE
107             INVENTORY-REPORT-FILE
108             SORTED-INVENTORY-FILE
109       STOP RUN.
110
111   2000-SELECT-INVENTORY-RECORDS.
112       MOVE "NO " TO WS-END-OF-FILE-SWITCH            INPUT
113       PERFORM 2800-READ-INVENTORY-RECORD             PROCEDURE
114       PERFORM 2200-SELECT-INVENTORY-RECORD
115           UNTIL END-OF-FILE.
116
117   2200-SELECT-INVENTORY-RECORD.
118       IF IR-INVENTORY-CLASS-CODE IS EQUAL TO "A"
119           PERFORM 2830-RELEASE-INVENTORY-RECORD      Input
120       END-IF                                         components
121       PERFORM 2800-READ-INVENTORY-RECORD.
122
123   2800-READ-INVENTORY-RECORD.
124       READ INVENTORY-FILE
125           AT END MOVE "YES" TO WS-END-OF-FILE-SWITCH
126       END-READ.
127
128   2830-RELEASE-INVENTORY-RECORD.
129       RELEASE SR-SORT-RECORD FROM IR-INVENTORY-RECORD.
130
131   3000-PROCESS-SORTED-RECORDS.
132       MOVE "NO " TO WS-END-OF-FILE-SWITCH            OUTPUT
133       PERFORM 3800-RETURN-SORTED-INV-RECORD          PROCEDURE
134       PERFORM 3200-PROCESS-SORTED-INV-RECORD
135           UNTIL END-OF-FILE.
136
137   3200-PROCESS-SORTED-INV-RECORD.
138       MOVE SR-SORT-RECORD TO SI-INVENTORY-RECORD     Output
139       MOVE SPACES TO RL-REPORT-LINE                  compo-
140       MOVE SI-WAREHOUSE-CODE TO RL-WAREHOUSE-CODE    nents
141       MOVE SI-PART-NUMBER TO RL-PART-NUMBER
142       MOVE SI-PART-DESCRIPTION TO RL-PART-DESCRIPTION
143       MOVE SI-INVENTORY-VALUE TO RL-INVENTORY-VALUE
144       PERFORM 3830-WRITE-SORTED-INV-RECORD
145       PERFORM 3890-WRITE-REPORT-LINE
146       PERFORM 3800-RETURN-SORTED-INV-RECORD.
147
148   3800-RETURN-SORTED-INV-RECORD.
149       RETURN SORT-FILE
150           AT END MOVE "YES" TO WS-END-OF-FILE-SWITCH
151       END-RETURN.
152
153   3830-WRITE-SORTED-INV-RECORD.
154       WRITE SI-INVENTORY-RECORD.
155
156   3890-WRITE-REPORT-LINE.
157       WRITE RL-REPORT-LINE
158           AFTER ADVANCING 1 LINE.
```

(c) The PROCEDURE-DIVISION—COBOL-85.

ENVIRONMENT DIVISION Coding

Because the programming specifications call for an output report-file, a file-control entry for the INVENTORY-REPORT-FILE has been specified. This means that four SELECT sentences are in the FILE-CONTROL paragraph of the ENVIRONMENT DIVISION: one each for the input-inventory file, the output-report file, the sorted inventory file, and the sort-work file.

DATA DIVISION Coding

An FD entry also must be established for the INVENTORY-REPORT-FILE. A record-description entry for the report-line format is coded.

In the record-description for the sorted output SI-INVENTORY-RECORD, observe that each field of the inventory record has been defined. Elementary field definitions are required because most of these fields must be moved to the output-report line. (As an alternative, the fields could have been defined in the SR-SORT-RECORD.)

PROCEDURE DIVISION Coding
The SORT Statement

In the SORTPP program, the GIVING phrase used in the two previous sort examples has been replaced by the OUTPUT PROCEDURE phrase.

The OUTPUT PROCEDURE Phrase.   To provide for processing of the sorted records, the OUTPUT PROCEDURE phrase must be specified. The SORT statement gives control to the output procedure after the sort has been completed. Figure 13-21 illustrates the OUTPUT PROCEDURE logic.

OUTPUT PROCEDURE processing and syntax are parallel to that of the INPUT PROCEDURE. The procedure-name specified is performed after the sort has been completed. Any output files created by the output procedure must be explicitly opened and closed by the programmer. For COBOL-74, output procedures introduce structured coding problems identical to those for input procedures. That is, an OUTPUT PROCEDURE can be referenced only by a SORT statement. Furthermore, within the output procedure, program control cannot be transferred to any procedure outside it and no SORT statements can be contained within it.

Figure 13-21   OUTPUT PROCEDURE logic: SORTPP program.

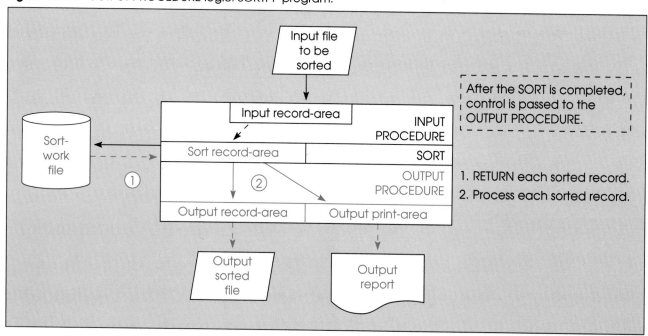

The OUTPUT PROCEDURE Logic

After the SORT statement coded within the 0000 mainline module has completed execution of the sorting process, the output module is performed. (This is the 3000-OP-PROCESS-SORTED-RECORDS SECTION in the COBOL-74 version and 3200-PROCESS-SORTED-RECORDS in the COBOL-85 version.) The logic of this procedure, which uses a priming-read (in the form of a priming-return), is as follows:

1. A record is returned from the sort-work SORT-FILE.

2. The SR-SORT-RECORD is moved to the output SI-INVENTORY-RECORD area.

3. The report-line is formatted by moving the fields to be printed from the SI-INVENTORY-RECORD area to the RL-REPORT-LINE area.

4. The SI-INVENTORY-RECORD is written to the output-sorted inventory file.

5. The RL-REPORT-LINE is written to the output-report file.

The above steps are repeated until all the records have been returned from the SORT-FILE. After end-of-file has been detected, program control returns to the next consecutive statement following the SORT statement. At that point, the files are closed and the run is stopped.

The RETURN Statement. The RETURN statement format is illustrated in Figure 13-22. It causes a record to be retrieved from the sort-work file and placed in the sort-work file record-area. Its function is similar to that of a READ operation from an input file. Like the READ statement, it has an INTO option. In accordance with our structured coding conventions for input/output operations, the RETURN statement should be coded as an independent module. The RETURN statement can be specified only within an OUTPUT PROCEDURE.

Observe that the WS-END-OF-FILE-SWITCH is used for both the input INVENTORY-FILE and the sort-work SORT-FILE. Normally, a separate end-of-file switch should be established for each input file. For this program, due to SORT statement handling, it would be impossible to process both of these files at the same time. Therefore, such multiple use is acceptable. Notice, however, that it is not only necessary to initialize the switch in the input procedure (the 2200-SELECT-INVENTORY-RECORDS module), but also mandatory that it be reset to "NO" in the output procedure (the 3200-PROCESS-SORTED-RECORDS module).

Notes Regarding the INPUT PROCEDURE

The INPUT PROCEDURE for the SORTPP program is identical in function to that of the SORTPRE program. Just to show an alternative approach, however, the RELEASE statement is coded with the FROM phrase.

Figure 13-22
RETURN statement format.

```
Format:

              RETURN file-name RECORD (INTO identifier)
                     AT END imperative-statement.


Example:

   RETURN SORT-FILE
       AT END MOVE "YES" TO WS-END-OF-FILE-SWITCH.

      or

   RETURN SORT-FILE INTO SI-INVENTORY-RECORD
       AT END MOVE "YES"" TO WS-END-OF-FILE SWITCH.
```

Recap of Sort Programs with Postprocessing of the Sorted File

Postprocessing of the sorted file is used when any one of the following program functions is required:

1. To create more than one sorted output file.

2. To select or summarize records after sorting and before writing them to a sorted output file.

3. To create additional records after sorting to be included in the sorted output file.

4. To change any characteristics of the sorted record (record length, field size, field location, field values, or the like) after the sort.

5. To validate, or edit, the records after sorting.

6. To list the sorted records (as is done in the SORTPP program).

7. To count the sorted records.

The OUTPUT PROCEDURE phrase must be coded within the SORT statement to provide for postprocessing of the sorted file.

Topic:	A Sort Program with Postprocessing of the Sorted File

Within a SORT statement, there are four possible combinations of USING, GIVING, INPUT PROCEDURE, and OUTPUT PROCEDURE phrases. Thus, to complete the sort-program coverage, an example of a sort program with postprocessing of the sorted file (but no preprocessing of the input file) is presented in this Topic. Programming documentation for the program is shown in Figure 13-23. Notice that the programming specifications call for the entire inventory file to be sorted (as was done in the SORTONLY program) and for the sorted records to be printed (as was done in the SORTPP program).

Figure 13-23   Programming documentation: Sort program with postprocessing of the sorted inventory file.

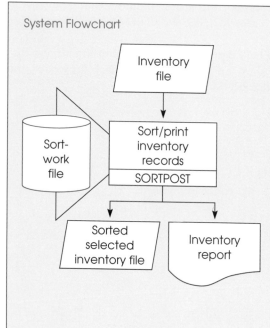

System Flowchart

Inventory file

Sort-work file

Sort/print inventory records

SORTPOST

Sorted selected inventory file

Inventory report

Programming Specifications

SORTPOST program operations:

1. Sort the inventory file in sequence according to the following sort key:

Major field:	Warehouse-code	(ascending sequence)
Intermediate field:	Inventory-value	(descending sequence)
Minor field:	Part-number	(ascending sequence)

2. After sorting, print each selected inventory record in accordance with the print-chart specifications for the selected inventory report.

   a. Accumulate the total inventory-value.

   b. After all inventory records have been printed, print a total line containing the total inventory-value from all records printed, in accordance with the print-chart specifications.

3. Write the sorted selected records to the sorted inventory file.

Figure 13-23 (continued)

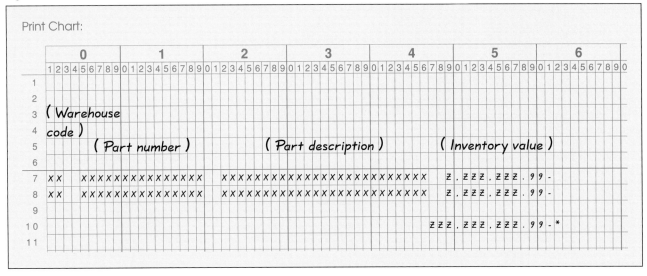

Print Chart:

This program is named SORTPOST (to indicate that it is an example of a sort program with postprocessing of the sorted file).

The SORTPOST Program

The structure chart for the SORTPOST program is shown in Figure 13-24; the program coding appears in Figure 13-25. The program logic is similar to that of the SORTPP program discussed in the last Topic. In accordance with the programming specifications, however, there is no need for an INPUT PROCEDURE, so the USING phrase is specified instead in the SORT statement.

The output procedure is similar to that for the SORTPP program, except that (1) additional logic is included to handle the report total, and (2) to show an alternative approach, the RETURN statement is coded with the INTO phrase.

Figure 13-24
Structure chart: Sort program with postprocessing of the sorted inventory file.

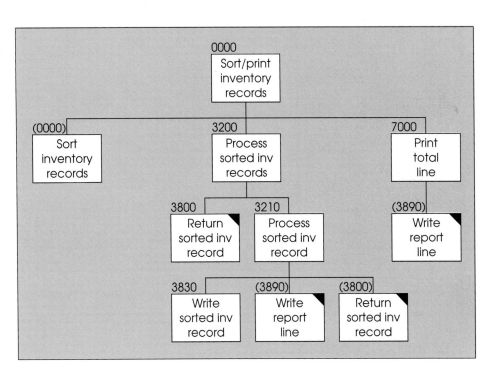

Figure 13-25
COBOL coding: SORTPOST
program.

```
 1              IDENTIFICATION DIVISION.
 2
 3         PROGRAM-ID.    SORTPOST.
 4         *              WRITTEN BY T. WELBURN.
 5         *              SILICON VALLEY MANUFACTURING COMPANY.
 6         *              MAR 28, 1986.
 7         *              REVISED 10/3/89 BY W. PRICE.
 8
 9         *         THIS IS A SORT PROGRAM WITH POSTPROCESSING
10         *              OF THE SORTED OUTPUT FILE
11
12         *         SORT STATEMENT PHRASES SPECIFIED ARE:
13         *              USING
14         *              OUTPUT PROCEDURE
15
16
17         ENVIRONMENT DIVISION.
18
19         CONFIGURATION SECTION.
20
21         SOURCE-COMPUTER.  (system dependent).
22         OBJECT-COMPUTER.  (system dependent).
23
24         INPUT-OUTPUT SECTION.
25
26         FILE-CONTROL.
27             SELECT INVENTORY-FILE
28                 ASSIGN TO (system dependent).
29             SELECT INVENTORY-REPORT-FILE
30                 ASSIGN TO (system dependent).
31             SELECT SORTED-INVENTORY-FILE
32                 ASSIGN TO (system dependent).
33             SELECT SORT-FILE
34                 ASSIGN TO (system dependent).
35
36
37         DATA DIVISION.
38
39         FILE SECTION.
40
41         FD  INVENTORY-FILE
42                 RECORD CONTAINS 54 CHARACTERS
43                 LABEL RECORDS ARE STANDARD.
44
45         01  IR-INVENTORY-RECORD.
46             05  FILLER                    PIC X(19).
47             05  IR-INVENTORY-CLASS-CODE   PIC X(1).
48             05  FILLER                    PIC X(34).
49
50         FD  INVENTORY-REPORT-FILE
51                 RECORD CONTAINS 132 CHARACTERS
52                 LABEL RECORDS ARE OMITTED.
53
54         01  RL-REPORT-LINE.
55             05  RL-WAREHOUSE-CODE         PIC X(2).
56             05  FILLER                    PIC X(2).
57             05  RL-PART-NUMBER            PIC X(15).
58             05  FILLER                    PIC X(2).
59             05  RL-PART-DESCRIPTION       PIC X(25).
60             05  FILLER                    PIC X(2).
61             05  RL-INVENTORY-VALUE        PIC Z,ZZZ,ZZZ.99-.
62             05  FILLER                    PIC X(71).
63
64         FD  SORTED-INVENTORY-FILE
65                 RECORD CONTAINS 54 CHARACTERS
66                 LABEL RECORDS ARE STANDARD.
67
68         01  SI-INVENTORY-RECORD.
69             05  SI-RECORD-CODE            PIC X(2).
70             05  SI-WAREHOUSE-CODE         PIC X(2).
71             05  SI-PART-NUMBER            PIC X(15).
72             05  SI-INVENTORY-CLASS-CODE   PIC X(1).
73             05  SI-PART-DESCRIPTION       PIC X(25).
74             05  SI-INVENTORY-VALUE        PIC S9(7)V99.
75
76         SD  SORT-FILE
77                 RECORD CONTAINS 54 CHARACTERS.
78
79         01  SR-SORT-RECORD.
80             05  FILLER                    PIC X(2).
81             05  SR-WAREHOUSE-CODE         PIC X(2).
82             05  SR-PART-NUMBER            PIC X(15).
83             05  FILLER                    PIC X(26).
84             05  SR-INVENTORY-VALUE        PIC S9(7)V99.
85
86         WORKING-STORAGE SECTION.
87
88         01  WS-SWITCHES.
89             05  WS-END-OF-FILE-SWITCH     PIC X(3).
90                 88  END-OF-FILE                       VALUE "YES".
91
92         01  WS-TOTAL-ACCUMULATORS.
93             05  WS-INVENTORY-VALUE-ACCUM  PIC S9(9)V99.
94
95         01  TL-TOTAL-LINE.
96             05  FILLER                    PIC X(46) VALUE SPACES.
97             05  TL-INVENTORY-VALUE        PIC ZZZ,ZZZ,ZZZ.99-.
98             05  FILLER                    PIC X(1)  VALUE " ".
99             05  FILLER                    PIC X(70) VALUE SPACES.
100
101
```

(a) The first three divisions.

Figure 13-25   (continued)

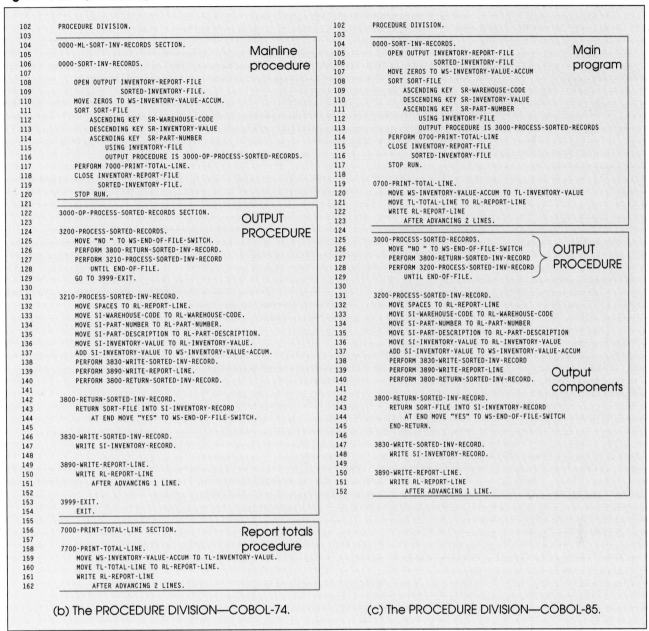

```
102   PROCEDURE DIVISION.
103
104   0000-ML-SORT-INV-RECORDS SECTION.          Mainline
105                                              procedure
106   0000-SORT-INV-RECORDS.
107
108       OPEN OUTPUT INVENTORY-REPORT-FILE
109                  SORTED-INVENTORY-FILE.
110       MOVE ZEROS TO WS-INVENTORY-VALUE-ACCUM.
111       SORT SORT-FILE
112           ASCENDING KEY  SR-WAREHOUSE-CODE
113           DESCENDING KEY SR-INVENTORY-VALUE
114           ASCENDING KEY  SR-PART-NUMBER
115               USING INVENTORY-FILE
116               OUTPUT PROCEDURE IS 3000-OP-PROCESS-SORTED-RECORDS.
117       PERFORM 7000-PRINT-TOTAL-LINE.
118       CLOSE INVENTORY-REPORT-FILE
119             SORTED-INVENTORY-FILE.
120       STOP RUN.
121
122   3000-OP-PROCESS-SORTED-RECORDS SECTION.     OUTPUT
123                                              PROCEDURE
124   3200-PROCESS-SORTED-RECORDS.
125       MOVE "NO " TO WS-END-OF-FILE-SWITCH.
126       PERFORM 3800-RETURN-SORTED-INV-RECORD.
127       PERFORM 3210-PROCESS-SORTED-INV-RECORD
128           UNTIL END-OF-FILE.
129       GO TO 3999-EXIT.
130
131   3210-PROCESS-SORTED-INV-RECORD.
132       MOVE SPACES TO RL-REPORT-LINE.
133       MOVE SI-WAREHOUSE-CODE TO RL-WAREHOUSE-CODE.
134       MOVE SI-PART-NUMBER TO RL-PART-NUMBER.
135       MOVE SI-PART-DESCRIPTION TO RL-PART-DESCRIPTION.
136       MOVE SI-INVENTORY-VALUE TO RL-INVENTORY-VALUE.
137       ADD SI-INVENTORY-VALUE TO WS-INVENTORY-VALUE-ACCUM.
138       PERFORM 3830-WRITE-SORTED-INV-RECORD.
139       PERFORM 3890-WRITE-REPORT-LINE.
140       PERFORM 3800-RETURN-SORTED-INV-RECORD.
141
142   3800-RETURN-SORTED-INV-RECORD.
143       RETURN SORT-FILE INTO SI-INVENTORY-RECORD
144           AT END MOVE "YES" TO WS-END-OF-FILE-SWITCH.
145
146   3830-WRITE-SORTED-INV-RECORD.
147       WRITE SI-INVENTORY-RECORD.
148
149   3890-WRITE-REPORT-LINE.
150       WRITE RL-REPORT-LINE
151           AFTER ADVANCING 1 LINE.
152
153   3999-EXIT.
154       EXIT.
155
156   7000-PRINT-TOTAL-LINE SECTION.             Report totals
157                                              procedure
158   7700-PRINT-TOTAL-LINE.
159       MOVE WS-INVENTORY-VALUE-ACCUM TO TL-INVENTORY-VALUE.
160       MOVE TL-TOTAL-LINE TO RL-REPORT-LINE.
161       WRITE RL-REPORT-LINE
162           AFTER ADVANCING 2 LINES.
```

(b) The PROCEDURE DIVISION—COBOL-74.

```
102   PROCEDURE DIVISION.
103
104   0000-SORT-INV-RECORDS.                     Main
105       OPEN OUTPUT INVENTORY-REPORT-FILE      program
106                   SORTED-INVENTORY-FILE
107       MOVE ZEROS TO WS-INVENTORY-VALUE-ACCUM
108       SORT SORT-FILE
109           ASCENDING KEY  SR-WAREHOUSE-CODE
110           DESCENDING KEY SR-INVENTORY-VALUE
111           ASCENDING KEY  SR-PART-NUMBER
112               USING INVENTORY-FILE
113               OUTPUT PROCEDURE IS 3000-PROCESS-SORTED-RECORDS
114       PERFORM 0700-PRINT-TOTAL-LINE
115       CLOSE INVENTORY-REPORT-FILE
116             SORTED-INVENTORY-FILE
117       STOP RUN.
118
119   0700-PRINT-TOTAL-LINE.
120       MOVE WS-INVENTORY-VALUE-ACCUM TO TL-INVENTORY-VALUE
121       MOVE TL-TOTAL-LINE TO RL-REPORT-LINE
122       WRITE RL-REPORT-LINE
123           AFTER ADVANCING 2 LINES.
124
125   3000-PROCESS-SORTED-RECORDS.          ] OUTPUT
126       MOVE "NO " TO WS-END-OF-FILE-SWITCH ] PROCEDURE
127       PERFORM 3800-RETURN-SORTED-INV-RECORD
128       PERFORM 3200-PROCESS-SORTED-INV-RECORD
129           UNTIL END-OF-FILE.
130
131   3200-PROCESS-SORTED-INV-RECORD.
132       MOVE SPACES TO RL-REPORT-LINE
133       MOVE SI-WAREHOUSE-CODE TO RL-WAREHOUSE-CODE
134       MOVE SI-PART-NUMBER TO RL-PART-NUMBER
135       MOVE SI-PART-DESCRIPTION TO RL-PART-DESCRIPTION
136       MOVE SI-INVENTORY-VALUE TO RL-INVENTORY-VALUE
137       ADD SI-INVENTORY-VALUE TO WS-INVENTORY-VALUE-ACCUM
138       PERFORM 3830-WRITE-SORTED-INV-RECORD
139       PERFORM 3890-WRITE-REPORT-LINE       Output
140       PERFORM 3800-RETURN-SORTED-INV-RECORD. components
141
142   3800-RETURN-SORTED-INV-RECORD.
143       RETURN SORT-FILE INTO SI-INVENTORY-RECORD
144           AT END MOVE "YES" TO WS-END-OF-FILE-SWITCH
145       END-RETURN.
146
147   3830-WRITE-SORTED-INV-RECORD.
148       WRITE SI-INVENTORY-RECORD.
149
150   3890-WRITE-REPORT-LINE.
151       WRITE RL-REPORT-LINE
152           AFTER ADVANCING 1 LINE.
```

(c) The PROCEDURE DIVISION—COBOL-85.

COBOL Sorts Versus Stand-Alone Sorts

On few COBOL subjects is there such a divergence of opinion as on the use of COBOL sorts versus stand-alone sorts. Those organizational standards and programmers that recommend use of stand-alone sorts contend that the stand-alone sorts (1) are quicker to write, (2) are easier to modify when sort-key specifications, field locations, record size, and/or blocking factors change, (3) require less main storage because the program storage requirements must be added to the sort storage requirements, (4) spare the time and effort required for the compilation of

COBOL programs, and (5) for COBOL-74, eliminate the adverse effect upon program structure introduced by the INPUT PROCEDURE and OUTPUT PROCEDURE phrases of the SORT statement.

COBOL sort advocates, on the other hand, argue that—unlike the stand-alone sorts—the COBOL sort specifications are standard and portable from one computer system to another. (Stand-alone sorts usually have different parameter specifications for each computer-operating system.) This standardization and portability has the dual effect of easing future conversions and reducing the need for programmer training and retraining. Further, when field locations, record size, or blocking factors change, the applicable COBOL programs must usually be modified and recompiled anyway; the sort modifications typically are handled almost automatically as a by-product of the required modifications.

Probably most important, those who favor COBOL sorts point out that use of the SORT statement with INPUT PROCEDURE and/or OUTPUT PROCEDURE phrases can improve input/output processing efficiency. That is because use of those phrases provides procedures in which the records can be processed "on the fly" to and/or from the sort-work area. Within a job stream of programs, this can have the effect of eliminating one read operation for each record when INPUT PROCEDURE is used and one write operation for each record when OUTPUT PROCEDURE is used. This situation is illustrated in the diagram and input/output operation comparison on the next page.

Currently, those who use COBOL sorts are probably in the majority. In many early COBOL compilers, the SORT statement was not available. As a result, early COBOL programmers became accustomed to and comfortable with the stand-alone sorts. Such programmers tend to be the ones who cling to the use of stand-alone sorts.

Many of the arguments against COBOL sorts are mitigated due to (1) increased main-storage availability, (2) generally faster COBOL compilations, and (3) elimination, in the COBOL-85 standard, of those requirements that had an adverse effect upon program structure. At the same time, contemporary views with regard to the importance of program portability and standardized, well-documented data-definition specifications auger well for the COBOL sorts. Further, the increased use of COBOL on microcomputers—whose operating systems do not typically contain a standard stand-alone sort—contributes to the trend away from the use of stand-alone sorts.

Example A: Stand-alone sort prior to COBOL report program

Input/output operation comparison

1. Read record from file to be sorted

2. Write record to sort-work file

3. Read record from sorted sort-work file

4. Write record to sorted file

5. Read record from sorted file

Example B: COBOL SORT in report program

1. Read record from file to be sorted

2. Write record to sort-work file

3. Read record from sorted sort-work file

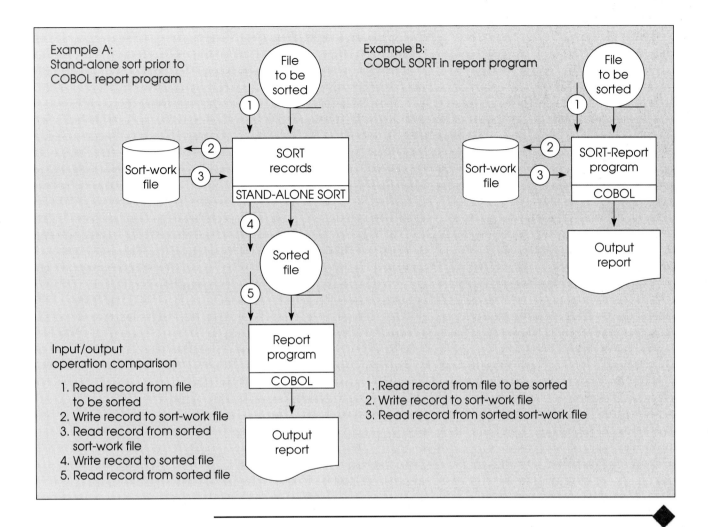

Example A:
Stand-alone sort prior to
COBOL report program

Example B:
COBOL SORT in report program

Input/output
operation comparison

1. Read record from file
   to be sorted
2. Write record to sort-work file
3. Read record from sorted
   sort-work file
4. Write record to sorted file
5. Read record from sorted file

1. Read record from file to be sorted
2. Write record to sort-work file
3. Read record from sorted sort-work file

Topic: **The MERGE Statement**

Merging Merging is the action of combining two or more files that are in the same sequence into one sequenced file. For instance, two sales transaction files might need to be combined into a single file. Or an accounts-receivable application for a department store might call for the merging of the month's charge transaction file and the cash-payments transaction file prior to preparing customer statements. (With the wide use of disk and the ease of using multiple files in an application, physical merging of files is not as significant as it was at one time.)

Utility sort programs are usually designed and written to handle the related function of merging. COBOL formats for those entries related to the MERGE statement are shown in Figure 13-26. To merge two or more files, remember that each file must already be in correct sequence according to the merge-key fields (those fields specified in the ASCENDING/DESCENDING KEY phrase of the MERGE statement).

As can be inferred from the similarity of the SORT and MERGE statements, merge programs follow the same general pattern as sort programs. However, there are two differences. Because a merge operation will always require at least two files, observe in the format notation that at least two files must be specified in the USING phrase. Notice also that the MERGE statement format does not offer an

Figure 13-26   MERGE-related formats.

```
MERGE Formats:

        ENVIRONMENT DIVISION.
        INPUT-OUTPUT SECTION.
        FILE-CONTROL.
                SELECT merge-file name
                ASSIGN TO implementor-name.


        DATA DIVISION.
        FILE SECTION.
   ⎡
   ⎢      SD merge-file-name
   ⎣
                 ⎡ RECORD CONTAINS [integer-1 TO] integer-2 CHARACTERS ⎤

                 ⎡          ⎧ RECORD IS   ⎫                                 ⎤
                 ⎢   DATA   ⎨             ⎬  data-name-1 [data-name-2] ... ⎥ .
                 ⎣          ⎩ RECORDS ARE ⎭                                 ⎦

                                                                   ⎤
              { record-description-entry } ...                     ⎥ ...
                                                                   ⎦


        PROCEDURE DIVISION.

            MERGE merge-file-name ON ⎧ ASCENDING  ⎫ KEY data-name-1 [data-name-2] ...
                                     ⎨ DESCENDING ⎬
                                     ⎩            ⎭
                         ⎡      ⎧ ASCENDING  ⎫                                 ⎤
                         ⎢  ON  ⎨            ⎬ KEY data-name-3 [data-name-4] ...⎥ ...
                         ⎣      ⎩ DESCENDING ⎭                                 ⎦

            USING file-name-1, file-name-2 [file-name-3] ...
                 ⎧ OUTPUT PROCEDURE IS section-name-1 ⎫
                 ⎨                                    ⎬
                 ⎩ GIVING file-name-4                 ⎭
            RETURN file-name RECORD [INTO identifier]
                AT END imperative-statement
```

INPUT PROCEDURE phrase—the USING phrase must be specified. This, in turn, means that the RELEASE statement—because it is limited to the INPUT PROCEDURE—is not applicable.

MERGE Statement Deficiency

The lack of an INPUT PROCEDURE imposes a serious limitation upon the MERGE statement: the number of records processed from each of the input files cannot be tallied. Good system control practices, however, generally mandate the need to count the records received from each file prior to a merge operation.

Merging with the SORT Statement

Because of this record-counting limitation (and also because the MERGE statement is not available on all compilers), a merge operation sometimes is handled instead by coding a SORT statement with either multiple USING files or multiple input files and an INPUT PROCEDURE phrase. A summarized program example of the latter is shown in Figure 13-27. Notice that this coding provides for the counting of records from each of the two input files. However, recognize that use of the SORT statement for merging operations will be less efficient in terms of processing time than the MERGE statement processing.

Figure 13-27   Example of merging through use of the SORT statement.

Example A: Merging by specification of multiple USING files

COBOL-74

```
SORT SORT-FILE
    ASCENDING KEY SR-SORT-KEY-FIELD
    USING FIRST-FILE
        SECOND-FILE
    GIVING MERGED-FILE.
```

COBOL-85

```
SORT SORT-FILE
    ASCENDING KEY SR-SORT-KEY-FIELD
    USING FIRST-FILE
        SECOND-FILE
    GIVING MERGED-FILE.
```

Example B: Merging with an INPUT PROCEDURE

COBOL-74

```
0000-ML-MERGE-TWO-FILES SECTION.

0000-MERGE-TWO-FILES.
    OPEN INPUT FIRST-FILE
            SECOND-FILE.
    SORT SORT-FILE
        ASCENDING KEY SR-SORT-KEY-FIELD
        INPUT PROCEDURE 2000-IP-MERGE-FILES
        GIVING MERGED-FILE.
    CLOSE FIRST-FILE
            SECOND-FILE.
    STOP RUN.

2000-IP-MERGE-FILES SECTION.
    MOVE "NO" TO WS-END-OF-FILE-SWITCH.
    MOVE ZEROS TO WS-FIRST-FILE-RECORDS
                WS-SECOND-FILE-RECORDS.
    PERFORM 2200-PROCESS-FIRST-FILE
        UNTIL END-OF-FILE.
    MOVE "NO" TO WS-END-OF-FILE-SWITCH.
    PERFORM 2210-PROCESS-SECOND-FILE
        UNTIL END-OF-FILE.
    GO TO 2999-EXIT.

2200-PROCESS-FIRST-FILE.
    PERFORM 2800-READ-FIRST-FILE-RECORD.
    IF NOT END-OF-FILE
        MOVE FF-FIRST-FILE-RECORD TO SR-SORT-RECORD
        ADD 1 TO WS-FIRST-FILE-RECORDS
        PERFORM 2830-RELEASE-MERGE-RECORD.

2210-PROCESS-SECOND-FILE.
    PERFORM 2810-READ-SECOND-FILE-RECORD.
    IF NOT END-OF-FILE
        MOVE SF-SECOND-FILE-RECORD TO SR-SORT-RECORD
        ADD 1 TO WS-SECOND-FILE-RECORDS
        PERFORM 2830-RELEASE-MERGE-RECORD.

2800-READ-FIRST-FILE-RECORD.
    READ FIRST-FILE
        AT END MOVE "YES" TO WS-END-OF-FILE-SWITCH.

2810-READ-SECOND-FILE-RECORD.
    READ SECOND-FILE
        AT END MOVE "YES" TO WS-END-OF-FILE-SWITCH.

2830-RELEASE-MERGE-RECORD.
    RELEASE SR-SORT-RECORD.

2999-EXIT.
    EXIT.
```

COBOL-85

```
0000-MERGE-TWO-FILES.
    OPEN INPUT FIRST-FILE
            SECOND-FILE
    SORT SORT-FILE
        ASCENDING KEY SR-SORT-KEY-FIELD
        INPUT PROCEDURE 2000-IP-MERGE-FILES
        GIVING MERGED-FILE
    CLOSE FIRST-FILE
            SECOND-FILE
    STOP RUN.

2000-IP-MERGE-FILES.
    MOVE "NO" TO WS-END-OF-FILE-SWITCH
    MOVE ZEROS TO WS-FIRST-FILE-RECORDS
                WS-SECOND-FILE-RECORDS
    PERFORM 2200-PROCESS-FIRST-FILE
        UNTIL END-OF-FILE
    MOVE "NO" TO WS-END-OF-FILE-SWITCH
    PERFORM 2210-PROCESS-SECOND-FILE
        UNTIL END-OF-FILE.

2200-PROCESS-FIRST-FILE.
    PERFORM 2800-READ-FIRST-FILE-RECORD
    IF NOT END-OF-FILE
        MOVE FF-FIRST-FILE-RECORD TO SR-SORT-RECORD
        ADD 1 TO WS-FIRST-FILE-RECORDS
        PERFORM 2830-RELEASE-MERGE-RECORD
    END-IF.

2210-PROCESS-SECOND-FILE.
    PERFORM 2810-READ-SECOND-FILE-RECORD
    IF NOT END-OF-FILE
        MOVE SF-SECOND-FILE-RECORD TO SR-SORT-RECORD
        ADD 1 TO WS-SECOND-FILE-RECORDS
        PERFORM 2830-RELEASE-MERGE-RECORD
    END-IF.

2800-READ-FIRST-FILE-RECORD.
    READ FIRST-FILE
        AT END MOVE "YES" TO WS-END-OF-FILE-SWITCH.

2810-READ-SECOND-FILE-RECORD.
    READ SECOND-FILE
        AT END MOVE "YES" TO WS-END-OF-FILE-SWITCH.

2830-RELEASE-MERGE-RECORD.
    RELEASE SR-SORT-RECORD.
```

In actual practice, the MERGE statement is seldom used because (1) merging requirements are encountered only occasionally (whereas sort processing is common) in commercial data-processing applications, (2) it lacks an input-procedure capability, and (3) a number of COBOL compilers do not provide the feature.

Chapter Summary

Record **sorting** can be handled either by (1) specifying **parameters** to a **stand-alone** (**external**) **sort**, or (2) coding a COBOL program that uses the SORT statement. When a **COBOL sort**—sometimes called an **internal sort**—is used, the sort-program processing will take one of four variations: (1) sort only, (2) sort with preprocessing of the input file, (3) sort with preprocessing of the input file and postprocessing of the sorted file, or (4) sort with postprocessing of the sorted file.

A **sort-only program** is coded by specifying the USING and GIVING phrases of the SORT statement.

A **sort program with preprocessing of the input file** is coded by specifying the INPUT PROCEDURE phrase (instead of the USING phrase) of the SORT statement. The RELEASE statement is used to transfer records to the sort-work file. This type of sort program is useful to (1) select and sort only certain records from the input file, (2) create additional records to be included in the sorted file, (3) make changes to the input record before sorting, (4) validate records prior to sorting, (5) list the input records before sorting, and/or (6) to count records prior to the sort.

A **sort program with postprocessing of the sorted file** is coded by specifying the OUTPUT PROCEDURE phrase (instead of the GIVING phrase) of the SORT statement. The RETURN statement is used to retrieve sorted records from the sort-work file. This type of sort program is useful to (1) create more than one sorted output file, (2) select or summarize records after sorting and before writing them to the sorted output file, (3) create additional records after sorting to be included in the output-sorted file, (4) make changes to the record after sorting, (5) validate the sorted records, (6) list the sorted records, and/or (7) count the sorted records. A **sort program with preprocessing of the input file and postprocessing of the sorted file** combines aspects of the sort programs of the preceding descriptions.

The MERGE statement can be used to combine two or more files according to a specified **merge key**. Each file must already be in the merge-key sequence. MERGE statement processing parallels that of the SORT statement, except that INPUT PROCEDURE processing is not available. Merge operations can alternatively be handled through SORT statement processing.

COBOL Language Element Summary

SORT/MERGE Statement ENVIRONMENT DIVISION Entries.   A file-control SELECT entry must be provided for the sort file named in each SORT statement (or for the merge file named in each MERGE statement).
Example:

```
SELECT SORT-FILE
    ASSIGN TO UT-S-SORTWORK.
```

For certain compilers, the implementor-name in the ASSIGN clause must conform to implementor-defined requirements.

SORT/MERGE Statement DATA DIVISION Entries.   An SD entry must be provided for each sort file (or merge file) named in a file-control entry. An SD entry is like an FD entry, except that the BLOCK CONTAINS and LABEL RECORDS clauses are not specified. Following the SD entry, a 01-level record-description entry describing the record to be sorted is specified.

Example:

```
SD  SORT-FILE
        RECORD CONTAINS 54 CHARACTERS.
01  SR-SORT-RECORD.
    05  FILLER                  PIC X(2).
    05  SR-WAREHOUSE-CODE       PIC X(2).
    05  SR-PART-NUMBER          PIC X(15).
    05  FILLER  PIC X(28).
    05  SR-INVENTORY-VALUE      PIC S9(7)V99.
```

■ The SD-name must match the name of the sort file (or merge file) selected in the ENVIRONMENT DIVISION file-control entry.

■ The 01-level record-description entry must contain a data-item description for each sort-key (or merge-key) field named in the KEY phrase(s) of the SORT (or MERGE) statement. The key fields may appear anywhere in the record and in any order.

■ Multiple record-descriptions may be specified, but the key fields must occupy the same relative positions within each record.

SORT Statement PROCEDURE DIVISION Entries.   The SORT statement is used to invoke the sort function.

Example:

```
SORT SORT-FILE
    ASCENDING KEY SR-WAREHOUSE-CODE
    DESCENDING KEY SR-INVENTORY-VALUE
    ASCENDING KEY SR-PART-NUMBER
        USING INVENTORY-FILE
        INPUT PROCEDURE IS 2000-IP-SELECT-INV-RECORDS
        GIVING SORTED-INVENTORY-FILE
        OUTPUT PROCEDURE IS 3000-OP-PROCESS-SORTED-RECORDS
```

Sort File.   The programmer does not code OPEN or CLOSE statements for the sort-work file.

KEY Phrase.   KEY fields are specified with the major field listed first. If there is more than one KEY field, additional fields are listed in order of decreasing significance—the minor field is last in the list.

ASCENDING KEY and DESCENDING KEY phrases may be mixed within the same SORT statement.

To ensure correct algebraic sequence, numeric sort-key fields containing both positive and negative values should be described as elementary signed numeric data-items within the SD record-description entry.

All KEY fields within the SD record-description entry must be described with the correct USAGE.

USING Phrase.   The USING phrase is specified to sort all records of an input file (or files).

When USING is specified, the SORT statement will cause the named file (or files) to be opened, transferred to the sort-work file, and closed. The programmer does not code OPEN or CLOSE statements for such files.

GIVING Phrase.   The GIVING phrase is specified to write all records of the sort-work file to an output-sorted file.

When GIVING is specified, the SORT statement will cause the named file (or files) to be opened, have the sorted records from the sort-work file transferred to it, and closed. The programmer does not code OPEN or CLOSE statements for such files.

INPUT PROCEDURE and OUTPUT PROCEDURE Phrases.   An INPUT PROCEDURE is specified to provide for processing of input records before they are sorted; an OUTPUT PROCEDURE is specified to provide for processing of the sort-work file records after they have been sorted.

An INPUT PROCEDURE or an OUTPUT PROCEDURE cannot contain a SORT or MERGE statement.

COBOL-74 restrictions:

■ The INPUT PROCEDURE and the OUTPUT PROCEDURE must be formed as sections.

■ The INPUT PROCEDURE and the OUTPUT PROCEDURE section-names must not be referenced, except by a SORT (or MERGE) statement.

■ Within an INPUT PROCEDURE or an OUTPUT PROCEDURE, program control cannot be transferred to procedures outside it.

MERGE Statement PROCEDURE DIVISION Entries.   The MERGE statement is used to invoke the MERGE function.

Example:

```
MERGE MERGE-FILE
    ASCENDING KEY SR-WAREHOUSE-CODE
    DESCENDING KEY SR-INVENTORY-VALUE
    ASCENDING KEY SR-PART-NUMBER
        USING INVENTORY-FILE-1
              INVENTORY-FILE-2
        GIVING SORTED-INVENTORY-FILE
        OUTPUT PROCEDURE IS 3000-OP-PROCESS-MERGED-RECORDS.
```

Syntactical requirements for the MERGE statement are the same as those for the SORT statement, except that:

■ The INPUT PROCEDURE phrase is not available.

■ At least two files are listed in the USING phrase.

RELEASE Statement.   The RELEASE statement is used to transfer a record to the sort file. (It is similar to a WRITE statement.)

Examples:

```
RELEASE SR-SORT-RECORD
```

or

```
RELEASE SR-SORT-RECORD FROM IR-INVENTORY-RECORD
```

The RELEASE statement can only be specified within an INPUT PROCEDURE.

The record to be released must be physically present (that is, moved to) the SD record-description area prior to issuing the RELEASE (the FROM option of the RELEASE statement may be coded to provide for this).

Because the MERGE statement does not contain an INPUT PROCEDURE phrase, the RELEASE statement cannot be used with a merge operation.

RETURN Statement. The RETURN statement is used to retrieve a record from the sort file after the records have been sorted. (It is similar to a READ statement.)
Examples:

```
RETURN SORT-FILE
    AT END MOVE "YES" TO WS-END-OF-FILE-SWITCH
```

or

```
RETURN SORT-FILE INTO SI-INVENTORY-RECORD
    AT END MOVE "YES" TO WS-END-OF-FILE-SWITCH
```

The RETURN statement can only be specified within an OUTPUT PROCEDURE.

Summary of COBOL-85 Differences

COBOL-85 does not require that the procedure names referenced by the INPUT PROCEDURE and OUTPUT PROCEDURE phrases be section names. The restriction that program control not be transferred out of an input or output procedure (section) thus becomes meaningless.

In COBOL-74, the relative arrangement—after sorting—of any records with duplicate sort keys was not defined. In COBOL-85, the optional WITH DUPLICATES IN ORDER phrase can be specified to ensure that records with duplicate sort-key values will be arranged in "first-in/first-out" order. The new SORT statement format is as follows:

$$
\underline{\text{SORT}} \text{ sort-file-name } \underline{\text{ON}} \left\{ \begin{array}{c} \underline{\text{ASCENDING}} \\ \underline{\text{DESCENDING}} \end{array} \right\} \text{KEY data-name-1 [data-name-2] } \dots
$$

$$
\left[\underline{\text{ON}} \left\{ \begin{array}{c} \underline{\text{ASCENDING}} \\ \underline{\text{DESCENDING}} \end{array} \right\} \text{KEY data-name-3 [data-name-4] } \dots \right] \dots
$$

[WITH <u>DUPLICATES</u> IN ORDER]

$$
\left\{ \begin{array}{l} \underline{\text{INPUT PROCEDURE}} \text{ IS procedure-name-1} \\ \underline{\text{USING}} \text{ file-name-1 [file-name-3] } \dots \end{array} \right\}
$$

$$
\left\{ \begin{array}{l} \underline{\text{OUTPUT PROCEDURE}} \text{ IS procedure-name-2} \\ \underline{\text{GIVING}} \text{ file-name-2} \end{array} \right\}
$$

Exercises
Terms for Definition

COBOL sort _____

external sort _____

intermediate field _____

internal sort _____

major field _____

merge key _____

merging _____

minor field _____

parameters _____

sort key _____

sorting _____

sort-work file _____

stand-alone sort _____

Review Questions

1. When a SORT or MERGE statement is specified in a COBOL program, a(n)

   _____ entry for the sort-work file is required in the
   ENVIRONMENT DIVISION.

2. When a SORT or MERGE statement is specified in a COBOL program, a(n)

   _____ entry for the sort-work file is required in the FILE
   SECTION of the DATA DIVISION.

3. Sort- and merge-key fields are specified in the _____ phrase
   of the SORT statement.

4. Specification of an input file to be sorted without preprocessing of the input

   records is handled by the _____ phrase of the SORT
   statement.

5. To create a sorted output file without postprocessing of the sorted records,

   the _____ phrase of the SORT statement is used.

6. To permit preprocessing of the input file to be sorted, the

   _____ phrase of the SORT statement must be specified.

7. To permit postprocessing of the sorted file, the _____ phrase
   of the SORT statement must be specified.

8. A RELEASE statement is similar in function to a(n) _____
   statement.

9. A RETURN statement is similar in function to a(n) _____
   statement.

10. Identify three items introduced by use of the COBOL-74 SORT statement that
    are in conflict with generally accepted structured coding conventions.

    a. _____

    b. _____

    c. _____

11. List six sort program requirements that call for specification of an INPUT
    PROCEDURE.

    a. _____

    b. _____

    c. _____

d. _____

e. _____

f. _____

12. List six sort program requirements that call for specification of an OUTPUT PROCEDURE.

a. _____

b. _____

c. _____

d. _____

e. _____

f. _____

13. When files are merged, each file must already be _____

_____.

14. In contrast to the SORT statement, the MERGE statement does not provide for

specification of a(n) _____ phrase.

Programming Assignments

Programming Assignment 13-1: Sort Vendor File

Background information:
For a better idea of how various vendors pay their bills, the financial officer of Tools Unlimited requires some reports in which the vendor file is by amount due within date due within vendor name.

Input file: Vendor file (VENDOR.DAT)

Input-record format:

Positions	Field	Data class	Comments
1–2	Record code	Alphanumeric	Code VM
4–11	Vendor number	Numeric	
12–17	Date due	Numeric	Format: *yymmdd*
18–37	Vendor name	Alphanumeric	
67–74	Amount due	Numeric	Dollars and cents

Output file: Sorted vendor file

Program operations:
1. Sort the vendor file.
   a. Arrange the records alphabetically in accordance with the value of the vendor-name field.
   b. Any records with matching vendor names are to be arranged in accordance with the date-due field (newest date first; oldest date last).

    c. Any records with matching vendor names and due dates are to be arranged in accordance with the amount-due field (highest amount first; lowest amount last).

2. Create a file of the sorted vendor records.

Programming Assignment 13-2: Select and Sort Inventory-Reorder Records

Background information:

The production manager of Tools Unlimited wishes to minimize her inventory cost. To that end, she needs some reports generated from the inventory file so that the records are sequenced by part number within reorder cost within inventory class.

Input file: Inventory file (INVEN.DAT)

Input-record format:

Positions	Field	Data class	Comments
1–2	Record code	Numeric	Code 44
4–13	Part number	Alphanumeric	
14–39	Part description	Alphanumeric	
40	Inventory class	Alphanumeric	
41–46	Unit cost	Numeric	Dollars and cents
48–51	Reorder point	Numeric	Whole number
52–55	Quantity on hand	Numeric	Whole number
56–59	Quantity on order	Numeric	Whole number
71–74	Reorder quantity	Numeric	Whole number
75–80	Other data		

Output file: Sorted parts file

Program operations:

1. Determine the reorder cost in accordance with the following:
   a. Calculate the quantity-available amount by subtracting the quantity-on-order amount from the quantity-on-hand amount.
   b. If the quantity-available amount is less than the reorder-point amount, calculate the quantity-to-order amount. The quantity-to-order amount is the reorder-quantity amount unless the quantity-to-order amount is greater, in which case it should be the next higher multiple of the reorder-quantity amount.
   c. If the quantity-available amount is not less than the reorder-point amount, set the quantity-to-order amount to zero.
   d. Multiply the quantity-to-order amount by the unit-cost field to equal the reorder cost.
2. Select and sort those records requiring a reorder (that is, a reorder-cost greater than zero).
   a. Arrange the records alphabetically in accordance with the value of the inventory-class field.
   b. Those records with matching inventory-class codes are to be arranged in accordance with the reorder-cost value (highest cost first; lowest cost last).
   c. Any records with matching inventory-class codes and reorder-cost values are to be arranged in ascending sequence in accordance with the value of the part-number field.
3. Create a file of the sorted selected inventory records.

Programming Assignment 13-3: Sort and Print Earnings File

Background information:

The payroll manager of Silicon Valley Manufacturing needs a report with output lines in sequence by employee name within year-to-date earnings within pay rate within pay code. Each record is to be printed in its sorted sequence together with the total number of hourly and salaried employees listed on the report. A sorted earnings file must be created on disk.

Input file: Earnings file (EARNINGS.DAT)

Input-record format:

Positions	Field	Data class	Comments
1–2	Record code	Alphanumeric	Code EM
20–31	Employee last name	Alphanumeric	
32–40	Employee first name	Alphanumeric	
41	Employee middle initial	Alphanumeric	
53	Pay code	Alphabetic	Blank or H
54–59	Pay rate	Numeric	99V9999 for Hourly
			9999V99 for Salaried
60–74	Other data		

Output files: Sorted earnings file
Earnings by pay-code report

Output-report format:

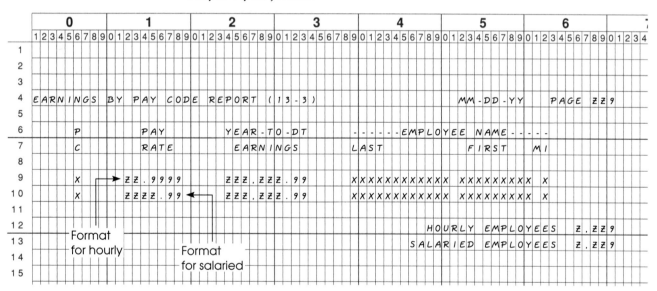

Program operations:

1. Sort the earnings file.
   a. Arrange the records alphabetically in accordance with the value of the pay-code field.
   b. Those records with matching pay-code values are to be arranged in accordance with the value of the pay rate field (highest rate first; lowest rate last).

c.   Those records with matching pay-code and pay-rate values are to be arranged in accordance with the value of the year-to-date earnings field (highest earnings first; lowest earnings last).
d.   Any records with matching pay-code, pay-rate, and year-to-date earnings are to be arranged alphabetically by employee name (last name first; first name, middle initial).
2. Make the following accumulations.
a.   Total number of hourly employees (pay-code field equal to "H").
b.   Total number of salaried employees (pay-code field equal to a blank space).
3. Create a disk file of the sorted earnings records.
4. Print each sorted earnings record on the earnings by pay-code report in accordance with the print-chart specifications.
a.   Single-space each detail line.
b.   Provide for a line span of 57 lines per page.

Programming Assignment 13-4: Classify, Sort, and Print Student Records

Background information:

The dean of instruction at Bayview Institute of Computer Technology makes periodic studies of student scholarship. A report is needed in which students are listed in order by student name within grade-point average within college-year status. The report must also include the total number of students in each college year. A disk file of the sorted records is to be created.

Input file: Student file (STUDENT.DAT)

Input-record format:

Positions	Field	Data class	Comments
1–2	Record code	Numeric	Code 22
12–25	Student last name	Alphanumeric	
26–35	Student first name	Alphanumeric	
39–41	Major code	Numeric	
45–47	Grade points	Numeric	
48–50	Units completed	Numeric	
51–70	Other data		

Output files: Student list by GPA by college year
Sorted student file

Output-report format:

```
        0              1              2              3              4              5              6              7
  1234567890 1234567890 1234567890 1234567890 1234567890 1234567890 1234567890 1234567890 12
 1
 2
 3
 4  STUDENT LIST BY GPA BY COLLEGE YEAR (13-4)                              MM-DD-YY      PAGE ZZ9
 5
 6  COLLEGE           STUDENT       ------STUDENT NAME-------         GRADE      UNITS
 7    YEAR            NUXBER            LAST        FIRST             POINTS      COMP.              GPA
 8
 9  XXXXXXXXX         999-99-9999   XXXXXXXXXXXXXX XXXXXXXXXX          ZZ9        ZZ9               9.99
10  XXXXXXXXX         999-99-9999   XXXXXXXXXXXXXX XXXXXXXXXX          ZZ9        ZZ9               9.99
11
12
13                                                                 FRESHMEN     ZZ,ZZ9
14     Print FRESHMAN,                                             SOPHOMORES   ZZ,ZZ9
15       SOPHOMORE,                                                JUNIORS      ZZ,ZZ9
16       JUNIOR, or                                                SENIORS      ZZ,ZZ9
17       SENIOR
18
```

Program operations:

1. Determine the college-year status for each student in accordance with the value of the units-completed field.
   a. Units completed from 0 to 29   = Freshman
   b. from 30 to 59   = Sophomore
   c. from 60 to 89   = Junior
   d. over 89   = Senior
2. Calculate each student's grade-point average by dividing the grade-points field by the units-completed field. Carry the quotient to two decimal places.
3. Sort the student records.
   a. Arrange the records in college-year order (seniors first; freshmen last).
   b. Those records with matching college years are to be arranged in accordance with the grade-point average (highest GPA first; lowest GPA last).
   c. Any records with matching college years and GPAs are to be arranged alphabetically by student name (last name first).
4. Accumulate the number of students in each of the four college years.
5. Create a disk file of the sorted student records.
6. Print the student list by GPA by college year in accordance with the print-chart specifications.
   a. Single-space each detail line.
   b. Provide for a line span of 57 lines per page.

Programming Assignment 13-5: Sorted Nurses' Telephone Directory

Background information:

The personnel director of Brooklawn Hospital needs a telephone directory of all non-supervisory nursing personnel in the hospital. The list is to be grouped with the parttime employees first and then fulltime employees. Within these two groupings, the list is to be in alphabetic sequence.

Input file: Nurses file (NURSES.DAT)

Positions	Field	Data class	Comments
3–25	Name (last, first, mi)	Alphanumeric	
26–32	Home telephone number	Alphanumeric	
33–46	Professional specialty	Alphanumeric	For example, Trauma Room
56	Employment code	Alphabetic	F—Fulltime employee P—Parttime employee
57	Supervisory code	Alphabetic	Y—Yes, N—No

Output-report format:

Program operations:

1. Select records for non-supervisory personnel only.
2. Sort the selected records.
   a. Group the records by employment code (parttime first followed by fulltime).
   b. Within each employment code group, sort the records alphabetically by name.
3. Create a disk file of the sorted records.
4. Print the sorted telephone directory file in accordance with the print-chart

specifications.

a. Print two heading lines on the first page and all subsequent pages; accumulate page numbers for the first line.

b. Start a new page to begin the fulltime employees (after the last parttime employee).

c. On the second heading line, print PARTTIME or FULLTIME as appropriate.

d. Double-space each detail line.

e. Provide for a line span of 25 lines.

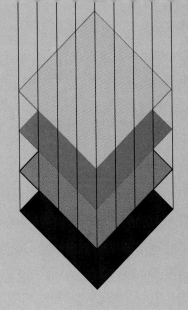

Appendixes

APPENDIX A   **The COBOL Report Writer Feature**   AA-1

APPENDIX B   **Other COBOL Clauses and Statements**   AB-1

APPENDIX C   **System Names for Selected COBOL Compilers**   AC-1

APPENDIX D   **Program Interruptions for IBM OS and DOS Systems**   AD-1

APPENDIX E   **Complete COBOL-74 Language Formats**   AE-1

APPENDIX F   **Complete COBOL-85 Language Formats**   AF-1

APPENDIX G   **COBOL Reserved Words**   AG-1

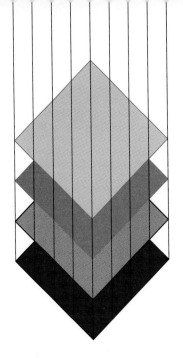

The COBOL Report Writer Feature

COBOL's Report Writer feature provides the ability to write report programs with a reduced amount of COBOL coding. PROCEDURE DIVISION coding is reduced because much of the report logic is handled through the specification of programming requirements in the RE-PORT SECTION of the DATA DIVISION. Coding requirements for the DATA DIVISION are sometimes also lessened because the need to define report control, accumulator, and FILLER fields is decreased. The Report Writer feature is not available on all COBOL compilers, however.

Figure AA.1 summarizes the coding differences when Report Writer is used. There are no coding differences for the IDENTIFICATION DIVISION or the ENVIRONMENT DIVISION. In the DATA DIVISION, the REPORT clause is introduced into the FD for the report file. Further, a completely new section—the REPORT SECTION—is coded after the WORKING-STORAGE SECTION. The Report Writer PROCEDURE DIVISION syntax contains three verbs: INITIATE, GENERATE, and TERMINATE.

Topic: AA-1: A Report with End-of-Report Totals

The REPORT Clause of the FD Entry

The REPORT SECTION
The RD Entry
 The CONTROL IS clause
 The PAGE LIMIT clause
01-Level Report Lines in the REPORT SECTION
 TYPE IS PAGE-HEADING
  The LINE and COLUMN clauses
  The SOURCE clause
 TYPE IS DETAIL
 TYPE IS CONTROL FOOTING FINAL
  The SUM clause
  SUM clause difference for IBM COBOL

The PROCEDURE DIVISION
The INITIATE Statement
The GENERATE Statement
The TERMINATE Statement

Figure AA. 1
Report Writer coding
differences.

Division	Report Writer differences
IDENTIFICATION	None
ENVIRONMENT	None
DATA	REPORT clause in FD-entry
	No 01-level record-description following the FD for the report-file in the FILE SECTION
	REPORT SECTION entries
PROCEDURE	INITIATE verb
	GENERATE verb
	TERMINATE verb
	USE BEFORE REPORTING statement
	SUPPRESS statement

Figure AA. 2 Payroll-report print chart.

In Chapter 6, you learned the details of report program coding via the PAYROLL program. The program documentation begins on page 283; the print chart defining the report format from that documentation is repeated here in Figure AA.2. The PAYROLL program itself is on pages 296, 299, and 300. A program to produce this report using the COBOL Report Writer feature is shown in Figure AA.3. Notice that this program, named RPAYROLL (for **R**eport Writer **payroll** program) is much shorter than the PAYROLL program presented in Chapter 6. On the RPAYROLL listing, key Report Writer entries are identified.

The REPORT Clause of the FD Entry

Figure AA.4 shows the FD-entry format for a Report Writer report file. It is identical to that for a regular printer file, except that the REPORT IS clause is coded to name the report file that will be described in the REPORT SECTION. (Observe that this REPORT IS clause introduces the need for another data-name. Hence, the file-name defined in the FD entry has been changed from PAYROLL-REPORT, as it was in the PAYROLL program, to PAYROLL-REPORT-FILE. PAYROLL-REPORT has been chosen as the report-name for the RD entry.)

When the REPORT clause is coded in the FD, no 01-level record-description entries are coded for that file in the FILE SECTION. Instead, the 01-level report-line records are described in the REPORT SECTION.

Figure AA. 3   Report Writer COBOL coding: RPAYROLL program.

```
001010 IDENTIFICATION DIVISION.
001020 PROGRAM-ID.    RPAYROLL.
001080*
001090*
001100*            THIS PROGRAM READS PAYROLL RECORDS,
001110*            COMPUTES THE GROSS PAY FOR EACH EMPLOYEE
001120*            AND PRINTS AN EMPLOYEE DETAIL LINE
001130*            FOR EACH PAYROLL RECORD.
001140*
001150*            AFTER ALL INPUT PAYROLL RECORDS HAVE BEEN
001160*            PROCESSED, A REPORT TOTAL LINE WILL BE PRINTED.
002010*
002020*
002030*
002040 ENVIRONMENT DIVISION.
002050*
002060*
002070 CONFIGURATION SECTION.
002080*
002090 SOURCE-COMPUTER.   IBM-3081.
002100 OBJECT-COMPUTER.   IBM-3081.
002110*
002120*
002130 INPUT-OUTPUT SECTION.
002140*
002150 FILE-CONTROL.
002160     SELECT PAYROLL-FILE
002170         ASSIGN TO UT-S-INFILE.
002180     SELECT PAYROLL-REPORT-FILE
002190         ASSIGN TO UT-S-PRTFILE.
003010*
003020*
003030*
003040 DATA DIVISION.
003050*
003060*
003070 FILE SECTION.
003080*
003090 FD  PAYROLL-FILE
003100         RECORD CONTAINS 80 CHARACTERS
003110         LABEL RECORDS ARE OMITTED.
003120*
003130 01  PAYROLL-RECORD.
003140     05  FILLER                    PIC X(80).
004010*
004020 FD  PAYROLL-REPORT-FILE
004030         RECORD CONTAINS 132 CHARACTERS
004040         LABEL RECORDS ARE OMITTED
004050         REPORT IS PAYROLL-REPORT.  ◄── REPORT clause
005010*
005020*
005030 WORKING-STORAGE SECTION.
005040*
005050*
005060 01  WS-SWITCHES.
005070     05  WS-END-OF-FILE-SWITCH     PIC X(3).
007010*
007020 01  WS-WORK-AREAS.
007030     05  WS-DATE-WORK              PIC 9(6).
007040     05  WS-DATE-REFORMAT REDEFINES WS-DATE-WORK.
007050         10  WS-YEAR               PIC 9(2).
007060         10  WS-MONTH              PIC 9(2).
007070         10  WS-DAY                PIC 9(2).
007080     05  WS-GROSS-PAY              PIC S9(5)V99.
007090     05  WS-CONSTANT-ONE           PIC S9(1)    VALUE +1.
020010*
020020 01  PR-PAYROLL-RECORD.
020030     05  PR-RECORD-CODE            PIC X(2).
020040     05  PR-SOC-SEC-NBR.
020050         10  PR-SOC-SEC-NBR-1      PIC 9(3).
020060         10  PR-SOC-SEC-NBR-2      PIC 9(2).
020070         10  PR-SOC-SEC-NBR-3      PIC 9(4).
020080     05  PR-EMPLOYEE-NAME          PIC X(24).
020090     05  PR-RATE-OF-PAY            PIC 9(2)V99.
020100     05  FILLER                    PIC X(5).
020110     05  PR-HOURS-WORKED           PIC 9(3)V99.
020120     05  FILLER                    PIC X(31).
```

```
030010*                                          REPORT SECTION
030020*
030030 REPORT SECTION.
030040*
030050*
030060 RD  PAYROLL-REPORT
030070         CONTROL IS FINAL
030080         PAGE LIMIT IS 57 LINES
030090         HEADING 1
030100         FIRST DETAIL 6
030110         LAST DETAIL 57
030120         FOOTING 57.
031010*
031020 01  TYPE IS PAGE-HEADING.                 Heading lines
031030*
031040     03  LINE 1.
031030         05  COLUMN 1   PIC X(18)  VALUE "UNIVERSAL BUSINESS".
031040         05  COLUMN 20  PIC X(16)  VALUE "SERVICES COMPANY".
031050         05  COLUMN 67  PIC X(14)  VALUE "PAYROLL REPORT".
031060*
031070     03  LINE 2.
031080         05  COLUMN 1   PIC 9(2)   SOURCE WS-MONTH.
031090         05  COLUMN 3   PIC X(1)   VALUE "/".
031100         05  COLUMN 4   PIC 9(2)   SOURCE WS-DAY.
031110         05  COLUMN 6   PIC X(1)   VALUE "/".
031120         05  COLUMN 7   PIC 9(2)   SOURCE WS-YEAR.
031130         05  COLUMN 73  PIC X(4)   VALUE "PAGE".
031140         05  COLUMN 78  PIC ZZ9    SOURCE PAGE-COUNTER.
031150*
031160     03  LINE 4.
031170         05  COLUMN 1   PIC X(11)  VALUE "S.S. NUMBER".
031180         05  COLUMN 21  PIC X(13)  VALUE "EMPLOYEE NAME".
031190         05  COLUMN 50  PIC X(4)   VALUE "RATE".
031200         05  COLUMN 61  PIC X(5)   VALUE "HOURS".
031210         05  COLUMN 72  PIC X(9)   VALUE "GROSS PAY".
033010*                                          Detail line
033020 01  DL-DETAIL-LINE
033030         TYPE IS DETAIL
033040         LINE IS PLUS 1.
033050     05  COLUMN 1    PIC 9(3)      SOURCE PR-SOC-SEC-NBR-1.
033060     05  COLUMN 4    PIC X(1)      VALUE "-".
033070     05  COLUMN 5    PIC 9(2)      SOURCE PR-SOC-SEC-NBR-2.
033080     05  COLUMN 7    PIC X(1)      VALUE "-".
033090     05  COLUMN 8    PIC 9(4)      SOURCE PR-SOC-SEC-NBR-3.
033100     05  COLUMN 18   PIC X(24)     SOURCE PR-EMPLOYEE-NAME.
033110     05  COLUMN 49   PIC ZZ.99     SOURCE PR-RATE-OF-PAY.
033120     05  COLUMN 60   PIC ZZZ.99    SOURCE PR-HOURS-WORKED.
033130     05  COLUMN 72   PIC ZZ,ZZZ.99 SOURCE WS-GROSS-PAY.
034010*                                          Total line
034020 01  TYPE IS CONTROL FOOTING FINAL
034030         LINE IS PLUS 3.
034040     05  COLUMN 20   PIC Z,ZZ9     SUM WS-CONSTANT-ONE.
034050     05  COLUMN 26   PIC X(15)     VALUE "TOTAL EMPLOYEES".
034060     05  COLUMN 57   PIC ZZ,ZZZ.99 SUM PR-HOURS-WORKED.
034070     05  COLUMN 71   PIC ZZZ,ZZZ.99 SUM WS-GROSS-PAY.
050010*
050020*
050030*
050040 PROCEDURE DIVISION.
050050*
050060*
050070 000-PRINT-PAYROLL-REPORT.
050080*
050090     OPEN INPUT PAYROLL-FILE
050100          OUTPUT PAYROLL-REPORT-FILE.
050110     INITIATE PAYROLL-REPORT.        ◄── Begins report
050120     PERFORM 100-INITIALIZE-VARIABLE-FIELDS.
050130     PERFORM 800-READ-PAYROLL-RECORD.
050140     PERFORM 200-PROCESS-PAYROLL-RECORD
050150         UNTIL WS-END-OF-FILE-SWITCH IS EQUAL TO "YES".
050160     TERMINATE PAYROLL-REPORT.       ◄── Ends report
050170     CLOSE PAYROLL-FILE
050180          PAYROLL-REPORT-FILE.
050190     STOP RUN.
100010*
100020*
100030 100-INITIALIZE-VARIABLE-FIELDS.
100040*
100050     MOVE "NO " TO WS-END-OF-FILE-SWITCH.
100080     ACCEPT WS-DATE-WORK FROM DATE.
200010*
200020*
200030 200-PROCESS-PAYROLL-RECORD.
200040*
200050     MULTIPLY PR-RATE-OF-PAY BY PR-HOURS-WORKED
200060         GIVING WS-GROSS-PAY ROUNDED.
200080     GENERATE DL-DETAIL-LINE.         ◄── Prints detail line
200090     PERFORM 800-READ-PAYROLL-RECORD.
800010*
800020*
800030 800-READ-PAYROLL-RECORD.
800040*
800050     READ PAYROLL-FILE INTO PR-PAYROLL-RECORD
800060         AT END MOVE "YES" TO WS-END-OF-FILE-SWITCH.
```

The REPORT SECTION

In the REPORT SECTION, a report-description (RD) entry is coded for each report to be prepared by the program.

The RD Entry

The RD-entry format is shown in Figure AA.5. Because most programs prepare a single report, just one RD entry is typically coded in a Report Writer program. The RD name—PAYROLL-REPORT in this case—must match the report-name specified in the FD entry. The RD entry contains two clauses: CONTROL IS and PAGE LIMIT.

Figure AA. 4
FD-entry format with the
REPORT clause.

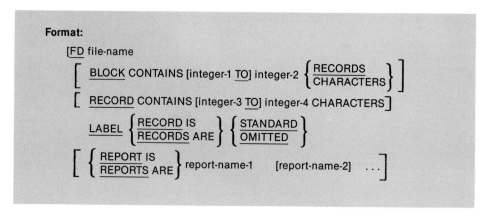

Format:

[FD file-name

　　　[<u>BLOCK</u> CONTAINS [integer-1 <u>TO</u>] integer-2 { <u>RECORDS</u> / <u>CHARACTERS</u> }]

　　　[<u>RECORD</u> CONTAINS [integer-3 <u>TO</u>] integer-4 CHARACTERS]

　　　<u>LABEL</u> { <u>RECORD</u> IS / <u>RECORDS</u> ARE } { <u>STANDARD</u> / <u>OMITTED</u> }

　　　[{ <u>REPORT</u> IS / <u>REPORTS</u> ARE } report-name-1　[report-name-2] ...]

Example:

```
004010*
004020 FD  PAYROLL-REPORT-FILE
004030         RECORD CONTAINS 132 CHARACTERS
004040         LABEL RECORDS ARE OMITTED
004050         REPORT IS PAYROLL-REPORT.
```

When the REPORT clause is coded,
no 01-level record-description entries
are coded after the FD entry.

Figure AA. 5
RD-entry format.

Format:

[REPORT <u>SECTION</u>.

[RD report-name

　　　[{ <u>CONTROL</u> IS / <u>CONTROLS</u> ARE } { data-name-1 [data-name-2] ... / <u>FINAL</u> [data-name-1 [data-name-2] ...] }]]

　　　[<u>PAGE</u> [LIMITS IS / LIMITS ARE] integer-1 [LINE / LINES]

　　　[<u>HEADING</u> integer-2]

　　　[<u>FIRST</u> <u>DETAIL</u> integer-3]

　　　[<u>LAST</u> <u>DETAIL</u> integer-4]

　　　[<u>FOOTING</u> integer-5] .

Example:

```
030010*
030020*
030030 REPORT SECTION.
030040*
030050*
030060 RD  PAYROLL-REPORT
030070         CONTROL IS FINAL
030080         PAGE LIMIT IS 57 LINES
030090            HEADING 1
030100            FIRST DETAIL 6
030110            LAST DETAIL 57
030120            FOOTING 57.
```

The CONTROL IS clause. The CONTROL IS clause is used to specify control-break hierarchies within the report. Because the payroll report program is a read-and-print program with only end-of-report totals (no control totals), CONTROL IS FINAL has been specified. The reserved word FINAL provides for the printing of final totals at the end of the report. (Actually, CONTROL IS FINAL is the default; if a report contains only final totals and no control totals, it is not necessary to explicitly code the CONTROL IS FINAL clause.)

The PAGE LIMIT clause. The PAGE LIMIT clause identifies the vertical line-span parameters to be used for the report. PAGE LIMIT IS 57 LINES has been coded because the line span of the report is 57 lines. Subordinate to the PAGE-LIMIT clause, additional line-span specifications are coded in the HEADING, FIRST DETAIL, LAST DETAIL, and FOOTING entries.

The HEADING entry is used to specify the line number at which the report headings will begin. HEADING 1 is typically coded so that the headings will begin on the first print line. The first detail line of the PAYROLL report is to be printed on the 6th print line, so FIRST DETAIL 6 has been coded. The last detail line is to be printed on the 57th print line of each page, so LAST DETAIL 57 has been coded. The last line at which the total, or footing, line is to be printed is also line 57, so FOOTING 57 has been specified.

01-Level Report Lines in the REPORT SECTION

The RPAYROLL program has three types of report lines: heading, detail, and final total. As a result, three 01-level report-group entries are coded after the RD entry, as shown in Figure AA.6. Each 01-level entry is identified as to what type of line it is. A report heading line is specified as TYPE IS PAGE-HEADING; a detail line is coded TYPE IS DETAIL; and a final total line is called TYPE IS CONTROL FOOTING FINAL.

TYPE IS PAGE-HEADING

```
031010*
031020 01   TYPE IS PAGE-HEADING.
031030*
031040      03   LINE 1.
031030           05   COLUMN 1    PIC X(18)   VALUE "UNIVERSAL BUSINESS".
031040           05   COLUMN 20   PIC X(16)   VALUE "SERVICES COMPANY".
031050           05   COLUMN 67   PIC X(14)   VALUE "PAYROLL REPORT".
031060*
031070      03   LINE 2.
031080           05   COLUMN 1    PIC 9(2)    SOURCE WS-MONTH.
031090           05   COLUMN 3    PIC X(1)    VALUE "/".
031100           05   COLUMN 4    PIC 9(2)    SOURCE WS-DAY.
031110           05   COLUMN 6    PIC X(1)    VALUE "/".
031120           05   COLUMN 7    PIC 9(2)    SOURCE WS-YEAR.
031130           05   COLUMN 73   PIC X(4)    VALUE "PAGE".
031140           05   COLUMN 78   PIC ZZ9     SOURCE PAGE-COUNTER.
031150*
031160      03   LINE 4.
031170           05   COLUMN 1    PIC X(11)   VALUE "S.S. NUMBER".
031180           05   COLUMN 21   PIC X(13)   VALUE "EMPLOYEE NAME".
031190           05   COLUMN 50   PIC X(4)    VALUE "RATE".
031200           05   COLUMN 61   PIC X(5)    VALUE "HOURS".
031210           05   COLUMN 72   PIC X(9)    VALUE "GROSS PAY".
```

PAGE-HEADING lines are printed on the first page of the report and at the top of each new page.

Only one 01-level TYPE IS PAGE-HEADING entry is permitted within an RD entry. Notice that no record-name was affixed to the 01-level TYPE IS PAGE-HEADING entry. A record-name is not required if the report-line record is not called out in the PROCEDURE DIVISION. Because PAGE-HEADING lines are seldom so referenced, record-names are usually omitted from their 01-level record-description entry.

Figure AA.7 shows the Report Writer data-item description format. The heading lines are coded by specifying the vertical LINE NUMBER on which the heading is to be printed and the horizontal COLUMN NUMBER at which the heading data is to begin. The reserved word NUMBER is optional after the words LINE and COLUMN; it is usually omitted.

Figure AA. 6
Report Writer 01-level report-line format.

```
Format:
        01   [data-name-1]
           ┌─                                                      ─┐
           │ LINE NUMBER IS  ┌ integer-1 [ON NEXT PAGE] ┐           │
           │                 └ PLUS integer-2            ┘           │
           └─                                                      ─┘
           ┌─                    ┌ integer-3       ┐ ─┐
           │ NEXT GROUP IS       │ PLUS integer-4  │  │
           │                     │ NEXT PAGE       │  │
           └─                    └                 ┘ ─┘
                                ┌─                                              ─┐
                                │  ┌ REPORT HEADING ┐                            │
                                │  │ RH             │                            │
                                │  ┌ PAGE HEADING ┐                              │
                                │  │ PH           │                              │
                                │  ┌ CONTROL HEADING ┐  ┌ data-name-2 ┐          │
                                │  │ CH              │  │ FINAL       │          │
                      TYPE IS   │  ┌ DETAIL ┐                                    │
                                │  │ DE     │                                    │
                                │  ┌ CONTROL FOOTING ┐  ┌ data-name-3 ┐          │
                                │  │ CF              │  │ FINAL       │          │
                                │  ┌ PAGE FOOTING ┐                              │
                                │  │ PF           │                              │
                                │  ┌ REPORT FOOTING ┐                            │
                                │  │ RF             │                            │
                                └─                                              ─┘
```

Example A: Page-heading line (01-level record-name typically omitted; because multiple heading lines are usually required, the LINE clause is typically coded at the next level)

```
031010*
031020 01   TYPE IS PAGE-HEADING.
```

Example B: Detail line (01-level record-name required)

```
033010*
033020 01   DL-DETAIL-LINE
033030         TYPE IS DETAIL
033040         LINE IS PLUS 1.
```

Example C: End-of-report total (01-level record-name typically omitted)

```
034010*
034020 01   TYPE IS CONTROL FOOTING FINAL
034030         LINE IS PLUS 3.
```

The LINE and COLUMN clauses. The LINE clause can be specified at either the group level or the elementary level. The COLUMN clause must be specified at the elementary level. Because most headings contain more than one line, it is typically convenient to specify the LINE clause at the group level and the COLUMN clause at the elementary level, as has been done in the RPAYROLL program.

In LINE 1 (and also LINE 4), notice that the constant data has been established by specifying the COLUMN number at which the field begins. Then, just as it would be in regular COBOL, the appropriate PICTURE and VALUE clauses are affixed.

The SOURCE clause. In addition to constant data, LINE 2 contains variable data—the run date. To introduce variable data into a Report Writer line, the SOURCE clause is used. The SOURCE clause specifies a field whose current value is to be placed in the field when it is printed. The field must either be defined in the DATA DIVISION or else be a special Report

Figure AA. 7
Report Writer data-item description format.

```
Format:
        Level-number [data-name-1]

        [ LINE NUMBER IS { integer-1 [ON NEXT PAGE] } ]
        [                { PLUS integer-2           } ]

        [ COLUMN NUMBER IS integer-3 ]

        { PICTURE }
        {         }  IS character-string
        { PIC     }

        {  SOURCE is identifier-1                                    }
        {                                                            }
        {  VALUE IS literal                                          }
        {  SUM identifier-2 [, identifier-3] ...                     }
        {                                                            }
        {     [ UPON data-name-2 [, data-name-3] ...] } ...          }
        {                                                            }
        {     [ RESET ON { data-name-4 } ]                           }
        {     [          { FINAL       } ]                           }
```

Example A: Group-level LINE clause and VALUE clauses

```
031030*
031040    03  LINE 1.
031030        05  COLUMN 1    PIC X(18)    VALUE "UNIVERSAL BUSINESS".
031040        05  COLUMN 20   PIC X(16)    VALUE "SERVICES COMPANY".
031050        05  COLUMN 67   PIC X(14)    VALUE "PAYROLL REPORT".
```

Example B: SOURCE clause

```
033100    05  COLUMN 18   PIC X(24)       SOURCE PR-EMPLOYEE-NAME.
```

Example C: SUM clause (can be used only on TYPE IS CONTROL FOOTING lines)

```
034050    05  COLUMN 20   PIC Z.ZZ9       SUM WS-CONSTANT-ONE.
```

Writer field. An example of the latter is shown in the SOURCE for COLUMN 57. PAGE-COUNTER is a special field provided by Report Writer that contains the current page number. The programmer does not define the PAGE-COUNTER field in the DATA DIVISION. The field is provided and the page count is tallied in it automatically.

TYPE IS DETAIL

```
033010*
033020 01  DL-DETAIL-LINE
033030         TYPE IS DETAIL
033040         LINE IS PLUS 1.
033050    05  COLUMN 1    PIC 9(3)     SOURCE PR-SOC-SEC-NBR-1.
033060    05  COLUMN 4    PIC X(1)     VALUE "-".
033070    05  COLUMN 5    PIC 9(2)     SOURCE PR-SOC-SEC-NBR-2.
033080    05  COLUMN 7    PIC X(1)     VALUE "-".
033090    05  COLUMN 8    PIC 9(4)     SOURCE PR-SOC-SEC-NBR-3.
033100    05  COLUMN 18   PIC X(24)    SOURCE PR-EMPLOYEE-NAME.
033110    05  COLUMN 49   PIC ZZ.99    SOURCE PR-RATE-OF-PAY.
033120    05  COLUMN 60   PIC ZZZ.99   SOURCE PR-HOURS-WORKED.
033130    05  COLUMN 72   PIC ZZ,ZZZ.99 SOURCE WS-GROSS-PAY.
```

As will be discussed when the PROCEDURE DIVISION code is explained, a TYPE IS DETAIL line is printed whenever a GENERATE statement naming that 01-level record-name is executed. There is no limit to the number of different TYPE IS DETAIL entries that may be coded.

Because the name of a TYPE IS DETAIL line must be referenced in the PROCEDURE DIVISION, a record-name—such as DL-DETAIL-LINE—is always required for a TYPE IS DETAIL line.

Instead of the absolute line numbers that normally apply to heading lines, relative line numbers are typically used for DETAIL lines to indicate single-, double-, or triple-spacing, and so forth. Relative LINE numbers are coded with the reserved word PLUS. So, because the payroll-report detail lines are to be single-spaced, LINE IS PLUS 1 has been coded as the line number for the DETAIL line. This will cause advancing of one line before each detail line is printed.

In the same manner as was coded for the heading lines, each field to be printed on the detail line is coded with a level number, a COLUMN number, a PICTURE clause, and either a SOURCE or a VALUE clause.

TYPE IS CONTROL FOOTING FINAL

```
034010*
034020 01   TYPE IS CONTROL FOOTING FINAL
034030           LINE IS PLUS 3.
034040     05   COLUMN 20   PIC Z,ZZ9        SUM WS-CONSTANT-ONE.
034050     05   COLUMN 26   PIC X(15)        VALUE "TOTAL EMPLOYEES".
034060     05   COLUMN 57   PIC ZZ,ZZZ.99    SUM PR-HOURS-WORKED.
034070     05   COLUMN 71   PIC ZZZ,ZZZ.99   SUM WS-GROSS-PAY.
```

A TYPE IS CONTROL FOOTING FINAL line is used for an end-of-report total line and is printed at the termination of the report, after all other lines have been printed. Like the PAGE-HEADING entry, only one TYPE IS CONTROL FOOTING FINAL entry is permitted within an RD entry. Also, like the TYPE IS PAGE-HEADING entry, the FINAL total line is not usually referenced in the PROCEDURE DIVISION, and thus a record-name is not usually coded in the 01-level record-description entry.

Because the report-total line is to be triple-spaced from the last detail line, the LINE clause is coded as LINE IS PLUS 3.

The SUM clause. To obtain totals in a CONTROL FOOTING line, the SUM clause is coded. The SUM clause causes Report Writer to establish a sum counter and to increment it each time a GENERATE statement is executed in the PROCEDURE DIVISION.

Therefore, to develop the total number of employees to be printed in COLUMN 20, the SUM WS-CONSTANT-ONE clause is coded. WS-CONSTANT-ONE is the name of a field in WORKING-STORAGE that contains a VALUE of +1. This means that each time a detail line is printed for an employee, the sum counter for the total number of employees to be printed in COLUMN 20 will be incremented by +1. When the total line is printed, the total number of employees accumulated in this sum counter will be printed. After the line is printed, Report Writer automatically sets the sum counter back to zero.

SUM counters have also been established to accumulate the total number of PR-HOURS-WORKED and the total WS-GROSS-PAY.

The SUM clause can be specified only in a TYPE IS CONTROL FOOTING line. A data-item that contains a SUM clause must have a numeric or a numeric-edited PICTURE.

The object of the SUM clause (the identifier coded after it) must be either (1) a numeric field specified as the object of a SOURCE clause, (2) the name of a REPORT SECTION field specified with the SUM clause (that is, another sum counter), or (3) a numeric field in the FILE SECTION or the WORKING-STORAGE SECTION.

SUM clause difference for IBM COBOL. IBM COBOL Report Writer adheres to the COBOL-68 standard rather than to the COBOL-74 or COBOL-85 standards. It does not permit the object of the SUM clause to be a field outside the REPORT SECTION (the third option listed above) unless the UPON clause is coded.

When the UPON clause is coded, the name of the detail line whose generation is to trigger incrementation is named after the reserved word UPON. Figure AA.8 contrasts the standard COBOL-74/85 and the IBM COBOL requirements to cause summation of the WS-CONSTANT-ONE field.

Figure AA. 8
SUM UPON clause for IBM OS
and DOS Report Writer.

The WS-CONSTANT-ONE field is in the WORKING-STORAGE SECTION:

* COBOL-68 requires that a field named in a SOURCE clause be either

    1. Named in a SOURCE clause, or

    2. The name of a SUM field at a lower level

To specify a WORKING-STORAGE field not named in a SOURCE clause or lower-level SUM clause, the UPON clause must be coded. The UPON clause must reference the name of the line for which, upon whose printing, summation is to take place.

COBOL-74 and COBOL-85 do not have the above requirement. Thus, WORKING-STORAGE SECTION fields not named in a SOURCE or lower-level SUM clause can be named in a SUM clause.

COBOL-74/85 example:

```
034050        05   COLUMN 20    PIC Z,ZZ9        SUM WS-CONSTANT-ONE.
```

COBOL-68 example (IBM OS and DOS Report Writer use the COBOL-68 standard):

```
034050        05   COLUMN 20    PIC Z,ZZ9        SUM WS-CONSTANT-ONE
                                                 UPON DL-DETAIL-LINE.
```

The PROCEDURE DIVISION

As shown in Figure AA.9, there are three main PROCEDURE DIVISION statements used with the Report Writer feature: INITIATE, GENERATE, and TERMINATE.

```
050010*
050020*
050030*
050040 PROCEDURE DIVISION.
050050*
050060*
050070 000-PRINT-PAYROLL-REPORT.
050080*
050090     OPEN INPUT PAYROLL-FILE
050100          OUTPUT PAYROLL-REPORT-FILE.
050110     INITIATE PAYROLL-REPORT.
050120     PERFORM 100-INITIALIZE-VARIABLE-FIELDS.
050130     PERFORM 800-READ-PAYROLL-RECORD.
050140     PERFORM 200-PROCESS-PAYROLL-RECORD
050150          UNTIL WS-END-OF-FILE-SWITCH IS EQUAL TO "YES".
050160     TERMINATE PAYROLL-REPORT.
050170     CLOSE PAYROLL-FILE
050180           PAYROLL-REPORT-FILE.
050190     STOP RUN.
100010*
100020*
100030 100-INITIALIZE-VARIABLE-FIELDS.
100040*
100050     MOVE "NO " TO WS-END-OF-FILE-SWITCH.
100080     ACCEPT WS-DATE-WORK FROM DATE.
200010*
200020*
200030 200-PROCESS-PAYROLL-RECORD.
200040*
200050     MULTIPLY PR-RATE-OF-PAY BY PR-HOURS-WORKED
200060          GIVING WS-GROSS-PAY ROUNDED.
200080     GENERATE DL-DETAIL-LINE.
200090     PERFORM 800-READ-PAYROLL-RECORD.
800010*
800020*
800030 800-READ-PAYROLL-RECORD.
800040*
800050     READ PAYROLL-FILE INTO PR-PAYROLL-RECORD
800060          AT END MOVE "YES" TO WS-END-OF-FILE-SWITCH.
```

The INITIATE Statement

The INITIATE statement begins Report Writer processing. The file named in the FD entry must be opened before the report named in the INITIATE statement can be initiated. The INITIATE statement sets all SUM accumulators to zero, sets the LINE-COUNTER to zero, and sets the PAGE COUNTER to 1.

Figure AA. 9
Report Writer PROCEDURE
DIVISION verbs.

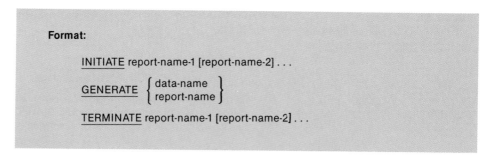

Format:

    <u>INITIATE</u> report-name-1 [report-name-2] . . .

    <u>GENERATE</u> $\left\{ \begin{array}{l} \text{data-name} \\ \text{report-name} \end{array} \right\}$

    <u>TERMINATE</u> report-name-1 [report-name-2] . . .

Examples:

```
050110      INITIATE PAYROLL-REPORT.     ◄──────── Initiates report processing

200080      GENERATE DL-DETAIL-LINE.     ◄──────── Prints detail line

050160      TERMINATE PAYROLL-REPORT.    ◄──────── Terminates report processing
```

**The GENERATE
Statement**

The GENERATE statement causes a detail line to be written to the report. The name of the
TYPE IS DETAIL line is typically coded as the object of the GENERATE verb.

When the GENERATE statement is executed, the Report Writer logic checks to see if a
PAGE-HEADING is required. If so, the report page is advanced and the heading lines are
printed before the detail line is processed.

**The TERMINATE
Statement**

The TERMINATE statement ends Report Writer processing. Before the report file is closed,
the report must be named in a TERMINATE statement. When the TERMINATE statement
is executed, a FINAL control break is triggered, which causes all TYPE CONTROL FOOT-
ING lines to be printed. After the TERMINATE statement is coded for the report, the CLOSE
statement for the report file should typically follow. As a result, the mainline module for a
Report Writer program will typically appear as follows:

```
OPEN files.
INITIATE report.
PERFORM initialize-variable fields.
PERFORM priming-read.
PERFORM process-input-record
   UNTIL end-of-file.
TERMINATE report.
CLOSE files.
STOP RUN.
```

Topic:	**AA-2: Reports with Control-Break Footings**

A Single-Level Control-Break Report
The CONTROL IS Clause
The LAST DETAIL and FOOTING Clauses
The TYPE IS CONTROL FOOTING Data-Name Option
The NEXT GROUP Clause
Generation of TYPE IS CONTROL FOOTING Lines

A Multiple-Level Control-Break Report
The RD Entry
   CONTROL IS clause
   PAGE LIMIT and FOOTING clauses
Generation of Control Footing Lines
The Rolling of Totals
PROCEDURE DIVISION Coding

A Single-Level Control-Break Report

The single-level sales report format that was introduced in Chapter 10 is repeated in Figure AA.10. Report Writer coding to produce the report, named RSCTLBRK (for **R**eport Writer **s**ingle-level **c**ontrol-**b**reak program) is shown in the program listing of Figure AA.11.

In addition to the Report Writer syntax presented in Topic AA-1 for a report with end-of-report totals, there are four other coding considerations for a single-level control-footings report: (1) the CONTROL IS clause in the RD entry, (2) the relationship between the LAST DETAIL and FOOTING clauses in the RD entry, (3) the TYPE IS CONTROL FOOTING data-name option in the 01-report-line entry, and (4) the NEXT GROUP clause in the 01-report-line entry. Each will be discussed, followed by an explanation of how the control footing lines are generated.

Figure AA. 10
Single-level sales-report print chart.

```
030050*
030060 RD  SALES-REPORT
030070         CONTROL IS FINAL
030080                SR-SALES-REP
030090         PAGE LIMIT IS 59 LINES
030100             HEADING 1
030110             FIRST DETAIL 7
030120             LAST DETAIL 57
030130             FOOTING 59.
```

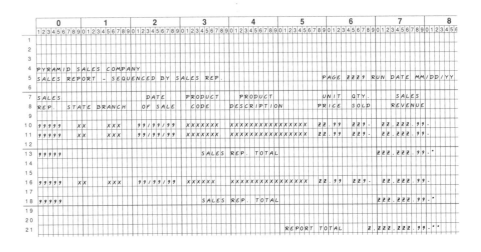

Figure AA. 11   Report Writer COBOL coding: RSCTLBRK program.

```
001010 IDENTIFICATION DIVISION.
001020 PROGRAM-ID.    RSCTLBRK.
001080*
001090*
001100*                  THIS PROGRAM READS SALES RECORDS,
001110*                  COMPUTES THE SALES REVENUE FOR EACH SALES RECORD
001120*                  AND PRINTS A SALES DETAIL LINE
001130*                  FOR EACH SALES RECORD.
001140*
001150*                  WHEN THE SALES-REP NUMBER CHANGES,
001160*                  A SALES-REP TOTAL LINE IS PRINTED.
001170*
001180*                  AFTER ALL INPUT SALES RECORDS HAVE BEEN PROCESSED,
001190*                  A REPORT-TOTAL LINE WILL BE PRINTED.
002010*
002020*
002030*
002040 ENVIRONMENT DIVISION.
002050*
002060*
002070 CONFIGURATION SECTION.
002080*
002090 SOURCE-COMPUTER.    IBM-3081.
002100 OBJECT-COMPUTER.    IBM-3081.
002110*
002120*
002130 INPUT-OUTPUT SECTION.
002140*
002150 FILE-CONTROL.
002160     SELECT SALES-FILE
002170         ASSIGN TO UT-S-INFILE.
002180     SELECT SALES-REPORT-FILE
002190         ASSIGN TO UT-S-PRTFILE.
003010*
003020*
003030*
003040 DATA DIVISION.
003050*
003060*
003070 FILE SECTION.
003080*
003090 FD  SALES-FILE
003100         RECORD CONTAINS 80 CHARACTERS
003110         LABEL RECORDS ARE OMITTED.
004010*
004020 01  SALES-RECORD.
004030     05  FILLER                     PIC X(80).
005010*
005020 FD  SALES-REPORT-FILE
005030         RECORD CONTAINS 132 CHARACTERS
005040         LABEL RECORDS ARE OMITTED
005050         REPORT IS SALES-REPORT.
006010*
006020*
006030 WORKING-STORAGE SECTION.
006040*
006050*
006060 01  WS-SWITCHES.
006070     05  WS-END-OF-FILE-SWITCH      PIC X(3).
006080         88  END-OF-FILE                        VALUE "YES".
009010*
009020 01  WS-WORK-AREAS.
009030     05  WS-DATE-WORK               PIC 9(6).
009040     05  WS-DATE-REFORMAT REDEFINES WS-DATE-WORK.
009050         10  WS-YEAR                PIC 9(2).
009060         10  WS-MONTH               PIC 9(2).
009070         10  WS-DAY                 PIC 9(2).
009080     05  WS-SALES-REVENUE           PIC S9(5)V99.
020010*
020020 01  SR-SALES-RECORD.
020030     05  SR-RECORD-CODE             PIC X(2).
020040     05  SR-STATE                   PIC X(2).
020050     05  SR-BRANCH                  PIC X(3).
020060     05  SR-SALES-REP               PIC X(5).
020070     05  SR-DATE-OF-SALE            PIC X(6).
020080     05  SR-PRODUCT-CODE            PIC X(7).
020090     05  SR-PRODUCT-DESCRIPTION     PIC X(16).
020100     05  SR-QUANTITY-SOLD           PIC S9(3).
020110     05  SR-UNIT-PRICE              PIC 9(2)V99.
020120     05  FILLER                     PIC X(32).
```

```
030010*  ───────────────────────────────────────
030020*                                          REPORT SECTION
030030 REPORT SECTION.
030040*
030050*
030060 RD  SALES-REPORT
030070         CONTROL IS FINAL
030080                 SR-SALES-REP
030090         PAGE LIMIT IS 59 LINES
030100         HEADING 1
030110         FIRST DETAIL 7
030120         LAST DETAIL 57
030130         FOOTING 59.
031010*  ───────────────────────────────────────
031020 01  TYPE IS PAGE-HEADING.                 Heading lines
031030     03  LINE 1.
031040         05  COLUMN 1    PIC X(21)  VALUE "PYRAMID SALES COMPANY".
031050*
031060     03  LINE 2.
031070         05  COLUMN 1    PIC X(20)  VALUE "SALES REPORT - SEQUE".
031080         05  COLUMN 21   PIC X(17)  VALUE "NCED BY SALES REP".
031090         05  COLUMN 59   PIC X(4)   VALUE "PAGE".
031100         05  COLUMN 64   PIC ZZZ9   SOURCE WS-PAGE-COUNT.
031110         05  COLUMN 69   PIC X(8)   VALUE "RUN DATE".
031120         05  COLUMN 78   PIC 9(2)   SOURCE WS-MONTH.
031130         05  COLUMN 80   PIC X(1)   VALUE "/".
031140         05  COLUMN 81   PIC 9(2)   SOURCE WS-DAY.
031150         05  COLUMN 83   PIC X(1)   VALUE "/".
031160         05  COLUMN 84   PIC 9(2)   SOURCE WS-YEAR.
031170*
031180     03  LINE 4.
031190         05  COLUMN 7    PIC X(5)   VALUE "SALES".
031200         05  COLUMN 23   PIC X(4)   VALUE "DATE".
031210         05  COLUMN 31   PIC X(7)   VALUE "PRODUCT".
031220         05  COLUMN 42   PIC X(7)   VALUE "PRODUCT".
031230         05  COLUMN 59   PIC X(4)   VALUE "UNIT".
031240         05  COLUMN 65   PIC X(3)   VALUE "QTY".
031250         05  COLUMN 74   PIC X(5)   VALUE "SALES".
031260*
031270     03  LINE 5.
031280         05  COLUMN 1    PIC X(4)   VALUE "REP.".
031290         05  COLUMN 7    PIC X(5)   VALUE "STATE".
031300         05  COLUMN 13   PIC X(6)   VALUE "BRANCH".
031310         05  COLUMN 22   PIC X(7)   VALUE "OF SALE".
031320         05  COLUMN 32   PIC X(4)   VALUE "CODE".
031330         05  COLUMN 40   PIC X(11)  VALUE "DESCRIPTION".
031340         05  COLUMN 58   PIC X(5)   VALUE "PRICE".
031350         05  COLUMN 65   PIC X(4)   VALUE "SOLD".
031360         05  COLUMN 73   PIC X(7)   VALUE "REVENUE".
034010*  ───────────────────────────────────────
034020 01  DL-DETAIL-LINE                        Detail line
034030         TYPE IS DETAIL
034040         LINE IS PLUS 1.
034050     05  COLUMN 1    PIC X(5)    SOURCE SR-SALES-REP.
034060     05  COLUMN 9    PIC X(2)    SOURCE SR-STATE.
034070     05  COLUMN 15   PIC X(3)    SOURCE SR-BRANCH.
034080     05  COLUMN 21   PIC XX/XX/XX SOURCE SR-DATE-OF-SALE.
034090     05  COLUMN 31   PIC X(7)    SOURCE SR-PRODUCT-CODE.
034100     05  COLUMN 40   PIC X(16)   SOURCE SR-PRODUCT-DESCRIPTION.
034110     05  COLUMN 58   PIC ZZ.99   SOURCE SR-UNIT-PRICE.
034120     05  COLUMN 65   PIC ZZ9-    SOURCE SR-QUANTITY-SOLD.
034130     05  COLUMN 71   PIC ZZ,ZZZ.99-  SOURCE WS-SALES-REVENUE.
035010*  ───────────────────────────────────────
035020 01  ST-SALES-REP-TOTAL-LINE               Control-total line
035030         TYPE IS CONTROL FOOTING SR-SALES-REP
035040         LINE IS PLUS 2
035050         NEXT GROUP IS PLUS 2.
035060     05  COLUMN 1    PIC X(5)    SOURCE SR-SALES-REP.
035070     05  COLUMN 34   PIC X(16)   VALUE "SALES REP. TOTAL".
035080     05  ST-SALES-REP-TOTAL
035090         COLUMN 70   PIC ZZZ,ZZZ.99-  SUM WS-SALES-REVENUE.
035100     05  COLUMN 81   PIC X(1)    VALUE "*".
036010*  ───────────────────────────────────────
036020 01  RT-REPORT-TOTAL-LINE.                 Report-total line
036030         TYPE IS CONTROL FOOTING FINAL
036040         LINE IS PLUS 3.
036050     05  COLUMN 51   PIC X(12)   VALUE "REPORT TOTAL".
036060     05  COLUMN 68   PIC Z,ZZZ,ZZZ.99-  SUM WS-SALES-REVENUE.
036070     05  COLUMN 81   PIC X(2)    VALUE "**".
050010*  ───────────────────────────────────────
050020*
050030*
050040 PROCEDURE DIVISION.
050050*
050060*
050070 000-PRINT-SALES-REPORT.
050080*
050090     OPEN INPUT SALES-FILE
050100         OUTPUT SALES-REPORT-FILE.
050110     INITIATE SALES-REPORT.
050120     PERFORM 100-INITIALIZE-VARIABLE-FIELDS.
050130     PERFORM 800-READ-SALES-RECORD.
050130     PERFORM 200-PROCESS-SALES-RECORD
050140         UNTIL END-OF-FILE.
050150     TERMINATE SALES-REPORT.
050160     CLOSE SALES-FILE
050170         SALES-REPORT-FILE.
050180     STOP RUN.
100010*
100020*
100030 100-INITIALIZE-VARIABLE-FIELDS.
100040*
100050     MOVE "NO " TO WS-END-OF-FILE-SWITCH.
100090     ACCEPT WS-DATE-WORK FROM DATE.
200010*
200020*
200030 200-PROCESS-SALES-RECORD.
200040*
300150     MULTIPLY SR-UNIT-PRICE BY SR-QUANTITY-SOLD
300160         GIVING WS-SALES-REVENUE ROUNDED.
300210     GENERATE DL-DETAIL-LINE.
300220     PERFORM 800-READ-SALES-RECORD.
800010*
800020*
800030 800-READ-SALES-RECORD.
800040*
800050     READ SALES-FILE INTO SR-SALES-RECORD
800060         AT END MOVE "YES" TO WS-END-OF-FILE-SWITCH.
```

The CONTROL IS Clause In the RPAYROLL program with end-of-report totals, CONTROL IS FINAL was specified in the RD entry For a control-break report, the CONTROL IS clause must also contain the name of the control field that triggers the control break. In this RSCTLBRK program, that control field is SR-SALES-REP, and thus it is specified after the reserved word FINAL (since a final end-of-report total is also desired).

When a data-name is specified in the CONTROL IS clause, that field must be defined in either the FILE SECTION or the WORKING-STORAGE SECTION of the DATA DIVISION. When more than one entry appears in the CONTROL IS clause, the entries must be listed in order of descending significance—that is, in major to minor sequence. Thus, FINAL is listed first and followed by the control field SR-SALES-REP.

The LAST DETAIL and FOOTING Clauses Because the RPAYROLL program had only end-of-report totals, both the LAST DETAIL and the FOOTING clauses of the RD entry were specified with the same line-number value. As mentioned in Chapter 10, however, it is generally considered poor form to print control totals at the top of a new report page that has no detail lines for that control group. In other words, if the last detail line on a page is also the last line for a control group, the control footings for that group should be printed on the same page.

Thus, in the RSCTLBRK report, LAST DETAIL 57 and FOOTING 59 have been specified. This will provide a line span of 57 lines per page except when the last detail line on a page is also the last record of a control group. When this occurs, the span should increase to 59 lines.

Remember that the control-break total line for the sales report is to be doublespaced from the last detail line of the control group. Hence, if the last record of a control group is printed at line 57, specification of the FOOTING 59 clause will permit the footing line to be printed on the same page at line 59.

Because the maximum number of lines to be printed on a page is 59, the PAGE LIMIT clause has accordingly been specified as PAGE LIMIT IS 59 LINES.

```
035010*
035020 01  ST-SALES-REP-TOTAL-LINE
035030         TYPE IS CONTROL FOOTING SR-SALES-REP
035040         LINE IS PLUS 2
035050         NEXT GROUP IS PLUS 2.
035060     05  COLUMN 1     PIC X(5)      SOURCE SR-SALES-REP.
035070     05  COLUMN 34    PIC X(16)     VALUE "SALES REP. TOTAL".
035080     05  ST-SALES-REP-TOTAL
035090         COLUMN 70    PIC ZZZ,ZZZ.99-  SUM WS-SALES-REVENUE.
035100     05  COLUMN 81    PIC X(1)      VALUE "*".
```

The TYPE IS CONTROL FOOTING Data-Name Option For end-of-report totals, the FINAL option is specified for the TYPE IS CONTROL FOOTING clause on the 01-level report-line description entry. For a control-break footing line, the data-name option is used.

The field of the input record that triggers the control break should be specified as the data-name. In the RSCTLBRK report, the SR-SALES-REP field is the control field. Hence, TYPE IS CONTROL FOOTING SR-SALES-REP is specified for the ST-SALES-REP-TOTAL-LINE. (The data-name must match a field specified in the CONTROL IS clause of the RD entry.)

(As mentioned in the previous topic, recognize that the record-name—ST-SALES-REP-TOTAL-LINE—need not have been affixed to this TYPE IS CONTROL FOOTING line. It has been done for this and the FINAL total line merely to facilitate comprehension of the program code.)

The NEXT GROUP Clause In the sales-report program, the first detail line for a new control group is to be triple-spaced from the control-total line. To accomplish this type of spacing, the NEXT GROUP clause is specified on the 01-level control-total footing line.

Observe that NEXT GROUP IS PLUS 2 has been specified in the RSCTLBRK program. One might think that PLUS 3 should be coded to obtain the triple-spacing. Remember, however, that the LINE IS PLUS 1 clause was specified on the detail-line description entry. The NEXT GROUP IS PLUS 2 will cause double-spacing after the control-total footing line is printed. The LINE IS PLUS 1 for the detail line will cause single-spacing before the detail line is printed. As a result, the desired triple-spacing will occur between the control-total footing line and the first detail line of the next group.

Figure AA. 12
Multiple-level sales-report
print chart.

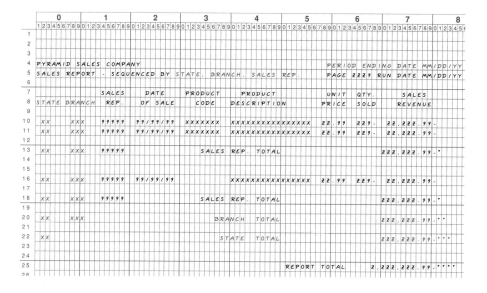

Generation of TYPE IS CONTROL FOOTING Lines

As mentioned in the last topic, detail lines are printed when the GENERATE statement is executed. When a TYPE IS CONTROL FOOTING data-name line is specified in the REPORT SECTION, Report Writer first—before generating the detail line—checks to see if a control break has occurred. If so, the control-total line is automatically printed. Hence, no PROCE-DURE DIVISION coding is required to produce the control breaks.

A Multiple-Level Control-Break Report

The multiple-level sales report that was introduced in Chapter 10 is repeated in Figure AA.12. Report Writer coding to produce the report, named RMCTLBRK (for **R**eport Writer **m**ultiple-level **c**ontrol-**br**eak program) is shown in the program listing of Figure AA.13. Those additional Report Writer considerations for a report with multiple-level controlbreak footings are shaded on the program listing.

In addition to the Report Writer syntax just covered for a single-level controlfootings report, there are three other major coding considerations for a multiple-level control-foot-ings report: (1) sequence of data-names in the CONTROL IS clause, (2) arrangement of 01-level lines in the REPORT SECTION, and (3) the rolling of totals.

The RD Entry

In the RD entry, the CONTROL IS clause has been expanded and the line span of the PAGE LIMIT and FOOTING clauses has been lengthened.

```
030050*
030060 RD   SALES-REPORT
030070          CONTROL IS FINAL
030080                   SR-STATE
030090                   SR-BRANCH
030100                   SR-SALES-REP
030080          PAGE LIMIT IS 63 LINES
030090             HEADING 1
030100             FIRST DETAIL 7
030110             LAST DETAIL 57
030120             FOOTING 63.
```

CONTROL IS clause. Because RMCTLBRK is a three-level control-break program with end-of-report totals, the reserved word FINAL plus the three control fields-SR-STATE, SR-BRANCH, and SR-SALES-REP—have been specified in the CONTROL IS clause.

Remember that the control fields must be listed in order of decreasing significance—that is, in major to minor field sequence. Hence, FINAL is specified first and the minor field—SR-SALES-REP—is coded last.

PAGE LIMIT and FOOTING clauses. To keep all control footing lines on the same page when the last detail line on a page is the last record of a major (SR-STATE) control group, the PAGE LIMIT and FOOTING clauses have been increased from 59 to line 63. (Line 57 will be the last detail line; line 59 will be the sales-rep control footing; line 61 will be the branch control footing; line 63 will be the state control footing.)

Admittedly, when line 63 is used, the margin for that page will be rather skimpy. However, for purposes of the text example, such specifications were used to maintain conformity with the single-level control-break program. (Recognize that it will be rare for the last detail line of a page to be the last record of a state control-group.)

Generation of Control Footing Lines

When the GENERATE statement is executed for a detail line, Report Writer first checks the control fields—as listed in the CONTROL IS clause—in major to minor sequence. When a control break is detected, the control footing lines are generated before the detail line is printed. The control footing lines are printed in minor to major sequence up to the level at which the control break occurred. That is, when a branch control break happens, first the sales-rep control footing line will be printed and then the branch control footing line. After that, the detail line for the record that triggered the control break—the first detail line for the next control group—will be printed.

In the RMCTLBRK program, observe that the control footing lines have been arranged in minor to major order; the sales-rep total line is coded first and the report-total line is coded last. As mentioned in Chapter 10, it is logical and therefore appropriate to arrange the 01-level report lines in this manner. However, such sequence is not required; remember that the CONTROL IS clause of the RD entry determines the printing sequence.

The Rolling of Totals

In the single-level RSCTLBRK program, the WS-SALES-REVENUE field was used to increment both the control-total and the report-total sales-revenue fields. This means that each time that a detail line was printed, two additions were made.

The same approach could be used in this multiple-level RMCTLBRK program. That is, the WS-SALES-REVENUE field could be listed in the SUM clause on all four control-total lines: sales-rep, branch, state, and end-of-report. This would mean that four additions would be made each time a detail line was printed.

As explained in Chapter 10, it is more efficient to provide for the **rolling of totals.** By doing so, only one addition—rather than four—is required as each detail line is printed.

```
035010*
035020 01   ST-SALES-REP-TOTAL-LINE
035030          TYPE IS CONTROL FOOTING SR-SALES-REP
035040          LINE IS PLUS 2
035050          NEXT GROUP IS PLUS 2.
035054      05  COLUMN 2    PIC X(2)        SOURCE SR-STATE.
035056      05  COLUMN 8    PIC X(3)        SOURCE SR-BRANCH.
035060      05  COLUMN 14   PIC X(5)        SOURCE SR-SALES-REP.
035070      05  COLUMN 34   PIC X(16)       VALUE "SALES REP. TOTAL".
035080      05  ST-SALES-REP-TOTAL
035090          COLUMN 70   PIC ZZZ,ZZZ.99-   SUM WS-SALES-REVENUE.
035100      05  COLUMN 81   PIC X(1)        VALUE "*".
036010*
036020 01   BT-BRANCH-TOTAL-LINE
036030          TYPE IS CONTROL FOOTING SR-BRANCH
036040          LINE IS PLUS 2
036050          NEXT GROUP IS PLUS 2.
036054      05  COLUMN 2    PIC X(2)        SOURCE SR-STATE.
036056      05  COLUMN 8    PIC X(3)        SOURCE SR-BRANCH.
036070      05  COLUMN 38   PIC X(12)       VALUE "BRANCH TOTAL".
036080      05  BT-BRANCH-TOTAL
036090          COLUMN 70   PIC ZZZ,ZZZ.99-   SUM ST-SALES-REP-TOTAL.
036100      05  COLUMN 81   PIC X(2)        VALUE "**".
036010*
036020 01   TT-STATE-TOTAL-LINE
036030          TYPE IS CONTROL FOOTING SR-STATE
036040          LINE IS PLUS 2
036050          NEXT GROUP IS PLUS 2.
036054      05  COLUMN 2    PIC X(2)        SOURCE SR-STATE.
036070      05  COLUMN 39   PIC X(11)       VALUE "STATE TOTAL".
036080      05  TT-STATE-TOTAL
036090          COLUMN 70   PIC ZZZ,ZZZ.99-   SUM BT-BRANCH-TOTAL.
036100      05  COLUMN 81   PIC X(3)        VALUE "***".
037010*
037020 01   RT-REPORT-TOTAL-LINE.
037030          TYPE IS CONTROL FOOTING FINAL
037040          LINE IS PLUS 3.
037050      05  COLUMN 51   PIC X(12)       VALUE "REPORT TOTAL".
037060      05  COLUMN 68   PIC Z,ZZZ,ZZZ.99-   SUM TT-STATE-TOTAL.
037070      05  COLUMN 81   PIC X(4)        VALUE "****".
```

Figure AA. 13   Report Writer COBOL coding: RMCTLBRK program.

```
001010 IDENTIFICATION DIVISION.
001020 PROGRAM-ID.    RMCTLBRK.
001080*
001090*
001100*              THIS PROGRAM READS SALES RECORDS,
001110*              COMPUTES THE SALES REVENUE FOR EACH SALES RECORD
001120*              AND PRINTS A SALES DETAIL LINE
001130*              FOR EACH SALES RECORD.
001140*
001150*              TOTAL LINES ARE PRINTED BY SALES-REP
001160*              WITHIN BRANCH WITHIN STATE.
001170*
001180*              AFTER ALL INPUT SALES RECORDS HAVE BEEN PROCESSED,
001190*              A REPORT-TOTAL LINE WILL BE PRINTED.
002010*
002020*
002030*
002040 ENVIRONMENT DIVISION.
002050*
002060*
002070 CONFIGURATION SECTION.
002080*
002090 SOURCE-COMPUTER.    IBM-3081.
002100 OBJECT-COMPUTER.    IBM-3081.
002110*
002120*
002130 INPUT-OUTPUT SECTION.
002140*
002150 FILE-CONTROL.
002160     SELECT SALES-FILE
002170         ASSIGN TO UT-S-INFILE.
002180     SELECT SALES-REPORT-FILE
002190         ASSIGN TO UT-S-PRTFILE.
003010*
003020*
003030*
003040 DATA DIVISION.
003050*
003060*
003070 FILE SECTION.
003080*
003090 FD  SALES-FILE
003100     RECORD CONTAINS 80 CHARACTERS
003110     LABEL RECORDS ARE OMITTED.
004010*
004020 01  SALES-RECORD.
004030     05  FILLER                      PIC X(80).
005010*
005020 FD  SALES-REPORT-FILE
005030     RECORD CONTAINS 132 CHARACTERS
005040     LABEL RECORDS ARE OMITTED
005050     REPORT IS SALES-REPORT.
006010*
006020*
006030 WORKING-STORAGE SECTION.
006040*
006050*
006060 01  WS-SWITCHES.
006070     05  WS-END-OF-FILE-SWITCH       PIC X(3).
006080         88  END-OF-FILE                       VALUE "YES".
009010*
009020 01  WS-WORK-AREAS.
009030     05  WS-DATE-WORK                PIC 9(6).
009040     05  WS-DATE-REFORMAT REDEFINES WS-DATE-WORK.
009050         10  WS-YEAR                 PIC 9(2).
009060         10  WS-MONTH                PIC 9(2).
009070         10  WS-DAY                  PIC 9(2).
009075     05  WS-PER-END-DATE             PIC X(6).
009080     05  WS-SALES-REVENUE            PIC S9(5)V99      COMP-3.
020010*
020020 01  SR-SALES-RECORD.
020030     05  SR-RECORD-CODE              PIC X(2).
020040     05  SR-STATE                    PIC X(2).
020050     05  SR-BRANCH                   PIC X(3).
020060     05  SR-SALES-REP                PIC X(5).
020070     05  SR-DATE-OF-SALE             PIC X(6).
020080     05  SR-PRODUCT-CODE             PIC X(7).
020090     05  SR-PRODUCT-DESCRIPTION      PIC X(16).
020100     05  SR-QUANTITY-SOLD            PIC S9(3).
020110     05  SR-UNIT-PRICE               PIC 9(2)V99.
020120     05  FILLER                      PIC X(32).
021010*
021020 01  DR-DATE-RECORD REDEFINES SR-SALES-RECORD.
021030     05  DR-RECORD-CODE              PIC X(2).
021040         88  DATE-RECORD                       VALUE "01".
021050     05  DR-PERIOD-ENDING-DATE       PIC X(6).
021060     05  FILLER                      PIC X(72).
```

```
030010*─────────────────────────────────────────────
030020*
030030 REPORT SECTION.                                    REPORT SECTION
030040*
030050*
030060 RD  SALES-REPORT
030070     CONTROL IS FINAL
030080             SR-STATE
030090             SR-BRANCH
030100             SR-SALES-REP
030080     PAGE LIMIT IS 63 LINES
030090         HEADING 1
030100         FIRST DETAIL 7
030110         LAST DETAIL 57
030120         FOOTING 63.
031010*─────────────────────────────────────────────
031020 01  TYPE IS PAGE-HEADING.                          Heading lines
031030     03  LINE 1.
031040         05  COLUMN 1   PIC X(20)  VALUE "PYRAMID SALES COMPANY".
031044         05  COLUMN 59  PIC X(17)  VALUE "PERIOD ENDING DATE".
031046         05  COLUMN 78  PIC XX/XX/XX SOURCE WS-PER-END-DATE.
031050*
031060     03  LINE 2.
031070         05  COLUMN 1   PIC X(20)  VALUE "SALES REPORT - SEQUE".
031080         05  COLUMN 21  PIC X(20)  VALUE "NCED BY STATE, BRANC".
031085         05  COLUMN 41  PIC X(13)  VALUE "H, SALES REP.".
031090         05  COLUMN 59  PIC X(4)   VALUE "PAGE".
031100         05  COLUMN 64  PIC ZZZ9   SOURCE WS-PAGE-COUNT.
031110         05  COLUMN 69  PIC X(8)   VALUE "RUN DATE".
031120         05  COLUMN 78  PIC 9(2)   SOURCE WS-MONTH.
031130         05  COLUMN 80  PIC X(1)   VALUE "/".
031140         05  COLUMN 81  PIC 9(2)   SOURCE WS-DAY.
031150         05  COLUMN 83  PIC X(1)   VALUE "/".
031160         05  COLUMN 84  PIC 9(2)   SOURCE WS-YEAR.
031170*
031180     03  LINE 4.
031190         05  COLUMN 14  PIC X(5)   VALUE "SALES".
031200         05  COLUMN 23  PIC X(4)   VALUE "DATE".
031210         05  COLUMN 31  PIC X(7)   VALUE "PRODUCT".
031220         05  COLUMN 42  PIC X(7)   VALUE "PRODUCT".
031230         05  COLUMN 59  PIC X(4)   VALUE "UNIT".
031240         05  COLUMN 65  PIC X(3)   VALUE "QTY".
031250         05  COLUMN 74  PIC X(5)   VALUE "SALES".
031260*
031270     03  LINE 5.
031280         05  COLUMN 1   PIC X(5)   VALUE "STATE".
031290         05  COLUMN 7   PIC X(6)   VALUE "BRANCH".
031300         05  COLUMN 15  PIC X(4)   VALUE "REP.".
031310         05  COLUMN 22  PIC X(7)   VALUE "OF SALE".
031320         05  COLUMN 32  PIC X(4)   VALUE "CODE".
031330         05  COLUMN 40  PIC X(11)  VALUE "DESCRIPTION".
031340         05  COLUMN 58  PIC X(5)   VALUE "PRICE".
031350         05  COLUMN 65  PIC X(4)   VALUE "SOLD".
031360         05  COLUMN 73  PIC X(7)   VALUE "REVENUE".
034010*─────────────────────────────────────────────
034020 01  DL-DETAIL-LINE                                 Detail line
034030     TYPE IS DETAIL
034040     LINE IS PLUS 1.
034050     05  COLUMN 2   PIC X(2)    SOURCE SR-STATE.
034060     05  COLUMN 8   PIC X(3)    SOURCE SR-BRANCH.
034070     05  COLUMN 14  PIC X(5)    SOURCE SR-SALES-REP.
034080     05  COLUMN 21  PIC XX/XX/XX SOURCE SR-DATE-OF-SALE.
034090     05  COLUMN 31  PIC X(7)    SOURCE SR-PRODUCT-CODE.
034100     05  COLUMN 40  PIC X(16)   SOURCE SR-PRODUCT-DESCRIPTION.
034110     05  COLUMN 58  PIC ZZ.99   SOURCE SR-UNIT-PRICE.
034120     05  COLUMN 65  PIC ZZ9-    SOURCE SR-QUANTITY-SOLD.
034130     05  COLUMN 71  PIC ZZ,ZZZ.99- SOURCE WS-SALES-REVENUE.
035010*─────────────────────────────────────────────
035020 01  ST-SALES-REP-TOTAL-LINE                  Sales-rep total line
035030     TYPE IS CONTROL FOOTING SR-SALES-REP
035040     LINE IS PLUS 2
035050     NEXT GROUP IS PLUS 2.
035054     05  COLUMN 2   PIC X(2)    SOURCE SR-STATE.
035056     05  COLUMN 8   PIC X(3)    SOURCE SR-BRANCH.
035060     05  COLUMN 14  PIC X(5)    SOURCE SR-SALES-REP.
035070     05  COLUMN 34  PIC X(16)   VALUE "SALES REP. TOTAL".
035080     05  ST-SALES-REP-TOTAL
035090         COLUMN 70  PIC ZZZ,ZZZ.99- SUM WS-SALES-REVENUE.
035100     05  COLUMN 81  PIC X(1)    VALUE "*".
036010*─────────────────────────────────────────────
036020 01  BT-BRANCH-TOTAL-LINE                        Branch total line
036030     TYPE IS CONTROL FOOTING SR-BRANCH
036040     LINE IS PLUS 2
036050     NEXT GROUP IS PLUS 2.
036054     05  COLUMN 2   PIC X(2)    SOURCE SR-STATE.
036056     05  COLUMN 8   PIC X(3)    SOURCE SR-BRANCH.
036070     05  COLUMN 38  PIC X(12)   VALUE "BRANCH TOTAL".
037010     05  BT-BRANCH-TOTAL
037020         COLUMN 70  PIC ZZZ,ZZZ.99- SUM ST-SALES-REP-TOTAL.
037030     05  COLUMN 81  PIC X(2)    VALUE "**".
037040*─────────────────────────────────────────────
037050 01  TT-STATE-TOTAL-LINE                          State total line
037060     TYPE IS CONTROL FOOTING SR-STATE
037070     LINE IS PLUS 2
037080     NEXT GROUP IS PLUS 2.
037090     05  COLUMN 2   PIC X(2)    SOURCE SR-STATE.
037100     05  COLUMN 39  PIC X(11)   VALUE "STATE TOTAL".
038010     05  TT-STATE-TOTAL
038020         COLUMN 70  PIC ZZZ,ZZZ.99- SUM BT-BRANCH-TOTAL.
038030     05  COLUMN 81  PIC X(3)    VALUE "***".
038040*─────────────────────────────────────────────
038050 01  RT-REPORT-TOTAL-LINE.                        Report total line
038060     TYPE IS CONTROL FOOTING FINAL
038070     LINE IS PLUS 3.
038080     05  COLUMN 51  PIC X(12)   VALUE "REPORT TOTAL".
038090     05  COLUMN 68  PIC Z,ZZZ,ZZZ.99- SUM TT-STATE-TOTAL.
038100     05  COLUMN 81  PIC X(4)    VALUE "****".
```

Figure AA. 13 (cont.)

Report Writer COBOL
coding: RMCTLBRK program.

```
050010*
050020*
050030*
050040 PROCEDURE DIVISION.
050050*
050060*
050070 000-PRINT-SALES-REPORT.
050080*
050090      OPEN INPUT SALES-FILE
050100          OUTPUT SALES-REPORT-FILE.
050110      INITIATE SALES-REPORT.
050120      PERFORM 100-INITIALIZE-VARIABLE-FIELDS.
050130      PERFORM 110-PROCESS-DATE-RECORD.
050150      PERFORM 200-PROCESS-SALES-RECORD
050160          UNTIL END-OF-FILE.
050170      TERMINATE SALES-REPORT.
050180      CLOSE SALES-FILE
050190          SALES-REPORT-FILE.
050200      STOP RUN.
100010*
100020*
100030 100-INITIALIZE-VARIABLE-FIELDS.
100040*
100050      MOVE "NO " TO WS-END-OF-FILE-SWITCH.
100090      ACCEPT WS-DATE-WORK FROM DATE.
110010*
110020*
110030 110-PROCESS-DATE-RECORD.
110040*
110050      PERFORM 800-READ-SALES-RECORD.
110060      IF DATE-RECORD
110070          MOVE DR-PERIOD-ENDING-DATE TO WS-PER-END-DATE
110080          PERFORM 800-READ-SALES-RECORD
110090      ELSE
110100          MOVE "YES" TO WS-END-OF-FILE-SWITCH.
200010*
200020*
200030 200-PROCESS-SALES-RECORD.
200040*
300150      MULTIPLY SR-UNIT-PRICE BY SR-QUANTITY-SOLD
300160          GIVING WS-SALES-REVENUE ROUNDED.
300210      GENERATE DL-DETAIL-LINE.
300220      PERFORM 800-READ-SALES-RECORD.
800010*
800020*
800030 800-READ-SALES-RECORD.
800040*
800050      READ SALES-FILE INTO SR-SALES-RECORD
800060          AT END MOVE "YES" TO WS-END-OF-FILE-SWITCH.
```

To provide for the rolling of totals, a data-name must be assigned to each sum counter, as shown on previous page. (Recognize that a data-name can be assigned to any data-item in the REPORT SECTION; few entries require one, however.)

Then, each higher-level sum counter references the field with the SUM clause at its immediately lower level. After each line is printed, the total field is thus added to the next higher level and the printed total is zeroed. Such coding will provide for the rolling of totals with Report Writer.

**PROCEDURE DIVISION
Coding**

The PROCEDURE DIVISION coding for the multiple-level RMCTLBRK report is identical to that for the single-level RSCTLBRK report except for the coding required to provide for the period-ending date.

Topic: AA-3: Other Report Writer Facilities

The RESET ON Clause

The GROUP INDICATE Clause

A Report with TYPE IS CONTROL HEADING Lines

Other Types of Report Writer Lines

A Report with Summary Group-Printed Lines

The USE BEFORE REPORTING Statement

The SUPPRESS Statement

Figure AA. 14   Example of the single-level sales report with cumulative totals.

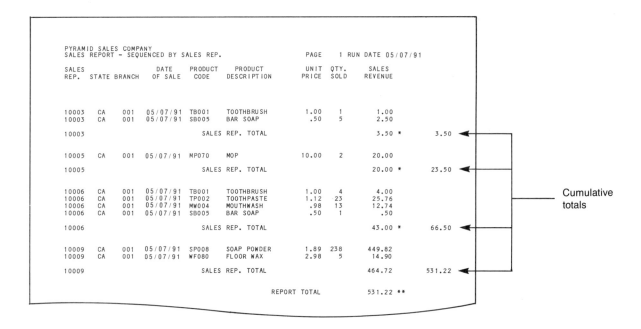

```
PYRAMID SALES COMPANY
SALES REPORT - SEQUENCED BY SALES REP.                    PAGE    1 RUN DATE 05/07/91

SALES                  DATE    PRODUCT   PRODUCT          UNIT  QTY.    SALES
REP.   STATE BRANCH    OF SALE CODE      DESCRIPTION       PRICE SOLD    REVENUE


10003  CA    001   05/07/91 TB001     TOOTHBRUSH          1.00  1        1.00
10003  CA    001   05/07/91 SB005     BAR SOAP             .50  5        2.50

10003                         SALES REP. TOTAL                           3.50 *       3.50  ◄

10005  CA    001   05/07/91 MP070     MOP                10.00  2       20.00

10005                         SALES REP. TOTAL                          20.00 *      23.50  ◄

10006  CA    001   05/07/91 TB001     TOOTHBRUSH          1.00  4        4.00
10006  CA    001   05/07/91 TP002     TOOTHPASTE          1.12  23      25.76
10006  CA    001   05/07/91 MW004     MOUTHWASH           .98   13      12.74
10006  CA    001   05/07/91 SB005     BAR SOAP            .50   1         .50

10006                         SALES REP. TOTAL                          43.00 *      66.50  ◄

10009  CA    001   05/07/91 SP008     SOAP POWDER         1.89  238     449.82
10009  CA    001   05/07/91 WF080     FLOOR WAX           2.98  5        14.90

10009                         SALES REP. TOTAL                          464.72      531.22  ◄

                              REPORT TOTAL                               531.22 **
```

Cumulative totals

Figure AA. 15
RESET ON clause format.

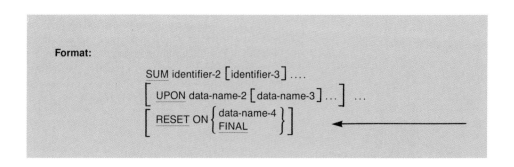

Format:

SUM identifier-2 [identifier-3] . . . .

[UPON data-name-2 [data-name-3] . . .] . . .

[RESET ON { data-name-4 / FINAL }]   ◄────────────

Example:

```
034140      05  COLUMN 84   PIC ZZZ,ZZZ.99- SUM WS-SALES-REVENUE
                                            RESET ON FINAL.
```

Besides those Report Writer features illustrated by the RPAYROLL, RSCTLBRK, and RMCTLBRK programs, there are a few additional provisions, and they will be covered in this topic.

The RESET ON Clause

SUM counters are normally zeroed after they are printed. Sometimes, however, **cumulative, or running, totals** are to be printed. Figure AA.14 shows an example of the single-level sales report with cumulative sales-revenue totals printed on each control footing line.

To override the automatic zeroing of sum counters, the RESET ON clause is specified after the SUM clause. Its format is shown in Figure AA.15. The identifier field must be a field (or the reserved word FINAL) named in a CONTROL IS clause. The identifier field must be a higher level of control—that is, major to—the group in which the RESET ON clause is coded.

Figure AA. 16   Example of the single-level sales report group indication.

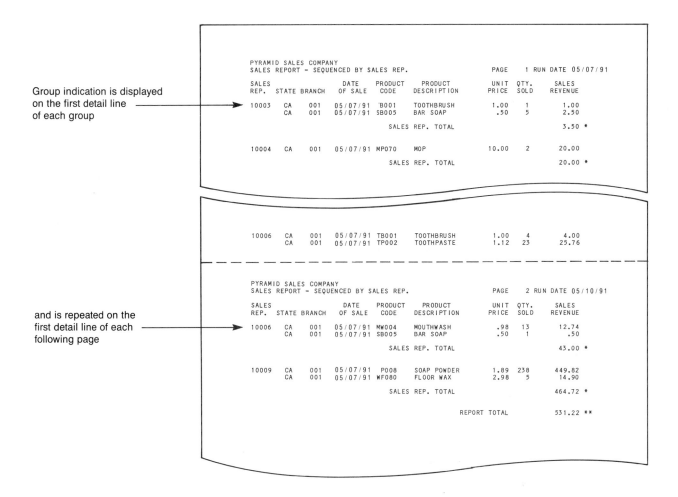

Group indication is displayed on the first detail line of each group

and is repeated on the first detail line of each following page

```
PYRAMID SALES COMPANY
SALES REPORT - SEQUENCED BY SALES REP.                    PAGE    1 RUN DATE 05/07/91

SALES                   DATE    PRODUCT   PRODUCT          UNIT   QTY.    SALES
REP.   STATE BRANCH   OF SALE    CODE     DESCRIPTION      PRICE  SOLD    REVENUE

10003    CA    001   05/07/91   B001     TOOTHBRUSH        1.00    1       1.00
         CA    001   05/07/91   SB005    BAR SOAP           .50    5       2.50

                                         SALES REP. TOTAL                  3.50 *


10004    CA    001   05/07/91   MP070    MOP              10.00    2      20.00

                                         SALES REP. TOTAL                 20.00 *
```

```
10006    CA    001   05/07/91   TB001    TOOTHBRUSH        1.00    4       4.00
         CA    001   05/07/91   TP002    TOOTHPASTE        1.12   23      25.76
```

```
PYRAMID SALES COMPANY
SALES REPORT - SEQUENCED BY SALES REP.                    PAGE    2 RUN DATE 05/10/91

SALES                   DATE    PRODUCT   PRODUCT          UNIT   QTY.    SALES
REP.   STATE BRANCH   OF SALE    CODE     DESCRIPTION      PRICE  SOLD    REVENUE

10006    CA    001   05/07/91   MW004    MOUTHWASH          .98   13      12.74
         CA    001   05/07/91   SB005    BAR SOAP           .50    1        .50

                                         SALES REP. TOTAL                 43.00 *


10009    CA    001   05/07/91   P008     SOAP POWDER       1.89  238     449.82
         CA    001   05/07/91   WF080    FLOOR WAX         2.98    5      14.90

                                         SALES REP. TOTAL                464.72 *


                                         REPORT TOTAL                    531.22 **
```

Figure AA. 17
GROUP INDICATE clause format.

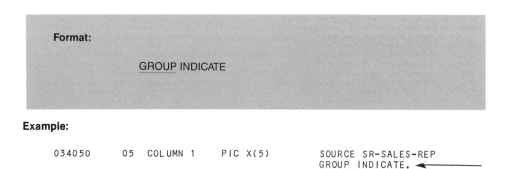

Format:

GROUP INDICATE

Example:

```
034050     05  COLUMN 1     PIC X(5)          SOURCE SR-SALES-REP
                                              GROUP INDICATE.
```

The GROUP INDICATE Clause

Group indication is used to enhance the readability of a report by eliminating repeated fields from adjacent report lines. When group indication is applied to a field, that field is printed only on the first detail line after a control break and on the first detail line of a fresh page. Figure AA.16 provides an example of the single-level sales report with group indication of the sales-rep number.

To provide such group indication with Report Writer, the GROUP INDICATE clause is used. Its format is shown in Figure AA.17. The GROUP INDICATE clause only can be specified with elementary fields within a TYPE IS DETAIL line.

Figure AA. 18   Example of the single-level sales report with control headings.

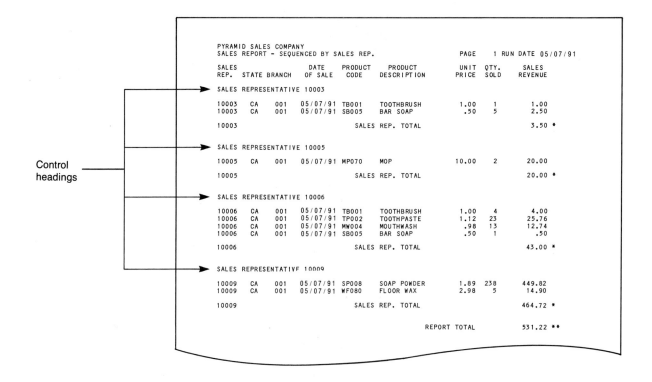

```
              PYRAMID SALES COMPANY
              SALES REPORT - SEQUENCED BY SALES REP.                    PAGE    1 RUN DATE 05/07/91

              SALES                    DATE    PRODUCT    PRODUCT         UNIT  QTY.    SALES
              REP.  STATE BRANCH     OF SALE    CODE      DESCRIPTION    PRICE  SOLD   REVENUE

              SALES REPRESENTATIVE 10003

              10003   CA    001    05/07/91  TB001     TOOTHBRUSH        1.00    1      1.00
              10003   CA    001    05/07/91  SB005     BAR SOAP           .50    5      2.50

              10003                                    SALES REP. TOTAL                3.50 *

              SALES REPRESENTATIVE 10005

              10005   CA    001    05/07/91  MP070     MOP              10.00    2     20.00
              10005                                    SALES REP. TOTAL               20.00 *

              SALES REPRESENTATIVE 10006

              10006   CA    001    05/07/91  TB001     TOOTHBRUSH        1.00    4      4.00
              10006   CA    001    05/07/91  TP002     TOOTHPASTE        1.12   23     25.76
              10006   CA    001    05/07/91  MW004     MOUTHWASH         .98    13     12.74
              10006   CA    001    05/07/91  SB005     BAR SOAP          .50     1       .50

              10006                                    SALES REP. TOTAL               43.00 *

              SALES REPRESENTATIVE 10009

              10009   CA    001    05/07/91  SP008     SOAP POWDER       1.89  238    449.82
              10009   CA    001    05/07/91  WF080     FLOOR WAX         2.98    5     14.90

              10009                                    SALES REP. TOTAL              464.72 *

                                                       REPORT TOTAL                  531.22 **
```

Control headings

Figure AA. 19
COBOL coding for a TYPE IS CONTROL HEADING report line.

```
033010 01  TYPE IS CONTROL HEADING
033020     LINE IS PLUS 2.
033030     05  COLUMN 1    PIC X(20)    VALUE "SALES REPRESENTATIVE".
033040     05  COLUMN 22   PIC X(5)     SOURCE SR-SALES-REP.
```

A Report with TYPE IS CONTROL HEADING Lines

Control heading lines are sometimes also used to enhance the readability of control-break reports. An example of a control heading line for each sales rep in the single-level sales report is shown in Figure AA.18. Control headings are sometimes used when it is necessary to conserve horizontal space on a report line; the control fields can thus be omitted from the detail line. The extra heading lines increase vertical line-space requirements, however.

Figure AA.19 shows an example of the coding for a TYPE IS CONTROL HEADING line. Like a control footing line, the identifier specified must be a field named in the CONTROL IS clause (or the reserved word FINAL).

Printing of control heading lines is triggered by the execution of the GENERATE statement. When a control break occurs, the control heading lines are printed—in major to minor order—after the control footing lines for the previous group and before the detail line for the current record. Control heading lines are also printed before the first detail line of the report is generated.

Other Types of Report Writer Lines

The following types of lines have been explained in this appendix:

- TYPE IS PAGE-HEADING

- TYPE IS CONTROL HEADING

- TYPE IS DETAIL

- TYPE IS CONTROL FOOTING

Figure AA. 20
Example of a summary
single-level sales report.

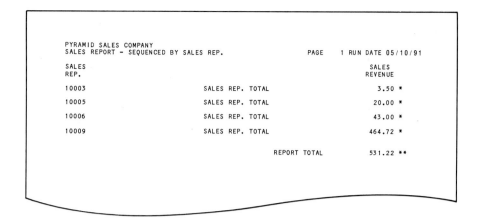

```
PYRAMID SALES COMPANY
SALES REPORT - SEQUENCED BY SALES REP.                    PAGE    1 RUN DATE 05/10/91

SALES                                                                     SALES
REP.                                                                      REVENUE

10003                           SALES REP. TOTAL                           3.50 *

10005                           SALES REP. TOTAL                          20.00 *

10006                           SALES REP. TOTAL                          43.00 *

10009                           SALES REP. TOTAL                         464.72 *


                                                   REPORT TOTAL          531.22 **
```

Figure AA. 21
Report Writer coding for a
summary report.

```
034010*
034020 01  DL-DETAIL-LINE
034030         TYPE IS DETAIL.  ◄──────────────── Dummy detail line
035010*
035020 01  ST-SUMMARY-LINE
035030         TYPE IS CONTROL FOOTING SR-SALES-REP
035040         LINE IS PLUS 2
035050         NEXT GROUP IS PLUS 2.
035060     05  COLUMN 1    PIC X(5)       SOURCE SR-SALES-REP.
035070     05  COLUMN 34   PIC X(16)      VALUE "SALES REP. TOTAL".
035080     05  ST-SALES-REP-TOTAL
035090         COLUMN 70   PIC ZZZ,ZZZ.99-  SUM WS-SALES-REVENUE
035095                                       UPON DL-DETAIL-LINE. ◄─┐
035100     05  COLUMN 81   PIC X(1)       VALUE "*".                │
```

SUM counters on the summary line
must be coded with the UPON clause.

Report Writer also provides for three additional—lesser used—types of report lines:

- TYPE IS REPORT HEADING

- TYPE IS PAGE FOOTING

- TYPE IS REPORT FOOTING

A TYPE IS REPORT HEADING line is printed at the beginning of a report, before any other lines. REPORT HEADING lines are used for prefatory material.

A TYPE IS PAGE FOOTING line is printed at the end of each page. It is sometimes used for footing descriptions, page numbers, and page totals. (However, remember that the SUM clause is limited to TYPE IS CONTROL FOOTING lines; page totals must be accumulated by PROCEDURE DIVISION logic.)

A TYPE IS REPORT FOOTING line is printed at the end of a report, after all other lines. REPORT FOOTING lines are used for legends and other report-ending material.

A Report with Summary Group-Printed Lines

A **summary,** or **group-printed, line** represents an accumulation of detail records. Summary lines are used to shorten the length of reports when the individual detail-entry information is not required.

A control footing line is, in effect, a summary line. Figure AA.20 shows the single-level sales report printed without detail lines to show an example of a summary report.

In order to accomplish the printing of summary lines without detail lines, a **dummy,** or **null, TYPE IS DETAIL line** must be coded. The dummy entry is required because the SUM counter incrementation is triggered by detail-line generation.

Figure AA.21 shows the coding that will produce a summary report. A dummy TYPE IS DETAIL line contains only the record-name-DL-DETAIL-LINE-and the TYPE IS DETAIL

Figure AA. 22
Example of the single-level
sales report with the total
number of sales
representatives.

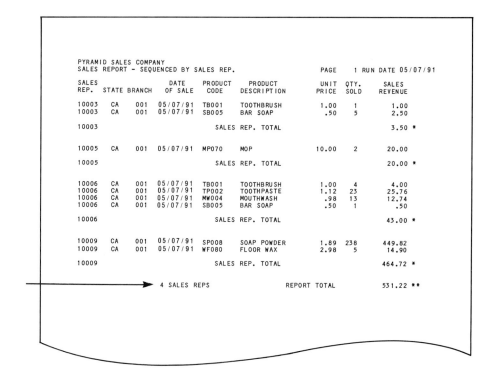

```
PYRAMID SALES COMPANY
SALES REPORT - SEQUENCED BY SALES REP.                    PAGE    1 RUN DATE 05/07/91

SALES                      DATE    PRODUCT    PRODUCT        UNIT   QTY.    SALES
REP.    STATE BRANCH    OF SALE     CODE     DESCRIPTION     PRICE  SOLD    REVENUE

10003    CA    001   05/07/91     TB001    TOOTHBRUSH        1.00    1       1.00
10003    CA    001   05/07/91     SB005    BAR SOAP           .50    5       2.50

10003                             SALES REP. TOTAL                          3.50 *


10005    CA    001   05/07/91     MP070    MOP              10.00    2      20.00

10005                             SALES REP. TOTAL                         20.00 *


10006    CA    001   05/07/91     TB001    TOOTHBRUSH        1.00    4       4.00
10006    CA    001   05/07/91     TP002    TOOTHPASTE        1.12   23      25.76
10006    CA    001   05/07/91     MW004    MOUTHWASH          .98   13      12.74
10006    CA    001   05/07/91     SB005    BAR SOAP           .50    1        .50

10006                             SALES REP. TOTAL                         43.00 *


10009    CA    001   05/07/91     SP008    SOAP POWDER       1.89  238     449.82
10009    CA    001   05/07/91     WF080    FLOOR WAX         2.98    5      14.90

10009                             SALES REP. TOTAL                        464.72 *


         4 SALES REPS                   REPORT TOTAL                      531.22 **
```

entry. No printing action will occur because no LINE clause, no fields, and no COLUMN clauses are coded.

Any SUM counters that are to be incremented for each detail item must be coded with the UPON clause as shown.

The USE BEFORE REPORTING Statement

Sometimes it is necessary to execute a routine before a certain report line is printed. Examples of such situations are (1) a table lookup before a control-heading line is printed, (2) arithmetic calculations other than summation that must be performed on a line, and (3) the need to count the number of control groups.

Suppose we wanted to count the number of sales representatives printed on the single-level sales report and to print the total on the end-of-report total line, as shown in Figure AA.22. Such a requirement requires use of the USE BEFORE REPORTING statement; it permits access to a report line after any SUM clauses within it are summed and before it is printed. Its format and the coding example are shown in Figure AA.23.

The USE BEFORE REPORTING statement is coded in a special PROCEDURE DIVISION area called DECLARATIVES. The DECLARATIVES must physically precede the rest of the PROCEDURE DIVISION. After the reserved words USE BEFORE REPORTING, the name of the report line that is to be accessed is coded. (A TYPE IS DETAIL line cannot be referenced in the USE BEFORE REPORTING statement. However, this restriction causes no problem. Detail-processing routines should be handled in the regular PROCEDURE DIVISION coding—between the READ statement and its following GENERATE statement.)

The number of sales representatives printed is the same as the number of control groups. Hence, USE BEFORE REPORTING ST-SALES-REP-TOTAL was coded. A USE BEFORE REPORTING module must be formed as a SECTION.

In the logic, a field defined in WORKING-STORAGE—WS-NBR-SALES-REPS—is incremented. Then, in the FINAL total line, the WS-NBR-SALES-REPS fields is coded as the object of a SOURCE clause.

The SUPPRESS Statement

Although it is a seldom-used facility, the SUPPRESS statement can be coded to inhibit the printing of a report group. As shown in Figure AA.24, the SUPPRESS statement must be coded in a USE BEFORE REPORTING module.

Figure AA. 23
The USE BEFORE REPORTING
statement.

Format:

USE BEFORE REPORTING identifier.

Example:

```
003040 DATA DIVISION.
          .
          .
006030 WORKING-STORAGE SECTION
          .
          .
009090      05  WS-NBR-SALES-REPS          PIC S9(4) VALUE ZERO.
          .
          .
030030 REPORT SECTION.
          .
          .
035010*
035020 01  ST-SALES-REP-TOTAL-LINE
035030         TYPE IS CONTROL FOOTING SR-SALES-REP
035040         LINE IS PLUS 2
035050         NEXT GROUP IS PLUS 2.
035060      05  COLUMN 1    PIC X(5)      SOURCE SR-SALES-REP.
035070      05  COLUMN 34   PIC X(16)     VALUE "SALES REP. TOTAL".
035080      05  ST-SALES-REP-TOTAL
035090          COLUMN 70   PIC ZZZ,ZZZ.99-  SUM WS-SALES-REVENUE.
035100      05  COLUMN 81   PIC X(1)      VALUE "*".
036010*
036020 01  RT-REPORT-TOTAL-LINE.
036030         TYPE IS CONTROL FOOTING FINAL
036040         LINE IS PLUS 3.
036042
036044      05  COLUMN 18   PIC ZZZ9      SOURCE WS-NBR-SALES-REPS.
036044      05  COLUMN 23   PIC X(10)     VALUE "SALES REPS".
036050      05  COLUMN 51   PIC X(12)     VALUE "REPORT TOTAL".
036060      05  COLUMN 68   PIC Z,ZZZ,ZZZ.99-  SUM WS-SALES-REVENUE.
036070      05  COLUMN 81   PIC X(2)      VALUE "**".
050010*
050020*
050030*
050040 PROCEDURE DIVISION.
050050*
050052*
050054 DECLARATIVES.
050055*
050056*
050060 TALLY-SALES-REPS SECTION.
050061      USE BEFORE REPORTING ST-SALES-REP-TOTAL-LINE.
050062*
050063 D010-COUNT-EACH-SALES-REP.
050064      ADD 1 TO WS-NBR-SALES-REPS.
050065*
050066 END DECLARATIVES.
050067*
050070 000-PRINT-SALES-REPORT.
050080*
          .
          .
          .
```

DECLARATIVES must be at the
beginning of the PROCEDURE DIVISION.

Modules must be formed as
SECTIONs within DECLARATIVES.

END DECLARATIVES must
terminate DECLARATIVES.

Figure AA. 24
SUPPRESS statement format

Format:

<u>SUPPRESS</u> PRINTING.

Example:

```
050010*
050020*
050030*
050040 PROCEDURE DIVISION.
050050*
050052*
050054 DECLARATIVES.
050055*
050056*
050060 OVERRIDE-SALES-REP-TOTAL SECTION.
050061    USE BEFORE REPORTING ST-SALES-REP-TOTAL-LINE.
050062*
050063 D010-OMIT-SALES-REP-TOTAL-LINE.
050064    SUPPRESS PRINTING.
050065*
050066 END DECLARATIVES.
050067*
050070 000-PRINT-SALES-REPORT.
050080*

                  •
                  •
                  •
```

Report Writer Summary

COBOL's **Report Writer** feature provides the ability to write report programs with a reduced amount of COBOL coding. The Report Writer feature is not available on all COBOL compilers, however.

Report Writer Language Element Summary

DATA DIVISION-FILE SECTION. The **REPORT IS clause** is coded in the FD entry to name the report file.

DATA DIVISION-REPORT SECTION. An **RD (report-description) entry** is coded in the REPORT SECTION for each report file named in an FD entry. The RD-name must match the report-name specified in the FD. The RD entry contains two clauses: CONTROL IS and PAGE LIMIT.

The **CONTROL IS clause** is used to specify control-break hierarchies within the report. Control fields (including the reserved word FINAL) must be listed in major to minor sequence.

The **PAGE LIMIT clause** identifies line-span parameters. The value specified after the reserved words PAGE LIMIT specifies the maximum line at which any line is to be printed on the report. The **HEADING entry** specifies the line number at which the report headings will begin. The **FIRST DETAIL entry** specifies the first line number at which the first detail line will be printed. The **LAST DETAIL entry** specifies the last line number at which a detail line is to be printed on each page. The **FOOTING entry** specifies the last line number at which a CONTROL FOOTING line is to be printed.

TYPE IS	Maximum number of 01-level entries permitted	Printing location	Printing triggered by	Comments
REPORT HEADING	One	At the beginning of the report	First execution of the GENERATE statement	
PAGE HEADING	One	At the top of each page before all other groups except the REPORT HEADING group	Full page upon execution of the GENERATE statement	NEXT GROUP clause cannot be used on a TYPE IS PAGE HEADING line (but the same effect can be achieved through appropriate specification of the FIRST DETAIL integer in the PAGE LIMIT clause)
CONTROL HEADING	One per identifier (including FINAL) named in the CONTROL clause	At the beginning of the control group for the corresponding identifier—in major to minor order	(1) First execution of the GENERATE statement (when FINAL is specified), and (2) control break for corresponding or more major CONTROL field upon execution of the GENERATE statement	
DETAIL	No limit	As the main body of the report	Each execution of the GENERATE statement	01-level entry must be assigned a record-name SUM clause is limited to TYPE IS DETAIL GROUP INDICATE clause is limited to TYPE IS DETAIL A TYPE IS DETAIL line cannot be named in a USE BEFORE REPORTING statement (but the same effect can be achieved through PROCEDURE DIVISION logic)
CONTROL FOOTING	One per identifier (including FINAL) named in the CONTROL clause	At the end of the control group for the corresponding identifier—in minor to major order	(1) Control break for corresponding or more major CONTROL field upon execution of the GENERATE statement, and (2) execution of the TERMINATE statement	
PAGE FOOTING	One	At the end of each page after all other groups except the REPORT FOOTING group	(1) Full page upon execution of the GENERATE statement, and (2) execution of the TERMINATE statement	NEXT GROUP clause cannot be used on a TYPE IS PAGE FOOTING line
REPORT FOOTING	One	At the end of the report after all other groups	Execution of the TERMINATE statement	NEXT GROUP clause cannot be used on a TYPE IS REPORT FOOTING line

01-level report-group entries are coded for each type of report line to be printed on the report.

The **LINE clause** is used to specify the vertical line-spacing requirements. It can be specified at either the group level or the elementary level. The LINE clause can be coded with either (1) an **absolute line number** or (2) a **relative line number** through specification of the reserved words LINE IS PLUS.

The **COLUMN clause** is used to specify the horizontal line positioning for each field to be printed.

The regular COBOL **VALUE clause** is used to store constant data into a REPORT SECTION field. To place variable data into a REPORT SECTION field, either a SOURCE or a SUM clause is specified.

The **SOURCE clause** requires specification of either (1) the name of a field or (2) the reserved word PAGE-COUNTER, which is a special Report Writer field that keeps track of the page number.

The **SUM clause** causes Report Writer to establish a **sum counter.** The SUM clause can be specified only in a TYPE IS CONTROL FOOTING line. The identifier coded after the reserved word SUM must be either (1) a numeric field specified as the object of a SOURCE clause, (2) the name of a REPORT SECTION field specified with the SUM clause (that is, another sum counter), or (3) a numeric field in the FILE SECTION or the WORKING-STORAGE SECTION.

Sum counters are automatically incremented when the GENERATE statement is executed. They are automatically zeroed after they are printed. To provide for the **rolling of totals,** a lower-level (more minor) sum counter is named in the SUM clause.

To override automatic zeroing of SUM COUNTERS, the **RESET ON clause** is coded. The **GROUP INDICATE clause** can be specified on TYPE IS DETAIL fields to provide for group indication.

For **summary (group-printed) reports,** a **dummy (null) TYPE IS DETAIL LINE** must be coded. A dummy TYPE IS DETAIL line contains only the record-name and the TYPE IS DETAIL entry. No detail-line printing action will occur because no LINE clause, no fields, and no COLUMN clauses are coded.

PROCEDURE DIVISION. The **INITIATE statement** begins Report Writer processing. The file named in the FD entry must be opened before the report named in the INITIATE statement can be initiated. The INITIATE statement handles the following processing:

■ All SUM counters are set to zero.

■ The LINE-COUNTER is set to zero.

■ The PAGE-COUNTER is set to 1.

The **GENERATE statement** causes a detail line to be written to the report. The name of the TYPE IS DETAIL line is typically coded as the object of the GENERATE verb. The first time the GENERATE statement is executed, the following processing occurs:

■ The REPORT HEADING group (if specified) is printed.

■ The PAGE HEADING group is printed.

■ CONTROL HEADING lines (if specified) are printed in major to minor order.

■ The first DETAIL line is printed.

For each GENERATE statement executed after the first, the following processing occurs:

■ Tests are made to see if a PAGE FOOTING group should be printed. If a PAGE FOOTING group is required during GENERATE processing, it is printed.

■ Tests are made to see if a PAGE HEADING group should be printed. If a PAGE HEADING group is required during GENERATE processing, it is printed.

- A test is made to see if one or more CONTROL FOOTING lines should be printed. If so, they are printed in minor to major order up to the most major level at which the control break occurred.

- A test is made to see if one or more CONTROL HEADING lines should be printed. If so, they are printed in major to minor order from the most major level at which the control break occurred.

- The DETAIL line is printed.

The **TERMINATE statement** ends Report Writer processing. Before the report file is closed, the report named in the TERMINATE STATEMENT must be terminated. When the TERMINATE statement is executed, the following processing occurs:

- Tests are made to see if a PAGE FOOTING group should be printed. If a PAGE FOOTING group is required during TERMINATE processing, it is printed.

- Tests are made to see if a PAGE-HEADING group should be printed. If a PAGE-HEADING group is required during TERMINATE processing, it is printed.

- All CONTROL FOOTING lines are printed, in major to minor order.

- The REPORT FOOTING group (if specified) is printed.

The **USE BEFORE REPORTING statement** can be coded in the DECLARATIVES area of the PROCEDURE DIVISION to enable the execution of a routine before a certain report line is printed. After the reserved words USE BEFORE REPORTING, the name of the report line that is to be accessed is coded. A TYPE IS DETAIL line cannot be referenced in the USE BEFORE REPORTING statement.

The **SUPPRESS statement** can be coded in a USE BEFORE REPORTING module to inhibit the printing of a report group.

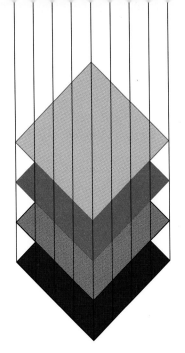

Other COBOL Clauses and Statements

A number of additional COBOL clauses and statements are either (1) not frequently used, (2) not in accordance with contemporary structured coding conventions, (3) outdated, or (4) part of the new COBOL-85 standard. Although this text does not cover clauses and statements used with COBOL's Relative I-0, Indexed I-0, Debug, Interprogram Communication, or Communication Modules, the following additional COBOL clauses and statements are covered in this appendix:

Division	Clause or statement
IDENTIFICATION	REMARKS (COBOL-68)
DATA	BLOCK CONTAINS clause
	OCCURS/DEPENDING ON
	66-**level** RENAMES
PROCEDURE	ACCEPT
	DISPLAY
	ALTER
	EXAMINE (COBOL-68)
	GO TO/DEPENDING ON
	INSPECT/CHARACTERS
	ADD CORRESPONDING
	SUBTRACT CORRESPONDING
	NOTE (COBOL-68)
	PERFORM/TIMES
	STRING
	UNSTRING
(All divisions)	COPY

IDENTIFICATION DIVISION

REMARKS Paragraph (COBOL-68)

The REMARKS paragraph was included in the COBOL-68 standards to provide the facility for general documentation in the IDENTIFICATION DIVISION. However, it was omitted from COBOL-74. The REMARKS paragraph can still be found in older programs and some programmers sometimes still use it. However, under COBOL-74 and COBOL-85, comment lines [an asterisk (*) in position 7] should be used rather than the REMARKS paragraph. Examples of the two methods are shown on the following page.

Format:

REMARKS.   comment-entry

Example:

```
REMARKS.   THE REMARKS PARAGRAPH WAS PROVIDED SO THAT
           OVERALL PROGRAM DOCUMENTATION COMMENTS
           COULD BE PROVIDED IN THE IDENTIFICATION DIVISION.
```

COBOL-74 and -85 method:

```
*          THE REMARKS PARAGRAPH WAS DROPPED FROM THE
*          1974 COBOL STANDARDS.  COMMENT LINES
*          (* IN POSITION 7) SHOULD NOW BE USED INSTEAD
*          OF THE REMARKS PARAGRAPH.
```

DATA DIVISION
BLOCK CONTAINS clause

Logical records stored on disk and tape media are commonly blocked into longer, physical record blocks. For instance, a file might be stored with 10 logical records stored as a single physical record. Such a file is said to have a **blocking factor** of 10. To provide for record blocking, the BLOCK CONTAINS clause is specified in the FD entry for the file. Notice in the following format that the BLOCK CONTAINS clause can be expressed with either the number of RECORDS (the blocking factor) in the block or the number of CHARACTERS (the block size) in the block. Specification of the number of RECORDS is usually more readily understandable and thus preferable to specification of the number of CHARACTERS.

Format:

$$\text{\underline{BLOCK} CONTAINS integer} \left\{ \begin{array}{l} \text{\underline{RECORDS}} \\ \text{CHARACTERS} \end{array} \right\}$$

Example:

```
FD SALES-TRANSACTION-FILE
RECORD CONTAINS 60 CHARACTERS
BLOCK CONTAINS 10 RECORDS
LABEL RECORDS ARE STANDARD.
```

OCCURS/DEPENDING ON Clause

The OCCURS/DEPENDING ON clause is not frequently used, but has two primary applications: (1) with variable-length records and (2) when the SEARCH statement is used with input-loaded tables. Variable-length records are beyond the scope of this text. An OCCURS/DEPENDING ON example with an input-loaded table application is shown below.

Format:

```
OCCURS integer-1 TO integer-2 TIMES

   DEPENDING ON data-name-1
```

Example:

```
*
 01  IT-TABLE-CONTROLS.
     05  IT-NBR-ENTRIES              PIC S9(4)      COMP SYNC.

*
 01  IT-ITEM-TABLE.
     05  IT-ITEM-ENTRY              OCCURS 1 TO 200 TIMES
                                    DEPENDING ON IT-NBR-ENTRIES.
         10  IT-ITEM-CODE           PIC X(8).
         10  IT-ITEM-DESCRIPTION    PIC X(20).
```

Notice that the IT-ITEM-TABLE is defined to hold a maximum of 200 table entries. Say, however, that there were only 45 table entries loaded. By keeping count of the number of table entries loaded—and storing that count in the object of the DEPENDING ON clause (IT-NBR-ENTRIES in the example)—table-lookup processing for unmatched entries is quicker. When a SEARCH statement does a lookup on the table, it will consider the table to be 45 entries long, rather than the 200 specified in the OCCURS clause. (The programmer should recognize, though, that the OCCURS/DEPENDING ON clause can provide inefficient processing and its use should be limited to appropriate situations.)

66-Level RENAMES Clause

The RENAMES clause is seldom used. It is similar to the REDEFINES clause in that it permits one or more fields to be assigned alternative data-names. It is different because (1) it does not provide for assigning a different PICTURE clause, (2) it allows multiple fields at the same level to be renamed, and (3) the clause must be placed at the end of the record-description to which it applies. Examples of the RENAMES clause are shown below.

Format:

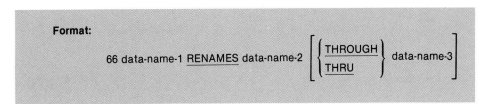

```
66 data-name-1 RENAMES data-name-2  [ { THROUGH } data-name-3 ]
                                      { THRU    }
```

Example:

```
*
 01  NA-NAME-AND-ADDRESS-RECORD.
     05  NA-FIRST-NAME    PIC X(10).
     05  NA-MID-INITIAL   PIC X(1).
     05  NA-LAST-NAME     PIC X(12).
     05  NA-ADDRESS       PIC X(24).
     05  NA-CITY          PIC X(13).
     05  NA-STATE         PIC X(2).
     05  NA-ZIP-CODE      PIC X(5).
*
     66  NA-FULL-NAME RENAMES NA-FIRST-NAME THRU NA-LAST-NAME.
     66  NA-STREET-ADDRESS RENAMES NA-ADDRESS.
     66  NA-DESTINATION RENAMES NA-CITY THRU NA-ZIP-CODE.
```

The following rules apply to the RENAMES clause:

■ It must be a level-number 66 entry and must be specified immediately following the record-description to which it applies.

■ It cannot be used to rename level-number 01, 66, 77, or 88 entries.

■ The identifiers being renamed cannot contain an OCCURS clause.

■ Data-name-3 (the THRU identifier) must physically follow identifier-2 in the record-description and cannot be subordinate to identifier-2.

PROCEDURE DIVISION
ACCEPT Statement

The ACCEPT statement obtains low-volume input data (such as dates, control numbers, etc.) from an input device or the computer-operator console. It is similar in function to a READ statement, but it differs because it does not require an FD entry (nor its associated SELECT file-control entry nor OPEN and CLOSE statements). ACCEPT statement examples are shown below.

Format:

        ACCEPT identifier [FROM mnemonic-name]

Example A: ACCEPT from input device

```
ACCEPT WS-PERIOD-ENDING-DATE.
```

Example B: ACCEPT from console

```
ENVIRONMENT DIVISION

    SPECIAL-NAMES.
        CONSOLE IS TYPEWRITER.


PROCEDURE DIVISION

    ACCEPT WS-PERIOD-ENDING-DATE FROM TYPEWRITER.
```

The identifier field can be either an elementary item of DISPLAY usage or a group item. The maximum length of the data transfer for each type of input device is defined by the particular COBOL compiler being used. (The maximum length is often set at 80 characters.) One physical record is read from the input device. If the data length of the transferred data is greater than the identifier length, the excess leftmost positions are truncated.

When the FROM phrase is used, the mnemonic name typically refers to the operator console.

Use of the ACCEPT statement for traditional batch processing is generally discouraged. It is better to use READ statements for normal high-volume input devices and to avoid accepting data from the operator console. Entry of data at the operator console tends to slow down operations and places a burden on the computer operator, who is typically tending to a number of operating requirements at any given time. Thus, to minimize the chance for error and to optimize computer run time, it is preferable to provide for the input of variable data (such as dates and starting check numbers) to be entered via a control record, which is prepared by personnel responsible for data control functions.

If you studied Chapter 9, you know that the ACCEPT is commonly used (non-standard) to accept data from a VDT device within on-line applications. Such interactive ACCEPT-statement syntax varies with different compilers.

DISPLAY Statement

The DISPLAY statement is the converse of the ACCEPT statement. It provides for the transfer of low-volume output data to an output device. It is similar in function to a WRITE statement, but it differs because it does not require an FD entry (nor its associated SELECT file-control entry nor OPEN and CLOSE statements). DISPLAY statement examples are shown below.

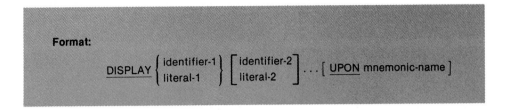

Format:

$$\underline{\text{DISPLAY}} \left\{ \begin{array}{l} \text{identifier-1} \\ \text{literal-1} \end{array} \right\} \left[\begin{array}{l} \text{identifier-2} \\ \text{literal-2} \end{array} \right] \ldots \left[\underline{\text{UPON}} \text{ mnemonic-name} \right]$$

Example A: DISPLAY upon output device

```
DISPLAY "RUN CANCELED DUE TO "  WS-ERROR-MESSAGE.
```

Example B: DISPLAY upon console

```
ENVIRONMENT DIVISION

SPECIAL-NAMES.
    CONSOLE IS TYPEWRITER.


PROCEDURE DIVISION

DISPLAY "ENTER PERIOD ENDING DATE" UPON TYPEWRITER.
```

The identifier field can be either an elementary item of DISPLAY usage or a group item. The maximum length of the data transfer for each type of output device is defined by the particular COBOL compiler being used. (The maximum length is often set at 120 or 132 characters.)

When the UPON phrase is used, the mnemonic-name typically refers to the operator console.

Use of the DISPLAY statement for traditional batch processing is generally discouraged. It is better to use WRITE statements for normal output devices and to avoid displaying data to the operator console. Many programmers use the DISPLAY statement while debugging, however, for temporary program statements to display the contents of fields and the like.

The DISPLAY statement is also used by certain COBOL compilers for VDT screen handling tasks within on-line applications. Such interactive DISPLAY-statement syntax varies with different compilers, however.

ALTER Statement

The ALTER statement modifies the path of program control. It is used in conjunction with the GO TO statement. There is a general consensus throughout the COBOL-programming community that the ALTER statement is a "bug-breeder" and hence should not be used. When the ALTER statement is coded, it is difficult to determine from the program listing exactly what procedure program control was or is to be transferred to at any given time. As a result, debugging is complicated and maintenance can be perplexing. The ALTER .statement has now been deleted from the language and is not present in COBOL-85.

The ALTER statement can sometimes be found in older COBOL programs, however. An example is shown on following page.

Format:

ALTER procedure-name-1 TO [PROCEED TO] procedure-name-2

[procedure-name-3 TO [PROCEED TO] procedure-name-4] . . .

Example:

```
*
*
 999-CONTROL-PROCEDURE.
*
     GO TO 999-PROCESS-DETAIL-RECORD.
*
*
 999-ANOTHER-PROCEDURE.
*
            .
            .
            .
     ALTER 999-CONTROL-PROCEDURE
           TO PROCEED TO 999-PROCESS-CONTROL-BREAK.
```

Procedure-name-1 must be paragraph containing only one GO TO staement, as is the case in the 999-CONTROL-PROCEDURE paragraph. After the ALTER statement is executed, the GO TO statement will transfer control to the 999-PROCESS-CONTROL-BREAK procedure rather than the 999-PROCESS-DETAIL-RECORD procedure. (There will typically be another ALTER statement elsewhere in the program to change control back to the 999-PROCESS-DETAIL-RECORD procedure when required.)

EXAMINE Statement (COBOL-68)

The EXAMINE statement of the COBOL-68 standards was superseded by the INSPECT statement introduced in COBOL-74. However, it can be found in many older programs and is still used by a number of programmers.

There are two EXAMINE statement formats: one with the TALLYING phrase and the other with the REPLACING phrase.

EXAMINE/TALLYING (Format-1). The Format-1 EXAMINE/TALLYING statement, together with examples, is shown on the following page. Execution of Example A will cause the XX-QUANTITY field to be examined—character by character—from left to right. The LEADING blank spaces present in the field will be counted and stored in a special COBOL field named TALLY. Whenever the TALLYING phrase is specified in a COBOL program, the TALLY field is automatically supplied; the programmer does not (and cannot) define the reserved word TALLY in the DATA DIVISION. [With many COBOL compilers, TALLY has the attributes of a five integer digit signed number field; that is, PIC S9(5).]

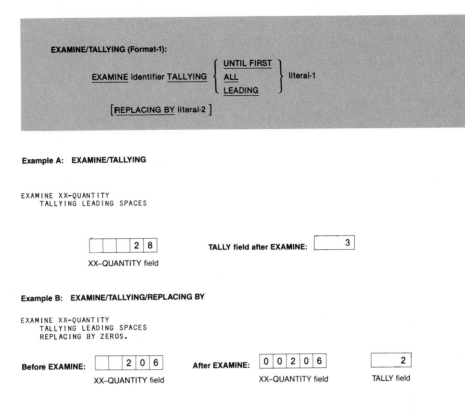

EXAMINE/TALLYING (Format-1):

EXAMINE identifier TALLYING { UNTIL FIRST / ALL / LEADING } literal-1

[REPLACING BY literal-2]

Example A: EXAMINE/TALLYING

```
EXAMINE XX-QUANTITY
    TALLYING LEADING SPACES
```

		2	8

XX–QUANTITY field

TALLY field after EXAMINE: | 3 |

Example B: EXAMINE/TALLYING/REPLACING BY

```
EXAMINE XX-QUANTITY
    TALLYING LEADING SPACES
    REPLACING BY ZEROS.
```

Before EXAMINE: | | | 2 | 0 | 6 |

XX–QUANTITY field

After EXAMINE: | 0 | 0 | 2 | 0 | 6 |

XX–QUANTITY field

| 2 |

TALLY field

TALLY is automatically initialized to zeros prior to each execution of an EXAMINE statement. (This is different from the processing for the tallying field of the INSPECT statement.)

When the optional REPLACING BY phrase is specified, as shown in Example B above, not only does the TALLYING occur but character replacement is also supplied. The tallied characters are also replaced by the value specified as literal-2. In Example B, the leading blank spaces are both counted and converted to zeros.

The identifier field specified in an EXAMINE statement must be of DISPLAY usage. Although it may be either a numeric or an alphanumeric field, the literals specified must be consistent with the data class of that identifier field. That is, literal-1 (and literal-2, if the REPLACING phrase is specified) must be a numeric digit if the identifier field is numeric.

Literal-1 and literal-2 must be a single character or digit. As shown in the examples, figurative constants can be used for the literals. When the identifier is a signed numeric field, the sign is not considered in the evaluation.

Notice that the TALLYING phrase has three options: ALL, UNTIL FIRST, and LEADING. ALL applies to all occurrences of literal-1 in the field. UNTIL FIRST begins at the leftmost position of the field and applies to all positions that precede the first occurrence of literal-1. LEADING, as shown in the examples, starts from the leftmost position of the field and applies to all occurrences of literal-1 that are present before any other character is encountered.

EXAMINE/REPLACING (Format-2). The EXAMINE/REPLACING statement provides for character replacement but not counting. An example is shown on the following page.

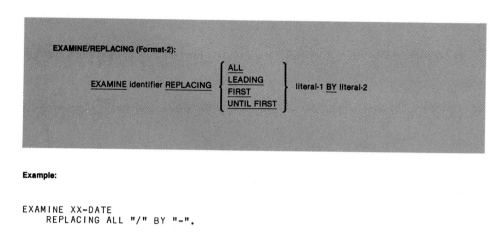

Example:

```
EXAMINE XX-DATE
    REPLACING ALL "/" BY "-".
```

Before EXAMINE: | 0 | 2 | / | 1 | 5 | / | 9 | 1 |
                                XX–DATE field

After EXAMINE: | 0 | 2 | - | 1 | 5 | - | 9 | 1 |
                                XX–DATE field

Syntactical rules regarding the identifier and the literals are the same as for the EXAMINE/TALLYING statement. An additional option—FIRST—is available. Although seldom used, the FIRST option causes replacement of only the leftmost occurrence of the value specified as literal-1.

The GO TO/DEPENDING ON Statement

The Format-1 GO TO statement was discussed in Chapter 13. The Format-2 GO TO statement contains the DEPENDING ON phrase and provides the ability to branch to various procedures depending on the value of a numeric identifier, as shown below.

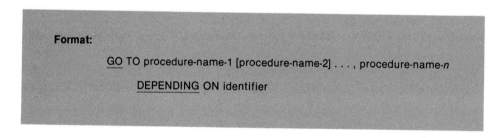

Example:

```
GO TO 999-PROCESS-RECORD-A
      999-PROCESS-RECORD-B
      999-PROCESS-RECORD-C
      999-PROCESS-RECORD-D
      999-PROCESS-RECORD-E
      DEPENDING ON WS-RECORD-CODE-FLAG.
```

The program branches to the relative procedure in conformance with the value present in the identifier field. That is, if the identifier field contains a 1, the program branches to the first procedure listed; if the field contains a 2, the program branches to the second procedure, and so forth. If the identifier field contains a value that is less than 1 or greater than the number of procedures listed, no branch is taken; the program instead continues to the next consecutive executable statement.

The GO TO/DEPENDING ON statement is seldom used because it has limited applicability and because, with structured coding, use of the GO TO statement is discouraged. However, use of the GO TO/DEPENDING ON statement to form a **case structure** is generally in accordance with structured coding conventions.

An example of a case structure is shown below. The group of modules is formed as a SECTION; the GO TO/DEPENDING ON statement is the first statement within the section. Observe that the case structure contains only one entry point and one exit point in accordance with structured coding principles.

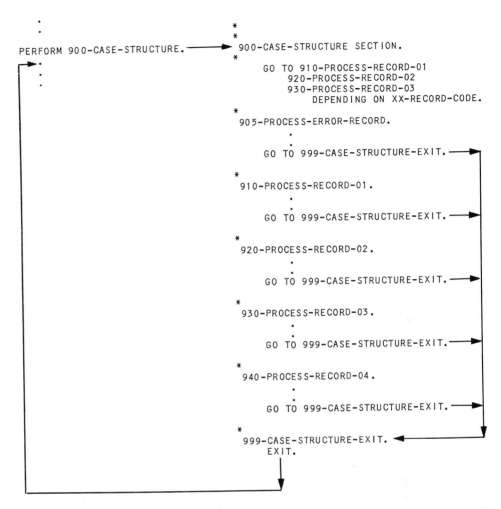

```
        .                           *
        .                           *
        .                           *
PERFORM 900-CASE-STRUCTURE. ─────▶  900-CASE-STRUCTURE SECTION.
  ┌──▶ .                           *
  │     .                             GO TO 910-PROCESS-RECORD-01
  │     .                                   920-PROCESS-RECORD-02
  │                                         930-PROCESS-RECORD-03
  │                                           DEPENDING ON XX-RECORD-CODE.
  │                                 *
  │                                 905-PROCESS-ERROR-RECORD.
  │                                       .
  │                                       .
  │                                     GO TO 999-CASE-STRUCTURE-EXIT. ──┐
  │                                                                      │
  │                                 *                                    │
  │                                 910-PROCESS-RECORD-01.               │
  │                                       .                              │
  │                                       .                              │
  │                                     GO TO 999-CASE-STRUCTURE-EXIT. ──┤
  │                                                                      │
  │                                 *                                    │
  │                                 920-PROCESS-RECORD-02.               │
  │                                       .                              │
  │                                       .                              │
  │                                     GO TO 999-CASE-STRUCTURE-EXIT. ──┤
  │                                                                      │
  │                                 *                                    │
  │                                 930-PROCESS-RECORD-03.               │
  │                                       .                              │
  │                                       .                              │
  │                                     GO TO 999-CASE-STRUCTURE-EXIT. ──┤
  │                                                                      │
  │                                 *                                    │
  │                                 940-PROCESS-RECORD-04.               │
  │                                       .                              │
  │                                       .                              │
  │                                     GO TO 999-CASE-STRUCTURE-EXIT. ──┤
  │                                                                      │
  │                                 *                                    │
  │                                 999-CASE-STRUCTURE-EXIT. ◀───────────┘
  │                                       EXIT.
  │                                          │
  └──────────────────────────────────────────
```

INSPECT/CHARACTERS Statement

The CHARACTERS BY phrase can be coded with INSPECT/TALLYING and INSPECT/REPLACING statements to tally or replace within a portion of the field. A few examples of this seldom-used feature are shown on the following page.

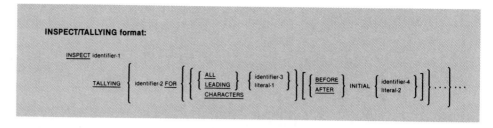

INSPECT/TALLYING format:

INSPECT identifier-1

TALLYING { identifier-2 FOR { { { ALL / LEADING / CHARACTERS } { identifier-3 / literal-1 } } [{ BEFORE / AFTER } INITIAL { identifier-4 / literal-2 }] } ... } ...

INSPECT/REPLACING format:

INSPECT identifier-1

REPLACING { { CHARACTERS BY { identifier-5 / literal-3 } [{ BEFORE / AFTER } INITIAL { identifier-4 / literal-2 }] } { { ALL / LEADING / FIRST } { { identifier-5 / literal-3 } BY { identifier-6 / literal-4 } [{ BEFORE / AFTER } INITIAL { identifier-7 / literal-5 }] } ... } } ... } ...

INSPECT/TALLYING examples:

		Contents of identifier-1	Contents of WS-TALLY after INSPECT statement executed (Initial value=0)

Example A. TALLYING/CHARACTERS option with BEFORE INITIAL phrase

```
INSPECT IN-SIGNED-AMOUNT-X
    TALLYING WS-TALLY
    FOR CHARACTERS BEFORE INITIAL "-".
```

-23712.38   0

Example B. TALLYING/CHARACTERS option with AFTER INITIAL phrase

```
INSPECT IN-SIGNED-AMOUNT-X
    TALLYING WS-TALLY
    FOR CHARACTERS AFTER INITIAL "-".
```

23712.3-8   1

INSPECT/REPLACING examples:

	Contents of identifier-1	
	Before INSPECT statement executed	After INSPECT statement executed

Example A. REPLACING CHARACTERS BY option with BEFORE INITIAL phrase

```
INSPECT IN-DECIMAL-AMOUNT
    REPLACING CHARACTERS BY "0"
    BEFORE INITIAL ".".
```

bbb403.28   000000.28

Example B. REPLACING CHARACTERS BY option with AFTER INITIAL phrase

```
INSPECT IN-DECIMAL-AMOUNT
    REPLACING CHARACTERS BY ZERO
    AFTER INITIAL ".".
```

bbb403.28   bbb403.00

Note: b = blank space

ADD CORRESPONDING and SUBTRACT CORRESPONDING Statements

You learned about the MOVE/CORRESPONDING statement in Chapter 5. The CORRESPONDING phrase can also be coded with the ADD and SUBTRACT statements. An example is shown on the following page. Of course, only those identical data-names with numeric PICTURE clauses will be included in the arithmetic. The CORRESPONDING option for the ADD and SUBTRACT statement has limited usefulness. As in the case of the CORRESPONDING option of the MOVE statement, its use is generally discouraged.

Formats:

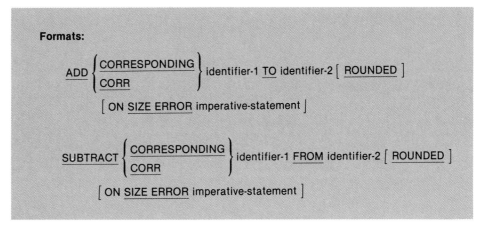

$$\text{ADD} \left\{ \begin{array}{l} \underline{\text{CORRESPONDING}} \\ \underline{\text{CORR}} \end{array} \right\} \text{identifier-1 } \underline{\text{TO}} \text{ identifier-2 } \left[\underline{\text{ROUNDED}} \right]$$

$$\left[\text{ON } \underline{\text{SIZE ERROR}} \text{ imperative-statement} \right]$$

$$\text{SUBTRACT} \left\{ \begin{array}{l} \underline{\text{CORRESPONDING}} \\ \underline{\text{CORR}} \end{array} \right\} \text{identifier-1 } \underline{\text{FROM}} \text{ identifier-2 } \left[\underline{\text{ROUNDED}} \right]$$

$$\left[\text{ON } \underline{\text{SIZE ERROR}} \text{ imperative-statement} \right]$$

Examples:

DATA DIVISION:

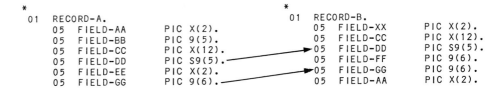

```
 *                                              *
 01  RECORD-A.                                  01  RECORD-B.
     05  FIELD-AA      PIC  X(2).                    05  FIELD-XX      PIC  X(2).
     05  FIELD-BB      PIC  9(5).                    05  FIELD-CC      PIC  X(12).
     05  FIELD-CC      PIC  X(12).          ───────→ 05  FIELD-DD      PIC  S9(5).
     05  FIELD-DD      PIC  S9(5).─────────┐         05  FIELD-FF      PIC  9(6).
     05  FIELD-EE      PIC  X(2).     ─────┼───────→ 05  FIELD-GG      PIC  9(6).
     05  FIELD-GG      PIC  9(6).──────────┘         05  FIELD-AA      PIC  X(2).
```

PROCEDURE DIVISION:

```
    ADD CORRESPONDING RECORD-A TO RECORD-B.

    SUBTRACT CORRESPONDING RECORD-A FROM RECORD-B.
```

NOTE Statement

The NOTE statement was present in COBOL-68 to permit inclusion of program comments in the PROCEDURE DIVISION. An example is shown below. The NOTE statement was removed from COBOL-74. Comment lines [an asterisk (*) in position 7] should currently be used in preference to the NOTE statement.

Format:

NOTE.   comment-entry

Example:

```
    NOTE.    THE NOTE STATEMENT WAS PROVIDED SO THAT EXPLANATORY
             PROGRAM DOCUMENTATION COMMENTS COULD BE PROVIDED
             IN THE PROCEDURE DIVISION.
```

COBOL-74 and -85

```
    *        THE NOTE STATEMENT WAS DROPPED FROM THE
    *        1974 COBOL STANDARDS.  COMMENT LINES
    *        (* IN POSITION 7) SHOULD NOW BE USED INSTEAD
    *        OF THE NOTE STATEMENT.
```

PERFORM/TIMES Statement

There are a number of variations of the PERFORM statement. The Format-1 PERFORM statement specifying a single-paragraph procedure and the Format-3 PERFORM/UNTIL statement were covered in Chapter 3. The Format-4 PERFORM/VARYING statement was discussed in Chapters 11 and 12. The Format-2 PERFORM/TIMES statement is probably the least used PERFORM statement option.

As shown below, the PERFORM/TIMES statement provides for performance of a procedure multiple times in accordance with the value of an integer number or the contents of an identifier field.

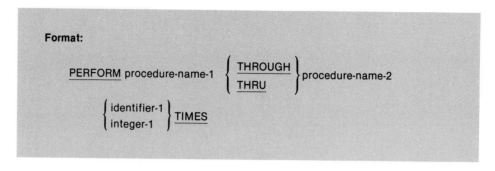

Format:

PERFORM procedure-name-1 { THROUGH / THRU } procedure-name-2

{ identifier-1 / integer-1 } TIMES

Example A: Integer option

```
PERFORM 999-PRINT-OUTPUT-FORM 2 TIMES.
```

Example B.   Identifier option

```
PERFORM 999-PRINT-OUTPUT-FORM WS-COPIES-REQUIRED TIMES.
```

STRING Statement

The STRING statement is a powerful character-manipulation statement. It can be used to join together different fields, or parts of different fields. It is a complex statement offering a number of options. Although it will not be covered fully here, an example of its use is shown on the following page in which a single full name field is assembled—with one blank space between names—from separate last, first, and middle name fields.

Format:

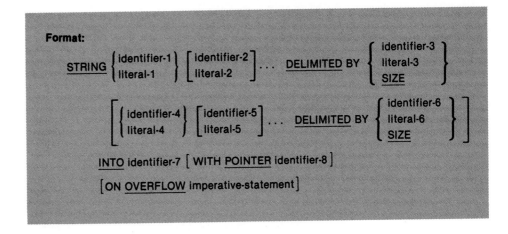

Example:

```
STRING IN-LAST-NAME DELIMITED BY " "
       " " DELIMITED BY SIZE
       IN-FIRST-NAME DELIMITED BY " "
       " " DELIMITED BY SIZE
       IN-MIDDLE-NAME DELIMITED BY " "
       " " DELIMITED BY SIZE
INTO OUT-FULL-NAME.
```

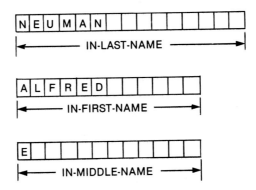

After STRING statement execution

UNSTRING Statement

The UNSTRING statement is the converse of the STRING statement. A powerful character-manipulation statement, it permits parts of a single field to be dispersed into one or more different fields. It too is a complex statement offering a number of options and will not be covered fully here. An example in which a single full name field (formatted with the last name first) is dispersed into separate last, first, and middle name fields is shown below.

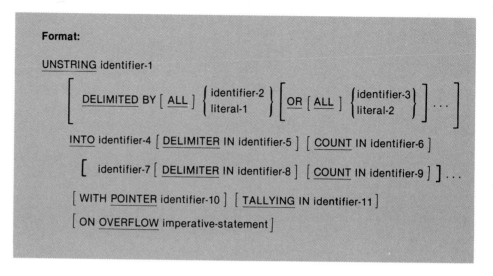

Format:

UNSTRING identifier-1

$$\left[\underline{\text{DELIMITED BY}} \left[\underline{\text{ALL}} \right] \left\{ \begin{array}{l} \text{identifier-2} \\ \text{literal-1} \end{array} \right\} \left[\underline{\text{OR}} \left[\underline{\text{ALL}} \right] \left\{ \begin{array}{l} \text{identifier-3} \\ \text{literal-2} \end{array} \right\} \right] \cdots \right]$$

$$\underline{\text{INTO}} \text{ identifier-4} \left[\underline{\text{DELIMITER}} \text{ IN identifier-5} \right] \left[\underline{\text{COUNT}} \text{ IN identifier-6} \right]$$

$$\left[\text{ identifier-7} \left[\underline{\text{DELIMITER}} \text{ IN identifier-8} \right] \left[\underline{\text{COUNT}} \text{ IN identifier-9} \right] \right] \cdots$$

$$\left[\underline{\text{WITH}} \underline{\text{POINTER}} \text{ identifier-10} \right] \left[\underline{\text{TALLYING}} \text{ IN identifier-11} \right]$$

$$\left[\underline{\text{ON}} \underline{\text{OVERFLOW}} \text{ imperative-statement} \right]$$

Example:

```
UNSTRING IN-FULL-NAME DELIMITED BY ALL " "
    INTO OUT-LAST-NAME
         OUT-FIRST-NAME
         OUT-MIDDLE-NAME.
```

After UNSTRING statement execution

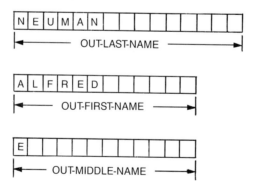

COPY Statement

The COPY statement is used to retrieve COBOL code that has been stored in the COBOL source-statement library. When a file-description, record-description, report-heading format, table, procedure, or other code segment must be used in multiple programs or by various programmers, it is desirable to store them in the source-statement library. Then, when programmers use the COPY statement to obtain the common code for their programs, four objectives are accomplished: (1) repetitious programmer coding is reduced, (2) standardization of data-names and procedures used in the programming installation is promoted, (3) coding errors are minimized, and (4) program revisions are simplified.

The COPY statement format, together with an example, is shown below. Observe that the statements acquired from the library are copied onto the next coding line following the COPY statement and are usually identified by the compiler with a symbol (commonly a "C," as in the example).

Format:

$$\underline{\text{COPY}}\ \text{text-name}\ \left[\ \left\{ \begin{matrix} \underline{\text{OF}} \\ \underline{\text{IN}} \end{matrix} \right\} \text{library-name} \right]$$

$$\left[\ \underline{\text{REPLACING}}\ \left\{ \left\{ \begin{matrix} == \text{pseudo-text} == \\ \text{identifier-1} \\ \text{literal-1} \\ \text{word-1} \end{matrix} \right\}\ \underline{\text{BY}}\ \left\{ \begin{matrix} == \text{pseudo-text-2} == \\ \text{identifier-2} \\ \text{literal-2} \\ \text{word-2} \end{matrix} \right\} \right\} \ldots \right]$$

Example:

Given that the following source statements have been cataloged as a source-statement library entry named NARECORD (notice that the 01-level record-name has been specified in the library as a comment-entry):

```
*01   NA-NAME-AND-ADDRESS-RECORD.
      05   NA-RECORD-CODE            PIC X(2).
      05   NA-NAME                   PIC X(20).
      05   NA-ADDRESS                PIC X(24).
      05   NA-CITY                   PIC X(13).
      05   NA-STATE                  PIC X(2).
      05   NA-ZIP-CODE               PIC X(9).
      05   NA-TELEPHONE-NUMBER       PIC X(10).
```

To incorporate the cataloged source statements into a program, the programmer codes the following statement in the source program:

```
01   NA-CUSTOMER-RECORD.   COPY NARECORD.
```

The following code is included in the source program:

```
    01   NA-CUSTOMER-RECORD.   COPY NARECORD.
C *01   NA-CUSTOMER-RECORD.
C        05   NA-RECORD-CODE            PIC X(2).
C        05   NA-NAME                   PIC X(20).
C        05   NA-ADDRESS                PIC X(24).
C        05   NA-CITY                   PIC X(13).
C        05   NA-STATE                  PIC X(2).
C        05   NA-ZIP-CODE               PIC X(9).
C        05   NA-TELEPHONE-NUMBER       PIC X(10).
```

Notice that the REPLACING phrase permits variations to be made in the copied code. However, some installation standards prohibit use of the REPLACING phrase because its use is counter to the usually desired standardization benefits offered by the COPY statement.

The methods that must be used to store or **catalog** the source statements in the library vary depending upon the operating system of the computer being used.

Many commercial data-processing installations do not use the COBOL source statement library but instead employ a proprietary library program product, such as *Panvalet* or *Librarian*. The proprietary products typically offer disk-storage, change control, and retention benefits. Such products have their own individual syntax.

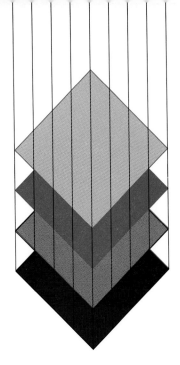

Systems-Name for Selected COBOL Compilers

This appendix presents computer-name and ASSIGN clause implementor-name formation rules for the following COBOL compilers:

- IBM OS/VS COBOL
- IBM DOS/VSE COBOL
- IBM Personal Computer COBOL by Microsoft
- DEC VAX COBOL
- HP COBOL-II/3000

IBM OS/VS COBOL

Computer-name (in ENVIRONMENT DIVISION SOURCE-COMPUTER and OBJECT-COMPUTER paragraphs)

Computer-name is a system-name of the form **IBM-*nnnn*** where *nnnn* identifies a three- or four-digit IBM mainframe model number.

Examples: SOURCE-COMPUTER. IBM 370.
OBJECT-COMPUTER. IBM-3081.

ASSIGN clause (in ENVIRONMENT DIVISION file-control entry)

<u>ASSIGN</u> to assignment-name

Assignment-name is formed in accordance with the class of file as follows:

- Physical sequential files (the type of file covered in this text): **[comments-] [S-] name**
- VSAM sequential files (not covered in this text): **[comments-] AS-name**
- VSAM indexed or relative files (not covered in this text): **[comments-] name**

The **comments** entry is optional, but is traditionally coded as it was originally required for earlier compiler versions:

- **UT** for utility (typically used for sequential input and output files)

- **UR** for unit record (seldom coded)

- **DA** for disk (typically used for direct-access disk files, which are not covered in this text)

The class **S** indicates a physical sequential file. It is an optional entry, but is traditionally coded because it was required for earlier compiler versions.

The **name** can contain up to eight characters. It can be composed of the letters A through Z and the numbers 0 through 9; the first character must be alphabetic.

Examples: ASSIGN TO UT-S-INFILE.
ASSIGN TO UT-S-PRTFILE.

IBM DOS/VSE COBOL

Computer-name (in ENVIRONMENT DIVISION SOURCE-COMPUTER and OBJECT-COMPUTER paragraphs)

Computer-name is a system-name of the form **IBM-*nnnn*** where *nnnn* identifies a three- or four-digit IBM mainframe model number.

Examples: SOURCE-COMPUTER. IBM-370.
OBJECT-COMPUTER. IBM-4341.

ASSIGN clause (in ENVIRONMENT DIVISION file-control entry)

<u>ASSIGN</u> to assignment-name

Assignment-name is of the form **SYS*nnn*-class-device-organization[-name]** where:

- *nnn* is a three-digit number from 000 through 240 inclusive. This field represents the symbolic unit to which the file is assigned.

- **class** indicates the device class and must be one of the following two-character abbreviations:

  UT for utility (typically used for sequential input files)
  UR for unit record (typically used for printer files)
  DA for disk (typically used for direct-access disk files, which are not covered in this text)

- **device** is a four- or five-character field that represents an IBM I/0 device number within the three device classes listed above. Present device numbers are as follows:

UT	UR		DA
2400	1442R	3211	2311
2311	1442P	3504	2314
2314	1403	3505	2319
2319	1404	3525R	3330
3330	1443	3525P	3340
3340	2501	3525W	3350
3350	2520R	3525M	3375
3375	2520P	3881	3540
3410	2540R	3203	FBA1
3420	2540P	5203	
3540	2560R	5425	
FBA1	2560P		
	2560W		

Note: R = reader
P = punch
W = printer
M = multiple line printer

- **organization** is a one-character field that identifies the file organization. For sequentially organized files—the only type covered in this text—the letter S is specified.

- **name** is a three- through seven-character field that identifies the external-name by which the file is known to the DOX/VSE operating system. It can be composed of the letters A through Z and the numbers 0 through 9; the first character must be alphabetic.

If this name field is coded, it must match the file-name specified in the filename field of the VOL, DLBL, or TLBL job control language statement. If not coded, the symbolic unit (SYS*nnn*) is used as the external-name. (The name field must be coded if more than one file is assigned to the same symbolic unit).

Examples: ASSIGN TO SYS012-UR-2501-S.
ASSIGN TO SYS014-UR-1403-S.
ASSIGN TO SYS001-UTFBA1-S-FILEOUT.

IBM Personal Computer COBOL by Microsoft

Computer-name (in ENVIRONMENT DIVISION SOURCE-COMPUTER and OBJECT-COMPUTER paragraphs)

Computer-name is a comments-entry.

Examples: SOURCE-COMPUTER. IBM-PERSONAL-COMPUTER.
OBJECT-COMPUTER. IBM-PC.

ASSIGN clause (in ENVIRONMENT DIVISION file-control entry)

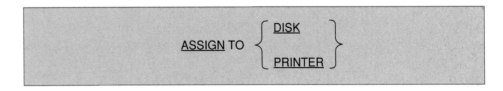

Either the system-name DISK or PRINTER must be chosen.

Examples: ASSIGN TO DISK.
ASSIGN TO PRINTER.

DEC VAX COBOL

Computer-name (in ENVIRONMENT DIVISION SOURCE-COMPUTER and OBJECT-COMPUTER paragraphs)

Computer-name is either a system-name of VAX-11 or a user-defined word.

Examples: SOURCE-COMPUTER. VAX-11.
OBJECT-COMPUTER. VAX11-735.

ASSIGN clause (in ENVIRONMENT DIVISION file-control entry)

ASSIGN to file-spec

File-spec is a nonnumeric literal of eight characters or less (enclosed in quotes) or a COBOL word formed according to the rules for user-defined names. It represents a partial or a complete file specification.

> Examples: ASSIGN TO "INFILE".
> ASSIGN TO SYS$OUTPUT

HP COBOL-II/3000

Computer-name (in ENVIRONMENT DIVISION SOURCE-COMPUTER and OBJECT-COMPUTER paragraphs)

Computer-name is a user-defined word with the restriction that the first character be alphabetic.

> Examples: SOURCE-COMPUTER. HP-3000.
> OBJECT-COMPUTER. HP-3000/64.

ASSIGN clause (in ENVIRONMENT DIVISION file-control entry)

ASSIGN to name

Name is the MPE file designator of the form **file/lockword.group.account,** and is coded as follows:

- **file** name is an MPE formal file designator. It may contain up to eight alphabetic or numeric characters; it must begin with an alphabetic character. The MPE designators $STDIN and $STDLIST may be used for standard input and standard list devices, respectively.

- **lockword** is specified if a lockword is assigned to the file.

- **group** must be specified if the file resides in a group other than your own. (However, you must be granted access to this group.)

- **account** must be specified if the file has an account other than your own. (However, you must be granted access to this account.)

> Examples: ASSIGN TO "INFILE".
> ASSIGN TO $STDLIST

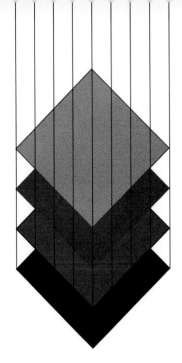

Program Interruptions for IBM OS and DOS Systems

With computers running IBM OS and DOS operating systems (IBM-370 system architecture), certain program interruptions will occur. Such an interruption is commonly referred to as an **abnormal ending** and nicknamed an **abend** (pronounced **AB**-end). An abend causes the system to terminate program processing and to cancel the program.

Two general types of program interruptions are (1) program checks and (2) other interruptions.

Program checks are the same for both the OS and DOS operating systems; the other interruptions are different for the two operating systems. This appendix covers program checks (that apply to both OS and DOS) and other interruptions for OS.

Program Checks

The IBM-370 system architecture diagnoses each machine-language instruction and the results of certain arithmetic operations to ensure that incorrect processing does not occur. When an obviously incorrect instruction is provided for execution (such as one containing an invalid operation code or an out-of-range storage address), a **program check** occurs.

There are 15 types of program checks as shown in Figure AD.1. With COBOL programs, most of them are seldom encountered. Those that occur most frequently are discussed below.

(The OS operating system assigns a three-digit system completion code to each program interruption. The OS system completion code is shown in parentheses after the name of each program check.)

Operation Exception (OC1)

COBOL programs that contain certain logic errors will trigger operation exceptions. Following are some typical causes:

- Attempting to READ or WRITE a file before it has been opened or after it has been closed.

- Failure to CLOSE files before the STOP RUN statement is executed.

- The identifier field of the AFTER ADVANCING phrase of the WRITE statement contains a value outside the range of permissible values (should be 0 to 99).

- Missing JCL statement for a file.

Protection Exception (OC4)

Although this error does not normally occur with COBOL programs on account boundary-protection errors, it may occur because of the following programming errors:

- Subscript or index not initialized prior to use.

- Incorrect ASSIGN clause system-name.

■ Assign clause system-name does not match the JCL statement system-name.

■ Missing JCL statement for a file.

■ Attempting to READ an unopened input file.

Addressing and Specification Exceptions (OC5 and OC6)

One of these exceptions may occur when one of the following programming errors is made:

■ Incorrect value in a subscript or index.

■ Improper exit from a performed procedure.

■ Attempting to refer to a field of an input record that is defined within the FILE section after the AT END phrase of the READ statement has been executed.

■ Attempting to refer to a field of an output record that is defined within the FILE section before the OPEN statement has been executed.

Figure AD. 1
Program interruptions.

Exception	Completion code (OS)	Cause
Operation	OC1	The computer has attempted to execute an invalid operation code.
Privileged-operation	OC2	An application program has requested the computer to execute an operation code that only the operating system supervisor program is permitted to execute.
Execute	OC3	Will not normally occur with a COBOL program.
Protection	OC4	The program has attempted to access or move data to an area of storage that does not belong to the program.
Addressing	OC5	The program has attempted to reference an address beyond the limit of the computer's physical storage.
Specification	OC6	A machine-language instruction address is invalid.
Data	OC7	The program has requested that a decimal arithmetic operation be performed on data that is not numeric.
Fixed-point-overflow	OC8	A calculated binary value is too large to be contained within a register.
Fixed-point-divide	OC9	The program has attempted to divide a binary field by zero or the quotient exceeds the register size.
Decimal-overflow	OCA	A calculated packed-decimal value is too large to be contained within the result field.
Decimal-divide	OCB	The program has attempted to divide a packed-decimal field by zero or the quotient exceeds the register size.
Exponent-overflow	OCC	Will not normally occur with a COBOL program.
Exponent-underflow	OCD	Will not normally occur with a COBOL program.
Significance	OCE	Will not normally occur with a COBOL program.
Floating-point	OCF	Will not normally occur with a COBOL program.

Data Exception (OC7)

This is probably the most commonly encountered program check and one that generally haunts beginning programmers. Its cause is simple: attempting to operate numerically on nonnumeric data with decimal arithmetic instructions. Fields that are being processed by decimal arithmetic instructions must contain a valid digit (0 through 9) in each digit position of the field, and a valid sign (plus, minus, unsigned assumed positive, or unsigned) in the sign position.

There are two general situations in which a data exception will occur.

The first situation is one in which the WORKING-STORAGE field is not initialized before it is used in the program. When the program begins, fields that are not properly initialized by VALUE clauses or PROCEDURE DIVISION statements contain either unpredictable values or, depending upon the operating system, binary zeros. (Binary zeros do not contain a valid decimal arithmetic sign.) Therefore, if the programmer neglects to initialize or improperly initializes a decimal arithmetic field, the field will probably contain data that is not valid for the decimal arithmetic instructions. Thus a data exception will occur.

A second situation is one in which input data is read into a program that does not contain decimal numeric data in a field that is specified with the picture symbol 9. For example, if a quantity field is input with blank spaces, a data exception will occur if the program attempts to ADD or otherwise operate numerically on those blank spaces with decimal arithmetic instructions.

The first situation described above is generally detected early in program testing. However, the second situation—because it is usually caused by input errors rather than programming errors—can happen long after a program has been tested and put into production unless proper validation of each input field is provided at some point in the program processing. This is why data validation programs are so important.

Note that errors in field specifications can also cause the second type of data exception. That is, if a 5-digit quantity field is defined as S9(6), a data exception may well result.

The COBOL programmer should recognize that, since COBOL uses arithmetic instructions for certain other verbs, a data exception can occur with the following statements:

- Arithmetic statements (ADD, SUBTRACT, MULTIPLY, DIVIDE, and COMPUTE) that operate on DISPLAY or COMP-3 fields.

- IF statement relation and condition-name conditions in which both the subject and object fields are numeric (and both are not of COMP usage).

- IF statement sign conditions in which the subject field is of DISPLAY or COMP-3 usage.

- MOVE statements from a DISPLAY or COMP-3 field to a COMP-3 or COMP field.

- MOVE statements to a numeric-edited field.

Following is a checklist of common data-exception causes:

- A numeric field was not initialized before it was used.

- A numeric field was incorrectly initialized.

  a. Moving ZEROS to a group field will produce invalid data for COMP and COMP-3 fields within the group, (ZEROS must be moved to the elementary COMP and COMP-3 fields.)

  b. Moving SPACES to either a group or elementary numeric field will produce invalid data for numeric fields.

  c. Moving 0 (a literal of a single zero) to a group field will produce invalid data for COMP and COMP-3 fields within the group. (This causes one zero to be moved to the first position of the group field and the remainder of the positions are padded with blank spaces.)

  d. Moving LOW-VALUES or HIGH-VALUES to a DISPLAY or COMP-3 field will produce invalid numeric data.

- A subscript or index was not initialized.

- A subscript or index contains an incorrect value.

  a. zero

  b. a negative number

  c. a number greater than the number of table-entry occurrences

- Invalid data was read into a numeric field.

  a. blank spaces

  b. certain nonnumeric characters

- Incorrect record-descriptions and/or data-item descriptions.

  a. wrong length specifications

  b. wrong usage specifications

Overflow Exceptions (OC8 and OCA)

This exception may occur if the result of a calculation exceeds the size of a register or the result field (and the statement does not contain an ON SIZE ERROR phrase). However, COBOL will normally not cause this interruption to be triggered with DISPLAY or COMP-3 fields. Instead, a result that is too long to be contained in the answer field will be truncated. The overflow error will not be identified (unless the ON SIZE ERROR phrase is specified).

Divide Exception (OC9 AND OCB)

According to the rules of mathematics, it is impossible to divide by zero. Thus, if a divisor field contains zero and a DIVIDE operation (without an ON SIZE ERROR phrase) is executed, a divide exception occurs. Before each DIVIDE statement, it is a good practice to validate the divisor field to ensure that it does not contain a zero. If the divisor field does contain a zero, either the DIVIDE statement should not be executed or, depending upon desired handling, the divisor should be changed to a value of 1. Such processing will eliminate divide exceptions.

Other Exceptions

When errors in subscript or index handling cause program data to overlay program instructions in storage, practically any program interruption can occur. In such cases, the type of program interruption that is identified is probably not meaningful.

Other Interruptions (OS)

Although there are numerous other interruptions, those system completion codes that the beginning COBOL programmer might encounter are discussed below.

I/O Error (001 through 008)

Completion codes that begin with two zeros (00x) indicate an I/O error. The error can be caused by either hardware malfunctions or coding mistakes. For beginning programmers and during the testing phase of program development, the usual problem—especially with completion codes 001, 002, and 004—is due to COBOL or JCL inconsistencies rather than hardware malfunctions. Common problems are summarized on the following page.

A wrong-length record has been read.

A record may erroneously be considered the wrong length if one or more of the following COBOL or JCL coding errors occurred.

■ The logical record length is incorrectly specified in the RECORD CONTAINS clause of the FD entry and/or the data-item description entries within a record-description entry.

■ The block length is incorrectly specified in the BLOCK CONTAINS clause of the FD entry.

■ The LRECL (logical record length) subparameter is coded in the DD statement and is incorrectly specified.

■ The BLKSIZE (block size) subparameter is coded in the DD statement and is incorrectly specified.

An attempt has been made to read beyond the end-of-file marker.

This might occur due to one of the following coding errors within the COBOL program.

■ A READ statement is incorrectly placed.

■ A program bug exists that causes a READ statement to be repeatedly executed.

■ The end-of-file switch is not properly set to indicate the end-of-file condition.

Reference has been made to a record or field within the FILE SECTION before the file has been opened or after the file has been closed.

This might occur due to one of the following coding errors within the COBOL program.

■ An OPEN or CLOSE statement is misplaced.

■ A MOVE statement exists that references a field within the FILE SECTION before the file is opened or after the file has been closed.

Unsuccessful Open (013 and 213)

File opening problems are identified by completion codes that end with 13 (xl3). Common problems are listed below.

Completion code 013.

The member-name specified for a partitioned data-set is not present within the PDS.

Check to ensure that both the data-set name and the member-name are correctly coded in the DSNAME parameter of the DD statement.

There is conflicting data-set control block information.

Information does not match between the program, the DCB (data-set control block) parameter of the DD statement, the data-set label, and/or the facilities generated for the operating system. Typical errors are as follows:

- The COBOL program specified BLOCK CONTAINS 0 RECORDS for an output file but no BLKSIZE subparameter was specified in the DCB parameter of the DD statement for the file.

- The BLKSIZE specified in the DCB parameter of the DD statement is not a multiple of the logical record length.

- The record format is fixed unblocked (either (1) no BLOCK CONTAINS clause is coded within the FD entry, or (2) the DCB parameter of the DD statement is coded RECFM=F) and the block length is not equal to the record length. (That is, the DCB parameter of the DD statement is specified with a BLKSIZE value that is not equal to either (1) the record length specified in the COBOL program, or (2) the LRECL value coded in the DCB.)

- The block length is greater than 32,767 bytes.

Completion code 213.

The file cannot be found.

This might be caused by one of the following:

- The data-set name is misspelled in the DSNAME parameter of the DD statement.

- A specific VOLUME was not specified and the data-set was not cataloged.

- The wrong volume is specified in the VOLUME parameter of the DD statement.

- The data set was inadvertently deleted, not cataloged, or uncataloged.

Job Cancelled (122, 222, 322, 522, and 722)

Completion codes that end in 22 (x22) signify that the job was cancelled.

Completion code 122: Job cancelled by operator (with dump).
When the computer operator cancels a job and requests a dump, completion code 122 is issued. Probable causes for an operator cancellation are as follows:

- The program is producing output (such as a high-volume of what appears to be repeated data) which leads the operator to believe that the program is in an endless loop.

- The operator was asked to mount a tape or disk volume which does not exist.

- The operator made a mistake and erroneously cancelled the job.

- Hardware resources were not available at the time the job was run.

- Resources are required for another purpose (such as to run a top-priority job or to perform maintenance).

- An attempt was made to read a nonlabeled tape as a tape with standard labels or vice versa.

Completion code 222: Job cancelled by operator (without dump). Completion code 222 is issued when the computer operator cancels a job but does not request a dump. Probable causes for the cancellation are the same as those listed above for completion code 122.

Completion code 322: Allotted time exceeded. When the execution time for a job or job step exceeds the time allotted, the system automatically cancels the job. Either the program contains a bug or the time allotment is insufficient for that particular run.

The program contains a bug.

Check the program for an endless loop.

The time allotment is insufficient.

An insufficient run time has been allotted by either a TIME parameter (in the JOB and/or EXEC statements) or by a default time limit specified in the job entry subsystem. (Remember that the TIME specified in the JOB statement for the complete job will override that specified in the EXEC statement for a particular step.) Increase the TIME value(s).

Completion code 522: Wait state limit exceeded. The system automatically cancels the job when a job step is in a wait state for more than 30 minutes. The typical cause for this occurrence is that the operator has failed to respond to a system request, such as to mount a volume.

Completion code 722: Output exceeds limits. When the number of output print or punch records exceeds the limit value, the system automatically cancels the job. The output record limit is specified in the OUTLIM parameter of the DD statement or, if not specified, the installation default value is used. A program bug in which a WRITE statement repeatedly gets executed is a common cause for the generation of excessive output.

Storage Unavailable (80A, 90A, and A78)

Storage problems are summarized below.

Completion code 80A: Insufficient storage. Completion code 80A is issued when more main or virtual storage is required than was available. This means that the REGION parameter of the JOB and/or EXEC statement(s) must either be specified with or increased to the required amount.

Completion code 90A and A78: Unable to release storage. These completion codes are issued when an attempt is made to release main storage that is not attached to the program. One reason for such a problem is an inadvertent attempt—in the COBOL program—to CLOSE an already closed file.

Requested Program Not Found (806)

Completion code 806 is issued when the load module requested in an EXEC statement cannot be found in the system library or in the JOBLIB or STEPLIB library. This might be caused by one of the following problems.

- The load module is not present in the load library.

- The load-module name is misspelled in the EXEC statement.

- The load-library name specified in the DSNAME parameter for a JOBLIB or STEPLIB DD statement is incorrect.

- During COBOL program compilation, failure to include a LKED.SYSLMOD DD statement to save the load module in a permanent load library.

- During COBOL program compilation, failure to specify the correct library-name and/or load-module name in the DSNAME parameter of the LKED.SYSLMOD (system load module) DD statement.

No Space Available on Volume (B37, D37, and E37)

Completion codes ending in 37 (x37) indicate that an output file requires more disk or tape space than is available.

Completion code B37: End of disk or tape volume—no more space available. Code B37 means that all the space has been used on the current volume and one of the following conditions existed.

- The volume could not be demounted (typically because it is a permanently resident volume).

- No additional volumes were specified in the SER, volume count, or REF subparameters of the VOLUME parameter of the DD statement.

- All 15 secondary allocations (specified in the SPACE parameter of the DD statement) were used.

Completion code D37: End of disk volume—no secondary allocation. Code D37 means that the primary allocation of disk space specified in the SPACE parameter of the DD statement was consumed and no secondary allocation was coded.

Completion code E37: End of disk or tape volume—no more volumes available. Code E37 means that additional volumes were required but could not be allocated because one of the following conditions existed.

- No additional volumes were supplied in the SER, volume count, or REF subparameters of the VOLUME parameter of the DD statement.

- For a partitioned data set, there was no additional space on the volume (a PDS must reside on a single volume).

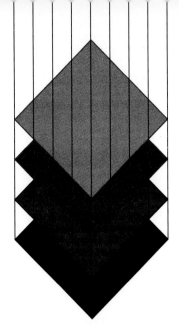

Complete COBOL-74 Language Formats

This appendix contains the composite language formats skeleton of the American National Standard COBOL (1974). It is intended to completely display all COBOL-74 language formats.

General Format for
IDENTIFICATION DIVISION

```
IDENTIFICATION DIVISION.

PROGRAM-ID.  program-name.

[AUTHOR.  [comment-entry ] ... ]

[INSTALLATION.  [comment-entry]  ...]

[DATE-WRITTEN.  [comment-entry]  ...]

[DATE-COMPILED.  [comment-entry]  ...]

[SECURITY.  [comment-entry ] ... ]
```

General Format for
ENVIRONMENT DIVISION

```
ENVIRONMENT DIVISION.

CONFIGURATION SECTION.

SOURCE-COMPUTER.  computer-name [WITH DEBUGGING MODE] .

OBJECT-COMPUTER.  computer-name

     ⎡            ⎧ WORDS      ⎫⎤
     ⎢, MEMORY SIZE integer ⎨ CHARACTERS ⎬⎥
     ⎣            ⎩ MODULES    ⎭⎦

     [, PROGRAM COLLATING SEQUENCE IS alphabet-name]

     [, SEGMENT-LIMIT IS segment-number ] .

[SPECIAL-NAMES.  [, implementor-name
```

$$\left\{ \begin{array}{l} \text{IS mnemonic-name } [\text{, ON STATUS IS condition-name-1 } [\text{, OFF STATUS IS condition-name-2}]] \\ \text{IS mnemonic-name } [\text{, OFF STATUS IS condition-name-2 } [\text{, ON STATUS IS condition-name-1}]] \\ \text{ON STATUS IS condition-name-1 } [\text{, OFF STATUS IS condition-name-2}] \\ \text{OFF STATUS IS condition-name-2 } [\text{, ON STATUS IS condition-name-1}] \end{array} \right\} \dots$$

$$\left[\text{, alphabet-name IS} \left\{ \begin{array}{l} \underline{STANDARD-1} \\ \underline{NATIVE} \\ \text{implementor-name} \\ \text{literal-1} \left[\left\{ \begin{array}{l} \underline{THROUGH} \\ \underline{THRU} \end{array} \right\} \text{literal-2} \\ \underline{ALSO} \text{ literal-3 } [, \underline{ALSO} \text{ literal-4}]\dots \right] \\ \left[\text{literal-5} \left[\left\{ \begin{array}{l} \underline{THROUGH} \\ \underline{THRU} \end{array} \right\} \text{literal-6} \\ \underline{ALSO} \text{ literal-7 } [, \underline{ALSO} \text{ literal-8}]\dots \right] \right] \end{array} \right\} \dots \right]$$

```
[, CURRENCY SIGN IS literal-9]
```

```
[, DECIMAL-POINT IS COMMA ] . ]

[INPUT-OUTPUT SECTION.

 FILE-CONTROL.

    {file-control-entry} ...

[I-O-CONTROL.
   ┌                                                                    ┐
   │ ; RERUN  ┌ ON  {file-name-1         }                             │
   │          └     {implementor-name}                                 │
   │                      ┌ ┌           ┌ REEL ┐ ┐                    │
   │                      │ │ [END OF]  │ UNIT │ │                    │
   │              EVERY   ┤ ┤           └      ┘ ├ OF file-name-2 ├ ...│
   │                      │ │ integer-1 RECORDS │ │                    │
   │                      │ integer-2 CLOCK-UNITS                      │
   │                      └ condition-name       ┘                    │
   └                                                                    ┘
   ┌           ┌ RECORD     ┐                                    ┐
   │ ; SAME    │ SORT       │ AREA FOR file-name-3 {, file-name-4} ... │ ...
   │           └ SORT-MERGE ┘                                    ┘
   ┌                                                                      ┐
   │ ; MULTIPLE FILE TAPE CONTAINS file-name-5 [ POSITION integer-3]     │
   │      [, file-name-6 [ POSITION integer-4]] ...  ] ...    . ]]
```

General Format for FILE-CONTROL Entry

FORMAT 1:

```
SELECT [OPTIONAL]  file-name

   ASSIGN TO implementor-name-1 [, implementor-name-2 ] ...

   ┌                    ┌ AREA  ┐ ┐
   │ ; RESERVE integer-1 │ AREAS │ │
   └                    └       ┘ ┘

   [; ORGANIZATION IS SEQUENTIAL ]

   [; ACCESS MODE IS SEQUENTIAL ]

   [; FILE STATUS IS data-name-1 ] .
```

FORMAT 2:

```
SELECT file-name

   ASSIGN TO implementor-name-1 [, implementor-name-2 ] ...

   ┌                    ┌ AREA  ┐ ┐
   │ ; RESERVE integer-1 │ AREAS │ │
   └                    └       ┘ ┘

   ; ORGANIZATION IS RELATIVE

   ┌                      ┌                                            ┐ ┐
   │ ; ACCESS MODE IS     │ SEQUENTIAL  [, RELATIVE KEY IS data-name-1]│ │
   │                      ┤ ┌ RANDOM  ┐                               ├ │
   │                      │ │ DYNAMIC │  , RELATIVE KEY IS data-name-1 │ │
   └                      └ └         ┘                               ┘ ┘

   [; FILE STATUS IS data-name-2 ] .
```

FORMAT 3:

```
SELECT file-name

   ASSIGN TO implementor-name-1 [, implementor-name-2 ] ...

   ┌                    ┌ AREA  ┐ ┐
   │ ; RESERVE integer-1 │ AREAS │ │
   └                    └       ┘ ┘

   ; ORGANIZATION IS INDEXED

   ┌                      ┌ SEQUENTIAL ┐ ┐
   │ ; ACCESS MODE IS     │ RANDOM     │ │
   │                      │ DYNAMIC    │ │
   └                      └            ┘ ┘
```

; <u>RECORD</u> KEY IS data-name-1

[; <u>ALTERNATE RECORD</u> KEY IS data-name-2 [WITH <u>DUPLICATES</u>]] ...

[; FILE <u>STATUS</u> IS data-name-3] .

FORMAT 4:

<u>SELECT</u> file-name <u>ASSIGN</u> TO implementor-name-1 [, implementor-name-2] ...

General Format for DATA DIVISION

<u>DATA</u> <u>DIVISION</u>.

[<u>FILE</u> <u>SECTION</u>.

[<u>FD</u> file-name

    [; <u>BLOCK</u> CONTAINS [integer-1 <u>TO</u>] integer-2 $\left\{\begin{array}{l}\underline{\text{RECORDS}}\\ \text{CHARACTERS}\end{array}\right\}$]

    [; <u>RECORD</u> CONTAINS [integer-3 <u>TO</u>] integer-4 CHARACTERS]

    ; <u>LABEL</u> $\left\{\begin{array}{l}\underline{\text{RECORD}}\text{ IS}\\ \underline{\text{RECORDS}}\text{ ARE}\end{array}\right\}$ $\left\{\begin{array}{l}\underline{\text{STANDARD}}\\ \underline{\text{OMITTED}}\end{array}\right\}$

    [; <u>VALUE</u> <u>OF</u> implementor-name-1 IS $\left\{\begin{array}{l}\text{data-name-1}\\ \text{literal-1}\end{array}\right\}$

        [, implementor-name-2 IS $\left\{\begin{array}{l}\text{data-name-2}\\ \text{literal-2}\end{array}\right\}$] ...]

    [; <u>DATA</u> $\left\{\begin{array}{l}\underline{\text{RECORD}}\text{ IS}\\ \underline{\text{RECORDS}}\text{ ARE}\end{array}\right\}$ data-name-3 [, data-name-4] ...]

    [; <u>LINAGE</u> IS $\left\{\begin{array}{l}\text{data-name-5}\\ \text{integer-5}\end{array}\right\}$ LINES [, WITH <u>FOOTING</u> AT $\left\{\begin{array}{l}\text{data-name-6}\\ \text{integer-6}\end{array}\right\}$]

        [, LINES AT <u>TOP</u> $\left\{\begin{array}{l}\text{data-name-7}\\ \text{integer-7}\end{array}\right\}$] [, LINES AT <u>BOTTOM</u> $\left\{\begin{array}{l}\text{data-name-8}\\ \text{integer-8}\end{array}\right\}$]]

    [; <u>CODE-SET</u> IS alphabet-name]

    [; $\left\{\begin{array}{l}\underline{\text{REPORT}}\text{ IS}\\ \underline{\text{REPORTS}}\text{ ARE}\end{array}\right\}$ report-name-1 [, report-name-2] ...].

[record-description-entry] ...] ...

[<u>SD</u> file-name

    [; <u>RECORD</u> CONTAINS [integer-1 <u>TO</u>] integer-2 CHARACTERS]

    [; <u>DATA</u> $\left\{\begin{array}{l}\underline{\text{RECORD}}\text{ IS}\\ \underline{\text{RECORDS}}\text{ ARE}\end{array}\right\}$ data-name-1 [, data-name-2] ...] .

{record-description-entry} ...] ...]

[<u>WORKING-STORAGE</u> SECTION.

$\left[\begin{array}{l}\text{77-level-description-entry}\\ \text{record-description-entry}\end{array}\right]$ ...]

[<u>LINKAGE</u> SECTION.

$\left[\begin{array}{l}\text{77-level-description-entry}\\ \text{record-description-entry}\end{array}\right]$ ...]

[<u>COMMUNICATION</u> SECTION.

[communication-description-entry

[record-description-entry] ...] ...]

```
[REPORT SECTION.

[RD   report-name

    [;  CODE literal-1]

    [;  {CONTROL IS  }  {data-name-1 [, data-name-2] ...          }]
        {CONTROLS ARE}  {FINAL [, data-name-1 [, data-name-2] ...])}

    [;  PAGE  [LIMIT IS  ]  integer-1  [LINE ]  [, HEADING integer-2]
              [LIMITS ARE]             [LINES]

         [, FIRST DETAIL integer-3]  [, LAST DETAIL integer-4]

         [, FOOTING integer-5 ] ].

{report-group-description-entry } ... ] ... ]
```

General Format for Data   *FORMAT 1:*
Description Entry

```
level-number  {data-name-1}
              {FILLER     }

    [;  REDEFINES data-name-2]

    [;  {PICTURE}  IS character-string]
        {PIC    }

    [;  [USAGE IS]  {COMPUTATIONAL}]
                    {COMP         }
                    {DISPLAY      }
                    {INDEX        }

    [;  [SIGN IS]  {LEADING }  [SEPARATE CHARACTER]]
                   {TRAILING}

    [;  OCCURS  {integer-1 TO integer-2 TIMES DEPENDING ON data-name-3}
                {integer-2 TIMES                                       }

         [{ASCENDING }  KEY IS data-name-4  [, data-name-5] ... ] ...
          {DESCENDING}

         [INDEXED BY index-name-1  [, index-name-2] ... ]]

    [;  {SYNCHRONIZED}  [LEFT ]]
        {SYNC        }   [RIGHT]

    [;  {JUSTIFIED}  RIGHT]
        {JUST     }

    [;  BLANK WHEN ZERO ]

    [;  VALUE IS literal ] .
```

FORMAT 2:

```
66  data-name-1; RENAMES data-name-2  [{THROUGH}  data-name-3 ] .
                                       {THRU   }
```

FORMAT 3:

```
88  condition-name;  {VALUE IS  }  literal-1  [{THROUGH}  literal-2]
                     {VALUES ARE}               {THRU   }

    [, literal-3  [{THROUGH}  literal-4 ]] ...  .
                   {THRU   }
```

General Format for
Communication
Description Entry

FORMAT 1:

CD cd-name;

$$\left[\begin{array}{l} \left[; \text{ SYMBOLIC } \underline{\text{QUEUE}} \text{ IS data-name-1}\right] \\ \quad\left[; \text{ SYMBOLIC } \underline{\text{SUB-QUEUE-1}} \text{ IS data-name-2}\right] \\ \quad\quad\left[; \text{ SYMBOLIC } \underline{\text{SUB-QUEUE-2}} \text{ IS data-name-3}\right] \\ \quad\quad\left[; \text{ SYMBOLIC } \underline{\text{SUB-QUEUE-3}} \text{ IS data-name-4}\right] \\ \quad\quad\left[; \underline{\text{MESSAGE }}\underline{\text{DATE}} \text{ IS data-name-5}\right] \\ \text{FOR } \left[\underline{\text{INITIAL}}\right] \underline{\text{INPUT}} \quad\left[; \underline{\text{MESSAGE }}\underline{\text{TIME}} \text{ IS data-name-6}\right] \\ \quad\quad\left[; \text{ SYMBOLIC } \underline{\text{SOURCE}} \text{ IS data-name-7}\right] \\ \quad\quad\left[; \underline{\text{TEXT }}\underline{\text{LENGTH}} \text{ IS data-name-8}\right] \\ \quad\quad\left[; \underline{\text{END }}\underline{\text{KEY}} \text{ IS data-name-9}\right] \\ \quad\quad\left[; \underline{\text{STATUS }}\underline{\text{KEY}} \text{ IS data-name-10}\right] \\ \quad\quad\left[; \text{ MESSAGE } \underline{\text{COUNT}} \text{ IS data-name-11}\right] \\ \left[\text{data-name-1, data-name-2, ..., data-name-11}\right] \end{array}\right]$$

FORMAT 2:

CD cd-name; FOR <u>OUTPUT</u>

$\left[; \underline{\text{DESTINATION }}\underline{\text{COUNT}} \text{ IS data-name-1}\right]$

$\left[; \underline{\text{TEXT }}\underline{\text{LENGTH}} \text{ IS data-name-2}\right]$

$\left[; \underline{\text{STATUS }}\underline{\text{KEY}} \text{ IS data-name-3}\right]$

$\left[; \underline{\text{DESTINATION }}\underline{\text{TABLE }}\underline{\text{OCCURS}} \text{ integer-2 TIMES}\right.$

$\quad\quad\left.\left[; \underline{\text{INDEXED}} \text{ BY index-name-1 } \left[, \text{ index-name-2}\right]...\right]\right]$

$\left[; \underline{\text{ERROR }}\underline{\text{KEY}} \text{ IS data-name-4}\right]$

$\left[; \text{ SYMBOLIC } \underline{\text{DESTINATION}} \text{ IS data-name-5}\right]$.

General Format for Report
Group Description Entry

FORMAT 1:

01 $\left[\text{data-name-1}\right]$

$\left[; \underline{\text{LINE}} \text{ NUMBER IS } \left\{\begin{array}{l}\text{integer-1 }\left[\text{ON }\underline{\text{NEXT }}\underline{\text{PAGE}}\right]\\ \underline{\text{PLUS}} \text{ integer-2}\end{array}\right\}\right]$

$\left[; \underline{\text{NEXT }}\underline{\text{GROUP}} \text{ IS } \left\{\begin{array}{l}\text{integer-3}\\ \underline{\text{PLUS}} \text{ integer-4}\\ \underline{\text{NEXT }}\underline{\text{PAGE}}\end{array}\right\}\right]$

$; \underline{\text{TYPE}} \text{ IS } \left\{\begin{array}{l}\left\{\begin{array}{l}\underline{\text{REPORT }}\underline{\text{HEADING}}\\ \underline{\text{RH}}\end{array}\right\}\\ \left\{\begin{array}{l}\underline{\text{PAGE }}\underline{\text{HEADING}}\\ \underline{\text{PH}}\end{array}\right\}\\ \left\{\begin{array}{l}\underline{\text{CONTROL }}\underline{\text{HEADING}}\\ \underline{\text{CH}}\end{array}\right\} \left\{\begin{array}{l}\text{data-name-2}\\ \underline{\text{FINAL}}\end{array}\right\}\\ \left\{\begin{array}{l}\underline{\text{DETAIL}}\\ \underline{\text{DE}}\end{array}\right\}\\ \left\{\begin{array}{l}\underline{\text{CONTROL }}\underline{\text{FOOTING}}\\ \underline{\text{CF}}\end{array}\right\} \left\{\begin{array}{l}\text{data-name-3}\\ \underline{\text{FINAL}}\end{array}\right\}\\ \left\{\begin{array}{l}\underline{\text{PAGE }}\underline{\text{FOOTING}}\\ \underline{\text{PF}}\end{array}\right\}\\ \left\{\begin{array}{l}\underline{\text{REPORT }}\underline{\text{FOOTING}}\\ \underline{\text{RF}}\end{array}\right\}\end{array}\right\}$

$\left[; \left[\underline{\text{USAGE}} \text{ IS}\right] \underline{\text{DISPLAY}}\right]$.

FORMAT 2:

```
level-number  [data-name-1]

        [; LINE NUMBER IS  {integer-1 [ON NEXT PAGE]}]
                          {PLUS integer-2          }

        [;  [USAGE IS]  DISPLAY ] .
```

FORMAT 3:

```
level-number  [data-name-1]

        [; BLANK WHEN ZERO]

        [; GROUP INDICATE ]

        [;  {JUSTIFIED}  RIGHT ]
            {JUST    }

        [; LINE NUMBER IS  {integer-1 [ON NEXT PAGE]}]
                          {PLUS integer-2          }

        [; COLUMN NUMBER IS integer-3]

         ;  {PICTURE}  IS character-string
            {PIC    }

        (  ; SOURCE IS identifier-1                           )
        (                                                     )
        (  ; VALUE IS literal                                 )
        {                                                     }
        {  {; SUM identifier-2  [, identifier-3]  ...         } ...
        (                                                     )
        (      [UPON data-name-2  [, data-name-3]  ...]}  ...  )
        (                                                     )
        (      [RESET ON  {data-name-4}]                      )
        (                 {FINAL     }                        )

        [;  [USAGE IS]  DISPLAY ] .
```

General Format for
PROCEDURE DIVISION

FORMAT 1:

```
PROCEDURE DIVISION  [USING data-name-1  [, data-name-2]  ...]  .

[DECLARATIVES.

{section-name SECTION [segment-number]  .  declarative-sentence

[paragraph-name. [sentence]  ...]  ...}  ...

END DECLARATIVES.]

{section-name SECTION [segment-number]  .

[paragraph-name. [sentence]  ...]  ...}  ...
```

FORMAT 2:

```
PROCEDURE DIVISION  [USING data-name-1  [, data-name-2]  ...]  .

{paragraph-name. [sentence]  ...}  ...
```

General Format
for Verbs

ACCEPT identifier [FROM mnemonic-name]

ACCEPT identifier FROM $\begin{Bmatrix} \text{DATE} \\ \text{DAY} \\ \text{TIME} \end{Bmatrix}$

ACCEPT cd-name MESSAGE COUNT

ADD $\begin{Bmatrix} \text{identifier-1} \\ \text{literal-1} \end{Bmatrix}$ $\begin{bmatrix} \text{, identifier-2} \\ \text{, literal-2} \end{bmatrix}$ ... TO identifier-m [ROUNDED]

    [, identifier-n [ROUNDED]] ... [; ON SIZE ERROR imperative-statement]

ADD $\begin{Bmatrix} \text{identifier-1} \\ \text{literal-1} \end{Bmatrix}$, $\begin{Bmatrix} \text{identifier-2} \\ \text{literal-2} \end{Bmatrix}$ $\begin{bmatrix} \text{, identifier-3} \\ \text{, literal-3} \end{bmatrix}$ ...

    GIVING identifier-m [ROUNDED] [, identifier-n [ROUNDED]] ...

    [; ON SIZE ERROR imperative-statement]

ADD $\begin{Bmatrix} \underline{\text{CORRESPONDING}} \\ \underline{\text{CORR}} \end{Bmatrix}$ identifier-1 TO identifier-2 [ROUNDED]

    [; ON SIZE ERROR imperative-statement]

ALTER procedure-name-1 TO [PROCEED TO] procedure-name-2

    [, procedure-name-3 TO [PROCEED TO] procedure-name-4] ...

CALL $\begin{Bmatrix} \text{identifier-1} \\ \text{literal-1} \end{Bmatrix}$ [USING data-name-1 [, data-name-2] ...]

    [; ON OVERFLOW imperative-statement]

CANCEL $\begin{Bmatrix} \text{identifier-1} \\ \text{literal-1} \end{Bmatrix}$ $\begin{bmatrix} \text{, identifier-2} \\ \text{, literal-2} \end{bmatrix}$ ...

CLOSE file-name-1 $\begin{bmatrix} \begin{Bmatrix} \underline{\text{REEL}} \\ \underline{\text{UNIT}} \end{Bmatrix} \begin{bmatrix} \text{WITH NO REWIND} \\ \text{FOR REMOVAL} \end{bmatrix} \\ \text{WITH} \begin{Bmatrix} \text{NO REWIND} \\ \text{LOCK} \end{Bmatrix} \end{bmatrix}$

    $\begin{bmatrix} \text{, file-name-2} \begin{bmatrix} \begin{Bmatrix} \underline{\text{REEL}} \\ \underline{\text{UNIT}} \end{Bmatrix} \begin{bmatrix} \text{WITH NO REWIND} \\ \text{FOR REMOVAL} \end{bmatrix} \\ \text{WITH} \begin{Bmatrix} \text{NO REWIND} \\ \text{LOCK} \end{Bmatrix} \end{bmatrix} \end{bmatrix}$ ...

CLOSE file-name-1 [WITH LOCK] [, file-name-2 [WITH LOCK]] ...

COMPUTE identifier-1 [ROUNDED] [, identifier-2 [ROUNDED]] ...

    = arithmetic-expression [; ON SIZE ERROR imperative-statement]

DELETE file-name RECORD [; INVALID KEY imperative-statement]

DISABLE $\begin{Bmatrix} \text{INPUT} \text{ [TERMINAL]} \\ \text{OUTPUT} \end{Bmatrix}$ cd-name WITH KEY $\begin{Bmatrix} \text{identifier-1} \\ \text{literal-1} \end{Bmatrix}$

DISPLAY $\begin{Bmatrix} \text{identifier-1} \\ \text{literal-1} \end{Bmatrix}$ $\begin{bmatrix} \text{, identifier-2} \\ \text{, literal-2} \end{bmatrix}$ ... [UPON mnemonic-name]

DIVIDE $\begin{Bmatrix} \text{identifier-1} \\ \text{literal-1} \end{Bmatrix}$ INTO identifier-2 [ROUNDED]

    [, identifier-3 [ROUNDED]] ... [; ON SIZE ERROR imperative-statement]

DIVIDE $\begin{Bmatrix} \text{identifier-1} \\ \text{literal-1} \end{Bmatrix}$ INTO $\begin{Bmatrix} \text{identifier-2} \\ \text{literal-2} \end{Bmatrix}$ GIVING identifier-3 [ROUNDED]

    [, identifier-4 [ROUNDED]] ... [; ON SIZE ERROR imperative-statement]

DIVIDE $\begin{Bmatrix} \text{identifier-1} \\ \text{literal-1} \end{Bmatrix}$ BY $\begin{Bmatrix} \text{identifier-2} \\ \text{literal-2} \end{Bmatrix}$ GIVING identifier-3 [ROUNDED]

    [, identifier-4 [ROUNDED]] ... [; ON SIZE ERROR imperative-statement]

DIVIDE $\begin{Bmatrix} \text{identifier-1} \\ \text{literal-1} \end{Bmatrix}$ INTO $\begin{Bmatrix} \text{identifier-2} \\ \text{literal-2} \end{Bmatrix}$ GIVING identifier-3 [ROUNDED]

REMAINDER identifier-4 [; ON SIZE ERROR imperative-statement]

DIVIDE $\begin{Bmatrix} \text{identifier-1} \\ \text{literal-1} \end{Bmatrix}$ BY $\begin{Bmatrix} \text{identifier-2} \\ \text{literal-2} \end{Bmatrix}$ GIVING identifier-3 [ROUNDED]

REMAINDER identifier-4 [; ON SIZE ERROR imperative-statement]

ENABLE $\begin{Bmatrix} \text{INPUT} \ [\text{TERMINAL}] \\ \text{OUTPUT} \end{Bmatrix}$ cd-name WITH KEY $\begin{Bmatrix} \text{identifier-1} \\ \text{literal-1} \end{Bmatrix}$

ENTER language-name [routine-name] .

EXIT [PROGRAM] .

GENERATE $\begin{Bmatrix} \text{data-name} \\ \text{report-name} \end{Bmatrix}$

GO TO [procedure-name-1]

GO TO procedure-name-1 [, procedure-name-2] ... , procedure-name-n

DEPENDING ON identifier

IF condition; $\begin{Bmatrix} \text{statement-1} \\ \text{NEXT SENTENCE} \end{Bmatrix}$ $\begin{Bmatrix} \text{; ELSE statement-2} \\ \text{; ELSE NEXT SENTENCE} \end{Bmatrix}$

INITIATE report-name-1 [, report-name-2] ...

INSPECT identifier-1 TALLYING

$\left\{ \text{, identifier-2 FOR} \left\{ \left\{ \begin{matrix} \underline{\text{ALL}} \\ \underline{\text{LEADING}} \\ \underline{\text{CHARACTERS}} \end{matrix} \right\} \begin{Bmatrix} \text{identifier-3} \\ \text{literal-1} \end{Bmatrix} \right\} \left[\begin{Bmatrix} \underline{\text{BEFORE}} \\ \underline{\text{AFTER}} \end{Bmatrix} \text{INITIAL} \begin{Bmatrix} \text{identifier-4} \\ \text{literal-2} \end{Bmatrix} \right] \right\} ... \right\} ...$

INSPECT identifier-1 REPLACING

$\left\{ \begin{matrix} \underline{\text{CHARACTERS}} \ \underline{\text{BY}} \begin{Bmatrix} \text{identifier-6} \\ \text{literal-4} \end{Bmatrix} \left[\begin{Bmatrix} \underline{\text{BEFORE}} \\ \underline{\text{AFTER}} \end{Bmatrix} \text{INITIAL} \begin{Bmatrix} \text{identifier-7} \\ \text{literal-5} \end{Bmatrix} \right] \\ \left\{ , \begin{Bmatrix} \underline{\text{ALL}} \\ \underline{\text{LEADING}} \\ \underline{\text{FIRST}} \end{Bmatrix} \right\} \left\{ , \begin{Bmatrix} \text{identifier-5} \\ \text{literal-3} \end{Bmatrix} \ \underline{\text{BY}} \begin{Bmatrix} \text{identifier-6} \\ \text{literal-4} \end{Bmatrix} \left[\begin{Bmatrix} \underline{\text{BEFORE}} \\ \underline{\text{AFTER}} \end{Bmatrix} \text{INITIAL} \begin{Bmatrix} \text{identifier-7} \\ \text{literal-5} \end{Bmatrix} \right] \right\} ... \end{matrix} \right\} ...$

INSPECT identifier-1 TALLYING

$\left\{ \text{, identifier-2 FOR} \left\{ \left\{ \begin{matrix} \underline{\text{ALL}} \\ \underline{\text{LEADING}} \\ \underline{\text{CHARACTERS}} \end{matrix} \right\} \begin{Bmatrix} \text{identifier-3} \\ \text{literal-1} \end{Bmatrix} \right\} \left[\begin{Bmatrix} \underline{\text{BEFORE}} \\ \underline{\text{AFTER}} \end{Bmatrix} \text{INITIAL} \begin{Bmatrix} \text{identifier-4} \\ \text{literal-2} \end{Bmatrix} \right] \right\} ... \right\} ... .$

REPLACING

$\left\{ \begin{matrix} \underline{\text{CHARACTERS}} \ \underline{\text{BY}} \begin{Bmatrix} \text{identifier-6} \\ \text{literal-4} \end{Bmatrix} \left[\begin{Bmatrix} \underline{\text{BEFORE}} \\ \underline{\text{AFTER}} \end{Bmatrix} \text{INITIAL} \begin{Bmatrix} \text{identifier-7} \\ \text{literal-5} \end{Bmatrix} \right] \\ \left\{ , \begin{Bmatrix} \underline{\text{ALL}} \\ \underline{\text{LEADING}} \\ \underline{\text{FIRST}} \end{Bmatrix} \right\} \left\{ , \begin{Bmatrix} \text{identifier-5} \\ \text{literal-3} \end{Bmatrix} \ \underline{\text{BY}} \begin{Bmatrix} \text{identifier-6} \\ \text{literal-4} \end{Bmatrix} \left[\begin{Bmatrix} \underline{\text{BEFORE}} \\ \underline{\text{AFTER}} \end{Bmatrix} \text{INITIAL} \begin{Bmatrix} \text{identifier-7} \\ \text{literal-5} \end{Bmatrix} \right] \right\} ... \end{matrix} \right\} ...$

MERGE file-name-1 ON $\begin{Bmatrix} \underline{\text{ASCENDING}} \\ \underline{\text{DESCENDING}} \end{Bmatrix}$ KEY data-name-1 [, data-name-2] ...

$\left[\text{ON} \begin{Bmatrix} \underline{\text{ASCENDING}} \\ \underline{\text{DESCENDING}} \end{Bmatrix} \text{KEY data-name-3 [, data-name-4] ...} \right]$ ...

[COLLATING SEQUENCE IS alphabet-name]

USING file-name-2, file-name-3 [, file-name-4] ...

$\left\{ \begin{matrix} \underline{\text{OUTPUT PROCEDURE}} \text{ IS section-name-1} \left[\begin{Bmatrix} \underline{\text{THROUGH}} \\ \underline{\text{THRU}} \end{Bmatrix} \text{ section-name-2} \right] \\ \underline{\text{GIVING}} \text{ file-name-5} \end{matrix} \right\}$

```
MOVE {identifier-1} TO identifier-2 [, identifier-3] ...
     {literal     }

MOVE {CORRESPONDING} identifier-1 TO identifier-2
     {CORR         }

MULTIPLY {identifier-1} BY identifier-2 [ROUNDED]
         {literal-1   }

     [, identifier-3 [ROUNDED]] ... [; ON SIZE ERROR imperative-statement]

MULTIPLY {identifier-1} BY {identifier-2} GIVING identifier-3 [ROUNDED]
         {literal-1   }    {literal-2   }

     [, identifier-4 [ROUNDED]] ... [; ON SIZE ERROR imperative-statement]

      ┌                                                                      ┐
      │ INPUT file-name-1 [REVERSED      ][, file-name-2 [REVERSED      ]]... │
      │                   [WITH NO REWIND]               [WITH NO REWIND]    │
OPEN  │ OUTPUT file-name-3 [WITH NO REWIND][, file-name-4 [WITH NO REWIND]]..│ ...
      │ I-O file-name-5 [, file-name-6] ...                                  │
      │ EXTEND file-name-7 [, file-name-8] ...                               │
      └                                                                      ┘

      ┌                                          ┐
      │ INPUT file-name-1 [, file-name-2] ...    │
OPEN  │ OUTPUT file-name-3 [, file-name-4] ...   │ ...
      │ I-O file-name-5 [, file-name-6] ...      │
      └                                          ┘

PERFORM procedure-name-1 [{THROUGH} procedure-name-2]
                         [{THRU   }                 ]

PERFORM procedure-name-1 [{THROUGH} procedure-name-2] {identifier-1} TIMES
                         [{THRU   }                 ] {integer-1   }

PERFORM procedure-name-1 [{THROUGH} procedure-name-2] UNTIL condition-1
                         [{THRU   }                 ]

PERFORM procedure-name-1 [{THROUGH} procedure-name-2]
                         [{THRU   }                 ]

     VARYING {identifier-2 } FROM {identifier-3 }
             {index-name-1 }      {index-name-2 }
                                  {literal-1    }

          BY {identifier-4} UNTIL condition-1
             {literal-3   }

     [AFTER {identifier-5 } FROM {identifier-6 }
            {index-name-3 }      {index-name-4 }
                                 {literal-3    }

          BY {identifier-7} UNTIL condition-2
             {literal-4   }

     [AFTER {identifier-8 } FROM {identifier-9 }
            {index-name-5 }      {index-name-6 }
                                 {literal-5    }

          BY {identifier-10} UNTIL condition-3]]
             {literal-6    }

READ file-name RECORD [INTO identifier] [; AT END imperative-statement]

READ file-name [NEXT] RECORD [INTO identifier]

     [; AT END imperative-statement]

READ file-name RECORD [INTO identifier] [; INVALID KEY imperative-statement]

READ file-name RECORD [INTO identifier]

     [; KEY IS data-name]

     [; INVALID KEY imperative-statement]

RECEIVE cd-name {MESSAGE} INTO identifier-1 [; NO DATA imperative-statement]
                {SEGMENT}

RELEASE record-name [FROM identifier]
```

```
RETURN file-name RECORD [INTO identifier] ; AT END imperative-statement

REWRITE record-name [FROM identifier]

REWRITE record-name [FROM identifier] [; INVALID KEY imperative-statement]

SEARCH identifier-1 [ VARYING {identifier-2  } ] [; AT END imperative-statement-1]
                              {index-name-1 }

        ; WHEN condition-1 {imperative-statement-2}
                           {NEXT SENTENCE        }

      [ ; WHEN condition-2 {imperative-statement-3} ] ...
                           {NEXT SENTENCE        }

SEARCH ALL identifier-1 [; AT END imperative-statement-1]

        ; WHEN {data-name-1  {IS EQUAL TO}  {identifier-3            }}
               {             {IS =        }  {literal-1               }}
               {                            {arithmetic-expression-1 }}
               {condition-name-1                                      }

                [ AND {data-name-2  {IS EQUAL TO}  {identifier-4            }} ] ...
                      {             {IS =        }  {literal-2               }}
                      {                            {arithmetic-expression-2 }}
                      {condition-name-2                                      }

               {imperative-statement-2}
               {NEXT SENTENCE        }

SEND cd-name FROM identifier-1

SEND cd-name [FROM identifier-1] {WITH identifier-2}
                                 {WITH ESI         }
                                 {WITH EMI         }
                                 {WITH EGI         }

    [ {BEFORE}  ADVANCING  {{{identifier-3} [LINE ]}} ]
      {AFTER }             {{{integer     } [LINES]}}
                          {{mnemonic-name}         }
                          {{PAGE         }         }

SET {identifier-1 [, identifier-2] ...}  TO  {identifier-3}
    {index-name-1 [, index-name-2] ...}       {index-name-3}
                                              {integer-1   }

SET index-name-4 [, index-name-5] ... {UP BY  }  {identifier-4}
                                      {DOWN BY}  {integer-2   }

SORT file-name-1 ON {ASCENDING }  KEY data-name-1 [, data-name-2] ...
                    {DESCENDING}

            [ ON {ASCENDING }  KEY data-name-3 [, data-name-4] ... ] ...
                 {DESCENDING}

        [COLLATING SEQUENCE IS alphabet-name]

        {INPUT PROCEDURE IS section-name-1 [ {THROUGH} section-name-2 ]}
        {                                    {THRU   }                 }
        {USING file-name-2 [, file-name-3] ...                         }

        {OUTPUT PROCEDURE IS section-name-3 [ {THROUGH} section-name-4 ]}
        {                                     {THRU   }                 }
        {GIVING file-name-4                                             }

START file-name [ KEY {IS EQUAL TO       }  data-name ]
                      {IS =              }
                      {IS GREATER THAN   }
                      {IS >              }
                      {IS NOT LESS THAN  }
                      {IS NOT <          }

        [; INVALID KEY imperative-statement]
```

$$\underline{STOP} \; \left\{ \begin{array}{l} \underline{RUN} \\ literal \end{array} \right\}$$

$$\underline{STRING} \; \left\{ \begin{array}{l} identifier-1 \\ literal-1 \end{array} \right\} \; \left[\begin{array}{l} , \; identifier-2 \\ , \; literal-2 \end{array} \right] \; \ldots \quad \underline{DELIMITED} \; BY \; \left\{ \begin{array}{l} identifier-3 \\ literal-3 \\ \underline{SIZE} \end{array} \right\}$$

$$\left[, \; \left\{ \begin{array}{l} identifier-4 \\ literal-4 \end{array} \right\} \; \left[\begin{array}{l} , \; identifier-5 \\ , \; literal-5 \end{array} \right] \; \ldots \quad \underline{DELIMITED} \; BY \; \left\{ \begin{array}{l} identifier-6 \\ literal-6 \\ \underline{SIZE} \end{array} \right\} \right] \ldots$$

$$\underline{INTO} \; identifier-7 \; \left[WITH \; \underline{POINTER} \; identifier-8 \right]$$

$$\left[; \; ON \; \underline{OVERFLOW} \; imperative-statement \right]$$

$$\underline{SUBTRACT} \; \left\{ \begin{array}{l} identifier-1 \\ literal-1 \end{array} \right\} \; \left[\begin{array}{l} , \; identifier-2 \\ , \; literal-2 \end{array} \right] \; \ldots \quad \underline{FROM} \; identifier-m \; \left[\underline{ROUNDED} \right]$$

$$\left[, \; identifier-n \; \left[\underline{ROUNDED} \right] \right] \; \ldots \; \left[; \; ON \; \underline{SIZE} \; \underline{ERROR} \; imperative-statement \right]$$

$$\underline{SUBTRACT} \; \left\{ \begin{array}{l} identifier-1 \\ literal-1 \end{array} \right\} \; \left[\begin{array}{l} , \; identifier-2 \\ , \; literal-2 \end{array} \right] \; \ldots \quad \underline{FROM} \; \left\{ \begin{array}{l} identifier-m \\ literal-m \end{array} \right\}$$

$$\underline{GIVING} \; identifier-n \; \left[\underline{ROUNDED} \right] \; \left[, \; identifier-o \; \left[\underline{ROUNDED} \right] \right] \; \ldots$$

$$\left[; \; ON \; \underline{SIZE} \; \underline{ERROR} \; imperative-statement \right]$$

$$\underline{SUBTRACT} \; \left\{ \begin{array}{l} \underline{CORRESPONDING} \\ \underline{CORR} \end{array} \right\} \; identifier-1 \; \underline{FROM} \; identifier-2 \; \left[\underline{ROUNDED} \right]$$

$$\left[; \; ON \; \underline{SIZE} \; \underline{ERROR} \; imperative-statement \right]$$

$$\underline{SUPPRESS} \; PRINTING$$

$$\underline{TERMINATE} \; report-name-1 \; \left[, \; report-name-2 \right] \; \ldots$$

$$\underline{UNSTRING} \; identifier-1$$

$$\left[\underline{DELIMITED} \; BY \; \left[\underline{ALL} \right] \; \left\{ \begin{array}{l} identifier-2 \\ literal-1 \end{array} \right\} \; \left[, \; \underline{OR} \; \left[\underline{ALL} \right] \; \left\{ \begin{array}{l} identifier-3 \\ literal-2 \end{array} \right\} \right] \; \ldots \right]$$

$$\underline{INTO} \; identifier-4 \; \left[, \; \underline{DELIMITER} \; IN \; identifier-5 \right] \; \left[, \; \underline{COUNT} \; IN \; identifier-6 \right]$$

$$\left[, \; identifier-7 \; \left[, \; \underline{DELIMITER} \; IN \; identifier-8 \right] \; \left[, \; \underline{COUNT} \; IN \; identifier-9 \right] \right] \ldots$$

$$\left[WITH \; \underline{POINTER} \; identifier-10 \right] \; \left[\underline{TALLYING} \; IN \; identifier-11 \right]$$

$$\left[; \; ON \; \underline{OVERFLOW} \; imperative-statement \right]$$

$$\underline{USE} \; \underline{AFTER} \; STANDARD \; \left\{ \begin{array}{l} \underline{EXCEPTION} \\ \underline{ERROR} \end{array} \right\} \; \underline{PROCEDURE} \; ON \; \left\{ \begin{array}{l} file-name-1 \; \left[, \; file-name-2 \right] \; \ldots \\ \underline{INPUT} \\ \underline{OUTPUT} \\ \underline{I-O} \\ \underline{EXTEND} \end{array} \right\} .$$

$$\underline{USE} \; \underline{AFTER} \; STANDARD \; \left\{ \begin{array}{l} \underline{EXCEPTION} \\ \underline{ERROR} \end{array} \right\} \; \underline{PROCEDURE} \; ON \; \left\{ \begin{array}{l} file-name-1 \; \left[, \; file-name-2 \right] \; \ldots \\ \underline{INPUT} \\ \underline{OUTPUT} \\ \underline{I-O} \end{array} \right\} .$$

$$\underline{USE} \; \underline{BEFORE} \; \underline{REPORTING} \; identifier .$$

$$\underline{USE} \; FOR \; \underline{DEBUGGING} \; ON \; \left\{ \begin{array}{l} cd-name-1 \\ \left[\underline{ALL} \; REFERENCES \; OF \right] \; identifier-1 \\ file-name-1 \\ procedure-name-1 \\ \underline{ALL} \; \underline{PROCEDURES} \end{array} \right\}$$

$$\left[, \; \begin{array}{l} cd-name-2 \\ \left[\underline{ALL} \; REFERENCES \; OF \right] \; identifier-2 \\ file-name-2 \\ procedure-name-2 \\ \underline{ALL} \; \underline{PROCEDURES} \end{array} \right] \; \ldots \; .$$

```
WRITE record-name [FROM identifier-1]

   ⎡ ⎧BEFORE⎫            ⎧⎧identifier-2⎫ ⎡LINE ⎤⎫ ⎤
 . ⎢ ⎨     ⎬ ADVANCING   ⎨⎩integer    ⎭ ⎣LINES⎦⎬ ⎥
   ⎣ ⎩AFTER ⎭            ⎩⎧mnemonic-name⎫      ⎭ ⎦
                          ⎩PAGE         ⎭

   ⎡    ⎧END-OF-PAGE⎫                     ⎤
   ⎢; AT⎨           ⎬ imperative-statement⎥
   ⎣    ⎩EOP        ⎭                     ⎦

WRITE record-name [FROM identifier] [; INVALID KEY imperative-statement]
```

General Format for Conditions

RELATION CONDITION:

```
⎧identifier-1          ⎫ ⎧IS [NOT] GREATER THAN⎫ ⎧identifier-2          ⎫
⎨literal-1             ⎬ ⎪IS [NOT] LESS THAN   ⎪ ⎨literal-2             ⎬
⎪arithmetic-expression-1⎪ ⎨IS [NOT] EQUAL TO    ⎬ ⎪arithmetic-expression-2⎪
⎩index-name-1          ⎭ ⎪IS [NOT] >           ⎪ ⎩index-name-2          ⎭
                         ⎪IS [NOT] <           ⎪
                         ⎩IS [NOT] =           ⎭
```

CLASS CONDITION:

```
identifier IS [NOT] ⎧NUMERIC   ⎫
                    ⎩ALPHABETIC⎭
```

SIGN CONDITION:

```
                            ⎧POSITIVE⎫
arithmetic-expression is [NOT] ⎨NEGATIVE⎬
                            ⎩ZERO    ⎭
```

CONDITION-NAME CONDITION:

```
condition-name
```

SWITCH-STATUS CONDITION:

```
condition-name
```

NEGATED SIMPLE CONDITION:

```
NOT simple-condition
```

COMBINED CONDITION:

```
condition ⎧⎧AND⎫ condition⎫ ...
          ⎩⎩OR ⎭          ⎭
```

ABBREVIATED COMBINED RELATION CONDITION:

```
relation-condition ⎧⎧AND⎫ [NOT] [relational-operator] object⎫ ...
                   ⎩⎩OR ⎭                                    ⎭
```

Miscellaneous Formats   **QUALIFICATION:**

```
⎧data-name-1   ⎫ ⎡⎧OF⎫          ⎤
⎨condition-name⎬ ⎢⎨  ⎬ data-name-2⎥ ...
⎩              ⎭ ⎣⎩IN⎭          ⎦

paragraph-name  ⎡⎧OF⎫             ⎤
                ⎢⎨  ⎬ section-name⎥
                ⎣⎩IN⎭             ⎦

text-name  ⎡⎧OF⎫            ⎤
           ⎢⎨  ⎬ library-name⎥
           ⎣⎩IN⎭            ⎦
```

SUBSCRIPTING:

$$\begin{Bmatrix} \text{data-name} \\ \text{condition-name} \end{Bmatrix} \text{ (subscript-1 } [, \text{ subscript-2 } [, \text{ subscript-3}]] \text{)}$$

INDEXING:

$$\begin{Bmatrix} \text{data-name} \\ \text{condition-name} \end{Bmatrix} \text{ (} \begin{Bmatrix} \text{index-name-1 } [\{\pm\} \text{ literal-2}] \\ \text{literal-1} \end{Bmatrix}$$

$$\left[, \begin{Bmatrix} \text{index-name-2 } [\{\pm\} \text{ literal-4}] \\ \text{literal-3} \end{Bmatrix} \left[, \begin{Bmatrix} \text{index-name-3 } [\{\pm\} \text{ literal-6}] \\ \text{literal-5} \end{Bmatrix} \right] \right] \text{)}$$

IDENTIFIER: FORMAT 1

$$\text{data-name-1 } \left[\begin{Bmatrix} \underline{OF} \\ \underline{IN} \end{Bmatrix} \text{ data-name-2} \right] \dots \left[\text{(subscript-1 } [, \text{ subscript-2} \right.$$

$$\left. [, \text{ subscript-3}]] \text{)} \right]$$

IDENTIFIER: FORMAT 2

$$\text{data-name-1 } \left[\begin{Bmatrix} \underline{OF} \\ \underline{IN} \end{Bmatrix} \text{ data-name-2} \right] \dots \left[\text{ (} \begin{Bmatrix} \text{index-name-1 } [\{\pm\} \text{ literal-2}] \\ \text{literal-1} \end{Bmatrix} \right.$$

$$\left. \left[, \begin{Bmatrix} \text{index-name-2 } [\{\pm\} \text{ literal-4}] \\ \text{literal-3} \end{Bmatrix} \left[, \begin{Bmatrix} \text{index-name-3 } [\{\pm\} \text{ literal-6}] \\ \text{literal-5} \end{Bmatrix} \right] \right] \text{)} \right]$$

General Format for COPY Statement

$$\underline{\text{COPY}} \text{ text-name } \left[\begin{Bmatrix} \underline{OF} \\ \underline{IN} \end{Bmatrix} \text{ library-name} \right]$$

$$\left[\underline{\text{REPLACING}} \quad \left\{ , \begin{Bmatrix} \text{==pseudo-text-1==} \\ \text{identifier-1} \\ \text{literal-1} \\ \text{word-1} \end{Bmatrix} \quad \underline{\text{BY}} \begin{Bmatrix} \text{==pseudo-text-2==} \\ \text{identifier-2} \\ \text{literal-2} \\ \text{word-2} \end{Bmatrix} \right\} \dots \right]$$

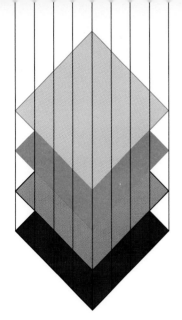

Complete COBOL-85 Language Formats

This appendix contains the composite language formats skeleton of the American National Standard COBOL (1985). It is intended to completely display all COBOL-85 language formats.

General Format for IDENTIFICATION DIVISION

```
IDENTIFICATION DIVISION.

PROGRAM-ID. program-name [IS {| COMMON |} PROGRAM]
                               |  INITIAL  |

[AUTHOR. [comment-entry] ...]

[INSTALLATION. [comment-entry] ...]

[DATE-WRITTEN. [comment-entry] ...]

[DATE-COMPLETED. [comment-entry] ...]

[SECURITY. [comment-entry] ...]
```

General Format for ENVIRONMENT DIVISION

```
[ENVIRONMENT DIVISION.

[CONFIGURATION SECTION.

[SOURCE-COMPUTER. [computer-name [WITH DEBUGGING MODE.]]

[OBJECT-COMPUTER. [computer-name

    ⎡                    ⎧ WORDS      ⎫ ⎤
    ⎢ MEMORY SIZE integer-1 ⎨ CHARACTERS ⎬ ⎥
    ⎣                    ⎩ MODULES    ⎭ ⎦

    [PROGRAM COLLATING SEQUENCE IS alphabet-name-1]

    [SEGMENT-LIMIT IS segment-number] . ]]

[SPECIAL-NAMES. [[implementor-name-1

    ⎧ IS mnemonic-name-1 [ON STATUS IS condition-name-1 [OFF STATUS IS condition-name-2]] ⎫
    ⎪ IS mnemonic-name-2 [OFF STATUS IS condition-name-2 [ON STATUS is condition-name-1]] ⎪ ...
    ⎨ ON STATUS IS condition-name-1 [OFF STATUS IS condition-name-2]                       ⎬
    ⎩ OFF STATUS IS condition-name-2 [ON STATUS IS condition-name-1]                       ⎭

    [ALPHABET alphabet-name-1 IS

        ⎧ STANDARD-1                                              ⎫
        ⎪ STANDARD-2                                              ⎪
        ⎪ NATIVE                                                  ⎪ ...
        ⎨ implementor-name-2                                      ⎬
        ⎪         ⎧ ⎡ THROUGH ⎤ literal-2 ⎤     ⎫                ⎪
        ⎪ literal-1 ⎨ ⎢ THRU    ⎥          ⎥ ... ⎬                ⎪
        ⎩         ⎩ ⎣ {ALSO literal-3} ... ⎦     ⎭                ⎭
```

$$\left[\underline{\text{SYMBOLIC}} \text{ CHARACTERS} \left\{\left\{\{\text{symbolic-character-1}\} \dots \left\{\begin{array}{l}\text{IS}\\\underline{\text{ARE}}\end{array}\right\} \{\text{integer-1}\}\dots \right\} \dots\right.\right.$$

$$\left.\left.[\underline{\text{IN}} \text{ alphabet-name-2}]\right\}\right] \dots$$

$$\left[\underline{\text{CLASS}} \text{ class-name IS} \left\{\text{literal-4} \left[\left\{\begin{array}{l}\underline{\text{THROUGH}}\\\underline{\text{THRU}}\end{array}\right\} \text{literal-5}\right]\right\} \dots \right] \dots$$

[CURRENCY SIGN IS literal-6]

[DECIMAL-POINT IS COMMA].]]]

[INPUT-OUTPUT SECTION.

FILE-CONTROL .

{file-control-entry} ...

{I-O-CONTROL .

$$\left[\left[\underline{\text{RERUN}} \left[\underline{\text{ON}} \left\{\begin{array}{l}\text{file-name-1}\\\text{implementor-name-1}\end{array}\right\}\right] \text{EVERY} \left\{\begin{array}{l}\left\{\begin{array}{l}[\text{END OF}]\left\{\begin{array}{l}\underline{\text{REEL}}\\\underline{\text{UNIT}}\end{array}\right\}\\\text{integer-1 }\underline{\text{RECORDS}}\end{array}\right\} \text{OF file-name-2}\\\text{integer-2 }\underline{\text{CLOCK-UNITS}}\\\text{condition-name-1}\end{array}\right\}\right] \dots\right.$$

$$\left[\left[\underline{\text{SAME}} \left[\begin{array}{l}\underline{\text{RECORD}}\\\underline{\text{SORT}}\\\underline{\text{SORT-MERGE}}\end{array}\right] \text{AREA FOR FILE-NAME-3 \{FILE-NAME-4\}} \dots \right] \dots\right.$$

[MULTIPLE FILE TAPE CONTAINS

{file-name-5 [POSITION IS integer-3] } ...] ... .]]]]

General Format for FILE-CONTROL Entry

SEQUENTIAL FILE:

SELECT [OPTIONAL] file-name-1

$$\underline{\text{ASSIGN}} \text{ TO} \left\{\begin{array}{l}\text{implementor-name-1}\\\text{literal-1}\end{array}\right\} \dots$$

$$\left[\underline{\text{RESERVE}} \text{ integer-1} \left[\begin{array}{l}\text{AREA}\\\text{AREAS}\end{array}\right]\right]$$

[[ORGANIZATION IS] SEQUENTIAL]

$$\left[\underline{\text{PADDING}} \text{ CHARACTER IS} \left\{\begin{array}{l}\text{data-name-1}\\\text{literal-2}\end{array}\right\}\right]$$

$$\left[\underline{\text{RECORD}} \underline{\text{DELIMITER}} \text{ IS} \left\{\begin{array}{l}\underline{\text{STANDARD-1}}\\\text{implementor-name-2}\end{array}\right\}\right]$$

[ACCESS MODE IS SEQUENTIAL]

[FILE STATUS IS data-name-2].

RELATIVE FILE:

SELECT [OPTIONAL] file-name-1

$$\underline{\text{ASSIGN}} \text{ TO} \left\{\begin{array}{l}\text{implementor-name-1}\\\text{literal-1}\end{array}\right\} \dots$$

$$\left[\underline{\text{RESERVE}} \text{ integer-1} \left[\begin{array}{l}\text{AREA}\\\text{AREAS}\end{array}\right]\right]$$

[ORGANIZATION IS] RELATIVE

$$\left[\underline{\text{ACCESS}} \text{ MODE IS} \left\{\begin{array}{l}\underline{\text{SEQUENTIAL}} [\underline{\text{RELATIVE}} \text{ KEY IS data-name-1}]\\\left\{\begin{array}{l}\underline{\text{RANDOM}}\\\underline{\text{DYNAMIC}}\end{array}\right\} \underline{\text{RELATIVE}} \text{ KEY IS data-name-1}\end{array}\right\}\right]$$

[FILE STATUS IS data-name-2].

INDEXED FILE:

```
SELECT [OPTIONAL] file-name-1

    ASSIGN TO  { implementor-name-1 } ...
               { literal-1          }

    [RESERVE integer-1 [ AREA  ]]
                       [ AREAS ]


    [ORGANIZATION IS] INDEXED

    [                    ( SEQUENTIAL )  ]
    [ ACCESS MODE IS     { RANDOM     }  ]
    [                    ( DYNAMIC    )  ]

    RECORD KEY IS data-name-1

    [ALTERNATE RECORD KEY IS data-name-2 [WITH DUPLICATES]] ...

    [FILE STATUS IS data-name-3].
```

SORT OR MERGE FILE:

```
SELECT file-name-1 ASSIGN TO    { implementor-name-1 } ... .
                                { literal-1          }
```

REPORT FILE:

```
SELECT [OPTIONAL] file-name-1
    ASSIGN TO { implementor-name-1 } ...
              { literal-1          }

    [RESERVE integer-1 [ AREA  ]]
                       [ AREAS ]

    [[ORGANIZATION IS] SEQUENTIAL ]

    [PADDING CHARACTER IS { data-name-1 }]
                          { literal-2   }

    [RECORD DELIMITER IS  { STANDARD-1         }]
                          { implementor-name-2 }

    [ACCESS MODE IS SEQUENTIAL]

    [FILE STATUS IS data-name-2].
```

General Format for DATA DIVISION

```
[DATA DIVISION.

[FILE SECTION.

[file-description-entry

{record-description-entry} ... ] ...

[sort-merge-file-description-entry

[report-file-description-entry] ... ]

[WORKING-STORAGE SECTION.

[77-level-description-entry   ]...]
[record-description-entry     ]

[LINKAGE SECTION.

[77-level-description-entry   ]...]
[record-description-entry     ]
```

```
[COMMUNICATION SECTION.

[communication-description-entry

[record-description-entry] ... ] ... ]

[REPORT SECTION.

[report-description-entry

{report-group-description-entry} ... ] ... ]]
```

General Format for File Description Entry

SEQUENTIAL FILE:

```
FD file-name-1

    [IS EXTERNAL]

    [IS GLOBAL]

    [BLOCK CONTAINS [integer-1 TO] integer-2 { RECORDS
                                               CHARACTERS }]

    [ RECORD { CONTAINS integer-3 CHARACTERS
               IS VARYING IN SIZE [[FROM integer-4] [ TO integer-5] CHARACTERS]
                   [DEPENDING ON data-name-1]
               CONTAINS integer-6 TO integer-7 CHARACTERS } ]

    [LABEL { RECORD IS   } { STANDARD }]
            { RECORDS ARE }  { OMITTED  }

    [VALUE OF { implementor-name-1 IS { data-name-2 }} ...]
                                       { literal-1   }

    [DATA { RECORD IS   } {data-name-3} ... ]
           { RECORDS ARE }

    [LINAGE IS { data-name-4 } LINES [WITH FOOTING AT { data-name-5 }]
               { intger-8    }                        { integer-9  }

        [LINES AT TOP { data-name-6 }] [LINES AT BOTTOM { data-name-7  }]]
                       { integer-10 }                    { integer-11 }

    [CODE-SET IS alphabet-name-1].
```

RELATIVE FILE:

```
FD file-name-1

    [IS EXTERNAL]

    [IS GLOBAL]

    [BLOCK CONTAINS [integer-1 TO] integer-2 { RECORDS
                                               CHARACTERS }]

    [ RECORD { CONTAINS integer-3 CHARACTERS
               IS VARYING IN SIZE [[FROM integer-4] [TO integer-5] CHARACTERS
                   [DEPENDING ON data-name-1]
               CONTAINS integer-6 TO integer-7 CHARACTERS } ]

    [LABEL { RECORD IS   } { STANDARD }]
            { RECORDS ARE }  { OMITTED  }

    [VALUE OF { implementor-name-1 IS { data-name-2 }} ...]
                                       { literal-1   }

    [DATA { RECORD IS   } {data-name-3} ...] .
           { RECORDS ARE }
```

INDEXED FILE:

```
FD file-name-1

    [IS EXTERNAL]

    [IS GLOBAL]

    [BLOCK CONTAINS  [integer-1 TO] ] integer-2    { RECORDS    }]
                                                   { CHARACTERS }

    [         { CONTAINS integer-3 CHARACTERS                              }
    [ RECORD  { IS VARYING IN SIZE [[FROM integer-4] [ TO integer-5] CHARACTERS] }
    [         {     [DEPENDING ON data-name-1]                            }
    [         { CONTAINS integer-6 TO integer-7 CHARACTERS                }  ]

    [ LABEL  { RECORD IS   }  { STANDARD }]
    [        { RECORDS ARE }  { OMITTED  }]

    [ VALUE OF  { implementor-name-1 IS  { data-name-2 }  }] ...]
    [                                    { literal-1   }      ]

    [ DATA  { RECORD IS   }  {data-name-3} ... ] .
    [       { RECORDS ARE }                     ]
```

SORT-MERGE FILE:

```
SD file-name-1
    [         { CONTAINS integer-1 CHARACTERS                             }
    [ RECORD  { IS VARYING IN SIZE [[FROM integer-2] [ TO integer-3] CHARACTERS] }
    [         {     [DEPENDING ON data-name-1]                            }
    [         { CONTAINS integer-4 TO integer-5 CHARACTERS                }  ]

    [ DATA  { RECORD IS   }  {data-name-2} ...] .
    [       { RECORDS ARE }                     ]
```

REPORT FILE:

```
FD file-name-1

    [IS EXTERNAL]

    [IS GLOBAL]

    [ BLOCK CONTAINS [integer-1 TO] integer-2  { RECORDS    }]
    [                                          { CHARACTERS }]

    [ RECORD { CONTAINS integer-3 CHARACTERS              }]
    [        { CONTAINS integer-4 TO integer-5 CHARACTERS }]

    [ LABEL  { RECORD IS   }  { STANDARD }]
    [        { RECORDS ARE }  { OMITTED  }]

    [ VALUE OF  { implementor-name-1 IS  { data-name-1 }  } ...]
    [                                    { literal-1   }       ]

    [CODE-SET IS alphabet-name-1]

    { REPORT IS   }  {report-name-1} ... .
    { REPORTS ARE }
```

General Format for
Data Description Entry

FORMAT 1:

```
level-number  [ data-name-1 ]
              [ FILLER      ]

    [REDEFINES data-name-2]

    [IS EXTERNAL]

    [IS GLOBAL]

    [ { PICTURE }  IS character-string ]
    [ { PIC     }                      ]
```

```
                    ⎡          ⎧ BINARY          ⎫ ⎤
                    ⎢          ⎪ COMPUTATIONAL   ⎪ ⎥
                    ⎢          ⎪ COMP            ⎪ ⎥
          [USAGE IS] ⎨ DISPLAY          ⎬
                    ⎢          ⎪ INDEX           ⎪ ⎥
                    ⎣          ⎩ PACKED-DECIMAL  ⎭ ⎦


          ⎡                 ⎧ LEADING  ⎫                        ⎤
          ⎢ [SIGN IS]       ⎨ TRAILING ⎬ [SEPARATE CHARACTER]  ⎥
          ⎣                 ⎩          ⎭                        ⎦


          ⎡ OCCURS integer-2 TIMES                                      ⎤
          ⎢                                                             ⎥
          ⎢    ⎡ ⎧ ASCENDING  ⎫                      ⎤                  ⎥
          ⎢    ⎢ ⎨ DESCENDING ⎬ KEY IS {data-name-3} ⎥ ...              ⎥
          ⎢    ⎣ ⎩            ⎭                       ⎦                 ⎥
          ⎢       [INDEXED BY {index-name-1} ... ]                      ⎥
          ⎢ OCCURS integer-1 TO integer-2 TIMES DEPENDING ON data-name-4⎥
          ⎢                                                             ⎥
          ⎢    ⎡ ⎧ ASCENDING  ⎫                      ⎤                  ⎥
          ⎢    ⎢ ⎨ DESCENDING ⎬ KEY IS {data-name-3} ⎥ ...              ⎥
          ⎣       [INDEXED BY {index-name-1} ... ]                      ⎦


          ⎡ ⎧ SYNCHRONIZED ⎫   ⎡ ⎡ LEFT  ⎤ ⎤ ⎤
          ⎢ ⎨ SYNC         ⎬   ⎢ ⎣ RIGHT ⎦ ⎦ ⎥
          ⎣ ⎩              ⎭                  ⎦

          ⎡ ⎧ JUSTIFIED ⎫       ⎤
          ⎢ ⎨ JUST      ⎬ RIGHT ⎥
          ⎣ ⎩          ⎭        ⎦

          [BLANK WHEN ZERO]

          [VALUE IS literal-1].
```

FORMAT 2:

```
          66 data-name-1 RENAMES data-name-2  ⎡ ⎧ THROUGH ⎫ data-name-3 ⎤  .
                                              ⎣ ⎩ THRU    ⎭             ⎦
```

FORMAT 3:

```
          88 condition-name-1 ⎧ VALUE  IS  ⎫ ⎧ literal-1  ⎡ ⎧ THROUGH ⎫ literal-2 ⎤ ⎫ ... .
                              ⎨ VALUES ARE ⎬ ⎨            ⎣ ⎩ THRU    ⎭           ⎦ ⎬
                              ⎩            ⎭ ⎩                                       ⎭
```

***General Format for
Communication
Description Entry***

FORMAT 1:

```
CD cd-name-1
                          ⎡                                            ⎤
                          ⎢ [[SYMBOLIC QUEUE IS data-name-1]           ⎥
                          ⎢                                            ⎥
                          ⎢   [SYMBOLIC SUB-QUEUE-1 IS data-name-2]    ⎥
                          ⎢                                            ⎥
                          ⎢   [SYMBOLIC SUB-QUEUE-2 IS data-name-3]    ⎥
                          ⎢                                            ⎥
                          ⎢   [SYMBOLIC SUB-QUEUE-3 IS data-name-4]    ⎥
                          ⎢                                            ⎥
                          ⎢   [MESSAGE DATE IS data-name-5]            ⎥
                          ⎢                                            ⎥
                          ⎢   [MESSAGE TIME IS data-name-6]            ⎥
                          ⎢                                            ⎥
                          ⎢   [SYMBOLIC SOURCE IS data-name-7]         ⎥
 FOR [INITIAL] INPUT      ⎢   [TEXT LENGTH IS data-name-8]             ⎥
                          ⎢                                            ⎥
                          ⎢   [END KEY IS data-name-9]                 ⎥
                          ⎢                                            ⎥
                          ⎢   [STATUS KEY IS data-name-10]             ⎥
                          ⎢                                            ⎥
                          ⎢   [MESSAGE COUNT IS data-name-11]]         ⎥
                          ⎢                                            ⎥
                          ⎢   [data-name 1, data-name-2, data-name-3,  ⎥
                          ⎢                                            ⎥
                          ⎢     data-name-4, data-name-5, data-name-6, ⎥
                          ⎢                                            ⎥
                          ⎢     data-name-7, data-name-8, data-name-9, ⎥
                          ⎢                                            ⎥
                          ⎣     data-name-10, data-name-11]            ⎦
```

FORMAT 2:

```
CD cd-name-1 FOR OUTPUT

    [DESTINATION COUNT IS data-name-1]

    [TEXT LENGTH IS data-name-2]

    [STATUS KEY IS data-name-3]

    [DESTINATION TABLE OCCURS integer-1 TIMES

        [INDEXED BY {index-name-1} ... ]]

    [ERROR KEY IS data-name-4]

    [SYMBOLIC DESTINATION IS data-name-5].
```

FORMAT 3:

```
CD cd-name-1
                            ┌                                    ┐
                            │ [[MESSAGE DATE IS data-name-1]      │
                            │                                    │
                            │   [MESSAGE TIME IS data-name-2]     │
                            │                                    │
                            │   [SYMBOLIC TERMINAL IS data-name-3]│
                            │                                    │
           FOR [INITIAL] I-O│   [TEXT LENGTH IS data-name-4]      │
                            │                                    │
                            │   [END KEY IS data-name-5]          │
                            │                                    │
                            │   [STATUS KEY IS data-name-6]]      │
                            │ [data-name-1, data-name-2, data-name-3,│
                            │                                    │
                            │    data-name-4, data-name-5, data-name-6]│
                            └                                    ┘


RD report-name-1

    [IS GLOBAL]

    [CODE literal-1]

    ┌[ CONTROL IS  ] { {data-name-1}  ...       }┐
    │[ CONTROLS ARE]  { FINAL [data-name-1]  ... }│
    └                                            ┘

    ┌     [ LIMIT IS  ]            [ LINE  ]                    ┐
    │PAGE [ LIMITS ARE] integer-1  [ LINES ] [HEADING integer-2]│
    └                                                          ┘

        [FIRST DETAIL integer-1] [LAST DETAIL integer-4]

        [FOOTING integer-5].
```

General Format for Report Group Description Entry

FORMAT 1:

```
01 [data-name-1]

    ┌                  { integer-1 ON NEXT PAGE] }┐
    │LINE NUMBER IS    { PLUS integer-2           }│
    └                                             ┘

    ┌                  ┌ integer-3       ┐┐
    │NEXT GROUP IS     { PLUS integer-4  }│
    │                  └ NEXT PAGE       ┘│
    └                                     ┘
```

$$\text{TYPE IS} \begin{Bmatrix} \left\{ \begin{matrix} \underline{\text{REPORT}} \ \underline{\text{HEADING}} \\ \underline{\text{RH}} \end{matrix} \right\} \\[4pt] \left\{ \begin{matrix} \underline{\text{PAGE}} \ \underline{\text{HEADING}} \\ \underline{\text{PH}} \end{matrix} \right\} \\[4pt] \left\{ \begin{matrix} \underline{\text{CONTROL}} \ \underline{\text{HEADING}} \\ \underline{\text{CH}} \end{matrix} \right\} \left\{ \begin{matrix} \text{data-name-2} \\ \underline{\text{FINAL}} \end{matrix} \right\} \\[4pt] \left\{ \begin{matrix} \underline{\text{DETAIL}} \\ \underline{\text{DE}} \end{matrix} \right\} \\[4pt] \left\{ \begin{matrix} \underline{\text{CONTROL}} \ \underline{\text{FOOTING}} \\ \underline{\text{CF}} \end{matrix} \right\} \left\{ \begin{matrix} \text{data-name-3} \\ \underline{\text{FINAL}} \end{matrix} \right\} \\[4pt] \left\{ \begin{matrix} \underline{\text{PAGE}} \ \underline{\text{FOOTING}} \\ \underline{\text{PF}} \end{matrix} \right\} \\[4pt] \left\{ \begin{matrix} \underline{\text{REPORT}} \ \underline{\text{FOOTING}} \\ \underline{\text{RF}} \end{matrix} \right\} \end{Bmatrix}$$

```
[[USAGE IS] DISPLAY].
```

FORMAT 2:

```
level-number [data-name-1]

    [LINE NUMBER IS {integer-1 [ON NEXT PAGE] }]
                    {PLUS integer-2           }

    [[USAGE IS] DISPLAY].
```

FORMAT 3:

```
level-number [data-name-1]

    {PICTURE} IS character-string
    {PIC    }

    [[USAGE IS] DISPLAY]

    [[SIGN IS]  {LEADING } SEPARATE CHARACTER]
                {TRAILING}

    [{JUSTIFIED} RIGHT]
     {JUST     }

    [BLANK WHEN ZERO]

    [LINE NUMBER IS {integer-1  [ON NEXT PAGE]}]
                    {PLUS integer-2           }

    [COLUMN NUMBER IS integer-3]
```

$$\begin{Bmatrix} \underline{\text{SOURCE}} \text{ IS identifier-1} \\[4pt] \underline{\text{VALUE}} \text{ IS literal-1} \\[4pt] \{\underline{\text{SUM}} \ \{\text{identifier-2}\} \ \dots \ [\underline{\text{UPON}} \ \{\text{data-name-2}\} \ \dots \ ]\} \ \dots \\[4pt] \qquad \left[\underline{\text{RESET}} \text{ ON } \left\{ \begin{matrix} \text{data-name-3} \\ \underline{\text{FINAL}} \end{matrix} \right\} \right] \end{Bmatrix}$$

```
[GROUP INDICATE].
```

General Format for PROCEDURE DIVISION

FORMAT 1:

```
[PROCEDURE DIVISION [USING {data-name-1}... ].

[DECLARATIVES.

{section-name SECTION [segment-number].

    USE statement.
```

```
[paragraph-name.

  [sentence] ... ] ... } ...

END DECLARATIVES.]

{section-name SECTION [segment-number].

[paragraph-name.

  [sentence] ... ]... }... ]
```

FORMAT 2:

```
[PROCEDURE DIVISION [USING {data-name-1} ... ].

{paragraph-name.

  [sentence] ... }... ]
```

General Format for COBOL Verbs

```
ACCEPT identifier-1  [FROM mnemonic-name-1]

                              ┌ DATE        ┐
                              │ DAY         │
ACCEPT identifier-2 FROM      ┤ DAY-OF-WEEK ├
                              └ TIME        ┘

ACCEPT cd-name-1 MESSAGE COUNT

ADD  { identifier-1 } ... TO {identifier-2 [ROUNDED]} ...
     { literal-1    }

  [ON SIZE ERROR imperative-statement-1]

  [NOT ON SIZE ERROR imperative-statement-2]

  [END-ADD]

ADD  { identifier-1 } ... TO { identifier-2 }
     { literal-1    }        { literal-2    }

  GIVING {identifier-3 [ROUNDED]} ...

  [ON SIZE ERROR imperative-statement-1]

  [NOT ON SIZE ERROR imperative-statement-2]

  [END-ADD]

ADD  { CORRESPONDING } identifier-1  TO identifier-2 [ROUNDED]
     { CORR          }

  [ON SIZE ERROR imperative-statement-1]

  [NOT ON SIZE ERROR imperative-statement-2]

  [END-ADD]

  ALTER  {procedure-name-1 TO  {PROCEED TO} procedure-name-2} ...

CALL { identifier-1 }  [USING { [BY REFERENCE] {identifier-2}... }... ]
     { literal-1    }         { BY CONTENT {IDENTIFIER-2}...     }
  [ON OVERFLOW imperative-statement-1]

  [END-CALL]

CALL { identifier-1 }  [USING { [BY REFERENCE] {identifier-2}... }... ]
     { literal-1    }         { BY CONTENT {IDENTIFIER-2}...     }

  [ON EXCEPTION imperative-statement-1]

  [NOT ON EXCEPTION imperative-statement-2]

  [END-CALL]

CANCEL    { identifier-1 } ...
          { literal-1    }
```

```
                       ┌                 ┌ { REEL } [FOR REMOVAL] ┐ ┐
SW   CLOSE  { file-name-1  │  { UNIT }              │ │ ...
                       │                 │ WITH { NO REWIND }    │ │
                       └                 └       { LOCK    }     ┘ ┘

RI   CLOSE {file-name-1 {WITH LOCK}} ...
```

COMPUTE {identifier-1 [ROUNDED]} ... = arithmetic-expression-1

   [ON SIZE ERROR imperative-statement-1]

   [NOT ON SIZE ERROR imperative-statement-2]

   [END-COMPUTE]

CONTINUE

DELETE file-name-1 RECORD

   [INVALID KEY imperative-statement-1]

   [NOT INVALID KEY imperative-statement-2]

   [END-DELETE]

DISABLE $\left\{ \begin{array}{l} \text{INPUT [TERMINAL]} \\ \text{I-O TERMINAL} \\ \text{OUTPUT} \end{array} \right\}$ cd-name-1 $\left[\text{WITH KEY} \left\{ \begin{array}{l} \text{identifier-1} \\ \text{literal-1} \end{array} \right\}\right]$

DISPLAY $\left\{ \begin{array}{l} \text{identifier-1} \\ \text{literal-1} \end{array} \right\}$... [UPON mnemonic-name-1 [WITH NO ADVANCING]

DIVIDE $\left\{ \begin{array}{l} \text{identifier-1} \\ \text{literal-1} \end{array} \right\}$ INTO {identifier-2 [ROUNDED]} ...

   [ON SIZE ERROR imperative-statement-1]

   [NOT ON SIZE ERROR imperative-statement-2]

   [END-DIVIDE]

DIVIDE $\left\{ \begin{array}{l} \text{identifier-1} \\ \text{literal-1} \end{array} \right\}$ INTO $\left\{ \begin{array}{l} \text{identifier-2} \\ \text{literal-2} \end{array} \right\}$

   GIVING {identifier-3 [ROUNDED]} ...

   [ON SIZE ERROR imperative-statement-1]

   [NOT ON SIZE ERROR imperative-statement-2]

   [END-DIVIDE]

DIVIDE $\left\{ \begin{array}{l} \text{identifier-1} \\ \text{literal-1} \end{array} \right\}$ BY $\left\{ \begin{array}{l} \text{identifier-2} \\ \text{literal-2} \end{array} \right\}$

   GIVING {identifier-3 [ROUNDED]} ...

   [ON SIZE ERROR imperative-statement-1]

   [NOT ON SIZE ERROR imperative-statement-2]

   [END-DIVIDE]

DIVIDE $\left\{ \begin{array}{l} \text{identifier-1} \\ \text{literal-1} \end{array} \right\}$ INTO $\left\{ \begin{array}{l} \text{identifier-2} \\ \text{literal-2} \end{array} \right\}$ GIVING identifier-3 [ROUNDED]

   REMAINDER identifier-4

   [ON SIZE ERROR imperative-statement-1]

   [NOT ON SIZE ERROR imperative-statement-2]

   [END-DIVIDE]

DIVIDE $\left\{ \begin{array}{l} \text{identifier-1} \\ \text{literal-1} \end{array} \right\}$ BY $\left\{ \begin{array}{l} \text{identifier-2} \\ \text{literal-2} \end{array} \right\}$ GIVING identifier-3 [ROUNDED]

   REMAINDER identifier-4

   [ON SIZE ERROR imperative-statement-1]

   [NOT ON SIZE ERROR imperative-statement-2]

   [END-DIVIDE]

ENABLE $\left\{ \begin{array}{l} \text{INPUT [TERMINAL]} \\ \text{I-O TERMINAL} \\ \text{OUTPUT} \end{array} \right\}$ cd-name-1 $\left[\text{WITH KEY} \left\{ \begin{array}{l} \text{identifier-1} \\ \text{literal-1} \end{array} \right\}\right]$

ENTER language-name-1 [routine-name-1].

```
EVALUATE  ⎧ identifier-1  ⎫       ⎡     ⎧ identifier-2  ⎫ ⎤
          ⎪ literal-1     ⎪       ⎢     ⎪ literal-2     ⎪ ⎥
          ⎨ expression-1  ⎬  ⎢ALSO ⎨ expression-2  ⎬ ⎥ ...
          ⎪ TRUE          ⎪       ⎢     ⎪ TRUE          ⎪ ⎥
          ⎩ FALSE         ⎭       ⎣     ⎩ FALSE         ⎭ ⎦

{{WHEN

    ⎧ ANY
    ⎪ condition-1
    ⎪ TRUE
    ⎨ FALSE
    ⎪          ⎧ identifier-3            ⎫ ⎡ ⎧ THROUGH ⎫ ⎧ identifier-4            ⎫ ⎤
    ⎩ [NOT] ⎨ literal-3                 ⎬ ⎢ ⎨ THRU    ⎬ ⎨ literal-4               ⎬ ⎥
             ⎩ arithmetic-expression-1 ⎭ ⎣ ⎩         ⎭ ⎩ arithmetic-expression-2 ⎭ ⎦

[ALSO

    ⎧ ANY
    ⎪ condition-2
    ⎪ TRUE
    ⎨ FALSE
    ⎪          ⎧ identifier-5            ⎫ ⎡ ⎧ THROUGH ⎫ ⎧ identifier-6            ⎫ ⎤
    ⎩ [NOT] ⎨ literal-5                 ⎬ ⎢ ⎨ THRU    ⎬ ⎨ literal-6               ⎬ ⎥ ... ⎬ ...
             ⎩ arithmetic-expression-3 ⎭ ⎣ ⎩         ⎭ ⎩ arithmetic-expression-4 ⎭ ⎦

imperative-statement-1} ...

[WHEN OTHER imperative-statement-2]

[END-EVALUATE]


EXIT


EXIT PROGRAM


GENERATE  ⎧ data-name-1   ⎫
          ⎨ report-name-1 ⎬


GO TO [procedure-name-1]


GO TO [procedure-name-1] ...  DEPENDING ON identifier-1


IF condition-1 THEN  ⎧ [statement-1] ...  ⎫ ⎧ ELSE {statement-2} ... [ END-IF ] ⎫
                     ⎨ NEXT SENTENCE       ⎬ ⎨ ELSE NEXT SENTENCE                ⎬
                                              ⎩ END-IF                            ⎭


INITIALIZE {identifier-1} ...

⎡           ⎧ ⎧ ALPHABETIC          ⎫          ⎧ identifier-2 ⎫   ⎤
⎢ REPLACING ⎨ ⎨ ALPHANUMERIC        ⎬ DATA BY  ⎨ literal-1     ⎬ ... ⎥
⎢           ⎪ ⎪ NUMERIC             ⎪          ⎩              ⎭   ⎥
⎢           ⎪ ⎨ APHANUMERIC-EDITED  ⎬                             ⎥
⎣           ⎩ ⎩ NUMERIC-EDITED      ⎭                             ⎦


INITIATE {report-name-1} ...

INSPECT identifier-1 TALLYING

⎧             ⎧ CHARACTERS ⎡ ⎧ BEFORE ⎫ INITIAL ⎧ identifier-4 ⎫ ⎤ ...              ⎫
⎪ identifier-2 FOR ⎨          ⎣ ⎩ AFTER  ⎭         ⎩ literal-2    ⎭ ⎦                 ⎬ ... ...
⎪             ⎪ ⎧ ALL     ⎫ ⎧ identifier-3 ⎫ ⎡ ⎧ BEFORE ⎫ INITIAL ⎧ identifier-4 ⎫ ⎤   ⎪
⎩             ⎩ ⎨ LEADING ⎬ ⎨ literal-1    ⎬ ⎣ ⎩ AFTER  ⎭         ⎩ literal-2    ⎭ ⎦... ...⎭


INSPECT identifier-1 REPLACING

⎧ CHARACTERS BY ⎧ identifier-5 ⎫ ⎡ ⎧ BEFORE ⎫ INITIAL ⎧ identifier-4 ⎫ ⎤ ...                                    ⎫
⎪               ⎩ literal-3    ⎭ ⎣ ⎩ AFTER  ⎭         ⎩ literal-2    ⎭ ⎦                                        ⎬ ...
⎪ ⎧ ALL     ⎫ ⎧ ⎧ identifier-3 ⎫    ⎧ identifier-5 ⎫ ⎡ ⎧ BEFORE ⎫ INITIAL ⎧ identifier-4 ⎫ ⎤ ...              ⎪
⎨ ⎪ LEADING ⎬ ⎨ ⎨ literal-1    ⎬ BY ⎨ literal-3    ⎬ ⎣ ⎩ AFTER  ⎭         ⎩ literal-2    ⎭ ⎦ ... ⎬ ...         ⎬
⎩ ⎩ FIRST   ⎭ ⎩ ⎩              ⎭    ⎩              ⎭                                                ⎭           ⎭
```

```
INSPECT identifier-1 TALLYING

⎧                      ⎧ CHARACTERS [[ {BEFORE}  INITIAL  { identifier-4 }] ...                                        ⎫
⎨ identifier-2 FOR ⎨              [[ {AFTER }            { literal-2    }]                                              ⎬ ...
⎩                      ⎪ ALL      ⎫ ⎧ { identifier-3 }  [[ {BEFORE}  INITIAL { identifier-4 }] ...} ...               ⎭
                        ⎩ LEADING ⎭ ⎩ { literal-1    }   [[ {AFTER }          { literal-2    }]                        


REPLACING

⎧ CHARACTERS BY { identifier-5 } [[ {BEFORE}  INITIAL  { identifier-4 }]                                                ⎫
⎨               { literal-3    } [[ {AFTER }           { literal-2    }]                                                ⎬ ...
⎪ ALL                                                                                                                   ⎪
⎪ LEADING ⎫ { { identifier-3 } BY { identifier-5 } [[ {BEFORE}  INITIAL { identifier-4 }] ...} ...                     ⎪
⎩ FIRST   ⎭ { { literal-1    }    { literal-3    } [[ {AFTER }          { literal-1    }]                              ⎭


INSPECT identifier-1 CONVERTING { identifier-6 } TO { identifier-7 }
                                 { literal-4    }     { literal-5    }

[[ {BEFORE}  INITIAL  { identifier-4 }] ...
 [ {AFTER }           { literal-2    }]

MERGE file-name-1 {ON { ASCENDING  } KEY {data-name-1} ...} ...
                       { DESCENDING }

    [COLLATING SEQUENCE IS alphabet-name-1]

    USING file-name-2 {file-name-3} ...

    ⎧ OUTPUT PROCEDURE IS procedure-name-1  [{ THROUGH } procedure-name-2 ] ⎫
    ⎨                                        { THRU    }                     ⎬
    ⎩ GIVING {file-name-4} ...                                              ⎭

MOVE { identifier-1 } TO { identifier-2 }
     { literal-1    }          ...

MOVE { CORRESPONDING } identifier-1 TO identifier-2
     { CORR          }

MULTIPLY { identifier-1 } BY {identifier-2 [ROUNDED]} ...
         { literal-1    }

    [ON SIZE ERROR imperative-statement-1]

    [NOT ON SIZE ERROR imperative-statement-2]

    [END-MULTIPLY]

MULTIPLY { identifier-1 } BY { identifier-2 }
         { literal-1    }    { literal-2    }

    GIVING {identifier-3 [ROUNDED]} ...

    [ON SIZE ERROR imperative-statement-1]

    [NOT ON SIZE ERROR imperative-statement-2]

    [END-MULTIPLY]

        ⎧ INPUT {file-name-1} [REVERSED      ]}... ⎫
        ⎪                     [WITH NO REWIND]     ⎪
S  OPEN ⎨ OUTPUT {file-name-2} [WITH NO REWIND]}... ⎬ ...
        ⎪ I-O {file-name-3} ...                     ⎪
        ⎩ EXTEND {file-name-4} ...                  ⎭

         ⎧ INPUT {file-name-1} ...  ⎫
         ⎪ OUTPUT {file-name-2} ... ⎪
RI OPEN ⎨ I-O {file-name-3} ...    ⎬ ...
         ⎩ EXTEND {file-name-4} ... ⎭

W  OPEN { OUTPUT {file-name-1 [WITH NO REWIND]} ... } ...
        { EXTEND {file-name-2} ...                  }

PERFORM [procedure-name-1  [{ THROUGH } procedure-name-2 ]]
                            { THRU    }

    [imperative-statement-1  END-PERFORM]
```

```
PERFORM  [procedure-name-1 { THROUGH } procedure-name-2 ]]
                            { THRU    }

         { identifier-1 } TIMES [imperative-statement-1 END-PERFORM]
         { integer-1    }

PERFORM  [procedure-name-1 [{ THROUGH } procedure-name-2 ]]
                            { THRU    }

    [ WITH TEST { BEFORE } ] UNTIL condition-1
                { AFTER  }

    [imperative-statement-1 END-PERFORM]


PERFORM  [ procedure-name-1 [{ THROUGH } procedure-name-2 ]]
                             { THRU    }

    [ WITH TEST { BEFORE } ]
                { AFTER  }

        VARYING { identifier-2 } FROM { identifier-3 }
                { index-name-1 }      { index-name-2 }
                                      { literal-1    }

            BY { identifier-4 } UNTIL condition-1
               { literal-2    }

          [ AFTER { identifier-5 } FROM { identifier-6 }
                  { literal-3    }      { index-name-4 }
                                        { literal-3    }

              BY { identifier-7 } UNTIL condition-2 ] ...
                 { literal-4    }

    [imperative-statement-1 END-PERFORM]


    PURGE cd-name-1


SRI READ file-name-1 [ NEXT] RECORD [ INTO identifier-1]

        [AT END imperative-statement-1]

        [NOT AT END imperative-statement-2]

        [END-READ]


R  READ file-name-1 RECORD [ INTO identifier-1]

        [INVALID KEY imperative-statement-3]

        [NOT INVALID KEY imperative-statement-4]

        [END-READ]

I  READ file-name-1 RECORD [ INTO identifier-1]

        [KEY IS data-name-1]

        [INVALID KEY imperative-statement-3]

        [NOT INVALID KEY imperative-statement-4]

        [END-READ]


    RECEIVE cd-name-1 { MESSAGE } INTO identifier-1
                      { SEGMENT }

        [NO DATA imperative-statement-1]

        [WITH DATA imperative-statement-2]

        [END-RECEIVE]


    RELEASE record-name-1 [ FROM identifier-1]


    RETURN file-name-1 RECORD [ INTO identifier-1]

        AT END imperative-statement-1
```

```
        [NOT AT END imperative-statement-2]

        [END-RETURN]


 S  REWRITE record-name-1 [FROM identifier-1]

RI  REWRITE record-name-1 [FROM identifier-1]

        [INVALID KEY imperative-statement-1]

        [NOT INVALID KEY imperative-statement-2]

        [END-REWRITE]


    SEARCH identifier-1  [VARYING {identifier-2 }]
                                  {index-name-1 }

        [AT END imperative-statement-1]

        {WHEN condition-1  {imperative-statement-2 }} ...
                           {NEXT SENTENCE          }

        [END-SEARCH]


    SEARCH ALL identifier-1  [AT END imperative-statement-1]

        WHEN  {data-name-1    {IS EQUAL TO}  {identifier-3            }}
              {               {IS =       }  {literal-1               }}
              {                             {arithmetic-expression-1 }}
              {condition-name-1                                       }

              [AND  {data-name-1 {IS EQUAL TO} {identifier-4            }}] ...
              [     {            {IS =       } {literal-2               }}]
              [     {condition-name-2          {arithmetic-expression-2 }}]

              {imperative-statement-2 }
              {NEXT SENTENCE          }

        [END-SEARCH]


    SEND cd-name-1 FROM identifier-1


    SEND cd-name-1 [FROM identifier-1] {WITH identifier-2 }
                                       {WITH ESI          }
                                       {WITH EMI          }
                                       {WITH EGI          }

        [{BEFORE}  ADVANCING {{identifier-3 }  [LINE ]}]
        [{AFTER }             {{integer-1    }  [LINES]}]
        [                     {                        }]
        [                     {{mnemonic-name-1 }      }]
        [                     {PAGE                     }]

        [REPLACING LINE]
    SET {index-name-1 }  TO  {index-name-2  }
        {identifier-1 }      {identifier-2  }
                             {integer-1     }

    SET {index-name-3} ... {UP BY  } {identifier-3 }
                           {DOWN BY} {integer-2    }

    SET {{mnemonic-name-1} ... TO {ON }} ...
                                  {OFF}

    SET {condition-name-1} ...   TO TRUE


    SORT file-name-1 {ON {ASCENDING }  KEY {data-name-1} ... } ...
                         {DESCENDING}

        [WITH DUPLICATES IN ORDER]

        [COLLATING SEQUENCE IS alphabet-name-1]
```

```
{ INPUT PROCEDURE IS procedure-name-1  [{ THROUGH } procedure-name-2 ] }
{                                        { THRU    }                    }
{ USING {file-name-2} ...                                              }


{ OUTPUT PROCEDURE IS procedure-name-3  [{ THROUGH } procedure-name-4 ] }
{                                        { THRU    }                    }
{ GIVING {file-name-3} ...                                             }


                    [       { IS EQUAL TO              }            ]
                    [       { IS =                     }            ]
                    [       { IS GREATER THAN          }            ]
START file-name-1   [ KEY   { IS NOT LESS THAN         } data-name-1]
                    [       { IS NOT <                 }            ]
                    [       { IS GREATER THAN OR EQUAL TO }         ]
                    [       { IS >=                    }            ]


    [INVALID KEY imperative-statement-1]

    [NOT INVALID KEY imperative-statement-2]

    [END-START]


STOP { RUN       }
     { literal-1 }


STRING { identifier-1 } ... DELIMITED BY { identifier-2 } ...
       { literal-1    }                  { literal-2    }
                                         { SIZE         }

    INTO identifier-3

    [WITH POINTER identifier-4]

    [ON OVERFLOW imperative-statement-1]

    [NOT ON OVERFLOW imperative-statement-2]

    [END-STRING]


SUBTRACT { identifier-1 } ... FROM {identifier-3 [ROUNDED]} ...
         { literal-1    }

    [ON SIZE ERROR imperative-statement-1]

    [NOT ON SIZE ERROR imperative-statement-2]

    [END-SUBTRACT]


SUBTRACT { identifier-1 } ... FROM { identifier-2 }
         { literal-1    }          { literal-2    }

    GIVING {identifier-3 [ROUNDED]} ...

    [ON SIZE ERROR imperative-statement-1]

    [NOT ON SIZE ERROR imperative-statement-2]

    [END-SUBTRACT]


SUBTRACT { CORRESPONDING } identifier-1 FROM identifier-2 [ROUNDED]
         { CORR          }

    [ON SIZE ERROR imperative-statement-1]

    [NOT ON SIZE ERROR imperative-statement-2]

    [END-SUBTRACT]


SUPPRESS PRINTING


TERMINATE {report-name-1} ...
```

UNSTRING identifier-1

[DELIMITED BY [ALL] {identifier-2 } [OR [ALL] {identifier-3 }...]
                     {literal-1   }   {literal-2   }

INTO [identifier-4 [DELIMITER IN identifier-5] [COUNT IN identifier-6]} ...

[WITH POINTER identifier-7]

[TALLYING IN identifier-8]

[ON OVERFLOW imperative-statement-1]

[NOT ON OVERFLOW imperative-statement-2]

[END-UNSTRING]

SRI USE [GLOBAL] AFTER STANDARD { EXCEPTION } PROCEDURE ON { {file-name-1} ... }
                                { ERROR   }   { INPUT   }
                                                             { OUTPUT   }
                                                             { I-O   }
                                                             { EXTEND   }

W USE AFTER STANDARD { EXCEPTION } PROCEDURE ON { {file-name-1} ... }
                     { ERROR   }   { OUTPUT   }
                                                  { EXTEND   }

USE [GLOBAL] BEFORE REPORTING identifier-1

USE FOR DEBUGGING ON { cd-name-1   }
                     { [ALL REFERENCES OF] identifier-1 } ...
                     { file-name-1   }
                     { procedure-name-1   }
                     { ALL PROCEDURES   }

S WRITE record-name-1 [FROM identifier-1]

[{ BEFORE } ADVANCING { {identifier-2} [LINE] }]
[{ AFTER }   { {integer-1   } [LINES] }]
[{   }]
[{ {mnemonic-name-1 }   }]
[{ PAGE   }   ]

[AT { END-OF-PAGE } imperative-statement-1]
[{ EOP   }   ]

[NOT AT { END-OF-PAGE } imperative-statement-2]
[{ EOP   }   ]
[END-WRITE]

RI WRITE record-name-1 [FROM identifier-1]

[INVALID KEY imperative-statement-1]

[NOT INVALID KEY imperative-statement-2]

[END-WRITE]

General Format for Copy and Replace Statements

COPY text-name-1 [{ OF } library-name-1]
                 [{ IN }   ]

[REPLACING { ==pseudo-text-1== } BY { ==pseudo-text-2== }]
[{ identifier-1   }   { identifier-2   }]...
[{ literal-1   }   { literal-2   }]
[{ word-1   }   { word-2   }]

REPLACE {==pseudo-text-1== BY ==pseudo-text-2==} ...

REPLACE OFF

General Format for Conditions

RELATION CONDITION:

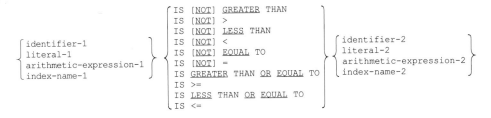

CLASS CONDITION:

```
                     ┌ NUMERIC          ┐
                     │ ALPHABETIC       │
identifier-1 IS [NOT]│ ALPHABETIC-LOWER │
                     │ ALPHABETIC-UPPER │
                     └ class-name-1     ┘
```

CONDITION-NAM CONDITION:

```
condition-name-1
```

SWITCH-STATUS CONDITION:

```
condition-name-1
```

SIGN CONDITION:

```
                            ┌ POSITIVE ┐
arithmetic-expression-1 IS [ NOT ]│ NEGATIVE │
                            └ ZERO     ┘
```

NEGATED CONDITION:

```
NOT condition-1
```

COMBINED CONDITION:

```
condition-1 { { AND } condition-2 } ...
            {   OR   }
```

ABBREVIATED COMBINED RELATION CONDITION:

```
relation-condition { { AND } [NOT] [relational-operator] object } ...
                   {   OR   }
```

Qualification **FORMAT 1:**

```
{ data-name-1      } { { { IN }  data-name-2 } ... [ { IN }  { file-name-1 } ] ]
{ condition-name-1 } { {   OF  }                    {   OF  } { cd-name-1   }   ]
                     {
                     { { IN }  { file-name-1 }
                     { {   OF  } { cd-name-1   }
```

FORMAT 2:

```
paragraph-name-1 { IN } section-name-1
                 {   OF  }
```

FORMAT 3:

```
text-name-1 { IN } library-name-1
            { OF }
```

FORMAT 4:

```
                      IN
LINAGE-COUNTER { IN } file-name-2 OF
               { OF }
```

FORMAT 5:

```
{ PAGE-COUNTER } { IN } report-name-2
{ LINE-COUNTER } { OF }
```

FORMAT 6:

```
            ┌ { IN } data-name-4 [ { IN } report-name-2 ] ┐
            │ { OF }             [ { OF }               ] │
data-name-3 ┤                                             ├
            │ { IN } report-name-2                        │
            └ { OF }                                      ┘
```

Miscellaneous Formats   **SUBSCRIPTING:**

```
                     ┌ integer-1                ┐
{ condition-name-1 } │ data-name-2 [{±} integer-2] │
{ data-name-1      } ( ┤                          ├ ... )
                     │ index-name-1 [{±} integer-3] │
                     └                          ┘
```

REFERENCE MODIFICATION:

```
data-name-1 (leftmost-character-position: [length])
```

IDENTIFIER:

```
                                      ┌ cd-name-1     ┐
data-name-1 [ { IN } data-name-2 ] ... { IN } │ file-name-1   │
            [ { OF }             ]     { OF } │ report-name-1 │
                                      └             ┘

    [({subscript} ... ) ] [(leftmost-character-position: [length])]
```

General Format for
Nested-Source
Programs

```
IDENTIFICATION DIVISION.

PROGRAM-ID. program-name-1 [IS INITIAL PROGRAM].

[ENVIRONMENT DIVISION. environment-division-content]

[DATA DIVISION. data-division-content]

[PROCEDURE DIVISION. procedure-division-content]

[[nested-source-program] ...

END PROGRAM program-name-1.]
```

General Format for Nested-Source-Program

<u>IDENTIFICATION</u> <u>DIVISION</u> .

<u>PROGRAM-ID</u>. program-name-2 [IS { | <u>COMMON</u> / <u>INITIAL</u> | } PROGRAM]

[<u>ENVIRONMENT</u> <u>DIVISION</u>. environment-division-content]

[<u>DATA</u> <u>DIVISION</u>. data-division-content]

[<u>PROCEDURE</u> <u>DIVISION</u>. procedure-division-content]

[nested-source-program] ...

<u>END</u> <u>PROGRAM</u> program-name-2.

General Format for a Sequence of Source Programs

{ <u>IDENTIFICATION</u> <u>DIVISION</u>.

<u>PROGRAM-ID</u>. program-name-3 [IS <u>INITIAL</u> PROGRAM].

[<u>ENVIRONMENT</u> <u>DIVISION</u>. environment-division-content]

[<u>DATA</u> <u>DIVISION</u>. data-division-content]

[<u>PROCEDURE</u> <u>DIVISION</u>. procedure-division-content]

[nested-source-program] ...

<u>END</u> <u>PROGRAM</u> program-name-3. ...

<u>IDENTIFICATION</u> <u>DIVISION</u>.

<u>PROGRAM-ID</u>. program-name-4 [IS <u>INITIAL</u> PROGRAM].

[<u>ENVIRONMENT</u> <u>DIVISION</u>. environment-division-content]

[<u>DATA</u> <u>DIVISION</u>. data-division-content]

[<u>PROCEDURE</u> <u>DIVISION</u>. procedure-division-content]

[[nested-source-program] ...

<u>END</u> <u>PROGRAM</u> program-name-4.]

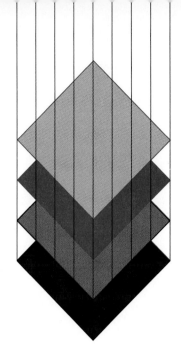

COBOL Reserved Words

ACCEPT	CLASS	DAY	END-EVALUATE
ACCESS	CLOCK-UNITS	DAY-OF-WEEK	END-IF
ADD	CLOSE	DE	END-MULTIPLY
ADVANCING	COBOL	r DEBUGGING	END-OF-PAGE
AFTER	CODE	DEBUG-CONTENTS	END-PERFORM
ALL	CODE-SET	DEBUG-ITEM	END-READ
ALPHABET	COLLATING	DEBUG-LINE	END-RECEIVE
ALPHABETIC	COLUMN	DEBUG-NAME	END-RETURN
ALPHABETIC-LOWER	COMMA	DEBUG-SUB-1	END-REWRITE
ALPHABETIC-UPPER	COMMON	DEBUG-SUB-2	END-SEARCH
ALPHANUMERIC	COMMUNICATION	DEBUG-SUB-3	END-START
ALPHANUMERIC-EDITED	COMP	a DEBUGGING	END-STRING
ALSO	COMPUTATIONAL	DECIMAL-POINT	END-SUBTRACT
ALTER	r COMPUTATIONAL-1	DECLARATIVES	END-UNSTRING
ALTERNATE	r COMPUTATIONAL-3	DELETE	END-WRITE
AND	r COMPUTATIONAL-4	DELIMITED	ENTER
ANY	r COMPUTATIONAL-6	DELIMITER	ENVIRONMENT
ARE	COMPUTE	DEPENDING	r EOF
AREA	r COMP-1	DESCENDING	r EOL
AREAS	r COMP-3	DESTINATION	a EOP
ASCENDING	r COMP-4	DETAIL	r EOS
ASSIGN	r COMP-6	DISABLE	EQUAL
AT	CONFIGURATION	DISPLAY	r ERASE
AUTHOR	CONTAINS	DIVIDE	ERROR
	CONTENT	DIVISION	ESI
r BEEP	CONTINUE	DOWN	EVALUATE
BEFORE	CONTROL	DUPLICATES	EVERY
BINARY	CONTROLS	DYNAMIC	EXCEPTION
BLANK	r CONVERT		EXIT
r BLINK	CONVERTING	r ECHO	EXTEND
BLOCK	COPY	EGI	EXTERNAL
BOTTOM	CORR	ELSE	
BY	CORRESPONDING	EMI	FALSE
	COUNT	ENABLE	FD
CALL	CURRENCY	END	FILE
CANCEL	r CURSOR	r END-ACCEPT	FILE-CONTROL
CD		END-ADD	FILLER
CF	DATA	END-CALL	FINAL
CH	DATE	END-COMPUTE	FIRST
CHARACTER	DATE-COMPILED	END-DELETE	FOOTING
CHARACTERS	DATE-WRITTEN	END-DIVIDE	FOR
			FROM

Notation: r = RM/COBOL-85 reserved word
             a = 1985 ANSI reserved word

GENERATE
GIVING
GLOBAL
GO
r GOBACK
GREATER
GROUP

HEADING
r HIGH
HIGH-VALUE
HIGH-VALUES

r ID
IDENTIFICATION
IF
IN
INDEX
INDEXED
INDICATE
INITIAL
INITIALIZE
INITIATE
INPUT
INPUT-OUTPUT
INSPECT
INSTALLATION
INTO
INVALID
IS
I-O
I-O-CONTROL

JUST
JUSTIFIED

KEY

LABEL
LAST
LEADING
LEFT
LENGTH
LESS
LIMIT
LIMITS
LINAGE
LINAGE-COUNTER
LINE
LINES
LINE-COUNTER
LINKAGE
LOCK
r LOW
LOW-VALUE
LOW-VALUES

MEMORY
MERGE
MESSAGE
MODE
MODULES
MOVE
MULTIPLE
MULTIPLY

NATIVE
NEGATIVE
NEXT
NO
NOT
NUMBER
NUMERIC
NUMERIC-EDITED

OBJECT-COMPUTER
OCCURS
OF
OFF
OMITTED
ON
OPEN
OPTIONAL
OR
ORDER
ORGANIZATION
OTHER
OUTPUT
OVERFLOW

PACKED-DECIMAL
PADDING
PAGE
PAGE-COUNTER
PERFORM
PF
PH
PIC
PICTURE
PLUS
POINTER
POSITION
POSITIVE
PRINTING
PROCEDURE
PROCEDURES
PROCEED
PROGRAM
PROGRAM-ID
r PROMPT
PURGE

QUEUE
QUOTE
QUOTES

RANDOM
RD
READ
RECEIVE
RECORD
RECORDS
REDEFINES
REEL
REFERENCE
REFERENCES
RELATIVE
RELEASE
REMAINDER
r REMARKS
REMOVAL
RENAMES
REPLACE

REPLACING
REPORT
REPORTING
REPORTS
RERUN
RESERVE
RESET
RETURN
r RETURN-CODE
r REVERSE
REVERSED
REWIND
REWRITE
RF
RH
RIGHT
ROUNDED
RUN

SAME
SD
SEARCH
SECTION
SECURITY
SEGMENT
SEGMENT-LIMIT
SELECT
SEND
SENTENCE
SEPARATE
SEQUENCE
SEQUENTIAL
SET
SIGN
SIZE
SORT
SORT-MERGE
SOURCE
SOURCE-COMPUTER
SPACE
SPACES
SPECIAL-NAMES
STANDARD
STANDARD-1
STANDARD-2
START
STATUS
STOP
STRING
SUBTRACT
SUB-QUEUE-1
SUB-QUEUE-2
SUB-QUEUE-3
SUM
SUPPRESS
SYMBOLIC
SYNC
SYNCHRONIZED

r TAB
TABLE
TALLYING
TAPE
TERMINAL
TERMINATE
TEST
TEXT

THAN
THEN
THROUGH
THRU
TIME
TIMES
TO
TOP
TRAILING
TRUE
TYPE

UNIT
r UNLOCK
UNSTRING
UNTIL
UP
r UPDATE
UPON
USAGE
USE
USING

VALUE
VALUES
VARYING

WHEN
WITH
WORDS
WORKING-STORAGE
WRITE

ZERO
ZEROES
ZEROS

r .
r ,
r ;
r (
r)
r "
r `
+
-
*
/
**
=
>
<
>=
<=
r :

Notation: r = RM/COBOL-85 reserved word
             a = 1985 ANSI reserved word

Index

Note: References to COBOL-85 features are printed in bold type.

A coding form area. *See* Area A
A picture symbol, 217, 238, 239
Abend, AD-1
Abeyance file, 392
Abnormal ending, AD-1
Absence check, 380
Absolute numeric data, 379
ACCEPT statement, 449,
    AB-3–AB-4, AE-7, **AF-9**
  ACCEPT/FROM format,
    301–302, 306, 307
  control-options, 449, 457–458,
    475
  FROM/DATE option,
    301–302, 306
  FROM/DAY-OF-WEEK
    option, **301–302, 306, 307**
  FROM/DAY option, 301, 306
  FROM/TIME option, 302, 306
Accumulating operation,
    154, 155
Accumulator, 154
ADD statement, 168–169, 193,
    AE-7, **AF-9**
  ADD/CORRESPONDING
    format, AB-12
  ADD/GIVING format,
    175–176
  ADD/TO format, 173–175
  when to use GIVING,
    186–187
Addend, 153
Addressing exception, AD-2
ADV compiler option, 75
ADVANCING:
  AFTER, 25, 120, 129, 303–304,
    307
  BEFORE, 120, 129
  output device and, 431, 432

AFTER:
  PERFORM/VARYING
    statement, 618–621
  WRITE statement, 25, 120,
    129, 303–304, 307
Algebraic numeric data, 379–380
ALL:
  INSPECT statement, 398–400,
    403–404, 431–432
  SEARCH statement, 586
ALPHABETIC class test,
    343–344
Alphabetic data class, 4
ALPHABETIC-LOWER class
    test, **344**
ALPHABETIC-UPPER class
    test, **344**
Alphanumeric data class, 4
Alphanumeric comparison,
    341–342
Alphanumeric data class, 4
Alphanumeric-edited data
    items, 227–228
Alphanumeric literals. *See*
    Nonnumeric literals
ALTER statement, AB-5, AE-7,
    AF-9
AND, 348–351, 360, 409
ANSI standards, 74, 118
APOST compiler option, 75
Apostrophe as delimiter, 118
Area A:
  common errors, 89–90, 135
  conventions and rules for,
    30, 31
  division headers and, 58, 61,
    64, 112
  FD and, 66

Area A (continued):
  paragraph headers and,
    112, 113
  01-level items and, 68–69
  77-level items and, 73
Area B:
  common errors, 89–90
  conventions and rules for,
    30, 31
  file-names and, 66
  level-numbers 02 through 49
    and, 68–69
  verbs and, 113, 129
Arguments in tables, 548,
    570–571, 606–615
Arithmetic operations, 153–154
  accumulating, 154, 155
  arithmetic statements,
    172, 193
  assumed decimal point for,
    152, 155
  COMPUTE vs. other verbs,
    187
  counting, 154
  data class for, 4, 6, 172
  field length and, 4
  GIVING usage guidelines,
    186–187
  hierarchy of, 184
  operator symbols, 183
  packed-decimal format for,
    190–192
  rounding off, 153, 155,
    174, 180
  scope terminators, **186, 194**
  signed numbers and, 4,
    151–152, 155
  size errors and, 174, 185–186
  subtracting, 154

Arithmetic operations
    (continued):
  terminology, 153
  truncation, 153, 155
  *See also specific arithmetic
    statements*
Arithmetic overflow. *See* ON
    SIZE ERROR
ASCENDING:
  MERGE statement, 673–674
  SEARCH statement, 584–585,
    588
  SORT statement, 652–653, 677
Ascending order, 483–485
ASCII, 150, 152, 155, 341–342
ASSIGN clause, 21, 62–64, 73,
    76, **453**
  for sort-work file, 650, 676
  system-names in,
    AC-1–AC-4
Assignment-name, AC-1–AC-2
Assumed decimal point,
    152, 155
  V picture symbol for, 168,
    192, 217, 218, 239
Asterisk (*):
  for blank lines, 56–57
  check protection and, 265–266
  comment lines and, 20, 56, 75
  COMPUTE statement and,
    183–185
  picture symbol, 218, 220, 238
Asterisks (**), 183–185
AT END:
  NOT operator for, **361**
  READ statement, 25, 121–123,
    129, **361**
  SEARCH statement, 581
Audit list, 389–390

Audit/error list, 390
Augend, 173–174
AUTHOR paragraph, 20, 60
AUTO, **461**
Auxiliary storage, 6–7, 431

B coding form area. *See* Area B
B picture symbol, 218, 222,
    227–228, 238, 240, 243
Batch validation, 388–389
BEFORE ADVANCING,
    120, 129
BELL, **475**
Bell, suppressing, 449
Binary digits, 150, 154
Binary search table lookups,
    552–554, 584–586, 587
Bits, 5, 150
Blank character, 5, 89
    absence check for, 380
    B picture symbol for, 218, 222,
        227–228, 238, 240, 243
    embedded-blank check for,
        383
    in numeric fields, 402–403
    See also Spacing
BLANK LINE, **461**, **475**
Blank lines, 56–57
BLANK REMAINDER, **461**, **475**
BLANK SCREEN, **458**, **475**
BLANK WHEN ZERO clause,
    229
BLINK:
    control-option, 448, 475
    screen-attribute, **461**, **475**
BLOCK CONTAINS clause,
    67, 650
Blocks:
    BLOCK CONTAINS clause,
        67, 650
    data addressing and, 6, 8
    floppy disk sectors and, 6
Body area, 256–257, 266
Boolean diagram, 348, 349, 350
Braces in format notation, 58
Brackets in format notation, 58
Bubble chart, 321–323
Buffers, initialization and, 119
BY:
    DIVIDE statement, 182–183
    MULTIPLY statement,
        179–180
Byte, 5, 8, 150, 154

CALL statement, AE-7, **AF-9**
CANCEL statement, AE-7, **AF-9**
Case structure, 356–357,
    AB-8–AB-9
Case (upper/lower), 470
CD entry, 65, AE-5, **AF-6–AF-7**
Chapin charts, 330
Chapin, Ned, 330
Character pitch, 257
Character testing, 378–380, 392.
    See also Class test; Sign test
CHARACTERS BY,
    AB-10–AB-11

Charge account program. *See*
    CHGACCT program
Charts and diagrams, 332–334
    Boolean diagram, 348, 349,
        350
    Chapin charts, 330
    data-flow diagrams (DFD),
        321–323
    HIPO, 322–325
    Jackson (JSP) diagrams,
        332–333
    Nassi-Shneiderman
        diagrams, 328–329
    print chart, 40–41
    program flowchart, 43–44, 49,
        104–106, 107, 325–328
    screen layout form, 450
    structure chart, 43–44, 49,
        102–103, 287–290, 321–322
    system flowchart, 41–42
    Warnier (and Warnier-Orr)
        diagrams, 331–332
    See also specific types of charts
Check digit, 384
Check protection, 265–266
CHGACCT program, 272–283
    flowchart for, 277–278
    listing, 279–280
    print chart for, 272
    programming specifications
        for, 273–274
    pseudocode for, 276
    record format for, 272
    structure chart for, 275
Class test, 343–344, 359, 378–379,
    AE-12, **AF-17**
    ALPHABETIC class test,
        343–344
    arithmetic signs and, 345
    NUMERIC class test, 343, 345,
        405, 412, 430
    user-defined, **361**
CLOSE statement, 25, 115, 128,
    129, AE-7, **AF-9**
    SORT statement and, 654, 677
COBOL-68, AA-8, AB-1–AB-2,
    AB-6–AB-8, AB-12–AB-13
COBOL-85 differences, 77
    ADD/GIVING statement,
        175, 194
    Area B limit, 30
    class condition, 343–344
    DAY-OF-WEEK, **301–302**,
        306, 307
    de-editing, **243**
    ENVIRONMENT DIVISION
        standard, 61
    EVALUATE statement,
        356–359, AB-5–AB-6
    FILLER, 70–71, 564–565
    IF statement, 281–283, 304,
        338–341, 343–346, 348–356,
        359–361
    INITIALIZE statement,
        282–283, 307,
        AB-9–AB-10
    INSPECT statement, 432

COBOL-85 differences
    (continued):
    LABEL RECORDS clause, 67
    packed-decimal format, 191
    PERFORM statement,
        466–467
    periods, 127, 129, 135, 339
    REDEFINES clause, 236, **243**
    relational operators, 340–341,
        359, 361
    reserved words, 54
    scope terminators, **127, 131,**
        186, 194
    SORT statement, 675, 679
    tables and table lookups, 565,
        567, 574, 577, 582, 583, 589,
        614–615, 628–629, 630
COBOL:
    COBOL-74 language formats,
        AE-1–AE-13
    COBOL-85 language formats,
        AF-1–AF-19
    coding conventions, 54–58,
        76–77
    coding forms, 28–30, 44, 45
    division structure, 16–26
    format notation, 57–58
    future standards, 61, 67
    language elements, 75–76,
        129, 587–588, 676–679,
        AA-24–AA-27
    overview, 12–34
    portability and, 191–192
    program execution, 26–27,
        113
    programming efficiency,
        191–192
    Report Writer feature,
        AA-1–AA-27
    structure summary chart, 130
    style summaries, 76–77, 129,
        243, 307, 360, 588
    See also Compiler (COBOL);
        Conventions and rules
COBOL sort, 644, 671–673
Code-existence check, 386
Coding forms, 28–30, 44, 45. *See
    also* Conventions and rules
Coding phase of program
    development, 36, 37, 44–48,
    49
COL (COLUMN), **458–460, 475**
Collating sequence, 341
COLUMN:
    Report Writer clause,
        AA-5–AA-6
    screen-attribute, **458–460, 475**
Column headings, 210–211,
    258–259
Combination check, 382
Combined IF conditions,
    348–351, 360, 409
    NOT operator in, 351–352
Comma (,):
    in format notation, 58
    picture symbol, 218, 220–221,
        238, 240
    punctuation character, 55–56

Comment-entry, 57, 60, 75
Comment lines, 20, 56, 75
Common modules, 275, 289
Communication description
    (CD) entry, 65, AE-5,
    AF-6–AF-7
COMP-3, 192
COMP, 569
COMP SYNC, 569
Compiler (COBOL), 45–46
    defined, 45
    diagnostics, 90–97, 136–141
    IBM compilers, 62–63, 90–94,
        136–138, 190–191,
        AC-1–AC-3
    Microsoft compiler, 63–64,
        AC-3
    options for, 75, 118
    packed-decimal format and,
        190–191
    Ryan-McFarland compiler,
        62–63, 94–97, 138–141,
        191–192, **453–455, 458–461**
    SOURCE-COMPUTER
        paragraph, 21, 61
    system-names, AC-1–AC-4
Compiling the program, 20–21,
    45–47
    clean compile, 48
    DATE-COMPILED
        paragraph, 60
    post-compile listing, 45–47,
        90–94, 137, 139–140
    syntax errors, 48, 135–136
    See also Debugging
Completion codes, AD-2
Compressed printing, 257
COMPUTATIONAL-3, 192
COMPUTE statement, 183–185,
    187, 193, AE-7, **AF-10**
Computer-names, 75,
    AC-1–AC-4
Condition-name condition,
    345–347, 360, 409–410,
    AE-12, **AF-17**
    NOT operator in, 351–352
    VALUE clause and, 346–347
Condition-names, 425, 454–455,
    AF-6
Conditional operations, 125–126
    AND operator, 348–351, 360,
        409
    class test, 343–344, 345, 359,
        361, 405, 412
    complex condition tests,
        350–351, 360
    condition-name condition,
        345–347, 360, 409–410
    general format, AE-12
    implied subjects and relation
        operators, 352–353
    NOT operator, 304, 342–343,
        351–353, **361**, 409
    OR operator, 349–351, 360,
        409
    parentheses in, 351
    relation condition, 340–343,
        359, 576

Conditional operations
(continued):
sign test, 344–345, 359,
379–380, 392, 412
CONFIGURATION SECTION,
20–21, 31, 61–62, 64, 73
OBJECT-COMPUTER
paragraph, 21, 62
SOURCE-COMPUTER
paragraph, 21, 61
SPECIAL-NAMES
paragraph, **361**
Consistency check, 382
Constants for page length, 305
CONTINUE statement, **AF-10**
Control break, 494, 496, 532
Control-break lines, 257,
260–262, 264–266
Control-break reports:
common errors, 496
control break testing, 496
end-of-page testing, 496–497
logic of, 494–497, 507–509,
513–516
multiple-level, 486–487,
509–532
Report Writer and,
AA-11–AA-17
single-level, 485–486, 487,
492–509
Control fields, 482, 485, 494
CONTROL FOOTING clause,
AA-8–AA-9,
AA-13–AA-14
Control groups, 485, 494, 532
CONTROL HEADING line,
AA-20
CONTROL IS clause,
AA-4–AA-5, AA-13,
AA-14
Control-options:
of ACCEPT statement, 449,
457–458, 475
of DISPLAY statement,
448–449, 456–457, 475
Conventions and rules:
Areas A and B, 30, 31
coding conventions, 54–58, 76
DATA DIVISION, 76–77
data-names, 70
ENVIRONMENT DIVISION,
76
format notation, 57–58
IDENTIFICATION
DIVISION, 76
indentation, 56, 68–70, 76, 340
independent module
conventions, 273
level-numbers, 23, 68–70
module-naming, 103
module-numbering, 104,
275–276, 658, 661
nonnumeric literals, 129
numeric literals, 171–172, 192
picture symbols, 239–243
PROCEDURE DIVISION, 129
REDEFINES clause, 236–237

SEARCH/VARYING
statement, 609–611
user-defined words, 54, 75
VALUE clause, 212–213, 347
CONVERTING, **432**
COPY statement, AB-15–AB-16,
AE-13, **AF-16**
CORRESPONDING:
ADD and SUBTRACT
statements, AB-12
MOVE statement, 234,
AB-11–AB-12
Counting, 154
CR (credit) picture symbol, 218,
223–224, 238, 241
Currency sign. See Dollar sign
($)
CURRENT-DATE, 302

Data:
alphabetic data, 4
alphanumeric data, 4
compression of, 190
display format for, 150–151
internal coding of, 150–151,
190–192
logical vs. physical
characteristics, 5–8
numeric data, 4, 6, 72,
151–153
table data storage, 557–558
test data, 143–144
See also Storage; Table(s)
Data class, 4, 8, 216
arithmetic operations and,
4, 6, 172
class test, 343–344, 345, 359,
378–379, 405, 412, AE-12,
AF-17
picture symbols and, 71–72,
228
Data compression, 190
Data-definition errors, 141–142
Data description entries. See
Data-item description
entries
DATA DIVISION, 6, 12, 17,
21–23, 31, 64–73
FILE SECTION, 21–23, 31,
65–72, 73
general format, AE-3–AE-6,
AF-3–AF-8
header, 64
new page for, 57
Report Writer and,
AA-2–AA-9,
AA-24–AA-26
SCREEN SECTION, **458–461**
WORKING-STORAGE
SECTION, 21, 23, 31, 72–73
Data element, 2
Data entry program. See
DATAENT program
Data exception, 401, AD-2,
AD-3–AD-4
Data-flow diagram (DFD),
321–323

Data-item description entries, 23
FILE SECTION data-names,
70
FILLER entries, 70
general format, AE-4,
AF-5–AF-6
indentation of, 68–70
level-numbers for, 68–70
PICTURE clauses, 70–72,
76–77
Data-names, 54, 70, 76, 135,
AF-6
qualification of, 234
table data-items, 570
DATA RECORDS clause, 67, 76
Data validation:
character testing, 378–380, 392
error handling methods,
391–392
field checking, 380–386, 392
field definition guidelines,
412
flowchart for, 402
INSPECT statement, 398–400
of numeric fields, 402–405
on-line vs. batch validation,
387–389
PICTURE clause and, 401,
404–405, 412
programs, 387–392
record checking, 386–387, 392
redefinition and, 401, 412,
426–427
screen input/output and,
472–474
variable subscripts and,
568–569
Data validation program. See
DATAVAL program
Database management system, 6
DATAENT program, 461–474
flowchart for, 465–466
listing, 468–469, 473
programming specifications
for, 462–463
pseudocode for, 464
SCREEN SECTION, **470–471**
structure chart for, 463
DATAVAL program, 400–431
field validation specifications
for, 402–403
flowchart for, 402, 417–419
listing, 401, 405–408, 410–411,
422–425
print chart for, 414
programming specifications
for, 412–413
pseudocode for, 416
record description for, 401
record layout for, 413
structure chart for, 415
system flowchart for, 413
DATE, 301–302, 306
Date check, 382–384
DATE-COMPILED paragraph,
60
DATE-WRITTEN paragraph, 60

Dates:
ACCEPT/FROM statement,
301–302, 306, 307
CURRENT-DATE, 302
date check, 382–384
formatting, 215–216, 221–222
period-ending date, 256
run date, 256
system date, 301–302
validating, 405–406
DAY, 92–96, 138
ACCEPT statement, 301, 306
DAY-OF-WEEK, **301–302, 306,
307**
DB (debit) picture symbol, 218,
224–225, 238, 241
De-editing, **232, 233, 243**
Debugging, 48–49, 88–97
common errors, 88–90, 496
data exception causes,
AD-3–AD-4
diagnostics, 90–97, 136–141
logic errors, 141–144
making corrections, 138, 141
program interruptions,
AD-1–AD-8
syntax errors, 48, 135–136
DEC VAX COBOL, AC-4
Decimal alignment, 174–175
Decimal-digit error, 401
Decimal-divide exception,
AD-2, AD-4
Decimal module numbers, 104
Decimal-overflow exception,
AD-2, AD-4
Decimal point, 166–168
assumed, 152, 155
for dollar and cent amounts,
188–189
numeric literals and, 171
as picture symbol, 218–219,
238, 241
REDEFINES clause and, 235
V picture symbol for, 168,
192, 217, 218, 239
Z picture symbol and, 220
DECLARATIVES area, AA-22
Deficient patron report
program. See PATDFCT
program
Deficient patron report program
with dollar and cents
amounts. See PATDFCT2
program
Deficient patron report program
with dollar and cents
amounts and column
headings. See PATDFCT3
program
DELETE statement, AE-7, **AF-10**
DEPENDING ON clause:
GO TO statement, AB-8–AB-9
OCCURS clause, AB-2
DESCENDING:
MERGE statement, 673–674
SEARCH statement, 584–585,
588
SORT statement, 652–653, 677

Descending order, 483–485
Design phase of program development, 36, 37, 43–44, 49
Detail diagrams (HIPO), 323–324
DETAIL line, AA-7–AA-8, AA-22
Detail lines, 14, 257
Device numbers, AC-2–AC-3
DFD (data-flow diagram), 321–323
Diagnostics, 90–97, 136–141
  IBM COBOL compiler, 90–94, 136–138
  RM-COBOL compiler, 94–97, 138–141
  See also Debugging
Diagonal. *See* Slash (/)
Diagrams. *See* Charts and diagrams
Difference, 153
DISABLE statement, AE-7, **AF-10**
Disk storage, 6–7, 431, AD-8
DISK system-name, AC-3
Displacement values, 579, 588
Display format, 150–151
DISPLAY statement, 448–449, AB-4–AB-5, AE-7, **AF-10**
  control-options, 448–449, 456–457, 475
  editing output, 455
  erasing the screen, 456–457
  positioning displayed items, 456
DISPTRA1 program, 450–458
  flowchart for, 452
  listing, 453
  programming specifications for, 450
  pseudocode for, 451
  structure chart for, 451
DISPTRA2 program, 458–461
Divide exceptions, AD-2, AD-4
DIVIDE statement, 168–169, 193, AE-7–AE-8, **AF-10**
  divide exceptions, AD-2, AD-4
  DIVIDE/BY/GIVING format, 182–183
  DIVIDE/BY/GIVING/ REMAINDER format, 182–183
  DIVIDE/GIVING format, 181
  DIVIDE/INTO format, 181
  DIVIDE/INTO/GIVING/ REMAINDER format, 182
  when to use GIVING, 186–187
Dividend, 153
Division headers, 20, 30, 58, 61, 64, 112
Divisor, 153
Documentation, 38–41. *See also* Charts and diagrams; IDENTIFICATION DIVISION

Dollar sign ($):
  foreign currency and, 225
  picture symbol, 218, 225, 226–227, 238, 242, 243
  in RM-COBOL diagnostics, 94
DOS:
  COBOL compilers, 63–64, AC-2–AC-3
  DOS/VS diagnostics, 90–94
  DOS/VSE COBOL, AC-2–AC-3
  program checks, AD-1–AD-4
Double quotes as delimiter, 118
Dummy end-of-table entry, 584
Dummy procedures, 144
Dummy TYPE IS DETAIL line, AA-22

E diagnostic category, 90
Early exit for serial search, 551–553, 582–584, 587
EBCDIC, 150, 152, 155, 341–342
Edit programs. *See* Data validation
Editing operations:
  alphanumeric editing, 227–228
  basic editing, 119–120, 214–216
  data class for, 6
  de-editing, **232, 233,** 243
  edit defined, 214
  hyphens and, 228
  MOVE statement for, 119–120, 215–216, 231–233
  numeric editing, 169–170, 187, 215, 217–229, 233
  for reports, 263–264
  zero suppression, 210–211, 215, 219–220, 229, 240
Efficiency of programs, 191–192
Elementary item, 23, 68
Elements:
  data, 2
  language, 75–76, 129, 587–588, 676–679
  PROCEDURE DIVISION, 112–114
  program, 12, 16–18
Elite pitch, 257
Ellipses in format notation, 58
ELSE, 281–282, **282–283,** 307
Embedded-blank check, 383
Embedded sign, 151, 155
ENABLE statement, AE-8, **AF-10**
END-ADD statement, **186, 194**
END-COMPUTE statement, **186, 194**
END-DIVIDE statement, **186, 194**
END-IF statement, **127, 129, 131, 282, 304**
END-MULTIPLY statement, **186, 194**
End-of-file (EOF) record, 7–8
  AT END and, 25, 121–123

End-of-file (EOF) record (continued):
  CLOSE statement and, 115
  condition-name for testing, 425
End-of-line (EOL), 456–457, 475
END-OF-PAGE, **361**
End-of-page test, 428–429, 496–497
End-of-screen (EOS), 456–457, 475
End-of-table dummy entry, 584
END-PERFORM statement, **467, 531–532**
END-READ statement, **127, 129, 131, 303**
END-SEARCH statement, **581–582**
END-SUBTRACT statement, **186, 194**
ENTER statement, AE-8, **AF-10**
ENVIRONMENT DIVISION, 12, 17, 20–21, 31, 61–64, 73
  CONFIGURATION SECTION, 20–21, 61–62, 64, 73, 361
  general format, AE-1–AE-2, **AF-1–AF-3**
  header, 61
  INPUT-OUTPUT SECTION, 21, 62–64, 73
EOF record. *See* End-of-file (EOF) record
EOL, 456–457, 475
EOS, 456–457, 475
Equal-key condition, 386–387
EQUAL TO, 126, 340–341
ERASE, 456–457, 475
Error-abeyance data validation, 391–392
Error codes in error list, 390
Error-line, 430–431
Error list, 390
Error messages:
  in error list, 390
  printing, 430–431
  in WORKING-STORAGE, 410–411
Error-rejection data validation, 391–392
Error-switch control logic, 427–428
Errors. *See* Debugging
EVALUATE statement, **356–359, 582–583, AB-5–AB-6, AF-11**
EXAMINE statement, AB-6–AB-8
Exceptions (interruptions), AD-1–AD-4
Execute exception, AD-2
Exercises:
  arithmetic operations, 155–157, 194–198
  CHGACCT program, 309–310
  COBOL overview, 31–34
  control-break programming, 488, 533–535

Exercises (continued):
  data storage, 8–10, 155–157
  data validation, 393–395, 433–435
  IDENTIFICATION, ENVIRONMENT, and DATA divisions, 77–80
  IF statement, 362–367
  PAYROLL program, 310–311
  PICTURE clause, 244–247
  PROCEDURE DIVISION, 131–132
  program development process, 49–51
  report programming, 267–269, 308–311
  screen input/output, 476–480
  sorting, 488, 679–681
  structured programming, 108, 334–335
  syntax/debugging, 97–99, 144–147, 196–198, 247–248, 366–367, 433–434, 592–593
  tables, 559–560, 589–593, 630–633
EXIT statement, 144, 647, 658, AE-8, **AF-11**
Explicit forms-control character allocation, 74–75
Exponent-overflow exception, AD-2
Exponent-underflow exception, AD-2
Exponentiation, 183, 187
EXTEND, 471
External sort, 644, 671–673

FALSE, **454–455,** 476
FD. *See* File-description (FD) entry
Field checking, 380–386, 392
  absence check, 380
  code-existence check, 386
  consistency check, 382
  date check, 382–384
  embedded-blank check, 383
  justification check, 382
  limit check, 381
  name-correspondence check, 385–386
  presence check, 380
  range check, 381, 412, 568–569
  reasonableness check, 381–382
  self-checking numbers, 384–385
Field(s), 3–4
  checking, 380–386, 392
  class test for, 343–345, 359, **361,** 378–379, 405, 412, AE-12, **AF-17**
  control fields, 482, 485, 494
  data class of, 4
  data-definition errors, 141–142
  defined, 2, 3, 8
  defining in data validation programs, 412

Field(s) (continued):
  duplicate names for, 234–237
  field checking, 380–386, 392
  group fields, 233
  indicative type, 482
  key field, 380, 386–387, 482
  length of, 4, 39–40, 569
  logical definition of, 5–6
  on reports, 258
  sign test for, 344–345, 359,
    379–380, 392, 412, AE-12,
    AF-17
  sort key, 482–485, 487, 644,
    650–651, 653–654
  sort-work file specifications,
    650–651
  table limit field, 574–576
  See also Initializing fields
Figurative constants, 117, 129,
    213
FILE-CONTROL paragraph, 21,
    62–64, 73, AE-2–AE-3, **AF-
    2–AF-3**
File-description (FD) entry,
    22–23, 65–67
  BLOCK CONTAINS clause,
    67, 650
  COBOL-85 formats, **AF-
    4–AF-5**
  DATA RECORDS clause, 67,
    76
  FD reserved word, 22, 65
  for indexed file, **AF-5**
  LABEL RECORDS clause, 67,
    114, 650
  for multiple-level control-
    break program, 524
  RECORD CONTAINS clause,
    66, 76, 650
  for relative file, **AF-4**
  for report file, **AF-5**
  REPORT IS clause, AA-2,
    AA-4
  for sequential file, **AF-4**
  See also CD entry; RD entry;
    SD entry
File-name:
  COBOL file-name, 62, 121,
    135
  physical file name, 62–64
FILE SECTION, 21–23, 31,
    65–72, 73
  data-names, 70
  file-description (FD) entry,
    22–23, 65–67
  implicit redefinition and, 170
  record-description entry,
    67–72
  VALUE clause and, 213
File(s):
  abeyance (suspense), 392
  COBOL file-name, 62, 121,
    135
  defined, 2, 8
  end-of-file (EOF) record, 7–8
  linkage between COBOL
    program and physical file,
    62–64

File(s) (continued):
  name length, 60
  physical file name, 62–64
  printer output as, 21
  program interruptions and,
    AD-4–AD-8
  for sort programs, 647–648
  sort-work file, 648–651,
    676–677
  VSAM files, AC-1
  See also CLOSE statement;
    OPEN statement; READ
    statement
FILLER, 23, 70, 564–565, 650–651
FINAL, AA-5
FIRST, 399, 432
FIRST DETAIL clause, AA-5
Fixed insertion characters, 218,
    223–225, 238, 241–242
Fixed insertion editing, 222–225
Fixed-point-divide exception,
    AD-2, AD-4
Fixed-point-overflow exception,
    AD-2, AD-4
Floating insertion characters,
    218, 225–227, 238, 242–243,
    266
Floating insertion editing,
    225–227
Floating-point exception, AD-2
Floppy disk format, 6–7
Flowcharts. *See* Charts and
    diagrams
FOOTING clause, AA-5, AA-13,
    AA-15
Foreign currency, 225
FROM:
  ACCEPT statement, 301–302,
    306, 307
  RELEASE statement, 660, **661**,
    667
  SCREEN SECTION, **460–461**,
    476
  SUBTRACT statement,
    177–178
  WRITE statement, 214
Front-end edit programs. *See*
    Data validation
FULL, **471**, **475**
Functions in tables, 548–549,
    570–571, 608–611

Garbage, 118, 378
GENERATE statement, AA-10,
    AA-20, AA-26–AA-27,
    AE-8, **AF-11**
GIVING, 172, 193
  ADD statement, 175–176
  DIVIDE statement, 181–183
  MULTIPLY statement,
    180–181
  SORT statement, 654, 677–679
  SUBTRACT statement, 178
  when to use, 186–187
GO TO statement, 647, 658,
    AB-8–AB-9, AE-8, **AF-11**
Grand-total area, 256–257, 266
GREATER THAN, 126, 340–341

GREATER THAN OR EQUAL
    TO, **340–341**, **343**
Gross pay report program. *See*
    GROSSPAY program
GROSSPAY program, 623–630
  listing, 627–628
  print chart for, 625
  programming specifications
    for, 624
  pseudocode for, 626
  record format and record
    layout for, 625
  structure chart for, 626
Group fields, 233
GROUP INDICATE clause,
    AA-19
Group item, 68
Group-printed lines,
    AA-21–AA-22

Hard-coded tables, 557–558, 564,
    588
Hard-copy output, 41
Headers. *See* Division headers;
    Paragraph headers; Section
    headers
Heading area, 256, 257–259, 266,
    296–298
HEADING clause, AA-5
Hierarchy:
  of arithmetic operations, 184
  for control-break testing, 514
  level numbers and, 22–23
Hierarchy plus Input-Process-
    Output. *See* HIPO
HIGH, 448, 475
High-order zeros. *See* Leading
    zeros
HIGHLIGHT, **461**, **475**
HIPO, 322–325
  detail diagrams, 323–324
  overview diagrams, 323–324
  visual table of contents
    (VTOC), 323–324
HP COBOL-11/3000, AC-4
Hyphen (-):
  common errors, 88–89, 135
  editing with, 228, 398–399
  in user-defined words, 54–55
  See also Minus sign (-)

I, coding convention for, 30
I-O reserved word, 114–115
I/O device numbers,
    AC-2–AC-3
I/O errors, AD-4–AD-5
IBM COBOL compilers, 62–63
  diagnostics from, 90–94,
    136–138
  DOS/VSE COBOL,
    AC-2–AC-3
  Microsoft COBOL for PCs,
    63–64, AC-3
  OS/VS COBOL, AC-1–AC-2
  packed-decimal format and,
    190–191
  Report Writer and, AA-8

IBM DOS/VSE COBOL,
    AC-2–AC-3
IBM OS program interruptions,
    AD-1–AD-8
  program checks, AD-1–AD-4
IBM OS/VS COBOL,
    AC-1–AC-2
IDENTIFICATION DIVISION,
    12, 17, 18–20, 31, 58–61, 73
  AUTHOR paragraph, 20, 60
  DATE-COMPILED
    paragraph, 60
  DATE-WRITTEN paragraph,
    60
  general format, AE-1, **AF-1**
  header, 58
  INSTALLATION paragraph,
    60
  obsolescence of optional
    entries, 61
  PROGRAM-ID paragraph, 20,
    60, 73
  REMARKS paragraph,
    AB-1–AB-2
  SECURITY paragraph, 61
Identifier format, 57, AE-13,
    AF-18
IF statement, 125–126, 128, 171,
    304, 336–376
  AND in, 348–351, 360, 409
  block IF statement, **282**
  class condition in, 343–344,
    345, 359, **361**
  combined IF conditions,
    348–351, 360, 409
  condition-name condition in,
    345–347, 360
  condition types for, 340
  configurations of, 338
  end-of-page testing, 304
  format, 126, AE-8, **AF-11**
  IF/ELSE format, 281–282,
    282–283, 307
  implied subjects and relation
    operators, 352–353
  indenting and, 340
  negated conditions, 351–352
  nested IF statements, 353–356,
    358, 360
  NEXT SENTENCE with,
    339–340
  OR in, 349–351, 360, 409
  overview, 125–126, 128,
    338–340
  relation condition in, 340–343,
    359
  relational operators for, 126
  sign condition in, 344–345,
    359
  style summary for, 360
  THEN with, **361**
Implementor-names, 75
Implicit forms-control character
    allocation, 74–75
Implicit redefinition, 170, 192,
    214

Implicit table argument, 551, 611–612

Implied relation operators, 352–353

Implied subjects for condition tests, 352–353

In-line PERFORM statement, **466–467**, **531–532**

Indentation, 56, 68–70, 76, 340

Independent data-item, 72–73

Independent module conventions, 273

INDEXED BY clause, 578–580, 613, 614

Indexed file, **AF-5**

Indexes, 578–580, 588, 609–611, AE-13

Indicative fields, 482

Initial-character printer forms control, 74–75

INITIALIZE statement, **282–283**, **307**, **AB-9–AB-10**, **AF-11**

Initializing fields:
  MOVE statement and, 118–119
  for table processing, 571–573, 577–578, 580, 582, 588, 610, 619, 621, 623
  VALUE clause and, 213–214, 347

INITIATE statement, AA-9–AA-10, AE-8, **AF-11**

INPUT, 114–115

Input-loaded tables, 557–558, 588, 622–623
  program example, 623–630

INPUT-OUTPUT SECTION, 21, 31, 62–64, 73

INPUT PROCEDURE, 657–660, **661–662**, 678

INSPECT statement, AB-10–AB-11, AE-8, **AF-11–AF-12**
  CONVERTING option, **432**
  REPLACING option, 398–399, 403–404, 431–432
  TALLYING option, 399–400, 432

Inspected field, 398

INSTALLATION paragraph, 60

Interactive processing, 448

Intermediate field, 483

Internal sort, 644, 671–673

INTO:
  DIVIDE statement, 181–182
  READ statement, 303, 306
  RETURN statement, 669, 671

IS [NOT] EQUAL TO, 126, 340–341

IS [NOT] GREATER THAN, 126, 340–341

IS [NOT] GREATER THAN OR EQUAL TO, **340–341**, **343**

IS [NOT] LESS THAN, 126, 340–341

IS [NOT] LESS THAN OR EQUAL TO, **340–341**

Jackson (JSP) diagrams, 332–333

Jackson, Michael, 332

Job cancelled, AD-6–AD-7

JSP diagrams, 332–333

Justification check, 382

KEY clause:
  MERGE statement, 673–674
  SEARCH statement, 584–585, 588
  SORT statement, 652–653, 677

Key field, 380, 386–387, 482. *See also* Sort key

Keyboard input. *See* Screen input/output

Keying the program, 45

L, coding convention for, 30

LABEL RECORDS clause, 67, 114, 650

LABELS program, 320–333
  Chapin chart for, 330
  data-flow diagram (DFD) for, 323
  flowchart for, 326–327
  HIPO for, 325
  Jackson (JSP) diagram for, 333
  Nassi-Shneiderman diagram for, 329
  programming specifications for, 320
  pseudocode for, 328
  structure chart for, 321
  Warnier-Orr diagram for, 331

Language elements, 75–76, 129, 587–588, 676–679, AA-24–AA-27

Language translator. *See* Compiler (COBOL)

LAST DETAIL clause, AA-5, AA-13

LCP (Logical Construction of Programs), 331

LEADING, 398–400, 431–432

Leading zeros:
  insertion of, 398–399, 403–405
  suppression of, 210–211, 215, 219–220, 229, 240

Leftmost zeros. *See* Leading zeros

Length:
  of fields, 4, 39–40, 569
  of file-names, 60
  page length constants, 305
  of reports, 259–260

LESS THAN, 126, 340–341

LESS THAN OR EQUAL TO, **340–341**

Level indicators, 65, 75

Level-numbers, 22–23, 68–70, 75, 76

Librarian, AB-16

Limit check, 381

LINE:
  control-option, 448–449, 456, 475
  Report Writer clause, AA-5–AA-6

LINE (continued):
  screen-attribute, **459–460**, **475**

Linear nested IF, 353–354, 360

Lines:
  blank, 56–57, **461**, **475**
  comment lines, 20, 56, 75
  control-break, 257, 260–262, 264–266
  detail, 14, 257
  error-line, 430–431
  output lines in WORKING-STORAGE, 214, 296–298
  report heading lines, 298, 305
  report-line span computation, 285, 426, 429
  screen input/output and, 448–449, 456, **459–460**, 475
  spacing on COBOL coding form, 56–57
  spacing on reports, 303–304, 307, 507–509
  summary line, 257, AA-21–AA-22
  total lines, 257, 260–262, 264–266
  01-level report lines, AA-5–AA-9

Linkage to physical file, 62–64

Listings. *See* Post-compile listings; Program listings

Literals:
  defined, 117
  MOVE statement and, 117
  nonnumeric literal delimiters, 117, 118
  numeric, 171–172, 192
  for screen display, **459**
  subscripts, 566–567, 587
  VALUE clause and, 212–213

Logic errors, 141–144

Logical Construction of Programs (LCP), 331

Logical operators, 348–351
  AND, 348–351, 360, 409
  complex conditions, 350–351
  OR, 349–351, 360, 409

Looping, 26, 105–106, 107

LOW, 448

Machine-independent language, 45

Machine language, 26, 113

Mailing labels program. *See* LABELS program

Mainline module, 24

Major control field, 513

Major sort field, 483, 487

Margins for reports, 259

MCTLBRK program, 509–532
  flowchart for, 518–521
  listing, 522–524, 527, 531
  print chart for, 509, 511
  programming specifications for, 509–510
  pseudocode for, 517
  record layouts for, 509, 511
  structure chart for, 516

Memory:
  dump, 295
  internal, 8
  reading records into, 15
  storage vs., 8
  See also Buffers; Storage

MERGE statement, 673–674, 676–677, 678, AE-8, **AF-12**

Merging, 673–676
  deficiency of MERGE statement, 674
  MERGE-related formats, 674
  SORT statement for, 675–676

Microsoft COBOL compiler, 63–64, AC-3

Minor control field, 513

Minor sort field, 483, 487

Minuend, 153

Minus sign (-):
  COMPUTE statement and, 183–185
  numeric fields and, 4, 151
  picture symbol, 218, 223, 225–226, 238, 241, 242
  as unary arithmetic operator, 185
  See also Hyphen (-)

Modules, 102–104
  common modules, 275, 289
  independent module conventions, 273
  mainline module, 24
  naming, 103
  numbering, 104, 275–276, 658, 661
  sections as, 644–646
  structure charts and, 287–290, 321–322
  table lookups and, 588

MOVE statement, 25, 116–120, 128, 129, 229–234, 237–239
  action of, 116
  alphanumeric operations, 231–232
  data validation and, 412, 429
  de-editing with, **232**, **233**
  figurative constants, 117
  format, 116–117, AE-9, **AF-12**
  group field operations, 233
  illegal moves, 230–231
  initializing fields with, 118–119
  literals, 117, 118
  MOVE/CORRESPONDING format, 234, AB-11–AB-12
  numeric editing and, 170, 215, 233
  numeric field to alphanumeric field, 233–234
  numeric operations, 232–233
  overview, 229–231, 237–239
  padding and, 231, 232
  simple editing with, 119–120, 215–216
  truncation and, 231, 232

MS-DOS. *See* DOS

Multiple-level control-break reports, 486–487, 509–532
  logic of, 513–516
  Report Writer and, AA-14–AA-17
Multiple-level control-break sales report program. See MCTLBRK program
Multiple-level tables, 556–557, 611–630
  input-loaded tables, 622–630
  PERFORM/VARYING/AFTER statement in, 618–621
  program example, 623–630
  three-level table processing, 616–618, 620–621
  two-level table processing, 611–615, 619–620
Multiplicand, 153
Multiplier, 153
MULTIPLY statement, 168–169, 193, AE-9, **AF-12**
  MULTIPLY/BY format, 179–180
  MULTIPLY/GIVING format, 180–181
  when to use GIVING, 186–187

Name-correspondence check, 385–386
Names:
  assignment-name, AC-1–AC-2
  COBOL file-name, 62, 121, 135
  computer-names, 75, AC-1–AC-4
  condition-names, 345–347, 351–352, 360, 409–410, 425, 454–455, **AF-6**
  data-names, 54, 70, 76, 135, 234, 570, **AF-6**
  implementor-names, 75
  name-correspondence check, 385–386
  physical file name, 62–64
  procedure-names, 24, 54, 103, 112, 128, 135
  program-name, 54, 60
  record-name, 120
  screen-names, **470**
  SORT-FILE, 650
  syntax errors and, 135–136
  system-names, 61, 75, AC-1–AC-4
  for table data-items, 570
  See also Reserved words
Nassi, Isaac, 328
Nassi-Shneiderman diagrams, 328–329
Negated conditions, 351–352
Negative numbers. See Signed numbers
NEGATIVE sign condition, 344–345

Nesting:
  IF statements, 353–356, 358, 360
  loops, **531–532**
  nested-source-program, **AF-19**
  OCCURS clauses, 611, 612–613, 616–617
  PERFORM statements, 513–515, **531–532**
  SEARCH statements, 614–615, 618
  source programs, **AF-18**
NEXT GROUP clause, AA-13
NEXT SENTENCE, 339–340
NO BEEP, 449, 457, 475
NOADV compiler option, 75
Nonlinear nested IF, 354–355, 360
Nonnumeric literals, 117, 118, 129, 212–213
NOT, 304, 342–343
  combined IF conditions, 352–353, 409
  exception phrases for verbs, **361**
  negated IF conditions, 351–352
NOT AT END, **361**
NOT END-OF-PAGE, **361**
NOT ON SIZE ERROR, **361**
NOTE statement, AB-12–AB-13
Null paragraphs, 647
NUMERIC class test, 343, 345, 405, 412, 430
Numeric comparisons, 341
Numeric data:
  absolute, 379
  algebraic, 379–380
  ASCII vs. EBCDIC handling of, 152
  assumed decimal point for, 152, 155
  check digit, 384
  class of, 4, 6
  class test for, 343, 345, 405
  data exceptions and, 401
  internal coding of, 190–192, 194
  packed-decimal format, 190–192
  picture symbol and, 72
  self-checking numbers, 384–385
  validating numeric fields, 402–405
  See also Dates; Signed numbers
Numeric-edited items, 169–170
  ADD/GIVING statement and, 175
  arithmetic operations and, 172
  GIVING and, 187
  MOVE statement and, 215
Numeric editing, 169–170, 217–227

Numeric editing (continued):
  BLANK WHEN ZERO clause, 229
  fixed insertion, 222–225
  floating insertion, 225–227
  GIVING and, 187
  hyphens and, 228
  MOVE statement and, 170, 215, 233
  picture symbols for, 218
  report guidelines, 263–264
  simple insertion, 220–222
  special insertion, 218–219
  zero suppression, 210–211, 215, 219–220, 229, 240
Numeric literals, 171–172, 192, 212–213, 566–567

O, coding convention for, 30
OBJECT-COMPUTER paragraph, 21, 62
Object program, 45–46
Occurrence numbers, 579
OCCURS clause, 587–588
  DEPENDING ON clause with, AB-2
  field length uniformity and, 569
  INDEXED BY clause and, 578–580, 612, 614
  KEY clause and, 584–585
  nested OCCURS clauses, 611, 612–613, 616–617
  table arguments and, 571
  table data and, 564–566, AB-2
  VALUE clause and, 213, 565, 589
On-line validation, 387–389
ON SIZE ERROR, 174, 185–186, 194, **361**
One (1), coding convention for, 30
OPEN statement, 25, 114–115, 128, 129, AE-9, **AF-12**
  EXTEND option, 471
  physical file names and, 62
  SORT statement and, 654, 677
Operation exception, AD-1, AD-2
OR, 349–351, 360, 409
Order of precedence, 184
ORGANIZATION clause, **453**
Orr, Kenneth, 331
OS (IBM Operating System), 62–63
  program interruptions, AD-1–AD-8
  system-names, AC-1–AC-2
OS/VS COBOL, AC-1–AC-2
Out-of-line procedure, 467
Out-of-line sequence, 26
OUTPUT, 114–115
OUTPUT PROCEDURE, 666–667, 678
Overflow exceptions, AD-2, AD-4
Overview diagrams (HIPO), 323–324

P picture symbol, 217, 239
PACKED-DECIMAL, 192
Packed-decimal format, 190–192
Padding, 231–232
Page eject code, 56–57, 75
Page-footing area, 257, 266
PAGE FOOTING line, AA-21
PAGE-HEADING line, AA-5–AA-7
Page headings, 256
Page length constant, 305
PAGE LIMIT clause, AA-4–AA-5, AA-15
Panvalet, AB-16
Paragraph headers, 20
  coding form area for, 30, 112, 113
  IDENTIFICATION DIVISION, 60–61
  periods and, 135
  PROCEDURE DIVISION, 112–113
Paragraphs:
  null paragraphs, 647
  periods and, 135
  PROCEDURE DIVISION, 112–113, 127–128
  procedures vs., 113
Parameters for sort utility, 644
Parentheses in condition tests, 351
PATDFCT program, 160–172
  flowchart for, 164–165
  listing, 166–167
  print chart for, 161
  programming specifications for, 162
  pseudocode for, 163–164
  record formats for, 160–161
  structure chart for, 163
PATDFCT2 program, 188–189
  listing, 189
  record format for, 188
PATDFCT3 program, 210–216
  listing, 211–212
  print chart for, 210
PATLIST program:
  flowchart for, 44
  listing, 18–20, 22, 24, 27–29
  pseudocode for, 44
  structure chart for, 44
PATLIST2 program:
  basic logic of, 126–127
  flowchart for, 105
  listing, 46–47, 65, 103
  programming specifications for, 42
  pseudocode for, 106
  structure chart for, 103
  system flowchart for, 42
Patron-address list program. See PATLIST program
Patron-address list program with under-target patrons identified. See PATLIST2 program

PAYROLL program, 283–305
  flowchart for, 292–293
  listing, 296, 299–300
  print chart for, 284–285
  programming specifications
    for, 286
  pseudocode for, 291
  record format for, 283
  structure chart for, 287–290
Payroll report program. *See*
  PAYROLL program
Payroll report with end-of-
  report totals program. *See*
  RPAYROLL report
PC-DOS. *See* DOS
Percentage calculation, 235
PERFORM statement, 26, 123,
  128, AE-9, **AF-13**
  GO TO statement vs., 647
  in-line PERFORM, **466–467,**
    531–532
  nested PERFORM/UNTIL
    statements, 513–515,
    531–532
  PERFORM/TIMES format,
    AB-13
  PERFORM/UNTIL format,
    26, 27, 123–126, 128, 129,
    572–576
  PERFORM/VARYING
    format, 576–578
  PERFORM/VARYING/
    AFTER format, 618–621
  scope terminator for, **467**
  table lookup and, 572–578
Period (.):
  AT END and, 122
  COBOL-85 and, **127, 129, 135,**
    339
  common errors, 88–89, 135
  division headers and, 58, 61,
    64, 112
  in format notation, 58
  OPEN statement and, 115
  paragraph headers and, 135
  procedure-names and, 112
  punctuation character, 55–56
  required periods, 135
  as scope terminator, 127, 135
  sentences and, 113
  See also Decimal point
Period-ending date, 256
Physical file name, 62–64
Physical record, 6
PIC, 22, 70–71, 76
  as screen-attribute, **460–461,**
    470–471, 476
Pica pitch, 257
PICTURE clause, 22–23, 70–72,
  76–77
  blank spaces and, 89–90
  data validation and, 401,
    404–405, 412
  date field editing and,
    215–216
  decimal points and, 168
  elementary items in, 23

PICTURE clause (continued):
  overview, 216–218, 227–228,
    237–243
  in SCREEN SECTION,
    460–461, 470–471, 476
  signed numbers and, 171, 178
  style considerations, 228, 243
Picture symbols, 71–72, 76, 151,
  217–228
  A, 217, 238, 239
  asterisk (*), 218, 220, 238, 240
  B, 218, 222, 227–228, 238, 240,
    243
  categories of, 216
  comma (,), 218, 220–221, 238,
    240
  CR, 218, 223–224, 238, 241
  currency sign ($), 218, 225,
    238, 242, 243
  data class and, 71–72, 228
  data validation and, 401,
    404–405, 412
  DB, 218, 224–225, 238, 241
  decimal point (.), 218–219,
    238, 241
  minus sign (-), 218, 223,
    225–226, 238, 241, 242
  overview, 217–218, 238,
    239–243
  P, 217, 239
  plus sign (+), 218, 223–224,
    226–227, 238, 241, 242
  S, 171, 178, 192, 217, 238, 239,
    412
  slash (/), 215–216, 218,
    221–222, 227–228, 238, 240,
    243
  V, 168, 192, 217, 228, 238, 239,
    412
  X, 71, 76, 151, 217, 227–228,
    238, 239, 401, 405, 412
  Z, 215, 218, 219–220, 238, 240
  0 (zero), 218, 222, 227–228,
    238, 240, 243
  9 (nine), 71–72, 76, 151, 238,
    239, 412
Pitch, 257
Plus sign (+):
  COMPUTE statement and,
    183–185
  numeric fields and, 4, 151
  picture symbol, 218, 223–224,
    226–227, 238, 241, 242
Portability of programs, 191–192
POSITION, 448–449, 456, 457,
  475
Positional addressing, 554–556,
  568
Positional table organization,
  550–551, 554–556
POSITIVE sign condition,
  344–345
Post-compile listings, 45–47,
  90–97, 137, 139–140
Presence check, 380
Priming read, 127
Print chart, 40–41. *See also*
  Screen layouts

Printer:
  printer forms control, 74–75
  RECORD CONTAINS clause
    and, 66
  specifications, 257
PRINTER system-name, AC-3
Printing. *See* WRITE statement
Privileged-operation exception,
  AD-2
PROCEDURE DIVISION, 6, 12,
  17, 23–26, 31, 110–131
  DECLARATIVES area, AA-22
  elements, 112–114
  general format, AE-6–AE-13,
    AF-8–AF-18
  header, 112
  new page for, 57
  paragraph headers, 30
  paragraph names, 24
  paragraphs, 112–113
  Report Writer and, AA-2,
    AA-9–AA-10,
    AA-26–AA-27
  sections, 112
  sections for sort programs,
    644–646, 658
  sentences, 113
  statements, 113
Procedure-names, 24, 54, 103,
  112, 128, 135
Procedures, 113, 144. *See also*
  Modules; Paragraphs
Product, 153
Program checks, AD-1–AD-4
Program development process,
  35–49
  coding phase, 36, 37, 44–48,
    49
  design phase, 36, 37, 43–44, 49
  specification phase, 36–43, 49
  testing phase, 36, 37, 48–49,
    143–144
Program flowchart, 43–44, 49,
  104–106, 107, 325–328
  basic structures for, 105–106,
    107
  drawbacks of, 328
  symbols for, 104–105
PROGRAM-ID paragraph, 20,
  60, 73
Program interruptions,
  AD-1–AD-8
Program listings:
  CHGACCT program, 279–280
  DATAENT program,
    468–469, 473
  DATAVAL program, 401,
    405–408, 410–411, 422–425
  DISPTRA1 program, 453
  DISPTRA2 program, 459
  GROSSPAY program,
    627–628
  MCTLBRK program, 522–524,
    527, 531
  PATDFCT program, 166–167
  PATDFCT2 program, 189
  PATDFCT3 program, 211–212

Program listings (continued):
  PATLIST program, 18–20, 22,
    24, 27–29
  PATLIST2 program, 46–47,
    65, 103
  PAYROLL program, 296,
    299–300
  RM-CTLBK program,
    AA-16–AA-17
  RPAYROLL report, AA-3
  RS-CTLBK program, AA-12
  SCTLBRK program, 502–503,
    508
  SORTONLY program, 649
  SORTPOST program, 670–671
  SORTPP program, 664–665
  SORTPRE program, 656
Program-name, 54, 60
Programming assignments:
  Account Balance Report
    (10-1), 536–537
  Accounts-Receivable Register
    (7-3), 370–371
  Accounts-Receivable Report
    (4-4, 5-4), 202–203, 251–252
  Aged Analysis Report (6-4),
    314–315
  Bookstore Inventory
    Application (2-7, 4-7, 5-7),
    85–86, 205, 253
  Budget Summary for
    Nurses—Single-Level
    Control Break (10-5),
    543–544
  Budget Summary for
    Nurses—Two-Level
    Control Break (10-6),
    544–546
  Classify, Sort, and Print
    Student Records (13-4),
    684–685
  Company Telephone
    Directory List (2-3), 82–83
  Complete Computers
    Corporation Vendor
    Lookup (11-6, 12-7),
    601–602, 640
  Computer Store Average
    Prices (6-7), 317–318
  Computer Store Product File
    (2-8), 86–87
  Customer-Record Display
    (9-4), 480
  Customer-Record Validation
    (8-4, 9-8), 440–442, 480
  Daily Cash Requirements
    Report (10-2), 537–539
  Degree-Program Lookup
    (11-2), 595–596
  Department-Name Lookup
    (11-1), 593–594
  Departmental Earnings
    Report (10-3), 539–541
  Earnings-Record Display
    (9-3), 480
  Earnings-Record Validation
    (8-3, 9-7), 437–440, 480

Programming assignments (continued):
Earnings Report (6-2), 312–313
Employee-Address Roster (2-4), 83–84
Federal Income Tax Computation (12-4), 636–637
Gross-Pay Report (4-3, 5-3), 201, 250–251
GROSSPAY modification (12-1), 633
International Mailing List Lookup (11-4), 598–599
Inventory Reorder Report (7-4), 371–372
Ledger-Record Display (9-1), 480
Ledger-Record Validation (8-1, 9-5), 435–436, 480
Load, Analyze, and Print Temperature Log (12-5), 637–639
Load Parts Table (12-3), 634–635
Nurses' Annuity Lookup (11-5), 599–601
Nurses' Duty Roster (2-5), 84–85
Nurses' File Validation (8-5), 442–445
Nurses' Salary Increase Projection (4-5, 5-5, 6-5, 7-5), 203–204, 252, 316, 372–374
Patron Address (1-1), 34
Patron Address/Contribution List (1-2), 34
Price List (6-1), 311–312
Region- and Territory-Name Lookup (11-3), 596–597
Sales Quota Report (6-3), 313–314
Salesperson List (2-2), 81–82
Salesperson Performance Report (4-2, 5-2), 199–200, 249–250
Select and Sort Inventory-Reorder Records (13-2), 682
Social Security Tax Report (7-2), 368–369
Sort and Print Earnings File (13-3), 683–684
Sort Vendor File (13-1), 681–682
Sorted Nurses' Telephone Directory (13-5), 686–687
Stock Brokerage Accounting (4-8), 205–206
Student List (2-1), 81
Sunsign Name Lookup (12-2), 633–634
Territory Sales Report (10-4), 541–543
Test Grades Report (7-1), 367–368

Programming assignments (continued):
Understocked Inventory Report (4-1, 5-1), 198–199, 248–249
Vehicle Insurance Lookup (12-6), 639–640
Vehicle Rental Application (2-6, 4-6, 5-6, 6-6), 85, 204, 252–253, 316
Vehicle Rental Summary Report (7-6), 374–375
Vehicle Rental Summary Report With Date Calculation (7-7), 375–376
Vendor-Record Display (9-2), 480
Vendor-Record Validation (8-2, 9-6), 436–437, 480
Programming specifications, 41–42
CHGACCT program, 273–274
DATAENT program, 462–463
DATAVAL program, 412–413
DISPTRA1 program, 450
GROSSPAY program, 624
LABELS program, 320
MCTLBRK program, 509–510
PATDFCT program, 162
PATLIST2 program, 42
PAYROLL program, 286
SCTLBRK program, 492
SORTONLY program, 649
SORTPOST program, 668
SORTPP program, 663
SORTPRE program, 655
PROMPT, 475
Protection exception, AD-2
Pseudocode, 43–44, 49, 106–107, 328
Punctuation rules, 55–56.
See also specific punctuation marks
PURGE statement, **AF-13**

Qualification of data-names, 234, AE-12, **AF-17–AF-18**
Quotation marks, 118, 172
QUOTE compiler option, 75
Quotient, 153

Random table organization, 549–550
Range check, 381, 412, 568–569
Range-step tables, 606–607
RD entry, 65, AA-3–AA-5, AA-14–AA-15, AE-5–AE-6, **AF-7–AF-8**
READ statement, 25, 121–123, 129, AE-9, **AF-13**
AT END, 25, 121–123, 129, **361**
effect of, 121–122
independent module convention for, 273, 306
INTO, 303, 306
physical file names and, 62
priming read, 127

Reasonableness check, 381–382
RECEIVE statement, AE-9, **AF-13**
Record checking, 386–388, 392
RECORD CONTAINS clause, 66, 76, 650
Record-description entry, 67–72
FILE SECTION data-names, 70
FILLER entries, 70
indentation of, 68–70
level-numbers for, 68–70
multiple entries, 170, 192
for multiple-level control-break report program, 527
PICTURE clauses, 70–72, 76–77
for sort-work file, 650–651
Record-image area, 390
Record layout forms, 38–39
Record-name, 120
Record sequence checks, 386–387
Record-set relationship checks, 387–388
Record(s):
data-definition errors, 141–142
DATA RECORDS clause, 67, 76
defined, 2, 8
end-of-file (EOF) record, 7–8
format definition for, 5–6, 22–23
LABEL RECORDS clause, 67, 77
layout forms, 38–39
physical, 6
record checking, 386–387, 392
RECORD CONTAINS clause, 66, 76
WRITE statement, 25, 120
See also Blocks
REDEFINES clause, 235–237, **243**
data validation and, 401, 412, 426–427
OCCURS clause and, 564–566, 569, 571
rules for, 236–237
VALUE clause and, 213
Redefinition. *See* OCCURS clause; REDEFINES clause
Reference modification, **AF-18**
Relation condition, 340–343, 359, AE-12, **AF-17**
alphanumeric comparisons, 341–342
end-of-table test, 576
NOT operator in, 342–343, 351–352
numeric comparisons, 341
Relational operators, 126, 304, 340–343, 576
Relationship check, 382
Relative file, **AF-4**
Relative indexing, 580, 588
Relative subscripting, **589**

Reasonableness check, 381–382
RELEASE statement, 660, **661**, 667, 678, AE-9, **AF-13**
REMAINDER, 182–183
Remainders, 153, 182–183, 187
REMARKS paragraph, AB-1–AB-2
RENAMES clause, AB-3
REPLACE statement, **AF-16**
Replacement-field value, 398
REPLACING:
COPY statement, AB-16
EXAMINE statement, AB-7–AB-8
INITIALIZE statement, **283**, **AB-9–AB-10**
INSPECT statement, 398–399, 431–432
Report file, **AF-5**
REPORT FOOTING line, AA-21
Report group description (RD) entry, 65, AA-3–AA-5, AA-14–AA-15, AE-5–AE-6, **AF-7–AF-8**
Report heading, 256
REPORT HEADING line, AA-21
REPORT IS clause, AA-2, AA-4
REPORT SECTION, AA-3–AA-9
RD entry, 65, AA-3–AA-5, AA-14–AA-15, AE-5–AE-6, **AF-7–AF-8**
report lines, AA-5–AA-9
Report Writer feature, AA-1–AA-27
DATA DIVISION, AA-2–AA-9, AA-24–AA-26
Report Writer Feature, IBM COBOL and, AA-8
Report Writer feature:
multiple-level control-break reports, AA-14–AA-17
other facilities, AA-17–AA-24
PROCEDURE DIVISION, AA-9–AA-10, AA-26–AA-27
rolling of totals, AA-15–AA-17
single-level control-break reports, AA-11–AA-14
summary, AA-25
Report Writer multiple-level control break program. *See* RM-CTLBK program
Report Writer single-level control break program. *See* RS-CTLBK program
Report(s):
body area, 256–257, 266
column headings, 210–211, 258–259
communicating the message, 189–190
control-break concepts, 485–487
defined, 38
design guidelines, 257–266, 267
editing guidelines, 263–264
fields on, 258

Report(s) (continued):
first heading line for, 305
grand-total area, 256–257, 266
heading area, 256, 257–259, 266
intercolumn space on, 262
margins, 259
multiple-level control-break reports, 486–487, 509–532
negative values on, 263
page-footing area, 257, 266
page length constant, 305
printer forms control, 74–75
printer specifications for, 257
program coding, 295–305, 306–307
program design, 283–295, 306
report-line span computation, 285, 426, 429
Report Writer feature, AA-1–AA-27
result-field size on, 260–262
single-level control-break reports, 485–486, 487, 492–509
spacing of lines on, 303–304, 307, 507–509
totals on, 260–262, 264–266
underlining on, 263
width and length of, 259–260
See also Print chart
REQUIRED, **471**, **475**
Reserved words, 20, 54, AG-1–AG-2
common misspellings, 90
diagnostics for, 92–96, 138
figurative constants, 117
format notation for, 57
for OPEN statement, 114
system-names, 61, 75
See also specific reserved words
RESET ON clause, AA-18
RETURN statement, 669, 671, 679, AE-10, **AF-13–AF-14**
REVERSE:
control-option, 448, 449, 456, 475
screen-attribute, **461**, 475
REWRITE statement, AE-10, **AF-14**
RM-COBOL compiler. *See* Ryan-McFarland COBOL compiler
RM-CTLBK program, AA-14–AA-17
listing, AA-16–AA-17
print chart for, AA-14
Rolling of totals, AA-15–AA-17
ROUNDED clause, 194
ADD statement, 174
MULTIPLY/BY statement, 180
Rounding off, 153, 155, 187
RPAYROLL report, AA-1–AA-10
listing, AA-3
print chart for, AA-2

RS-CTLBK program, AA-11–AA-14
listing, AA-12
print chart for, AA-11
Rules. *See* Conventions and rules
Run date, 256
Runtime errors, 142–143
Ryan-McFarland COBOL compiler, 62–63
diagnostics from, 94–97, 138–141
packed-decimal format and, 191
portability and, 191–192
SCREEN SECTION, **458–461**
SELECT statement, **453**
SET statement, **454–455**

S picture symbol, 171, 178, 192, 217, 238, 239, 412
Sales-transaction display program. *See* DATAENT program; DISPTRA1 program; DISPTRA2 program
Sales-transaction validation program. *See* DATAVAL program
Scope terminators, **127**, **129**, **131**, **135**, **282**
arithmetic scope terminators, **186**, **194**
of PERFORM statement, **467**
period as, 127
of SEARCH statement, 581–582
Screen-attributes, **458–461**, **471**, **475–476**
Screen input/output, 448–476
ACCEPT statement, 449, 457–458
data validation, 472–474
DISPLAY statement, 448–449, 455–457
editing output, 455
erasing the screen, 456–457
positioning displayed items, 456
SCREEN SECTION, **458–461**, **468**, **470–471**
SELECT statement and, **453**
SET statement and, **454–455**
Screen layouts, 41, 450–451
Screen-names, **470**
SCREEN SECTION, **458–461**
overview, **461**
PICTURE clause in, **460–461**, **470–471**
screen-attributes in, **458–461**, **471**
screen control and positioning in, **468**
SCTLBRK program, 492–509
flowchart for, 499–501
listing, 502–503
print chart for, 493

SCTLBRK program (continued):
programming specifications for, 492
pseudocode for, 495, 498
record layout for, 493
structure chart for, 497
SD entry, 65, 650, 676–677
Search argument, 548
Search-field value, 398
SEARCH statement, AE-10, **AF-14**
ALL clause, 586, 588
AT END, 581
Format-1 (serial), 581–582
Format-2 (binary), 585–586
KEY clause and, 584–585
nested SEARCH statements, 614–615, 618
table lookup and, 578–582, 584–586, 588, 609–611
for three-level table lookup, 617–618
for two explicit arguments, 614–615
VARYING option for, 609–611
WHEN, 581, 586, 614–615
Searching. *See* Table(s)
Section headers, 30
Sections, 112, 644–646, 658
Sectors on floppy disk, 6–7
SECURITY paragraph, 61
SELECT clause, 21, 62–64, 73, 76, **453**
for sort-work file, 650, 676
Selection flowchart structure, 105–106, 107
Selection object, 356
Selection subject, 356
Self-checking numbers, 384–385
Semicolon (;):
in format notation, 58
punctuation character, 55–56
SEND statement, AE-10, **AF-14**
Sentences, 113, 128
Separate-character sign, 151–152
Sequence flowchart structure, 105–106, 107
Sequence of source programs, **AF-19**
Sequential access, 121
Sequential file, **AF-4**
Sequential table organization, 549–550, 552–553
Serial table lookups, 551–553, 571–584, 587
with early exit, 551–553, 582–584, 587
logic of, 572, 578
PERFORM/UNTIL statement driver, 572–576
PERFORM/VARYING statement driver, 576–578
SEARCH statement driver, 578–582
SET statement, 454–455, 580, AE-10, **AF-14**
Shneiderman, Ben, 328

Sign test, 344–345, 359, 379–380, 392, 412, AE-12, **AF-17**
Signed numbers, 4, 151–152, 155
class test and, 345
defining fields for, 171
numeric literals, 172
reports and, 262–263
S picture symbol for, 171, 178, 192, 217, 239
sign test, 344–345, 359, 379–380
sort-key fields and, 653
SUBTRACT statement and, 178–179
Significance exception, AD-2
Simple insertion editing, 220–222, 227–228
Single-level control-break reports, 485–486, 487, 492–509, 532
control break testing, 496
end-of-page testing, 496–497
logic of, 494–497, 507–509
Report Writer and, AA-11–AA-14
Single-level control-break sales report program. *See* SCTLBRK program
Single quote as delimiter, 118
SIZE ERROR, 174, 185–186, 194, **361**
Slash (/):
COMPUTE statement and, 183–185
page eject code, 56–57, 75
picture symbol, 215–216, 218, 221–222, 227–228, 238, 240, 243
replacing by hyphen, 398–399
Soft copy, 41
Sort file, 648–651, 676–677
Sort-file Description (SD) entry, 65, 650, 676–677
Sort key, 482–485, 487, 644, 650–651, 653–654
Sort-merge file, **AF-5**
Sort-only program. *See* SORTONLY program
Sort program with postprocessing. *See* SORTPOST program
Sort program with preprocessing. *See* SORTPRE program
Sort program with preprocessing and postprocessing. *See* SORTPP program
SORT statement, 651–654, 676–678, 679
ASCENDING/DESCENDING KEY, 652–653, 677
COBOL-74 vs COBOL-85 and, 679
format, 652, AE-10, **AF-14–AF-15**
GIVING, 654, 677–678

SORT statement (continued):
INPUT PROCEDURE,
657–660, **661–662**, 678
merging with, 675–676
OUTPUT PROCEDURE,
666–667, 678
related formats, 645
RELEASE statement and, 660,
661, 667, 678
RETURN statement and, 669,
671, 679
USING, 654, 677
Sort-work file, 648–651, 676–677
Sorting:
COBOL-74 and, 644–647
COBOL sort (internal), 644,
671–673
defined, 482
EXIT statement, 647, 658
field type for, 482
GO TO statement, 647, 658
postprocessing program,
668–671
preprocessing and
postprocessing program,
663–668
preprocessing program,
654–663
PROCEDURE DIVISION
sections and, 644–646, 658
RELEASE statement, 660, **661**
sort key, 482–485, 487, 644,
650–651, 653–654
sort-only program, 648–654
SORT-related formats, 645
sort-work file, 648–651,
676–677
stand-alone sort (external),
644, 671–673
See also Merging
SORTONLY program, 648–654
listing, 649
programming specifications
for, 649
record layout for, 647
system flowchart for, 649
SORTPOST program, 668–671
listing, 670–671
print chart for, 669
programming specifications
for, 668
record layout for, 647
structure chart for, 669
system flowchart for, 668
SORTPP program, 663–668
listing, 664–665
print chart for, 663
programming specifications
for, 663
record layout for, 647
structure chart for, 664
system flowchart for, 663
SORTPRE program, 654–663
listing, 656
programming specifications
for, 655
record layout for, 647

SORTPRE program (continued):
structure chart for, 655
system flowchart for, 655
SOURCE clause, AA-6–AA-7
SOURCE-COMPUTER
paragraph, 21, 61
Source programs, 45–46,
AF-18–AF-19
SPACE (SPACES), 117, 213,
404–405
Spacing:
blanks in records, 5
of COBOL lines, 56–57
of COBOL words, 55–56, 89
common errors, 135
of lines on reports, 303–304,
307, 507–509
Special characters, 4
Special insertion numeric
editing, 218–219
SPECIAL-NAMES paragraph,
361
Specification exception, AD-2
Specification phase of program
development, 36–43, 49
Stand-alone sort, 644, 671–673
START statement, AE-10, **AF-15**
Statements. *See* Verbs
Stepdown-key condition,
386–387
STOP statement, 113, 116, 129,
AE-11, **AF-15**
RUN option, 26, 116
Storage:
auxiliary storage media, 6–8,
431
data characteristics, 3–4
dump, 295
logical vs. physical data
entities, 5–8
memory vs., 8
multiple record description
entries and, 170
principles of data storage, 1–8
program interruptions and,
AD-7, AD-8
table data storage, 557–558
See also Memory
STRING statement,
AB-13–AB-14, AE-11,
AF-15
Stroke. *See* Slash (/)
Structure chart, 43–44, 49,
102–103, 321–322
designing, 287–290
intermodule communication
flow on, 321–322
module-numbering
conventions and, 104
Structured flowchart, 328–329
Structured programming,
101–107
case structure, 356–357,
AB-8–AB-9
flowcharting, 104–106, 107
INPUT PROCEDURE and,
657–658

Structured programming
(continued):
modules, 102–104, 107
overview, 102
pseudocode, 106–107
structure charts, 102–103
See also Charts and diagrams
Structured walkthroughs, 43, 49,
143
Stub testing, 144
Style summaries, 76–77, 129,
243, 307, 360, 588
Subfield, 3
Subscriber mailing labels
program. *See* LABELS
program
Subscripts, AE-13, **AF-18**
defined, 566
indexes vs., 578–580, 588
literal, 566–567, 587
range validation for, 568–569
relative subscripting, **589**
for separately defined
arguments and functions,
609
USAGE COMP clause for, 569
variable, 568–569, 587
Subtotal lines, 257, 260–262,
264–266
SUBTRACT statement, 168, 193,
AE-11, **AF-15**
negative differences and,
178–179
SUBTRACT/
CORRESPONDING
format, AB-12
SUBTRACT/FROM format,
177–178
SUBTRACT/GIVING format,
178
when to use GIVING,
186–187
Subtracting, 154
Subtrahend, 153
Sum, 153, 173
SUM clause, AA-8–AA-9
Summary line, 257,
AA-21–AA-22
SUPPRESS statement,
AA-23–AA-24, AA-27,
AE-11, **AF-15**
Suppression of leading zeros,
210–211, 215, 219–220, 229,
240
Suspense file, 392
Symbols:
arithmetic operators, 183
common modules, 275
program flowchart symbols,
104–105
See also Picture symbols
SYNC (SYNCHRONIZED), 569
Syntax errors, 48, 135–136.
See also Debugging
System date, 301–302
System flowchart, 41–42

System-names, 61, 75,
AC-1–AC-4

Table(s):
arguments, 548, 570–571,
606–615
binary search lookups,
552–554, 584–586, 587
column, 611
default entry, 570
defined, 548
dummy end-of-table entry,
584
early exit for serial search,
551–553, 582–584, 587
entries, 548
establishing in WORKING-
STORAGE, 564–565,
569–571, 574–576, 588, 612
field length uniformity in, 569
functions, 548–549, 570–571
hard-coded, 557–558, 564, 588
implicit argument for, 551,
611–612
index for, 578–580
initialization for, 571–573,
577–578, 580, 582, 588, 610,
619, 621, 623
input-loaded, 557–558, 588,
622–630
loading, 623, 629
multiple-level tables, 556–557,
611–630
naming table data-items, 570
OCCURS clause for, 564–566,
569, 571, 587–588, AB-2
organization methods,
549–551
positional addressing of,
554–556
range-step tables, 606–607
row, 611
search argument, 548
separately defined arguments
and functions, 608–611
serial lookups, 551–553,
571–584, 587
style summary for, 588
subscripts for accessing,
566–569
summary of organization and
lookup methods, 556
table limit field, 574–576
three-level table processing,
616–618, 620–621
two-level table processing,
611–615, 619–620
USAGE COMP clause for, 569
See also Multiple-level tables
TALLY, AB-6–AB-7
TALLYING, 399–400, 432
EXAMINE statement,
AB-6–AB-7
Tallying field, 400
Tape storage, 6–7, 431, AD-8
TERMINATE statement, AA-10,
AA-27, AE-11, **AF-15**

Test data, 143–144
Testing phase of program development, 36, 37, 48–49, 143–144
THEN, 361
TIME, 302, 306
Time:
  ACCEPT/FROM TIME statement, 302, 306
  remainders and, 182
TIMES, AB-13
TO:
  ADD statement, 172, 173–175, **175, 194**
  SCREEN SECTION, **461, 476**
Top-down design, 287
Top-down stub testing, 144
Total lines, 257, 260–262, 264–266
Tracks, floppy disk, 6–7
TRUE, **454–455, 476**
Truncation, 153, 155, AD-4
  alphanumeric MOVE operations and, 231
  COMPUTE statement and, 187
  MULTIPLY/BY statement and, 180
  numeric MOVE operations and, 232
Two (2), coding convention for, 30
TYPE IS:
  CONTROL FOOTING, AA-8–AA-9, AA-13–AA-14
  CONTROL HEADING, AA-20
  DETAIL, AA-7–AA-8, AA-22
  PAGE FOOTING, AA-21
  PAGE-HEADING, AA-5–AA-7
  REPORT FOOTING, AA-21
  REPORT HEADING, AA-21

Unary arithmetic operator, 185
Underlining on reports, 263
UNSTRING statement, AB-14–AB-15, AE-11, **AF-16**
Unstructured program, 102

UNTIL, 26, 27, 123–126, 128, 129, 572–576
UPDATE, 449, 457–458
UPON, AB-5
USAGE clause, 192, 569
Usage-frequency table organization, 549–550
USE BEFORE REPORTING statement, AA-22–AA-23, AA-27, AE-11, **AF-16**
USE statement, AE-11, **AF-16**
User-defined class condition, **361**
User-defined words, 21, 54–55
  COBOL file-name, 62, 121, 135
  data-names, 54, 70, 76, 135, 570
  format notation for, 57
  procedure-names, 24, 54, 103, 112, 128, 135
  program-name, 54, 60
  record-name, 120
  rules for, 54, 75
USING:
  SCREEN SECTION, **460–461, 476**
  SORT statement, 654, 677

V picture symbol, 168, 192, 217, 238, 239
  data validation and, 412
  decimal point editing symbol vs., 218
  parentheses and, 228
Validation. See Data validation
VALUE clause, 118, 212–214, 360
  for condition-names, 346–347
  conventions and rules for, 212–213
  for initializing fields, 213–214, 347
  OCCURS clause and, 213, 565, 589
  for report heading lines, 298
  tables and, 564–565
VALUE OF FILE-ID clause, 63–64
Variable subscripts, 568–569, 587

VARYING:
  PERFORM statement, 576–578, 618–621
  SEARCH statement, 609–611
VAX-11 system-name, AC-4
Verbs, 24, 128, 129
  branching verbs, 113
  formats, AE-7–AE-12, **AF-9–AF-16**
  verb-adjective-object names, 103
Vertical alignment, 56
Vertical forms-control, 74–75
Vertical spacing of COBOL lines, 56–57
Virgule. See Slash (/)
VSAM files, AC-1
VTOC (visual table of contents) of HIPO, 323–324

W diagnostic category, 90
Walkthroughs, structured, 43, 49, 143
Warnier (and Warnier-Orr) diagrams, 331–332
Warnier, Jean-Dominique, 331
WHEN:
  EVALUATE statement, **583**
  SEARCH statement, 581, 586, 614–615
Width of reports, 259–260
Words (system architecture), 150
WORKING-STORAGE SECTION, 21, 23, 31, 72–73
  error messages in, 410–411
  implicit redefinition and, 170
  output lines in, 214, 296–298
  style for, 295–298, 307
  table establishment in, 564–565, 569–571, 574–576, 588, 612
  VALUE clause in, 212–214
WRITE statement, 25, 120, 129, AE-12, **AF-16**
  AFTER ADVANCING, 25, 120, 129, 303–304, 307
  AFTER ADVANCING PAGE, 304
  BEFORE ADVANCING, 120, 129

WRITE statement (continued):
  independent module convention for, 273, 281
WRITE/FROM format, 214
writing records to disk or tape, 431

X picture symbol, 71, 76, 151, 217, 227–228, 238, 239
  data validation and, 401, 405, 412

Z picture symbol, 215, 218, 219–220, 238, 240
Zero (0):
  BLANK WHEN ZERO clause, 229
  coding convention for, 30
  figurative constants for, 117, 213
  insertion of leading zeros, 398–399, 403–405
  picture symbol, 218, 222, 227–228, 238, 240, 243
  sign test for, 344–345
  suppression of leading zeros, 210–211, 215, 219–220, 229, 240
ZERO sign condition, 344–345
ZERO (ZEROES, ZEROS), 117, 213

0. See Zero (0)
1, coding convention for, 30
01-level record-description entry. See Record-description entry
01-level report lines, AA-5–AA-9
2, coding convention for, 30
9 picture symbol, 71–72, 76, 151, 217, 238, 239, 412
10-pitch, 257
12-pitch, 257
66-level RENAMES clause, AB-3
77-level independent data-items, 72–73
88-level condition-names. See Condition-name condition; Condition-names

Special offer on
RM/COBOL–85!

See previous page
for details.